MW00784680

Choral Constructions in Greek Culture

Why did the Greeks of the archaic and early classical periods join in choruses that sang and danced on public and private occasions? This book offers a wide-ranging exploration of representations of chorality in the poetry, art and material remains of early Greece in order to demonstrate the centrality of the activity in the social, religious and technological practices of individuals and communities. Moving from a consideration of choral archetypes, among them cauldrons, columns, Gorgons, ships and halcyons, the discussion then turns to an investigation of how participation in choral song and dance shaped communal experience and interacted with a variety of disparate spheres that included weaving, cataloguing, temple architecture and inscribing. The study ends with a treatment of the role of choral activity in generating epiphanies and allowing viewers and participants access to realms that typically lie beyond their perception.

DEBORAH TARN STEINER is the John Jay Professor of Greek in the Classics Department of Columbia University; her work focuses on archaic and early classical Greek poetry, art and architecture and treats intersections between the different media. Earlier publications include articles on lyric poetry and archaic artefacts and books on metaphor in Pindar, myths and images of writing in early Greece, representations of sculpted images in Greek poets, philosophers and prose writers and a commentary on two books of the *Odyssey*.

Choral Constructions in Greek Culture

The Idea of the Chorus in the Poetry, Art and Social Practices of the Archaic and Early Classical Periods

DEBORAH TARN STEINER

Columbia University, New York

CAMBRIDGE
UNIVERSITY PRESS

CAMBRIDGE
UNIVERSITY PRESS

University Printing House, Cambridge CB2 8BS, United Kingdom

One Liberty Plaza, 20th Floor, New York, NY 10006, USA

477 Williamstown Road, Port Melbourne, VIC 3207, Australia

314–321, 3rd Floor, Plot 3, Splendor Forum, Jasola District Centre,
New Delhi – 110025, India

79 Anson Road, #06–04/06, Singapore 079906

Cambridge University Press is part of the University of Cambridge.

It furthers the University's mission by disseminating knowledge in the pursuit of
education, learning, and research at the highest international levels of excellence.

www.cambridge.org
Information on this title: www.cambridge.org/9781107110687
DOI: 10.1017/9781316275436

© Deborah Tarn Steiner 2021

This publication is in copyright. Subject to statutory exception
and to the provisions of relevant collective licensing agreements,
no reproduction of any part may take place without the written
permission of Cambridge University Press.

First published 2021

A catalogue record for this publication is available from the British Library.

ISBN 978-1-107-11068-7 Hardback

Cambridge University Press has no responsibility for the persistence or accuracy of
URLs for external or third-party internet websites referred to in this publication
and does not guarantee that any content on such websites is, or will remain,
accurate or appropriate.

In memory of my mother, Zara Steiner, and to my daughters, Rebecca and Miriam, with all my love and thanks

Contents

Illustrations

Preface and Acknowledgements

This book had its origins in the idyllic landscape of Delphi where, in the early summer of 2009, I participated in a conference organized by Richard Martin and Natasha Peponi. It was on my return journey home on the airplane, after having exhausted my stock of novels, snacks and the films on offer, that the outlines of this study – a review of what I call 'archetypal' or 'paradigmatic' choruses, groups of singer-dancers on whom the historical choruses of archaic and early classical Greece modelled themselves and whose identities they took on during their performances – began to emerge. Since that now-long-ago transatlantic flight, the project has, rather hydra-like, grown and multiplied, turning into the undeniably bulky patchwork of topics and themes, many very far from the subject as originally conceived, that make up the finished book. It is my hope that what is presented here does not show too many signs of the oxygen-short atmosphere in which it was originally formulated and looks more to the glorious Delphic landscape than to the airport terminal.

Like any work that has taken far too long and that draws on heterogeneous sources and crosses many disciplinary boundaries, this book has gained immeasurably from the publications, help and observations of more friends and colleagues than I can name, and what follows is no more than a partial list. I owe particular thanks to those individuals who have generously read some of the chapters, and offered comments and, most importantly, corrections of sometimes glaring errors. Leslie Kurke has been a guiding presence from the first, repeatedly allowing me to draw on her insights, sharing yet to be published work and supplying detailed annotations of several parts of the book; deep thanks too to Mark Buchan, Susan Edmunds, Clemente Marconi, Sheila Murnaghan, Alexandra Pappas, Anna Uhlig and Ruth Webb, who have taken the time and trouble to read several of the chapters and whose expertise has filled out my often too sketchy knowledge of the sources and material treated here. The book has been enriched by many others, some originally strangers who have now become friends, who have willingly sent copies of their articles, some still unpublished or shortly to appear, supplied me with images and offered all sorts of other types of guidance. Among them are Peter Agócs, Rosa Andújar, Natasha Binek, Ewen Bowie, Jesús Carruesco, Joseph Day, Gloria Ferrari, Renaud Gagné, Hanna Golab, Richard Gordon, Mark Griffith (who, among other things, set me right on the gender of a particular horse), Christina Gunth, Guy Hedreen, Alessandra Inglese, Barbara Kowalzig, Pauline LeVen, Sarah Morris, Richard Neer, Sarah Olsen, Ian Rutherford, Michael Squire, Vicky Vlachou and Naomi Weiss. For those numerous occasions when he sparked a new idea or prompted me to rethink what I thought I understood concerning choral lyric (and much else), I know that I owe particular thanks to Andrew Ford, whose work on ancient Greek song has been very much a touchstone from the first. Footnotes throughout the study will record the particular nature of the debts that I owe several of these individuals, and I offer apologies in advance to others whose names are not included on this list, but whose observations and responses to lectures and conferences where I have presented parts of this work have proved invaluable. Any errors, of course, remain very much my own, and I hope adequately to have documented my borrowings and not to have neglected too many kindnesses.

I have many other debts to record, chief among them to the Center for Ballet and the Arts in New York where, under the truly inspiring leadership of Jennifer·Homans, I was among the fellows in the spring of 2017; earlier that academic year, a fellowship at the Institute for Advanced Studies in Princeton allowed me the necessary time and space to complete portions of the book, and Angelos Chaniotis made the community of classicists a particular vibrant one. The Lodge Fund in the Department of Classics at Columbia has also provided critical financial help at different stages of the project, and I could not imagine writing this book without the presence of my Columbia students and colleagues, with particular thanks to Francesco de Angelis, Marcus Folch, Helene Foley, Joe Howley and John Ma and to the graduates and undergraduates in my Greek Survey classes.

Michael Sharp has been an exemplary editor throughout, supplying a judicious mixture of guidance, tolerance, patience and an occasional dose of pragmatism and economic good sense, and I am also much indebted to my two anonymous readers for the Press, who first read the proposal that I submitted, and then the finished book, and whose suggestions and corrections have been a source of guidance during the revision process. Thanks too to Simone Oppen, who proofread an earlier version of the manuscript, and to Cecilia Mackay, my truly invaluable picture researcher, with whom I have worked over the last year; I could not have brought this project to completion without her.

Substantial portions of different chapters, in particular parts of Chapters 2, 5, 8 and 9, have appeared as pieces in other volumes or journals, and I have much benefitted from the editors and readers who have commented on and, most frequently, trimmed the various submissions. Chapter 2 draws on my 'From the Demonic to the Divine: Cauldrons, Choral Dancers and Encounters with Gods' in F. Lissarrague and F. Prost (eds.), *Construire le dieu en images* (Lille, 2015) and the final section of Chapter 5 as well as part of the discussion in Chapter 9 develop material from 'Lists in Performance: Maritime Catalogues, Naval Inventories and Choral Song and Dance in the Archaic and Classical Period', which appeared in *Mètis* 16 (2018). The early parts of Chapter 8 overlap with the discussion in 'Sleights of Hand: Epigraphic Capping and the Visual Enactment of *Eris* in Early Greek Epigrams', in C. Damon and C. H. Pieper (eds.), *Eris vs. Aemulatio: Competition in the Ancient World* (Leiden, 2018), and arguments and material in Chapter 9 had an earlier sounding in 'Choruses and Catalogues: The Performative and Generic Context of the Asopids in the Hesiodic Catalogue of Women', in C. Tsagalis (ed.), *Poetry in Fragments: Studies in the Hesiodic Corpus and Its Afterlife* (Berlin, 2017). Portions of this chapter also reappear in 'Girls in Lines: Generic Exchanges in Early Greek Hexameter Poetry and Choral Lyric', in M. Foster, L. Kurke and N. Weiss (eds.), *Genre in Archaic and Classical Greek Poetry: Theories and Models* (Leiden, 2020). None of this already published work is identical to the chapters as they now stand, and all have been revised, expanded or reshaped in various ways.

It only remains to record debts of a more personal kind. Of deep importance to the book have been the friendships that I have enjoyed throughout the decade of writing, and to Emily Gowers, Andrea Nightingale, Jackie Wullschläger and Froma Zeitlin, as well as to many in the lists above, special thanks. The dedication cannot reflect what I owe to my mother, who I very much hoped would see this book in print, and to my daughters, who have given me more than words can say; and apologies to them for having too frequently shut my study door. Finally, my husband Andrew Feldherr: although he has not read one word of this book, and may have only the vaguest sense of what I have been working on over these many years, he has been with me, perhaps unwittingly, at each and every moment of the project, anticipating where my thoughts were going, supplying books and articles I never thought I would need only to discover their centrality to my work and providing the multiple forms of companionship and support which make me feel that the book belongs to him.

Introduction

τί δεῖ με χορεύειν;[*]

'We do not know how the ancient Greeks danced. Of the 95,140 combined body movements which have been laboriously calculated to have existed in their dances, we still haven't the vaguest idea how they looked in action. But we do know some of the reasons why the Greeks danced, and that is perhaps more important than how they danced.'[1]

1 Introduction and Book Overview

On one of the four sides of an Attic red-figure astragalos of ca. 470–450 B.C.E. from the workshop of Sotades, a man stands positioned next to a rock-like structure or open-mouthed cave (Fig. 0.1).[2] With one arm raised up high and the other pointing forward, he looks towards a file of three maidens performing a ring dance while directing the girls' (and external viewer's) attention to the scene that fills the remaining three sides of the vessel: here ten maidens dance in mid-air, executing a variety of motions and steps (Fig. 0.2). As Gloria Ferrari's rich reading of the image confirms,[3] the original publisher of the vase correctly identified that ethereal chorus: they are the constellations of the Pleiades and Hyades, both originally maiden collectives then catasterized, who form among the principal archetypal parthenaic choruses in the Greek sources; it was they, according to a scholion to Theocritus (Σ ad Theoc. Id. 13.25 Wendel), who were the inventors of choreia and of the παννυχίς, the all-night dance performed under the star-filled sky. As the astragalos painter presents the link between the earth-bound and celestial ensembles, and in accordance with the pointing gesture of the man within the scene, the former are invited to perform following the example of

[*] 'Why should I take part in the chorus?' Henrichs 1994/95 also uses the line sung by the chorus at Soph. OT 896 as the title for his article.
[1] Highwater 1996, 42, also cited by Smith 2016, 145.
[2] London, British Museum E 804; ARV² 765.20.
[3] Ferrari 2008, 2–5. Ferrari also uses the astragalos as an introduction to the themes of her study. For a very different reading of the vase, see Budelmann and Power 2015, 285.

Fig. 0.1 Attic red-figure astragalos from the workshop of Sotades, ca. 470–450 B.C.E. London, British Museum E 804. Photograph © The Trustees of The British Museum.

Fig. 0.2 Attic red-figure astragalos from the workshop of Sotades, ca. 470–450 B.C.E. Second side. London, British Museum E 804. Photograph © The Trustees of The British Museum.

the dancers up above. Texts that both pre- and postdate the astragalos amply attest to the ubiquity of the notion of the constellations as choral dancers, astral bodies moving in eternal circles in the night sky, and whom mortal choristers cite in their songs while dancing down below.[4]

If maidens-turned-stars offer poets and artists one paradigmatic grouping for their representations of *choreia*, that particular institution of song (*ôidê*) and dance (*orchêsis*) as Plato defines it at *Laws* 654b3–4, then these luminous bodies are only one among a much broader set of choral prototypes apparent in the literary, visual and material record from archaic and early classical Greece and on whom real-world chorus members model or 'project' themselves. To sample the poetic evidence, Bacchylides 17 introduces in rapid succession a company of dolphins, Nereids circle-dancing beneath the waves and the seven *parthenoi* whom Theseus escorts to Crete, accompanists to their paean-singing male counterparts whom the sea echoes with its strain; these several ensembles all appear within what is variously categorized as a paean or dithyramb performed by an actual troupe of young Ceians on Delos, home to the famed Deliades, exemplary singer-dancers from the *Homeric Hymn to Apollo* through Pindar, Euripides and beyond, and who furnish another regularly evoked model-worthy collective. A Nereid, a chorus-leading ship equipped with oars plied rhythmically, the sounding, eddying waves, dolphins, choruses at the Spartan festival of the Hyakinthia, cranes and equine *chorêgoi* moving along a 'horsey' path of song through dancing stars populate a single choral song in Euripides' *Helen* (1451–511), each one of these an assemblage with its own choric antecedents already visible in the lyric and archaic hexameter tradition.

Vase painters from the late eighth century on, offer matching depictions of these and other choral aggregates, using a variety of devices to alert viewers to the role of the phenomena as exemplars for the real-world singer-dancers who share the vessels' surfaces. In some instances, artists juxtapose choruses of *parthenoi* with water birds positioned in parallel alignments so as to signal affinities between the avian flocks and dancing maidens (Fig. 0.3),[5] or place a choral procession of men advancing in orderly fashion immediately below a company of horses, whose carefully coiffed manes and trappings visually echo those of the marchers on the

---

[4] For these, see chiefly Miller 1986, Ferrari 2008, Csapo 2008 and the many examples also treated in this study. Throughout the book, I use the term chorister, at the risk of evoking its more religious contemporary associations, interchangeably with 'choreute' or 'chorus member'.

[5] Argos, Argos Archaeological Museum C 229. Both this and all the subsequent examples cited here receive detailed treatment and more extensive documentation in the chapters that follow.

Fig. 0.3 Late Geometric krater from Argos. Argos, Archaeological Museum C 229. Photograph courtesy of the École française d'Athènes à Argos, inv. C 229. Cliché 27381, EFA/Emile Sérafis.

lower register of the vessel (Fig. 4.4).[6] Dolphins, on occasion equipped with feet (complete with the instep that characterizes dancers) gambol, typically in circular formations, to the music of an aulos-playing companion,[7] accompany komast dancers or, transformed by Dionysus from piratical sailors into maritime form, leap about the god's 'choregic' ship as though performing a ring dance.[8] Cranes striking balletic poses decorate the foot of the sixth-century François Vase, visual reminders of the *geranos*, the so-called Crane Dance, performed by Theseus and his 'twice seven' shown on the topmost band of the pot (Figs. 0.4, 0.5).[9] And if the Cyclades derive their name from their circular layout in the sea, then one vase painter anticipates the choral character that they explicitly assume in later poetic sources (Callimachus' *Hymn to Delos* most strikingly): an Attic red-figure cup attributed to the Eretria Painter of ca. 430–420 displays two maenad-like dancers whom the inscriptions name as Delos and Euboea, here shown dancing with the satyr Lemnos and their mother Tethys alongside other nymphs or maenads and silens and satyrs with musical names (Fig. 0.6).[10] The choral motif recurs on the tondo of the cup, where the nymph dancing with a satyr is labelled Choro, choral dance personified (Fig. 0.7).

[6] Formerly Berlin, Antiquarium A 42, with discussion in Ferrari 1987.
[7] Rome, Villa Giulia 64608.
[8] Munich, Antikensammlungen 8729; *ABV* 146.21, 686. For other instances and illustrations, see Csapo 2003, 78–90.
[9] Florence, National Archaeological Museum 4209; *ABV* 76.1, 682.
[10] Warsaw, National Museum 142458; *ARV*² 1253, 58.

Fig. 0.4 Black-figure volute krater ('François Vase') signed by Kleitias and Ergotimos, ca. 570 B.C.E. Florence, Museo Archeologico Etrusco 4209. Photograph © Soprintendenza Archeologia della Toscana – Firenze.

Fig. 0.5 Black-figure volute krater ('François Vase') signed by Kleitias and Ergotimos, ca. 570 B.C.E. Florence, Museo Archeologico Etrusco 4209. Detail of Theseus' disembarkation on Crete. Photograph © Soprintendenza Archeologia della Toscana – Firenze.

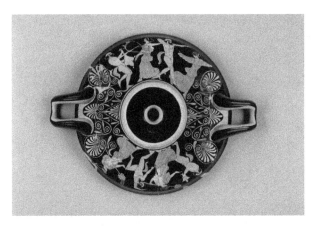

Fig. 0.6 Attic red-figure cup attributed to the Eretria Painter, ca. 430–420 B.C.E. Exterior. Warsaw, National Museum 142458. Photograph © Ligier Piotr/Muzeum Narodowe w Warszawie.

Fig. 0.7 Attic red-figure cup attributed to the Eretria Painter, ca. 430–420 B.C.E. Interior. Warsaw, National Museum 142458. Photograph © Ligier Piotr/Muzeum Narodowe w Warszawie.

While recent scholarship has treated several of these archetypes, chiefly stars and dolphins,[11] this book's first half aims to provide a more synoptic,

---

[11] See, particularly, Csapo 2003 and 2008 and Ferrari 2008; to avoid repeating their insights, I do not devote self-standing chapters to these two models. Weiss 2018 offers a more recent treatment of the theme of *choreia* and some of its paradigms focused on Euripides.

albeit still partial, account of the diverse collectives apparent in the early
visual and poetic sources (a more complete 'catalogue' would include,
among others, monkeys whose malformed bodies and ungainly motions
mirror the buttock-slapping padded choruses at symposia and parody the
activities performed by those present at the occasion).[12] Beyond simply identifying the heterogeneous and frequently surprising phenomena – whether
Gorgons, cauldrons, bovines, ships or the seemingly static column – which, in
the Greek imaginary, lay behind and, to some extent, gave form and fashion to
the choral ensemble and to its representation by poets, prose-writers and
artists in a variety of media, each chapter investigates the reasons prompting
a particular selection and observes connections between the varied *comparanda*. Determined at once by the myths and popular lore that supplied these
templates with their aitiologies and signal properties, by the rituals and
topographies framing them, and by developments in technology, music,
song and dance, each one of these model choruses carries its own dense
substrate and 'back history' and simultaneously responds to the political, social
and cultural contexts conditioning its appearance within a particular poem,
inscription or visual account and the time and place of that object's production, performance and viewership.

Following the excavation of these choral archetypes, the book's second
portion reverses the question posed in the earlier chapters. In place of
asking what paradigms the Greeks of the archaic and early classical periods
looked to when thinking about and depicting *choreia*, the discussions in
Chapters 6 through 10 explore how chorality served as a both real and
symbolic 'construction' which drew on and in turn shaped other areas of
communal experience, whether social and religious practices or technological pursuits. To cite just one example of the types of intersections
treated here, an anecdote preserved in the Pindaric *Apophthegmata* reports
that on his arrival at Delphi the poet was asked what he had come to
sacrifice: his succinct response, 'a paean'.[13] The exchange nicely taps into
the affinity between song and dance spectacles and other tributes, among
them sacrificial offerings and votive goods, tendered to the gods who were
worshipped at the civic and extra-urban sacred sites where choruses typically performed. Also manifesting the chorus-dedication kinship, the
parthenaic chorus members of Euripides' *Phoenissae* compare their choral
service to Apollo to that supplied by the precious donations at the sanctuary: 'I became a handmaiden (λάτρις) to Phoebus, just like his *agalmata*

---

[12] For these, see Steiner 2016a.
[13] Kurke 2012, 220 also cites the story in her discussion of the chorus as a locus of value.

Fig. 0.8 Karyatid from the Siphnian Treasury, Delphi, ca. 530–525 B.C.E. Delphi, Archaeological Museum. Photograph © Luisa Ricciarini/Bridgeman Images.

fashioned in gold' (220–21); a later passage, in which the chorus styles itself 'the first fruits of the spear' dedicated to Apollo (282), reiterates the singer-dancers' self-alignment with inanimate offerings.

The continuity between females who render song and dance tribute at shrines, votive artefacts and choruses finds fresh expression in architectural innovations visible from the sixth century on: the so-called 'karyatids', marble statues of long-robed women erected at the Siphnian Treasury at Delphi (Fig. 0.8) and elsewhere.[14] These figures not only 'serve' by propping up the lintel and making offerings with their outstretched hands,[15] but, as their name suggests, they may have been conceived as permanent stand-ins for the occasional choruses that performed at the sites, themselves reconfigurations of an originary choric ensemble: the eponymous

[14] Delphi, Archaeological Museum; many standard treatments suggest that the Knidian Treasury of ca. 550 also originally featured karyatids but, as Marconi 2007, 17 notes, the downdating of the sculptural figures traditionally assigned to the building makes this impossible.

[15] Here I echo Neer 2001, 316, who details this form of structural service.

Fig. 0.9 The south porch of the Athenian Erechtheion with the six replica karyatids as seen from the south-east, ca. 421–406 B.C.E. London, British Museum 1816, 0610.128 (Greek and Roman Sculpture 407). Photograph Harrieta171/Wikimedia CC BY-SA 3.0.

Karyatids were the maidens who supplied a standing chorus at the cult of Artemis Karyatis in Sparta. Chorality similarly informs the libation-making columnar maidens (who would originally have held *phialai* in their hands) of the Erechtheion; according to a fragment from Euripides' *Erechtheus* (fr. 370.77–80 K), the girls' self-sacrifice on behalf of their polis received mimetic commemoration and celebration in cult in the shape of choruses performing 'sacred maiden dances', these perhaps revisualized in the six Ionic columns fronting the building (Fig. 0.9)[16] that form two semi-choruses, each one stepping in the opposite direction around the structure. The presence of a maiden chorus in commemorative rites for the daughters of Erechtheus has a 'choral logic' of its own. Catasterized for their service to the city, these Erechtheids became none other than the celestial Hyades visible on the astragalos cited earlier, whose dance the three maidens encircling the fourth-century Acanthus Column in Delphi (Fig. 0.10), according to a revisionary reading, lastingly re-enact.[17]

---

[16] London, British Museum 1816, 0610.128 (Greek and Roman Sculpture 407).

[17] Delphi, Archaeological Museum 466, 1423, 4851; for this reading, see Ferrari 2008, 141–47; note too Power 2011, 75 n. 21.

Fig. 0.10 Fourth-century Acanthus Column from Delphi. Delphi, Archaeological Museum 466, 1423, 4851. Photograph © Luisa Ricciarini/Bridgeman Images.

2   Structure and Themes

As this rapid overview and sampling of the book's contents and concerns makes evident, both the diversity of objects and practices and the hetero- geneity of the sources gathered here, some written, others painted or worked in stone, wood, metal or cloth,[18] pose major organizational chal- lenges, and ones that I do not claim more than partially to have solved. In the first half of the study, both a loose chronology and the broader taxonomy to which a choral ensemble belongs determine the order of the chapters. Developing the discussion in Chapter 1 of the sequence of

[18] Even the book page can, in post-classical times, become its own *orchestra* or ornamented dancing floor.

'choralized' objects forged by Hephaestus in *Iliad* 18, Chapter 2 takes as its focal point a proto-Geometric vase (Fig. 2.0)[19] that reprises the Orientalizing cauldrons imagined by Homer as the first of the god's wondrous dancing and vocalizing metallic products. Chapters 3, 4 and 5 variously treat the choral collectives inhabiting the sky, land and sea in investigations of flocks of birds, singing-dancing animals and the choruses of aquatic nymphs who populate rivers, springs, fountains and the ocean, a space they share with the ships that, together with their crews, furnish additional choral paradigms. Manufactured objects return in Chapter 6 – which serves very much by way of pivot between the book's two halves and introduces a further choral archetype while simultaneously broaching the questions taken up in the subsequent discussions – in the form of the embodied columns from whom dancers, reaching from choruses in archaic Ionia through to Isadora Duncan, have taken choreographic cues.

Disrupting these divisions between the discrete groupings, however, are the many texts and images that combine several archetypal choruses within a single frame, making repetition and cross-referencing unavoidable. Pindar's fragmentary *Paean* 8 presents just such a portmanteau composition: within the better-preserved portion of the papyrus, which describes the third fantastical temple built at Delphi, the poet imagines an uncanny rooftop chorus fashioned out of gold, acroteria-like ornaments that simultaneously recall the singing-dancing avian Sirens of the lyric and visual repertoires and the costly objects of dedication with which choruses in other works equate themselves. Adding to the medley, these so-called 'Charmers', divas endowed with fatally attractive vocal powers, stand on the gable of a building whose bronze columns and walls possess the *rhythmos* that characterizes the choral dancer. Nor are Orientalizing tripod-cauldrons absent from the intermix: in the plausible view of Nassos Papalexandrou,[20] Pindar has modelled his metallic singers after the Siren attachments used to decorate the precious votive vessels.

The same structural principles inform the design of the volume's second half, whose individual discussions treat diverse technological and social practices. Here too each chapter seeks to some degree to build on the preceding one: the frequent analogies between the arts of weaving and writing established in our sources facilitate the shift from a chapter on cloth-making to one on 'choreo-graphy' (the interactions between alphabetic writing and a chorus in performance) and the early use of writing in

---

[19] Eleusis, Archaeological Museum 2630.   [20] Papalexandrou 2003/04.

the drawing up of lists connects epigraphic practices to the exploration of correspondences between choruses and oral and written catalogues that follows. But here too plentiful boundary crossing occurs both between the discrete investigations and across the book's thematic divide. The François Vase, cited in Chapter 3 for its pertinence to choruses of cranes, returns several times in the study's latter portions, both because it visualizes Ariadne as a spinner-weaver and because it features a series of *dipinti*, these presented in the manner of a catalogue, that accompany the choral dancers on its topmost band. The choralized columns explored in Chapter 6 not only furnish models for the troupes that danced and sang at the civic and domestic sites demarcated by these structures, but also exemplify exchanges between *choreia* and technical developments in building practices and temple architecture. In visual accounts and the archaeological record, columns can, furthermore, delineate the sites where women weave and spin; and with their fluting and bases as prime surfaces for inscriptions, they additionally accommodate the epigraphic dances treated in Chapter 8. The penultimate chapter also includes material that the book's earlier discussion of aquatic and maritime choruses already introduced, returning to the naval armadas that are not only portrayed as participants in choral spectacles, but also furnish the items inventoried in the lyric catalogues delivered by choral dancer-singers and in inscriptions documenting Athens' seagoing resources.

This medley-making notwithstanding, there is both chronological progression within the volume's overall design and thematic continuities between its individual parts. I begin with a close reading of the earliest of my poetic sources, the account of Thetis' visit to Hephaestus' forge in *Iliad* 18, and end with a detailed consideration of a passage from Philostratus' *Imagines*, where the gallery guide exactingly describes a painting of a choral performance. Certain central motifs or consistent choral 'constructions' also emerge. One theme extending from start to close, and already signalled in the examples cited above, concerns the equivalence between the richly decorated *agalmata* that supplied votives, guest-gifts and heirlooms, and the chorus, this similarly conceived as a 'factured' assemblage that, like the top-rank objects, advertised its radiance, preciosity, desirability, dynamism and capacity to unite multiple elements into a single harmonious composite. By way of correlate, the *chorêgos* and/or composer of a work assumes the role of the craftsman who designs, welds, hammers, constructs, glues and weaves together words, voices, instrumentation and the choreutes' movements; we will witness Daedalus, master architect, metallurgist and statue-maker, turning choreographer and teaching the art of *choreia* to

Theseus, who in turn creates a woven fabric from his fourteen dancers, a textile freshly realized, perhaps, in the repeated artistic motif of parthenaic choruses enveloped in a single pattern-woven cloth. The chorus members are not just the passive matter with which the *chorêgos* works, but active participants in the crafting process, taking on their leader's task now as builders, now as weavers and, in one instance, as those who 'drill' (τόρευε) or, if we adopt a widely accepted alternate reading, turn their song on a lathe (τόρνευε, Ar. *Thesm.* 986).[21]

Choral morphology, understood, following the pioneering work of Claude Calame,[22] as including the make-up of the chorus, the relations between its members and the configurations in which it processes and dances,[23] proves another constant in the chapters, and both the structure of the choral group and the formations adopted by its dancer-singers find, I suggest, their reflections in writing, weaving and cataloguing practices as well as in the archetypal choruses proposed by the sources. While vase images present performers in the v-shapes that characterize the flight patterns of migrating cranes, some of the earliest *abecedaria* adopt the same configuration in instances where their painters and potters show the letters travelling from the opposite ends of the pot and converging at a central point; this deployment invests the graphic notations with the movements and patterning characteristic of a dancing troupe. Other archaic inscriptions celebrating prize-winning choruses and their star performers circle around the vessels on which they are painted or incised, emulating the ring-dances enacted by the chorus members, and/or reproduce through letter placement the rise and fall of their voices and the up-down motion of their feet.

This sustained attention to affinities between the design of the phenomena informing visual and textual depictions of choruses and the sounds and particularly the movements of the choral performers also unites the discussions, which return many times to the vexed issue of choreography. Granted, neither the early texts nor images allow us accurately to reconstruct this lost element (although performance spaces supply some clues),

---

[21] The emendation is that of Bentley.   [22] Calame 1997.

[23] While some may question my extension of the notion of choral dance to processional movement, here I follow both the ancient sources and more recent theorists such as Naerebout 1997 and 2006 in defining dance as 'rhythmical', 'patterned' and 'mostly stereotyped' motion; note too Mylonopoulos 2006. For the processional structure of the typically circular dithyrambic chorus, see Hedreen 2013. Also following these accounts, indications of context, particular elements pointing to ritual occasions and the presence of spectators and other scenes included on the pots, may help distinguish the performances from more routine, secular forms of activity and group movement.

and the fifth- and fourth-century treatises on dance to which later sources
refer are all but wholly missing, known to us from little more than the titles
cited by later authors.[24] Equally problematic, with some exceptions,[25] are
attempts to tease out from the language of choral poetry indicators of actual
schêmata (the dancer's poses) and the steps in between these moments of
arrest. Rather than seeking to remedy this gap, or to suggest a one-to-one
relationship between what the sources describe and what actually occurred
when choruses performed, this study advances a different claim: that the
diction, imagery and poetological or meta-performative discourse in the
literary sources read in conjunction with the iconography of the visual and
epigraphic records furnish a means of recovering not the spectacle as once
staged, but that performance as filtered through both *aisthêsis*, the powerful
sensual response activated by music, song and dance,[26] and the collective
imaginaries of composers, performers, artists and their public. The performance theorist Richard Schechner offers a model for this 'restored
nonevent' (as he styles it): in his suggestion, the reconstruction of an earlier
performance stands as a recreation of the conceptualized original spectacle,
and not that spectacle itself, a reflection not of its historicity but of its
historical significance at the moment of its composition and execution.[27]

My focus on reception and response prompts a further suggestion
central to my approach: that an audience would process and react to the
performance not with the senses alone, but with intellection too. Balthasar
de Beaujoyeulx, the choreographer of *Le Balet comique de la Royne* of 1581,
a multimedia masque created for the occasion of the marriage between the
Valois Anne, duc de Joyeuse and Mademoiselle de Vaudemont, comments
on these several interconnected dimensions in his preface to the libretto of
the work.[28] In his account, poetry, music and dance together were audible
and visible manifestations of the harmony that emerges from strife,
a critical ideological concern of that period and one that was central to
the image of monarchy that the king, Henri III, was currently propagating.
This harmony, Beaujoyeulx further remarks, powerfully impacts on the

---

[24] See Naerebout 2006 for these.
[25] The 'binding song' of the Furies in Aeschylus' *Eumenides* supplies one compelling example of
a chorus that seems directly to describe its movements on the stage; see Prins 1991 for rich
discussion. At several points I do suggest a form of mimesis between the language of a passage
and the movements performed by the choral dancers, but the correspondence is never direct.
See too below, where I return to this question.
[26] Indeed, as Franko 1993, 95 postulates for the court ballets of the French baroque, a choral
performance 'is its own effects'.
[27] Schechner 1985, 35–116.
[28] My account draws from the illuminating analysis of Franko 1993, 34–51.

emotions and creates an audience uniquely primed to receive the sense impressions generated by the spectacle. What the preface terms *l'esprit*, the spirit or mind, is deeply implicated too, responding to harmony by a variety of actions that the choreographer describes as a mental 'tightening, loosening or expanding' ('*resserrant ou desserrant ou accroissant*'). But the intellect's involvement in the performance does not end there: in apprehending music, song and dance, viewers would also engage in inference making, drawing analogies between the spectacle and other phenomena and concepts.

The view expressed by the sixteenth-century ballet master points us back to Aristotle's alignment of the intense, participatory and engaged act of watching spectacles, what he terms *to theôrein*, with the drawing of analogies, a practice that occurs when we look at paintings and at dramas on the stage (their choral elements presumably included) and that involves the two-step progression outlined at *Poet.* 1448b10–17:

ἃ γὰρ αὐτὰ λυπηρῶς ὁρῶμεν, τούτων τὰς εἰκόνας τὰς μάλιστα ἠκριβωμένας χαίρομεν θεωροῦντες, οἷον θηρίων τε μορφὰς τῶν ἀτιμοτάτων καὶ νεκρῶν. αἴτιον δὲ καὶ τούτου, ὅτι μανθάνειν οὐ μόνον τοῖς φιλοσόφοις ἥδιστον ἀλλὰ καὶ τοῖς ἄλλοις ὁμοίως, ἀλλ' ἐπὶ βραχὺ κοινωνοῦσιν αὐτοῦ. διὰ γὰρ τοῦτο χαίρουσι τὰς εἰκόνας ὁρῶντες, ὅτι συμβαίνει θεωροῦντας μανθάνειν καὶ συλλογίζεσθαι τί ἕκαστον, οἷον ὅτι οὗτος ἐκεῖνος·

With regard to those things that we look at with pain, the most accurate representations cause us delight when we look attentively at them, such as the shapes of the basest of beasts or corpses. And the reason for this is that learning is the most pleasurable thing not only for philosophers but for others too, except that they take part in it briefly. It is for this reason that people delight in looking at images, because it happens that by looking attentively at them, they learn and they infer about what each one is, namely that this one is that.

As the passage makes clear, although the 'unmarked' act of sight, *to horan*, is the precondition for a more attentive or contemplative type of spectatorship, the latter arises not from the object itself, but from its representation or image (*eikôn*); it is only at this secondary stage that comparison and association occur. A comment later in the discussion, concerning the way in which metaphor should be fashioned, picks up on and reframes this earlier claim. As the philosopher remarks at 1459a7–8, to construct a successful metaphor is the same as practising this heightened or concentrated mode of viewing: 'for successful metaphor making is the apprehension of the similar (τὸ γὰρ εὖ μεταφέρειν τὸ τὸ ὅμοιον θεωρεῖν ἐστιν)'. When we hear and grasp the meaning of a metaphor or a simile, which Aristotle treats on several occasions as interchangeable (e.g. *Rhet.* 1406b), we necessarily become those who deal in images and secondary representations.

Aristotle's equation of *theôria* with metaphor-making proves pertinent to a further area of continuity within my discussions, which on many occasions take their points of departure from the imagery used by the sources for evocations of *choreia* and its different elements. In the case of the literary sources, metaphors and similes form the focus of many of the close readings presented here; where the painted and plastic media are concerned, the iconographical elements that Ferrari describes as 'figures of speech'[29] and Burkhard Fehr terms *schêmata*[30] supply visual correlates to the verbal devices. Again, these features are not direct reflections of an objective reality, but constructions that respond to current conventions, ideologies and concerns. As Ferrari comments, 'the [visual] image is a representation. Its task is to depict not what exists but what is conceivable, the notions according to which reality takes its shape in a given society ... an artificial creation whose relationship to actual reality is indirect and immensely complex'. As Ferrari also observes here and in another discussion, these visual figures are analogous to and sometimes reflections of the metaphors used in contemporary literary sources, which they in turn illuminate and underwrite; both are 'projection[s] of thought'.[31]

The very term *metapherein* selected by Aristotle, which means quite literally to carry across and move from one place to another, already implies this transformative process and can be mapped onto the several 'translations', changes and shifts integral to *choreia*. The first of these concerns the passage from what is said to its embodiment in the dancers' motions. Dance, at least in the Platonic and later view, takes on the attributes of the voice, supplying a visible projection and manifestation at the corporeal level of what is heard and its transfer from one medium to another; as the Athenian Stranger of the *Laws* explains, the art of dancing (τὴν ὀρχηστικήν ... τέχνην) is the 'imitation through *schêmata* [bodily postures, gestures] of what is being said' (*Leg.* 816a5).[32] Since in the Greek view this mimesis describes an act of representation rather than

---

[29] The expression serves as the title for Ferrari 2002; for the citations that follow, see pp. 20–21 of her study.

[30] Fehr 2009, 129–30.   [31] Ferrari 2002, 71.

[32] Plutarch would later spell out the point more plainly still, declaring, in a reformulation of Simonides' celebrated equation of poetry and painting, that dance is silent poetry and poetry 'vocalized dance' (φθεγγομένην ὄρχησιν, *Mor.* 748a3–10). See too his similar characterization of a particular genre of choral lyric, the riddling hyporcheme (for which see Chapter 3), as an 'imitation through poses (*schêmata*) and words' (*Mor.* 748b1).

one of direct imitation,[33] the transference does not involve an exact repli-cation but rather an associative relationship or, as Frank Hoff formulates it in a discussion of different media combining dance and song, Japanese Noh and Kabuki, the type of more oblique connections and exchanges that metaphoric language involves: '[significant] movement in dance is not an equivalence, that is, a metaphor for certain verbal meanings of the song … movement is not exclusively mimetic, not literal nor directly illustrative of a text. Rather it is suggestive'.[34] A similar account appears in the earlier reflections of Paul Valéry as he describes, in a freeform and visually dynamic type of verse, his poem-in-the-making, *La Jeune Parque*:

> Poetry is dance. This is the analogical principle which must keep us from confusing poetry with prose.
>   Verse is a way of speaking as dance steps are a way of moving.
>   This dance feigns speech and thought (by metaphor). It is more or less *figurative*.[35]

Already for the ancient sources, the linguistic changes set into play by verbal images stand in the dense relation to the movements of the dance that Valéry would suggest. In Quintilian's twofold definition of *figura*, the rhetorician introduces a somatic analogy, first applying the term to 'any form in which thought is expressed' and comparing it to the shape and outward form of human bodies, 'which, whatever their composition, must have some appearance' (*quibus, quoquo modo sunt composita, utique habitus est aliquis*). He then goes on to single out a specialized usage of *figura*, for which he preserves the Greek noun *schêma*: 'in the second and specialized sense, in which it is called a *schêma*, it means a rational change (*mutatio*) in meaning or language from the ordinary and simple form, that is to say a change analogous to that involved by sitting, lying down on something or looking back' (*Inst.* 9.1.10–11). Concluding the discussion, Quintilian notes that *schêmata* may also be defined as what can be termed 'postures of language' (*quasi gestus sic appellandi sunt*) and distinguishes between language that is devoid of figures, which he calls ἀσχημάτιστον, and one adorned with figures, or ἐσχηματισμένην (9.1.13). Since in his formulation these 'postures' undergo change, from the upright, static body to one differently positioned and in motion, then, continuing and extending Quintilian's analogy, the introduction of figurative language necessarily requires a move from one *schêma* to another, the striking of

---

[33] As forcefully argued in Nagy 1990, 42–45, 373–75; see too Halliwell 2002.
[34] Hoff 1976, 1. With thanks to Naomi Weiss for pointing me to Hoff's discussion.
[35] From the *Notebooks* of Valéry, trans. J. Lawler.

a fresh pose.[36] What the passage describes is comparable to the sequence that makes up the movements of the choral dance: a series of changing postures, interspersed by the steps that propel the choreute from one to the next.

The metaphors and similes used by the sources to conjure up the choral spectacle, no less than their accounts of its choreography, are also central to my discussions insofar as they serve as reflections of the social and political ideologies that, as noted above, further play a role in conditioning the ancient viewers' response. While politics remain a subsidiary theme in this book, the civic choruses, the ritual behaviours and the technological activities featured here are necessarily embedded in the context of the cities (in both their public and more private spaces) and extra-urban shrines, some local and others panhellenic, in which these practices occurred. The co-presence of egalitarian and hierarchical structures within the choral ensemble, and the similar stratifications that position a single horse, heifer or bird as the leader of the larger collective or set one weaver over the rest in her cloth-making group, implicitly and explicitly address questions of relations in the civic sphere, where conflicts between members of the elite or between individuals occupying the political spotlight and the demos are an ever present threat.[37] Where Leslie Kurke's acute reading of Pindar's second *Partheneion* composed for a maiden chorus performing at the Daphnephoria at Thebes adopts precisely this perspective by placing the song within its contemporary political setting,[38] I look more to the paradigms and analogies cited in Pindar and other choral poets and suggest that these provide other avenues for acknowledging and resolving ongoing tensions within the body politic. Exemplary of the way in which a cohesive group may accommodate variegation and individuality and constitutes a 'plural singularity',[39] a chorus in its various iterations can supply a model for how a city composed of heterogeneous elements and divergent groups may nonetheless form a unified community. The weaving imagery so ubiquitous and highly developed in choral lyric supplies an instance of the intersections between *choreia* and civic harmony: the *kerkis* (shuttle or more properly 'shed bar'), as Plato's Socrates recognizes at *Cratylus* 388a–b, is at once an instrument which allows the weaver to

---

[36] For this, see Franko 1993, 16.

[37] The discussion of the institution of *chorêgia* in Wilson 2000 remains fundamental here. For an account of how writers of the imperial period treated *choreia* as a 'microcosmic marker of traditional Greek political behaviour' and a model for relations between the ruler and the ruled and those among citizens of the polis, see Bowie 2006 (the citation is from p. 75).

[38] Kurke 2007; see too Kurke 2015.   [39] The expression belongs to Franko 1993, 35.

separate the different threads and divide the warp from the weft, and simultaneously furnishes the means of creating the cohesive fabric, a dimension of the art that Plato would explore shortly after in his discussion of how to achieve social harmony in the city-in-formation in the *Politicus*. Correspondingly, the disrupted relations between the various members of a bovine or avian collective, or moments when their orderly motions go 'off track' (as do those of the vulture pair at Aesch. *Ag.* 50–51) offer reflections of social and political fractures and dislocations.

Chorality, as several chapters argue, also supplies a vehicle for articulating and manifesting exchanges between different cities, each with its own concerns and designs. As inhabitants of the rivers that connect one region and polis of Greece to another in patterns of affiliation and genealogy, and as eponyms of the springs that occur first in one locale and then bubble up in another distant civic space, the singing-dancing nymphine daughters of Asopos and Danaus fulfill a role not unlike that of choruses participating in *theôriai*, the sacred embassies that travelled from their homes to other cities and to extra-urban panhellenic shrines where they established and affirmed relations of intra-polis amity and renewed connections with their colonies and *metropoleis*. On other occasions, a paradigmatic chorus introduced by the performers of a song might serve to assert one city's supremacy over others in the region or within the alliance to which it belonged. Bacchylides 17 notoriously positions the Athenian hero Theseus as the ur-*chorêgos* whose leadership of the 'twice seven' to Crete and then to Delos effectively displaces Apollo leading his band of Cretans to Delphi; in the view of several scholars,[40] this Atheno-centric song performed by the now-tributary Ceians allowed the increasingly hegemonic city to use an opulent choral display visibly and audibly to declare its choral-cum-political primacy shortly after its assumption of the leadership of the Delian League.[41] Choral activity also lies at the origins of the long-standing rivalry between Corinth and Samos, whose polemical relations stemmed, in Herodotus' account (3.48), from the help given by the Samians to some Corcyrean boys imprisoned by the Corinthians; seeking to feed the prisoners, the Samians devised a ritual in which choruses of youths and maidens brought sesame and honey cakes to the prisoners held at the temple of Artemis. Choral weaving is, again, implicated, albeit with a more positive outcome, in

---

[40] See, most recently, Pavlou 2012 with older bibliography.

[41] In a much more wholesale act of cultural imperialism through chorality, Alexander presents the imposition of Greek *choreia* on India as part of his Hellenization of the East, declaring 'I want victorious Greeks to dance (ἐχορεῦσαι) in India'; for this, see Plut. *De Alex. Fort.* 1.332a–b Nachstädt.

a second such political rivalry. The Elean Heraia, a festival founded to mark the end to the protracted conflicts between Elis and Pisa, included among its rites both the weaving of a robe for the tutelary goddess and coming-of-age dance performances by female choruses drawn from the different cities that had negotiated the settlement of hostilities; weaving and choral dance are activities whose corollary role as statements of cohesion and unity, sometimes following periods of disjunction, our sources variously indicate.

If watching choruses from other city-states formed part of the 'viewership' with which civic ambassadors, styled *theôroi*, were charged, then the chorus more generally supplies a prime site for thinking about visuality, spectatorship and the singular nature of the relations between choral singer-dancers and those who witness the performance, a give-and-take in which distinctions between performers and their audiences break down.[42] Many of the chapters address different dimensions of this theme, whether in investigations of the phrase all but unique to choral lyric 'to show the song',[43] or close readings of passages that exemplify the visionary powers attributed to chorus members and their leaders and/or illustrate the quasi-magnetic impact of a choral spectacle on its audience. Also considered in this study are the several ways in which vase painters position choruses as witnesses to the mythological event that they 'presentify' to internal and external viewers through the modality of song-dance. Among our earliest inscriptions, a significant number, whether the Dipylon jug or the graffiti at Thera cut into rock surfaces that record and similarly commemorate skilled dancing (both illustrated in Chapter 8), practise what I call 'readerly visuality',[44] inviting viewers and readers to attend as much to the look of the letters as to their contents and to apprehend, in the manner of their original audiences, in these alphabetic assemblages schematized re-evocations of a bygone spectacle. As the concluding chapter proposes, by Hellenistic and later times, the rhetorical device of *enargeia*, 'visual vividness', had come to describe the transformation of a hearer or reader into a spectator, the process that is already operative in these archaic examples, while *phantasiai* became the term of choice for the mental images of the unseen that the speaker practising *enargeia* transmits to his audience.

---

[42] States 1996, 25 offers a succinct expression of this effacement of boundaries, terming it 'the collapse of means and ends into each other, the simultaneity of producing something and responding to it in the same behavioral act'. Bierl 2009, 5 also cites this theorist, together with Schechner 1985, 14–16.

[43] See Nikolaev 2012 for the expression 'to show the song', and Swift 2016 for choral performance as a chiefly visual phenomenon.

[44] The expression is borrowed from Esrock 1994.

This emphasis on the capacity of choral song to make manifest events now remote in space, time and ontology, and the 'artefactual' quality of a chorus and the spectacle staged both suggest that issues of preservation, transmission and reperformance are a central concern of choral poets from very early on, and in no small part determine the practices and archetypes on which they draw. Although transience and ephemerality are conditions native to all oral poetry, composers of choral lyric, the individual chapters propose, seem to devise their metaphors and conceits in a particularly concentrated and sustained effort to counter this in-built obsolescence. Perhaps because of the occasional and 'one-off' character of many lyric compositions, and because they depend as much on the music, dance and the sensory impressions generated by the event as on their verbal elements, the songs repeatedly introduce scenarios which imagine and facilitate performances in other venues and on future occasions with different participants. Pindar's choice to equate his *chorodidaskalos*, one Aineas, with a *skutalê* (*Ol.* 6.90–91), a message stick used for the transmission of coded communications, allows him to position this secondary individual as the bearer of an accurate 'script' of the ode and the one who can oversee its repeat and regularized performance at the festival of Hera Partheneia at Stymphalia. Likening a choral spectacle to a votive object complete with the inscription whose enunciation re-enacts the original presentation of the gift does much the same, while a chorus that projects its identity onto the Pleiades or Deliades assumes the character and status of these mythological and real-world groups whose performances are recurrent and even part of an atemporal and cosmic order.

If the approach and thematic concerns outlined here risk adopting a 'totalizing' lens and reading chorality into each and every space the Greeks frequented – the oceans they crossed in their choregic ships equipped with dancing oars, the springs and fountain houses from which they fetched their water, the cultivated fields where they ploughed strophic and antistrophic furrows – and in all manner of heterogeneous routine activities and practices, then the central position that the chorus held in daily life goes some way to justifying this perspective. As others have demonstrated, virtually every individual in a community, male and female, young and old, would have danced and sung as a member of a choral group and/or have watched the performances that formed a regular part of civic and panhellenic rituals and took place in more private contexts too. For many youths and maidens, participation in choral dance-and-song was tantamount to a *rite de passage*, an occasion for the transmission of shared traditions and values and a declaration of their readiness for citizenship, participation in the fighting ranks and/or marriage; for the fifth-century dramatists and Plato after them, *choreia* also supplied the social 'glue' that held together the well-functioning polis and allowed its citizens to act as members of a single community. The multiple interconnections between *choreia* and other facets of the world inhabited by the Greeks of the archaic and early classical periods argued for here result from the centrality, near ubiquity and familiarity of the institution and its practice.

3 Earlier Scholarship

Confronted with the topic of this book, a would-be reader might well experience a sense of *déjà-lu* and legitimately wonder whether there is space for yet another treatment of the ancient Greek chorus. The last three decades have seen a resurgence of interest in choral lyric and *choreia* more generally, with scholars adopting a variety of approaches and drawing on the many other disciplines and methodologies that have similarly shaped my discussions and readings of the sources. Following the pioneering work of Calame, first published in English in 1997, and Eva Stehle's book of the same year,[45] many have documented how participation in choral dancing was essential to the socialization and acculturation of maidens and youths, while others have called attention to the broader sociopolitical functions of chorality, its role in community-building, in the creation and reinforce-ment of political hierarchies, and in negotiating local identities and the relations between competing city-states.[46] Performance studies have also influenced current understanding of *choreia*, which, in Barbara Kowalzig's compelling account, provided the main model for ritual as performative action in archaic and early classical Greece.[47] Other topics of repeated inquiry have been the exchanges between choral lyric (itself involving mimesis in the form of 'ritual re-enactment' or 'reliving through ritual')[48] and its redeployment on the Attic stage,[49] with particular attention to the device of 'choral self-referentiality' and 'choral projection' deployed by the

---

[45] Calame 1997, Stehle 1997.

[46] E.g. Nagy 1990, Wilson 2000, 2007, Kowalzig 2004, 2007, Kurke 2005, 2007, Ferrari 2008, Fearn 2007, 2011.

[47] Kowalzig 2007; see too Bierl 2009.

[48] The terms belong to Nagy, who discusses the notion in publications extending from Nagy 1990 and 1994/95 to Nagy 2013.

[49] See, among others, Swift 2010 and 2011, the essays in Gagné and Hopman 2013 and numerous studies by Calame (e.g. Calame 1994/95, 2004 and 2013).

dramatic choruses.[50] A volume edited by Anastasia-Erasmia Peponi, whose work has done much to illuminate the dance element in choral lyric,[51] views chorality from a philosophical angle, detailing its place in Plato's *Laws*,[52] and the collection overseen by Lucia Athanassaki and Ewen Bowie gathers articles featuring many of these and other approaches, including a focus increasingly apparent in recent scholarship on the reperformance and dissemination of choral lyric.[53] Another volume highlights the importance of visuality in choral poetry and treats the relations between the contents of the songs and the public and private sites where they were performed,[54] a topic more narrowly addressed in an earlier collection of articles, which explores the device of deixis so liberally used by composers in the lyric genres.[55] Other works adopt a very particularized perspective in their investigations of individual choral genres, with the paean and dithyramb attracting particular attention,[56] and several choral poets, among them Pindar,[57] Bacchylides,[58] and Stesichorus,[59] are the subjects of recent monographs. Since Peter Wilson's path-breaking account of the Athenian *chorêgia*, scholars are also increasingly attentive to the 'nuts and bolts' of choral activity, its financing, the make-up of an individual ensemble and the regulations surrounding the institution,[60] and more recent discussions are now taking the story forward, detailing the continued presence of choral lyric in performance and other forms in the fourth century and beyond;[61] central to their accounts are the changes brought about when a once living spectacle of song and dance is transferred to the written page.[62] Looking still further afield, Lauren Curtis explores the place of the chorus within Augustan poetry and the essays gathered by Joshua Billings, Felix Budelmann and Fiona Macintosh variously address how the ancient ritual practice has found a place in post-classical philosophy,

---

[50] Henrichs 1994/95, 1996, Wilson 1999/2000, Csapo 1999/2000, 2004, Swift 2013.

[51] Peponi 2007, 2009; see too Crowhurst 1963, Lonsdale 1993, Naerebout 1997 and Connelly 2011.

[52] Peponi 2013.   [53] Athanassaki and Bowie 2011.   [54] Cazzato and Lardinois 2016.

[55] Felson-Rubin 2004.

[56] For the paean, see, among others, Rutherford 2001, Ford 2006; for dithyrambic song, Zimmermann 1992, Lavecchia 2000, Kowalzig and Wilson 2013. Increasingly, scholars are also seeking to illuminate the still enigmatic hyporcheme (e.g. Andújar 2018).

[57] Currie 2005, Maslov 2015 and Phillips 2016. A very recent work by Kurke and Neer (2019) focused on Pindar appeared too late for me to consult.

[58] Fearn 2007.   [59] Davies and Finglass 2014.

[60] Wilson 2000; on the more pragmatic aspects of choral performances, see, for example, Currie 2011 and Hubbard 2011.

[61] See, for example, LeVen 2014 and the collection of articles in Wilson 2007 and Bosher 2012.

[62] LeVen 2014, Phillips 2016; for the epigraphic evidence, the numerous publications by Chaniotis (e.g. Chaniotis 2006 and 2007) prove essential.

aesthetics, drama, opera, politics and, most recently, the Broadway musical.[63]

As this necessarily partial round-up of recent trends and areas of inquiry reveals, while the present study is very much heir and even a latecomer to a more than crowded and diversified choral table, no existing account covers the ground traversed here nor poses the types of questions that I raise. Beyond the more synthetic approach to the material observed above and the close focus on the archaic period which has attracted less notice than the classical age, distinctive to the book (although Ferrari, Csapo, Carruesco, Wilson and Kurke and Neer do in different ways anticipate me here)[64] is the attempt to give equal space to the literary, visual and epigraphic records and to interweave images, both painted and sculpted, other *realia* and texts in mutually illuminating ways. In my exploration of these diverses media, I also pay close attention to the materiality of the sources, their physical fabric, the manner in which they were viewed and used, and the social and spatial contexts in which encounters with them occurred. Whereas many other studies privilege the verbal element of *choreia* more readily accessible to us, and approach choral poems primarily as texts rather than as ongoing performances before an audience (although the tide is unquestionably shifting), my discussions aim more fully to accommodate their visual, choreographic and musicological dimensions, albeit in the secondary reconstructions offered by the sources.

The chief dividends to this book are, I hope, threefold. First, a novel and enhanced understanding of the centrality of choral performances to Greek society and patterns of thought in the archaic and early classical periods and of their impact on other practices, religious, artistic, artisanal, topographic and 'graphological' among them. Second, fresh readings of a range of artefacts, sites, images and literary texts, some very familiar, others much less well known and even recently disinterred, that are designed both to cast new light on the objects of discussion and to demonstrate connections between these works and the environments in which they were produced and disseminated. And third, the creation of a type of 'thick description' of the ways in which the Greeks of the periods under investigation thought about song-dance practices, a recreation that can come about through an investigation of the imaginary as well as real worlds inhabited by those who variously participated in, viewed and fashioned – in words, paint, metal, clay, thread, wooden tablets, papyrus rolls, and their own corporeal engagement – the choral performances treated here.

---

[63] Curtis 2017, Billings, Budelmann and Macintosh 2013.
[64] Ferrari 2008, Csapo 2003, Carruesco 2016, Wilson 2007, Kurke and Neer 2014 and 2019.

Choreia at the Forge: Tripod Cauldrons, Golden
Maidens and the Choral Dancers on Achilles'
Shield in *Iliad* 18

Introduction

On the penultimate ring of Achilles' shield, Hephaestus fashions an image
of a chorus of youths and maidens, metallic bodies miraculously moving,
whose appearance and dance figures the poet minutely describes
(*Il.* 18.590–605, cited below).[1] The making of the shield stands as the
capstone in a concatenation of smaller episodes that begins with Thetis'
arrival at Hephaestus' home at 18.369, and then moves from the reception
room of the house to the god's forge nearby. My primary purpose in singling
out this segment of book 18 is to suggest a thematic logic and broader
trajectory to its sequence of scenes, and more particularly to the triad of
objects, tripods, golden girls and the armour for Achilles, selected by the poet
for detailed description in each portion of Thetis' visit. As my close reading
demonstrates, the representation of the chorus on the shield offers the fullest
realization of the template already informing the other works of art created
by Hephaestus, each constituting a group of figures that moves and, on
occasion, may also sound out and/or sing in the manner of a chorus.

My choice of the Iliadic episode as the focal point for this opening
chapter has a second aim. Not only will the account of the divine foundry
privilege several of the objects (buildings, parthenaic ensembles, textiles
and tripod-cauldrons among them) to which the subsequent discussions
return in more particularized fashion, but here too I introduce a theme
that, as noted in the introductory chapter, many later portions of the study
take up: the intimate relations between craftsmanship, *choreia* and the
action of the *chorêgos*. In the equivalences that the sources establish
between these different spheres, singer-dancers and the spectacles they
stage offer the consummate expression of the properties that belong to

---

[1] While this is the band whose description the poet places in the next to last position in his
narrative, we cannot be sure of its actual location on the shield; the distribution of the scenes, and
their positions relative to one another, remain very vague and defy reconstruction in schematic
form; for this, see Squire 2013, and Lynn-George 1988, 174–200.

the most fully realized works of art and that depend, in no small part, on the presence of a master craftsman's hand.[2] Standing counterpart to the artisan who forges, assembles, weaves and adorns his materials into the finished product is the individual responsible for marshalling, arranging and orchestrating – this in the fullest sense of determining the contents of the performers' song, their music, 'look' and choreography – the choral ensemble.

1   The Twenty Tripods

From the very outset of the episode, the theme of mobility, and its absence, punctuates the poet's account. Lines 369–71 announce the start of Thetis' visit as she arrives at the craftsman god's home:

> Ἡφαίστου δ' ἵκανε δόμον Θέτις ἀργυρόπεζα
> ἄφθιτον ἀστερόεντα μεταπρεπέ' ἀθανάτοισι   370
> χάλκεον, ὅν ῥ' αὐτὸς ποιήσατο κυλλοποδίων.

> Silver-footed [or 'silver-sandaled'] Thetis came to the house of Hephaestus, imperishable, starry and conspicuous among the immortals, and made of bronze, which he himself, club-footed, had made.

Nothing but formulaic diction here, but two aspects of this opening description nonetheless stand out: first the choice and placement of the epithets given to the pair of gods, the first styled 'silver-footed/sandaled', the second characterized by the handicap that impairs his feet;[3] each isometric adjective occupies the final position in the lines that begin and complete this three-line period and both fill the last two metrical slots in the hexameter. Lending further significance to Thetis' epithet and giving it a more than merely 'ornamental' status is the recapitulation of the metallic quality of the goddess' feet or footwear in the attributes of Hephaestus' home; also metal-fashioned, the house sparkles with the radiance underscored by the adjective ἀστερόεντα. For all that it is made of static bronze, the house assumes a dynamic quality by virtue of its 'starry' nature,[4] and is invested with the radiance that, as Thetis' epithet already suggests, Homer particularly assigns to things that emit light as they move (indeed, ἄργυρος

---

[2] For this concept, I owe much to the work of Day 2010, Power 2011, Kurke 2012 and 2013.

[3] Rinon 2006, 9 also notes the proximity of the epithets; as he goes on to point out, some of the manuscripts repeat Thetis' epithet at the end of 381 while two lines later the term ἀμφιγυήεις is used of Hephaestus.

[4] For more on the motion of the stars, see Section 3; for buildings in explicitly choral motion, see Section 2.

is cognate with ἀργός, an adjective that, much like our term 'quicksilver', describes both brilliance and rapid motion). Similarity and counterpoint run through the lines: while Thetis possesses attributes that assimilate her to the products of the god's craftsmanship, her twinkling feet both anticipate and contrast with Hephaestus' deformed limbs. In keeping with this distinction, and developing it too, where the visitor's first action involves movement (she 'arrives'), her host is introduced in his capacity as the one whose business it is to 'make', an opposition repeated at lines 380–81.

The poet then goes on to detail the objects that Hephaestus is currently forging, twenty tripods equipped with wheels (373–81):

> τρίποδας γὰρ ἐείκοσι πάντας ἔτευχεν
> ἑστάμεναι περὶ τοῖχον ἐϋσταθέος μεγάροιο,
> χρύσεα δέ σφ' ὑπὸ κύκλα ἑκάστῳ πυθμένι θῆκεν,   375
> ὄφρά οἱ αὐτόματοι θεῖον δυσαίατ' ἀγῶνα
> ἠδ' αὖτις πρὸς δῶμα νεοίατο, θαῦμα ἰδέσθαι.
> οἳ δ' ἤτοι τόσσον μὲν ἔχον τέλος, οὔατα δ' οὔ πω
> δαιδάλεα προσέκειτο· τά ῥ' ἤρτυε, κόπτε δὲ δεσμούς.
> ὄφρ' ὅ γε ταῦτ' ἐπονεῖτο ἰδυίῃσι πραπίδεσσι,   380
> τόφρά οἱ ἐγγύθεν ἦλθε θεὰ Θέτις ἀργυρόπεζα.

He was fashioning twenty tripods which were to stand along the wall of his strong-founded palace, and he had set golden wheels beneath the base of each one in order that of their own motion they could enter into the immortal *agôn*, and come back to his house again, a wonder to behold. These were so far finished, but he had not yet added on the cunningly wrought ear handles. He was arranging these, and he was beating out the chains. So he was expending labour with his knowing wits. Meanwhile the goddess silver-footed Thetis approached him.

Objects of perennial fascination, and later picked out for special mention by Aristotle (*Pol.* 1253b36), these wheeled artefacts stand ready to self-propel from Hephaestus' workshop into the *agôn* of the gods, and back again. As archaeologists have noted, their fantastical nature notwithstanding, there are real-world analogues for these mobile tripods, the Cypriote bronze wheeled stands that are attested both in the archaeological record and in literary texts (see particularly the description of the bronze stands fashioned by Hiram for King Solomon at I Kings 7.27; Ugaritic texts furnish additional examples).[5] Cauldrons with openwork stands have

---

[5] Four certain complete examples have been found in Cyprus, all four-sided and whose walls are decorated with a variety of figural and geometric motifs; feet or wheels are attached and the stands are topped with rings. They are typically dated to the twelfth and eleventh centuries.

been found in several sites from the Geometric period; one, possibly of Corinthian origin, comes from Ithaca (a find spot particularly suggestive when set against the description of the gifts bestowed on Odysseus by the Phaeacians, including a 'surpassingly beautiful cauldron and tripod', at *Od.* 13.217, which the hero stores in the Cave of the Nymphs); another, whose stand probably dates from the eighth century, was buried in an Etruscan tomb at Capodimonte. Both Delphi and the Idaean cave on Crete have also yielded fragments of wheeled stands.[6]

But questions of provenance and historical paradigms aside, my concern is with the latent chorality of these objects, and with the poet's choice of diction and motifs that invite his audience to see in them anticipations of the activities and properties that would similarly characterize the more explicitly choral fabrications in the later scenes. We might begin with the space to which the tripods will proceed. Following an observation made by Nassos Papalexandrou,[7] who notes the spatial meaning that *agôn* can carry and suggests that we should imagine the objects moving into an assembly or location set aside for the staging of a spectacle, I would propose a possible connection between the site to which Hephaestus' cauldrons travel and the spaces where dance performances occur. On two occasions in the *Odyssey*, *agôn* refers explicitly to the venue where *choreia* takes place, the first when the Phaeacian stewards prepare a dancing area within an *agôn* where Demodocus will sing while around him youths 'beat the wonderful dance with their feet' (8.258–65; see Chapter 7 for detailed discussion). This performance done, the two premier Phaeacian dancers then entertain the company with their skilled display while the other chorus members 'standing about the *agôn* stamped out the time' (379–80). Another archaic usage supports Papalexandrou's suggestion: in Alcman's third *Partheneion*, the choral voice declares itself 'eager to hear the voice of girls singing a beautiful melody ... and bids me to go to the *agôn*, where I shall rapidly shake my yellow hair ... soft feet' (fr. 3.1–3 *PMGF*).

Agôn recurs again in a passage where the language of chorality is nothing if not over-determined.[8] In his celebration of the victor's uncle Alexidamos in *Pythian* 9, Pindar recalls how this earlier athlete had won his bride by participating in a courtship contest modelled on the mythical prototype staged by Danaus so as to find husbands for his forty-eight maiden daughters. As the poet describes the original event, Danaus 'caused the whole chorus to stand at the finish line [or 'turning place'] of the *agôn*, and gave

[6] See Coldstream 2003, 283 and Morris 1992, 10–11 for these.
[7] Papalexandrou 2005, 32 and n. 73.   [8] See Myers 2007 for detailed discussion.

orders to decide by the trials of feet which daughter each hero would win' (ἔστασεν γὰρ ἅπαντα χορόν / ἐν τέρμασιν αὐτίκ' ἀγῶνος· / σὺν δ' ἀέθλοις ἐκέλευσεν διακρῖναι ποδῶν, / ἄντινα σχήσοι τις ἡρώων, 114–16). Here the father appears (as he would do in Aeschylus' *Suppliants*)[9] as *chorêgos*, preparing his daughterly troupe to take part in what is effectively a courtship dance in the performance space set aside for them.

There is a second overlap between the Homeric and Pindaric passages. The expression used at *Pyth.* 9.114 for Danaus' actions, ἔστασεν γὰρ ἅπαντα χορόν, is drawn from the technical language of *choreia*, and variously refers in archaic and classical sources to 'leading', 'forming' or 'establishing' a chorus as a permanent institution.[10] The same term returns at the event which Antaios organizes for the betrothal of his daughter, whom he 'caused to stand on the line' (ποτὶ γραμμᾷ ... στᾶσε, 117–18), once more positioning her in preparation for what will be as much, again, a courtship dance as the running race superimposed on that spectacle. An earlier choral song, which anticipates the Pindaric doubling of race and dance, offers another example of this language: in Alcman's first *Partheneion*, the maidenly chorus members describe how Agido, the leader of their band, is 'outstanding, as if someone were to make stand (τις ... στάσειεν) among a grazing herd a perfect horse, a prize winner with resounding hooves' (46–47). Whether recalling a preliminary moment in the ongoing spectacle, or figuring the action occurring in the here-and-now, the image should, in Peponi's compelling suggestion, be read as 'meta-performative': the 'someone' here is none other than the *chorodidaskalos* who places the troupe's *chorêgos* at the centre of her surrounding performers.[11] Homer's own account of the entertainment that Alkinous masterminds for Odysseus on Scheria supplies a still earlier usage: after the dance floor has been readied, Demodocus moves to the midpoint of the space before the young dancers assume their (here circular) stand, waiting for him to strike up: ἀμφὶ δὲ κοῦροι / πρωθήβαι ἵσταντο (*Od.* 8.262–63).

Back in Hephaestus' foundry, we witness the moment still preliminary to this 'stationing' of the performing ensemble: the god is currently fashioning his tripods 'so as to make [them] stand (ἑστάμεναι) against the wall', intending to line up his products prior to their perhaps processional entry into the *agôn*.[12]

---

[9] Murnaghan 2005 explores how Aeschylus exploits the pre-dramatic choral character of the Danaids within the language and action of the play. See further Chapter 5.

[10] See Myers 2007 for this.   [11] Peponi 2004, 315. Later chapters return to these lines.

[12] Power 2011, 69 n. 48 cites a presentation by Mark Alonge at the 2008 Chicago APA that exactly anticipates my point: according to the abstract of his discussion of a series of Euripidean choruses, '*stantes* describes the choristers getting into position prior to, and in anticipation of, their dancing; other examples of *histantai* used by itself to describe choral formation can be cited to support of this interpretation (e.g. *Odyssey* 8.263)'.

A fourth-century text reworks the tripod-chorus analogy suggested by the god's actions, affirming that vessels, even utilitarian culinary receptacles (the original function of cauldrons prior to their elaboration), bring a choral ensemble to mind not only for the orderly deployment intended by Hephaestus, but for their possession of the *kinêsis* or potential mobility that necessarily belongs to objects invested with *rhythmos*: so Xenophon, replacing ἵστημι with κεῖμαι which, like its verbal counterpart, can mean 'to be placed in position' or 'set up', comments at *Oec.* 8.19–20:

> καλὸν δὲ καὶ ὃ πάντων καταγελάσειεν ἂν μάλιστα οὐχ ὁ σεμνὸς ἀλλ' ὁ κομψός, [ὅτι] καὶ χύτρας [φησὶν] εὔρυθμον φαίνεσθαι εὐκρινῶς κειμένας · – τὰ δὲ ἄλλα ἤδη που ἀπὸ τούτου ἅπαντα καλλίω φαίνεται κατὰ κόσμον κείμενα· χορὸς γὰρ σκευῶν ἕκαστα φαίνεται, καὶ τὸ μέσον δὲ πάντων τούτων καλὸν φαίνεται, ἐκποδὼν ἑκάστου κειμένου· ὥσπερ καὶ κύκλιος χορὸς οὐ μόνον αὐτὸς καλὸν θέαμά ἐστιν . . .

> no serious man will smile when I claim that there is beauty in the order even of pots and pans set out in regular (lit. well-rhythmed) and well-regulated order . . . There is nothing, in short, that does not gain in beauty when set out in order. For each set looks like a *choros* of utensils, and the space between the sets is beautiful to see, when each set is kept clear of it, just as a circular chorus is a beautiful spectacle in itself . . .

Pindar's maiden choruses, no less than Xenophon's harmonious assemblage (the kitchen pots are deployed κατὰ κόσμον), intersect with the Iliadic description on an additional count. So as to heighten the attractions of his daughter, privileged in the manner of the chorus leader as the fairest of the fair, the Libyan king decks her out (κοσμήσαις, 118) as he stands her in the line. Even so does Hephaestus prepare to add the final ornamental touches to his tripods, fashioning (ἤρτυε) the 'ears' that, like the elaborate handles that appear on the three vessels shown on an early sixth-century cylindrical terracotta tripod kothon from Thasos (Fig. 1.0) or those that top the tripods on a proto-Corinthian oinochoe from the Kerameikos,[13] will be finely wrought and intricate. With the choice of ἀρτύω, signalling the preparation of something that requires skill on the craftsman's part, the poet introduces a term that would subsequently enter choral diction. The author of the *Homeric Hymn to Artemis* selects an alternate form of the verb for the action of the goddess as she likewise 'fits out' or 'puts in order' her choral ensemble, here made up of the Muses and Graces, prior to their performance (καλὸν χορὸν ἀρτυνέουσα, 27.15); a second cognate verb, ἀρτίζω,

---

[13] Athens, National Archaeological Museum 17874; Athens, Kerameikos 1267; for additional examples, see Wilson Jones 2002, 367, fig. 16.

Fig. 1.0 Early sixth-century tripod kothon from Thasos. Athens, National Archaeological Museum 17874. Photograph Demetrios Gialouris © Hellenic Ministry of Culture and Sports/National Archaeological Receipts Fund.

describes another set of archetypal dancers, the Nymphs, as they 'deck out' or 'array' their dance in the waters of the spring at Theoc. 13.43. As Calame observes, these several terms, all derived from the root *ἀρ, point to the assemblage of an orderly and carefully articulated product, one 'constructed according to a certain plan'.[14] More broadly, their presence in these very different areas, metalworking and the readying of the chorus (in both the *Iliad* and the *Homeric Hymn* the action occurs at the preliminary stage, before the tripods are completed or the troupe actually performs), gives expression to the underlying affinity this chapter highlights: the fabricated or 'factural' quality of the chorus, a manifestation of its maker's artisanal expertise.

The projected addition of these decorative handles not only evokes the tripods' accessorizing, the last 'touch up' before the performance begins, but further gives them the anthropomorphism that will become more pronounced with the golden automata, the next set of objects crafted by Hephaestus. Just like pottery endowed with human features, whether outsized eyes, a projecting foot by way of a base or a nipple (the so-called *mastoi* jugs) or phallos, the Homeric οὔατα ('ears') span the realms of object and body, giving to the latter the 'constructivist' or 'artificed' dimension so pronounced in the choral representation on Achilles' shield. Already invested with the uniquely

[14] Calame 1997, 41.

human capacity for dynamic motion (see below), the tripods' acquisition of 'ears' will further grant them the faculty of hearing, allowing them to listen and respond to their divine maker's directives.[15]

A second feature to be fastened to the objects, the 'bands' that Hephaestus is currently cutting, contributes to the tripods' high visual appeal and promotes their likeness to living bodies. Not so much the chains that would allow the transport of the vessels (self-moving objects would have no need of these, and the detail seems gratuitous insofar as no other Homeric tripods include such elements), these instead furnish additional embellishment.[16] Exactly in this manner, the ropes formerly used for the transport of large-scale storage jars become the decorative and necklace-like incised, stamped, and stippled bands that encircled relief pithoi (Fig. 1.1),[17] another set of valuable, high-status objects featuring a wealth of ornamentation and that date from the early

Fig. 1.1 Late Minoan relief pithos with band decoration. London, British Museum A 739. Photograph © The Trustees of The British Museum.

---

[15] See Pind. *Pyth.* 1.1–4 for a chorus whose capacity to listen is intimately related to, and even located in, its mobile and dancing feet.

[16] Edwards 1991 *ad loc.* interprets these fastenings as 'rivets' to fasten the handles to the tripod body; however, the term is never used in that sense elsewhere, and when the identical phrase recurs at *Od.* 8.275, δεσμοί are unmistakably 'chains'. I will be returning to connections between chains and ropes and *choreia* in several later chapters.

[17] London, British Museum A 739. See Steiner 2013b for these.

archaic age on. Much like the necklaces worn by women dressed up in their finery, many of these bands occur below the rim or base of the neck, or beneath the upper row of handles. An episode in Odyssey 8, where Arete directs the hero carefully to fasten a bond or strap around the coffer that he should use to store the gifts given him by the Phaeacian queen, confirms the ornamental quality that a δεσμός may possess: the fastening that Odysseus casts about the chest is styled ποικίλος (448), just the term that is used of the gold-and-amber necklace that Eurymachus presents to Penelope at *Od.* 18.295.

Before noting additional areas where tripods and dancers coincide, it is worth lingering, as the poet does, on the κύκλα that allow Hephaestus' vessels to self-propel. I earlier suggested that from the start of the Homeric episode, limbs and feet form a leitmotif. The very name for the objects on which Hephaestus is labouring, τρίποδες, of course means 'with three feet' or, in a still more pertinent usage first found in Hesiod, 'going on three feet' (*Erg.* 533), and representations of the vessels from the archaic period on regularly show them standing on feet-like elements, some shaped like lions' paws, others with the instep distinctive of human feet; the numerous examples include the tripod cauldrons displayed on a black-figure dinos of ca. 570 (Fig. 1.2) and a terracotta plaque from Kythnos, also from the early sixth century, where lion-pawed tripods alternate with riders.[18] The golden κύκλα on the Homeric tripods (and note the only other usage of κύκλα for 'wheels' at *Il.* 5.722, where they are again elaborately configured and objects of wonder),[19] no less than 'silver-footed' Thetis, have a direct connection to the choreute and make good sense when we view the vessels as potential performers: from Homer onwards, evocations of choral performers draw attention not just to their feet,[20] but to the expressly metallic sheen that these emit. When the chorus of Phaeacian youths dances, it is the 'gleamings of their feet' (μαρμαρυγάς ... ποδῶν, 8.265) that elicit *thauma* in Odysseus, the same response that Homer invites his audience to experience at his description of the motions of Hephaestus' gold-wheeled tripods. These terms recur in the *Homeric Hymn to Apollo*: as the god gives the lead to the chorus of Muses, he is imagined 'stepping handsomely and high (ὕψι); and a radiance shines about him, even the

[18] Paris, Musée du Louvre E 875; Paris, Musée du Louvre MNP 579.
[19] These wheels belong to the chariot on which Hera and Athena descend to the battlefield, an extraordinary vehicle that takes ten lines to describe. The κύκλα occupy the major portion of the account: their felly is styled imperishable (ἄφθιτος) and the fashion in which it is joined to the running rim constitutes in and of itself a θαῦμα ἰδέσθαι (725).
[20] Note Hes. *Th.* 3–4, Alcm. fr. 3 *PMGF* and Bacch. 17.103–08, as well as the numerous examples cited in later chapters.

Fig. 1.2 Attic black-figure dinos, ca. 570 B.C.E. Paris, Musée du Louvre E 875.
Photograph © RMN-Grand Palais (Musée du Louvre)/Hervé Lewandowski.

gleaming of his feet (μαρμαρυγαί τε ποδῶν) and well-spun chiton'
(201–03).[21] On at least one occasion, that dazzle depends on the choreutes'
sandals: trumping the silver footwear given Thetis by the Iliadic poet,
Euripides pictures the Muses performing at the goddess' wedding as they
'beat the ground with their gold-sandaled foot' (*IA* 1042–43).

Nothing better affirms the familiarity of the notion than the way in
which Sappho varies the perhaps too hackneyed topos. In fr. 16 V., very
plausibly composed as an epithalamium performed by a parthenaic
chorus,[22] the poetic ego recalls the appearance of Anaktoria (the
chorêgos or lead dancer at this earlier event?) as she danced together
with her companions; singled out for special mention are the maiden's
'lovely step and the bright sparkle of her face' (ἔρατόν τε βᾶμα /
κἀμάρυχμα λάμπρον . . . προσώπω, 17–18), an expression that transposes
the radiance normally assigned to the dancer's feet to her countenance
instead. The conjunction of Anaktoria's step and the ἀμάρυγμα of her
face give this sparkle its full range of meanings. At once cognate with
μαρμαίρω, which describes the glint or gleam of metal and highly polished stone, ἀμάρυγμα also belongs to objects in rapid motion, wrestlers

---

[21] Note too Bacch. 17.103–08, where the source of the radiance is the limbs of the Nereids as they
dance: 'for from their twinkling limbs shone out a radiance as of fire . . . and they were
delighting their hearts by dancing with liquid feet'.

[22] Lardinois 1996.

or horses performing their moves (Bacch. 9.36, Ar. *Av.* 925); as one discussion defines this flash, it is 'brightness as moving light'.[23]

An epinician song by Bacchylides performed at Syracuse makes tripods the source of the self-same radiance that emanates from choral dancers' feet within a passage that constructs dense relations between the objects and the spectacle being enacted by the celebrants visualizing those far-off offerings. In a description of the famous Deinomenid dedications set up on the eastern terrace of the temple of Apollo at Delphi, the choral voice observes how 'gold shines out with the flashings of highly wrought tripods standing before the temple' (λάμπει δ' ὑπὸ μαρμαρυγαῖς ὁ χρυσός, / ὑψιδαιδάλτων τριπόδων σταθέντων / πάροιθε ναοῦ, 3.17–19). If, as a later chapter proposes, the *agalmata* so regularly featured in epinician poetry serve in part to emblematize the chorus and its song and dance, then Bacchylides' performers and the tripods all but perfectly coalesce. Mapping the Syracusan venue where the chorus delivers its musical and choreographic tribute onto the Delphic site selected by Hieron to raise a golden tripodic monument next to that of Gelon in commemoration of and thanksgiving for a military victory,[24] the chorus members – perhaps even in linear formation and decked out in rich ornaments while, Apollo-like, stepping high – represent in animated form those precious, tall-standing and enduring dedications permanently displayed before the Apolline temple; indeed, supposing that the Syracusan choreutes performed before the sixth-century temple of Apollo in their native city, a typical venue for the staging of such public spectacles, the correspondence between the moving, erect and radiant bodies of the dancers and the votives likewise funded by and celebratory of Bacchylides' *laudandus* would be closer still. This linear arrangement of tripods occurs elsewhere: at the cult site for the hero Ptoion adjacent to Akraiphia in Boeotia, the tripods were, unusually, not set up at the perimeter of the temple, but aligned the length of the avenue leading to the sanctuary, while Plato's Socrates refers to the tripods of Nikias and his brothers 'standing in a row' (ἐφεξῆς ἑστῶτές) in the Dionysion' (*Gorg.* 472a6–7; see too Chapter 3 for the adverb in an explicitly choral context).

Returning to the Iliadic forge, the very term chosen by the poet for the wheels that Hephaestus' tripods possess is significant in itself. Much more common than the plural κύκλα found in this passage is the singular κύκλος,

---

[23] Brown 1989, 8. Cf. Σ BPQV *ad Od.* 8.265: '*marmarugê* denotes the emission of light and the sort of brilliance that derives from intense movement'. Very similar vocabulary returns in Plato's description of the 'dance of the stars' at *Tim.* 68a and of the viewer's response to it, with discussion in Nightingale 2018.

[24] For this coalescence between Delphi and Syracuse, see further Chapter 6.

the noun regularly used to describe a ring or circle, a meaning then instantly actualized in the 'circuit' completed by the tripods as they depart from Hephaestus' home only to return again (αὖτις πρὸς δῶμα νεοίατο, 377). As I detail in Section 3, linearity – the formation in which Hephaestus intends his vessels first to stand – and circularity are the defining configur-ations of the phenomena depicted on the rounded surface of the shield as well as the two principal structures in which both the metal-forged youths and maidens on its penultimate band and archaic and classical choruses dance.[25] On this score too, the tripods offer an early sounding of the language and motifs that find their most extended expression not just in the choral spectacle on the shield, but in the entire make-up, verbal, factural and poetic, of this final artefact: respecting the god's larger design, in which bands depicting Okeanos bracket all the other scenes, the exegesis of the shield's contents takes the form of a ring composition whose circularity the tripods' corresponding movements first intimate.[26]

While the subsequent chapter documents many additional intersections between the highly worked tripods of the archaic age and choral dance and song, here I move on to the closing of this preliminary portion of Thetis' visit and to the individual, Hephaestus' wife Charis, whom Homer now brings onto the scene. Charis' presence and marital role give commentators pause; for the Odyssean poet, Aphrodite is spouse to the god, and that second partnership figures much more commonly in later texts. But the larger thematics of an episode so centrally focused on the properties of intricately worked and alluring objects explain the apparent anomaly. As Willem Verdenius remarks, Charis personifies the charm of Hephaestus' metalwork,[27] the brilliance that also here adheres to the goddess' 'sleek-shining veil' (the Homeric hapax λιπαροκρήδεμνος, 382). Hesiod's account, which calls the god's wife by the name that belongs to one of the three Graces, Aglaïa (Th. 945), resembles the *Iliad*'s insofar as it too pairs Hephaestus with an instantiation of a prime quality of the goods fashioned by the craftsman. Both designations point to what is perhaps the most fundamental property of any work of art that models itself after the divine

---

[25] For a much later, and particularly elaborate, description of a chorus that alternates between circular and linear motions, see Stat. *Achill.* 1.827–34 with its clear description of how the dancers sometimes face off in straight lines (*obvia versae*) and then spin about in a ring (*orbe*). They also seem to perform more circuitous or serpentine motions as they 'wind about'.

[26] Largely beyond the scope of this chapter is the theme treated by so many discussions of the shield: the intimate relations between Hephaestus' manufactured object and the poet's own 'poietic' composition.

[27] Verdenius 1987, 104, cited by Day 2010, 256 with additional material. Edwards 1991 *ad* 382 notes *Od.* 6.234, where Hephaestus' products are styled χαρίεντα ἔργα.

prototypes: as countless descriptions attest, objects crafted by the supremely skilled artist, metalworker or image-maker are radiant, endowed with that sheen, brilliance and play of shifting, rapidly moving light that Aglaïa and terms cognate with her name signal.[28]

2 Hephaestus' Golden Automata

After informing his wife of the origins of the debt that he owes to Thetis, Hephaestus then puts his work aside before moving to the door, now with a retinue attending him in his halting and belaboured passage. In the lines describing the limping god accompanied by what turn out to be fresh products of his craftsmanship, the poet presents a second 'incipient'[29] or proto-choral group, and again invites us to assimilate dancing bodies and metallic objects. And while the tripods were invested with properties that broadly distinguish choreutes, regardless of their age or gender, the golden automata present a more specifically *maiden* chorus, characterized by the attributes that, as later chapters additionally spell out, poets and artists regularly associate with parthenaic ensembles. As the discussion of this portion of the larger episode also illustrates, the relations that Homer constructs between this second set of artefacts and their divine maker anticipate later accounts of the hierarchies and relations structuring a choral group.

But first the lines (410–21):

ἀνέστη   410
χωλεύων· ὑπὸ δὲ κνῆμαι ῥώοντο ἀραιαί.
φύσας μέν ῥ' ἀπάνευθε τίθει πυρός, ὅπλά τε πάντα
λάρνακ' ἐς ἀργυρέην συλλέξατο, τοῖς ἐπονεῖτο·
σπόγγῳ δ' ἀμφὶ πρόσωπα καὶ ἄμφω χεῖρ' ἀπομόργνυ
αὐχένα τε στιβαρὸν καὶ στήθεα λαχνήεντα,   415
δῦ δὲ χιτῶν', ἕλε δὲ σκῆπτρον παχύ, βῆ δὲ θύραζε
χωλεύων· ὑπὸ δ' ἀμφίπολοι ῥώοντο ἄνακτι
χρύσειαι, ζωῇσι νεήνισιν εἰοικυῖαι.
τῇς ἐν μὲν νόος ἐστὶ μετὰ φρεσίν, ἐν δὲ καὶ αὐδὴ
καὶ σθένος, ἀθανάτων δὲ θεῶν ἄπο ἔργα ἴσασιν.   420
αἳ μὲν ὕπαιθα ἄνακτος ἐποίπνυον·

---

[28] *aglaïa* also frequently describes brilliance in the context of the dance (e.g. Pind. *Pyth.* 1.2, frr. 75.7, 148, 199 S.-M.). For further discussion, see Mullen 1982, 61, 82–86, 222. See too Ar. *Ran.* 335–36.
[29] I borrow the term from Power 2011, 75.

limping, he stood up; but his slender limbs moved beneath him. He set the
bellows away from the fire, and gathered all the tools with which he
laboured in a silver chest. Then with a sponge he wiped his face and
both hands and mighty neck and shaggy chest, and put on a tunic, and
took up a thick stick and went limping to the doorway. And in support of
their master moved his maidservants, golden and in appearance like to
living young girls. There is intelligence in their wits, and there is speech
and strength in them, and from the immortal gods they know tasks/deeds.
They bustled about in support of their master.

Just as in the earlier passage, but at greater length, the poet begins by
flagging the contrast between those endowed with the power of rapid,
fluid and synchronized motion and the crippled smith, a difference made
emphatic by the reuse of the same verb, ῥώοντο (411, 417) in the identical
metrical position in the lines. For all that Hephaestus and the maids
perform the same action, the repetition draws attention to the disparity
in the movements described: where Hephaestus' 'narrow shanks', themselves the locus of his limbs' weakness, form a piece with χωλεύων in the
verse-initial position, the handmaidens who appear immediately after are
unimpeded in their passage and, indeed, have motion to spare: they 'bustle
about', ἐποίπνυον, at the close of the account (see below for more on the
term). The contrast between uninterrupted and regular movements and
the god's own hobbled gait also includes a glance back to the tripods. In the
visualization of the stick-equipped Hephaestus, the poet portrays him
moving on the same 'three legs' (in the Hesiodic account at *Erg.* 533,
τρίπους explicitly refers to an aged man walking with a stick) that were
the defining features and eponyms of the earlier objects. But where the
tripods' wheels guaranteed those products an even, cohesive and even
continual mobility, Hephaestus' three legs do the precise opposite.

There is more to the use of ῥώοντο in reference to the golden girls.
Elsewhere in the *Iliad*, the verb describes a second company of maidens, the
nymphs who 'move nimbly' around the river Achelous (24.616).[30] The poet
most likely intends his audience to understand the deities as engaged in
dancing, performing their signature activity at the sites they so regularly
frequent. In the *HHVen.* 261, Aphrodite portrays these same mountain-
dwelling nymphs unequivocally as choral dancers, maidens who 'move in
the lovely dance with the immortals' (καλὸν χορὸν ἐρρώσαντο). Hesiod
anticipates that usage, selecting the verb, here in compound form, for the

[30] Much like the fast-moving maids in Hephaestus' forge, the nymphs in book 24 appear
juxtaposed with a figure whose want of mobility their contrasting action underscores; in the
very next line, the poet depicts the eternally mourning Niobe petrified by grief (617).

archetypal dancing Muses of the *Theogony* proem (8), where it comes qualified by the detail so commonplace in accounts of choral dancers: these maidens 'move rapidly with their feet' (ἐπερρώσαντο δὲ ποσσίν).[31]

Used in conjunction with ῥώοντο in the Iliadic scene, the preposition ὑπό invites us to imagine that the automata actually support or even carry the debilitated god, and this is the meaning that commentators typically assign the phrase. The picture strikingly resembles the scenario presented in a seventh-century citharodic proem, explored in much greater detail in Chapter 3, where a maiden chorus again occupies centre stage; in the view of one Hellenistic reader at least, Alcman's fr. 26 *PMGF* would (unwittingly) redescribe exactly the arrangement that the Iliadic poet suggests, this in an image designed to express the limb-weakened *chorêgos'* desire to overcome his debility so as to move together with his parthenaic chorus. Cited here are the lines preceded by Antigonus Carystus' later gloss:[32]

> τῶν δὲ ἀλκυόνων οἱ ἄρσενες κηρύλοι καλοῦνται· ὅταν οὖν ὑπὸ τοῦ γήρως ἀσθενήσωσιν καὶ μηκέτι δύνωνται πέτεσθαι, φέρουσιν αὐτοὺς αἱ θήλειαι ἐπὶ τῶν πτερῶν λαβοῦσαι. καὶ ἔστι τὸ ὑπὸ τοῦ Ἀλκμᾶνος λεγόμενον τούτῳ συνῳκειωμένον· φησὶν γὰρ ἀσθενὴς ὢν διὰ τὸ γῆρας καὶ τοῖς χοροῖς οὐ δυνάμενος συμπεριφέρεσθαι οὐδὲ τῇ τῶν παρθένων ὀρχήσει·
>
> οὔ μ' ἔτι, παρσενικαὶ μελιγάρυες ἱαρόφωνοι,
> γυῖα φέρην δύναται· βάλε δὴ βάλε κηρύλος εἴην,
> ὅς τ' ἐπὶ κύματος ἄνθος ἅμ' ἀλκυόνεσσι ποτήται
> νηδεὲς ἦτορ ἔχων, ἁλιπόρφυρος ἱαρὸς ὄρνις.

Male halcyons are called ceryli. When they become weak from old age and are no longer able to fly, the females carry them, taking them on their wings. What Alcman says is connected with this: weak from old age and unable to whirl about with the choruses and the girls' dancing, he says:

No longer, honey-toned, strong-voiced [or 'holy-voiced'] girls, can my limbs carry me. If only, if only I were a cerylus, who flies along with the halcyons over the flower of the wave with resolute heart, strong [or 'holy'], sea-blue bird.

---

[31] That the motion of the Hesiodic goddesses takes the form of a dance an earlier line confirms; when we first glimpse the Muses, they are 'dancing around the violet spring on tender feet' (περὶ κρήνην ἰοειδέα πόσσ' ἁπαλοῖσιν / ὀρχεῦνται, 3–4).

[32] As Power 2010, 202–03 n. 43 comments, the topos of the speaker's weakened legs 'must thematize the fact that the citharist typically moves less actively than the choral dancers he accompanies', precisely the contrast that Homer's juxtaposition of the automata and Hephaestus more explicitly articulates.

Even if we concur (as I think we should) with the many recent readers who have questioned Antigonus' equation of the ornithological marvel with Alcman's lines and observe that nothing in the text suggests anything more than the speaker's wish to join the company of the 'halcyons', that is, to gain admission to the maidens' dance, this rather less vivid representation still stands in close relation to the Homeric account: in both scenes, young girls figured as dancers appear in company with an older man whose mobility is impaired, and in both the ensemble supplies an escort for the enfeebled individual. The preposition used by Homer at 417 allows this 'weaker' reading too; while most readers see in ὑπό a reference to actual physical support or 'propping up', the term can also refer to the act of accompaniment, musical on occasion, or, of equal relevance to my suggestion that Homer positions Hephaestus as *chorêgos* to his golden girls, to relations of subordination or dependence. Viewed this way, the phrase would describe how the handmaidens escort Hephaestus or are obedient to his lead,[33] much as parthenaic choruses perform under the direction of the individual musician/poet/chorus-leader orchestrating their song and motions. Indeed, the very capacity to move made emphatic in lines 417 and 421 of the Iliadic representation proves a direct result of the 'quickening' properties given the girls by the god, and signals their dependence on their fashioner: without the σθένος that Hephaestus grants them, these automata would remain static.

Consistent with this representation of Hephaestus not just as *chorêgos*, but as the craftsman who endows his products with vivifying motion is a passage from the later lyric corpus, significantly located at the very outset of Pindar's *Nemean 5*. Here the poetic ego begins by declaring himself 'no sculptor so as to fashion *agalmata* standing idling on their very base' (οὐκ ἀνδριαντοποιός εἰμ᾽, ὥστ᾽ ἐλινύσοντα ἐργάζεσθαι ἀγάλματ᾽ ἐπ᾽ αὐτᾶς βαθμίδος / ἑσταότ᾽, 1–2) and goes on to contrast these inert figures with his travelling, sounding song.[34] While the conceit allows the poet to promote the powers of his medium over those of the maker of the victory images that were the second chief (and, as Pindar initially construes them here, rival) means for celebrating and memorializing athletic triumphs, it also gestures towards Pindar in his role as *chorêgos* who sets the still stationary choral bodies in motion (so ἑσταότ᾽ in emphatic verse-initial position at line 2; the verb ἐλινύω can also specifically describe cessation or rest from movement). Only by virtue of the chorus-leader's preliminary

---

[33] Edwards 1991 *ad* 420–22 notes that among the possible meanings for the prepositional expression would be 'under his commands'.

[34] Cf. *Isthm.* 2.45–46, again with the 'artisanal' verb ἐργάζομαι.

'quickening' intervention can the choreutes supply the subsequent performance. Insofar as he animates his 'statuesque' performers mounted on their bases, the initiator of the song-dance takes on the role played elsewhere by Hephaestus and his legendary double Daedalus, to whom sources from the fifth century on ascribe the power to endow their images with movement (they can also speak), and more specifically to get down from their pedestals and walk about.[35]

But time now to turn to the other properties granted by Hephaestus to the serving girls, and that, along with their motion-giving σθένος, transform these metallic bodies into sentient beings. While far from exclusive to the choral paradigm, the faculties that the Homeric narrator lists are fully consistent with the typology used for maiden dancing groups. Most obvious, of course, is the servants' parthenaic status as flagged by νεήνισιν (418), and their evident collective identity, another defining feature of the morphology of the archaic chorus.[36] Also singled out for mention by the Homeric poet is the gold used to fashion the automata. This not only recalls the golden wheeled tripods, a similarly undifferentiated aggregate, but simultaneously gives the serving girls the metallic preciosity, sparkle and radiance so typical of choral performers, and of maidenly ones in spades; so the hair of Hagesichora, the *chorêgos* of Alcman's first *Partheneion*, 'blooms with gold' (53–54) and the same metal reappears in the snake-like bracelets worn by the young girls in her charge (66–67); the feature recurs in the poet's third parthenaic song, where Astymelousa, the chorus leader here, resembles a branch of gold (fr. 3.68 *PMGF*). Significant too is the sequence of properties assigned to these handmaidens, first their age status, then the gold used to fashion them, and positioned immediately after these, their strength and powers of articulation: as the next chapter explores, metallic voices exist in close combination with parthenaic ensembles and typically belong to the paradigmatic choruses on whom real-world dancer-singers model themselves.

While the 'voice and strength' doublet that the poet includes first and foremost signals the fact of vivification (cf. Hes. *Erg.* 61–62),[37] and together with the line that follows – the maids 'know *erga* from the immortal gods' (420; cf. Hes. *Erg.* 64) – equates these automata with other divine creations

---

[35] For examples, see Steiner 2001, 139.   [36] Calame 1997, 30–33 discusses choral 'collectivity'.

[37] Hephaestus endows others of his creations with the property of voice, most obviously at Hes. *Th.* 584, where the beasts adorning Pandora's diadem are 'like to living animals with voices'. For the overlaps between these and the Homeric automata, and additional examples of Hephaestus' animated products (although none apart from Pandora and the animals on her crown have voices), see Faraone 1992, 18–22 and 101.

whom the gods endow with the capacities of sentient beings, the phrase that closes the description at 421 might nuance an audience's understanding of the particular properties given the girls. Where the ὑπό of the account's start specified the manner in which the maidservants moved in relation to Hephaestus, when the preposition, here in the expanded form ὕπαιθα (421), returns at the passage's close, it belongs to a different action, and one that looks less to motion than to speech. Regularly translated 'bustling about' (the verb is also used of Hephaestus at *Il.* 1.600), ποιπνύω is formed by reduplication from the root of πνέω, and is cognate with πέπνυμαι, which properly indicates the intake of breath by the speaker or singer before beginning an address or performance.[38] Although it is Hesiod, not Homer, who famously establishes the particular relation between the act of 'in-spiration' and the performance of poetry, this when he recalls how the Muses first 'breathed divine song into him' (ἐνέπνευσαν ... αὐδήν, *Th.* 31–32), the Iliadic poet's choice of verb similarly suggests that the maidens not only dance under the direction of their lordly *chorêgos*, but that, by virtue of the αὐδή he has granted them, they also give 'support' in the form of vocal accompaniment.

If we understand the phrase at 421 as a pointer to the automata's powers of articulation, and even of song, then the detail concerning the kind of voice they possess is very well suited to this characterization. As noted above, the doublet 'strength and voice' may simply be a formulaic phrase deployed in object-vivification scenes. But, as scholars have observed,[39] and as the line from the *Theogony* just cited exemplifies, epic diction reserves *audê* for a distinctive type of voice or speech. Used by the gods only when they seek to communicate with men, it is the means by which the gap between the divine and human realms, each with its own language and forms of vocalization, can be bridged. It is because the term occupies this intermediate status that *audê* also describes the voice that divinities give to mortal bards, and, as we will see, to choral collectives too. Even as the Hesiodic singer has *audê* breathed into him, so both Phemius and Demodocus are (in a formulation used of these two alone in Homer) 'like gods with respect to their *audê*' (*Od.* 1.371, 9.4).

Also cohering with these other suggestions that the golden girls can sing is their capacity to 'know the deeds of the gods'. Again, this formulaic phrase is very much at home in animation episodes, and perhaps signifies nothing more than that these fabrications, well versed in their household

---

[38] See the detailed discussion in Clarke 1999, 84–86.
[39] See particularly Clay 1974, Ford 1992, 177–79, Collins 1999, Goslin 2010, 356.

duties, can fulfill their allotted tasks (cf. *Il.* 9.128). But ἔργα in Homeric diction has a broader referential range, and encompasses not just domestic chores, but 'deeds' performed in war or other enterprises, and 'works' of any kind. In combination with the verb and preposition here, the expression can also indicate that the golden girls know deeds that are derived from, or whose source or origin is the gods.[40] This type of knowledge belongs to another parthenaic collective, whom the Homeric poet famously invokes in book 2 for its all-knowingness; so, in his address to the Muses at the start of the Catalogue of Ships, he declares that by virtue of their omnipresence, the divinities 'know everything' (ὑμεῖς γὰρ θεαί ἐστε, πάρεστέ, τε ἴστέ τε πάντα, 485). The Muses' pan-cognizance and ability to transmit to men knowledge of the doings of the divinities as well as those of mortals also forms a motif that punctuates the prelude of Hesiod's *Theogony* (see 25, 26, 101, 105, 114), likewise making an appearance in the paradigmatic Olympian choral scene in the *Homeric Hymn to Apollo*, where the chorus of Muses sings of the 'gifts of the gods' (190). Although none of these passages expresses the idea of the goddesses' knowledge in the diction used of the golden girls at *Il.* 18.420, a phrase at *Od.* 1.338 comes very close to the formulation here: when Penelope urges the bard Phemius to change his song, she remarks, 'since you know many other deeds of mortals and of gods (οἶδας / ἔργ' ἀνδρῶν τε θεῶν τε), which are a source of enchantment, and which singers celebrate, sing one of these' (337–39). The formulaic epithet 'divine' given Phemius at 336 succinctly declares the source of the bard's cognitive expertise; this is epic's shorthand way of saying that he has received his song from the Muses. Read against these templates, might the golden girls who accompany Hephaestus in his 'poietic' labours likewise be celebrants and memorialists of the doings of (and here the products crafted by) divinities?[41]

   The fact that these artefacts are 'envoiced' not only forms part of the progression that the poet traces out – where the tripods could only move and maybe hear,[42] the golden girls have powers of articulation as well – but adds another piece to the ongoing imbrication of *chorêgos* and craftsman. As several passages in Pindar make clear, the choristers' ability to vocalize, no less than their capacity to move, directly depends on the presence of

---

[40] Indeed, Power 2011, 77 translates the phrase in just the way I am proposing: 'they know the deeds of the immortal gods'.

[41] Frontisi-Ducroux 2002 offers a very suggestive discussion of the parallels between Hephaestus' characterization and the powers deployed by the Homeric poet.

[42] The next chapter will, however, suggest that cauldrons are also phenomena that can speak and sing.

their leader. Nowhere is this more apparent than at the opening of *Nemean* 3, where the speaker enjoins the Muse to come to the aid of the still silent, and static too (so μένω, a verb which regularly describes 'standing still' or 'fixedly'; cf. Aesch. *Ag.* 854) youths who will perform the ode: 'for by the water of Asopos are waiting (μένοντ') the builders of honey-sounding revels, young men who desire your voice' (3–5). In the event it is not the Muse, but Pindar who supplies the necessary vocal impetus; arriving with the hymn, he proposes to 'impart it to the voices [or 'discourse']' of the members of the silent *kômos* (κείνων τέ νιν ὀάροις . . . κοινάσομαι, 11–12), allowing them to realize their own tectonic powers as they go on to build the celebratory song and dance.

A second Pindaric work likewise combines the several strands visible in the Homeric account of the automata, offering its own version of how a divine craftsman grants golden objects that form an explicitly choral collective a voice that allows for the articulation and channelling of divine knowledge. In a version of events that may owe as much to the poet's invention as to his elaboration of a pre-existing but no longer extant tale, Pindar describes the third temple of Apollo that Athena and Hephaestus built at Delphi, a metallic structure fashioned out of bronze and topped by acroteria-like golden figures.[43] While the text is lacunose, enough remains of the third and fourth triads (?) of *Paean* 8 (fr. 52i.65–90 S.-M.= B2 102–27 Rutherford) to discern the nature of the building and its adornments. Appealing to the Muses to furnish a description of this *ergon*, the poet then goes on to transmit the contents of the goddesses' response:

το<ῦ> δὲ παντέχ[νοις   65
Ἁφαίστου παλάμαις καὶ Ἀθά[νας
τίς ὁ ῥυθμὸς ἐφαίνετο;
χάλκεοι μὲν τοῖχοι χάλκ[εαί
   θ' ὑπὸ κίονες ἔστασαν,
χρύσεαι δ' ἒξ ὑπὲρ αἰετοῦ   70
ἄειδον Κηληδόνες.
ἀλλά μιν Κρόνου παῖ[δες
κεραυνῷ χθόν' ἀνοιξάμ[ε]νọ[ι
ἔκρυψαν τὸ [π]άντων ἔργων ἱερώτ[ατον

γλυκείας ὀπὸς ἀγασ[θ]έντες,   75
ὅτι ξένοι ἔφ[θ]<ι>νον
ἄτερθεν τεκέων

---

[43] I return to this passage in Chapter 3 and several later portions of the study. For detailed discussion, and consideration of possible antecedents or parallels, see Rutherford 2001, 210–32.

ἀλόχων τε μελ[ί]φρονι
αὐδ[ᾷ θυμὸν ἀνακρίμναντες· επε[
λυσίμβροτον παρθενίᾳ κε̣[80
ἀκηράτων δαίδαλμα [
ἐ̣νέθηκε δὲ Παλλὰς ἀμ[
φωνᾷ τά τ' ἐόντα τε κα[ὶ
πρόσθεν γεγενημένα
        . . . . . .]ται Μναμοσύνᾳ[85
⌣.]παντα σφιν ἔφρα[σ.ν

⌣]ᾳ̣ιον δόλον ἀπνευ[−⌣
⌣−]. γὰρ ἐπῆν πόνος
⌣−−]. ἀρετα[   ]
⌣⌣−] καθαρὸν δ[.].[90

But what, o Muses, was the *rhythmos* that the temple showed forth
through the all-skilled hands of Hephaestus and Athena? Bronze were
the walls, bronze pillars stood beneath, and six Golden Charmers sang
above the gable. But the sons of Cronus opened the ground with
a thunderbolt and hid it, the most sacred of all works . . .

. . . astonished at the sweet voice, that foreigners wasted away apart from
children and wives, hanging up their spirits as a dedication to the voice
that is like honey to the mind, the man-releasing/destroying contrivance
of pure (words?) in the maiden's . . . and Pallas put in . . . to the voice and
Mnemosyne (and the Muses?) told them everything that is and was
before . . . (making) breathless a cunning contrivance (of old) for toil
was incumbent . . . excellence . . . pure

Commentators both ancient and modern highlight the Siren-like nature of
these gold-fashioned singers,[44] and several early readers invested the
Charmers with the wings typical of representations of the Sirens from the
sixth century on. But, as Power notes in passing, there are also marked
affinities with Hephaestus' serving girls in *Iliad* 18.[45] Assuming that the
adjective παρθενίᾳ in line 80 describes some feature of the Keledones, then
they are maidens too, and have been given the same *audê* as their Homeric
antecedents.[46] Also in keeping with the paradigm that Hephaestus' other
vivified artefacts supply – although Athena, not the craftsman god, serves
as the chief agent here – the singers' powers of articulation seem (the text is

---

[44] See, already, Paus. 10.12 and Philostr. *VA* 6.11 for the parallel.   [45] Power 2011, 77.
[46] Pindar uses two other terms, each with its own valence, of the Keledones' vocalizations,
    a seeming redundancy that aims both to capture the hybridity of these creatures, Muses and
    monsters, human, bestial and divine, images and living things, and to underscore what is most
    remarkable about them.

uncertain at this point) to have been 'put into' (ἐνέθηκε) them. The source of their Muse-like knowledge is, again, the gods, the instructors, I suggested, of Hephaestus' golden maids: 'Mnemosyne (and the Muses?) told them everything that is and was before'. Although the papyrus becomes too fragmentary at this point for any sure reconstruction, also intriguing is the reference to 'breathlessness' (ἀπνευ[-) at 87. If the term does apply to the Keledones and describes their condition following the withdrawal of their singing powers that occurs on the temple's destruction, then they lose that capacity for 'in-spiration' that Hephaestus' 'bustling/breathing' attendants lastingly retain.

3   The Dancers on the Shield

Before turning to the creation of the third and final object that will emerge from Hephaestus' foundry, the shield, the poet pauses to detail the bellows used to heat the fire in which the metal will be forged (468–73):

> βῆ δ' ἐπὶ φύσας·
> τὰς δ' ἐς πῦρ ἔτρεψε κέλευσέ τε ἐργάζεσθαι.
> φῦσαι δ' ἐν χοάνοισιν ἐείκοσι πᾶσαι ἐφύσων   470
> παντοίην εὔπρηστον ἀϋτμὴν ἐξανιεῖσαι,
> ἄλλοτε μὲν σπεύδοντι παρέμμεναι, ἄλλοτε δ' αὖτε,
> ὅππως Ἥφαιστός τ' ἐθέλοι καὶ ἔργον ἄνοιτο.

And then [Hephaestus] went to the bellows, which he turned towards the fire and gave them orders to work. And the bellows, all twenty of them, blew on the hollow melting places, sending forth their well-blowing breath this way and that, as he hurried to be in one place, and then in another, wherever Hephaestus might wish them to blow, and the work might be completed.

This depiction of these implements essential to the metalworker neatly recapitulates properties of both the tripods and the golden girls. The bellows number twenty like the vessels first introduced, and are apparently self-moving too; there is no clear demarcation of subject and agent here, and once the god has 'turned' the tools in the direction he desires, they seem to perform their other tasks without his intervention, following their master in his passage from place to place as the automata did. Also reminiscent of the serving maids, the bellows act as collective helpers to the god; their task is to 'work', ἐργάζεσθαι, at his behest and to match their movements to his.

Featured here too, as it was in the account of the maidens, is the tools' possession of a property that demarcates living beings, and that is not only the stuff of life, but, as proposed above in my reading of ἐποίπνυον, permits the production of sound and voice. 'Breath', here underscored by the addition of the adjective εὔπρηστον modifying ἀϋτμή and which gives the action an almost aesthetic cast, is what Achilles retains until the moment of his death (so *Il.* 9.609), while the verb used of the bellows' exhalations, ἐξανίημι, offers a compound of the verb repeatedly chosen by Hesiod for the Muses' performance of their song in the *Theogony* prelude (e.g. 10, 42, 65). The relationship between Hephaestus and the moving, blowing bellows has a further choral resonance; by virtue of the lead supplied by their divine *chorêgos*, whose own regularized side to side passage the equally balanced phrase ἄλλοτε μὲν ... ἄλλοτε δ' conveys, the tools acquire the requisite synchronicity even as their emissions retain the 'manifoldness' or multiplicity (παντοίην, 471) that Pindar regards as a prime quality of the best music and song.[47]

The images on the shield that emerge from the conjunction of the bellows and their overseer present the site where chorality most unmistakably declares itself as an epiphenomenon of craftsmanship. Even before the extended description of the performance on the object's penultimate band, choruses and dance motions executed by a heterogeneous cast of characters and objects occur in the other tableaux devised by Hephaestus, keeping the motif before the audience's eyes. This choral note is struck at the very outset as the god fashions on the first of the rings the heavens festooned with stars, among which the poet names the sun, moon, Arctos (the Bear), Orion, and the Pleiades and Hyades.[48] As noted in the introductory chapter, Ferrari and Csapo have detailed the motif of what Plato would style the 'dances of the stars' (*Tim.* 40c2–3), and have traced the intimate relations between astral groups and maiden dancers (a theme this study also takes up in Chapters 4 and 6); as they demonstrate, both visual and textual accounts present heavenly bodies as models for earthly parthenaic choruses,[49] and among such paradigms, the several fashioned by the divine

---

[47] E.g. *Pyth.* 12.19 and 23, *Nem.* 5.25; also common in Pindar is the notion of the breath of music or song, for which see, *inter alia*, *Nem.* 3.79. To press the analogy further, it is almost as if these windy emanations provide the soundtrack that accompanies the making of the shield. For the affinity of the bellows to the flute, see this chapter's final discussion.

[48] 'He made ... on it all the constellations that wreathe the heavens, the Pleiades and the Hyades and the strength (σθένος) of Orion and the Bear, to whom men give also the name the Wagon, who turns about in a fixed place and observes Orion' (483–88). My understanding of this and subsequent passages has been much enhanced by the discussion of Carruesco 2016.

[49] See the Introduction together with Ferrari 2008 and Csapo 2008; see too Miller 1986, 55–99.

craftsman on the shield occupy pride of place. Not only do the sun and moon regularly take the form of those who lead the company of other stars in their choral round, but each of the subsequent constellations cited by the Homeric narrator is similarly implicated in this celestial dance. As Ferrari shows, later sources privilege the Pleiades and Hyades in their accounts of dancing maidens-turned-stars on whom mortal parthenaic groups project their choral identity,[50] a motif made explicit in the reference to the 'heavenly choruses (χοροί), Pleiades, Hyades' in a song sung by a maiden chorus at Eur. *El.* 467–68, while Orion is the hunter whose endless pursuit of the Pleiades prompts their metamorphosis into starry form. The aetiology of the Bear recapitulates these maidens' trajectory. Pursued by her son Arcas (who himself becomes a star), this one-time nymph, formerly designated Callisto, who dances among her fellow *parthenoi* in choruses of Artemis, again escapes by means of catasterism.[51] Also indicative of the connections between this opening shield panel and the dancing group pictured on the fifth of the rings is the reprise of the language used for the balletic constellations in the visualization of the choral performers; even as the stars 'crown' (ἐστεφάνωται, 485) the sky, so the maidens in their choruses are decked out in their more microcosmic diadems (στεφάνας, 597).[52]

A second overlap depends on the emphasis both tableaux include on circular motion, one among the repeated links between the scenes placed on the shield's surface and its own rounded shape centred about an oceanic ring that, as suggested above, is both factural and poetic. This circularity first occurs in Homer's account of the Bear as she 'turns about in a fixed place' (ἥ τ' αὐτοῦ στρέφεται, 488), enacting a cyclical motion that later theorists of *choreia* would equate with the sequence of strophe and antistrophe executed by choral dancers, and whose turns and counterturns

---

[50] For the relevant sources, see Ferrari 2008, 2–3 and 89–91.

[51] Ferrari 2002, 172–73 argues for the link between this and the dance, perhaps in imitation of a bear, performed by young girls at the sanctuary of Artemis Brauronia. Striking too for its choral implications is the poet's careful demarcation of two types of motion, apparent in the way in which he differentiates the gyrations of the Bear from those of the other constellations; in Plato's later account of the 'dances of the stars' in the *Timaeus* and *Laws*, he similarly singles out circular rotation about a fixed point (this, in a patently artisanal image, likened to 'circular things turned on a lathe' at *Leg.* 898a4–5, 898b1–2) as the most perfect form of movement.

[52] These adornments might even be imagined in the form of the headdress styled *kalathiskos* so commonly worn by dancers in vase paintings from the archaic period on, and which takes the form of a broad band encircling the wearer's head with thin spikes radiating from it; again, I follow Ferrari 2008, 135–50 in viewing this crown as the rayed halo or starry nimbus that assimilates the mortal dancer to the astral bodies (shown by painters in personified form with the same crowns about their heads) performing their choreographic figures in the sky. For a much later instance of this 'crown' in conjunction with a star chorus, see *AP* 9.270.

were themselves aligned with the movements of the planets.[53] The verb στρέφω not only appears in Attic drama for the movements of one such chorus (Pl. Com. fr. 99 K.-A.; cf. Soph. *Trach.* 220), but further suggests the site occupied by the star vis-à-vis the other constellations in what we might, following Pindar's *Paean* 8, call the shield's overall ῥυθμός, its patterned-cum-choreographed design. Nicander's *Alexipharmaka* calls the same Bear 'bossed' or '*omphalos*-like' (ὀμφαλόεσσαν, 7), an expression for which a scholion to the line supplies two possible explanations: Arctos is so called either because it is circumpolar or 'on account of the chorus of stars that surrounds it'. Positioned here, and in the 'gloss' that Nicander's epithet supplies for the Iliadic account, Arctos also resolves an anomaly in Hephaestus' construction: unlike the standard Homeric shield, this one alone seemingly lacks an *omphalos* or boss, a centrepoint that supports the other elements.[54] The later scene of *choreia* will present a very similar arrangement, motion around a single fixed point.

A more earthly chorus follows shortly on, in the context of the wedding celebration moving through the city streets on the shield's next to be described ring. To the sound of the bridal *hymenaios*, a song that is just the first among the many contemporary choral genres sampled in the ecphrasis, a chorus of youths re-enacts the motions of the heavenly bodies; as the performers engage in similarly eddying movements (ἐδίνεον, 494), now pipes and lyres additionally accompany their dance. A second choral motion, the linear, processional step of those who lead the brides (ἠγίνεον, 493), frames the turns as the dancers pass through the streets.[55] The response of the women watching the performance, who 'wonder' (θαύμαζον, 496) at the spectacle, recurs numerous times in subsequent accounts of choral spectatorship,[56] pinpointing that heightened sensation of awe and even reverence elicited by phenomena that partake of the divine (epiphanies similarly prompt *thauma*) and that works of virtuosic crafts-manship likewise generate.[57] Although displayed earlier in the sequence of rings, this wedding scene more properly presents the aftermath to the dance in the penultimate representation:[58] the adjective ἀλφεσίβοιαι (593) used of the maidens in the later panel, no less than their brilliant dress,

[53] Mullen 1982, 225–30 offers full documentation of this; see too Briand 2009, 100.
[54] See Buchan 2012, 73–74 for this missing boss.
[55] Cf. the more elaborated choral performance at [Hes.] *Sc.* 270–85, where the term *kômos* also appears for the first time.
[56] Among early examples, see *Od.* 8.265, *HHAp.* 156.
[57] E.g. Hes. *Th.* 581, the brooch of Odysseus (*Od.* 19.235), the shield tableaux (*Il.* 18.549) and the earlier noted wheels of Hephaestus' cauldrons.
[58] As observed by Lonsdale 1995, 274.

designates them objects of courtship who display themselves in their finery before the eyes of potential grooms. In an anticipation of the wedding celebration on the earlier-positioned band, these prenuptial choruses move in both lines and circles, spinning about and running towards each other 'in lines' or 'ranks' (ἐπὶ στίχας, 602).

Fresh conjunctions of lines and circles recur in the countryside, albeit here with 'dancers' of a very different kind. Figured on the field that the subsequent circle displays are ploughmen driving teams of oxen to and fro (earthly versions of that ever-circling Wagon of 487), their actions described in verses that include no less than three evocations of circular motion: 'circling their teams about as they drove in one direction and then the other' (ζεύγεα δινεύοντες ἐλάστρεον ἔνθα καὶ ἔνθα, 543), each ploughman receives a cup of wine as he reaches the furrow's end and then wheels about (στρέψαντες, στρέψασκον, 544, 546). The circuits of the oxen and their drivers result not merely from the logic of their 'boustrophedic' activity, but also from the material constraints imposed by the circular shield;[59] bumping up against the physical-cum-poetic boundary of the ring by which they are contained (lines 544 and 546 place the limit of the furrow in verse-final position, reflecting the movement of the composition as it must travel backwards to the next line's start), the labourers, like Arctos before them, are compelled to 'turn around in place'.

Read against later lyric poetry and performative traditions, this representation gains its own choral underpinnings and looks forward to the performers positioned on the penultimate band. In Pindar's *Pythian* 6, the chorus members begin by describing themselves as 'ploughing up again (ἀναπολίζομεν) the field of glancing-eyed Aphrodite and of the Graces' (1–3; cf. *Nem.* 6.32, 7.104), reconfiguring the agricultural task as a choral metaphor which equates the field with the dancing floor, the regular haunt of the Graces (e.g. *Pyth.* 12.26–27; for a more literal cultivated field turned *orchestra*, see Hdt. 1.66, with discussion in several later chapters). The action of the Pindaric singer-dancers turning over the ground time and again as they proceed towards a (metaphoric) sacred site – a treasure house of song – also draws attention to the dynamics of the ongoing performance and synchronizes its several stages into one set of repeated motions within a setting both imaginary and real. As this opening conceit goes on to suggest, much like the ploughman first traversing the field in linear fashion and then circling about in repeated boustrophedic turns, the choristers initially advance (προσοιχόμενοι, 4) in a processional formation towards the performance space; arriving there, they

[59] Buchan 2012, 81.

then will regroup in the circular structure required by the ring dance, turning first one way and then the other in the successive strophes and antistrophes (ἀναπολίζομεν nicely conveys both this linear incipience and the regular back-and-forth) in what seems a no less unending circuit than that imposed on the metallic labourers.

Both Homer's choice of subject matter and the Pindaric conceit might also carry, at least for later audiences, a more particularized choral charge, or perhaps remind them of a dance drawn from their festal practices. Although there is no determining whether the so-called *karpaia* performed in Northern Greece and detailed by Xenophon at *Anab.* 6.1.7–11 was already familiar in archaic times, nor how widespread such types of dances might have been, the historian's report closely dovetails with the Homeric scene.[60] As Xenophon presents the spectacle, one of the two participants 'puts down his weapons and starts to sow grain and drive a team, constantly turning this way and that (πυκνὰ δὲ στρεφόμενος)', while the other takes on the role of robber whom the ploughman must fight to prevent his oxen's theft; later in the performance, one of the dancers, now equipped with a shield, 'whirls about' (ἐδινεῖτο) prior to turning a somersault, weapon and all.

Closer in time to the composition of the *Iliad*, the coincidence of choral dancing and the agricultural activity chosen by Hephaestus for his representation supplies the subject for the painter of an Attic black-figure Siana cup of ca. 575–550 from Kamiros on Rhodes (Figs. 1.3, 1.4).[61] On its obverse the vessel shows a sacrifice and choral dance, while two men, one sowing and the other ploughing with his team of oxen, appear on the reverse side. Both scenes present activities that belong to the sphere of Demeter and that celebrate her

Fig. 1.3 Attic black-figure band cup, ca. 575–550 B.C.E. Side A. London, British Museum 1906.12–15.1. Photograph © The Trustees of The British Museum.

---

[60] Eckerman 2014 cites the dance in the context of his discussion of the ploughing image in *Pyth.* 6.
[61] London, British Museum 1906.12–15.1; *ABV* 90.7.

Fig. 1.4 Attic black-figure band cup, ca. 575–550 B.C.E. Side B. London, British Museum 1906.12–15.1. Photograph © The Trustees of The British Museum.

powers; the goddess is represented by the veiled figure seated at the far left-hand side of the choral performance and before whom five women and a boy dance towards an altar where a priestess stands holding a winnowing fan. On the other face, the men working the land are also doing the 'work of Demeter'. The first man whom the goddess had taught to plough was one Bouzyges, ancestor of the Athenian family of the Bouzygai, and every year members of this family performed a ploughing ceremony – the so-called triple 'sacred ploughings' – at the foot of the Acropolis, the rite perhaps commemorated on the cup.[62]

Since this event seems to have occurred around the time of the celebration of the Thesmophoria at Athens, scholars tend to associate the choral scene on the obverse of the vase with the exclusively female choruses that danced for Demeter and Kore at the agricultural festival, performances to which Aristophanes' *Thesmophoriazusai* directly refers in a seeming re-enactment on the stage (947–1000).[63] Particularly evocative of the deployment of the chorus on the Siana cup are lines 953–58, where the Aristophanic singers issue self-directed instructions as to how precisely

---

[62] For the cup and its significance, see Simon 1983, 20–21, Connelly 2007, 66, 81–82 and the discussion in *LIMC* s.v. 'Bouzyges'. In keeping with the great majority of images treated in this passage, the visual account postdates Homer by more than a century.

[63] For discussion, see Parker 2005, 280–82, who notes the problematic presence of the youth included in the chorus line; Ashmole 1946 identifies him as the *pais amphithalês* who figured on the third day of the festival. For women's choruses at the Thesmophoria, with passing reference to the vase, see too Budelmann and Power 2015, 279–80 and n. 81.

their dance should be performed, complete with both a mention of the linked hands included on the cup and the suggestion of haste joined with rhythmic motion no less evident in the visual account:

> ὅρμα χώρει, κοῦφα ποσίν, ἄγ᾽ εἰς κύκλον,
> χερὶ σύναπτε χεῖρα, ῥυθμὸν χορείας
> ὕπαγε πᾶσα. βαῖνε καρπαλίμοιν ποδοῖν. ἐπισκοπεῖν δὲ
> πανταχῇ κυκλοῦσαν ὄμμα χρὴ χοροῦ κατάστασιν.

> Get started, get moving, move lightly on your feet into a circle, join hand to hand, set the rhythm of the dance to motion, step it up with nimble feet. And our choral formation must turn an eye circlewise and look everywhere. (text and trans. Sommerstein modified)

If Athenian women dancing on behalf of Demeter Thesmophoros seem very remote from the world conjured up by Hephaestus' crafting skills on this portion of the shield, uniquely populated by male ploughmen and youths who will reap the harvest, then there are several interfaces with the scenes shown on the Siana cup. Not only is the Iliadic field expressly designated 'thrice ploughed',[64] suggesting that the oxen teams perform three circuits each, but the agricultural activity presented on the vessel's reverse stands in close relation to the constellations featured in the opening tableaux on the shield (this temporal conjunction also informs the shield's own seasonal or almanac-like design). In Hesiod's account of the synchronic relations between the movement of the stars and the sequence of tasks which he charges the canny farmer to perform, the dawn rising of the Pleiades (which occurs mid-May) signals the moment when he should cease from digging his vineyards so as to harvest his grain (*Erg.* 383–84, 571–73); the late June dawn rising of Orion indicates the point at which he must winnow the sown grain (597–600).

More conventional is the dance performed on the 'single path' (565) to the vineyard occupying a fresh area of the shield, and whose configuration, for all that it is placed on a circular surface, must be linear. To the music of the lyre-playing youth 'in their middle' (ἐν μέσσοισι, 569) youths and maidens (a pairing that anticipates the choral band) bearing baskets of grapes advance 'skipping with their feet' (ποσὶ σκαίροντες; cf. ἐπισταμένοισι πόδεσσι of line 599) as they whistle along with the kitharist's song (569–72).

---

[64] The epithet returns at *Od.* 5.127, here in reference to an event in which Demeter is directly implicated; for the term again, and a clear reprise of the Odyssean lines, see Hes. *Th.* 971. Particularly suggestive is Pind. *Nem.* 7.104, with a reference to triple ploughing in the ode's final epode; could we read the image as meta-poetic, a reference to the cessation of the turns and counterturns the dancers have been performing?

This representation not only rehearses the penultimate choral scene (there too Hephaestus' tableau distinguishes between the dancers and the individual who, in amongst the group, accompanies them, with music and song),[65] but, in its exactly medial position in the verbal account, serves as a bridge between the opening depiction of the starry heavens and the chorus at the close. While most commentators suppose that the youth singing the Linus song is performing a lament, according to several ancient sources, the mythical musician composed not *thrênoi*, but 'a cosmogony, the course of the sun and moon' (DL 1.4),[66] the two constellations forged at the outset by Hephaestus on the first of the shield bands (484). If the vineyard scene does glance back to that opening representation, then the troupe of grape-pickers re-enacts the celestial ballet that supplies the master paradigm. Intriguingly, both the diction and the larger portrayal of the cosmos in Stobaeus' extended 'citation' of Linus' song at 1.10.5, in a chapter titled 'On the origins and principles (*stoicheia*) of all things', reads almost like a commentary on the contents of several of the other panels on the Achillean shield. Here the poet of the composition declares the emergence of all things 'from the whole', describes the 'limits' (πείρατ'; cf. *Il.* 18.501) that both constrain and are transcended by these things, and observes that, in the end, 'deathless death hides all things … but what has already existed, with unfamiliar images and with figures/postures of shape (σχήμασι μορφῆς), will change direction, and vanish from the sight of all' (1.10.5.1–14).

In a turn to the pastoral domain, Hephaestus then crafts a seemingly peaceful bucolic scene of cattle being driven to pasture.[67] Accompanying the animals are four herdsmen forged in gold, their motion described with the verb στιχάομαι (ἐστιχόωντο, 577), a term reserved in Homeric diction for those drawn up in ranks or rows and/or advancing in regular formation. While the lions' attack that follows does not develop this pointer to the synchronized motion of the foursome, exactly such an arrangement recurs on the penultimate band where the dancers performing their runs are similarly arranged in ranks, ἐπὶ στίχας (602). As Calame's detailed treatment of the term demonstrates,[68] while the core meaning of *stichos* is that of an 'ordered line', it also appears in association with the processional

---

[65] For this, see n. 93. According to Athenaeus' account at 1.15b (cited in section 4), the performance here, with its division of song and dance, is a hyporcheme.

[66] A point for which I am much indebted to my student Caleb Simone, whose paper delivered at CAMWS detailed the evidence.

[67] For additional discussion of this band, see Chapter 4.

[68] Calame 1997, 39–40; see too Carruesco 2016.

movement of the chorus as the performers move towards their destination. The earliest instance describes the dancing-singing Muses descending from the Heliconian heights at Hes. *Th.* 10 (στεῖχον), and many later accounts of choral motion include both the noun and its verbal form (e.g. Xen. *Eph.* 1.2.3). Apollonius may have these choral associations in mind when he redeploys the verb in his account of how Orpheus' performance on the lyre causes the oak trees to accompany him (A.R. 1.28–30); responding to the lead of what the poet describes as the 'directions of his song and dance' (σήματα μολπῆς, cf. Pind. *Pyth.* 1.3), the trees move off in the wake of their musician/*chorêgos* in their ranked, processional arrangement (στιχόωσιν).[69]

On the Homeric shield, and very much in keeping with the combination of (choral) motions enacted in earlier panels, the herdsmen's rectilinear formation coincides with the circles described by the other figures in the scene; as the nine swift-/bright-footed dogs (κύνες πόδας ἀργοί), who at the outset of the account were 'following' (ἕποντο) just as the skipping grape-pickers did on the preceding band (572),[70] now move to attack the lions preying on the herd, they first advance and then, growing fearful, turn aside (ἀπετρωπῶντο), coming to a standstill (ἱστάμενοι) before resuming the sequence anew (585–86). These canine rushes and retreats again anticipate the scene soon to follow; just as the rows of choral dancers will switch off from their lines into circles, so the dogs first move in and out towards the midpoint supplied by the two lions ravening on their prey (note the two tumblers in the dancers' midst, and the larger group of spectators surrounding them). In the static pose the dogs then assume, they rehearse a series of movements and stances that, in later accounts, belongs to the lyric chorus as it performs strophe, antistrophe (turning about) and epode, in which the performers supposedly stood in place.[71]

Capping these multiple choruses – stars, youth and maiden dancers, ploughmen, cow-driving herdsmen and canines – is the performance on the penultimate ring (590–605):

> ἐν δὲ χορὸν ποίκιλλε περικλυτὸς ἀμφιγυήεις, 590
> τῷ ἴκελον οἷόν ποτ' ἐνὶ Κνωσῷ εὐρείῃ
> Δαίδαλος ἤσκησεν καλλιπλοκάμῳ Ἀριάδνῃ.
> ἔνθα μὲν ἠΐθεοι καὶ παρθένοι ἀλφεσίβοιαι
> ὠρχεῦντ', ἀλλήλων ἐπὶ καρπῷ χεῖρας ἔχοντες.

---

[69] Chapter 6 returns to the passage.
[70] For the verb in the context of the choristers following their leader, see Chapter 5.
[71] Mullen 1982 offers extensive discussion of this account, applying it to Pindar's triadic odes.

τῶν δ' αἳ μὲν λεπτὰς ὀθόνας ἔχον, οἳ δὲ χιτῶνας   595
εἴατ' ἐϋννήτους, ἦκα στίλβοντας ἐλαίῳ·
καί ῥ' αἳ μὲν καλὰς στεφάνας ἔχον, οἳ δὲ μαχαίρας
εἶχον χρυσείας ἐξ ἀργυρέων τελαμώνων.
οἳ δ' ὁτὲ μὲν θρέξασκον ἐπισταμένοισι πόδεσσι
ῥεῖα μάλ', ὡς ὅτε τις τροχὸν ἄρμενον ἐν παλάμῃσιν   600
ἑζόμενος κεραμεὺς πειρήσεται, αἴ κε θέῃσιν·
ἄλλοτε δ' αὖ θρέξασκον ἐπὶ στίχας ἀλλήλοισι.
πολλὸς δ' ἱμερόεντα χορὸν περιίσταθ' ὅμιλος
τερπόμενοι· δοιὼ δὲ κυβιστητῆρε κατ' αὐτοὺς
μολπῆς ἐξάρχοντες ἐδίνευον κατὰ μέσσους.   605

And on it the very famous one with crooked limbs was elaborately crafting a *choros*, like to the one that once in broad Knossos Daedalus fashioned for lovely locked Ariadne. And there the young men and girls who bring many oxen to their parents were dancing, having their hands upon one another's wrists. And of these, the girls had fine garments of delicate linen, and the youths had chitons that were well-spun and softly glistening with oil; and the girls had beautiful diadems and the youths had golden knives (hanging) from belts of silver. And at times they were running on well-skilled [or 'knowledgeable'] feet, very smoothly, as when a potter who is seated tests the wheel fitted to his hands, to see if it runs; and at others they were running in rows up to one another. And a great throng was standing about the desirous chorus taking delight. And two tumblers among them gave the lead to the song and dance and were whirling about in their midst.

Unmistakable in this account are the properties of dancers already signalled, their radiance and sheen made literal by the metal from which they, no less than the accessories that the poet details, are forged. Indeed, the verb which initiates the passage already encompasses this luminosity; in Françoise Frontisi-Ducroux's gloss, ποίκιλλε, used for the first and only time within the ecphrasis and unique to this penultimate act of craftsmanship (the blander terms *teuchô*, *poieô* and *tithêmi* appear at the outset of the earlier rings), not only describes an ultra-refined and elaborate artistry but carries connotations of 'une luminosité bigarrée et ... scintillement'.[72] If

---

[72] Frontisi-Ducroux 2002, 465. Edwards 1991 *ad* 490–92 comments that the verb perhaps 'hints that this picture is more in the nature of a decorative frieze, like the rows of identical figures on Geometric vases'. One might particularly think of the dancers on relief pithoi of the period, frequently decked out in elaborate garments and accessories; on patterned textiles and chorality, see Carruesco 2016, 89. As Power 2011, 80 n. 36 observes, the adjective ποικίλος appears as a technical term in Hero's account of the making of automata (*Pneum.* 1 *proem.* lines 15, 346). In a very different domain, Plato's *Timaeus*, as though bringing together the astral and choral

the oil-slicked garments, diadems, knives of gold and silver sword-belts combine with their wearers' spins to fill the scene with the bedazzling, motion-filled play of variegated light heralded by the verb, then Hephaestus is also more than fabricant here; as Stephen Lonsdale observes,[73] the craftsman acts as the *chorêgos* who – like Antaios, the father of the bride claimed in a courtship dance, 'decking out' (κοσμήσαις, 118) the girl prior to placing her in the chorus line in Pindar's *Pythian* 9 – adorns his dancers before he sets them moving. Although examples of the usage long postdate the Homeric poet, later Greek linguistic practice registers the confluence of *chorêgos* and metalworker intimated here; in an expression first found in Demosthenes, the chorus-leader is the one who 'welds together' (συγκροτεῖν, 21.17.5) his chorus (see Section 4).[74]

A fresh intersection of crafting and dancing occurs shortly afterwards, in the simile that figures the chorus' smooth and rapid 'whirls'. Likening their motions to those of the wheel that the potter tests by spinning, the poet additionally describes this *trochos* as 'fitted' (ἄρμενον) to its user's hands.[75] The participle does more than just fill out the hexameter line. From the verb ἀραρίσκω, it both suits the craftsman-god who is joining disparate elements together into a harmonious whole (a sense already present in ἤρτυε at 380, there used of Hephaestus 'fitting' the tripods with their daedalic handles) and bears more narrowly on the action of the choral dancer, the βητάρμων of *Od.* 8.250 and 383.[76] Glossed by Hesychius as a combination of the terms βαίνω and ἀραρίσκω (more recent etymologists concur), it styles the dancer as the one who fits his or her steps together and highlights 'the craftsmanlike skill required to order the steps of the dance'.[77]

The notion of the assemblage of disparate elements into a cohesive and aesthetically pleasing whole as realized in a choral performance extends beyond the dance and into the totality of the choral experience, its verbal as well as choreographic dimensions. Trying to explain that wondrous

---

scenes on the Homeric shield, would repeatedly attribute the *poikilia* particular to Hephaestus' chorus to the stars performing their complex and variegated dances, describing circles, spirals and moving together and apart; note particularly the description of the 'movements of these [astral] bodies as wonderously variegated (πεποικιλμένας δὲ θαυμαστῶς)' at 39d, with the discussion of Nightingale 2018, 347.

[73] Lonsdale 1995, 273.

[74] Cf. Pind. *Nem.* 7.77–79, where the poet describes the Muse who 'fastens together' gold, ivory and coral into the wreath that stands figure for the choral performance. The verb κολλάω can variously be used of objects that are glued, joined or even, when metal is involved, welded together.

[75] For this detail, see the observations of Kurke 2012, 230.

[76] A point made by Lonsdale 1995, 274.

[77] The citation is from Lonsdale 1995, 274. See too Power 2011, 81–82 with his n. 45.

phenomenon whereby each member of the audience is made to imagine
him- or herself the singer-dancer as the chorus of Deliades performs, the
poet of the *Homeric Hymn to Apollo* makes this quasi-magical transference
depend on the beauteous coordination and integration of different parts that
occurs when diverse bodies, motions and voices are joined into the unity that
is the choral group: 'so beautifully is their song fitted together' (οὕτω σφιν
καλῇ συνάρηρεν ἀοιδή, 164).[78] Where the poet can only convey the verbal-
cum-musical harmony of the Delos ensemble's performance by observing its
impact on its auditors, a later red-figure lebes gamikos from Delos of ca. 470
attributed to the Syriskos Painter may offer an account of the corresponding
visual impression made by these wondrous Delian singer-dancers, whose
appearance and the choreography of their complex line-dance unite intricacy
with an overall orderliness.[79]

A fragmentary piece by Pindar, generally classified as a paean or hyporcheme, more forcefully brings out the expressly artisanal craftsmanship that
choral performances involve when, comparing a paean composed by the
Locrian Xenocritus to a finely wrought chariot, the singers style the vehicle/
song 'fitted' and 'fitting' both (ἄρμενον, fr. 140b.11 S.-M.) to its recipient, the
god Apollo; the participle not only echoes the ἁρμονία used at the poem's
opening, where it referred to the compositional skills of the choral poet
Xenocritus, but encompasses a familiar noun for chariot, the ἄρμα, a term
omitted by Pindar – he uses the [ὄ]χημα instead – precisely because the other
expressions audibly and thematically signal its presence. As the Pindaric
speaker describes Xenocritus' musical technique, its artisanal *choreia*
involves acoustic, material and choreographic properties: it is at once 'shrill',
λιγ[ύ, and (if the supplement is sound) 'well-woven', εὐπλεκές.[80]

The Homeric narrator's verbal representation of the choral dancers
offers its own exact reflection of this harmonious arrangement of parts.
The interlocking word order of 603, which introduces the circle of viewers
surrounding the chorus, mimics the regular patterns of the performers'
linear and circular movements. With the adjective and its corresponding
noun bracketing the phrase (and the final sounds of πολλός and ὅμιλος
create an audible balance), the χορός occupies the very middle of the line, its

---

[78] See Kurke 2012 for further discussion. As Kurke observes at 230, the potter's wheel is 'itself an
object of skilled crafting (since it has to be perfectly balanced and symmetrical to run smoothly)
and the means to craft other symmetrical and harmonious artifacts'. For more on the passage,
see Chapter 10.

[79] Mykonos, Mykonos Archaeological Museum 970; *ARV*² 261.19. For the view that the image
may feature the Deliades, see Marconi 2010, 132.

[80] For detailed discussion of the fragment, see Steiner 2016b; I return to the weaving imagery here
in Chapter 7.

intermediate position reflecting the arrangement of viewers around the object of spectatorship.[81] A different type of coordination exists between the two groups whom the single line encompasses; ἱμερόεντα means both 'desired' and 'desiring'. In a transfer or symbiosis like that experienced by the spectators of the Delian performers in the *Hymn*, the future amorous relations between the members of this mixed choral group (this is a courtship dance) generate the same sentiments in those who act as audience.

Reinforcing the idea of the jointure essential to craftsmanship is the gesture that the metallic dancers perform. Visual representations of choruses from the archaic period on regularly show participants with their hands on one another's wrists, as on a black-figure lekythos by the Amasis Painter of ca. 550–530 (Fig. 7.11).[82] Here several groups of girls circle around the shoulder of the vase, performing a wedding dance that complements the nuptial procession shown on the body of the pot; in one of the groups the dancers clasp hands while in another they grasp their neighbour by the wrist. Both gestures supply a small-scale expression of a *harmonia* that the two scenes on the lekythos broadcast in more whole-sale fashion: for the parthenaic chorus on the shoulder, the 'fitting together' of hands or hands and wrists forms part of the concordant assemblage of parts that choral dancing manifests and that the presence of Harmonia in the dance of the gods on Olympia in the *Homeric Hymn to Apollo* (182–206) similarly articulates; for the newly married couple, the 'hand on wrist' clasp of the dancers re-enacts the moment when the groom performed the gesture so as to claim his new bride. Again, Pindar's ninth *Pythian* offers a clear expression of how the 'fitting together' gesture assigned to the Homeric potter as he cups his hands around his wheel stands in close relation to choral dancing and to marriage; just prior to imagining Antaios 'decking out' his daughter for the subsequent choral performance, Pindar declares the father's aim of 'matching' (ἁρμόζων, 117) a groom to the would-be bride.[83]

If the juxtaposition of potter and dancers flags the equivalence between their activities and the 'artefacts' both create, then the proximity between

---

[81] As observed by Kurke 2012, 226.

[82] New York, Metropolitan Museum of Art 56.11.1; *Para.* 66.

[83] Note that following his success in the courtship competition, the victor Alexidamos then claims his prize by taking her by the hand (χερὶ χειρὸς ἑλών, 122). Both this gesture, and the fitting of the bride to the groom point us back to the early stages of the song, where a finely fashioned artefact is included in the scene; at lines 10–11, the poet imagines Aphrodite, goddess of the union between Apollo and his new-won bride Cyrene, 'as she laid her hand on [Apollo's] divinely wrought chariot'.

the two is still more narrowly defined. Sounding a theme already introduced in the opening stages of Thetis' visit, the design of lines 599 and 600
juxtaposes the 'knowing feet' of the chorus with the potter's hands
(παλάμῃσιν) cupping his wheel, each of the two body parts occupying the
final position in the verse; where the first is the site of motion and
the second the agent that initiates the wheel/chorus' turns, the skill that
the dancers' feet possess is also that exercised by the craftsman's 'fitting'
hands, which are, in the endless loop created by this correspondence, the
instigators of the turning motions that the choristers' feet take up. And
where the start of the episode suggested relations of opposition between
silver-footed Thetis arriving at the god's home and the lame divinity
engaged in craftsmanship, now that contrast between moving and making
(or more properly 'handi-craft') is resolved, each act dependent on or
realized in its counterpart. The poet's use of παλάμη for the potter's
hands reinforces the affinity between *choreia* and the work of the artisan
and recapitulates the idea of the special and coextensive expertise that both
dancer and pot-maker deploy: more specific in meaning than χείρ, παλάμη
is the noun of choice in epic diction for the individual engaged in creating
a work of skilled artistry (e.g. *Il.* 15.411, Hes. *Th.* 580, here used of
Hephaestus; cf. Pind. fr. 52i.66 S.-M.).[84]

Lines 599–602, which form their own internal ring marked by the
repetition of θρέξασκον in verse-identical position, establish a further correspondence between the chorus' movements and those that the potter
requires of his 'running' wheel. As noted earlier, dancing and running are
proximate activities in the Greek sources, whether juxtaposed as separate
events on ritual occasions, where racing regularly occurred, or conflated
within the choreography of the dance. A fragment from Sophocles'
Thamyras spells out the equivalence expressed by the conjunction of the
dancers and *trochos* on the shield as the dramatic chorus observes how the
trochaic rhythm of the musical accompaniment turns its dance into
a headlong run: 'these melodies in which we celebrate you get the feet
forward, a running step (τρόχιμα βάσιμα) with hands and feet' (fr. 240 R.).

Also apparent in the Homeric simile are links back to the items featured
in the earlier scenes at the forge, the wheeled tripods and the golden girls.
Even as, in an overlap signalled earlier, the back-and-forth journeys of the
tripods anticipated the motions that the potter here imparts to his wheel,
connections also exist between the κεραμεύς and Hephaestus as the tripods'

---

[84] Note too [Hes.] *Sc.* 219, 320. In fifth-century Greek, παλάμη succinctly designates a crafted
object or work of art.

maker. As Mark Buchan points out, it is as though 'the potter is not simply trying to make a pot, but an object that can "run" autonomously',[85] exactly, I would add, what Hephaestus succeeds in doing in equipping the tripods with the power to self-propel (αὐτόματοι, 376), and what he effects anew when he sets the dancers in their perpetual and no less regular choral motions. The symmetry between the turning wheel and dancing feet also confirms the latent chorality suggested for the tripods' golden κύκλα, and their correspondence to the body part that so many scenes of *choreia* – the one on Achilles' shield among them – privilege.

Nor are the overlaps between the activity of the potter and the scene on the shield limited to the turnings of the wheel. Although the simile makes no mention of what this ceramicist plans to fashion, the type of pot he will throw on his *trochos*, Homeric audiences would be very familiar with one among the most common figurative motifs on contemporary Geometric vases: a line of dancers forming a continuous frieze that circles around the vessel. More broadly, the technique of an archaic κεραμεύς would closely correspond with that which, as the Homeric narrator's description invites us to suppose, Hephaestus uses in forging the shield: in making pithoi and other large-scale vessels, the potter would build up his pot in coils, first one band and then another stacked on top. Frequently painted or incised with figurative and non-figurative designs, these bands would incorporate repeated, interconnected and independent motifs. The François Vase, which commentators have frequently proposed as a *comparandum* for the Iliadic shield design, both echoes its choral theme, presenting no fewer than three archetypal choruses (the 'twice seven', the Muses and a flock of cranes, all treated in later chapters) on different regions of the pot, and includes depictions of events, whether a marriage or scenes of warfare, that find their analogues on the divine artefact.

If the potter's wheel recalls the twenty tripods, then a still more immediate connection exists between the Hephaestus-forged chorus and the serving girls earlier described. Several discussions signal the perhaps deliberate ambiguity of the term χορός at 590 and, following an interpretation already found in Pausanias (9.40.3), propose that Homer invites us to understand Daedalus as creator not of an intricately worked space set aside for the dance, but of an actual sculpted chorus or group in relief which, by virtue of the legendary craftsman's notorious capacity to endow his products with powers of motion, comes to life before our eyes (when

---

[85] Buchan 2012, 76.

χορός is repeated at 603, it clearly refers to the dancers).[86] Viewed this way, these objects are, in Kurke's rich account, moving images, 'a "chorus" of animated statues that moved and danced in unison, wrought of precious metal just like the dancers on Hephaestus' shield'.[87] If the Homeric passage allows this second meaning, then the earlier automata supply exact counterparts to these choral dancers and the metal maidens before them, similarly granted powers of synchronized motion. There is a further confluence of Daedalus' roles as craftsman and *chorêgos* here: the verb used for the master craftsman fashioning the chorus or dancing floor, ἀσκέω, recurs later in another choral context: in Pindar's fr. 94b.71–72 S.-M., one Andaisistrota 'equips' (ἐπάσκησε) or decks out the girl who heads the line of parthenaic choristers setting out to dance in the Theban Daphnephoria.

We owe to a scholiast's comment on this unique appearance of Daedalus in the Homeric corpus one further conjunction between the creation or preparation of a chorus and skilled craftsmanship.[88] According to the ancient reader, the dance performed on the Homeric shield is none other than the so-called *geranos* or Crane Dance, first executed by Theseus and the fourteen Athenian youths and maidens following their escape from the Cretan labyrinth; as our commentator further explains, this was the occasion when Daedalus 'devised the craft of *choreia* (τῆς χορείας τὴν ἐμπερίαν ... ἐποίησεν) and showed it to the dancers', and whose prompt Theseus followed when, as leader of the chorus line, 'he wove (ἔπλεκεν) such a χορός in a circular formation'.[89]

But Homer's description of the choral tableau forged by Hephaestus, following Daedalus' *poiêsis*, does not end with the crowd encircling the dancers and delighting in the spectacle they stage; instead the account closes by making place for a pair of 'tumblers' (κυβιστητῆρε, *Il.* 18.605) who also whirl (ἐδίνευον) about, executing their acrobatic moves at the midpoint of the chorus whose performance they lead off (κατ' αὐτοὺς / μολπῆς ἐξάρχοντες, 605–06). In Richard Neer's compelling reading,[90] these metal-crafted figurines, along with their several 'living' counterparts in

---

[86] On this, see Kurke 2012, 230 and 2013, 157–58, Power 2011, 81 with his n. 38, Frontisi-Ducroux 2002, 482–83 and Frontisi-Ducroux 1975/2000, 135–37, citing Callistratus, *Stat.* 3.5 (χορὸν ἤσκησε κινούμενον Δαίδαλος), Lucian, *Salt.* 13, Philostratus, *Imag.* 10. As Power 2011, 81 comments, read this way, ἔνθα at 593 would refer to the position on the shield where the chorus dances.

[87] Kurke 2013, 158.   [88] Σ in Venetus A *ad Il.* 18.591–92a.

[89] For detailed discussion, see Chapter 7. Callimachus also evokes weaving in the context of the Geranos, now relocating it to the Delian altar of Apollo 'woven' out of horns around which Theseus and the fourteen escapees performed the dance; for this, see *H.* 2.61 and *H.* 4.312–13.

[90] Neer 2018, 476–80.

choral scenes in the *Odyssey* (4.15–19, 8.370–80), could be aligned with a still extant and near contemporary object, which allows us to witness at first hand the confluence between an intricately wrought, precious artefact and the all-radiant choral performance that Achilles' shield holds up for show. An ivory statuette, dated to the final quarter of the seventh century and found in a votive deposit at the Samian Heraion, depicts a youth, nude but for his patterned belt, earrings and elaborately worked crown, spring-ing up with his legs tucked up behind him and his arms hanging by his sides.[91] Enhancing the ivory's lustre, the maker of this diminutive leaper (it measures some 14.5cm) would additionally have picked out the figure's eyes, brows, earrings and pubic hair with a bright inlay while decorating its circlet with gleaming amber disks, of which four still remain. Originally one of a set of two, the pair of statuettes would have formed the sidepieces for the sound box of a wooden kithara or phorminx, serving by way of handles for the instrument.[92] On many counts, as Neer observes, this radiant figure, its dazzle further multiplied as it, together with its double on the other side, would have moved along with the lyre as the kitharode plucked the strings and plied his instrument as he processed or danced along with his choral band, recalls the Iliadic dancers and acrobats. Emitting the same 'flashings', *marmarugai*, that typically emanate from choral dancers' feet in archaic accounts, and similarly adorned with shining metallic accessories, this leaping youth can be understood as a reified image of one of the lead members of the youthful choral ensembles whose performances in the Samian sanctuary the resplendent instrument would once have accompanied;[93] dancing in celebration of Hera, these choral troupes might themselves have perceived in the rhythmically leaping and shimmer-ing statuettes their paradigms and enduring doubles.[94]

4 The Dancing Hephaestus

If, as suggested above, the scenes in *Iliad* 18 offer an extended and ever-fuller exploration of the affinity between a choral performance and the products of craftsmanship, then my argument begs a larger question: what underlies this equivalence and, as corollary to this, why does it find expression in the person of Hephaestus, whose crippled limbs make him

[91] Vathy, Archaeological Museum 1665. For illustration and discussion, see Neer 2018, 477–80 and Connelley 2011, 330–31.
[92] For a reconstruction, see Connelley 2011, 331 and Neer 2018, 278.   [93] Connelley 2011, 331.
[94] Neer 2018, 480.

prima facie quite the most unlikely candidate for a link with *choreia*? For Power and Kurke,[95] advancing an argument to which this study is much indebted, the kinship between chorality and the scintillating objects produced in the divine foundry depends on the properties that song and dance spectacles and highly wrought artefacts (*agalmata*) share – *charis*, radiance, *poikilia* and erotic allure – and both result from the skilful joining and synchronization of heterogeneous and valuable elements into a harmonious, patterned or 'rhythmed' whole.[96] Common too are the sensations and responses elicited in those who play audience to elaborately fashioned works of art and to choral occasions: *terpsis*, awed wonder (*thauma*),[97] attraction, identification and the sensation of being in the presence of something that partakes of the divine.

  Implicit in this account is one answer to my second question and to the topic addressed in this concluding section of the chapter: the intimate relations between Hephaestus and *choreia* would have their origins in his particular prerogatives and sphere of excellence. As the not-to-be surpassed craftsman, he is necessarily implicated in chorality, which requires the same expenditure of expertise, display of intricate artistry and mastery of diverse media (voice, words, instrumental music, choreography, the 'look' of the choreutes) as the manufactured goods created by the divine artisan. In the succinct formulation of Françoise Frontisi-Ducroux, 'la danse est un modèle de l'art total, à la fois visuel, figurative, cinétique, vivant et musical'.[98] But missing from these several discussions is due consideration of what defines the divinity as much as his handiwork and the characteristic that stands, particularly in archaic and classical visual accounts, in such close relations to his signal powers: the impaired limbs and feet so emphasized through the course of the episodes already treated, and that, I suggest, are no less bound up with Hephaestus' creation of the sequence of choral archetypes in these scenes. While Chapter 3 will explore how participation in *choreia* supplies an antidote and corrective to the debility afflicting the god, here I follow a different line of argument. Beginning with a second

---

[95] Power 2011; Kurke 2012 and 2013.

[96] Indeed, as Grand-Clément (2015, 415) observes, *poikilia*, which chiefly describes variegation and complexity, is also conducive to cohesion insofar as it results in the creation of 'strong connections' and can 'bind dissimilar elements'. Note too Pl. *Tim.* 40c where the motions performed by the chorus of stars, repeatedly characterized as variegated, include moments when the astral bodies come together in clusters (συνάψεσιν).

[97] See Neer 2010 for full exploration of this element.

[98] Frontisi-Ducroux 2002, 482. Her argument, unlike mine, pertains chiefly to relations between Hephaestus' craftsmanship as manifested in the creation of the shield, and that of the Homeric poet, also a producer of images encompassing all realms of experience that the audience may wonder at.

Homeric episode in which Hephaestus' handicap is, once again, integral to a choral spectacle currently being staged, I then turn briefly to the mythical, artistic, textual and ritual spheres so as to sample (in what is a very partial and scattershot account) some other expressions of the god's affinity with the practice of song-dance. In the proposal made here, Hephaestus' curiously configured anatomy does not so much render him unfit for choral dancing as manifest his possession of a power that is as critical to the chorus members' practice of their art as it is to his craftsmanship.

For a fresh expression of Hephaestus' involvement with song and dance, we need to turn from *Iliad* 18 to the *Odyssey* and to the period spent by Odysseus on Scheria, an island distinctive for the presence of two interlinked phenomena: a series of supremely beautiful, precious, dazzling and even miraculously animated objects ornamenting its landscape – Alkinous' palace, the gold-and-silver guardian dogs at its threshold, these fashioned by Hephaestus, two golden torch bearers (all described in 7.80–102) – and an unrivalled mastery of the art of dancing (see 8.250–53, 382–84). An episode in book 8 not only narrowly intercalates Hephaestus' craftsmanship, his lameness and a choral performance, but implicitly comments on and sets out to surpass the same god's creation of the scene on the penultimate shield band in *Iliad* 18: here the Odyssean poet, with the polemical intent typical of his reworkings of the rival and anterior composition, reverses the passage from words to images devised by Hephaestus and completes the work of vivification that the divinity's artistry could only partially (as the Iliadic narrator repeatedly reminds us) achieve. The events displayed synchronically on the shield – the dancing chorus, the singer with his lyre[99] and the two tumblers who, 'leading off the dance were whirling about in the middle' (μολπῆς ἐξάρχοντες ἐδίνευον κατὰ μέσσους, 18.606) – form the triplet of performances (albeit with the absence of maiden dancers) in this portion of *Odyssey* 8. And just as the frame of Demodocus' story looks back to the choral image forged by the god in the earlier poem, so its contents tessellate with several other of the motifs that run through the sequence of Iliadic scenes explored above.[100]

Just to set the scene: following Alkinous' instructions, Demodocus is summoned from the palace while nine chosen individuals prepare the

---

[99] Here, following the persuasive arguments of Revermann 1998, I assume the inclusion of the frequently omitted lines at 18.603–06, which introduce the lyre-playing *aoidos* in the dancers' midst. As Revermann observes, the Odyssean scene supplies a compelling reason for following the ancient authors who cite the lines.

[100] Extraneous to my discussion is the relevance of the song to its primary auditor, Odysseus. For a recent succinct treatment of this and earlier bibliography, see Hedreen 2016, 138–42.

space of the *agôn*, smoothing down the surface where the *aoidos* and chorus will perform. In the passage cited earlier, the Phaeacian youths, the best among the dancers, take up their stance, surrounding the bard positioned at their centre, and proceed to stage their *thauma*-provoking performance (262–66). While more recent commentators debate whether this dance occurs prior to Demodocus' second song, whose recitation will then be followed by the two-person ball dance afterwards (witness the two tumblers on the shield),[101] or whether the poet imagines a single 'narrative dance',[102] effectively a choral performance with song accompanied by a chorus of dancers, Athenaeus' commentary on the episode clearly assumes the second scenario. Observing Homer's familiarity with the practice of 'dancing with song accompaniment', he goes on to cite the moment when 'Demodocus sang while young boys danced', proposing by way of analogue the vineyard scene on the shield band where 'a boy played the lyre while others opposite him frisked about to the song and the dance' (1.15d). Following Athenaeus' lead, I assume a choral performance and read this in relation to a motif so central both to Demodocus' narrative and to the depiction of the god in *Iliad* 18: his deformity and the impeded motion that results.

There is no need to dwell on how Demodocus' second story foregrounds Hephaestus' ill-shaped anatomy, repeatedly juxtaposing his malformed limbs and feet with the facility for motion that Ares, his opposite number and rival, enjoys. The cuckolded husband himself spotlights the contrast, noting ruefully that while Aphrodite shuns him on account of his being lame (χωλόν, 308), she has chosen Ares as paramour, 'because he is good-looking and nimble of foot (ἀρτίπος)' (310), a remark that prefaces his account of how the deformity came about. As Chantraine glosses the first element in the compound adjective at 310,[103] it designates something that 'adapts' itself, creating an exact fit or join, and is cognate with other terms built from the root *αρ that, as noted above, appears in such artisanal terms as ἀραρίσκω.[104] So characterized, Ares recalls the individuals that the poem

---

[101] Cf. *Od.* 4.15–19, where, in a kind of conflation of the shield scene and the sequence described in *Od.* 8, a lyre-equipped *aoidos* accompanies two tumblers who 'whirled about through their midst, leading off the *molpê*'.

[102] Murray 2008, 166. See too Mullen 1982, 13 who views Demodocus as 'a leader with voice and lyre presiding over some kind of elaborate mime'. The term αὐτάρ at 266 allows both interpretations.

[103] Chantraine 1999, s.v. ἄρτι.

[104] In keeping with the unmistakably ribald and even off-colour quality of the entire narrative, it seems likely that the term carries sexual connotations (so the 'foot' repeatedly appears as a slang term for the phallos in the comic poets). The problem, from Hephaestus' perspective, is that Ares' foot is too good at 'fitting in' while his own deformed feet serve as an expression of

very recently introduced, the βητάρμονες (8.250; so too 383), those youths ideally suited to the dance by virtue of their preeminence in fitting together their steps. And if dancing seems an unlikely talent for a god of war, this is not the only place that the Homeric poet suggests a connection between Ares and the (choral) art. For all the contrast between the fighter and dancer regularly drawn in the *Iliad* (see Chapter 3), in one instance at least, the skills required of the two coalesce: Hector, boasting of his mastery of the art of warfare, remarks to Ajax, 'I know how to dance-and-sing in the close combat for raging Ares' (οἶδα δ' ἐνὶ σταδίῃ δηΐῳ μέλπεσθαι Ἄρηϊ, *Il.* 7.241).[105]

Invested with this artisanal/choreographic significance, Ares' fitting or adaptable 'footwork' stands as counterpart and in opposition to the skill concentrated in the divine craftsman's hands, a pairing made apparent in the poet's account of the confrontation that directly pits Hephaestus' manufacturing expertise against Ares' feet. Indeed, following the lame god's defeat of the most well-footed of the Olympians, a triumph he scores by rendering Ares' limbs still more immobile than his own (οὐδέ τι κινῆσαι μελέων ἦν οὐδ' ἀναεῖραι, 298), one of the divine witnesses to the adulterous pair's discomfiture spells out this antithesis, making Hephaestus' powers of craftsmanship a direct function of his pedal deformity (329–32).[106] More indirectly, the correspondence between Ares and those currently perform-ing their choral dance – young like him and lithe of movement – while (or before) the song is sung suggests Hephaestus' necessary exclusion from the activity for which his limbs and feet are so ill suited, making him more analogous to the other no less physically impaired participant in the performance: the blind Demodocus, whose compositional powers find their reflection in the divinity's technical artistry.

As the Iliadic and Odyssean poets' several alignments of Hephaestus with scenes of choral dancing themselves suggest, the god's relations to *choreia* may be closer and more complex than they might immediately seem, and images on vases, myths and ritual practices from the archaic period on confirm his several-faceted involvement in this performative mode. Among the diverse expressions of that interface belongs the much

---

his sexual deficiencies (viz. his failed attempt to have intercourse with the virginal Athena and vexed marital relations with Aphrodite).

[105] The verb selected here is exactly that used for choral dancing at *Il.* 16.182 and *HHP* 19.21. For Ares as participant in a choral dance, cf. *HHAp.* 200–01, where the god performs a kind of *pas de deux* with Hermes. Commenting on the lines, Richardson 2010 *ad loc.* likens the pair to the tumblers featured on the Iliadic shield at 18.604–05.

[106] κιχάνει τοι βραδὺς ὠκύν, / ὡς καὶ νῦν Ἥφαιστος ἐὼν βραδὺς εἷλεν Ἄρηα, / ὠκύτατόν περ ἐόντα θεῶν, οἳ Ὄλυμπον ἔχουσι, / χωλὸς ἐών, τέχνῃσι·

discussed corpus of komast vases which, beginning in seventh-century Corinth, and then appearing in many other parts of Greece through to the sixth century's second half, typically feature fat-bellied, bottom-slapping dancers with protruding buttocks who perform singly and in choruses and frequently engage in forms of riotous behaviour, drinking to excess, brawling and having sex among them.[107] Most surprisingly for figures whose signature activity is their vigorous dancing, a striking proportion of these revelers have feet that are twisted about, unnaturally elongated or otherwise misshapen, features that seem to form part of their overall costuming rather than actual deformities.[108] The overlaps with Hephaestus go well beyond the (real and feigned) lameness that the god and dancers share. Although the komasts appear in a variety of different contexts, where setting can be determined, painters regularly position them at symposia, where, like Hephaestus who serves out wine/nectar from the krater and diverts the divine feasters with his buffoonery at the close of *Iliad* 1, they supply comic entertainment for the company and, located in proximity of the mixing bowl, seem similarly involved in the dispensing (as well as consumption) of drink.[109]

But most intriguing are the several sources that more directly connect the komasts and the god by including the two within representations of a single event. A lost play by the late sixth- or early fifth-century Sicilian comic dramatist Epicharmos, most probably turning about the well-known story of Hephaestus' return to Olympus following his expulsion some nine years earlier, is variously titled *Komastai* or *Hephaistos*, a double nomenclature which, following other such examples, suggests that the revelers, taking on the chorus' role, would have appeared alongside the god.[110] Antedating the play, several black-figure vases include komast dancers within representations of the Return scene (see too below), depicting them as members of the procession that escorts Hephaestus back to his Olympian home.[111] On the earliest of these, a Middle Corinthian amphoriskos dated to ca. 600–585,[112] two padded dancers accompany the lame god mounted on his mule; from

[107] For the most comprehensive recent discussion with earlier bibliography, see Smith 2010.

[108] In the Corinthian corpus alone, almost 40 among the 300 listed in Seeberg 1971 include the malformations, while lame dancers would reappear on pots from Athens, Boeotia and possibly East Greece; see Smith 2009 and 2010 for these.

[109] Smith 2009, 79. In a further overlap, one of the Iliadic versions of Hephaestus' ejection from Olympus describes how Zeus grabbed him by the foot so as to hurl him out (*Il.* 1.590–94); in what could be a replay of the motif, several komast vases show figures seizing a companion by the leg or foot as though to pull him down; for these, see Steiner 2009, 262.

[110] Smith 2009, 75.   [111] For comprehensive discussion, see Hedreen 1992 and 2004.

[112] Athens, National Archaeological Museum 664, with Smith 2009, 75 and 2010, 28.

about a decade later comes a Corinthian krater of ca. 575–550 attributed to the Orphelandros Painter[113] that again portrays two revellers, one of whom carries the drinking horn that so frequently appears as a defining attribute of these bibulous figures. A third, albeit less immediate pairing supplies the decorative programme for a mid-sixth-century Boeotian skyphos;[114] one side of the cup displays the Return, showing the god as he reaches for a drink from the wineskin carried by one of the pair of non-komastic figures preceding him; a miniature komast scene appears on the other face, and places among its hetero- and homosexual copulating couples a komast who supports himself on a visibly deformed foot.

In Tyler Jo Smith's reading of the evidence, the lame padded dancers should be understood as costumed impersonators of the god, 'Hephaistoi' as she styles them, whose outsider status, association with the symposium and wine (beyond Hephaestus' appearance in *Iliad* 1, Dionysus notoriously brings about his return to Olympus by giving his fellow god too much to drink), misshapen anatomy and role as self-styled buffoon they mimic.[115] But for my purposes, these affinities more simply point to an association between the god and the art of choral dancing – the komasts frequently appear as part of larger groups, performing the same gestures and steps and moving in synchronic fashion – in a link that echoes the motif already visible in Homeric epic.

Adding to this concatenation are several sets of mythical figures with much more direct connections to Hephaestus, and who combine their participation in choral dancing with metallurgic skills. Among these belong the Kabeiroi, first mentioned by Herodotus who identifies them as sons of the god (3.37); among the traits they inherit are their father's malformed limbs and dwarfish appearance as well as his supremacy in metalworking.[116] On the island of Lemnos, the chief cult site of Hephaestus and the place where the god fell to earth following his ejection from Olympus, the Kabeiroi again appear as sons of the deity, and are depicted on coins wearing the felt cap and hammer that form part of their progenitor's iconography. Very closely related to the Corybantes, these best

---

[113] London, British Museum 1867.5–8.860.

[114] Thebes, Archaeological Museum 31.187, with Smith 2009, 82 and 2010, 157, 170, 172.

[115] Smith 2009, 79.

[116] In many accounts, these demonic beings are elided with the figures represented on the more than 300 drinking vessels from the fifth and fourth centuries found at the Kabeirion some six miles west of Thebes, whom art historians also regularly view as heirs of the earlier komast dancers (see Smith 2009, 91 and 2010, 151–52). Like the padded komasts, they display grotesque and deformed anatomies, some with exaggerated bellies, protruding buttocks and prominent phalloi, and on occasion adopt the postures and gestures of dancers. However, as Mitchell 2009, 254 cautions, the two sets of figures exist in two separate traditions and have quite different associations.

known for their invention and performance of a whirling dance in armour performed about the infant Zeus, the Kabeiroi participate in the orgiastic dances that formed part of the rituals celebrated on behalf of the Great Mother at her sanctuary in Samothrace. The manufacture of the metallic goods in which the Kabeiroi are variously involved exhibits a more straightforward link to choral dances, particularly those associated with the orgiastic rites celebrated on behalf of the Phrygian Cybele and Dionysus; so the bronze gifts at Arkalokhori and other early sanctuaries stand witness to the 'intimate relationship between dance rituals and the smith who makes bronze cymbals and other percussion instruments' used to accompany the performances.[117]

Hesychius further identifies the Kabeiroi as crabs, the commonly styled *karkinoi* whose name not only supplies the *vox propria* for the blacksmith's tongs[118] but also occurs in the context of the 'crab dance' staged by the sons of the eponymous Karkinos at the close of Aristophanes' *Wasps*. In keeping with their larger mythical typology, a diminished stature seems to have been a defining element of this historical foursome (so *Vesp.* 1510, *Pax* 790 and a scholion to *Vesp.* 1502c, citing Pherecrates) no less than their skill as dancers. As spectators to their performance, the chorus leader and his troupe minutely describe the performers' mode of locomotion: they first enter in a perhaps scuttling processional formation (forms of προσέρπω appear at 1509 and 1531) and then abandon linearity for circle dancing, spinning around (κυκλοσοβεῖτε, 1523; παράβαινε κύκλῳ, 1529) while kicking out one leg in a step called a 'Phrynichus kick' and slapping their bellies.

Among other mythical groups who similarly combine metallurgic expertise with participation in choral dancing are the Phrygian Daktyli, iron miners, magicians and craftsmen, often ten in number, whose name succinctly declares their skilled artisanship. Closely related to the Corybantes in later rationalizing accounts,[119] they appear alongside the Argonauts in a ghost-calming ritual at Kyzikos, where they perform a leaping armed dance, whirling about as they strike their shields with their swords (A.R. 1.1123–31). Other facets of the Daktyli reinforce their centrality to the musical dimensions of *choreia*: they were credited with the introduction of the aulos into Greece, and with having arranged the clash

---

[117] Lonsdale 1995, 280.   [118] For the ancient sources, see Detienne and Vernant 1978, 269.
[119] Strabo 10.3.7 sees the Daktyli as essentially identical to the Kabeiroi, Corybantes, Kouretes and Telchines, all armed figures who participate in dances.

and bang of bronze. In Lucian's account, Priapus, who teaches Mars to dance, is a Daktyl or a Titan (*Salt.* 19–21).[120]

A different dimension of Hephaestus' biography, already mentioned, proves relevant to his proximity to the dancers who populate his myths and images. While no visual or verbal representation goes so far as to show the god as an active participant in a dancing chorus, the numerous Attic vase images (almost 130 of them are extant, with the earliest representation, included on the François Vase, dated to the sixth century's first half) featuring the god's return to Olympus position him in the midst of a Dionysiac *kômos* that, more typically than the komast dancers treated above, is made up of satyrs playing music and dancing. On some pots, an Attic red-figure calyx krater from ca. 440–420 assigned to the Group of Polygnotos and an Attic red-figure pelike by the Lugano painter of ca. 430–390 among them,[121] the very donkey on which Hephaestus so frequently rides seems to perform dance figures, and/or to form part of a larger chorus line.[122] A red-figure calyx krater attributed to the Kleophrades Painter of ca. 500 (Fig. 1.5)[123] draws a more particularized connection between the god's metallurgic skills and the satyrs' komastic activity. Positioned beneath one of the handles a line of four satyrs appears, the two in the middle dancing to the music supplied by the aulos-playing leader of the group; an outsized set of leather bellows also equips the musician-satyr. As Lissarrague points out,[124] the pipes and bellows visually and verbally echo one another: the aulos' double tubes find their counterpart in the single piece of piping that hangs down from the bellows, this too sometimes called an aulos. As Pindar's *Pyth.* 12.25, analysed in detail in Chapter 2, reminds us, the instrument is itself made of hammered bronze, and so a product of the forge and of the bellows used in creating metallic goods. Both Kleophrades' krater and other images of the triumphal return do more than just establish the place of metalworking in scenes of choral dancing and Hephaestus' capacity to generate the objects that set others in

---

[120] Note too the equation of their name with the dactylic rhythm, this first attested in the first century B.C.E. For these different characteristics, see Solinus 11.4–6; Clem. Alex. *Stromat.* 1.15.132; [Plut.] *De mus.* 5.1132; Alexander Polyhistor, *FGrH* 263 F 77; Lucian, *Salt.* 19–21. I owe these references to Blakeley 2006, 15 on whose extensive study this section is largely based.

[121] Munich, Antikensammlungen 2384; *ARV²* 1057.98, *Para.* 445; Munich, Antikensammlungen S68; *ARV²* 1347.1, *Para.* 482.

[122] E.g. an Attic black-figure band cup of the second half of the sixth century; New York, Metropolitan Museum of Art 7.230.5. For recent discussion of many of the images, see Hedreen 2004 and Fineberg 2009.

[123] Cambridge, MA, Harvard Art Museums 1960.236; *ARV²* 185.31.

[124] Lissarrague 1990, 43–44.

Fig. 1.5 Attic red-figure calyx krater attributed to the Kleophrades Painter, ca. 500 B.C.E. Cambridge, MA, Harvard Art Museums 1960.236. Photograph Harvard Art Museums © President and Fellows of Harvard College.

motion. Much as in the Iliadic foundry, the god whose deformity excludes him from the dance surrounds himself with figures for whom constant, rapid and unchecked motion is a signature activity.[125]

The frequent portrayals of the return of Hephaestus bear directly on the sequence of points with which this chapter concludes, and that initially take us back to the scene in *Odyssey* 8 featuring the pronounced presence of Hephaestus and of a choral dance. As the formation of the Phaeacian youths who surround Demodocus clearly demonstrates, the chorus that accompanies (or supplies the 'warm-up' act for) his second song executes a circle dance, conforming to what sources from the fifth century on would call the κύκλιος χόρος or circular chorus. Intriguingly, both visual and textual sources indicate the presence of these dances in the context of the Hephaisteia, the festival celebrated on the god's behalf in Athens, and reorganized and augmented in scale in 421/0 so as to accommodate a team torch race, lavish sacrifices, a procession and musical competitions involving choruses that danced in circles.[126] A volute krater attributed to Polion and dated to ca. 420 supplies a visual account of the event (Figs. 1.6, 1.7),[127] while also pairing the occasion with a variety of other elements pertinent to my discussion. Immediately

---

[125] See Lissarrague 1993 and 2013, 165–70 with comments on satyrs' inability to remain still.
[126] *IG* I³ 82; for the musical element, *IG* I³ 82.14.
[127] Ferrara, Museo Nazionale di Spina T 127; *ARV*² 1171.1, 1685, *Para.* 459.

Fig. 1.6 Attic red-figure volute krater attributed to Polion, ca. 420 B.C.E. Side A. Ferrara, Museo Nazionale di Spina T 127. Photograph courtesy of the Archaeological Superintendency of Ferrara.

below the rim of the jar and circling around its neck, the artist positions a *lampadedromia*, the torch race that formed part of the Hephaisteia, and whose connection to the god and his cultic celebration is confirmed by the depiction of the return of Hephaestus on the obverse of the body of the pot. Also visible in this second scene are the themes of music and dance, this possibly of the same circular kind featured at Hephaestus' festival; depicted in the image is a reclining, kantharos-equipped Dionysus – whose cult regularly included performances of the dithyramb, the song sung and danced by the same circular-type choruses that competed at the Hephaisteia – together with his retinue of satyrs and maenads, some equipped with torches while one of the maenads carries a lyre. The figure of Hera, seated on a chair and carrying a sceptre, no less than the presence of wine at this sympotic occasion, succinctly introduce motifs that allude to the larger story surrounding the craftsman god's readmission into Olympus.

The episode depicted on the krater's reverse side freshly expresses that musical element even as it may gesture again towards the ritual occasion placed on the neck; here we witness a performance by Thamyris, dressed as a professional musician complete with long robes and his concert kithara. The presence of the instrument-carrying Muses, playing the role of audience, clearly alludes to the unhappy dénouement of the encounter as first narrated in *Il.* 2.599–600: following Thamyris' challenge of their musical pre-eminence, the goddesses will maim the rival kitharode and deprive him of his singing powers. In one likely interpretation of the vase's visual programme, this scene evokes a now-lost dithyramb (or more properly a song accompanied by a circular chorus) telling the story of Thamyris that would have been

Fig. 1.7 Attic red-figure volute krater attributed to Polion, ca. 420 B.C.E. Side
B. Ferrara, Museo Nazionale di Spina T 127. Photograph courtesy of the Archaeological
Superintendency of Ferrara.

performed on the occasion of the Hephaisteia and formed one among the
pieces in the musico-choral *agônes* at the event.[128] If that reading is correct,
this portion of the krater furnishes visual evidence for the choral competitions
recorded in our epigraphic sources concerning the festival.

Putting all this together in the context of Demodocus' second song,
which turns about and celebrates the defining attribute of Hephaestus as
displayed through his scoring a victory in an *agôn* with a seemingly invin-
cible rival deity, might the Phaeacian bard be performing a composition in
honour of the god accompanied by a choral ring dance, a kind of anticipation of the choruses that performed at the Hephaisteia? This is the scenario
we witness in the *Homeric Hymn to Apollo* 156–59, where the Deliades sing

---

[128]   See Bundrick 2005, 130 for discussion.

and dance what looks very like a paean on behalf of the god celebrated at the Delia, and whose song the *Hymn* incorporates into its own hexameter tradition. Indeed, in a fresh display of acumen and agonistic 'filling in' of the elements omitted by his Iliadic counterpart in his earlier poem, the composer of the *Odyssey* may even make his current audience hear the song that the *aoidos* forged by Hephaestus on his shield band performed: that nameless singer was none other than Demodocus, singing in celebration of the divinity to whom he owed his lasting representation.

But this perhaps fanciful suggestion of some kind of Phaeacian Hephaisteia *avant la lettre* aside, my chief concern is with the relations of likeness and opposition between the god and his torch race. A *lampadedromia*, a contest that requires its participants to exercise both speed (the property the Homeric god seems so singularly to lack in the Odyssean episode) and dexterity so as to keep the torch burning while they run, is eminently suited to a god whose role it is to preside over, and even embody, the medium of fire, on whose control and deployment Hephaestus' activity at his forge so clearly depends. It is fire, its nature and channelling into a contained, productive and creative form, that proves central to a second reading of the connection between Hephaestus and the choral dance. As the groundbreaking article by Detienne and Vernant first demonstrated,[129] representations of the god with his seemingly misshapen legs and feet more properly offer a bifurcated account: while some images and texts treat these malformations as indices of his lameness, the artistic and mythical traditions also use the anatomical irregularity so as to suggest Hephaestus' bipedalism, his capacity for rapid changes of motion and for moving simultaneously, in the manner of the crabs whose progenitors he is, in two directions. So equipped, the god is not only ideally suited to the mastery of that swiftest, most volatile of elements that, once illuminated, moves so rapidly and unstoppably, but he also exemplifies the kinetic qualities (and the dazzle too, visible in the torches carried by the participants in the wedding song and dance included on the shield) that, as later chapters will further demonstrate, belong among the most fundamental attributes of a choral dancer, and that are chiefly concentrated in his or her 'knowing' limbs and feet.

---

[129] Detienne and Vernant 1978, 259–75.

2 | From the Demonic to the Divine: Gorgons, Cauldrons and Choral Dance

Introduction

A well-known Protoattic neck amphora from Eleusis by the Polyphemus Painter dated to ca. 670–650 preserves the largest extant vase painting (Fig. 2.0).[1] On its central field, two Gorgons, presented frontally as they move away from the headless body of their sister who seemingly floats horizontal in mid-air, pursue Perseus fleeing around the damaged curve of the vase. The vessel fascinates scholars for any number of reasons: not only do its dimensions outstrip those of other amphoras for the period (it measures some 1.42 m in height), while its decoration offers 'the most complete example known of the Black and White style';[2] it also features our earliest visual representation of Perseus' flight and among the first depictions of the Polyphemus episode on its neck. On this pot too Athena makes her début in Attic vase painting. While some studies focus chiefly on the meaning of the vessel's rich iconography and detail its innovatory artistic techniques,[3] others are more concerned with reconstructing its 'biography';[4] indeed, the Eleusis amphora has become what one scholar calls a 'poster child' for the need to address not just the aesthetic issues but also the social questions that arise from early Greek pottery and to consider the life history of an object as discernible from its archaeological and cultural contexts.[5]

My aim in revisiting this familiar object is to explore what is perhaps the most arresting feature in the representation of the Gorgons, the artist's choice to model the monsters' heads after the Orientalizing bronze protome cauldrons, originally derived from Urartian or Neohittite models, made by metalworkers and used as dedications in Greek sanctuaries from ca. 700 on. In the interpretation formulated here, I suggest that the vase's central scene offers an example of, and indeed unites, two choral archetypes treated in this study: not just the tripod cauldrons that, as the previous

---

[1] Eleusis, Archaeological Museum 2630.   [2] Morris 1984, 11.
[3] Hurwit 1977, 24–25; Osborne 1988; Giuliani 2013, 70–78; Haug 2012, 497.
[4] Langdon 2001, 600; see too Whitley 1994, 63–64.   [5] Langdon 2001, 579.

Fig. 2.0 Protoattic neck amphora by the Polyphemus Painter, ca. 670–650 B.C.E.
Eleusis, Archaeological Museum 2630. Photograph: Sarah C. Murray/Wikimedia CC
BY-SA 2.

chapter suggested, the Homeric poet already introduces in *Iliad* 18 as
a proto-chorus, but also the monstrous triad of Gorgon sisters, whom
our early visual and textual sources likewise propose as a paradigmatic
dancing ensemble and whose representation on the amphora newly articulates the notion identified in Chapter 1: the 'factural' quality of a choral
ensemble. The discussion's first part explores how the Polyphemus Painter,
in keeping with other archaic visual and textual sources, figures the three
sisters as members of a dancing chorus, and cites additional evidence –
topographic, functional and thematic – to demonstrate how cauldrons
intersect with the practice of *choreia*. Section 2 seeks to accommodate
this 'choral' reading of the cauldrons on the Eleusis vase within
a reconstruction of the 'biography' of the pot by identifying, albeit speculatively, the ritual event that it may be designed to commemorate and that
further explains its reuse as a burial jar for a child aged between ten and
twelve. In Section 3, I propose that the amphora cauldrons are invested
with the same sonorous dimension that such vessels exhibit in other
accounts, and that grants men access to a type of voice that characterizes
not just immortal choristers, whether demonic or divine, but their human

counterparts, chiefly *parthenoi*, possessed of just such suprahuman vocal properties and efficacy. More broadly, my analysis suggests, the amphora painter chooses to include the Orientalizing cauldrons in the image so as to acculturate the foreign, threatening and uncanny and to draw it into the compass of one among the principal Greek ritual practices designed to 'presentify' the gods, that of choral dance and song.

1   Choral Gorgons and Dancing Pots

I begin with the artist's striking depiction of the Gorgon heads, fashioned after the bronze cauldrons that, chiefly derived from N. Syrian and Urartian prototypes, Greek metalworkers begin to imitate and modify from ca. 700 and that served as prestige votive goods, and place these objects within the larger visual typology used to depict Medusa's sisters. As several recent studies of Gorgons in Geometric art demonstrate, the earliest images imagine them not just (nor even so much) as the repellent and terrifying monsters of later accounts, but, more surprisingly, as a parthenaic chorus.[6] To cite just two examples detailed by Susan Langdon,[7] on a Late Geometric two-handled flask from Cretan Andromyloi, two shoulder panels juxtapose lines of dancers; in one panel, a mixed line of men and women appears; in the other, four Gorgons complete with shoulder snakes dance and/or pursue the girls and boys. These monsters' iconographic similarity to the pair on the Eleusis amphora confirms their Gorgon identity. In a second instance of the typology, an ivory seal of the same period found in the Argive Heraion portrays two identical Gorgons side by side, complete with outsized heads, broad double skirts and open-mouthed snakes sprouting from their shoulders (Fig. 2.1);[8] the position of their feet, turned towards one another, mirrors the arrangement found in other early representations of dancers.

Two articles by Kathryn Topper situate these and other representations of the monsters within the larger morphology of maiden choruses as delineated by Calame.[9] Not only do the three sisters form a collectivity of same-age *parthenoi* united at once by kinship ties and by locality, but one

---

[6] This characterization is also intimated by Hurwit 1985, 167, who describes the two figures on the Eleusis amphora as 'a chorus line'.

[7] Langdon 2008, 6–7, with her fig. 0.4, and 112–13.

[8] Athens, National Archaeological Museum 14047.

[9] Topper 2007 and 2010, drawing on Calame 1997.

Fig. 2.1 Ivory seal from the Argive Heraion. Athens, National Archaeological Museum 14047. Drawing after R. Hampe, *Frühe griechische Sagenbilder in Böotien* (Athens, 1936), p. 65, fig. 26.

of their members is, *chorêgos*-like, singled out from the rest.[10] Medusa, frequently described as beautiful, alone is mortal and attracts first the amorous desires of Poseidon and then the fatal, but also potentially erotic attentions of Perseus. In the familiar mythico-choral scenario, both god and hero 'abduct' this pre-eminent maiden from the dancing group (an abduction that, in the second instance, results in the death so frequently conflated in myth and imagery with this quasi-nuptial rite of passage). The Eleusis amphora depicts the Gorgon sisters in a manner consistent with this template on many counts and the scene's location is just the first of the several areas of correspondence. In the account supplied by Hesiod of Poseidon's 'choral snatch',[11] the episode occurs in a flowery meadow (*Th.* 279) and flowers also figure prominently on the occasions when Persephone, Helen and other chorus-leading heroines are similarly carried off from the company of their fellow dancers. Flowers in the form of rosettes belong among the motifs that appear repeatedly in the representation of the Gorgons on the amphora where they serve a double function: while situating us in the meadow landscape where parthenaic choruses typically dance, they also create visual correspondences between the different portions of the pot, supplying one of the elements (both figurative and

[10] As Topper 2007, 87 observes, on the Eleusis amphora Medusa is bigger and has a more rounded torso than her sisters; we might further note that, like these Gorgons, maiden choruses frequently come in threes: the Charites and, according to some sources, the Sirens and Muses also form a triad.

[11] A phrase I borrow from Boedeker 1974.

ornamental) that reappear in the lion attack shown on the shoulder and in the blinding of Polyphemus featured on the neck. In Carruesco's reading,[12] these rosettes may bear still more directly on the choral dance, supplying stylized depictions of the linear, circling and other movements created by the choreographic design executed by the performers.

Also oscillating between a figurative and largely ornamental significance, and a second motif that unifies the vessel's different parts (its decorative bands as well as the figural scenes), are the wave-like lines prominently placed beneath the Gorgons' feet and then again above their heads, where they visually echo the shape formed by the snakes most immediately below them. Many discussions view these motifs as evocative of water, and the feature is again typical of the lush landscape that choral dancers on early Argive pottery regularly occupy. In these scenes, as an indicator of the maidens' budding fertility, a body of water forms an integral part of the flowery meadow setting framing the parthenaic chorus.[13] Exemplary of this topography is a krater fragment with a row of four branch-holding female figures dancing either above or beyond a series of lines – more angular and forming zigzags in this instance – also suggestive of water and that positions the chorus along what Langdon identifies as 'a pebbly beach or riverbank' (Fig. 4.0, with discussion in Chapter 4).[14] The presence of a fish and water bird reinforces that watery dimension.

The Gorgon sisters' pursuit of Perseus also has a place within this scheme, albeit with deformations of the normative account; here the monsters play the counterparts to the sisters or companions of the abducted maiden who, more typically, flee, run to their father or exhibit signs of distress. As Topper remarks in her review of visual accounts of the scene, the 'painters have exploited the ambiguity of the [Gorgons'] poses in order to mark them simultaneously as pursuers of the hero and as the sisters of the violated maiden'.[15] Although Topper does not make the point, the fact that the sisters run again draws on the choral paradigm. While Section 2 illustrates the co-presence of running races and choral dancing at ritual events, here I would note that these activities are coextensive and all but indistinguishable in a comparable context. A Corinthian black-figure krater dated to ca. 560 offers one of the earliest extant representations of Peleus' abduction of Thetis,[16] shown here together with her sister Nereids

---

[12] Carruesco 2016, esp. 87–101.   [13] See Langdon 2008, 158, 168 with examples.

[14] Argos, Archaeological Museum C 240, with Langdon 2008, 165–66.   [15] Topper 2007, 85.

[16] Paris, Musée du Louvre E 639. For detailed discussion of this and the other objects cited below, see Barringer 1995, 72–73 and 83–87.

Fig. 2.2 Attic red-figure cup by the Poseidon Painter, ca. 510–500 B.C.E. London, British Museum E 15. Photograph © The Trustees of The British Museum.

who form one of the archetypal choral ensembles this study explores (see Chapter 5). With their split skirts and arms held away from their bodies, the maidens not only resemble the Eleusis Gorgons, but, depending on whose reading we follow, are variously interpreted as running or dancing. The indeterminacy occurs again on a number of vessels from the later sixth century on portraying the same scene; on an Attic red-figure cup from ca. 510–500 by the Poseidon Painter, four Nereids flank Peleus and Thetis locked in their struggle (Fig. 2.2); those on the left side run away, while those on the right seem to dance.[17] The Polyphemus artist's choice of visual schema for his Gorgons' legs – one kicked out to the right, the other set straight on the ground – further equates them more with dancers than with those who run, and whose distinctive pose typifies later accounts of the Gorgon pursuers.[18] Among these 'runners' belong the Gorgons on the Protoattic amphora by the Nessos Painter from ca. 660:[19] there, like Medusa herself in other scenes and sculptural representations, the sisters assume their now-characteristic *Knielauf* position.

A closer look at details of the Eleusis image, many of which are also visible in broadly contemporary portrayals of the Gorgons, reveals fresh facets of the artist's adherence to choral iconography, even as he adapts it to

[17] London, British Museum E 15; cf. London, The Victoria and Albert Museum 4807.1901.
[18] See Osborne 1988, 3 for this.
[19] Athens, National Archaeological Museum 1002; cf. the dinos by the Gorgon Painter (Paris, Musée du Louvre E 874).

his monstrous subjects and infuses the familiar with an outlandish and distorted quality. Typical of female choral dancers in Geometric art are the triangular shaped skirts complete with trailing hemlines worn by the Gorgon sisters; these dragging hemlines are first visible on choreutes of the late eighth century,[20] and particularly close to the Eleusis amphora is a fragmentary Protoattic amphora or hydria found in a well in the Athenian agora and dated to the third quarter of the seventh century.[21] Here a line of three women dances to the music supplied by a flute player, their hemlines trailing to the ground while their feet are left exposed.[22]

But in the Eleusis amphora's design of the skirt, split all the way to the thigh, the Polyphemus artist also introduces a marked departure from normative choral dress (see, however, the black-figure krater in Paris with Nereids cited above, where just such skirts appear). These split garments, a fashion modelled after Oriental and more particularly Assyrian sartorial practices, serve early artists as one way of singularizing monstrous females, Amazons on a terracotta shield from Tiryns[23] and an aryballos from Samothrace among them.[24] The style similarly appears on a Gorgon depicted as Mistress of Animals on a plate from Rhodes of ca. 600,[25] where the monster not only wears a split skirt, but kicks out her exposed leg much in the manner of the Eleusis pair (note too the trailing hemline), while the Medusa depicted on a terracotta plaque of ca. 580–570 that belonged to the Temple of Olympian Zeus at Syracuse conspicuously displays her bared legs.[26]

Robin Osborne's reading of the amphora scene sees the revelation of the leg that the split allows as part of the more broadly transgressive character of these particular maidens who, like Amazons, confuse proper gender classifications.[27] Whereas nudity is usually reserved for men and clothing demarcates the female, here the Gorgons mingle aspects of masculinity and femininity, exposing their legs in exactly the manner of the two Gorgons on the Nessos amphora just cited. Nor is this the only feature confusing the choral pair on the Eleusis amphora with their male counterparts; the artist, Jeffrey Hurwit observes, has lavished particular attention on the Gorgons'

---

[20] Crowhurst 1963, no. 1.   [21] Brann 1961, 307–08 and pl. 71.

[22] Crowhurst 1963, 2 suggests that this visual scheme may be an artistic convention that allows painters simultaneously to show the dancer's feet while signalling that the skirt reached to the ground.

[23] For this, see Langdon 2008, 56–57 and her fig. 2.1.   [24] Ahlberg-Cornell 1992, fig. 174.

[25] London, British Museum GR 1860.4–4.2.

[26] Syracuse, Museo Archeologico Regionale 'Paolo Orsi', 34540, 34543, 34895, with discussion and earlier bibliography in Marconi 2007, 54.

[27] Osborne 1988, 3.

limbs, allowing dark, cursive strokes to show through the white paint, a technique that gives them 'unprecedented volume and corporality'.[28] A glance to the figures shown on the vessel's neck confirms the masculine quality of this feature; exactly the same device is used for the bare legs of Odysseus, whose pronounced thighs and slimmer calves echo those of the Gorgons below.

The vigorous movement, one foot thrust in front of the other, performed by the crew members lined up behind Odysseus further links the two scenes. Whereas female dancers tend to take small, mincing steps, the wide stride common to the Eleusis monsters and to their counterparts in the representation of the episode by the contemporary Nessos Painter are more typical not just of men but of male choristers, whether shown with their legs spaced wide apart or actually leaping. Without going so far as to read the figures deployed in linear fashion in the blinding scene on the upper register of the Eleusis vessel as an iteration of the choral theme (although Odysseus' feat would be the matter treated in Philoxenus' dithyrambic *Cyclops*, where a chorus could have danced out the episode), the position of the hero's two followers invites the viewer to compare them with the Gorgon sisters who appear almost directly below them. Visual parallelism between male choristers and the Gorgons informs a black-figure kothon from Boeotia, dated to the second quarter of the sixth century (Fig. 2.3).[29] Here Perseus appears together with the monster decorating the different panels on the legs while a frieze running around the vessel's side depicts five komast dancers with an aulos-player. A glance from the dancing figures with their left legs thrust vigorously before them to the elevated and outstretched limbs of the Gorgons flanking them on one side confirms their participation in a common typology. These visual details all contribute to the larger gender anomaly in which the tripod cauldron is implicated. While epic poetry, the archaeological record and many social and ritual practices unequivocally associate these highly worked and monumentalized objects with aristocratic 'male behaviour and spheres of action', particularly in their role as prizes in athletic competitions and status-declaring votive goods, the vessels also occur in the female and domestic spheres, most markedly in the ceramic models found in women's graves and the use of female figures as tripod attachments (see below).[30]

The snakes that sprout so vividly from the sides of the figures' heads and shoulders on the Eleusis amphora also suit the artist's bifurcated model in

---

[28] Hurwit 1985, 168.   [29] Berlin, Antikensammlung, Schloss Charlottenburg F 1727; *ABV* 29.1.
[30] For this, with the evidence, see the nuanced discussion of Langdon 2008, 270–86. The citation is from p. 270.

Fig. 2.3 Black-figure tripod-kothon by the Painter of Berlin F 1727, ca. 570 B.C.E. Berlin, Antikensammlung, Schloss Charlottenburg. Photograph © 2019. Scala, Florence/ bpk, Bildagentur für Kunst, Kultur und Geschichte, Berlin.

a different respect. Replacing the luxurious locks typical of maiden dancers in the Geometric visual repertoire, and here integral to the terrifying aspect of the sisters, the beasts also have an established place in visual representations of parthenaic choruses. Langdon documents the frequent presence of serpentine elements in images of dancing maidens and, arguing against assigning the creatures the purely funerary significance assumed in most accounts, points to their close association with the meadows where girls dance.[31] So on an Argive krater from Corinth four large white snakes circle around the lower body of the bowl beneath three dancing women wearing belted skirts (Fig. 2.4),[32] while two seals from the Argive Heraion similarly present female dancers and a snake.[33] Eva Brann aptly styles the neck and shoulder fragment from the Attic amphora or hydria of ca. 700, with its series of women in ornamented gowns dancing delicately to the music supplied by a piper, 'snake-draped',[34] and the motif also appears in Alcman's first *Partheneion*, albeit in the more muted form of the 'snake-like' ornaments worn by the parthenaic choristers (fr. 1.67 *PMGF*).

---

[31] Langdon 2008, 156–58.   [32] Corinth, Archaeological Museum T 2545.
[33] Langdon 2008, 156–57 and her fig. 3.15.   [34] Brann 1961, 307.

Fig. 2.4 Late Geometric Argive krater from Corinth. Corinth, Archaeological Museum T 2545. Photograph from C. Blegen, H. Palmer and R. Young, *Corinth XIII* (Princeton, 1964), pp. 35–36, pl. 9, 47–1, courtesy of Ino Ioannidou and Lenia Bartzioti, American School of Classical Studies at Athens, Corinth.

The snakes equipping the Eleusis Gorgons return us to the proto-type used for the design of their heads, and to the artist's simultaneous and very exact adherence to the Orientalizing cauldron paradigm even as he draws on choral iconography. Not only do the beasts sprouting from the head and shoulders of the Gorgon on the right curve around as though forming one half of the handles on the bronze vessels of the period,[35] but the structural composition of the monsters narrowly reproduces the design of cauldrons on contemporary pots in a more wholesale manner. To cite one example, a Protocorinthian lekythos-oinochoe of ca. 700 in New York depicts an Oriental-style cauldron that, like the Gorgons, is tripartite in form (Fig. 2.5);[36] while its topmost portion, complete with snake-like protomes and zigzags at the rim much like the 'growth' topping the Eleusis amphora Gorgons, matches the two sisters' heads, the middle unit presents a bulbous

[35] See Payne 1971, 214.　　[36] New York, Metropolitan Museum of Art 23.160.18.

Fig. 2.5 Protocorinthian conical lekythos-oinochoe, ca. 700 B.C.E. New York, Metropolitan Museum of Art 23.160.18, Rogers Fund 1923. Photograph © The Metropolitan Museum of Art.

diamond equivalent to the Gorgons' torsos; the vessel's triangular base in turn forms the counterpart to their skirts.[37]

Nor is the cauldron motif limited to the dancing duo. The body of Medusa, now in the prone position, offers a reiteration of the cauldron scheme, with a further element added to the pronounced 'factural' motif. With the monster's head already in Perseus' possession, the rounded cauldron belly is now shifted downwards to the torso while again the skirt recalls the vessel's base. The rendering of Medusa's garment reworks, with a difference, the equation between her sisters' heads and a highly ornamented artefact: echoed here is the form of the amphora on which the monster's body appears, complete with its strikingly elongated shape that tapers off at its end. The more small-scale and free-form designs on the skirt reconfigure the vessel's dense ornamentation and repeat some of the motifs included on its surface. The artist has also taken pains with the rendering of the torso, whose scale- or mesh-like decorative features might put a viewer

[37] It is fascinating to observe how, in the Sutton Movement Writing system developed as a notation to record the motions and poses of dances, several of the stylized pictograms exactly match the tripartite cauldron shape; for a particularly suggestive example, see Høgseth 2013, 101, fig. 10.12.

in mind of the hammered and incised ornamental elements on breast plates and other types of the metal-forged objects already evoked by her sisters.[38]

But how do we fit these cauldrons into the larger choral scheme? Many existing discussions of the concern simply identify the artist's model while neglecting to comment on why he chooses to include cauldrons in the composition; others, seeking to explain the vessels' presence, observe that the beast protomes invest the sisters with the requisite uncanny, outlandish and demonic air. So, in Herrmann's view, the attachments inspire 'Schrecklichkeit',[39] while the suggestive account by Papalexandrou interprets the decorations on the vessels' rims, and Orientalizing cauldrons more broadly, as indices of the 'new, dangerous, and uncontrollable dimension of the world' that the Greeks were encountering in their trading and colonizing ventures of the period.[40] The very choice of incident for the body of the Eleusis amphora, Perseus' encounter with the Gorgons, is, of course, in and of itself a locus of terror and anxiety, and the artist's presentation of the monsters and of their heads in particular magnifies this fearsome dimension in several respects. With their faces presented frontally – in the manner of the *gorgoneia* used as temple antefixes from the seventh century on – the Gorgons' eyes meet those of the amphora viewer, a device replicated by the topmost snake protomes on their heads. As rendered by the painter, these snakes come complete with 'savagely glaring' eyes (cf. [Hes.] *Sc.* 236) and take their impetus from real world cauldron models, whose attachments typically accentuate the beasts' (apotropaic?) powers of sight by equipping them with just such bulging eyes; these often take the form of inserts in another metal whose sparkle further draws the viewers' gaze and risks exercising the Gorgon's own 'transfixing' power.

The issue of visuality – its possibility and foreclosure at the moment of death – is not only, in Osborne's compelling reading, the leitmotif that links the amphora's several figural scenes and gives the vessel its thematic significance, but also directs us back to the Iliadic tripods. As noted in the earlier discussion, they too are view-worthy, awe-inspiring objects, whose wheels, gleaming, precious and moving attachments yet to be fixed on, the poet styles *thauma idesthai* (*Il.* 18.377). An artist seeking to draw his viewers' attention to one among the chief innovatory aspects of his undoubtedly high-priced vessel, and to convey what may be his central motif, can do no better than to portray figures that are conceived in the likeness of these manufactured goods, designed from the *Iliad* on to compel

---

[38] For additional affinities between metalwork and textiles, see Chapter 7.
[39] Herrmann 1979, 141.   [40] Papalexandrou 2005, 170; see too Marconi 2007, 213.

audiences – whether Thetis, or the visitors to sacred sites and the gods to whom the objects are so often dedicated – to look and marvel at their highly worked appearance and to register the requisite sensations of admiration for the craftsman and wonder (*thauma*) at the product.

The pronounced visuality given to Medusa's sisters' cauldron heads is likewise implicated in the larger episode chosen by the artist for his central scene: Perseus' slaying of the monster and his escape with the head, the locus of its too potent eyes.[41] A concern with an exchange of looks and the capacity of the outward facing gaze to instigate a response, now primarily of horror but also of fascination and aesthetic appreciation in the one who meets the fashioned or painted eye, is apparent in the treatment of the *gorgoneion* in the *Iliad*; here, at 11.33–40, the monster, 'looking grimly', appears in company with Terror and Fear on the topmost portion of Agamemnon's shield with its fantastical 'twenty gleaming bosses of white tin'. Complete with the three-headed enamel snake wound around its strap, the design of the hero's metallic shield also transforms the Gorgon into a richly ornamented manufactured object, which anticipates the amphora's representation of the sisters' heads as just such metal-forged artefacts, here additionally 'materialized' by being placed on a finely decorated terracotta vessel. Early vase painters adopt the same Gorgon motif for their representations of Achilles' shield, following not just the literary precedent in *Iliad* 11, but also that of contemporary shields and their intricately wrought bands, where the same blazon and sometimes, in the latter instance, the Gorgons' encounter with Perseus occurs.[42] On the reverse side of an Attic black-figure neck amphora in Boston attributed to the Camtar Painter and dated to ca. 550,[43] Thetis presents the hero with his new shield, here distinguished by its 'Boeotian' design, on whose surface the artist has placed a frontal *gorgoneion*; in this instance, the face is a blank, but the multiple snakes topping the head and forming the two shoulder blades beneath the chin come complete with staring eyes, the latter two shown frontally.[44] As though to underscore the singularity of the motif, on the vessel's other side the artist positions six hoplite warriors, equipped with more workaday circular shields with geometric patterns.

---

[41] As much explored by Osborne 1988 and Mack 2002.

[42] For discussion, see Squire 2013, 167 and for the shield bands, see Marconi 2007, 145. Note too the [Hesiodic] *Scutum* cited in section 3 (a description of Heracles' shield), and Eur. *El.* 459–60, where the encounter between Perseus and Medusa similarly forms one among the scenes forged on this revisionary account of the Iliadic precedent.

[43] Boston, Museum of Fine Arts 21.21; *ABV* 84.3, *Para.* 31.

[44] For this and other examples, see Squire 2013, 167 with additional bibliography in his n. 93.

But appeals to the terror, awe and fascination informing the attachments on the Orientalizing cauldrons on the Eleusis amphora and other uses of the Gorgon motif more generally, and the contribution of this scene and its rendering to the larger 'ocular' theme that gives the pot its coherence, only go some way to explaining the Polyphemus Painter's choice of design.[45] So rather than limiting my reading to these interpretative routes, I propose at least in part to resolve the puzzle of the Gorgons' protome-cauldron heads by looking once again to the choral paradigm also shaping the monstrous triads' presentation and by developing the suggestion already introduced in Chapter 1 concerning the multifaceted association between cauldrons and choral dancing. Where my analysis of the tripods wrought by Hephaestus in his Iliadic forge focused on the aesthetic and kinetic properties shared by the artefacts and choristers performing their song and dance, and noted intersections between the vocabulary used for the manufacture of the wondrous objects and the formation and deployment of choral ensembles, here I document the chiefly ritual practices that offer close analogues to the combination of dance and cauldrons on the Eleusis amphora and suggest continuities between the representation of caul-drons and of choreutes in visual accounts. As I go on to detail, the arrangement devised by the Polyphemus Painter makes much better sense when read in the context of depictions of these occasions in the texts and vase imagery of the archaic period and in the later sources that retroject sometimes current rites back to an earlier and often myth-ical age.

First the convention very apparent in the seventh-century visual reper-toire of equipping (uniquely) female dancers with a variety of vessels carried on their heads. A work known as the Flowery Ornaments stand, also assigned to the Polyphemus Painter, features two choral ensembles.[46] A procession with nine warriors fills the lower portion of the conical stand together with a single figure wearing a chiton and shorter himation and prancing with his heels lifted. Matching these marchers is a second proces-sion of twelve women on the upper bowl of the stand, their mouths open as if in song, balancing protome cauldrons on their heads; these vessels are painted white to signal the metal's gleam. As Sarah Morris comments, the placement of the female figures just below the rim 'suggests a conscious

---

[45] *Contra* the view of Papalexandrou 2005, 170–73, there were many other markers available for signalling foreignness and female monstrosity, the dancers' split skirts among them, and the sources supply no evidence for the new objects of dedication provoking the largely negative response that Papalexandrou assigns to them.

[46] Berlin, Antikensammlung A 41 and 44. See the discussion in Morris 1984, 46–47.

allusion to the now-lost clay (or metal?) cauldron supported on the stand' and positioned directly above the dancers' heads,[47] offering an instance of the practice of that 'skeuomorphism' whereby metal goods are reconfigured into terracotta versions. In another instance, an eighth-century bronze statuette from Olympia shows a female figure dressed in a robe with incised designs, her right arm raised to support the biconical vessel on her head.[48] The figure may originally have served as a fixture on a tripod cauldron, a counterpart to the warriors and horses that supply the more usual attachments. From dancers carrying pots on their heads to pot-headed dancers, and from vessel-carrying bronze females topping cauldrons to (painted) bronze cauldrons on the heads of females, it seems a short enough step.

A second link between cauldrons and choral dancing depends on the vessels' role as focal elements in the space where choruses staged their ritual song and dance. According to Himerius (*Or.* 48.10–11 = Alc. fr. 307c V.), Alcaeus composed a paean, probably for performance at Delphi, celebrating Apollo. In Himerius' gloss of the no longer extant work, 'the citizens of Delphi . . . composing a paean accompanied by music and staging dances of youths around the tripod, invoked Apollo to leave the land of the Hyperboreans and to come to them'. A tripod-circling choral event might plausibly have occurred in the context of a ritual at a second sacred and oracular site. Plentiful attestations exist for a ceremony involving an annual theoric procession in which Boeotians carried a tripod for dedication at the sanctuary of Zeus at Dodona (on which, see section 3), and Proclus' catalogue of religious choral compositions lists a 'tripod-carrying song' (τριποδοφορικὸν μέλος, *Chrest.* 321[b]33) performed by way of escort and of which Pindar's fr. 59 S.-M. may be our sole remaining example.[49] Granted, the very lacunose fragment includes no mention of dancing in association with the procession, and refers only to tripods and to something that 'shares in the lyre', but it is tempting to conjecture that the chorus performing the piece might also have executed a dance around the vessel once it reached its destination.

Other early classical and later songs imagine and, I would propose, restage this association between tripods and the choral dance and align the chorus members and vessels still more closely. The previous chapter cited the proem to Bacchylides' third ode, where the song's performers

---

[47] Morris 1984, 47.

[48] Athens, National Archaeological Museum 6218. See Langdon 1998, 259–60 and fig. 10, whose interpretation I follow here. See too Langdon 2008, 273–74.

[49] For the fragment, see Rutherford 2001, 427–29.

prompt their audience to visualize two sets of renowned and opulent tripod cauldrons (one, in my speculative suggestion, currently on display near to the performance site) and modelled themselves after these longer-lasting votive goods set up at Syracuse and Delphi, while the chorus in Euripides' *Ion* echoes the event recorded by Alcaeus when it celebrates in song and dance the Delphic site, 'where Phoebus' umbilical hearth of the earth offers oracles near the tripod circled by dances' (χορευομένῳ τρίποδι, 461–64). A later hymn to Hestia by Aristonous of Corinth, preserved in an inscription dated to ca. 334/3, offers a second such dense and imagistic interplay between the chorus performing the ode and the Delphic tripods (*SIG* 449.1–17):

> ἱερὰν ἱερῶν ἄνασσαν
> Ἑστίαν ὑμνήσομεν, ἃ καὶ Ὄλυμπον
> καὶ μυχὸν γαίας μεσόμφαλον ἀεί
> Πυθίαν τε δάφναν κατέχουσα
> ναὸν ἀν' ὑψίπυλον Φοίβου χορεύεις   5
> τερπομένα τριπόδων θεσπίσμασι,
> καὶ χρυσέαν φόρμιγγ' Ἀπόλλων
> ὁπηνίκ' ἂν ἑπτάτονον
> κρέκων μετὰ σοῦ θαλιάζον-
> τας θεοὺς ὕμνοισιν αὔξῃ.   10
> χαῖρε Κρόνου θύγατερ
> καὶ Ῥέας, μούνα πυρὸς ἀμφιέπουσα
> βωμοὺς ἀθανάτων ἐριτίμους,
> Ἑστία, δίδου δ' ἀμοιβάς
> ἐξ ὁσίων πολὺν ἡμᾶς   15
> ὄλβον ἔχοντας ἀεὶ λιπαρόθρονον
> ἀμφὶ σὰν θυμέλαν χορεύειν.

Let us hymn holy Hestia, queen of the holy ones, who holds forever sway over Olympus and the navel in the recesses of the earth, and the Pythian laurel, you who dance in the high-gated temple of Phoebus, taking delight in the oracular voices of tripods, and Apollo's golden seven-stringed phorminx, whenever he plays it to exalt, with you, the feasting gods in his hymns. Hail, daughter of Cronus and Rhea, who alone brings fire to the honoured altars of the immortals; Hestia, give us, in exchange for our prayers, prosperity without impiety and to sing and dance around your bright-throned altar for ever.

Although, in the closing lines, the altar supplies the centrepoint about which the choristers wish perpetually to sing and dance, the earlier part

Fig. 2.6 Attic black-figure skyphos from the Kerameikos, ca. 735–720 B.C.E. Interior. Athens, National Archaeological Museum 874. Photograph Giannis Patrikianos © Hellenic Ministry of Sport/Archaeological Receipts Fund.

of the *Hymn* explicitly connects Hestia's paradigmatic performance to tripods and further associates her dance with the vessels' voices, investing them with the capacity to speak, and, in this instance, perhaps to sing.[50] Apparent here too is the choreutes' self-projection onto the divine song and dance within the sacred recess: figuring Hestia's action as a specifically choral dance (χορεύεις, 5), they map their own activities onto hers as they describe themselves engaged in just that activity (χορεύειν, 17). Rounding out the picture of a divine choral performance is the presence of Apollo, the ur-*chorêgos* equipped with his lyre, accompanying Hestia in their joint celebration (ὕμνοισιν) of the other immortals; even so do the latter-day celebrants hymn (ὑμνήσομεν, 1) the goddess with their song of tribute.[51] The internal rings created by these repetitions, which link deities and the chorus first in one direction, and then in its reverse, might perhaps reflect the movement of the dancers: just as Hestia turns about the tripod in the manner described by the *Ion* chorus, so they circle around the altar at the shrine.

A Geometric skyphos from the Kerameikos portrays a performance of just this kind, positioning tripod cauldrons as the objects around which the choral dancers turn and turn about (Figs. 2.6, 2.7).[52] Here three choruses of men and women, hands joined in a cyclical dance executed to the music of

[50] Section 3 focuses on this dimension of the tripod cauldron.
[51] For these echoes, see LeVen 2014, 298–99.
[52] Athens, National Archaeological Museum 874.

Fig. 2.7 Attic black-figure skyphos from the Kerameikos, ca. 735–720 B.C.E. Exterior. Athens, National Archaeological Museum 874. Photograph Giannis Patrikianos © Hellenic Ministry of Sport/Archaeological Receipts Fund.

the lyre-player, fill the interior of the vessel while a frieze of eight tripod cauldrons encircles its outer surface. The deployment of the tripods may reflect the spatial dynamic of a dance performed on behalf of Apollo by choruses on the Athenian Acropolis,[53] a site that displayed a rich cache of such objects from the Late Geometric period on. As Papalexandrou comments, 'the visual distinction between "exterior" (tripods-phenomenal backdrop) and "interior" (dance) corresponds to an inverse spatial arrangement in pragmatic circumstances . . . the tripods on the pot may stand as the ritual epicentre around which the choral event on the interior takes place'.[54]

In the conventional reading of the Kerameikos skyphos, the artist includes the vessels because they would have served as prizes in the dancing contests occurring on the inside of the cup. Some would situate the scenes more narrowly, seeing in the motifs' combination a representation of the choral event at the Thargeleia, on whose second day the winners of the dithyrambic competition would dedicate the tripod they had won at the sanctuary of Apollo.[55] A second vase from the Kerameikos (Fig. 2.8),[56] an object whose upper part is shaped in the manner of a tripod cauldron complete with ring handles positioned on the rim, portrays among its dense figurative scenes a dance performed by five youths; large scale Orientalizing cauldrons (as high as the choreutes, and whose overall configuration is suggestive of the dancers' own shape) with animal protomes on highly decorated stands flank the performers on either

---

[53] Karouzou 1954, 9, taken up by Papalexandrou 2005, 196–97.

[54] Papalexandrou 2005, 196–97.

[55] Karouzou 1954, 9 and Borell 1978, 66, whose views many later scholars follow. For the Thargeleia, see Wilson 2007.

[56] Athens, National Archaeological Museum 810.

Fig. 2.8 Late Geometric funerary krater from the Kerameikos. Athens, National Archaeological Museum 810. Photograph Irini Miari © Hellenic Ministry of Culture and Sports/Archaeological Receipts Fund.

side.[57] This dance, in J. N. Coldstream's view, would have formed one among the agonistic events at funeral games celebrated on behalf of the aristocrat buried in the grave where the object was disinterred.[58] The textual repertoire amply confirms the use of cauldrons as prizes in musical competitions from the late eighth or early seventh century on (see Hes. *Erg.* 656–67), but more specific to a victory-winning choral dance is the no longer extant bronze tripod cauldron dedicated on the Athenian Acropolis in the first decades of the fifth century, whose inscribed base (*IG* I³ 833 *bis*) reads:

[νικέ]σας hό[δε πρõ]τον Ἀθένεσ[ιν χο]ρõι νδρõ[ν] |
[ἀσκε]τẽς σοφ[ίας τόνδ' ἀνέθε[κ]εν hόρον |
[εὐχσ]άμενο[ς· π]λείστοις δὲ [χ]οροῖς ἔσχο κατὰ φῦ[λα] |
[ἀνδ]ρõν νι[κẽ]σαί φεσι π[ερ]ὶ τρίποδος.

---

[57] See Pernice 1892, 206–07, who demonstrates that the handles consciously imitate the round handles of hammered bronze tripods even as the painted horses on the handles follow the model of bronze horses on Geometric tripods.

[58] Coldstream 2003, 119. Or, in keeping with the skyphos, the scene might attest to the dead man's participation in choral dancing, for which this very lavishly decorated vessel with its unusual shape and wealth of heroizing scenes might have been the prize.

[having won] first with a chorus of men at Athens this man dedicated this
horos of (lovely? practised?) poetic skill as he had vowed to; and he claims to
have won with very many choruses of men overseas among nations for the
honour of a tripod. (text and translation, with modifications, after Bowie
2010)

In my return to the inscription in Chapter 8, I propose that the expression
π[ερ]ὶ τρίποδος in the final line reflects not just the role of the vessel as
commemorative prize, but another tripod-encircling performance.

As the evidence just reviewed suggests, tempering the seeming singularity of the depiction of the Gorgons on the Eleusis amphora are more
recognizable elements drawn from Greek ritual and agonistic practices.
This mix of the familiar and outlandish exists alongside a second coincidence of contrasting spheres: even as the sisters' appearance highlights
their monstrous and fearsome qualities, the presence of objects so valuable,
precious and highly worked that they belong in the world of gods as well as
that of men reinforces the already charged character of the Gorgons'
activity, their performance of the choral dance that in and of itself bridges
the divine and mortal spheres. As numerous texts, the *Homeric Hymn to
Apollo* and Pindar's epinicia most emphatically, demonstrate, when youths
and maidens join hands in the dance they engage in a gesture that
momentarily assimilates them and their audiences to the ever-dancing
gods, making them, in the Homeric hymnist's words as he deploys
a doublet normally reserved for the Olympians alone, 'immortal and
unaging' (151). In Section 2 of the discussion, I aim to show how the
Eleusis amphora restages and reconceives such a moment of assimilation
in a further respect, calling to mind two ritual acts which would have
brought the pot's youthful occupant into the presence of the divine even
as it aggrandizes and celebrates that individual for his quasi-heroic feat.

2   Contextualizing the Eleusis Amphora

In the argument presented in section 1, the Polyphemus Painter's portrayal
of the Gorgon sisters' heads in the manner of Orientalizing protome
cauldrons has its impetus in more than just a search for the exotic, alarming
and rococo. Instead it follows from both the visual conventions used for
representations of choruses of dancing maidens and their status as fabu-
lously 'factured' goods, and from the multiple ritual connections, some also
embedded in early artistic practice, between cauldrons and the dance. In

what follows, I aim to integrate the reading developed so far within
a possible reconstruction of the 'life history' of the amphora, showing
how the presence of the cauldrons in the Gorgon scene could illuminate
the choral context for which the vessel might originally have been designed
while also explaining its subsequent selection as the container for the body
of the youthful deceased.[59]

While several fine accounts have associated the Eleusis amphora's iconography with its role as burial vessel,[60] this reading fails to reckon with the
fact that the pot seems not primarily designed for a funerary purpose.[61]
Instead there is an indicator of a shift in role: its lower half had to be severed
off so as to introduce the body of the dead and the amphora was then
clamped back together with lead before being placed on its side in the grave
in the west cemetery of Eleusis.[62] Also arguing against a purely funerary
function is the fact that narrative mythical scenes such as those displayed
on the amphora decorate fewer than a quarter of the pots used for child
burials in Attica; the singularity of its iconography thus makes the vase
idiosyncratic rather than an expression of a common *mentalité* and shared
notion of death that, in some accounts, its selection of images variously
articulates.[63]

Taken together, these several factors should alert us to the amphora's
more variegated history and to the several functions it could have filled
at different points in its trajectory from the potter's workshop to the
cemetery. In the interpretation developed here, in accordance with
the practice of using Protoattic pottery in the context of 'liminal'
events, moments of importance in the social life of individuals, and

---

[59] By way of caveat, I grant that my reconstruction of the pot's trajectory is only one among many
     stories that could be told, but the evidence presented gives the 'career' suggested here additional
     plausibility.

[60] Most particularly that of Osborne 1988.

[61] Morris 1984, 11 and Morris 1998, 30–32. As one of my readers notes, this scission neatly
     recapitulates the decapitation shown on the vase.

[62] As Langdon 2001, 580, comments, 'in an archaeological context, shifts in meaning may be
     detected more readily when an object demonstrates movement in time or space through some
     visual sign of dislocation', among them a break mended.

[63] See Morris 1998, 31; Whitley 1994, 56. As Whitley also documents, contrary to the earlier view,
     'Protoattic was not exclusively a funerary style', and could be found in a variety of contexts. One
     final element makes the amphora stand out and argues for its membership of a class of pottery
     associated not expressly with death, but with other moments of importance in the social life of
     individuals: its emphatically Orientalizing elements, visible not just in the form of the cauldrons
     with their snake protomes, but also in the rosettes on the thighs of Odysseus' men. Whitley has
     demonstrated the relative resistance of Dark Age Attica to Orientalizing motifs and the tenacity
     of the Geometric style on painted pottery compared with the readiness with which Euboea,
     Crete and even neighbouring Aegina welcomed the foreign and exotic style.

of deploying pots and other manufactured goods in the rituals accompanying these events and/or as commemorative markers of the same, the Eleusis amphora would have celebrated and served as lasting testimony to the dead boy's earlier participation in some kind of maturation rite. It would then have been chosen as funerary vessel because it could both 'signify the life stage last attained' and 'bring an incomplete social state to posthumous closure'.[64] One caveat does, however, need to be observed: although the dead child is regularly identified as a boy, some ten to twelve years of age, the gender of young bones remains hard to determine. A different story line – although one that still featured liminal moments in the life of the deceased and even choral dancing – would have to be reconstructed in the case of a young girl.[65]

The presence of the Gorgons, and of Odysseus' confrontation with Polyphemus too,[66] allows us, albeit speculatively, to reconstruct the first stage of this vessel's heterogeneous career. As many discussions have shown,[67] Perseus' encounter with Medusa and her sisters was a central myth in the maturation rites celebrated in different parts of Greece, in which youths on the cusp of manhood would participate in a variety of symbolic trials, several featuring re-enactments of the hero's encounter with the monsters and the pursuit that followed.[68] To cite just some among the scattered pieces of evidence, grotesque, Gorgon-like masks found at Tiryns and at the sanctuary of Artemis Orthia in Sparta, a site closely associated with initiation rituals for both boys and girls,[69] may have been worn by dancers in dramatized contests featuring 'frightful female creatures' opposed by a heroic young man, representative of a larger group of

---

[64] Langdon 2001, 584.

[65] Langdon 2001, 598 also comments that 'Geometric child burials are not clearly gendered male or female'.

[66] While I fully recognize that a more complete reading of the vase such as Osborne 1988 supplies would accommodate this and the third figurative scene too (the lion attack), my discussion focuses all but exclusively on the Gorgon image.

[67] Particularly influential is the article of Jameson 1990; see too Marinatos 2000, 59–61, Langdon 2008, 74–76 and Carter 1987.

[68] It may be objected that Attica has supplied no evidence for the practice of the types of maturation rites explicitly connected with Perseus and/or with Gorgons such as were staged at Mycenae, Tiryns and Sparta, and that the Perseus myth and its celebration and re-enactment in the choral songs and the ritual events where the pieces were performed are much more prominent in the cities of the Argive plain and Sparta (see Kowalzig 2007, 129–80 for these); however, the archetypal role of Perseus as a successfully maturing youth would have been sufficiently widespread to guarantee its familiarity to and suitability for the Eleusis amphora's more local audience.

[69] Carter 1987; Langdon 2008, 74–76.

initiates,[70] while a sixth-century inscription from Mycenae notes the appointment of judges, the 'recorders of sacred matters for Perseus' as arbiters 'in the place of parents', seemingly a reference to the appointees' adjudication of contests among young boys participating in maturation rites.[71] In a widely cited article treating the inscription, Michael Jameson connects the Mycenaean ritual with the masks at Tiryns and elsewhere, and further postulates Perseus' role as 'patron of the institution whereby boys took their place in the archaic community of Mykenai'.[72]

The amphora artist's choice to depict a dance and pursuit combined fits neatly into this ritual frame. As noted in the previous chapter, the choral dancers on the Hephaestus-forged shield of *Iliad* 18 already unite the two activities as they alternate between running (θρέξασκον, 599) and circle dancing, a sequence immediately reconfigured in the simile of the potter's wheel that the ceramicist spins 'to see if it might run (θέησιν)' (601). The two exist in tandem in historical rituals too; whether we look to the Spartan Karneia, or to the rites performed by maidens at the coming-of-age festival of the Heraia at Elis, or to the festival celebrated at the sanctuary of Artemis Brauronia, youthful initiates of both sexes participate in a combination of choral dancing and running races, actions that Alcman's first *Partheneion* and the finale of Pindar's ninth *Pythian* conflate into one or present side by side.[73] In the first of the Spartan poet's choral songs, a horse race is used by way of figure for the actions of the two *chorêgoi* leading the maiden performers (58–59), and in one reading of lines 8–9 of his *Parth.* 3, the singers' description of how, following their participation in an *agôn* (πεδ' ἀγῶν), they will subsequently '(rapidly) shake my yellow hair' suggests first a race and then a dance.[74] The association occurs anew in Theocritus' transposition of the once live choral occasion to the written page: the

---

[70] See Jameson 1990, 217; the youth was perhaps equipped with one of the sickles that have also been found at Tiryns. The reconstruction is not unproblematic, particularly because the Tiryns masks lack many of the characteristics that Gorgons regularly display (the artefacts have deeply furrowed faces, grinning mouths with protruding tusks, huge ears and bulging eyes). But, as Marinatos 2000, 61 concludes, for all that the rituals may have preserved different regional identities, there is no denying the link between the initiation mask and the *gorgoneion*, and the relevance of Perseus to the maturation scenario. In addition to the finds at Tiryns and the sanctuary of Orthia, excavators discovered an early seventh-century bronze votive mask at the Theban Kabeirion with round eyes, open mouth displaying sharp teeth and snaky locks; the similarity of the material found at this site to that of Kato Syme, where initiation rites did occur, suggests that the mask served a similar purpose.

[71] *IG* IV 493, with discussion in Jameson 1990.   [72] Jameson 1990, 215.

[73] These examples receive more detailed discussion in other chapters.

[74] Hamilton 1989, 467–68; note that the next phrase legible on the papyrus refers to the girls' 'soft feet', which further suggests a dance; for shaking the hair in the dance, see the close parallel in Eur. *IT* 1145–50.

maiden chorus that, within the 'originary' epithalamic occasion conjured
up in *Idyll* 18 now celebrates Helen with a wedding song and dance, recalls
how formerly it would race together with its *chorêgos*-now-turned-bride by
the banks of the Eurotas, an activity that serves as precursor/rehearsal for
its current performance.[75] Strikingly, and whether in reality, or more likely
in the constructions projected onto them by artists and writers, celebrations of the Arkteia were occasions on which maidens might run/dance
with their limbs – and more – exposed; so a series of images on *krateriskoi*
from Brauron dated to the first half of the fifth century depict girls either
nude or in short dresses sometimes running, sometimes dancing, and, on
occasion, headed towards an altar.[76] Two vessels supply evidence for more
formalized group choral dancing at the Brauronia. A fragmentary black-
figure pyxis disinterred at the site depicts three women holding hands and
arranged in a choral formation, accompanied by a piper facing them;[77]
a female aulete, seated in this instance, provides the music for the dance
performed by an ensemble of women who dance around the lid of
a fragmentary red-figure pyxis lid also recovered from Brauron.[78]

No less relevant is the gesture performed by the individual at the
successful completion of at least some of these rites, the dedication of
a tripod cauldron. In their accounts of the Theban Daphnephoria, where
a youth of good family, attractive physique and flourishing health served as
priest of Apollo Ismenios for a year, and whose initiatory character for both
girls (who participated in choral dances at the event) and boys Calame has
documented,[79] both Pausanias and Proclus observe that it became customary for the parents of the *daphnephoros* to dedicate a cauldron on the
youth's behalf to Apollo, this placed in the Ismenion when the term of
office was done.[80] Indeed, in one plausible reading, the famous inscribed
Mantiklos statuette of ca. 700–675,[81] with its request to Apollo for a *charis*-
filled return, would have been just such a cauldron attachment.[82] The
figurine would have adorned a vessel designed to commemorate in permanent metallic form Mantiklos' participation in the Theban ritual. If the
dedication of a cauldron not only signalled the terminus to the rite but, in
the context of a boy's admission into the society of adult men, also

[75] See Hamilton 1989, 468 with his n. 68.
[76] For recent discussion, with older bibliography, see Ferrari 2002, 167–76.
[77] Brauron, Archaeological Museum of Brauron 527 (A 3).
[78] Brauron, Archaeological Museum of Brauron 276 (A 50).   [79] Calame 1997, 103–04.
[80] Paus. 9.10.4, Proclus *apud* Photius, *Bibl.* Cod. 239, p. 321a Bekker; for discussion, see Kurke 2007, esp. 71–84.
[81] Boston, Museum of Fine Arts 03.997, with further discussion in Chapters 7 and 8.
[82] Papalexandrou 2005, 84–86.

articulated a claim to an elevated social status,[83] the selection of the opulent and outsized Eleusis amphora could similarly enhance and affirm the boy's position in his new group of peers.

The Orientalizing elements in the design and iconography of the cauldrons depicted by the Polyphemus Painter and that are visible elsewhere on the vessel too, have additional pertinence to the social status advertised by the vessel. Several scholars have addressed the question of the use of objects with Orientalizing features, as opposed to those of more indigenous and traditional design, as dedications and grave goods, and have tracked the rate at which the different regions of Greece embraced the new style.[84] Since, following Whitley's analysis (see n. 63), Attica proved singularly resistant to this 'exotic material culture',[85] the deployment of an Orientalizing pot at Eleusis would have been a considered and deliberate choice on the part of the object's commissioner. But accounts of the significance of that choice differ from one discussion to the next. For Ian Morris,[86] Orientalizing metal offerings are statements of prestige, broadcasting the dedicator's status-conferring links to the East, and are also invested with the heroizing associations of the cauldrons and tripods that featured as top-rank prizes and gifts in Homeric song. As noted in Section 1, Papalexandrou prefers to view the Orientalizing tripod as 'an alternative means for registering the same kinds of claims to power and authority as those assertively manifested by the revered, age-old tripod',[87] but by a different group. Citing Herodotus' report that one Kolaios marked the conclusion of his successful eastern trading venture with the dedication of a monumentalized bronze cauldron, complete with a 'row of continuous griffin heads around its rim ... and supported on three kneeling figures in bronze, eleven and a half feet high' (4.152) at the Samian Heraion, Papalexandrou suggests that such artefacts represented an attempt on the part of these *nouveaux riches* to claim a share of the social prestige that the existing elite enjoyed.

The Eleusis amphora could be accommodated within each of these accounts; a player in the local prestige 'sweepstakes' in which seventh-century aristocrats engaged, it would declare the prominence of the boy's

---

[83] As suggested by Papalexandrou 2005, esp. 149–88.

[84] Whitley 1994, Morris 1998, Papalexandrou 2005.

[85] Whitley 1994, 60 explains this on the grounds of the social structure of Athens and the surrounding area, where aristocrats jealously guarded their symbolic privileges and resisted artistic novelties because 'their style and iconography cannot easily be fitted into the existing symbolic order, an order which relates directly to material needs'.

[86] Morris 1998, 276–79.   [87] Papalexandrou 2005, 171.

family and the high position he could claim in his community of peers, or serve as an assertion of the wealth that a successful trader had acquired through the course of his travels in distant parts, and that he was now parlaying into 'symbolic capital' on his son's behalf on his more native ground. But the object also admits a further and less self-seeking reading. If the amphora had been commissioned and purchased to celebrate a boy's participation in maturation rites, then the heads are not just visual reminders of that successful rite of passage; in a display of how the foreign and dangerous can be tamed and mastered in Greek hands and stripped of its threatening and even monstrous properties, the Orientalizing cauldrons are here assimilated into indigenous practices and myths, and much like Medusa's own head that finds its home on Athena's protective shield, made into articles that have a role in community-building rituals and that can play a part in acts of piety towards gods in local contexts.

The amphora cauldrons may possess a further significance and commemorative potential. Since choral dancing and races at maturation rites were competitive in character, the vessels could bring to mind a tripod-winning performance by the youth and his age mates on the original festive occasion. The vase in Athens cited earlier (Fig. 2.8) that combines tripods and dancers seems to possess much of the mnemonic character suggested here: its upper portion has the form of a cauldron, a shape that would visually recall the metal version that was the prize at the event, while the pot features what is unmistakably a chorus of dancing *youths* – witness their shoulder-length hair and well-toned legs.[88] That these large-scale metal prizes also served as votives whose dedication would, on occasion, be *de rigueur*, a remark by Herodotus affirms; as he notes, 'long ago', the bronze tripods won by athletes at the Games of Apollo Tropaion were awarded only on condition that they not be taken away but be 'dedicated on the spot to the god' (1.144). The inscribed tripod cauldron dedication from Athens cited earlier celebrates and commemorates the victory of the choristers and of their poet/*chorêgos* in a dithyrambic competition.

In my necessarily tentative reconstruction of the amphora's biography, then, its iconography would be a means of gesturing towards and reflecting on a critical event in the life course of an individual. In representing the Gorgon sisters, the painter has combined an archetypal myth of maturation (or rather two, when place is made for the Polyphemus scene) with elements drawn from the type of ritual event that staged its re-enactment, showing at once Perseus' triumph over Medusa and his subsequent success

---

[88] See Papalexandrou 2005, 197 for detailed discussion of this point.

in the race against his pursuers, these invested with that choral identity which protagonists in the rituals would similarly assume. Recalling the deceased's participation in a coming-of-age festival, here projected onto the fantastical realm that such events brought into play, the depiction of the Gorgon dancers with their cauldron heads additionally evokes the dedication of a bronze vessel on the youth's behalf. Perhaps inscribed with an epigram of the type found on such vessels at sacred sites and that compel divine attendance each time the text is read out loud, the original metallic object would lastingly restage for its viewers the moment of exchange between men and gods and the piety and glory of its giver at this crucial moment of 'passage'. The painted amphora, which might have been displayed at the youth's home, could supply a secondary recollection of that moment, prompting its own celebratory revisiting of the earlier event. The amphora's markedly Orientalizing iconography suits this account: as noted above, Protoattic and Orientalizing pottery frequently occur in the context of such 'liminal' occasions.

The selection of the vessel as a funerary container would follow on from its commemorative potential. Already implicated in the youth's life history, and integral to the fashioning of his social persona, it would take its place in another rite of passage where it continued to shape and propagate its occupant's identity. Not only would the pot stand testament to the transition from boyhood to young adulthood which the youth had successfully negotiated, and together with the scene on its neck, perhaps preview the 'heroic' career that he would have gone on to enjoy; by effecting the boy's integration into the timeless world of myth and displaying two acts of heroism in which individuals successfully withstand death-dealing monsters, male and female both, the amphora recommends itself for its funerary role by virtue of its capacity to suggest that the deceased may transcend the limits of his own mortality. It is to this realm of atemporality and the overcoming of death's arresting power that the third section of the discussion returns.

3   Voices of Bronze

In the suggestion of the earlier sections of this chapter, cauldrons evoke chorality on two particular counts: first, because they, like the choral dancers, are offerings designed to summon the gods into the world of men on ritual and more casual occasions, 'presentifying' them for participants and audiences attending the events; and second, because the vessels, like other *agalmata* explored elsewhere in this study, share in the luminosity, grace, opulence, artisanal and gaze-compelling aspect, and even the swift and synchronized motion characteristic of choristers. In this third section of the discussion, I add to the equation a further attribute that creates fresh links between the motifs on the Eleusis amphora (the Gorgon heads chief among these, but elements elsewhere on the pot too), *choreia* and cauldrons: the acoustic dimension, and the singular powers of vocalization common to singing choruses, the artefacts and Gorgons both here and more generally.

It should, at the outset, be noted that sound is fundamental to Gorgon ontology. Scholars derive the sisters' name from the Sanskrit root *garg, itself cognate with terms signifying guttural and gurgling sounds and the gullet or throat; the pendulous tongue that so many representations of Gorgons and *gorgoneia* display – among the many instances, we might look to the pediment of the Syracusan Temple of Apollo of ca. 590–580 or a second such probably pedimental *gorgoneion* from Molino a Vento at Gela of just ten years earlier – prohibits all articulate speech, while the distended mouth magnifies the monsters' terrible shriek.[89] Their incoherence notwithstanding, accounts of the monsters' encounter with Perseus equip the episode with a fearsome soundtrack, with snakes in the starring role. Noise (along with the fixating gaze mentioned more in passing) is already a standout feature of the representation of the Gorgons in the Pseudo-Hesiodic *Scutum*, where the animated snakes again appear participating in the pursuit of Perseus as depicted on the shield's adamantine surface (232–37):

βαινουσέων ἰάχεσκε σάκος μεγάλῳ ὀρυμαγδῷ
ὀξέα καὶ λιγέως· ἐπὶ δὲ ζώνῃσι δράκοντε
δοιὼ ἀπῃωρεῦντ' ἐπικυρτώοντε κάρηνα·
λίχμαζον δ' ἄρα τώ γε, μένει δ' ἐχάρασσον ὀδόντας   235
ἄγρια δερκομένω· ἐπὶ δὲ δεινοῖσι καρήνοις
Γοργείοις ἐδονεῖτο μέγας φόβος.

As they ran, the shield resounded sharply and piercingly with a loud noise. At their girdles, two serpents hung down, their heads arching forward; both of them were licking with their tongues, and they ground their teeth with strength, glaring savagely. Upon the terrible heads of the Gorgons, fear raged hugely [or 'raised a terrible commotion' in the form of a 'buzz' or other loud sound].

---

[89] See Howe 1954, 210–12, Segal 1998, 86–87 and Frontisi-Ducroux 1994, 258.

In his second *Dithyramb*, Pindar imagines the no less noisy beasts now incorporated into Athena's aegis that 'rings out with the hisses of myriad serpents' (μυρίων φθογγάζεται κλαγγαῖς δρακόντων, fr. 70b.18 S.-M.), while in Euripides' rendering, 'a hundred-headed shriekings/hissings (ἰαχήμασι) of snakes' accompany the Gorgon, also styled μαρμαρωπός, 'of glittering eyes', as she joins with Lyssa in maddening Heracles (*HF* 880–84). These loud-voiced serpents also recall the archetypal clamorous and incoherent monster Typhoeus, on whose shoulders sprout 'a hundred heads of a snake, a terrible dragon's, licking with their dark tongues ... And there were *phonai* in all his terrible heads, sending forth all kinds of sounds' (Hes. *Th.* 824–30).

On the Eleusis amphora, sound also plays a critical role: while Polyphemus opens his mouth as if to scream in pain, and the lion's mouth gapes to emit a roar,[90] the animal protomes – mixed in with the snakes are other types of beast whose heads resemble that of the lion shown in the register between the two mythical episodes – add to the cacophony. Just as early bronze griffins on Greek cauldrons have wide-open mouths and protruding, pointed tongues, and lion-headed griffins have distended jaws (Fig. 2.9), so too do the Polyphemus Painter's protomes;[91] also familiar to the viewer would be the full sets of teeth that some of the extant cauldron beast attachments still exhibit, suggestive of the tooth-grinding sound described in the [Hesiodic] *Scutum*. The amphora design relocates these teeth to the rounded cauldron body, where tooth-shaped sets of lines appear exactly where the mouth, complete with its full dentition, would normally be positioned. On the acoustic count too, the monstrous sisters distort the choral paradigm. Where typically depictions of choral dancers in Geometric art include a lyre-player or aulete, here the brazen vessels have become the source of the primitive music to which the Gorgons, much as the crazed Euripidean Heracles would do (*HF* 871, χορεύσω, 879, χορευθέντ'), perform their (choral) dance.

But sound is not limited to the painted protomes and to the cauldron heads of which they form a part; it is also very much apparent in accounts of cauldron-tripods in myth and cult, which register the vessels' surprising capacity for emitting sounds and even types of speech and song that most

---

[90] As noted by Hurwit 1985, 169 and Osborne 1988, 2.

[91] Cambridge, MA, Harvard Art Museums 1963.130. For additional illustrations, and protomes with full dentition, see Hopkins 1960 and Goldman 1960. The impact of these protomes would be similar to that achieved by the diadem that Hephaestus forges for Pandora in the *Theogony*; all but transcending the limits of artistic representation, it is topped with 'monsters ... similar to animals endowed with speech' (Hes. *Th.* 584).

Fig. 2.9 Griffin protome from a cauldron, ca. 650 B.C.E. Cambridge, MA, Harvard Art Museums/Arthur M. Sackler Museum, Gift of Frederick M. Watkins 1963.130. Photograph Harvard Art Museums © President and Fellows of Harvard College.

frequently occur in a more or less explicit choral context. Most fully detailed in sources, probably from the late fourth century on, are events at Dodona, whose possible association with choral dancing was noted in Section 1. As ancient exegetes agree, the proverbial expression 'Dodonian bronze' refers to those who talk a lot and is derived from a phenomenon at the shrine of Zeus at Dodona; lacking walls, the site has a series of cauldrons placed close to one another so as to form a fence-like circle (similar in shape to the choral formation assumed by those who dance around an altar or other sacred structure), 'so that if one touches one of them, it sends on the resonance to all the others through the contact, and the echo endures until one touches the first one again' (St. Byz. s.v. Δωδώνη).[92] Much like the choral Muses of hexameter poetry, whether those of the *Iliad* singing antiphonally (ἄειδον ἀμειβόμεναι ὀπὶ καλῇ, 1.604) or their Odyssean counterparts who, in company with the Nereids, perform the dirge at the funeral of Achilles (the same phrase is used of them at *Od.* 24.60), or the choruses of archaic lyric song taking up from the citharodic proomion supplied by the poet/*chorêgos*, these Dodonian vessels 'sing' responsively or in antiphonal

---

[92] For this, see Kowalzig 2007, 331. The fullest discussion remains that of Cook 1902.

fashion, each one re-sounding the note issued by the preliminary 'choregic' tripod; by the time the circuit reaches completion, all are emitting the same sound concordantly.

Speech as well as song belongs to these vessels, and this of a very particular kind. Post-classical sources associate the sonorous cauldrons with the famed Dodonian Doves, the name given to the priestesses at the shrine who issued oracles. According to the Christian authors, when the god wished to give an oracle, these ministrants 'prophesied what the divinity threw into them' after they had been 'filled with the harmonic sound of a ringing cauldron', and we owe to these same attacks on pagan practices the claim that it was the vessels' 'harmonious' (*enharmonios*) ringing that brought about the priestesses' states of ecstasy.[93] No mere Christian construct designed to discredit the famed oracular shrine, the tradition is already familiar to Lucan, who refers to 'the sounds Dodona makes with the bronze cauldron of Jupiter' (*BC* 6.427; cf. Philostr. *Imag.* 2.33.3, where the term ἠχοῦν occurs of the bronze 'sounding out').

Nor are the Dodonian cauldrons the only instance of vessels that emit sounds associated with prophetic speech. Lucan's mention of their acoustic properties comes in a passage that simultaneously refers to 'the Delian tripods' and 'Pythian chasms' (*BC* 6.425), and Himerius' gloss on Alcaeus' paean cited earlier substitutes for these *antra* a set of resonant bronzes: the return of Apollo from the Hyperboreans to Delphi occurs when the god 'thought it was time that the tripods of Delphi should ring out (ἠχῆσαι)', an event contemporaneous with the performance of the paean and the execution of dances around the central tripod; the conjunction suggests a scenario in which the vessels supply the background music to the young dancers' 'tripodic' performance. The discussion in Section 1 already flagged a further instance of choral performances in combination with the sounding and expressly prophetic vessels in Aristonous' juxtaposition of the 'oracular voices' of the Delphic tripods with the dance of Hestia as emulated by the hymn's real world performers; as in Alcaeus' lost paean, the speaking vessels are multiple here, suggesting that the Apolline tripod from which the Pythia issued her pronouncements has shared its role with the other votive tripods at the shrine. From the late second century comes a paean by Limenius, preserved in an inscription on the south wall of the Athenian Treasury at Delphi tentatively dated to 106/5 B.C.E. (*FD* 3.2.47 =

---

[93] See Nonnus the Abbot quoting Gregory of Nazianzus, Migne *PG* 36.1405a; Cosmas of Maiuma, *Spicilegium Romanum* 2.172; Maximus of Tyre, *Lecture* 8.1b, with other sources given in Cook 1902, 20–21 and Johnston 2008, 65–67.

SIG^3 711L.12);[94] lines 19–21 of the composition move from a reference to the song's performers and composers, members of the Dionysiac *technitae* at Athens, to an invocation of the addressee, Apollo, who controls 'the tripod where [oracles] are sung' (χρησμῳδὸν ... τρίποδα). The perhaps deliberately elliptical phrasing allows the numinous object to be the agent here.

The brazen voices ascribed to tripods at Delphi and Delos recur in another, very different context, now reassigned to the maidenly choral performers at these sites. In Pindar's second *Paean*, dated to ca. 490 B.C.E., the Abderite singers performing the piece describe two other choruses, these made up of *parthenoi*, appearing at Delos and Delphi: 'choral songs and dances are resounding throughout fragrant Delos, and among the high rocks of Parnassus again and again (*thama*) the *parthenoi* of Delphi with shining headbands form a swift-footed chorus and sing a sweet strain with brazen voice' (χαλκέᾳ ... αὐδᾷ, fr. 52b.96–102 S.-M.). This metallic voice characterizes other maiden singers too, who, either directly or more partially take the form of artefacts invested with the capacity for enduring (note *thama* above) and/or uncanny utterances. Pindar is again the source for the mysterious maiden chorus of Keledones or Charmers in his eighth *Paean* (fr. 52i.67–84 S.-M.) introduced in Chapter 1; this sixfold golden group sings with 'honey-sweet voice' (γλυκείας ὀπός) atop the god-built bronze Temple of Apollo at Delphi.[95] While the precise form that Pindar imagined for his Charmers remains enigmatic – are they acroterial maidens, as in the standard view earlier cited, or even, according to one revisionary account, Siren-like figures modelled after the protomes arranged about the ring of the bronze tripod cauldrons that have been discovered at the site[96] – there is no mistaking the *Paean* singers' joint focus on the figures' vocalizations and their metallic character.[97] While the Charmers are

---

[94] Rutherford 2004, 79. Bélis 1988 dates the performance of the song to 128 B.C.E.

[95] See the fuller citation in Chapter 1.

[96] For the first, Power 2011; for the second, Papalexandrou 2003/04, 157. Following Papalexandrou's view, not only in both instances do we have the marked conjunction of tripods and sound, but the Keledones, who sing of past, present and future from the cauldron's rim, exercise the same oracular role that ancient commentators assign to the Dodonian tripods and that many also link to the avian prophetesses in the oak tree that utter their pronouncements. Some ancient sources think that the Keledones had wings (see Power 2011, 73–74 for evidence), and Philostratus claims that they took the form of wrynecks, ἴυγγες (*VA* 6.11); earlier in the text, Philostratus describes a set of the golden spinning disks that hung from the ceiling of a royal room in Persia. The kings' magi were responsible for keeping them 'harmonically tuned' (*harmottesthai*), and the objects supposedly also possessed the 'tongues of gods'.

[97] Rutherford 2001, 220 attractively suggests that we are to suppose that the Charmers' song was a paean, although he then goes on to note that a more Siren-like composition, featuring 'universal knowledge', is equally likely.

fashioned from gold, and not from the bronze used for tripods, that second metal occupies pride of place in the anaphoric description of the temple just a few lines earlier (χάλκεοι μὲν τοῖχοι χάλκ[εαί θ' ὑπὸ κίονες ἕστασαν, 69). The rhetorical device not only 'draws attention to the material of the third temple while evoking its metallic resonance',[98] but prepares the way for the no less resonant song that issues from the metal-made Keledones. The term ῥυθμός in line 67 also anticipates the appearance of these tuneful singers, offering, as noted in Chapter 1, a preview of a quality that belongs to any choral group executing its song and dance. A Pindaric hapax, the expression properly describes a 'flowing motion',[99] but following Power's discussion, I would also assign to ῥυθμός 'sonoric and kinetic meanings'[100] and see in it a reference to that vocalic-cum-choreographic 'order in movement' that is, according to Plato, a defining property of choral song and dance (*Leg.* 655a; cf. 673d). For an audience present at the performance of Pindar's work, the verbal conceit would find confirmation in the spectacle before them, a chorus of moving, sounding dancers, creating audible and visual patterns through their vocalizations and steps.

Nor is Pindar the first poet to invest the expressly parthenaic and choral voice with a metallic (and omniscient) resonance. Instead, in a well-known passage from book 2 of the *Iliad*, Homer offers an intriguing precedent for the conceit when the narrator confesses himself unable to recite the numbers and names of those who came to Troy, not even if 'there were within me ten tongues and ten mouths, and an unbreakable voice and heart of bronze' (φωνὴ δ' ἄρρηκτος, χάλκεον δέ μοι ἦτορ ἐνείη, 490).[101] While in another context these multiple tongues and mouths might recall the monstrous, polycephalic Typhoeus or Cerberus, here the vocal proliferation carries an entirely positive weight. Departing from formulaic convention,

---

[98] Papalexandrou 2003/04, 151. Another 'bronze maiden' conceit cited by Power (2011, 109) is also suggestive in the light of the Siren-like nature of the Charmers: the speaker of the opening line of the so-called Midas epigram (cited in DL 1.89–90) declares itself 'a maiden of bronze' and goes on to proclaim its capacity for eternal vocalization: 'remaining on this very spot, over this much bewept tomb, I will announce to passers-by that Midas is buried here'. The figure topping the grave monument was most likely a Sphinx or, more apposite to my argument, a Siren. For more on the Sirens, see Chapter 3 and for discussion of the epigram, Ford 2002, 101–05.

[99] Rutherford 2001, 219 for this.

[100] Power 2011, 79. His view is that these singing golden statues represent a prototypical standing chorus at Delphi, their materiality an expression of the 'super-occasional potential of choral performance' (112).

[101] For more on this second proem, see the detailed discussion in Chapter 9. Very pertinent to my argument is the view cited there that the catalogue that follows is the epic poet's transformation of a choral dirge into hexameter song.

the bronze normally applied in epic diction to the amplified voices of monsters, gods and the occasional god-like hero is now reassigned to the heart, while the epithet 'unbreakable', chiefly reserved by Homer for artefacts, many made of metal and of Olympian manufacture, belongs to the voice instead. Indeed, there may be a return to the conceit, if the reconstruction is sound, in Sappho 31.9 V, where the all too mortal poetic voice declares that its 'tongue is broken'. Famously the introduction of a hiatus between noun and verb makes the singers (and here I follow those who consider this a work most likely composed by Sappho for choral performance) re-enact that scission with their voice, a counterpart to the 'hiatal glitch' used in Pindar's *Paean* 8.78–79 to suggest the difference between a flesh-and-blood chorus and the uncanny singers on the temple roof, whose golden constitution means that they never need pause to catch their breath.[102] Establishing fresh relations of likeness and contrast between the Iliadic Muses' 'unbroken' voice evocative of a bronze or metal forged object and the Sapphic tongue is the lyric poet's †ἔαγε; in Homeric diction, the verb regularly describes the moment when weaponry made from bronze and other metals – shields, swords and spears most typically – shatters, splintered into fragments under the force of an opposing blow.

Read with these later works in mind, the singularity in diction noted for the passage in *Iliad* 2 may be deliberate, and the poet's means of alerting his audience to the fact of a vocal permanence both wondrous and divine. The possession of an unbroken voice together with another internal organ mortal-forged, the innovatory phrasing suggests, would require the poet's acquisition of properties that variously belong to the divine and demonic, to extraordinary metallic goods and, on occasion, to the mortal (and chiefly parthenaic) chorister, and his or her transformation into a plurality of singers that could go on vocalizing unceasingly for all time. Framed by the twofold invocation to his patron goddesses, here, for the first time in the composition and in a departure from the initial invocation in the proem's opening line, addressed as a plurality,[103] Homer's *adynaton* additionally implies that the Muses, insofar as they could fulfill the designated task if so they chose, must possess just the type of vocal organs that the lines propose. If my interpretation is correct, then the passage supplies the earliest instance of the trope of the durability and permanence that song and speech achieve when they are joined with and channelled through a metal medium,

[102] Here I follow the interpretation and phrasing of Power 2011, 92. See too the discussion in Chapter 10.
[103] On this switch to a plurality, see the discussion in Chapter 9.

which Homer here associates with the archetypal parthenaic chorus of the ever-singing, dancing Muses.[104] That some sources assigned Muse-like prophetic qualities to the Dodonian, Delian and Delphic cauldrons' echoings, and to the Keledones too, is fresh confirmation of the proximate qualities that these diverse sonorous phenomena – bronze vessels and choruses – both possess.

Returning to the Eleusis amphora, my suggestion is that the cauldron heads of Medusa's sisters may visually articulate the idea of a suprahuman, transcendent and unceasing choral voice that has the quality of an object made of bronze. Invested with these properties, the artist's choice to integrate the vessels into the image proves very much in accordance with the larger impetus behind the Gorgons' design. Just as the changes he rings on choral dance iconography both preserve the monsters' uncanny and fearsome aspects and render them benign by assimilating them to maidens performing in celebration of the gods within the context of civic rituals, so too the amphora's acoustics transmute the terrifying hisses of the snakes into the sweeter (metallic) strains of eternally resonant maiden voices, able lastingly to commemorate the vessel's object of celebration and, now, occupant too.

In effecting these several transformations, the scene depicted on the body of the pot closely anticipates the act of musical-cum-choral acculturation and the conversion of the transient into something of *longue durée* described in a later poetic account of the same event, the Gorgons' pursuit of Perseus. To celebrate the victory of Midas of Akragas, who took first prize in the auletic competition at the Pythian games in 490 B.C.E., Pindar's *Pythian* 12 selects a story that, fittingly enough, recovers the origins of the art in which the *laudandus* has triumphed. According to the probably innovatory version given by Pindar here, the auletic art was first invented by Athena, who created the new *technê* by 'weaving [into music] the fierce Gorgons' deathly dirge that she heard dripping forth from under the unapproachable snaky heads of the maidens in their direful toil' (οὔλιον θρῆνον διαπλέξαισ᾽ Ἀθάνα· / τὸν παρθενίοις ὑπό τ᾽ ἀπλάτοις ὀφίων κεφαλαῖς / ἄϊε λειβόμενον δυσπενθέϊ σὺν καμάτῳ, 8–10).

Following a synoptic account of Perseus' encounter with the monstrous triad and a brief glance at the hero's subsequent feats, Pindar then rounds out the mythical portion of his song by returning to the goddess' invention, now detailing both the nature of the composition that she played upon the

[104] Curiously, many of the same tropes are used of the castrati of the early modern period; in one contemporary account, 'the castrato was considered a sort of virtuoso instrumentalist of the larynx, rather than a singer in the sense we understand the term; he was an infallible singing machine' (*LRB* 8 October 2015, 13).

new-made instrument and the object's mode of construction and contemporary functions. As the poet declares at 19–27, by way of marking the triumph of her protégé, Athena additionally devised a particular melody:

> παρθένος αὐλῶν τεῦχε πάμφωνον μέλος,
> ὄφρα τὸν Εὐρυάλας ἐκ καρπαλιμᾶν γενύων   20
> χριμφθέντα σὺν ἔντεσι μιμήσαιτ᾽ ἐρικλάγκταν γόον.
> εὗρεν θεός· ἀλλά νιν εὑροῖσ᾽ ἀνδράσι θνατοῖς ἔχειν,
> ὠνύμασεν κεφαλᾶν πολλᾶν νόμον,
> εὐκλεᾶ λαοσσόων μναστῆρ᾽ ἀγών ων,
>
> λεπτοῦ διανισόμενον χαλκοῦ θαμὰ καὶ δονάκων,   25
> τοὶ παρὰ καλλίχορον ναίοισι πόλιν Χαρίτων
> Καφισίδος ἐν τεμένει, πιστοὶ χορευτᾶν μάρτυρες.

the maiden fashioned a melody with every sound for pipes, so that she might imitate the far-shrieking wail that was forced from the fast-moving jaws of Euryale. The goddess invented it, but invented it for mortals to have, and she called it the tune of many heads, famous reminder of contests where people flock, the tune that often passes through the thin bronze and the reeds which grow by the Graces' city of beautiful dancing places in the precinct of Kephisos' daughter, faithful witnesses of choruses.

As these lines make clear, for all their heterogeneity in time, space and genre, the Eleusis amphora and epinician composition cohere very closely in their themes and motifs, both using the same mythological event to address a common set of issues and incorporating the Gorgons, acoustics, choral dancing and metallic products requiring high-calibre artisanal skill in their treatment of the broader concerns articulated in their works. Several acute readings of *Pythian* 12 have detailed how, within the Pindaric version of the story, the poem transforms the unbounded, bestial, feminine and cacophonous mourning cry of Medusa's sisters and the victim's dying plaint into a 'cultural act' and replaces the ghastly howl of pain from the Gorgon's distended mouth with 'a pleasing sound [that] emerges from an artificial channel, whose constricted passage produces the "many-headed song" at all-male contests of art and athletics'.[105] Indeed, sound, and its mutation from the discord of lament and suffering to the harmonious melody played upon the pipes in a celebratory, ritual and, as detailed below, expressly choral context,[106] is the focus of the account,

---

[105] Segal 1998, 90; for the process of acculturation within the song, see too Clay 1992, 519–24 and Frontisi-Ducroux 1994.
[106] Chapter 3 takes up this theme.

which downplays the visual powers of Medusa's head the better to highlight the auditory element more relevant to Midas' present victory. A similar process of 'acoustic acculturation' occurs by virtue of the incorporation of the Gorgons' cauldron heads on the Eleusis amphora. Even as the bronze artefacts maintain the fearsome aspects of the 'music' to which the sisters dance, they concurrently harness the monsters' primitive and bestial hisses, clangs and gnashes to an object that was the epitome of the metalworker's manufacturing art, a prestige and costly good already associated with the master craftsman Hephaestus in the *Iliad*, and that constituted a supremely intricate, decorated and daedalic piece in the Geometric age.

Particularly relevant to the Eleusis amphora are lines 25–27, where Pindar turns his focus from auletics to the aulos, an invention that depends on the products of both nature and culture, bronze and the reeds that here, as elsewhere, the poet links to the city over which the Graces preside. In his description of the instrument's trajectory, Pindar not only invests the aulos-music with that brazen and factured quality ascribed elsewhere to the choral voice and makes the instrument a product of craftsmanship, but twice associates the maiden deities with chorality, and in so doing completes Athena's task of civilizing transformation. By replacing the triadic monsters of the ode's beginning, whose traditional choral character I earlier tracked, with the winsome Graces, goddesses of all festive delights and particular patrons and practitioners of choral dance (see below), he introduces a second archetypal trio of eternally dancing maidens.

Sources both textual and visual unequivocally establish the Graces' signature connection with *choreia*. They dance together with the Horai, hands on each others' wrists, in the *Homeric Hymn to Apollo* (194–96), and the chorus of *mystae* in the *Frogs* invites Iacchos to participate in the dance 'that has the greatest share of the Charites' (334; cf. *Od.* 18.194, *Thesm.* 121–22); so too Euripides gives them the epithet χοροποιοί (*Phoen.* 788). Artists similarly deploy dance iconography to represent the maidens, regularly showing the goddesses with their hands linked. The François Vase of ca. 570 already signals the Graces' character by placing the sisters together with three Horai and three dancing nymphs, while on an early fifth-century relief from Paros, the deities dance with their right hands raised and their left pulling on their skirts.[107] Scholars variously identify the triad of dancing maidens – Charites, Horai or Aglaurids? – who link wrists and follow a flute player on a late archaic relief from the Athenian Acropolis, and we meet the triplet again on an archaizing relief by

---

[107] Munich, Glyptothek 241.

Callimachos dated to the first century, where they dance on tiptoe as they follow Pan's lead.[108] Pindar's own familiarity with the goddesses' sponsorship of the practice also declares itself in *Ol.* 14, where he assigns them special authority over the dance, declaring that 'not even the gods arrange choruses or feasts' in their absence (8–9) and then invoking Thalia, 'lover of song and dance' (16), whom he requests to look with favour on the current *kômos* as it performs its own dance figures (κοῦφα βιβῶντα, 17).[109] *Pythian* 12 exploits the theme afresh, now giving to the newly urbanized musical activity an additional level of solemnity. Although the epigraphic evidence belongs only to the second and first centuries B.C.E., Orchomenos played host to auletic, dramatic and poetic contests on the occasion of the Charitesia, a festival celebrated on the Graces' behalf and that probably dates to much earlier times;[110] as Pindar's text suggests, choral performances are likely to have been included among the rites addressed to the divinities.

But beyond recasting the Gorgons in this delightful, most civilized and aesthetically pleasing form, there is an additional explanation for the introduction of the Orchomenos choruses here. The θαμά of line 25 points to the regularized nature of these celebrations, the constant recurrence of the dances in the sacred calendar. Inasmuch as the Boeotian choruses furnish counterparts to the performers executing *Pythian* 12 in the here-and-now, most probably at Akragas, the Pindaric celebrants engage in a stratagem familiar from both choral lyric and later Attic drama, the act of 'choral projection' in which the chorus currently dancing and singing assimilates itself to another group of performers, whether real, legendary or divine. The rationale that Power gives for the use of this projection in Bacchylides 13 works very well for the Pindaric celebration too.[111] In Bacchylides' piece, the poet grants legitimacy and a recurrent, civic character to his *ad hoc* group of performers, an Aeginetan chorus praising a one-time victor without distinguished heritage, by having his singers map their identity onto that of a standing maiden chorus celebrating the island's eponymous nymph and her heroic descendants in periodic civic festivals.[112] In much the same fashion, Pindar's introduction of choruses on Orchomenos' dancing floor endows the performers celebrating Midas' victory (in an event that Pindar eulogizes on no other occasion, and won by

---

[108] See *LIMC* for these.

[109] See too Pindar's extremely fragmentary third *Paean* (with discussion in Rutherford 2001, 275–80), where he includes the Graces, the bronze flute and choral performances.

[110] For the festival, see Schachter 1981, 140–44.   [111] Power 2000, 67–81.

[112] This work receives more extended discussion in several later chapters.

an individual whose lack of patronymic and whose name hint at his obscure, even foreign, origins) with an authority and long-standing character that transforms the transient victory and its musical/choral commemoration into something more permanent, inscribing it within the regular ritual round. One element of Bacchylides' extended description of his local chorus particularly resembles Pindar's strategy in *Pythian* 12: at line 86, Bacchylides uses ταρφέως, 'regularly, continuously', of the movement of the *chorêgos,* an indicator of the iterative nature of the performance visualized here.[113] The θαμά of *Pythian* 12.25 does much the same.

Reinforcing the repeated and established character of the festival celebration evoked at the close of Pindar's ode is the description given the Graces, now styled μάρτυρες, both memorialists and perpetual witnesses to the choruses that perform in the sacred space.[114] By virtue of their introduction into the epinician celebration as infallible (πιστοί) record-keepers, they preserve the memory of the performance currently enacted in Akragas, and in so doing can guarantee the song future performances. The bronze protome cauldrons on the Eleusis amphora – if my conjecture that the successful completion of a maturation rite, perhaps capped by a tripod-winning choral performance, lies behind its central image is correct – fulfill a corresponding end: using the visual rather than verbal medium, the artist includes evocations of the object dedicated by the family of the now deceased to mark the youth's success, and, insofar as it offered proof of his participation in the *agôn,* could serve as the catalyst for future commemorations of his achievement at the event.

---

[113] Power 2000, 81.   [114] For more on the term in choral contexts, see Chapter 10.

3 | Flying with the Birds: Avian *Choreia* and Bird Choruses in Art and Text

Writing about the choreographer Elizabeth Streb's 'Human Fountain', Alec Wilkinson remarks of the piece's climactic conclusion, when all twenty-one dancers are in the air, 'it is like watching swallows dipping over rooftops, at that moment when, wings folded and falling, they are merely forms'.

New Yorker 29 June 2015

Introduction

On a Late Geometric krater from Argos (Fig. 3.0),[1] two panels with lines of female dancers appear above a band of birds, likewise arranged in a linear and collective formation. Even as the birds' design follows the conventions regularly used for portraying avians in Geometric art, their bent limbs simultaneously mirror the legs peeking out from the skirts of each dancer above, suggesting relations of equivalence between the flock and choral group, whose members also move from left to right around the body of the bowl. Among the abstract shapes used to depict the birds are the wavy lines that recur in the zigzag decorative motifs in the adjacent bands and panels. As stylized representations of bodies of water, these elements both position the choruses in the verdant landscape that, as noted in Chapter 2, typically supplies the backdrop for maiden dancers in the archaic visual and textual accounts and cohere with the artist's portrayal of the birds: as their iconography makes clear, these are water birds, the ornithological species with whom our sources (as examples cited in this chapter illustrate) most regularly associate choral performers.

In its pairing of birds and choral ensembles, the Argive bowl forms part of a more extensive group of vessels from the same period. A krater fragment from the Agamemnoneion at Mycenae, where a line of four birds occupies the panel immediately below the maiden choral dancers, presents a similar

---

[1] Argos, Archaeological Museum C 229; from grave T45 in Argos.

Fig. 3.0 Black-figure oinochoe from Pithekoussai, ca. 700–680 B.C.E. London, British Museum 1849, 0518.18. Drawing from H. B. Walters, *Catalogue of Greek and Etruscan Vases in the British Museum* (London, 1912), Vol. 1, Part 2.

juxtaposition,[2] while the three figurative friezes that ornament the different portions of an oinochoe from Pithekoussai, dated to ca. 700–680 and identified as the work of a Euboean artist (Fig. 3.0),[3] offer a more emphatic rendering of the motif. On the neck of the vase, a single bird, whose elongated neck and beak suggest a water bird, variously identified as a heron or crane, appears together with a mixed group of five male and female dancers. Balanced on one leg between a vigorously moving youth (his back leg also raised off the ground) and a maiden in the chorus line, the bird seems very much a member of the ensemble: not only does its crest offer a counterpart to the locks of the two maidens, but at first glance its long pointed beak appears to be the extension of the adjacent dancer's arm. The animal frieze around the shoulder includes two more birds, very similar in configuration to the one on the neck; the artist positions this pair in the space that exactly coincides with the central figures – the man partnering the wreath-carrying maiden – in the dance above.

Echoing these images, and uniting the three portions of the oinochoe, is the representation decorating the jug's lowest portion. All but identical in design to the bird included in the chorus are the avian figures circling around the base, each one enclosed within a circular element which interlocks with the one adjacent to it and forms part of a larger dotted chain or garland. If, following Carruesco's proposal cited in an earlier chapter,[4] we can read such non-figurative devices as a kind of

---

[2] See Langdon 2008, fig. 3.18 for this.

[3] London, British Museum 1849, 0518.18. I later address the question of whether, as Coldstream 1968 first suggested, the artist shows Theseus and Ariadne dancing the *geranos* here.

[4] Carruesco 2016, 90–105.

choreographic notation, then these frames would further coordinate the birds with the movements of the dancers above.

A fragment from the Argive Heraion largely repeats the oinochoe design by integrating a large water bird shown *en pointe* into the mixed chorus line:[5] now the long-necked creature stands between a male dancer performing an athletic leap and a second figure with his feet on the ground standing to the bird's left. Flanking them on either side are lines of polos-wearing female choristers, who process or dance from left to right.[6] A second water bird of similar design appears on the sherd that forms the fragment's companion piece, here placed to the left of a man and a woman, the latter dressed in exactly the same manner as the female figures in the chorus. Together the pair grasps a branch, identical to that held by one of the choral maidens in the line on the rim, as well as the pomegranate twig that frequently equips female dancers in visual accounts. The co-presence of the birds unites the two scenes, suggesting relations of continuity between the choreutes and the couple, one or both of whose members would have been recent participants in the ongoing performance.[7]

In a better state of preservation is a Clazomenian slim amphora found in Egypt, dated to ca. 540–525 and attributed to the Petrie Group (Fig. 3.1).[8] On the obverse of the vase's body (the design on the reverse is no longer visible, but may have shown the same scene), four similarly dressed women process in a measured step while below them on the base five long-necked birds appear with their wings outstretched. A large-sized sphinx occupies the neck area immediately above the procession. While the purple paint used to accentuate details of the sphinx, the women's garments and the forepart of the birds' elaborately decorated wings gives visual continuity to the different registers, there might also be a thematic unity to the three scenes: even as the birds beneath the marchers' feet suggest the creatures' capacity for dance-like motions, the sphinx, a figure imagined by Sophocles as ποικιλῳδός, 'of intricate song', and a 'rhapsode' (*OT* 130, 391) and to

---

[5] See Langdon 2008, 185–86 and her figs. 3.27 and 3.28. Langdon suggests a representation of performances at the Heraia, the chief Argive festival in honour of the goddess.

[6] As examples in later chapters will further illustrate, there is a strong tradition of female choral dancers (and a karyatid) wearing poloi in the visual and architectural records; see, among others, the Corinthian women in the *Frauenfest* scenes discussed in Chapter 7, and note too the similarly topped female dancers on the frieze from the Samothrace Hall of Choral Dancers, dated to the second half of the fourth century, with their low and slightly flaring poloi.

[7] Might we have a hint in this of the courtship or abduction scenario so frequently depicted on Argive pottery? For this, see Langdon 2008, esp. 230–33.

[8] London, British Museum 1888.2-69a, b.

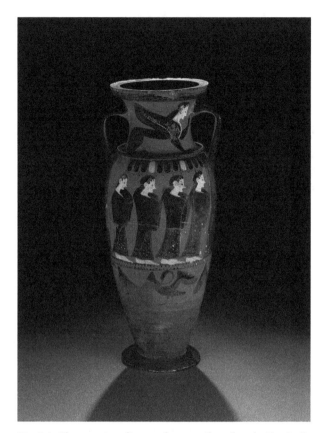

Fig. 3.1 Clazomenian slim amphora attributed to the Petrie Group, ca. 540–525 B.C.E. London, British Museum 1888.2-69a, b. Photograph © The Trustees of The British Museum.

whom Euripides similarly attributes song, *melos* (*Phoen.* 1506–07; cf. *El.* 471–72), adds in the melic element absent from the silent ensemble.[9]

While the very ubiquity of birds as decorative devices, mere space-fillers and commonplace occupants of the friezes decorating pots in the early visual record, stands in the way of any attempt to situate the avian motif within a more unified reading of these and other vessels and to grant a thematic significance to the birds' presence within a larger iconographical programme, the material presented in this chapter goes some way to supporting my claim for a (sometimes) deliberate pairing of choruses and flocks of birds in archaic vase painting. In each of its three sections, the discussion singles out one of the species most privileged in that association:

---

[9] Cf. a second Clazomenian black-figure amphora in Berlin (Berlin, Antikensammlung 4530).

first halcyons, then cranes and, lastly, doves or thrushes (the two are frequently treated as interchangeable).[10] Focusing in each instance principally on a single text or a passage within a larger composition and the visual material that complements its account, and drawing on the mythology, ornithological lore and ritual practices framing each type of bird, I explore some of the reasons that determine its selection as choice choral *comparandum*. In the closing discussion, I return to my point of departure, the combination of birds and dancing ensembles in vase imagery, and look at the evolution of the archaic motif through to the late sixth and fifth centuries.

1 Halcyons

We owe the preservation of Alcman fr. 26 *PMGF* to the third-century B.C.E. author Antigonus Carystus, who, in the lines already cited in Chapter 1, introduces the fragment in the context of his description of an ornithological wonder (*Mirabilia* 23 = *De animalibus* fr. 54b Dorandi):

> τῶν δὲ ἀλκυόνων οἱ ἄρσενες κηρύλοι καλοῦνται· ὅταν οὖν ὑπὸ τοῦ γήρως ἀσθενήσωσιν καὶ μηκέτι δύνωνται πέτεσθαι, φέρουσιν αὐτοὺς αἱ θήλειαι ἐπὶ τῶν πτερῶν λαβοῦσαι. καὶ ἔστι τὸ ὑπὸ τοῦ Ἀλκμᾶνος λεγόμενον τούτῳ συνῳκειωμένον· φησὶν γὰρ ἀσθενὴς ὢν διὰ τὸ γῆρας καὶ τοῖς χοροῖς οὐ δυνάμενος συμπεριφέρεσθαι οὐδὲ τῇ τῶν παρθένων ὀρχήσει·

> οὔ μ᾽ ἔτι, παρσενικαὶ μελιγάρυες ἱαρόφωνοι,
> γυῖα φέρην δύναται· βάλε δὴ βάλε κηρύλος εἴην,
> ὅς τ᾽ ἐπὶ κύματος ἄνθος ἅμ᾽ ἀλκυόνεσσι ποτήται
> νηδεὲς ἦτορ ἔχων, ἁλιπόρφυρος ἱαρὸς ὄρνις.

Male halcyons are called ceryli. When they become weak from old age and are no longer able to fly, the females carry them, taking them on their wings. What Alcman says is connected with this: weak from old age and unable to whirl about with the choruses and the girls' dancing, he says:

No longer, honey-toned strong-voiced [or 'holy-voiced'] girls, can my limbs carry me. If only, if only I were a cerylus, who flies along with the halcyons over the flower of the wave with resolute heart, strong [or 'holy'], sea-blue bird.

---

[10] See too Chapter 10 for a brief consideration of swallows in the context of choral performances in pre-Greek art.

Discussions of the fragment tend to concentrate on two points.[11] Older
scholars debate the question of whether the Spartan poet does indeed refer
to the phenomenon that the Hellenistic writer describes: is the speaker,
probably the poet himself, or more properly his poetic ego, really imagining
that, to overcome his weakened state, the *parthenoi* addressed here might
carry him as the halcyons do the aged male, and does Antigonus Carystus
correctly view the lines as illustrative of the natural curiosity, evidence that
Alcman was versed in a piece of avian lore only attested in much later
times?[12] For more recent readers, the lines' interest lies principally in the
overlap between their language and the fragment's central theme,
the debility of old age and the speaker's consequent inability to join in
the activities of young girls, and Sappho fr. 58 V. (this supplemented by the
'New Sappho' of the Cologne papyrus); like Alcman, here the singer regrets
her loss of the youth and the agility that once was hers in an address to a
choral group.[13]

My concern with the fragment is more straightforward: why, among any
number of possible bird species, does the poet liken his *parthenoi* to
halcyons, mythical creatures whom scholars usually equate with the king-
fisher, and what do these particular birds have to do with the poem's
diction and preoccupations? Beyond casting new light on the lines that
our Hellenistic source preserves, an investigation of the rich cache of
myths and images surrounding halcyons yields two chief dividends: first,
it offers insights into Greek notions of *choreia*, its earliest manifestations,
unique powers, relations to the divine and bearings on cosmology; and
second, and picking up on one of the previous chapter's strands, it illustrates the several properties that the sources view as particular to and
uniquely concentrated in the parthenaic choral voice. With Alcman's
lines by way of entry point, my discussion begins with the halcyon's place
in the story that the Greek sources fashion concerning the origins of choral
song, where the monodic, pre-cultural and 'naturalistic' lament of the
typically (fr. 26 *PMGF* notwithstanding) female bird gives rise to the

---

[11] Vestrheim 2004 surveys earlier discussions.

[12] As dissenters observe, the phenomenon described by Antigonus is entirely absent from all
earlier sources, and poets through the Hellenistic period make no reference to it. I do, however,
assume (with Plutarch, Aelian and other ancient sources) that the cerylus is the male of the same
species as the halcyons (Arist. *HA* 593b8–12 is in the minority in regarding it as a separate
species). For the birds, see the fascinating material gathered by Thompson 1936, 46–51 and
139–40.

[13] Among those who have noted the correspondence, Calame 1983, 474; Gronewald and Daniel
2004, 7; Bernsdorff 2004, 33–34; Hardie 2005, 28; Lardinois 2009, 51–52; Nagy 2009, 191. These
accounts variously signal proximity and contrast between the works while all agreeing on the
common nature of the theme.

complex composition that the ensemble of singer-dancers performs. As argued here, it is the halcyon's role as mourner *par excellence* that most especially recommends it for its originary or ur-choral role.

1.1 Mourning Becomes the Halcyon

As both the syntax and conceit shaping Alcman's opening declaration in fr. 26 *PMGF* suggest, the speaker's utterance takes the form of a lament. Among later discussions of the phrase βάλε δὴ βάλε, the *EM* defines it as belonging to the language of those in dire straits, precisely the situation in which Callimachus' Hecale, bewailing her current outcast and penurious condition, pronounces the same phrase: εἰμὶ λιπερνῆτις· βάλε μοι, βάλε τὸ τρίτον εἴη (fr. 254.2 Pf.). Also defining the earlier poem's exclamation as mourning discourse is the wish that the larger phrase expresses, and which echoes or anticipates those many instances in which individuals – whether the Homeric Penelope (*Od.* 19.515–23) or Aeschylus' Cassandra (*Ag.* 1146–48) or the singers of the so-called 'escape odes' of Euripidean tragedy (see *Andr.* 862, *Ion* 796–98, *IT* 1138–42, *Hipp.* 732–51 and *Hel.* 1478–79)[14] – bewailing a present unenviable state equate themselves with birds and/or express longing for transformation into winged form so that they might escape their current sufferings.

While nightingales figure prominently in the trope, halcyons are if anything more commonplace. The hexameter sources already cast the bird, whose very name is, in eponymous fashion, bound up with its signature mode of song, as an archetypal mourner. Describing Kleopatra's mother Marpessa, the Iliadic Phoenix recalls how the hero Idas was willing to confront Apollo 'for the sake of the fair-ankled maiden, a girl whom her father and honoured mother had named in their palace Alkyone, sea-bird, as a byname, since for her sake her mother with the sorrow-laden cry of a sea-bird wept because far-darting Phoebus Apollo had taken her' (*Il.* 9.560–64). If we follow one possible interpretation of the rather puzzling phrase, and assume that Kleopatra (and not her mother) is named Alkyone so as to recall Marpessa's sorrow on being snatched from Idas,[15] then 'Alkyone' stands filial testament to the grief of one member of the amorous pair separated from her spouse.[16] And just as the nightingale's song takes the

---

[14] See the additional half dozen passages cited by Barrett 1964 *ad* 1290–93.

[15] The pronoun in the Homeric phrase is ambiguous, and could refer to either Marpessa or Kleopatra. For full discussion, see Gresseth 1964, 19–20.

[16] For a different possible reading of the exemplum, with Kleopatra as the object of Apollo's abduction, see Heiden 2008a, 135–36 with further discussion below.

form of the constantly reiterated name of Procne's son Itys, whom the now-avian mother eternally laments with her tuneful cry, so the halcyon's 'ceyx, ceyx' is viewed as a ceaseless expression of its grief for its lost mate, already identified as one Ceyx in the [Hesiodic] account (fr. 10d M.-W.).[17] Indeed, the reiterative phrasing in line 2 of Alcman, βάλε δὴ βάλε, annexes what may be just such an unintelligible, pre-musical bird-like call, this reminiscent of the halcyon's own signature song.[18] As Andrew Ford remarks, repetition is the 'characteristic mode of lament',[19] a point confirmed by one among the ancient etymologies for *elegos*, in its later fifth-century sense of 'sung lament', that derives it from the cry ἒ ἒ λέγειν.[20]

[Hesiod's] presentation of Alkyone, whom the poet sets within an aetiological narrative that explains the origins of the bird, highlights a different facet of the heroine's 'biography'. According to the existing fragment cited above, Zeus transformed the spousal pair into a halcyon and tern because they addressed each other as Zeus and Hera as an expression of their outstanding (viz. hubristic) conjugal passion. While the mourning motif is absent from this tale, a second version of the story, albeit attested only in later texts,[21] makes lamentation central to the metamorphosis and replaces the gods' punitive action with one prompted by compassion instead. Nicander is our earliest source for the tale of how Ceyx dies in a shipwreck and Alkyone mourns so inconsolably that the gods take pity on the bereaved wife and turn her into a halcyon by way of release.[22]

Whatever the reason for Alkyone's change in shape, Homer's description of the bird, where its characteristic plaint supplies the keynote to the story, finds ample elaboration in fifth-century sources. Euripides' *IT* reprises the theme at the start of an ode performed by the maiden singers making up its chorus. The song begins, together with an intriguing

---

[17] Dionysius (*De Avibus* 2.7) reports that, 'if the male happens to die, the [females] mourn for a long time, abstaining from food and drink, and perish, and when they are about to stop singing, they utter ceyx, ceyx at frequent intervals, and then fall silent'. Lucian, *Halc.* 1 calls the bird πολύθρηνος καὶ πολύδακρυς.

[18] In the lines from Eur. *IT* 1089–95, the halcyon's song of lament is only intelligible to those who already know its impetus; this too might indicate its preverbal character.

[19] Ford 2010, 297.

[20] For this, see Bowie 1986, 25. See too the repeated use of the refrain derived from the Linus melody, αἴλινον αἴλινον εἰπέ, in the parodos of Aeschylus' *Agamemnon* and Pind. fr. 128 S.-M.

[21] As Forbes Irving 1992, 239–40 argues, passing allusions in Homer and Euripides to the halcyon suit this second story better than the punitive rationale given by [Hesiod], suggesting not that the [Hesiodic] account underwent a later change, but the priority of the 'remedial' version of events.

[22] For Nicander's version, see Proclus G 1.399; cf. Ov. *Met.* 11.410–748, Lucian, *Halc.* 2, Dionys. *De Av.* 2.8, Hyg. *Fab.* 65.

suggestion of a choral *agôn*, albeit with one singer set against the group, by apostrophizing the halcyon, 'who by the sea's rocky cliffs sadly sing your song of lament, crying with meaning plain to those who know that you are singing those incessant songs for your mate, I match myself with you (σοι παραβάλλομαι) as I lament, an unwinged bird … ' (1089–95).[23] Indeed, Euripides seems to have made the mourning halcyon something of his calling card, so familiar to Athenian audiences that Aristophanes' 'Aeschylus' sees fit to riff on it in the *Frogs*: in his pastiche of his opponent's lyrics, the older dramatist begins his mock-Euripidean song of lament with an appeal to the halcyons (1309–12) modelled on a passage from the *Hypsipyle.*

While spousal misfortunes often generate the halcyon's lament, other types of losses, typically that of its offspring, also afflict the calamity-prone bird. The Homeric Marpessa already appears as mother of a daughter, and, as one discussion of the passage notes,[24] if it is the mother who acquires the name Alkyone, as the syntax also allows, then, under this identity, she must be mourning the loss of her child who forms the object of Apollo's amorous designs and whom her father Idas subsequently recovers from the god. After mentioning the female's willingness to carry her aged spouse that Antigonus describes (and citing fr. 26 *PMGF*), Plutarch goes on to detail at enormous length the admirable care with which the halcyon constructs its nest, this as a function of the bird's 'love for her offspring and care for their preservation' (*Mor.* 983b). But the motherhood writ so large in these accounts is, once again, bound up with lamentation. According to the myth informing the period of midwinter calm named for the halcyon, pity for the grief of the bird following the loss of her fledglings when her nest was carried off by the waves prompts Aeolus to still the winds; the bird's plaintive cry, in this account, articulates her maternal sorrow.

If mourning becomes the halcyon, then it also stands as the mode of song from which, a variety of sources propose, choral composition takes its departure point. Herodotus notes how the musical lament can diversify and be transformed into multiple other strains. In his remarks concerning the genesis of song, the Egyptian *thrênos* stands ancestor to all subsequent vocal genres, the very first *aoidê* from which heterogeneous later Egyptian and Greek forms develop (2.79).[25] Pindar makes the *thrênos* even more originary to his choral poetry. In the trajectory traced out in *Pythian* 12, and detailed in the previous chapter, it is the lament emitted by the

---

[23] That same competitive note returns in the Helen parodos considered below, where Helen uses the term ἁμιλλαθῶ (165) for her lament; for this, see Weiss 2018, 154.

[24] Gresseth 1964, 90.   [25] See Ford 2002, 151–52 for discussion of the passage.

Gorgons mourning the death of their sister that serves as the catalyst for Athena's invention of the pipes and of the auletic music that accompanies contemporary choruses as they sing and dance.[26]

Alcman's lines anticipate the evolution that these later authors describe, making the audience witness to the transition from the solitary lament of the cerylus to the collective performance. In the view of commentators, fr. 26 *PMGF* supplied the citharodic prooimion, itself thought to belong among the oldest forms of lyric by fifth- and fourth-century sources,[27] to the choral song about to be enacted by the singer-dancers poised to join their leader. So contextualized, the words are not just 'performative' insofar as they effect precisely the action they describe, the moment when the poet-musician-*chorêgos* takes his place in the company of his maidenly group, whether they just dance while he plays and sings, or sing along with him, or assume the voice that formerly was his, but 'meta-performative'. In a scenario closely revisited in later texts, Alcman presents the cries of the solitary mourner as the foundational and pre-cultural form of song that precedes all 'artified' versions of the same and whose transition into fully developed *choreia* depends on the presence of a plurality of singers who take up and musically and generically transform the lamenting monodic avian voice into choral form.[28]

The story that fr. 26 *PMGF* tells concerning the origins of the highly worked, complex choral piece performed by a singing, dancing ensemble proves anything but idiosyncratic. Two songs in Attic drama observe just this trajectory, sounding variations on the threnetic and bird motifs so prominent in Alcman's lines. In the parodos of Euripides' *Helen*, the play's heroine begins with a three-line introduction whose two dactylic hexameters followed by a pentameter are designed to sound much like a citharodic proem (164–66).[29] Following this prelude, whose initiatory or originary character the expression καταβαλλομένα, 'laying a foundation', suggests,[30] Helen then sings in lyric metres. In her opening strophe, also ground-laying insofar as these are the first lyrics to appear in the drama, she directs

---

[26] See too my more extended treatment in Steiner 2013a.   [27] Ford 2010, 286 with his n. 14.

[28] Cf. Lucian, *De luctu* 20, where, in a different configuration, a figure styled a *chorêgos* transforms the *thrênoi* of 'simpletons', which consist of nothing but cries of 'alas', into a song which he 'leads off' and accompanies with melody.

[29] Willink 1990, 78; Ford 2010, 286. My account of the parodos and of the hoopoe's song from Aristophanes' *Birds* that follows owes much to Ford's rich analysis. See too Weiss 2018, 144–56.

[30] ὢ μεγάλων ἀχέων καταβαλλομένα μέγαν οἶκτον / ποῖον ἀμιλλαθῶ γόον ἢ τίνα μοῦσαν ἐπέλθω / δάκρυσιν ἢ θρήνοις ἢ πένθεσιν; αἰαῖ (164–66). See Ford 2010, 286 n. 12 for the foundational aspect of this. Cf. Pind. *Pyth.* 7.1–3 where, at the outset of the ode and here in an architectural image, the chorus 'sets down' (βαλέσθαι) the foundation for the coming performance.

an appeal to the chorus of parthenaic Sirens (of whom more below), explicitly identified as birds, whom she asks to aid, iterate and complement her in a lament that would call to mind a 'patterned threnody' (167–78):[31]

> πτεροφόροι νεάνιδες,
> παρθένοι Χθονὸς κόραι,
> Σειρῆνες, εἴθ' ἐμοῖς
> †γόοις μόλοιτ' ἔχουσαι Λίβυν   170
> λωτὸν ἢ σύριγγας ἢ
> φόρμιγγας αἰλίνοις κακοῖς†
> τοῖς ἐμοῖσι σύνοχα δάκρυα,
> πάθεσι πάθεα, μέλεσι μέλεα,
> μουσεῖα θρηνήμα-
>   σι ξυνῳδά, πέμψαιτε
> Φερσέφασσα †φονία χάριτας†   175
> ἵν' ἐπὶ δάκρυσι παρ' ἐμέθεν ὑπὸ
> μέλαθρα νύχια παιᾶνα
> νέκυσιν ὀλομένοις λάβῃ.

> Winged girls, maiden daughters of Earth, Sirens, would that you would come having the Libyan lotus-flute or pan pipes to my wails of woe; and would that tears in accord with [my tears], sufferings with sufferings, songs with songs, a deadly concert hall sounding in unison with dirges, Persephone might send, so that as a thanks-offering she may receive from me with my tears in her halls of night a paean for the dead that are gone.

Included in Helen's summons are the several different forms of the 'supplementation' (in Ford's account)[32] that must occur for her lament to undergo transformation into the choral performance that the chorus members' appearance initiates: passage from a solitary to a collective voice,[33] musical accompaniment and, with the term μουσεῖα, although here usually read as a reference to the singers rather than to their performance site, a hint of a transfer to a more formal, public setting.[34] Like the halcyons addressed by Alcman, the Sirens' twofold association with mourning and with music (often of an expressly choral kind, as detailed later), as well as their parthenaic character, makes them 'ideal partners' for Helen's lament.[35]

[31] Willink 1990, 78. [32] Ford 2010, 285.

[33] Weiss 2018, 148 suggests an anticipation of 'musical reciprocity' in the repetitions in 173 and the terms σύνοχα and ξυνῳδά.

[34] Ford 2010, 288–89.

[35] The phrase is from Allan 2008 *ad* 167–69. These aspects of the mythical singer are already visible in Alcman fr. 30 *PMGF*, ἁ Μῶσα κέκλαγ' ἀ λίγηα Σηρήν, of which there may even be a hint in the Euripidean lines. Equating Siren and Muse, the earlier poet also attributes to both the

In place of the winged singers invoked by the heroine, an actual chorus of maidens appears and responds to Helen's lyrics in lines that emphasize the merely noisy, inarticulate character and naturalistic setting of her just-heard solitary plaint (179–90):

κυανοειδὲς ἀμφ' ὕδωρ
ἔτυχον ἕλικά τ' ἀνὰ χλόαν   180
φοίνικας ἁλίῳ
πέπλους χρυσέαισιν
<τ' ἐν> αὐγαῖς θάλπουσ'
    ἀμφὶ δόνακος ἔρνεσιν·
ἔνθεν οἰκτρὸν ὅμαδον ἔκλυον,
ἄλυρον ἔλεγον, ὅτι ποτ' ἔλακεν   185
<‒‒◡> αἰάγμασι στένουσα νύμφα τις
οἷα Ναῒς ὄρεσι †φυγάδα
νόμον† ἱεῖσα γοερόν, ὑπὸ δὲ
πέτρινα γύαλα κλαγγαῖσι
Πανὸς ἀναβοᾷ γάμους.   190

By the dark-blue water I happened to be drying along the verdant tendril the purple garments in the golden rays upon the shoots of the reeds, whence I heard a piteous din, a song of grief not fit for the lyre, which she once shrieked out with an *aiai* cry, a Nymph groaning, such as a Naiad in flight sends out to the mountains, a mournful strain, and in accompaniment with the shrieks, the rocky vales shout aloud the nuptials of Pan.

As the chorus members freshly note, absent from this pre-natural sound is the necessary musical accompaniment, not that of the rustic pipes cited by Helen, but of the lyre, an instrument that, unlike the aulos, ill suits the lament. Answering her monodic plaint with a song and dance performed in unison, the troupe of captive women supplies the audience with the properly polished and artistic version of what is retrospectively defined (this despite the elegant and complex character of the opening strophe) as little more than unrefined, inarticulate (a mere *aiai* sound) and unacculturated cacophony. As Ford points out,[36] the singers' recall of how they heard Helen's cry as they were drying freshly laundered clothes in the sun further serves to highlight the choral character of the ongoing parodos and to define the relations between the different participants; the detail points

same sound, the κλαγγή used by the chorus for Helen's utterance in its responsive characterizing of her cries. The adjective used by Alcman for the Siren is also regularly found in epic and later descriptions not only of the Muses' voice, but also of the mourner's.
[36] Ford 2010, 294.

back to the episode in *Od.* 6 where, embarked on another laundry expedition and with the clothes spread out to dry, Nausikaa acts as chorus leader for her maidservants (99–109). So Helen, the reference intimates, will stand as *chorêgos* to this latter-day band of singer-dancers.[37]

In another monodic song from a drama staged just two years earlier, and that many regard as directly influencing the *Helen* parodos,[38] Aristophanes' *Tereus*, now a hoopoe, invites Procne, his nightingale mate, to perform a summons to the other birds (*Av.* 209–22):

> ἄγε σύννομέ μοι, παῦσαι μὲν ὕπνου,
> λῦσον δὲ νόμους ἱερῶν ὕμνων,   210
> οὓς διὰ θείου στόματος θρηνεῖς
> τὸν ἐμὸν καὶ σὸν πολύδακρυν Ἴτυν,
> ἐλελιζομένη διεροῖς μέλεσιν
> γένυος ξουθῆς. καθαρὰ χωρεῖ
> διὰ φυλλοκόμου μίλακος ἠχὼ   215
> πρὸς Διὸς ἕδρας, ἵν' ὁ χρυσοκόμας
> Φοῖβος ἀκούων τοῖς σοῖς ἐλέγοις
> ἀντιψάλλων ἐλεφαντόδετον
> φόρμιγγα θεῶν ἵστησι χορούς·
> διὰ δ' ἀθανάτων στομάτων χωρεῖ   220
> ξύμφωνος ὁμοῦ
> θεία μακάρων ὀλολυγή.

> Come, sharer of my musical pieces [or 'habitat'], cease from sleep, emit the nomes of sacred hymns, lamenting through your godlike lips for my child and yours, much mourned Itys, quivering in the liquid melodies of your oscillating throat. Pure the echo goes apace through the well-tressed bryony to the seat of Zeus, where golden-haired Phoebus listens and for your elegy plucks in response the ivory-inlaid lyre and sets up divine choruses. And from the mouths of the immortals proceeds together [with it] and in harmony the godlike cry of joy of the blessed ones.

Tereus' invocation twice identifies Procne's spontaneous and natural bird cry as a lament (211–12, 217), and then imagines the response it will meet among the Olympians, where Apollo supplies the lyre accompaniment and sets up a chorus (the expression is from the technical language describing the formation of a chorus, and sometimes its very first establishment) which sings 'in perfect harmony' (221) with the nightingale down below.

---

[37] As Weiss 2018, 146, observes, by way of underpinning for the role she assumes, Euripides can draw on Helen's traditional position as chorus-leader in archaic and classical Greek myth and ritual. For this, see too Chapter 9.

[38] For bibliography, see Ford 2010, 290 n. 30. See too Weiss 2018, 165–66 for the overlaps.

Where in Euripides' drama Helen's call for a divine bird chorus to accompany her song is answered by the advent of the Sirens' fully human counterparts, in Aristophanes much the opposite occurs: instead of Apollo and his Olympian chorus, an actual avian ensemble takes the stage. That Aristophanes had fr. 26 *PMGF* in mind when composing Tereus' more extended summons seems likely; lines 250–51 patently recall the opening of the earlier song, and a scholion to the passage identifies Alcman as the source for Tereus' phrasing in his address to the halcyons. As Nan Dunbar remarks, the phrase ἐπὶ πόντιον οἶδμα θαλάσσης is a 'hyper-heroical equivalent' of Alcman's ἐπὶ κύματος ἄνθος, while the very next phrase, μετ' ἀλκυόνεσσι, all but echoes its archaic precedent.[39]

Add to the presence of birds and of 'supplemental' choruses a third feature that the two songs in Attic drama share with fr. 26 *PMGF*: a capacity for generic mutation that turns out to be integral to the lament. While there is no identifying the type of performance which would have followed Alcman's prooimion, and lament figures within any number of different melic compositions and within *partheneia* most particularly, exactly this generic instability belongs to the two passages cited above: Helen signals the shifting and protean quality of her cry by restyling the 'woeful wails' a paean (176),[40] while in Aristophanes, the Muses emit an ὀλολυγή (222), the shout that regularly accompanies a moment of triumph and joy and paeans too,[41] as Apollo re-plays Procne's lament on his lyre.

1.2 *Halcyons, Marriageable Maidens and the Parthenaic Voice*

Taken together, the cluster of halcyon myths and images reviewed so far privileges certain recurrent themes: conjugal love, maternity and solitary grieving for a lost family member, be they husband, daughter or collective progeny. To these motifs, although here I rely chiefly on post-classical sources, I would add two further interconnected concerns: first, passage from the season of maidenhood to that of wife, and second, participation in the parthenaic choral groupings integral to that earlier time of life.

An epigram composed by Antipater (*AP* 6.160) illustrates the halcyon's place in reflections on the transition that the *parthenos* confronts: here a maiden performing the customary dedications to Kore on the eve of

---

[39] Dunbar 1995 *ad loc.* Both Pucci 1997, 71 n. 62 and Silk 1980, 101 allow for a common source.

[40] See Allen 2008 *ad loc.* for this.

[41] Barker 2004, 192 comments on the unstable and shifting nature of what Procne sings: 'it is too many things at once. It is a νόμος, a ὕμνος, a θρῆνος, an ἔλεγος'. See too the discussion of the characterization of the lament of Penelope *qua* nightingale in Nagy 1996, esp. 7–38.

marriage terms her votive shuttle 'the halcyon of Pallas' loom', a formulation that succinctly brings together the bird-like, shrill sound that the
implement makes as it passes through the threads,[42] and the sorrowful
nature of this valedictory gesture as the speaker bids farewell to her unwed
state. A second epigram similarly unites maidenhood, mourning and the
halcyons when it places the birds in company with the parthenaic Nereids
whom they join in bewailing the fall of Corinth: in the maritime nymphs'
declaration that 'we alone ... remain *korai* and lament, like halcyons, your
sorrows' (*AP* 9.151.7–8), the Nereids' status as unwed girls together with
their role as singers of laments prompt their identification with the birds.

Visible in this last example is the bird not as solitary mourner, but as
member of a threnetic ensemble. The Nereid-halcyon-choral link occurs
again in Theocritus, *Id.* 7.59–60, where the poet calls the birds 'most dear' to
the Nereids as they sing in choruses; as Csapo makes clear, since these sea
nymphs typically function as paradigmatic choral performers, fifty identical
maidens executing what sources from the sixth century on frequently describe
as dithyrambic-style circular dances that match the eddying of their native
waves,[43] the pairing with the halcyon maps the Nereids' choral identity onto
the birds. This facet of the halcyon's profile manifests itself in another myth of
avian metamorphosis, where again the bird *qua* chorister assumes its quintessential mourning role. As a scholion to *Il.* 11.20 reports and Eustathius
confirms, Kinyras, king of Cyprus, has fifty daughters – the number repeatedly
found in association not just with the Nereids but with other archetypal choral
groupings too –[44] who leapt into the sea and became halcyons. Lament
continues to inform these Cyprian *parthenoi*-turned-birds: their change of
shape occurs because of the maidens' grief at the death of their father at the
hands of Apollo, against whom Kinyras had matched himself in a musical
contest, while Kinyras' own name is cognate with κινυρός, meaning 'lament'.[45]
The fifty birds' tuneful utterances thus function both as a choral memorializa-
tion of their father's musical skills and as a *thrênos* for his death. The fanciful
myth may embroider on a more historical musico-choral phenomenon; our
sources also identify this Cyprian king as the ancestor of the priestly guild of
Kinyradai, who presided over the rites of Aphrodite at her Greco-Phoenician

---

[42] In the view of Thompson 1936, 48, the poet does not have sound in mind, but rather the rapid
   movement of the shuttle and its resemblance to the 'flash' of the brightly coloured bird.
[43] Csapo 2003; I return to the Nereids in Chapter 5.
[44] This receives fuller treatment in Dowden 1989, 158, where the author documents both real and
   mythical choruses made up of fifty members.
[45] Forbes Irving 1992, 241; Franklin 2015, esp. 189–92, with the detail that in Hellenistic texts
   κινύρεσθαι functioned as a shorthand way to refer to the mourning songs of halcyons, swallows
   and other sorrowing birds.

temple at Paphos. These 'sons of Kinyras' may belong to a tradition of lyre-playing ensemble singers visible in ritual contexts in the Near East,[46] while Kinyras' halcyon daughters are also recognizable in the threnodic and other choruses that appear among instrumentalists and dancers on Cypro-Phoenician bowls.[47]

Together, this thematic cluster supplies a second answer to the question posed at the outset of the discussion of fr. 26 *PMGF*: why halcyons? As several readings of Alcman's first *Partheneion* and of a series of poems by Sappho and Corinna have shown, the stories and symbols included in works expressly composed for choruses of *parthenoi* are in part selected for the lessons they contain – both for the performers and for an audience that would include other young girls and their would-be suitors – concerning female desirability, its dangers (frequently resulting in abduction scenarios) and delights and the mechanisms for its control, marriage most centrally.[48] While the myths narrated in these compositions offer more extended explorations of such concerns, images and metaphors in the songs can serve as more succinct expressions of the same, perceptible to audiences familiar with these thematic and symbolic registers. Consistent with this model, the prefatory lines of fr. 26 *PMGF* deploy a conceit tailor-made for the preoccupations most central to its maidenly performers. Indeed, if, as some propose, the piece was designed to be danced and sung within the context of a marriage celebration (although this section's closing argument suggests a second possible performance frame), then its evocation of a bird that stands symbol of conjugal devotion, fidelity and maternal care becomes more apposite still.

While this feature of archaic *partheneia* is well-travelled ground, a less-explored 'maiden' theme also visible within these choral songs exhibits a fresh connection to the halcyon and to the mythical complex surrounding the bird. Even as performances by parthenaic ensembles supply self- and community-directed lessons, their ability to command a hearing depends on the singular quality and powers that Greek sources ascribe to the virginal choral voice and which guarantee it the necessary authority and impact on its audience. Among these distinctive attributes belongs a property that accounts of the halcyon make native to the species: its ability to calm the winds and bring about that period of calm that is the *sine qua non* for song's reception.

[46] Franklin 2015, 279–319, 401–24. Pindar's mention of Kinyras in *Pyth.* 2.15–18 features a choral performance by some anonymous Cyprian singers, but here their song is one of praise not lamentation.

[47] Franklin 2015, 191 and 289.   [48] Ingalls 2000, with earlier bibliography; Stehle 1997.

For the clearest expression of the halcyons' power to lull the blustering winds and waves, we need again to look forward to Theocritus' seventh *Idyll*, where Lykidas describes how the birds 'lay to rest the waves and the deep, the south wind and the east, that stirs the seaweed in the lowest depth' (57–59). Where other authors credit the period of calm during the 'halcyon days' to Aeolus' compassionate intervention (see above), or make that fortnight merely contemporaneous with the season when the birds bear their young, Theocritus' singer posits the meteorological phenomenon as the direct result of the halcyons' vocalizations.[49] Lykidas' designation of the birds as 'most dear to the green-grey Nereids' (60) confirms the relation of cause-and-effect; from Hesiod on, the sea-dwelling nymphs similarly enjoy the capacity to 'soothe the blasts of the raging winds' (*Th.* 253–54; cf. Hdt. 7.191), and it cannot be fortuitous (although the singers do not spell out the link) that in Euripides' *Helen*, the eponymous Nereid Galaneia (Calm) gives her directions to the rowers on the ship carrying Helen home when the sea 'is windless of breezes' (1455–57). That stillness neatly allows us to hear not just the Nereid's voice, but the ongoing parthenaic choral song which, performed in the dramatic here-and-now, channels her words.

The association between a maritime calm and the halcyons has a rich pre-Theocritean history, and one that, in roundabout fashion and with the Sirens once again added to the ornithological medley, circles back to Alcman's fr. 26 *PMGF*. In an exploration of the particular powers of what turns out to be a choral, virginal and avian song, a fragment from an epinician by Simonides preserved by Plutarch (*Mor.* 722c) records a second occasion on which the winds are still: 'for then arose no leaf-shaking blast of the winds which might have spread abroad and prevented the honey-sweet voice (μελιαδέα γᾶρυν) from fastening (ἀραρεῖν) on the ears of mortals' (fr. 595 *PMG*).[50] Both the manner in which Plutarch introduces the lines, cited in the context of a discussion of the acoustic conditions optimal for sound to carry, and Simonides' own diction unmistakably allude to the canonical encounter between Odysseus and the Sirens. Not only does Simonides' μελιαδέα γᾶρυν recall the μελίγηρυν used by the Sirens of their voice at *Od.* 12.187, but Plutarch prefaces the quotation by noting how sound carries during a 'windless calm' (νηνημία ... καὶ γαλήνη), a phrase that incorporates two terms from *Od.* 12.168–69, where the winds fall still as the hero's boat approaches the Sirens' shores (αὐτίκ᾽ ἔπειτ᾽ ἄνεμος μὲν ἐπαύσατο ἠδὲ γαλήνη / ἔπλετο νηνεμίη).[51] As recent studies have shown,

---

[49] Hunter 1999 *ad loc.* Cf. A.R. 1.1085.

[50] See Poltera 2008 for a recent commentary on the fragment.

[51] Alcman's μελιγάρυες may similarly include an echo of the Homeric term for the Sirens' voice.

not only do post-Homeric poets, Alcman in his first *Partheneion* and Apollonius among them, and artists from the sixth century on present these enchantresses as an archetypal parthenaic chorus (this already suggested by their Odyssean location in a 'flowery meadow' at 12.159), and bird-women to boot,[52] but their appeal to the Homeric hero incorporates diction and metrical devices more typical of the lyric than hexameter register, presenting something of a generic challenge and threat to the epic's course.[53] Reminiscent of the wind-stilling properties assigned by Simonides to the voice described in fr. 595 *PMG*, and making its parthenaic and choral qualities explicit, is the claim voiced by the Theban choristers performing Pindar's near contemporary second *Partheneion*: in an instance of choral self-projection, the singers declare that they will 'imitate in my songs to the accompaniment of lotus pipes the Sirens' loud song (κόμπον), which silences the swift blasts of Zephyr, and whenever with the strength of winter chilling Boreas rages swiftly over the sea . . .' (fr. 94b.13–19 S.-M.).[54] The lines allude, again, to the Homeric singers and to *Od.* 12.168–69 cited above.

With the curious verb placed in verse-initial position of line 3, ἀραρεῖν, Simonides freshly suggests the Sirenic property within the vocalizations. Where Homer more implicitly tropes the 'fixative' quality of the Sirens' song (and the very name of the singers is cognate with the Greek term for rope, *seira*) through the cables binding Odysseus to the mast, Simonides' term makes the motif more emphatic: the song seemingly fastens or affixes itself to its audiences' ears, a kind of earbud *avant la lettre*.[55] The auditory

---

[52] Alcman fr. 1.96–99 *PMGF*, Pind. fr. 94b.8–17 S.-M., A.R. 4.891–99; among the visual representations belongs a late sixth-century black-figure oinochoe (New York, Collection of Gregory Callimanopulos; *Para.* 183.22 *bis*).

[53] For detailed discussion of the chorality and 'lyricism' of the Sirens, see Peponi 2012, 76–80 and Weiss 2018, 150–53; note too Bowie 2011, 54–56 and 57–59.

[54] Pindar adds an additional element to the Sirenic appeals that further guarantees them a hearing: the sheer volume implicit in the κόμπος (as noted by Peponi 2012, 84). Alcman may also gesture towards this facet of his choristers' voice in the adjective used of the halcyon-performers at the opening of fr. 26 *PMGF*, ἱαρόφωνοι, whose first element, cognate with the form *ἶρος, endows the girls' song with strength as well as a privileged relation to the gods (*pace* Calame 1983, 476).

[55] Again, Pindaric poetry supplies its own version of the conceit: as noted in my earlier discussions, there is no mistaking the Odyssean model behind the Keledones, whose vocalizations are endowed with the irresistible appeal of the Sirens' song and who similarly prevent the visitors to the temple from returning home (indeed, Pindar's evocation of auditors perishing apart from their wives and children patently echoes *Od.* 12.42–43, while the sweetness of the Charmers' αὐδή dovetails with the 'honeyed' quality of the Sirens' voice). In an uncanny figuration of the adhesive powers that likewise belong to the singers featured in fr. 595 *PMG*, albeit with the roles reversed, Pindar's metallic choristers make their audience 'attach' themselves to their vocalizations.

organ becomes just one more element in the composite choral song, itself the result of the 'fitting together' process detailed in earlier chapters.

While fr. 595 *PMG* omits all mention of the halcyons, the birds make their entry into a second Simonidean fragment that, as several older discussions suggest and a more recent demonstration of the two fragments' metrical responsion affirms,[56] belongs to the same composition. The lines preserved by Aristotle take the form of a simile, which includes our first extant reference to the halcyon days (fr. 508 *PMG* = Arist. *HA* 542b):

>   . . . ὡς ὁπόταν
> χειμέριον κατὰ μῆνα πινύσκῃ
> Ζεὺς ἤματα τέσσαρα καὶ δέκα,
> λαθάνεμον δέ μιν ὥραν
> καλέουσιν ἐπιχθόνιοι   5
> ἱερὰν παιδοτρόφον ποικίλας
> ἀλκυόνος.

> as when in the winter month Zeus admonishes fourteen days, and mortals call it the holy season which forgets the winds, the season of child-rearing for the dappled halcyon.

With his introduction of the halcyons, Simonides suggestively redeploys the adjective twice used in Alcman for the property of the bird and its voice: ἱερὰν is the term applied in fr. 508 *PMG* to the season in which the bird produces its offspring, a reworking, with *variatio*, of Alcman's phrasing in lines 1 and 4 of fr. 26 *PMGF*. Although it remains impossible to determine the exact relation between the two Simonidean fragments, and what role the Sirens and halcyons played in the larger piece, both citations unmistakably include the period of windless calm.[57] Worth noting too is Simonides' introduction of the halcyon days within the context of a simile; might the poet's epinician singers, in the manner of the *parthenoi* of Pindar's fr. 94a.13–19 S.-M., be likening the impact of their song, or that of some other more paradigmatic parthenaic ensemble onto whom they are projecting their identity, to the stillness that prevails when the halcyons raise their voices?

---

[56] Führer 2007; see too the additional points made by Poltera 2008, 311.

[57] Indeed, in one solution to the crux in line 2 of fr. 508 *PMG*, where the regular meaning of πινύσκω, 'I advise' or 'make wise', does not fit the context, Clarke 1997/98 emends the text to ἀπινύσκῃ. If that correction is right, then Simonides imagines Zeus 'losing his breath', an expression that, following the identification of the god with atmospheric phenomena, indicates that he ceases to blow the winds; it is this withholding of a rival source of sound that again guarantees the avian singers the conditions optimal for song to impress itself on an audience.

1.3 Choreia *and Rejuvenation*

Closely connected with the seasonality that informs the halcyons' breeding practices is the final piece in the complex of myths surrounding the birds that may have prompted Alcman's particularized choice of metaphor: the halcyons' participation in the astral-cum-agricultural round and their link to that moment when the year renews itself and winter yields to the generative months of spring. As argued here, like choral dancing, which in the Greek imaginary offers participants the possibility of rejuvenation and of regaining or permanently inhabiting the season of youth, halcyon mythology grants the birds the analogous capacity for rebirth and the recapture of a bygone time. This section begins with Sappho's so-called Tithonus poem, a composition that, as noted above, stands in particularly close relation to Alcman's fr. 26 *PMGF* [58] and that more patently takes up the theme of *choreia*'s power to reverse senescence,[59] before exploring the halcyon's pertinence to this regeneration scheme; building on these several elements, my closing suggestion concerns a possible performance context for Alcman's song.

In place of the Spartan poet's halcyons, Sappho's fr. 58 V., this now supplemented by *P. Köln* 21351 and 21376, cites the myth of Tithonus' abduction by the winged Eos and his airborne travel overseas, narrating the tale within a lament about old age and the poetic ego's inability to join the youthful dancing chorus members in whose midst she locates herself:

ὔμμες πεδὰ Μοίσαν ἰ]οκ[ό]λπων κάλα δῶρα, παῖδες,
σπουδάσδετε καὶ τὰ]ν φιλάοιδον λιγύραν χελύνναν·
ἔμοι δ᾽ ἄπαλον πρίν] ποτ. [ἔ]οντα χρόα γῆρας ἤδη
ἐπέλλαβε, λεῦκαι δ᾽ ἐγ]ένοντο τρίχες ἐκ μελαίναν·
βάρυς δέ μ᾽ ὁ θ]ῦμος. πεπόηται, γόνα δ᾽ [ο]ὐ φέροισι,
τὰ δή ποτα λαίψηρ᾽ ἔον ὄρχησθ᾽ ἴςα νεβρίοισι.
τὰ ⟨μὲν⟩ στεναχίσδω θαμέως· ἀλλὰ τί κεν ποείην;
ἀγήραον ἄνθρωπον ἔοντ᾽ οὐ δύνατον γένεσθαι.
καὶ γάρ π[ο]τα Τίθωνον ἔφαντο βροδόπαχυν Αὔων
ἔρωι φ αθεισαν βάμεν᾽ εἰς ἔσχατα γᾶς φέροισα[ν,
ἔοντα [κ]άλον καὶ νέον, ἀλλ᾽ αὖτον ὔμως ἔμαρψε
χρόνωι πόλιον γῆρας, ἔχ[ο]ντ᾽ ἀθανάταν ἄκοιτιν.

---

[58] See n. 12.

[59] For a second expression of this idea in combination with the flight motif, see, among others, Eur. *HF* 637–700; the pronounced dithyrambic inflection of the song coincides with the commonplace view that participation in the rites of Dionysus supplies an antidote to time's passage; for this, see Ar. *Ran.* 345–48, Eur. *Bacch.* 184–90, Pl. *Leg.* 666a2–c7, which reworks Euripides' language in the *HF*.

Pursue the violet-laden Muses' handsome gifts, my children, and the loud-voiced lyre so dear to song; but me – my skin which once was soft is withered now by age, my hair has turned to white which once was black, my heart has been weighed down, my knees give no support which once were nimble in the dance like little fawns. How often I lament these things. But what to do? No being that is human can escape old age. For people used to think that Dawn with rosy arms and loving murmurs took Tithonus fine and young to reach the edges of the earth; yet still grey age in time did seize him, though his consort cannot die. (text and translation after D. Obbink)

Much as Alcman does, Sappho opens by establishing a sharp contrast between the speaker and the members of her chorus, the *paides* whom the first two lines address and whom she seems to urge to cultivate 'the beautiful gifts' that belong to 'violet-breasted' goddesses. The consensus is that Sappho describes the benefactions of the Muses here, but in accordance with what follows, I would instead suggest the Graces, patrons not just of music and song, but more particularly of choral dance.[60] The speaker, afflicted by old age, then explains that her weakened limbs prohibit her from joining in the dance. And yet, for all that the poem rules the escape from time that would permit participation in the choristers' activity out of court, the subsequent lines' appeal to the Eos and Tithonus myth keeps that idea of everlasting youth,[61] and more strictly rejuvenation in the context of *choreia*, very much in play. Even as the seemingly sorry tale of the youthful abductee stands proof of the assertion that old age is an ineluctable human lot, the poem's description of how Dawn carried off her beloved to 'the ends of the earth' evokes a potentially different outcome. Not only is this the site where Okeanos flows, into whose waters the Sun sinks down prior to its renewal and rebirth at dawn of each new day;[62] here too Eos has her 'house and χοροί' (*Od.* 12.3–4), these last both the dancing spaces and astral

---

[60] See Schlesier 2011 for the same suggestion. For the Graces and their particular patronage of the dance, see Chapter 2.

[61] Schlesier 2011 suggests that the use of the Tithonus story would call to mind the more unequivocally positive exemplum with which it was paired in the (probably) seventh-century *Homeric Hymn to Aphrodite* (which many commentators see as a reference point for Sappho's own song), where Ganymede achieves not just immortality, but the eternal youth that Eos forgets to request for Tithonus. Janko 2005 sees the Tithonus paradigm as potentially positive insofar as the character's transformation into an eternally singing cicada supplies 'an ideal image for the aged poetess herself (Sappho), with her well-attested wish to have her poetry win glory beyond the grave'; see too Greene 2009, 158.

[62] Nagy 1973, 156: 'The movements of the sun suggest the theme of death and rebirth. With the waning of the day, the old sun submerges beyond the horizon into the west Okeanos; then, after night has passed, a new sun emerges from the east Okeanos'.

choruses over which the goddess presides.[63] As Anton Bierl proposes, in the land of Aiai, the site to which Tithonus is transported by the winged goddess, we should imagine Dawn acting as *chorêgos* to her company of dancing stars, leading them in performance as they enact their movements in the sky each break of day. Still following Bierl, insofar as Sappho models herself on Eos no less than Tithonus[64] – she too is captivated by the sight of her παῖδες and their youthful bodies, and is herself possessor of χοροί, over whom the mortal *chorêgos*, like her divine counterpart, presides – the goddess offers a model for just that rejuvenation or renewal that the poetic ego, 'being human', declares out of reach.

The overlap with Alcman's poems is several-fold: not just the obvious departure of strength from the speaker's limbs that prohibits choral dancing, but, in more subtle fashion, the notion of a winged passage (and even, if we allow that Antigonus may have got things right, actual transportation by a female winged vector such as Eos supplies for Tithonus) overseas to some fantastical site and the rejuvenation, with the additional choral aspect indicated by Bierl, that this could entail.[65] In each instance, there is the possibility of endlessly prolonging that particular youthful activity from which the poetic ego finds him- or herself excluded and of allowing mortals, no less than divinities, to enjoy an existence resembling that imagined by the *Homeric Hymn to Aphrodite* informing Sappho's work.[66] Here the miraculously mortal but ever-unaging Nymphs introduced in lines 259–60 exhibit precisely the conjunction that Sappho, gesturing towards that song here as elsewhere in the composition, deems unattainable. Further linking the two pieces is the signature activity assigned the Nymphs by the hymnist: they are choral dancers (καλὸν χορὸν ἐρρώσαντο, *HHVen.* 261). If Sappho wishes listeners to have in mind not just the *Hymn*, but the element that its rendition of the Tithonus story omits (viz. Tithonus' transformation into a cicada) but alludes to at several sites,[67] then the Lesbian singer's seemingly negative but designedly open-ended exemplum has, in fact, a happy resolution: the Trojan youth undergoes metamorphosis into a cicada, whose practice of sloughing off its old skin and acquiring a new carapace each year offers a model for perpetual

[63] Here I follow Bierl 2016, 321; for more on these star choruses, see later in this chapter.
[64] Bierl 2016, 320–21.
[65] As noted in the conclusion to this section's discussion, such sites often combine a quasi-eternal and blessed mode of existence with the motif of choral dancing.
[66] Rawles 2005 makes a very cogent case for this composition as Sapphic intertext; while most discussions focus only on the relations between Sappho's version of the Eos–Tithonus story and that in the *Hymn*, the allusions, Rawles demonstrates, extend well beyond this single passage.
[67] See Rawles 2005, 6 for the evidence.

revitalization. Tithonus' change of state is relevant to Alcman's fr. 26 *PMGF* on a final count; it is by becoming both a singer and a creature endowed with wings, the equipment with which the insect produces its everlasting song and also flies, that individuals escape unenviable conditions, whether old age or some other form of suffering. Those same wings, furthermore, make the erstwhile Trojan beloved the mirror image of his divine abductor.

If all this seems remote from the halcyons central to Alcman's fr. 26 *PMGF*, then a handful of ancient sources reveal the place of the birds in rejuvenation/regeneration scenarios. Among these belongs a scholion to Pindar, *Nem.* 2.16, which states that Alkyone is one among the seven Pleiades (information that our commentator attributes to Hesiod), the star cluster whose members constitute that archetypal parthenaic chorus explored in other chapters. As Olga Levaniouk notes, in ancient astronomical schemes, the rising of the Pleiades marked the vernal equinox, considered the moment when the sun began its yearly circuit; the winter solstice then coincides with their culmination.[68] While there is no determining the point at which the Alkyone–Pleiades link entered the complex of stories surrounding the bird, or of knowing whether Alcman and his audience were familiar with this byway of 'avianology', fr. 26 *PMGF* includes a possible pointer to the halcyon as a harbinger of seasonal change. If we preserve the penultimate word in the final line of the fragment as the codices transmit it, then the designation of the halcyon as εἴαρος, 'of springtime',[69] would associate the bird not only with that prime season of youth but with this point of renewal in the annual round, when, as later sources attest, fair weather returns (so A.R. 1.1086). Aristotle's gloss on Simonides fr. 508 *PMG*, the lines discussed earlier, confirms the bird's place within these astral dynamics; as the philosopher explains, the halcyon breeds at the time of the winter solstice, and hence the calm weather seven days before and seven after it, called the halcyon days. In a comment shortly afterwards, Aristotle refers to the Pleiades: 'the halcyon is the most rarely seen of all birds. It is seen only about the time of the setting of the Pleiades and the winter solstice' (*HA* 542b21–23).

If we can assume that the halcyons' association with seasonal change and, more particularly, with the vernal equinox existed already in the early archaic age,[70] then the overseas flight proposed by the speaker of

[68] Levaniouk 1999, 121.
[69] For discussion, see Calame 1983 *ad loc.* with arguments for and against the term. ἔαρ appears with the nightingale at Sappho fr. 136 V. and of the swallow at Sim. 597 *PMG*. See too the arguments in favour of the codices' reading in Giangrande 1971, 105.
[70] Hes. *Erg.* 561–63 already refers to the vernal equinox.

fr. 26 *PMGF* would carry with it a promise similar to that which Eos' transport of Tithonus/Sappho to her faraway home includes, that of a winged passage to a paradisiacal type of existence free from old age and all the other miseries of mortal life. One marker of this blessed state is the prolongation of a phenomenon that, in the view of most commentators, Hesiod includes in his mention of the spring equinox, a point of the year when 'nights and days are no longer unequal' (*Erg.* 562). In a passage in *Olympian* 2, where Pindar imagines the pleasures that await the ἐσλοί after death, he assigns them not only a life free from toil but one in which they have 'sunshine in equal nights and in equal days' (61–62), a condition that he then equates with the idyllic lifestyle of the inhabitants of the Isles of the Blessed (71–74); this site is characterized by its golden, brilliant vegetation and the garlands and crowns that its inhabitants pass their time in weaving. Other texts seem likewise to attribute a state of permanent light/dark equipoise to the fantastical and faraway lands where blessed or exceptionally favoured peoples dwell. Lucian's account of the city of these happy few combines the equinox with the absence of old age; here 'it is neither night among them nor yet very bright day' (*VH* 2.12), but a kind of perpetual penumbra in which light and dark exist in equal measure. No wonder that this same state, featuring six-month days and nights, exists in the land of the supremely good-fortuned Hyperboreans (Pomponius Mela, *De chorographia* 3.36),[71] a race also distinctive for a life filled with *choreia*. As Pindar's *Pythian* 10 observes, 'and the Muse is no stranger to their ways, for everywhere choruses of maidens, sounds of lyres, and pipes' shrill notes are stirring. With golden laurel they crown their hair and feast joyfully. Neither sickness nor accursed old age mingles with that holy race' (37–42); the picture painted here closely resembles that of *Ol.* 2.71–74.

Nor does this link to the Pleiades exhaust the 'celestial' dimension of the Alkyone myth. The halcyons are involved not only, whether in association with or independent of the star cluster, with the winter solstice and spring

---

[71] In Pliny's account (*HN* 4.12.89), this fabled land, whose population lives a life free from all sickness, hunger and pain, is home to a second and related cosmological/astral wonder: here, he reports, some locate 'the pivots of the universe and the extreme limits of the circuits of the stars, with six months of daylight at the turning round of the sun, not, as the ignorant affirm, from the spring equinox to autumn. The sun rises for them once a year, at the solstice, and sets once at the winter solstice.' The turning points of the sun, the place on the horizon where the sun was seen to rise on the midsummer and midwinter day, mark the moment when the solar body reverses its course at the solstices, and that together with the equinoxes, signal the change of the seasons.

equinox, but with the dawn of each new day. According to Lucian's version of the story (*Hal.* 2), both Alkyone and her husband Ceyx are descended from the morning star, the 'light-bringer' (Phosphoros) who puts an end to night and was believed to lead the sun back from the underworld at the start of day. Ovid's earlier account in *Met.* 11.410–748 proposes a rather different scenario, but already includes the astral associations visible in Lucian: for the Latin poet, Alkyone is the daughter of Aeolus, married to Ceyx, son of Lucifer, the light-bringing morning star. Following Ovid's narrative, when Alkyone discovers the body of Ceyx, who has lost his life at sea, she jumps off a jetty and becomes a halcyon.[72] Uttering her now-avian cry of lament and touching the corpse with her wings as she skims the surface of the waves, the grieving heroine, through the agency of the compassionate gods, turns her spouse into a second bird so that their loving partnership may endure. Where Levaniouk connects this story with the motif of the frustrated or desirous lover who seeks relief by leaping from a rock into the ocean,[73] I would focus instead on the act of metamorphosis, resuscitation and renewal with which the episode ends; consonant with her association with the morning star (albeit through her husband here), and with the time-reversing powers of avian metamorphosis, Alkyone leads Ceyx back from the death that his immersion in the water signals and to a feathered existence free from sorrow. While this story, so redolent of a Hellenistic sensibility, long postdates Alcman, the Spartan poet's choice of the halcyon could still draw on the bird's pre-existing role in heralding and promoting vernal renewal and the rebirth of day as marked by the sun's return to its starting point following its diurnal passage through the sky. That journey, in which the stellar body ages and then, sinking down into the waters of Okeanos, 'dies' prior to its regeneration at the light-bringing dawn, stands paradigm for the outcome that Alcman's poetic ego seeks.

The halcyon's link with the Pleiades, with the morning star and with moments of seasonal and daily renewal and change bear on fr. 26 *PMGF* in one final respect. Taking my cue from Ferrari's discussion of Alcman's first *Partheneion*, a song whose emphatic astral symbolism, she argues, suggests its performance at the Spartan Karneia, a festival marking a point of seasonal turnabout when the stars exhibit a particular configuration in the sky,[74] I would situate fr. 26 *PMGF* within a similarly season-marking and festive frame and propose that it too reflects and choreographically enacts events currently occurring in the arrangement of the stars. Just as the

---

[72] Although Ovid omits this element, a scholion to Ar. *Av.* 250 reports that Ceyx was turned into a cerylus.
[73] Levaniouk 1999, 124–25.   [74] Ferrari 2008.

imagery of the first *Partheneion* invites its audience to look upwards to where the constellations perform their nocturnal dance, so here the equation of the maiden chorus with birds flying overhead (ποτῆται, a frequentative, indicates the recurrent, regularized nature of the birds' activity) directs attention to the medium inhabited by the halcyons (and stars) on whom the dancers, through movement and voice, are invited to model themselves.

The conjunction between the birds' seemingly rare appearances and specific moments in the year might allow us still more precisely to pinpoint the event for which fr. 26 *PMGF* was designed, a ritual celebration which should coincide with the return of fair weather and a moment of transition in the agricultural year. The Spartan Hyakinthia, an early summer festival that was firmly established by the end of the eighth century,[75] seems the most obvious occasion for the song, and exhibits two further features particularly apposite to fr. 26 *PMGF*. First, the role given to maiden choruses whose performances during a night-time ritual Calame's detailed reconstruction of the festival documents[76] and whose presence the third stasimon of Euripides' *Helen* likewise evokes (1469–70); and second, the myth commemorated by the rite, and that turns about several of the themes visible in the scant four remaining lines of Alcman's song.

In a story first attested in the *Helen* (1469–73), but doubtless of older provenance given the antiquity of the pre-Greek cult, Apollo accidentally kills his beloved Hyakinthos, whose body his sister Polyboia (depicted as a *parthenos* on the tomb of Hyakinthos at Amyklai dated to the mid-sixth century)[77] then recovers and takes up to heaven. After a short period of death, the youth is reborn together with his sibling and heroized.[78] The element of regeneration observed by scholars in the sequence of the three days of the festival re-enacts this process, from the funereal atmosphere of the first day dedicated to Hyakinthos, to the joyous musical and sacrificial festivities that occurred on days two and three: as Calame comments, 'from the annihilation of the old order, from death and mourning, we pass to a

---

[75] For detailed discussion, see Pettersson 1992, 19–41 and Calame 1997, 174–85. Several later chapters return to the festival.

[76] Calame 1997, 174–85; Calame's discussion also suggests Alcman as composer of a song for performance by a parthenaic chorus on this occasion: fr. 10a *PMGF*, which features the *chorêgos* Agesidamos and the chorus of Dymainai includes a mention of Amyklai, prompting Calame's suggestion that Alcman (or someone else) composed the song for performance at the Hyakinthia.

[77] Among the scenes on the tomb, according to Paus. 3.19.4, was a representation of the hero and his sister being led up to the sky by a series of goddesses.

[78] Pettersson 1992, 29–37 discusses the existence of two conflicting representations of Hyakinthos, sometimes as a mature man, sometimes as a youth and *erômenos*.

new life marked by the joy of resurrection'.[79] Placed in this context, the opening of Alcman's song reflects, on a microcosmic and personal level, the concerns of the myth around which the festival revolves: since Greek sources do not strictly distinguish rejuvenation from rebirth (as the tales of Pelops and Jason, among others, illustrate), and the 'restoration of life to the dead and of youth to the old are variants of each other',[80] the tale of Hyakinthos suggests that the aged singer's wish for rejuvenation might, at least in part, be realized through his participation in the festival as *chorêgos*.

We might press the analogy further and, following Calame, see in the παρσενικαί featured in fr. 26 *PMGF* instantiations of the maidenly Polyboia (whom Pausanias identifies as a *parthenos* at 3.19.4), her brother's helper, restorer and sharer in immortalization in the myth, whose identity the adolescent members of the choral group assume as they (together with their limb-weakened *chorêgos*) are 'born again on the second day to a new life, for which they expressed their thanks to Apollo'.[81] This regeneration would extend beyond the youthful segment of the population; for the older celebrants too (and the Spartans turned out *en masse* for the procession to Amyklai), the story of death and rebirth, celebrated at a critical point in the seasonal cycle when the year renewed itself, held out the hope of reversing and negating the passage of time, of returning to the 'springtime' of their youth; for these individuals, Alcman's *persona loquens* would stand proxy. Again, *choreia* is a central element here: as fr. 26 *PMGF* affirms, and as the choral dances performed 'in the old/traditional style' at the Hyakinthia visibly demonstrate,[82] participating in dancing groups proves the medium through which this recovery of past time, rebirth and the defeat of senescence may occur.

2 Cranes

In his extended account of halcyons (*Hal.* 1.620–22), Oppian cites a second bird species for its choral character, styling a flock of cranes in flight a χορός. As this section's discussion aims to illustrate, the association between cranes and choruses that this late source observes draws on a well-established topos

---

[79] Calame 1997, 182, with a review of earlier accounts.
[80] Scodel 1980, 308. As Scodel comments, the two ideas appear in tandem in the second stasimon of the *Heracles*: here the second youth that the aged singers long to achieve is granted to those who 'after dying, would return to the light of the sun' (660–61).
[81] Calame 1997, 182.
[82] According to Polykrates (*FGrH* 588 F 1 = Athen. 4.139e), dancers at the Hyakinthia performed in the traditional style (κίνησιν ἀρχαικήν) to the music of the pipes; for more on this, see below.

that dates back to archaic visual and poetic sources and that pairs these supremely 'gregarious' birds with singer-dancers in a variety of public and more private settings.[83] My account of the role of cranes as a paradigmatic choral collective onto whom performers in images and texts regularly map their identities takes as its focal point the second strophe in the third stasimon of Euripides' *Helen* – a song performed by the maiden chorus as Helen and Menelaus make their way towards the Egyptian shore and the boat that will take them back to Greece – and already cited for its reference to Spartan cult practices and events at Amyklai. In keeping with the design of Section 1, I both illustrate the extended traditions in earlier poetry and art in which the singers' appeal to the cranes is embedded, and then offer an account of the birds' particularized place within this ode and their bearing on musico-choral concerns in late fifth-century Athens.

2.1   Crane Flight, Dance Formations and the Bird's Signature Cry (Eur. Hel. 1478–87)

First, then, the opening portion of the second strophe:

δι' αἰθέρος εἴθε ποτανοὶ
γενοίμεθ' ὅπαι Λιβύας
οἰωνοὶ στολάδες[84]   1480
ὄμβρον χειμέριον λιποῦσαι νίσονται πρεσβυτάτου
σύριγγι πειθόμεναι
ποιμένος, ἄβροχά θ' ὃς
πεδία καρποφόρα τε γᾶς   1485
ἐπιπετόμενος ἰαχεῖ.
ὦ πταναὶ δολιχαύχενες,

If only we could fly through the air to where the birds in array from Libya go, leaving the wintery rain behind, obedient to the panpipes of the eldest, their shepherd, who calls out as he flies over the rainless and fruit-bearing plains of the earth. O long-necked birds . . .

The lines' initial appeal to the cranes returns us to already familiar ground. Like Alcman, the song expresses a longing to escape from a current plight (the girls' exile in Egypt), and to do so by means of an avian transformation that would allow those uttering the wish to traverse the seas.[85] Reminiscent

---

[83]   In the view of Arist. *Pol. HA* 488a3–4, cranes are ἀγελαῖοι, birds who flock together.

[84]   Note the variant used by Diggle's *OCT*, στιχάδες. Here I use the text of Allan 2008.

[85]   More narrowly, and as Weiss 2018, 184–85 notes, the motif of music-making birds already appears in the drama's parodos and first stasimon.

of Alcman too, the affinity between the dramatic chorus performing on stage and this flock draws on traditional representations of the birds, and, in this instance, on the principal and interlinked characteristics granted the species from archaic texts and images on: their singular ability to dance, their distinctive flight-formation and their loud and piercing cry.

In their self-association with cranes in flight (a species cited in no other Euripidean escape ode nor in frequent wishes for metamorphosis into feathered form, whether in drama or the older lyric and epic accounts), the choristers immediately take up an analogy already visible at several points in the *Iliad*. Whether or not the Greeks had witnessed something like the remarkable group dance that Demoiselle cranes pausing in their migratory flights perform,[86] in the suggestive argument of Leonard Muellner the crane/dancer kinship already underlies a sequence of similes in *Iliad* 3.[87] The book begins by likening the mustered Trojan army to migrating cranes *en route* to their battle with the pygmies (2–7; note too the emphasis on the birds' distinctive sound, the thrice repeated κλαγγή that furnishes the pivot on which the comparison turns), and later likens Paris to the individual who has just quitted not the χῶρος of battle (315, 344) but the χορός that is the dancing space or chorus (393). Linking the two similes, and underpinning the very anomalous depiction of the cranes at the book's opening (typically the *Iliad* paints the species as meadow-dwelling herbivores who cluster and feed on the ground, and not as predators but prey) is the corresponding displacement of Paris from his wonted sphere and role: from dance floor to battlefield, from choral dancer to warrior.

Latent in the crane-dancer equivalence that the sequence constructs, Muellner further argues, is Homer's familiarity with the so-called *geranos* or Crane Dance, identified by the scholia as the dance performed by the chorus of youths and maidens on the penultimate ring on Achilles' shield (*Il.* 18.590–606). According to ancient commentators, this was the dance that Theseus first instituted with a chorus made up of the seven maidens and seven youths whom he rescued from the labyrinth, after Daedalus had 'devised the craft of *choreia* ... and showed it to the dancers'.[88] Where the scholia imagine the performance occurring immediately at the exit of the maze, with Daedalus as chorus-instructor and Theseus as *chorêgos*,

---

[86] Pliny (*HN* 10.39.60) records the phenomenon. See too Muellner 1990, 92, and this description from the website of the International Crane Foundation: 'In Demoiselle Cranes, the female initiates the display and utters one call for each male call. All cranes engage in dancing, which includes various behaviors such as bowing, jumping, running, stick or grass tossing, and wing flapping'.

[87] Muellner 1990.   [88] Σ AB *ad* Hom. *Il.* 18.590.

Callimachus, our earliest sure literary source for the *geranos*, locates it, with
Plutarch and Pollux after him, on Delos instead;[89] there the Theseus-led
performance subsequently becomes the mythological model for the choral
dance still executed in imperial times as part of the ritual celebration of the
Aphrodisia, where dancers circled around the goddess' horned altar.

The crane-choral dancer association only implicit in Homer finds more
direct expression in the visual tradition, and already, perhaps, in the
interpretation first advanced by J. N. Coldstream,[90] in the image on the
London oinochoe cited at the outset of this chapter (Fig. 3.0), where cranes
(if this is the species depicted here) appear in the three figural friezes on the
pot. Several features of the representation might locate the topmost scene
on Crete and point to a performance of the *geranos* on Theseus' arrival or
just prior to his departure: the male dancers hold oars, the girls wear
Minoan-style flounced dresses and open bodices, and one of the female
figures, tentatively identified as Ariadne, appears with what could be her
signature crown or a victory-cum-bridal wreath anticipating – or celebrating – Theseus' defeat of the monstrous hybrid and the marriage which
should follow her departure with the hero. Coldstream draws attention to
the interaction between the Ariadne figure and the man immediately
adjacent to her in the line, Theseus perhaps. Forming the central pair,
they alone do not link hands; instead the male figure places his hand on the
maiden's breast.[91]

The early sixth-century François Vase includes a more unmistakable
association of cranes and choral dancers, presenting both collectives in a
stacked design that recalls the oinochoe.[92] As though to confirm the
character of the performance portrayed on the upper register, where
Theseus heads the line of his 'twice seven', a second image located at the
very base of the pot, on its foot, depicts the Geranomachy, the mock-heroic
battle of the pygmies and the cranes already evoked in the simile in *Iliad* 3
(Figs. 0.5, 0.6). The probably parodic relation of the two images notwithstanding (while the supremely martial Theseus dances up above, the

---

[89] *Hymn* 4.310 Pf., Plut. *Thes.* 21, Poll. 4.101.

[90] Coldstream 1968. A crane similarly appears adjacent to a group of choral performers on a
bronze Phoenician bowl, also dated to the late eighth century (Paris, Louvre AO 4702; for this,
see Langdon 2008, fig. 3.29 and my discussion in Chapter 4).

[91] Note too the Late Geometric Attic krater (London, British Museum 1899, 0219.1), which may
represent the actual departure and Ariadne's abduction

[92] Here I develop a passing suggestion in Muellner 1990, 92–93; see too Hedreen 2016, 194–97 also
citing Muellner. In a modern revisiting of the theme, with an astral element too, during the
construction of Renzo Piano's Stavros Niarchos Foundation Cultural Center in Athens in 2014,
the choreographer Renato Zanella staged a fifteen-minute 'dance' performance of the ten giant
cranes on the construction site set to the music from Holst's *The Planets*.

pygmy, typically a dancer, on the base has forsaken his proper activity to do battle with the cranes in a patent deformation of an epic-style combat), the artist Kleitias has given viewers several prompts for reading the scenes in tandem. He has portrayed fourteen birds, their number matching the canonical 'twice seven' would-be tribute victims on the neck; and in marked contrast to the misshapen and corpulent pygmies mounted on the backs of goats, the cranes, some standing tall on the ground, others with their wings outspread as they swoop in flight, have all the grace, agility and stature of the choral dancer.

Two additional vases offer fresh instances of the pairing of dancing and the crane in the early visual corpus. The artist of an archaic black-figure handleless bowl in Athens, painted in a style that anticipates the later parodic Kabeiric vases, gives the association a passing glance (Figs. 3.2, 3.3).[93] On one side of the pot, a Dionysus-like figure holding a crane by its neck appears, while dancing komasts and a seated aulos-player surround the pair on either side. The same komasts return on an Attic black-figure hydria in Rome, now in conjunction with the Geranomachy (Figs. 3.4, 3.5).[94] On the body of the pot we witness a riotous dance whose performers raise their legs to waist height, their arms outstretched and legs bent back

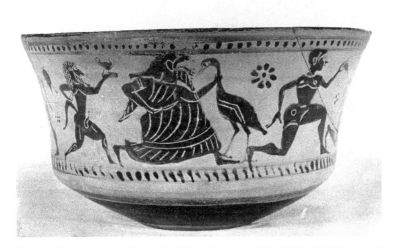

Fig. 3.2 Boeotian black-figure handleless bowl, ca. 500–480 B.C.E. Side A. Athens, National Archaeological Museum 418. Photograph © National Archaeological Museum, Athens.

---

[93] Athens, National Archaeological Museum 418.   [94] Rome, Villa Giulia 50425.

Fig. 3.3 Boeotian black-figure handleless bowl, ca. 500–480 B.C.E. Side B. Athens, National Archaeological Museum 418. Photograph © National Archaeological Museum, Athens.

Fig. 3.4 Attic black-figure hydria. Body of vase. Rome, Museo Nazionale di Villa Giulia 50425. Photograph Mauro Bennedetti © MiBAC. Museo Nazionale Etrusco di Villa Giulia.

Fig. 3.5 Attic black-figure hydria. Shoulder of vase. Rome, Museo Nazionale di Villa Giulia 50425. Photograph Mauro Bennedetti © MiBAC. Museo Nazionale Etrusco di Villa Giulia.

and forward; positioned immediately above on the shoulder is the battle of the pygmies and cranes. Even as the pygmies' poses mirror those of the dancers below, the cranes likewise participate in the 'dance'; one appears to be standing on the tips of its toes as it stretches wide its wings.

With the Homeric text and a rich artistic tradition reaching back to the early seventh century as backdrop to his stasimon, Euripides achieves one of his several ends: the suggestion that this unmistakably dithyrambic-style and musico-chorally novelizing ode[95] currently being performed on stage does no more than return us to a much earlier and canonical mode of *choreia*, which variously combined choristers, cranes and the paradigmatic *geranos*. The ode's subsequent mention of the syrinx-playing avian leader does much the same insofar as it too retrojects one of the chief participants in the ongoing spectacle back to a much earlier, mythically sanctioned and even Iliadic frame of reference. Implicit in the choice of instrument is its association with the primitive, agrarian sphere, a rusticity reinforced by the equation of the crane-musician with a 'shepherd', typically a presence in a

---

[95] See Steiner 2011 for detailed discussion of the song's 'New Musical' character and debt to dithyrambic-style compositions. As demonstrated there (2011, 310), the very introduction of birds forms part of Euripides' incorporation of dithyrambic elements since composers of dithyrambs were supposedly obsessed with avian/aerial phenomena.

pre-cultural domain.[96] The syrinx's properties are already on display in one
of the term's two appearances in Homer, this, once again, on Achilles'
dance-themed shield, where herdsmen play the pipes (*Il.* 18.525–26; for the
chorality implicit in the scene, see Chapters 1 and 4). While the instrument
has a place in what seems to be a cluster of interrelated motifs characterizing Euripides' choral songs featuring both choral projection and dithy-
ramb-inspired New Musical elements,[97] the glance back to the canonical
Homeric source would here reinforce the archaizing, traditionalist veneer
that the dramatist gives his musician, 'naturalizing' and reinserting the
figure into the epic realm.

But this same traditionalism, it turns out, also allows Euripides to
endorse the very innovations that the Homeric references and mythical
associations seemingly mute. Both the suggestion of a re-enactment of
Theseus' foundational *geranos* at the dawn of the 'craft of *choreia*' and
the privileging of the syrinx-equipped musician engage with ongoing
controversies surrounding the so-called New Music, and most particularly
with debates concerning changes in choral formation and kinetics, the role
of instrumentalists and the pipes and their relation to the verbal elements of
choral song. On the first of these several flash points, the Crane Dance and
more particularly its choreography has a direct bearing. While some
question the scholia's identification of the dancers on Achilles' shield
with the Cretan/Delian performers, most scholars grant some kind of
parallel between the motions of choruses performing the *geranos* and
those of the birds in flight. Marcel Detienne associates the dance with the
crane's migration routes which encircle the globe,[98] while Louis Séchan
offers two suggestions as to why the *geranos* might have been so designated:
'either because the dancers advanced with head high and necks extended,
waving their linked arms as if they were wings; or rather, more probably,
because the most characteristic arrangement of the line suggested the idea
of the triangular flight of a flock of cranes'.[99] Several Greek authors, and
modern readers after them, view the dance figures as evocations of the
maze from which the rescued band emerged. In Plutarch's account,
the *geranos* presents a *mimêma* of the twists and turns of the labyrinth,

---

[96] The expression also harks back to traditional Homeric diction, where the *basileus* serves as
shepherd of his flock. The parodos of Euripides' *Phaethon*, where an instance of choral
projection is similarly surrounded with references to natural and archetypal forms of musical
activity, includes the pan pipes (fr. 773.71–72 K.). See Csapo 2008, 275–76 for the passage. Weiss
2018 includes several insightful discussions of the syrinx in Euripides.
[97] See, again the parodos of *Phaethon* (fr. 773.63–86 K.).   [98] Detienne 1989, 22–23.
[99] Séchan 1930, 120.

with the dancers moving in a syncopated rhythm that features alternating, spiral-like motions (παραλλάξεις καὶ ἀνελίξεις, *Thes.* 21).

For my purposes, what matters is not so much how the *geranos* got its name as what ancient sources observe about the formation in which it was performed. Both textual and visual accounts offer two rather different descriptions (sometimes in a single passage), one featuring a circle, the other a processional and linear type of dance. The Delian performance, where the dancers circle about the altar, clearly takes the former shape and terms for 'centre' and 'circle' occur frequently in Callimachus, and in Plutarch and Pollux's reconstructions.[100] But rectilinear formations are prominent in the sources too: Pollux says that the chorus members formed a line 'each behind the other' (ἕκαστος ὑφ' ἑκάστῳ κατὰ στοῖχον) with a *chorêgos* at the end of each (4.101); according to Hesychius' *Lexicon*, the title γερανουλκός, literally 'the one who pulls the crane', was given to the two chorus leaders, which suggests the division of the chorus members into two lines, perhaps in the shape of a *lambda* with a leader at the head of each.[101] Visual images present a similarly bifurcated view: while many artists portray a circular chorus,[102] the François Vase shows the dancers in a line and a Little Master black band cup in Munich also imagines a processional or linear type formation, representing the chorus in an exact 'v' shape (Fig. 7.9).[103] The epigraphic evidence inclines towards linearity: inscriptions from Delos mentioning the use of a rope – apparent too in Hesychius' gloss – during the performance of the *geranos* suggest that the performance may have resembled the 'rope dances' which are visible in both the textual and visual record and to which Section 3 of this chapter returns; in these instances, a rope linking the chorus members keeps them strictly aligned.[104]

Explaining this heterogeneity, Calame refers us back to the Homeric account of the dance on the shield of Achilles where the dancers run towards each other 'in lines' or 'ranks', ἐπὶ στίχας (*Il.* 18.602), a description that suggests 'two "procession type" semichoruses heading towards each other'.[105] Alternating with this formation are the circles that the youths and maidens, spinning like the potter's wheel, also execute. If the *geranos*, like

---

[100] As noted by Calame 1997, 54.

[101] Hesychius s.v. γερανουλκός. See too Diels 1890, 91–92, Latte 1913, 68–69.

[102] Calame 1997, 54 discusses some of these, together with bibliography.

[103] Munich, Antikensammlungen 2243; *ABV* 163.2, 160.2; *Para.* 68. See the discussion in Crowhurst 1963, 295, who interprets this as a representation of circular movement.

[104] For these, and the inscriptional evidence, see Langdon 2008, 176 and fig. 3.23; for the rope, see Lawler 1946, 125–26 and Pindar fr. 70b.1–2 S.-M.

[105] Crowhurst 1963, 295.

the dance on Achilles' shield with which ancient readers paired it, features this interchange between circles and lines, then the motions of the Euripidean dancers on the stage could do the same as the performers, now whirling, now aligned and ranked, re-enacted the movements of the Delian- and/or Cretan-located chorus, whose canonical status would be further enhanced by its Homeric and even Hephaestean ancestry.[106]

That choral formation and changes from the line to circle are important in the third stasimon, the second strophe's opening line already indicates. As William Allan comments, the term στολάδες 'denotes ordered movement', prompting us to envision the familiar v or double-v formation characteristic not just of the birds in their triangular flight, whose structure, our sources report, resembles that of a *lambda* or *delta*[107] with the leader of the group at the apex of the triangle,[108] but of choruses from the archaic period on. In the arrangement suggested by a number of early images, the musician, whether a player on the pipes or lyre, would stand at the middle of the two converging groups – just the arrangement visible on a Protoattic loutrophoros in Paris that shows a mixed chorus in this v-formation.[109]

In showcasing both lines and the more circular structure also assigned to the *geranos*, a combination similarly found in the opening strophe where the forward trajectory of the Greece-bound ship occurs even as dancing dolphins circle around the vessel, Euripides has his cake and eats it too: he both endorses what turns out to be a prime object of contemporary choral contestation – the dithyrambists' fondness for 'whirling' dances and for diction and conceits indicative of it[110] – while integrating into the second strophe an earlier, more traditional formation. The debate is actually older than the late fifth- and fourth-century critics of what they (mis)represent as an innovation allow, and has an earlier sounding in the opening lines of Pindar's second *Dithyramb* (fr. 70b S.-M.).[111] Here the poet describes how the dithyrambic chorus, earlier 'stretched out like a line', later assumed circular form (this, the song indicates, is the Pindaric preference as the *persona loquens* disparages the earlier arrangement as *dépassé*), a change

---

[106] See the remarks in Calame 2009b, esp. 131–33, on references to the *geranos* and, more broadly, linear and circular elements in Bacch. 17 (discussed in several chapters here), a work which Calame classifies as a dithyramb. See too Calame 2009a.

[107] This prompts Philostr. *Her.* 33.10–12 and Hyg. *Fab.* 277 to ascribe to cranes the invention of the alphabet. For the v-formation in which cranes fly, see, among others, Plut. *Mor.* 967b8–c2, Ael. *NA* 3.13, Philostr. *Her.* 33.11. Weiss 2018, 186 suggests that the Euripidean chorus would choreographically re-enact that structure.

[108] The variant preferred in the *OCT*, στιχάδες, also indicates the structured quality of cranes' flight.

[109] Paris, Musée du Louvre CA 2985.   [110] See Csapo 1999/2000 and 2008.

[111] For detailed discussion of the lines, see D'Angour 1997 whose argument I summarize.

that may have been first introduced by the sixth-century composer and musician Lasos, seeking to improve choral coordination and vocal clarity and more particularly to avoid poorly synchronized and badly articulated sibilants. In a fragment whose precise date (early or late fifth century?) and generic character (is it from a satyr drama, or a hyporcheme, as Athenaeus defines it, or a dithyramb?) remain topics of debate, Pratinas roundly critiques the new deployment, perhaps taking direct aim – as he does elsewhere – at Lasos: when the satyr chorus performing the lines objects that 'song was made queen by the Pierian: so let the pipe dance in second place; he is servant' (fr. 708 *PMG*), it is calling for a return to an older choral structure, with the musician bringing up the rear.

This novel arrangement would have had a further impact on *choreia*, also registered in critical vein in Pratinas' lines. By enhancing the musician's visibility and audibility to dancers and audience alike, it would 'focus attention on his musical leadership and instrumental prowess'.[112] The second strophe in Euripides' ode follows just this template: as noted above, the lines promote to starring role the syrinx player who gains the lead position among the migratory flock – and even in the manner of a *basileus* – at whose apex or midpoint he flies, and whose instrument supplies the music to whose accompaniment the cranes travel through the air. Again, the strophe reiterates a feature of new-style choral compositions and their manner of performance already introduced in the stasimon's opening visualization: by inviting his audience to envision the ship complete with a piper sounding out the beat to which the rowers plied their oars, and positioning that vessel as the source of the music to which the dolphin-choristers surrounding it danced, Euripides situated, whether merely in the song's words, or in the actual formation on stage, the musician at the midpoint of the circle of the maritime and real-world dramatic choruses.

Confronting contemporary broadsides against not just the piper but his ever-more-extravagant feats on his instrument, the double aulos so frequently assailed by critics of the New Music for its politically charged 'manyness' and negatively freighted polyphony and *poikilia*,[113] Euripides deploys the crane's signature call as part of his demonstration of auletic versatility, putting its heterogeneity directly on display and so promoting the innovations introduced by Lasos and those who followed his lead by further expanding the range of the pipes.[114] By casting the accompanist as

---

[112] D'Angour 1997, 342–43.

[113] See Steiner 2011 and 2016b for the primary sources and earlier bibliography.

[114] [Plut.] *De mus.* 1137a–b and 1141b–c spell out the link between Lasos and these innovations.

the syrinx-playing crane, the chorus already draws audience attention to the aulos' tonal versatility as the piper, in a feat of musical mimeticism, sounds out a note evocative of the rustic device.[115] This imitation of one instrument by another not only belongs among the features of the New Music singled out for stricture in Pl. *Leg.* 700b, but points back again to musical innovations ascribed to Lasos, credited with giving to the kithara the same multiplicity of sounds that the aulos already possessed.

With the compound adjective δολιχαύχενες (1487), Euripides' strophe additionally flags notorious crane acoustics (cf. the phrase assigned the dithyrambist and New Musician parodied in Aristophanes' *Birds*: οἰωνῶν ταναοδείρων, 1394) and in so doing newly signals the aulos' tonal reach, its capacity to shift rapidly across the full bandwidth of sound. The birds' characteristic long necks accommodate their distinctive elongated wind-pipes, 'with which they produce [the] piercing, sonorous, trombone-like sounds'[116] already highlighted in the simile at the outset of *Iliad* 3. This deeper pitched note proves quite the opposite of the shrillness regularly described as the sound of the syrinx heard by the Euripidean audience just a few instants earlier. Reproducing the birds' signature call no less than that of the pan pipes, the piper's virtuosic display produces sounds that blend with the crane-ventriloquizing choral voice singing out the lines. For Pratinas' satyr chorus' recognition of what they regard as part and parcel of the offensive qualities of the aulos and new modes of playing, the compound λαλοβαρύοπα stands witness: juxtaposed in the single composite is the chattering or twittering native to those with high voices with depth of sound, and that exactly catches the instrument's tonal heterogeneity.

2.2   Cranes, Stars and Seasonality (Eur. Hel. 1487–94)

ὦ πταναὶ δολιχαύχενες,
σύννομοι νεφέων δρόμου,
βᾶτε Πλειάδας ὑπὸ μέσας
Ὠρίωνά τ᾽ ἐννύχιον,   1490
καρύξατ᾽ ἀγγελίαν
Εὐρώταν ἐφεζόμεναι,
Μενέλεως ὅτι Δαρδάνου
πόλιν ἑλὼν δόμον ἥξει.

O long-necked winged ones, partners of the racing clouds, go beneath the Pleiades in mid-course and Orion in the night. Announce the tidings as

---

[115] As also observed in Weiss 2018, 186.   [116] Muellner 1990, 74.

you come to land by the Eurotas that Menelaus will come home having
taken the city of Troy.

Line 1488 adds a fresh group of figures to the dance, partnering the cranes
in flight with the swift-paced clouds. With this short phrase, Euripides
looks not just to the several facets of *choreia*, its music, song and dance, but
also to the dithyramb and to the Spartan ritual practices featured in the first
antistrophe. While Allan assigns a generalizing sense to σύννομοι, 'partners
with',[117] the expression can also mean 'sharer of νόμοι', where νόμοι signify
nomes, 'musical pieces'; σύννομος has just this meaning when applied to
another winged singer, the nightingale at Ar. *Av.* 203 cited earlier.[118] If, as
the mockery of Strepsiades at Ar. *Nub.* 333–38 illustrates, aerial phenomena, and clouds especially, were hallmarks of the 'nephelous' compositional
style and insubstantial verbiage of the dithyrambs now in vogue (cf. Ar. *Av.*
1384, *Nub.* 333, *Pax* 830 and 831), then the choral expression pairs the
cranes with the elements that, for the Aristophanic jokes to work, must
have been a feature of these musical extravagances that was no less familiar
than their predilection for all things ornithological.

The term δρόμος at the line's end is also rich in associations, linking this
avian flock with the Spartan choruses who, in the earlier verses, stood in
mimetic relationship to the dancers on the stage. Again, it turns out, an
embrace of dithyrambic poetics finds its counterweight in a nod to a
tradition-sanctioned event and more pointedly still to the most 'fossilized'
form of *choreia* practised in Euripides' own age. Ritualized races, as noted in
Chapter 2, figure in the passage from Theocritus' *Epithalamium*, where the
maiden singers describe the running contests (δρόμος, *Id.* 18.22) in which
they raced in their bands of sixty by the banks of the Eurotas, the very spot
where Euripides' cranes are about to land (1492). Calame locates these races
at the site which the sources name Dromos, a famous exercise ground
adjacent to the Spartan sanctuary of Helen where the choruses described in
the song at the end of Aristophanes' *Lysistrata* celebrate their rites (1309–15).
In conflating racing and choral activity, Euripides, like Theocritus after him,
follows a well-established (Spartan) tradition; the leaders of the chorus in
Alcman's first *Partheneion* are already likened to race-horses whose running
the poet signals (δραμήται, 59) and who, as I go on to illustrate here and in
the subsequent chapter, are themselves associated with birds.

The fresh pointer to choro-ritual events at Sparta is anything but uncon-
sidered, and allows the dramatist once again to chart his careful path
between an embrace of the innovatory in music and choreography and

---

[117] Allan 2008 *ad loc.*   [118] See Barker 2004, 192 for the use of the expression here.

adherence to all that is most tradition bound. In fr. 708 *PMG* Pratinas'
satyrs address, once again in bilious vein, the recent style of dancing that
the pipes' elevation and repositioning has brought about: 'what are these
dance steps (χορεύματα)?' The aulos' new primacy, they declare, spoils not
just the verbal element but also ῥυθμός, a term that refers principally to the
movements of the body. Rejecting these novelties, the singer-dancers close
by declaring their fidelity to the choreography traditionally associated with
Dionysiac/dithyrambic dancing: 'here you will have the proper tossing of
hand and foot, ivy-tressed lord of the triumphant dithyramb; hear now the
Dorian dance song that is mine'.

Scholars puzzle over the adjective Dorian in Pratinas' phrase, since the
Spartan tradition of dancing in choruses for Dionysus (conspicuously
absent from Laconian iconography) seems to have been comparatively
weak.[119] But the term may carry a more 'ideological' and musicological
than religious charge: by allying themselves with Dorian *mousikê*, the satyrs
declare themselves not so much promoters of an old-style Dionysiac
worship as unreconstructed musical and choreographic traditionalists. In
Euripides' third stasimon, the first antistrophe engaged directly with the
issue that the passing reference to 'racing' more succinctly reintroduces
here: in their evocation of and self-equation with the choruses dancing at
the Hyakinthia and by citing this and other Spartan cults at 1465–70, the
ode's performers suggested that they too danced in the manner native to
the Spartans, viz. a long-standing and temporally sanctioned one. Not only,
in a comment preceding a reference to a saying by Pratinas, does the
speaker in Athenaeus more generally remark, 'of all the Greeks, the
Spartans have most faithfully preserved the art of music ... Even to this
day they carefully guard the ancient songs, and are very well taught in them
and exact in holding to them' (14.632f), but a further citation preserved by
Athenaeus narrows this fidelity to earlier practices to choral choreography:
according to Polykrates (*FGrH* 588 F 1 = Athen. 4.139e), dancers at the
Hyakinthia performed in the traditional style (κίνησιν ἀρχαικήν) to the
music of the pipes. The opening of the second strophe in Euripides'
drama returns to this sticking point; even if the dancers were displaying
the new-style choreography complete with the swift-changing and heterogeneous steps and poses required by its no less rapid shifts in metre, they
dodge the bullet and mount a spirited response to the critics of dithy-
rambic/New Musical style dancing: projecting their innovatory kinetics

---

[119] See Constantinidou 1998 for discussion.

onto the tradition-bound Spartan choruses and primordial dance of the cranes, they annul the charges of novelty and corruption.

The term δρόμος is suggestive on one further count, looking both back to the previous antistrophe and forward to the chorus' account of the cranes' passage through the sky so precisely detailed in the next two lines. In Euripides' *Phaethon*, Helios gives directions for the path that the hero should observe as he drives the solar chariot through the sky: 'go, keeping to the course (δρόμος) that leads to the seven Pleiades' (fr. 779 K.). The crane-choreutes of *Helen* follow what is more properly a choreographic 'track' (and we know of lines marked out on the *orchestra* floor to guide the dancers' movements)[120] that, in analogous fashion, takes them beneath 'the Pleiades in midcourse and Orion in the night' (1489–90).

With this mention of the Pleiades, one final and supremely archetypal chorus joins the group that already includes dolphins (and sailors metamorphosed into dolphins), Nereids, Spartan dancers, the several performers on Achilles' shield and the cranes still present in this most recent picture. According to the ancient sources, the constellations in the night sky are dancing choruses of maidens, and among these stars, as Ferrari so clearly documents, the Pleiades claim pride of place.[121] As noted in my introductory chapter, a scholion to Theocritus 13.25 (Wendel), citing Callimachus, styles them the inventors of *choreia* and of the παννυχίς, the all-night dance performed under the star-filled sky (note the adjective ἐννύχιον used of Orion by Euripides' chorus, also a look back to the Hyakinthia described as νύχιον in 1470), when they were still maidens and prior to their being catasterized.

The equation of these dancing constellations – Pleiades and others – with the choral bodies moving onstage is a commonplace in fifth-century drama, and frequently sounded in Euripides and his fellow dramatists.[122] In an earlier instance of choral projection, Sophocles' chorus invokes Dionysus as '*choragos* of the fire-breathing stars' (*Ant.* 1146) and in their description of the shield of Achilles, the chorus of Euripides' *Electra* designates the Pleiades, together with their sisters the Hyades, choral dancers.[123] In the *Ion* (further explored in the subsequent section), this cosmic dance encompasses the entire sky (1078–80). The same notion of

---

[120] Hesychius s.v. *grammai*.
[121] Ferrari 2008, 3 *et passim*. For 'star choruses', and their connection with mystery cults in the ancient sources, see Csapo 2008.
[122] For a complete list of the relevant passages, see Csapo 2008, 264 n. 8.
[123] 'In the middle of the shield the bright circle of the sun was shining on winged horses, and the heavenly choruses of stars, the Pleiades, Hyades' (464–68). For choral Pleiades, see too Hyg. *Poet. astr.* 2.21, Hor. *Carm.* 4.14.21, Prop. 3.5.36 and Csapo 2008, 266.

stellar *choreia* figures in a fragment of Critias (fr. 4 *TrGF*), and, at greater length, in Plato and Aristotle,[124] and where these sources detail the motions of the dancing stars, they are inevitably circular. The astragalos of ca. 470–450 from the workshop of the Athenian painter Sotades cited at this study's start (Fig. 0.1) further confirms the ubiquity of the notion. Set within this context, the description of the cranes in their (linear) flight beneath the (circling) constellations presents the audience with two choruses hierarchically arranged: the birds beneath, the stars on top.[125]

Nor does this exhaust the significance of the Pleiades-crane association. In uniting birds and stars in a single image, the singers assign the cranes their familiar role as the heralds of seasonal change. For Hesiod, the sight of the birds as they migrate south to the river valleys of Sudan and Ethiopia marks the advent of the late autumn or early winter ploughing season (*Erg.* 448–51). Should the farmer miss this first indicator, he can still observe a second one; as two other Hesiodic passages affirm, this is also the moment when the Pleiades and Orion enact their autumnal setting (*Erg.* 383–84, 615–17). West's note on lines 383–84 dates this occurrence to 31 October, when the stars, now situated on the darker side of the sky, are visible 'just before sunrise'.[126] Hesiod's by now perhaps canonical almanac allows Euripides' audience to pinpoint the exact moment when the cranes are passing through the sky, which, the chorus observes, occurs when the Pleiades and Orion are midcourse.[127] If, following West's reconstruction, the settings of these stars take place respectively in late October and the start of November, and their risings in late June and early July, Euripides' cranes perform their journey sometime in late summer and early autumn, arriving by the Eurotas' banks just at the setting of the Pleiades and Orion.[128] Hesiod confirms this 'timetable': Perses should harvest his grapes 'when Orion and Sirius are come to the middle of the sky (ἐς μέσον ... οὐρανόν)', (*Erg.* 609–610), a task that immediately precedes the next item in the calendar, ploughing the fields at the setting of the Pleiades and Orion.

But why does Euripides insert these precise seasonal indicators? Chorality, and more particularly traditional Spartan *choreia* may again be

---

[124] For these and other passages, see the material collected in Miller 1986, 1–55, with further discussion in Ferrari 2008, 5–7 and Csapo 2008, 264–67.

[125] Perhaps relevant to the star/crane pairing is the fact that the Cretan/Delian *geranos* was performed at night and, according to some interpretations, offered a mimesis of the movements of the heavenly bodies along the zodiac; for this, see Lawler 1946, 117–18.

[126] West 1978 *ad loc.*

[127] Cf. Eur. *Ion* 1152–53: 'the Pleiades were passing through midheaven and so was Orion with his sword'.

[128] These are, of course, two of the constellations featured at *Il.* 18.486.

at issue here. As already noted, in her reading of Alcman's first *Partheneion*, Ferrari argues that the song performed by the Spartan maidens maps the political order which the mythical portion of the composition describes onto the cosmic order as it manifests itself in 'a momentous event in the night sky', the setting of the Pleiades and Hyades at the turn of the year.[129] Alcman's composition, she further proposes, would be sung and danced as part of the *pannychis* that occurred during a major state festival, the nine-day Karneia held in honor of Apollo (also celebrated in the vicinity of the Dromos and the temple of the Dioskouroi), designed to mark this moment of seasonal, agricultural and cosmic change. In Ferrari's interpretation, the words and movements of Alcman's chorus recapitulate the astral dance that the singers invite their audience to witness.[130] A passage from *Alcestis* confirms that Euripides and his public knew of the event: there the chorus projects itself onto the role of singers who celebrate the heroine 'in songs unaccompanied by the lyre when at Sparta the cycle of the season of the month of Karneia comes circling round, and the moon is on high the whole night long, and also in rich, gleaming Athens' (447–52). If this can be taken as sufficient evidence that the Karneia included choral performances, then a glance to the festival would be in keeping with the privileging of forms of traditional, archetypal and cultic *choreia* in the stasimon so far, and with the backward-looking *mousikê* of Spartan musico-choral culture.

2.3   The Cranes of Ibycus

By way of coda to the consideration of the crane-chorister equation focused on the *Helen* stasimon, I end with what may be a further instance of the pairing and evidence of its more widespread and enduring currency. In the well-known anecdote told about the death of Ibycus, first found in texts of the Hellenistic period, and reported by sources as varied as Antipater of Sidon (*AP* 7.745) and, among later authorities, Plutarch (*Mor.* 509e–f) and the *Suda*, the poet is captured by bandits in a deserted place; spotting a flock of cranes flying overhead, he declares that the birds will be his avengers. Following their murder of the poet, and return to the city of Corinth, one of the thieves catches sight of some cranes, and remarks, 'Look, the avengers of Ibycus'. His ill-judged words prompt the subsequent discovery of the crime and the retribution that Ibycus had predicted before his death.

---

[129]   Ferrari 2008, 17, with a summary of the book's larger argument.
[130]   Ferrari 2008, 87; for the evidence concerning the Karneia, see Ferrari 2008, 28–35 together with Pettersson 1992, chapter 3.

While some ancient sources would connect the story with Ibycus' name –
suggestive of the bird known as the ἴβυξ – there is little reason to equate the
two bird species, and the presence of the cranes requires a different explanation. Read in the context of the much earlier references to the birds reviewed
above, and which invite us to see cranes as paradigmatic chorus members, the
anecdote makes better sense: could we understand the avenging flock as an
instantiation of the performers who danced and sang the poet's compositions,
and who, in keeping with several of the other choruses detailed through this
and other chapters, support, aid and maintain their *chorêgos* in the tight
relations of reciprocity that bind the singing-dancing group into a single
body? While the mode in which Ibycus' poems were performed remains a
matter of debate, and some prefer to see him principally as a composer of
monodies, there is plentiful evidence to suggest that, at least in the earlier part
of his musical career, he participated actively in the vigorous citharodic and
choral culture native to southern Italy.[131] A scholion to the poet's fr. 296 *PMG*
identifies the lines as derived from a dithyramb,[132] and another fragment, fr.
290 *PMG*, concerns Meleager, the subject of a dithyrambic composition by
one Cleomenes of Rhegium (838 *PMG*) active a century later. Other sources
suggest that Ibycus composed choral lyric in the manner of Stesichorus, and
Power reads a curious story preserved in Himerius, *Or.* 22.5, in which the poet
while *en route* to the older poet's home town of Himera falls from his chariot
and breaks his wrist, an accident that forces him to suspend his musical
activity, as 'a narrativization of Ibycus' stylistic debt to his Himerian
predecessor'.[133] These several indications of choral activity make more likely
the role of avenging cranes as chorus members loyal even after death to their
erstwhile leader, and the potential of Ibycus' choral compositions for reperformance independent of their original poet/*chorêgos*.

3 Doves

A model shrine from Cyprus, tentatively dated to seventh century, displays
four figures placed around the perimeter of what commentators identify as a
'dovecote', a central fenestrated pillar topped by doves that serves as an

---

[131] Timaeus describes a competition between the citharodes Eunomos of Locri and Ariston of
Rhegium (*FGrH* 566 F 43), and Pausanias cites the choruses of boys who came from Messina to
Rhegium to perform at a festival there (5.25.2–3).

[132] Although Fearn 2007, 167 n. 13 disagrees with the characterization.

[133] Power 2010, 240. A mention of Stesichorus immediately precedes Himerius' report of the
anecdote.

iconic representation of Aphrodite, the deity most closely associated with the birds.[134] Three of the four figures dance, turned inwards so as to face the shrine to which they address their act of worship, while the fourth, accompanying them on his lyre, faces outward, drawing viewers of the object into the ritual event. Where here the doves serve as stand-ins for the goddess, whose epiphanic presence in response to the ongoing performance they presage, in the Greek hexameter, lyric and dramatic sources the pairing of the birds and choral dancers proves much more intimate. As my reading of three passages from archaic and classical texts, with a fourth example from the early imperial period included to demonstrate the longevity of the motif, goes on to illustrate, poets typically align flocks of doves with young, female dancer-singers, these frequently positioned as the victims of male aggression.

3.1 *Maids All in a Row (Od. 22.465–73)*

My discussion of the dove/chorister association in a passage in *Odyssey* 22 (whose logistics no less than tone have provoked critique and condemnation on many commentators' part) takes its cue from two points in an interpretation of the lines owed to Sheila Murnaghan.[135] First, that the twelve of Penelope's serving maids who have betrayed their mistress and slept with the interlopers in their master's house form an 'anti-chorus' that distorts conventional relations between their *chorêgos* (Penelope) and the *parthenoi* making up her choral ensemble and replaces the tight and symbiotic bonds of affection and even eros between leader and choreutes and among the members of the group with internal fractures, betrayal and hostility; and second, that in keeping with this inversion, the mode of death inflicted on the dozen renegades involves a travesty of a cultic choral dance, whose proper execution archaic textual and visual sources record. My discussion builds on Murnaghan's account in several ways, first by demonstrating how closely the language and dynamics of the description of the maidens' dispatch conform to choral diction and practices found in Homer and later sources, and second by developing the point on which Murnaghan's reading touches only in passing: the comparison between the girls at the moment of their death and doves, an equivalence more fully explored in the lyric and dramatic texts also featured here.

The contested passage occurs immediately after Odysseus' killing of the suitors and in the context of his efforts to cleanse the now-polluted dining

---

[134] Paris, Musée du Louvre AO 22.221; see Franklin 2015, 236–38 whose reading I follow.
[135] Murnaghan 2018. I am most grateful to the author for sharing her work with me before its publication and allowing me to draw on its insights.

hall while preventing outsiders from discerning the slaughter within. When the newly victorious hero further directs his son to kill the maids with the sword in the area outside the house, Telemachus objects to this 'clean death' (462). Instead, in the action the youth then performs, the girls are strung up in a line in the manner of birds and left suspended until they die (465–73):

ὣς ἄρ' ἔφη, καὶ πεῖσμα νεὸς κυανοπρώροιο   465
κίονος ἐξάψας μεγάλης περίβαλλε θόλοιο,
ὑψόσ' ἐπεντανύσας, μή τις ποσὶν οὖδας ἵκοιτο.
ὡς δ' ὅτ' ἂν ἢ κίχλαι τανυσίπτεροι ἠὲ πέλειαι
ἕρκει ἐνιπλήξωσι, τό θ' ἑστήκῃ ἐνὶ θάμνῳ,
αὖλιν ἐσιέμεναι, στυγερὸς δ' ὑπεδέξατο κοῖτος,   470
ὣς αἵ γ' ἑξείης κεφαλὰς ἔχον, ἀμφὶ δὲ πάσαις
δειρῇσι βρόχοι ἦσαν, ὅπως οἴκτιστα θάνοιεν.
ἤσπαιρον δὲ πόδεσσι μίνυνθά, περ οὔ τι μάλα δήν.

So he spoke, and taking the cable of a dark-prowed ship, fastened it to the high pillar, and cast it about the round-house, stretching it out up high, so that none could reach the ground with her feet, and like long-winged thrushes, or doves, who have fallen into a snare set up for them in a thicket, trying to find a roosting place, but the sleep that received them was hateful; so they held their heads all in a line, and each had her neck caught fast in a noose, so that they might die most piteously. They struggled with their feet for a little, not for very long.

The problems that vex commentators are manifold: first, Telemachus, showing unwonted initiative, goes against the direct instructions of his father in unprecedented fashion in devising the penalty;[136] and second, the gruesome punishment inflicted here is unparalleled in Homer or any other extant source. Also undermining the episode's authenticity are the confused mechanics of Telemachus' device, a bizarre contrivance several of whose elements run counter to the laws of physics and common sense (all amply discussed by Fernandez-Galiano); dictional anomalies and the later usages that the passage includes only compound its contested status.

While both the mode of death (hanging typifies so many female deaths in Greek myth and is particularly well suited to those guilty of sexual crimes, Epikaste in *Od.* 11.271–80 among them), and the episode's place in the work's larger structure (a doublet to the no less horrible mutilation of Melanthius in the subsequent incident) are sufficient grounds for the lines' inclusion, my concern is with how they draw attention to the maidservants'

---

[136] See the comments of Fernandez-Galiano 1992 *ad* 441–73.

(anti)choral character and bring a dance to mind. A grasp of the choral paradigm underlying the victims' death in part depends – and here I round out Murnaghan's account –[137] on reading the incident in conjunction with the scenes that bracket it on either side, first the cleansing of the *megaron* and its rearrangement for a still undefined purpose, and then the activity for which those preparations were intended, whose fulfillment the poet postpones until the early stages of book 23. After washing down the tables and chairs, Telemachus and his helpers then 'scrape the floor of the well-constructed house with shovels' (λίστροισιν δάπεδον πύκα ποιητοῖο δόμοιο / ξῦον, 455–56). Two hapaxes in the phrase alert us to the significance of what is going on: the 'shovel' is cognate with terms like λίς and λισσός that refer to things that are 'even, smooth, polished', and the verb ξύω belongs to a family of technical terms for 'smoothing, polishing, planing, shaving down'.[138] An audience familiar with the poem's earlier events would recall a similar scene featuring just this mode of action: before the Phaeacian youths in book 8 can dazzle spectators with their choral display, special 'stewards of the course stood up ... who on every occasion set in good order the grounds for dance performances, and they smoothed the dancing floor (λείηναν δὲ χορόν) and broadened all the ground' (258–61).

Confirmation of the correspondence between events on Scheria and those now occurring in Odysseus' more workaday home and in the same sympotic context follows shortly on. With his account of the contemporaneous death of the faithless maidservants sandwiched in between, the poet returns to the *megaron* where the hero is giving orders for a mock-celebration designed to hide from passers-by the carnage he has wreaked. In what has been read as an evocation of the choral dance performed on the occasion of a wedding (and of course, the second-time groom and bride are about to be (re)united before heading off to the nuptial chamber), Odysseus, in the choregic-role,[139] directs both men and women – presumably the remaining female servants, Penelope's loyal 'troupe', since none from outside the palace have been admitted in – to make themselves ready, washing and adorning themselves as choral dancers routinely do in epic and beyond, to entertain the company with their dancing (23.141–47):

ὣς ἔφαθ', οἱ δ' ἄρα τοῦ μάλα μὲν κλύον ἠδ' ἐπίθοντο.
πρῶτα μὲν οὖν λούσαντο καὶ ἀμφιέσαντο χιτῶνας,
ὅπλισθεν δὲ γυναῖκες· ὁ δ' εἵλετο θεῖος ἀοιδὸς
φόρμιγγα γλαφυρήν, ἐν δέ σφισιν ἵμερον ὦρσε

---

[137] Murnaghan 2018, esp. 180.   [138] Fernandez-Galiano 1992 *ad loc.*
[139] For Odysseus as *chorêgos*, or, as she styles him, *chorodidaskalos*, see Murnaghan 2018, 172.

μολπῆς τε γλυκερῆς καὶ ἀμύμονος ὀρχηθμοῖο.   145
τοῖσιν δὲ μέγα δῶμα περιστεναχίζετο ποσσὶν
ἀνδρῶν παιζόντων καλλιζώνων τε γυναικῶν.

So he spoke and they listened carefully to him and obeyed. First they
washed themselves, and put on their tunics, and the women decked
themselves out. But the divine singer took his hollow lyre and stirred up
within them the desire for the sweet song and the excellent dancing. Now
the great house resounded all about to the footsteps of the men dancing
there and of the fair-girdled women.

The occasion includes additional echoes of that earlier Phaeacian scene,
albeit with a mixed rather than exclusively male choral ensemble: not only
did the anticipatory performance take place within an episode filled with
courtship and marital undertones (is Odysseus to claim Nausicaa as the
bride she hopes to be?), but there too a lyre-playing *aoidos*, Demodocus,
initiates the movements of the dancers, who likewise strike the ground with
their feet (πέπληγον δὲ χορὸν θεῖον ποσίν, 8.264).

What happens to the maidservants, and their configuration as a distorted choral collective, should be read against the normative performance
that the actions inside the house first presage and then go on to stage. No
sooner is everything 'set in good order' (διεκοσμήσαντο, 22.457)[140] within
than we witness the synchronic and very different sequence of preparations
occurring in the space in the dining hall's immediate proximity, the
courtyard to Odysseus' home. Taking on his father's role as impresario/
chorêgos, Telemachus, together with his helpers, 'leads out' (ἐξαγαγόντες,
441)[141] the guilty twelve of the original fifty-strong group[142] and directs the
maids' motions. He and his henchmen proceed to 'pen them up' in a
narrow space, the inverse of the broad expanse required by the Phaeacian
youths and their counterparts in Odysseus' *megaron*. And for the mode of
death earlier proposed, whereby each girl would be killed in turn,
Telemachus substitutes a method exactly suited to the collective and
undifferentiated character of a troupe of singer-dancers; for all that
Fernandez-Galiano sensibly objects that 'it would surely be simpler to
string the girls up one by one' (*ad* 441–73), the choral character shaping
the group requires that all die 'concordantly'.

---

[140] For the verb in an expressly choral context, see Chapter 9.
[141] Again, as later chapters demonstrate, a term used in choral contexts; Murnaghan 2018, 180 also
notes the choice of verb.
[142] As Murnaghan 2018, 179 observes, both numbers have 'strong choral associations'.

As for the death itself, as Murnaghan comments, the girls' formation once strung up recalls that of the chorus line, its members similarly arranged sequentially, one after the other (ἐξείης). Of significance too, she observes, is the poignant focus on the victims' feet,[143] moving about convulsively in their death throes in a perversion of the regular motion that other Odyssean descriptions of choral dance spotlight. Cited above were the visualizations of the chorus of Phaeacian youths and the corresponding group dancing in Odysseus' halls, and in both instances the poet – as so many poetic evocations of choral dancers would do after him (see Chapter 1) – privileges the performers' feet, whether their synchronicity, swiftness, shape or sparkle.

The acrobatic ball dance also performed on Scheria in book 8 supplies another precedent, and not just for the attention paid to the action of the two star dancers' feet, here displaying their swift and skilful interchanges (372–79):

> οἱ δ' ἐπεὶ οὖν σφαῖραν καλὴν μετὰ χερσὶν ἕλοντο,
> πορφυρέην, τήν σφιν Πόλυβος ποίησε δαΐφρων,
> τὴν ἕτερος ῥίπτασκε ποτὶ νέφεα σκιόεντα
> ἰδνωθεὶς ὀπίσω· ὁ δ' ἀπὸ χθονὸς ὑψόσ' ἀερθεὶς   375
> ῥηϊδίως μεθέλεσκε, πάρος ποσὶν οὖδας ἱκέσθαι.
> αὐτὰρ ἐπεὶ δὴ σφαίρῃ ἀν' ἰθὺν πειρήσαντο,
> ὀρχείσθην δὴ ἔπειτα ποτὶ χθονὶ πουλυβοτείρῃ
> ταρφέ' ἀμειβομένω·

After they had taken the beautiful purple ball in their hands, which skilled Polybos had made, one of them would throw it up to the shadowy clouds bending far over backwards; but the other rising up on high from the ground easily would catch it again before his feet came back to the ground. Then, after they had played their game with the ball thrown upward, these two performed a dance on the man-nourishing earth, with rapid changes of position.

Strikingly, this earlier passage draws attention to one of the marvels of this dance, that the ball is caught before the catcher even touches the ground with his feet (ποσὶν οὖδας ἱκέσθαι). In analogous fashion, Telemachus designs his device so that, in a phrase that echoes the earlier diction, the maidservants' feet cannot reach the ground (μή τις ποσὶν οὖδας ἵκοιτο). The opening of line 467 includes another (inverted) parallel to that wondrous performance: where the youth 'stretches out the rope high in the air', the Phaeacian ball-dancers take turns elevating their bodies (ὑψόσ' ἀερθείς).

---

[143] Murnaghan 2018, 180.

Before following Murnaghan anew in defining the precise dance traves-
tied by the maids, first two possible analogues for the expressly choral and
collective death-by-hanging endured by the faithless girls. Although the
account belongs uniquely to a source at many centuries' remove from the
Odyssey, to Lactantius' commentary on Statius' *Thebaid* (*ad* 4.225), this
much later text supplies a second instance of a chorus that hangs itself, here
the self-inflicted fate suffered by a very well-established and archetypal
parthenaic troupe. The incident occurs at the shrine of Artemis Karyatis on
the border between Arcadia and Laconia where, as many earlier reports
confirm,[144] dances by the standing epichoric Karyatids were a central
feature of the annual feast and sacrifices in celebration of the goddess.
While most versions of the incident record an attack on the shrine by the
Messenians and their leader Aristomenes' abduction of the maiden choreutes, subsequently ransomed following some soldiers' attempt to violate
them, Lactantius follows what may be a different tradition: presaging some
future misfortune, the girls take pre-emptive action, and seeking refuge in a
nut tree, proceed to hang themselves.[145]

A second parthenaic chorus might be added to the group, the Danaid
maidens making up the chorus in Aeschylus' *Suppliants*. A later chapter
(Chapter 5) will explore the all but unique choral self-consciousness of
these figures and their marked self-modelling after the parthenaic choruses
that belong to religious cults rather than to the Attic stage, but for now just
the mode of death that they threaten to visit on themselves and their bird-
like characterization: as they warn the Argive king Pelasgus, should he
refuse their supplication and fail to grant them protection from their
Egyptian cousins, who would impose on them what the maidens regard
as an enforced marriage, they will hang themselves from the divine images
in the sanctuary where they have taken refuge (463–65; cf. 160). A simile
used earlier by Danaus of his daughters, emphatically depicted as a collective here, also recalls the representation of the 'choralized' maidservants of
the *Odyssey*; bidding the girls adopt a suppliant posture, he likens them to a
'flock of doves' (ἑσμός ... πελειάδων, 223) pursued by the predatory bird
that stands figure for their Egyptian cousins. While the girl-helpless-dove
equation is something of a poetic commonplace, together the choice of

---

[144] See particularly Paus. 3.10.7 and 4.16.9, with the detailed discussion in Calame 1997, 149–56.
For the Karyatids, see Chapter 6.
[145] For a second self-administered and collective death chosen by another choral group of
maidens, see Paus. 4.4.2–3. Although Pausanias does not identify the girls as choral dancers,
several other sources report that dances on behalf of Artemis occurred at the site of the
incident, the shrine of Artemis Limnatis. Absent from the *testimonia*, however, is any
indication of the manner in which the girls killed themselves.

species and the self-hanging that the Danaids propose prove consistent
with their larger parthenaic-cum-choral profile, which frames them as the
innocent victims of (sexual) aggression. Like the Karyatids, the Danaids
belong within the normative narrative from which Penelope's maidservants deviate: not only do they seem willingly to have accepted the suitors'
advances and surrendered their virginity, but, far from choosing their
mode of death, they must endure it by way of punishment.

Now to the Odyssean 'dance', and to Murnaghan's further insight:[146] that
the dying girls perform a distorted version of an actual cult dance and one, I
would add, that is attested in our very earliest visual sources and in later texts.
In Section 2 of this chapter, I noted the evidence for 'rope dances' in the
context of the *geranos* and the apparent use of ropes – if that is the correct
meaning of the ῥυμοί cited in two Delian inscriptions –[147] for the Crane
Dancers' performance and which, their practical value in guaranteeing group
coordination and guiding the chorus' motions apart, point back to the myth
of the escape from the labyrinth. Two images included on a Polledrara
hydria in London dated to ca. 575–550 (Fig. 7.7, with further discussion in
Chapter 7) make the rope rather than the more conventional thread integral to
Theseus' rescue of the Athenian youths and maidens and give it a prominent
place in this pictorial representation of events in Crete.[148] On the upper zone
of the vase the hero slays the Minotaur while in the area beneath Theseus and
Ariadne again appear, the youth playing the lyre as Ariadne leads a choral
dance performed by four women. Equipping the first of the dancers is what
appears to be a thick, long cord identical to that carried by Ariadne in the
upper register, which the image shows rising in a spiral between the legs of the
Minotaur.

A number of images from the Geometric period, depicting performers
aligned through the use of ropes tying each one to the next, attest to the
antiquity of the practice. Among the pottery finds from the sanctuary of
Athena Alea, a kourotrophic deity worshipped in Tegea, are not just two
krater sherds with maiden dancers, but fragments of cylindrical pyxides
depicting, in Langdon's account, groups of male and female performers

---

[146] Murnaghan 2018, 181.
[147] There is little consensus concerning the inscriptions' usage of the term that elsewhere variously
refers to a chariot pole, a trace or a log or block of wood. In several accounts, however, and
when read in conjunction with both the γερανουλκός or 'crane-puller' cited in Hesychius and
the derivation of the noun from ἐρύω 'to draw or drag', the term would describe the ropes held
or used by the dancers to maintain coordination and guide them through the figures of the
dance; see further Lawler 1946, 125–26.
[148] London, British Museum 1850, 0227.50 with discussion in Smith 1894.

segregated by gender who dance 'with a cord connecting their waists'.[149] Telemachus' substitution of the ship's cable for the ritually sanctioned and traditional rope would both suit the thematics of the poem and the maritime world of Odysseus' adventures and point to a fresh subversion of the conventional dance in the maidservants' death. A second detail also skews the paradigm: where actual rope-dancers are linked at the waist, a hanging death requires that the cord be placed around the neck (a device that further prevents the victims from uttering a sound, or even singing, if songs accompanied these rope dances).[150]

The Tegean evidence is important on a further count. As Lawler notes,[151] we seem to have an allusion to just this dance in the oracle given to the Spartans as they prepared to make war on Tegea; in Herodotus' report of the Pythia's response at 1.66.13, the oracle declares, 'I shall give you Tegea to dance in, and her fair plain to measure with a rope (σχοίνῳ διαμετρήσασθαι)'. Inevitably, the recipient of the message mistakes its meaning; as it turns out, the Spartans, defeated and placed in fetters, are forced to work the Tegean land with shackles about their feet, thereby measuring out the plain in a distorted form of the cult dance more properly performed in the sacred space of the Artemis precinct there. The penalty resembles the Odyssean scene insofar as it too stages a transgressive performance of what in this instance is a local form of choral celebration, and turns that ritual dance into a collective punishment.

The term used by Herodotus for the rope, *schoinos*, proves relevant not just to the distorted dance of the dying Odyssean handmaids, but to another allusion to the rope in an explicitly choral context. Pindar's programmatic second *Dithyramb* (fr. 70b S.-M.) opens with what, in a recent view and as noted in the preceding discussion, is a reference to the linear formation of dithyramb-performing choruses prior to their rearrangement into the circular structure that the performers would then more regularly assume (1–2):

[149] See Langdon 2008, 176 and her fig. 3.23; cf. Livy 27.37.13–15 for just such rope dances by maidens in honour of Juno: *tum septem et uiginti uirgines, longam indutae uestem, carmen in Iunonem reginam canentes ibant, illa tempestate forsitan laudabile rudibus ingeniis, nunc abhorrens et inconditum si referatur; uirginum ordinem sequebantur decemuiri coronati laurea praetextatique. a porta Iugario uico in forum uenere; in foro pompa constitit et per manus reste data uirgines sonum uocis pulsu pedum modulantes incesserunt.* For more on the rope dance, see Chapter 7.

[150] Note that in Eurykleia's later description of events to Penelope, she describes hearing the groan (στόνον, 23.40) emitted by the dying girls; this sound takes the place of the joyous songs of celebratory choruses.

[151] Lawler 1946, 129.

Πͅρὶν μὲν ἔρπε σχοινοτένειά τ᾽ ἀοιδά
   διθͅυράμβων . . .

Formerly the song of dithyrambs came forth stretched out like a measuring rope . . .

Without engaging with all the questions surrounding the shape of the dithyramb, or the previously mentioned issue of who first devised that circular formation, I would note the coincidence between Pindar's phrasing and that of both the Odyssean and Herodotean accounts. Where the oracle tells the Spartans that they will measure out the plain with the *schoinos* – and elsewhere in the historian, the term refers to a construction device used by the Persians both for measuring distances and for guaranteeing that building elements are properly aligned – and Pindar imagines the dancers in their earlier linear formation, Telemachus 'stretches out' (ἐπεντανύσας) the cable to be used as the hanging device.

3.2   *Alcman, fr. 1.60–63* PMGF

Finally, and by way of bridge to the very different context in which Alcman's chorus of Spartan maidens sang and danced, there is the simile used by the Homeric narrator of the dying girls, likened to doves or thrushes. While thrushes also suit a choral band insofar as the birds are another species that aggregate (see Ar. *Av.* 591: ἀγέλη μία κιχλῶν), it is doves that demonstrate much tighter links with the dancing groups in other poetic genres. Best known, of course, is the much debated appearance of the term Peleiades in Alcman's first *Partheneion* (fr. 1.60–63 *PMGF*):

ταὶ Πεληάδες γὰρ ἅμιν   60
Ὀρθρίαι φᾶρος φεροίσαις
νύκτα δι᾽ ἀμβροσίαν ἅτε σήριον
ἄστρον ἀυηρομέναι μάχονται·

For against us [or, on our behalf] the Peleiades contend, as we carry the robe [or plough or torch] to Orthria, rising up like Sirius in the ambrosial Night

The questions surrounding both these Peleiades and the activities described (as well as the syntax of the lines) are legion, and commentators continue to advance divergent interpretations: are the Peleiades doves or the constellation of the Pleiades (the more common view in recent discussions); does the term refer to the two *chorêgoi*, Agido and Hagesichora, to a rival chorus (a now-discredited position) or to the star cluster; what is being carried here, when and for whom; and if that object is a robe, then does the Sirius comparison apply to that garment or to the Peleiades? Without entering these disputes, my concern is uniquely with the (possible) evocation of doves in reference to a collective of choral performers and with the several ways in which these particular birds prove pertinent to the *Partheneion*, its diction, themes and systems of imagery.

Diction first. The participle ἀυηρομέναι well suits an avian flock, and Peponi strengthens the argument for the doves' presence by citing epic analogies and further noting passages in the *Iliad* where the same vocabulary of elevation chosen by Alcman for the birds appears in descriptions of racing horses.[152] Insofar as the formulation builds on the Homeric equivalence between the equine and avian realms,[153] it supplies a natural 'follow on' to the conceit that has just described the two *chorêgoi*, whom the singers imagined in the likeness of prize-winning coursers competing in races. Just as at the funeral games of Patroclus Diomedes' team 'are lifted high up (ὑψόσ' ἀειρέσθην) as they make their swift passage' (23.501), so too are Alcman's doves-in-flight. Even as the birds would suit the immediate context and neatly look back to the image just deployed, they also claim a place within the poem on their own behalf. Towards the papyrus' end birds, here in their more common capacity as singers, reappear when the choristers compare, in self-denigrating fashion, their vocalizing skills to those of the screech owl (87); as they declare, only the avian Sirens outmatch Hagesichora, whose powers of song are also those of the divaesque swan (96–101). Coincidentally, doves and a Siren appear in company on an Attic black-figure lekythos of ca. 550–500 in a private collection in Zurich;[154] here a single Siren stands positioned between several doves forming a group encircling the figure.

Reinforcing the suitability of doves is their conformity to one of the poem's larger concerns, first sounded in the mythical section of the song that features the story of the struggle between the Hippocoontidae and Castor and Polydeuces. Sidestepping, once again, the difficulties surrounding the seemingly innovatory version of the story followed by Alcman here, suffice to say that the most likely nub of the dispute between the youths turns about the abduction of either Helen or the Leukippidae,[155] the two

---

[152] Peponi 2004, 304–06. Note too the use of the phrase ἀειρόμενοι χθ[ον in a (likely) reference to horses at Eur. fr. 752f.39 K.

[153] See Eur. *IT* 1138–47 for another instance of the pairing.   [154] *ABV* 457.2, *Para.* 199.

[155] See Robbins 1994.

mythical heroines, also dubbed πῶλοι in cult practice, whose personas Agido and Hagesichora would re-enact. If the second all but lost myth also included in the piece recounted the Giants' attempt to assault goddesses, as several commentators propose, then the singers would sound anew a theme so apposite to the dangers to which their parthenaic condition and own incipient sexuality exposed them, and Calame cites a series of tales where maidens who suffered abduction were transformed into doves, the species whom our sources (Aeschylus' *Suppliants* is just one of many examples) frequently associate with the virginal state. One such story, albeit only preserved in a late author (Ant. Lib. 1.1, with Nicander as the source), tells of the nymph Ktesylla, whom we first meet dancing in a chorus for Apollo (χορεύουσαν Πυθίοις παρὰ τὸν βωμὸν τοῦ Ἀπόλλωνος) and whose father had betrothed her, under oath, to Hermochares; after a narrative imbroglio, the divinities help Hermochares seduce the maiden, who then dies in childbirth, and the story ends with Ktesylla's metamorphosis into a dove and the institution of cult worship on her behalf. The dove's broader profile as an object of pursuit by a larger bird makes the species particularly apt for the role of maiden as victim of a sexual aggressor.

Nor is there any reason to rule out a simultaneous reference to the stellar Pleiades, whom sources archaic, classical and later repeatedly associate with doves. The fullest account belongs to Athenaeus who, in 11.489f-91d, exhaustively quotes a series of earlier writers who make the linkage clear and introduces the citations in the context of a prolonged analysis of the description of Nestor's cup at *Il.* 11.632–35, a grandiose vessel, 'pierced with golden studs (χρυσείοις ἥλοισι πεπαρμένον)', whose other decorative elements include a pair of golden doves shown feeding on each of its four handles (οὔατα δ᾽ αὐτοῦ / τέσσαρ᾽ ἔσαν, δοιαὶ δὲ πελειάδες ἀμφὶς ἕκαστον / χρύσειαι νεμέθοντο). According to the account supplied by the speaker Nestoris, the birds forming a circle around the cup's rim stand counterpart to the stars on Nestor's more broadly 'cosmic' object – its shape reproducing that of the larger world – whose studs are nothing other than the constellations; among these, Nestoris explains, Homer privileges the Pleiades, intending us to understand the doves topping the handles as figures for the astral cluster, an assertion that he goes on to support by appealing to those several earlier authors who equate the Pleiades and the birds. According to Moero, one of the 'authorities' cited here, the Odyssean doves that supposedly carry ambrosia to Zeus at *Od.* 12.62–63 are really the Pleiades, better suited for that privileged role.

A variety of other sources, some cited in Athenaeus, others independent of his discussion, freshly combine the star cluster and doves, sometimes eliding the two. A scholion to *Il.* 18.486 explains that the constellations shown on Achilles' shield fleeing from Orion were originally the seven maiden daughters of Atlas and the nymph Pleione, whom Zeus first turned into doves, and only subsequently into the Pleiades. There are traces of the ambiguity in lyric and dramatic sources too, again in reference to the tale of Orion: so a mention of the hunter and the Pleiades in Pind. *Nem.* 2.11–12 may well, in the explication of another scholion, simultaneously evoke doves (here described as mountain dwellers) and stars, while a fragment of Aeschylus puns on the near homonyms (fr. 312 R.):

> And the seven maidens who bore the name of Atlas wept for their father's great task of upholding the roof of the heavens, as a result of which they now have the form of things that appear in the night, the wingless Doves (ἄπτεροι Πελειάδες).

Read against this patchwork of accounts, Alcman's Peleiades seem likely candidates for their double role, that of both birds and stars, in an intercalation no less visible in the figure of Alkyone, the eponymous halcyon and one of the constellation of the Pleiades treated in Section 1 and whose place in the mythological complex the poet may have drawn on in fr. 26 *PMGF*. There too the bird, one among the larger flock, stands figure for the maiden chorus performing the song.

3.3 Euripides, *Ion* 1196–208

A passage from Euripides' *Ion* offers an additional, and, in keeping with the Odyssean description of the maidservants' death, distorted reiteration of the dove-chorister nexus, combining the sympotic setting framing the girls' dispatch in the hexameter text with the astral element important to Alcman's redeployment of the ornithological conceit. In the Euripidean servant's detailed narrative of events at the celebratory banquet staged by Ion in a tent at Delphi, it is a dove, one among a larger flock, that first alerts the company to the presence of the poisoned chalice from which the youthful hero is supposed to drink. The birds appear at the very moment when the contents of the just mixed wine-bowls stand ready for distribution (1196–208):

κἀν τῷδε μόχθῳ πτηνὸς ἐσπίπτει δόμους
κῶμος πελειῶν (Λοξίου γὰρ ἐν δόμοις
ἄτρεστα ναίουσ'), ὡς δ' ἀπέσπεισαν μέθυ

ἐς αὐτὸ χείλη πώματος κεχρημέναι
καθῆκαν, εἷλκον δ' εὐπτέρους ἐς αὐχένας.   1200
καὶ ταῖς μὲν ἄλλαις ἄνοσος ἦν λοιβὴ θεοῦ·
ἣ δ' ἕζετ' ἔνθ' ὁ καινὸς ἔσπεισεν γόνος
ποτοῦ τ' ἐγεύσατ' εὐθὺς εὔπτερον δέμας
ἔσεισε κἀβάκχευσεν, ἐκ δ' ἔκλαγξ' ὄπα
ἀξύνετον αἰάζουσ'· ἐθάμβησεν δὲ πᾶς   1205
θοινατόρων ὅμιλος ὄρνιθος πόνους.
θνῄσκει δ' ἀπασπαίρουσα, φοινικοσκελεῖς
χηλὰς παρεῖσα.

While we were busy with this task, a winged *kômos* of doves alighted in the dwelling (for they inhabit Loxias' house without fear), and since some wine had been poured away, into this they lowered their beaks in want of drink, and drew it up into their well-feathered throats. And for all the rest the libation for the god was harmless, but the bird which landed where the new son had poured his drink, having tasted it, at once shook its well-feathered body and began to play the Bacchant, and, bewailing, screeched out an unintelligible cry. And the whole company of feasters was astounded at the labours of the bird. Panting heavily, it expired, letting its red-limbed talons go slack.

Euripides' language immediately brings out the choral character of this flock. Suited to the sympotic milieu framing their advent is the birds' depiction as a *kômos*, and one that takes part in wine consumption too,[156] which also anticipates the sounding of the Bacchic motif in ἐβάκχευσεν and the role of drink as instigator of the poisoned dove's dance (see *Od.* 14.463–65 for the wine-dance linkage). The detailed description of the bird's motions in response to the draught is doubly suggestive of its participation in a choral-komastic paradigm: shaking its body whose feathers resemble a maiden's locks, the dove performs the head-swaying gesture characteristic of dancing maenads (cf. Ar. *Lys.* 1311–12, used of choral dancers) and 'plays the Bacchant' insofar as it enacts the extravagant, unbridled movements native to the Dionysiac *thiasos*.[157] Adding in a vocal element, albeit in a further deformation of proper choral practice, the bird 'screeches' in its death throes, substituting for the desired harmonious and intelligible utterance performed by a typical ensemble this un-acculturated, pre-linguistic and

[156] Note the ubiquitous presence of wine in depictions of komast dancers, most typically equipped with drinking horns. See too Aesch. *Ag.* 1186–90, treated below.
[157] Cf. Anacr. 356a *PMG*; 'to play the Bassara' while drinking would involve the speaker's analogous self-transformation into a female follower of Dionysus.

solitary cry of pain, or even, in keeping with this chapter's earlier discussion, lament.[158] The final visualization signals the close of this 'death dance' as, in terms that recall the Odyssean account of the maidservants' demise (*Od.* 22.473, ἤσπαιρον δὲ πόδεσσι), the dove's talons, suggestively bright-hued in the manner of the colourful sandals a choreute might wear, relax from the tensile position more typical of the dancer. That the description should focus exclusively on the motions and the voice of just one among the larger flock again nods towards more by-the-book depictions of choral performances while registering its departures. If the spotlight regularly falls on the *chorêgos* and her pre-eminence in dance and song, place is also made for the collective aspects of the spectacle, its cohesion and unity; this dove, instead, stages a solo performance, the singular object of the audience's attention.[159]

For all that the 'Bacchic' conduct of this komastic dove seems ill-suited to its unmistakably feminine gender, and the very characterization of the larger flock as the *kômos* that arrives desirous of drink suggests anything but a proper maiden chorus such as audiences witnessed in non-dramatic ritual events,[160] the picture drawn by the servant nonetheless proves broadly consistent with representations of women's choral activities in other texts, dramatic and otherwise, of the period.[161] In his choice of diction and portrayal of the bibulous birds, Euripides echoes the description earlier given by Aeschylus' Cassandra when she terms the Furies a blood-drunk *kômos* that will not quit the house where it has made its home and that sings its ill-omened song (*Ag.* 1186–92; Cassandra's nightmarish vision of these discordant and intemperate presences comes immediately before her report of the transgressive symposium hosted by Atreus for Thyestes). Like the dove that 'screeches' at Ion's gathering, the maiden chorus that sings and dances at the festival portrayed at Eur. *Hcld.* 777–83 'shouts' (ἰαχεῖ) as it raises the noisy *ololugê*, adopting its own more

---

[158] The earlier mention of the birds' 'well-feathered throats' already draws attention to their capacity for vocalization; cf. Hes. *Erg.* 203 in reference to the nightingale as singer/*aoidos*.

[159] On the privileging of choral dance over the individual display in archaic and later Greek sources, see Olsen (unpublished).

[160] Cf. Alcibiades' 'komastic' arrival at Agathon's symposium in search of drink at Pl. *Symp.* 212d–e. Normative visual representations of komasts include only men, although nude women do appear on a Corinthian psykter of ca. 570–550 (Brussels, Musées Royales d'Art et d'Histoire R 248), which may well be an image that belongs more to fantasy than reality.

[161] Much of the material that follows derives from the discussion of Budelmann and Power 2015, esp. 280–87, concerning the slanted nature of representations of female choral activity by Athenian sources. As the authors note at 281, the female ensembles are generally portrayed as 'sub-choral', and, in a point particularly apposite to the *Ion* scene, ancient authors are chary of describing them with the term *choros* and its derivatives. For this and other examples of female figures among komast dancers, see Smith 2010, 26–27.

boisterous and wordless form of vocalization in place of joining in the (articulate) songs (ἀοιδαί) concurrently performed by the youthful male choreutes.[162] Even the choral ensemble participating in the state-administered Hyakinthia (a Spartan rather than Athenian festival, and therefore 'foreign') in the *Helen* stasimon treated earlier receives a twofold designation: Helen will join with the female celebrants 'in their choruses or in the *kômoi* . . . for night-time merrymaking' (1468–70).

Other poetic and prose sources of the fourth century follow suit, repeatedly painting (in their doubtless filtered accounts) women's choral activity as a deviation from and deformation of the formalized, orderly and structured choruses in which youths and grown men were more regularly portrayed as participating in contemporary Athens. In comic fashion, Kallipides, a character in Menander's *Dyskolos*, anticipates another drink-seeking female chorus, whose condition will require that they leave it to the men at the wedding party to supply the necessary epithalamic song and dance (856–60); when one of the now-drunken maidens does try to initiate the choral dance, she must hide the 'bloom' of her countenance, perhaps an attempt to conceal the ruddiness caused by an excessive intake. Typical of this larger trend is the Athenian Stranger's depiction of female choruses in Plato's *Laws*. There the speaker's equation of the songs and motions with which mothers lull their restless newborns to sleep with the actions of women officiating at curative Corybantic rituals and what he designates their 'wild Bacchic rites' (*Leg.* 790d–e) is an anything but neutral account. In his later discussion of the broader category of 'Bacchic *orchêsis*' of which these Corybantic songs and dances form a part, the Stranger further remarks that the chorus members imitate 'Nymphs and Pans and Silens and drunken satyrs', actions that he distinguishes from the well-regulated and more sanctioned forms of *choreia* at Magnesia (815c–d).

The larger setting of the Euripidean scene supplies additional grounds for the introduction of an avian chorus. As a later chapter proposes (Chapter 6), the textiles used for the construction of the tent erected by Ion to replace the more conventional sympotic space, and whose designs the same prolix servant has closely detailed in an earlier portion of his report (1133–65), turn the entire dwelling into a manifestation of a cosmic dance, whose performers are the constellations circling about the night sky just before the break of dawn. What, then, could be more suited to this woven backdrop than the flight of doves who, attracted by the pictorial simulation of their

---

[162] Cf. the very similar division in the much earlier Bacch. 17.125–26: the maidens sound the *ololugê* while the youths perform the paean with 'lovely voice'.

aerial habitat,[163] then join in company with the homonymous Pleiades, picked out for special mention at 1152, and the other stars in the astral spectacle orchestrated here? Might an audience even imagine that one portion of the already quasi-animate astral designs, that Pleiad cluster, had come to life, and been transformed – albeit briefly – from fabric-image to reality, transmuted into the form of an actual flock of dancing doves?

3.4 *Strabo 6.1.8*

A passage in Strabo, preserving one of the several distasteful anecdotes told of the notorious late fifth-century tyrant, Dionysius of Syracuse, and of his conduct at the symposia that the now-exiled despot would host, offers a suitable point of closure for the preceding discussion on two grounds. Not only does Strabo's tale stand witness to the persistence of the archaic and classical pairing of dove and choral dancer on into the imperial age, but it more narrowly echoes several of the principal concerns addressed in earlier usages of that coupling. As the narrative reports, in an attempt to divert the company in novel ways, Dionysius

> συναγαγὼν δὲ τὰς ὡραίας παρθένους περιστερὰς κολοπτέρους ἐν τοῖς συμποσίοις ἠφίει, κἀκείνας ἐκέλευσε θηρεύειν γυμνάς, τινὰς δὲ καὶ σανδάλια ὑποδουμένας ἄζυγα, τὸ μὲν ὑψηλὸν, τὸ δὲ ταπεινόν, περιδιώκειν ἔφασαν τοῦ ἀπρεποῦς χάριν.

> would gather together the girls who were ripe for marriage, let loose doves with cropped wings upon them in the midst of the banquets, and then bid the girls chase them in a state of nudity, and also bid some of them, shod with sandals that were not matched (one high and the other low), pursue the doves all around in order to make themselves appear more unseemly. (trans. Jones modified)

Much as in the earlier accounts, Strabo's language alerts us to the model that the tyrant's innovations so roundly subvert, the dance that should – and does, in the Odyssean juxtaposition of the maidservants' punishment with the performance in Odysseus' dining hall – form part of the regular sequence of entertainments that symposia accommodated. Introducing respectable *parthenoi* into this all-male gathering from which they should properly be excluded, Dionysius already cuts a *chorêgos*-like figure as he

---

[163] Cf. the famous anecdote told of the contest between the artists Parrhasius and Zeuxis in which each displayed his powers of verisimilitude. Zeuxis paints a basket of grapes that looks so real that birds, deceived by the picture, come down to peck at the fruit (Pliny, *NH* 35.36 supplies a detailed account).

'leads together' (cf. ἐξαγαγόντες at *Od.* 22.441) the nubile members of his troupe whose movements and appearance he has minutely and anomalously scripted. In place of the dance that *parthenoi* stage in cultic and other settings, and most typically in their 'coming out' rites when they reach marriageable age, these performers turn predators instead and hunt down the very birds to whom maidens are so frequently likened. Further conforming to his directing and 'stage manager' role, Dionysius divides his ensemble into two semi-choruses, expressly ordering one group to conduct a circular pursuit (περιδιώκειν) around the room, a travesty of the ring dance that is the parthenaic chorus' most typical performance mode.

On several other counts, Dionysius skews the sanctioned practice of the *chorêgos*. Contrary to the impresario who decks out and accessorizes his performers so as to heighten their visual appeal, these girls are stripped of the richly decorated garments that characterize the public appearances of maidenly chorus members, and some are additionally made to wear the most curious and unparalleled of shoes: where dancers in other sources display embroidered and gleaming sandals, drawing the viewers' gaze to this locus of their skill, here the same footwear, one shoe elevated, one low, forces the maidens to perform the ungainly, hobbling steps that undermine the seemly and well-rhythmed motions that characterize the choral dance. Consonant with this is the indignity visited on the objects of pursuit: their wings are clipped, impeding their capacity for flight and making their flailing attempts to achieve their normally rapid and smooth passage through the air a counterpart to their pursuers' stumbling steps. More broadly, and very much in keeping with the episode from the *Odyssey* from which my discussion began, here a fresh set of parthenaic choristers must submit to a male overlord and are forced to engage in an anti-*choreia* that features a scrambling and disambiguation of the dove-dancer paradigm.

4 Bird Choruses in Attic Vase Imagery

The chiefly textual sources explored in this chapter should, the introduction suggested, be read alongside visual images dating from the seventh and sixth centuries that variously juxtapose and intermingle choral dancers with birds both individual and in flocks. Athenian artists from the very early fifth century on inherit and transform the motif, more closely realizing the equivalence between the avian and male and female ensembles proposed by their predecessors in a series of vase representations showing groups of singer-dancers whose costumes actually transform them into birds.

Fig. 3.6 Attic black-figure oinochoe by the Gela Painter, ca. 500–490 B.C.E. London, British Museum B 509. Photograph © The Trustees of The British Museum.

First in this sequence of well-known images is an Attic black-figure oinochoe by the Gela Painter (Fig. 3.6).[164] Dated to ca. 500–490, the jug shows two bearded men dressed as cock-like birds (their 'crests' stand erect) dancing to the music of the aulos-player on their left. As Rothwell notes, by virtue of the wings and feathered tights with 'feet' attached to their knees, the costumed individuals 'would look as if they were flying'.[165] Indeed, the artist takes pains to replicate the bird-like movements of the dancers: one of the performers has his wings extended and the other stretches out one leg while his arms are carefully positioned, one up, one down.

Both similar and different from the figures on the oinochoe are the so-called Berlin birds on a black-figure amphora from ca. 480, where a piper

---

[164] London, British Museum B 509; *ABV* 473, *Para.* 214. For detailed treatment of this and the other vases in the series, see Rothwell 2007, esp. 52–58 and Green 1985.

[165] Rothwell 2007, 52.

Fig. 3.7 Attic black-figure amphora, ca. 480 B.C.E. Berlin, Antikensammlung F 1830. Photograph © 2019. Scala, Florence/bpk, Bildagentur für Kunst, Kultur und Geschichte, Berlin.

marching to the right leads two men dressed as birds (Fig. 3.7).[166] While the upright crests on these choristers' heads identify them, like the oinochoe figures, as cocks, these birds are static. Still muffled up in their near floor-length *himatia* – which they would presumably remove as they began to dance in more vigorous fashion, thereby revealing the bird costumes below – the two are portrayed at the moment when they make their processional entrance in the linear formation that precedes the full-scale performance.

From the final quarter of the fifth century (the vase is now dated to ca. 425) comes a red-figure calyx-krater in Naples with two more men dressed as birds, here positioned on either side of the piper shown frontally at the composition's centre; the instrumentalist, very much the focal point of the image and the figure to whom the costumed dancers are turned, further commands attention for his richly woven cloak, patterned with geometric motifs and chariots, winged horses, hares and deer.[167] Like the two

---

[166] Berlin, Antikensammlung F 1830.

[167] Naples, Museo Nazionale 205239, with illustration and discussion in Rothwell 2007, 54 and pl. IV; for such woven fabrics, and the suggestion that the complex weaving design evokes the correspondingly intricate nature of the choral song and dance, see Chapter 7.

oinochoe birds, these figures dance, and, again, their costumes most closely equate them with cocks. The dominance of the cock, a bird type absent from the discussion so far, in these representations could have a variety of causes, among them the species' well-known agonism, which would suit the competitive theatrical frame in which these avian dancers have, in older accounts, typically been situated (the date of several of the vases also broadly coincides with Themistocles' supposed introduction of the cock-fight into the theatre to commemorate the defeat of the Persians). But both the martial and other features of the cock are no less pertinent to the proto-dramatic and non-theatrical sympotic context where more recent discussions locate these scenes.[168] Not only, in keeping with the much documented pederastic dimension to the drinking party, do the birds furnish one among the love gifts that the *erastês* typically offers his beloved (the costumed figures' open 'beaks', bent knees and prominent erect phalloi, whose shape finds an echo in the piper's double aulos, invite an erotic engagement on the viewer's part), but images dating to the sixth and early fifth century introduce cocks into representations of komast dancers or other *kômos* scenes and/or place them alongside satyrs and maenads similarly engaged in lively dancing. To cite an example of the first of these pairings, the reverse face of an Attic black-figure Tyrrhenian Group amphora dated to ca. 570–560 positions two cocks on either side of four naked dancing youths;[169] Two of the dancers stand facing the birds, each with one arm around the neck of the cock next to him as though to include it in the performance. The artist of a black-figure skyphos of ca. 525–475 in Taranto introduces cocks equivalent in size to the adjacent figures into the line of satyrs and maenads dancing around the body of the pot;[170] in this instance the birds appear to be more spectators than participants in the revelry.

One final vase close to the start of the series completes this cluster of ornithological choruses, although it features a different arrangement and a different species of bird. On the reverse side of a black-figure skyphos by

---

[168] For the association of cocks in fifth-century Athens, and the context of the vases, see Rothwell 2007, 55–57.

[169] London, British Museum 1897, 0727.2; *ABV* 97.27, 683; *Para.* 37. Perhaps the cock simile introduced in the final passage in Pindar's *Olympian* 12, a work composed on behalf of a victor in the running race, Ergoteles of Himera, might offer a fresh example of the bird as choral dancer. In likening their *laudandus* to a cock ('truly, son of Philanor, the honour of your feet would not have shed its leaves ingloriously like a cock fighting indoors at its native hearth . . .', 13–14), the celebrants not only fold a reference to Ergoteles' enforced exile into praise of his recent 'pedal' glory, but could be glancing to their own emulative and cock-like motions as they perform.

[170] Taranto, Museo Archeologico Nazionale 4590; *ABV* 623.6.

Fig. 3.8 Attic black-figure skyphos of the Heron Group, ca. 490–480 B.C.E. Side B. Boston, Museum of Fine Arts 20.18. Gift of the Heirs of Henry Adams. Photograph © 2020, Museum of Fine Arts, Boston.

the Heron Group in Boston of ca. 490–480 are six riders mounted on birds, whom art historians routinely identify as ostriches, with an aulos-player facing the line (Fig. 3.8); immediately in front of the piper, and also facing the chorus line, a bearded, cloaked pygmy appears in a pose reminiscent of a dancer's.[171] The scene forms the counterpart to the six dolphin riders on the other side (Fig. 3.9), these likewise accompanied by a musician (although no additional figure joins the group),[172] and the artist has taken pains to establish visual continuities between the two ensembles; in both instances the six riders wear garments picked out with white dots, the dolphins' curved and bifurcated tails substitute for the ostriches' two legs, and the prominent white strip that accentuates the birds' upraised necks

---

[171] Boston, Museum of Fine Arts 20.18; *ABV* 617. For the question of why ostriches, see Rothwell 2007, 72–73, whose several suggestions I echo, although he recognizes the absence of any clear explanation for the painter's choice. For all that it departs from the standard reading, I would suggest (following Naomi Weiss *per litteras*) that the pairing of the birds with the dancing (?) pygmy might put a viewer in mind of the Geranomachia, and that these might not be ostriches, but cranes instead. Granted, only the former were credited with being of a size to carry youths on their backs (Opp. *Cyn.* 3.482 and 3.490–91), but they lack the cranes' close link with dance.

[172] For more on this image, see Chapter 8.

Fig. 3.9 Attic black-figure skyphos of the Heron Group, ca. 490–480 B.C.E. Side A. Boston, Museum of Fine Arts 20.18. Gift of the Heirs of Henry Adams. Photograph © 2020, Museum of Fine Arts, Boston.

has its counterpart in the identically coloured and also curved line drawing attention to the underbellies of the maritime creatures. Presented with each image in its turn, the viewer witnesses two choruses at once similar and disparate: both depict hybrid species, the first a seagoing mammal, the second a bird that did not fly and had cloven hooves, one land-based, the other a traveller of the seas, and both variously credited with the ability to carry men on their backs.

As noted, connections with dramatic choruses dominate older discussions of the vases, and are undoubtedly relevant to some of the still extant images.[173] Scholars have suggested connections between the oinochoe cocks and Magnes' *Birds*, a comedy similarly dated to the early decades of the fifth century following the formal introduction of the genre into the City Dionysia in 486, while Aristophanes' *Birds* of 414 B.C.E. and his *Clouds*, where the duelling *Logoi* were, according to a scholion, displayed

---

[173] Beyond the scope of my discussion is the larger problem of whether we can link the images with specific dramas. Among the more comprehensive treatments of the issue, although with an emphasis on tragedy rather than comedy, see Taplin 1993 and particularly his even-handed framing of the debate at 22–28.

in wickerwork cages fighting like cocks, could have supplied the impetus for the red-figure calyx-krater of the late fifth century that is broadly contemporary with the dramatist.[174] We also have fragments of Aristophanes' *Storks*, tentatively dated to the 390s, a *Nightingales* and *Ants* by Cantharus, and a third *Birds* by a fourth-century dramatist who shares the name of an earlier author of comedies, Crates. But lost in these discussions of birds on the Attic stage and in what may be their pre-dramatic, sympotic settings is due consideration of creatures' place within the poetic and visual traditions that preceded and recognizably shaped the later ensembles, and whose avian imagery and motifs the later choruses draw on and 'spectacularize' even as they refashion them to different ends. In a further turnabout encountered in several other portions of this study, where the early poets and vase painters chiefly propose analogies between maiden choruses and flocks of birds, and most noticeably when halcyons and doves furnish the *comparanda*, the gendered quality of the alignment undergoes a shift in both comedy and the visual tradition: now it is choruses of men that present themselves in the likeness of the birds, introducing fresh species to the equations imagined by the earlier sources, some more apposite to male spheres of activity and concerns. Euripides' *Helen*, where, in more-traditional fashion, a maidenly chorus suggests its likeness to a flock of cranes, contributes an additional wrinkle: it is male choreutes who assume the twofold identity of the maidens-turned-cranes.

The story this chapter has aimed to reconstruct is necessarily incomplete, and lacks the 'prequel' that can be recovered from earlier sources that lie largely outside this study's temporal scope. Painted images and artefacts from Minoan and Mycenaean culture already include birds, most typically swallows, in scenes featuring companies of dancers, singers and musicians engaged in rites of veneration addressed to the gods. The advent of these winged creatures signals the realization of the end for which the ritual performance is designed: through their sounds and motions, and sometimes their self-assimilation with birds, the mortal celebrants seek to simulate and stimulate the advent of the god, who may manifest him or herself in the avian guise that both Greek and pre-Greek divinities so frequently adopt. The continuing 'epiphanic' dimension of *choreia* and the central role of collective song and dance in bridging the spatial and ontological divide between men and gods is a topic, complete with its 'ornithological' orientation, taken up in the concluding chapter of this study.

---

[174] Naples, Museo Nazionale 205239. On the question of which Aristophanic comedy is most closely related to the image, see Rothwell 2007, 54.

4 | The Carnival of the Animals: Dancing in Herds

'There are principal dancers and they'll step out, but they go back into the group. It almost seems like it's lonely out there. You want to go back into the herd' – the former New York City Ballet soloist Craig Hall, commenting on the choreography of Justin Peck's ballets.

New York Times 10 May 2018

Introduction

A fragment of Pindar preserved and identified by Athenaeus as a hyporcheme (14.631c = fr. 112 S.-M.) describes a Spartan parthenaic troupe (if the text is sound) as an ἀγέλα or 'herd'. The term recurs in a second Pindaric composition, fr. 122 S.-M., where it again refers to a troupe of maidens, these expressly figured as cows, who take part in a choral-style performance *en route* to a sacrifice.[1] In a third usage of the expression in fr. 70b.22 S.-M., the Pindaric performers of this dithyramb apply it to the herd of wild beasts, their species undefined, whose collective dancing in a cacophonous chorus made up of gods, nymphs, animals and other sonorous objects is said to 'enchant' Dionysus (ὁ δὲ κηλεῖται χορευοίσαισι κα[ὶ θηρῶν ἀγέλαις); in this instance the scene imagined by the singers stands as the template and paradigm for their own more earth-bound *choreia*, similarly staged by way of tribute to the god as they participate in his signature choral genre.

In designating two expressly choral ensembles 'herds', and in using the term χορεύω for the action of the dancing animals, Pindar succinctly expresses the particular analogy or instance of 'choral mapping' that this chapter, which moves from the sky back down to land, explores: the role of animal aggregates as analogues for or figurations of choruses and their song-dance. As I go on to demonstrate, poetic and visual sources from the early archaic period on regularly introduce groups of domesticated and

[1] A reading I suggest in Section 2.

untamed beasts – horses, cows and deer are the species that each of the chapter's three sections treats –[2] both as exemplars of the qualities most characteristic of and prized in dancing ensembles and, in some instances, as their reverse: in several of the texts singled out for discussion here, the animal aggregates, and bovines most particularly, furnish negatively freighted models whose evocation signals distortions in the properties and function of ritual choral ensembles and for whom the actual performers of the choral song-dance must act as corrective.

1 Equines and Choristers

In a series of passages in his treatise on horsemanship, Xenophon applies to the movement and poses adopted by horses a vocabulary more typically found in association with dance, and directly likens the equine to the dancer. So, the writer explains at *Eq.* 7.10.2, 'if the horse should carry his head too low, let the rider hold his hands up higher; if too high, lower down; for in this way he will arrange it in the most graceful pose (οὕτω γὰρ ἂν μάλιστα κοσμοίη τὸ σχῆμα)'. *Schêma*, the term that most regularly describes dance postures in the Greek sources, appears in its verbal form in a second passage, where it describes the horse's natural inclination to assume beautiful poses so as to instigate erotic desire in its (female) audience (10.4.1–5.1):

> ὅταν γὰρ αὐτὸς σχηματοποιεῖσθαι θέλῃ παρ' ἵππους, μάλιστα δὲ ὅταν παρὰ θηλείας, τότε αἴρει τε τὸν αὐχένα ἄνω καὶ κυρτοῖ μάλιστα τὴν κεφαλὴν γοργούμενος, καὶ τὰ μὲν σκέλη ὑγρὰ μετεωρίζει, τὴν δὲ οὐρὰν ἀνωτάτω ἀνατείνει.

> whenever [the horse] chooses to strike poses before horses, and especially before mares, he raises his neck highest and arches his head to the uttermost, looking fierce; he lifts his pliant legs up off the ground and tosses his tail up.

A third passage, at 11.6.1–7.1, newly introduces the analogy, here with a simile that more explicitly likens horse and dancer and attributes naturally graceful postures to both:

---

[2] A more comprehensive and extended consideration would take in several other animal kinds, choral monkeys (see Steiner 2016a), dogs (those of the *Oresteia* and Sophocles' *Ichneutae* most particularly), goats and donkeys among them. Bears at the Arkteia also belong in a more complete account. My discussion limits itself to the species privileged by the sources.

ἃ μὲν γὰρ ὁ ἵππος ἀναγκαζόμενος ποιεῖ . . . οὔτ᾽ ἐπίσταται οὔτε καλά ἐστιν,
οὐδὲν μᾶλλον ἢ εἴ τις ὀρχηστὴν μαστιγοίη καὶ κεντρίζοι · πολὺ γὰρ ἂν πλείω
ἀσχημονοίη ἢ καλὰ ποιοίη ὁ τοιαῦτα πάσχων καὶ ἵππος καὶ ἄνθρωπος.
ἀλλὰ δεῖ ἀπὸ σημείων ἑκόντα πάντα τὰ κάλλιστα καὶ λαμπρότατα
ἐπιδείκνυσθαι.

For what a horse does under constraint ... he does neither with understanding nor beautifully, and with no more grace than a dancer would
show if he were whipped and goaded. Being treated thus, both horse and
man will rather do what is more lacking in good pose than what is
beautiful. But of his own inclination, a horse must willingly make the
most graceful and brilliant appearance of his own and with directions.

A text from the imperial age returns to the pairing, and even suggests that
horses, and cows too, can surpass their human counterparts not just as solo
dancers but as members of larger ensembles. After earlier noting the
particular responsiveness of horses to the music of the syrinx and pipes –
the instruments that so frequently accompany choral performances – and
remarking that deer share in the characteristic and can similarly be
'charmed' (κῆλουνται) by the instruments' sound, Plutarch goes on to
comment that foals may, with practice, learn how to 'process in rhythm'
(βαδίζειν ἐν ῥυθμῷ). Extending the parallel, he observes how 'in the theatres,
horses and cows go through an exact routine in which they lie down, or do
dances (χορείας) or hold a precarious pose or perform movements not at all
easy for men' (*Mor.* 961e, 992a–b; trans. W. C. Hembold modified).[3]

1.1   Horses, Chorêgoi *and Chorus Members in Epic, Lyric and Drama*

In equating the poses and movements that the horse performs with those of
the dancer and chorus member displaying his or her grace, beauty and skill,
Xenophon and Plutarch, most probably unwittingly, rework a motif
already visible in archaic sources, and that more particularly pertains to
the choral troupe: whether positioned as leader to the larger 'herd' (usually
made up of mares), or as one among those subordinate members subject to
another's control, these equines furnish poets and artists with handy figures
for the human ensembles. Before turning to the several more secure
occurrences of the combination in post-Homeric texts and visual images,
I begin with a passage where the epic poet incorporates traditional choral
diction, conceits and concerns into a simile aligning a warrior with a horse.
This example also introduces several of the chief areas where the

---

[3]   See Griffith 2006b, 317–18 for several of these citations and discussion.

morphology and properties of choruses and the vocabulary devised for their expression most closely intersect with at least four prime aspects of ancient horsemanship and Greek thinking about equids: the nature of the herd and relations between its different members, the attributes most valued in a steed, horse grooming and adornment and the animals' taming and further training.[4]

In an abrupt shift from the mood of pathos in the preceding episode, where Hector and Andromache meet for their final leave taking, book 6 of the *Iliad* closes by spotlighting Paris as he joyously returns from Helen's bedchamber to the field of battle from which he was removed some three books back (505–14):[5]

> σεύατ' ἔπειτ' ἀνὰ ἄστυ, ποσὶ κραιπνοῖσι πεποιθώς.   505
> ὡς δ' ὅτε τις στατὸς ἵππος, ἀκοστήσας ἐπὶ φάτνῃ,
> δεσμὸν ἀπορρήξας θείῃ πεδίοιο κροαίνων,
> εἰωθὼς λούεσθαι ἐϋρρεῖος ποταμοῖο
> κυδιόων· ὑψοῦ δὲ κάρη ἔχει, ἀμφὶ δὲ χαῖται
> ὤμοις ἀΐσσονται· ὃ δ' ἀγλαΐηφι πεποιθώς,   510
> ῥίμφά ἑ γοῦνα φέρει μετά τ' ἤθεα καὶ νομὸν ἵππων·
> ὡς υἱὸς Πριάμοιο Πάρις κατὰ Περγάμου ἄκρης
> τεύχεσι παμφαίνων ὥς τ' ἠλέκτωρ ἐβεβήκει
> καγχαλόων, ταχέες δὲ πόδες φέρον·

> Then he hastened through the town, trusting in his swift feet, as when a stalled horse well-fed at the manger, having broken his chain, runs across the plain stamping with his hooves, wont to bathe himself in the well-flowing river, exulting. And he holds his head high, and his mane darts out over his shoulders. Trusting in his brilliance, his knees carry him lightly to the haunts and pastures of horses; even so did the son of Priam, Paris, all-shining in his armour like electrum, go from the citadel rejoicing, and his swift feet were carrying him.

A comparison between this passage and a second simile featuring two horses, this time unequivocally positioned as counterparts to the pair of *chorêgoi* heading the maiden troupe currently performing Alcman's first *Partheneion*, brings out the latent chorality in the Homeric representation. The property of the courser that the epic poet first observes is the swiftness of its feet, the site, in Homer and later sources, of the choral dancer's skill

---

[4] In what follows, I am particularly indebted to Griffith 2006a and 2006b; the author closely details these facets of the horse and other types of equines in the Greek sources.

[5] It may be objected that this same simile is used of Hector at *Il.* 15.262–70, where the meaning I assign to it in book 6 has no relevance. But, in a different context and applied to a different character, the thematic import of the comparison can change.

and of the fleetness that audiences wonder at (as earlier chapters have detailed). It is this same attribute that, in part, underpins Alcman's simile: so the characterization of Agido, one of the two leaders, as a horse who is 'prize-winning with resounding hooves' (ἀεθλοφόρον καναχάποδα, 48), victorious in the running race in which lines 58–59 imagine the *chorêgoi* as participants. Also common to Homer and Alcman is the evocation of the sonic dimension of these rapidly plied hooves-cum-feet and that would, in performance, correspond to the sound raised by the dancer as he or she struck the ground. The Homeric κροαίνων conveys this audible element,[6] while Alcman's choice of adjective for the racing animal similarly integrates the sonorous beat into his account.

Picked out for special emphasis in the Homeric simile is the horse's mane 'streaming over its shoulders' as it races across the plain and that matches Paris' flowing locks, a particular source of the hero's visual and erotic appeal (*Il.* 3.55), outspread in his swift passage. Again, the equation between a resplendent mane and hair recurs in the *Partheneion*, used by the singers when describing one of their two leaders: Hagesichora's tresses, here designated with the noun χαίτη that does double service, referring at once to horse and human hair,[7] 'shines forth like unalloyed gold' (ἐπανθεῖ / χρυσὸς [ὡ]ς ἀκήρατος, 53–54). And while the epic poet does not assign metallic brilliance to the steed of the simile, that same gleam belongs to the hero's weaponry that, like Hagesichora's locks, is compared to a radiant substance; Homer cites *electôr* in this instance, a term regularly used of the beaming sun, the constellation with which Agido was equated in the lines first introducing her (40–41).

The term *aglaïa* chosen by the Iliadic narrator in the subsequent phrase as the audience witnesses the stallion 'placing its trust in its brilliance' forms a natural pendant to the description of the mane, finding its echo in Xenophon's characterization of a horse's mane, forelock and tail as gifts from the gods to the species 'for the sake of splendour' (ἀγλαΐας, *Eq.* 5.8.2). But there is a further dimension to this property; built on the root *gl-* common in terms describing radiance and luminosity, it both anticipates the shine emanating from Paris' all-gleaming armour and is a *sine qua non* for the impression made by the choral dancer, whose own hair, jewellery

[6] The verb, used by the Homeric poet only here and in the reuse of the simile in book 15, puzzled ancient readers, but is most commonly glossed 'beating with the feet' (according to Aelian, *NA* 2.10, among the sources of a stallion's notorious pride and *hauteur* is 'the clang of its hooves'). Homer's own depictions of choral dancing register this sound on several occasions.

[7] Indeed, as Griffith 2006b, 308–09 observes, with the exception of lions' manes, the manes and tails of horses uniquely attract the same terminology as that found in descriptions of human tresses, nouns such as χαίτη, κόμη, ἔθειρα and θρίξ.

and other accessories are the sources of this sparkling, moving light (see Chapter 1). Alcman's *Partheneion* makes explicit mention of these features in the lines in which the choristers dwell on their allure, even as they belittle their own sources of bedazzlement in contrast to the outstanding properties of their *chorêgoi*; among the accoutrements singled out are an all-gold bracelet and a headdress styled an '*agalma* of violet-eyed maidens' (68–69). As Day observes of the *agalma*, it most probably derives from the same family as the nouns, adjectives and verbs denoting brilliance, among them *aglaïzô*, *aglaïa* and *aglaos*.[8]

Further linking the epic and lyric passages is the characterization of the equine herd, in the hexameter passage the group that occupies the 'haunts and pasturage' to which the stallion is headed, in the *Partheneion* a set of grazing beasts. In Ferrari's suggestion, Alcman's puzzling equation of the equine *chorêgos* with one of the dreams 'beneath the rock' may cohere with her membership of the pasturing herd: Moschus' *Europa* similarly draws on the conceit when the poet describes 'the race of dreams that grazes' (ποιμαίνεται, 5).[9] The epic simile ends with a mention of the horse's destination as the still solitary animal seeks to rejoin the larger company and take its place among them.[10] In a point to which I will return, these other horses form, like the ἀγέλη that describes the Pindaric choral performers in the fragments noted above, an undifferentiated aggregate, subordinate to the one – and here explicitly gendered male – pre-eminent animal, the counterpart to the *chorêgos* or leader/trainer of the band.

A fresh reason for seeing the simile through a choral lens and Paris as a *chorêgos*-like figure resuming his place as leader of the troupe becomes apparent when the passage is read as a sequel or point of closure to the events initiated in book 3, which detailed the hero's last appearance prior to his re-emergence from the domestic space of book 6. Now, in the closing lines of the urban intermezzo, Paris rejoins the martial sphere that he had quitted in less than glorious fashion in the earlier book where, rescued at the eleventh hour from defeat in his duel with Menelaus, he was whisked to safety by Aphrodite and set down in his bedchamber. Summoning Helen to her lover, the disguised goddess likens her male protégé to the individual

---

[8] Day 2010, 91.   [9] Ferrari 2008, 74.

[10] For one ancient reader at least, Vergil in his all-but-verbatim replication of the simile at *Aen.* 11.492–97, the herd populating the site to which the hero – Turnus here – gallops is made up explicitly of mares (*equarum*, 494). If that implication is already present in the Homeric lines, then this larger group even more closely resembles the grazing herd in Alcman's *Partheneion*, which stands in for the maidens performing the song. The horse's trajectory, *en route* to rejoin the feminine herd, also echoes Paris' pronounced sexual proclivities.

who, 'gleaming in beauty and his clothing' (κάλλεϊ τε στίλβων καὶ εἵμασιν, 3.392) just as choral dancers do (cf. *Il.* 18.596, where στίλβοντας again describes the choristers' garments), has just quitted the χορός. As Deborah Boedeker's analysis of the lines observes,[11] this sequence of events interweaves several motifs from a familiar scenario, albeit with the gender roles inverted: Paris' removal from the battlefield recalls a maiden's abduction by a typically male god or lover (and the term used for Aphrodite's 'snatch' of Paris at 3.380 is ἁρπάζω, the abduction verb *par excellence*), while the reference to the χορός – whether this is just the dance, the dancing space or an actual chorus – also borrows from the scheme, which regularly depicts the *parthenos* abducted from the chorus line where she performs together with her age mates. In keeping with that model too, and with the goddess once again playing the part of male divinity or would-be human lover, the spectacle of Paris as dancer instigates Aphrodite's desire, here channelled, as Helen recognizes in the taunting words she addresses to the divinity (406–09), through the person of her human surrogate who replaces the goddess in Paris' bed.

The earlier characterization of Paris *qua* choral dancer in his appearance in book 3 (and there is no mention of him in the intervening books) also helps explain a further element of the equine simile in book 6, the presence of the 'fair-flowing river' in which the horse wishes to bathe. As one commentary remarks,[12] the detail seems out of place since generally horses do not wash themselves nor does it correspond to any of Paris' actions in the scene. But if the poet draws on existing notions of chorality in his ongoing characterization of the previously chorus-dancing hero turned warrior here, then the line makes better sense. While, as noted in previous chapters, indicators of a watery landscape are almost *de rigueur* in images showing maiden choruses on Argive Geometric vases, the particular act of bathing figures in textual accounts of the activities of and milieus surrounding parthenaic dancers. Already the archetypal Muses in the proem of Hesiod's *Theogony* bathe in the spring or river prior to forming their χορός (5), while Nausikaa and her maidens, their laundry spread out to dry on the riverbank, bathe and anoint themselves with oil (*Od.* 6.96) before turning to their meal and commencing their choral ball dance. And if the mistress and her maids only wash themselves in the interests of hygiene following their exertions at the tubs, then Theocritus closely integrates the 'bathing places' by the Spartan Eurotas (παρ' Εὐρώταο λοετροῖς, *Id.* 18.23) into his account of the race-cum-dance in which the four choral bands of

---

[11] Boedeker 1974, 61–63.   [12] Graziosi and Haubold 2010 *ad loc.*

sixty maidens participate; perhaps also relevant is the coupling of 'warm baths' and the dance, albeit along with other pleasures, in the account that Alkinous gives of the Phaeacian life style at *Od.* 8.248–49 (for further examples, see Chapter 5).

If the Homeric simile does anticipate Alcman's song in many respects, that lyric representation also exploits the chorister-horse equation in ways quite independent of the epic passage. The extensive use of the motif in the text's second part may be in part determined by the ritual context inform- ing the composition. As Alexander Garvie first suggested, the *chorêgoi* Agido and Hagesichora might have served as the priestesses of the Spartan cult of the two Leukippidae, Phoebe and Hilaeira, who were originally courted by both the Hippocoontids – the sons of Horseman – enumerated at the poem's start and the Dioskouroi, whom myth repeatedly depicts as riders (Polydeuces also appears in the first line of the extant portion of the poem); according to the ancient sources, these priestesses were styled πῶλοι, foals, and were two in number.[13]

The equine image developed in the description of the two chorus leaders also recurs later in the song. Although fragmentary, lines 92–95 introduce the σηραφόρος (the 'trace-horse') as well as the helmsman, two figures who assume the same directing and path-determining functions. The metaphor proves tailor-made for an evocation of the relations between our two pre- eminent *chorêgoi* and the maidenly aggregate subordinate to their guidance and expertise. As visual accounts of chariot teams in the black- and red- figure repertoire illustrate,[14] these typically consist of four horses, fre- quently shown frontally. Within these groups, the horse on the extreme right was designated the trace-horse (or 'out-runner', παρήορος) and was allowed to run unharnessed and free from the yoke, attached only by the 'traces'. Its role was to set the pace for the remaining three around the turns, where heightened dexterity and authoritative leadership were at a premium. The four-horse team might also have two privileged members whose greater stature, signalling dominance, corresponds to that of the single trace-horse in other foursomes. In the arrangement visible in the black-figure repertoire, the two middle horses often form a pair, sometimes rubbing noses to demonstrate their bond, while the two on the outside are shown interacting with the human figure in the scene – a driver or attend- ant – or looking outward for guidance. Examples include a black-figure column krater of ca. 525–475 with a four-horse chariot positioned frontally

---

[13] For the ancient evidence, see Garvie 1965; cf. Robbins 1994, Nagy 1990, 346.
[14] For more detailed discussion and the examples that follow, see Griffith 2006b, 333–35.

on each of its two handles, iterations of the chariots also depicted on the vase's two faces.[15] In distinction to their two teammates, who have their heads turned aside, these innermost and identical horses look into one another's eyes and incline their heads so that their noses intersect. On a black-figure neck amphora from the late sixth century, the artist locates another four-horse team, absent a chariot, on each shoulder, here positioned between two eyes;[16] while the two trace-horses' heads are painted in profile, facing to the right, the two yoke horses have frontal faces and noses that overlap and touch.

Again, we can map this visual scheme onto the relations imagined for Alcman's parthenaic choruses: just like the two inside horses depicted by artists, Agido and Hagesichora form a tight-knit unit. But also like the steeds that frame the internal pair on a red-figure column krater attributed to the Painter of Bologna 228 of ca. 460,[17] whose necks are raised higher than those of their companions in an indication of their superiority and perhaps leading, course-determining role, the two *chorêgoi* outmatch the rest of their troupe in speed, singing powers and beauty and anticipate the trace-horse cited later in the song.[18] Linguistic usage reflects the hierarchical structures visible in both these visual equine collectives and the choral ensemble. As already noted, the term 'herd', ἀγέλη, could describe a group of typically youthful choristers; among these, one of the maidens or youths would, in addition to an adult leader, act as trainer of the group, and, in language drawn from the sphere of horse and bovine management, could be designated βουαγός or ἀγελάτης.[19]

Among the variety of relations between the members of a horse team – that may comprise two, three or four members – there are other configurations that readily correspond to those already on display in Alcman's choruses in the first and third *Partheneia* and that pertain to choruses more generally. Just as equality among the subordinate chorus members, undifferentiated in the third song, and presented as a chiefly homogeneous unit in the first, where none is privileged above the rest but all are

[15] Private Market, Christie's Sale Catalogue 18.10.2005, 104–05, no. 119.
[16] Champaign, Krannert Art Museum, University of Illinois at Urbana-Champaign 70.8.2. Griffith 2006b, 333 n. 84 cites a number of other examples.
[17] New York, Metropolitan Museum of Art 29.131.7; *ARV*² 511.4, *Para.* 382.
[18] As Griffith observes (2006b, 334–35), the asymmetrical relations visible in the equine group on the krater are freshly played out in the two warriors also shown in the scene, whose eyes and (horsehair) helmet plumes are depicted in a manner that recalls the horses' eyes and manes. In the human pairing, it is the figure equipped with shield and spear, and positioned in front of his companion, the driver of the team, who is marked out as the superior in age and status – a warrior as opposed to a mere charioteer.
[19] Griffith 2006b, 331.

introduced by the same dismissive οὔτε formula in 64–72, so team members are supposed to be evenly matched, all of similar 'age, size, strength, speed, and looks'.[20] Two terms used of equine groups bring out their unity, σύζυγοι and ὁμόζυγες; the first of these recalls the representation of the paradigmatic choral triad made up by the ever-dancing Graces, whom Euripides describes as the συζύγιαι Χάριτες (*Hipp.* 1148).

A composition by Anacreon, his familiar 'Thracian filly' poem (417 *PMG*), makes ample use of the image of the horse engaged in several of the actions assigned the steeds in Homer and Alcman and, for all the absence of any mention of a larger ensemble of choreutes, the poet's reintroduction of diction and conceits already familiar from choral typology invite us to see the inamorata as the lead member of a parthenaic ensemble.[21] Addressing the object of his desire as a πῶλε Θρηκίη, the speaker goes on to claim that he could easily bridle the girl and gain control of her motions (4–6):

> ἡνίας δ᾽ ἔχων στρέφοιμί σ᾽ ἀμφὶ τέρματα δρόμου·
> νῦν δὲ λειμῶνάς τε βόσκεαι κοῦφά τε σκιρτῶσα παίζεις·   5
> δεξιὸν γὰρ ἱπποπείρην οὐκ ἔχεις ἐπεμβάτην.

> and holding the reins I could turn you round the turning posts of the racecourse. But now instead you graze in the meadow skipping lightly as you play, since you have no skilled horseman to ride you.

Discussions of the lines rightly observe the ambiguity of the verb παίζω in the context of a poem concerned with achieving sexual mastery of the desired maiden currently placed – like Herotime in Anacreon's fr. 346 *PMG* who similarly disports herself in a meadow 'where the Cyprian tethered her (lovely?) horses freed from the yoke' –[22] in an erotically charged landscape redolent of budding female sexuality (a theme that the similes in Homer and Alcman evoke more glancingly with their references to equines that, like Anacreon's, are grazing). But in combination with 'skipping', the verb also preserves its more innocent meaning, describing not so much a readiness for amorous dalliance (συμπαίζω more fully implies that) as participation in the dance. Here, as the filly-cum-dancer

---

[20] Griffith 2006b, 333.

[21] My suggestion is not that Anacreon's song would be chorally performed (like his other compositions, fr. 417 *PMG* is a monody), but more simply that its language and imagery draw on the existing notion of the dancer and *chorêgos* as a member of a herd of horses.

[22] For παίζω and its compounds, see Rosenmeyer 2004. Herotime could be read as a figure who begins as a participant in a typically equine choral troupe in a bucolic setting, and who subsequently forsakes her fellow dancers and subverts the initial paradigm by becoming a solo – and debased – performer.

performs the same movements as the youths and maidens making their way from the vineyard and skipping to the lyre-playing of a youth in one of the pastoral scenes on the Homeric shield of Achilles (*Il.* 18.567–72), she simultaneously recalls Alcman's lead choristers, these likewise dancers depicted among the larger equine group at pasture.

Consonant with this choral and performative shading is the term στρέφοιμι in the first line. As subsequent examples will show, the 'turn' that the speaker wishes the filly to carry out also characterizes the chorus' movement at the strophic breaks of the song. In this instance, the 'rider' acts as the *chorêgos* who directs the lead performer's steps in the running 'race', equine and otherwise, that Greek sources, as the first *Partheneion* already illustrated, so regularly conflate with choral dancing. Where Alcman's account presents Agido and Hagesichora as prize-winning horses, coursers who compete in an *agôn*, the Anacreontic ego additionally boasts of his skill in guiding the filly around the turning post, the moment which more than any other determines the outcome of the race.

The image of the race, and the agonistic motif attendant on it introduced by Alcman and Anacreon both occupy centrestage in the first of the several fifth-century examples of the equation between the choral dancer and the horse. In a fragment of a Pindaric hyporcheme, whose genre and extended set of animal images are much more fully treated in Section 3, the speaker urges on the dancing group by directing it to take its cue from either a horse or dog (fr. 107a S.-M.):

> Πελασγὸν ἵππον ἢ κύνα
> Ἀμυκλαίαν ἀγωνίῳ
> ἐλελιζόμενος ποδὶ μιμέο καμπύλον μέλος διώκων,

> imitate the Pelasgian horse or dog from Amyklai as you whirl with your competing foot and impel forward the curving song . . .

In John Franklin's acute reading of these lines,[23] the 'curve' described by the *melos* has a threefold sphere of reference: most immediately evocative of the animals' limbs that bend as they run and of the *kampê* or *kamptêr*, the goal or turning point in a race that supplies the song's larger imagistic frame, it also has a meta-musical/performative dimension insofar as it can describe the 'metrical turning point and melodic change' within a composition.[24] Numerous texts from the later fifth century describe

---

[23] Franklin 2013, 228–29.

[24] Among the examples handily gathered in Restani 1983, terms referring to turns and bends are used by or of Phrynis, Aristophanes, Eupolos, Agathon, Pherecrates, Kinesias, Timotheos and Telestes.

and endlessly parody the vogue for 'bending' or 'turning' – i.e. harmonic modulation within strophes[25] – among the so-called New Musicians (chiefly composers of dithyrambs), and notorious is the charge levelled against these by the Aristophanic Socrates, who dubs the charlatans 'song-benders of circular choruses' (κυκλίων τε χορῶν ἀσματοκάμπτας, *Nub.* 333); in another attack on stylistic innovations, Pherecrates' *Cheiron* brings on stage none other than Mousikê herself to complain of the (sexual) violence done to her by the New Musicians and their instruments, singling out for special rancour the 'exharmonic twists' (ἐξαρμονίους καμπάς, fr. 155.9 K.-A.) introduced by the dithyrambic poet Kinesias. But as Franklin and others have argued, such modulation and shifts between the different *harmoniai* were already practised by the avant-garde choral poets/musicians and pipe-players of the late sixth and early fifth century, and Pindar belongs very much among them.[26] In Franklin's further suggestion concerning fr. 107a S.-M., 'it is tempting to suppose that the passage occurred just before a strophic boundary'.[27] The animal's course that follows the song's twists and turns involves its own internal circular motions; in describing the choreutes' feet as 'whirling', Pindar uses the reduplicated epic form of ἐλίσσω, the verb that Euripides would later privilege in his evocations of the circle dances performed by choruses and which came to be most closely associated with Dionysiac cult.[28]

Greek drama, both tragedy and comedy, furnishes several additional manifestations of the dancer, sometimes solo, but more frequently as participant in a chorus, *qua* horse. Our earliest instance belongs to Aeschylus and, in the first of the drama's two uses of the equine conceit pertinent to choral dancing, to the *Choephoroi*'s second stasimon, where the singers imagine Orestes in the likeness of a youthful racehorse, 'the orphaned colt yoked to the chariot (ἅρμασιν)' (794–95). Invoking Zeus, they then ask the god that this still unregulated foal might achieve more order and rhythmic discipline to temper his movements (796–99):

> ἐν δρόμῳ
> προστιθεὶς μέτρον, κτίσον
> †σωζόμενον† ῥυθμόν,
> τοῦτ' ἰδεῖν δάπεδον ἀνόμενον
> βημάτων ὄρεγμα.

---

[25] As Franklin 2013 demonstrates, in contrast to the later practice, earlier composers such as Pindar introduced modulations only at strophic boundaries and not within the strophes.

[26] Franklin 2013, Steiner 2013a and 2016b, with earlier bibliography.   [27] Franklin 2013, 229.

[28] Csapo 1999/2000, 422.

on his strides in the race impose a measure and a steady rhythm, that this
ground may see the swift striving of his steps reach the end of the course.

The analogies with dance and its expression in *choreia* are evident. In
Plato's later definition of *rhythmos* in the *Philebus*, it is an attribute of
movements which are 'numerically regulated (δι' ἀριθμῶν μετρηθέντα) and
which must be called rhythms and measures (ῥυθμοὺς καὶ μέτρα)' (17d).
This same vocabulary reappears in a performative context when, in the
Laws, the Athenian Stranger seeks to trace the origins of man's unique
capacity for choral dance. Alone of all species, innate to the human is the
development of a sense of order, *taxis*, in motion, which the speaker further
defines as *rhythmos*. It is the union of this regulated movement and the
same good order in vocal sounds that constitutes *choreia*, song-dance
(664e–665a). In the speaker's later account of the new *mousikê*, which he
so harshly critiques at 669c–e, among the many musico-choral sins laid at
the door of contemporary dithyrambic composers is their propensity to
'divorce rhythm and movement from the tune' and to produce songs and
choreography ill-suited to citizen performers. Athenaeus would later find
fault with choral composers on related grounds, disparaging those who
failed to observe orderliness (whose contrary he styles *ataxia* in the immediately preceding phrase) in choreographing the movements that their
dancer-singers will perform, and who 'put together dance figures without
regulation (ἀμέτρως)' (14.628e).

In the *Choephoroi* account, the dance/choral frame introduced by the
reference to rhythm and metre continues in the 'steps' that Orestes should
stretch out so as to achieve victory in the race.[29] βῆμα may also describe the
motions of the dancer performing in a choral group, as in Sappho's
recollection of the 'fair step' that belonged to Anaktoria (fr. 16 V.,
ἐρατὸν ... βᾶμα) as she used to lead the Sapphic chorus.[30] The expression
appears earlier still, forming part of the compound applied by the Homeric
poet to the Phaeacian dancers at *Od.* 8.250 and 383: they are βητάρμονες,
those who fit (ἀραρίσκω) their steps together. The chorus' visualization of
Orestes as the chariot-yoked colt includes a glance to the verbal portion of
the compound noun: to achieve victory with the ἅρμα, the horse's movements must manifest the same 'fitting together' and coordination implicit
in the noun and its etymological underpinnings.

---

[29] Behind the metaphor lies the racing/choral dancing equivalence visible in coming-of-age
practices and particularly appropriate to Orestes, depicted in the play as undergoing his own
maturation rite.

[30] See too Chapter 1.

For Aeschylus' audience, the assimilation of the foal with the choral performer would be much more self-evident. It seems plausible that, as in the other instances cited below, the expressions chosen by the *Choephoroi* choristers might be self-referential and draw attention to their enactment of the movements that, in their *dramatis personae*, they recommend for the youthful hero.[31] Maintaining due measure in their dance and displaying the requisite metrical and musical orderliness in their song, they offer themselves as models for *choreia* properly performed.

The image of Orestes as participant in a chariot race and his alignment with the racing horse recur in the drama's closing moments, where the dance-cum-choral element latent in the second stasimon comes more fully to the fore. In his final moments of lucidity following the matricide, and just before his vision of the Furies, Orestes returns to the conceit chosen by the chorus as he first imagines himself in the likeness of the charioteer who drives his team off the track and then suggests that he, no less than the horses, is the victim of a series of disordering forces, these internally located and all-mastering (1021–25):

> ἀλλ' ὡς ἂν εἰδῆτ', οὐ γὰρ οἶδ' ὅπη τελεῖ,
> ὥσπερ ξὺν ἵπποις ἡνιοστροφῶ δρόμου
> ἐξωτέρω· φέρουσι γὰρ νικώμενον
> φρένες δύσαρκτοι, πρὸς δὲ καρδία φόβος
> ᾄδειν ἕτοιμος ἠδ' ὑπορχεῖσθαι κότῳ.   1025

> But so that you might know – for I do not know the end point, just as one who guides the chariot with horses, I am driving somewhat off the track. For my mind is almost out of control and carries me along, overpowered, and fear is near my heart ready to sing and to dance along to wrath's tune.

The two portions of this extended simile-turned-metaphor form a composite, both evoking Orestes' sense of internal disarray, which is figured in each instance as a type of vigorous and distorted motion, whether that of a chariot driver veering off course or of a dance-and-song performed under the dictates of the external and irresistible force of avenging anger. Although Orestes does not spell out the nature of fear's *choreia*, Euripides' Lyssa – the wolfish rage-cum-madness that stands equivalent to the wrath cited by the hero – would exactingly depict that sensation's impact on the motions and sounds performed by the individual held in its ineluctable grasp;[32] following her portrayal of Hercules as he

---

[31] Weiss 2018, 197 n. 21 makes the same suggestion.

[32] Euripides may even have the Aeschylean passage in mind. Note particularly the reference to racing in the lines from the later drama.

'shakes his head at the starting point of his race, whirls his turned-aside and fierce-eyed pupils (διαστρόφους ἑλίσσει ... γοργωπούς κόρας) in silence, and is not master of his breathing ... he bellows terribly' (*HF* 867–70), Lyssa addresses her victim directly and predicts still worse to come: 'I shall soon make you dance the more and I shall play on you the pipes of fear (χορεύσω καὶ καταυλήσω φόβῳ)' (871).[33]

That fear's performance takes choral form in Aeschylus, the quasi-technical language used by Orestes to describe it unmistakably establishes: this is a hyporcheme (so ὑπορχεῖσθαι, 1025), a lyric genre given a variety of sometimes contradictory definitions in the ancient sources and whose sole explicit mention in extant Attic tragedy occurs here.[34] Each part of the twofold phrase, whose focus on the turmoil experienced within the speaker's mind-and-body reinforces the continuity structurally flagged by πρὸς δέ, conditions the other. While the reference to a choral performance retroactively turns the movements of the charioteer into just such a spectacle gone awry, the team's departure from the track allows us to understand the disorderly quality of the singing and dancing occurring adjacent to the hero's heart. If, as the Pindaric fragment cited above and Plutarch's account at *Quaest. conv.* 9.748a–b (a hyporcheme involves 'a *mimêsis*, through poses and words') indicate,[35] a pronounced mimetic element characterizes this song-dance, then the juxtaposition of the chariot team and the speaker's representation of fear's *choreia* as belonging to the hyporchemic genre proves particularly significant: the charioteer's veering course becomes the dance generated by wrath's music-making.

It is Euripides who furnishes several additional examples (treated in thematic rather than chronological order here) of representations of the horse as *chorêgos* or as a member of the larger ensemble. The parodos of the *Iphigenia at Aulis* returns to the chariot-horse and racing imagery so prevalent in the earlier sources as the chorus, having travelled from

[33] For fresh dance language in the subsequent description of the result of Lyssa's intervention, see 978.

[34] As Andújar 2018, 271 suggestively observes, Orestes' representation of his 'performance' conforms with the description that Lucian would give of a chorus of youths performing a hyporcheme at Delos, some of whom dance while others sing (*Salt.* 16); so too Orestes distinguishes fear's song from the dance element. As to the highly elusive hyporchematic genre, all our knowledge of its character is filtered not only through an Alexandrian sensibility, but, at still further remove, through those imperial and later authors who preserve the views of Hellenistic editors and savants in later commentaries and brief citations. I am also indebted to an unpublished discussion of the genre by Peter Agócs who kindly shared a text of his talk with me.

[35] The language returns in Athen. 1.15d: the hyporcheme is here defined as a type of *orchêsis* that involves 'an imitation of acts that can be interpreted by words'.

Chalcis for the express purpose of playing viewer (171, 189–92), treats the audience to a full account of the spectacle it witnesses at Aulis.[36] Perceiving Achilles on the beach below, the singers dwell on his appearance as he races against a quadriga driven by Eumelos, whose horses also receive an extended description in this first non-strophic epode (206–30):[37]

> τὸν ἰσάνεμόν τε ποδοῖν
> λαιψηροδρόμον Ἀχιλλέα,
> τὸν ἁ Θέτις τέκε καὶ
> Χείρων ἐξεπόνησεν,
> ἴδον αἰγιαλοῖς παρά τε κροκάλαις   210
> δρόμον ἔχοντα σὺν ὅπλοις·
> ἅμιλλαν δ’ ἐπόνει ποδοῖν
> πρὸς ἅρμα τέτρωρον
> ἑλίσσων περὶ νίκας·   215
> ὁ δὲ διφρηλάτας ἐβόατ’
> Εὔμηλος Φερητιάδας,
> οὗ καλλίστους ἰδόμαν
> χρυσοδαιδάλτοις στομίοις
> πώλους κέντρῳ θεινομένους,   220
> τοὺς μὲν μέσους ζυγίους
> λευκοστίκτῳ τριχὶ βαλιούς,
> τοὺς δ’ ἔξω σειροφόρους
> ἀντήρεις καμπαῖσι δρόμων
> πυρσότριχας, μονόχαλα δ’ ὑπὸ σφυρὰ   225
> ποικιλοδέρμονας· οἷς παρεπάλλετο
> Πηλεΐδας σὺν ὅπλοισι παρ’ ἄντυγα
> καὶ σύριγγας ἁρματείους.   230

And he who is equal to the wind in his feet, swift-running Achilles, whom Thetis bore and Cheiron formed by instruction, I saw him having a race in armour along the seashore. And he was labouring at the contest on feet against the four-horsed chariot, wheeling round for victory. And the charioteer was shouting, Eumelos, grandson of Pheres, whose supremely fair colts I could see with intricately worked golden bridles as they were struck by the goad, the yoked ones in the middle, dappled with white-speckled hair, and the trace-horses on the outside facing the bends of the race, with flame-coloured hair, piebald beneath their single-footed ankles.

---

[36] The parodos receives additional treatment in Chapters 5 and 9. Issues of authenticity raised by commentators concerning the portion of the passage focused on here lie outside the scope of my discussion.

[37] Weiss 2018, 195–98 offers a reading that coincides with mine on several points.

> Alongside them the son of Peleus was leaping in his armour beside the
> chariot rail and its hub-wheels.

As Euripides' chorus danced on stage while singing the lines, the analogies
between the performing company and the contestants in this race, one on
foot, the other driving his four-horse team, become apparent on several
fronts. First, through the choristers' use of terminology filled with the
motifs so familiar from the numerous textual and visual representations
of *choreia* cited in this and other chapters. Patently in sync with by-the-
book evocations of paradigmatic choral performances are the speed, metallic dazzle, colourful variegation, striking coiffure, intricate craftsmanship,
ornamentation, skilled footwork, youth (horses and heroes both), expenditure of labour and agonism visible in both Achilles and the colts against
whom he competes; taken up here too is the commonplace elision of
running, typically in a race, and dancing, already apparent in the epic (so
Il. 18.601) and lyric corpora.[38]

The quasi-technical terms included in the description that look to
choreography and musical accompaniment give a choral dimension to
the singers' more patent glance to both the race in full armour and the
pyrrhiche, the 'weapon dance' that formed part of the programme of
competitive events at the Panathenaia by the late fifth century. As the
images of leaping dancers in archaic vase paintings already illustrate, and
the two star Phaeacian acrobatic-dancers in *Odyssey* 8 affirm, Achilles
performs his winning moves much like the lead dancer(s) – and in some
instances prize-winner – of the larger troupe.[39] The verb παραπάλλομαι,
a Euripidean hapax, appears in uncompounded form in the context of
dancing, sometimes choral, elsewhere in Euripides (see *El.* 435, 477, *Tro.*
325), and again in the passage from Aristophanes' *Lysistrata* treated at this
section's close. If Achilles plays the pre-eminent dancer performing his
winning stunt solo, then Eumelos, who directs the undifferentiated members of the equine team, acts as *chorêgos* to his more numerous ensemble
participating in the competitive event.

Equally apposite to the motions of the quadriga and the chorus is
Euripides' inclusion of his verb of predilection for the rotating motions
of dithyrambic-style circle dancing, ἐλίσσω, here applied to Achilles as he
'whirls' together with the chariot, whose 'bends', the καμπαί similarly
figured in the Pindaric hyporcheme, fashion a second and matching circle.

---

[38] For this, see Chapter 2 and Weiss 2018, 196–97.
[39] As also noted by Weiss 2018, 198 n. 25 with additional examples. Cf. the corresponding picture
of Achilles 'light in the leap of his feet' at Eur. *El.* 206–07, for which, see Chapter 5.

Placed in the context of this display of Euripidean 'New Musicality' (so, among other features, the recherché vocabulary, proliferation of compound terms and pleonasms in the lines), the first of the two terms flags the song's embrace of the novelizing composers' fondness for references to whirling, spinning motions[40] while the second recalls the harmonic shifts that were a hallmark of contemporary dithyrambic compositions.

Issues of *harmonia* and musical modulation might even be written into the dramatist's choice to portray Achilles in this manner and most particularly in his detailing of the chariot. A curious passage from Glaucus of Rhegium's *On the Ancient Poets and Musicians*, cited by [Plutarch] (*De mus.* 7.1133e–f), names the aulete Olympos as author of a *Harmateios* or 'Chariot' *nomos*, one among the modes that Euripides' 'variegated' epode might sample here.[41] Nor is the sonic ambience absent from the lines. As Andrew Barker notes in a different context, the syrinx cited by the chorus in the closing phrase has meta-musical connotations, calling to mind not just the aulete accompanying the song but also the shrill sound emanating from the nave of the chariot wheel as it rotates.[42]

Read against my earlier discussion of the configuration of the four-horse team and the relations of hierarchy and equality and leadership and subordination brought out in textual and visual representations, additional 'cross-overs' between the scene focalized in the epode and the Euripidean chorus singing and dancing out the song become evident. Stratification among the initially collective colts introduces fresh divisions, with differentiation between those in the middle and the more important trace-horses positioned on the outside, whose tawny manes associate them with the flame-coloured head and helmet of the Iliadic Achilles. The triple-run of adjectives used for these more expert coursers additionally distinguishes them from the two tyros in the foursome, who receive only a single descriptive term. It is tempting, of course, not only to map the morphology of these steeds onto the Euripidean chorus, under the tutelage of a *chorodidaskalos*,[43] but to see a meta-performative dimension to the language used of the horses and of Achilles' movements: the dancer-singers on the stage do not so much imitate or reproduce the actions of the horses turning about the posts and Achilles' leaps and twirls as engage

---

[40] For a more explicit reference to circular movement, see the description of the Nereid figureheads on the ships in the second strophe (231–41), with discussion in Chapter 5.
[41] This is a matter I take up in Steiner 2016b in reference to Pindar's fr. 140b S.-M.
[42] Barker 1984, 61 n. 27. See too the discussion of the syrinx in the second stasimon of the *Helen* and its 'New Musical' associations in Chapter 3.
[43] See later chapters for textual and visual examples of choruses that include less practised members.

in sequences of steps and gestures suggestive of what their words describe.[44]

Quite independent of the chariot team that has been integral to several of the passages considered so far are the choralized Dioskouroi introduced in the third stasimon of Euripides' *Helen*. Where the previous chapter focused on the cranes in the second strophe of the ode, these birds in flight find companion dancers not just in the Pleiades earlier detailed, but in the pair of horsemen-cum-riders introduced in the answering antistrophe concluding the song (1495–500):

> μόλοιτέ ποθ' ἵππιον οἶμον   1495
> δι' αἰθέρος ἱέμενοι,
> παῖδες Τυνδαρίδαι,
> λαμπρῶν ἀστέρων ὑπ' ἀέλλαις οἳ ναίετ' οὐράνιοι,
> σωτῆρε τᾶς Ἑλένας   1500

> Come rushing through the air along the equine course, o children of Tyndareos, you who dwell in the heavens beneath the whirlings of the brilliant stars, saviours of Helen

The divine twins summoned by the chorus here are, of course, thoroughly at home in the Spartan cult scene that the stasimon has already featured; as noted earlier, south of Sparta was the Dromos where youths would train for races under the tutelage of the Dioskouroi, who were worshipped in conjunction with Helen at her cult site on the opposite bank of the Eurotas where the cranes of the earlier verses will come to land. The equine element so prevalent in textual and visual representations of these 'horsey' twins[45] also points back to the first antistrophe and to the Leukippidae presented there, the latter-day priestesses and chorus-leaders who took on the role of the original two sisters and Dioskouroi brides and were known as πῶλοι.

But there are narrower continuities too. The description of the horse-mounted youths as dwellers 'in the heavens beneath the whirlings of the brilliant stars' not only includes a reminder of the twins' stellar identity; it also offers an exactly matching panel to the picture in the preceding stanza. Where the cranes traced a linear path through the sky populated by the dancing circles of the Pleiades and Orion, now the divine riders also follow their trajectory through the night-time heavens in the midst of the gyrating stars, astral bodies depicted in a manner that maintains the choral identity

---

[44] Here I differ from Weiss 2018, 196–97 who assumes a more direct mimeticism.
[45] See Allan 2008 *ad* 1495–96 for a sampling of the evidence.

earlier claimed by the Pleiades. The representation of the horsemen's swift passage along the horse-trod track has a choreographic element too: insofar as moving in the manner of the steed is regularly equated with the motions of the dance, here the chorus imagines the twins as dancers as well as riders. A passage from Euripides' *Iphigenia at Tauris* offers a second and more explicit sounding of that equivalence in lines that feature in quick succession horses, stars, birds and an unequivocally choral performance:[46] no sooner does the parthenaic chorus declare its desire to 'step along the shining horse-courses (λαμπροὺς ἱπποδρόμους βαίην), where the fire of the sun goes' (1139–40) than, having reformulated that wish into a longing for metamorphosis into an avian form, it ends with its third yearning: to 'stand up in the choruses' (χοροῖς δ' ἐνσταίην) that whir about (ἑλίσσω once again) in epithalamic dances (1143–46). The two verbs' syntactical correspondence (βαίην/ἐνσταίην) reinforces the parallels and complementary relations between the concluding ring dance and the opening linear/processional equine passage.

In positioning the divine twins among the radiant constellations, the invocation in the *Helen* suggests a choral as well as cosmic structure. The term ὑπό chosen by the singers for the location of the riders vis-à-vis the stars can mean 'under', as in line 1489, or, used with the dative here, 'in the company of'. Read this way, the phrase imagines the twins standing to the constellations much as the pre-eminent crane/chorus leader or piper stood to the larger avian flock. The affinity between the horse-mounted Dioskouroi and stars finds its reflection in contemporary visual culture. Artists as well as poets regularly imagine the principal stellar bodies – Night, Moon, Dawn and the Sun – riding horses, or carried across the sky in horse-drawn chariots,[47] and here Euripides extends that conceit to the divinized and starry brothers.

Consistent too with the second strophe, and with the formation just proposed is the musical element in the antistrophe's first line. At the literal level, the 'equine course' at 1495 must refer to the track on which the mounted brothers ride.[48] But already in archaic poetry, οἶμος signifies the 'path of song' that a composer/singer travels in creating and performing his composition.[49] That such a work can be 'hippic', the parallel Pindaric

---

[46] On the lines, see too Weiss 2018, 29–30.

[47] Ferrari 2008, 95–96; I return to this in Chapter 6. Note too Eur. *Andromeda* frr. 114 and 124 K.; the play was produced alongside *Helen*.

[48] οἶμον is itself a conjecture for the divergent ms. readings, οἶμα (the spring or swoop of an animal), and ἅρμα.

[49] See *HHMerc*. 451 and Pind. *Ol*. 9.47; cf. the Homeric usage of οἴμη (e.g. *Od*. 8.481, 22.347), the 'way of song', and Ar. *Av*. 1374, where Kinesias flies on the 'path of song'.

expression ἱππίῳ νόμῳ (*Ol.* 1.101) used for a song composed to celebrate a victory on a horse affirms and a second Pindaric coinage introduced in an ode for a charioteer, Καστόρειον (*Pyth.* 2.69), is also apposite to the chorus' phrase:[50] what then could be more fitting than for the twins to travel by means of a 'horsey song' or 'equestrian tune' which they, in the role of *chorêgoi*, lead off to the accompaniment of the dancing of the stars/chorus members on the stage? This musical interpretation suits a second term, which, taken together with οἶμος, gives lines 1495–96 a different but no less fitting sense. Since ἵημι regularly describes the projection of sound, speech or song, the phrase can be construed as an invitation to the Dioskouroi to 'come through the sky, emitting an equine song', again much as the lead crane did before.[51] Figured in these terms, the divine rescuers assume the likeness of the choralized horses and leaders of their herds apparent in earlier sources.

If equines furnish paradigmatic *chorêgoi* in the *Helen* account, the horse, on this occasion just a juvenile or πῶλος, cited in the final epode of the parodos of the *Bacchae* forms part of the larger herd made up of Bacchants, currently singing and dancing in celebration of Dionysus. Standing representative of the group, the filly appears in a phrase that is nothing if not traditional in its choice of diction (164–66):

> ἡδομέ-
> να δ᾽ ἄρα πῶλος ὅπως ἅμα ματέρι φορβάδι κῶλον ἄγει ταχύπουν
> σκιρτήμασι βάκχα.   165

joyfully, then, like a foal together with its grazing mother, the Bacchant moves her swift-footed limb in her skippings.

To note first the obvious continuities with the earlier sources, as in Alcman (and note too Anacreon fr. 417 *PMG*, which more obliquely draws on the terminology of choral dancing for the representation of the 'filly' at play) the female dancer is figured as the young horse that grazes, here together with its mother, under whose protection it still remains (most likely a reference to the presence of married women as well as *parthenoi* among the maenadic bands in both the *dramatis personae* taken on by the

---

[50] Cf. Pind. *Isthm.* 1.16.

[51] If, following Lucian's description of the chorus of boys who performed during sacrifices at Delos (*Salt.* 16), the hyporcheme was a genre in which some choreutes sang while others danced, then the ὑπό, reflected in the name of this performance type, might be a pointer to Euripides' use of a hyporcheme-type song here. There could have been a separation between those chorus members who took on the role of the twins, and those performing as stars (see Andújar 2018, 272 for this division). It is curious to find so many horses in passages from the lyric and tragic corpus that match ancient accounts of *hyporchêmata*.

Euripidean chorus and in ritual practices). In keeping with the epic and Pindaric coursers, the representation also highlights the rapid motion of this youthful horse and the skips distinctive of that age group. It is tempting to assume, as in Pindar, Aeschylus and the other Euripidean examples, a correlation with the chorus' own choreography, its corresponding emulation of the horse in the motion of the dancers' legs and rapid footwork: the extensive visual evidence for Bacchic dancing repeatedly demonstrates how participants performed just the types of vigorous movements described in line 165.[52]

Two passages from Aristophanes illustrate the comic dramatist's redeployment of the 'choral horse' motif as he combines equines with terms that have a now-established valence in the traditional vocabulary of *choreia*. The first usage belongs to the lines performed by the vagrant poet who visits Cloudcuckooland in the *Birds* and couches his appeal for Pisthetaerus' patronage with a florid address that patently riffs on a hyporcheme composed by Pindar for Hieron (fr. 105a S.-M.). Embarking on his sample encomion of this new city-founder, the visitor begins with the standard invocation to his tutelary divinities (924–25):

> ἀλλά τις ὠκεῖα Μουσάων φάτις
> οἷάπερ ἵππων ἀμαρυγά.   925

> Nay, the voice of the Muses' is swift, in the manner of the flashing of horses' hooves.

Eliding together sound and motion in the conceit, the poet gives to the immortal voice the distinctive sparkle cognate with the 'twinkling' (μαρμαρυγή) that, from Homeric poetry on and through the lyric corpus, the choral dancer's rapid footwork and position changes emit, selecting out a property particularly well-suited to the genre of the hyporcheme from which his pastiche draws. Very much in the spirit of another Pindaric hyporcheme, the earlier explored fr. 107a S.-M., is the characterization of the horse as choral dancer, together with the also familiar substitution of the hooves for the choreute's sounding feet.

The closing of Aristophanes' *Lysistrata* supplies a fitting end to this sampling of the evidence insofar as it clearly points back to the text treated at this section's outset, Alcman's first *Partheneion*, as well as to Euripides'

---

[52] In a frustratingly vague reference to choral dancing in classical drama, Plutarch also notes the movements (*phorae*) executed by the dancers that culminate in representational positions or pauses called *schêmata* 'in which dancers compose their bodies in the attitude of Apollo or Pan or a Bacchant, and then retain that aspect like a figure in a picture' (*Quaest. conv.* 9.747c).

song in the *Helen* produced just one year earlier. In a call, most likely issued by the Spartan ambassador, to the Spartan chorus, the speaker summons the Muse while also addressing the dancers as the drama concludes (1296–315):

> Ταΰγετον αὖτ' ἐραννὸν ἐκλιπῶά,
> Μῶά μόλε, <μόλε,> Λάκαινα, πρεπτὸν ἁμὶν
> κλέωά τὸν Ἀμύκλαις σιὸν
> καὶ Χαλκίοικον Ἀσάναν,
> Τυνδαρίδας τ' ἀγασώς,   1300
> τοὶ δὴ πὰρ Εὐρώταν ψιάδδοντι.
> εἶα μάλ' ἔμβη,
> ὢ εἶα κοῦφα πᾶλον,
> ὡς Σπάρταν ὑμνίωμες,   1305
> τᾷ σιῶν χοροὶ μέλοντι
> καὶ ποδῶν κτύπος,
> <ὅχ'> ἆτε πῶλοι ταὶ κόραι
> πὰρ τὸν Εὐρώταν
> ἀμπάλλοντι, πυκνὰ ποδοῖν   1310
> ἀγκονίωαί,
> ταὶ δὲ κόμαι σείονται
> ἅπερ Βακχᾶν θυρσαδδωᾶν καὶ παιδδωᾶν.
> ἀγῆται δ' ἁ Λήδας παῖς
> ἀγνὰ χοραγὸς εὐπρεπής.   1315

Come back again from lovely Taygetus, Spartan Muse, and come, Laconian Muse, and in a manner befitting us, celebrate the god of Amyklai, and Athena of the brazen house and the noble sons of Tyndareos who sport alongside the Eurotas; hey there, step it up, hey, prance lightly, that we may hymn Sparta, which delights in choral dances in honour of the gods and the beat of feet and where beside the Eurotas, the maidens frisk like fillies, raising clouds of dust with their feet and their locks are tossed like those of bacchants who sport and ply the *thyrsos*. And they are led by Leda's daughter, the pure and comely chorus leader.

Bierl has documented the many elements, whether repeated diction, shared motifs or common sites and casts of characters both mythical and divine, that Aristophanes draws from Alcman, among them the prominent assimilation of the dancer to the horse,[53] but many of these features also belong to the broader set of representations of horses and fillies as choral dancers considered here: the focus on the hair/mane, the sound raised by

---

[53] Bierl 2011, 433–34.

the strike of the feet-turned-hooves, the presence of the river and the singling out of the pre-eminent animal and *chorêgos*. As in the previous instances too, the kernel of the equation between the horse and the dancer depends on the capacity for rapid movement, leaps and prances, albeit synchronized in the cohesive choral performance, that the filly possesses and that the chorus must here emulate. The visual evidence presented below confirms the kinetic properties highlighted in the textual representations as well as clearly delineating both the 'regulating' role of the *chorêgos* and the broader affinities between the make-up of the chorus and that of the equine herd.[54]

1.2 Choruses and Horses in the Visual Account

If poets composing songs for choruses find equines eminently 'good to think with', then artists of the archaic and classical periods (although this latter group to a lesser degree) also variously draw attention to the equivalence between horses and the performing groups. While others have explored vases that combine visual representations of the animals, both singly and as members of larger companies, with choral activity,[55] and have noted the ways in which the juxtaposition of the two motifs within a single image or through their spatial proximity on an object bear on social constructions of gender and most particularly of maidenhood and marriage, my discussion aims to present a more nuanced account of the evidence by setting it against the textual accounts just reviewed. Approached from this standpoint, we can see how these vessels invest the horse-choral dancer pairing with meanings that both correspond to and differ from those proposed in the verbal representations, which they both inform and draw on, and how, much like the written sources, these images evolve and change through time.

In keeping with the birds treated in the previous chapter, horses prove among the earliest and most commonplace figurative motifs introduced by vase painters, and regularly serve more as 'space fillers' than as active

---

[54] Absent from this discussion, in large part because it has received a recent detailed treatment in Weiss 2018, 211–24, is one further instance of a 'horse-chorus', to which the singers in Euripides' *IA* refer (1058–66), and which Weiss reads as a pointer towards the play's grim outcome and Iphigenia's wedding manqué. I would only add that the description of the 'horse-mounted *thiasos*' as it arrives at the wedding feast of Hippodameia, and its movement towards 'the mixing bowl of Bacchus' not only introduces a Bacchic and marriage-transgressing dimension to the occasion, but also styles the Centaur troupe a late-arriving *kômos* in search of drink. Consistent with this is the loud shout emitted by the newcomers (ἀνέκλαγον).

[55] Langdon 2008 offers the most extensive discussion.

players in the construction of the larger messages articulated by a vessel's iconographic programme and the 'cultural themes and social attitudes'[56] that it propagates. But, like the bird images too, some alignments and juxtapositions seemingly result from more conscious choices on their artists' part, and among these belongs the very earliest extant Argive depiction of a choral performance on a fragment of an unattributed Late Geometric krater of ca. 750–730 (fig. 4.0).[57] Here a man drives a bridled horse across what looks like a stone-strewn piece of ground (if that is what the dots indicate) with a water bird positioned to its left. Zigzag lines fill the space adjacent to the bird and beneath the horse's feet, perhaps a stylized representation of the body of water that the driver seeks to make it cross. Immediately above the horse, but in more diminutive form and located so

Fig. 4.0 Late Geometric krater from Argos, ca. 750–730 B.C.E. Argos, Archaeological Museum C 240. Photograph © École française d'Athènes à Argos, inv. C 240. Cliché 27380 EFA/Emile Sérafis.

---

[56] Hurwit 2002, 2.

[57] Argos, Archaeological Museum C 240; for discussion, see Moore 2004, 50 and Langdon 2008, 165–66.

as to correspond to the space between the horse's rump to just beyond the tip of its muzzle, a chorus of four women dances in a row; the figures wear short, multi-string belts, carry branches in their hands and move in the same direction as the animal. Various elements, figurative and non-figurative, link the different registers; a branch identical to those carried by the dancers rises from the top of the driver's head, and one of the two reins that extends from the man's hand to just below the horse's neck recalls the strings of the belts also pointing from left to right. The horse's spiky tail and the upright lines that form its mane further echo the design of the maidens' branches.

A different dimension of the parallelism depends on the artist's portrayal of the horse-driver, so positioned as to make him span the two scenes; not only do the figure's larger dimensions mean that he encompasses both, but the branch extending from his head ends just at the point where the final dancer's equivalent branch appears; also linking the two portions of the panel is one of the driver's reins, which describes a sinuous line whose topmost point almost forms the ground line for the feet of the same last dancer and whose rise and declivities suggest that the chorus members are likewise in motion. The man's involvement in both spheres and the common direction in which both the horse and maidens move allow him to fulfill two functions: not just the driver of the horse but also the one who directs the chorus. The etymology of χορηγός unites two separate notions pertinent to the combination of activities visible on the krater. Following Chantraine's discussion of words ending in -αγός and -ηγός, Calame comments that 'the evolution of the meaning of ἄγω, "to push", replaced by ἐλαύνω, "to lead", "to conduct", which then competes with ἡγέομαι, has resulted in a semantic contamination of the two terms'.[58]

To adopt the interpretation that Langdon suggests for this and several other Argive vases of the period, we might read the two images in tandem, and see in the driver's mastery of his rein-driven horse a pointer to the stage of life which will shortly claim the maiden dancers: performing in the choruses so characteristic of the lifestyle of *parthenoi* on the cusp of maturity, they are poised to enter the state of marriage with all the submission to male control that the transition entails. As Langdon remarks, 'the recurrent image of horse taming evokes a language of husbandry that is not

---

[58] Calame 1997, 44. For the chorus leader as the one who stands at the end of the line and drives the performers forward, we have Pollux's description of the choreography of the *geranos* in which, in his account, the chorus formed two lines, one behind the other, and at the end of each of the lines was a *chorêgos* (4.101). A *melos* can also be driven forward as in Pind. fr. 107a.3 S.-M., treated in Section 3.

meant for the horse alone'.[59] The artist's choice to depict an animal of unmistakably male gender poses no stumbling block to this reading: although we cannot assume a one-to-one equation between the dancing maidens and horse, mastering the latter requires the exercise of the proximate and sometimes coercive skills that the man must use in domesticating his bride.

The combination of horses and maiden dancers observed for the krater occurs not only in the Argive repertoire but on vessels from Mycenae too, and Langdon counts no fewer than eight instances of their joint appearance in Geometric vase painting.[60] A skyphos fragment of ca. 725–700 from the Argive Heraion makes the connection very clear (Fig. 4.1);[61] here a man leading a horse simultaneously stands at the head of a line of dancers, three still visible on the fragment; they are again dressed in long skirts, have multi-string belts and carry branches in their hands. The man's arms and hands are positioned so as demonstrate the analogous 'leading' role that he fulfills vis-à-vis both horse and maidens. Exactly like the dancers and perhaps modelling the gesture for the troupe, he holds his elbows crooked and hands pointing upward while simultaneously tugging with one hand on the muzzle of the horse and clasping the hand of the maiden at his right with the other.

Horses and choral dancers coincide elsewhere, although each artist chooses a different way of formulating their relations. The decorative scheme on a second Late Geometric krater, also from the Argive

Fig. 4.1 Skyphos fragment from the Argive Heraion, ca. 725–700 B.C.E. Cambridge, MA, Harvard Art Museums, Arthur M. Sackler Collection 1935.35.17. Photograph © President and Fellows of Harvard College.

---

[59] Langdon 2008, 164.   [60] Langdon 2008, 162.
[61] Cambridge, MA, Harvard Art Museums, Arthur M. Sackler Collection 1935.35.17.

Heraion,[62] emphatically reiterates the equine motif, surrounding a representation of maiden dancers with scenes of horses being led by men. On the bowl's upper register a large-sized horse appears, whose extended neck and head arch over the man who directs it towards the right; on the other side of a panel filled with diagonal zigzag lines, a virtual mirror image of this scene occurs, which again positions a man in front of a horse, which he now leads leftwards as though to meet his fellow driver. In the panel immediately below the first of these two horse leaders, maidens dressed in typical fashion, again with long skirts and stringed belts, dance in a line while joining hands; placed to the dancers' right and in a separate panel, a man stands between two horses which he holds by their bridles. These depictions of figures engaged in directing and controlling horses framing the choral dancers bring out at least partial analogies between the different activities: again, just as the animals are made to submit to the mastery of their male leaders, drivers and tamers, so too, perhaps, will the girls currently dancing without such 'leadership' in their chorus line (much as the horses in Anacreon fr. 346.7–8 *PMG* still do).

An outsized oinochoe (it measures some 78cm in height) found adjacent to a woman's grave at the southern end of the plain of Marathon (Fig. 4.2),[63] and also dated to the late eighth century, illustrates the interplay between choral dancing and horsemanship in particularly sustained fashion and introduces into its visual scheme a clear reference to the aftermath of the performances positioned above and below it. The vessel displays two sizable choruses, the first just below the lip, where forty girls and youths link hands and carry leafy boughs, the second around the bottommost band, where forty-three maidens perform a ring dance, also with their hands joined. Very unusual in the already standardized choral iconography is the stylized tree that appears at the midpoint of this second group and around which the figures circle. This tree motif recurs in one of the six figural panels on the midsection of the oinochoe (Fig. 4.3), where both members of a male-female pair hold a branch in one hand while from their other hands – these clasped together – a tree very similar in appearance to that shown in the choral scene seems to sprout. The circlet enclosing the figures' joined hands, as well as their gesture, declares their status as newlyweds, with the tree perhaps standing symbol for the fertility that their union will bring about.

---

[62] Argos, Archaeological Museum C 210, with illustration in Langdon 2008, fig. 3.17.
[63] Marathon, Archaeological Museum K2209, with full discussion in Vlachou 2016.

Fig. 4.2 Late Geometric giant pitcher from Marathon, ca. 720–700 B.C.E. Marathon, Archaeological Museum K2209. Photograph courtesy of Vicky Vlachou, used by permission of the Ephorate of Antiquities of Eastern Attica. © Hellenic Ministry of Culture, Education and Religious Affairs/Archaeological Receipts Fund.

Fig. 4.3 Line drawing of central frieze on giant pitcher from Marathon. Marathon, Archaeological Museum K2209. Drawing courtesy of Vicky Vlachou, used by permission of the Ephorate of Antiquities of Eastern Attica. © Hellenic Ministry of Culture, Education and Religious Affairs/Archaeological Receipts Fund.

Immediately adjacent to the bridal pair, a man astride a horse occupies a second panel. Like the couple, he too carries leafy boughs, one in each of his upraised hands. The painter offers two more iterations of the equine motif, the first in the form of the winged horse that appears in the third of the three panels on this side of the vase, the second on the opposite face, where a centaur, like the rider, is equipped with two branches. Through the repetition of these tree and branch motifs, the painter establishes visual parallels between riding, choral dancing and matrimony, a nexus whose elements appear in various combinations on other objects of the same period; so the artist of a black-figure oinochoe places a female dancing chorus around the pitcher's lip while decorating the body with four square panels, two of which show single horses, one a centaur with branches, and the fourth a female figure again equipped with branches and a wreath.[64] Viewed in its entirety, the Marathon oinochoe presents in schematic fashion a narrative programme that traces out the passage (perhaps that once performed by the occupant of the grave) from the state of maiden-hood, where a girl dances with her age mates in bucolic settings, to the mixed-cum-courtship dance following the moment when she becomes fully nubile, to the occasion of her marriage.[65]

The socio-cultural reading proposed above for the chorus/horse analogy is just one of several meanings that the pairing might in part convey. In other instances the focus falls not so much on the idea of 'taming' and acculturation but more, as in many of the poetic instances already cited, on the horse as exemplar of the motions that the dancing group performs as well as on its coordination, conditioning and beauteous adornment. On a potsherd from Argos, a horse's leg overlaps a dancer's skirt while another shows a dancer placed beneath a horse's neck.[66] On the Protoattic hydria by the Analatos Painter in Paris,[67] a mirroring relationship may exist between the orderly procession of two-horse chariots driven by standing male figures on the body of the vase and the mixed-gender chorus on the neck, also circling round the circumference with men alternating with the female dancers.

A troupe of animals, now complete with riders, can more exactly convey the regulated, disciplined motion likewise required of choristers. In one instance, a representation of choral *eutaxia* (to borrow a term used by Xenophon) also suggests that requisite masculine and civic value. The conical portion of the Protoattic 'Menelas' stand found on Aegina and probably by the Polyphemus Painter shows five men wearing white-dotted black mantles

---

[64] Athens, National Archaeological Museum 29838, with Vlachou 2016, 137.
[65] Cf. the shield of Achilles in *Iliad* 18, which includes three such interrelated scenes. Lucian (and several authors before him; see [Hes.] *Scut.* 272–79; Pl. *Leg.* 771e–772a) similarly regards such boy-girl choral dances as critical to the 'pairings off' that form the preliminaries to marriage; for this, see *Salt.* 12.
[66] Argos, Archaeological Museum C 4574; C 4168.　　[67] Paris, Musée du Louvre 2985.

Fig. 4.4 'Menelas Stand'; conical portion of the Protoattic 'Menelas Stand' from Aegina, ca. 680–650 B.C.E. Formerly Berlin, Antiquarium A 42. Illustration after *CVA* Berlin I, pl. 33.

over long patterned gowns walking with a measured step and equipped with spears in their hands (Fig. 4.4);[68] each has the identical, carefully arranged hairstyle held in place by a headband. Alongside one of the five the name Menelas appears. As Ferrari has demonstrated,[69] the inscription does not identify this individual as the Homeric hero; rather the choice of the Doric form (the dialect used in choral lyric) of Menelaus' name, and close parallels with other images from the Late Geometric period showing processions of men, sometimes clearly engaged in singing or accompanied by a musician (see below), allow us to recognize in the marchers members of a chorus and in the dipinto a suggestion of the words or subject of their song.

Immediately above this processional line the artist has filled a narrower zone with a frieze of horses goaded on by staff-carrying jockeys dressed in decorated fabrics. Each of the three still fully visible finely groomed horses has a luxuriant mane and advances with its legs extended so as to cover a space slightly larger than the men below; like the marchers' feet, the horses' hooves rest on the ground line demarcating this image from the one beneath. Inviting viewers to read the two registers together are the repeated figural and non-figural designs and motifs in each band. The goads carried

---

[68] Formerly Berlin, Antiquarium A 42, with discussion in Ferrari 1987.

[69] Ferrari 1987. While many subsequent discussions adopt Ferrari's suggestion, Immerwahr 1990, 10 n. 7 registers dissent.

by the riders echo the spears similarly held in each of the marchers' right hands, and the thick lock of hair hanging braid-like down each man's back offers a counterpart to the horse tails above; divided into three thick strands, the arrangement also replicates the design of the equine manes, these too carefully demarcated and extending over the horses' powerful chests, whose contours match those of the marchers below.

While Ferrari plausibly proposes that the stand was designed to serve as a 'commemorative piece' for a particular choral performance in the context of a civic festival (even the Panathenaia in her suggestion) and that the jockeys may be participants in the horse races that formed part of the agonistic programme, the choice to pair the procession of men with the riders would do more than supply a lasting snapshot of an actual event. That same combination reappears on a mid-sixth-century Attic black-figure cup-krater in Paris (Fig. 4.5),[70] where thirty-four well-dressed men, some with beards and some without, stand in a single file before an aulos-player, their choral character additionally confirmed by the dancing

Fig. 4.5 Attic black-figure krater by the BMN Painter, ca. 550 B.C.E. Paris, Musée du Louvre CA 2988. Photograph © RMN-Grand Palais (Musée du Louvre)/Hervé Lewandowski.

---

[70] Paris, Musée du Louvre CA 2988.

dolphins on the inside of the rim. On this occasion, riders fill the band beneath the marchers, moving in the opposite direction to those above, and with their mounts depicted in running motion, their bodies fully extended and front hooves off the ground. The parallels and distinctions between the two vessels offer a window into the meanings that the pairing of riders and masculine chorus members can carry. In both instances the equestrian scene supplies a reiteration of the elite activity already visible in the depiction of the richly dressed participants in the choral spectacle; the ownership of horses and mastery of riding skills are limited to those belonging to the upper social echelons, and participation in horse (and chariot) races, the top rank agonistic activities, further typifies aristocratic mores. On the Menelas stand, the artist proposes relations of equivalence between the stately motion of the men processing from left to right and the horsemen who also move with regimented step and regularity, advancing in the same direction at what is clearly a walking pace; on the cup, where indicators of a performance within a Dionysiac milieu appear and the procession may form part of the dithyramb staged by the chorus,[71] the riders' speed and the dynamism and the unchecked power of their mounts signal the more spirited and 'movemented' nature of celebrations on behalf of Dionysus whose presence the dancing dolphins also convey.

Two more images act by way of bridge, both chronologically and subject-wise, between the Menelas stand and the final vase considered here. First, a Siana cup in Amsterdam attributed to the Heidelberg Painter, dating to the second quarter of the sixth century (Fig. 4.6).[72] On the obverse face, a line of dancers dressed in long tunics with short chitons on top is positioned to the left and right of an aulete. While each of the chorus members also wears a cap equipped with ear flaps and a fillet picked out in white, the artist configures these headpieces differently: those of the three dancers on the left and the piper have two black horse ears rising from the headband, a feature missing from the caps of the triad on the right, who also perform a livelier step than their counterparts. As H. A. G. Brijder observes, the design of the ears resembles that of many satyrs, also equine in shape and similarly pointing backwards.[73]

A second image, a black figure hydria attributed to the Circle of the Lydos likewise dated to ca. 560 (Figs. 4.7, 4.8),[74] resembles the Amsterdam cup in many respects and further reinforces the 'equine' element that the Heidelberg Painter restricts to the headgear worn by just some of his chorus members.

---

[71] For discussion of the processional dithyramb, see Hedreen 2013.
[72] Amsterdam, Allard Pierson Museum 3356.   [73] Brijder 1986, 73 with parallels.
[74] New York, Metropolitan Museum of Art 1988.11.3. For detailed discussion, see Moore 2006.

Fig. 4.6 Attic black-figure Siana cup, ca. 560–550 B.C.E. Amsterdam, Allard Pierson Museum 3356. Photograph courtesy of the Allard Pierson Museum.

Fig. 4.7 Attic black-figure hydria attributed to the Circle of the Lydos, ca. 560 B.C.E. Shoulder detail. New York, Metropolitan Museum of Art 1988.11.3. Photograph © The Metropolitan Museum of Art, The Bothmer Purchase Fund, 1988.

The shoulder of the vase shows four male choristers facing an aulos-player who stands to their left; again the dancers, depicted with one foot raised in the air and their arms tucked up to their shoulders, wear fillets with horses' ears (the artist omits the second ear of each pair), this time painted in black. Picking up on the motif is the image that fills the body of the vase, where we see the departure of a hoplite walking behind his horse-mounted squire, who leads a second horse belonging to his master.[75] Beyond the presence of equine elements, the use of the same black, red and white colours to highlight details,

---

[75] Moore 2006, 36 notes how the slender legs and small hooves give the horse a 'dainty aspect'.

Fig. 4.8 Attic black-figure hydria attributed to the Circle of the Lydos, ca. 560 B.C.E. Body of vase. New York, Metropolitan Museum of Art 1988.11.3. Photograph © The Metropolitan Museum of Art, The Bothmer Purchase Fund, 1988.

and the decorative motifs that ornament the hoplite's armour, the horse's gear, the squire's cloak and the chitons worn by the dancers, one further detail suggests at least some continuity between the two scenes: corresponding to the horse ears topping the fillets is the mounted horse's topknot protruding from its head and the horsehair crest that decorates the hoplite's helmet.

Both images may be juxtaposed with a third and later representation exhibiting a still closer combination of chorus and riders. A well-known black-figure amphora in Berlin of ca. 550–540 attributed to the Painter of Berlin 1686 shows a formally dressed aulos-player on the left facing three men in horse costumes (their bearded faces still visible beneath their masks), each carrying another man on his shoulders (Fig. 4.9);[76] all three riders wear breastplates over short chitons and helmets with distinctive

---

[76] Berlin, Antikensammlung F1697; *ABV* 297.17, *Para.* 128. For discussion, see Hedreen 1992, 136–38, Osborne 2008, 403 and Rothwell 2007, 37–38.

Fig. 4.9 Attic black-figure amphora attributed to the Painter of Berlin 1686, ca. 550–540 B.C.E. Berlin, Antikensammlung F1697. Photograph © 2019. Scala, Florence/bpk, Bildagentur für Kunst, Kultur und Geschichte, Berlin.

crests, the first with upright donkey ears standing perpendicular to the wearer's head, the middle with a crescent-shaped, horn-like addition and the last with a circle intersected by four spokes. In between the riders and the piper is an inscription made up of the letters EIO together with mere squiggles, which may convey the sound of the song performed by the chorus, perhaps, appropriately, a kind of 'giddy up'.

A second choral event occupies the reverse of the amphora; here three naked ithyphallic satyrs and two maenads dressed in tight-fitted short tunics stand waiting in a single file for the satyr piper facing their company to give the signal to begin the performance. In addition to the obvious links between the images on the object's two sides (each shows figures in a line, uniform in their motions, and both groups confront an aulos-player), the satyr musician has the horse's legs that point back to the costumed figures on the obverse; where the chorus members can only dress like horses, and perform horse-like activities when they turn themselves into mounts, the Dionysiac aulete achieves a more-perfect hybridity, acquiring equine features and displaying that 'horsiness' frequently assigned to satyrs. In keeping with this occlusion between the real (or performative) realm and the more-imaginary world in which satyrs and maenads dwell, the five-strong chorus lacks all obvious signs of costuming.

While the amphora has generated a variety of readings, my concern is with the ways in which it recombines the riders, horses and chorus members shown separately on the Menelas stand, and whose affinities the

Amsterdam and New York vessels suggest in more muted fashion. In the first instance, choral participation in a civic ritual is depicted as belonging to the same sphere of activity and social stratum as equestrianism, with the horses reflecting the elite character of the chorus members, their good order, bodily conditioning and regulation. The spears the marchers carry also remind the viewer of their membership in the military ranks, whether the cavalry or hoplite line for which dancing in choruses can train a man. On the Berlin amphora, all these elements are scrambled so as to provide an image of the world 'turned upside down', as would suit a vase produced for the sympotic setting where just such inversions can occur. Within this bounded and demarcated 'other' space, adult men may abandon the erect posture that typifies the literally upstanding citizen and forfeit their very humanness along with their well-shaped physiques so as to take on the role of beasts of burden mounted by the more youthful riders, this itself a reversal of the usual hierarchical relations between adult and younger man. These riders are moreover anything but exemplars of skilled and well-ordered activity; they sit awkwardly on their 'horses' (the first in line seems particularly unsteady and might put a viewer in mind of a participant in those competitive sympotic games that required the symposiasts to stay upright and maintain their balance after a night of heavy drinking)[77] whose manes they hold with one hand – absent the bridles and reins frequently symbolic of progress to a more civilized state – while needing to balance themselves with the other arm raised behind. The projections from the helmets occur on a handful of Chalcidian and Corinthian helmets shown on vases from the sixth through to the fourth centuries, but perhaps the curious headdresses, one of which has animal ears pointing up between two curved horns, worn by the symposiasts reclining in the open air on a Heron Class black-figure skyphos from the Athenian agora of ca. 525–475, supplies a better parallel, and points us to the sympotic milieu framing the amphora chorus.[78]

In a discussion of the Berlin amphora and other images, Robin Osborne cautions against treating these scenes as reflections of actual practices;[79] rather, the artists may 'literalize' the similes and metaphors used by poets, and we should be cautious in assigning them the performative reality that the poetic compositions enjoyed. In considering these representations

---

[77] Cf. the black-figure amphora of ca. 540–530 by the Swing Painter showing five costumed men on stilts; a Centauromachy occurs on the other side (Christchurch, Logie Collection of the University of Canterbury 41.57; *Para.* 134.31 *bis*).

[78] Athens, Agora Museum P 32413 with discussion in Topper 2012, 44.

[79] Osborne 2008, esp. 402–13.

alongside the texts cited in this section's first half, the discussion has aimed to follow the interpretative route proposed by Osborne: what these images may chiefly be showing is the visual realization of the long-standing equation between choral singer-dancers and horses and equestrians that performances could further activate by means of the sounds and choreography integral to *choreia*.

2 Bovine Choruses

A Phoenician bronze bowl, reportedly found in Sparta and dated to the late eighth century (Fig. 4.10),[80] features two scenes whose elements at once recall the avian focus of the preceding chapter and introduce the second of the several paradigmatic choral groupings considered here. In the outermost of the two friezes in the bowl's interior, seven poloi-wearing women

Fig. 4.10 Interior of a Phoenician bronze bowl from the late eighth century. Paris, Musée du Louvre AO 4702. Drawing reproduced from R. Dussaud, 'Coupe de bronze chypro-phénicienne trouvée en Grèce', *ABSA* 37 (1936/1937): 94.

---

[80] Paris, Musée du Louvre AO 4702.

with the interlinked hands and synchronized movements suggestive of a choral ensemble move towards a seated goddess. Also taking part in the procession are four musicians, three playing lyre-like instruments, and several other female figures, some holding flowers and one with an outsized piece of cloth. A large-bodied crane appears between this cloth-carrier and the women making up the chorus. The innermost frieze shows six cattle circling around the floral element at the bowl's centre; together their processional movement, ring structure and the way in which each animal's horn seems to reach out so as to touch its neighbour's tail much as the dancers clasp their hands rework elements in the design of the surrounding scene, and position the cows as one among the tributes, together with the cloth and performance of music and dance, being offered to the goddess at this ritual event.[81]

The juxtaposition of choral activity with a troupe of bovines recurs on a near contemporary and more notional object, the Iliadic shield of Achilles whose scenes I have treated from a variety of perspectives in earlier parts of this study, and whose similarity to and possible modelling after Phoenician metal-work and its motifs discussions routinely acknowledge. Nearing the end of his description, the narrator pauses to detail three among the final bands forged by Hephaestus. In the first of the sequence, youths and maidens process in a line from the vineyard where the grapes stand ready to be harvested, skipping to the music and song supplied by a youthful lyre-player (*Il.* 18.567–72); in the second, cows are driven out to pasture by herdsmen and their dogs, their progress interrupted by an attack by two lions (573–86);[82] and closing out the triad is a full-scale choral performance, with youths and maidens as the dancers (590–604). Where the discussion in Chapter 1 called attention to the continuities between the several bands' structure and design, and suggested that the cows form part of a processional advance complete with choregic cowherds and dogs, here I would additionally note that, like the Phoenician metalworker, the Homeric poet has surrounded his bovines with occasions that include choral dancing. Indeed, for an audience familiar with epic diction and the traditional referentiality of its terms, the light bounds performed by the grape-pickers might even point forward to the subsequent appearance of the cattle; in a simile at *Od.* 10.410–14, the calves to whom Odysseus' men rejoicing at their leader's return are compared 'skip in roundabout fashion

---

[81] As Langdon 2008, 189–90 proposes, a Greek patron might have (mistakenly) seen in the combination of a line of cattle, a female chorus and an offering of a cloth a reference to events at the Argive Heraia, a festival that included maiden choral dancers, the sacrifice of the cattle that joined in the procession towards the altar and the presentation of a new robe to Hera, a ritual to which this section returns.

[82] A brief three-line description of a herd of 'white sheep' also out at pasture in the glens follows, reinforcing the animal motif.

all together' (περὶ … πᾶσαι ἅμα σκαίρουσιν, 410–12), encircling their mothers as they come back from grazing in the pasture.[83]

If neither the bowl nor Iliadic shield does much more than spatially to align a troupe of cows with choral activity, then the sources of the later archaic and early classical period would take up the pairing visible on these objects and propose fresh and narrower continuities between frequently youthful and typically maidenly chorus members and the animal group-ings. As the two texts selected here illustrate, and as this chapter's intro-duction already noted, where horses typically supplied positive paradigms whom the singer-dancers in the here-and-now may take as their models, assimilation with cows works in more variegated and even negative fashion;[84] for *choreia* to fulfill its normative functions in ritual and civic contexts, a group may have to cast off the bovine identity whose initial assumption signals its alienation from its proper cohesion-building role.

2.1 *Bacchylides 11.40–112*

Bacchylides' eleventh ode, composed on behalf of Alexidamus from the southern Italian city of Metapontion, the victor in the boy's wrestling event at Delphi,[85] exhibits an unusually dense structure that encompasses three interconnected myths. My reading is principally concerned with the most extended of these narratives, which tells the tale of Proitus' daughters, their initial offence against Hera, their punishment and their subsequent release from their maddened condition following their father's supplication of Artemis (40–112). Others have traced the dense relations between this story and its epinician frame, demonstrating the many verbal and thematic echoes that tie the narrative of the Proitids to the other mythical accounts in the ode, and also much explored is the idiosyncratic quality of Bacchylides' version of the girls' punishment, and its overlaps with and deviations from other extant sources.[86] Unique to the ode's account is the omission of the seer Melampous, who more regularly performs the thera-peutic intervention here assigned in part to Proitus, Artemis' own starring role in effecting the cure and her curious exchange of prerogatives with

[83] Note too how at *Od.* 10.413 the calves, lowing all the while, 'run around' (μυκώμεναι ἀμφιθέουσι) the maternal cows. The intimation of dancing bovines would find its full realization in Theoc. *Id.* 6.45, where, at the sound of the pipes and syrinx, the calves in the herdsmen's care instantly begin to dance.
[84] See too the portrayal of Deianeira as heifer in Soph. *Trach.* 530, with discussion in Chapter 10.
[85] The date of the victory is unknown.
[86] For good discussions, see Carey 1980, Seaford 1988, Dowden 1989, 73–95, Cairns 2005 and 2010, 268–99, Kowalzig 2007, 268–97; my reading variously draws on these several accounts.

Hera and the departure from the (prototypical) dénouement of the story found in other versions, where two of the Proitids are married off to Melampous and to his brother Bias. As discussions of the conduct and characterizations of the Proitids further demonstrate, Bacchylides' account – like that of later sources – shares much with more familiar Dionysiac myths concerning women, whether the daughters of Cadmus or those of Minyas, who, following their rejection or disparagement of the god, are afflicted with madness, abandoning their homes and cities to engage in maenadic-type activities in the mountains.

In keeping with this chapter's larger theme, my discussion focuses on the marked bovine presence and assimilation of the Proitids to a herd of cows in Bacchylides' piece (this consonant with other versions of the story) and aims to trace the relations between this 'cow-centrism' and a different element also privileged in the song, chorality. *Choreia* informs the ode in three principal respects. First, as my account illustrates, Bacchylides depicts the Proitids both implicitly and explicitly as a both normative and, at times, distorted choral collective; second, side by side with the maiden group are the several other choruses within the piece, some in its mythical portions and others in the epinician frame; and third, recoverable from the narrative are exchanges and correspondences between these internally evoked performers and the choreutes presenting the current work, whose motions and formations might take their cue from the events that their words describe. The Proitids' likeness to and even assimilation with the bovine herd interacts with these several elements and bears directly on the chorus' self-referentiality and its moments of choral projection.

The choral motif declares itself very early on. Following an opening invocation to the goddess Nike, Bacchylides observes hymnal and epinician convention in making the deity sponsor for the current citywide celebrations (9–14):[87]

σέθεν δ' ἕκατι
καὶ νῦ[ν Μετ]απόντιον εὐγυίων κ[ατέ]χουσι νέων   10
κῶμοί τε καὶ εὐφροσύναι θεότιμον ἄστυ·
ὑμνεῦσι δὲ Πυθιόνικον παῖδα θαητ[ὸ]ν Φαΐσκου.

[87] Heath and Lefkowitz 1991, 190 see this as a reference not to the current performance but to the more generalized context that frames it. But as Cairns 2010 *ad* 11–12 notes, the fact that these revellers are singing in praise of Alexidamus unmistakably unites the description within the lines with the ongoing ode. Bacchylides further equates the two, as Cairns suggests, by embedding the victory announcement within the account of the songs of the *kômoi*, the point I go on to develop.

By your favour now the *kômoi* and festivities of fine-limbed youths prevail in Metapontion, the god-honoured city; they sing in praise of a victor at the Pythian games, the resplendent son of Phaiscus.

The lines read very much like a self-reflexive description of the actual performance that has just begun. *Kômos* is not just the term regularly deployed by Bacchylides and Pindar for the group that sings and dances the ode, but the revellers' activity and the nature of their song further equates them with the chorus members visible to the audience: like the Bacchylidean celebrants, they sing a *hymnos* in praise of Alexidamus' win and one which includes the information that the encomion-in-performance must supply, an embedding that allows the poet to assign delivery of the chief of his 'required elements' to the singers internal to his verse. In the sample of the komasts' song of praise relayed here, the proclamation of the site of the win and name of the victor's father reproduce the contents of the victory announcement originally pronounced by the sacred herald at the games as the athlete stepped up to claim his prize, the moment now re-enacted in the epinician song. As Bacchylides' chorus adds its voice to this expanding sequence of re-articulations of the *angelia*, it echoes and amplifies the critical information, further diffusing Alexidamus' renown. Self-referentiality and self-projection onto the Metapontine komastic groups may also determine the choice of adjective for the youthful revellers: drawing attention to the body part most important for the chorister, 'fine-limbed' simultaneously highlights the current performers' corresponding agility. This exemplary chorus of youths furnishes the paradigm from which the ensemble of Proitid *parthenoi* will, until the ending of their tale, so sharply deviate.

A second, more oblique glance to choral dancing occurs in the first epode, here alongside the first sounding of the bovine motif. Immediately following mention of Alexidamus' return to his 'heifer-raising (πορτιτρόφον) Italian homeland' (30) comes the balancing epithet that qualifies the place where the youth has scored his many victories, the 'land of fine choruses/dancing spaces' (χθονὶ καλλιχόρῳ, 32). As Jebb noted,[88] among the reasons for accepting the textual supplement Ἰταλίαν (Platt) in the first of the two phrases is the implicit presence of cows in the toponym, which revisits the adjective just used: Bacchylides may be playing on a popular etymology that derived *Italia* from ϝιταλός, 'ox' or 'calf'. The second noun-epithet phrase has a more general frame of reference that can encompass both Delphi, the site of the most recent win, and,

---

[88] Jebb 1905 *ad loc.*

perhaps, the victor's native ground. Set within the performative frame, it both freshly calls attention to Bacchylides' chorus members' participation in this tradition of 'fair-dancing' that links the southern Italian city with the Greek homeland and gestures to the site of the performance, the space set aside for the dance-and-song.

Further on in the epode a second divine presence appears, Artemis, whose favour both Alexidamus and his city enjoy. Typically, a relative pronoun supplies the pivot from the goddess in her tutelary role to her participation in the first of the myths. Beginning – as so many epinician narratives do – with the moment that marks the culmination of the story about to be narrated, Bacchylides' singers recall how it was for Artemis that 'the son of Abas once founded an altar for many supplications, along with his fine-robed daughters'.[89] Moving ever further back in time, the poet then recounts the starting point of the tale, the Proitids' disparagement of Hera, the punitive madness she inflicts on them and their departure from their father's house and city, Tiryns. Even in this introductory portion, Bacchylides intimates the maidens' affinity with cattle: in what also acts as a nod to Hera's role as goddess of marriage, the one who 'yokes', and as an indication of the goddess' curious departure from her wonted activity insofar as she diverts the girls from the marital trajectory over which she normally presides,[90] the divinity is imagined 'yoking' (ζεύξασ', 46) the Proitids to their alienating madness.

Consonant with this suggestion of Proitus' daughters' now-animalized status is the description of the maidens as they flee to the mountains at the second strophe's end: they depart 'emitting terrible cries' (σμερδαλέαν φωνὰν ἱεῖσαι, 56). Like several other sources that pre- and postdate Bacchylides, the poet gestures towards what some Latin authors would explicitly record: the girls' belief that they had become cows or their actual transformation into the animals. Where Bacchylides' Proitids do no more than utter possibly beast-like sounds, in the [Hesiodic] *Catalogue* their bovine aspect depends on the disfigurement that Hera brings about: 'for onto their heads she poured a dread itch, for a scabby illness (ἀλφός) seized hold of all their skin' (fr. 133 M.-W.). Defined as 'leprosy' by Philodemus

---

[89] As Carey (1980, 236) points out, Bacchylides postpones alerting us to the reason for the dedication of the altar until the very close of the myth, before detailing its further relevance to the current victory.

[90] As noted above, and in a point developed in other readings, there is a simultaneous exchange and overlap of roles between Hera and Artemis. Where Hera, already designated in her conjugal capacity at the 'wife of Zeus', has driven the girls into the wilds where Artemis Agrotera more naturally presides, Artemis as Hemera brings them back, taming them in preparation for the marital rite which lies in Hera's domain.

(*De pietate* B 6529–33 Obbink), this skin disease causes a white blotchiness that, as commentators note, would give the Proitids the appearance of dappled cows. The merely implicit assimilation in the Greek sources would be spelled out by Servius; commenting on the maidens' mental delusion in his note on Vergil's *Eclogue* 6.48, he describes how Hera makes the girls think themselves cattle and depart for the woodland pastures uttering moos and 'fearing the yoke' (*illa irata hunc errorem earum inmisit mentibus, ut se putantes uaccas in saltus abirent et plerumque mugirent et timerent aratra*). The grammarian Probus' remarks on the line in the *Eclogues* follow the same version of the tale: in his citation of [Hesiod]'s fr. 133 M.-W., Proitus' daughters leave Argos because they thought themselves cows.[91]

As discussions also observe, the 'logic' of the affinity becomes more apparent in light of the rituals celebrated on behalf of Hera at the Argive Heraion, a cult site not only located in Proitus' original home and that he supposedly took over when he moved to Tiryns, but one that, almost equidistant between the two cities, historically served both communities. White cows figured prominently in the great procession that made its way from Argos to the sanctuary on the occasion of the goddess' festival, when the priestess would be taken to the shrine in a wagon drawn by a brace of the animals; several descriptions of the *pompê* additionally mention the presence of white heifers for sacrifice while white-clad maidens also process.[92] Scattered in the ancient visual and textual sources are some suggestions that maiden choruses also played a role in the celebrations.[93] The surest pointer is a passage in Euripides' *Electra* (173–80), where the parthenaic chorus invites the drama's heroine to join with the other Argive maidens in their processional departure for the shrine, a summons refused by Electra on account of her want of the finery required to participate in choral dancing (οὐδ' ἱστᾶσα χορούς, 178). A series of vase fragments from the Heraion dated to the Geometric period depict choruses of female figures, but there is no determining whether the participants are girls or

---

[91] See Dowden 1989, 94–95.

[92] See Seaford 1988, 122–23, Kowalzig 2007, 280. Ovid, *Amores* 3.13 describes a festival of Juno at Falerii where there are white heifers for sacrifice and maidens 'veiled in white clothes in the ancient Greek fashion'; Ovid also comments that the style or look (*facies*) of the procession is Argive; as Seaford 1988, 122 notes of Seneca, *Med.* 364–66, the dramatist 'combines the themes of freedom from the yoke, sacrifice, marriage and the whiteness of the cattle in the context of Argive Hera', going on to conclude that the white-robed Argive maidens in procession to the Heraion seem associated with white unyoked cattle. For a further explicit conjunction of 'slayings of cows' and 'sacred maiden dances', see Eur. fr. 370.77–80 K. discussed in Chapter 6.

[93] For more detailed discussion, see Calame 1997, 119–20; see too Chapter 5.

older women.[94] Finally, Dionysius of Halicarnassus compares a rite celebrated on Hera's behalf complete with epichoric maiden choruses singing hymns at Falerii to the Argive festival, but does not detail where the specific correspondences lie (*Ant. Rom.* 1.21.2; see too n. 93).

In describing the girls' flight to the wild spaces of the woods (a visualization that returns in similar terms on two later occasions, at 83–84 and 93–94), the Bacchylidean singers not only depict the Proitids in the likeness of a Dionysiac-type *thiasos* uttering ritual cries as it heads for the unacculturated spaces beyond the civic realm, but use vocabulary that bears on the maidens' chorus-like conduct. Commentators variously interpret the meaning of line 54, in which Hera casts into the Proitids' hearts 'a thought that turned them round' (παλίντροπον ... νόημα). For Herwig Maehler and Douglas Cairns,[95] the νόημα describes the madness that drives the girls from their home; but objecting that the spatial sense of the adjective would then logically indicate the maidens' return to their father's house, Richard Seaford understands Hera as reversing that intention, and impelling the Proitids to adopt the contrary course that is her alienating design.[96] A focus on the 'kinetic' dimension of the adjective yields a different interpretation of the phrase, and suggests that this 'back-turning' thought finds realization in a more literal turnabout, a movement in which the maidens reverse their previous trajectory and circle about.[97] Accompanying their gyrations with terrible vociferations, the Proitids engage in a distorted version of the ring dance that maiden choruses most regularly stage.

Postponing the sequel to the Proitids' youthful folly until the return to the story at the end of the second epode (see below), the song then segues from the girls' departure from Tiryns into its second narrative, this nested in the more extended Proitid myth. Taking a fresh step back in time, the poet rehearses the catalyst for Tiryns' foundation, the quarrel between Proitus and his brother Acrisius, for which Bacchylides is our earliest extant source. In lines 64–67, the poet briefly sketches in the origins of the dissension (a version that may deliberately suppress some of the darker elements in the story found in later sources):

---

[94] Argos, Archaeological Museum C 229.   [95] Maehler 1982–97 *ad loc.*, Cairns 2010 *ad loc.*
[96] Seaford 1988, 119.
[97] A parallel to this 'back-turning' has already occurred in the first antistrophe in the context of the victor's own unfortunate reversal. An earlier defeat at the Olympic games is here ascribed to some kind of irregularity in the judgement. Had someone not 'diverted the path of justice from the straight' (δίκας κέλευθον / εἰ μή τις ἀπέτραπεν ὀρθᾶς, 26–27), Alexidamus' return home on that occasion would have been every bit as glorious as his current advent.

νεῖκος γὰρ ἀμαιμάκετον
βληχρᾶς ἀνέπαλτο κασιγνητοῖς ἀπ' ἀρχᾶς   65
Προίτῳ τε καὶ Ἀκρισίῳ·
     λαούς τε διχοστασίαις
ἤρειπον ἀμετροδίκοις μάχαις τε λυγραῖς.

For a quarrel not to be resisted had leapt up from a small beginning
between the brothers Proitus and Acrisius, and they had been ruining the
people with lawless feuds and dismal battles.

As Cairns' account well brings out,[98] multiple points of contact link this
mini-myth to both the framing Proitid narrative and Alexidamus' career.
But visible here too is a fresh expression of what the maidens' story already
intimated, the presence of a series of negative choral paradigms internal to
the ode, which act as foils for the current performance and the more
regularized ritual to which the poem will ultimately tie it. The term chosen
for the dissension, διχοστασία (uniquely in the plural here), occurs several
times in the context of civil strife in the sixth-century elegiac poets and
gives what begins as a fraternal conflict broader political and citywide
implications. But the expression also carries choral associations, sounding
a theme common in lyric and later sources, which regularly link correctly
functioning *choreia* and civic good order. Derived from the root of the verb
ἵστημι, the second element in διχοστασία can have both a transitive and
intransitive sense, most usually meaning the act of 'setting up, establishing',
but also cognate with 'standing, stature, station, position'; as previously
noted, in phrases such as χορούς ἱστάναι, it serves as the technical term for
the institution or formation of a chorus. Stasis can also occur in other
compound forms, again with choral connotations that encompass
a political meaning. In Aeschylus' *Suppliants*, the Danaid choristers address
their father – who explicitly dictates their movements and actions and,
outside the fictional world of the drama, serves as *chorêgos* – as στασίαρχος
(11),[99] a designation that reworks one of the elements in another expression for the chorus-leader already found in Alcman, [χο]ροστάτις (fr. 1.84
PMGF). A paraphrase offered by the scholion describes Danaus as ὁ τῆς
συστάσεως ἄρχων, and the term σύστασις occurs in tragedy of individuals
forming collectives, in one instance explicitly circular (Eur. *Andr.*

---

[98] Cairns 2005.

[99] As Kavoulaki 2011, 374 points out, 'ἄρχω – ἀρχός (the second element in *stasi-archos*) is
equivalent to ἄγω – ἀγός (the second part of the compound χοραγός/χορηγός) and both stems
can express the aspect of command and leadership'. For more on the Danaids, see Chapter 5.

1088–89); the noun can also refer to a group that stands juxtaposed with or in opposition to another.

In his discussion of the patterns of division within a choral grouping, Gregory Nagy suggests a compelling means of uniting the two very different areas to which *stasis* belongs, one pertaining to choruses, the other to community conflict: 'I would argue that *stasis* in the negative sense of "conflict" is a metaphor ... for the ritualised interpersonal divisions that are acted out in the process of establishing or constituting choral performances; this constitution is in turn achieved through the literal divisions into which chorus members are systematically assigned when the chorus was organised'.[100] This well explains the term chosen by Bacchylides, which presents the feuds that divide citizens as occasions in which groups of individuals 'stand apart' or in opposition to one another. Once again, we might, perhaps, imagine a correspondence between the Bacchylidean singers' diction and their ongoing performance, even a self-reflexive element; a particular dance motion or divided choral formation might create its own suggestive representation of the moment of separation that stands in contrast to the refashioned communal unity, expressed through a second use of ἵστημι that Bacchylides reserves for the ode's end.

The singers' return to the Proitid myth is neatly orchestrated, with Tiryns, Proitus' new foundation, serving as the point from which the 'black-haired untamed (ἄδματοι) daughters rushed away and fled' (82–84). This passing reminder of the maidens' likeness to a herd of cattle – the term ἀδμής belongs exclusively to the unwed girl and unbroken animal – is coupled with the second statement of the fact of their flight. The third evocation of the period that the Proitids spend in the wilds in the next strophe fills out the account: 'for full thirteen months they wandered about the dusky woods and fled through the whole of sheep-nourishing Arcadia' (92–94).[101] Later sources detail what occurred in these uncultivated and/or pastoral spaces, and while we cannot know whether Bacchylides and his audience would have been familiar with other versions of events, or the degree to which these result from subsequent cross-contaminations between the Proitid story and different, often Dionysus-centred resistance myths, the ode's threefold evocation of this liminal period gives it a particular narrative weight. Our fullest description of what transpired

---

[100] Nagy 1990, 366–67.

[101] Several commentators point to the Dionysiac elements in these accounts, but Dowden 1989, 90 also suggests a ritual significance to the 'thirteen months' in which the maidens occupy the liminal realm before their reintegration at Lousoi; if the myth found its re-enactment in ritual form, then 'the year of the Proitids' myth denotes a status lasting from one festival to the next'.

during the time belongs to Apollodorus, who draws on a medley of sources
to cobble together a tale in which Melampous plays a central role: following
the worsening of the maidens' malady and the compact Melampous made
with Proitus, the seer 'with the help of the most able-bodied youths pursued
the women with shouting (ἀλαλαγμοῦ) and a sort of possessed dancing
from the mountains into Sikyon' (2.29.1).[102] In Ken Dowden's view,
'shouting and dancing by youths implies a dance-group, a chorus of male
age-group corresponding to our maidens preparing for marriage',[103] and
he reads Apollodorus' phrase describing the youths' dance, τινος ἐνθέου
χορείας, as the author's attempt to gloss a technical term that described this
particular form of *choreia* no longer familiar to him or to his readers.[104]
Also significant is the detail that Apollodorus includes concerning the
corresponding behaviour of the girls: they were 'running through the
deserted places in a manner entirely disorderly' (μετ' ἀκοσμίας ἁπάσης
διὰ τῆς ἐρημίας ἐτρόχαζον, 2.27.3). Properly executed, choral dancing is
distinctly orderly and *eukosmia* even characterizes the performance of
Euripides' chorus of Bacchants (*Bacch.* 693; cf. the distinction between
'noble' dances, characterized by *kosmos*, and 'shameful ones' that lack the
property at Athen. 14.628d).[105]

Absent any indication of an actual hunt or pursuit in Bacchylides'
narrative,[106] and the poem's focus simply on the fact of flight (φεῦγον is
repeated three times, on each occasion in verse-initial position), there are
scant grounds for suggesting that the ode evokes a type of ritual re-
enactment of the mythical events in the form of a choral *agôn* between
two rival groups of singing, dancing choristers, one made up of youths, the
other of maidens, which Apollodorus' account more readily accommodates. And while running, racing and pursuit are integral to several initiation rituals, and the visual record offers multiple instances of maidens

---

[102] As Seaford 1988, 134–35 observes, this is a corruption of the *ololugê* appropriate for sacrifice;
the *alalagê* is masculine and martial in character, often a cry of triumph in warfare, and forms
part of the maidens' assumption of the male, active role as hunters/hoplites. It is also worth
observing the equine analogy that other versions of the myth include; according to Serv. *ad*
Verg. *Ecl.* 6.48, two of the Proitids are named Lysippe and Hipponoe, while [Hes.] fr. 37.13 M.-
W. describes Bias as 'horse-tamer' (ἱππόδαμος).

[103] Dowden 1989, 86: 'To lead this chorus, to be its *exarchos*, would be the sort of distinction
amongst one's contemporaries . . . This is the position Melampous reflects, probably having
displaced a local figure . . . If the female group is "mad", then they too are a chorus performing
a corresponding wild and noisy dance'.

[104] Dowden 1989, 86.

[105] But note Budelmann and Power 2015, whose discussion I cited in Chapter 3.

[106] Kowalzig 2007, 281 assumes a hunt, but nothing in the language of the ode or even the
characterization of Artemis, so regularly described as huntress, points to this.

whose action can be read either as running or dancing sometimes in the context of a pursuit scenario,[107] Bacchylides' Proitids simply 'wander about' (ἠλύκταζον, 93) during their period of alienation.[108]

But parthenaic initiation rites bear on the Proitids' behaviour in another respect. As events at the Arkteia celebrated on behalf of Artemis at Brauron and Mounychia, where maidens styled *arktoi* or Bears 'share the animal-esque resonances of the Proitids',[109] attest, emulation of or assimilation to an untamed animal is integral to the actions in which girls engage as they pass from one age state to another. Our sources emphasize the premarital character of these ritual role-playings and their direct relation to a girl's readiness for marriage, explaining how, in the view of the ancient sources, participation in such rites acts in a cathartic manner, which effectively 'releases them from savagery' before marriage (Bekker, *Anecd. Gr.* i.445; Σ *ad* Theoc. *Id.* 2.66).[110] As Bacchylides will similarly make clear in the resolution of the story at Lousoi, this prenuptial dimension has a distinctly civic aspect, preparing the youthful initiates for their role as wives and mothers of the citizens of the polis overseeing the occasion. According to the report in the *Suda* concerning the rites at Brauron, 'the Athenians voted that no maiden could be married unless she had been a bear for the goddess'.[111]

The Arkteia again proves relevant to the events that Bacchylides positions at the end of the Proitid myth, where the ode also includes a final and emphatic restatement of the bovine and chorality motifs and their inter-connections. After Proitus' self-purification in the waters of the 'fair-flowing Lousos' where, in a moment suggestive of Bacchylides' knowledge of the skin-whitening disease suffered by the Proitids cited by the [Hesiodic] *Catalogue*, the king washes his skin (95–98), he calls on Artemis 'to lead out (ἐξαγαγεῖν) his children from wretched, insane frenzy' (102–03). Audible in the verb, as Anne Pippin Burnett and Seaford note, is the 'leading off' so frequently performed by the groom as he claims his bride in marriage (e.g. *Il.* 13.379, Pind. *Pyth.* 9.123, Eur. *IA* 693), and Seaford further comments of the term that it intimates the girls' passage from maidenhood to the state of wife, while also making Artemis – and not Hera, as we would expect – responsible for that transition.[112] The nod to

---

[107] A point taken up in Chapters 2 and 5.
[108] Although discussions of the myth regularly cite the Agrionia at Orchomenos – a ritual re-enactment of the tale of Minyas' daughters who offended Dionysus, went mad and were pursued either by other maenads or their husbands – in the context of the Proitid story, Bacchylides' 11 conforms to this tale only in the broadest sense.
[109] Kowalzig 2007, 283.   [110] Cited by Seaford 1988, 121.
[111] Again noted in Seaford 1988, 122.   [112] Burnett 1985, 112; Seaford 1988, 120.

marriage is also entirely apposite if, as suggested above, the king's ablutions are a reworking of the Proitids' own therapeutic bath after their disfigurement. The bathing serves more than a purely curative end (and several places in the Peloponnese claimed the privilege of being the site where the healing occurred); it is also prenuptial and a marker of the girls' belated submission to Hera.[113]

But there may be a further significance to the 'leading out'. As Kowalzig nicely expresses it, the transformation of the Proitids and arrival at Lousoi marks the 'time for the girls to cease their existence as a troupe of wild animals and to change into a cast of choral dancers. Artemis' part . . . is to put the libertine maidens into a well-ordered choral formation – to change the beasts into the sacred herd belonging to the goddess'.[114] The verb chosen by Bacchylides would suit this reading of Artemis' role, and make her intervention still more specifically 'choral'. The notion of 'leading out' proves critical to the action of the *chorêgos* or *exarchôn*, the latter the term chosen by Hesychius for the individual who initiates the choral performance and gives the signal for the dance-and-song to begin.[115] A scholion to *Od.* 6.244 introduces a verb very similar to Bacchylides' by way of preface to a citation of Alcman's fr. 81 *PMGF*, albeit with the preposition changed; according to the ancient commentator, the poet/*chorêgos* had his ensemble deliver the quoted line while he was 'leading in' (εἰσάγων) the *parthenoi*. Bacchylides' formulation, which may deliberately conflate a marital and choral meaning, positions Artemis in a very customary role, as leader of the choral group, on some occasions made up of mountain-dwelling nymphs, on others of the Muses and Graces. For a full representation of Artemis as *chorêgos*, there is the visualization in the longer of the goddess' two *Homeric Hymns*, where, following her appearance as huntress, she travels to Delphi in order to lead the dance (ἐξάρχουσα χορούς, 27.18; cf. *HHAp.* 194–99 and *Od.* 6.101–06). In leading the Proitids out of their frenzied state – this complete with the disorderly motions described by Apollodorus – Artemis takes her place as the conductor and organizer of the group that assumes a likeness to these more normative and paradigmatic choruses.

---

[113] Larson 2001, 115.

[114] Kowalzig 2007, 282 somewhat questionably assumes that the 'sacred herd' referred to by Polybius at 4.18.10–12 and 4.19.4–5 should be viewed as the permanent herd pastured at Artemis' shrine. But Sinn 1992 argues that this just refers to the practice of placing cattle under the protection of the goddess as a temporary expedient when the animals risked being carried off by enemy troops.

[115] Hesych. s.v. χορηγός. See Calame 1997, 43 and 1983, 563.

Critical to the Proitids' change of state is, of course, the sacrifice that Proitus promises to Artemis, the 'twenty red-haired unyoked (ἄζυγας) oxen' (104–05) that he will offer up in thanks for his daughters' release from their frenzy. Seaford and Kowalzig both identify the cattle as a substitutional sacrifice;[116] as counterparts to the 'untamed' (ἄδματοι) maidens to whom the cattle clearly correspond, this offering plays the same role fulfilled by the animal stand-ins for virgin sacrifices to Artemis at the Arkteia and elsewhere, while also functioning as the *proteleia*, or preliminary sacrifice before marriage.[117] But this forms only one part of the thanks rendered to the goddess; in Kowalzig's formulation, the girls' wild and untamed aspect is 'given for the deity's consumption',[118] while their now-tamed condition makes them ripe for participation in the choral dances that they go on to institute on Artemis' behalf as the poem moves out of the world of myth and into that of current ritual practice (110–12):

τοὶ δ' αὐτίκα οἱ τέμενος βωμόν τε τεῦχον,   110
χραῖνόν τέ μιν αἵματι μήλων καὶ χοροὺς ἵσταν γυναικῶν.

> And they straightaway made her a precinct and altar and stained it with the blood of sheep and established choruses of women.

While the 'blood of sheep' must correspond to the reality of the present-day rite, where participants sacrifice sheep in place of the cattle given by Proitus as expiatory payment for his daughters, the choral dances supply their own corresponding form of tribute and 'corrective' to the Proitids' distorted *choreia* earlier in the song. The emphatic γυναικῶν at the antistrophe's end, as Cairns points out,[119] marks the girls' transition from their earlier parthenaic stage (so designated at 47–48) to full-grown status and suggests that the choral dances still celebrated at Lousoi, and attested by the presence of terracotta dancing groups found at the sanctuary,[120] were performed by adult women as well as unwed maidens. Just as choral projection marked the opening of the ode, so it occurs anew at its close, but with a difference. Whereas the *kômoi* singing and dancing in praise of Alexidamus perform on this single occasion, now the Bacchylidean choristers, in a fashion visible also in the poet's Ode 13,[121] equate their activity with that of more regular standing choruses celebrating Artemis at her

---

[116] Seaford 1988, 123, 124; Kowalzig 2007, 281 notes the parallel with Iphigenia, also replaced by an animal.
[117] Seaford 1988, 119.   [118] Kowalzig 2007, 283.   [119] Cairns 2010 *ad loc.*
[120] See Jost 1985, 421 for these.   [121] For more on this piece, see Chapter 5.

festivals, choruses that, moreover, have their antecedents in the venerable and atemporal mythical world.

But the projection involves a further element. Insofar as the initial performers in the dances were the Proitids themselves, and the present-day participants assume the role of these originary dancers, Alexidamus' celebrants also become one with, or project their identity onto, this mythical group, whose praise of Artemis to whom the *laudandus* owes thanks for his win forms a piece with the Proitids' song of gratitude for an earlier divine benefaction.[122] These choral rituals at Lousoi may, perhaps like the performance of Bacchylides' choristers, have included some kind of ritual re-enactment of the myth, even the maidens' assumption of the bovine elements in the Proitids' behaviour. In Dowden's attractive reconstruction, much like the girls in the Attic Brauronia who, dressed in their saffron robes, assume the role of bears, so the Tyrnithian girls who danced at Lousoi change 'audibly and visibly into dappled cows afflicted with blotchy skin disease, using daub to white themselves out'.[123] Among the functions that Artemis fulfills at Lousoi are indications of the parallelism between her roles in regard to the young and to cattle: now styled θεροσκόπος (107) in Bacchylides' ode, she is also implicitly *kourotrophos*, an identity revealed by the nature of the votive offerings at the shrine.[124]

In the reparation of the earlier disorderly choruses effected by the closing of the victory song, the poet once again selects standard terminology for the institution or setting up of a chorus, χορούς ἵσταν (112), a phrase that glances briefly back to the moment of civic-cum-choral διχοστασία earlier described. Whereas in that portion of the myth a family dispute threatened the destruction of communal activity and provoked the division of citizens into rival and contending groups that ended in the dissolution of the original civic collective, the establishment of rites on behalf of Artemis offers a paradigm for the re-formation of social bonds.[125] If the parthenaic choral performers at Lousoi are participating in some kind of 'coming out' ceremony, then marriage between members of

---

[122] Cairns 2010 *ad* 112 notes the connection between the resolution of the Proitid myth and 'the joyful *kômoi* in honour of the victory that Alexidamus owes to Artemis'.
[123] Dowden 1989, 82 and 88 cites by way of analogy the 'sooty' men in the Agrionia.
[124] As the goddess' tutelary role vis-à-vis the youthful Alexidamus demonstrates, she also plays this role in Metapontion.
[125] Other repeated diction ties together this moment with the earlier myth: Proitus' supplication of Artemis in the concluding portion of the myth stands parallel to the Argives' appeals to Proitus and Acrisius, and Zeus's own intervention, which brings an end (παῦσαι) to the civic dispute, narrowly anticipates Artemis' action when she also puts a stop (παῦσεν) to the Proitids' madness.

the civic group and the propagation of future citizens is also in the air, a guarantor of the city's harmonious endurance.[126] The more polis-centred and topological implications of the foundation of these choruses receive confirmation in the final stanza: clearly parallel to the establishment of the Lousion precinct and the choruses that perform at the site is the 'desirable grove beside the Casas with its abundant waters' (118–19)[127] which the 'Achaean men dear to Ares' (113–14; viz. Proitus' 'breakaway faction' also described in martial terms) established as part of their foundation of Metapontion. It is tempting to assume, as Cairns suggests,[128] a performance at the Metapontine Artemision which now completes the full chain of re-enactments: through choral projection, Bacchylides' singer-dancers meld their identity with that of the Lousion choruses that themselves take on the role of the Proitid maidens, first a frenzied troupe of bovine singer-dancers, and subsequently the original parthenaic chorus to perform at the shrine.[129]

2.2 Pindar fr. 122 S.-M.

According to our ancient sources' reconstructions of the circumstances for which Pindar composed fr. 122 S.-M., the now-fragmentary work celebrates the occasion when one Xenophon of Corinth made a thanks-offering to Aphrodite at the goddess' shrine in the unlikely form of a group of prostitutes. Earlier discussions of the piece have chiefly concentrated on the question of whether or not it serves as proof of the institution of sacred prostitution at the goddess' Corinthian shrine, but my angle of approach is a different one; like Bacchylides' celebration of Alexidamus, I suggest, Pindar's piece assimilates a group of young girls to a herd of cattle while investing them with choral properties in ways that both resemble and depart from the Bacchylidean handling of the Proitid myth:[130]

πολύξεναι νεάνιδες, ἀμφίπολοι
Πειθοῦς ἐν ἀφνειῷ Κορίνθῳ,

---

[126] Cairns 2010, 128: 'the *kômos* of strong-limbed youths suggests a chorus of Alexidamus' age-mates, and these might be imagined as potential husbands for the maidens of the community who, with the help of Artemis, take the message of the Proitid myth to heart'.

[127] We naturally think back to the ablutions of Proitus in the 'fair flowing' Lousos (96); see Cairns 2010 *ad* 119.

[128] Cairns 2010, 128.

[129] Fascinatingly, and in a way that might indicate his knowledge of Bacchylides' poem, Catullus develops the heifer-choral dancer analogy in his poem 64; see particularly lines 27–34, well discussed by Curtis 2017, 65–70, although the author does not observe the Greek precedent.

[130] For a differently oriented discussion of the piece, see Chapter 6.

αἵ τε τᾶς χλωρᾶς λιβάνου ξανθὰ δάκρη
θυμιᾶτε, πολλάκι ματέρ’ ἐρώτων
   οὐρανίαν πτάμεναι
νοήματι πρὸς Ἀφροδίταν,   5

(Β′) ὑμῖν ἄνευθ’ ἐπαγορίας ἔπορεν,
ὦ παῖδες, ἐρατειναῖς <ἐν> εὐναῖς
μαλθακᾶς ὥρας ἀπὸ καρπὸν δρέπεσθαι.
σὺν δ’ ἀνάγκᾳ πᾶν καλόν . . .   9
***

(Γ′) ἀλλὰ θαυμάζω, τί με λέξοντι Ἰσθμοῦ   13
δεσπόται τοιάνδε μελίφρονος ἀρχὰν
   εὑρόμενον σκολίου
ξυνάορον ξυναῖς γυναιξίν.

(Δ′) διδάξαμεν χρυσὸν καθαρᾷ βασάνῳ   16
***

ὦ Κύπρου δέσποινα, τεὸν δεῦτ’ ἐς ἄλσος   23?
φορβάδων κορᾶν ἀγέλαν ἑκατόγγυι-
   ον Ξενοφῶν τελέαις
ἐπάγαγ’ εὐχωλαῖς ἰανθείς.

Young girls who welcome many guests, handmaidens of Persuasion in rich Corinth, you who burn the yellow tears of fresh incense, often fluttering in thought to the heavenly mother of desires, Aphrodite. To you, children, she has granted without the possibility of refusal to cull (or 'to have culled')[131] the fruit of soft youth in delightful couchings. With necessity, all is lovely . . .

But I wonder what the lords of the Isthmus will say of my devising such a beginning of a honey-minded *skolion*, partner to women common to all.

We teach the quality of gold on a pure touchstone

O mistress of Cyprus, here into your precinct Xenophon has brought a hundred-limbed herd of girls to graze in gladness at the fulfillment of his prayers.

The opening line defines the young girls as 'hospitable' handmaidens whose service takes the form of making ritual offerings to their divine *despoina*. But by the poem's end, these same ministrants have acquired

---

[131] The verb may be construed two different ways; if read as a middle-passive, as several commentators suggest, then the girls are virgins; Burnett 2011, 58, however, takes issue with this 'misreading'.

a fuller profile and more diverse 'overlords'.[132] In the song's third strophe, the poet takes the *korai* from the sacred context originally framing them to the more secular sphere where he reimagines the group acting 'in partnership' (ξυνάορον) with the current song. The term chosen here looks simultaneously to two spheres, both equally apposite to the performance milieu.[133] In Homer and elsewhere in Pindar, συνάορος occurs in musical/performative contexts, variously designating the lyre that accompanies the feast (*Od.* 8.99) or the praise sung to the music of that lyre (Pind. *Nem.* 4.5); in fifth-century usage, it can also refer to a sexual partner, albeit not a courtesan or other type of lover, but a legitimate husband or wife. In styling the *skolion* both an 'accompaniment to' and 'consort of' the maidservants, whom the line's end then redefines as 'women shared in common', Pindar makes this female group a partner in the performance of his innovatory song, itself an object in which all might share as the different symposiasts took it up in turn, while simultaneously pointing the way to the girls' subsequent change in status.[134] Presented with this re-jigged account, the audience is prompted to envision the youthful ensemble as a chorus participating not in a sacred rite but in the musical entertainment at the symposium even as its members provide sexual gratification to the Isthmian symposiasts playing audience to the song.[135]

But as Kurke's acute reading brings out, the *amphipoloi* undergo yet another change in state, and one that, as a later chapter argues,[136] is fully consistent with the performative role they have just assumed as choral partners to the Pindaric song as well as Aphrodite's *therapnai*. Noting how the 'hundred-limbed herd' evokes the Homeric hecatomb (and in Homer ἀγέλη with only one exception always designates herds of oxen and cattle), Kurke observes that the girls 'have become sacrificial victims, adorned and led to [Aphrodite's] grove in fulfillment of a vow'.[137] While Burnett objects that the *skolion* includes 'no reference to sacrifice, formal dedication, or temple',[138] Kurke's interpretation more accurately follows at least one

---

[132] Kurke 1996, 58 notes the repetition of the term δεσπόται in δέσποινα.

[133] This *double entendre* follows immediately on from the poet's designation of his song as a *skolion*, a work whose 'skewed' nature may consist in part of the twist in sense or twofold meaning its terminology – and particularly language that carries sexual innuendoes – can include. For problems of defining the genre, see Liberman 2016, 54–60.

[134] Burnett 2011, 52–54 draws attention to how the girls' role as purveyors of sexual pleasure is already visible in the language of the opening, where many of the terms used there occur elsewhere in erotic contexts.

[135] The repetition of the prefix ξυν emphasizes the link between the notion of partnership and the girls' sexual status. For the debated issue of the context for which the song was designed, see Liberman 2016, 55–56 with earlier bibliography.

[136] See Chapter 6.   [137] Kurke 1996, 58.   [138] Burnett 2011, 59; see too Budin 2008, 125.

ancient reading of the lines. In Athenaeus' preface to his citation of the piece, he gives a detailed account of the occasion for its performance, reporting that Pindar's *skolion* 'was sung at the sacrifice (θυσίαν)' in which Xenophon was accompanied by women who were being offered to Aphrodite (13.573e–f).[139] The poet's description of how Xenophon 'has led' (ἐπάγαγ') the herd into the goddess' precinct 'in gladness at the fulfillment of his prayers' amply explains why Athenaeus or his source, correctly or not, would assume a votive frame.

Pindar's choice of diction in the lines also develops, and indeed reinforces, the choral connotations just observed. As this chapter's introduction noted, the poet uses the term ἀγέλα on several occasions explicitly to describe a group of choral performers, and very similar to the κορᾶν ἀγέλαν featured here is the 'Laconian herd of *parthenoi*' (Λάκαινα μὲν παρθένων ἀγέλα) of his fr. 112 S.-M.; again, according to Athenaeus, who cites the lines at 14.631c, the reference is to a choral performance, that of a hyporcheme. Also consistent with the choral characterization of the Corinthian group is the role assigned to Xenophon, who presents his ensemble within the sacred and here bucolic space that would also furnish the site for choral performances (as in Bacch. 11.118; see above).[140] Viewed through the choral lens, the use of ἐπάγω for this act of introduction offers another compound verb built about the notion of choral 'leading in' to add to those previously cited and presents the votary in the role of *chorêgos* bringing in his troupe at the start of a performance that celebrates the divine occupant of a shrine.

What is important for my purposes is the coincidence between this witty and light-hearted sympotic piece and Bacchylides' much weightier myth of the Proitids. The divergences between the stories and the very different functions each poem fulfills notwithstanding, they overlap on several counts: in both a group of maidens takes on the character of a choral collective imagined as a bovine herd; and in both these 'cattle' form the counterparts or doubles for an actual sacrificial offering, one to Aphrodite, the other to Artemis. Common too are the roles of the men in the Pindaric and Bacchylidean works, who act as the initiators and presenters/sponsors of the offerings. As detailed above, Proitus promises the sacrifice of the twenty unyoked cows that stand proxy for his daughters, while Pindar's

---

[139] Athenaeus is in turn citing Chamaeleon fr. 31 Wehrli. As Liberman 2016, 55 notes, Chaemeleon bases his observation not on external evidence, but on the contents of the poem itself.

[140] The herd is an expressly 'grazing' one, a detail that recalls the characterization of the 'horsey' ensembles treated earlier in this chapter.

Xenophon is the one who acts on his promise with his own possibly maidenly, and so suitably pure, 'herd'.

3 Deer, Particularly Fawns

In a stasimon in Euripides' *Alcestis*, the chorus addresses Apollo, recalling that he once assumed charge of Admetus' herds and played 'hymeneal songs' for the animals at pasture (βοσκήμασι σοῖσι συρίζων / ποιμνίτας ὑμεναίους, 576–77). Under the charm of his lyre and syrinx, wild animals come to join the domesticated groups (579–87):

> σὺν δ' ἐποιμαίνοντο χαρᾷ μελέων βαλιαί τε
>   λύγκες,
> ἔβα δὲ λιποῦσ' Ὄθρυος νάπαν λεόντων   580
> ἁ δαφοινὸς ἴλα·
> χόρευσε δ' ἀμφὶ σὰν κιθάραν,
> Φοῖβε, ποικιλόθριξ
> νεβρὸς ὑψικόμων πέραν   585
> βαίνουσ' ἐλατᾶν σφυρῷ κούφῳ,
> χαίρουσ' εὔφρονι μολπᾷ.

> In joy at his songs, both spotted lynxes were shepherded, and leaving the vale of Othrys, a pride of tawny lions, and the dapple-haired fawn danced in choruses about your kithara, stepping with its light ankle beyond the fir trees with lofty foliage, rejoicing in your joyous song and dance melody.

The evocation of this pastoral idyll, I suggest, offers just one instance of the final pairing explored here, in which choruses equate themselves with deer and more particularly with fawns, and through their language, choreography and the accompanying music, take on the likeness of these wild, undomesticated creatures, traditionally reclusive dwellers of a sylvan setting. The animal's configuration as a member of a dancing troupe is principally restricted to lyric and dramatic compositions, whose representations of the deer diverge sharply from that found in Homeric epic. Where for the poet of the *Iliad* and *Odyssey* the creatures are typically timorous and/or cowardly, and act as the helpless victims of lions and other more powerful beasts in the similes in which they all but uniquely appear,[141] in

---

[141] The Homeric depiction does extend to the lyric corpus and is also visible in Archil. fr. 196a W. and Anacr. 408 *PMG*; both representations foreground the animals' fear and hesitancy, and make these the hinges on which the comparison between maiden and deer chiefly turns.

choral and dramatic texts, as the citation from Euripides suggests, they instead frequently become exemplars of the speed and balleticism, the capacity to leap high and turn nimbly, so valued in the dancing ensemble and particularly in the leader of the troupe.

3.1   Deer in Choral Lyric and Attic Drama

Sappho fr. 58 V. is the first extant piece to introduce, in no more than glancing fashion, the deer-choral dancer trope, and here the animals are positioned by way of contrast and counterpoint to the *chorêgos* of the chorus performing Sappho's poetry. Calling on the members of her group to join the dance, the speaker then laments her exclusion from the activity because of the weakness of her knees, 'which were once swift to dance like young fawns' (τὰ δή ποτα λαίψηρ' ἔον ὄρχησθ' ἴσα νεβρίοισι, 6). In my discussion of the lines in Chapter 3, I highlighted their resemblance to Alcman fr. 26 *PMGF*, similarly concerned with the aged poet/chorus-leader's inability to take his former place in his parthenaic chorus. There is no mistaking the many indicators of the choral context for which Sappho's lines were designed, and the verb ὀρχέομαι chosen by the poet in line 6 suits this larger ambience. In a fragment generally attributed to Sappho (*inc. auct.* 16), the poet recalls how: 'Cretan women indeed once thus gracefully with their tender feet danced (ὄρχηντ') around the lovely altar'.

A more extended passage in Bacchylides would redeploy the simile in reference to a maiden who performs in local choral celebrations of the Aiakids and of their island home, Aegina (13.84–95):[142]

καί τις ὑψαυχὴς κόρα
    – –⏑⏑–⏑⏑]ραν   85
πόδεσσι ταρφέως
ἠΰτε νεβρὸς ἀπεν[θής
    ἀνθεμόεντας ἐπ[' ὄχθους
κοῦφα σὺν ἀγχιδόμ[οις
    θρώσκουσ' ἀγακλειτα[ῖς ἑταίρα]ις·   90

ταὶ δὲ στεφανωσάμε[ναι φοιν]ικέων
ἀνθέων δόνακός τ' ἐ[πιχω-
    ρίαν ἄθυρσιν
παρθένοι μέλπουσι τ[εὸν λέχο]ς, ὦ
    δέσποινα παγξε[ίνου χθονός,   95

---

[142]   For additional treatment of the passage, see Chapter 5.

> And many a high-vaunting maiden sings in praise of your [might], rapidly on feet [...] as she leaps lightly like a carefree fawn onto the flowery [banks] with her illustrious [companions] from close neighbours' homes. Crowning themselves with their local adornment of crimson flowers and reeds, the maidens sing and dance of your [marriage bed], o mistress of the all-hospitable land.

In Bruno Gentili's view,[143] the simile looks back to two passages in Anacreon, the first fr. 408 *PMG*, where the fearful girl and object of desire is likened to a fawn, the second fr. 417 *PMG*, whose 'Thracian filly' likewise anticipates several of the traits displayed by this Aeginetan maiden. But, as Cairns notes,[144] Bacchylides' cervine chorister displays nothing of the fear so prominent in the first of the fragments, while the patently erotic element and emphasis on male mastery writ so large in the second is also missing here. Instead the comparison serves primarily to underscore the graceful and lithe motions of the fawn *qua* dancer even as its haunts, the flowery banks, presage the subsequent depiction of the choral celebrants, who crown themselves in 'crimson flowers and reeds' (91–92). Also tying the tenor to its vehicle is the intimation of the leaping fawn in the hapax used to describe the maiden dancer, here styled 'high-vaunting', a compound which already carries the sense of height or elevation, perhaps conveyed in both vocal-cum-musical pitch and/or amplification, and is then transferred to the physical sphere and embodied with the introduction of the leaping deer. The near dwelling 'companions' who appear immediately after in the phrase most obviously refer to the performer's fellow chorus members who are not only, as I argue in Chapter 5, stand-ins for the original parthenaic Asopid sorority (hence the glorifying epithet, 'famed') but, with the simile still in play, also counterparts to the herd of deer that accompanies the leader of the animal collective.

From the same period comes the deer that figures in a fragmentary Pindaric hyporcheme (fr. 107a S.-M.), whose opening lines I cited in Section 1 of the chapter and whom the poet positions in company with the horse and dog. Much as the cranes would do in Euripides' *Helen* stasimon (see Chapter 3), Pindar's three animals, my more ample reading here suggests, become the means through which the poet declares his embrace of compositional and choreographic innovation and virtuosity, and each in turn furnishes a visible and audible demonstration of the positions he stakes out in current musico-choral debates. In the extant lines, as preserved by Plutarch, *Mor.* 748b, the poetic I/*chorêgos* (or, less likely, all the choreutes in a performative

---

[143] Gentili 1958, 122–23.   [144] Cairns 2010 *ad loc.*

self-exhortation)[145] first calls on the chorus to act in the manner of the fleet horse or hound as it chases down the object of pursuit, perhaps another hyporcheme staged by a real or notional rival ensemble, and then goes on more fully to characterize the prey that it must track down:

> Πελασγὸν ἵππον ἢ κύνα
> Ἀμυκλαίαν ἀγωνίῳ
> ἐλελιζόμενος ποδὶ μιμέο καμπύλον μέλος διώκων,
> οἷ᾽ ἀνὰ Δώτιον ἀνθεμόεν πεδί-
>   ον πέταται θάνατον κεροέσσα
> εὑρέμεν ματεῖσ᾽ ἐλάφῳ·   5
> τὰν δ᾽ ἐπ᾽ αὐχένι στρέφοι-
>   σαν {ἕτερον} κάρα πάντ᾽ ἐπ᾽ οἶμον ...

imitate the Pelasgian horse or dog from Amyklai as you whirl with your competing foot and impel forward the curving song, even as it flies over the flowery Dotian plain, seeking to find death for the horned deer; and as she turns her head on her neck (the dog pursues?) her on every path.

The genre of the composition bears narrowly on this rare reference to a directly mimetic relation between the chorus members and the several animals included in the lines.[146] As Athenaeus' account of the hyporcheme observes, 'this variety of dance is an imitation of acts which can be interpreted by words' (1.15d), that is, dances that use mimesis for narrative ends, and its invention was assigned to the seventh-century Thaletas of Gortyn (Σ Pind. *Pyth.* 2.127), who supposedly devised it to accompany the highly mimetic weapon dances performed by the Kouretes.[147] In fr. 107a S.-M., Pindar closely interweaves the properties of horses, dogs and deer as protagonists in a race-cum-hunt with those of the ongoing performance in its verbal, musical and choreographic aspects, beginning with the correspondence between the limbs of the racehorse bending as it runs around the track and those of the currently circling singer-dancers, whose legs (as earlier noted) would assume or corporialize the shape of the melodic turns audible in the vocal and instrumental portions of the piece.

To focus more fully on the appearance of the deer in fr. 107a S.-M., the attributes of the animal allow for additional and narrower affinities between the object of pursuit and the ongoing choral spectacle and its

---

[145] See Poltera 2008, 432 for this.

[146] Cf. Pind. fr. 140b.15 S.-M. for a second instance of this act of imitation, here in reference to the dolphin.

[147] Elsewhere this dance is made the innovation of the Dioskouroi, for whom, see the discussion of the choral horse and, again, the scholion to *Pyth.* 2.127.

performers. In keeping with his focus on circuits and bends in the preceding lines, the poet depicts the deer as it turns (στρέφοισαν) its neck, an act
that can emblematize not just the melodic changes but the choreutes as they
reverse their course. The position of the deer's neck, which draws the
viewer's eye upward, takes in other aspects of the performers' action;
while vase painters regularly show chorus members turning their necks
and heads so as to glance back to the dancer following them in the line or
circle, the gesture is no less typical of deer in the Geometric visual repertoire and persists as a motif in later representations. The well-known
Dipylon amphora has a subsidiary frieze of just such 'regardant' deer
while an oinochoe also in Athens similarly includes such back-looking
deer;[148] an Attic neck amphora attributed to the Antimenes Painter now
in Munich offers a third instance of the gesture on black-figure vases.[149]
Among the many later examples, on a red-figure amphora of ca. 525–475
a dog attacks (pertinently enough to the Pindaric song) a deer whose neck is
bent back so as to describe a curve,[150] and from the same period comes an
Attic red-figure cup fragment attributed to Oltos with a finely rendered
deer in the tondo (Fig. 4.11).[151] This animal still more closely resembles the
visualization in fr. 107a S.-M.: again looking backwards and with the turn
of the neck emphasized by the curving *kalos* inscription that redescribes its
shape, this animal rises high off the ground line with its two bent front legs
in a pose suggestive of its running, leaping motion.

The final phrase in the Pindaric fragment, πάντ' ἐπ' οἶμον, includes
a further intersection between the race/pursuit and the work's musicological concerns. Pointing to the literal path on which the hunting dog or
horse and deer run, it also accommodates the current contestants' ability to
produce an ever-changing, modulating and travelling song that can keep
up with and match the variegated and multi-directional course of the deer
as it seeks to throw its pursuers off their musical track, the tradition-
sanctioned οἴμη or path of song. In using the expression, Pindar succinctly
equates the kinetic, instrumental and rhythmic properties of his composition not so much with what its words describe as with its formal verbal
design: the phrase effectively circles back to the earlier reference to the
melos as the object that is 'driven' or 'pursued' and recalls the agonistic
element also sounded in that phrase. For a poet seeking to gain an edge in
a musical marketplace, the race conceit would supply a handy way of

---

[148] Athens, National Archaeological Museum 804 and 152.
[149] Munich, Antikensammlungen J 145.
[150] Tübingen, Institut für Klassische Archäologie, Eberhard Karls Universität S101629; *ARV* 14.
[151] New York, Metropolitan Museum of Art 06.1021.300; *ARV*² 64.99.

Fig. 4.11 Attic red-figure cup fragment attributed to Oltos, ca. 525–475 B.C.E. Interior. New York, Metropolitan Museum of Art 06.1021.300. Photograph © The Metropolitan Museum of Art, Rogers Fund, 1906.

asserting primacy, and nothing better suggests the conventional and even shopworn quality that the motif would later acquire than Choerilus' choice, in his new epic narrative on the Persian wars, to turn the figure on its head by simply withdrawing from the contest (*SH* 317):

> ἆ μάκαρ, ὅστις ἔην κεῖνον χρόνον ἴδρις ἀοιδῆς,
> Μουσάων θεράπων, ὅτ' ἀκήρατος ἦν ἔτι λειμών·
> νῦν δ' ὅτε πάντα δέδασται, ἔχουσι δὲ πείρατα τέχναι,
> ὕστατοι ὥστε δρόμου καταλειπόμεθ', οὐδέ πη ἔστι
> πάντῃ παπταίνοντα νεοζυγὲς ἅρμα πελάσσαι.

> O blessed he who was skilled in song, a servant of the Muses, at that time when the meadow was still undefiled; but now when everything is distributed, and there are boundaries to the arts, we are left behind as the last in the race, nor is there any way for me, although I peer in every direction, to steer a newly yoked chariot.

Pindar's display of compositional primacy by virtue of his novelizing practices may extend to the choreography of this hyporcheme,[152] a type of

---

[152] As remarked in passing by Franklin 2013, 228 who does not pursue the topic; he also notes the context of the Pindaric citation, the point I develop further here.

song-dance where, as noted above, the emphasis seemingly falls more on
the dancers' elaborate mimetic movements than on the accompanying song
(the name, which literally means a piece 'danced to an accompaniment',
indicates as much).[153] The context of Plutarch's citation of this and fr. 107b
S.-M. is important here: the speaker introduces both sets of lines as proof of
his contention that 'dancing and poetry are fully associated, and the one
involves the other', a conjunction that, in his view, exists most especially
'when they combine in that type of composition called hyporcheme, in
which the two arts taken together effect a single work, a representation by
means of poses and words' (748a–b). The reference to the equine or canine
chorister's 'whirling foot' revisited in the deer's zigzagging course spans
these several facets of the performance; used elsewhere by Pindar of the
vibrations of the lyre (*Ol.* 9.13, *Pyth.* 1.4, though both instances include
a secondary reference to the dancers' motions), the participle flags the
gyrations of the chorus members and the feet that power their steps as
they compete against rival ensembles in the ongoing *agôn*.[154] As the
discussion in Chapter 3 of circling movements in the third stasimon in
Euripides' *Helen* and of Pratinas' earlier critique of the innovatory choral
formation in dithyrambic dancing (fr. 708 *PMG*) illustrated, the turning
steps in performances of a ring dance could themselves become a source of
controversy.[155]

    Although the animal and hunting imagery so foregrounded in fr. 107a
S.-M. is absent from the lines that plausibly formed part of the original
piece and which Plutarch goes on to cite as evidence that Pindar 'is not
ashamed to praise himself as much for his dancing as for his poetry' (*Mor.*
748c), continuities in diction and theme argue for fr. 107b S.-M.'s link with
what precedes it; read together, the two pieces demonstrate the ways in
which the dog, horse and deer of the first set of lines can again supply

[153] For this reading of the preposition ὑπό as equivalent to μετά, see Proclus *ap.* Phot. *Bibl.*
320b33ff., and Chapter 3. The name hyporcheme first appears in Pl. *Ion* 534c. For much of
what follows, I am indebted to Peter Agócs, who kindly shared the text of a paper he delivered
on the topic.

[154] According to the definition of the hyporcheme given in the *EM* s.v. προσῴδιον, it involves
performers 'dancing and running in a circle around the altar as the sacrifices burned'.

[155] Placed in this context, the song's localization of the 'hunt' on the 'Dosian plain' may do more
than suggest the uncultivated and wild regions of the primeval landscape of Thessaly (its plain
the site of another type of 'contest', that between the gods and Titans). According to our
sources, and the archaeological and epigraphic evidence, Thessaly was home to several cults of
Dionysus, which seem likely to have involved dithyrambic-style performances. The city of
Larisa included celebrants of the god named *archousai*, the term found in an inscription from
the first century, and Lucian notes that the 'leading men' of Thessaly, the προστάται, were also
called προορχηστῆραι on account of their status as dancers (*Salt.* 14). For the evidence, see Mili
2015, 117–18.

a means of eliding the animal realm with more properly performative and meta-musical concerns (107b):

> ἐλαφρὸν ὄρχημ' οἶδα ποδῶν μειγνύμεν·
> Κρῆτα μὲν καλ<έο>ντι τρόπον, τὸ δ' ὄργανον Μολοσσόν.

> I know how to mix my steps in the light-footed dance; they call the manner Cretan, but the instrument Molossian.

The term that opens this second fragment, ἐλαφρόν, audibly recalls the all but identical sounding ἔλαφος featured in fr. 107a S.-M. and endows the dance with which it is now coupled with the nimbleness that the near homonymous animal has just displayed. In a second and more direct return to the earlier vocabulary, Pindar again draws attention to the foot plied in the dance, engaged here too in a circle-style movement as it is 'mixed' (a favourite Pindaric metaphor for song composition and the creation of a cohesive but multifaceted product; cf. *Ol.* 3.8) with the steps of the other performers and with the tuneful and verbal elements of the spectacle. In addition to its musical (and sympotic) associations, the verb additionally suggests the vogue for heterogeneity which later critiques of the New Music would so roundly stricture and for which Plato would use the synonymous and here derogatory κεράννυμι (*Leg.* 700d; cf. [Plut.] *De mus.* 1132e). To Telestes belongs a further reference to this mixing in his Pindaric-inflected (see *Ol.* 6.91) image of the sympotic 'mixing bowl' of song in which, albeit implicitly, musical modes may be combined in a single 'container' or poetic work (810.1 *PMG*).[156] As suits the genre of fr. 107b S.-M., a competition where victory – formal or more informal – depends in large part on the complexity of the dance figures, Pindar uses the conceit for the chief domain in which this performance might outstrip its rivals.

A further glance back to the pursuit staged in fr. 107a S.-M. informs the opening of the second line of the perhaps follow-on fragment. Even as the noun *tropos* allows the poet to revisit the literal turns and bends described by the several actors in the preceding piece, the deer with its bent-back neck among them, it simultaneously maintains the focus on the technical aspects of the current composition. In identifying the musical mode or *harmonia* of the piece as Cretan, the specification might look both to the ur-hyporcheme performed by the Cretan Kouretes on the birth of Zeus and to the metre that gave the dancers their rhythmic cues. According to Hephaestion, who cites a line of Bacchylides made up of five cretic feet by way of evidence (*Ench.* 16 Consbruch), the Kouretes were also the

---

[156] See LeVen 2014, 105 for the suggestion.

inventors of the cretic metre commonly used in composing hyporchemes. If novelty and an eye-arresting performance style are Pindar's
prime concerns here, then the preceding mention of 'pedal mixing'
alerts the viewer to the medley-making of the poet's compositional
design, his refusal to limit himself to the conventional (?) cretic
scheme. As modern commentators note, the fragmentary hyporchemes
assigned to the poet (the Alexandrian bookrolls of Pindar supposedly
contained two books of works in the genre) do not observe a regular
cretic metre, although some deploy a cretic/cretic-paeonic rhythm, and
the most recent editor of fr. 107a S.-M. aptly calls the piece 'poly-
metric', identifying in it iambic, trochaic and aeolic elements.[157]
A flaunting of the observance of a simpler and more unitary metrical
design may also inform Pratinas' attack on new-fangled practices in fr.
708 *PMG*; not only should the aulos 'dance behind', but it should be
roundly beaten for its taste for extending its stride across metrical
distinctions (παραμελορυθμοβάταν, 13). According to Athenaeus
(14.617c), and suitable to its ongoing emphasis on the dance, fr. 708
PMG belongs not, as critics have more frequently proposed, to
a dithyramb or satyr drama, but to a hyporcheme.[158]

Much in keeping with Pratinas' (contemporary?) concern with the aulos'
new sovereignty is the remainder of the second line of fr. 107b S.-M., where
the composition now nods to the instrument accompanying the performance, the ὄργανον that in Melanippes, Telestes and others after them
unequivocally refers to the pipes, the 'clever instrument' (σοφόν ...
ὄργανον) as Telestes styles it in his account of its invention at fr. 805
PMG. Particularly pertinent to what I suggest motivates the diction of the
Pindaric lines is Plato's later choice of ὄργανον in his broadside directed at
the practices that he routinely lays at the door of the New Musicians: as he
remarks at *Rep*. 399d3–5, the music of the pipes, an *organon* again, is the
dernier cri in all that is variegated, modulated, hybrid, mimetic and (implicitly) undesirable, and neither the instrument maker nor its players should
be allowed into the ideal city-state. In fr. 107b S.-M., as in the later
examples, the term seems to carry with it the associations with novelty
and the mingling of heterogeneous elements showcased in the lines. As for

[157] Poltera 2008, 430.
[158] For a good summary of the debate, see Griffith 2013, 273. Another of Pratinas' strictures, its
generic provenance unknown, closely echoes the language of fr. 107a S.-M. in a rejection of
Ionian tuning or style: 'don't pursue (δίωκε) the tight-strung Muse, nor the slack Iastian' (712
PMG). Pratinas' choice of verb here, read together with the same expression's appearance at the
start of fr. 107a S.-M., suggests that it had meta-musical associations.

the closing adjective 'Molossian' modifying the noun, this might involve an additional point of continuity with the animals so dominant in fr. 107a S.-M. According to our ancient sources, Molossian hounds were skilled in the hunt.

A visual representation that predates Pindar's hyporcheme by more than a century already supplies an artistic rendering, albeit in exaggerated and parodic form, of the broad and almost pantomime-like manner of performance (complete with musical accompaniment) that frr. 107a and b S.-M. might have put on show. Decorating the lower portion of an Early Corinthian alabastron of ca. 620–595 in Paris are several komast dancers seemingly out hunting (Fig. 4.12);[159] one of the figures is being attacked by a panther while another komast with a crooked foot takes part in the action. Pointing to a performative frame are the two komast-musicians who also appear, one equipped with a kithara, the other with a diaulos, and signalling the perhaps sympotic and proto-dramatic nature of the scene is an outsized bust of Dionysus (regularly associated with komasts on other vases) positioned immediately beneath the lyre.[160] While the patently ungainly nature

Fig. 4.12 Early Corinthian alabastron, ca. 620–595 B.C.E. Paris, Musée du Louvre S 1104. Photograph © RMN-Grand Palais (Musée du Louvre)/Tony Querrec.

---

[159] Paris, Musée du Louvre S 1104.
[160] Steinhart 2007, 204–06 also connects the alabastron with fr. 107a S.-M. As he notes, this is our only extant hunting scene with komasts.

of these dancers' movements, conveyed by their protruding backsides and stomachs bulked out with extra padding and by the crippled foot that would seemingly forestall any choreographic virtuosity, is a far cry from the Pindaric composition's showcasing of its dancers' skill, both the fragment and vase share the hunting context and the focus on the mimetic qualities of the ongoing performance.

Two passages from Euripides' choral lyrics, in addition to the one cited at this section's start, supply recapitulations of and allusions back to the deer and fawns as dancers in these earlier accounts. In *Electra* 859–65, the chorus bids Electra join in their dance-song to celebrate Orestes' anticipated 'victory' in the slaying of Aegisthus:

> θὲς ἐς χορόν, ὦ φίλα, ἴχνος, ὡς νεβρὸς οὐράνιον
> πήδημα κουφίζουσα σὺν ἀγλαΐᾳ.   861
> νικᾷ στεφαναφόρα κρείσσω τῶν παρ' Ἀλφειοῦ
>   ῥεέθροις τελέσας
> κασίγνητος σέθεν· ἀλλ' ὑπάειδε
> καλλίνικον ᾠδὰν ἐμῷ χορῷ.   865

> Set your step to the dance, dear friend, like a fawn making light sky-high leaps with festive splendour. Your brother has achieved a crown-bearing victory greater than those by the streams of the Alpheus. But come sing the *kallinikos* song as accompaniment to my dance.

Besides incorporating the now-standard mention of the animal's lightness and facility for leaping high, the chorus also draws on the depiction of the fawn as the joyous creature visible in earlier texts. And if the representation seems familiar, it is because, as Martin Cropp has already observed,[161] Euripides may well be pointing his audience back to Bacchylides 13. Not only does the fawn imagined by the dramatic chorus perform the motions and display the temperament of its epinician predecessor, but the context of Bacchylides' simile and its explicitly celebratory tenor give the appropriation a broader significance: in the ongoing conceit of Euripides' drama, Orestes is a participant in an athletic *agôn*, and his murder of Aegisthus stands as nothing less than his victory in the Olympian games. Style, diction, metre (dactylo-epitrites with alternating sequences of dactyls and iambo-trochaics, which recall the rhythm frequently chosen by Pindar and Bacchylides) and imagery, including the positioning of a simile at the start of the strophe, the use of ἀγλαΐα, the term that more than any other signals the radiance and joy of victory in epinician song while also characterizing

---

[161] Cropp 2013 *ad loc.*

its choral celebration, and periphrasis all bring Pindar and Bacchylides to mind and anticipate the moment when Orestes will receive the victory ribbons from his sister when he returns onstage.[162]

But epinician is not the only lyric genre that the Euripidean chorus samples here. Reminiscent of the hyporchemes just discussed is the lines' foregrounding of the choreographic dimension, complete with the vigorous dancing and animal mimesis noted in other examples. Electra's role is expressly to supply the verbal-vocal component to an already ongoing dance as though, in accordance with the account given by Lucian of a hyporcheme performed by a chorus of youths at Delos, where one segment of the ensemble dances while another sings (*Salt.* 16), the performance envisaged in the lines assumes a separation of the singer from the dancers.[163] The heroine's explicit refusal to participate as vocal accompanist (note the particularized ὑπάειδε at 864), delivered in the iambic lines which replace the antistrophe expected by the audience, threatens to put an abrupt end to the performance; instead of singing along, Electra proposes that the chorus interrupt its current activity and go indoors to fetch garlands with which to crown Orestes (866–72). Much as she declined an earlier invitation in the parodos to act as *chorêgos* for the parthenaic chorus processing to the festival in celebration of Hera on account of her shabbiness (174–80),[164] so here Electra will not join in the victory song and dance. In the event, it is Electra who departs the stage in search of the wreaths, while the chorus announces its intention to continue with a performance defined, with emphatic pleonasm, principally by its dance component (although note the 'shout' added on at 879): 'but we shall dance our dance (χωρήσεται … χόρευμα) which is dear to the Muses' (874–75).

Euripides again combines *choreia* with the fawn in a passage in the *Bacchae*, now replacing the foal that figures in the drama's parodos (see Section 1) with this second paradigmatic dancer and adding on the hunt conceit by casting the animal as the object of pursuit. As others have noted, the association is a natural one in light of the *Bacchae*'s repeated mentions of the fawn skins that belong to conventional maenadic dress (to which I return below), and that would presumably have been worn by the

---

[162] On the epinician character of the ode, see Swift 2010, 156–70 and Carey 2012, 22–25.
[163] Andújar 2018 reads the passage in similar fashion, and offers additional evidence to support this account.
[164] That earlier passage contributed to the ongoing intimation of Electra's estrangement from the choral group; as Weiss 2018, 61–62 notes, the heroine enters the stage performing a strophic song that is more extended than the subsequent shared parodos and that stands out for its 'extraordinarily self-referential focus' on the singer's solitary song and dance, which stands in strict opposition to the chorus' own.

choreutes enacting the dramatic role, but it carries additional significance
for the singers' performance. The extended reference begins at the outset of
the third stasimon, a song that occurs just after Dionysus has suggested that
Pentheus go spy on the maenads, and is sustained through the course of the
first strophe (862–74; trans. Seaford):

ἆρ' ἐν παννυχίοις χοροῖς
θήσω ποτὲ λευκὸν
πόδ' ἀναβακχεύουσα, δέραν
αἰθέρ' ἐς δροσερὸν ῥίπτουσ',   865
    ὡς νεβρὸς χλοεραῖς ἐμπαί-
    ζουσα λείμακος ἡδοναῖς,
ἁνίκ' ἂν φοβερὰν φύγῃ
θήραν ἔξω φυλακᾶς
εὐπλέκτων ὑπὲρ ἀρκύων,   870
θωύσσων δὲ κυναγέτας
συντείνῃ δράμημα κυνῶν,
μόχθοις δ' ὠκυδρόμοις ἀελ-
    λὰς θρῴσκῃ πεδίον
παραποτάμιον, ἡδομένα
βροτῶν ἐρημίαις σκιαρο-   875
    κόμοιό τ' ἔρνεσιν ὕλας;

Shall I ever in the all-night dances set my white foot in Bacchic revelry,
tossing my throat to the dewy air of heaven, like a fawn playing in the
verdant pleasures of the meadow, when it escapes the terrifying hunt,
beyond the guard, over the well-woven nets, and the hunter with a cry
intensifies the running of the hounds, and it bounds, storm swift with fast-
running efforts, to the plain by the river, rejoicing in the wilderness
without mortals and the shoots of the shady-leaved forests?

Again, much in the description takes us back to earlier accounts. Like the
fawns before it – and several of the horses or foals in the lyric corpus – this
one is depicted in a verdant and hence springtime flowery meadow and
watery milieu. Surmounting the nets that would hold it in and breaking
loose from man-made constraints and enclosures, it performs the leaps and
bounds native to the animal. The hunting and pursuit imagery and the
emphasis on the fawn's fleetness of foot is particularly reminiscent of the
Pindaric hyporcheme, and also harking back to that fragment is the second
locale described by the maenadic singers, the same plain (πεδίον) on which
that deer's flight occurred. But in a departure from the lyric precedent,
where the animal ran for its life, this young creature is fancy-free, its
insouciant quality consonant not only with the foal of the parodos (and,

as commentators observe, the fawn further resembles a horse insofar as it is 'storm swift', a description that matches the adjectives ἀελλόπος or ἀελλοδρόμας regularly applied to racehorses), but with Bacchylides' epinician portrayal of the joyful *nebros*. Bringing the tenor and vehicle of the simile still closer together is the participle ἐμπαίζουσα, a term that simultaneously refers to generalized play and to the dance.

As Albert Henrichs notes,[165] and in keeping with the choral projection onto the foal in the epode of the parodos, the song is also self-referential in its focus on the motions of the fawn, whose play-cum-dance draws attention to the choreographic moves on stage.[166] Nor does this exhaust the diction's suggestion of choral kinetics. In Helene Foley's account,[167] the stasimon 'pairs a concrete strophe that evokes Dionysiac dance with a more abstract antistrophe', a sequence in which the first stanza describes fleet and light-footed movement while the second 'contemplates the slow and inescapable workings of divine justice ... which hunts down the unholy and eventuates in the release provided by belief'. Building on Foley's insight, we might note the terms used in 888–90, which both echo and contrast with the vocabulary of the strophe. Referring to the delayed but inexorable exactions of the divine, the singers describe how these 'conceal in complex ways the long foot of time and hunt down the impious one' (κρυπτεύουσι δὲ ποικίλως / δαρὸν χρόνου πόδα καὶ / θηρῶσιν τὸν ἄσεπτον). Rhythm and metre do their share in bringing out the shift; although James Diggle finds suspicious the response of the normal glyconic at 867 and a 'dragged' one at 887 with the three long syllables at the line's end, the alternation nicely captures the change from the carefree and untrammelled fawn to the eventual victim of divine justice. My suggestion is that here, as elsewhere, the appearance of the fawn signals a 'meta-performative' moment, where we are invited to be attentive not so much to the dramatic narrative as to the reflexive relations between language, choreography and the mediating role of metre and rhythm within the spectacle currently being staged.

It comes as no surprise to discover one final evocation of the choral dancer as leaping fawn in the same passage that I treated earlier, the exit-song in Aristophanes' *Lysistrata*. Just a few lines after the Spartan delegate has enjoined the dancers to emulate the prancing filly and shake their hair

---

[165] Henrichs 1994/1995, 88.
[166] See too Bierl 2013, 222–23, who comments 'just as with the foal in the parodos, so the fleeting and jumping deer is projected as an image of dance in the third stasimon. In the performative future tense, the chorus speaks about its actual choral performance.'
[167] Foley (unpublished).

in the manner of bacchants led by Artemis as *chorêgos*, he addresses the
chorus more directly in the closing moments of the drama (1316–21):

ἀλλ' ἄγε, κόμαν παραμπύκιδδε χερί, ποδοῖν τε πάδη
ἃ τις ἔλαφος · κρότον δ' ἁμᾶ ποίη χορωφελήταν,
καὶ τὰν σιὰν δ' αὖ τὰν κρατίσταν Χαλκίοικον ὕμνη   1320
τὰν παμμάχον. . .

> But come, make your hand into a band for your hair, and let your feet leap
> like a hind and clap your hands as well to help the dance along and sing in
> praise of the all-vanquishing goddess, the Lady of the Bronze House.

References to Euripides' reflections on choral dancing in the third stasimon
of the *Helen* are visible here in the glance to the song and dance performances staged by the Leukippidae and the Spartan maidens at Amyklai before
the temple of Athena Chalkioikos (*Hel.* 1465–68, with discussion in Chapter
3), an allusion that well suits the 'Spartan' character of this song. But choral
self-referentiality is also very much at issue in the lines as the dramatic chorus
performing in the theatre of Dionysus enacts the steps and hand motions
signalled by the speaker in its emulation of a Spartan-style *choreia*.

3.2 *Deer and* Choreia *in the Visual Repertoire*

Where the Geometric and later archaic repertoire offered numerous
examples of the combination of horses and choral dancers, and even
their conflation into one and the same individual on the several pots
showing chorus members as equines, there is little to suggest any considered choice on the artist's part when deer and choruses appear in
proximity or participate in a single scene. Further telling against any link
between the two motifs is the ubiquity of the animal on Geometric and later
vases, whether it is portrayed, together with other animals, in continuous
friezes where it typically grazes or adopts a recumbent position, or in any
number of other contexts: deer may regularly serve as the victims of attacks
by lions, panthers and men, and as the companions of gods, heroes and
mortals; they also appear in courtship scenes, at fountain houses and even
as presences in rustic-style symposia. A Late Geometric hydria with female
dancers on its neck has a panel of three grazing deer beneath the vertical
handle directly next to this portion of the vase,[168] but the contiguity is likely
to be pure happenstance as the artist reaches for one among his conventional stock of animal fillers.

[168] Rome, Villa Giulia 1212.

For all the absence of any demonstrable thematic significance underpinning the combination of the deer and choral motifs, two subsets in the
broader category of archaic and early classical vase paintings depicting
the animals may have some bearing on the poetic accounts. Anticipating
the pairing of Apollo and fawns who come to dance as the god plays on the
kithara and pipes in the lines from Euripides' *Alcestis* cited at this section's
start, artists from the second quarter of the sixth century through to the
fifth regularly position a deer immediately behind or next to the lyre-
equipped god. While on many of these vessels (large numbers of which
are still extant) the presence of Artemis readily explains the animal's
appearance, and in many instances no choral activity is discernible, some
vase painters not only include within the scenes the Muses, whom they
represent as the dancing-singing followers of Apollo Musagetes, but additionally suggest the deer's particularized kinship with the ensemble.
Among the several examples, an Attic black-figure hydria originally from
Rhodes of ca. 525–475 shows two pairs of female figures generally identified as Muses who stand on either side of Apollo as he plays on his lyre;[169]
for all that they are still static at this point, the krotala they carry in their
hands distinguish them as dancers. Located to Apollo's right, and facing the
god, the deer has its head turned so as to look back at one of the pairs, as
though linking the *chorêgos* to his ensemble and inviting the dancers to
follow the god's musical lead. On a white-ground lekythos by the Sappho
Painter from ca. 500 (Fig. 4.13),[170] the krotala equipping the female figures
combined with their poses and gestures more unequivocally declare them
dancers. Unlike their counterparts on the hydria, these four women,
including the one who carries a second lyre, move to the rhythm of the
clappers in their hands, bending their knees and inclining their bodies. One
of the foursome uses her free hand to lift up her garment so as to expose the
foot as it rises off the ground. Accentuating the movement, and suggesting
that these choristers sing as well as dance, are the nonsense inscriptions that
follow their contours; curving about each figure, and separating one from
the next, they stand in for the words that complete the ongoing performance. Again a deer accompanies Apollo, now looking back at the god while
facing one of the members of the group circling around the pot; here, as on
the amphora, it serves as bridge between the musician and his troupe.

In some instances, other gods and goddesses (Hermes frequently participates in these scenes) appear together with the deer-accompanied, lyre-

---

[169] London, British Museum B 346. Cf. the similar arrangement on a black-figure neck amphora
(Agrigento, Museo Archeologico Regionale R 138).
[170] Paris, Musée du Louvre MNB 910.

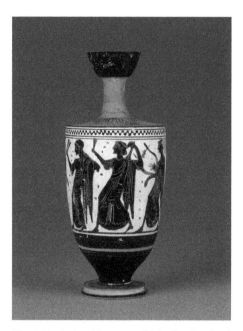

Fig. 4.13 Attic white-ground lekythos by the Sappho Painter, ca. 500 B.C.E. Paris, Musée du Louvre MNB 910. Photograph © RMN-Grand Palais/Hervé Lewandowski.

playing god, replacing the Muses or joining them so as to form a larger group. While these images again omit any reference to choral activity, their artists frequently pair them with a second scene on the pot's other side, this one showing Dionysus accompanied by dancing satyrs and/or maenads. On an Attic black-figure amphora dated to ca. 510–500, the obverse depicts Apollo playing his kithara in company with Hermes, Athena and a deer; Dionysus appears on the reverse, holding a kantharos and flanked by a dancing maenad and satyr.[171] A second amphora also from ca. 510 selects two similar scenes, presenting Apollo standing with a deer between female figures as he plays his kithara on one of the two sides; satyrs dance with a maenad on the other face.[172] Maenads are the dancers on the reverse of a third black-figure neck amphora, companions to Dionysus with his kantharos;[173] on the vessel's obverse, a deer (complete with antlers) stands behind Artemis, who is placed to the left of the kithara-equipped Apollo; the animal gracefully raises one of its front hooves, matching the movement performed by the maenad dancing to Dionysus' right on the reverse.

---

[171] Toledo, Museum of Art 29.48; *Para.* 146.15 *bis.*
[172] New York, Brooklyn Museum 62.147.2; *Para.* 166.163is.
[173] Budapest, Hungarian Museum of Fine Arts 50.612; *Para.* 149.19 *bis.*

Since deer accompany other gods (and heroes too) engaged in actions that have nothing to do with music, dance and song, I would do more than suggest that the painters of the pots just cited may, like the poets of the archaic and early classical age, have links between the chorus member and the deer in mind. More plausibly perhaps, the animal is shown responding, as choral dancers also do, to Apollo's music-making, and plays audience on the vessels to the ongoing performance, modelling an external viewer's similar engagement in and responsiveness to the scene. But a second set of vessels, now coupling deer directly with dancing satyrs and maenads, integrates the animal much more closely into the music-and-dance motifs and, on occasion, looks towards its role as a participant and partner in the activity.

There is no need to reiterate the numerous links between satyrs and cervines: satyrs hunt deer, copulate with them, sniff them, ride on their backs and also wear *nebrides* as they dance, sometimes all but transformed into the animals when the animal skins preserve their heads and feet. On an Attic red-figure neck amphora attributed to the Kleophrades Painter of ca. 525–475, two maenads dance on either side of a pipe-playing satyr who holds his body as though striking a pose as he performs to the music of his diaulos.[174] The deerskin still complete with head and feet that he wears about his shoulders appears as much a participant in the event as garment. Shown with open eyes and ears pricked up, the animal seems to be listening to the music, responding, as Plutarch would later suggest in the remark cited in Section 1, to the charm exercised by the piping, held spellbound as its limbs go slack.

Deer enter into no less close relations with maenads; again Dionysus' female followers make the animals the targets of their hunt, tear their victims apart and, most characteristically, wear their skins as they perform a variety of activities. Most suggestive of the deer as participant in a chorus are the scenes where the animals are imagined as partnering the maenads as they dance. An Attic red-figure neck amphora from the mid-fifth century offers a particularly vivid realization of the conceit (Fig. 4.14):[175] here a maenad carrying a snake and bending her body towards the elongated *thyrsos* which she uses by way of prop leans down towards a spotted fawn whose markings echo those on her garment, a deer or panther skin; the animal rises up to meet the maenad, returning her gaze with its upturned head while lifting its two front legs high in the air in a graceful pose. From the first quarter of the fifth century comes an Attic white-ground lekythos showing a comparable

---

[174] Munich, Antikensammlungen 8732; *ARV²* 182.6, 1632.
[175] Brussels, Musées Royaux d'Art et d'Histoire R255; *ARV²* 670.4.

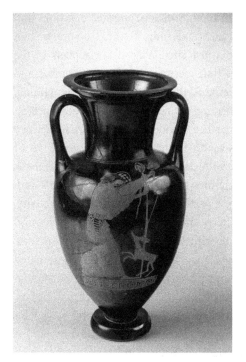

Fig. 4.14 Attic red-figure amphora, ca. 475–425 B.C.E. Brussels, Musées Royaux d'Art et d'Histoire R255. Photograph © MRAH, Brussels.

pas de deux:[176] here the deer, positioned so as to face a dancing maenad equipped with krotala and an ivy sprig in her hands, follows the figure's motions, its extended front left leg offering a visual match to the maenad's back-thrust left limb and raised foot. Very frequently the deer furnishes an accessory in maenadic dancing, an article that like the snake or *thyrsos*, the Bacchant holds out in her hand or carries on her person; moving with the dancer, the animal acquires something of the figure's dynamism. On the reverse of a black-figure neck amphora attributed to the Diosphos Painter from the late sixth century, two maenads dance in ecstatic fashion;[177] while one restrains a lion (perhaps poised to attack the deer) by its tail, her companion hoists a deer high on her shoulder, its legs positioned so as to echo those of its bearer. The dancing maenad on an Attic red-figure lekythos of the mid-fifth century extends both her arms as though to maintain her balance;[178] the deer she holds in her right hand forms the counterpart to the ivy sprig in her left while seeming to impel the maenad forward as it gambols in its airborne pose.

[176] London, Market, Bonhams 14.5.2003,99, no. 266.
[177] Mississippi, University of Mississippi, University Museums 77.3.58; *Para.* 248.136.
[178] Vienna, Kunsthistorisches Museum 3209; *ARV*² 659.53.

Other examples of these combinations of deer and Dionysiac dancers, whether satyrs, maenads or even men and women who take on the mythical celebrants' roles in ritual and sympotic settings,[179] could be cited without resolving the question of the degree to which an individual painter intends to integrate the animal within the choral dance typology. So, once again, the safest course is to leave the matter open and to assume a variety of viewer responses: familiarity with the many examples of deer that appear as chorus members in the lyric and dramatic repertoires might condition one vessel user and viewer to set the animal within a choral frame and to perceive relations between the animal and a dancing ensemble; reversing the trajectory, for a symposiast, a participant in a ritual or a member of a theatre audience that watches a chorus perform a song that cites a deer, prior exposure to the visual motif might allow a more instant grasp of the verbal conceit. For others, the two realms would doubtless remain distinct, each existing within its own independent network of associations.

[179] An Attic black-figure lekythos (Eleusis, Archaeological Museum 2409) from the early fifth century shows women dancing at the Lenaia in maenad-like poses, moving around a post with a mask of Dionysus; a deer also in lively motion appears behind the post.

5 | Water Music: Nymphs, Ships and Choral Aquatics

Introduction

Pindar's sixth *Paean* opens with a declaration of the 'orphaned' state of the performance site at Delphi, a condition that the arrival of the speaker with his chorus will put to rights (fr. 52f.1–11 S.-M.):

> πρὸς Ὀλυμπίου Διός σε χρυσέα
>   κλυτόμαντι Πυθοῖ,
> λίσσομαι Χαρίτεσ-
>   σίν τε καὶ σὺν Ἀφροδίτᾳ,
> ἐν ζαθέῳ με δέξαι χρόνῳ   5
> ἀοίδιμον Πιερίδων προφάταν·
> ὕδατι γὰρ ἐπὶ χαλκοπύλῳ
>   ψόφον ἀΐων Κασταλίας
> ὀρφανὸν ἀνδρῶν χορεύσιος ἦλθον
> ἔταις ἀμαχανίαν ἀ[λ]έξων   10
>   τεοῖσιν ἐμαῖς τε τιμ[α]ῖς·

> golden Pytho, famed for seers, I beseech you by Olympian Zeus, with the Graces and Aphrodite, receive me, the interpreter of the Pierides, famed in song, at the sacred time. For having heard, at the water of Castalia with its gate of bronze, its sound bereft of the dancing of men, I have come to ward off helplessness from your townsmen and my privileges.

As Alex Hardie points out, the syntax of lines 5–6 can be construed in several ways.[1] While most commentators assume that it is the sound of the fountain, its plashing waters, that lacks the accompaniment of the dance, a different sense emerges if we read ὕδατι with Castalia and ψόφον with ἀνδρῶν: 'for having heard, at the bronze-gated water of Castalia, a noise – bereft of males – of dancing ... '. Read in this manner, the sound belongs not to the fountain, but to that made by the choral dancers as they perform.[2] In Hardie's view, the syntactical ambiguity may be deliberate:

---

[1] Hardie 1996, 220.

[2] As Hardie 1996, 220 also notes, Callimachus twice uses ἄψοφος of the absence of the beat made by the feet of choral dancers (*H.* 2.12, 4.302) and other sources similarly refer to the sound of the

drawing on the commonplace equation between the noise made by water and that of choral dance, Pindar intends us to understand the ψόφος heard by the speaker as belonging both to the fountain and to the dancers, these of an expressly non-masculine kind.

The identification of these performers comes just a few lines on when, in the passage announcing the arrival of the poetic ego at the precinct of Apollo, a chorus of maidens duly appears (15–18):

τόθι Λατοΐδαν   15
θαμινὰ Δελφῶν κόραι
χθονὸς ὀμφαλὸν παρὰ σκιάεντα μελπ[ό]μεναι
ποδὶ κροτέο[ντι γᾶν θο]ῷ

> where the maidens of Delphi often sing to Leto's son at the shady navel of the earth and beat the ground with rapid foot

These female dancers are the standing chorus of the Delphides whom Pindar and other poets frequently include in paeans and who, like so many parthenaic ensembles, are the more permanent celebrants of the god (hence θαμινά) on whom the occasional male performers, newcomers to the shrine, model themselves. As Hardie comments, 'the action (and the verb κροτέοντι in particular) suggests the noise denoted by ψόφος. Given the association between ψόφος and χόρευσιος at 8f., it is hard to believe that Pindar did not intend an internal cross reference between the two passages and thus the two noises ... the noise of Castalia may correlate in some positive way with the noise of the dance of women'.[3] Assuming that the story preserved only in much later sources already existed in the early fifth century, then Pindar's audience would also know the Castalian fountain's back history: originally a nymph, the daughter of the river god Achelous (or of the Phocian river god Kephisos, depending on whose version we follow), she took on her present aquatic form when she dived into a well to escape Apollo's pursuit.

It is the correspondence between bodies of water, their properties, inhabitants and those who typically frequent them, and *choreia* that is the topic of this chapter and of its (selective) account of the associations

---

footfall as a ψόφος, which properly describes the sound of one thing striking against another. The detail of the 'gate of bronze' contributes to the emphatically 'aqueous' scene; according to the scholia, here the poet evokes the bronze lions through whose mouth the Kephisos river flowed into the Castalian spring, and a site where ritual lustrations may have occurred prior to entry into the sanctuary.
[3] Hardie 1996, 222.

between the springs, wells, rivers and maritime spaces in the real and mythical Greek land- and seascapes and troupes of singer-dancers. Most simply, and as the lines that open *Paean* 6 illustrate, choral poets exploit the affinity between the sounds and motions, these regularly described as 'eddying', made by water and those emitted and executed by choristers as they sing, clap their hands and tread sonorous, circling measures with their feet. Springs, pools, fountain houses and the rest also enter into close relations with choruses insofar as they, as also visible in the *Paean* proem, are prime sites where choral performances are staged, can serve as sources of the water critical to the ritual events of which *choreia* forms a part (purification in the Delphic instance) and furthermore prove central to the myths recounted by the performers.

Intersections between choruses and the aquatic sphere are apparent in several further areas. Choral projection regularly occurs when choristers model themselves after the mythical occupants of these watery sites, the nymphs who are paradigmatic dancers and sponsors of choral activity. More oblique, but also of significance, are the roles common to seas and water courses and choral collectives; even as the first two fashion vectors of transport and of communication that allow communities to interact, so choral song and dance and its practitioners supply the means for creating links between individual *poleis* and other cities both nearby and more far-flung. Whether choruses literally travel by land and sea from one place to the next as part of sacred embassies, or whether they remain strictly home-based institutions, the springs, rivers and oceans cited in the myths and legends that they tell can not only ground a one-off performance in the more long-standing substratum of local traditions, rituals and aetiology-rich topographies, but additionally allow the performers to construct, 'explain' and negotiate connections between a city and the larger Greek world, making it a player on a regional or panhellenic stage.

My investigation of these diverse exchanges limits itself to five different choral companies, the last something of an outlier, but with pronounced connections to the rest. Following a consideration of the many links between water sources, choruses and nymphs – the larger category to which the first four of my dancer-singers belong – I go on to explore a series of nymphine sororities, one river-based, one exhibiting particularly intimate relations with springs, the third maritime, and the fourth a troupe that performs well-side. The final discussion turns to another ensemble that populates the waters of the sea, the companies of ships on whose formations, motions, acoustics and crews choruses regularly model themselves.

1   Dancing Nymphs and Water Sources

When Odysseus belatedly returns to Ithaca, the narrator pauses to intro-duce the audience to the geography of the island. Adjacent to the harbour is a cave, 'that is shaded, pleasant and sacred to the nymphs who are called the Nymphs of wellsprings, Naïads' (*Od.* 13.103–04); inside there are stone mixing bowls, jars and looms, 'and there is water ever flowing' (109). Walking from Eumaeus' peripheral hut to his palace, Odysseus interrupts his journey at a fountain on the edges of the city where the townspeople come to fetch their water; around the stone structure are black poplars 'all in a circle' and an altar to the nymphs to whom passersby make sacrifice (17.205–11). These Odyssean instances are just two indicators of the multiple and ubiquitous connections, whether genealogical, topographic or etymological, between nymphs and watery spaces. So the Okeanids, Asopids, Nereids and the offspring of Achelous all belong among the several sets of nymphs who are the daughters of the sea and rivers, and the names given these and others of their kind frequently include the element *naïs* (cognate with *naô*, to flow) or end with the suffix *rhoê*, indicative of the motion and sound made by water.[4] Whether in accord-ance with their heritage, or independent of parentage, nymphs are also eponymous with springs, fountains and sources of water, as well as the discoverers and replenishers of these; Amymone, Castalia, Arethousa and Dirke are just some among the numerous examples. Indeed, so ubiquitous is the association that by Hellenistic times the term *nymphê* can simply designate water.

Other mentions of the nymphs from Homer on feature their prime activity, which typically occurs in association with a river or in the prox-imity of a body of water. At *Il.* 24.615–16, Achilles describes Mount Sipylos, where there are 'the couching places of the nymphs that dance around Achelous'; making landfall in Thrinakia, Odysseus and his crew drag their ship into a cave adjacent to the harbour, 'where the nymphs had their beautiful dancing places' (*Od.* 12.317–18). In the *Homeric Hymn to Aphrodite*, where Anchises initially wonders whether the disguised Aphrodite is 'one of the nymphs … who haunt this lovely mountain and the springs of rivers' (97–99), the same nymphs appear later in the piece, here depicted as participants in a choral dance (καλὸν χορὸν ἐρρώσαντο, 261). Dancing of an expressly choral kind is made explicit in the *Homeric*

---

[4] Larson 2001, 4; I have drawn extensively on her study in this chapter. Nymphs also figure prominently in my discussion of weaving in Chapter 7.

Hymn to Pan, usually dated to the early fifth century, which celebrates the god as 'roaming through wooded meadows with the nymphs who delight in choral dancing' (19.3–4),[5] while a further hexameter source, the *Cypria*, sounds a variation on the choral scheme, combining it with a watery site; in company with the Graces, the nymphs sing 'beautifully on Mount Ida of the many springs' (fr. 6 M.-W.).[6] From other sources, chiefly inscriptions and reports of cult activity, come renewed indicators of the nymphs' participation in choruses; at sites in Thasos, Phokis, Cyrene, Attica and Siros, Apollo is designated *Nymphagetês*.[7]

Material evidence combined with topography amply bears out the association of nymphs with water and *choreia*, two aspects of the maidens' identity that, as in the poetic sources, are often closely conjoined at their cult sites. The places set aside for rites addressed to the deities are, in the majority of instances, characterized by fresh water, this derived not just from the rivers and springs already cited, but also from natural water sources within the caves that typically accommodate nymph cults; these may include man-made additions to facilitate access to the much sought after resource, whether by means of channels and basins built to receive water, or wells and fountains. In Athens, a small cave on the south side of the Acropolis containing a spring and home to the nymphs became part of a fountain house in the third century, but the association between the goddesses and these increasingly elaborate structures dates back to the sixth century, when building a view-worthy fountain house might form part of a tyrant's embellishment of his cityscape. The highly decorated fountain house at Megara supplied by Theagenes, which incorporated the fountain that was home to the Sithnid nymphs, was still standing in Pausanias' day, when it earned the visitor's commendation (1.40.1). Votive deposits at these sites include large numbers of loutrophoroi, the vessels used to gather water for the prenuptial bath and that served as part of the offerings, the *proteleia*, made prior to marriage.

Additional evidence for the nymphs' aquatic orientation comes from the vase paintings affirming their predilection for bathing. Among the best-known of the scenes is a black-figure amphora by the Priam Painter of the late sixth century showing seven swimming nymphs in a grotto with two fountains (Fig. 5.0);[8] the artist includes a diving block and the maidens' clothes and aryballoi hanging in the trees surrounding the pool. Participants in rituals addressed to

---

[5] The epigraphic evidence confirms Pan's function as νυμφηγέτης, the 'leader of the Nymphs'; see *IG* IV² 1.130.15–16; cf. Aristid. *Or.* 53.4, where the god is so named.

[6] Later authors supply additional evidence for the activity: see Men. *Dysk.* 950–53 and Alciphron 4.13.12.

[7] Larson 2001, 96.   [8] Rome, Villa Giulia 2609; *Para.* 146.8*ter*.

Fig. 5.0 Attic black-figure amphora by the Priam Painter, ca. 520 B.C.E. Rome, Museo Nazionale di Villa Giulia 2609. Photograph Mauro Bennedetti © MiBAC. Museo Nazionale Etrusco di Villa Giulia.

the nymphs re-enacted the actions of the goddesses, likewise bathing in the waters frequented by the deities; at the so-called Grotta Caruso in Locri, where votives to the nymphs were found, excavations also uncovered a basin that could be filled with water brought through a system of canals from an internal spring. Positioned in the basin was a rock which would have been submerged when the cavity was filled with water; as Bonnie MacLachlan suggests,[9] those performing the prenuptial rites indicated by the presence of *proteleia* among the offerings would descend to the basin by a set of stairs and sit on the rock so as to take a purificatory bath.

The archaeological record also confirms the account given in the literary sources for the nymphs' choral identity, particularly in the form of the many votive plaques found at their cult sites. Typically these terracotta

---

[9] MacLachlan 2009.

pinakes show the deities, frequently displayed as a threesome, with their hands joined in the ring dance and stepping sideways. Two painted wooden plaques from the Pitsa cave near Corinth of ca. 540–530, which portray three females with overlapping bodies covered by a single mantle, belong at the start of the extant series;[10] an inscription on one of them records that the votive was dedicated to the nymphs. A second frequent iconographic scheme on Attic nymph reliefs shows a slightly diminutive male figure – his size indicative of his mortal status – who holds hands with the nymphs as he seems to join them in their dance.

Other three-dimensional votives offer fresh evidence for the place of choral dancing in the ritual activities practised on the nymphs' behalf. A common type of dedication dating from the archaic to the Hellenistic period arranges dancing figures around the circumference of a terracotta disk with a musician at its centre; from this category comes a spoked wheel on whose perimeter a group of female figures in floor-length garments join hands so as to dance around a syrinx-playing Pan standing at the midpoint of the object (Fig. 5.1).[11] Dated to ca. 450, the disk was discovered at the

Fig. 5.1 Terracotta disk from Corcyra, ca. 450 B.C.E. Delphi, Archaeological Museum 16678. Photograph courtesy of École française d'Athènes. © Hellenic Ministry of Culture and Sports/Archaeological Receipts Fund.

---

[10] See Larson 2001, 260 and her fig. 5.18. I return to the single mantle theme in Chapter 7.

[11] Delphi, Archaeological Musuem, no. 16678, See Larson 2001, 236–38 for discussion. An earlier such representation, with four dancers, comes from the Charalavi Trypa cave in Leukada (Leukada, Archaeological Museum of Leukada no. 3365).

Corycian cave sacred to the nymphs located above the temples at Delphi, a site where evidence of ritual activity dates back at least to the sixth century. A black-figure plaque from the same cave varies the motif, showing nymphs dancing together with their frequent companions, the silens.[12]

When led by Hermes, Pan or Dionysus, the figures on these plaques and disks represent the deities themselves engaged in choral dancing; absent these indications of divine identity, the dancers may be mortal worshippers, who emulate the activity of choice of the recipients of their choral tribute. Jennifer Larson plausibly suggests that the articulated dolls in the form of female figurines, some equipped with *krotala* and *tympana* and that later sources refer to as *nymphai*, may be representations of the nymphs (the poloi worn by some of the dolls would signal divine status) or of their votaries, dedicated by young girls to mark a rite of passage (Fig. 7.1).[13] The holes visible in the bodies of the figurines suggest that they would be dangled on a string, an arrangement designed to reinforce their likeness to those moving in the dance, a point detailed later in this study.

Some extant examples also accommodate a watery element in the iconographic scheme. Plaques depicting dancing nymphs from Attica regularly include the river god Achelous, who appears either in the form of a bull with a human face, his front portion protruding into the cave framing the scene, or as a mask-like face set against one wall,[14] and from a cave on Kephallenia comes a unique disk with three Pan-led nymphs carrying hydriai on their heads.[15] In a fresh combination of water and the choral dance, a relief found in a cave near Eleusis, where miniature loutrophoroi also formed part of the votive deposit, depicts Pan and female dancers; the central piercing in the object indicates that the object also served as a waterspout.[16]

The dancing floors discovered at spaces set aside for the cult of the nymphs supply fresh evidence for their character as participants in and sponsors of *choreia*, and additionally suggest that service to the deities took the form of choral performances. Just as the *Odyssey* speaks of the nymphs' καλοὶ χοροί, so at the cave of Vari at the south end of Mount Hymettos a platform built on a layer of stone and identified as a dancing floor was unearthed on the lowest stratum of the site; it may date to the sixth century or even earlier.[17] Confirmation for the existence of a place for dancing at

---

[12] Larson 2001, 235.
[13] London, British Museum 1865.0720.35; see discussion in Larson 2001, 106–07. I return to these figures in Chapter 7.
[14] Larson 2001, 99–100.   [15] Larson 2001, 241.   [16] Larson 2001, 248 with her fig. 5.12.
[17] Schörner and Goette 2004, 213.

this site, albeit from a later period, depends on an inscription of ca. 400 recording the service of one Archedamos, who emigrated from Thera to Attica and seems to have been a particular devotee of the nymphs (in one inscription, *IG* I³ 980, he styles himself νυμφόληπτος); among his acts of architectural piety, he refurbished the cave at Vari at the end of the fifth century.[18] Depending on how *IG* I³ 977 B is restored, Archedamos either constructed 'a dancing place for choruses', a site where dances on behalf of the Nymphs could be performed, or in another reading, took part in the choral dancing that celebrated the divinities: 'Archedamos of Thera and a dancer in choruses (χο(ρ)ον ὀ(ρ)|χεστ[ε]ς) built [this] up for the Nymphs'.

Examples of the nymphs' connections with water and choral dance could be multiplied and instances cited from many parts of Greece from the archaic period through to imperial times. But my concern is chiefly with the poetic sources' deployment of these motifs and with the ways in which they draw on myth, cult practices, topography and iconography as they intertwine nymphs, water sources and *choreia* in their songs. As my readings aim to illustrate, it is a conjunction that serves several ends: while highlighting the dynamics of an ongoing performance, it can additionally promote the thematic and political agendas informing a work and demonstrate the particular powers of choral dance and song, its capacity uniquely to supply an enduring record of past events both historical and mythical, to anchor a community to its local (sometimes contested) space and, as already noted, to create frequently self-serving narrative connections between different city states.

2   Fathers and Daughters: The Asopids

2.1   Pindar fr. 52f.124–37 S.-M.

Circling back to the opening, the final epode of *Paean* 6 introduces a fresh maiden collective dancing in proximity to a body of water.[19] Here, hailing the island of Aegina as an astral body, the performers imagine her receiving their praise and answering their choral tribute by recounting the story of her abduction from her paternal home (125–29):

[18] Bowie 2010, 331–32 offers a recent account of the inscriptions; see further Chapter 6.
[19] The much debated question of the identity of the performers of the final portion of the *Paean* lies largely outside the scope of my argument; see n. 32.

νᾶσος, [ὦ] Διὸς Ἑλ-   125
     λανίου φαεννὸν ἄστρον.
οὕνεκεν οὔ σε παιηόνων
ἄδορπον εὐνάξομεν, ἀλλ᾽ ἀοιδᾶν
ῥόθια δεκομένα κατερεῖς . . .

island, o shining star of Zeus Hellanios, wherefore we shall not put you to
bed without a supper of paeans; rather, as you receive waves of song, you
will recount . . .

After fresh celebration of the island, the chorus then gives Aegina's 'biography' in a narrative that refigures what was earlier a toponym into a
waterside nymph (134–36):

ὑδάτ<εσσ>ι δ᾽ ἐπ᾽ Ἀσ[ω-
ποῦ π[οτ᾽ ἀ]πὸ προθύρων βαθύκολ-   135
πον ἀνερέψατο παρθένον
Αἴγιναν·

and by the waters of the Asopos [Zeus] once carried off from the forecourt
the deep-bosomed maiden Aigina.

There is some confusion among our sources (and modern discussions
register their own puzzlement) as to the place where this abduction
occurred, an enigma that stems from the very multiplicity of water courses
bearing the name Asopos and that gives the whole 'rivery' myth what turns
out to be a handy and exploitable plasticity. According to one version of
events, and that Pindar follows in *Isthm.* 8.16–24, Zeus abducted Aegina
from the banks of the Asopos that passed through the territory of Plataea
and formed the southern boundary of Boeotia, and relocated her in the
eponymous island where, now carrying the offspring of the god, she gave
birth to the Aeginetan hero Aiakos. According to a second myth, visible in
an epinician song by Bacchylides treated below, the deed occurred on the
banks of the Phliasian Asopos, a river that traced its course through
the north-eastern Peloponnese, passing through Phleious and into the
Corinthian Gulf at Sicyon.[20] The lines could also refer to a third Asopos,
this one, whose particular status I also detail below, located on Aegina
itself.[21]

---

[20] This version of events, known to us from Diodorus 4.72, was unacceptable to the Thebans (so
Paus. 2.5.3). There is actually a fourth Asopos; Hdt. 7.199–200 mentions the existence of a
Thessalian river named Asopos that flowed into the Gulf of Malis.

[21] In the view of Fearn (2003, 359), the lines from *Paean* 6 could refer to the Theban river, but 'it is
much more likely that in the Aeginetan version Aegina already lived by the river on the island'.

Visible in this extended salutation are two interconnected themes: first water, whether in the form of the literal sea over which Aegina presides, the metaphoric 'waves' of song addressed to her or the Asopos river, progenitor of the addressee, and second, although more obliquely, chorality. Typically of Pindaric ring-composition, the opening lines of the final epode point back to the opening of the *Paean* cited earlier, and establish multiple connections with that passage at the level of diction, imagery and syntax. As the choristers give Aegina the promised sustenance in the form of the 'pulsing waves (ῥόθια) of song' (128–29), they select a term for their performance that reworks the combination of sound and motion apparent in the opening description of the noise emanating from the waters of Castalia and the accompanying and complementary beat of the Delphides' feet: ῥόθια connotes not just the waters of the ocean, but those waves' audible tumult and the rushing, dashing and plashing motion of the breakers, a counterpart to the choreutes' rapid footwork and strike on the ground. And just as the *persona loquens* of the poem's start arrived so as to remedy a lack, and further presented himself at the first triad's end in the act of performing a libation of song (58–61), so too the singers at the performance's close style themselves givers of necessary sustenance, here both a liquid tribute ('waves of song') and a supper of paeans.

It is Hardie once again who draws attention to more narrow dictional and syntactical parallels between the opening and close:[22] so lines 134–35, ὑδάτ<εσσ>ι δ' ἐπ Ἀσ[ω-/ποῦ echo 7–8, ὕδατι ... ἐπὶ ... / ... Κασταλίας, and within both scenes the singers introduce not just water but 'gates' or 'doors' and identify features of the landscape. Still following Hardie, but developing his argument, this final vignette may also accommodate the chorality motif highlighted at the start.[23] For an audience well versed in abduction stories, and, of course, witnessing the choral dance as performed before their eyes, the account of how Zeus bore Aegina off from the portico of her natal home with her 'father' Asopos in close proximity would recall the scenario so ubiquitous in visual and literary representations of such 'choral snatches' in the archaic and classical age: that of a pre-eminent maiden with whom a man or god falls in love and whom he abducts while she dances in the company of her kin/age mates,[24] a company made up, in

---

[22] Hardie 1996, 228 and 230.

[23] Hardie 1996, 229–31: 'The possibility that Pindar characterizes the "choric nymph" Aegina and her association with water in such a way as to clarify the association between the Delphides and Castalia deserves serious consideration'.

[24] Polymele, the disguised Aphrodite, Persephone with the Okeanids, the Karyatids and Helen are among the many examples cited through the course of this study. For additional instances, see Hardie 1996, 230.

this instance, of Aegina's sister Asopids. On several occasions too, just such a
paternal figure stands close by, and the dance occurs in a watery locale. Even
the 'portico' fits the bill; the forecourt of the house is precisely the site where
real-world parthenaic and other choruses perform (see Pind. *Pyth.* 3.78 and
later chapters). A series of vase representations clustered chiefly in the early
fifth century – there are over thirty extant examples in the corpus – show the
abduction of Aegina, many including her sisters on either side of the maiden
as they witness the act; as in the parallel depictions of Peleus' abduction of
Thetis detailed in Section 4, the artists imagine the Asopids in poses that are
suggestive not so much of flight as of an ongoing dance.

The subject also appears in statuary, and may well have been the episode
shown on the now-lost bronze statue groups that Pausanias saw at Olympia
and Delphi (5.22.6, 10.13.6), the former clearly depicting Aegina together
with her sisters.[25] In describing this monument, Pausanias names Nemea,
Harpina, Corcyra and Thebe, with Asopos seemingly positioned last in the
line:

> ἀνέθεσαν δὲ καὶ Φλιάσιοι Δία καὶ θυγατέρας τὰς Ἀσωποῦ καὶ αὐτὸν
> Ἀσωπόν, διακεκόσμηται δὲ οὕτω σφίσι τὰ ἀγάλματα. Νεμέα μὲν τῶν
> ἀδελφῶν πρώτη, μετὰ δὲ αὐτὴν Ζεὺς λαμβανόμενός ἐστιν Αἰγίνης, παρὰ δὲ
> τὴν Αἴγιναν ἕστηκεν Ἅρπινα . . ., μετὰ δὲ αὐτὴν Κόρκυρά τε καὶ ἐπ' αὐτῇ
> Θήβη, τελευταῖος δὲ ὁ Ἀσωπός.

> The Phliasians also dedicated a Zeus and the daughters of Asopos and
> Asopos himself: the images are divided and marshalled thus: Nemea is the
> first of the sisters and after her comes Zeus seizing Aegina; next to Aegina
> stands Harpina . . . after her is Corcyra with Thebe next; last of all comes
> Asopos.

The language of the passage, complete with the term διακοσμέω, used in
much earlier sources for the marshalling-cum-arraying of formations of
both troops and choral dancers, leaves no doubt as to the group's linear
presentation. Perhaps reading off each name inscribed beneath the successive images, Pausanias effectively presents the daughters as though they
were drawn up in a chorus line, with Asopos positioned as *chorêgos* who,
viewing the figures from left to right, would head the troupe. We might
compare to this the well-known family grouping from a monument usually
dated to ca. 560–550, dedicated by one Geneleos at the Samian Heraion
(Fig. 8.7),[26] and consisting of six marble statues set up on a base with their

[25] For fresh consideration of Pausanias' account, see Chapter 9.
[26] Vathy, Archaeological Museum of Samos 768; one of the original six, the maiden inscribed
Ornithe, is currently in Berlin (Berlin, Staatliches Museum 1739).

names inscribed on their bodies. Presented one after the other, the sculptor has fashioned three standing *korai*, whose stance indicates a processional or even dancing movement. Several scholars propose that the sculptor imagines Geneleos' daughters as performers in dances in honour of Hera in which these named maidens once participated, with the music supplied by the aulos-playing son also included in the group.[27]

Still more significant for *Paean* 6 was the sculpture group originally designed for the east pediment of the temple of Aphaia on Aegina, commissioned ca. 500 at the same time as the construction of the building, and which featured Zeus's abduction of the eponymous nymph.[28] Although the Aeginetans apparently rejected and replaced the image sometime in the next decades – there is debate as to precisely when, but most prefer the 480s – excavators have unearthed the fragmentary remains from the site where the pedimental components were then exhibited, the stoa-like structures on either side of the Altar Court in front of the temple. There is no way of knowing whether the original scene included Asopos' other daughters, but, in the light of contemporary vase images and pedimental design, it seems likely enough that they formed part of the representation. Maiden choruses that performed in the vicinity of the temple (see below) could then have modelled themselves after the sorority depicted on the pediment as first conceived.

Korai found on the island supply additional evidence for such performances.[29] Among the extant four, three, all dated to the first half of the sixth century, come from the Aphaia sanctuary; one, dressed in a tight-fitting chiton and belt, was found below the eastern terrace; another, from the north-east slope outside the temenos has the same type of gown, with a central vertical maeander pattern border that runs between the legs. The third wears a belted chiton arranged so as to make the tips of her shoes visible, together with earrings and a taenia holding her distinctively styled hair. As many readings of *korai* suggest, these stone maidens dressed in their finery serve as the offerings that lastingly represent *parthenoi* as they appeared decked out in rich garments and jewellery when participating in choral processions and dancing; their continued presence in the shrine, and in proximity to latter-day performances, commemorates and eternalizes their tributes to the deity. Other artefacts from the sanctuary can help identify the nature of the rituals framing these spectacles; pointing to the Aeginetans' practice of the coming-of-age rites over which Aphaia, in her role as patroness of childbirth and *kourotrophos*, would

[27] See Karakasi 2003, 28–29 with earlier bibliography.
[28] For discussion, see Sinn 1987 and Watson 2011. According to Pausanias 2.30.3, Pindar composed a cult song for the sanctuary.
[29] For documentation, illustrations and discussion, see Karakasi 2003, 109–12 and Chapter 8.

have presided are the rolls of ribbons discovered at the site, once used by maidens to attach offerings of hair as markers of their passage from one age group to the next.[30] Dances require dancing spaces, and the sanctuary included just such a dancing floor. According to Ulrich Sinn's reconstruction, a smoothed rock surface that supplied a stage for the performance of ring dances stood between the propylon and buildings in the south-east, while the colonnaded porch of the propylon and hall of the so-called Amphipoleion might have offered seating for spectators of the display.[31]

For the Aeginetans gathered at the Delphic *theoxenia*, lines 134–35 of *Paean* 6 might thus not only recall a much celebrated local monument and its (once intended) decorative programme, but would create a still tighter amalgam between the site of the current performance, where the Pindaric chorus – whether one made up of Delphians, of Aeginetans or comprising two choruses, the second from Aegina picking up where the first had left off –[32] now dances and sings, and choral activity back home. Reinforcing the correlation between the waters of Castalia where *Paean* 6 situates itself and the Asopid banks, the space where, as a series of passages in Pindar and Bacchylides cited below inform us, choral performances regularly occurred, the brief evocation of Aeginetan topography contributes another localizing element. The purpose is twofold: more broadly, the move serves to bridge the distance between the distant, peripheral island together with its local traditions and the panhellenic sanctuary and to buttress what the song has been doing all along, affirming the place of Aegina as integral to the Greek community and holding up its myths and heroes as central to the well-being of the Hellene collectivity; more narrowly, and using the device of choral projection to equate the current occasion with ritual events back home, it posits relations between the dancing Delphides visible at the poem's start and their Aeginetan counterparts, the Asopids and those maidens now taking on the mythical sorority's role in performances at the island's shrines.

2.2 *Pindar, Nem. 3.1–16*

Perhaps most closely comparable to *Paean* 6 is the *mise en scène* at the start of Pindar's *Nemean* 3, where, in diction reminiscent of the *Paean*'s

---

[30] See Sinn 1988.

[31] According to the suggestion offered by Sinn (1988, 154–57), festivals celebrated on the goddess' behalf would also have taken place not in the walled temenos but on a 'festival meadow' located to the west and south of the sanctuary. This would certainly accommodate choral dancing in which local girls would have performed, perhaps re-enacting the myth of the foundational rape.

[32] For discussion, see Kurke 2005, esp. 86–95 and Rutherford 2001, 331–38.

opening, the poet invites us to imagine a situation equivalent to that at
Delphi, where Castalia awaits the arrival of the Pindaric *kômos* to supply
the missing male choral dance. Following an initial invocation/invitation to
the Muse to visit Aegina, the site of the current song, the speaker goes on to
describe a state of lack and explains the pressing need for the presence of
the goddess (3–7):

ὕδατι γάρ

μένοντ᾽ ἐπ᾽ Ἀσωπίῳ μελιγαρύων τέκτονες

κώμων νεανίαι, σέθεν ὄπα μαιόμενοι.   5

διψῇ δὲ πρᾶγος ἄλλο μὲν ἄλλου,

ἀεθλονικία δὲ μάλιστ᾽ ἀοιδὰν φιλεῖ,

for by the waters of Asopos the builders of honey-sounding revels are
waiting, young men desirous of your voice. Different deeds thirst for
different rewards, but victory in the games loves song most of all . . .

In almost imperceptible fashion, the water that initially constitutes the
literal substance of the river becomes the flowing matter of the voice
emitted by the Muse, thereby satisfying the metaphoric 'thirst' currently
afflicting both the song-less *kômos* and still uncelebrated victory. But, the
metaphor notwithstanding, the scene presented by the poetic (or choral)
ego all but exactly corresponds to the song's performative reality. As
G. Aurelio Privitera proposed, and in a suggestion recently developed by
David Fearn,[33] the reference to the waters of the Asopos would point not, as
the scholia perplexed by the apparent absence of a river by that name on
Aegina assumed, to the Phliasian Asopos that runs to the west of the site of
the Nemean games, but to a spring on Aegina; the chosen designation
formed part of the efforts by the island-dwellers to establish, through water,
a connection with the mainland river Asopos and his daughters whom they
claimed as progenitors. According to Fearn's hypothetical reconstruction,
some time in the sixth century the Aeginetans would have built an under-
ground watercourse (or, in Privitera's suggestion, an aqueduct) following
the route of a dry riverbed on the island so as to carry water from the region
of Mount Panhellenios in the southern part of their territory to the central
town. The *Etymologicum Magnum* (s.v. Ἀμφιφορίτης) mentions just such an
'Asopid spring', or Ἀσωπίδα κρήνη, in reference to an *agôn* located at the
site, a running race styled the Ἀμφιφορίτης (an event also named the
Ἀμφορίτης), in which participants had to carry an amphora filled with

---

[33] Fearn 2007, 102–05 with Privitera 1988.

water (from the spring?).[34] According to the Alexandrian scholar Kallistratos (Σ *ad* Pind. *Nem.* 3.1c, iii.42 Dr.), these waters are to be identified with a daughter of Asopos, evidently the nymph Aegina herself.[35]

These features of Aeginetan topography and ritual do much to shape the subsequent lines of *Nemean* 3, where the speaker imagines how he will share his Muse-derived hymn with the waiting *kômos* (12–16):

> χαρίεντα δ᾽ ἕξει πόνον
> χώρας ἄγαλμα, Μυρμιδόνες ἵνα πρότεροι
> ᾤκησαν, ὧν παλαίφατον ἀγοράν
> οὐκ ἐλεγχέεσσιν Ἀριστοκλείδας τεάν   15
> ἐμίανε κατ᾽ αἶσαν ...

> And it [the hymn] will have graceful toil as an adornment of the place where the Myrmidons formerly dwelled, whose ancient-famed agora Aristocleidas did not stain with reproaches in accordance with your allotment ...

Following the language and conceits used by Pindar in other Aeginetan odes, where the epinician *choreia* takes the form of just such a 'graceful' offering and even styles itself a votive garland dedicated by the chorus members to Aiakos at his shrine (e.g. *Nem.* 5.53–54, 8.13–16),[36] Fearn's view that the Asopos featured at the poem's start would have been adjacent to the Aiakeion in the agora where the epinician is now staged makes very good sense.[37] Although no ancient source identifies the site of the shrine, nor have archaeological excavations determined its exact location, Pausanias records that it stood in the city's 'most visible spot' and close to the port (2.29.6), both likely enough places for an agora; it may even have been a fresh provocation that the Athenians, involved in disputes with the island, chose to build their rival late sixth-century shrine to Aiakos in Athens' own agora.

If the spring, shrine and agora form a single complex and all draw attention to the space where the chorus now performs, then the notional *agalma* constructed by the youthful ensemble furnishes, in typical Pindaric fashion, an equivalent and double of the actual Aiakeion. When set side-by-

[34] *EM* s.v. Ἀμφιφορίτης. The passage is cited by Pfeijffer 1999, 247, who also identifies the 'Asopid waters' as a reference to the Asopid 'well or stream' on Aegina. On this *agôn*, see below.
[35] See Nagy 2011, 75. The identification between a nymph and spring is also commonplace; according to one of the two etymologies that Stephanus of Byzantium supplies for another nymph-turned-place, Cyrene, her name was derived 'from the native spring Cyra'.
[36] Here I follow Kurke 2013, 156 and her suggestion that the 'graceful toil' refers to the work of the chorus fashioning its song and dance.
[37] Fearn 2007, 104.

side, the scene imagined at the start of *Nemean* 3 and the decorations on the building visible to the Pindaric audience and whose iconographic programme Pausanias details at 2.29.7–8 offer mirroring representations:

> Fashioned in relief at the entrance are the envoys whom the Greeks once dispatched to Aiakos. The reason for the embassy given by the Aeginetans is the same as that supplied by the other Greeks. A drought had for some time struck Greece, and no rain fell … until at last they sent envoys to Delphi to ask the cause and to seek release from the evil. The Pythian priestess told them to appease Zeus, and said that it was necessary, were he to listen to them, for the one to supplicate him to be Aiakos. And so they sent envoys from each city in order to ask Aiakos. By sacrifice and prayer to Zeus Panhellenios, he caused rain to fall upon Greece, and the Aeginetans made these likenesses of those who came to him.

It takes little effort to link the sculpted scene with the opening of Pindar's song and its recasting of the mythical events in their epinician frame: the Greeks seeking water correspond to the singers yearning for the Muses' liquid voice that slakes the thirst that now belongs to the victory in need of praise. In a somewhat self-promoting move, the *persona loquens* actually reverses the scene depicted on the Aiakeion;[38] rather than the waterless Greeks arriving at Aegina in search of Zeus-given rain, now a mainland dweller (playing an Aiakos-like role) comes with the Muse-sourced draught (perhaps even from the Theban Asopos?) that he shares, in a quasi-sympotic image, with the needy islanders – a return, perhaps, for their earlier watery benefaction to the Greeks. The end of the song confirms and enhances the liquid nature of the poet's gift, now conceived as a 'mixed drink', a cocktail of song and aulos that takes the form of a milk and honey libation (76–79). The 'honey-sounding' revels that the *kômos* has yet to supply at the ode's opening have been not only realized but rendered more elaborate as we witness the delivery of the complex mellifluous offering.

Pindar incorporates one final piece of local colour into this 'riverine' opening, further sustaining the initial focus on water in Aeginetan topography, myth and ritual practice. In the description of the agora where the choristers' performance fashions its pleasing *agalma*, the speaker notes the presence of the Myrmidons as early inhabitants of Aegina and so creates the expectation that their story might follow.[39] More than just a display of familiarity with the island's 'history', this passing reference connects the

---

[38] As Fearn 2007, 104 notes, Isocrates reports that the Aiakeion was built at the spot where Aiakos supplicated Zeus for rain (9.14–15).

[39] Pfeijffer 1999, 270.

feat achieved by the victor Aristocleidas in the pankration at Nemea with a
more home-based *agôn* that also took place in proximity of the Aiakeion
and so constructs fresh links between the mainland site and the island. It is
Apollonius whose *Argonautica* gives the first extant account of the aetiology of the Ἀμφιφορίτης at the Asopid spring (4.1765–72): in the poet's
report, the practice derives from the Argonauts, who, on arrival on the
island,

> contended in blameless strife about the fetching of water, who first should
> draw it and come to the ship. For both their need and the ceaseless breeze
> urged them on. There even until now do the Myrmidon youths take up on
> their shoulders the filled-up jars and with light feet (κούφοισιν ...
> πόδεσσιν) strive for victory in the race.

Again, the prelude of the Pindaric song glances towards a tale that turns
about a pressing need for water and links the present celebration of an
epinician victory with the island's glorious mythical beginnings and its
heritage in ritual as well as monumental form. It might not be too whimsical to see in the Aeginetan youths performing Pindar's ode counterparts
or reconfigurations of the *kouroi* who, 'nimble-footed', contended in the
original running race, regularly re-enacted in the form of the Ἀμφιφορίτης;
as so often, choral dancing would be a counterpart to running, both actions
dependent on the speed and skill of the participants' footwork. The localizing detail that the performance of the ode occurs in the 'Nemean sacred
month' at line 2 supports this connection to the ritualized *agôn*, and lends a
synchronicity to events. According to some ancient sources, the competition took place in the month Delphinion and/or in honour of Apollo
Delphinios, much worshipped on Aegina, and was contemporary with
the biennial celebration of the Nemean games.[40]

Just as the final epode of *Paean 6* presented events on Aegina in a
manner designed to highlight the parallels between the island and Delphi
and the choral activity that both sites accommodated, so written into the
reference to the waters of the Asopos at the outset of *Nemean 3* is a long
chain of associations that bind the Nemean victory to the Aeginetan
landscape, its myths, rituals, architectural landmarks and history, and
that turn the performers – mainland poet and civic chorus both – into
multiforms of key players in the island's self-fashioned narrative. Indeed,
the confusion of the scholia and of many commentators after them with

---

[40] Σ Pind. *Nem.* 5.81b cited by Privitera 1988, 68. Since the 'Dolphin god' featured prominently in
the coming-of-age rituals aimed at boys, the name of the month points to the nature of the
ritual.

regard to the location of the Asopos named at the ode's start forms part and parcel of the Pindaric agenda, that of conjoining Nemea and the island seeking to augment (and ameliorate) its status within the larger Greek community. Two pictures are superimposed and blended together: the celebration of Aristocleidas' victory at the Asopos in the territory of Nemea, and the present-day restaging of those celebrations at the Asopid site that hosted the more cyclical re-enactments and commemorations of a second athletic victory, one that occurred at the very same point in the local ritual calendar. A 'mixed drink' indeed.

2.3   Bacchylides 13.77–95

To understand the full relevance of these several Pindaric references to the waters of the Asopos and the degree of choral projection going on within these compositions, we need to turn to two works by Bacchylides, where the focus falls less on the father-figure than on his daughters. In his *Ode* 13, composed for Pytheas, another Aeginetan athlete and also a victor in the pankration at Nemea, the singers follow their praise of the celebrant and description of his home return crowned with his victory garland with an invocation to their native island (77–95):

ὦ ποταμοῦ θύγατερ
    δινᾶντος Αἴγιν' ἠπιόφρον,

ἦ τοι μεγάλαν [Κρονίδας
    ἔδωκε τιμάν   80
ἐν πάντεσσι ν[εορτόν]
πυρσὸν ὡς Ἕλλ[ασι νίκαν
φαίνων· τό γε σὸν [κράτος ὑμ]νεῖ
καί τις ὑψαυχὴς κόρα
    [στείχουσ' ἀνὰ γᾶν ἱε]ράν   85
    πόδεσσι ταρφέως
ἠΰτε νεβρὸς ἀπεν[θής]
ἀνθεμόεντας ἐπ[' ὄχθους]
κοῦφα σὺν ἀγχιδόμ[οις
    θρῴσκουσ' ἀγακλειτα[ῖς ἑταίρα]ις·   90

ταὶ δὲ στεφανωσάμε[ναι φοιν]ικέων
ἀνθέων δόνακός τ' ἐ[πιχω-]
    ρίαν ἄθυρσιν
παρθένοι μέλπουσι τ[εὸν λέχο]ς, ὦ
    δέσποινα παγξε[ίνου χθονός   95

> Daughter of the eddying river, gentle-minded Aegina, truly (the son of
> Cronus) has given you great honour, showing forth among all the Greeks
> (a new victory) like a beacon; and some high-vaunting girl sings in praise
> of your (power/fame), (walking on sacred soil?), time and time again
> lightly springing with her feet, like a carefree fawn to the flowery banks
> with her illustrious near dwelling (companions); and garlanded with the
> local adornment of crimson flowers and reeds those maidens sing, queen
> of an all-hospitable land, of your (marriage bed) . . .

As others have established, there is no mistaking the tight connection that
Bacchylides establishes between the internal parthenaic chorus that these
lines introduce and the performers of the composition being enacted in the
here-and-now: both are engaged in song and dance (μέλπω is used of each
chorus at 94 and 190), the maiden *choragos* performs a *hymnos*, the term
which describes the epinician song at 223, and both ensembles praise the
prowess of the objects of their celebration, the *kratos* of Aegina standing
counterpart to Pytheas' 'strength' already cited in line 75. Even the maidens'
garlands can be equated with the wreaths most likely worn by the
Bacchylidean chorus and by their *laudandus* Pytheas, returning with his
'crowns of all flourishing flowers' at 69–70.[41] Bacchylides also lays special
emphasis on the choral character of the Aeginetan maidens: not only are the
members of the group tied by bonds of locality and defined as *hetairai*,[42] the
term used by Pindar for the *parthenoi* who sing a nuptial song for Coronis
(*Pyth.* 3.17–19),[43] but, as the previous chapter explored, the self-comparison
by maiden choruses to fawns was already a (parthenaic) choral topos. Where
Power's illuminating reading considers this embedded performance an
instance of choral projection, and views the celebrants of Pytheas' one-off
victory, in a bid to enhance their local status, as identifying their *choreia* with
that of a standing maiden chorus that regularly sang and danced in honour of
their founding nymph and her offspring,[44] Fearn additionally argues that the
girls' performance – and that of the chorus of youths delivering Bacchylides'

---

[41] Power 2000, 72 details these points; as he goes on to observe, the very invocation of Aegina
together with the celebration of Aegina's descendants that follows can be read as the utterance
of the maiden singers now channelled through the Bacchylidean chorus. For the garlands and
flowers, cf. Pindar's own celebration of Pytheas – or more properly his ancestor – in *Nem.* 5.54,
where the final moments of the song describe the dedication of 'grassy crowns of flowers' (by the
victor and the chorus members?) at the Aiakeion.

[42] This depends on a broadly accepted textual reconstruction.

[43] Also noted by Calame 1997, 33.

[44] See too Stehle 1997, 106; while she grants the reality of such choral performances by *parthenoi*,
she draws attention to the element of fantasy in the visualization, its creation of an 'ideal scene'.

Abb. 1. Halsbild der Hydria A 1
Vgl. Taf. 1, 1 und 2

Fig. 5.2 Protoattic black-figure hydria, late eighth century. Berlin, Antikensammlung 31573. Drawing in *CVA* Berlin I, pl. 40. Photograph courtesy of Barbara Kowalzig.

corresponding composition – takes place on the banks of the Asopos.[45] As he notes, the reference to 'reeds' would be a passing nod to that riverine site. A second term in the lines cited above looks to the same space; the fawn to which the *chorêgos* is compared is headed not, as many translations suggest, to the hills but to the flowery banks of the Asopos.

Material evidence in addition to the pediments and *korai* excavated at the temple of Aphaia and cited in the discussion of Pindar's sixth *Paean* supplies proof for the presence of female choral activity on Aegina. Four archaic vases with representations of choral dancers were found on the island, the first of which appears on a late eighth-century hydria now in Berlin (Fig. 5.2).[46] Nine women led by a male lyre-player and aulete circle around the vessel's neck. Absent any indication of the chorus members' identity, there is no establishing whether the artist sought to portray a particular or generic ensemble, nor, if he had a specific group in mind, who these figures might be. But given the frequency with which Aeginetan choruses map their identity onto the Asopids, it is tempting to see these nine female choristers as representing that sorority. As though in anticipation of Bacchylides' embedding stratagem, where male and female choruses are superimposed one on the other, a procession of twelve men moving to the right occupies the neck's lower zone; here too an aulos-player (preceded by a musician equipped with a cithara) leads the line. The male ensemble

---

[45] Fearn 2007, 116.   [46] Berlin Antikensammlung 31753, with Calame 1997, 100 n. 31.

differs from the maidens above in several respects; not only in number, but also in the more vigorous motions that two of the choreutes perform, depicted as though rising up on their toes; and where the girls carry the branches so common in representations of parthenaic choruses, the men are empty handed, with their arms bent as though preparing to perform a clapping gesture.[47] Both separate and juxtaposed, the two choruses suggest the relations of equivalence but not identity that Bacchylides' later song also stages.

Returning to Bacchylides 13, my suggestion is that this local maiden chorus may similarly model its activity after that of the Asopids and that its location by the banks of the (Aeginetan) Asopos promotes the equation between these contemporary dancers and their mythical archetypes, the sorority that, whether on Aegina or mainland Greece, also once performed waterside. Retelling the story of the progenitor of its island, the latter-day band recalls the foundational abduction by drawing attention to its chorus leader, whom it singles out from her companions, the stand-ins for the sisters of the nymph-and-bride. The introduction of this standing chorus multiplies the levels of choral 'mapping'; even as the more occasional performers of the praise of Pytheas augment their authority and the enduring quality of their song by assimilating themselves to the chorus of Aeginetan *parthenoi* engaged in the more ritualized celebration of Pytheas' native land,[48] so those maidens on the cusp of marriage take as their templates the ever-singing-dancing Asopids, these too destined to leave the group in turn as brides to illustrious men.

2.4 *Bacchylides 9.39–65*

Bacchylides 13 does not exhaust references to Asopos and his daughters in the poet's epinician songs. As already noted, in addition to the Boeotian and Aeginetan rivers, yet another Asopos flowed through Phleious, a region in proximity of Nemea, and on into the Gulf of Corinth. In Bacchylides' ninth ode, composed on behalf of the Nemean victory of Automedes from Phleious, this river and his daughters receive explicit praise in lines 39–65, as the singers rehearse how the fame of the Asopos has travelled to the far points of the earth, further stoked by the renown of his numerous daughters. First introduced as the marker of the site to which Automedes returns following his pentathlon triumph, the Asopos goes on to take centrestage:

> ἵκετ᾽ [Ἀσωπὸ]ν πάρα πορφυροδίναν·
> τοῦ κ[λέος π]ᾶσαν χθόνα   40

---

[47] Crowhurst 1963, 36.   [48] See Power 2000 for this reading.

ἦλθε[ν καὶ] ἐπ' ἔσχατα Νείλου,
ταί τ' ἐπ' εὐραεῖπόρῳ
οἰκεῦσι Θερμώδον[τος, ἐ]γχέων
ἴστορες κοῦραι διωξίπποι'. Ἄρηος,

σῶν, ὦ πολυζήλωτε ἄναξ ποταμῶν,   45
ἐγγόνων γεύσαντο, καὶ ὑψιπύλου Τροίας ἔδος.
στείχει δι' εὐρείας κελε[ύ]θου
μυρία πάντα φάτις
σᾶς γενεᾶς λιπαρο-
        ζώνων θυγατρῶν, ἃς θε[ο]ί   50
σὺν τύχαις ᾤκισσαν ἀρχα-
        γοὺς ἀπορθήτων ἀγυιᾶν.

τίς γὰρ οὐκ οἶδεν κυανοπλοκάμου
        Θήβας ἐΰδμα[τον πόλι]ν,
ἢ τὰν μεγαλώνυ]μον Αἴγιναν, μεγ[ίστ]ου Ζην]ὸς [ἃ πλαθεῖσα λ]
        ἔχει τέκεν ἥρω   55

. .]δε σω[. . . . . . .]ου,
[ὃς γ]ᾶς βασά[νοισιν Ἀχ]αιῶν
        ]υ[   ]α.

τ[--◡---◡--]   60
α[......]ω[......ε]ὕπεπλον [..].[]

ἡ[δὲ Πειράν]αν ἑλικοστέφανον]
        κ[ούραν, ὅ]σαι τ' ἄλλαι θεῶν
ε[ὐναῖς ἐδ]άμησαν ἀριγνώτ[ο]ις π[α]λαι.[οῦ]
[παῖδες αἰ]δο[ῖ]αι ποταμοῦ   65
        κε[λ]άδοντος·

[Automedes] came back to the purple-eddying Asopos, of whom the fame has gone over the whole earth and even to the far reaches of the Nile. And those who dwell by the fair-flowing Thermodon, skilled in the spear, daughters of horse-driving Ares, have had a taste of your descendants, o much envied king of rivers, as has the seat of high-gated Troy. On a wide path travel in all directions the countless reports of your progeny, the shining-girdled daughters whom the gods with good fortune have settled as rulers of unsacked streets. For who does not know of the well-built town of dark-haired Thebe or of the renowned Aegina, who (came to) the bed of great Zeus and bore the hero ... who the land of the Achaeans by the tests ... ? ... fair-robed ... and (Peirene the maiden) of the twirling garland, and all those others who won glory when bedded by gods, venerable daughters of the ancient resounding river.

Here the river serves, as so often, as the perfect means of establishing a 'natural' connection between the victor's home town and the larger Greek world, acting as a trajectory between one region and the other, while Asopos' several daughters extend their father's reach and make the local topographical feature the literal source of familiar sites in far-flung places.[49] As my reading of this and the immediately surrounding passages of the composition illustrates, Bacchylides punctuates these several sections with diction and conceits designed to fashion intersections between the chief actors in each scene and to frame the multiple protagonists – the river, his nymphine daughters and Automedes himself – in ways that position them as participants in a *choreia* that prefigures and models that of the Bacchylidean chorus.

This choral motif makes its initial showing in the vividly realized description of the victor as he performed his winning feats in the pentathlon (27–36):

πενταέθλοισιν γὰρ ἐνέπρεπεν ὡς
    ἄστρων διακρίνει φάη
νυκτὸς διχομηνίδο[ς] εὐφεγγὴς σελάνα·
τοῖος Ἑλλάνων δι' ἀπ[εί]ρονα κύκλον   30
φαῖνε. θαυμ[α]στὸν δέμας
δίσκον τροχοειδέα ῥίπτων,
καὶ μελαμφύλλου κλάδον
ἀκτέας ἐς αἰπεινὰν προπέμπων
αἰθέρ' ἐκ χειρὸς βοὰν ὤτρυνε λαῶν·   35

ἢ τε[λε]υτάσας ἀμάρυγμα πάλας

> for he was conspicuous among the pentathletes as the bright moon in the mid-month night outshines the light of stars; even so in the endless circle of the Greeks did he display his wondrous form casting the wheel-shaped discus and when, sending forth the dark-leaved branch of the elder into the lofty sky from his hand, he aroused the shout of the people or as he completed the flashing moves of the wrestling.

For an audience familiar with depictions of choruses in earlier epic and lyric sources, both the language and imagery of the opening lines would readily align Automedes with a *chorêgos* surrounded by the (lesser) members of his troupe. Just as Nausikaa stands out (μετέπρεπε, *Od.* 6.109) among her serving maids as she leads them in their dance, and the singers of Alcman's first *Partheneion* style their chorus leader Agido 'pre-eminent' (ἐκπρεπής, 46), so the present-day *laudandus* surpasses his fellow

---

[49] I return to this passage in Chapter 9.

contestants. Pointing to the same set of choral conventions is the astral simile that follows, and which, in the view of Fearn and others,[50] echoes the famous conceit in Sappho fr. 96.6–10 V. Since the individual whom Sappho likens to the brilliant star outshining her companions in Lydia is singularized for her special delight in *molpê* (5), the poet seemingly characterizes the absent woman as an erstwhile lead dancer of the Lesbian group she has now left behind. As other chapters have shown, the equivalence between the *chorêgos* and supremely radiant star both pre- and postdates Sappho, reaching from the Homeric shield of Achilles through to the 'shining star (αἰγλά[ε]ντος ἀστήρ)' that stands figure for the Astymelousa in Alcman's third *Partheneion* and on into Attic drama.

Additional pointers to chorality depend on the spatial design that Bacchylides invites us to envision for the athletic *agôn*. Positioned at the epicentre of his fellow pentathletes, themselves surrounded by the 'boundless circle' of spectators shouting out their acclaim, Automedes appears much as do the two Phaeacian star dancers performing their ball dance while their fellow chorus members look on, raising an approbatory din with their clapping hands. Representative of the larger company forming the second tier of bystanders and viewers, Odysseus already acknowledges the wonder (σέβας) that the spectacle elicits in him (*Od.* 8.372–84) much as the epinician chorus registers the *thauma* that belongs to the performer-athlete's outward form.[51] Bacchylides' description privileges choral circularity in smaller ways too: the victor makes his cast with the 'wheel-shaped discus', executing a move in which the body would describe an arc. And if the Homeric account of the choral dance on the shield of Achilles reflects traditional notions and conceits, then the spins of the moving wheel, included there by way of *comparanda* for the dancers' footwork (*Il.* 18.599–601), would supply a familiar metonym for the rapid turns that a chorus member performed.

One final term at the description's close also draws on diction regularly found in the context of choral performances. Where the passage began with an evocation of the moon's radiance, so it ends with more flashing light (ἀμάρυγμα, 36), this time emitted by Automedes' moves in the wrestling bout. If the opening simile draws on Sappho fr. 96 V., then ἀμάρυγμα appears in another of that poet's songs, which, like fr. 96 V., recalls a girl as

---

[50] Fearn 2003, 362–63; Cairns 2010, 254 questions the claim.

[51] Cf. the *thauma* aroused in Odysseus by the earlier choral dance (8.265) and Bacchylides' use of θαυμαστόν for Automedes' body. For a similar tripartite structure, see the choral scene on Achilles' shield.

2 Fathers and Daughters: The Asopids

she once danced as *première* in a chorus:[52] there, in a recollection of the now-departed Anaktoria, the speaker declares her longing to see 'the brilliant sparkle of her face' (κἀμάρυχμα λάμπρον ... προσώπω, fr. 16.18 V.). Bacchylides' choice of noun works particularly neatly here: since ἀμάρυγμα offers a variation on the noun μαρμαρυγή regularly used in epic accounts of the sparkle generated by choral dancers' feet, it seems particularly apt for a wrestler whose skill in part resides in his no less expert and rapidly shifting feet, the pedal twists and turns that guarantee him victory (cf. Pind. *Nem.* 4.93).

Choral terminology, which allows Bacchylides' audience to see in the ongoing performance a re-enactment of the past events, both mythical and historical, that the singers call to mind, continues to manifest itself in the subsequent passage, where the poet focuses on the Asopos and goes on to celebrate his daughters. Positioned just after the depiction of Automedes' winning cast, the striking hapax πορφυροδίναν, 'with purple eddies', used of the river revisits the idea of circularity, and preserves in the present-day landscape the movements integral to the athlete's earlier triumph. Such whirling motion then returns in the subsequent description of the Asopids, whom Bacchylides invests with the radiance, sparkle and elements of circularity that characterized both Automedes and the Asopos. First intro-ducing the sorority, the poet styles them 'shining-girdled' (λιπαροζώνων, 49–50) while Peirene (?) is distinguished by her 'twirling garland' (ἑλικοστέφα[νον], 62), an epithet which also assigns her the circular wreath that earlier crowned Automedes (23).[53]

Closing out this mythical excursus is a return to the Asopos and its waters, whose mention supplied the point of departure for the embedded narrative. Where earlier the poet alerted us to the river's swirls, he now highlights its audibility as it emits a κέλαδος (65), the noise made by running water that can also describe the singing of epinician compositions (see Bacch. 14.21) and musical sound, usages that invest the term with metapoetic significance. Confirming this anticipatory pointer to the cur-rent enactment of the ode, and turning the resounding Asopid waters into one among the diverse celebrants of the victory, just such instrumental music returns as the subject of the lacunose phrase that appears three lines

---

[52] Also cited by Fearn 2003, 364 in passing; see too Cairns 2010, 256. For this reading of fr. 16 V., see Chapter 1.

[53] The reference to Aphrodite and the Erotes in the fragmentary passage at 66–76 seems further to draw the mythical heroines and victor together. Understood by commentators as a nod to the victor's youth, loveliness and still unwed state, these attributes would make him, like the Asopids who aroused divine desire, a focus of erotic attention.

on, where the singers cite the 'shouts' of the typically vociferous pipes (αὐ]
λῶν βοαί, 68), which quite likely accompanied the ongoing performance.
With the river's clamour now transposed to the vocal and musical registers,
Bacchylides promotes the confluence of the multiple scenes, each filled
with choral sounds and kinetics. The metaphoric vocalizations of the
instruments loop back not just to the river but to the much earlier shout
of the spectators (βοάν, 35) witnessing the victory of Automedes, whose
skillful moves find an enduring model in the eddying Asopos and, at the
more microcosmic level, in the accessories that deck out his daughters. If
the role of *choreia* is in no small part to meld together present, past and
mythical events, and to demonstrate continuity through time and space,
then Bacchylides' arrangement of his chosen scenes and protagonists has
amply satisfied the composer's brief.

2.5   *Corinna fr. 654* PMG

Pindar and Bacchylides are not the only fifth-century poets to feature the
Asopids as an archetypal chorus ready for emulation and modelling in their
choral songs. My final instance, a work by the Boeotian poet Corinna
(whom the anecdotal tradition, extrapolating from Pindaric elements in
her compositions, imagines as rival to that poet, whom she supposedly
defeated five times in competition), seems newly to introduce the sorority
as analogues for what, in this instance, is in and of itself a maiden chorus.
Of course any mention of Corinna comes surrounded by unresolved
debates concerning the poet's date, the manner in which her songs were
performed and their intended audience, and two assumptions, more carefully argued for by other scholars,[54] underpin the reading that follows: first,
that Corinna belongs to the fifth century, and second, that her poems were
most likely composed for choruses of *parthenoi* in Tanagra and perhaps
elsewhere in Boeotia. Among the more extensive remaining fragments
belongs the so-called 'Daughters of Asopos', a work whose extant portion
occupies columns II to IV of fr. 654 *PMG*. The nymphs appear quite early

---

[54] Here I follow, among others, Stehle 1997, esp. 101–04, Larson 2002, Collins 2006, 19–20 (with
an overview of the argument), Lardinois 2011, 165–68. The case for the choral character of
Corinna's poetry rests on admittedly slender grounds. Fr. 655.1–16 *PMG*, which opens with an
invocation to Terpsichora ('she who delights in choruses') and is spoken in the voice of a poet or
that of the collective chorus, which announces that it proclaims the legends of its homeland,
Tanagra in Boeotia, offers the most compelling evidence. In Stehle's reading, the fragment
suggests that Corinna addresses two audiences for whom different songs are performed: first the
collective audience made up of the women of Tanagra, and second the *parthenoi* with whom the
stories 'from our fathers' time' seem to be connected.

in what remains of the poem, introduced in a list focused on their role as brides and abductees of the gods:[55]

ὧν Ἥγ[ιναν γε]νέθλαν
Δεὺς[　　　ἀ]γαθῶν
πατρο[　　ἐ]ς,
Κορκού[ραν δὲ κὴ Σαλαμῖ-]
ν' εἰδ[' Εὔβοιαν ἐράνναν]　　　　　　　　　　　　　5

Ποτι[δάων κλέψε πα]τείρ,
Σιν[ώπαν δὲ Λατοΐδα]ς
Θέσ[πιαν τ' ἔστιν ἔχων·

Of these (daughters) Zeus, giver of good things, (took) his child Aegina . . . from her father's . . . while Corcyra (and Salamis) and (lovely Euboea) (were stolen) by father Poseidon, and (Leto's son) is in possession of Sinope and Thespia . . .

Where many discussions of the piece observe the overlaps between its subject matter, theme and structure and those found in the [Hesiodic] *Catalogue of Women*, which in standard reconstructions devoted a considerable portion of book 4 to the Asopid heroines, Corinna's piece may simultaneously tap into the chorality associated with the Asopids. With Tanagra likely concluding what takes the form of an enumerative review,[56] the initial list seems to feature an ascending scale, where the performers single out that final city for the closing and privileged position, as though granting it the pre-eminence owed to the *chorêgos*; its end location allows the poet to give it the requisite expanded space and elaboration. Since Tanagra supplies the site for what seem to be choral performances of Corinna's poetry by *parthenoi* in fr. 655 *PMG*, the passage might offer a fresh instance of choral projection, with the role of the Asopids here assumed by the latter-day ensemble of local maidens also on the threshold of marriage and even performing before an audience including potential grooms.[57] To speculate a little further, might the lead dancer of Corinna's troupe be the one assigned the privilege of assuming Tanagra's part, and,

[55] For the catalogue structure of the passage, see the discussion in Chapter 9.
[56] For this suggestion, see Page 1953, 26, Bowra 1938, 213 and, more recently, Kousoulini 2016, 86–87.
[57] Beyond that fragment, we have no references to choral activity in Tanagra, whether by *parthenoi* or other groups, although Calame 1997, 135 n. 131, citing Schachter 1981, 79–80 and 185–86, proposes that it might have been the site for an Agrionia, complete with a re-enactment of the race (for this festival and its choral connotations, see Chapter 4).

like other such *chorêgoi*, be the object of the praise and distinction that her fellow chorus members give to her?

The argument made in this section for the Asopids' status as a paradigmatic parthenaic chorus runs up against one major stumbling block: among all the representations cited, whether visual or textual, none explicitly grants the Asopids the character of a troupe of singer-dancers. For this we need instead to wait for a passage in the third stasimon of Euripides' *Heracles*, where the chorus, rejoicing at the death of Lycus, invites the whole Theban topography to join in the epinician-style dance and song being performed on the Attic stage (781–89):

> Ἰσμήν’ ὦ στεφαναφόρει
> ξεσταί θ’ ἑπταπύλου πόλεως
> ἀναχορεύσατ’ ἀγυιαὶ
> Δίρκα θ’ ἁ καλλιρρέεθρος,
> σύν τ’ Ἀσωπιάδες κόραι   785
>   πατρὸς ὕδωρ βᾶτε λιποῦσαι συναοιδοὶ
> Νύμφαι τὸν Ἡρακλέους
> καλλίνικον ἀγῶνα.

Be wreathed o river Ismenus, and you polished streets of seven-gated Thebes, start the dance, and you fair-flowing Dirke, and you maidens, daughters of Asopos, leave your father's waters and come, Nymphs, to join in singing of the contest Heracles gloriously won.

Here the Asopids' classification as 'nymphs' goes some way in predetermining their participation in the celebration as they engage in the prototypical activity, dancing, routinely assigned to these demi-gods in myth, cult and the visual tradition. But, in the proposal made here, Euripides also draws on the more specific and long-standing association between the daughters of Asopos and choral activity. Once again, a male chorus – and one whose dramatic identity is that of aged men – equates itself with this exemplary youthful maidenly ensemble and in so doing achieves the form of rejuvenation through *choreia* detailed in the drama's second stasimon.

3 Danaids

Notorious for killing their husbands on their wedding night, and for their sorry fate in the Underworld where they eternally carry water in leaky pithoi, the Danaids have a more auspicious and beneficent early and expressly Argive history, one centred about a tight connection with water that only turns punitive in what seems the later account. As my discussion traces out, several of our earliest sources imagine the maidens not in their man-slaying character but first and foremost as spring and river nymphs,[58] intimately involved in bringing water to regions where there was none before, and, insofar as they are guarantors of human as well as natural fertility, as sponsors of the powers of propagation of young maidens turning wives (*nymphai*). My concern is with the interplay between these aqueous-cum-nymphine aspects of the Danaids and their depiction in art and texts from the archaic through to the early classical age as a paradigmatic chorus, a collective with whom current-day ensembles may align themselves as they restage the performances of their mythical counterparts and draw on the powers traditionally assigned to them.[59]

3.1   The Argive Danaids

By the time the fifth-century sources introduce the Danaids, the heroines already carry with them a complex mythology that offers several templates from which individual authors can select. The earliest mention of the daughters of Danaos occurs in fr. 128 M.-W. of the [Hesiodic] *Catalogue of Women*, which Strabo cites (8.6.8), where the 'watery' element in their profile forms the focal point of the account. For the author of the *Catalogue*, the maidens, or their father, are responsible for irrigating Argos: the Danaids transformed the arid region into a land of springs. Homer is also familiar with at least some portion of the story: 'thirsty' is the epithet given Argos (πολυδίψιον Ἄργος) in the poet's formulaic diction. Apollodorus fills in the details at 2.1.4, attributing the desiccated condition of the land to a divine contretemps. Called in to adjudicate a dispute between Hera and Poseidon, Inachos, a son of Okeanos and Tethys and the earliest king of Argos as well as the eponymous river of the Argolid, decided that Hera should be the local deity.[60] In pique at the slight, Poseidon dried up the region's rivers. Waterless it remained until, when

---

[58] For the Danaids as nymphs, see Kaempf-Dimitriadou 1979, 28 n. 210; *LIMC* s.v. Danaides nos. 337–71, Amymone nos. 742–52; on springs and Danaids, see Detienne 1989 165, 168–70; on Amymone as river, see Dowden 1989, 151–53.

[59] While I focus on positive representations of the sisters, the Danaids may also, like the Proitids of the previous chapter (with whom their story shares several themes and motifs), appear alienated from both their choral and nymphine role, as they patently do in Aeschylus' *Suppliants*. Since both the nymphine and choral dimensions of the Aeschylean characters have received ample discussion in several excellent readings (see, in particular, Murnaghan 2005, Kavoulaki 2011, Swift 2010, Bachvarova 2009 and Dowden 1989), the drama does not figure in my discussion.

[60] Paus. 2.15.5 tells almost the same story, but has Inachos judge together with two other rivers, Kephisos and Asterion.

Danaos became king in turn, he sent his daughters out in search of water, an enterprise that corresponds to the historical sinking of wells.[61]

Visible in this dimension of the narrative is the link between the Danaids' role in the re-hydration of the Argolid and their status as archetypal brides, this second element manifest both in their personal histories and in the place of water, whether carried or deployed, in the ritual acts preceding marriage. Through the course of her quest, Amymone, typically shown in fifth-century vase representations equipped with a hydria or other jug for carrying the water that is both the object of her search and, as it turns out, prenuptial too,[62] rouses a sleeping satyr who pursues her until Poseidon comes to her rescue, claiming her in turn; by way of wedding gift, he reveals the sources of the Lerna and so reverses his earlier punishment. Pausanias reports the presence of a spring and the river it fed called Amymone at Lerna (2.37.1), on the boundaries of the land whose fertility its never-failing waters guaranteed, while a second water source known by the same name was located in the city of Argos; there it coexisted with three other springs important to the cult of Hera and similarly identified with the Danaids.[63]

These same four springs are eponymous with four among the Danaids who, combining their role as personified waters with that of local heroines and nymphs, appear in two passages from Callimachus' *Aetia*. Presumably basing his accounts on Argolid myths from much earlier times, the poet makes the springs Amymone, Physadeia, Hippe and Automate, all described as daughters of Danaos, the subjects of the now-fragmentary lines that introduce them in the context of purification rites.[64] Fr. 66 Pf., the more extensive of the two extant fragments, opens by invoking its four addressees as 'heroines' (ἡρῶσσαι), a term that can be used of local goddesses as well as of girls or women of special status in myth.[65] The next line focuses on Amymone, whose love-story provided the *aition* for one of the springs; now described as a 'water (ἐφυδριάς) … nymph', the maiden's

---

[61] Larson 2001, 150. Strabo 8.6.8 finds the account inapposite due to the ubiquity of rivers, lakes, marshes and wells in the region and the many wells in the city of Argos, whose discovery, Strabo tells us, was ascribed to the Danaids. He proposes various emendations to the Homeric phrase.

[62] The scene is particularly popular on fifth-century lebetes gamikoi, an indication of its pertinence to the nuptial rite.

[63] For these, see Apollod. 2.1.4 and Strabo 8.6.8.

[64] As Larson 2001, 150 plausibly concludes, 'Amymone, then, and at least some of her sisters were probably water nymphs attracted into the Danaid saga'. Call. *H.* 5.47–48 instructs slaves to carry water from springs on the day of Athena's bath, mentioning specifically Physadeia and Amymone, 'the (daughter) of Danaos'.

[65] Harder 2012 *ad loc.*

aquatic dimension is brought to the fore and here directly coupled with her status as bride.[66]

By line 6 of the passage, Amymone has unmistakably become the water that supplies the wherewithal for the ritual that the fragment records: those engaged in weaving the sacred garment for Hera must first purify themselves with the substance furnished by the spring, which then appears as the subject and addressee of the phrase: 'truly it is not allowed that girls whose task it is to weave Hera's sacred garment stand at the loom before they have poured your water on their head, sitting on the holy rock around which you run on both sides (τὸν μὲν σὺ μέσον περιδέδρομας ἀμφίς)' (2–6). The penultimate phrase, which bids farewell to the four water sources, which it names and designates the 'venerable homes of nymphs', takes a more rationalizing stance: these springs, fountains or wells are named after the Danaids, whose habitation they also provide. The final extant line, 'flow sleek / fertility-bringing Pelasgian girls' (λιπαραὶ ῥεῖτε Πελασγιάδες, 9) equivocates between the several possible identities; these girls are at once the Danaid maidens, complete with parentage, and irrigating springs.

Also suggestive here is the link to the purification rite performed under the auspices of Hera, introduced by Callimachus in lines 2–6, and which those charged with weaving the goddess' special robe must undertake.[67] The poet designates the garment with the term *patos*, a noun unattested elsewhere and glossed by grammarians as a peplos or *enduma*. Such purificatory bathing was central to Hera's role as paradigmatic bride; in one instance of the practice, our sources describe the periodic bath that the goddess' image received in Argive cult, for which special priestesses known as the Eresides carried the water.[68] As many assume, this bath has a prenuptial character and may well have preceded a *hieros gamos* similar to that included in the mysteries of Hera at the spring of Canathus in Nauplia. In Pausanias' account of the Nauplian rite at 2.38.2–3, the goddess became a *parthenos* again after bathing in that spring each year.[69] The robe woven by the Argive maidens in Callimachus' lines thus forms a piece with the celebrants' own bath in their local spring; while their immersion in the waters re-enacts Hera's corresponding action, the cloth they will go on to weave can supply both the bridal robe and a covering for the marriage bed.

[66] As Larson 2001, 53 notes, ἐφυδριάς is an adjective that is used elsewhere of nymphs.
[67] The two extant lines of fr. 65 Pf. also record a purification rite that interlinks female fertility (here women who have just gone through childbirth), one of the Danaids, Automate, and the stream that bears her name (Αὐτομά[της] εὐναὲς ἐπών[υμον, 'with fair flowing stream, called after Automate').
[68] Larson 2001, 115 with n. 73.
[69] For comparable rites in festivals of Hera, see Steiner 2001, 110.

This nuptial motif may even extend to the rock on which participants in the rite must sit, a detail that looks not to Hera but to Amymone's earlier 'history'; in textual accounts, Poseidon strikes a rock so as to restore the Argive water sources when he bestows his gift on his new-won bride.[70] Reinforcing this complex of activities is the poet's choice of epithet for the 'Pelasgian girls', λιπαραί. The waters are so styled not just for their radiance but also for the richness and fruitful quality of the springs, promoters of the fertility of the Argolid and its brides.

Within this group of myths and ritual practices are several possible pointers to the Danaids' role as practitioners and sponsors of the maidenly *choreia* that forms part and parcel of their character as nymphs and that figures prominently in the earlier text detailed in the next section of the discussion. John Scheid and Jesper Svenbro propose that the festival for which Hera's robe is being woven in fr. 66 Pf. is the Argive Endumatia,[71] to which we have only one very passing and late reference. In a passage describing the early establishment (the term is *katastasis*) of choral lyric in different parts of Greece, [Plutarch] names three composers, Thaletas of Gortyn, Xenocritus of Locri and Polymnestus of Colophon, as responsible for the reorganization of musical institutions at Sparta; among the festivals for which they composed their works in other parts of Greece was the Feast of the Endumatia at Argos, here cited alongside the Spartan Gymnopaidia and the Feast of Apodeixeis in Arcadia (*De mus.* 1134c). A fragment of Sosibius (cited in Athen. 15.678b–c) gives an account of choral events at the Gymnopaidia while Xenocritus was variously credited with the composition of paeans and dithyrambs, both of which would suit rites that included choral performances. If just such spectacles of song and dance occurred at this Argive festival – as they did at the Heraia at Elis that also combined the weaving of a robe for Hera, ritual purification in a spring, choral dances and initiation rites for young girls in the form of running races (Paus. 5.16.2–8)[72] – then the Danaids, waters and maidens both, would also supply paradigms for the *parthenoi* who danced at Hera's festival.

While the Callimachean fragment includes no mention of the aftermath of the ritual described, and the extant lines do not specify the festival for which the garment is destined, the preparation of a robe designed for a

---

[70] In the visual tradition, several artists include a rock in the encounter between Poseidon and Amymone; see Larson 2001, 115 and a red-figure pelike in Agrigento (Agrigento, Museo Archeologico Regionale 1586) showing the scene.

[71] Scheid and Svenbro 1996, 31 and 77, with notes.

[72] Later chapters return to this event on several occasions.

hieros gamos corresponds with what we know of the large-scale rite celebrated in the Argive Heraion, variously called the Heraia or Hekatombaia,
and that, in Burkert's view, is the occasion that the poet has in mind in
describing the pre-weaving purification rite.[73] According to standard
reconstructions, the high point of the Heraia ritual involved first the
presentation of a peplos to the goddess and then the celebration of the
sacred marriage for which the garment had been woven. As the sources
make clear, parthenaic choruses participated at the event and may even
have performed as the cloth was delivered. Our clearest indication of their
presence belongs to a passage from Euripides' *Electra* noted in the previous
chapter, where the local maidenly chorus invites the protagonist to join its
procession (so στείχειν at 174) to the shrine where the celebrants will
perform their choral dances. But Electra, citing her lamentable want of
finery, declines their invitation (178–80):

> οὐδ' ἱστᾶσα χορούς
> Ἀργείαις ἅμα νύμφαις
> εἱλικτὸν κρούσω πόδ' ἐμόν.   180

> Nor will I, taking my position in the chorus together with the Argive
> maidens, strike my whirling foot.

Calame cites several other references to such choral activity at the Heraia,
both textual and visual,[74] while Pausanias makes passing mention of the
purification rite practised by some of the chief actors in the sequence of
events (2.17.1); the priestesses who performed the sacrifices integral to the
ritual would cleanse themselves in the waters of a spring in the vicinity of
the shrine called the Eleutherion.

Connections between the members of the Danaid sorority and the
Heraia leave their trace in another source. Several scholars have suggested
that Aeschylus' Danaid trilogy might have furnished an aetiology for the
festival, particularly in light of the tradition that Hypermnestra (and Io
before her, in Hellanikos' chronological account)[75] became priestess of
Hera at Argos.[76] At the Heraia, the real-world priestess of the goddess, an
important civic presence whose tenure of service was used to date cult
matters and historical events,[77] held a place of honour, mounted on an ox-
drawn cart and driven in the sacrificial procession that made its way to the
temple. Assuming that the parthenaic choruses would have accompanied

[73] Burkert 1983, 163.
[74] Calame 1997, 119–20; for visual accounts, see Crowhurst 1963 nos. 50, 56, 92, 93, 95, 96 and 100.
[75] *FGrH* 4 F 74–83.   [76] See Belfiore 2000, 59.
[77] For details, see Connelly 2007, 57 and 69–72.

this pre-eminent individual and latter-day counterpart to Hypermnestra, we would witness a scenario familiar from other choral rites: an ensemble made up of local maidens charged with taking on the roles of the original Danaid dancers, companions and subordinate to the individual who served as the *chorêgos*-like figure, much as Hypermnestra (she who is 'much wooed') once did.

Whatever place the Danaids did or did not hold at the Heraia, the nymphs' status as a paradigmatic chorus on whom maiden Argive ensembles might fashion themselves can be discerned in other facets of their characterization. Calame observes how the suffix -*id* in the sisters' name and the fact of their collectivity aligns them with a series of similarly designated mythical and historical choruses, whether the Nereids, Deliades or Okeanids;[78] significant too is the number fifty, which reappears in other groups of singer-dancers including the Nereids, the daughters of Kinyras (see Chapter 3), and actual dithyrambic choruses of men and boys. It was, in another instance, a mixed chorus of fifty youths and maidens that the Megarians sent yearly to Corinth to perform laments for the daughter of the Megarian Klytias, who had died after her marriage to the Bacchiad king of Corinth.[79]

Early visual evidence may also exhibit the Danaids in their choral role. Several art historians have identified the parthenaic choruses so commonplace on Argive Geometric pottery and more particularly on vessels found in proximity of the Heraion located midway between Argos and Mycenae (over half of the extant examples come from the shrine) as Danaids, or, as I would suggest, local maidens reperforming the dances first enacted by their mythical antecedents. The Danaid identification makes good sense of a distinctive feature of this corpus: in her review of these representations, Langdon remarks that 'in Geometric art, maiden dancers are regularly associated with water only in the Argolid', a singularity she then plausibly explains by suggesting that 'Geometric artists might find no better way to evoke the Danaids than a line of identical maidens surrounded by their gift of water'.[80] Their veils, belts and the dancers' repeated pairing with horses being tamed additionally anticipate the maidens' (eventual) submission to the necessity of marriage, which the latter-day choristers now model for the viewer, whether other nubile girls in attendance at the rite, or youths perusing these potential wives and mothers.

---

[78] Calame 1997, 30.   [79] For these, see Dowden 1989, 158.   [80] Langdon 2008, 158 and 165.

3.2 *Pindar*, Pyth. *9.105–20*

Langdon's interpretation of these dancing *parthenoi* as Danaids about to undergo a change in status closely matches the unequivocal depiction of the maidens as a chorus in Pindar's ninth *Pythian*, a work already cited in Chapter 1 for its choral terminology. In an ode among whose central preoccupations are marriage and, as corollary to this, fertility and human and natural 'ripeness', and whose chief mythical paradigm is the nymph Cyrene whom Apollo must win as bride, the poet concludes the song with a turn to the victor's ancestors, who came along with many others to seek the hand of the daughter of the Libyan Antaios. In the Pindaric version of events in lines 112–20, the maiden's father chooses to adopt the device earlier deployed by Danaos to dispose of his forty-eight daughters on a single occasion (the number neatly pinpoints the stage in the myth at which the contest occurs: Amymone has already been claimed by Poseidon and Hypermnestra, unlike her remaining sisters, has spared her Egyptian husband).[81] In Pindar's visualization of the event,

> Δαναόν ποτ' ἐν Ἄργει
> οἷον εὗρεν τεσσαράκοντα καὶ ὀκ-
>   τὼ παρθένοισι πρὶν μέσον ἆμαρ, ἑλεῖν
> ὠκύτατον γάμον· ἔστασεν γὰρ ἅπαντα χορόν
> ἐν τέρμασιν αὐτίκ' ἀγῶνος·
> σὺν δ' ἀέθλοις ἐκέλευσεν διακρῖναι ποδῶν,   115
> ἄντινα σχήσοι τις ἡρώ-
>   ων, ὅσοι γαμβροί σφιν ἦλθον.
>
> οὕτω δ' ἐδίδου Λίβυς ἁρμόζων κόρᾳ
> νυμφίον ἄνδρα· ποτὶ γραμμᾷ μὲν αὐτὰν
>   στᾶσε κοσμήσαις, τέλος ἔμμεν ἄκρον,
> εἶπε δ' ἐν μέσσοις ἀπάγεσθαι, ὃς ἂν πρῶτος θορών
> ἀμφὶ οἱ ψαύσειε πέπλοις.   120

Danaos once in Argos had devised such a means to gain a most swift marriage for his forty-eight daughters before noon; straightaway he placed the whole chorus at the finish line of the contest and ordered that there be a decision by the trials of a foot race to determine which daughter each hero would have, of those who came as bridegrooms for them. In this manner the Libyan made an offer for matching a groom to his daughter.

---

[81] Pindar is not our only source for the story. According to Paus. 3.12.2, the foot race for the suitors organized by Danaos serves as the paradigm for the same-style contest arranged by Penelope's father for the selection of the groom.

> Having decked her out, he stood her at the line, to be the final goal, and he
> said in their midst that whoever first leaping forward should touch her
> garment would lead her off with him.

As the discussion by Micah Myers argues, and as an earlier chapter noted, previous readers of the lines have neglected to observe how Pindar depicts the courtship event not so much as an athletic competition as an enterprise that inscribes the race within the frame of a parthenaic choral dance.[82] Using an expression drawn from the technical language of *choreia*, χορὸν ἵστημι, Danaos assumes the role of the *chorêgos* who arranges the maidenly aggregate in the performative arena, or more specifically, the 'dancing place' which the term ἀγών selected here not infrequently describes.[83]

As Myers further proposes, Pindar's evocation of a performing chorus then carries over into the more 'historical' courtship contest in which the victor's ancestor Alexidamos participated. Although his discussion does not develop the point, both the structural design of this closing portion of the ode and the poet's diction prompt the superimposition of the Danaid scene onto the later occasion, and invite us to continue to hold two contexts – a running race and choral performance – simultaneously in mind. In the architecture of the passage, Alexidamos' victory in the *agôn* flanks the Danaid episode on either side, while the details of that 'historical' courtship coincide with and reinforce the choral dimensions of its mythical precedent: not only is the emphatic declaration of Antaios' daughter's beauty (θαητὸν εἶδος, 108) consistent with descriptions of the pre-eminent loveliness that a single maiden in the group, and leader of the rest, displays in other choral poetry, but we witness a replay of the familiar scenario whereby that same outstanding individual is abducted or departs in marriage from the company of her fellow maidens while dancing in a chorus. Consonant too with this choral colouring is Antaios' conduct here. Even as his mythical prototype arranges his plurality of daughters for their dance, so this father similarly acts in the choregic manner as he 'decks out' (κοσμήσαις, 118) the bride-to-be in the finery that parthenaic choreutes display; in a further correspondence noted earlier, when Antaios 'positions' the nubile maiden 'on the line' (γραμμᾷ ... στᾶσε, 118),[84] his gesture mirrors that of Danaos 'placing' his daughters on the equivalent markers or *termata*, not just the terminus of the race but also the 'turning points' that can demarcate the site at which a dance reverses itself prior to

---

[82] Myers 2007.   [83] See Chapter 1.
[84] Note too that the term *gramma* is used of lines traced out in the theatrical *orchestra* to guide the movements of the chorus.

redescribing its choreographic course.[85] Bivalence similarly belongs to the verb that Pindar uses for the action that the winner is to perform: inviting the would-be groom to 'leap' (θορών, 119) so as to touch the girl's (nuptial) peplos, Antaios' language calls to mind not just the consummation of Alexidamos' erotic designs,[86] but also the motion familiar from many Geometric and late archaic depictions of both exclusively male and mixed choruses. On a Corinthian aryballos showing a group of youths dancing in a contest, the lead dancer performs an acrobatic leap (Fig. 8.2),[87] and the move occurs a second time on a rim fragment from the Argive Heraion in a depiction of youths and maidens performing in a single space; while the latter dance demurely with small steps, a single male facing them jumps up high.[88]

On one further count Antaios' daughter takes on elements elsewhere associated with the Danaids. Emphatic in the depiction of the much courted maiden from whom the suitors are eager to 'cull the blooming fruit (καρπὸν ἀνθήσαντ' ἀποδρέψαι) of gold-crowned Hebe' (109–10) and whose marriage her father literally 'plants' (φυτεύων, 111) is the reprise of the floral and fertility imagery that is so dominant a motif in the ode's earlier retelling of the story of the nymph Cyrene and her relocation to Libya, where she promotes the flourishing of plants, crops and flocks. The language of the lines describing the latter-day suitors' sentiments and actions contain clear echoes of that opening myth: the audience has already heard Apollo ask whether he may legitimately 'lay his hand' (36; cf. χειρὸς ἑλών, 122) on Cyrene and 'reap the honey-sweet flower (κεῖραι μελιαδέα ποίαν, 37)' from the bridal bed. Insofar as the Danaids as nymphs are sponsors not just of marriage, but also of the fertility that results from their re-irrigation of Argos and their broader 'nymphine' links with water-filled sites, they have a natural place among these other bloom-instigating and blossoming brides.

Reading the Danaids and Antaios' daughter, their stand-in at her own courtship competition, as versions of or counterparts to Cyrene also makes sense of the shading in Pindar's introduction of Apollo's bride-to-be in lines 13–16: there the poet names her the daughter of Hypseus, 'a hero second in descent from Okeanos whom ... Kreousa, the Naïd daughter of

[85] Also suggestive is the Libyan father's position ἐν μέσσοις (119) as he issues his instructions to the suitors: the expression suggests a circular formation, with the *chorêgos* located in the middle of his dancers.
[86] Used transitively, in Attic tragedy θρώσκω regularly means to 'mount, impregnate'.
[87] Corinth, Archaeological Museum C 54.1, with detailed discussion in Chapter 8.
[88] For this, see Langdon 2008, 185 and her fig. 3.27; see too the material collected in Crowhurst 1963 for more leaping dancers.

Gaia, bore having found love in the marriage bed of Peneios'. Granddaughter of a water nymph who was married to the personification of the principal Thessalian river,[89] Cyrene possesses all the aquatic and riverine associations of the Argive maidens. Like her Danaid counterparts too, she is also, in a tradition familiar to our later sources, eponymous with a Cyrenean spring from which the city may have taken its name. Stephanus of Byzantium offers two possible etymologies for that designation, either 'city of Libya, from Cyrene, the daughter of Hypseus, or from the native spring, Cyra', a duality that Callimachus already exploits by identifying the sacred spring of Apollo in the city as Cyra.[90]

Cyrenean traditions, topography and rituals are also apposite to the mapping of a running race onto a choral dance visible at the close of *Pythian* 9. As the epigraphic and literary evidence makes plain, Cyrene was host to a rich and expansive choral culture that supposedly reached back to mythical times and to the very occasion that lies behind the Pindaric visualization of Alexidamos' courtship of the Libyan maiden, which the poet here embeds in a celebration of a victory at the games at the Pythian sanctuary of Apollo. According to Callimachus' *Hymn to Apollo* (which draws on Pindar's fifth *Pythian* and its references to Karneian Apollo), the Cyrenean founder Battos built the temple of Apollo Karneios at Azilis, where the Cretans (newcomers too) danced at the Karneia for the first time with the local Libyan women (85–87). Intriguingly, one vase image offers evidence for a girl-youth dance at a celebration of this same Apolline festival: on the reverse of a Lucanian red-figure volute krater dated to ca. 420–400 (Fig. 5.3),[91] in a scene showing the preliminary stages of a choral performance, a girl and boy dance together near a pillar inscribed with the word Karneios. The designation locates the event at a sanctuary of Apollo Karneios, most likely the one at Sparta, although nothing on the vase confirms the site. Epigraphic evidence belonging to the second half of the fourth century also attests to dithyrambic choruses that performed in rituals at Cyrene, again, according to the most recent account, in the celebration of Apollo Karneios.[92]

The closing visualization in *Pythian* 9 thus brings together and creates tight connections between the event in which the Cyrenean Telesikrates

---

[89] In the Hesiodic tradition of the *Catalogue of Women*, Cyrene simply lives 'beside the waters of the Peneios' ([Hes.] fr. 215 M.-W.).

[90] St. Byz. s.v. Κυρήνη; Call. *H.* 2.88–90. For discussion, see Dougherty 1993, 147.

[91] Taranto, Museo Nazionale Archeologico 8263; for analysis, see Ferrari 2008, 135–37 and Ceccarelli and Milanezi 2007, 199.

[92] Ceccarelli and Milanezei 2007, 196–99.

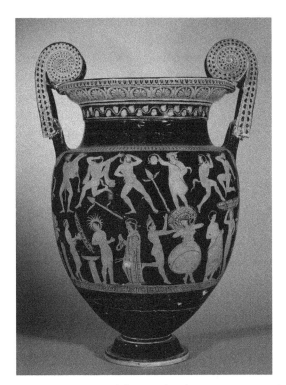

Fig. 5.3 Lucanian red-figure volute krater, ca. 420–400 B.C.E. Taranto, Museo Nazionale Archeologico 8263. Photograph © 2019. White Images/Scala, Florence.

carried off his prize – the running race at the Delphic games – and the current celebration of that win, a choral song and dance that identifies itself with a more regular ritual event at his native city also performed in Apollo's honour (and that, to boot, occurred at the temple of the god that dates back to the sixth century, and whose location was determined by the sacred spring at the site, the so-called Spring of Apollo).[93] Insofar as Pindar's internal *choros* of Argive Danaids finds its counterpart in the actual Cyrenean performers, the members of the encomiastic group follow a consistent motif in the ode where traditional gender lines are blurred, and where Telesikrates himself is equated with the *parthenos* Cyrene.[94] More broadly consistent with the compositions of Pindar and Bacchylides, and as already noted in Section 1, a choral work performed by an ensemble of youths takes its cue from an internal maidenly collective, which further displays the attributes that the current dancer-singers should exhibit: the

[93] It seems plausible that the performance of *Pythian* 9 occurred at the same location.

[94] For the intriguing suggestion that the dancers at the Karneia involved just such gender switches, see Ferrari 2008, 147–51.

cohesion or good order and harmony apparent in the Danaids' alignment and in the *kosmos* assigned their Libyan counterpart.

Nor is it the choral dance alone that associates the Pindaric performance to the Karneia. Although there are no sure attestations of racing at the Cyrenean version of the festival, a foot race involving some of the youths, designated *staphylodromoi* or 'grape-runners', was one among the principal elements of the Karneia as celebrated in Sparta, Cnidos and Thera.[95] Pindar may even nod towards that Cyrenean event, together with the presence of choruses, when, in a more prolonged visit to the city, he reports that Aristoteles, in his role as founder, 'laid down a road straight-cut and level for the processions (πομπαῖς) of Apollo' (*Pyth.* 5.90–91), a space well suited to both processional choruses and to runners.[96] The co-presence of racing and choral dancing and the tight relations between them is a theme explored at other points in this chapter and in the broader study, and one of particular relevance to both the *laudandus* of *Pythian* 9 and those now celebrating his success in song and dance. It was precisely youths on the brink of adulthood, the age group to which Telesikrates belongs, who would participate in these two activities and whose conduct the Pindaric chorus members re-enact as they revisit those historical, mythical and ritual races verbally and, perhaps, kinetically too in the choreography of their dance.

4 Nereids

My third choral grouping retains many of the characteristics already observed for the Danaids. Among the several indicators of the Danaid-Nereid proximity belong the names that the members of the two collectives share: Glauke, one of the four daughters of Danaos born to him by Europa along with Automate, Amymone and Scaea (Apoll. 2.1.5), also figures as a Nereid in Homer and Hesiod (*Il.* 18.39, *Th.* 244). More broadly suggestive of their joint participation in the single overarching typology is the Nereids' morphology and signature activity: they too are a fifty-strong sorority (the number becomes canonical, although their size fluctuates in the early sources) and dancing chorus that regularly performs not only the laments observed in Chapter 3, but prenuptial dances too, most typically on the occasion of the loss of their leader Thetis to the mortal Peleus, who claims

---

[95] See Burkert 1985, 234–35 for detailed discussion.

[96] Granted, the poet goes on to observe that the road was designed 'to echo with horses' hoofs'.

her in marriage. Following Corinthian artists who first take up the motif,
Attic vase painters of the sixth and fifth century repeatedly portrayed
Nereids in the context of this abduction scene (there are over one hundred
such images),[97] where the would-be ravisher variously stalks, pursues or
struggles with his intended bride. While interpretations of the Nereids'
action on these occasions differs, Judith Barringer makes a compelling case
for reading the postures adopted by the nymphs on two early Corinthian
and Attic pots – both dated to ca. 560[98] – as that of dancers rather than of
maidens in flight, and she also cites an Attic red-figure cup by the Poseidon
Painter of ca. 510–500 (Fig. 2.2),[99] where the artist clearly differentiates
between the two sets of nymphs in the abduction scene: while the Nereids
on the left of the struggling pair run with long strides and vigorous arm
movements, the gestures of those on the far right are characteristic of
dancers in other visual accounts.[100] To Barringer's evidence I would add
a still earlier seventh-century representation, a fragment from a 'Melian'
amphora dated to ca. 630–600 from Neapolis.[101] Positioned on the neck is a
depiction of Peleus' abduction of Thetis, whom he grasps by the wrist so as
to draw her away from the company of her fellow Nereids. Two of the
company that surrounds the pair again exactly conform to dancer typology;
with their lead foot raised up in the air, and the hand of one located so as to
lift up the richly patterned skirt that she, like her companions, wears, they
betray no signs of haste or alarm as they circle around the surface of the
vase. Unequivocal evidence for artistic representations of Nereids as dancers comes in the form of the well-known black-figure Little Master lip cup
from Tarquinia of ca. 550 (Fig. 5.4) more fully discussed below.[102]

Literary accounts likewise imagine Nereids as choral dancers, an activity
realized on the Attic stage in Aeschylus' no longer extant *Nereids*, whose
chorus took on the role of the nymphs, and a detailed discussion by Csapo
both reviews the evidence and argues for the sisters' more specific delineation as dithyrambic performers.[103] As he also shows, Nereids regularly
appear in the company of dolphins, whom our sources make integral to the
origins of the dithyrambic genre and who, like the Nereids, 'dance' in
circular formations in maritime settings. While the circular chorus does

[97] Barringer 1995 offers a rich survey.
[98] Paris, Musée du Louvre E 639; Munich, Antikensammlungen 8966.
[99] London, British Museum E 15; *ARV²* 136.1, 1705.   [100] Barringer 1995, 72–77 and 83–85.
[101] Kavala, Kavala Museum 1086; see Langdon 2008, 228 and her fig. 4.19.
[102] Tarquinia, Museo Nazionale Tarquinese RC 4194.
[103] Csapo 2003. Barringer 1995 further presents several scenes in which the Nereids' movement
    strongly resembles that of dancing maenads, with whom the Nereids also share links to
    Dionysus.

Fig. 5.4 Attic black-figure Little Master lip cup, ca. 550 B.C.E. Tarquinia, Museo Nazionale Tarquinese RC 4194. Photograph De Agostini Picture Library/G. Nimatallah/ Bridgeman Images.

not invariably indicate the execution of the dithyramb, and recent scholars have demonstrated the more catch-all nature of the designation *kuklioi choroi* found in fifth-century and later sources, the Nereids' presence in a series of Euripidean choral lyrics (most particularly in *Ion*, *Helen* and *Electra*, all treated in this and other chapters) which advertise their debt to the dithyrambs composed by the 'New Musicians' confirm that the Nereid-dithyrambic link exists in at least some instances. Post-classical sources offer fresh representations of dancing Nereids, among them the choruses of nymphs in an epigram by Philodemus (*AP* 6.349), a picture cited by Philostratus where Galateia dances with Nereids and choral dolphins (*Imag.* 2.8) and a passage from Nonnus' *Dionysiaca*, where the nymphs circle the god in a wedding dance (*Dion.* 48.192–94).

Rather than duplicate Barringer and Csapo's illuminating treatment of these and other sources, my discussion's first part restricts itself to a single text that these scholars cite only in passing, Bacchylides 17, in which the *choreia* of the Nereids plays a pivotal role and serves by way of template for the chorus currently performing the piece. Part two then turns to a series of images which, I suggest, offer matching accounts, similarly presenting the maritime nymphs as paradigms for latter-day ritual choruses, whose functions and interactions with the audience they likewise 'script'. In both instances too, the poet and artists highlight not just the choral character of the underwater dancers, but assign them the twofold function that parthenaic choruses generally claim: they are both objects of spectatorship for the viewer witnessing the performance, and, in a motif more amply treated in the final chapter of this study, the privileged channels or focalizers who can grant access to sights and events that would remain otherwise unapprehended; as such they mediate between the world of myth and that inhabited by audiences, whether those who view the vases or attend the choral spectacle.

4.1   Bacchylides 17.97–116

At the dramatic high point of the story narrated in Bacchylides 17, a poem dated to the opening decades of the fifth century and performed by a chorus of Ceians at the Delia,[104] Theseus responds to Minos' challenge and performs his daring dive into the waves. Escorted by a company of dolphins to Poseidon's maritime palace, the hero then witnesses the dance of a chorus of Nereids and receives tokens of his incipient manhood from Amphitrite (100–16):

ἔμολέν τε θεῶν   100
μέγαρον· τόθι κλυτὰς ἰδὼν
ἔδεισ᾽ ὀλβίοιο Νη-
ρέος κόρας· ἀπὸ γὰρ ἀγλα-
ῶν λάμπε γυίων σέλας
ὧτε πυρός, ἀμφὶ χαίταις   105
δὲ χρυσεόπλοκοι
δίνηντο ταινίαι· χορῷ δ᾽ ἔτερ-
πον κέαρ ὑγροῖσι ποσσίν.
εἶδέν τε πατρὸς ἄλοχον φίλαν
σεμνὰν βοῶπιν ἐρατοῖ-   110
σιν Ἀμφιτρίταν δόμοις·
ἅ νιν ἀμφέβαλεν ἀϊόνα πορφυρέαν,

κόμαισί τ᾽ ἐπέθηκεν οὔλαις
ἀμεμφέα πλόκον,
τόν ποτέ οἱ ἐν γάμῳ   115
δῶκε δόλιος Ἀφροδίτα ῥόδοις ἐρεμνόν.

---

[104] Although the date is disputed, most commentators place the work after Athens assumed leadership of the Delian League headquartered on the island in 478/77.

And then he came to the palace of the god. And there, seeing the famed daughters of blessed Nereus, he felt fear. For from their radiant limbs there shone a blaze as of fire and the gold-woven ribbons whirled about their hair. And they were delighting their heart in their supple [lit. 'liquid'] feet.[105] And he saw the dear reverent wife, cow-eyed, of his father, Amphitrite, in the beauteous house. And she cast about him the purple cloak and set on his curling hair the blameless wreath, dusky with roses, which once wily Aphrodite gave her at her marriage.

The appearance of the Nereid chorus has, in some respects, been anticipated in the events immediately preceding this encounter. As noted above, the dolphins that convey the hero to his father's home regularly appear together with the nymphs, participants not just in episodes in which Nereids play a major role but also in their dances. While seven south Italian vases from ca. 470 on simply show Nereids on dolphin back typically engaged in bringing arms to Achilles, a mid-sixth-century Etruscan amphora by the Paris Painter more explicitly presents the two ensembles as choral dancers:[106] here dolphin men turn in one direction around the shoulder of the pot while four Nereids perform the same movement in reverse. Dolphins and Nereids would coalesce again, here in company with a similarly dancing hero, in the first stasimon of Euripides' *Electra*, 'a paradigm of Euripides' dithyrambic ... or "New Musical" style',[107] where the singers address the Troy-bound ships 'with countless oars escorting dances together with the Nereids, where the pipe-loving dolphin was leaping, winding in circles at the dark-blue-rammed prow, conveying the son of Thetis, buoyant in the leap of his feet (κοῦφον ἅλμα ποδῶν), Achilles' (433–39). In similar fashion, and here underscoring the Nereids' presence through a reduplication of the motif, a choral ode in Euripides' *Helen* surrounds a description of the 'fair-dancing dolphins' encircling the ship conveying Helen and Menelaus to Sparta with a twofold mention of the underwater sorority, first in the shape of the nymphs' father Nereus (1452) and then by naming one of the fifty, 'Galanea, daughter of the grey Sea' (1457–58).[108] Arion was credited with authorship of a poem that he supposedly had inscribed on the dolphin statuette dedicated by the

---

[105] The expression conveys at once the dancers' maritime identity, their lithe motions, the watery element that so often accompanies maiden choruses in Geometric art and the common conceit of moving water as dancing nymphs.

[106] Rome, Musei Capitolini 9, with discussion and illustration in Csapo 2003, 83–85 and his fig. 4.7.

[107] Csapo 2003, 72.

[108] With discussion in Steiner 2011. I return to the lines in Section 5, while other chapters explore different facets of the stasimon.

musician following his rescue-by-dolphin from the waves, a composition that probably belongs to the late fifth century ([Arion] 939 *PMG*). Incorporating all the stylistic hallmarks of the New Musical dithyrambs currently in vogue in Athens, the poet imagines how dolphins styled 'nurselings of the daughters of Nereus' dance in a circle 'with buoyant tossings of their lightly leaping feet' (χορεύουσι(ν) κύκλῳ / κούφοισι ποδῶν ῥίμμασιν / ἐλαφρ' ἀναπαλλόμενοι, 5–7).[109]

But if Bacchylides' dolphin convoy looks forward to the subsequent introduction of the Nereids, the poet chooses to reserve the choral motif for these underwater dancers.[110] Sounding all the usual tropes found in descriptions of paradigmatic choruses – the Nereids are literally bedazzling, richly adorned in the radiant accessories that match the brilliance of their flashing limbs – they also possess the pliant feet privileged in other accounts of dancing girls. Apparent in the visualization too is a suggestion of the ring or circular dance typical of maidenly ensembles;[111] so the Nereids' gold-interwoven hair ribbons whirl about, replicating not just the motions of their wearers, but those of the eddying liquid medium – as the term ὑγροῖσιν reminds us – in which the dancers stage the spectacle.[112] Written into this account is also the response that choral performances regularly elicit, the *terpsis* that in this instance belongs not to Theseus who, for all that he acts as internal viewer here, is so wonderstruck that he feels fear, but to the performers themselves, and which should find its match in the sensations of the spectators witnessing the Ceians' ongoing display.

Seemingly contemporaneous with the choral dance is Amphitrite's bestowal of the gifts with which she greets her youthful visitor, the purple cloak and wreath of roses (note the imperfect used for the more atemporal dance in contrast to the aorist describing the one-off action). The garland can be read in many ways: at once a token of the victory that Theseus achieves over the Cretan *hegemôn*, first in this diving challenge and then again on Cretan ground where he will rescue the 'twice seven' whom he escorts as tribute for the Minotaur, it is also an indicator of the youth's

---

[109] See Csapo 2003, 74–77 for the piece.

[110] But note that Theseus' dolphin ride might bring to mind a series of near contemporary images showing dolphin-mounted choruses of men wearing the same hoplite armour that characterizes the Bacchylidean hero. For these, see Rothwell 2007, 58–71.

[111] The question of whether this is an explicitly dithyrambic dance is beyond the scope of my discussion, and I do not weigh in on the much debated question of whether the composition is a dithyramb or a paean.

[112] Pavlou 2012, 535 also notes the feature and its Dionysiac associations, but relates it chiefly to the *geranos*, which she views the Nereids as performing here.

readiness to assume the part of Ariadne's groom.[113] But striking too in the lines are the parallels between the wreath and the dance preceding it: doubling for the interwoven (χρυσεόπλοκοι) ribbons entwining the Nereids' hair (and recall that taeniae can also be the fillets awarded agonistic victors) is the expressly woven circlet (πλόκον), whose roses replace the gold interlacing; and just as the streamers adorn the nymphs' locks (χαίταις), so Amphitrite now places the garland about Theseus' hair (κόμαισι), again assimilating his appearance to that of the nymphs.[114] Typical of the larger set of concerns that go together with membership of the category of water-based *nymphai*, the Nereids' performance at this rehearsal of Theseus' bridal role, and their anticipatory fulfillment of the part of the hymeneal choruses in the rite, looks to their broader participation in moments of transition from the unwed state, both that of maidens and of youths, to marriage on other occasions: as the visual sources just reviewed suggest, the Nereids not only stand witness to Peleus' abduction of Thetis from their sorority, but dance as the hero claims his not-always-unwilling bride.

Reinforcing the connections between the Nereids and Theseus in Bacchylides' account is the hero's appearance when he then emerges from the waves and rejoins those still waiting in alarm on board the ship (122–24):

> μόλ' ἀδίαντος ἐξ ἁλὸς
> θαῦμα πάντεσσι, λάμ-
>   πε δ' ἀμφὶ γυίοις θεῶν δῶρ',

> he came unwet from the sea, a marvel for all, and the gods' gifts shone about his limbs ...

Reminiscent of the depiction of the nymphs is the sparkle emanating from Theseus' limbs (in an instance of polyptoton, the poet reuses the terms λάμπε and γυίων applied earlier to the maidens) and the response that his advent garners: not just pleasure but now the *thauma* that, as other chapters have detailed, characterizes the sensation experienced by those attending supremely skilled and intricately factured choral performances. In this moment both internal and external audiences – and πάντεσσι can have a generalized reference – witness for a second time the sparkling light

---

[113] See Chapter 7 for discussion of vase images that show Ariadne holding the wreath that styles her bride-to-be even as she prepares to bestow it on Theseus on his successful escape from the labyrinth.

[114] For Calame 2009b, 122 and 144–46 these overlaps form part of the 'feminization' of Theseus in both Bacchylides and artistic representations of the hero.

that belonged to the performers in the earlier underwater spectacle (although our vision of Theseus is at two removes; first seen by the Athenian youths and maidens, he is then redescribed by the Ceian choristers). Insofar as the hero replicates features of the Nereids' dance, he serves as mediator between the submerged realm and the world above ground.

The result of this mediation appears immediately afterwards, when a further canonical mythical chorus, this also made up of *parthenoi*, now takes up the nymphs' performance and re-enacts it on board ship (124–28):

> ἀγλαό–
> θρονοί τε κοῦραι σὺν εὐ-   125
> θυμίᾳ νεοκτίτῳ
> ὠλόλυξαν, ἔ–
> κλαγεν δὲ πόντος·

> and the resplendent-throned maidens cried out with new-found joy, and the sea rang out.

Maehler's note on 125 registers the confusion that 'resplendent-throned' might cause:[115] more naturally applicable to the Nereids, the epithet here belongs to the Athenian maidens raising the *ololugê*. A different interpretation of the compound adjective would still more closely link the mortal performers and Nereids: since, in many archaic and later instances, the term *throna* describes robes woven with flowers, Bacchylides might be prompting his audience to picture the ship-board girls dressed in richly embroidered garments, counterparts to the gleaming ribbons displayed by the underwater dancers. The precise meaning of the adjective aside, Bacchylides' overall intent in conflating the archetypal maritime nymphs with their parthenaic counterparts above the waves is clear: by virtue of the elision, he invests the *korai* with the choral character of the Nereids even as his Ceian choristers (in a fresh blurring of gender lines) appropriate the Athenian maidens' role. Included in this penultimate moment before a final return to the here-and-now is also an appeal to the audience's ears as well as eyes: where earlier the poet privileged the kinetic aspect of *choreia*, here the cry of joy together with the κλαγγή emitted by the sea contribute the sound missing from the first of the sequential dances.

Nor does the 'representational' role of that Ceian troupe end here. In the concluding lines of the song, the singers audibly integrate the female *ololugê* just sounded into the larger song performed by the youths in the Theseus-led Athenian company in lines 128–29: 'and nearby the youths

[115] Maehler 2004, 188.

sang the paean with lovely voice' (ἠΐθεοι δ' ἐγγύθεν / νέοι παιάνιξαν ἐρατᾷ ὀπί). The final phrase, the prayer that Apollo might grant success to the ongoing performance ('Delian god, rejoicing in your heart in the Ceian choruses,[116] grant a god-sent fortune of blessings'), concludes the series of links between the mythical event beneath the waves, the Athenian maidens and youths, and the present-day occasion, blending past and present and myth and reality as the Ceian chorus revoices the paean song that, whatever its time or setting, is designed to elicit Apollo's favour. A passing dictional echo completes this work of amalgamation as it prompts an audience to see in the site where the performance is now being staged the deck of the Crete-bound ship: just as in lines 90–92 it was a favouring breeze that sped the rapidly conveying vessel (ὠκύπομπον δόρυ, 90) on its god-determined course, so now that auspicious wind has become the benefaction of Apollo, here styled 'god-sent' or θεόπομπον.

4.2 Nereids as Choral Mediators in Visual Accounts

In choosing to include a Nereid chorus as witness to Theseus' heroic feat, and in intercalating the nymphs' performance with the several other choruses that the latter portion of the composition introduces, Bacchylides constructs a multi-layered account that has precedents in representations of the Nereids in late archaic vase painting. On the tondo of the mid-sixth-century Little Master lip cup in Tarquinia cited above (Fig. 5.4), seventeen dancing Nereids surround another hero achieving victory over an aggressor, this time Heracles struggling with Triton. Much as in Bacchylides' composition, where the Nereids' performance stands in close relation to the ongoing event, viz. Amphitrite's bestowal of tokens of manhood on Theseus, the dancers on the cup seem to translate the wrestling match into their gestures and choreography: the hero's grasp as he holds his victim tight finds its visual analogue in the joined hands of the surrounding Nereids, while the geometric bands surrounding both pictures, and which freshly fashion a *periplokê*, reproduce the clasped hands motif common to the two figurative scenes.[117] An audience familiar with the many overlaps between dance and combat sport would have little trouble in recognizing the continuity. On an Athenian red-figure psykter

---

[116] As Calame 2009b, 131 observes, the evocation of plural 'choruses' leaves space for all the other choral performers the poem has introduced. As he further suggests, the Ceian choristers also recall the many groups of Ionians featured in the *Homeric Hymn to Apollo* who, like the current performers, dance and sing in praise of Apollo.

[117] As observed by Carruesco 2016, 101.

dated to ca. 525–475,[118] athletes, some depicted as boxers and others wrestling, appear in company with a piper, evidence that an aulete might accompany the exercises no less than he did choral lyric. The proximity between the different spheres is also visible on a black-figure pelike in New York of ca. 510 by the Acheloos Painter;[119] here two boxers train to the accompaniment of music played on a double aulos, whose melody supplies a means of regulating the rhythmic motions of their hands and feet.

A fifth-century text taps into the association in more subtle fashion while newly demonstrating the reflective and transmitting roles that *choreia* fulfills on the Tarquinia cup. In the first stasimon of Sophocles' *Trachiniai*, a chorus made up of local maidens narrates the all-out struggle between the two rivals for Deianeira's hand, Heracles and the monstrous Achelous, in a vivid verbal recreation of what is effectively a mixture of a wrestling and boxing match, something most closely akin to the pankration. In their description of the antagonists' gestures, so closely coordinated and synchronized that the hero and monster are all but indistinguishable, the singers use diction that elsewhere – albeit in much later sources, and clustered chiefly in Athenaeus, but some of it dependent on citations from the earlier dramatists – appears in reference to the *schêmata* of dancers. Particularly evocative of choreography are the specific wrestling moves assigned the contestants in lines 517–21:

> τότ᾽ ἦν χερός, ἦν δὲ τόξ-
>   ων πάταγος,
> ταυρείων τ᾽ ἀνάμιγδα κεράτων·
> ἦν δ᾽ ἀμφίπλεκτοι κλίμακες,   520
> ἦν δὲ μετώπων ὀλόεντα πλήγματα . . .

> Then was the clash of fists and bows, in confusion with that of bull's horns,
> and there were interwoven grapplings, and deadly blows of foreheads . . .

Even as the dancers' arms and limbs might offer a stylized representation of the ἀμφίπλεκτοι κλίμακες, apparently a move in which one wrestler or participant in the pankration jumped on his opponent's back and wrapped his legs around his waist, the 'interwoven' quality of the contestants' limbs

---

[118] Zurich, Zurich University 4039; *ARV²* 1621.3 *bis*.

[119] New York, Metropolitan Museum of Art 49.11.1; *ABV* 384.19. Other references to the presence of the pipes in wrestling schools occur in textual sources, including one in Plutarch's *Pelopidas*: in a discussion of the Theban Sacred Band – the city's elite fighting corps – the author explains that the lawgivers in the city introduced both eros and the aulos at the site so as to 'remove and mollify the spirited and untempered nature' and 'blend together the characters of young men' in pursuit of Harmonia (19.1).

looks again to the dancers' footwork and interlinked hands. Among the choreographic moves recorded in Athenaeus and Pollux is also the so-called *therma(u)stris*, in which the dancer jumped up and crossed his legs in the air.[120] The affinity of foot and hand motions and wrestling stratagems finds further expression in Aristoxenus' discussion of the Spartan *gymnopaidikê*, a dance in which the youthful participants would perform 'various rhythmic movements and various figures with their arms in a gentle manner, and thus depict scenes from the wrestling school and the pankration, moving their feet in rhythm' (Athen. 14.631b). The expressions chosen by the Sophoclean chorus allow the audience not just to hear the blows exchanged by the combatants but visually to apprehend them too; the phrase πάμπληκτα παγκόνιτα already introduced in the opening strophe (505) with its repeated 'p's is richly onomatopoeic, and the multiplication of the sound and reuse of terms derived from πλήσσω, to 'strike' or 'smite', in the epode charts the struggle's growing intensity as the blows grow ever more frequent; accompanying the description are the matching rhythmic 'strikes' of the dancers' feet, both audible and visible to the eye.

Where the dramatist can work with sounds and bodies in motion to achieve this choral re-enactment of a bygone event, the artist of the Tarquinia cup has other means of promoting connections between the chief actors in the scene and the Nereid chorus so as to underscore the mimetic potential of the nymphs' performance. In distinction to Triton wholly enclosed in the tondo, Heracles breaches the spatial boundary as the elbow of his left arm, depicted in a manner that the Nereids' own crooked arms redescribe, extends into the lines that demarcate the limits of the wrestling scene. Still more pronounced is the way in which the hero's left foot reaches from the centre of the tondo into the space of the surrounding dance, where it all but meets the foot of one of the Nereids. Shown with one foot advanced and raised aloft and the other planted on the ground line supplied by the first of the black bands, Heracles further resembles the choreutes, turning the combat into a dance even as the Nereids' performance reflects the *agôn* in which the hero is involved. The central image may include a further pointer to the Nereids' ongoing *choreia*. The dolphins encircling the lower portion of the wrestling scene not only succinctly declare its maritime setting but are, as noted earlier in this section, quintessential choral dancers and the regular companions of the Nereids.

My discussion of the Bacchylidean passage highlighted how the Nereid chorus mediated between the sequence of mythical events and the current

---

[120] Athen. 14.630a, Pollux 4.102, Hesych. s.v.

performance by the Ceians on Delos, a role that the dancers on the cup also fulfill. Situated so as to surround the struggling pair, the Nereids supply the audience for the combatants and even stand surrogate for the cup viewer. For Mark Stansbury-O'Donnell, a direct link exists between the nymphs' role as spectators and their expressly choral character; as he suggests, the mythical dancers 'serve as an index for the choruses of young women who would perform songs before the city's population about heroes and gods in public festivals',[121] a reading that he then extends to the numerous depictions from the archaic and early classical corpus that place groups of spectators in symmetrical, synchronized and orderly formations on either side of a scene of combat, whether one waged by two unnamed warriors or by familiar figures from the world of myth. In these instances, the onlookers, who may display various degrees of involvement or detachment from the events they view, represent those who provide a narrative and re-enactment of the paradigmatic events, recounting and modelling in their words and dance what belongs to the mythical, bygone and timeless realm. The representation of the Nereid choristers may still more closely articulate their 'intermedial' function as those who sing and dance the event into being. In her discussion of the figures, Pauline Ghiron-Bistagne identifies them as 'young men dressed as women', performing a 'farandole accompanied by a song narrating one of the hero's exploits'.[122]

A second cup not cited by Stansbury-O'Donnell shows the same scene as the Tarquinia cup, and makes evident the Nereids' role both as spectators and as chorus members. Here, on an Attic black-figure band cup dated to ca. 550 in Atlanta (Fig. 5.5),[123] the maidens are positioned to either side of Heracles and Triton – not so much wrestling on this occasion, but with the hero depicted more as though he were riding on the monster's back.[124] Immediately to the left of the figures stands Poseidon, his left hand raised so as to gesture towards the pair, drawing our attention to the object of his spectatorship; balancing him on the right is one of the group of Nereids encircling the pot, all of whom look back at the encounter and freshly model the spectator's role. While most discussions read the Nereids as fleeing from the scene, there seems little reason for consternation, and here too, as in other instances, they are better understood as dancers who,

[121] Stansbury-O'Donnell 2006, 90.
[122] Ghiron-Bistagne 1976, 269. I have been unable to examine the actual cup, but photographs suggest that this identification of the dancers as costumed men is correct.
[123] Atlanta, Michael C. Carlos Museum, Emory University 2000.1.2.
[124] The reverse offers a closely matching scene, with the Nereids positioned on either side of Peleus as he makes off with Thetis.

Fig. 5.5 Attic black-figure band cup, ca. 550 B.C.E. Atlanta, Michael C. Carlos Museum, Emory University 2000.1.2. Photograph courtesy of Michael C. Carlos Museum, Emory University/Bruce M. White 2008.

internal and external to the central event, recreate what they witness in their motions and song. As on its Tarquinian counterpart, on this cup too Heracles' elongated feet seem to meet the foot of a Nereid, and the fish included in the image supply further 'liminal' elements that unite performers and protagonists; while Triton holds one fish in his left hand, its free-floating pair, whose curvature reiterates the shape of the band enclosing the scene and the circular nature of the performance, appears between Poseidon and a Nereid. The sinuous Triton, his body covered in intricate 'eye'-like motifs, offers a larger-scale evocation of the movements of the dancers, and perhaps, in its surface *poikilia*, a statement of their choreographic intricacy too.

Both the Atlanta and Tarquinia cups use an additional device to put an audience in mind not just of a choral dance but of the singing also integral to it. In each instance the representations include nonsense inscriptions that serve to complement the gestures and motions that the various actors perform, highlighting the movements of their legs and arms. On the Little Master vase, these dipinti take the form of rows of closely placed tiny dots that run from below the Nereids' arms and travel down their bodies,[125] while those on the second cup not only similarly align themselves with the dancers, again suggesting the contents of their song, but additionally appear above and below the curving body of the Triton, as though further to unite the spectators with the object of their gaze. Counterparts to this design appear on the well-known psykter by Oltos with its chorus of armed men mounted on dolphins,[126] where the now-coherent words 'upon the dolphin' inscribed retrograde in front of the mouth of each hoplite both sound out the line recited by the chorus and describe the downward dives of the animals on which they ride.

These visual depictions of another feat performed by a second hero help clarify the role of the Bacchylidean Nereids, and suggest that they belong to a longer tradition in which the daughters of Nereus assume the role of a choral collective that, perhaps by virtue of the liminal status more broadly accorded to nymphs who stand poised between mortal and immortal (as detailed at *HHVen.* 259–72), transmits the invisible mythical event to present-day choruses performing before their fellow citizens. While there are no grounds for claiming that these and other images of the Nereids would in any way have shaped Bacchylides' piece, these independent poetic and visual accounts nonetheless share common ground: like the artists before him, the poet presents the maidenly troupe as an archetype for the chorus that performs his song, positioning them both as objects worthy of our gaze and as viewers and displayers of the unseen.

5   The Daughters of Celeus in the *Homeric Hymn to Demeter*

The participants in my final 'watery' sorority, the daughters of the Eleusinian king Celeus who figure largely in the *Homeric Hymn to Demeter* (a work conventionally dated to ca. 650–550 B.C.E.), do not have an explicitly nymphine identity and so stand outside the category as more formally defined. Instead they merit inclusion here because, like the Asopids, Danaids and Nereids, their role as a foundational parthenaic chorus coexists with their pronounced connection with water, and more particularly, in keeping with the first two collectives, with hydraulics and the maintenance of a community's access to the life- and crop-sustaining

---

[125] The arrangement offers a perfect depiction of how the dancer corporializes the contents of his or her song, turning its words and modes of expression into the form of bodily motions.

[126] New York, Metropolitan Museum of Art 1989.281.69; *ABV*² 1622.7 *bis*; *Para.* 326, 259, with further discussion in later chapters.

substance. Just as the daughters of Asopos performed by the banks of the paternal river, and a water-rich milieu framed the activity of the other two groupings, so too these Eleusinian maidens dance at a water source with which they are closely associated and where they too enact the originary performance that historical choruses will take up, thereby guaranteeing that the fertility that depends on the irrigation of the land will continue. Celeus' daughters resemble these other nymphs on a further count: like the daughters of Danaos, and those of Asopos too, their story is intertwined with the topography and architectural features of their community and with its chief ritual event.

No sooner has the disguised Demeter arrived at Eleusis than, according to the Homeric hymnist's version of the story, the daughters of the local ruler Celeus come to draw water from the well, the so-called Parthenion, at which Demeter sits. The poet gives the girls a brief introduction, and, as is typical in such catalogues, singles out the last of the four for special mention (*HHCer.* 108–10; cf. 145–46):[127]

> τέσσαρες ὥς τε θεαὶ κουρήϊον ἄνθος ἔχουσαι,
> Καλλιδίκη καὶ Κλεισιδίκη Δημώ τ' ἐρόεσσα
> Καλλιθόη θ', ἣ τῶν προγενεστάτη ἦεν ἁπασῶν·   110

> four in number, like to goddesses in the flower of their youth, Callidice, Clisidice, lovely Demo and Callithoe, the eldest of them all.

Following their conversation with the newcomer, and report of the encounter to their mother, Metaneira sends her daughters back to summon Demeter to their home. In just a few lines, the poet describes their return journey to the well, evoking their swift departure from the house with a simile (174–78):

> αἱ δ' ὥς τ' ἢ ἔλαφοι ἢ πόρτιες ἤαρος ὥρῃ
> ἄλλοντ' ἂν λειμῶνα κορεσσάμεναι φρένα φορβῇ,   175
> ὣς αἱ ἐπισχόμεναι ἑανῶν πτύχας ἱμεροέντων
> ἤϊξαν κοίλην κατ' ἀμαξιτόν, ἀμφὶ δὲ χαῖται
> ὤμοις ἀΐσσοντο κροκηΐῳ ἄνθει ὁμοῖαι.

> Just as deer or heifers in the season of spring leap through the meadow sated with fodder, so they, lifting up the folds of their lovely garments, darted down the hollow wagon-track, and their hair streamed out on their shoulders like to a crocus flower.

---

[127] See Chapter 9 for detailed discussion of choruses presented as catalogues.

The poet's choice of imagery needs little explanation; deer and calves, as the previous chapter emphasized, signal both the litheness and grace of the girls as they rush off to carry out their mission, and the maidens' youthfulness too. The reference to the season of spring in the first simile and mention of the crocus bloom in the second draw attention to the particular stage of life occupied by this winsome quartet: maidens are, of course, associated with flowery meadows, symbols of their budding sexuality, and the adjective 'desire-causing' describing their robes, here hoisted up so as to expose their ankles, glances to the erotic allure that goes with their springtime burst of bloom.

In these lines too we get a first sounding of the maidens' role as mortal counterparts to the daughter whom Demeter has lost. As Helene Foley notes in her commentary,[128] their resemblance to flowers and to goddesses underscores their kinship with Persephone, already described as 'flower-faced' at line 8 of the *Hymn*.[129] When we first meet that maiden in the opening lines of the piece, she is placed in a landscape that narrowly anticipates the spot where the poet locates the fawn and heifer of his simile, a flowery meadow from which she plucks the crocus flower mentioned again at 179, and also forms one of a group of maidens, the Okeanids with whom she 'plays' or 'dances' (παίζουσαν, 5).[130] As for the Eleusinian girls' Persephone-like readiness for marriage, Demeter herself observes this when she voices the wish that they may find husbands to whom they will bear children (136; cf. 145).

The poet's choice of tropes whose associations with *choreia* other chapters have explored notwithstanding, there is nothing in this introductory account to intimate a future choral role for Celeus' daughters, nor does the poet press the resemblance of this Callithoe-headed quartet to Persephone dancing with her Okeanid companions. But a detail in the scene of the encounter between the goddess and maidens would already have introduced the choral motif and drawn on the audience's familiarity – if the *Hymn* was designed for performance at Eleusis –[131] with the rites whose aetiology and location in the local landscape the song goes on to describe. Critical here is the site of that initial meeting, and the confusion in the sources concerning where exactly Demeter first takes her seat. According

---

[128] Foley 1994 *ad* 98–112 and 169–89.

[129] In reference to the comparison of the girls to goddesses, Richardson 1974, 184 points us to Nausikaa likened to Artemis at the moment when she, like the divinity, leads the dance at *Od.* 6.101–09.

[130] Calame 1997, 92 does not hesitate to understand the verb as a reference to a dance perhaps performed in honour of Artemis.

[131] This remains an object of debate, well summarized in Foley 1994, 169–78.

to Callimachus' sixth *Hymn*, the goddess sits not at the Parthenion, the location named by the archaic hymnist at 99, but at a different well, this called the Kallichoron or 'Lovely Dance' (15–16), a structure still visible near the eastern corner of the Greater Propylon just outside the entrance to the Eleusinian sanctuary. The archaic poet is also acquainted with that well, but postpones mention of it until the ritual centrepoint in his account, when the goddess prescribes her rites to the Eleusinians: 'but now let all the people build me a great temple . . . on the rising hill above the Kallichoron' (271–72). Scholars explain the disaccord in several ways, most proposing that the Parthenion, a well mentioned only in the *Homeric Hymn* and that has never been located, is the same as the Kallichoron, or that the name of the Parthenion was replaced by Kallichoron after the filling in of the second water source. According to Nicholas Richardson's detailed account,[132] the Parthenion would have been identical to a well mentioned by the epic poet Pamphos, who styles it Anthion (see Paus. 1.39.1), a name perhaps later transferred elsewhere, while this same well was also called Kallichoron.

But there may be a different and more thematic way of understanding the multiplication of well names in the *Hymn*. The Kallichoron, as its designation suggests, is the structure that several extant sources flag as the site where female choruses sang and danced in commemoration of the fact 'that there the women of Eleusis first organized a chorus and sang to the goddess' (Paus. 1.38.6; cf. Apollod. 1.5.1; Call. fr. 611 Pf.; Nic. *Ther.* 484–87; Eur. *Supp.* 392, 619). The name itself figures repeatedly as an epithet used of choral dancing,[133] and, as Csapo further notes,[134] in adjectival form, it more particularly appears at moments of choral projection, whether in the 'dithyrambic' third stasimon of Euripides' *Helen*, used on that occasion of the dolphins circling about the ship (1453), or, in an instance more specific to Eleusinian ritual, in Euripides' *Ion* (1075–86; see below). Aristophanes also includes the expression in his account of the actions of the chorus of Mystae in the *Frogs* as it celebrates the Eleusinian rites in the Underworld: departing for the *pannychis* (371), the all-night dance performed when the initiates first arrived at Eleusis, the chorus members declare that they will 'play/dance in our special manner with most beautiful dances (καλλιχορώτατον)' (450–52), a phrase whose diction may incorporate a reference to the well. In Richardson's plausible suggestion, which accords with my proposal here, if the actual choral celebrations included performances by *parthenoi*, this would readily explain the name Parthenion given by the hymnist to the well where

---

[132] Richardson 1974, 326–28.   [133] Henrichs 1996, 51–52.   [134] Csapo 2008, 268.

Celeus' daughters go and acknowledge the place of more juvenile participants among the women dancers in the historical rites.

Several of the dramas just cited more narrowly observe the presence of
maidens among the larger female groupings that danced at the Kallichoron.
Just prior to the lines from the *Frogs*, which elide the name of the well with
the performances located there, the chorus leader announces his intention
to go to the site of the celebration of the *pannychis* together with the 'girls
(κόραις) and women' (445); already earlier in the parodos the singers steal a
look at a young girl whom they designate a συμπαιστρία (411), a 'playmate'
or 'fellow dancer', and with whom Dionysus, teasing apart the two meanings of παίζω, wants expressly to 'play and dance in a chorus (παίζειν τε καὶ
χορεύειν)' (407). More the stuff of fantasy, in the choral projection in the
Ion (1078–89) we find among the dancers participating in the Eleusinian
celebration the virginal Nereids. Embedded in the events and diction of the
Hymn to Demeter is, I suggest, already an anticipation and even foretaste of
these parthenaic choral celebrations.[135]

Immediately after the scene in which the goddess specifies the site where
the Eleusinians are to perform their propitiatory rituals (ἱλάσκοισθε, 274),
which, she announces, they should conduct 'above the Kallichoron', the
poet describes the atmosphere of trepidation at Celeus' house that follows
Demeter's self-revelation and epiphanic departure. Having tried in vain to
comfort the infant Demophon, distraught at the loss of his divine nurse,
Celeus' daughters then spend 'the entire night trying to propitiate
(παννύχιαι ... ἱλάσκοντο) the glorious goddess, trembling (παλλόμεναι)
with fear' (292–93). Both the temporal adjective and the participle suggest a
rehearsal of the more formalized (and joyous) ritual dances that these
maidens, and those after them, are to perform in proximity of the well in
celebration of Demeter: 'all night long' exactly corresponds to the time
frame of the *pannychis*, while πάλλω would come to be used, in simple and
compounded form, for the leaps and bounds performed by choral dancers
in Attic drama, some expressly female.[136] Most pertinent to the context in
which the hymnist selects the verb are two evocations of 'leaping' female
choruses in Aristophanes, the first made up of young girls, the second
referring to the larger company celebrating the women-only rites at the

---

[135] Budelmann and Power 2015, 271 n. 52 make the same suggestion, and further propose that the
lines anticipate the broader trajectory of the Eleusinian rites, in which initial sensations of 'fear
and awe [are] transmuted to choral joy'.

[136] The verb is used twice of dancing dolphins (Eur. *El.* 435, Ar. *Ran.* 1317) and, in an expressly
human choral context, at Eur. *Troad.* 325; cf. Eur. *IA* 227, with discussion in Chapter 4. See too
Naerebout 1997, 281–82.

Thesmophoria.[137] The Spartan giving directions to the women at the close
of the *Lysistrata* tells them to 'leap' in the manner of the fillies and maidens
(πῶλοι ταὶ κόραι) gathered by the Eurotas, who 'leap up' in turn (*Lys.* 1304,
1307–10), and the verb recurs at *Thesm.* 985, here, most appositely, in
reference to the movements of a female chorus celebrating not just
Demeter and Persephone (so 948) but Dionysus too, the god whose rites
had undergone syncretism with those of the two female divinities and who
had his own intimate connections with choral dancing.[138]

In his note on the earlier description of the girls' departure after their
initial encounter with the goddess at the well (*ad* 169–88), Richardson
observes additional foreshadowings of Eleusinian ritual. Even as the twice-
mentioned (107, 170) vessels carried by the girls on their water-fetching
expedition reflect the prominent place of different types of jars carried by
women in Eleusinian cult, whether the hydriai that served as votives in
miniaturized or full-size form and may also have been used in an actual
procession of *hydrophoroi*, or the specialized vessel variously called a kernon
or plemochoe perhaps carried in an (albeit unattested, see below) *kernophoria* included in the *pompê* and from which water would be poured out in
the final moments of the rite,[139] so 'the scene of the girls running down the
road, and leading Demeter to Eleusis, may reflect part of the ceremonies at
Eleusis, that is, a procession or ritual dance, led by the priestesses, of whom
the daughters of Celeus may be the prototypes'.[140] One enigmatic piece of
visual evidence, and that long postdates the *Hymn*, could illustrate the
presence of such vessel-carrying female processors/dancers in the
Eleusinian rites. On a red-figure votive pinax of ca. 370 dedicated by a lady
named Ninnion and now in Athens (Fig. 5.6),[141] we can see, among the other
figures, women with *kernoi* attached by strings to their heads who are
variously viewed as walking or dancing; the scene includes an aulos-player,
who at least confirms the presence of a musical accompaniment, and the
figure on the far left stands elevated on her toes with the billowing skirt

---

[137] This may be the chorus shown on the Attic black band cup (London, British Museum 1906.12–15.1) treated in Chapter 1.
[138] See Bierl 2009, 110 for the observation that this connection extends to all the gods invoked in the song.
[139] On a possible *kernophoria*, see the discussion of Mitsopoulou 2011, 192 and her n. 20. According to Athen. 11.496a–b, on the last day of the Mysteries participants 'filled two plemochoai and set them up, one to the east, one to the west, and then overturned them, saying mystic words as they did so'.
[140] Richardson 1974, 201. It should, however, be noted that these priestesses, the so-called Hierophantides, who carried the *hiera*, the sacred objects, in special baskets in the procession, were two in number, one for Demeter, the other for Kore; they were also married women.
[141] Athens, National Archaeological Museum 11036.

Fig. 5.6 Attic red-figure votive plaque, ca. 370 B.C.E. Athens, National Archaeological Museum 11036. Photograph Spyros Tsavdaroglou © Hellenic Ministry of Culture and Sports/Archaeological Receipts Fund.

characteristic of the dancer in other visual accounts.[142] Interpreted either as showing the arrival of the Eleusinian procession at the Telesterion or as the performance of the *pannychis* following this, the plaque may support Richardson's idea of a processional dance performed by women. Also pertinent to the role of the Eleusinian vessel-bearers as dancers is a reference in several late sources to a kernos-carrying dance (κερνοφόρον ὄρχημα),[143] while the technical expression used of the heinous crime of betraying the secret rites more broadly observes the centrality of dance in the course of the Eleusinian occasion: those guilty of the crime were charged with 'dancing out' (ἐξορχεῖσθαι) the Mysteries.[144]

A second visual representation of events at the sanctuary seems not only to acknowledge the place of vessel-carrying in the Eleusinian *pompê* but additionally to accommodate the well that figures in the ritual as the site of choral dancing. Two narrow golden strip bands, their provenance unknown, of ca. 300 mirror one another (Fig. 5.7).[145] In each of the symmetrical compositions

---

[142] Her posture is not unlike that of the *kalathiskos* dancer on the Lucanian volute krater participating in the Karneia discussed in the previous section.

[143] Pollux 4.103, Athen. 14.629d. Neither author gives a ritual context for the dance.

[144] See LSJ for examples.

[145] Athens, National Archaeological Museum St. 342a-6; my discussion largely follows that of Mitsopoulou 2011, 195–204, with additional illustrations of the bands.

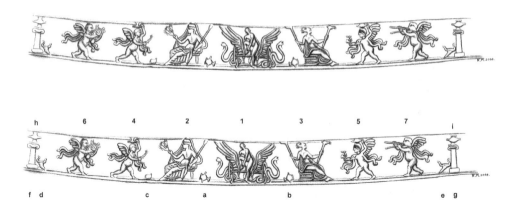

Fig. 5.7 Gold strip bands, ca. 300 B.C.E. Athens, National Archaeological Museum St. 342a-6. Drawing by Katarina Mavraganis courtesy of C. Mitsopoulou.

made up of seven figures, Demeter and Kore are seated on either side of the centrally placed Triptolemos preparing to depart on his chariot on the final day of the Mysteries; approaching each goddess are two Erotes, one of whom carries a myrtle branch, the other a musical instrument (the diminutive figure on the left plays a lyre, his double on the right the diaulos). Two overturned vessels flank Triptolemos' winged vehicle, and the two lead Erotes raise one hand so as to steady the pot each carries on his head. If the two vessels by the chariot look to the final moments of the rites when, as Athenaeus reports (see n. 139), the plemochoai were emptied and cast prone on the ground, then the Erotes point to an earlier moment in the sequence of events and serve as stand-ins for the women who would process with jars on their heads. As for the role played by the well, the wellhead on which Demeter appears to sit recalls the location of the initial meeting with her future initiates and/or the site of their choral dance.

The scenario suggested here, whereby latter-day ritual choruses re-enact the roles and activities attributed to the first participants and celebrants of the rites, Celeus' daughters, and whose lead dancer could even assume the part of the eldest of the sisters, finds further corroboration in a second element in Pausanias' report: at 1.38.3 he remarks that the maidens, here given different names, first performed the sacred rites on behalf of the two goddesses together with Eumolpos ('Beautiful Song/Dance'), the original Priest of the Mysteries. As Richardson details,[146] the girls then received honours after their death and, in his further reconstruction, would have

---

[146] Richardson 1974, 183–84.

served as prototypes for the two (albeit married) priestesses, the Hierophantides, who figured prominently at Eleusis and were members of the Eumolpid clan.[147] Although we have no clear indication of the make-up of the female choruses that danced at the Kallichoron in historical times, Pausanias' account may indicate that the daughters of the Eumolpidae, an elite Eleusinian family, played a leading role in the performances.[148] Following this model, the suitably named Eumolpos assumes the part of the father-*chorêgos* responsible for marshalling and leading a choral troupe headed by his daughters to the performance site.

The emphasis on water-fetching that in the *Hymn* motivates the initial visit of the daughters of Celeus to the well (106), and whose execution the narrator observes in his return to the activity at 169–70, not only reflects the central place of water in the ritual attested in our visual and textual sources, but more narrowly suits the assignment of the task to the sorority, whose parthenaic status makes them ready emblems of the agricultural growth and fecundity that depend on abundant water, whether in the form of rain or as channelled through natural and man-made structures; although commonplace, the expression used by the hymnist on introducing the girls, 'having the flower of youth' (108), signals this element from the outset. As the representations of maidens at fountain houses which appear with great frequency in the black- and red-figure repertoires – especially on hydriai, where they achieve maximum popularity in the decades between ca. 530 and 480 – attest, water-fetching is among the activities that artists particularly associate with *parthenoi*.[149] Like the daughters of Celeus, the water-fetchers on the vases are typically of noble bearing, 'well-groomed and elegantly dressed',[150] and among the names with which inscriptions on the vases identify them are not only pointers to the beauty signalled by the hymnist's Callidice and Calliope (so Callippe on one vase and also the term *kalê* simply added to the name in some instances) but references to flowers too (Rhodon, Elanthis, Anthyle, Rodopis).[151] Some carry a flower which they raise to their face, an accessory and gesture that has been variously interpreted as a glance to the nuptial sphere (brides also carry flowers) or to the festival of the Anthesteria, on

---

[147] As such, the role of these latter-day celebrants would resemble that of the Leukippidae at the sanctuary of Amyklai in Sparta. As noted in the discussion in Chapter 4, the identities of these once-mythical maidens would have been taken over by the two performers who led the parthenaic choruses that danced in rituals performed at the site.

[148] As suggested by Budelmann and Power 2015, 271.

[149] For recent discussion and bibliography, see Ferrari 2003a and Sabetai 2009, on whose accounts I have principally drawn; note too Trümper 2012.

[150] Ferrari 2003a, 45.   [151] See Ferrari 2003a, 45 for these.

Fig. 5.8 Attic black-figure hydria by the Priam Painter, ca. 520 B.C.E. Boston, Museum of Fine Arts 61.195, William Francis Warden Fund. Photograph © Museum of Fine Arts, Boston.

whose second day (the Hydrophoria) a ritual took place that involved pouring water into a chasm. More vegetation appears in the form of the branches that the girls carry in their hands, exactly as did the parthenaic choristers in the Geometric vases.

Also consonant with the 'testimony' of the Homeric hymnist is the suggestion, although I grant that this is just one possible reading of the scenes, of dancing at the well, and the indications of ritual that some artists further include. A black-figure hydria by the Priam Painter from the last quarter of the sixth century shows five girls at a fountain house (Fig. 5.8);[152] the second figure from the right raises her arms in a pose adopted by dancers on contemporary pots and turns her head so as to look back at her neighbour in the line, a gesture also regularly included in visual representations of dancing groups. On a black-figure skyphos also of the late sixth century,[153] the fountain-house motif is integrated into a scene showing a

152 Boston, Museum of Fine Arts 61.195.
153 Athens, National Archaeological Museum 12531; see Sabetai 2009, 109 for this and other references to Dionysus, and, for choruses at the Anthesteria, Wilson 2000, 32.

procession *en route* to perform a sacrifice before two herms, perhaps a ritual in honour of Hermes and Dionysus, who were both celebrated at the Anthesteria, a festival where choral dancing, some of it featuring women, also seems to have occurred; here one of the women performs a jump identifiable as the dance step executed by (albeit male) dancers in other scenes.[154]

Alongside the daughters of Celeus, other water-based maidens, the Nymphs themselves, also claim a place in Eleusinian ritual. An inscription on the edge of a well beside the Dipylon gate, the point at which the procession to Eleusis started, not only includes the water-bestowing divinities alongside Pan, the god who typically leads them in the dance, but also rehearses the ritual formula that the initiates will pronounce: 'O Pan, o men, be of good cheer, beautiful Nymphs, rain, conceive, overflow'.[155] Still more patent is the presence of one of the three collectives of Nymphs treated in this chapter among those who perform at the site of the Kallichoron well where, in the argument advanced here, Celeus' daughters initiated the choral dances included in the Mysteries. In a lyric song in Euripides' *Ion* already mentioned in passing above, the singers visualize that spectacle (1075–86):

> αἰσχύνομαι τὸν πολύυ-
>   μνον θεόν, εἰ παρὰ Καλλιχόροισι παγαῖς   1075
> λαμπάδα θεωρὸς εἰκάδων
> ἐννύχιον ἄυπνος ὄψεται,
> ὅτε καὶ Διὸς ἀστερωπὸς
> ἀνεχόρευσεν αἰθήρ,
> χορεύει δὲ σελάνα   1080
> καὶ πεντήκοντα κόραι
> †Νηρέος αἱ κατὰ πόντον
> ἀεναῶν τε ποταμῶν†
> δίνας χορευόμεναι
> τὰν χρυσοστέφανον κόραν   1085
> καὶ ματέρα σεμνάν·

I feel shame before the much sung god were a sleepless spectator to see, beside the springs of the Kallichoron, the torch of the month's twentieth day that burns through the night, when the starry ether of Zeus has led off the dance and the moon dances and the fifty daughters of Nereus celebrate in choral dance on the sea and the eddies of the ever-flowing rivers the golden-crowned maiden and her reverent mother.

---

[154] So Ferrari 2003a, 47.   [155] See Mylonas 1961, 270 for this.

Here, in their own dance and song, the choreutes playing the part of the maidservants of Creusa (slaves who nonetheless highlight their identification with Athens) restage the paradigmatic choral dance at the well, a performance now attributed not to the Eleusinian girls, but to the archetypal Nereids instead who dance together through the night with the other constellations.

6 Ship Choruses

Ships have already figured in the discussion, whether in reference to Aegina and her 'ship-ruling fortune' (Pind. fr. 52f.130–31 S.-M.) or in the shape of Theseus' Crete-bound craft in Bacchylides 17. But, as this closing discussion seeks to establish, oar-powered vessels play more than ancillary or supporting roles in these accounts: in texts and images from the archaic through to the classical period and beyond, painters, poets and prose writers regularly draw parallels between sailing and rowing ships and participating in choral troupes, now equating the seagoing fleets with performing ensembles, now mapping those plying the oars and their boatswains onto chorus members overseen by their *chorêgoi*. The association may take on a political inflection too: in fifth-century Athens, the ability to dance in a chorus and to row a trireme become, for better or more typically for worse, two corresponding facets of a man's larger service to his polis. Exemplary of this is [Xenophon's] distempered observation concerning the payment now given to the demos in a variety of spheres, where once citizens served voluntarily: 'the people expect to get paid for singing, running, dancing and sailing on ships (ὀρχούμενος καὶ πλέων ἐν ταῖς ναυσίν) in order that they may have the money' (*Ath. Pol.* 1.13.8–9); patent here is the pairing of choral participation with the obligation to man the city's boats.

6.1 Choral Ships in Vase Painting

My first example concerns a scene already cited in other chapters, the topmost band of the François Vase with its representation of Theseus' disembarkation from the boat beached on the Cretan shore (Fig. 0.5). While most accounts largely ignore the ship and its crew,[156] the painter Kleitias, I suggest, invests

---

[156] A notable exception is Olsen 2015, who also integrates the shipboard scene into her reading. Where she contrasts the movements of the chorus and crew, viewing the former as the acculturated, ritualized and collective form of the random and disordered motions and

these with a choral dimension to be much more fully realized by the 'twice seven' choreutes following their musician-leader. The design of the last member of the chorus line, one Phaidimos, shown striding onto *terra firma* as though trying to catch up with the remainder of the troupe,[157] not only forms a bridge between the vessel and processional dance but echoes the depiction of the craft: the double rudder protruding from the ship's two sides reaches out so as to overlap or appear coextensive with Phaidimos' feet, thereby equipping the boat with its own set of 'legs' that similarly move in rhythmic fashion, first up, then down.

If the ship participates in the choral spectacle, then it also furnishes a dancing floor. Just as the closing scene in Bacchylides 17 turns that chorus-bearing boat into a maritime *orchestra*, so here a more impromptu type of joyful and even proto-choral celebration seems to be occurring on deck, an anticipation of the formalized and perhaps more socially circumscribed performance adjacent to it.[158] Two figures with their arms outstretched move in unison, and in front of them stands another youth whose posture, with his arms raised on high, resembles that of dancers about to leap. Towards the front of the boat, two sailors reach out to one another, as though seeking to link their hands in the manner of the chorus members towards whom they look. In a phenomenon already touched on in the earlier discussion, and sometimes styled 'kinesthetic contagion',[159] these spectator figures seem to experience that form of reciprocity and mutuality that unites singer-dancers with their viewers: so compelling is the spectacle seen and heard by the members of the crew that they find themselves re-enacting in more individualized and freestyle fashion the performers' own movements and interactions. Their heterogeneity in dress and pose and their lack of cohesion or leader-like figure notwithstanding,[160] the rowers nonetheless constitute a second chorus, shown rehearsing the paradigmatic dance.

The single ship on the François Vase joins a more numerous maritime company on a bilingual cup attributed to the Painter of London E 2 and, near the Antiope Painter of ca. 510–500.[161] In the interior of the vessel (Fig. 5.9), a

---

gestures made by those excluded from the chorus, I see the crew members, together with their ship, more as a 'proto-chorus', participants in a rehearsal for what takes place on land.

[157] For the 'late arrival' motif in depictions of choruses in vase paintings, see Crowhurst 1963, 243. As he comments, this figure always seems to be male.

[158] Giuliani 2013, 129 suggests that the men on board are unidentified because the privilege of a name is granted only to 'the aristocratic protagonists of the story'; on the distinctions between the two groups, see Olsen 2015. For more on the dipinti in the image, see Chapter 8.

[159] A point I owe to Olsen 2017, with good discussion of this phenomenon.

[160] Olsen 2015 details this.

[161] London, British Museum 1843.11–3.29; *ARV²* 225.1, 1636; *Para.* 151.

Fig. 5.9 Bilingual cup attributed to the Painter of London E 2 and near the Antiope Painter, ca. 510–500 B.C.E. Interior. London, British Museum 1843.11–3.29. Photograph © The Trustees of The British Museum.

frieze of four boats complete with crews circle around a black-glaze band that represents the sea; interspersed between each, groups of two and three dolphins leap downwards into the water. A ram in the shape of a boar's head forms each ship's prow, and a helmsman sits in front of the rowers, whose heads act as the supports for the ships' rails[162] and seem moving parts of the larger wooden structures. The juxtaposition of the boar prows and dolphins facing one another serves to unite the ships and their dolphin partners, both occupants of the animal world, while the presence of the rowers with their lines of neatly aligned and downward-facing oars suggests that they produce the strike or rhythm to which the dolphins and 'animalized' boats both move.

Reinforcing the connections with this Dionysiac-inflected dance as signalled by the dolphins' presence is the cup's exterior (Fig. 5.10), which simultaneously looks back to the red-figure youth lifting a pointed amphora in the tondo. The obverse face shows two youths, one equipped with an oinochoe, dancing around a second pointed amphora; the reverse

---

[162] See the discussion in Cohen 2006, 42.

Fig. 5.10 Bilingual cup attributed to the Painter of London E 2 and near the Antiope Painter, ca. 510–500 B.C.E. Side A. London, British Museum 1843.11–3.29. Photograph © The Trustees of The British Museum.

recapitulates the scene, now assigning one of the two dancing youths the vessel closely linked with Dionysus, the drinking horn. The wine motif unites the several surfaces of the cup: when filled with the liquid, the ships and dolphins would appear to travel across the medium (the 'wine-dark' sea) while the amphorae on the tondo and exterior are also bound up with the theme since jars of this shape were regularly used in the transport of wine.[163] But insofar as the youths celebrate a *kômos*, dance supplies a second overarching element, recalling, perhaps, how Dionysus, embarked on a ship, transformed his crew into a chorus of dancing dolphins, the original celebrants of the dithyramb.[164]

Another sympotic vase of the same period proposes a different combination of choral and maritime activity. On the interior rim of an Attic black-figure

---

[163] Cohen 2006, 42.

[164] As depicted in the tondo of the well-known black-figure cup by Exekias of ca. 540, where Dionysus reclines on board his ship while the piratical crew whom he has turned into dolphins gambol around the vessel (Munich, Antikensammlungen 2044; *ABV* 146.21, 686; *Para.* 60). Although in part conditioned by the pictorial space available, Exekias' choice to position the animals so that they form a partial circle around the vessel (and together with the seven grape clusters hanging from the mast in parallel formation, they describe a full circle) may be read as a pointer towards the dolphins' role as the original dithyrambic chorus. In Exekias' visualization, the ship has an unmistakably dolphin shape, with dolphins as decorative devices on its body by way of metonymic prompt. Viewed this way, Dionysus is not only *chorêgos*, the one who marshals the performance, but the central dolphin-rider too.

Fig. 5.11 Attic black-figure dinos, ca. 525–475 B.C.E. Interior rim. Würzburg, Martin von Wagner Museum L 527. Photograph Christina Kiefer © Martin von Wagner Museum der Universität Würzburg.

dinos fragment from Tarquinia of ca. 525–475 (Fig. 5.11),[165] the artist depicts a ship with rowers and a helmsman, who holds up one hand before his mouth and tips his head back; the pose, which resembles that adopted by singers on vases of the same period, might suggest the 'tuneful' directions that he issues as he calls out the beat for the oarsmen to follow. As though in answer to his summons, to the ship's right an outsized octopus appears; leaping above the waves, it holds its two rows of legs aloft, each one symmetrically deployed on either side of its body with tentacles extended and curving around at their tips. The octopus' design not only echoes that of the ship, this too equipped with parallel banks of oars; also consistent with these oars plied rhythmically in response to the vocalizing helmsman, the creature seems to move to the rhythm observed by the vessel.[166] The scene on the fragment's external ring (Fig. 5.12) plainly spells out the choral motif informing the interior. Here Hephaestus appears, accompanied by satyrs, maenads and men all dancing so as to form an unbroken ring: both at land and at sea, the Dionysiac wine mixed

---

[165] Würzburg, Martin von Wagner Museum L 527.

[166] Might this leggy octopus be performing the dance figure to which an albeit much later source refers (see Athen. 14.629f), which was called the *keleustês*, the term that more typically describes the coxswain-like individual who determines the speed of the rowers' strokes? See Weiss 2018, 182, with further details in Lawler 1944, 31–33, who associates this set of actions with the 'nautical dance' (*orchêsis nautikê*) to which Libanius (64.14) and Pollux (4.101) refer.

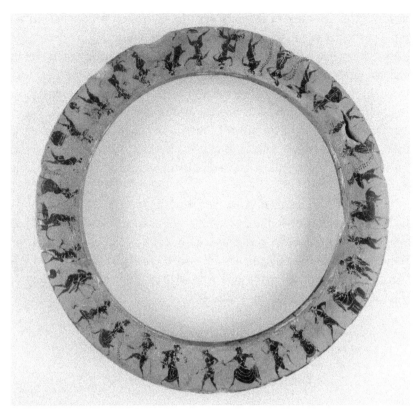

Fig. 5.12 Attic black-figure dinos, ca. 525–475 B.C.E. Exterior rim. Würzburg, Martin von Wagner Museum L 527. Photograph Christina Kiefer © Martin von Wagner Museum der Universität Würzburg.

in the bowl would set the world a-dancing (see Eur. *Bacch.* 21), turning ships and crews into members of performing ensembles.

6.2 *Nautical* Choreia *in Poetry and Prose*

The transformation of the ship equipped with rowers into a participant in a choral performance visible on the vases just reviewed finds its later counterpart in a series of chiefly fifth-century texts, whose authors variously juxtapose choruses and vessels, sometimes singly and sometimes as members of larger armadas, in ways that suggest equivalences between the two.[167] As these sources illustrate, boats not only transport and/or accompany choruses travelling from one place to another; through the actions of

---

[167] See Chapter 9, where I suggest that the ships enumerated in *Iliad* 2 are already conceived of as a choral ensemble.

those on deck or seated at the oars, and the vessels' own motions, formations, participation in spectacularized displays, musicality or decorative
features, they may join in, instigate or fashion choral performances for an
audience of viewers. The concentration of these references in fifth-century
Athenian sources is anything but fortuitous; increasingly dependent on its
fleet to maintain and defend its hegemony, the city was also the site where
choruses, whether in the theatre of Dionysus, in polis rituals or at the more
distant locations where Athens sent its troupes to dance and sing, were
central to the city's self-image and a dominant presence on the panhellenic
stage.

A passage from the opening of Pindar's fifth *Isthmian* supplies among
the first fifth-century soundings of the confluence between a nautical
company and a chorus in performance. In an ode composed for a victor
from the maritime city of Aegina, the poet begins by hailing the goddess
Theia and saluting her as the one who sheds her lustre on a variety of
spheres, both at land and sea (4–6):

> καὶ γὰρ ἐριζόμεναι
> νᾶες ἐν πόντῳ καὶ ὑφ᾽ ἅρμασιν ἵπποι   5
> διὰ τεάν, ὤνασσα, τιμὰν ὠκυδινά-
>   τοις ἐν ἁμίλλαισι θαυμασταὶ πέλονται·

and then too when ships are vying in rivalry on the sea or horses yoked to
chariots, it is through your honour, o queen, that they become wondrous
to behold in swift-spinning competitions.

Several terms signal the paradigmatic role of these ships, whose display
imagistically mirrors and models that of the Pindaric chorus: not only are
these vessels engaged in competitions, pointers both to the formalized
contents framing so much choral activity and to Pindar's abiding concern
with outmatching potential epinician rivals, but the compound adjective
ὠκυδίνητος, a Pindaric hapax, calls to mind the swift spins that the dancers
invite their audience to visualize and project onto their movements. ἅμιλλα,
as passages from Sophocles and Euripides would illustrate,[168] regularly
describes a circular choral performance, while the 'wonder' attendant on
the boats' display (an acknowledgement too of the Aeginetans' maritime
expertise) recalls the *thauma* regularly inspired by skilled displays of song
and dance.

---

[168] Soph. *Trach.* 218–22, Eur. *IT* 1144–51. For ἅμιλλα used more generally of other choral
competitions, see Aesch. *PV* 129, Philod. *Paean* 132–34, Pl. *Leg.* 834e, Xen. *Mem.* 3.3.12.

For Aeschylus, the equivalence between maritime activity and choral dancing turns more narrowly on the particular hand motions of his choreutes – the *cheironomia* or 'hand dance' for which one of this dramatist's actors was, apparently, celebrated (see Athen. 1.21f) –[169] and which he twice makes equivalent to those of rowers.[170] In the more extended instance, the chorus of the *Septem*, mourning the fratricidal struggle at the city walls, describes itself as replicating Charon's actions as he plies the oars in ferrying Eteocles and Polyneices to the Underworld (854–57):

ἀλλὰ γόων, ὦ φίλαι, κατ' οὖρον
ἐρέσσετ' ἀμφὶ κρατὶ πόμπιμον χεροῖν   855
πίτυλον, ὃς αἰὲν δι' Ἀχέροντ' ἀμείβεται,
τὰν ἄστονον μελάγκροκον ναύστολον θεωρίδα,

But, o friends, along the wind of lamentation, row with your hands about your head the oar's escort-giving stroke, which is always going across the Acheron, the theoric sea-faring vessel, black sailed and without groans . . .

Exploiting the twofold meaning of ἐρέσσω, both to 'row' and to 'ply' or to 'put in rapid motion', the chorus equates the threnetic blows it delivers to its head with the strike of the rower's oars (note the alliterative and rhyming sound structure and interlacing word order of κρατὶ πόμπιμον χεροῖν / πίτυλον) and, through words and gestures, transforms the theatre's dance floor into the Acheron-crossing ship, propelled by the hand motions performed by the ensemble. Further equating the maritime *orchestra* with a chorus-bearing ship is the vessel's designation as a black-sailed θεωρίς, the noun typically reserved for the theoric vessel – supposedly the very boat used by Theseus on his return from Crete when he put in at Delos for the original performance of the *geranos* – dispatched by Athens for the yearly Delia, and used to transport its choral troupe (see below for more on this). Since the conceit of the 'fair wind' of song was a commonplace in the broadly contemporary choral songs of Pindar (e.g. *Pyth.* 4.1–4, *Nem.* 6.28b–29), the phrase accommodates the music supplied by the pipes that would both accompany the dramatic performance and be played during funerary rites. The *Persae* offers the second conflation of rowing with the gestures of lament performed by the chorus currently on stage. Here, at 1046, the defeated Xerxes acts in the manner of the *chorodidaskalos* as he

---

[169] In Athenaeus' report, Telestes, a famed actor-dancer, could act the entire *Septem* through such hand gestures.

[170] See Weiss 2018, 41–42, who also comments on these two instances; our readings coincide on several points.

instructs his aged councillors in the dance and song appropriate to the occasion: 'row (ἔρεσσ'), row, row and groan on my behalf'.

Several decades on, Euripides not only echoes the precise parallel introduced by Aeschylus, correlating the beating gestures of his grieving chorus members with the rower's strikes (*Troad.* 1236), but in no fewer than three lyric interludes offers multiple variations on the analogy between maritime travel, boats and their crews and those who sing and dance on stage. The earliest of the triad belongs to the first stasimon of *Electra* (432–86), in a song positioned between Electra's initial exchange with the disguised Orestes and the scene of the siblings' recognition. The stasimon, whose New Musical features Csapo has documented,[171] begins with a visualization of the Trojan armada that crossed the seas (432–41):

> κλειναὶ νᾶες, αἵ ποτ' ἔβατε Τροίαν
> τοῖς ἀμετρήτοις ἐρετμοῖς
> πέμπουσαι χορεύματα Νηρῄδων,
> ἵν' ὁ φίλαυλος ἔπαλλε δελ-   435
>   φὶς πρῴραις κυανεμβόλοι-
>   σιν εἱλισσόμενος,
> πορεύων τὸν τᾶς Θέτιδος
> κοῦφον ἅλμα ποδῶν Ἀχιλῆ
> σὺν Ἀγαμέμνονι Τρωίας   440
> ἐπὶ Σιμουντίδας ἀκτάς.

Famous ships who once went to Troy with countless oars, conducting choral dances with the Nereids, where the aulos-loving dolphin leaped and whirled at your dark-blue prows, conveying the son of Thetis, light in the leap of his feet, Achilles, with Agamemnon to the banks of Trojan Simois.

There are no fewer than three internal choruses in the opening five lines: the dancing ships, the company of Nereids and the dolphin (the single animal standing in for the larger group) that leaps and whirls in the circle dance that complements that of the nymphs. In an arrangement also visible in the third stasimon of Euripides' *Helen* (see below), the gyrating Nereids and dolphin perform their ring dances in conjunction with the linear trajectory of the plural ships, offering a mix of those lines and circles that suggest the shifting formations that a dramatic chorus might adopt. On board ship, Achilles is still a light-hearted dancer (a few lines on, at 451, as the mood begins to darken, the hero's foot assumes the swiftness that it displays in his pursuit of Hector prior to the Trojan's death), even the star

---

[171] Csapo 2003, 72. See too the detailed discussion in Weiss 2018, 78–85 in a reading that similarly highlights the choral self-referentiality apparent in the singers' diction and conceits.

performer of the naval troupe whose nimble leaps take their cue from those of the dolphin.[172]

In place of the armada featured in the *Electra* ode, the third stasimon of *Helen* introduces the single vessel as the first in a sequence of participants in the kind of 'ur-*choreia*' presented by the song. Again, the ship appears in the invocation that opens the first strophe (1451–64):[173]

Φοίνισσα Σιδωνιὰς ὦ
ταχεῖα κώπα, ῥοθίοισι Νηρέως
εἰρεσία φίλα,
χοραγὲ τῶν καλλιχόρων
δελφίνων, ὅταν αὐ-   1455
    ρᾶν πέλαγος ἀνήνεμον ἦι,
γλαυκὰ δὲ Πόντου θυγάτηρ
Γαλάνεια τάδ’ εἴπη·
κατὰ μὲν ἱστία πετάσατ’, αὔ-
    ρας λιπόντες εἰναλίας,   1460
λάβετε δ’ εἰλατίνας πλάτας
ὦ ναῦται ναῦται,
πέμποντες εὐλιμένους
Περσείων οἴκων Ἑλέναν ἐπ’ ἀκτάς.

O swift Phoenician ship from Sidon, oarage dear to the surging waves of Nereus, chorus leader of the fair-dancing dolphins, whenever the sea is without the breezes' wind, and the gray-eyed daughter of Nereus, Galaneia, speaks thus, 'unfurl the sails, leaving the sea-breezes out of the reckoning, take up the oars of fir, o sailors, sailors, escorting Helen to the well-harboured shores of Perseus' home'.

In a rich display of its 'New Musical' elements, whether the 'floating apostrophe' typical of contemporary dithyrambic composers who embraced innovation, or the anadiplosis at 1462, another hallmark of that style of composition, or the twofold use of circumlocution or synecdoche for the larger vessel as the lines evoke the 'oar' and 'oarage dear to the waves of Nereus', the song hails the ship as 'chorus-leader' whom

---

[172] Predating the drama by over a century is an Attic black-figure amphora of ca. 540 (London, British Museum B 240) that anticipates the 'leaping' Achilles in a scene that combines the hero, oar-rowed ship and dolphin, here a member of a larger company. For discussion, see Barringer 1995, 53–54 and pl. 62.

[173] Again, there is much overlap between my discussion and the more extended reading of Weiss 2018, 180–89, whose valuable account adds much to the more narrowly focused treatment here.

'beautifully dancing' dolphins surround.[174] Where earlier I noted the presence of the Nereids in the lines, pride of place is granted to the vessel and to its thrice-mentioned oars. The sustained focus on these objects promotes the mimetic quality of the singers' account: in the spectacle currently presented to the theatre audience, the *auletês*, the new 'star performer' in New Musical compositions, would assume the role of the *triêraulês*, whose piping served to set the rhythm for the oarsmen.[175] In popular belief, it was also the music emitted by his pipes that attracted the dolphins and instigated their dance. By virtue of this musical dimension, the exchanges and conflations between the chorus' performance and the maritime scene that its words conjure up become still tighter: just as the dolphins leap to the beat generated by the rowers in accord with the playing of the instrumentalist, so the chorus members dance to the music supplied by their piper, who also determines the rhythm to which the internal oars are plied.

In the third Euripidean instance, the parodos of the *Iphigenia at Aulis*, the chorus of local women describes a scene that directs the audience back to the early stages of the Trojan War and to the Achaean army and fleet gathered on the beach at Aulis.[176] Making their processional entrance onto the stage, the choristers begin by introducing the two objects of their earlier spectatorship (164–73):

> ἔμολον ἀμφὶ παρακτίαν
>   ψάμαθον Αὐλίδος ἐναλίας,   165
> Εὐρίπου διὰ χευμάτων
> κέλσασα στενοπόρθμων,
> Χαλκίδα πόλιν ἐμὰν προλιποῦσ',
> ἀγχιάλων ὑδάτων τροφὸν
> τᾶς κλεινᾶς Ἀρεθούσας,   170
> Ἀχαιῶν στρατιὰν ὡς ἐσιδοίμαν
> Ἀχαιῶν τε πλάτας ναυσιπόρους ἡ-
>   μιθέων,

I came to the sandy seashore of Aulis on the coast, and put in having left Chalcis, my city which feeds the waters of famed Arethusa near the sea, and passing through the narrow stream-poured straits of the Euripus, in order that I might see the army of the Achaeans and the sea-faring oars of the demigods.

---

[174] See Henrichs 1996, 51 for treatment of the expression καλλιχόρων; he views this as evocative not only of choral dancing in general, but of the tragic choruses for which Athens was famous – including the dancing of the chorus currently using the term on stage.

[175] See Eur. *Hel.* 1575–76, where the term ῥόθια, an acoustical expression already used at 1452, and evocative of the plashing of the oars, also reappears.

[176] Again, for a more sustained and similarly oriented reading, see Weiss 2018, 193–204.

Following their description of a series of the leaders of the Greeks engaged in leisure-time activities remote from warfare, the chorus then turns to the second sight that it sought out on arriving at Aulis, and, in a patent echo of the invocation to the Muses prefacing the Catalogue of Ships in *Iliad* 2,[177] declares that it came 'for the count of ships ... and wondrous (lit. 'unspeakable') spectacle (ναῶν δ᾽ εἰς ἀριθμὸν ... καὶ θέαν ἀθέσφατον, 231–32)'.[178] Like the Homeric bard before them, the Euripidean singers will overcome the ineffable quality of the sight they would transmit, treating the audience to a description which imagines the ships as so many participants in a choral spectacle, now re-enacted by the dramatic chorus that sings and dances on the stage. Where the earlier portions of the parodos depicted the Greek heroes equipped with objects and engaged in motions that the dancers could reprise,[179] now, in the three pairs of strophes and antistrophes making up its second part, the correspondences principally belong to the equivalence between the naval and choral formations, the boat insignia selected by the singers for special mention and the presence of *chorêgoi*-like leaders who, again like their Homeric precedents, conduct and arrange their nautical ensembles.

First in the list are Achilles' fifty vessels – and here the dramatist specifies that these are penteconters (238), galleys with fifty oars corresponding to a fifty-strong choral troupe – adorned with golden figures of Nereids who 'stood/were positioned at the extremity (κατ᾽ ἄκρα ... ἔστασαν), on the sterns' (239–41). All the elements privileged in the account establish parallels between these reified and *agalmata*-like figures and the members of the smaller parthenaic ensemble that, in the dramatic fiction, recalls the scene: this fifty-strong company of Nereids is visually brilliant, stands upright and is located at one end of the drawn-out line described by the fleet extending over the Trojan plain. Also fifty in number are the Argive ships that, once again, are 'made to stand' (243) next in the right-to-left formation that the chorus continues to fashion as it dances out and verbally scans the mental image of the scene it recollects. With the appearance of the Athenian contingent, the ships are given a leader, Theseus' son, who, fulfilling the role of *chorêgos*, 'is conducting (ἄγων) the sixty vessels next in the line (ἑξῆς)' (247–49). The Boeotian contingent takes its place adjacent

[177] See Chapter 9 for detailed discussion of the Homeric Catalogue.
[178] Commentators continue to question the authenticity of the second portion of the parodos, a debate not pertinent to my discussion.
[179] Note, particularly, the two Ajaxes playing at draughts in 'much woven forms' (196, with Chapter 7), the running and leaping of Achilles as he races on the shore (207, 226) and Eumelos' 'lovely steeds', yoked to the chariot that is 'whirling' (ἑλίσσων) as it competes with Achilles (213–20). See Weiss 2018, 195–98 for several of these and other dance-inflected terms.

to the Athenian levy, this one made up of vessels that are, like Achilles' Nereid ensemble, personified and additionally furnished with their own internal leader. Noting that these ships are 'dressed' or 'adorned' (ἐστολισμένας, 255) with decorative devices, the singers also recollect that at their forefront stands Cadmus, positioned on the stern. Much as in Alcman's first *Partheneion*, where the three adornments cited first in the catalogue of chorus members stand in for their wearers, so here the descriptions of the decorative features of each vessel could prompt an audience to look closely at the costumes and accoutrements of the choristers, perhaps also differentiated one from the other in the details of their dress.

Following the account of the insignia that accessorize other contingents in the fleet, the singers conclude their review with lines that still more emphatically underscore the choral character of the naval spectacle and cast the vessels as consubstantial with the performers' actions and persons (288–98):

> Αἴας δ' ὁ Σαλαμῖνος ἔντροφος
> †δεξιὸν κέρας
> πρὸς τὸ λαιὸν ξύναγε   290
> τῶν ἆσσον ὥρμει πλάταισιν†
> ἐσχάταισι συμπλέκων
> δώδεκ' εὐστροφωτάταισι ναυσίν. ὡς
> ἄιον καὶ ναυβάταν
> εἰδόμαν λεών·   295
> ᾧ τις εἰ προσαρμόσει
> βαρβάρους βάριδας,
> νόστον οὐκ ἀποίσεται,

Ajax, the nurseling of Salamis, was bringing together his right wing to the left of those near whom he was positioned with the oars weaving together with the last twelve well-twisted ships, as I heard and saw the crew. So that if someone were to fit a foreign vessel to it, that ship would not obtain a safe return . . .

As suits the final spot, the diction reflects the closing of the ring structuring the catalogue as Ajax, another *chorêgos*-like figure, adds the final element that proves no less necessary for the list's completion than for the simultaneous closure of the naval-cum-chorus line. Suited to the choral dance is the weaving terminology that depicts Ajax interspersing individual ships in the larger formation so as to fashion a unified structure, a textile made of boats, and continuing that cloth-making conceit so common in choral lyric is the very curious adjective used of the crafts, 'well-twisted', that calls a spinning, rotating motion to mind in what may also be a glance to the cables. Reflective of the ongoing performance too is the verb assigned the enemy vessel that hazards an encounter with Ajax's ships: although an antagonist, it nonetheless 'fits itself' to the ship with which it engages. By virtue of the chosen term, the ship, denied a return to its home, becomes just another piece in the longer line, a 'concordizing' that reflects the larger harmony displayed by the song and dance; even once hostile elements can be accommodated in the ordering and cohesive institution of *choreia*.

Bypassing fifth-century comedy, where dramatists seem freshly to propose parallels between dancing in choruses and serving on board an Athenian trireme,[180] I turn to two prose accounts, both of whose descriptions of historical events introduce ships within implicit and explicit choral frames. The first of these is Thucydides' celebrated account of the Athenian fleet gathered at the Piraeus prior to its departure at the start of the Sicilian expedition in book 6, which lingers exhaustively on the different vessel types and their crews. From the outset of his report, as commentators note, the historian underscores the visible brilliance and view-worthy nature of the outsized fleet, punctuating his account with terms for sight and spectatorship and impressing on his reader the outstanding comeliness of the display (so εὐπρεπεστάτη at 31.2.1, a term repeated at 31.3.13).[181] Several discussions have also brought out the ways in which each ship and its crew members, both extravagantly equipped and brilliantly decked out so as to surpass rivals in the remainder of the naval company, resemble nothing so much as contestants engaged in a festival *agôn*, watched by a crowd seeking out an eye-pleasing piece of pageantry.[182] But the adherence to that performance format is more particularized than scholars have recognized. Much as those tapped as *chorêgoi* in fifth- and fourth-century Athens would vie with one another in equipping their chorus members with visually arresting and innovative costumes, so the trierarchs treat their ships and the men on board, also caught up in the rivalry, in the manner

---

[180] See particularly the view articulated in the *agôn* between Dionysus and the *Frogs*' amphibian troupe, where the physical conditioning and dexterity that participation in dramatic and other ritual choruses requires is the *sine qua non* for rowing in the city's fleet; Aristophanes' fragmentary *Babylonians* and Eupolis' *Taxiarchs* may also have included the motif. A patent equivalence between choral dancing and rowing occurs in a much later instance: see A.R. 1.536–41, where the Argonauts rowing in time to Orpheus' lyre are likened to youthful choristers honouring Apollo at Delphi, Delos and 'by the waters of the Ismenus'.

[181] See 31.1.4, 31.1.5, 31.4.3 and 31.6.2.

[182] See Jordan 2000, 62–65, Kallet 2001, 48–66 (note particularly 63), Steiner 2005, 412–14. More specifically, the description seems designed to call to mind the boat race at the Piraeus that formed part of the sequence of contests at the Panathenaia.

of such chorus members on whom they expend effort and financial largesse (31.3.9–4.2):

τῶν <δὲ> τριηράρχων ἐπιφοράς τε πρὸς τῷ ἐκ δημοσίου μισθῷ διδόντων τοῖς θρανίταις τῶν ναυτῶν καὶ ταῖς ὑπηρεσίαις καὶ τἆλλα σημείοις καὶ κατασκευαῖς πολυτελέσι χρησαμένων, καὶ ἐς τὰ μακρότατα προθυμηθέντος ἑνὸς ἑκάστου ὅπως αὐτῷ τινι εὐπρεπείᾳ τε ἡ ναῦς μάλιστα προέξει καὶ τῷ ταχυναυτεῖν, τὸ δὲ πεζὸν καταλόγοις τε χρηστοῖς ἐκκριθὲν καὶ ὅπλων καὶ τῶν περὶ τὸ σῶμα σκευῶν μεγάλῃ σπουδῇ πρὸς ἀλλήλους ἁμιλληθέν. ξυνέβη δὲ πρός τε σφᾶς αὐτοὺς ἅμα ἔριν γενέσθαι,

and the trierarchs both put into [the ships] the most select rowers, and besides the wages of the state, they gave something of their own to the *thrantiae* [the rowers on the uppermost bank] and regular rowers, and bestowed great cost otherwise every one upon his own galley, both in the painted decorations and expensive fixtures, each one striving to the utmost to have his ship, in fair appearance and also in swiftness, exceed in beauty the rest. And as for the land forces, they were levied with exceedingly great choice, and every man endeavoured to surpass his fellow in the zealousness of his arms and the gear that belonged to his person. And there came about as a result competitive striving between them …

The affinity between the naval assemblage and the choruses that performed at civic festivals extends beyond their shared competitive striving (ἁμιλληθέν, ἔριν). Reminiscent of the public-private partnership that allowed *chorêgoi* to put on such financially ruinous shows is the mode of financing in which the trierarchs supplement the pay given by the polis to the sailors, and deploy their own resources for the more 'decorative' elements. Apparent here too are the metonymic relations between the vessels and those on board: the trierarchs' lavish and agonistic decking out of the vessels with their painted devices and rigging stands parallel to the self-accessorizing of the men – here specifically the land forces embarked on the convoy – striving to outdo one another in their opulent weaponry and armour.

More narrowly too, the vocabulary chosen by Thucydides can be matched with terms found in earlier and contemporary descriptions of choruses and their performances. With the choral frame in place, the (albeit commonplace) verb used for the initial leading out of the ships, ἀνάγω (30.2.1; cf. 32.1.3), gains in significance: it is the term that Thucydides, following hexameter and dramatic precedents (e.g. [Hes.] *Scut.* 280; cf. Eur. *Troad.* 329) had earlier used at 3.104.4.1 in his report of how the cities that dispatched choruses to the Delia 'led out' their ensembles. Choral terminology recurs at 31.3.4: ἐξαρτύω, the compound of a verb that can refer in poetic genres to equipping choruses, here designates that same activity, now directed towards the ships and their crews.[183] Such painstaking preliminaries, viz. the *ponos* (31.3.5) expended by the city and trierarchs on the fleet's showiness,[184] contribute to investing the participants in this spectacle with the heightened visibility, luxuriant adornment and brilliance (so λαμπρότης at 31.6.2) so regularly assigned to choruses, their leaders and singer-dancers, in descriptions that, as other chapters have explored, begin in *Iliad* 18.590–604, run through Alcman, Sappho and other archaic lyric poets, and appear anew in Pindar, Bacchylides and the fifth-century dramatists. That same razzle-dazzle characterized Alcibiades earlier in book 6, when, in his account of his appearance as the cynosure of all eyes, he served as *chorêgos* in a manner that 'outshone' (λαμπρύνομαι, 6.16.3.2) the displays of his rivals. The response of the crowd gathered at the Piraeus, and of those who simply hear of the event, is no less apposite to a choral performance: where the latter typically elicits *thauma* or *sebas* (awe) in those who watch, the Sicilian expedition prompts the fleet-viewers to experience the analogous *thambos* (31.6.2).

But it is in the final stages of the description that, on both thematic and linguistic grounds, events at the Piraeus most closely dovetail with the choral model. In the moments before the ships set sail, and where ἀνάξεσθαι appears again, Thucydides establishes the soundscape appropriate to a choral performance, before adding in the ritual acts and choreography that occasions featuring *choreia* similarly include. The sounding of the trumpet gives the signal for the pouring of libations and the singing of the (choral) paean,[185] with the herald supplying the cue for the song and the crews and spectators responding in unison to his lead off. The paean completed, the ships then adopt the two most standard choral formations sequentially: first setting off in a column that recalls a chorus' processional departure to its performance site,[186] they subsequently engage in a competitive display, perhaps with a suggestion of a shift to the ring structure frequently assumed by not just by dithyrambic choruses, but also by choral ensembles performing in other genres (32.2.2–5):

> παιανίσαντες δὲ καὶ τελεώσαντες τὰς σπονδὰς ἀνήγοντο, καὶ ἐπὶ κέρως τὸ πρῶτον ἐκπλεύσαντες ἅμιλλαν ἤδη μέχρι Αἰγίνης ἐποιοῦντο.

---

[183] See *HH* 27.15, of Artemis as *chorêgos* (καλὸν χορὸν ἀρτυνέουσα); cf. the cognate verb, ἀρτίζω, describing another set of archetypal dancers at Theoc. 13.43. For discussion, see Chapters 1 and 2.

[184] For *ponos* of a choral performance, see Pind. *Nem.* 3.11–12, with Kurke 2012, 229–30.

[185] Cf. Aesch. *Pers.* 386–405.   [186] As noted by Gomme, Andrewes and Dover 1992 *ad loc.*

And when they had sung the paean and ended the libations, they put out to sea; and having at first gone out in a long file, galley after galley, they after went in a competition for superiority by Aegina.

The chorus of cavalrymen in Aristophanes' *Knights* adopts the same con-figurations when Demosthenes, acting like a *chorêgos*, directs its members first to advance in a column (κέρας), and then to 'wheel around' (κἀπαναστρέφου, 243–44) as they regroup into a circle. As already observed in my discussion of Pindar's fifth *Isthmian*, in fifth-century sources ἄμιλλα regularly describes the circle dance.

Where Alcibiades is the mastermind behind the Sicilian expedition, it is his rival Nikias who plays the leading role in the more patently choral spectacle that the statesman-general mounted (most probably) just a few years prior to the Piraeus event.[187] Among Nikias' signal achievements detailed by Plutarch (*Nik.* 3.5.1–3.7) was the *theôria* that he conducted from Athens to Delos, and which rapidly gained notoriety for a splendour far surpassing what had been done before. Integral to the display, in the biographer's report, was the manner in which the chorus disembarked in what Nikias evidently designed as a replay of the event pictured on the topmost band of the François Vase and in later visual and textual accounts, with his own person now in the Theseus role:

μνημονεύεται δ' αὐτοῦ καὶ τὰ περὶ Δῆλον ὡς λαμπρὰ καὶ θεοπρεπῆ φιλοτιμήματα. τῶν γὰρ χορῶν, οὓς αἱ πόλεις ἔπεμπον ᾀσομένους τῷ θεῷ, προσπλεόντων μὲν ὡς ἔτυχεν, εὐθὺς δ' ὄχλου πρὸς τὴν ναῦν ἀπαντῶντος ᾄδειν κελευομένων κατ' οὐδένα κόσμον, ἀλλ' ὑπὸ σπουδῆς ἀσυντάκτως ἀποβαινόντων ἅμα καὶ στεφανουμένων καὶ μεταμφιεννυμένων, ἐκεῖνος ὅτε τὴν θεωρίαν ἦγεν, αὐτὸς μὲν εἰς Ῥήνειαν ἀπέβη, τὸν χορὸν ἔχων καὶ τὰ ἱερεῖα καὶ τὴν ἄλλην παρασκευήν, ζεῦγμα δὲ πεποιημένον Ἀθήνησι πρὸς τὰ μέτρα καὶ κεκοσμημένον ἐκπρεπῶς χρυσώσεσι καὶ βαφαῖς καὶ στεφάνοις καὶ αὐλαίαις κομίζων, διὰ νυκτὸς ἐγεφύρωσε τὸν μεταξὺ Ῥηνείας καὶ Δήλου πόρον, οὐκ ὄντα μέγαν· εἶθ' ἅμ' ἡμέρᾳ τήν τε πομπὴν τῷ θεῷ καὶ τὸν χορὸν ἄγων κεκοσμημένον πολυτελῶς καὶ ᾄδοντα διὰ τῆς γεφύρας ἀπεβίβαζε.

It is a matter of record also how brilliant and worthy of the god [Nikias'] outlays at Delos were. The choruses whom cities would send thither to sing the praises of the god had been used to put in at the island in haphazard fashion. The crowd of worshippers would meet them at the ship and bid them sing, not according to *kosmos*, but as they were, disembarking hastily and not in ranks [i.e. not in battle order, disorderly],

---

[187] The date remains uncertain, but Hornblower 2008, 518 assigns it to 421 or 417.

and while they were actually putting on their wreaths and garments. But when Nikias conducted the festal embassy, he first landed on the neighbouring island of Rheneia, with his chorus, sacrificial victims and other equipment. Then, with a bridge of boats that he had brought along with him from Athens, where it had been made to measure and signally adorned with gildings and dyed stuffs and garlands and tapestries, he spanned during the night the strait between Rheneia and Delos, which is not wide. At break of day he led his festal procession in honour of the god, and with his chorus arrayed lavishly and singing as it marched, across the bridge to land.

Particularly pertinent to my discussion, and reminiscent too of the Thucydidean account, is the evident parallelism between the bridge of ships and the chorus processing over it. In Plutarch's depiction, those vessels in their line are effectively 'dressed' in the garments that the earlier chorus members were hastily assuming even as they performed and are adorned in a manner that, in diction and syntactical structure, anticipates the account of the choral group just a few lines on (compare κεκοσμημένον ἐκπρεπῶς and κεκοσμημένον πολυτελῶς). The phrase πρὸς τὰ μέτρα applied by Plutarch to the 'made-to-measure' vessels is no less applicable to the *metra*-observing song and regulated motion of the Athenians as they cross onto dry land in such well-ordered fashion. Invested with their festive attributes and observing the regularity that a choral performance requires, the ships thus supply metonyms for or reflections of the chorus members, identical in appearance and in their observance of kinetic good measure.

The topmost band on the François Vase showing the very scene that Nikias' Delian spectacle aims to re-enact and that furnishes the mythical paradigm informing the latter-day theoric chorus visually anticipates not just the continuity between the chorus line and the ships suggested by Plutarch's report, but also the narrower correspondence between the bridge of boats and the choruetes' formation. The ships that Nikias links together so as to form a chain supply the counterpart to the Theseus-led performers who process with interlinked hands that similarly join the individual members into an unbroken line in their progression from ship to shore. The construction of a chain is an element more explicitly brought out in earlier versions of how Rheneia and Delos were joined; in Thucydides' report at 3.104, Polykrates links the two islands not with a bridge of boats, but with a golden chain. Nikias' boats and choristers, fresh displays by an imperial power and no less visually brilliant than the nautocrat's chain would have been, recreate this linkage in a novel naval-cum-choral form.

6 | A Chorus of Columns: Pindar's *Agalmata* and the Architectural Chorus

'She made a gesture completely related to the columns' – the photographer Edward Steicher on photographing Isadora Duncan in the portals of the Parthenon in 1920.

Introduction

Pindar opens his sixth *Olympian* with characteristic hyperbole and éclat (1–9):

> χρυσέας ὑποστάσαντες εὐ-
>   τειχεῖ προθύρῳ θαλάμου
> κίονας ὡς ὅτε θαητὸν μέγαρον
> πάξομεν· ἀρχομένου δ' ἔργου πρόσωπον
> χρὴ θέμεν τηλαυγές. εἰ δ' εἴ-
>   η μὲν Ὀλυμπιονίκας,
> βωμῷ τε μαντείῳ ταμίας Διὸς ἐν Πίσᾳ,   5
> συνοικιστήρ τε τᾶν κλεινᾶν Συρακοσ-
>   σᾶν, τίνα κεν φύγοι ὕμνον
> κεῖνος ἀνήρ, ἐπικύρσαις
>   ἀφθόνων ἀστῶν ἐν ἱμερταῖς ἀοιδαῖς;
>
> ἴστω γὰρ ἐν τούτῳ πεδί-
>   λῳ δαιμόνιον πόδ' ἔχων
> Σωστράτου υἱός.

Setting up golden columns beneath the well-walled porch of our dwelling, we will fix in the ground, as it were, a hall to be gazed at with wonder; when a work is begun it is necessary to make its forefront far-shining. If someone should be an Olympic victor and a steward of the mantic altar of Zeus at Pisa and co-founder of famous Syracuse, what hymn could he escape, a man such as that, falling in with townsmen ungrudging in lovely song? Let the son of Sostratos know that he has his blessed foot in such a sandal.

For those familiar with the poet's encomiastic style, this is vintage Pindar. In the epinician odes, and in his other choral poetry too, the composer regularly introduces so-called *agalmata*, grandiose, luxury and highly worked artefacts that feature most prominently in elite gift exchange and as votive objects dedicated to the gods, as *comparanda* for his songs.[1] Where older discussions viewed these metaphors as figures for the poem itself, the composition as a work made up of words, recent readings have moved away from this strictly 'logocentric' perspective: instead they identify the tenor of the image not as the text, but as the performance being enacted before an audience, a spectacle that through its music, words, song and dance has an auditory, visual, kinetic and somatic appeal; it is this totality that elicits the viewer and listener's aesthetic response, the pleasure and mimetic engagement at the physical and psychic levels that unites audience and performers at the occasion.[2] And while, in this revisionary approach, the 'pay-off' of the *agalma* conceit remains the same – the transformation of the one-off performance of a work into a thing reified, precious, typically sacrosanct and of *longue durée*, complete with the potential for re-enactment – the foregrounding of the poems' performative dimensions allows us to witness the precise and multiple levels at which this equivalence or more properly union between the choral spectacle and the artefact occurs.

This substitution of *choreia* for the text involves more than just a tweaking of the relations between poems and *agalmata* as earlier conceived, and perhaps nowhere more than in the question of the distance or proximity of the metaphor's two terms. If the precious object emblematizes the choral performance, then the gap between the tenor and the vehicle all but disappears. Choruses resemble or stand as counterparts to high-value goods-cum-offerings not only because, as Mary Depew and Joseph Day have amply detailed,[3] the singers describe their roles, attributes and activities in language used in inscriptions and in other texts for the dedication of a votive to a god, and similarly call attention to their visibility, 'skills, beauty, virtue, or lavish display' and mnemonic powers.[4] More

---

[1] For a concise and still definitive treatment of *agalmata*, see Gernet 1981, 73–111.
[2] This shift is most visible in Day 1994, 2000 and 2010, Depew 1997 and 2000, Kowalzig 2007, Power 2011, Kurke 2012 and 2013. Throughout this chapter, I use the terms 'tenor' and 'vehicle' as defined in the work of Richards 1973, where the former refers to the subject to which various attributes and properties are ascribed, and the latter to the object from which these elements are derived.
[3] See n. 2.   [4] Day 1994, 70.

fundamentally, this equivalence results from the manner in which, like the votive, the choral ensemble is conceived in and of itself as a highly wrought and valuable phenomenon, the product of its maker and performers' *sophia* and *technê* that represents and even replaces in vivified form the *agalma* evoked through its words.[5] But the relationship between tenor and vehicle does not travel in this single direction alone: just as the Pindaric conceits take their impetus from the already 'factured' character of choruses and the ways in which both they and their *choreia* fulfill ornamental, celebratory, commemorative and votive ends, so too the poet seems frequently to choose his *agalmata* with an eye to their 'incipient chorality',[6] whether this depends on traditions concerning the objects' origins and back histories and/or on their existing links to sites and occasions where choristers sing and dance and the gestures they perform.

This chapter presents an attempt to trace out just one instance of this two-way exchange, with a discussion focused chiefly on a single object and three texts. Using the golden pillars of *Ol.* 6 as a starting point (and with a glance towards the objects as they recur in the same author's eighth *Paean*), its first section explores the close connections between columns, choreutes and *choreia*, and demonstrates the multiple relations between the architectural elements and singer-dancers in Pindar and other early sources. In Section 2, I turn to a second Pindaric composition, the so-called *Hymn to Zeus*, and examine the role given to the still more fantastical columns presented in that song and their connections with three other both familiar and less common choral paradigms: stars (frequently figured in many other images and texts), islands and trees. And while columns receive no mention in the last of my examples, Callimachus' *Hymn to Delos*, Section 3 of the chapter argues that the Hellenistic poet makes explicit the choral motif already visible in the Pindaric precedent and, through his revisionary account of the Delian history already central to the *Hymn to Zeus*, transforms Pindar's columnar ensemble into the multiple choruses that punctuate his piece, several of which again take stellar, island and arboreal form. The discussion ends with Section 4's briefer reading of two additional works, one a passage from Attic tragedy, the other a fourth-century votive artefact, that likewise conjoin columns and choruses and integrate several of the other choral phenomena present in the Pindaric and Callimachean texts.

---

[5] As argued in Chapter 1.

[6] The handy expression I have taken from Power 2011, 75 in other portions of this study.

1   *Olympian* 6.1–9: Embodied Columns and Columnar Choruses

Back, then, to the golden supports that the singer-dancers raise on high at the opening of *Ol.* 6 and to my suggestion that these columns supply multiforms or doubles of the performers at the outset of the piece, furnishing a display whose opulence and glamour matches the choreutes' own. Configuring and paralleling the choristers' gestures, position, function, qualities and the nature of the spectacle they present, the pillars are also 'fixatives': from a single transitory event, the celebration of Hagesias' victory in choral song becomes, quite literally, a lasting feature of the landscape, a representation in monumentalized form which can work as both a catalyst and a performance site for future reiterations of the ode. My argument begins by highlighting the dedicatory frame within which both these columns and the Pindaric performance belong before treating some more particularized associations of choral performances and columns in the architectural record.

1.1   *The Votive Frame*

Postponing mention of the object of its action, the chorus opens by declaring that it is 'raising up' something made of gold. ὑποστάσαντες might already call the act of dedication to mind, and belongs together with the several other 'tectonic' terms in the passage that align the two sets of practices that the prelude describes: setting up a votive offering and participating in a choral dance. Although most typically ἀνατίθημι describes the dedication of an object to the god, ἵστημι supplies a regular alternative in the archaic and later epigraphic repertoire. Two early fifth-century inscriptions, the first from a base in the Piraeus that probably supported a herm (*CEG* 316), the second the well-known lines on the base of a bronze statue from Halicarnassus (*CEG* 429), furnish examples of the convention:

> Πύθων Ἑρμῆ ἄγαλμα Ἑρμοστρά[το Ἀβδηρίτης
>   ἔστησεμ πολλὰς | θησάμενας πόληας.
>   Εὔφρων ἔ|ξεποίησ' οὐκ ἀδαὴς Πάριος.

> Python son of Hermostratus from Abdera set up for Hermes the object of delight after gazing on many cities. Euphron fashioned it, not unskilled, from Paros.

αὐδὴ τεχνήεσσα λίθου, λέγε τίς τόδ᾽ ἄ[γαλμα]|
στῆσεν Ἀπόλλωνος βωμὸν ἐπαγλαΐ[σας]. |
Παναμύης υἱὸς Κασβώλλιος εἴ μ᾽ ἐπ[οτρύνεις]|
ἐξειπεῖν, δεκάτην τήνδ᾽ ἀνέθηκε θε[ῷ].

'Voice crafted of stone, tell who set up this object of delight, bringing
delight to the altar of Apollo.' 'Panamyes, son of Kasbollis, if you urge me
to speak out, dedicated this tithe to the god.'

While these inscriptions advertise the merits of the statues supported by the
bases, a column might be a self-standing object of dedication whose eye-
catching character deserves epigraphic mention and commendation. An
early sixth-century inscription prominently situated on the top step of the
foundations of the colossal temple of Apollo at Syracuse, just beside the
stairway leading up to the temple's east façade, makes clear that its pillars
were also votive goods, worthy of praise and record (*IG* XIV 1; *SEG*
XXXI 841):

Κλεο[. . .]ες ἐποίεσε τὸπέλονι ho Κνιδιε[ί]δα κ᾽ Ἐπικ[λ]ἔς (σ)τύλεια καλὰ
ϝέργα.

Kleomenes the son of Knidieidas made (the temple) for Apollo, and
Epikles the columns, beautiful works.[7]

These were special columns indeed: forming two rows of four at the
building's front, and some 7.98 m in height, the sharply tapered stones
may have been the commissioner's unexpected addition and, in a break
with the Dorian building traditions of the area, of Ionic design. The temple
of Artemis at Ephesus built by Kroisos sometime before 547 B.C.E. offers a
second sixth-century example. Fragments of the inscribed base moulding
on four of the five sculpted column drums attest to the contribution made
by the Lydian, each one reading βα[σιλεὺς] Κρ[οῖσος] ἀν[έθηκ]εν (King
Kroisos dedicated this);[8] the placement of the text on the astragals at the
bottom of the shafts is consistent with the practice of positioning votive
inscriptions on the base on which a gift was displayed.[9] The Hellenistic
potentates who contributed to the temple's reconstruction in the second
half of the fourth century may have followed suit; Pliny expressly notes that

---

[7] Because the inscription is badly worn, its exact meaning remains a matter of debate; in another
possible reading, the dedication declares that 'Kleomenes, the son of Knidieidas, made it for
Apollo, and Epikles, son of Tyletas, finished it, beautiful works'. See, most recently, Hurwit 2016,
51–52 for discussion and a third possible reading. It also remains hard to determine whether
Kleomenes is the actual builder or more the one who financed and oversaw the temple's
construction.

[8] *IEphesos* 1518; *Syll.*³ 6; London, British Museum B 16.   [9] As observed by Umholtz 2002, 265.

several kings financed the colossal pillars (*NH* 36.29.95), information that he, or his source, might well have derived from inscriptions included on the objects. A fluted marble column-shaft is styled an *agalma* in a late sixth-century Melian graffito on its surface, where it declares itself the fulfillment of a vow made to the 'child of Zeus' and dedicated by Ekphantos (*SEG* III 738)[10] while (Pyth?)odoros calls his column offering of ca. 470 in the precinct of Aphrodite Pandemos in Athens 'a first offering from the good things (he has received)' (*CEG* 268). Antedating both of these is a modest stub column from Sangri on Naxos, dedicated to Apollo Alexitidês in the late seventh or early sixth century, whose votive inscription appears on its abacus.[11]

But dedicatory associations form only one facet of the Pindaric chorus' double-valent verb. As sources from the archaic and later periods demonstrate, and as Chapter 1 detailed with examples from the Homeric and lyric repertoire, ἵστημι is also the *vox propria* for the action of 'leading off', 'setting up' and 'permanently instituting' a chorus,[12] and can refer to the positioning and stance of the dancers and/or their *chorêgos* just before the performance begins. Much like the start of *Nemean* 5 with its call to the choreutes to quit their static poses and to begin their dance, the opening of *Ol.* 6 offers a variation on the familiar tableau: here the chorus members, whose declaration that they are 'raising' verbally describes what their movements enact, viz. their initial 'standing up in a chorus', are self-directed.

While the choreographic relevance of the upright stance implicit in the verb and in the reference to the columns that follows is a point to which I return, also striking in the proem is the tight confluence between the choristers' motions and the viewers' experience of the building whose erection they are invited to witness: confronted with the type of structure visualized at the outset of the ode, the eye travels in a linear manner,[13] following the upward thrust of the columns before encountering what is positioned at its top. Column flutings, whose lines run up and down the surface, encourage this impression of verticality. Even so does the verbal description point upwards before turning back to the column base, firm

---

[10] See Chapter 8 for more on this. For discussion see Jeffery 1961, 320.

[11] Naxos, Archaeological Museum of Naxos MN 8.

[12] In addition to the examples earlier cited in previous chapters, note too Pind. fr. 52b.99 S.-M. and Bacch. 11.112.

[13] Porter 2010, 440 likewise notes the 'soaring verticality' written into the description of the pillars in *Paean* 8 treated later in this section. The upward motion of the text and eye is all the more striking since, as Marconi 2014/15, 189 points out, Pausanias, perhaps reflecting common practice, tends to describe buildings from their top down.

fixed in the ground, only then to ascend anew in the reference to the 'forefront'. This verbal juxtaposition of upward movement and an anchoring in the ground, accentuated by the verse-initial position of πάξομεν, well serves the ongoing visualization of the temple whose elements are still taking shape and assuming their positions: through the use of entasis (see below) Greek architects and builders made the columns seem firmly fixed in place.

This extended description of the building-in-construction develops the dedication scenario already initiated in line 1 while continuing to draw attention to the ongoing performance. The objects that the chorus members-cum-donors erect are situated in a 'well-walled' porch. Again, the corpus of fifth-century epigrams attests to the practice of placing votives in exactly this location. So in this mid-fifth-century example, the votary, one Lysistrate, a priestess of Demeter and Kore, sets up (ἵστημι again) an offering as an 'ornament' of the portico (*CEG* 317):[14]

[ἀ]ρρῆτο τελετῆς πρόπολος σῆς, πότνια Δηοῖ,|
   καὶ θυγατρὸς προθύρο κόσμον ἄγαλμα τόδε|
ἔστησεν στεφάνω Λυσιστράτη, οὐδὲ παρόντων|
   φείδεται ἀλλὰ θεοῖς ἄφθονος εἰς δύναμιν.

The attendant of your secret ritual, lady Deo, and of your daughter's, set up this object of delight as an adornment of the porch, two crowns, nor was she, Lysistrate, sparing of what she had, but for the gods she was unstinting as far as was in her power.

Actual votive practice informs Pindar's *Nemean* 5, where in lines 53–54 the poet envisions his Aeginetan choristers dedicating the victor's crown in the forecourt of the shrine that belongs to the local hero Aiakos:

προθύροισιν δ' Αἰακοῦ
ἀνθέων ποιάεντα φέρε στεφανώ-
ματα σὺν ξανθαῖς Χάρισσιν.

And to the porch of Aiakos' temple bring the leafy crowns of flowers in the company of the fair-haired Graces.

Just as votives would jostle for space in the area before a temple or sacred shrine, so too, if Pindar accurately reflects current practice, this forecourt

---

[14] In a much later instance, Posidippus draws on the familiar practice when, in his famous epigram on Lysippus' image of Kairos (19 *HE* = *AP* 16.275), the statue describes how it was dedicated ἐν προθύροις, in the forecourt; a second piece, possibly by the same author, likewise commemorates a dedication – on this occasion of spurs, whips and a rein – 'on the portico' (*AP* 5.202).

was the site where choruses regularly staged their performances. At *Pyth.* 3.78–79, the poet describes maidens 'who often sing and dance before my porch (παρ' ἐμὸν πρόθυρον) at night' in honour of a deity, and at *Isthm.* 8.1–4, the *kômos*, Pindar's standard term for the chorus that performs the odes, likewise appears 'at the resplendent porch' of the victor's father Telesarchos. As the previous chapter argued, the account of how Zeus abducted Aegina from the portico of her father's home (fr. 52f.135–36 S.-M.) would call a familiar scenario to mind, where an amorous deity or hero snatches up the object of desire as she dances together with her sisters or age mates in proximity of her native home.[15] While the porticos in these examples form part of domestic, secular space, the lines from *Nemean 5* visualize the arrival of the Pindaric chorus at a cult site, the Aeginetan Aiakeion.

The injunction within the lines from the fifth *Nemean* offers another example of the tight connections between votive practice and choral dance-and-song, here so intertwined that the two are all but indistinguishable. The offering that the chorus members are making is at once the crown that the victor has won and that, following regular protocol, he would dedicate at the shrine of a god or tutelary hero on his home return, and the different dimensions of the performance as witnessed by the audience; the leafy garlands correspond to the accessories of the singer-dancers, frequently wreathed, while simultaneously furnishing, in the Pindaric repertoire of images, a figure for the ever-verdant song.[16] The Graces introduced at the close of the chorus' self-exhortation are no less suited to the spectacle presented in the here-and-now. Pindaric poetry repeatedly summons or includes the goddesses as personifications of the particular delights of the performance put on by the chorus,[17] and in the opening lines of *Paean 6*, the speaker calls on Delphi 'to receive (δέξαι) me with the Charites and Aphrodite at the holy (festival) time' (fr. 52f.1–5 S.-M.). As Day, noting the dedicatory force of the injunction 'to receive', remarks of the *theoxenia* for which this paean was composed, 'it is a ritualized occasion of offering, and the performers in all the grace, charm, and allure of their song and dance provide the main gift'.[18] Summons to the Charites to lend the delight that they emblematize to a performance extends well beyond Pindar; in 871

---

[15] Hardie 1996, 229–31. I return to the passage in Section 2.

[16] A Pindaric dithyramb discussed in Chapter 10 uses much the same language as it dedicates its performance to the gods whom it invites to 'take your part of the violet-bound crowns and spring-picked flowers, and [to] look upon me moving forward, from Zeus, with *aglaïa* of song' (fr. 75.6–8 S.-M.).

[17] See the examples listed in Day 2010, 245 n. 51.   [18] Day 2010, 249.

PMG, the chorus of Eleian women invite Dionysus to come 'with the Graces (σὺν Χαρίτεσσιν)', a phrase that may refer not only to the goddesses but also to the women's grace-filled choral tribute, a realization of all that the Charites represent.[19]

The poetic conflations of dedicatory language and gestures with the staging of a choral spectacle in these Pindaric works reflect and draw on the regular co-presence of the two activities within a single 'real-world' sacred space that extends beyond the portico. Excavations of the northern sector of the Hellenistic sanctuary of Apollo on the Cyprian island of Geronisos have unearthed a large circular platform of pale yellow marine silt (laboriously transported from the shore) enclosed by two concentric ring walls, this identified as a dance floor used by youths who underwent initiation rites at the site; located in the innermost wall were two limestone pinakes with holes at the upper corners, proof that votives were also dedicated there.[20] These plaques might plausibly exhibit a closer connection to the ritual performances of the boys; since many pinakes from Eleusis and elsewhere depict dancing figures, the Geronisos dedications could visually (and perhaps in writing too) commemorate and perpetuate the dancer/votaries' performative tribute to the god.

Commemoration of service rendered in the form of dance well predates the Hellenistic age and seems the intention of Archedamos of Thera, the worshipper of the Nymphs already introduced in earlier chapters, who, according to *CEG* 321, 'worked over' (ἐξηργ|άζατο) their cave at Vari at the end of the fifth century and recorded his architectural endeavours in a series of dedicatory inscriptions in the remodelled space. If we adopt the first of the two possible readings of *IG* I³ 977 B cited in the previous chapter, and assume that Archedamos advertises his construction of a dancing floor for the goddesses, then the link between votive activity and ritual performances is particularly close: the dancing space fashioned for dances to celebrate the Nymphs constitutes the offering, recorded as such adjacent to the newly built space.

But, in a way that surpasses many of the examples cited so far, the proem of *Olympian* 6 selects for the vehicle of its metaphor an object that creates a still closer bond between the performance and the votive good. Just as donors regularly proffered gifts that served as miniaturized and enduring representations of ritual acts – dancing among them – performed in honour of the god and that might depict the votaries engaged in that

---

[19] So Stehle 1997, 111 and Chapter 10 for more on these examples.
[20] See Connelly 2010 for detailed discussion of the site.

activity, so the poet devises an *anathêma* consubstantial with its donors, lastingly manifesting the ongoing spectacle and the particular character and appeal of these dancer-singers presenting their choral offering. Occupying pride of place in the account and, perhaps, still the subject of lines 3–4,[21] the pillars are the chief carriers of this identity between the material object and *choreia*. The first element in this fusion is the place of the columns within the ode's larger design. Positioned at the very start, they both correspond to the performance's incipient status as it gets underway and to the no less frontal location of the elements in building designs. As the chorus in Euripides' *Ion* 184–87 attests, columns are what first strike the eye when a temple or other sacred structure comes into view, and it cannot be fortuitous that these architectonic 'preludes' appear, as in Pindar, in the opening phrase of the Euripidean parodos. Pindar's choice of verb may also signal the double status of the columns, their literal and performative facets; indicating the raising of the actual supports which must be set in place before any further construction can occur,[22] ὑφίστημι can also mean 'to begin with', a usage regularly found in Attic drama.[23]

Tipping us off to the notional or figurative quality of the pillars is the gold from which they are made. While this aggrandizing detail corresponds to no contemporary building practices and rather points to the realm of the fantastical,[24] it perfectly suits the performers' appearance. As detailed in Chapter 1, choruses regularly draw attention to their radiance and luminosity, and to the precious ornaments, some of gold and silver, which they wear. Whether the πρόσωπον continues to refer to the pillars that 'front' the building or directs us upwards to the pediment (see below), its 'far-shining' quality maintains the focus on the sparkle that is the particular attribute of the choral dancer. Again, the phrase at lines 3–4 carries a double referent as it plays off the several meanings that πρόσωπον includes. The façade of a monumental structure, an ἔργον, should be resplendent, as was the Alcmaeonid-funded pediment of the sixth-century temple of Apollo at Delphi famously finished in marble; and if the description still dwells on the pillars, then the term is equally à propos, a reminder of the

---

[21] While most commentators are probably correct in assuming that πρόσωπον refers to the building's pediment, Pindar's language is sufficiently general that the term can also include the pillars. For a similar ambiguity, see Eur. *Ion* 185–89 cited below; there is no consensus concerning the referent for the πρόσωπα mentioned there.

[22] For a further example, see the final section of the chapter.

[23] In later fifth- and fourth-century authors, ὑφίστημι also comes to mean 'to substitute' one thing for another, or 'to set before oneself as model'; for Plotinus, it describes hypostatization.

[24] See *Od.* 7.89 for the silver pillars of Alkinous' palace, a building whose metallic walls, columns and other elements anticipate the structure imagined in Pindar's *Paean* 8 considered below.

gleam of the supports that, in contemporary practice and as detailed later on, might also be fashioned from marble, the most translucent of stones.

But the radiance evoked in *Olympian* 6 does not belong to the building alone: it is also the particular attribute of the choral dancer's πρόσωπον or face, which draws the eye of the audience and elicits special mention. So in Alcman's first *Partheneion*, the chorus members first hail their leader Agido, wondering at her 'silvery face' (τό τ' ἀργύριον πρόσωπον, 55), and Sappho fr. 16 V. registers the same sparkle on Anaktoria's countenance; as the maiden dances with her age mates, her bedazzling countenance is one of the two features that the poetic ego most longs to see: βολλοίμαν … κἀμάρυχμα λάμπρον ἴδην προσώπω (17–18). As Kurke points out, the cognate term *marmarugê* that appears repeatedly of choral performers in the archaic repertoire has the same root as the word for marble, investing the dancers with the luminosity of the stone used for the manufacture of precious goods and registering the play of light on its surface.[25]

If the opening lines of Pindar's composition principally focus on the choreutes' movements and eye-catching appearance, then the prelude also accommodates the song that *choreia* necessarily includes. As noted above, the 'far-shining façade' on which the passage lingers may point the audience upwards towards the pediment or perhaps the architrave topping the columns, a portion of the building on which, the *persona loquens* remarks, the architect-performers should expend particular care. The lines that follow this gnomic-style recommendation explain the importance accorded these structural elements. Identifying the subject and recipient of their choral tribute, and recording the Olympian victory that caps Hagesias' previous achievements, the singer-dancers incorporate into the dwelling they are constructing the 'victory announcement' that is one of the required components of epinikia. In accordance with a practice visible in other Pindaric songs featuring *agalmata*, the poet here not only transforms the once-spoken proclamation into the inscribed dedication that the material votive would typically include, but is careful to position that 'inscription' in the location where it was likely to appear. Where buildings are concerned, the pediment or architrave frequently supplied the necessary writing surface. *Pythian* 6, which famously opens with the conceit of

---

[25] Kurke 2012, 228. Very pertinent to this is the remark by an ancient commentator on the Homeric description of the Phaeacian dancers (Σ BPQV *ad Od.* 8.265): '*marmarugê* denotes the emission of light (*apostilpsis*) and the sort of brilliance (*lampêdôn*) that derives from intense movement'. Note too Pl. *Tim.* 68a, where the same term is defined as the sensation of bedazzlement experienced by a viewer confronted with the sight of something 'brilliant and glittering'.

the treasure house of song, the thesauros already built at Delphi, makes similar use of its prosôpon, more clearly indicating its role in hosting the inscription which will propagate the victor's glory (14–18):

> In the pure daylight the façade (πρόσωπον), Thrasyboulos, on behalf of your father and of your genos will announce (ἀπαγγελεῖ) a victory with the chariot, famous in man's speech, shared by your father and your clan.

The mid-sixth-century marble Ionic treasure house that the Knidians built at Delphi anticipates the poetic conceit; running in a single line from near the left-hand edge of the architrave with a short boustrophedon turn at the line's end, its now very fragmentary inscription declared that 'the demos of the Knidians dedicated this treasury and the statues to Pythian Apollo as a tithe'.[26] If the prosôpon of Olympian 6 belongs to the column, describing the frontal area on which the viewer's eye would dwell, then this too could accommodate the dedication. The small-scale (it measures only 1.05 m) column from Sangri cited above records its votive status on its abacus placed between the incised volutes while Iphidike, erecting a marble votive column of ca. 510–500 on the Athenian Acropolis, had the words 'Iphidike dedicated me to Athena, protectress of the city' inscribed from right to left along its flutes (Epigraphical Museum inv. 6241; CEG 198). As both these real-world examples and the lines from Pindar's Pyth. 6 demonstrate, the epigraphic syntax grants the inanimate structure the ability to speak. In much this manner, the declaration of Hagesias' win included in the proem of Ol. 6 may be understood as the inscribed message that the columnar choreutes now enunciate in their song.

Pindar's lacunose eighth Paean, also discussed in previous chapters, adds a fresh dimension to the column as dancer-singer conceit that opens Hagesias' ode and suggests an engagement with the analogy on Pindar's part that extends beyond the sixth Olympian. Turning its attention to the third in the sequence of temples to Apollo built at Delphi, this one of divine manufacture, the chorus asks (fr. 52i.65–68 S.-M.):

> το<ῦ> δὲ παντέχ[νοις   65
> Ἁφαίστου παλάμαις καὶ Ἀθά[νας
> τίς ὁ ῥυθμὸς ἐφαίνετο;
> χάλκεοι μὲν τοῖχοι χάλκ[εαί
>   θ' ὑπὸ κίονες ἔστασαν,

---

[26] Pouilloux and Roux 1963, 68. Here I follow the restoration proposed by Roux.

what was the *rhythmos* shown by the all-fashioning skills of Hephaestus and Athena? Bronze were the walls and bronze the columns that stood beneath . . .

Rhythmos, a Pindaric hapax, would not appear again in an explicitly architectural context until the work of Philo Mechanicus (ca. 200 B.C.E.), when, at *Syntaxis* 4.4 (ed. Schöne), the writer on mechanics and technology remarks, 'it was not possible at the very beginning to establish the forms (ῥυθμούς) of works of architecture without engaging in prior experimentation'. Philo uses the term in slightly altered fashion later in the passage, now invoking the notion of *eurhythmia* ('the quality of being well-shaped'),[27] in what may be a reference to the widespread practice – visible already in buildings of the sixth century, and used for the Doric columns of the Parthenon's peristyle – of departing from the strict geometrical regularity through entasis (the slight swelling in the column shafts' outline) and other forms of tapering and curvature so as to factor in the distortions created by the viewer's eye:[28] 'by a process of trial and error, adding to [the parts of the buildings'] bulk and again subtracting from them . . ., architectural forms are produced which are suited to the vision and have the appearance of being well-shaped (εὔρυθμα)'. In Strabo, *eurhythmia* is the overall impression created by the temple of Artemis Leukophryene at Magnesia-on-the-Maeander (14.1.40), whose sacred enclosure surpasses that of the Artemision at Ephesus owing to 'the well-designed quality (εὐρυθμία) of its appearance' (inscriptions from the late third century on indicate that the temple, built on the site of an earlier foundation, accommodated performances by choruses of maidens participating in the quadrennial Artemision).[29] Edmund Thomas suggests that what impressed Strabo was the structure's much admired eustyle colonnade, 'with two and a quarter column diameters for each intercolumniation', and further proposes that Strabo's report may have informed Vitruvius' use of *eurhythmia*, which the Roman architect makes a *sine qua non* of building practice and defines as 'the commodious look of the body in the arrangement of its limbs' (1.2.3).[30] In a direct application of the concept of 'shapeliness' to pillars, Heron of Alexandria approvingly cites the architect who employs entasis and other structural devices in his column designs so as to 'devise remedies against

[27] For discussion of this term, see Wilson Jones 2015, 51–53. As his discussion well brings out, the concept of *eurhythmia* involved a subjective element, comprising the relationship 'between composition and aesthetic pleasure' and aiming to generate visual delight.

[28] For these, see the detailed account of Haselberger 1999, 22–30.

[29] *SIG* II 695.28ff., with Calame 1997, 96–97.   [30] Thomas 2015, 275–76.

the deceptions of the eyes, aiming not at true equality and *eurhythmia*, but at what appears to be so' (*Def.* 135.13).

But does the Pindaric use of *rhythmos* of the temple columns and other elements already have the technical ring that these later architectural discussions would give to it? Commentators have puzzled over the *Paean*'s introduction of the term, variously used in seventh- and sixth-century sources for the 'disposition' of an individual, the 'pattern' of human life or perhaps a man's alternation from one condition to another. Post-Pindaric fifth-century authors give the noun the meaning 'shape', 'form' and 'configuration', and also apply it to regular, repeated movement, whether that observed in marching or, at Aristophanes, *Thesm.* 985, in choral dancing (πάλλ', ἀνάστρεφ' εὐρύθμῳ ποδί). Although the term's etymology remains unresolved, some deriving it from ῥέω, 'to flow', others from ἐρύω, 'to pull, draw', Kowalzig's recent discussion follows, in some-what modified form, Benveniste in placing motion and fluidity at the concept's centre: '*rhythmos* designates the form when it is moving', and refers to, in Benveniste's phrase, 'a configuration of movements organized in time';[31] so too, according to Jerome Pollitt, 'a single, well-chosen *rhythmos* could, in fact, convey the whole nature of movement'.[32] Following this 'dynamic' interpretation, the reference to 'flowing movement' in *Paean* 8 may describe the impression of a mobile structure generated by the play of light on the metallic surface.[33]

But, as Power proposes, Pindar most likely chooses *rhythmos* because it succinctly unites two different spheres, the architectural, as visible in later accounts, and the musico-choral, and already invests the temple with the 'kinetic and sonoric' dimensions to be more fully realized in the choral ensemble of Keledones topping the structure, whom the very next lines introduce;[34] Siren-like beguilers, their song supplies the music and sets the cadence to which the structural components just detailed dance.[35] Eugen Petersen's much earlier discussion of *rhythmos* observes that link with dancing also visible in the expression used by Aristophanes cited above, and suggests that *rhythmoi* would originally – and in a usage on which Pindar may be drawing – have described the 'positions' or *schêmata* repeatedly assumed by the body in the course of the dance.[36]

---

[31] Kowalzig 2013, 182 and 184 citing Benveniste 1971, 281–82.   [32] Pollitt 1972, 57.
[33] This is the explanation of Rutherford 2001, 219.   [34] Power 2011, 79.
[35] Cf. Hes. *Th.* 40–43 for an account of a building that responds to a choral performance, albeit in this instance with pleasure rather than motion. On hearing the 'lily-like voices' of the chorus of Muses, 'the halls of loud-thundering Zeus laugh with joy'.
[36] Petersen 1917; Kowalzig 2013, 182, without referring to the piece, modifies that view, pointing out that *schêmata* describe static and rigid poses, and not the movements between them.

Commenting on this view, Pollitt notes that the synchronization of dance and music would mean that 'the recurrent positions taken by the dancer in the course of his movements also marked distinct intervals in the music; the *rhythmoi* of the dancer thus became the *rhythmoi* of the music';[37] indeed, the 'raising' (*arsis*) and 'placing, downbeat' (*thesis*) of the dancer's foot (*pous* or *basis*) become the bases for the generation of rhythm and metre in music and poetry and for their aesthetic impact on the audience (cf. Aristides Quintilianus, *De musica* 1.13). In Plato, *rhythmos* expressly describes the measured motions of the chorus, these demarcated and enunciated by the voice performing the words and melody, and by the strike of the choristers' feet.

The two facets of the term – one architectonic, the other choreographic – may also come together in another quite early fifth-century source, the sole extant fragment (fr. 78 R.) from Aeschylus' satyr drama (?) *Thalamapoioi* (the title, 'Chamber-makers', itself suggests a tight relation between build-ing and the chorus members):

> ἀλλ᾽ ὁ μέν τις Λέσβιον φατνώματι
> κῦμ᾽ ἐν τριγώνοις ἐκπεραινέτω ῥυθμοῖς

> But let someone complete on the coffered ceiling a Lesbian wave-mould-ing with its triangular patterning

The 'wave-moulding' or *cyma reversa* applied to the ceiling here refers to the horizontal bands of decoration with projecting profiles, whose contours the carved and painted designs signalled and which served to create shadowed light and to articulate transitions. This type of moulding occurs as a feature of both wall and pillar design closely associated with the Ionic order, and is used as the uppermost element in a cornice which itself forms a patterned sequence of repeated elements. The fragment invites us to 'see in'[38] the satyr-chorus members' dance something equivalent to the action that their words describe: performing a sequence of steps in synchronized and repetitive manner and perhaps adopting the v-formation suggestive of the 'triangular patterning' in the lines, they corporeally bring about the completion of the ceiling and fashion their own embodied structure.

That the pillar conceit of *Olympian* 6 combines the auditory and verbal as well as the visual, kinetic and even tactile dimensions of the chorus' performance,[39] its multi-sensory 'architecture', a later reader of Pindar suggests. In his attempt to characterize the style of Pindaric poetry, what

---

[37] Pollitt 1974, 139.   [38] I borrow the term 'seeing in' from Wollheim 1987.
[39] See Thomas 2015, 284 on this tactile element in architecture.

he designates its signature 'austere harmony', Dionysius of Halicarnassus
employs an architectonic image, figuring each word of the poem in the
manner of something wrought out of stone that stands on its own, separated by an interval from its neighbour, and able to be apprehended –
audibly, but the description encompasses visual perception too – in the
round:[40]

> ἐρείδεσθαι βούλεται τὰ ὀνόματα ἀσφαλῶς καὶ στάσεις λαμβάνειν ἰσχυράς,
> ὥστ᾽ ἐκ περιφανείας ἕκαστον ὄνομα ὁρᾶσθαι, ἀπέχειν τε ἀπ᾽ ἀλλήλων τὰ
> μόρια διαστάσεις ἀξιολόγους αἰσθητοῖς χρόνοις διειργόμενα· τραχείαις τε
> χρῆσθαι πολλαχῇ καὶ ἀντιτύποις ταῖς συμβολαῖς οὐδὲν αὐτῇ διαφέρει, οἷαι
> γίνονται τῶν λογάδην συντιθεμένων ἐν οἰκοδομίαις λίθων αἱ μὴ εὐγώνιοι καὶ
> μὴ συνεξεσμέναι βάσεις, ἀργαὶ δέ τινες καὶ αὐτοσχέδιοι· μεγάλοις τε καὶ
> διαβεβηκόσιν εἰς πλάτος ὀνόμασιν ὡς τὰ πολλὰ μηκύνεσθαι φιλεῖ· τὸ γὰρ εἰς
> βραχείας συλλαβὰς συνάγεσθαι πολέμιον αὐτῇ, πλὴν εἴ ποτε ἀνάγκη
> βιάζοιτο.

> It requires that the words should be firmly planted and placed in strong
> positions, so that each word should be seen on every side, and that the
> parts should be at appreciable distances from one another, being separated
> by perceptible intervals. It does not mind admitting harsh and dissonant
> collocations, like blocks of natural stone placed together in building, with
> their bases not cut square or polished smooth, but remaining unworked
> and rough-hewn. It has a general liking for expansion by means of long
> words that extend over a wide space, because restriction to short syllables
> is repugnant to it, except if necessity sometimes compels. (*Comp.* 22;
> trans. Usher modified)

Many of the terms chosen by Dionysius well suit the Pindaric pillars, not
least the idea of something firmly fixed (cf. the Pindaric πάξομεν) and the
notion that the verbal object is both conspicuous (as in τηλαυγές) and can
be viewed on all sides as the viewer circles around it. The terms στάσεις,
διαστάσεις and βάσεις are entirely apposite to the notional 'supports' of the
incipient ode: so Greek building inscriptions frequently refer to the 'positioning of the pillar', στάσις τοῦ κίονος, and βάσις describes the foundation
or base on which that pillar stands. Even the 'harshness' and 'dissonance'
that Dionysius makes integral to his 'austere harmony', and that seem to
run counter to the description of the pillars in the Pindaric piece (and the
bases of the real-world columns would necessarily be 'squared off') can, at
least by Dionysius' time, be part of a building's appeal and of its architect's

---

[40] It is tempting to suppose with Fitzgerald 1987, 171–72 that Dionysius had the pillars at the start
of *Olympian* 6 in mind here. Note too Benediktson 2000, 112.

original design: unworked stones might be included so as to achieve a
'rusticated' effect, this sought after precisely because the contrast would
enhance the impression made by the more finished elements, heightening
their impact on a viewer.[41] Like Dionysius, Apuleius' tongue-in-cheek
dismissal of his own highly worked-over rhetorical style likens it to an
accumulation of such unfinished masonry, which lacked the desired regularity and alignment (*De deo Socr.* pr. 3). Anticipating an effect familiar to
Dionysius' audience, Pindar's discordant acoustics, in the view of a latter-
day audience, actually promote the aesthetic merits of his compositions.

Reading Dionysius' description against the Pindaric precedent, a second
dimension becomes apparent in a (doubtless unwitting) demonstration of
how closely architectonic and choral terminology may intersect. As in the
Pindaric columns, these words-cum-stones take on the character of living
bodies that move in relation to one another even as they issue sound. Like
the members of a chorus line, whose brilliantly decked-out bodies would
circle about, permitting viewers to apprehend them from all sides, they are
also spaced out at regular intervals, each one individualized. In much this
manner, a detail of dress, bodily feature, stance or accessory singularizes
each participant in the '*corps de ballet*' introduced in lines 64–76 of
Alcman's first *Partheneion*, while multiple vase images from the
Geometric period likewise include small variations which interject elements of heterogeneity into the collective choral group. Indeed, perceptible
in Dionysius' account of the 'austere style' is the tension already on display
in the early artistic repertoire, and most fully realized by the comic choruses
of fifth-century Attic drama: as Renaud Gagné remarks of the choristers
who take on the role of the twenty-four letters of the Ionic alphabet (see
Chapter 8 for full discussion), their 'performance could exploit the double
nature of the individualized chorus in old comedy, a collective composed of
distinct individuals'.[42] Two terms in Dionysius acknowledge this overall
cohesion and the verbal columns' membership of a single ensemble. The
verb that describes the 'placing together' of the stones (συντιθεμένων)
appears in other sources in the context both of combining diverse elements
in an oral or written composition and of choreographing a dance, whose
different motions must be linked together. Also indicative of participation
in an overarching and unified superstructure is Dionysius' concession in
the final phrase of the passage; under space constraint – a small plot of land,
a restricted performance site – the individual elements can be 'brought

---

[41] Thomas 2015, 282; Thomas also cites the passage from Apuleius referred to below.
[42] Gagné 2013, 309.

together', the gaps between them narrowed and their 'self-standing' quality minimized.

For all the seeming fixity and stability of the components of Pindar's verbal construct and the lapidary character that Dionysius perceives in it, the peristyle building imagined by the later rhetorician further resembles a chorus insofar as it moves and sounds. *Kinêsis* is implicit in διαβαίνω, which means to stride or walk with the legs wide apart as well as to take up a stance, and gives the impression that these stones are both 'firm planted' and capable of motion; we witness the same paradox of dynamism and fixity at the outset of *Olympian* 6 and again in Pindar's eighth *Paean*. διαστάσεις combines movement and sound with the visual perception of extension or expansiveness:[43] it can refer both to a musical interval and to the 'rests', the ἠρεμίαι, that exist in any movement, that perceptible moment of stillness of particular concern to fifth-century statue-makers (and on display in the sculptures of the Aeginetan temple of Aphaia) and adopted in the postures of dancers before they move again. ἀντίτυπος freshly comprises the audible and kinetic: principally indicative of the force of repulsion, it also describes sounds that echo or answer to one another. Again, the stones are simultaneously at variance and parts of a single unit, each taking up the voice of the next one in the line, but issuing a contrasting sound.

As for the unfinished rupestral elements observed by Dionysius, these too find their counterpart in choral aesthetics. In her discussion of the quality of *rhythmos* cited above, Kowalzig notes how its opposite, the fracturing of regularity (*arrhythmia*), is visible in the depiction of the chorus of women found in a tomb at Ruvo, and dated to the fourth century:[44] as she remarks, the different colouration of the dress worn by the second dancer from the left marks her out, 'while the dark braid continuing into the dress of her neighbour sutures her back into the collective strung together by the dancing movement'. In the view of the imperial rhetoricians, an excessive regularity or refinement in verbal composition, which resulted from things being well joined and harmonized, could actually produce satiety in an audience, whose taste for the 'charming and refined' (so *Rhet. ad Her.* 1.23.32) or what the Romans called *concinnitas* – also used of buildings in Cicero's description of his brother's estate (*Ad Q. fr.* 3.1.5) – was soon exhausted. Both architecture and chorus members are subject to this principle.

---

[43] Note the Latin term *amplitudo*, which can apply to the sphere of building (e.g. Pliny, *Ep.* 10.49.1) and to rhetoric; for discussion, see Thomas 2015, 279.

[44] Naples, Museo Nazionale 9352–57, with Kowalzig 2013, 189.

1.2   The Karyatid Chorus

Returning to the archaic context, this portion of the discussion suggests that the notion that the columns of a building might perform in the manner of a moving and singing choral ensemble is not pure whimsy and rococo on Pindar's part. Instead the column-chorister analogy is on display in the sacred landscape of late archaic and classical Greece, and in buildings that predate *Ol.* 6 by several decades. Adorning the forefront of the Siphnian Treasury at Delphi, dated to ca. 530–525, were several pairs of columnar women (Fig. 0.8), figures that conform to what sources from the fourth century on term 'karyatids', generally defined as marble statues of long-robed women used in the place of columns. About a century later Athens would erect six such figures, identified not as 'karyatids' but simply as *korai* in the building inscriptions, on the south porch of the Erechtheion (Fig. 0.9). As current discussions of karyatids routinely note,[45] Vitruvius' account of the origins of the motif – the first karyatids, he explains, were designed to recall some Carian matrons taken into slavery when their city was punished for medizing during the Persian Wars (1.1.5–6) – seems to get things very wrong.[46] In distinction to telamons, whose heads are bowed and bodies bent to shoulder their heavy load (witness those on the Olympeion at Akragas), there is nothing downtrodden or subservient about these richly dressed female figures, their heads erect and gaze forward-directed, and whose overall design aims to minimize the impression of weight-bearing; as Ione Shear remarks, the polos crown worn by the Siphnian karyatids 'served visually to lighten the load carried by the maidens'.[47]

Both etymology and building practices suggest a very different origin for the karyatids. According to many Greek and Roman sources, Vitruvius aside, the term in its primary usage described the members of the standing maiden chorus at the shrine of Artemis Karyatis ('Artemis of the Walnut Tree') and the Nymphs in Sparta, whose annual celebration of the goddess featured dances performed in her honour.[48] Pausanias and Plutarch both refer to the dancing Karyatids: according to Pausanias the maidens performed in the local style, ἐπιχώριος ὄρχησις, and Pliny mentions among the works of Praxiteles three sets of images which he seems to group together because they all show choruses of female dancers – maenads, Thyiads and

---

[45] For good recent discussion, see Ridgway 1999, 145–50, Rykwert 1996, 134–35 and Shear 1999.
[46] Vitruvius seems the originator of this particular aetiology.
[47] Shear 1999, 77. My discussion also draws on the illuminating account in Neer 2001, 315–18.
[48] See Calame 1997, 149–56 for more extensive discussion of the cult.

Karyatids.[49] Athenaeus mentions a drama produced by Pratinas with the title Karyatides – the logical inference is that the chorus assumed the identity of the maiden dancers at the shrine – and for Pollux the verb derived from the noun, καρυατίζειν, describes 'dancing in a stately way' or 'doing a ring dance'.[50]

The architectural record confirms, via a different route, the extended connection between karyatids and choruses of women performing ritual and specifically round dances. In Shear's persuasive account, Greek architects erecting the columnar women at mainland sites would have taken their impetus and model from the vast marble temples in Asia Minor complete with their supersized and ornately sculpted column drums.[51] At the mid-sixth-century temple of Artemis at Ephesus, such drums stood on tall bases mounted on plinths. On the lower drums of the columns on the east façade, decorative rounded and squared reliefs show participants in a religious festival, a sequence of figures made up not only of long-robed men and horses but also of elaborately carved women likewise shown in profile,

Fig. 6.0 Female figure on column drum from Ephesus, ca. 550–520 B.C.E. London, British Museum B 91. Photograph © The Trustees of The British Museum.

---

[49] Paus. 3.10.7, 4.16.9, Plut. *Artax.* 18.2, Pliny, *NH* 36.4.23; see too Lucian, *Salt.* 10.
[50] Athen. 9.392f, Pollux 4.104.
[51] Shear 1999 with full bibliography for earlier discussions of the drums.

Fig. 6.1 Column drum from Kyzikos, ca. 540 B.C.E. Istanbul, Archaeological Museum 5370. Photograph courtesy of Livius.org/Jona Lendering.

one of whom carries an offering and another of whom appears to dance (Fig. 6.0); positioned just above the eye level of the viewer and richly clad in layers of fabric they form 'a continuous frieze of sculptured figures'.[52] At Kyzikos to the north, also dated to the mid-sixth century, one such sculpted drum carries a veiled maiden in a tight-fitting chiton with a deep overfold (Fig. 6.1);[53] flanking her on both sides are naked youths whose hands she reaches out to take as though to perform a ring dance. Where, in Joan Connelly's attractive reading, 'the dance may be set in the mythical past when the first youths and maidens of Kyzikos established a tradition of choral performances that was perpetuated in the historical ritual',[54] an actual ritual event may still more closely inform the decorative motif, turning the temple columns' architectural fabric into a record of and model for an event in which viewers may themselves have participated.[55]

Best preserved are the sculpted columns at the temple of Apollo at Didyma, dated to ca. 540–525, where reliefs of nearly life-sized young women encircle the shafts of the drums rising directly from the base of the pronaos (Fig. 6.2).[56] The column flutings descend between the figures, both demarcating the intervals between them as they stand facing forward,

---

[52] Shear 1999, 78.   [53] Istanbul, Archaeological Musum 5370.   [54] Connelly 2007, 124.

[55] For the 'mirroring' role of temple architecture, see Marconi 2013.

[56] Berlin, Antikensammlung SK 1721.

Fig. 6.2 Column drum fragment from Didyma, ca. 540–525 B.C.E. Berlin,
Antikensammlung SK 1721. Photograph Ingrid Geske. Photo © 2019. Scala, Florence/
bpk, Bildagentur für Kunst, Kultur und Geschichte, Berlin.

their backs pressed up against the shaft, and, perhaps, mirroring the folds of
the floor-length garments the maidens would, like their Ephesian counterparts, have worn; in this formal sense, the stone-cutters create a direct
visual parallel between the ornamental figurative sculptures and the
columns.[57] Still visible are the rich ornaments that these evidently high-
status figures wear: dressed in their chitons, himatia and veils, one figure
has a rounded ribbon or crown holding her veiled headdress in place, while
others display wreaths surrounding their veils.[58] Most plausibly, the figures
offer stylized representations of participants in the annual procession that

[57] The equivalence works in both directions; the *korê* dedicated by Cheramyes at the Heraion on
Samos wears a chiton whose descending pleats resemble column flutes; as Wilson Jones 2014,
143 comments, 'the almost cylindrical lower part and the way it flares to meet the plinth recalls a
column'.
[58] For details, see Connelly 2007, 122–23 and Marconi 2007, 26.

would make its way from the Delphinion in Miletus to Didyma, a route
punctuated by stops for ritual activity at designated sites, with sacrifices
and maybe choral performances too; dances would be particularly appropriate at the sanctuary of the Nymphs on that processional route, also the
find spot for *korai*, whose presence confirms the votive activity that went
on there.[59] Firmer evidence for a link between women's participation in
ritual dancing and votive maidens comes from the Didymaion itself. Close
by the figures circling the columns of the pronaos stood the so-called
Round Altar, a structure surrounded by six bases; while interpretations of
the bases' purpose differ, one view identifies them as supports for the *korai*
discovered at the site.[60] Like the figures arranged around the nearby
ornamented drums, the maidens positioned in circular formation would
lastingly re-enact one of the most characteristic forms of female ritual and
dedicatory activity, the performance of ring dances in service of the god.
Consonant with a choral character are two additional features of the
Didyma column women. With their hands extended, they may make
offerings,[61] both the actual gifts they present to the god and the less-
tangible tribute that their *choreia* involves; they also exhibit the homogeneity and equality as well as epichoric identity that defines chorus members.

Back on the Greek mainland, the karyatids adorning sacred structures
variously preserve the link with choral dance exhibited at the Ionian
temples. The still extant figure from the Siphnian Treasury wears a thin
chiton with wavy folds beneath her mantle and also reaches out her hand in
a gesture of offering. Although her posture is stiff, even 'hieratic',[62] one
feature of the figure might call a dancer to mind: as some of the extant *korai*
also do, she gathers up her long robe with her missing left hand so as to pull
it tight across her lower body. Although this gesture has a more generalized
significance, indicating the observance of proper social behaviour and
decorum as practised by elite women, it is also an action, Lawler has
suggested, typical of the Ionian women who took part in choral dancing,
and whom our sources regularly describe as dressed in their floor-length
garments;[63] so at the archetypal festival for Apollo at Delos evoked in the
sixth-century *Homeric Hymn to Apollo*, the 'long-robed Ionians' (147–48),

---

[59] See Karakasi 2003, 41–44 for some possible indications of this.   [60] Ibid.

[61] See Neer 2001, who nicely emphasizes this idea of service at 316–17. However, caution is
necessary with regard to the figures on the Didyma columns; although some restorations (see
Gruben 1963) suggest that each holds a sacrificial offering, the more recent discussion of
Marconi 2007, 26 regards this as unlikely.

[62] So Themelis 1992, 53; following Ridgway 1977, 109 he views the figure as a divine image, a
Nymph.

[63] Lawler 1943.

husbands and their wives, are in attendance, and both perform in choruses to celebrate the god. As Lawler further notes, the ample chiton that Herodotus also assigns to Ionian women (5.88) would have hindered mobility unless the dancers could make the 'graceful manipulation' of the garment into a stylized feature of their performance.[64] Maintaining the association with the dance is one of the scenes in high relief on the basket-shaped polos that the Siphnian karyatid balances on her head.[65] On the better preserved back part of the crown, three satyrs and two nymphs or maenads appear; one of the satyrs raises his right leg as he dances, perhaps performing on the now-lost aulos with which he may originally have been equipped. The action of the remaining figures is harder to discern; what some interpret as a group of dancers can also be read as an abduction scene (although the two activities are far from incompatible). If the artist did show a Dionysiac *thiasos* engaged in its characteristic orgiastic dance, then the image would project onto the timeless world of myth and nature the performances in which the Siphnian women who formed part of the delegation sent by the city to the festival of Apollo at Delphi participated, albeit in more restrained and decorous form and in service to a different god.

More patently 'choral' are the Erechtheid *korai*, whose posture and appearance suggest not just their votive role – the figures originally held phialai in their right hands, vessels that would style them libation-pourers – but their character as a dancing group, even one divided into two semi-choruses.[66] On the left side of the building, the *korai* might seem to step lightly with their right foot bent while those on the right, their left foot bent, advance in the opposite direction; just like the choruses performing in contemporary Athens in the *orchestra* of the theatre of Dionysus, who on occasion divide in two, depart in different directions and then reunite on their return, so the two lines of stone maidens would circle around the

---

[64] Lawler 1943, 64. Lawler also cites a variety of votive figures of dancers from Ionia – the dancing women on a relief from the Branchidae and one on a relief from Gjölbaschi – who gather up their skirts in this way, as do participants in the ritualized processions whose movements our sources view as a form of dance (see Athen. 1.20f–21a, Dion. Hal. 7.68.3–6). For the reliefs, see Richter 1970, figs. 466 and 516.

[65] For discussion and the problems in reconstruction of the scenes, see Themelis 1992, 54–64.

[66] Here I draw on the suggestion of Karvouni 1997, 204. For a later parallel, see the frieze of female dancers from the Hall of the Choral Dancers at Samothrace from the fourth century's second half (with detailed discussion in Marconi 2010). Depicted in a frieze that would have encircled the entire building along with the rest of the entablature, the more numerous maiden dancers (over 900 in a recent count) may likewise have been shown as two processions, a shorter one to the left, and a longer one to the right, which converged at the middle of the frieze on the building's central façade.

building before meeting up at its centre. One small detail of the karyatids'
appearance, the sandals peeking out from beneath the hems of their long
Ionian robes, might freshly promote their association with dancing. While
elaborately worked sandals seem more generally to enhance a real and
sculpted maiden's charms, the sixth- and fifth-century sources cited in the
earlier discussion of the feature in Chapter 1 detail fancy sandals in
accounts of the accessories equipping choral dancers.

This chapter's second section treats further instances of 'choralized'
sandals relevant to both the Erechtheid portico and to Pindar's columnar
choreia, but first one final aspect of the Athenian maidens fronting the
temple. Many scholarly accounts view these *korai* as generic, most broadly
alluding to the idea of female service proffered to the divinities and hero
(Athena Polias and Poseidon-Erechtheus) whose cults were celebrated inside
the building that the columnar girls supported and adorned. But there may
be a reference to a more historical set of maidens here and to the ritual
dances that they performed in late fifth-century Athens. In the story of
Erechtheus presented in Euripides' drama of that name (and supplementing
its fragments with later versions of the tale), the mythical early king leads the
Athenians against the Eleusinians, these championed by the Thracian
Eumolpus, a son of Poseidon. An oracle from Delphi made victory in battle
contingent on the sacrifice of one of Erechtheus' three daughters, who
conjointly swear an oath that, were one to die in the required manner, the
others would then kill themselves. The sacrifice and suicide duly occur, and
after Erechtheus defeats Eumolpus in battle, Poseidon avenges his son's
death by slaying the Athenian king with his trident; Athena then sets up a
cult for Erechtheus and Poseidon (now restyled Poseidon-Erechtheus), who
shared an altar and a priest, in her own temple. Most relevant to the karyatid
porch is the fragment of Euripides' play where the goddess enjoins the
Athenians to commemorate and celebrate Erechtheus' daughters in cult,
and declares that, rather than descending to Hades, the sisters will take up
residence in the sky where they will become the 'divine Hyakinthids'.[67]
Directing her citizens to create a precinct for the maidens, Athena further
commands the Athenians to worship the Erechtheids with annual sacrifices
and choral dancers (fr. 370.77–80 K.):

τοῖς ἐμοῖς ἀστο[ῖς λέγ]ω
ἐνιαυσίαις σφας μὴ λεληϲμ[ένους] χρονῳ

[67] The suggestion of catasterization receives a second sounding in the very fragmentary v. 107; see too Σ Aratus 172 (p. 166 Martin), with its identification of the Hyakinthids with the Hyades, a familiar stellar cluster.

θυσίαισι τιμᾶν καὶ σφαγαῖσι [βουκ]τόνοις
κοσμοῦντας ἱ]εροῖς παρθένων [χορεύ]μασιν·   80

> I (instruct) my citizens to honour them, not ever forgetting this over time, with annual sacrifices and slayings of oxen, adorning these rituals with sacred maiden dances.[68]

Athena's language not only demonstrates anew the tight link between a material offering and a choral dance, imagining *choreia* as a *kosmos*, precisely the term used in *CEG* 317 (see above) for a votive good and similarly selected by Pindar for a choral offering turned *agalma* in fr. 194 S.-M., but also curiously anticipates the Erechtheid portico, whose construction began one or two years after the date of 423/22 usually assigned to the play. While it is possible that plans for the structure may already have been circulating – architects in Athens would make public 'exhibition pieces' of their projected designs – more probably the relationship travels in the opposite direction: the building makes the commonplace poetic equation between votive offering and choral dance literal, realizing the metaphor in tangible form and depicting the maiden choruses as just such *agalmata*, beautiful and enduring representations of the dances they performed. Indeed, the marble *korai* may not be the only manifestation of the dancers whom the fragment describes. Just as at the Ionian Didymaion the women encircling the column drums stood in close proximity to a set of votive *korai*, so the largest number of the cache of Acropolis *korai* – some thirty-two – were discovered in the vicinity of the Erechtheion, in the area to the north-west of the building.[69]

  Choral dancing requires a performance space, and the area adjacent to the temple may well supply just such a site. As excavations have revealed, a rectangular space opens up between the north porch of the Erechtheion to

---

[68] Wilson 2000, 326 n. 165 notes the several discussions that interpret the fragment differently and question the existence of these maiden choruses; however, as he observes, most accept the '"fact" of female *choreia*'. See too the discussion in Budelmann and Power 2015, 257–58; in their view, these choral dances might plausibly have been performed during the *pannychides* of the Panathenaia and would not have formed part of a self-standing and independent cult.

[69] Granted, to suggest a connection between these votive maidens and choral dancers begs the larger and highly vexed question of the function of the *korai* dedicated at Athens and elsewhere, and there are any number of competing readings, including the discussion by Keesling 2003, who challenges the widespread view that they are generic figures or representations of women serving as sacred personnel. But another site does allow for a tighter bond between choral maidens and the dedications that adorned a shrine. The chief find spot for the *korai* from Delos was in the area of the Artemision, and the inscription on the Nikandre *korê* confirms that some of these figures were dedicated to Artemis. According to one reading, the dedications originally stood in the space around the cult centre of the sanctuary, the Altar of Horns, where the sources locate choral dances in honour of Apollo and Artemis; for discussion, see Karakasi 2003, 73–78.

the west, a broad staircase to the east and the three steps of the crepidoma facing south. In Connelley's reconstruction,[70] this 'plaza', whose floor was already paved over in very early times and which would have afforded the necessary protection from wind and external noise, 'would have been an ideal location for choral singing and dancing'. Here, as Connelley suggests, festival-goers could gather to attend performances staged by choruses of youths and maidens, singing and dancing in the manner of the troupes evoked in a choral song in Euripides' *Heracleidai* 777–83: as the singers recall, on these occasions the 'windswept' hill of the Acropolis would resound with the ritual cries and beating feet of *parthenoi* as they accompanied the hymns to Athena sung by the youths.

This chapter's final section will return to the Erechtheid maidens, and to one further columnar artefact displaying them as dancers and dedications, but for now my focus remains on karyatids. Confirmation of the objects' votive character comes from a dedicatory inscription connected with the building of the Knidian Treasury, where the figures are called *agalmata*,[71] their highly worked and ornamented appearance, like that of the Athenian maidens, freshly exemplifying the qualities most likely to gain divine attention and an answering *charis*. The design of the girls on the Erechtheion porch seems further to highlight their dedicatory character even as it masks their architectural role; not only, as noted, were they equipped with vessels containing offerings in their now-missing right hands, the phialai with whose ornamental egg-and-dart design their capitals display a pronounced likeness,[72] but the omission of the volutes that usually formed part of the capitals of Ionic pillars and the placement of the columnar-*korai* against a solid wall give them the appearance of self-standing objects of dedication.[73] Like the Athenian karyatids, the Siphnian figures also trope their role as gifts as they participate in the larger votive role that the Treasury fulfills; with their right hands extended, they are gift-bearers, visibly and enduringly re-enacting the gesture of the Siphnian delegates whose precious donations to Apollo the building housed.[74] Indeed, as Richard Neer acutely observes, the very structural

---

[70] Connelley 2011, 332–33, whose description I follow.

[71] See Themelis 1992, 51 for the inscription and discussion.

[72] Wilson Jones 2014, 169; his account also notes how the capital of the karyatid usually assigned to the Knidian Treasury also assimilates the characteristic ribbing of the phiale.

[73] So Shear 1999, 83.

[74] Neer 2001, 317–18 addresses the paradox of women, excluded from the civic life of the polis, serving as representations of Siphnians, a phenomenon that might be compared to the practice of having male choruses project their identity onto maiden dancers. His analysis usefully offers a possible answer to the conundrum: servitude to the god allows them to assume this public role.

purpose of these figures freshly signals their votary and concomitantly 'servile' character: the columnar women 'serve' not only because they are gift-givers, but also, and still more patently, because they support the lintel, a function that 'shows them to be the *therapnai* of the deity'.[75]

This conjunction of serving maiden, votary and *agalma* (ornament and offering both) recurs in the self-characterization of a group of maidens who unmistakably form a choral ensemble.[76] Reflecting on their ritual career past and future, the choreutes of Euripides' *Phoenissae en route* to Delphi remark (220–25):

> ἴσα δ' ἀγάλμασι χρυσοτεύ-   220
> κτοις Φοίβῳ λάτρις ἐγενόμαν·
> ἔτι δὲ Κασταλίας ὕδωρ
> περιμένει με κόμας ἐμᾶς
> δεῦσαι παρθένιον χλιδὰν
> Φοιβείαισι λατρείαις.   225

> There I became the handmaiden of Phoebus, like to his offerings fashioned in gold. But as yet the water of Castalia is waiting for me to wet the maiden glory of my locks for the service of Phoebus.[77]

The expression equates the ministration that the girls render to Apollo with the role of the golden offerings at his Delphic site, and in so doing invites us to see the richly attired singer-dancers on the stage as just such *agalmata* or precious votives in the making. The maidens' anticipated role at Delphi both recapitulates their ornamental and glittering character – χλιδή is derived from a root term referring to that brilliance and gleam that is so integral to a gift's capacity to please the god – and additionally looks to the choral dances to be performed on Apollo's behalf:[78] as noted in Chapter 5, the opening of Pindar's sixth *Paean*, composed for a choral delegation sent in sacred pilgrimage to Delphi, identifies the water of Castalia, currently 'bereft of men's choral dancing' (ὀρφανὸν ἀνδρῶν χορεύσιος, fr. 52f.9 S.-M.), as the very spot where the Pindaric chorus will stage its performance, and then goes on to glance towards the maiden choruses dancing adjacent to the spring. The idea of service also bears more narrowly on the column even

---

[75] Neer 2001, 316.

[76] This is true of the chorus members whether they are considered in their internal dramatic role, or in their own persons, as participants in a ritual *choreia* in the theatre of Dionysus.

[77] Power 2011, 76 also cites the lines.

[78] Cf. the evocation of a choral dance in the song of another Euripidean parthenaic chorus (*IT* 1144–52): 'If only I could take my place in choruses where once as a girl at illustrious weddings … in rivalry of grace (χλιδᾶς) and richly luxuriant finery rousing myself for the contest as I threw about me richly worked robes and locks.'

independent of karyatids: in the lines from Euripides' *Ion* discussed above, the chorus designates the 'well-columned courts of the gods and altars' that the maidens see on their approach to Delphi as structures 'in the service' (θεραπεῖα, 187) of Apollo Agyieus. Although the θεραπεία refers in generalized fashion to the ritual activity that goes on at the site, it also illustrates how the architectural features of a building may participate in the service that votaries and the physical fabric of the sanctuary jointly render to the god.

One final set of karyatids reiterates the association between the columnar figures and the dance, combining them in another dense set of relations, at once visual, mythical and ritual. Designed by Bathycles in the mid-sixth century, the elaborate throne of Apollo at his sanctuary at Amyklai in Sparta included karyatids serving as supports. Above these, the reconstructions suggest, stood curious 'hybrid' columns, Doric on one side and Ionian on the other. Decorating other portions of the throne were two sets of archetypal choral *parthenoi*, a pair of Graces and another of the Horai, who, in both visual and literary accounts, regularly dance in ensembles (e.g. *HHAp.* 194–96; Pind. *Ol.* 4.2). Most intriguingly, according to Pausanias' detailed description of the structure at 3.18.9–19.5, Bathycles depicted the Magnesian workmen who carried out the project in the form of a dancing chorus; with their hands linked, they present a line of moving figures at the very top of the throne. The representation would answer to another scene of choral dancing set among the forty-five reliefs that adorned the complex, this one showing that ur-*choreia* of the Phaeacian youths performing to the song and music of Demodocus in *Od.* 8. Bathycles' assimilation of craftsmen-builders and choral performers nicely answers to the intersections between other mythical and legendary 'constructors' (Hephaestus and Daedalus principally; for Demodocus, see Chapter 7) and the fashioned choruses treated in this and other chapters, and gives the throne that overall *rhythmos* that Pindar's paeanic temple similarly displays.

When framed by the rituals celebrated on behalf of Apollo at the shrine, the emphasis on chorality in the throne's iconographical programme seems particularly well chosen. During the course of the three-day Hyakinthia,[79] and following the musical and dance performances in which choruses executed what our ancient authors describe as 'traditional dances', a grand procession would make its way from the city of Sparta to the Amyklaion, with maidens riding in special wickerwork chariots prominent among the participants.[80] Several different sources suggest that these girls

[79] See the more detailed discussion of the festival in Chapter 3.
[80] Calame 1997, 175–77 reviews the evidence and concludes that 'the part played by Spartan girls at the Hyakinthia ... included choral dancing'; see too Pettersson 1992.

then performed choral dances in honour of Apollo and the hero Hyakinthos buried at the sanctuary. In addition to the third stasimon of Euripides' *Helen* detailed in Chapters 3 and 4, Calame cites Jerome's mention of how Aristomenes abducted the Spartan *parthenoi* dancing in choruses at the site (Hier. *Jov.* 1.41, p. 284 Migne). Intriguingly Jerome has moved this incident from the festival of Artemis Karyatis, where the abduction more usually occurs. Among the artefacts excavated from the Amyklaion, which included many terracotta female figurines, was a stele dated to the third century; the scenes carved on it show a sacrifice and a choral dance, with five figures including a dancing woman and two female musicians with pipes and a plectrum.[81]

1.3 The Embodied Peristyle

But time to leave the service-rendering and votive karyatid chorus behind, and to propose that the analogy between the pillar and chorister may predate these sixth-century columnar figures. In the very speculative but intriguing argument of Maria Karvouni,[82] the peristyle so distinctive of the archaic and classical Greek temple, and the feature that chiefly set it apart from its Minoan and Mycenaean predecessors, was nothing less than a stylized and abstract representation of a chorus celebrating the god housed within, each column the equivalent of one chorus member. Well-grounded in the sources is the correspondence between the different elements of the pillar – whether used for secular or religious buildings – and the human body.[83] Iphigenia's report of the dream she had of Orestes closely tracks the parallels (Eur. *IT* 46–54):

> χθονὸς δὲ νῶτα σεισθῆναι σάλῳ,
> φεύγειν δὲ κἄξω στᾶσα θριγκὸν εἰσιδεῖν
> δόμων πίτνοντα, πᾶν δ᾽ ἐρείψιμον στέγος
> βεβλημένον πρὸς οὖδας ἐξ ἄκρων σταθμῶν.
> μόνος δ᾽ ἐλείφθη στῦλος, ὡς ἔδοξέ μοι,   50
> δόμων πατρῴων, ἐκ δ᾽ ἐπικράνων κόμας
> ξανθὰς καθεῖναι, φθέγμα δ᾽ ἀνθρώπου λαβεῖν,
> κἀγὼ τέχνην τήνδ᾽ ἣν ἔχω ξενοκτόνον
> τιμῶσ᾽ ὑδραίνειν αὐτὸν ὡς θανούμενον,

---

[81] Calame 1997, 177.
[82] Karvouni 1997; cf. Ach. Tat. 1.15.1 for the realization of the notion in his χορὸς κιόνων.
[83] For the more fundamental equation between the human body and something that is constructed in the manner of an artefact, see Karvouni 1999.

The earth's surface seemed to be shaken by a tremor. I fled and standing outside seemed to see the cornice of the house falling and the whole roof, from the tops of columns down, thrown down in ruins to the ground. One pillar was left, as it seemed to me, from the ancestral dwelling, and from its head it seemed to grow tawny hair and take the voice of a human. So I, honouring this stranger-killing art that I have, sprinkled it with water as though it were about to die.

Drawing on the traditional notion of the guardian/ruler of the house or city as a pillar (see Pind. *Ol.* 2.6–7, 81–82; Aesch. *Ag.* 897–98), an image for all that is strong, steadfast and gives support, Iphigenia's speech might include a more exact equation between the stylos and the human form. In Mary Stieber's view,[84] here Euripides prompts us to imagine Orestes as a Corinthian column, the most ornate of the three orders and one further distinguished by its capital elaborately decorated with acanthus leaves and maybe even gilded (so Orestes' golden hair).

But rather than see in this highly wrought and personified prop a glance to the innovatory Corinthian columnar form, the first example of which, in standard accounts, belongs to the temple of Apollo at Bassai and whose date remains a topic of dispute, I would look to a much earlier sounding of the pillar-body equivalence. This is already visible in Odysseus' familiar description of the wondrous bed he constructed on the occasion of his marriage and that serves as the token of identity that Penelope still seeks before she will formally recognize her spouse (*Od.* 23.184–204). If the Greek sources imagine the human body as a constructed object, one assembled, shaped, joined together and fashioned into a coherent whole,[85] then the *kiôn* expressly cited by the hero at line 191 as analogue for the 'massive' or bulky tree trunk (πάχετος δ᾽ ἦν ἠΰτε κίων) that he cuts, shapes, planes, polishes and richly ornaments proves the *sêma* for his laboriously reconstructed self (as well as that of Penelope fashioned into the hero's bride).[86] When read against these archaic and classical sources, Vitruvius' much later demonstration of a point-by-point correspondence between the parts of the human body and the different column orders (the Doric column is the male body; the Ionic and Corinthian the female; the different elements of the Ionic column make reference to the female form, the volutes the hair, the base the shoes, the fluting the folds of women's dress),[87] seems no more than an elaboration of a very long-established notion. Nor is this a literary conceit alone: already in the technical

---

[84] Stieber 2011, 41–48.

[85] For the Greek 'constructivist' view of the human body, see Karvouni 1999.

[86] For more on the arboreal quality of the column, see Section 2.2.   [87] Vitr. 4.1.6–7.

vocabulary developed by the Greeks, the *sphondylos* referred both to the spinal column and to the column drum.

But for Karvouni, the columns in the peristyle temple stand in much more intimate relation to the chorus member. As she notes, perhaps the fundamental act of worship, and one reaching back to Minoan and Mycenaean times, involved celebrants dancing around an altar, statue or house of the god, surrounding and encompassing the sacred site even as they marked it off (one terracotta Minoan goddess, in her view, even has a chorus depicted on her decorated skirt, its members literally dancing around the circular surface as they celebrate the idol in their midst).[88] The singers of the traditional Cretan cult song found at Palaikastro, the Hymn of the Kouretes, give a verbal account of the action that accompanies their invocation to Zeus (6–10): 'come and delight in the dance-song that we pluck for you on lyres, mixing it together with pipes, and which we sing, taking up position (στάντες ... ἀμφί) around your well-fenced altar'. Much the same vocabulary occurs in Sappho fr. 154 V. where, in what may plausibly be an evocation of a *pannychis*, the all-night dance in service of a deity, 'the women stood about the altar (περὶ βῶμον ἐστάθησαν)' as the full moon rose in the sky. This act of encirclement and enclosure is precisely the role that the columns perform;[89] as Karvouni remarks, the physical structure of the peristyle becomes 'an architectural metaphor of a religious act',[90] a visible reconfiguration of the chorus' own prior *peristasis* as it 'stands around' the object of its worship. And if the circular dance is the most typical form that the gesture of worship took, the rectangular structure of the colonnade is also evocative of a choral formation surrounding a central point. Already in the Homeric poet's account of the chorus of youths and maidens on Achilles' shield, the choreutes are arranged in what could be quadrilinear ranks, *stichoi* (*Il.* 18.602), as well as in circles as they perform around the tumblers (and most likely the singer too) at the midpoint of their dance; in classical times, a chorus is no less frequently

---

[88] Karvouni 1997, 104. For another such figure, see Chapter 7.
[89] Cf. Pindar's description of Heracles' foundational act at Olympia in *Ol.* 3 and 10; this begins when the hero measures out and fences in the Altis as a sacred temenos (*Ol.* 10.44–46); at *Ol.* 3.24 he decides further to demarcate the space by planting trees from the land of the Hyperboreans around it. For the tree-column equivalence, see below. There is a further coincidence between this enclosed space and the dancing floor; both were the objects of special attention, sometimes specially paved; so the Geronisos dancing floor already cited, and the area of worship at the ninth-century sanctuary of Artemis Orthia; for this second space, see Karvouni 1997, 39.
[90] Karvouni 1997, 88. See too her comment on p. 53, 'The altar surrounded by suppliants is replaced by the temple surrounded by columns as if the actual ritual had been substituted by an embodiment of it, the peripteral temple'.

tetragônos, four-square, as circular, and the rectangle was the shape regularly assumed by the choral dancers performing tragedy and comedy in the theatre of Dionysus.[91]

Suggestive too, as Karvouni observes, is the coincidence between the chorus' votary character and the structure of the column, its different elements refiguring in abstract and materialized form the gesture of offering performed by its members both individually and as an ensemble. Consonant with the celebrants' votive role is the capital (an element which is styled, as in the passage from the *IT* just cited, the *epikranion*, a term regularly used for the female headdress), whose rounded middle part Vitruvius calls the *echinus*. The ancient commentators observe its ritual function; glossing the term, they liken it to the chytra, the earthenware pot used for libations and foodstuffs presented to the gods. In Vitruvius' fanciful account of the origins of the Corinthian column at 4.1.9–10, the idea for the design came to its 'inventor' Callimachos on witnessing a grave monument topped by a basket containing objects particularly dear to the *parthenos* who, having died a premature death, was buried beneath. Vitruvius designates that basket a kalathos, the term whose diminutive (*kalathiskos*) describes the headdress that women participating in choral dances so frequently wore on their heads. As earlier noted, capitals whose *echinus* was decorated with convex ribs or fluting or with the floral schemes visible at the archaic temple of Hera at Paestum and elsewhere assimilate ornamental motifs frequently used for the libation dish, the phiale. The service-rendering character of the column capital extends to the abacus (the Greek sources call it a *plinthos*) on its top: the slab's flat surface recalls the table or altar on which an offering would be placed and turns each individual column into a votary. When viewed as an ensemble, the service performed by the peristyle is shared among all its members alike: together they support the entablature resting on their topmost elements.[92]

Terminology for the column's other parts exhibits the same pertinence to the chorus member, and even suggests that in describing these features the later sources may have drawn on the existing language common to *choreia* and votive practice. So *basis*, which, as earlier illustrated, is used in imperial sources for a statue pedestal or more specifically for the column

[91] Note, again, Simonides' characterization of the 'truly good' man at fr. 542.3 *PMG*, also imagined as an artisanal 'construct': he is 'fashioned (τετυγμένον) four-square (τετράγωνον) with regard to his hands, feet and mind'. As the formulation suggests, the structural design has ethical implications.

[92] Karvouni 1997, esp. 176–91 details several of the points summarized here.

base, describes the measured step and motion of the choral dancer in fifth-century sources. Even before Aristophanes refers to the χορείας . . . βάσιν at *Thesm.* 968, Pindar paints an archetypal choral scene in which the dancer's footstep, βάσις again, 'harkens to' the notes issued by the lyre (*Pyth.* 1.1–4). Since, for Euripides at least, the same term can refer to the print of a sandal (*El.* 532), we might imagine that Pindar has in mind the moment when the sandalled foot strikes the floor in accord with the rhythm of the music. The text explored below turns the linguistic overlap between the column base and the shoe-clad foot into its own poetic reality.

2   Pindar's *Hymn to Zeus*: Columns, Islands and Stars

So far I have focused principally on relations between the column and the dancing body, specifically that of the maiden participant in a chorus. But the richness and complexity of the prelude of *Olympian* 6 depends not only on the singers' appeal to the golden pillars as figures for their own persons and activities, but on the repeated conjunction, semantic and syntactic, of motion and fixity that supplies one of the composition's leitmotifs. No sooner does the song describe the raising of the architectural elements than these columns are set fast in the ground, a sequence recapitulated when the *laudandus* Hagesias, now fleeing the hymn in hot pursuit, then falls in with the Syracusans singing in praise of his win, his movement arrested by the sandal which holds his foot. This same concern with motion and stasis is critical to the second Pindaric text explored here, the (possibly misnamed)[93] *Hymn to Zeus* and to its evocation of what I suggest is a further set of anthropomorphized columns freshly associated with *choreia*.

2.1   *Another Choral Temple*

In what may be an innovative version of the story, Pindar's *Hymn* introduces among its different elements the performance of Apollo and the Muses at the Theban wedding of Cadmos and Harmonia, an occasion regularly cited as a paradigmatic *choreia* that acts by way of frame and model for the here-and-now occasion witnessed by the audiences for this and other choral works.[94] The context in which the *Hymn* was performed

[93] For this, see D'Alessio 2009, who also surveys the history of reconstructions of the fragmentary text.

[94] The wedding of Peleus and Thetis at which the Muses also performed provides another such 'modelling' *choreia* for the lyric poets.

confirms this reflective or framing relationship: commentators propose that Pindar composed the work for a Theban chorus presenting its song and dance either at the Ismenion during ritual celebrations of Apollo at his sanctuary in Thebes, or possibly at another Apolline cult space, the Theban-controlled Delion near Tanagra.[95] Among the narratives included in the Muses' wedding song is the tale of Apollo's birth on Delos, which just prior to the nativity was turned from a free-floating island into a site so immobile that the ancient sources celebrated its invulnerability to earthquakes. According to Pindar's fantastical account, this transformation occurs when four adamantine pillars spring up spontaneously from the seabed, rooting the island raised aloft on their tops (fr. 33d.1–9 S.-M.):

ἦν γὰρ τὸ πάροιθε φορητὰ
    κυμάτεσσιν παντοδαπῶν ἀνέμων
ῥιπαῖσιν· ἀλλ' ἁ Κοιογενὴς ὁπότ' ὠδί-
    νεσσι θυίοισ' ἀγχιτόκοις ἐπέβα
    νιν, δὴ τότε τέσσαρες ὀρθαί   5
πρέμνων ἀπώρουσαν χθονίων,
ἂν δ' ἐπικράνοις σχέθον
πέτραν ἀδαμαντοπέδιλοι
κίονες,

For previously it [Delos] was carried on the waves by the blasts of winds of all sorts. But when Koios' daughter, frantic with the pains of approaching birth, set foot on it, then did four upright columns with adamantine sandals rise from their foundations in the earth and on their capitals support the rock . . .

As commentators note, the structure imagined here would call to mind a piece of sacred architecture, a peristyle temple, with Delos in the role of the entablature that rests on the column capitals. The specification that the pillars number four makes this match up still more exact: four pillars form the corners of the tetragonal colonnade.[96] But a temple is not the only analogy that Pindar's language evokes: these Delian columns' properties also suggest a living figure, one that combines the mobility and fixity likewise exhibited by the golden supports in the prelude of *Olympian 6*;

[95] See D'Alessio 2009, 142–44 for this last suggestion.

[96] By the time of the Athenian Parthenon at least, builders would distinguish these four pillars by making them broader in diameter (as was the case for the Parthenon) than the rest so as to create the optical illusion of exact homogeneity between the structural elements of the colonnade.

and like those columns too, the *Hymn*'s four props display several features that parallel those of choral dancers.

First the adjective initially applied to the supports: they are 'upright'. Nothing untoward here as Pindar conveys an essential quality of the pillar whose fluting draws attention to its straightness and upright stance. The property appears again in metaphors that liken individuals to columns, an index of their moral 'rectitude'. So in *Ol.* 2.81, Hector is the 'steadfast pillar' (ἀστραβῆ κίονα) of Troy; the adjective's literal meaning is 'untwisted', a term that recurs in a building inscription in reference to a pedestal or some kind of column base (βάσις, *IG* VII 3073.104). But when ὀρθός is read together with the earlier appearance of the same term within the *Hymn*, this in a report of the *mousikê* (the totality of the Muses' arts comprising music, song and dance) that Apollo performs to accompany the Muses' delivery of the tale of Delos and of other narratives, Pindar's characterization of the columns acquires additional meaning: in fr. 32.1 S.-M., the god appears 'making a display of upright *mousikê*', ἐπιδεικνυμένου μουσικὰν ὀρθάν. With the adjective's reassignment to the pillars, the structures become the materialized embodiments of that Apolline *mousikê* as manifested in the *choreia* of both the Muses and the Theban chorus who, in the *Hymn*'s synchronic design, are both narrating the story of Delos' transformation.

Set within its performance context, 'straightness' also seems particularly apposite: an upright stance is precisely the quality required of the dancer, whose pleasing and skillful performance depends on the correct alignment of the spine, back, shoulders and abdomen. Plato makes explicit the bond between posture in choral dancing and the ethico-musical register when, describing the dances of war and peace performed by civic choruses, the Athenian Stranger remarks at *Leg.* 815a–b:

> τό τε ὀρθὸν ἐν τούτοις καὶ τὸ εὔτονον,[97] τῶν ἀγαθῶν σωμάτων καὶ ψυχῶν ὁπόταν γίγνηται μίμημα, εὐθυφερὲς ὡς τὸ πολὺ τῶν τοῦ σώματος μελῶν γιγνόμενον, ὀρθὸν μὲν τὸ τοιοῦτον, τὸ δὲ τούτοις τοὐναντίον οὐκ ὀρθὸν ἀποδεχόμενον.

> In these [dances] the quality that is upright (*orthon*) and well-strung – given that it is in imitation of good bodies and souls, and the limbs of the bodies are for the most part in good alignment (lit. running in a straight line) – is the quality that is considered correct (*orthon*) and its opposite incorrect.

---

[97] The adjective can also refer to the well-pitched voice (e.g. Arist. *GA* 786b8).

In Plutarch's view at *Mor.* 397a–b, the rectitude common to the spectacle staged by Apollo and the Delian pillars looks not to dance, but to the particular quality of Pindar's musical design; rejecting the innovatory melodic modulations or bends favoured by other contemporary choral composers, the poet declares himself in favour of the 'straight' as opposed to the 'sinuous' (ἐπικεκλασμένην).[98]

Pindar attributes a further and much more singular property to these pillars at line 8 where, anthropomorphizing the structures, he equips them with sandals of adamant. Even as the representation revisits the paradox of the moving and static pillars of *Ol.* 6 (the Delian columns that surged up just a moment before now acquire footwear made from the hardest and most immovable of all matter), it endows the props with a feature expressly associated, both in Pindar's other songs and the sources cited in Chapter 1, with *choreia*. With the exception of *Pyth.* 4.95–96, where Jason, as myth requires, is 'single-sandalled', Pindaric poetry uses πέδιλον exclusively in musico-choral contexts, and often with a meta-performative dimension. On an occasion also noted in earlier chapters, sandals equip the choral dancer, the *chorêgos* who appears 'stepping on sandals' as she leads her maidens to their Theban performance site in the second *Partheneion* (fr. 94b.70 S.-M.); and when in *Ol.* 6 the flight of Hagesias ends with his encounter with the *kômos* performing the celebratory ode, the reminder to the victor that his foot is 'destined for this sandal' indicates not only that he has fulfilled the conditions just spelled out by the singers; in more literal fashion, the image suggests an exact 'fit' between the subject and the song's rhythmical measure or foot beat. It is as though Hagesias has actually joined the dancing band, one of this group of celebrants by virtue of his ability to accommodate his steps to their music and the motions of their dance.

The sandal included in the opening lines of *Olympian* 3 appears in a passage no less evocative of song-dance, its musical and choreographic components here combined with its visual as well as auditory appeal (1–6):

> Τυνδαρίδαις τε φιλοξείνοις ἁδεῖν
> καλλιπλοκάμῳ θ' Ἑλένᾳ
> κλεινὰν Ἀκράγαντα γεραίρων εὔχομαι,
> Θήρωνος Ὀλυμπιονίκαν
> ὕμνον ὀρθώσαις, ἀκαμαντοπόδων
> ἵππων ἄωτον. Μοῖσα δ' οὕτω ποι παρέ-

---

[98] Hardie 2000, 33 cites Plutarch's reading in his discussion of the Pindaric account. If this flies in the face of Pindar's innovatory compositions discussed in other chapters, it is because by Plutarch's time the poet had been assigned the role of strict musical traditionalist.

στα μοι νεοσίγαλον εὑρόντι τρόπον
Δωρίῳ φωνὰν ἐναρμόξαι πεδίλῳ   5

ἀγλαόκωμον·

> I pray that I may please the hospitable Tyndaridae and fair-tressed Helen
> in celebrating famed Akragas by setting up an Olympic victory hymn for
> Theron, the finest reward for horses with untiring feet. And for that
> reason, I believe, the Muse stood beside me as I found a newly shining
> musical style to fit into the Dorian sandal, a voice that gives lustre to the
> *kômos*.

First invoking a series of deities native to the site, the singers draw on
language and tropes familiar from epigrams as, here too, the song takes on
the character of a precious offering (perhaps even an equestrian monument
as would suit the victory being celebrated here), a votive 'raised up high' so
as to please its divine and human recipients.[99] The term ἄωτον, coupled
with the εὔχομαι of the opening, offers a hyperbolic variant on the standard
epigraphic formula εὐξάμενος/-αμένη δεκάτην or ἀπαρχήν. Following this
equation of *choreia* and *agalma*, the singers then present a more detailed
and densely compacted account of the character and qualities of their
materialized performance (with the Muse as overseer and participant),[100]
which further blends the tenor and vehicle of the metaphor. Ancient and
modern commentators variously interpret the statement in lines 4–6. For
those who understand the sandal as a variant on the more commonplace
pous, 'foot',[101] there is a reference to metre here, as Pindar advertises his
perhaps innovatory use of dactyloepitrites, signalling that this is the first
instance of his choice of that metrical scheme for an ode. For those who see
a pointer to melody, the combination of *tropos* and Dorian sandal looks
rather to the song's mode or *harmonia*.[102]

Musical and vocal concerns are just some of the facets of the choral
spectacle featured in the phrase. To 'fit' (ἐναρμόξαι) not only signals, for a
professional composer or musician, the 'tuning' of the choral voice to the
corresponding rhythm or melodic structure (cf. *Isthm.* 1.16), while also
casting the poet/choristers in that artisanal role that suits the opening
architectonic conceit. But coupled with the sandal worn by the chorus

[99] See further the discussion of this terminology in Pindar's *Ol.* 7 in Chapter 8.
[100] With the verb παρίστημι, the poet imagines the goddess actually standing alongside the chorus members.
[101] Anderson 1994, 99 intriguingly proposes that the πέδιλον may stand for the *kroupedzai* (or *kroupezai*), a clapper device worn by the aulete beneath his foot.
[102] For discussion of the possible meanings in ancient and modern readings, see Prauscello 2012, 77–78.

members, and which, in the epic commonplace, is 'fitted' to the foot, the verb additionally accommodates the dance steps forming part of the ensemble. Since the audible strike of the dancers' sandals on the ground coincides with the 'beat' of their song, demarcating the rhythmic and spatial patterns described by the choreography, the performers direct the audience to their skilled footwork and to its con-sonance with other elements of the ongoing spectacle. Nor is the visual-cum-material aspect of the epinician tribute forgotten here; in a synaesthetic blend typical of Pindar, the terms νεοσίγαλον and ἀγλαόκωμον both evoke the lustre that votive goods share with choral offerings and assign the visual sparkle that regularly emanates from the artefacts and choreutes alike to the vocal and instrumental aspects of this votive *choreia*.[103]

Viewed together with the 'choralized' shoes that Pindar introduces on these three other occasions, the Delian pillars' adamantine sandals not only humanize the structures, but suggest their likeness to participants in an ongoing choral song and dance on behalf of Delos, whom they celebrate and, in the manner of the choral karyatids just reviewed, literally serve by providing her with their unwavering support. If this reading seems overly fanciful, a number of ancillary factors may render it more plausible. First, the appearance of the pillars in the *Hymn* exactly coincides with the moment when Leto sets foot on the island in the very throes of birth (3–4). As plentiful other depictions of this moment in Pindar, Simonides and the hymnic tradition detail, a whole company of birth attendants trad-itionally presides at the event, celebrating the advent of the immortal infant with their song and dance.[104] In the *Homeric Hymn to Apollo*, female deities are at the scene, announcing the moment of delivery with their *ololugê* (119); Pindar's twelfth *Paean* also registers the shout raised by Eileithyia and Lachesis, here accompanied by a group of local women who respond in kind (fr. 52m.16–20 S.-M.).[105] Simonides' version of events in 519 *PMG*, fr. 32 turns the nativity into an unmistakably choral performance; even as Leto is giving birth, an unspecified set of celebrants 'set up a fair [dance in the] meadows; for now [the goddess] was burdened with the private toils of

---

[103] In uncompounded form, σίγαλον frequently describes gleaming garments and other ornamented objects; here it makes the sound of the music to which the choristers sing and dance coextensive with their appearance. As Prauscello 2012, 78 observes, ἀγλαόκωμον also 'refers to the fictionalized generic status of the choral performance as embedded in the epinicians and it is the voice of the chorus which has to be tuned to a corresponding harmony'.

[104] Kowalzig 2007, 60–68 supplies a detailed treatment of the extant texts with earlier bibliography.

[105] Whether these so-called ἐγχώριαι did more than simply utter a shout proves impossible to tell since the fragment breaks off here.

birth ... cried out ... of the ... divine, and sent forth ...'; in a second paeanic depiction by Simonides, the hymnists are the Deliades, the archetypal celebrants of Apollo (519 *PMG*, fr. 55). As Kowalzig reconstructs the fragmentary song, 'the paean thus summons the girls in the same role as the "goddesses" mixed with "local women" who appear in [Pindar's] *Paean* 12, at the transition between the mythical and performative parts of the song'.[106]

Beyond the particular occasion framing the pillars' appearance, the tableau formed by Delos and her supports maps onto a second dimension of *choreia*, articulating and visualizing in materialized form both the unity of the members of the collective and the hierarchical relationships that stratify a choral group. Just as choristers provide both attendance and praise for their *chorêgos*, around whom they may be deployed in circular or rectangular formations, and whom, in several early poetic accounts, they more literally 'support' (see the discussion of Hephaestus and his golden maidservants and the analysis of Alcman fr. 26 *PMGF* in Chapters 1 and 3), so these columns raise up and carry Delos on their tops. Indeed, it might not be too much of a stretch to see in the conceit of these load-bearers a figure for a feature of choral dance and song that appears on several occasions in Pindar and other authors, the (willingly proffered) *ponos* that it requires of its performers. Acknowledging their exertions, and in what Kurke identifies as a reference to the dance, the singer-dancers of *Nemean* 3 – just styled 'craftsmen of revels' (4) – describe how their performance 'will have graceful (χαρίεντα) *ponos* as an *agalma* of the place' (12–13).[107] As in the *Hymn*, the choral-cum-structural toils of the Aeginetan group result in the generation of a building, on this occasion the more historical shrine of the local hero Aiakos that stands as a lasting testament to the qualities of their more transient 'constructivist' performance.

A third and more particularized element within the *Hymn* promotes and facilitates the correspondence between Delos as a peripteral temple and Pindar's Theban chorus. In the passage immediately preceding fr. 33d S.-M. (and considered in greater detail below), the singers address Delos directly, calling her 'god-built', θεοδμάτα (fr. 33c.1 S.-M.). The adjective recurs a second time in the composition, in the only extant line from fr. 35c S.-M., where an audience 'listening to the god-built strain of melodies' (νόμων ἀκούοντες θεόδματον κέλαδον) appears. The phrase could refer to any number of musical performances, but, like fr. 33d S.-M., may plausibly

---

[106] Kowalzig 2007, 65.

[107] Kurke 2012, 229–30 (with her n. 19) cites Pind. fr. 70c.16 S.-M. and Eur. *Bacch.* 64–67 for other uses of *ponos* for choral labour. Add to this Pindar's *Paean* 7b (fr. 52h.22 S.-M.) with the discussion at Rutherford 2001, 249 n. 18.

look back to that presented by Apollo and the Muses at the marriage of Cadmos and Harmonia.[108] Much as the 'upright' character of the Delian columns suggested their status as monumentalized and enduring displays of the quality of the *mousikê* 'shown forth' by Apollo, so their more broadly divine origins and properties reconfigure the similarly fashioned melodies produced by the god and to which the chorus of Muses sings and dances.

The likely performance context for the *Hymn* would add one further element to the 'anagogical' chain suggested here, which serves to link the current occasion to a series of mythical events and the 'auditoria' where they (notionally) occurred. If Pindar's Theban chorus was staging the work at or in proximity of the Ismenion, then its present location not only encompasses a material reminder of a second mythical marriage, that between Apollo and the local nymph Melia (who is introduced together with the Ismenion at the outset of the *Hymn*, at fr. 29.1 S.-M.), whose nuptial bed the shrine preserved, but adds a third dancing space to the two already associated here: joining the real-world Theban site and the place where once Apollo led the Muses at the wedding of Cadmos and Harmonia is the ground of Delos from whose ground the dancing pillars first leapt up (πρέμνων ἀπώρουσαν χθονίων, fr. 33d.6 S.-M.) as they rendered tribute to their island-temple *laudanda*. And if the Ismenion, or a space nearby, did supply the Pindaric chorus with its performance grounds, then the elision between the imaginary Delian and actual Theban landscapes would be still more complete: even as the singers introduced the four pillars rising in their maritime locale, an audience would have in its sight lines the more numerous fluted columns (remains of which excavators have unearthed) that belonged to their own Doric peristyle temple, a structure that dates back to archaic times. A passage from *Pythian* 11 affirms Pindar's familiarity with the building; invoking the daughters of Cadmos and Harmonia at the outset of the piece, he bids them 'join Melia at the treasury of the golden tripods, which Loxias honoured before all others and named the Ismenion' (4–6).[109]

[108] Pindar uses θεόδματος of Delos another time, at *Ol.* 6.59; if the poet has the four adamantine supports in mind (so Bing 2008, 100 n. 16), then the term would introduce a second set of fantastical columns to the ode. Aristides suggests that the Pindaric *Hymn* might have extended the 'factural' conceit to the activity of the Muses who perform in the composition (*Or.* 45.106): 'Pindar … says in the marriage of Zeus, that when he asked the gods whether they needed anything, they requested that he make for himself some gods [i.e. the Muses] who would adorn (κατακοσμήσουσι) with words and music all those great works and all the arrangements of his'.

[109] Like the *Hymn*, *Pythian* 11 introduces a mythical parthenaic chorus by way of counterpart to its own performers; in the subsequent lines, Apollo is imagined as he summons 'the local band of heroines to gather together' and be present at the celebration.

For all the fantastical quality of Pindar's Delian columns, they turn out to be integral to the larger thematics of the song. In Hardie's detailed cosmological reading of the *Hymn*,[110] the poet's choice to represent Delos as a temple made up of pillars and an entablature figures the island as a miniaturized model of the larger arrangement of the cosmos which, in accordance with accounts in earlier textual and visual sources,[111] the poet envisages as a sky supported by a column, whether those that Atlas bears at *Od.* 1.52–54, or the silver columns that Hesiod positions between Tartarus and the heavens at *Th.* 779, these in turn connected to the pillar to which Atlas is bound earlier in the composition.[112] The moment when Delos is lastingly fixed in place by virtue of her four supports thus rehearses the larger narrative of the *Hymn*, which tracks the process whereby Zeus gradually imposes stability on the previously disordered cosmos, and reiterates one of the moments integral to this transition: just as Delos will rise on her vertical pillars, so in fr. 30.2–4 S.-M. Themis, herself the guarantor of regularity and good order, goes up to the sky to become the wife of Zeus, similarly ascending 'from the streams of Okeanos along a shining road [i.e. the Milky Way] to the holy ladder of Olympus'. As Hardie also notes, 'the "straight columns" represent a vertical axis between sea floor and surface; and their straightness suggests contrast with the circularity of the cosmos'.[113] Placing the poem in its choral context adds a meta-performative element to the arrangements that the *Hymn* describes: lines and circles map onto standard choral formations, while, as I have proposed, the 'straightness' of the pillars models the stance of the performers of the piece.

Particularly suggestive in this regard is the cosmological model that Anaximander supposedly constructed, and where the earth, conceived as a cylinder in the shape of a column drum (κίονι λίθῳ παραπλήσιον, Hippolytus, *Ref.* 1.6.3), was suspended at the centre. In his written account, the cosmographer noted that it was 3 x 1 in dimensions, observing the rules of proportion followed by contemporary architects in designing the columns for the monumental Doric temples currently under construction in Ionia.[114] The pillar's role in cosmology extends to the visual tradition; a mid-sixth-century Laconian cup by Arkesilas imagines Prometheus column-bound, unable to ward off the eagle plucking at his liver; facing him is

[110] Hardie 2000.

[111] Hardie 2000, 28 also cites Ibycus fr. 336 *PMG* and the Laconian cup by the Arkesilas Painter of ca. 550 treated below.

[112] See West 1966 *ad Th.* 779 and 522.   [113] Hardie 2000, 27.

[114] For sources and discussion, see Couprie et al. 2003, 173 with n. 12 and McEwen 1993, 27.

Atlas, his body positioned so as to underscore his similarity to his brother while he holds up a starry sky.[115] As a discussion of the cup observes,[116] the feet of both Titans rest on an expressly Doric column from which flowers grow, as though it too both sprang from and represents the earth. As I go on to suggest, the organic quality of this pillar proves very pertinent to Pindar's later structures and again brings their latent chorality into play.

2.2   Choruses, Columns and Trees

A further feature of the Delian columns completes this kaleidoscopic picture of material structures and dancing bodies engaged in the celebration of and service to the object of their praise. In the line describing the pillars springing up from the ground, Pindar selects for their foundations a noun more typically at home in the arboreal sphere: πρέμνον primarily refers to the bottom of the tree trunk or to the trunk itself, a meaning very much in sync with the verb ἀπορούω immediately following it, and which invests the columns with the movement that belongs to something organic and animate.[117] The tree-like quality of these structures makes sense on several counts. First because, as Pindar's account of Heracles' gesture at Olympia, where the hero plants his Hyperborean-sourced trees 'around the twelve-lap turn of the hippodrome' (*Ol.* 3.33–34) makes clear,[118] trees could assume the 'demarcating' function at sacred sites that pillars acquired later on.[119] And second, and more critically for my purposes, because early columns would have been made of wood not stone. It is this aspect of the objects that Neer observes in his discussion of the relations between tree trunks, columns and archaic statuary, *korai* in particular,[120] but already, I suggested, on display in the Odyssean simile treated earlier, where the olive tree chosen by the hero for his marriage bed is likened to the pillar in its

---

[115]   Rome, Vatican 16592.   [116]   Yalouris 1980, 313–14.

[117]   Cf. *Ol.* 7.61–63, a description of the birth of Rhodes from the sea. In this account, the island, 'rising up from the ground (αὐξομέναν πεδόθεν)' and simultaneously gilded with a golden shower (34–37), is syntactically and thematically aligned with the synchronic birth of Athena: 'when, by the skills of Hephaestus, with the stroke of the bronze-forged axe, [Athena] sprang forth (ἀνορούσαισ', 37) from her father's head'. Like the Delian structure imagined by the *Hymn*, both goddess and island are at once animate, kinetic phenomena and the result of a process of craftsmanship.

[118]   Reminiscent of the chorus is not only the suggestion of circularity in these trees' formation (περὶ τέρμα), but the detail that, on first spotting them in their distant locale, the hero wonders (θάμβαινε, 32) at them, and is seized with desire (ἵμερος ἔσχεν, 33) to carry them off to mainland Greece.

[119]   Both also seem to have been objects of worship in Minoan and Mycenaean times. Note too Pliny, *HN* 12.2.3, 'trees formed the first temples of the gods'.

[120]   Neer 2010, 34–35.

breadth or bulk. Like that notional column, many archaic images were fashioned out of wood, a paradigm still visible in the design of the sixth-century *korai* from Samos, whose cylindrical shape looks back to the trunks from which their predecessors would have been carved. Their very 'trunki-ness', as Neer also remarks, makes these *korai* 'resemble Ionic columns, which likewise are stone versions of wooden architectural members'.[121] Something of the pillar's original tree-like character also persists in the design of the Corinthian column, whose capital is covered in acanthus leaves (see Section 4 for more on these features).[122] According to Vitruvius' whimsical account of the origins of the order at 4.1.9–10, the decorative device was inspired by the actual leaves and shoots growing from the acanthus root on whose top the nurse of the dead Corinthian maiden had, unknowingly, placed her commemorative basket.

Columns and trees coexist in a variety of other media, both verbal and visual. The Niobid Painter combines the two elements on a red-figure volute krater in Boston of ca. 460, whose upper register shows Peleus (or maybe Theseus) pursuing Thetis accompanied by one of her Nereid sisters;[123] demarcating the space in which the pursuit occurs is an altar with a palm tree on the far left, and a column on the right.[124] Other vessels use the same two elements in tandem or as alternatives, now pairing the palm with a column to balance it in scenes of erotic pursuits, now introducing either one or the other to indicate the setting of the encoun-ter, whether the courtyard of a house or a sanctuary. Both, as we have seen, are sites where parthenaic choruses perform, and that, sometimes precisely because they furnish dancing floors, are the locations for abduc-tions such as we witness on the krater, where Thetis appears together with one of the larger Nereid company. As Christiane Sourvinou-Inwood argues in her exploration of these images,[125] the palm tree also has particularly close associations with Artemis – evoked in passing in fr. 33c.1–2 S.-M., where Pindar salutes Delos as the 'shoot (ἔρνος) most desirable to the children of Leto with shining tresses' – and with the

---

[121] According to Neer (2010, 34), this arboreal character does not extend to *kouroi*, generally more 'blocky' than 'trunky' in character.

[122] In Rykwert's suggestion, the prototype for the tree or plant conceit may be found in the Near East: here reliefs and other objects from Babylon and Sumer include columns which Rykwert 1980, 290 designates 'artificial trees', and he cites a Babylonian relief featuring a column whose shaft resembles a palm trunk and ends in a palm-bud capital.

[123] Boston, Museum of Fine Arts 33.56; *ARV*[2] 600.12.

[124] Sourvinou-Inwood 1987, 192 cites the vase together with other examples.

[125] Sourvinou-Inwood 1987.

coming-of-age rites, choral dancing prominent among them, in which
maidens participated under the goddess' tutelage.

The choral implications of trees, shoots and the palm tree in particular
are apparent in other texts and images depicting maidens dancing. At the
most literal level, the associations look to the realia of the performance.
Representations of choruses of *parthenoi* on Argive and Attic pots from the
Geometric period typically show each dancer with a stiff branch in her
hand,[126] and the equation of Astymelousa, the lead performer in Alcman's
third *Partheneion*, with a 'golden shoot' (χρύσιον ἔρνος, 68) may reflect the
actual foliage carried by the maiden; in similar fashion, the choristers of
Pindar's second *Partheneion* have their hands equipped with a 'shining
branch (ὄρπακ' ἀγλάον)' of laurel (fr. 94b.6–7 S.-M.). The term ἔρνος used
of Astymelousa and of the Pindaric Delos too recalls an earlier account of a
young choral dancer, positioned, like Alcman's performer, as a potential
object of desire. So in the eros-fuelled encounter between Odysseus beleaguered on the shore of Scheria and Nausikaa, who has just left off leading
her serving girls in their ball dance, the hero first observes how the sight of
the maiden participating in *choreia* will rejoice the heart of onlookers; in
the phrase he uses of that imagined scene, Nausikaa is 'a shoot entering the
dance' (θάλος χορὸν εἰσοιχνεῦσαν, *Od.* 6.157). A variant on that leafy
growth appears just a few lines on: praising the girl's loveliness, Odysseus
now compares her to a tree that he once saw growing at the Delian altar of
Apollo (most likely the famous date palm clasped by Leto as she gave birth;
so *HHAp.* 117, ἀμφὶ δὲ φοίνικι βάλε πήχεε), which he describes as the 'young
sprout shooting up' (νέον ἔρνος ἀνερχόμενον, 163). W. B. Stanford's note on
the term of comparison anticipates my suggestion here: 'With its shapely
columnar trunk, it makes a charming comparison for a tall, slender girl,
with a hint of archaic sculptural style to it'.[127] Together the shoot-like
dancing maiden and girl as date palm sprout are participants in the sphere
of Artemis, with whom, as noted above, the tree was closely affiliated and
whom the Homeric poet has already introduced when he likened Nausikaa
as *chorêgos* to the goddess leading her band of Nymphs in their choral
dance (6.102–06).[128]

---

[126] Langdon 2008, esp. 153–56, supplies many examples with detailed analysis of the meaning of
the branch.

[127] Stanford 1965 *ad loc.*

[128] Later Attic vase painting regularly positions a maiden standing by a palm tree, a conjunction
that signals how the individual enjoys Artemis' protection as she passes from girlhood to the
state of marriage.

A later fifth-century text revisits this long-standing combination of tree and dancer-cum-chorus leader. Longing to return to Greece, the parthenaic chorus of Euripides' *IT* visualizes itself participating in choral dancing at the sanctuary of Artemis Lochia on Delos, a site distinguished by the 'date palm with its luxuriant tresses' (φοίνικα … ἁβροκόμαν, 1099). As in the earlier Pindaric *Hymn* and the vase images cited above, the tree with its abundant locks offers a reconfiguration of the maiden dancers who, in a reprise of the terms used at 1099, exactingly describe their appearance in the nuptial dance evoked at the closing of their song: it was on that occasion that, decked out in their 'luxurious finery' (ἁβροπλούτοιο … χλιδᾶς, 1149),[129] they would perform their circling dance, their locks (πλοκάμους, 1151) shading their cheeks as they spun about.[130]

Section 3 will offer additional evidence for trees taking on a choral role, but here I would point back to the earlier discussion of the Karyatides, and to a variant in the mythical traditions surrounding the parthenaic chorus at the shrine of Artemis 'of the Nut Tree' (a cognomen, a late source reports, derived from the *karya* or 'nut tree' growing at the site).[131] While one version of the story has the maidens, threatened with abduction, take refuge in a nut tree and hang themselves, in another the three daughters of Dion, the king of Sparta, were the original occupants of the shrine, where they practised the gift of divination given them by Apollo. As Servius, our only source for this sequence of events, reports,[132] the god fell in love with one of the sisters, named Karya, and claimed her as his own. Confronted with her sisters' opposition, he turned them into stones while Karya, his beloved, is changed into the eponymous tree. If the historical Karyatides commemorated and re-enacted the roles of the earlier triadic sorority, then that oracular girl-turned-tree now appears in the shape of a choral performer (perhaps the pre-eminent figure of the troupe) and realizes just that chorister-tree equivalence I have suggested for Pindar's arboreal pillars.

2.3 Island and Star Choruses

In accordance with and even preparatory to the choral aspect of the Pindaric pillars, their role as figures or precursors for the Theban celebrants

---

[129] Note the original ms. reading χαίτας; the term was rejected both because it is unmetrical and because the adjective seemed ill-suited to hair. See Langdon 2008, 145–51 for the abundant locks typical of maiden choruses in Geometric art.

[130] Indeed, Euripides may even intend an allusion to Pindar's composition in the lines describing that 'delicate-haired palm … so dear to Leto's offspring' (1099–1102).

[131] Lact. *ad* Stat. *Theb.* 4.225, with discussion in Calame 1997, 152–53.

[132] Serv. *ad* Verg. *Ecl.* 8.29 with Calame 1997, 153.

in the here-and-now, is the imagery used in the *Hymn*'s earlier description
of Delos. Read together, these two fragments, the first picturing the island
as pre-eminent chorus leader, the second introducing the pillars as the
members of her ensemble, present a recasting in quite literally material
form of a scenario familiar from Alcman, Sappho and elsewhere in which a
group of singers exalts their *chorêgos* for her beauty, skill and grace. While
we cannot know what occurred between the still extant lines of frr. 33c and
33d S.-M., in the first of the two passages the singers, perhaps channelling
the voice of the Apollo-led Muses, invoke the island:

> χαῖρ᾽, ὦ θεοδμάτα, λιπαροπλοκάμου
> παίδεσσι Λατοῦς ἱμεροέστατον ἔρνος,
> πόντου θύγατερ, χθονὸς εὐρεί-
>   ας ἀκίνητον τέρας, ἄν τε βροτοί
> Δᾶλον κικλήσκοισιν, μάκαρες δ᾽ ἐν Ὀλύμπῳ   5
>   τηλέφαντον κυανέας χθονὸς ἄστρον.

> Hail, o heaven-built island, offshoot most desirable to the children of
> shining-haired Leto, daughter of the sea, immobile marvel of the broad
> earth, whom mortals call Delos, but the blessed gods on Olympus call the
> far-shining star of the dark-blue earth.

Already apparent here are the two chief identities that Delos combines;
called Asteria, the starry one, before her change in state, she is also styled an
island. But in good Pindaric fashion, these two facets prove all but indistinguishable as the poet invites us to consider the island from a double
perspective, now human and now divine. What appears to men looking
along a land-based, horizontal axis as an immobile island set within the
watery expanse simultaneously presents itself to the gods, from their top-
down vantage point, as a constellation framed by the terrestrial realm down
below. Hence Pindar's unparalleled description of the earth as 'dark-blue';
choosing an epithet that more typically belongs to the sea, he presents land
and water as an undifferentiated mass, illuminated by the star suspended
above it.

While the invocation makes no explicit reference to the island's choregic
role, the terms selected here are nonetheless well grounded in the imagery
regularly applied to the chorus leader. Strikingly, the star as well as the
shoot is a *comparandum* of choice for the choristers of Alcman's third
Partheneion in their exaltation of Astymelousa, whom they liken to 'some
star flying through the twinkling heavens' (τις αἰγλά[ε]ντος ἀστήρ / ὠρανῶ
διαιπετής, fr. 3.66–67 *PMGF*). The astragalos by the Sotades Painter (Fig.
0.1) showing the chorus director as he invites the members of his band to

model their ring dance after that of the Hyades and Pleiades portrayed on the vessel's other three sides revisualizes the sequence of similes in Alcman's song: two of the dancers in the sky carry just such leafy branches. Like the no less radiant *ernos* evoked in the subsequent line of Pindar's *Hymn*, the astral body, as other chapters have explored, belongs to the traditional vocabulary of *choreia* and draws on the paradigmatic stellar ensembles visible from Homeric poetry on. In Alcman's maiden song, the image not only offers a generalized reference to the brilliance that is the *sine qua non* of choral dancers and the spectacles they stage, but might more directly correspond to Astymelousa's appearance here: could she be wearing the distinctive headdress – not, as scholars long believed, a 'little basket' but a starry crown – worn to perform the common *kalathiskos* dance?[133]

The Pindaric *Hymn*'s foregrounding of Delos' astral identity also coheres with a familiar episode in the island's larger 'metamorphic' story, perhaps mentioned in some lost portion of the song, and featured in Pindar's *Paean* 5: Delos' abduction by Zeus. As Peter Bing notes in his discussion of that piece,[134] when the poet uses the periphrasis Ἀστερίας δέμας for the island at fr. 52e.41 S.-M., the expression offers a capsule allusion to how the island was formerly a nymph who leapt into the sea so as to escape Zeus's amorous pursuit. While there is no suggestion in the extant versions of this event that Delos was dancing in a chorus, Pindar's sixth *Paean* not only presents a very similar conjunction of elements in reference to Aegina – island, star and abductee of Zeus – in its final epode (fr. 52f.124–37 S.-M.), but, as already argued in Chapter 5, there gestures towards this framing choral event:

> ὀνομακλύτα γ᾽ ἔνεσσι Δωριεῖ
>   μ[ε]δέοισα [πό]ντῳ
> νᾶσος, [ὦ] Διὸς Ἑλ-   125
>   λανίου φαεννὸν ἄστρον.
> οὔνεκεν οὔ σε παιηόνων
> ἄδορπον εὐνάξομεν, ἀλλ᾽ ἀοιδᾶν
> ῥόθια δεκομένα κατερεῖς
>   πόθεν ἔλαβες ναυπρύτανιν   130
> δαίμονα καὶ τὰν θεμίξενον ἀρετ[άν.
> ὁ πάντα τοι τά τε καὶ τὰ τεύχων
>   σὸν ἐγγυάλιξεν ὄλβον
> εὐρύο[πα] Κρόνου παῖς, ὑδάτ<εσσ>ι δ᾽ ἐπ᾽ Ἀσω-
>   ποῦ π[οτ᾽ ἀ]πὸ προθύρων βαθύκολ-   135

---

[133] For details of this, see Ferrari 2008, 135–50.   [134] Bing 2008, 98–99.

ποῦ ἀ<u>ν</u>ερέψατο παρθένον
Αἴγιναν·

> island whose name is famous indeed, you live and rule in the Dorian sea, o
> shining star of Zeus Hellanios, wherefore we shall not put you to bed
> without a supper of paeans; rather, as you receive waves of song, you will
> recount whence you got your ship-ruling prerogative and the virtue of just
> regard for strangers. Truly the far-seeing son of Cronus who accomplishes
> all things, both this and that, has placed prosperity in your hands, and by
> the waters of the Asopos he carried off from her portal the deep-bosomed
> virgin, Aegina.

Here, in more elaborated fashion, Aegina exhibits the same multiple
identities and roles that Delos combines: even as she is the object of the
choral praise (the 'waves of song'), the island is concomitantly a 'shining
star' before freshly modulating into a nymph, daughter of the river Asopos,
whom Zeus abducted from the forecourt of her natal home. The depiction
of Aegina in choral poetry supplies a counterpart to that of Delos on a
second count: as the earlier chapter also detailed, following her evolution
from abducted nymph to island, she becomes the object of celebration by
the choruses of Aeginetan girls whose activity recalls that in which she
would formerly have engaged.

Her previous history aside, there is perhaps a more fundamental reason
for seeing the Delos of the Pindaric *Hymn* as a (proto-)participant in
choreia and as the leader of her maidenly troupe: her Cycladic identity.
Although the explicit depiction of the island as chorus leader and as the
midpoint around which the Cyclades perform their circle dance must wait
until the Callimachean *Hymn* discussed in Section 3, the notion of the
dance of the islands, and even of Delos as the privileged member of the
performing ensemble, seems already to have existed in fifth-century
Greece, perhaps arising in conjunction with the newly prominent Delian
League and as a result of the intense choral activity that came to be focused
on the island from the archaic period on.[135] Granted, the first attestation of
dancing islands appears only on an object that postdates Pindar by several
decades: an Attic red-figure cup attributed to the Eretria Painter of ca. 430–
420 displays two maenad-like dancers whom inscriptions name as Delos
and Euboea, here shown dancing with the satyr Lemnos and their mother
Tethys alongside other nymphs or maenads and silens and satyrs with

---

[135] There is no establishing the date of composition for the Pindaric *Hymn*.

musical names (Figs. 0.6, 0.7).[136] Although Beazley suggests that the artist has borrowed his notion from a now-lost poetic work,[137] it remains impossible to determine whether there was a pre-existing source for the artistic conceit, or whether the painter is the innovator here. What is securely attested is the choral ambience surrounding Delos from the archaic sources on: the sixth-century *Homeric Hymn to Apollo* already chooses to position the most fully detailed choral celebration of the god on that island, and the earlier cited paeans by Pindar and Simonides follow suit in their accounts of the choral performances hailing Apollo's birth. The motif resurfaces, although in a different manifestation, on the Eretria Painter's vase, where the nymph dancing with a satyr in the tondo is designated Choro, choral dance herself.

The dance of the islands may also have become sufficiently familiar to make an appearance on the Attic stage: an [Aristophanic] drama has the title *Nesoi*, perhaps a reference to a chorus of islands that danced and sang. A second possible pointer to the conceit occurs in a passage from Aristophanes' *Clouds*, where Socrates invokes the nephelous choristers as they 'draw up the holy *choros* with the nymphs in the gardens of father Okeanos' (271). Although some commentators identify these maidens as the Okeanidai, the very similar picture that Callimachus would present of the parthenaic islands as they process to precisely this site to perform their choral dances (*H.* 4.19–20; see below) could indicate that the dramatist had a mixed chorus of dancing clouds and nymphs-turned-islands in mind. Well suited to this second chorus is the locale specified by the Aristophanic Socrates, the verdant space of the garden or κῆπος that Ibycus fr. 286.3–4 *PMG* expressly assigns to *parthenoi* and where, in art as well as text, troupes of maidens stage their choral dances.

3 Callimachus' *Hymn to Delos*: From Pillars Back to Choristers

As noted in this chapter's introduction, the last of my three principal texts, Callimachus' *Hymn to Delos*, a work that acknowledges its debt to its several Pindaric precedents and the *Hymn to Zeus* very much among

---

[136] Warsaw, National Museum 142458; *ARV*² 1253.58. See Smith 2011, 35 for discussion and Chapter 8 of this study. A much later depiction of an island as chorus member belongs to a votive relief of ca. 100, where the last figure in the line of dancers, differentiated from the rest by being shown as a small child, has the name Tilos, an island in the Dodecanese (Naples, Museo Nazionale 6725).

[137] Beazley 1928, 63.

them, lacks all mention of the pillars that have been my principal focus so far. But for all their absence, the composition proves pertinent to my argument in several ways: not only does the choral theme only latent in the fragments of Pindar's *Hymn* come unmistakably to the fore and supply one of the text's leitmotifs,[138] but the choregic character that Pindar intimates for the island also becomes explicit here. Visible too in the Callimachean piece is the redistribution of the role of choristers assigned the pillars in the *Hymn to Zeus* and its reiteration within a sequence of choral ensembles fantastical, legendary and historical that include among them islands, trees and stars.

3.1 'Nesiotic' Choruses and the Conjunction of Islands and Stars

Opening his tribute to the birthplace of Apollo, Callimachus offers several snapshot characterizations of the island, first acknowledging the immobility that defines the quintessentially stable Delos. In lines 11–14, which style the site literally un-turnable (ἄτροπος) for all the waves that swirl about and beat its surface, the poet twice intimates Delos' soon-to-be-developed role as both *chorêgos*-like centrepoint and dancing floor: so ἁλιπλήξ (11), 'sea-beaten', whose second element the description of maiden dancers in the final stages of the hymn will revisit as they strike the island's 'steadfast surface' (αἱ δὲ ποδὶ πλήσσουσι χορίτιδες ἀσφαλὲς οὖδας, 306); and ἑλίσσων (13), the term used of the sea foam's whirligigs, is similarly echoed at 321 (ἑλίξαι), where a final chorus of mariners performs a series of circular motions around the island's altar.

The very next passage realizes the first of these previewed functions as Delos unequivocally appears in the role of island-*chorêgos*, leading her troupe made up of the other Cyclades in processional formation – the sequential arrangement of her followers' names visibly conveys their linearity – to their performance site. In lines 17–18, the poet addresses the subject of his composition in his description of how 'whenever the islands assemble at the house of Okeanos and Tethys you journey going as *exarchos*' (ἔξαρχος ὁδεύει)'. With ἔξαρχος, Callimachus selects the technical term for chorus leader while his depiction of the islands travelling one after the other in Delos' tracks or steps (ἴχνια, 19) coheres with any number of

---

[138] Extraneous to my discussion is the whole riddling issue of the agenda (addressed by other accounts) behind the Callimachean focus on choral performance within the *Hymn*: does the poet attempt merely to make his readers experience the written work as something actually danced and sung as such works would once have been, or is there actually a performative context for the piece?

earlier accounts of choruses progressing on journeys both short and more extended: recall Pindar's maidenly band conducted by the father of their lead member, who immediately follows him on the road to the performance site (fr. 94b.66–70 S.-M.).

No sooner does Callimachus picture this moving line than he replaces it with a representation that highlights the island's stability and, I suggest, reworks in typically polemical fashion Pindar's account of Delos with her four supportive, protective and surrounding pillars (23–27):

> κεῖναι μὲν πύργοισι περισκεπέεσσιν ἐρυμναί,
> Δῆλος δ' Ἀπόλλωνι· τί δὲ στιβαρώτερον ἕρκος;
> τείχεα μὲν καὶ λᾶες ὑπὸ ῥιπῆς κε πέσοιεν   25
> Στρυμονίου βορέαο· θεὸς δ' ἀεὶ ἀστυφέλικτος·
> Δῆλε φίλη, τοῖός σε βοηθόος ἀμφιβέβηκεν.

> Those ones [the islands] are fenced by the towers that screen them all around, but Delos by Apollo; for what is a more mighty enclosure? Walls and stones may fall beneath the blows of the Strymonian Boreas; but the god is always unshaken. Beloved Delos, such a source of help walks around you.

Granting the other Cyclades the material quality assigned by Pindar to Delos, the lines invert the 'adamantine' status of the earlier pillars, declaring instead the vulnerability of all such structures, whether towers, stones or walls; instead it is the impregnable god who acts as Delos' mighty ἕρκος (24), the fence and 'enclosure' for a sacred site that demarcates and safeguards it. And although the towers 'covering all around' suggest the circular or rectangular deployment of these and the other devices enumerated here (cf. περικίων used at Eur. *IT* 405 and fr. 369.5 K. of the colonnade of the peripteral temple), the god's protecting and encompassing gesture goes one better insofar as it takes mobile form: like a chorus, he 'circumumambulates' (ἀμφιβέβηκεν, 27), transforming a static architectural formation into a moving one.

A second nod towards the choralized islands occurs when Callimachus then takes us back to the earliest stages of Delos' history and to the moment when she and the other Cyclades were first created. Like so many choruses, these islands emerge from an artisanal process, first fashioned (εἰργάζετο, 32) by the tool-equipped Poseidon. His craftsmanship completed, the god then uses a lever to hoist up his products and to 'roll' (εἰσεκύλισε, 33) them into the sea, investing them with that rotational movement written into their name and that more patently defines the collective when it makes its third and final appearance at the *Hymn's* close. In place of their earlier processional formation, the Cyclades, now explicitly designated a *choros*, are imagined dancing circle-wise around Delos (300–03). The phrase at 267, περιναίετε νῆσοι, already presages this structure, and the prefix returns at 300, here reinforced by the twice used ἀμφί:

Ἀστερίη θυόεσσα, σὲ μὲν περί τ᾿ ἀμφί τε νῆσοι   300
κύκλον ἐποιήσαντο καὶ ὡς χορὸν ἀμφεβάλοντο·
οὔτε σιωπηλὴν οὔτ᾿ ἄψοφον οὖλος ἐθείραις
Ἕσπερος, ἀλλ᾿ αἰεί σε καταβλέπει ἀμφιβόητον.

Fragrant Asteria, around and about you the islands have made a circle and place themselves around you as a chorus. Nor are you silent nor without the sound of dancing when curly-haired Hesperos looks down on you, but always surrounded by sound.

This final account of the islands' dance includes a fresh amplification of the Pindaric account: where the earlier poet only suggested an association between Delos' twofold identity, at once a land mass in the sea and a star, Callimachus reworks the pairing in these lines' diction and design. The introduction of Hesperos in 303 picks up on Delos' already sounded astral identity – hence the choice of Asteria, 'starry one', to designate her here – and calls to mind the corresponding dance-and-song of the stars that, from the account in *Il.* 18.488–89 on (the Homeric lines include a reference to the 'look' of one of the circling constellations, there assigned to Arktos 'that circles around … while looking warily at Orion') regularly turn about a single fixed body in the sky. The structure of the passage, visible to a reader and audible to the individual who, perhaps, attends the performance that it might have received, aligns events in the sky and sea: Asteria and Hesperos both stand in verse-initial position, supplying the frame and paradigm for the dance of islands down below. And while the last two lines chiefly emphasize the music and song of the performance, ἄψοφον draws attention to the sound of these island-dancers' feet.[139]

Later sources continue to associate islands and stars. Where Aelius Aristides merely presents the two as corresponding decorative ensembles (Zeus 'adorns the whole sky with stars just as the sea with islands', κοσμήσαις μὲν ἄστροις τὸν πάντα οὐρανόν, ὥσπερ ταῖς νήσοις τὴν θάλατταν, *Or.* 43.13), Plutarch's report of Timarchus' vision at the oracle of Trophonius at *Mor.* 590c–f imagines islands (albeit not the Cyclades) taking part in what resembles a grand cosmological choral performance, complete with music and the circular motions characteristic of dancers. In

---

[139] As detailed in the previous chapter.

his glimpse of cosmic reality, Timarchus can perceive 'islands illuminated by one another, taking on now one colour, now another . . . And he fancied that their circular movement made a musical whirring in the aether. In their midst lay spread a sea or lake, through whose blue transparency the colours passed in their migrations; and of the islands a few sailed out in a channel and crossed the current, while many others were carried along with it, the sea itself drifting around, smoothly and evenly in a circle'.[140] As commentators explain, in this cosmology the sea represents the Milky Way, the astral path that, in Hardie's view, Pindar included in his *Hymn*, while the islands are the planets crossing the zodiac, here in the form of the channel; those that must be carried by the motions of the water are the constellations that occupy a fixed position in the sky.

3.2   A Dancing Arboretum

The 'feet' implicit in the term ἄψοφον in Callimachus' Delian *Hymn* are not confined to this closing account (note too the 'foot prints', ἴχνια, at 19), but characterize both Delos and her fellow Cyclades earlier in the work, where they form part of the third choral identity given to these maritime formations: not just an island chorus, nor one of stars, but, again consistent with the Pindaric precedent, a collectivity composed of trees. No sooner have we registered the islands' artisanal quality than the polymorphic picture changes again; as the poet goes on to explain, the dynamism of the Cyclades depends on Poseidon's having 'uprooted them from their bases' (πρυμνόθεν ἐρρίζωσε, 35), thereby destroying the features that formerly anchored his products to the seabed. The diction of the phrase prompts us to envision the islands complete with the roots more usually characteristic of trees and recalls the Pindaric representation at fr. 33d.6 S.-M., where the pillars rose from their 'trunks', the πρέμνων (reused by Callimachus at 322) that may be cognate with the similar sounding πρυμνό- selected by the Hellenistic poet.[141] ῥίζα also possesses a more direct link to the column: in fourth-century texts, the term appears as an equivalent to *basis*, and in later usage can refer to a column base.[142]

But where her fellow islands seem to lose their roots, Delos still retains and uses them at the moment when she exchanges her mobility for a steady

---

[140] Hardie 2000, 26 cites both this and the passage from Aelius Aristides.
[141] See Benveniste 1969 s.v. πρέμνον for this.
[142] See the examples cited in LSJ. Apposite to this pillar-vegetation link is the acanthus root that lies beneath the monument raised to the Corinthian maiden and whose leaves Callimachos' Corinthian column seeks to reproduce.

state. No longer reliant on the columns that in Pindar allowed her to cease her peregrinations, the Callimachean Delos is the sole agent of her transformation, putting down the 'roots of her feet' into the sea: ἐνὶ πόντου / κύμασιν Αἰγαίοιο ποδῶν ἐνεθήκαο ῥίζας (53–54). The mention of the island's feet, a curious collocation with roots, may further gesture towards the most distinctive feature of the pillars in the Pindaric account, the sandals with which those anthropomorphized and arboreal structures were shod.

When trees return in more explicit fashion later in Callimachus' *Hymn*, they do so in an expressly choral context, and one that advertises the intimate links between nymphs, one among Delos' several identities, trees and maiden dancers. As Mount Helicon flees from the advent of Leto, empathy and a symbiotic bond with her arboreal correlate compel Melia, the 'ash-tree nymph' (another glance to the Theban orientation of the Pindaric *Hymn*, which names Melia in the opening line of fr. 29 S.-M.), to quit the chorus in which she has been ring-dancing (ἡ δ' ὑποδινηθεῖσα χοροῦ ἀπεπαύσατο νύμφη, 79). Melia's fear on behalf of her dislocated oak prompts the narrator's appeal to the Muses to confirm the story that the Hamadryads, who make up the nymph's choral company, are coeval with oak trees (82–83).[143] A passage from Apollonius' *Argonautica* cited in a previous chapter suggests that Callimachus is drawing on a conceit already familiar to his readers. There the oak trees also privileged in the *Hymn to Delos* appear among the audiences for the performance of Orpheus as he plays upon his lyre and, observing the rhythm that the musician sets, then follow his lead (1.28–31):

φηγοὶ δ' ἀγριάδες κείνης ἔτι σήματα μολπῆς
ἀκτῇ Θρηκίῃ Ζώνης ἔπι τηλεθόωσαι
ἑξείης στιχόωσιν ἐπήτριμοι, ἃς ὅγ' ἐπιπρό   30
θελγομένας φόρμιγγι κατήγαγε Πιερίηθεν.

To this day the wild oaks, the configurations [or 'symbols', 'directives'] of [Orpheus'] choral song, that flourish on the Thracian shore of Zone, still draw themselves up in interwoven ranks one after the other, the ones which, charmed by his phorminx, onwards he conducted down from Pieria.

---

[143] At *HHVen*. 261, the nymphs' defining activity is their participation in choral dancing with the 'immortal gods'; at 266–67, the trees – whose life and death measure out the nymphs' own lifespan – rise up to form sacred precincts (τεμένη) for the same *athanatoi*, inviting us to imagine the dances taking place within that marked-off space.

Visible in the account are a series of terms that emphasize the trees' choral character and assign them the properties and behaviours typical of the ensembles in earlier accounts. Flagging the oaks' ranked and rectilinear movement as they deploy themselves in the *stichoi* that belong among the prototypical choral formations, Apollonius adds a localizing detail, 'down from Pieria', that links the trees to the similarly processing Muses (στεῖχον, 11) whom Hesiod introduces in the proem of the *Theogony* and whom he will subsequently recast as Pierian in the opening lines of the *Works and Days*. Apollonius additionally chooses to describe the oaks with the adjective ἐπήτριμος, which belongs to the weaving vocabulary that, as Chapter 7 details, is so regularly applied to choral song and dance. Consistent with Pindar's *Pyth.* 1.3, where the performers' footsteps hearken to the 'signals (σάμασιν)' issued by the lyre-playing Apollo preparing to lead his Muses in their song and dance, these trees observe Orpheus' musical and choreographic direct-ives before processing under the leadership that defines the *chorêgos* and that the designation itself articulates (cf. the 'chorus-leading [ἁγησιχόρων] preludes' at *Pyth.* 1.4). But this is not just a one-off performance. Exploiting the several meanings of σῆμα, the poet sug-gests that these now firmly situated trees continue physically to embody and make manifest that original choral music, song and dance in the location to which their *chorêgos* once conducted them, now forming a standing chorus that perpetually re-enacts the moment of their institution.

4 Pillars, Trees and Stars

The several works reviewed in the previous sections, I have argued, estab-lish close connections between choruses and a series of interrelated phe-nomena similarly conceived as singing-dancing ensembles, whether columns, trees, islands or stars. This final section more briefly treats two artefacts, the first a purely imaginary creation (albeit one that recalls real-world analogues) depicted in a passage from Attic drama, the second a votive object still visible today, that offer fresh combinations of at least three of these four paradigms and create new alignments between their different elements.

4.1 Celestial Fabrics in the Ion

In the episode that follows the third stasimon in Euripides' *Ion*, a temple attendant enters and exhaustively details the manner in which the drama's protagonist fashioned the elaborate tent-like building in which Ion intends to host his valedictory and civic-style (the entire population of Delphi will participate) feast.[144] The narrative begins by introducing the four supports that Ion erects, not columns, strictly speaking, but structures described as 'orthostates', which nonetheless serve much in the manner of columns here; with the props in place, the youth then measures out ten thousand square feet for the enclosed area within. Together with its four supports – assuming one for each side of what the attendant describes as a squared-off rectangle (1137) and demarcated space – the design of the expressly 'wall-less' structure resembles nothing so much as that of a peripteral temple, open on all sides.[145] But as the speaker goes on to detail the pictures woven on the textiles that Ion drapes over the pre-built frame, the orthostates assume the more cosmological dimensions familiar from the texts already cited: what they supply the girding for is nothing less than a 'textile planetarium',[146] a night sky festooned with stars (1147–58):

Οὐρανὸς ἀθροίζων ἄστρ' ἐν αἰθέρος κύκλῳ·
ἵππους μὲν ἤλαυν' ἐς τελευταίαν φλόγα
Ἥλιος, ἐφέλκων λαμπρὸν Ἑσπέρου φάος·
μελάμπεπλος δὲ Νὺξ ἀσείρωτον ζυγοῖς   1150
ὄχημ' ἔπαλλεν, ἄστρα δ' ὡμάρτει θεᾷ·
Πλειὰς μὲν ᾔει μεσοπόρου δι' αἰθέρος
ὅ τε ξιφήρης Ὠρίων, ὕπερθε δὲ
Ἄρκτος στρέφουσ' οὐραῖα χρυσήρη πόλῳ·
κύκλος δὲ πανσέληνος ἠκόντιζ' ἄνω   1155
μηνὸς διχήρης, Ὑάδες τε, ναυτίλοις
σαφέστατον σημεῖον, ἥ τε φωσφόρος
Ἕως διώκουσ' ἄστρα.

Heaven was assembling the stars in the circle of the sky; Helios was driving his horses to their flaming goal, dragging after him the brilliant light of Hesperos. Black-cloaked Night swung her chariot onwards, drawn by a pair with no trace-horses, and the stars accompanied the goddess. The Pleiades moved on a path through the middle of the sky as did Orion with

---

[144] See Chapter 3 for a differently oriented discussion of the scene.
[145] As Schmitt Pantel 1992, 218–21 observes, the vast dimensions of the space, unusual for a tent designed for a public feast, might prompt the audience to think of the sixth-century Hekatompedon on the Acropolis, a temple to Athena of one hundred feet, for which, see below.
[146] The expression is that of Shapiro 1980, 268.

his sword, and above them was the Bear turning at the pole with its golden tail. The full circle of the moon darted her beams upward at mid-month, and the Hyades, the clearest sign to sailors, were there, while light-bearing Dawn put the stars to flight.

While many of the terms in the description recall the shield band that the Iliadic poet positions at the start of his account of the Hephaestus-forged artefact at *Il.* 18.483–89, and preserves the circle motion so visible in the earlier representation, Euripides also devises a new arrangement, depicting the Pleiades travelling along a path through the centre of the sky in Orion's company and giving greater emphasis to the moon, whose temporal aspect he also details. In the penultimate line of the passage, Dawn appears as a bearer of illumination.

The full significance of this detailed report, as Froma Zeitlin comments,[147] depends on the fabric design's look back to the choral ode immediately preceding it and which acts by way of anticipatory doublet. Here, at 1074–88,[148] the chorus declares the shame that it would feel were a foreigner (i.e. Ion) to witness the rites celebrated at the Eleusinian Mysteries, and specifically the choral dances, both human and celestial, that these include:

> αἰσχύνομαι τὸν πολύυ-
>   μνον θεόν, εἰ παρὰ Καλλιχόροισι παγαῖς   1075
> λαμπάδα θεωρὸς εἰκάδων
> ἐννύχιον ἄυπνος ὄψεται,
> ὅτε καὶ Διὸς ἀστερωπὸς
> ἀνεχόρευσεν αἰθήρ,
> χορεύει δὲ σελάνα   1080
> καὶ πεντήκοντα κόραι
> †Νηρέος αἱ κατὰ πόντον
> ἀεναῶν τε ποταμῶν†
> δίνας χορευόμεναι
> τὰν χρυσοστέφανον κόραν   1085
> καὶ ματέρα σεμνάν·
> ἵν' ἐλπίζει βασιλεύ-
> σειν ἄλλων πόνον ἐσπεσὼν
> <ὁ> Φοίβειος ἀλάτας.

I feel shame before the much sung god if by the streams of Kallichoros a sleepless spectator will look on the torch of the twentieth day which burns all night, when even the starry-faced aether of Zeus has led off the dance and the moon dances, and the fifty daughters of Nereus by the sea and the eddies of the ever-flowing rivers are also dancing in honour of the golden-

---

[147] Zeitlin 1996, 319.   [148] The previous chapter also treated the passage in a different context.

crowned maiden and her revered mother. It is here that he hopes to reign, the vagabond of Phoebus, attacking the *ponos* of others.

In an instance of choral projection, the chorus of serving maids equate the dance they currently perform before the (licit) spectators in the theatre of Dionysus, this no less a song-dance *ponos* in honour of the deity, with the familiar nocturnal choral dances that celebrated Demeter and Kore at the Kallichoron witnessed by the outsider.[149] But there is a second choral model visible here and a further object of the hero's imagined *theôria*, the all-night dance that simultaneously occurs in the starry sky up above. Coming so shortly after the stasimon, the scene on the tapestries, which redeploys several of the terms from that song and reintroduces some of the same astral bodies, offers a second representation of a night-time sky made luminous with the circling constellations.

The relevance of the tent pillars to the star-studded spectacle and the thematic relations been the structure's different parts become more evident in the light of a pyxis lid in Berlin dated to ca. 430–420, where the winged figure of Night drives a four-horse chariot (Fig. 6.3).[150] Selene follows her, mounted on horseback while looking back towards Eos, who rides in a two-horse chariot. The figures circle around the surface, racing towards a Corinthian column with partly gilded volutes, topped by a second, narrower and slightly tapered pillar that rises from some downward curving leaves. In Ferrari's interpretation, the image 'plays on the extended metaphor of the astral bodies' trek across the sky as a racecourse by visualizing the point at which they "turn" as a *terma* of a hippodrome',[151] and portrays this turning point in the shape of the column which fulfills just this function in images picturing the less-fantastical chariot and horse races in which men compete.[152] Earlier I noted the lines in Pindar's third *Olympian* where, anticipating the role that pillars would play, Heracles planted the olive trees he had brought back from the land of the Hyperboreans which delimited the racecourse and, as the expression 'twelve-turned *terma* for the racecourse for horses' (*Ol.* 3.33–34) makes clear, also served as the turning posts in the races. But the pillar on the pyxis lid does more than set these constellations within an ethereal *agôn*; insofar

---

[149] These same Eleusinian dances, but not localized at the well, are the target of a choral projection in the second stasimon of Euripides' *Helen*. For the syncretism between Eleusinian and Dionysiac cults, see Csapo 2008, 267.
[150] Berlin, Antikensammlung F 2519.   [151] Ferrari 2008, 145.
[152] E.g. Paris, Musée du Louvre E 875; *ABV* 104.123; Karlsruhe, Badisches Landesmuseum B 2423; *ABV* 100.65.

Fig. 6.3 Attic red-figure pyxis lid, ca. 430–420 B.C.E. Berlin, Antikensammlung F 2519. Photograph © 2019. Scala, Florence/bpk, Bildagentur für Kunst, Kultur und Geschichte, Berlin.

as it supplies the *terma* of the course and the marker around which the charioteers and rider must circle, it taps into the familiar notion of the dance of the stars and the rotational motions that they eternally perform. Choral poems that predate the pyxis, and detailed in earlier chapters, integrate this turning post into their diction and imagery, whether in Pindar's *Pythian* 9, where Danaus, acting as *chorodidaskalos*, positions the maiden chorus of his daughters ἐν τέρμασιν (114), both the point around which the *parthenoi* will reverse their course as they dance and the finish post for the suitors who compete in a running race so as to win their brides, or in the conceit of the *kampulon melos*, used in a hyporcheme by the same poet (fr. 107a.2–3 S.-M.); here, drawing on the *kampê* or *kamptêr* that is the turning post in the diaulos or two-stade foot race, Pindar devises a phrase exactly suited to a chorus engaged in a competitive performance.[153]

Returning to the post-and-fabric structure constructed by Ion, the role of the supports vis-à-vis the spectacle woven into the textiles becomes clear: determining the limits of the celestial *orchestra* within whose compass this

---

[153] See Chapters 1 and 4 for these, together with the inscription on the choregic monument discussed in Chapter 8.

stellar chorus stages its display, they supply the turning posts which the astral charioteers and their fellow chorus members must encircle in their dance. Two details of the attendant's account reinforce the idea of rotational passage around a boundary marker. Noting the care with which Ion selects the position for his props, the speaker explains that the tent will be neither fully exposed to the rays of the sun nor so located that it occupies the spot where these rays 'end their life's course (τελευτώσας βίον)' (1136), this last a reference to the point – described in the *Odyssey* as the τροπαὶ ἠελίοιο (15.404) – at which the sun reverses its diurnal and seasonal passage prior to making the same movements in reverse. More circles around a post occur within the fabric itself, which includes among its images Arktos 'turning about its pole', the πόλος that is the physical axle or pivot of the wheel; the adjective 'golden' used of this midpoint declares its materiality here.

My suggestion, then, is that in building his cosmic tent, complete with its moving constellations and the posts that function as the turning points for their circles in the sky,[154] Ion transforms the astral dance onto which the chorus projected its performance in the preceding choral song into a woven and architectonic frame, a counterpart constructed with wood and cloth to that live and ever-recurrent celestial event. With the Delphic population gathered inside the tent as audience to his textile-ballet, and prior to his departure for Athens, the protagonist stages his more transient version of the Eleusinian rite on Delphic ground by conjuring up a starry chorus of his own.[155] The pillars that support this second choral dance add a cosmological element absent from the earlier account and integrate the choral performance into a broader model of cosmic harmony.

But there is a second template informing the attendant's account, which aligns Ion's makeshift banqueting hall with a different and strictly earthbound space at a site where *choreia* occurred. There is no mistaking the specialized language that fills the initial report of how Ion went about

[154] Note the passing evocation of this idea of a cosmic track with boundaries at 1135–36; as Lee 1997 comments *ad* 1147ff., 'the Servant's eye sweeps from one edge of the roof-tapestry, where Sun is about to set, through to the pole at the centre and then to the other edge with the approach of Dawn'.

[155] Indeed, the quasi-technical language used for the construction of the tent very much suits not just the professional builder, but the individual who leads or sets up a chorus. In the instructions Xouthos issues, the youth should 'erect with the labour of craftsmen a well-fitting *skenē*' (ἀμφήρεις μένων σκηνὰς ἀνίστη τεκτόνων μοχθήμασιν, 1128–29). Derived from ἀραρίσκω, as Stieber 2011, 303 suggests, the adjective used of the tent also appears in the description of the Deliades' choral song, beautifully 'put together' (συνάρηρεν, *HHAp.* 164), while Pindar's third *Nemean* presents the choristers as 'builders' (τέκτονες) of the epinician performance (4); previous chapters have cited evidence for the labour that *choreia* exacts.

designing the site for his tent, a structure that is, as Xouthos first directs, to be 'joined all round' (ἀμφήρεις, 1128) and whose four exactingly squared-off corners the pleonastic phrase 'measured out the length of the distance so as to form a rectangle' (πλέθρου σταθμήσας μῆκος εἰς εὐγωνίαν, 1137) indi-cates. Further details concerning the tent's dimensions follow, as though the attendant came equipped with an actual building plan. These numerical specifications – Ion measures out one hundred feet on each side – might put an audience in mind of an actual building with which they were familiar, the archaic temple erected on the north slope of the Acropolis and identified in the accompanying inscriptions as the Hekatompedon, 'of one hundred feet'. Insofar as Ion's tent resembles a sacred dwelling of this type (albeit a building in the shape not of a rectangle but a square), and one whose construction details would be preserved in inscriptions using the vocabulary that Euripides draws on here,[156] it supplies a fitting site for the dance displayed on the tapestries.

4.2 The Acanthus Column at Delphi

The Delphic setting of Ion's tent accommodates one final and still extant conjunction of dancers, pillars and stars. The famous fourth-century Acanthus Column discovered in the sanctuary of Pythian Apollo at the site consists of five column drums, with a capital rising from a base of acanthus leaves at its top (Fig. 0.10);[157] additional acanthus leaves encircle the base of each drum and completely cover the capital. Surrounding the two-metre high shaft supported by that capital, this freshly covered with acanthus, are three *kalathiskos* dancers, their feet raised off the ground as though the figures were suspended in mid-air. Like the karyatids earlier reviewed, they raise their right arms, palms upwards, so as to help support the tripod that originally topped the dedication (this gesture, styled *sima*, is variously enacted in prayer, dancing and in temple architecture, where it refers to the topmost element at the edge of the roof which turns upwards as though in supplication).[158] Again, I would follow the recent revisionary interpretation of the column proposed by Ferrari:[159] the figures, evocative of stars by virtue of their *kalathiskos* crowns of rays and their suspension off the ground, are the three daughters of Erechtheus, who were catasterized

---

[156] See Stieber 2011, 305–07 for details. [157] Delphi, Archaeological Museum 466, 1423, 4851.
[158] As observed by Karvouni 1997, 122–23. [159] Ferrari 2008, 141–47.

and turned into the Hyades;[160] according to our ancient sources, the Hyades are, together with the Pleiades, the inventors of the night-time dances performed by mortal choruses. Ferrari reads the column which the figures surround as a cosmic landmark, the celestial *terma* or turning point and site at which the sun reverses its course and that in ancient sources delimits the circuit of the stars.[161]

If this identification is correct, then the fourth-century votive to Apollo offers a visual manifestation of the same myth cited in Section 1 and depicts the self-sacrificing maidens in their now-eternal state as constellations in the sky. As such it supplies a smaller-scale reworking of many of the elements that came together in the design of the earlier Erechtheid portico, where the mythical maidens assumed lithified and columnar form as they performed their choral dances while marking out the sacred enclosure within. Like their Eleusinian counterparts, these figures in Athens form part of a larger votive object and furnish models for the actual choruses that may have performed in the space adjacent to the temple in commemoration and celebration of the maidens' civic self-sacrifice. At Delphi, the equivalence between the monument, complete with the original tripod that topped the column, and the real-world performances would have been no less evident to the visitors to the shrine. In Chapter 2, I cited some of the several passages describing choral dancing around the Delphic tripod, a well-attested practice that would condition a viewer's encounter with the Acanthus Column: having, perhaps, attended or participated in one of these events, he or she would understand the Erechtheid maidens circling the tripod as monumentalized reconfigurations of the dancers turning around the oracular vessel.

The Pindaric 'dancing' columns of *Ol.* 6 supplied this chapter's point of departure, and it is with another combination of columns and choral dancers, those that stage the final dance performance on Achilles' shield in *Iliad* 18, that I would end. Dated to the late first century B.C.E. or early first century C.E. (with one tablet from the Antonine period), the twenty-two miniature ivory tablets known as the *Tabulae Iliacae* include among their heterogeneous images depictions of scenes from the *Iliad* on their

---

[160] The identification is more problematic than Ferrari grants; Eur. fr. 370 K., cited earlier for its mention of the choral performances that the Athenians should establish in memory of Erechtheus' daughters, also indicates their divinization in the form of the Hyakinthids (71–74). According to a scholion to Aratus, *Phaen.* 172, Euripides further identifies the Erechtheids/ Hyakinthids with the Hyades, the star cluster to which the dramatist refers in a very fragmentary line (170) in Athena's speech.

[161] See Franks 2009, 464–65 for further discussion, and corroboration of the location of this *terma* among the Hyperboreans.

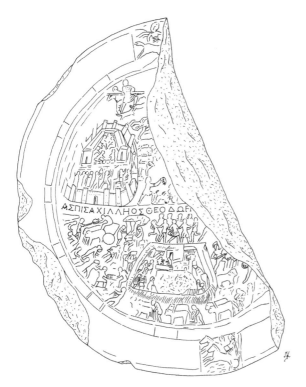

Fig. 6.4 *Tabula Iliaca Capitolina* 4 N Rome, first century C.E. Rome, Musei Capitolini 83a. Drawing courtesy of Michael Squire.

front, with transcriptions of passages from Homer, in a variety of visual pictograms, on their back.[162] Two of the tablets, 4 N and 5O, focus particularly closely on the scenes forged on Achilles' shield, the first of these in a much better state of preservation. Replicating the circular, three-dimensional form of Hephaestus' model, 4 N places the images on the different bands seemingly at random on its surface, forcing the viewer to restore the Homeric sequence by moving his eye from one scene to the tableau that follows it in the poem and which may be located at some distance from it in the tablet's design. The choral dance occupies the upper middle register of the lower section, positioned immediately beneath the inscription that identifies the craftsman as Theodorus (Fig. 6.4);[163] perhaps in acknowledgement of the superlative quality of Hephaestus' penultimate

---

[162] Squire 2011 offers the most detailed treatment; see too Squire 2013, 170–79.
[163] Rome, Musei Capitolini 83a.

band, and of Homer's pyrotechnic verbal counterpart, the name of the artist/stone-cutter exactly spans the space filled by the performers.

Looking at the outer rim of the tablet, which takes the place of the Homeric Okeanos that forms the outermost band and contains the rest, the viewer encounters a fresh wonder: the tiny squiggles that Theodorus seems to substitute for the ever-flowing stream turn out to be made up of alphabetic letters and words, a transcription of the entire text of *Il.* 18.438–608, broken up into a series of columns, each one containing between ten and thirteen lines of verse. As Michael Squire notes, these columnar texts, originally ten in all (six still survive), are 'circulating . . . wheeling round the object in anticlockwise order',[164] while the passage describing the chorus completes the circle. Bifurcating the pictorial representation that these textual columns surround is another pillar, this one outsized, carrying many lines of text, while many of the individual shield scenes include other more small-scale pillars as well as structures in circular formations (so, in accordance with the Homeric account, the choral dancers have their hands joined and move circle-wise).[165] Much in keeping with Pindar's ode, a choral performance has been reified, now in the form not of a building, but of an ivory shield. But where the columns of the encomiastic song are vivified in the living, moving persons of the dancers, here, in accordance with his time and place, Theodorus' experience of *choreia* comes in the form of a text that supplies the matter with which he builds.

---

[164] Squire 2013, 177.

[165] The tradition of presenting texts in column form would have a long *Nachleben*; for one outstanding example, still more amazing than the *Tabulae Iliacae*, see the micrographic engravings by Matthias Buchinger (1674–1739), a German artist born without hands and feet. His largest surviving *Decalogue*, measuring twenty-one inches in height, transcribes the Ten Commandments onto tablets framed by elaborate Corinthian columns in a sanctuary, while the family trees of two aristocratic patrons take the form of texts on scrolls pinned to the trunks of two columnar trees (this image is twelve inches high).

From an item in *Vogue* from March, 2016: 'At her New York launch of her
new fashion label, Amanda Phelan had the Vim Vigor dance company
perform a piece inspired by the machines used to create her print-heavy
textural collection.'

Introduction

Among the artefacts distinct to Boeotia are a series of female terracotta
figurines dressed in bell-shaped skirts, these fashioned on the potter's
wheel and flattened while still malleable; all are Late Geometric or sub-
Geometric and were found in the graves of women and children from the
tenth to the eighth century or in votive deposits associated with these.
Designs evocative of weaving decorate many of their garments,[1] and the
most highly ornamented of the figurines, dated to the late eighth century,
comes complete with locks of hair, a necklace, sandals and a frieze of
dancing females circling around her richly patterned skirt; the dancers
are similarly dressed in woven textiles (Fig. 7.0).[2] J. N. Coldstream's brief
discussion notes in passing that the motifs on the garment are 'perhaps
indicating a textile pattern',[3] an affinity brought out by the way in which the
dancers' crooked arms visually replicate the zigzag pattern that appears at
the top of the doll's garment, which makes figurative and non-figurative
elements part of a single woven design and products of the same art.[4]
Although no other representations of patterned fabrics in the visual record
include dancers among their often complex figural designs,[5] the presence

[1] The presence of these textile-like decorations can already be seen on the early Bronze Age
'goddess of Myrtos' figurine (Agios Nikolaos, Archaeological Museum of Agios Nikolaos).
[2] Paris, Musée du Louvre CA 623.97.   [3] Coldstream 2003, 202.
[4] The overlap is not surprising; see Barber 1991, 197 and 312–13 and the discussion at the end of
this chapter's Section 2.
[5] The so-called 'Lady of Sibari', a seventh-century Etruscan terracotta figurine, furnishes a possible
analogue: one of the woven bands of her richly decorated skirt features five maidens standing in a

Fig. 7.0 Boeotian terracotta figurine, ca. 700 B.C.E. Paris, Musée du Louvre CA 623.97. Photograph © RMN-Grand Palais/Hervé Lewandowski.

of the performers on the woven skirt of the Boeotian statuette might already point to a connection between weaving and choral activity, particularly that associated with women and girls.

A text, dated to the second half of the eighth century, supplies fresh evidence for the intercalation of elaborately patterned cloth and choral dance in archaic Greece. As noted earlier in this study, in introducing the penultimate image that receives detailed description in the account of the forging of Achilles' shield, the tableau depicting a dancing chorus, the Iliadic poet selects a verb very different from the more humdrum terms earlier used for Hephaestus' activity: not ποιέω, τίθημι, or τεύχω but ποικίλλω (*Il.* 18.590), a verb derived, like the adjective ποικίλος, from the root **peik-*, and whose core meaning is 'to make things [be] varied'. Frequently translated 'to work in various colours', in several other Homeric passages where ποικίλλω or its cognates appear the

line with their hands interlinked; like on the Boeotian example, the patterning on the girls' skirts repeats the cross-hatched design on the fabric covering the larger figure's torso, while immediately beneath the maidens we see a second possible 'chorus', this one made up of four youths similarly aligned and with their hands linked. For other figural designs on textiles, see n. 8.

term also carries a more specific frame of reference, describing the technique of 'pattern-weaving' so as to create an elaborately decorated textile.[6] In *Il.* 22.440–41, Andromache weaves a cloth in which she 'sprinkles' (ἔπασσε) or interweaves 'flowers that were varied' (θρόνα ποικίλ') in precisely the design so common on the flower-decorated garments worn by the figures who populate the vase imagery of this and later periods. The passage plainly echoes an earlier account in the poem; when we first encounter Helen, the poet portrays her weaving a no less elaborate textile, whose figurative elements are not flowers, but the many 'struggles' (ἀέθλους, 3.126) endured by the Achaeans and Trojans in the course of the ongoing war. According to the scholia b and AT on 22.441, πάσσειν is the Cypriot term for ποικίλλειν, and similarly describes the process of introducing complex decorations into a woven fabric. The use of the cognate noun, ποίκιλμα, at 6.294 supplies fresh evidence for this cluster of terms; here too the referent is a richly woven peplos, the gleaming garment offered by the Trojan women to Athena in the hope of warding off destruction from their city. Sappho fr. 1.1–2 V. introduces a divine pattern-weaver to add to the human company when, at the outset of the song, the *persona loquens* makes her appeal to 'wile-weaving' (δολ[όπλοκε) Aphrodite, whose skill in achieving variegation at the loom the opening epithet πο]ικιλόθρο[ν, 'of the multicoloured [inwoven] flowers/throne' (an adjective more commonly translated 'of the multi-patterned throne', but the first rendering is equally correct) might indicate. From the mid-sixth century comes Pherecydes of Syros' cosmogonic account of how, at his wedding to Chthonie, Zas (i.e. Zeus) clothes his bride in a peplos which clearly consists of an elaborately pattern-woven cloth (fr. B 2 DK); as the mythographer describes the event, the groom interweaves (ποικίλλει) into the garment a depiction of Ge, Ogenos and the halls of Ogenos. One much later text, albeit a standalone, circles back to the eighth-century image with which I began and suggests a counterpart to the design on the skirt of the figurine: in an epigram by Antipater of Sidon, three maidens dedicate a cloth they have woven for Artemis with a border at whose centre one Bitie has 'wrought these maidens flourishing in the dance' (τάσδε χοροιθαλέας κάμε κούρας) performing besides the streams of the 'winding Maeander', a phrase suggestive not only of the choreography of the performance, but of the weaver's motion too (*AP* 6.287).[7]

---

[6] See Nagy 2010a, 273–310 for detailed discussion of the point and for several of the examples cited here. As he and others demonstrate, ποικίλλω describes not embroidery, something that would be superimposed on an already woven textile, but the technique of weaving designs 'into' the cloth as it is being made.

[7] The demonstrative pronoun suggests that the cloth offers a representation of the girls themselves as, in their triad, they danced on behalf of the goddess. The verb here, however, is not ποικίλλω but ὑφαίνω.

Read together, the Boeotian figurine, the passage in *Iliad* 18 and the Hellenistic epigram pose the question that this chapter addresses: why the association between the fabrication of intricately woven textiles and *choreia*, and how might we account for what turns out to be an enduring and multifaceted link between cloth-making and the composition and performance of choral song and dance? In each of its four parts, my discussion looks at one of the chief areas where that correspondence receives its most frequent expression. In Section 1, I treat the early visual sources (presented in loose chronological sequence, and buttressed on occasion with textual material) where artefacts in a variety of media already combine participation in choruses with weaving and cloth working and with the fabrics that these generate. Section 2 turns to a series of texts that bear out the material evidence; as archaic poetry and fifth-century drama illustrate, choral song and dance and weaving are not just proximate activities performed in the course of ritual and other events by the same groups of individuals and at one and the same life stage, but both linguistic usage and the morphology of the choral ensemble, its gestures, steps and accessories, can be much more narrowly aligned with the production of patterned textiles. In Section 3, I suggest an underlying rationale for the coincidence and synchronization of the two activities, grounding their relation in actual techniques used by those engaged in the 'pattern-weaving' featured in the examples cited in the earlier sections. Section 4 concludes by drawing together the different media so as to identify some of the central concerns that the confluence of weaving and *choreia* articulates: both, I suggest, look to the creation of *harmonia* in the related spheres of the *oikos* and polis, the bringing together of disparate elements through a process that involves both division and recombination, stratification and cohesion.

1 Weaving and Choral Dancing in the Early Visual Account

1.1 Terracotta Figurines and the Nymphs

Returning to the Boeotian terracotta for a moment, I would propose a more specific way of understanding the painter's choice to depict a frieze of dancers circling about the skirt, a design, as noted, all but unparalleled in other representations of fabrics no less elaborately interwoven with figurative elements in the visual record.[8] Like other such figurines, the legs of this doll would have been made separately and attached beneath the skirt by a wire or cord, allowing it to move when the figure was suspended or dangled on a string as was originally intended; on one such image in Boston,[9] dated to the fourth century, the body has holes on the sides to allow the legs to be fastened and many such dolls were discovered with their limbs detached and placed elsewhere in both the early and later periods. Other evidence suggests that beyond their capacity to move, these figures were conceived as dancers. In several instances, the dolls carry musical instruments in their hands, *tympana* and the castanets that marked the rhythm and beat of the performers' feet as they danced their measures (Fig. 7.1).[10] More indirectly, Plato's extended use of the figure of the puppet

Fig. 7.1 Mould-made terracotta doll, ca. 350 B.C.E. London, British Museum 1865, 0720.35. Photograph © The Trustees of The British Museum.

---

[8] Among other examples, the goddess arriving at the wedding of Peleus and Thetis on the François Vase wears a garment decorated with a pattern of stacked chariot friezes, while a Demeter on a red-figure skyphos by Makron of ca. 490 (London, British Museum E 140; *ARV²* 495.3) displays a cloak woven with dolphins similarly aligned.

[9] Boston, Museum of Fine Arts 18.460. The doll has an earring, a fillet holding her hair and shoes on her feet.

[10] London, British Museum 1865, 0720.35.

at *Leg.* 653c7–654a5, as Kurke's reading explores,[11] assimilates the figure on the string to the choral dancer, its limbs now slack, now pulled upright under its divine *chorêgos'* direction (see below).

Provenance further situates these figures in a choral frame. Many of the extant examples were found among the votives in caves sacred to the nymphs – such as in the fourth-century deposits from a cave at Locri, the Grotta Caruso – with spaces expressly set aside for the maiden participants in the rites to perform choral dances, along with other prenuptial activities, in celebrations of the ever-dancing deities.[12] Best known perhaps is the cave at Vari at the south end of Mount Hymettos in Attica, where among the many inscriptions by the self-identified Archedamos, one signals his devotion to the Nymphs and another the central place of dancing in rituals celebrated on the deities' behalf;[13] on the cave's lower stratum, excavators uncovered an earth platform built on a layer of stone, regularly interpreted as a dancing floor in accordance with Archedamos' message. The votives excavated here, dating from ca. 500–150, include three articulated dolls. Another such figurine, of Corinthian manufacture and from the fifth century, is patently a choral dancer (Fig. 7.2).[14] Wearing a short chiton decorated with bands filled with chevrons, zigzags and short dashes whose stacked arrangement suggests a woven design, and with articulated legs and arms, she is also equipped with the headdress that, in conjunction with her chitoniskos, identifies her as a performer in the *kalathiskos* dance. For Jennifer Larson the dress, instruments and moving limbs 'reflect both the mythic idea of a dancing, musical nymph and the young girl's expectation that one day she would emulate the nymphs by becoming a member of a chorus'.[15]

Votives like these are not alone in celebrating the Nymphs, as well as other female deities, in their capacity as choral dancers. Among the objects found in votive deposits dating from the late sixth through to the fourth century are a series of terracotta plaques depicting draped women or maidens, invariably in triads. Very schematic, the figures adopt a frontal pose and stand side by side. On one plaque from Amyklai,[16] the three individuals are holding hands as if dancing, and six plaques from the Panagopoulos plot show a similarly draped and dancing trio; another, also from Amyklai, equips the figures with wreaths, and with their right

---

[11] Kurke 2013; see too Pl. *Quaest. conv.* 9.748b-c for the puppet/choral dancer analogy.

[12] See Chapter 5 for detailed discussion.   [13] See Chapters 5 and 6 for the inscriptions.

[14] New York, Metropolitan Museum of Art, Rogers Fund 1944.11.8.   [15] Larson 2001, 106.

[16] For the first plaque, Athens, National Archaeological Museum 16464, with good discussion in Connelly 2007, 170–71.

Fig. 7.2 Fifth-century Corinthian mould-made terracotta doll. New York, Metropolitan Museum of Art, Rogers Fund 1944.11.8. Photograph © The Metropolitan Museum of Art.

arms raised.[17] If divinities are the subjects here, then several threesomes come to mind; the dancing figures are on occasion identified as the Graces or, more frequently, Nymphs (absent an inscription, nothing permits us to distinguish the two), and some propose the Horai. When Hermes or Pan

---

[17] Salapata 2009, 325 and 327 details these.

accompanies the dancers, and/or when the plaques and stone reliefs come from cave sanctuaries, the Nymphs can be more securely recognized. Several discussions substitute mortal worshippers for deities, with the votaries perhaps emulating and celebrating the objects of their veneration by performing the same actions.

Read in this context, we can see how the woven design on the Boeotian image's skirt might supply a visual and lasting record of the actual dances celebrated for the (nymphine?) divinity to whom the figure was dedicated. The chorus on the garment stands in mimetic relation to its wearer, who is conceived as a paradigmatic participant in just the type of dance that her votaries now lastingly perform in her service as they circle about their *chorêgos*-like figure. Weaving, the art evoked by the doll's skirt, is doubly appropriate here: not only because, as detailed in this chapter, it is conceived as a corollary and counterpart to *choreia*, but because, from the *Odyssey* on, Nymphs, the deities with whom these terracottas are particularly closely connected, are similarly adept at working the loom.[18] Most famously, the cave sacred to the Nymphs on Ithaca accommodates the stone looms on which they weave sea-purple cloth (13.107–08), and two more individualized figures, Circe and Calypso, form part of Homer's larger company of weaving nymphs. Quintus of Smyrna, drawing on the epic precedent, includes in his *Posthomerica* a description of a Paphlagonian cave complete with stone images of the site's inhabitants, 'Pans and charming nymphs', alongside looms and spindles (6.480–81).

Just as the dances performed by their votaries reproduce one of the Nymphs' two signature activities, so other dedications recognize the deities in their role as weavers. Archaeologists have found loom weights in votive deposits in caves typically associated with their cults, among them at the cave of Daskalio, situated in the bay of Vathy, with its sixteen whole or fragmentary weights. Loom weights similarly appear among the votives dedicated at the so-called Casino Macri, which belongs to the series of grotto-nymphaea excavated in Locri; the structure also contains fragments of a hip bath, evidence for the practice of the water rituals commonly associated with Nymphs and very much apparent at another Locrian cave featuring dedications to the deities, the Grotta Caruso. Weaving, nymphs and prenuptial bathing coincide again in Callimachus' account of rituals celebrated on behalf of Hera in Argos in fr. 66 Pf. of the *Aetia*, a piece already treated in Chapter 5 and to which I return in Section 2.[19]

---

[18] See too *Cypria* fr. 5.

[19] It is in this fragment that the poet includes a term unattested elsewhere, πάτος, and whose meaning the ancient grammarians gloss as equivalent to the *enduma*, the ceremonial woven

1.2 Corinthian Choruses

The coincidence of weaving and choral dancing in the examples already cited manifests itself again, invested with a rather different significance, in a series of representations on Corinthian vases; dated from the last quarter of the seventh to the mid-sixth century, these show women engaged in ritual activity, or *Frauenfest* scenes.[20] The depictions occur on flasks, phialai, pyxeis and wine cups, and, on one occasion, on a krater, and come from grave and votive deposits, among them the votives at the shrine of Hera at Perachora and that of Demeter and Kore at Acrocorinth.[21] On a pyxis in Paris by the Skating Painter,[22] which may have been found in a grave between Corinth and Sicyon, women advance in a measured processional step towards a figure, perhaps a cult image, while others carry votive objects for the deity, spindles among them. On another pyxis in Munich, also attributed by some to the Skating Painter and in a poor state of preservation, two similar groups of women are seated, holding what is variously seen as a child, or child statue, or a spindle;[23] the same action appears on the lower portion of the pot, now combined with women displayed in an orderly chorus line with their hands joined, and with others who carry a basket or goat (Fig. 7.3). A female aulete completes the second group, confirming that a dance performance accompanies the presentation of other gifts. A Corinthian flask from the first quarter of the sixth century belongs to the same series (the Skating Painter is again cited as artist here); women holding wreaths with linked hands dance around the vessel, positioned above a second band where one of the figures carries a ritual basket, the *kanoun*, on her head (Fig. 7.4).[24] Participants on these and other *Frauenfest* vessels wear the special 'festival mantle' typical of depictions of women taking part in ritual events; a standout from more workaday woven garments, it is one among the elaborately patterned clothing displayed on these occasions.[25]

These images propose a variety of relations between participating in choruses and cloth-making, the second forming, as Elizabeth Pemberton comments, an ancillary motif on many of the vases.[26] In a note observing that Corinthian women, like those in other cities, presented goddesses with

---

garment attested for a ritual of Hera at Olympia (Paus. 5.16.2–8); might this be a variant or deformation of the noun παστός, the term that the scholia cited earlier derived from πάσσειν?

[20] For a discussion on which I have drawn, see Pemberton 2000.   [21] See Dillon 2002, 14.
[22] Paris, Bibliothèque Nationale 94.   [23] Munich, Antikensammlungen 7741.
[24] Baltimore, Walters Art Gallery 48.192.   [25] For detailed treatment, see Roccos 1995.
[26] Pemberton 2000, 94: 'women dancing, processions of women and young girls, references to weaving, all these are appropriate themes for any female deity of the household, the family, the female community'.

Fig. 7.3 Corinthian black-figure pyxis attributed to the Skating Painter, ca. 600–570 B.C.E. Munich, Antikensammlungen 7741. Photograph Renate Kühling © Staatliche Antikensammlungen und Glyptothek München.

Fig. 7.4 Corinthian black-figure flask attributed to the Skating Painter, ca. 600–570 B.C.E. Baltimore, Walters Art Gallery 48.192. Photograph © Walters Art Museum, Baltimore.

ritually woven fabrics, Pemberton makes the further suggestion that this chapter takes up:[27] that the cultural product generated by the activity would stand by way of analogue to the ordered dance also figured on the pots, and, I would add, freshly expressed in the elaborate garments all but fully covering some of the women's bodies. The representation of Artemis in *HH* 27.15–18 articulates the connection between the *kosmos* that choral dance (and song) puts on show and the well-woven cloth; having gone to Apollo's Olympian home so as to 'organize the Muses' and Graces' lovely chorus (καλὸν χορὸν ἀρτυνέουσα)',[28] the goddess leads the ensemble 'having a graceful (χαρίεντα) *kosmon* about her body', viz. the garment that she wears and whose orderly and grace-imbued design forms a correlate to or metonym for the no less beauteous chorus, complete with the Charites themselves, that Artemis now arranges or 'fits out'.[29]

Since all the objects and activities depicted on the Corinthian vases involve the types of gifts proffered and the mode of work performed by women and young girls in their service to female deities, nothing permits us to identify the particular immortal celebrated here; Hera, Demeter and Kore, and Artemis are among the candidates most frequently proposed. But more secure is the provenance of about sixty terracotta spindles, as well as bobbins and loom weights, discovered at the coastal sanctuary of Hera at Perachora near Corinth, evidence for the donors' self-identification as spinners and as weavers in Hera's cult. A quite recently published fragmentary black-figure skyphos now in Athens (Fig. 7.5),[30] also found at the sanctuary and dated to 600–550, confirms the co-presence of female choral dancing at the shrine. On the recombined fragments, four almost complete figures appear, all dressed in short-sleeved chitons or belted peploi; remains of a fifth are also visible. Several sherds found nearby also feature the women, and the vase's publisher, Nassi Malagardis, suggests ten female figures in all, five on each side of the skyphos.[31] There is no

[27] Pemberton 2000, 94 n. 43.

[28] For discussion of the verb and its factural connotations, see Chapter 1.

[29] Even as the vases construct a link between female choruses and their role in cloth-making, they also register a key distinction between the two activities, thereby mitigating the potentially problematic aspect attendant on women's participation in the public rituals shown here and on objects designed, in several instances, for male as well as female viewers: with this display of their all but exclusively domestic enterprise in the civic sphere, the choristers simultaneously hide their bodies from exposure by wrapping them in their self-produced textiles, effectively 'privatizing' the site of their performances and turning it into an extension of the *oikos* where they more normally remain, a theme to which this chapter returns. With thanks to Sheila Murnaghan for this point.

[30] Athens, National Archaeological Museum 3637.

[31] Malagardis 2008, whose analysis I follow.

Fig. 7.5 Fragmentary black-figure skyphos, 600–550 B.C.E. Athens, National Archaeological Museum 3637. Photograph Irini Mauri © Hellenic Ministry of Culture and Sports/Archaeological Receipts Fund.

mistaking the ensemble's choral character. The figures move in a single file, travelling to the right, each executing the almost identical rhythmic and vigorous step; their arms, crooked at the elbows, and the pairs in which they are arranged, the members of each set turning their heads towards the one behind, freshly point to a representation of a dance. These choristers are singers too: five identical inscriptions appear between the figures, each made up of the letters YOYO that gradually disappear, as though the sound becomes fainter as it travels. The notations are not alphabetic nonsense, but rather the onomatopoeic transcription of the cry enunciated by the dancers as they perform the *ololugê*, the ritual shout regularly raised by female choruses in festival contexts and attested in many textual accounts of this and later periods (e.g. Sappho fr. 44.31 V., Bacch. 17.126, Eur. *Hcld.* 780–83). If the vase did originally show ten figures, then the same number appears in three visual depictions of female choruses from the end of the eighth to the mid-fifth century as well as in archaic poetry.[32] As documented in Chapter 4, our textual sources bear out the evidence of the skyphos and make choral dancing central to the rites of Hera,

---

[32] See Calame 1997, 22 for the images and textual evidence.

particularly in rituals addressed to the goddess in her capacity as Hera Akraia and Limenaia.

A different set of artefacts depicting women participating in ritual events makes woven textiles a prominent feature of choral activity at Corinth and elsewhere. Corinthian vase painters are among the first to deploy the very common, but much debated iconographic scheme that exhibits a group of female figures (numbers range from two to nine) beneath a single mantle, depicted, in many instances, as a supersized cloth with a richly patterned design.[33] Boeotian, Attic and Chalcidian artists, responding to Corinthian influence, take up the motif, which first appears at the start of the sixth century and remains popular through to its final quarter. The fact that many of these images occur on alabastra (although kraters seem likewise to attract the draped ensembles, particularly when several such groups appear) suggests that women would have been among the intended audiences and that the vessels served at least in part to reflect rituals in which their users participated or were familiar with as spectators to the event. The eye-catching and large-scale mantles, whose extended dimensions would have required particular skill and an expenditure of labour on their collective weavers' part, seem to call attention to the figures' role as textile producers.

Although there is a wide divergence in opinion on the significance of the motif (complicating things further are representations of men, sometimes with one or more women, sometimes with another male, beneath the cloth), most scholars grant the cultic or more broadly religious context framing at least some of the single-mantled female groups. The regularity and orderliness of the movements these enveloped figures perform suggests a processional and, on occasion, a dance formation suited to a chorus, as does their clearly collective nature emphasized by their being gathered under a single garment; so H. G. Buchholz describes the cloaked women on a Boeotian black-figure alabastron originally in East Berlin as a female chorus performing a 'festlicher Tanz', engaged, aptly enough, in making a peplos offering.[34] Also coinciding with the iconography regularly associated with choruses of maidens in archaic images are the branches that these figures frequently carry; the accessory appears not just on the Berlin alabastron but again on a second alabastron from the same region, now in Lund, from the first half of the sixth century, where two maidens (with

---

[33] For discussion and review of the objects, see Koch-Harnack 1989, Buchholz 1987 and Guarducci 1928–29.

[34] Berlin, Staatliches Museum 3158, with Buchholz 1987, 28.

unbound hair) process from left to right beneath a single mantle.[35] In the representation of the Horai also united beneath the shared garment on the François Vase, the divinities' coordinated hand motions suggest their rhythmic progress and participation in a less lively form of the dance that Dionysus, positioned immediately in front of them with bent arms and legs, more visibly performs.

Unique among the twenty versions of the processional arrangement listed by Buchholz is a black-figure cup of ca. 600–590, whose lead figure holds up a wreath (Fig. 7.6).[36] Here no fewer than nine maidens make up the group of closely clustered and overlapping figures, each of whom wears a diadem, necklace and patterned gown partly visible beneath the single richly woven fabric that covers the ensemble and reaches from their shoulders to knee-length. The number of the line members naturally brings the Muses to mind, but there is little about the scene to suggest divinities – the bystander figures have nothing godly about them – and in the nearly exact reiteration of the motif on the cup's other side, the group includes only seven girls. The wreath held up by the lead maiden in each instance

Fig. 7.6 Black-figure cup, ca. 600–590 B.C.E. Berlin, Antikensammlung F 3993. Photograph © 2019. Scala, Florence/bpk, Bildagentur für Kunst, Kultur und Geschichte, Berlin.

---

[35] Lund, Universitätssammlung (Buchholz no. 31). See too Boston, Museum of Fine Arts 18.490 and Bonn, Akademisches Kunstmuseum 573 (Buchholz nos. 34 and 38) for more branch-carrying women beneath the single cloth.

[36] Berlin, Antikensammlung F 3993.

recalls those that equip *chorêgoi* in other visual and textual examples, while the finely decorated mantle enveloping all the figures alike suggests another instance of the coincidence between pattern-weaving and participation in choral ensembles. Here, as in the other instances explored above, the garment with its highly regularized woven design not only imposes order on the body around which it is wrapped, but offers a statement about the nature of the wearers' activity: a procession in which each member forms one unit in the larger composite made up by the group is invested with the same *kosmos* as the cloth even as it offers a visualization of the *poikilia* so characteristic of the highly worked textile, a quality that results from the use of heterogeneous elements to create a cohesive whole.

1.3 Parthenoi *in Scenes of Weaving and Choral Dance*

If rites performed by women at Corinth and elsewhere incorporated weaving implements in choral dancing, involved the participants' display of the fruits of their industry in their choice of dress and/or featured offerings of cloths and textile-making tools from the donors' domestic handiwork presented at the sites where they also processed and danced,[37] then the association between weaving and the chorus is particularly pronounced, as the earlier discussion of the Nymphs suggested, in representations of the lifestyle of *parthenoi*; and, further in keeping with other rituals celebrated in the goddesses' cults, nowhere is their twofold presence more emphatic than when a maiden is about to turn bride.

Among the earliest images to introduce the bride-to-be as spinner/ weaver into a choral context is the François Vase of ca. 570. The topmost scene (Fig. 0.5), in which Theseus leads the 'twice seven' in what may be read as an anticipatory representation of the 'Crane Dance' performed on the band's escape from the labyrinth, presages future events on another count; behind the figure of the nurse stands a richly dressed Ariadne equipped with the ball of thread that will allow Theseus to find his way out from the maze and that more broadly declares its holder possessed of the skills necessary for her soon-to-occur transition to the marital state.[38] But the presence of the thread also suggests narrower continuities between the maiden and the choral dance occupying much of this frieze; in the accounts of the *geranos* discussed in Chapter 3, the sources style the *chorêgos* the one who 'pulls the crane' (γερανουλκός, Hesch. s.v.) and

---

[37] See below for other rituals where the two activities are combined.
[38] Here I draw on the reading in Hedreen 2011.

mentions of ropes have been found among the Delian inventories, perhaps for the very purpose of pulling the line of dancers in some way or another. Plutarch's description of the motions of that Delian chorus includes the term ἀνελίξεις (*Thes.* 21.2), literally an unrolling or motion in reverse that evokes both circularity and the unspooling of the thread or wool already rolled up by the spinner around the distaff; Pherecydes uses it in precisely this way in *FGrH* 3 F 148.[39] For some ancient sources, and modern interpreters too, the movements of the dance were designed to evoke the twists and turns of the labyrinth, whose winding passages the escapees negotiated by virtue of the thread spun by Ariadne.[40]

Also proposing connections between the skein of wool, here configured rather differently, and the choral performance is the Polledrara hydria cited in Chapter 3, a vase found at the Grotta of Isis at Vulci and dated to ca. 575–550 (Fig. 7.7).[41] On the upper frieze, Ariadne, who watches Theseus' struggle with the Minotaur, lifts up her all-enveloping (future) bridal mantle with one hand while in the other she holds not the more usual ball of thread, but a thick cord (itself a woven object) which touches the ground at Theseus' left foot before twisting upwards between the monster's limbs. This cord reappears on the lower frieze, again associated with Ariadne, who holds it up in her hand. To her left is a chorus of six female figures (Fig. 7.8), moving towards the right and headed by a lyre-carrying figure, Theseus again.

Fig. 7.7 Polledrara hydria, ca. 575–550 B.C.E. Upper register. London, British Museum 1850, 0227.50. From C. Smith, 'Polledrara Ware', *JHS* 14 (1894): pl. 7.

---

[39] See the discussion of the *skutalê* in Chapter 8. Euripides' Electra chooses the verb in uncompounded form when directing the chorus of maidens to 'turn back' their foot and return the way they came: πάλιν ἀνὰ πόδα σὸν εἰλίξεις / μεθεμένα κτύπου (*Or.* 171–72). Since elsewhere Euripides applies the term expressly to choral dancing, and κτύπος can refer to the beat of the dancers' feet, it seems likely that Electra is telling the choreutes to perform their same dance steps in reverse.

[40] It is Plutarch again who explains the *geranos* as an 'imitation of the goings around and pathways of the labyrinth' (μίμημα τῶν ἐν τῷ Λαβυρίνθῳ περιόδων καὶ διεξόδων ἔν τινι ῥυθμῷ, *Thes.* 21.1).

[41] London, British Museum 1850.0227.50 with discussion in Smith 1894.

Fig. 7.8 Polledrara hydria, ca. 575–550 B.C.E. Lower register. London, British Museum 1850, 0227.50. From C. Smith, 'Polledrara Ware', *JHS* 14 (1894): pl. 7.

The scholion to the description of the dance on Achilles' shield band confirms the relevance of textile production to these scenes: as noted in earlier chapters, Theseus 'weaves' his chorus of fourteen into the *geranos* dance (Σ AB *ad* Hom. *Il.* 18.590). Mapping this comment onto the scenes on the vases, the hero becomes the one who realizes the practice for which Ariadne's thread is intended, creating a textile of dancers. Indeed, the scholiast's remark places weaving at the foundational moment of choral dance: it was on this very occasion that Daedalus first 'devised the craft of *choreia* . . . and showed it to the dancers'. It is not only that, as Power notes, the legendary craftsman has turned choreographer;[42] taking his cue from Daedalus, Theseus also particularizes the sculptor-builder's originary 'poietic' act with his pattern-weaving and in so doing supplies the model for Hephaestus, who then interweaves a chorus on the shield band.

The earliest extant representation of Theseus' confrontation with the Minotaur, on a Cycladic relief pithos of ca. 650 in Basel,[43] already presents the yarn as 'determinant' of the subsequent choral perform-ance. On the neck of the jar, Theseus, accompanied by two boys and three girls, confronts the monstrous quadruped. All members of the group carry rocks in one raised hand while grasping with the other the thread or rope linking them together;[44] holding onto the means by which they will make it safely out of the maze and whose circuitous course their movement on the pithos observes, they 'rehearse' the victory dance that immediately follows their emergence. Already here, and then in reperforming the maze's twists and turns in the *geranos*, the 'twice seven' activate both meanings of the bivalent term *choros* as it appears in *Il.* 18.590 and 603; even as they turn the space of the labyrinth into the floor of the dance (*choros*), they realize their nature

---

[42] Power 2011, 80–81.   [43] Basel, Antikenmuseum BS 617.
[44] For dancers linked together by a waist-level rope, see Chapter 3.

as a troupe of dancers, also styled a *choros*. As Indra McEwen remarks, 'the dancing floor seems to emerge with the dancing of the youths and maidens',[45] whose alternating circular and linear steps preserve variegation while imposing order and regularity on what was random and heterogeneous before – precisely the transformation, as numerous examples in this chapter will exemplify, that *choreia* and weaving bring about both separately and in tandem. The same circles and rectilinear movements featured in the *geranos* appear in visual depictions of the Cretan maze from antiquity through to the Renaissance and in later garden design: whereas the textual sources stress the labyrinth's indecipherability, the absence of coherent shape or discernible morphology, artists render the structure as a series of regular squares, or as concentric rings, one fitted within the other.[46] These shapes exactly match the two choreographic sequences assigned by the Iliadic poet to his (*geranos*?) dancing chorus on Achilles' shield.[47]

Back on the François Vase, Ariadne is equipped with a second 'signifying' object: the Cretan princess holds a wreath. Appropriate to the frequently garlanded choral dancer, and to the crowning of the victor that Theseus will shortly become, the object also offers additional affirmation of the maiden's role as pattern-weaver: to make a wreath, as the sources cited in Section 2 demonstrate, is to interweave the multiple elements that go into the composition of *choreia*. The artist of an Attic black-figure band cup of ca. 550–540, signed by the potters Archikles and Glaukytes (Fig. 7.9),[48] expresses the mirroring relationship between Ariadne's wreath and the lyre also equipping the chorus-leading Theseus on the François Vase. On the cup, Athena appears immediately behind Theseus as he fights the Minotaur, holding the instrument that the hero must have given her so as to free his hands for the struggle. Lined up behind the goddess are four Athenian maidens and three youths watching the fight, arranged in the same linear formation that they assume on the François Vase of just two decades before; static here, they are nonetheless shown in the manner of a chorus line, first

[45] McEwen 1993, 63.

[46] For examples, see McEwen 1993, 60–61. From the fifth century on, coins from Knossos regularly displayed rectangular, circular and swastika-shaped labyrinths.

[47] The coalescence between group dancing and the labyrinth has a very rich post-classical history; see Greene 2001 for the action of treading a maze in dance as exemplified by the labyrinth dances in Renaissance England and France; Greene's discussion begins by citing the lines spoken by Gonzalo in Shakespeare's *Tempest*, which prove wonderfully apposite to the ancient evidence: 'here's a maze trod indeed through forth-rights and maeanders!'.

[48] Munich, Antikensammlungen 2243; *ABV* 163.2, 160.2; *Para.* 68.

Fig. 7.9 Attic black-figure cup signed by Archikles and Glaukytes, ca. 550–540 B.C.E. Munich, Antikensammlungen 2243. Photograph Renate Kühling © Staatliche Antikensammlungen und Glyptothek München.

girl, then boy, a deployment which, together with the lyre, anticipates the dance they will shortly perform.[49] Also reminiscent of the François Vase is the figure of Ariadne standing immediately behind the monster, in parallel position to Athena; in her outstretched right hand she carries the ball of wool, and in her left a wreath. The artist creates visual affinities not only between the lyre and the ball of wool, but between the goddess and maiden as leaders of their respective 'chorus lines', with Athena acting as stand-in for Theseus. Even as the moving figure of the nurse brings a dancer to mind, Ariadne's wreath signals her potential as *chorêgos* and/or *première danseuse*, invested with the attribute that in both textual and visual accounts distinguishes the maiden who heads the chorus. The accessory, visible again on the black-figure cup from Argos described earlier in this chapter (Fig. 7.6),[50] and which similarly equips the *chorêgos* in Alcman's third *Partheneion* (πυλεῶν' ἔχοισα, 65),

---

[49] While the pose of the nurse, the next in line after Ariadne and shown with knees bent, leaning back and arms upraised, is often read as an indication of excitement and alarm, her configuration also resembles that used for choral dancers on archaic vases; compare the red-figure column krater in the Mannerist style of ca. 500–490 (Basel, Antikenmuseum BS 415), showing six chorus members with their arms and legs in very similar fashion. See too the discussion of 'spectator figures' in Chapters 3 and 10.

[50] Berlin, Antikensammlung F 3993.

may also have a Delian connection. In Lawler's view, the 'great *hormos*, strung with threads of gold, seven cubits long' (*HHAp.* 103–04) promised by Iris to Eileithyia may refer to a Delian 'cult dance in which a large garland, *hormos*, was carried in solemn procession by youths and maidens, alternating in a line'.[51]

The obverse of a black-figure neck amphora from ca. 560 offers a further and particularly emphatic manifestation of the parallelism between the spinner's art and the wreath, both multiplying the motif and, perhaps, gesturing towards the triumphal *geranos* in which the struggle between Theseus and the Minotaur will end.[52] Flanking Theseus and his antagonist, who flees to the right to escape the hero's outstretched sword, are seven maidens, three on one side and four on the other, making up the canonical seven. Replacing the wreaths carried by three of the quartet on the right are the distaffs, whose individual threads form a carefully rendered pattern of criss-crosses that match the hatching on the headdresses worn by the three maidens on the left. Although, again, there is no hint that these 'spectator figures' are engaged in a choral performance, the intricate design of the threads wound about the distaffs anticipates the complex but orderly choreography of the dance, whose execution the maidens 'rehearse' as they twine their wool about the cone-shaped stick.

For both Luca Giuliani and Hedreen,[53] matrimony is very much the underlying message of the scene on the François Vase, a motif taken up – at its later stage – in the depiction of the wedding of Peleus and Thetis on a lower band on the pot. By showing his mastery of the lyre and his leadership and stewardship of *choreia*, Theseus declares himself a suitor while Ariadne responds with a demonstration of her nubility and industry by virtue of her ball of thread. A courtship dance seems similarly to lie behind other early representations of the *geranos*. On the shield of Achilles, dowered brides-to-be dance together with their male wooers in a performance that the poet explicitly links with Ariadne and the myth's Cretan provenance; the invariably equal number of the Athenians whom Theseus escorts, seven of each gender, also suggests this 'pairing off'. Courtship and matrimony likewise inform the so-called 'necklace' dance described by

---

[51] Lawler 1948, 4; cf. Hedreen 2011, 500 and Weiss 2018, 68, who connects this object with the golden chains evoked by Electra (Eur. *El.* 176) in the context of her refusal to join in choral dancing.

[52] Tokyo, Matsuoka Museum of Art 172.

[53] Giuliani 2013, 155–57, 195–96; Hedreen 2011, 498–501.

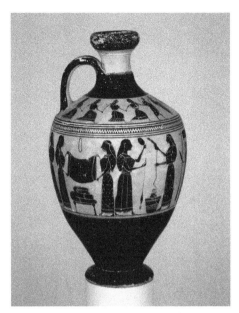

Fig. 7.10 Black-figure lekythos by the Amasis Painter, ca. 550–530 B.C.E. New York, Metropolitan Museum of Art 1931.11.10, Fletcher Fund, 1931. Photograph © The Metropolitan Museum of Art.

Lucian (*Salt.* 12), a circular dance performed by ephebes and maidens in which their respective qualities are 'woven' together (see Section 4). Nonnus echoes the notion when he describes marriage hymns that 'weave the choruses' (χοροπλεκέων ὑμεναίων, *Dionys.* 6.49).

Our most complete pictorial account of wool-working and weaving techniques appears on a well-known vase by the Amasis Painter of ca. 550–530 (Fig. 7.10).[54] On the body of the diminutive lekythos the artist shows nine women engaged in a variety of tasks: three weigh out the wool while a second group of four spins it into yarn. In a dominating position at the centre of the representation, two women work at a very large upright loom, passing the shuttle through the threads. On the shoulder of the vase, we witness the sphere for which this cloth-in-production is directed and the object that results from the collective labours of the group below: here a bride dressed in a peplos and seated on a throne displays the nuptial mantle in the 'bridal gesture' while holding out a wreath; on either side and approaching the newly married figure are two groups of four made up of her former companions – at the loom as well as

---

[54] New York, Metropolitan Museum of Art 1931.11.10; *ABV* 154.57, 688; *Para.* 64.

Fig. 7.11 Black-figure lekythos by the Amasis Painter, ca. 550–530 B.C.E. New York, Metropolitan Museum of Art 1956.11.1, Purchase Walter C. Baker Gift, 1956. Photograph © The Metropolitan Museum of Art.

in the chorus – who dance with linked hands. Numerical parity reinforces the continuities between the scenes on the lekythos' body and shoulder: nine women down below, and now, following the loss of the erstwhile member of their chorus and perhaps, *chorêgos*, four and four dancers plus one bride.

Steven Lonsdale compares the lekythos to a second vessel by the Amasis Painter found together with it, identical in shape and size, and with a decorative scheme similarly divided between the shoulder and the body (Fig. 7.11).[55] As on the weaving vase, this companion piece exhibits in the upper register a scene of nuptial dancing: nine women, once again divided into two groups, here of three and six, perform a ring dance to the accompaniment of a lyre-player and aulete. The members of the trio place their hands on the wrist of the next dancer in the line, perhaps, in this context, recapping the gesture required of the groom as he claims his new wife. Depicted on the body of the vase is a central moment of the marriage rite as the newly wed pair, seated in a cart and accompanied by two women and a man walking in procession, travel towards the bridegroom's

---

[55] New York, Metropolitan Museum of Art 1956.11.1; *Para.* 66.

home, where his mother waits to receive them. Like the seated figure on
the shoulder of the lekythos with the weaving scene, the bride is veiled and
carries a wreath. As Lonsdale notes, the dances on the shoulder of the first
of the two vessels 'should be seen as a celebration of the presentation of
the wedding dress to the bride as she is about to leave her old status
(represented by the band of maidens making wool) and undergo the
transition to married life depicted on the companion vase', where we
now witness the dances that accompanied the actual matrimonial rite.[56]
While others have documented the central role of textiles in the maiden's
passage into marriage, whether in the form of the cloths included in her
dowry, the blanket spread over the nuptial bed or the garments with
which the bride is decked out and which may then be used as coverlet,[57]
Lonsdale understands the weaving in which the girls participate on the
first lekythos as a signifier of the existence that their companion now
leaves behind.

Other visual accounts offer combinations and juxtapositions of parthenaic choral dances with girls as producers of textiles, both spinners and
weavers – whether in the generic here-and-now, or in the world of myth –
and invite viewers to understand how quickly the young fabric-maker
may turn dancer. A very lovely white-ground phiale of ca. 450 in Boston,
its provenance unknown, integrates wool-working into one such scene
(Fig. 7.12).[58] Circling around the interior of the libation bowl, seven
maidens identically dressed in chitons and pink mantles turn about an
altar while another girl at the head of the line playing the aulos directly
faces the structure. To the right of the altar is a wool basket, positioned
immediately below a ribbon or sash suspended from the border of the
image. Should we read the basket as just an indicator of another occupa-
tion typical of the girls, or does its presence designate their participation
in a different form of 'weaving' – the choral dance which they currently
perform?

As for the ribbon, the article not only points in a general manner to
feminine toilettes, but stands in a much narrower relationship to wool-
working, spinning, weaving and the maidens on the phiale. Even as the
dancers wear fillets in their hair, the loop of the fringed cloth on the wall
reconfigures the more pronounced circles and spirals of the band (or more
probably a strand of yarn) that winds around the upper portion of the

---

[56] Lonsdale 1993, 217–18.
[57] For a particularly detailed exploration, see Scheid and Svenbro 1996, 53–107.
[58] Boston, Museum of Fine Arts 65.908. For more on this image, see below.

Fig. 7.12 White-ground phiale, ca. 450 B.C.E. Interior. Boston, Museum of Fine Arts 65.908, Edwin E. Jack Fund Photograph © 2020, Museum of Fine Arts, Boston.

basket immediately beneath it;[59] the altar with which the basket shares the centrepoint of the dance recapitulates that object's shape, complete with the spiralling curlicues that likewise decorate its topmost element. Diction also reflects the close relations between wool-working, the fillet and the ritual event occurring on the phiale, as indicated by the presence of the altar; according to Pollux 4.116, the *agrênon* refers to the hank of wool that has been carded but not yet spun and that might serve as a votive good or supply the fillets wrapped around sacred objects. The ribbon as an accessory which unites weaving, wreaths and parthenaic choral dancers, and these in a prenuptial context, belongs to the passage in Bacchylides explored in Chapter 5; here the dazzling Nereids witnessed by Theseus *en route* to Crete perform their circle dances adorned with 'fillets interwoven with gold' that 'whirl about' (χρυσεόπλοκοι / δίνηντο ταινίαι, 17.106–07). Just a moment later, these same adornments reappear in the rose-interwoven

---

[59] The *kalathos* is itself a woven object, commonly made out of willow plaited rods; when potters from the Geometric age on reproduced *kalathoi* in clay, they would decorate the vessels with patterns evocative of their woven character, even, on occasion, including triangular perforations that recalled the spaces visible in textiles. For discussion and examples, see Trinkl 2015, 192.

plokon given to the hero by Amphitrite in anticipation of his role as Ariadne's groom; so contextualized, the Nereids' be-ribboned performance becomes a proleptic nuptial dance.

Ferrari's close analysis of vases showing girls engaged in fabric-making identifies another feature of these scenes, alerting us to the distinctions that artists introduce between groups of *parthenoi* and women represented spinning, weaving or carrying the tools of their craft.[60] These include demarcations in pose (who is seated, and who stands), clothing and ornaments; some cloth-makers are more elaborately or richly adorned than their otherwise similar companions, while others signal their status by their centrality, surrounded by those who play the attendant role. An oversized wool basket included on an Attic red-figure pyxis in Athens showing the Nereids adorning the lead member of their company introduces weaving into the context of what turns out to be a hierarchical mythical sorority:[61] while Thetis sits at the centre, mirror in hand, some of her sisters play an also quite prominent role as they approach her holding a variety of accessories for her (bridal?) beautification. Several others of the group are distinguished by more subtle means; some wear mantles over their gowns, others do not. On an early classical Attic red-figure pyxis of ca. 460,[62] whose figures are labelled Helen, Clytemnestra, Cassandra, Iphigenia and Danae, Helen sits with her wool basket at her side while the remainder stand, again carrying items to deck out the bride; the first three wear the chiton and mantle, but the latter two do not. The other figures on the pyxis are unnamed, further indicating their lower position in the stratified group. The white-ground phiale already cited for its combination of a wool basket and parthenaic chorus includes a parallel device for distinguishing between the troupe's older, more expert members and the tyros, here singularized not for their lesser cloth-making skills but for their status as newcomers to the dancing group. Positioned almost at the line's end, two maidens whose hair is still unbound look not at one another like the other pairs, but at the older figure bringing up the rear; occupying the spot sometimes reserved for the *chorêgos*, she can supply the directions these unseasoned choreutes still require.[63]

---

[60] Ferrari 2002, 43–45.   [61] Athens, Ephoria Athinon A 1877.
[62] London, British Museum E 773; ARV^2 805.89.
[63] Connelly 2007, 30. To go further afield, several Etruscan artefacts showing women engaged in spinning and weaving – among them those on the eighth-century Throne of Verucchio and a Daunian stele dated to the seventh to sixth century, where some weavers sit while others stand – suggest similar stratifications. For these, see Gleba 2008, 28 and 30.

This privileging of some members of both weaving and choral ensembles in vase imagery finds its earliest precedent in Homeric epic, and in the figures of Helen and Penelope, both of whom take on the interconnected roles of *chorêgos* and leader/overseer of the perhaps younger and socially inferior members of their cloth-making troupes.[64] Not only do both act as the instigators and lead-off singers of choral laments, to whom the rest of the undifferentiated chorus responds in kind (e.g. *Il.* 24.761, *Od.* 4.715–21), but the poet also more minutely suggests their superior expertise at the spindle and loom: for Helen, in distinction to the rest, the narrator reserves the weaving of the elaborately patterned 'double' (δίπλακα) cloth in *Il.* 3.125–28,[65] while he also equips her, in *Od.* 4.125–35, with a richly decorated silver wool basket, golden distaff and skein of distinctively 'violet-dark' yarn. Theocritus would subsequently elaborate on the epic account; in his *Epithalamium*, detailed in Section 2, it is Helen once again whose superiority depends on her unchallenged star status as both chorus-leader and weaver. Like the Spartan queen, Penelope is also a uniquely skilled practitioner of her craft: it is she alone who seems to fashion (and unequivocally to unravel) the large-scale shroud for Laertes quite independent of her maids. The artist of a much cited mid-fifth-century red-figure skyphos from Chiusi,[66] where a mourning Penelope sits at her weaving in Telemachus' presence, fills out what the Homeric account leaves us to imagine: displayed on the large standing loom complete with loom weights positioned behind her is an elaborately pattern-woven cloth, whose intricate border design, featuring winged horses, a Medusa-like figure and griffins, attests to her expertise.

Also consistent with the morphology of the chorus as delineated by Calame,[67] the maidens engaged in wool-working may be sisters – so the Nereids or the Graces who weave the robe for Aphrodite at *Il.* 5.338 – or companions who belong to the same life stage. In an epigram from the *Greek Anthology* (6.174), the three maidens who dedicate a wool basket, spindle and *kerkis* to Pallas style themselves 'three girls of the same age

---

[64] For Helen as a choregic figure, and most particularly the leader in laments, see Martin 2008 and for her complementary function as director of her maidservants' handiwork, see Karanika 2014, 25–41 and Murnaghan 2018, 170. Murnaghan, whose argument I build on here, then goes on persuasively to apply this typology to Penelope in the *Odyssey*.

[65] Cf. *Od.* 19.241 for a second use of the term; although normally translated 'double-folded', the doubleness could also refer to a technique possibly used by Greek weavers to create a double weave: when the cloth was turned to its other side, both the pattern and its colours would appear in reverse.

[66] Chiusi, Museo Archeologico Nazionale 63.564; *ARV*² 1300.2, 1689; *Para.* 475.

[67] Calame 1997, 21–30.

(τρισσαί ... ἅλικες)', uniting their trio with the term regularly used of members of choral bands; in Pindar's *Pyth.* 3.17, the maidens who sing the wedding song at Coronis' nuptials are likewise ἅλικες and the designation reappears, here applied to the chorus performing on behalf of Aegina, in a textual variant in an ode by Bacchylides (13.89). These groups attend their leader in a variety of activities, among them wool-working, weaving and choral dancing. As Ferrari, drawing together the different elements found in the scenes of textile production, remarks, it is precisely these practices that characterize that category of '*parthenoi aidoiai*, who live together in nymphlike community, sharing simple tasks and pleasures, such as working wool, gathering flowers and making garlands, playing ball, and dancing'. As she also observes, citing the examples of the Charites, Nereids and Calypso with her attendants, 'the mythical thiasos, the band of companion girls all of the same age, also consists of wool-workers'.[68]

Together the visual and textual evidence point to one final element that creates parallels between cloth-makers and choral dancers: their co-location within the same architectural space. As other chapters have demonstrated, the forecourt or *prothuron* of the house or palace supplies a choice site for maiden groups – and youths as well – to dance, a liminal area neither fully in nor out but one that bridges the divide between the private and public spheres. At *Pyth.* 3.77–79, Pindar presents the coeval maidens singing and dancing in celebration of the Mother and Pan in nocturnal performances located 'before the door':

> ἀλλ' ἐπεύξασθαι μὲν ἐγὼν ἐθέλω
> Ματρί, τὰν κοῦραι παρ' ἐμὸν πρόθυρον σὺν
>   Πανὶ μέλπονται θαμά
> σεμνὰν θεὸν ἐννύχιαι.

> But I wish to make a prayer to the Mother, for whom, together with Pan, the girls before my door sing and dance frequently, the venerable goddess, in night time performances.[69]

Also, perhaps, indicative of this same location is a passage in Pindar's second *Pythian*, where the singers elide their current musical celebration of Hieron with the choral tribute paid both by Locrian maidens

---

[68] Ferrari 2002, with citations from 57 and 58.
[69] As usual, the θαμά points to a regularized choral performance in what resembles a *pannychis*.

and, by way of mythical precedent, by the Cyprians to their king
Kinyras (15–19):

κελαδέοντι μὲν ἀμφὶ Κινύραν πολλάκις   15
φᾶμαι Κυπρίων, τὸν ὁ χρυσοχαῖτα προ-
        φρόνως ἐφίλησ’ Ἀπόλλων,

ἱερέα κτίλον Ἀφροδίτας· ἄγει δὲ χάρις
        φίλων ποί τινος ἀντὶ ἔργων ὀπιζομένα·
σὲ δ’, ὦ Δεινομένειε παῖ, Ζεφυρία πρὸ δόμων
Λοκρὶς παρθένος ἀπύει,

The voices of the Cyprians frequently celebrate Kinyras, whom golden-
haired Apollo eagerly loved, the priestly darling of Aphrodite, for grace
with reverence goes forth in some way in return for someone’s dear deeds.
But you, o son of Deinomenes, the *parthenos* of Western Locri invokes in
front of her house ...

An ambiguity – perhaps deliberate – surrounds both the maiden and
the location of her performance. Bruno Currie’s meticulous discussion
offers three possible interpretations for this enigmatic Locrian girl: the
account ‘may refer to a single maiden before her house. Or, as a
collective singular, it may refer to individual maidens, each before
her house. Or, again, it may as a collective singular refer to a chorus
of maidens at one location’.[70] Drawing attention to the passage’s use
of diction reminiscent of the description of the Cyprian chorus in the
preceding antistrophe, Currie concludes that the solitary *parthenos*
should be understood as a stand-in for the larger choral ensemble.
As for the performance space, is this ‘house’ a private home in front of
which the Locrian maidens sing or a public temple? Angela Bellia
prefers the second site, connecting the Pindaric account to a cult
involving young girls and attested at Locri at the sanctuary of
Centocamere, which dates from the end of seventh century;[71] other
sources indicate a more domestic context: Hephaestus already fashions
maidens who sing nuptial songs, having perhaps issued from the forecourt
of their houses on Achilles’ shield (*Il.* 18.490–96). By blurring distinctions
between the home and sacred space, Pindar, typically, suggests a variety

[70] Currie 2005, 268–72. This last suggestion follows the lead of a scholion to the lines, which
    already recognizes in the maiden singing solo the community of Locrian *parthenoi*.
[71] Bellia 2012, 83–91.

Fig. 7.13 Attic red-figure pyxis by the Painter of the Louvre Centauromachy, ca. 475–425 B.C.E. Paris, Musée du Louvre CA 587. Photograph © RMN-Grand Palais/Les frères Chuzeville.

of venues for the (re)performance of his choral song, which models itself on these more regular and venerable renditions.[72]

Visual accounts no less frequently position weaving and other tasks involved in cloth production in the domestic forecourt. As recent studies argue, these activities went on not, as previously believed, within the secluded quarters and women's chambers of the home, but in its portico, the *prothuron*, as indicated by the presence of columns or other indications of spatial location in the images. A red-figure pyxis by the Painter of the Louvre Centauromachy dated ca. 475–425 shows two women with a distaff and handloom (Fig. 7.13);[73] standing next to the open door of the bedchamber, they perform their tasks in the courtyard outside. The same arrangement occurs on a second pyxis by the Phiale Painter, where a woman spins together with a second figure equipped with an alabastron and small chest;[74] here too the open *thalamos* door through which a

---

[72] Cf. the reference to an epinician sung 'before the house (προδόμοις)' at Bacch. 6.14–15. The location indicated could be the temple of Zeus in Olympia or a reperformance at the victor's home.

[73] Paris, Musée du Louvre CA 587; *ARV*[2] 1094, 1682; *Para.* 449.

[74] Vienna, Kunsthistorisches Museum 3719. For these and the examples that follow, see Bundrick 2008, esp. 314.

couch is visible locates our spinner outside the home, while the handloom present in the scene indicates the next step in the cloth production, the weaving of the new-spun thread into fabric. On the New York pyxis by the Painter of Philadelphia 2449,[75] columns, which may separate the portico from the courtyard, situate the six women, including one carding wool, in the exterior space, and two columns similarly demarcate a portico on a hydria by the Leningrad Painter, which includes two seated spinners among the five shown.[76] Excavations of private houses at Olynthos, which have unearthed the presence of holes for loom posts together with loomweights on the floor of the courtyard, the *aulê* (or *pastas*, as it was frequently designated) of several homes, including some sixteen from the forecourt of one of the houses, confirm that weaving occurred in these spaces.[77] Practical considerations determined the site: weavers required a good source of light and an outdoor area would provide the necessary illumination.

The phiale in Boston previously cited for its depiction of a round dance and the wool basket in the scene offers our best evidence for the confluence of choral dancing and wool-working in the portico, and the significance of the activities' spatial correspondence. While the column and altar could position the dancers in a public area, the wool basket and hanging ribbon suggest a more private walled enclosure where textile production takes place.[78] This transitional site exactly suits these maiden dancers' betwixt-and-between status: still *parthenoi*, they, or one of their group, is about to quit the domestic setting and enter into matrimony following this halfway exposure to the public view. No wonder that, as the example of Aegina in Pindar's sixth *Paean* illustrates,[79] abduction (perhaps, in this and other instances, from the chorus in which the maiden dances) frequently occurs precisely in this liminal location.

2 *Choreia* and Weaving in Textual Accounts: Genre, Diction and Imagery

Textual sources contemporary with the images just reviewed offer some-times matching, sometimes very different reflections of affinities between choral performances and textiles. My discussion of just some of the

---

[75] New York, Metropolitan Museum of Art 06.1117; *ARV²* 815.3.

[76] San Simeon, Hearst Collection 529.63; *ARV²* 571.81.

[77] See Cahill 2002, 74–193 for this and other houses.   [78] Ferrari 2002, 43.   [79] See Chapter 5.

examples from the archaic and early classical period falls broadly into three parts. First, most simply, I present several (far from all) passages juxtaposing or combining weaving and choral dancing in much the manner of the vases and which variously express the continuities between the two practices. Part two explores the commonplace and all but hackneyed confluence between weaving and poetic composition, and textiles and finished songs in the imagery of archaic and early classical poetry, and seeks to locate the generic underpinnings of the conceit with close readings of two scenes in Homeric epic. In part three, I further detail the diction common to both *choreia* and cloth-making in passages from the lyric and dramatic repertoires, with a particular focus on terms that belong simultaneously to the design of lyres and looms and those that describe processes and techniques used both to create textiles and to compose and perform choral poetry; as several more extended passages from the choral poets who exploit these overlaps demonstrate, their works employ the polysemous vocabulary so as to articulate both the nature and properties of their compositions and to figure an ongoing song and dance in the likeness of a broad variety of woven goods, from clothing to garlands, patterned sandals to baskets and braided hair.

2.1   Weavers Are Also Choral Dancers

Just as vase painters represent choristers and weavers or spinners in scenes placed in proximity with one another on the surface of the pot, or include briefer references to wool and cloth-making in images of choral dancing, so poets present the two activities in tandem or link them more narrowly through diction repeated from one passage to the next. In straightforward fashion, and famously, Aristophanes' *Lysistrata* gives weaving and membership of a chorus joint star billing when the *chorêgos* cites first one, and then the other, in the course of listing the various ritual roles that girls and women fulfill in Athenian cult practices (641–46): mention of Brauron, where girls participated in dancing and racing in celebrations of Artemis, comes hard on the heels of service at the Arrhephoria, in which sequestered girls wove the sacred peplos for Athena each year.[80]

Intersections between weaving and *choreia* are also commonplace in Euripides. In the first stasimon of the *Hecuba*, the captive Trojan chorus maps its identity onto that of the ensemble of Deliades, the perennial

---

[80]   The two activities – specifically the weaving a sacred garment for a deity, Hera here, and dancing in choruses – recur at the festival for Hera at Elis, detailed in Section 4.

celebrants of Apollo and Artemis in dance and song, in a wish that it might hymn the goddess in concert with these 'Delian maidens' (463–64). The stanza that immediately follows proposes a second no less desirable scenario, that of an encounter with the young girls in the service of Pallas Athena prior to the Panathenaia, and anticipates the choristers' co-participation in the Arrhephoria that preceded the celebration of the event (466–72):

> ἢ Παλλάδος ἐν πόλει
> τὰς καλλιδίφρους Ἀθα-
>   ναίας ἐν κροκέῳ πέπλῳ
> ζεύξομαι ἆρα πώ-
>   λους ἐν δαιδαλέαισι ποι-   470
>   κίλλουσ᾽ ἀνθοκρόκοισι πή-
>   ναις ἢ Τιτάνων γενεάν,

Or shall I after all in the city of Pallas pattern-weave colts yoked to beautiful chariots into the saffron peplos of Athena or [am I to weave] with variegated flower-coloured spun threads the race of Titans …

As Stieber notes,[81] Talthybius' choice then to address the chorus as *korai* (485), for all these womens' widowed state, is not so much 'belittling' as an acknowledgement of their self-projection onto the still maidenly figures of weavers and dancers. The dramatist uses this same framework for a passage in the *IT* where Iphigenia, narrating her past history, refers again to serving Pallas Athena *qua* weaver, this time in conjunction with a second festival, the Heraia celebrated at Argos with its maiden choruses, whose leadership the heroine would naturally assume (see Chapters 4 and 5, with Eur. *El.* 171–80). Contrasted with this is the distorted form of *choreia* over which Iphigenia must now preside, here closely combined with her loss of her status as weaver (221–28):

> οὐ τὰν Ἄργει μέλπουσ᾽ Ἥραν
> οὐδ᾽ ἱστοῖς ἐν καλλιφθόγγοις
> κερκίδι Παλλάδος Ἀτθίδος εἰκὼ
> <καὶ> Τιτάνων ποικίλλουσ᾽, ἀλλ᾽
> †αἱμορράντων δυσφόρμιγγα   225
> ξείνων αἱμάσσουσ᾽ ἄταν βωμοὺς†
> οἰκτράν τ᾽ αἰαζόντων αὐδὰν
> οἰκτρόν τ᾽ ἐκβαλλόντων δάκρυον.

---

[81] Stieber 2011, 322.

> I do not sing in honour of Hera at Argos nor pattern-weave with my *kerkis*[82] on the fair-voiced looms the likeness of Attic Pallas and of the Titans; no, rather, bloodying the altar, I inflict a blood-besprinkled death on many strangers, a death unfit for the lyre, who wail with piteous voice while casting out their piteous tear.

Both diction and imagery bring out the parallels between the two forms of service: the singing of the celebrant leading her choral company is echoed by the 'fair voice' of the looms, as though these objects were participating in their own form of melodic offering. Both are activities performed as part of larger ensembles – the looms are plural – whose joyous sound stands in opposition to the singular, discordant and mournful voice of the victim of the rites now practiced by Iphigenia, currently displaced from her proper ritual choregic and weaving roles and in a distant land. More implicit in the passage, I suggest, is the familiar equivalence between the loom and lyre and the more particular alignment of the *kerkis* and plectrum, implements that are both used to pluck or strum the threads of their respective objects and that generate a twanging sound;[83] absent the loom, the lyre that produces concordant song has also gone missing.

The *Bacchae* reverses the usual tight relations between weaving and choral performance, with the emphasis on dancing here, and positions the latter, in the inverted world of extra-urban Dionysiac cult, as the antithesis to working the loom. As they perform the parodos, the maenadic choreutes imagine the whole Theban land set a-dancing as its population follows the example of the women who have abandoned the city and specifically their looms (114–19):

> αὐτίκα γᾶ πᾶσα χορεύσει,
> Βρόμιος εὖτ' ἂν ἄγῃ θιάσους   115
> εἰς ὄρος εἰς ὄρος, ἔνθα μένει
> θηλυγενὴς ὄχλος
> ἀφ' ἱστῶν παρὰ κερκίδων τ'
> οἰστρηθεὶς Διονύσῳ.

[82] This term is regularly, and erroneously, translated as 'shuttle'. The shuttle is properly the object that carries the weft wound about it (three such 'bobbins' are visible on the Amasis lekythos with the large-scale loom) and is passed through the warp threads. The *kerkis* is, in modern terminology, the 'pin beater' or 'weaving pin', whose original shape and size in Greece remain largely unknown, and which has several different functions. It beats the weft upward into place or 'strums' the warp in order to even out the weaving. For detailed discussion, see Barber 1991, 273–74 and Edmunds 2012, who modifies Barber on several points. I owe a major debt of gratitude to Susan Edmunds, who corrected me on this and several other technical points, and who kindly demonstrated how to weave on her reconstructions of a warp-weighted loom.

[83] See Barber 1991, 273. I return to the 'tuneful' *kerkis* later in the chapter.

> Straightaway the whole land will dance in choruses whenever Bromios leads the *thiasos* to the mountains, to the mountains, where waits the female throng having quit the loom and the pin beater under Dionysus' goad.

But perhaps the choruses' estrangement is not as complete as the statement would suggest; on the mountain, the Bacchants engage in a 'natural' form of weaving that shuns technological devices and requires only the action of the hands: among the 'pleasant *ponoi*' they perform, according to the messenger's report at 1053–55, is the restoration of the decoration that 'wreathes' or 'crowns' (ἐξαναστέφω) their depleted *thyrsoi*, a task that involves re-garlanding the staff with foliage. As though the glance to the wreath necessarily carried in its wake a reference to *choreia*, the dramatist no sooner visualizes the re-weaving than we witness the group singing a cult song in antiphonal fashion (βακχεῖον ἀντέκλαζον ἀλλήλαις μέλος, 1057).

The relations between choral activity and weaving acquire particular intricacy in the last Euripidean example cited here. Appropriately enough, in a drama where textiles play so critical a role, the dramatist introduces the motif already in the parodos of the *Ion*, where the chorus of maidens processes onto the stage while describing the wondrous sight that it encounters on its visit to Delphi. Among the scenes on the metopes at which the singers marvel is a depiction of Heracles lopping off the Hydra's head, an exploit with which they are already familiar from having told it 'in my threads' (παρὰ πήναις, 197); the reference must be either to storytelling while weaving or, more likely, to the portrayal of the hero's feat in a story-cloth (perhaps woven into the fabric even as the myth was being told). Assuming the second scenario, that figured textile becomes the substance of the choral performance witnessed by the theatregoers, a cloth now rewoven by the dancers through their steps, gestures and poses. In the subsequent description of the Gigantomachy that follows the chorus' recognition of Athena on another metope, the intersection between a cloth, a mythological event and the song and dance currently being staged continues: there is no knowing whether the girls now are viewing two different metopes, one displaying the goddess, the other the battle between the gods and Giants, or whether they still look at Athena, whose peplos was patterned with the story of the battle between gods and Giants, a second woven fabric now vocalized in choral fashion.[84]

---

[84] A further reference to working the loom occurs in the epode of the first stasimon, again combined with storytelling (507); cf. *IA* 788–90 for the same conjunction.

These poetic associations are well-grounded in the ritual occasions familiar to the dramas' audiences. Festivals celebrating a variety of deities featured both weaving and/or the presentation of textiles and choral dancing in their ritual events. Fr. 66 Pf. from Callimachus' *Aetia*, discussed in Chapters 4 and 5, describes how in Argos the maidens who are to weave the robe for Hera must first purify themselves by bathing in the waters of Amymone; dancing choruses formed part of the celebration of the goddess in the festival at her central Argolid sanctuary, the Heraion. We owe to Pausanias (3.16.2) the only information we have concerning the weaving of a robe for Apollo as a ritual element at the Hyakinthia at Amyklai in Sparta; in his report, the townswomen wove a tunic for the god in a special room, called the Chiton, set aside for the task. Calame suggests a location in or near the sanctuary of Hilaeira and Phoebe, and proposes that the garment was brought to Amyklai during the procession from Sparta to the sanctuary.[85] Chapter 3 already detailed the prominence of choral dancing, including performances by young girls, at the festival, and the running races included at the event.

Nor do the two activities rub shoulders uniquely in Attic drama and in cult. Offering a more drawn-out and self-conscious demonstration of the overlap, the maiden chorus celebrating Helen in Theocritus' *Epithalamium* singles out two accomplishments of the bride-to-be for special mention: even as the dancers are performing a prenuptial dance with 'interwoven feet' (ποσσὶ περιπλέκτοις, *Id.* 18.8), they praise Helen as both cloth-maker and, I suggest, their erstwhile *chorêgos*, musician and lead-singer both (32–37):

> οὐδέ τις ἐκ ταλάρω πανίσδεται ἔργα τοιαῦτα,
> οὐδ' ἐνὶ δαιδαλέῳ πυκινώτερον ἄτριον ἱστῷ
> κερκίδι συμπλέξασα μακρῶν ἔταμ' ἐκ κελεόντων.
> οὐ μὰν οὐδὲ λύραν τις ἐπίσταται ὧδε κροτῆσαι   35
> Ἄρτεμιν ἀείδοισα καὶ εὐρύστερνον Ἀθάναν
> ὡς Ἑλένα,

none from her basket winds off such yarn as she, nor at her patterned loom interweaves with her *kerkis* and cuts from the tall loom-beams a closer weft. Nor yet is any so skilled as Helen to strike the lyre and hymn Artemis and broad-breasted Athena ...

---

[85] Calame 1997, 172.

While the reference may be to Helen singing her hymn in monodic fashion, the sequence of images suggests a choral performance: first the intricate weaving patterns described by the chorus' footwork, then Helen's excellence at the loom, where she fashions a tight-woven cloth, and in final position, her primacy in 'striking' the lyre, an action that equates her with the weaver who strums the warp threads into place with her pin beater, thereby similarly generating sound.[86] The account of Helen as weaver and lyre-player thus stands as counterpart to the ongoing 'woven' performance; as the bride makes her cloth, so do the maidens interweave their *choreia*; they are both choral dancers and the weaving attendants to their leader's song whose cloth production they re-enact.

With his choice of the verb κροτέω, Theocritus not only looks to the gestures and musicality that weaving and lyre-playing share, but still further narrows the gap between the attendants' performance and the actions of their *laudanda*: Pindar's fr. 194 S.-M., treated in the subsequent section, uses the expression to figure the song and dance in performance as arising from an act of manufacture, and in fourth-century sources, the compound συγκροτέω describes the *chorêgos* charged with 'welding together' his troupe.[87] The recherché expression πηνίζομαι, to wind off a reel for the woof, also promotes the actions' complementarity: it evokes the performers' circling motions as they follow the choreographic-cum-musical cues of the lead-musician's weaving implements turned lyre. And should his audience have missed the motif, Theocritus sounds it again in the singers' glance to a second action: previewing the celebration on the following day, they describe how they will gather 'woven' (πλέξασαι, 44) garlands to honour the bride.

2.2   The 'Web of Song' and Its Generic Milieu

In an influential discussion of the conceit of the 'web of song' so commonplace in texts from the archaic period on, Jane Snyder grounds the image chiefly in the affinity between the lyre and loom visible in the passage from Theocritus' *Epithalamium* just cited.[88] As she spells out the analogy, just as the loom consisted of a large upright device with two posts and a crossbar

---

[86]   The privileging of the *kerkis* in this and other passages already cited is a further nod to Helen's outstanding skill. As Edmunds 2012 comments, no other aspect of weaving seems to require so much expertise as that of 'placing the weft across the warp so that it is neither too tight nor too loose', mistakes that the correct manipulation of the pin beater can prevent. It is the beating in of the weft, and the pin beater's use in separating and combining the threads, that sets the skilled weaver apart and distinguishes her cloth from that of lesser fabricants.

[87]   See Chapter 1, and the discussion in 7.2.2.   [88]   Snyder 1981, 194–95.

to which the warp threads were attached, so the lyre included two arms and a crossbar from which the strings were similarly suspended. Vase representations and particularly images of handlooms, whose spoon-like shape so closely resembles that of the hand-held instrument, bring out the resemblance, and texts register the correspondence too. This loom-harp kinship may inform Critias' commemoration of Anacreon, so regularly imagined as a player on the stringed barbiton, as the individual 'once weaving songs of womanly melodies' (γυναικείων μελέων πλέξαντά ποτ' ᾠδάς, Athen. 13.600d = *PMG* 500). The image would, at once, bring to mind the poet's composition of his songs and, perhaps, exploiting the twofold meaning of μέλος, both song and limb, celebrate him as *chorêgos*, the one whose music and melodies wove women's limbs into the dance.

Before detailing further examples of such overlaps between weaving and song-making, some grounded in similarities in the function and design of the tools required, many reflected in the diction shared by the two activities, I would suggest reframing Snyder's account. In her view, and that of many other scholars, the notion of weaving the woven composition dates back to hexameter epic and, beyond that, to the Indo-European tradition informing it, where the poet *qua* weaver and his textile song already appear.[89] The *locus classicus* is, of course, the moment in *Iliad* 3 when we first encounter Helen as she works at her loom, creating a sumptuous purple double-sided cloth that exactly mirrors, in diction as well as subject matter, what the bard is simultaneously narrating; so 3.127 (Τρώων θ' ἱπποδάμων καὶ Ἀχαιῶν χαλκοχιτώνων), which describes the figures whom Helen pattern-weaves into her web, is identical to 131, where the poet incorporates into his song the contents of Iris' report concerning the ongoing conflict on the battlefield. But, this possible stumbling block aside,[90] I propose that the song-as-textile conceit more properly belongs to choral lyric, and this on several counts. Not only, as I argue, does archaic epic, in contrast to choral lyric, where the analogy becomes a virtual cliché, never refer directly to the web of song, but it is the properties distinctive of choral poetry, and the very features that demarcate it from monody, that explain why the 'web of song' finds its more natural home in this particular genre.[91]

---

[89] See Tuck 2006, 545 for examples and older bibliography.

[90] As already noted, Helen can be read as fulfilling the role of chorus-leader; for more on this, see Chapter 9.

[91] More narrowly, where Snyder 1981 makes the lyre-loom equivalence fundamental to her account, the song-fabric correspondence is not exclusive to compositions accompanied by stringed instruments, but is no less commonly found in works danced and sung to the pipes. As examples later in the discussion demonstrate, the sources also imagine the aulos as both a woven object and a weaver.

An observation made by John Scheid and Jesper Svenbro offers an entry point into understanding why choral productions seem so largely to monopolize weaving imagery.[92] As they note, distinctions exist between cloth-making as a figure deployed in epic and in the later lyric poets, and more particularly between the linguistic expressions privileged by composers in each of the two genres. While Homer regularly uses ὑφαίνω to describe the fashioning of subtle words, plans and tricks, neither he nor Hesiod has recourse to the term when referring to poetic composition and performance, nor exploits a possible or supposed etymological link between ὑφαίνω and the ὕμνος on which lyric sources like to play (e.g. Pind. *Ol.* 1.8 considered below and, more unmistakably, Bacch. fr. 5.9–10, ὑφάνας / ὕμνον). Moreover, when epic song does configure itself as a textile, it looks to a later stage in cloth production, the stitching that occurs with the already completed fabrics. So fr. 357 M.-W. of [Hesiod] refers to *aoidoi* as those 'stitching a song in new *hymnoi*' (ἐν νεαροῖς ὕμνοις ῥάψαντες ἀοιδήν), a representation taken up by Pindar in *Nem.* 2.2, where he names the epic-singing Homeridae the ῥαπτῶν ἐπέων ... ἀοιδοί.

In contrast to this, choral composers not only repeatedly introduce the singer-weaver image and devise any number of metaphors that extend and ring variations on the analogy, but generally (although there are exceptions to the rule) favour πλέκω and its cognates over ὑφαίνω. As Scheid and Svenbro pinpoint the difference between the verbs, the latter is the unmarked term, while the former more particularly describes the process of 'interweaving' (what I have been calling 'pattern-weaving') and plaiting, and highlights the combination of different elements so as to generate a complex, variegated product.[93] The choral performance, whose conjunction of music, song, dance and its multiple participants distinguishes it from monodic song, seems a prime candidate for the processes evoked by πλέκω. A second technological image, which choral lyric also presses into service, turns out similarly to be drawn from weaving: at *Pyth.* 3.113–14, Pindar speaks of 'words that ring out, such as skilled craftsmen joined' (τέκτονες ... ἅρμοσαν) and more unequivocally linked to the choral performance is the statement at *Nem.* 3.4–5: here these same *tektones* are fabricants of the sweet-voiced *kômos*. The root *teks from which *tektôn* and cognate

---

[92] Scheid and Svenbro 1996, 114–19.   [93] Scheid and Svenbro 1996, 118 with their n. 26.

terms are derived, and also of Indo-European origin, means not just to
'construct' but also to 'weave'.[94]

But in emphasizing the distinction between epic and lyric song, Scheid
and Svenbro bypass the two passages in the Homeric poems that, para-
doxically, may already support their argument. The opening of this
chapter cited the first of these, noting the Iliadic poet's choice of
ποικίλλω to describe the forging of the shield band showing the dancing
chorus. While Frontisi-Ducroux well observes that the term calls attention to the special quality of this image, whose interplay of light and
motion creates the variegation and changeability that the adjective
ποικίλος describes, and which gives to the tableau its surpassing dazzle
and luminosity,[95] there may be a simpler explanation: determining the
verb's selection is the subject of the representation, the choral performance complete with dancers and the musician in their midst,[96] that is
already conceived of as a woven object.

The equivalence would be readily comprehensible to an archaic
audience: just as the motifs, objects of representation and band divisions used on early pottery seem, in part, to take their impetus from
textiles, so there is a mutual give-and-take between the decoration,
both figurative and non-figurative, of metal goods and those on cloths,
which introduce the designs that are visible on contemporary and
earlier shield bands, jewelry and other metallic artefacts.
Metalworkers are also the borrowers here, incorporating scenes from
the woven cloths and picturing individuals dressed in patterned garments into their figural scenes.[97]

As Nagy points out,[98] ritual practices in several parts of Greece also
variously united textile production and forging: the weaving of the
patterned peplos for Athena – a practice, he argues, already familiar to
the Homeric poet – began at the Chalkeia, a festival that celebrated the
master-forger Hephaestus and Athena, the goddess who presides over

[94] See Woodard 2014, 230. Among the derivates he cites are the Latin *texo*, 'to weave, plait' and High German *dehsen*, 'to beat flax' and *dehse*, 'spindle'. Note the tradition, mentioned by Pausanias at 10.5.10 concerning the second temple of Apollo at Delphi, 'interwoven (διεπλέξαντο)' by its builders out of fern stalks.
[95] Frontisi-Ducroux 2002, 465.
[96] Here I follow Revermann 1998, with Nagy 2010a, 300 n. 87, in retaining the presence of the bard in 604–05.
[97] E.g. the rosettes so common on decorative golden goods dating to the eighth century, and the mid-sixth-century shield band from Olympia where Athena, shown helping Perseus slay Medusa, wears a pattern-woven garment (Olympia, Museum at Olympia B 975).
[98] Nagy 2010a, 291–93.

Fig. 7.14 Late seventh-century Etruscan bronze tintinnabulum. Bologna, Arsenale Militare, Tomba degli Ori. Photograph courtesy of Museo Civico Archeologico, Bologna.

the weaver's craft, while the Gigantomachy woven on that cloth (at *Euthphr.* 6b–c Plato uses the term καταποικίλλω for the technique used to produce the scene) is the mythological event that Pheidias selects as decoration for the gold-overlaid bronze shield of Athena. No surprise, then, that in Euripides' *Electra*, the Argive chorus participating in the Heraia – a festival where the goddess received a ritually woven peplos, choruses performed (see *El.* 171–80, noted above) and athletes won shields of bronze – chooses to relate the tale of Achilles' divinely forged shield that Thetis presented to her son on his departure for Troy (432–86). Beyond the Greek mainland, metalworking and textiles coincide on the late seventh-century tintinnabulum found in a tomb in Bologna's Arsenale Militare (Fig. 7.14).[99] Made up of two bronze sheets joined at their edges, each side displays two scenes in which women variously prepare the distaffs to spin and weave the finished thread; with its repoussé technique, the rattle's surface is itself suggestive of the design on the garments worn by the several figures and that the cloth they prepare may reproduce.

A series of vase images cited by Nagy in service of a different argument proves freshly relevant to the woven character of the shield and to

---

[99] Bologna, Museo Civico Archeologico.

Fig. 7.15 Attic black-figure hydria attributed to the Tyrrhenian Group, ca. 575–550 B.C.E. Paris, Musée du Louvre E 869. Photograph © RMN-Grand Palais/Les frères Chuzeville.

Hephaestus' metal-weaving.[100] On an Attic black-figure column krater in Berlin attributed to the Painter of London B 76 from ca. 575–525,[101] Achilles receives his arms from Thetis; behind the goddess stand two Nereids, similarly clothed in elaborate pattern-woven garments and carrying garlands. Even as the decorations on the nymphs' skirts recapitulate the ornamental border on the shield, which overlaps and meshes with the topmost area of Thetis' garment, so the wreaths recall the floral motif at the shield's centrepoint. Still more pronounced is the continuity between the garland and shield on an Attic black-figure hydria attributed to the Tyrrhenian Group dated to the same period and similarly showing the new panoply's delivery (Fig. 7.15):[102] on this occasion Thetis carries both the wreath and shield, while two Nereids holding other pieces of armour follow after her. There is no mistaking the similarity between the two objects that the goddess gives her son; the garland complete with flowers is positioned immediately above the shield, whose shape mirrors, on a larger scale, that of the circlet. As on the Berlin bowl, the armour's design also stands in close relation to the woven fabrics worn by the several female figures. The

[100] Nagy 2010a, 293–95.   [101] Berlin, Antikensammlung 3763; *ABV* 87.17, *Para.* 32.
[102] Paris, Musée du Louvre E 869; *ABV* 106.2, *Para.* 43.

colouration of the boss matches Thetis' skirt while the shield's decorative rim, painted in black with white circles outlined in black, replicates the borders of the skirts worn by the two Nereids: these too are black with white tracery. Like the garments, the prominently placed wreath results from a process of interweaving, whereby the floral elements and foliage are plaited or intertwined, or, in the words of an Iliadic scholion, 'wound up together' (συνεστραμμένας).[103]

The second Homeric instance of choral weaving belongs to an episode in *Odyssey* 8 where the poet seemingly recalls and vivifies the scene forged by the Iliadic Hephaestus and more fully develops the *choreia*-weaving analogy already intimated in that passage. As part of the entertainment staged for Odysseus by Alkinous, the Phaeacian king bids his herald summon Demodocus and place him in the middle of what has been turned into a *choros*, or temporary dance floor. Youths 'well-versed in dancing', having taken up their circular formation around the bard, then 'strike the divine dance/dance floor' (πέπληγον δὲ χορὸν θεῖον, 264) with their feet, executing the flashing, varied and rapid steps that elicit wonder in Odysseus. Even as this performance is ongoing,[104] the bard 'strikes up' (ἀνεβάλλετο, 266) the prelude on his lyre before embarking on his tale of how Hephaestus caught Ares and Aphrodite *in flagrante*.

Taking my cue from Carruesco's reading of the scene,[105] I would suggest close connections between Hephaestus' ruse for entrapping the adulterous pair, which turns about forging, webs and weaving and the choral performance presented by the youths and Demodocus accompanying them with his phorminx and song. First setting up his anvil, the cuckolded husband proceeds to beat out the chains (κόπτε δὲ δεσμούς, 274) for his *dolos*. Although the particular verb chosen by the poet here never appears of a choral song and dance,[106] the 'striking' or 'knocking' action it describes both echoes the sound raised by the dancers' feet as they continue to 'strike' the ground in sync with the musician's notes on the finger-plucked instrument, and belongs to a larger complex of terms referring to acts of hammering,

---

[103] Σ D *ad Il.* 17.51, cited by Nagy 2010a, 295–96.

[104] *Pace* Garvie 1994 *ad* 256–65, who argues that the choral dance and Demodocus' song are two separate events, the bard's narrative providing an 'interlude' in the dancing; but see, for a different view, among others, Murray 2008, 166.

[105] Carruesco 2016, 81.

[106] One genre, the *kommos*, does suggest a possible link. For this, see *Choeph.* 423–29, where, in a passage filled with terms for beating and striking, the chorus recalls and perhaps recreates audibly and through gesture the sung laments it performed at the death of Agamemnon. The phrase with which the passage begins, ἔκοψα κομμόν, calls attention to the relation between the act of lamentation and cutting or beating; etymologically, *kommos* is derived from κόπτω insofar as it is something that beats or is beaten out.

forging and striking metal that are simultaneously used of choral performances.[107] A fragmentary Pindaric work composed for a Theban chorus (fr. 194 S.-M.) deploys the analogy; even as the performers figure their celebration as a golden pedestal that has been 'hammered out (κεκρότηται) for holy songs', an audience would hear the choreutes' feet striking the ground in the action made explicit by the same poet's fr. 52f.17–18 S.-M.: there, evoking the *choreia* of the archetypal Delphides by way of model for its own, the Pindaric chorus pictures the maidens 'dancing and singing as they beat the ground with rapid feet' (μελπ[ό]μεναι / ποδὶ κροτέο [ντι γᾶν θο]ῷ).[108]

Events internal to Demodocus' song and its visual, audible and choreographic execution by the bard and chorus merge again in the description of how Hephaestus 'pours the chains all in a circle' (χέε δέσματα κύκλῳ ἀπάντῃ, 278) around the bedposts while suspending others from the roof beams of the bed chamber (ἐξεκέχυντο, 279). The pouring action visualized here is well suited to the deity in his capacity as smith: among the very few extant signatures on Greek metalwork is that of one Pasikles, whose monumental bronze astragalos dedicated to Apollo at his temple in Didyma sometime in the third quarter of the sixth century reads 'Pasikles the son of Kydimenes cast (EXHEE) these'.[109] But forging is only one of the several activities evoked by the phrase. If later usage reflects more traditional notions of *choreia*, then Hephaestus' action simultaneously gestures towards the ongoing performance of song and dance: in Euripides' *Suppliants*, Adrastos anticipates the *molpê* that he will enact on the dead's behalf, figuring this song-dance as something he will (perhaps with the

---

[107] Cf. the Spartan prisoners in Herodotus' account of the punishment inflicted on them by the Tegeans, viz. being forced to 'measure out' the Tegean plain – this described in the oracle received prior to the attack as 'foot-struck' (ποσσίκροτον, 1.66.12) – as they worked the land in chains in their anomalous version of a choral cult dance. Of particular relevance to Demodocus' song are the fetters worn by the prisoners, and which are later 'hung up around the temple' of Athena Alea as a dedication (1.66.21–67.1). Although Herodotus does not draw the connection, the stamp of foot predicted by the Pythia anticipates the sound made by the chains first beaten on the anvil and now, wound about the captives' feet, striking the ground. Several compound terms found in later sources use κροτέω in expressions which refer to the special sandals, variously called *kroupezai* and *kroupala*, worn by dancers for the purpose of marking out the rhythm; Pollux's description of the *kroupeza* clearly indicates the role of these sandals in the choral dance, which, in his gloss, are fashioned for the sounding of 'the prelude of the chorus' (7.87).

[108] I owe this point to Power 2011, 111. In this category of 'beating', 'striking' and 'clapping' verbs, κτυπέω holds a particularly important place; among the many meta-musical passages where the verb occurs, see Aesch. *Sept.* 100–03 and Eur. *Tro.* 1306, 1325 and fr. 752f.27–28 K.

[109] See Hurwit 2016, 99 for discussion.

funerary libation, a common conceit for song, also in mind) likewise 'pour out' (ἐκχέω, 773).

If, as proposed above, the Phaeacian episode does look back to the penultimate shield band fabricated by Hephaestus in *Iliad* 18, then the poet's detailed account of the circular and linear structures into which the deity arranges the new-forged chains freshly indicates the reflexive relations between the action in Demodocus' narrative and the ongoing performance. Read against that earlier Iliadic tableau, where the metal-forged choreutes switch off between rotational motions as they spin about and the ranked formations they adopt as they regroup in their lines (ἐπὶ στίχας, 18. 602), the complex pattern generated by the bonds' circular and linear deployment exactly corresponds to that of the choral dance. The δεσμός in conjunction with a dancing chorus would return unmistakably in the famous Binding Song – *hymnos desmios* – performed by the Furies in Aeschylus' *Eumenides* (307–96), where word arrangement and metre turn that dance-and-song into a fresh circular device to entrap its victim. A bond is in itself not just a forged object, but something that is complex and interwoven and an artefact that, in later usages, 'forms a connection' between disparate elements, whether the linked dancer's hands – the Furies join hands before starting to dance (χορὸν ἅψωμεν, 307) – or the decorative knot that accompanies so many Geometric vase images of dancers.[110]

If the depiction of Hephaestus attaching the chains in a horizontal and vertical manner might recall the setting up of a loom as the weaver prepares the warp and woof threads, and the criss-crossing structure that the forged objects fashion over and around the bed similarly resemble a web, then a direct reference to that woven device follows immediately on. Even as Demodocus plays on his phorminx, which like a loom has strings suspended from a central bar, so his divine counterpart manipulates those cord's metal-forged counterparts, now described as 'delicate like those of a spider's web' (ἠΰτ' ἀράχνια λεπτά, 280).[111] Together with the glance to the bard's musicianship, the audience might hear in the adjective a passing reference to Demodocus' voice: back on the Iliadic shield, the phorminx-equipped youth accompanying the dancers on

---

[110] See Carruesco 2016, 90–91 for this. The δεσμός returns later in *Od.* 8 when, in curiously emphatic and detailed fashion, Arete directs Odysseus carefully to fasten the treasure chest she has given him, and to 'throw a fastening bond (δεσμὸν ἴηλον) around it' (443). When Odysseus follows Arete's instructions, the fastening he places on the chest is *poikilos* (448).

[111] Cf. an advertisement by Dupont promoting the first nylon stockings, made of 'filaments as strong as steel, as fine as a spider's web'. For more spiders' webs in a choral context, see the text discussed at this section's end.

their return from harvesting the grapes sings, in cognate fashion, 'with delicate voice' (λεπταλέη φωνῇ, *Il.* 18.571).[112]

Sound and voice aside, the Odyssean simile more immediately makes room for the multimedia spectacle, serving to reinforce the audience's sense of the performance as a cloth-in-production, whose makers generate the fabric with their dance. Very commonly applied in Homeric diction to woven fabrics, λεπτός distinguishes products that are not only finely spun and delicate, but also, with the addition of oil, possess a heightened suppleness and brilliance, qualities they share with choral dancers. It is just such garments that the dancers on the Iliadic shield wear (λεπτὰς ὀθόνας, *Il.* 18.595) and that, closer to the Phaeacian choristers' home, are produced by the weavers adjacent to Alkinous' palace, whose expertise at the loom Odysseus lingered to observe: exactly like those worn by the Iliadic performers, the cloths woven by these women are 'delicate and fine-spun' (λεπτοὶ ἐΰννητοι, 7.97), and shimmer with their oil appliqué (107).

Following the success of his contrivance, Hephaestus then calls together his fellow Olympians to witness the spectacle of the web-caught adulterers – effectively the Phaeacian youths' dance lastingly reified in this metal-made textile. The gods' concluding act of spectatorship (325–27) contributes one final point of juncture between the performance and events internal to its narrative: in the prelude to the song and dance, when the Phaeacians danced without Demodocus' accompaniment, Odysseus similarly looked attentively, not laughing in this instance, but wondering at this parallel display of expertise (264–65).

2.3 *Choral Weaving in the Lyric Repertoire*

These Homeric passages aside, it is the choral poets who develop and expand the weaving conceit, drawing on a much fuller range of textile-making techniques to supply figures for their acts of composition and the performances that result. In some instances the analogy depends on nothing more than the presence of a single term that simultaneously belongs to the weaving and musico-choral milieus and so can give a song its 'fabricated' character; elsewhere, and particularly in the densely metaphoric poetry of Pindar, the lyricist introduces extended and elaborate images that may accommodate several facets of cloth-making and a variety of

---

[112] By the late fifth century, λεπτός would regularly be used of the voice and sound (e.g. Eur. fr. 773.67 K., Ar. *Av.* 235).

woven goods. In the review that follows, I look both at the overlapping diction that allows poets to activate the image and at the range of textiles and articles, many of these additionally worn or carried by chorus members as they perform, that the weaving practices cited in the songs generate.

Among the most intricate of the images that draw on dictional, structural and functional parallels between cloth-making and song composition belongs to Pindar's fr. 215a.6–7 S.-M., where the poetic voice's declaration that it is obliged '['to adorn'?/'to praise'?] my ancient fatherland with a comb of the Pierides (κτενὶ Πιερίδ[ων), like the yellow hair of a maiden' looks to a stage prior to weaving. The κτείς is not just an article that equips the *parthenos* at her toilette, but serves as the comb for carding wool, which could then be fashioned into the long fluffy rolls ready for spinning.[113] Here associated with the Muses and poetic-cum-musical celebrations, the comb evokes a third and possibly currently visible object, the lyre complete with its plectrum or pick that accompanies the goddesses' archetypal *choreia* emulated by the chorus here. The combination of hair-combing and lyre-playing does not become explicit until Roman poetry, where Horace imagines Paris doing both in a single phrase (*C.* 1.15.14–15) and where the *pecten* explicitly refers at one and the same time to the hair comb, the weaving implement and the plectrum used to pluck the strings of the lyre on which the hero plays.[114] But Pindar may anticipate this later trope and linguistic turn. In this simile, combing replaces the weaving imagery so ubiquitous in his and Bacchylides' poetry so as to describe a stage prior to the combination of different elements, whether that of warp and woof or of word, music and dance, into the single song-cloth. As I go on to demonstrate, the *chorêgos* must divide and distinguish the chorus members prior to their coming together in the composite performance.[115]

---

[113] These rolls are visible in the hands of the weavers and in the wool baskets shown on the Amasis lekythos (fig. 7.9), with discussion in Edmunds 2012.

[114] Examples of the *pecten* used in lyre-playing include Verg. *Aen.* 6.647, where Orpheus accompanies the chorus of Thracian singers on his lyre; see too Persius 6.2. In her discussion of terms cognate with the Greek τέκειν, Barber 1991, 261 observes that the action originally described would not be that of combing, but more of plucking, as when the wool was plucked from a moulting sheep.

[115] A curious passage from Statius' *Achilleis*, it should be noted, would give the 'comb' an entirely different and intriguing choral significance. In a description of the dance performed by the girls of Skyros on Achilles' and Diomedes' arrival on the island (*Achill.* 1.827–34), the dancers seem to alternate between linear and circular movements, sometimes turning to 'face another in an Amazonian comb (*obviae versae / pectine Amazonio*)'. As a commentator observes (Dilke 2005 *ad* 832), this may be a reference to an otherwise unattested 'comb dance' in which two rows of dancers are interlaced like the teeth of a comb.

The seemingly recherché image would also find its reflection in the 'visuals' of the choral performance. If, as the object cited by the speaking voice suggests, fr. 215a S.-M. belonged to a *partheneion* or other type of composition designed for a maiden chorus, then audiences would witness the performers' elaborately styled and adorned hair, so characteristic of dancers in art and text, and that sometimes features the intricate braids belonging to many *korai*, which require the separation of the locks prior to their recombination.[116] The match between the poetic conceit and the ongoing spectacle informs the 'comb of the Pierides' in a further respect. As several pieces in the *Greek Anthology* (e.g. 6.211) and the objects found in votive deposits amply illustrate, a comb, often highly worked and designed in costly materials, was a suitable parthenaic dedication. Even as the comb might delight and adorn the deity to whom it is offered, so Pindar's choral gift, typically presented here as an *agalma*, does much the same.

The Pindaric 'comb of the Muses' may encompass one third and no less critical facet of this compositional, spectacular and tributary offering, its verbal artistry. In a later instance of the kinship between weaving, hair styling and literary production, Dionysius of Halicarnassus compares the care lavished by Plato on the arrangement of the words that make up his dialogues to the attention necessary for achieving an elaborate coiffure: 'and Plato did not stop combing (κτενίζων) and curling his own dialogues and weaving/plaiting (ἀναπλέκων) them in every way', thereby creating texts consisting of words 'transposed in varied (ποικίλως) woven patterns' (*Comp.* 25). Just as Pindar's singer-dancers unite their painstaking hair combing with the woven quality of their song, so Dionysius imagines a similar process reflected in the interwoven nature of the once spoken and now written words and phrases of the Platonic texts.

With the wool plucked, washed, combed and spun, cloth-makers could then proceed to the loom, whose design and accompanying implements again suggest numerous parallels to the art and act of choral composition. As already exemplified by the passage from Theocritus, the correspondences between the plectrum and pin beater (*kerkis*) promote affinities between weaving, music making and the performance of song. The verb κρέκειν, literally 'to strike', focuses on the auditory sphere: used, perhaps, in its primary instance of the weaver beating the weft into place or strumming

---

[116] See the very suggestive mention of hair plaiting or combing in the context of the song-dance performance framing that reference at Eur. *Hec.* 923–24; here the chorus recalls how it once 'arranged/composed (ἐρρυθμιζόμαν) my hair in a tied-up headband', as though the coiffure that resulted exhibited some kind of musical or choreographic quality.

the warp to even out the woven portion,[117] it also refers to the player on the lyre or harp who plucks the strings with the plectrum. A fragment of Alcman (fr. 140 *PMGF*) provides among the earliest instances of the crossover; as a later etymologist explains the expression κερκολύρα, the noun is equivalent to the variant κρεκολύρα, best rendered as 'lyre beater', an onomatopoetic coinage for the sound made by the plectrum plucking at the strings which corresponds to the pin beater's action and to the twang, 'thump or tinkling' that the implement produces.[118] In our absence of firm knowledge regarding the shape and size of the *kerkis* used by the Greek weavers, we can only conjecture as to its physical similarity to the plectrum; in his evocation of the implement, Aeschylus describes its action as 'the strokes of the weaving sword (σπάθης τε πληγάς)' (*Choeph.* 232), devising an image in which the weapon has assumed the role that the pin beater would more normally play in pattern weaving.[119]

Sappho also draws on the parallel. Near the opening of her fr. 99 V., the words χόρδαισι ... διακρέκην, 'to strike/weave on the strings', are legible, a notion more evidently taken up in fr. 102 V., where the poetic ego's self-avowed loss of her ability to weave stands in relations of likeness and opposition to the ongoing performance.

> γλύκηα μᾶτερ, οὔτοι δύναμαι κρέκην τὸν ἴστον
> πόθῳ δάμεισα παῖδος βραδίναν δι' Ἀφροδίταν

> sweet mother, I am not able to strike the loom, overcome with desire for a youth on account of slender Aphrodite

As in the better known fr. 31 V., the force of desire seemingly robs the speaker of her musical and compositional powers, here not so much to sing as to play upon the lyre, even as the performance audibly and visibly continues before the audience in what, I suggest, is a chorally delivered piece.[120] A paean by Athenaios dated to 128/27 B.C.E. varies the long-lived

---

[117] As Barber 1991, 273 remarks, the double usage is grounded in 'the verbal root *krek-*, which has to do with hitting strings noisily with sharp instruments. From looking just at the Greek, one has trouble telling whether the meaning began with weaving or with playing a stringed instrument, but since all the cognates outside Greece have to do with weaving, we can assume weaving as the semantic base for Greek too'.

[118] The latter description comes from Jørgensen 2013, 131.

[119] I draw these terms from Edmunds 2012.

[120] For this, see Lardinois 1996. Euripides would also frequently exploit the song-issuing *kerkis* trope and the 'strike' common to musicians and weavers; see, among other instances, fr. 528a K. from the *Meleager*, which refers to the 'concerns of the singing *kerkis*' and, more fully, the remark by Hypsipyle in fr. 752f.9–11 K. More succinct is the expression κερκίδος ἀοιδοῦ at fr. 528a K., and note too *IT* 222–23 and *IA* 788–90. Sophoclean shuttles are more generally

conceit, transferring κρέκειν from the kithara to the pipes while postponing a reference to the expected stringed instrument. In lines that focus on the acoustics of their performance, the singers declare: 'and the clear, roaring aulos-reed strikes (κρέκει) a song with variegated melodies, and the golden, sweet-voiced kitharist sings out a prelude to the hymns' (14–16). In all these usages, the weaving-playing affinity extends to the visual dimension: the action of strumming the threads with the pin beater or hand stands parallel to the gestures of the musician as his or her fingers travel over the instrument.

Other weaving terms deployed in choral poetry depend not only on the audible and verbal aspects of the composition, but on the arrangement of the dancers who perform the song, whether they move in formation or strike poses. Weaving and the stringed instrument share the μίτος, the thread/string essential to both the loom and lyre's design and whose double usage articulates anew the objects' affinity. Homer already uses the noun for the thread of the warp through which the shuttle is passed at *Il*. 23.762 while later sources apply it of the lyre string;[121] so the author of an epigram (*AP* 6.83.5–6; cf. Philostr. Jun. *Imag.* 6) describes his debilitated state:

> ἠιθέοις μελέτω κιθάρης μίτος· ἀντὶ δὲ πλήκτρου
> σκηπανίῳ τρομερὰς χεῖρας ἐρεισάμεθα.

> Let the string of the lyre be the concern for young men, while I support my shaky hands with a staff in place of the plectrum.

But it is a further usage of μίτος, although one not attested before the mid-fifth century, when the comic dramatist Pherecrates includes the expression (fr. 156.7 K.-A.), that is more specifically apposite to a choral performance insofar as it refers to the formation adopted by the chorus and already visible in much earlier visual accounts; just as archaic vases regularly show youths and maidens dancing in their linear deployments, so to arrange something κατὰ μίτον, literally 'connected by one thread', is to present it 'continuously', 'in an unbroken order'.[122]

---

invested with powers of communication and a speaking voice. In the *Tereus*, writing, weaving and the issuing of words all come together in the phrase cited by Aristotle from the drama (fr. 595 R.): κερκίδος φωνή not only points to the shrill sound supposedly made by the pin beater, but to its powers of verbalization as the act of weaving is turned into a generator of speech. Other examples include Soph. fr. 890 R. with *P.Oxy.* 4807, κερκίδος ὕμνοις.

[121] Pherecydes *FrGrH* 3 F 14 uses the term of the 'clue' given to Theseus by Ariadne; it may also describe the web of the spider (*AP* 6.39; cf. Eur. fr. 369 K. considered below).

[122] See the later discussion of Pindar's fr. 70b S.-M.

A related activity is the stringing together of heterogeneous elements so as to produce a necklace or a wreath. Regularly used of precious necklaces in Homer (e.g. *Od.* 18.296, 15.460), εἴρειν, 'to string together', reappears in a Pindaric reference to the creation of a woven crown, here fashioned with three rare and valuable materials that stand figure for the 'combinatory' song currently performed by the choristers, plausibly equipped with rich headwear of their own (*Nem.* 7.77–79):

> εἴρειν στεφάνους ἐλαφρόν, ἀναβάλεο· Μοῖσά τοι
> κολλᾷ χρυσὸν ἔν τε λευκὸν ἐλέφανθ' ἁμᾶ
> καὶ λείριον ἄνθεμον ποντίας ὑφελοῖσ' ἐέρσας.

> The stringing of crowns is easy; strike up the prelude. Indeed the Muse joins fast together gold and white ivory and the lily flower of the sea.[123]

Where most commentators interpret the 'flower of the sea' as a periphrasis for coral, Boedeker understands it as a reference to the sea-purple dye used in fabric-making and suggests that weaving lies behind the larger conceit; what the Muse fashions is 'a woven headband of cloth dyed purple and ornamented with gold and ivory'.[124] Literary and material evidence featuring textiles with golden threads, sometimes combined with other strands of dyed purple, support this reading and turn the Pindaric image into something more closely resembling real-world precious cloths: in addition to the corselet interwoven with gold threads dedicated to Athena Lindia by the Egyptian Amasis (Hdt. 3.47), two pieces of fabric woven in gold and purple were among the goods found in the fourth-century 'Philip's tomb' in Vergina, which were additionally decorated with floral motifs.[125]

The verb εἴρειν, now in composite form (and again in combination with a golden thread or cord), recurs in a still more patently choral context in Plato's investigation of the nature and origins of *choreia*; here, at *Laws* 654a1–5, the joining or 'stringing together' of individuals in a single performing ensemble lies at the very origins of the institution:

> ἡμῖν δὲ οὓς εἴπομεν τοὺς θεοὺς συγχορευτὰς δεδόσθαι, τούτους εἶναι καὶ
> τοὺς δεδωκότας τὴν ἔνρυθμόν τε καὶ ἐναρμόνιον αἴσθησιν μεθ' ἡδονῆς, ᾗ δὴ
> κινεῖν τε ἡμᾶς καὶ χορηγεῖν ἡμῶν τούτους, ᾠδαῖς τε καὶ ὀρχήσεσιν ἀλλήλοις
> συνείροντας, χορούς τε ὠνομακέναι παρὰ τὸ τῆς χαρᾶς ἔμφυτον ὄνομα.

---

[123] The verb can also be used of glueing and forging.   [124] Boedeker 1984, 94.

[125] See Gleba 2008, 80–82 for these and other examples. For a cloth discovered in Koropi near Athens with silver-gilded threads for embellishment, see Spantidaki 2015, 37.

To us, however, have been given the gods whom we spoke of as fellow dancers, and they have given us pleasing perception of rhythm and harmony. Using this, they move us and lead us in choruses, stringing us together one with another by means of songs and dances; and that is why they bestowed the name 'choruses', from the joy that is native to these activities.

Much as the 'necklace' dance later recorded by Lucian (effectively a courtship dance resulting in matrimony) is made up of its male and female choreutes placed on a single thread so as to form a *hormos*, a description then immediately followed by a glance to the chorus forged by Hephaestus performing the *geranos* (*Salt.* 12–13),[126] so these individuals become a unity when strung together as a troupe. Reading the Platonic passage, as Kurke proposes,[127] together with the closely preceding account of how the education that men have received 'grows slack' over time so that the gods are needed to set individuals 'upright again' (653c7–d2), we can understand how the puppet imagery first introduced by the Athenian Stranger at 644d7 permeates the formulation here. In that earlier account, the speaker observes that the string connecting the choristers and making them all move together as if in a puppet chorus is the 'golden and sacred pull of *logismos*' (645a) that he earlier described. Even before the explicit turn to the chorus, the Stranger's diction is apposite to these choral 'mechanics' and to the implements involved in the execution of the dance. Just as the *chorêgos* in other accounts is the individual who 'pulls the line' or stands at the head of his roped-together followers, so here the language of 'dragging' or 'pulling' anticipates the leading function assigned to the Platonic divinities (644e1–645a5):

> τόδε δὲ ἴσμεν, ὅτι ταῦτα τὰ πάθη ἐν ἡμῖν οἷον νεῦρα ἢ σμήρινθοί τινες ἐνοῦσαι σπῶσίν τε ἡμᾶς καὶ ἀλλήλαις ἀνθέλκουσιν ἐναντίαι οὖσαι ἐπ' ἐναντίας πράξεις, οὗ δὴ διωρισμένη ἀρετὴ καὶ κακία κεῖται. μιᾷ γάρ φησιν ὁ λόγος δεῖν τῶν ἕλξεων συνεπόμενον ἀεὶ καὶ μηδαμῇ ἀπολειπόμενον ἐκείνης, ἀνθέλκειν τοῖς ἄλλοις νεύροις ἕκαστον, ταύτην δ' εἶναι τὴν τοῦ λογισμοῦ ἀγωγὴν χρυσῆν καὶ ἱεράν, τῆς πόλεως κοινὸν νόμον ἐπικαλουμένην, ἄλλας δὲ σκληρὰς καὶ σιδηρᾶς, τὴν δὲ μαλακὴν ἅτε χρυσῆν οὖσαν, τὰς δὲ ἄλλας παντοδαποῖς εἴδεσιν ὁμοίας. δεῖν δὴ τῇ καλλίστῃ ἀγωγῇ τῇ τοῦ νόμου ἀεὶ συλλαμβάνειν·

---

[126] The topmost frieze of the François Vase (showing the *geranos*?) exactly illustrates just such a necklace dance; reading the haphazardly positioned crew still on the boat, as Olsen 2015 does, as a proto-chorus that lacks the requisite regulation, we can see in the orderly and strung-together twice seven an instance of a paradigmatic ensemble.

[127] See Kurke 2013, 124–35 for the interpretation followed here.

> This we know, that the affections within us, like sinews of cords, drag us
> along, and being opposed to each other, pull one against the other to
> opposite actions; and this is where the division between virtue and
> wickedness lies. For, as our reasoning states, there is one of these pulling
> forces which every man should always follow, and in no respect leave hold
> of, counteracting thereby the pull of other sinews, and this is the golden
> and sacred leading cord of reasoning, designated the civic law common to
> all; and whereas the other cords are hard and steely and of every possible
> formation, this one is soft in as much as it is gold. This fairest leading of
> the law we must always take hold of.

Threads and threading together and the role of the *chorêgos* as line-
regulator are very much at issue in one further term that spans weaving and
choreia. Building on an etymological foundation, Bernard Gallet's little-
cited study proposes a connection between the nouns καῖρος, a technical
weaving term already attested in one of the Pylos tablets (Pylos UB 1318),
where *ka-r-oi* seemingly refers to a fringe on a cloth, and then again in *Od.*
7.107, there used of woven linen (καιροσέων δ' ὀθονέων), and καιρός,
regularly translated as 'due measure', 'seasonability', 'the critical time' or
'the opportunity' that must be seized.[128] As Barber explains,[129] καῖρος, the
equivalent of the modern 'shed bar', and the rod clearly visible in the mid-
section of the loom shown on the first of the Amasis lekythoi cited earlier
(Fig. 7.9), 'functions partly as a template to which the immovable half of the
web is bound . . . to keep it in its proper place and width as the warp threads
of the other shed are pulled past. That is, it serves also to regulate the
warp'.[130] Leaving aside Gallet's painstaking reconstruction of how the
functions fulfilled by this feature of loom design inform the probably
later καιρός (first attested in Hes. *Erg.* 694), my concern is with the ways
in which the ancient sources connect the second and abstract noun with
weaving, and how the several roles assigned the shed bar bear on choral
morphology and on the actions that occur preliminary to and as part of the
performance.

Among the many passages that Gallet cites from Pindar and other
authors that seem to incorporate and build on the etymological link and/

---

[128] Gallet 1990, 9–75.

[129] Barber 1991, 271; see too her fig. 3.27 for a clear illustration of the place of this bar on the warp-
weighted loom. A shed is the space between the warp threads through which the weft passes,
and is created by a shedding device. All weaving requires the creation of at least two different
sheds.

[130] In an earlier discussion on p. 82, Barber describes the καῖρος as a rod that 'can be stuck into the
warp in such a way that every second thread passes over the rod while the threads in between
pass under'.

or homonymity between the two differently accented nouns, *Pyth.* 9.76–79 offers a particularly compelling example. Midway through an ode preoccupied with the fleeting nature of time and that transient 'ripe moment' that the athlete and young maiden must simultaneously seize to achieve their respective ends, agonistic victory and marriage, the poetic ego offers a reflection on what makes for a successful epinician, both in its composition and performance (note the presence of the audience of 'hearers'):

> ἀρεταὶ δ' αἰεὶ μεγάλαι πολύμυθοι·
> βαιὰ δ' ἐν μακροῖσι ποικίλλειν
> ἀκοὰ σοφοῖς· ὁ δὲ καιρὸς ὁμοίως
> παντὸς ἔχει κορυφάν.

> Great virtues are always rich in songs. To create variegation (lit. 'to pattern-weave') in a narrow space among things that are long drawn out is matter for the wise to hear. But *kairos* holds the summit (or 'choicest') of all alike.

Gallet's suggestion that the coincidence of καιρός with ποικίλλειν not only activates the derivation of the noun and its relation to καῖρος, but that weaving technology shapes the larger statement too, makes excellent sense of lines that have prompted the widely divergent interpretations reviewed in his discussion.[131] The role of the 'shed bar' well conforms – albeit without a one-to-one correspondence – to the actions described here: the καῖρος holds some of the warp threads firmly in place, allowing them to remain fixed as the other warps are pulled past, and so plays a critical role in the creation of the complex and compacted textile. Not only, furthermore, do the 'fixative' functions (ἔχει) of the καῖρος coincide with the ode's larger concern with arresting the transient, but neatly too, the shed bar occupies the mid-section of the loom, positioned halfway between the top and bottom of the uprights, and thus is equivalent in location to its homonym, introduced exactly half way through Pindar's ode.

Typically the passage also includes a 'meta-performative' dimension that draws attention to the dynamics and structure of the ongoing spectacle and the roles of the participants. What Gallet renders the 'fil conducteur' and 'régulateur' corresponds to the functions of the *chorêgos*, whether the chorus trainer or lead musician or dancer of the troupe and the one responsible for determining the arrangement of its members, whom he

---

[131] See Gallet 1990, 83–101.

or she might group together into pairs or variously distance from one another (see Chapter 8 for examples); even so does the shed bar create the spaces between the warp threads attached to it and keep these properly aligned. The mention of the κορυφή further shines the spotlight on the chorus leader. Referring to the apex, the site where two lines converge, it could also describe the meeting point between two choral groups in v-formation that come together under the leadership of the single *chorêgos*, the individual who, according to the *Suda*, 'likes to be placed at the head (ἄκρος) of the chorus'.[132]

A second occurrence of καιρός at *Pyth.* 1.81–82, here in a phrase that includes several terms that look directly to the weaver's art, while again endorsing brevity or compression over prolixity, further supports Gallet's view that Pindar intends a syllepsis between the two forms of the noun:[133]

> καιρὸν εἰ φθέγξαιο, πολλῶν πείρατα συντανύσαις
> ἐν βραχεῖ, μείων ἔπεται μῶμος ἀνθρώ-
>   πων·

> If you were to speak to the point, drawing the strands of many things into a small space, less censure of men would follow.

Since the cord or tie belongs among the primary meanings of πεῖραρ, something that fastens one thing to another and that itself forms a loop or circle, the process envisioned here readily brings the action of the weaver to mind. So Ann Bergren, observing the underlying analogy, although with no reference to the καῖρος, explains, 'intertwining the strands of many things (πολλῶν) but in a short space (ἐν βραχεῖ) (i.e. the little space between the strands) would produce a fabric small in size but very closely knit' –[134] just the type of tightly compacted cloth that Helen, the master weaver, would produce in Theocritus' *Epithalamium* (πυκινώτερον, *Id.* 18.33). For an audience familiar with the actions of the weaver, the moment when the warp threads of the other shed are pulled past the warps fastened to the shed bar might come to mind. More broadly, the image corresponds to the gestures that go into the creation of the best kind of cloth, one that has its weft placed across the warp so that it is neither too tight nor too loose, a positioning that

---

[132] *Suda* s.v. ψιλεύς.   [133] Gallet 1990, 103–115 discusses the example.

[134] Bergren 1975, 151. Visible in some ancient textiles are the gaps between the different threads, perhaps the products of less skilled weavers.

the weaver can achieve through beating the weft into place with the *kerkis*.[135]

Here too choral morphology and the role of the *chorêgos* are discernible in a passage that may simultaneously comment on what the audience is looking at as the singers deliver the gnomic remark. Assuming the kinship between the chorus-leader and καῖρος suggested above, the speaker draws attention to that individual – and φθέγγομαι can mean 'to name, tell of, celebrate' – and observes how he 'draws together' the formerly 'spread out' choristers into a close-compacted space, regulating the distances between them. Pindar is no stranger to the challenge of spacing chorus members so as to achieve the most pleasing kind of vocalization, and on one occasion takes issue with an old-style arrangement in which the choreutes were positioned at too great intervals from one another. The opening of fr. 70b S.-M., a dithyramb, critiques this deployment, declaring it a too long drawn-out *schoinos* (itself a plaited, woven rope) that creeps along (ἕρπε σχοινοτένεια, fr. 70b.1 S.-M.). In Pindar's stricture, this deployment results in an undesirable spatial extension, drawing things out excessively (the line-expanding compound hapax σχοινοτένεια audibly mimics this distension), while the lack of the sought-after vocal coordination is a further consequence of the over-distancing of one chorister from the next. Recommending the more compact arrangement that a circular formation allows, Pindar goes on to describe the requisite mixture of spacing and cohesion: the singer-dancers are now 'spread out (διαπέπ[τ]α[νται) in their well-centred circles (εὐο]μφάλ[οις κύ]κλοισι)' (70b.4–5).[136]

Gallet goes on to cite a whole series of other passages in which καιρός evokes a process whereby disparate elements are combined in orderly fashion, including a brief glance to *Ol.* 9.35–39 where several additional terms untreated in his discussion but again pertinent to weaving appear.[137] In a further reflection on what makes for the best song composition, the speaker cautions himself to abandon a potentially impious tale involving Heracles' attack on the gods:

> ἀπό μοι λόγον   35
> τοῦτον, στόμα, ῥῖψον·
> ἐπεὶ τό γε λοιδορῆσαι θεούς

---

[135] For discussion and demonstration of the several actions required, see Edmunds 2012 and her fig. 36.

[136] For this interpretation and restoration of the lacunose lines, and the issue of vocal coordination as the lines' concern, see D'Angour 1997.

[137] Gallet 1990, 136.

ἐχθρὰ σοφία, καὶ τὸ καυχᾶσθαι παρὰ καιρόν

μανίαισιν ὑποκρέκει.

> Cast that story away from me, my mouth, since to badmouth the gods is a
> hateful skill and to boast in untimely fashion (or 'excessively') is to sound
> out in accompaniment with madness.

While commentators typically understand ὑποκρέκει as referring to an
outsized sound, κρέκω, as noted earlier, regularly describes the audible
act of beating the weft threads into place and strumming the warp with
the *kerkis* so as to achieve the proper spacing. Again, the use of the verb
recalibrates the meaning of καιρός, drawing it into the weaving sphere, and
allowing an audience to understand in the final line a nicely detailed
account of how *not* to fashion fabric on the loom, itself the parallel *sophia*,
the expertise or 'know-how' at risk of distortion here.[138] Although the
καῖρος *qua* shed bar may do no more than activate the line's imagistic
dimension, there may be some significance to the expression παρὰ καιρόν;
like the misjudged speech act, perhaps the shed bar is similarly misplaced.

   Vocal coordination and matters of harmony may also be at issue here;
the incorrect placing and spacing of the thread-like chorus members will
yield discordancy, the unpleasant sound that fr. 70b.3 S.-M. describes when
it declares that singers in their older linear formation issued from their
mouths a *san* deemed 'false' (κίβδηλον). Euphony might be the product not
only of the choreutes now positioned in their neatly spaced-out circles, but
of the correct use of the *kerkis* or perhaps, as Edmunds additionally
proposes, of a stick which could strike the warps 'so that they shake
themselves into orderly rows'.[139]

   One final term found in Pindar similarly refers to a practice as familiar to
early weavers and the wearers of their products as to composers of choral
lyric: the *prooimion*.[140] Commonly used to describe the opening of a song,
the prelude that precedes the actual path of the song (*oimê*), or, later, the
exordium of a speech, the expression can, in an etymological sense, mean
the 'initial threading'.[141] This is a process that produces the *exstasis* or
heading band designed to prevent the cloth from unravelling,[142] the ribbed

---

[138] ῥῖψον, a verb stronger in intensity than βάλλω, already introduces the motif of dis-measure and
evokes the gesture required here to correct a potential 'overcast' on the speaker, musician or
weaver's part as he or she mis-throws the shuttle and misses the threads.

[139] Edmunds 2012.

[140] Pindar unequivocally uses the term in reference to the practice of the Homeridae as they 'stitch'
together their songs at *Nem.* 2.3, but it never appears in hexameter poetry or other monodic
genres.

[141] Nagy 2008/09, 292.   [142] Barber 1991, 270 and 271.

strip visible, as Barber comments, on the portion of fabric thrown over the left arms of several figures on the Parthenon frieze and on the garments worn by other fifth-century images. On several occasions, Pindaric *prooimia* seem to glance towards this secondary frame of reference while integrating it into an image positioned, fittingly, at the outset of a song. In the appeal to the lyre that begins Pythian 1, the singers imagine the instrument in the hands of Apollo, the ur-*chorêgos*, as he leads the Muses in dance and song (1–4):

> χρυσέα φόρμιγξ, Ἀπόλλωνος καὶ ἰοπλοκάμων
> σύνδικον Μοισᾶν κτέανον· τᾶς ἀκούει
>   μὲν βάσις ἀγλαΐας ἀρχά,
> πείθονται δ' ἀοιδοὶ σάμασιν
> ἀγησιχόρων ὁπόταν προοιμίων
>   ἀμβολὰς τεύχῃς ἐλελιζομένα.

> Golden phorminx, rightful possession of Apollo and the violet-tressed Muses, to you the footstep listens as it begins the splendid celebration, and the singers obey your signals whenever you, being made to vibrate, fashion the striking up of the chorus-leading *prooimia*.

The description succinctly acknowledges every facet of the spectacle, its instrumentation, dance and song, and vividly evokes the divine choreutes responding to Apollo's opening notes even as the Syracusan dancer-singers represent their steps, sounds and submission to their musician's lead in their more earth-bound performance. If the choice to style these opening moments the *prooimia* aims to equate them with the preparatory stages of cloth-making, then the combination of lyre, footstep, a verb of facture (τεύχῃς) and the vibrations that Apollo's action generates are well suited to a weaving enterprise and to the initial threading preliminary to the creation of the larger fabric. According to this second model, the golden phorminx stands as a grandiose equivalent to the similarly shaped loom at which mortals work, while Apollo as player on its threads acts as master weaver here, the one whose plying of the plectrum-pin beater dictates the actions performed by the remainder of the troupe; following his directions, they – Muses and Syracusans both – execute the steps that might correspond to the weaving attendants' horizontal passage from left to right and back again as they move across the upright loom.

ἐλελίζω may prove pertinent to the same weaving scenario. As noted earlier, striking the warp threads with a stick would cause them to vibrate and shake themselves out into a row. The quivering motion that the

Pindaric verb describes could also evoke a second action on the weaver's part; in attempting to explain the term *rhodanê* used of the weft, Barber hypothesizes that it was cognate with the adjective *rhodanos*, which means 'flickering, wavering' and refers to the visual impression made by the weft as it travels over and under the warp threads.[143] The expression *rhodanê* occurs just once in Homer, at *Il.* 18.576, when, in the depiction of the bucolic landscape through which the cows on the Hephaestus-forged shield are driven to pasture, the term describes the movements of the reeds. These more speculative suggestions aside, with the 'heading band' of the first *Pythian* now in place, the weavers' 'fabrication' at the loom can proceed.

The *prooimion* as an initial threading, or the 'heading band' fashioned by that process, may inform a second image placed again by way of preface to a song. In a celebration of an equestrian victory by Megakles, a member of the once-dominant Alcmaeonid clan, the poet leads off with what has been read exclusively as a building conceit (*Pyth.* 7.1–3):

κάλλιστον αἱ μεγαλοπόλιες Ἀθᾶναι
προοίμιον Ἀλκμανιδᾶν εὐρυσθενεῖ
γενεᾷ κρηπῖδ᾽ ἀοιδᾶν ἵπποισι βαλέσθαι.

The great-city Athens is the fairest *prooimion* for the widely powerful clan of the Alcmaeonidae to be cast as a foundation of horse-honouring songs.

Bringing to mind both the creation of a structure rising on its foundations and the victory image to be set up on its pedestal in commemoration of the win, the metaphor may simultaneously present the performers as weavers. Athens, the *fons et origo* in Pindar's telling, of the victor's family, supplies the fitting 'heading band' that must be fashioned before the weavers pursue their encomiastic task. Patterned cloths included horses among their figural designs: already on the François Vase, among the immortals attending the wedding of Peleus and Thetis, one of the female figures wears a dress with horizontal friezes of chariots and horses, a motif that reappears on the cloak worn by Demeter on an early fifth-century skyphos by Makron;[144] winged horses are the more fantastical creatures decorating Penelope's unfinished cloth on the red-figure skyphos from Chiusi cited earlier.

Textiles are far from the only woven objects featured in Pindaric and other choral poetry; instead they belong to a broader category of artefacts that possess the intricacy and complexity characteristic of the genre in which they occur and that composers seek to highlight through

---

[143] Barker 1991, 273.   [144] London, British Museum E 140; *ARV²* 495.3.

the introduction of these real and more notional crafted goods. One Pindaric piece, most likely a paean or hyporcheme, underscores the 'conjunctive' element signalled by πλέκω. In a metaphor likening the song to a finely fashioned chariot, the singers describe the vehicle as both shrill, λιγ[ύ, and 'well-woven', εὐπλεκές (fr. 140b.8–9 S.-M.).[145] Following what may then be the additional equation of this musical creation with a dedication (the fragmentary nature of the text forbids certainty here),[146] the weaving terminology draws attention to the 'factural' and harmoniously composite and compacted quality that choral poetry and votives share and so anticipates the restatement of these properties in ἄρμενον, the term that closes the opening section of the work. Pindar has already introduced the notion of a design that brings a diversity of materials into harmonious concordance when he presented the Locrian Xenocritus at the song's start as the inventor of a new *harmonia* for the flutes (2), thus making the motif of 'fitting together' two or more things, as the weaver does with warp and weft, bracket the entire description. That a *harmonia* is itself a woven thing, the invocation to the lyre at *Nem.* 4.44–45 – albeit in a phrase that selects ὑφαίνω for its verb – demonstrates:

ἐξύφαινε, γλυκεῖα, καὶ τόδ᾽ αὐτίκα, φόρμιγξ,
Λυδίᾳ σὺν ἁρμονίᾳ μέλος . . .   45

Weave out straight forth, sweet lyre, this song too in the Lydian mode . . .[147]

Where *Nemean* 4 features the lyre as one among the ode's several weavers, in fr. 140b S.-M. the 'well-woven' quality of the chariot turns out equally to suit the (double) pipes for which Xenocritus designs his new *harmonia* and whose twice-repeated presence in the song may glance towards the musical accompaniment to which the piece was performed. In Andrew Barker's

---

[145] Although the second term is the (widely accepted) conjecture of Fileni 1987, it seems likely on many grounds. Not only is the adjective used by Homer and [Hesiod] of a chariot (*Il.* 23.436; *Sc.* 306, 370), but Pindar applies it to songs at fr. 52e.12 S.-M.

[146] See Steiner 2016b for a close reading of the fragment and this emendation.

[147] Approaching the ode's end, the *persona loquens* sounds the weaving conceit a second time. Celebrating Melesias, the trainer of the victor in the wrestling event being fêted here, the speaker declares that only an individual who was 'unthrowable in speech' could praise a man of this kind, an encomiast who, with skills parallel to Melesias' own, 'weaving his words (ῥήματα πλέκων), would twist (στρέφοι) in the strife' (93–94). Again, πλέκω draws attention to the ode's complexity, its shifting, twisting, turning and variegated character that mirrors the moves performed by the victorious wrestler. 'Twisting' also brings spinning to mind, the process that precedes weaving.

view, the instrument itself involves the act of interlacing insofar as it produced a complex sound made up of two separate lines combined so as to create a form of dialogue.[148] The instrument as integral to the several woven facets of *choreia* is made patent in another Pindaric piece, *Pythian* 12,[149] whose account of the invention of the music of the aulos concludes with a mention of the piped melody that accompanies the choral dancing that occurred at the festival of the ever-dancing Graces at Orchomenos (25–27). Aiming to imitate the death plaint of Medusa and the cries of her grieving sisters, these in turn accompanied by the hissing of the snakes sprouting from the Gorgons' heads, Athena 'interweaves' (διαπλέξαισ', 8) the three different sounds on her newly invented instrument.[150]

A focus on the intertwining of heterogeneous elements returns at *Ol.* 6.86–87, where the poetic ego presents himself 'weaving a variegated song for spear-wielding men' (ἀνδράσιν αἰχματαῖσι πλέκων / ποικίλον ὕμνον). The conceit is newly taken up in fr. 179 S.-M., a fragment in which the task at hand is again that of fashioning a poetic ornament, now a woven headband for the sons of Amythaon (ὑφαίνω δ' Ἀμυθαονίδαισιν ποικίλον / ἄνδημα). In both passages the adjective underscores the composite quality that Pindar would make exclusive to his choral compositions. Variegation figures again in *Nem.* 8.15, in the dedication of another head ornament – on this occasion for the image of Aiakos at Aegina – whose musical element is foregrounded: Λυδίαν μίτραν καναχηδὰ πεποικιλμέναν ('a Lydian headband ornamented/interwoven with ringing sound'). Examples of headbands in the material record bear out the intricacy assigned this choral gift; that worn by the Mantiklos Apollo[151] not only combines different techniques, metal-forging and incising, and several geometric patterns, but repeats in more miniaturized fashion two 'woven' features of the larger image, first the figure's braided hair whose diagonal lines it replicates, and second, the writing on the legs which, viewed purely as decorative elements, replaces the ornamented textiles worn by figures in other media.

If ποικίλος – as its repeated usage from Homer on in the context of intricately woven garments suggests –[152] is closely bound up with pattern-weaving, then Pindar's several turns to the expression ποικίλος ὕμνος would succinctly call attention to the woven character of a song. In a statement whose precise valence, whether positive, negative or both at once, is hard to

---

[148] Barker 1995, 45–46.   [149] For the text and discussion, see Chapter 2.

[150] See Steiner 2013a for detailed discussion.

[151] Boston, Museum of Fine Arts 03.997, with further discussion in Chapter 8.

[152] The presence of the Mycenaean equivalent *po-ki-ro-nu-ka* on a tablet concerning textiles pushes that association still further back.

gauge, *Ol.* 1.29 declares that *muthoi* 'ornamented with intricately/duplici-tously fabricated lies' (δεδαιδαλμένοι ψεύδεσι ποικίλοις) deceive their listeners. But this decorative weaving that adorns to a superlative and perhaps delusory degree returns in unequivocally affirmative fashion at the song's end, where the encomiast declares it his intention to 'deck out [Hieron] in the famed folds of song' (κλυταῖσι δαιδαλωσέμεν ὕμνων πτυχαῖς, 105), viz. the folds of the woven robe that the poet has been fashioning in this ode, and will rework on a future occasion to accommo-date his patron's further victory. Woven goods may have had a preliminary appearance in the ode, already underpinning the conceit at lines 8–9. In the curious image of how 'the much spoken song (ὁ πολύφατος ὕμνος)' is cast around the wits (μητίεσσι) of poets', Pindar selects an adjective for the *hymnos* that, in Robert Renehan's observation, audibly introduces the idea of weaving;[153] perhaps contributing to that secondary meaning is the frequent combination in Pindar and sources that predate him of weaving and *mêtis*.

In the more standard interpretation of the proem's expression,[154] the lines primarily refer to the act of crowning with a wreath, an adornment that unites the sympotic celebrants and the object of their praise, the victorious Hieron turned host, in the symbiotic bond characteristic of relations between the Pindaric celebrant and his paymaster. The associ-ation between weaving and wreathing or garlanding is commonplace in the poet's encomia. As the image of the 'variegated crown' or circlet so ubiquitous in the odes suggests, the head ornament is itself a woven or plaited object: fr. 179 S.-M., cited above, invests the adornment with just this property, while the speaker at *Isthm.* 8.66–67 declares, 'let one of his comrades in honour of the pankration weave (πλεκέτω) for Kleandros a luxurious crown of myrtle'. The plaited garland of foliage can, in a further step of combination and fitting one thing to another, involve its intermingling with an additional element; a phrase at *Isthm.* 7.39 imagines this secondary process when the piece figures itself as engaged in 'fitting/harmonizing the hair with wreaths' (ἀείσομαι χαίταν στεφάνοισιν ἁρμόζων).

On other occasions in choral song, ornamental wreaths, headbands and garlands appear hard on the heels of a weaving allusion or metaphor (as occurred in the sequence of activities punctuating Theocritus' later *Epithalamium*). No sooner does Bacchylides picture the poetic ego

---

[153] Renehan 1969, 219–21, who would understand the ode as a tunic woven by the poet.
[154] See Nisetich 1975; his view is followed by later discussions.

'weaving a *hymnos*', a musical tribute earlier described as an *agalma* sent by the Muses (3–10), at the outset of his fifth ode than the speaker professes himself the '*therapôn* of Urania with her golden headband' (χρυσάμπυκος Οὐρανίας, 13–14); it is as though the poet were presenting his tutelary goddess with a second woven ornament, that which the song is concurrently creating, to match her already existing headdress. A second Bacchylidean passage links the woven garland or headdress expressly to the movement of the dancers internal and external to the song. Section 1 cited fr. 17.101–08 S.-M., where the audience can witness, through the eyes of Theseus, the circle dance performed by the Nereids adorned with whirling and gold-interwoven hair ribbons that anticipate the rose-twined πλόκος then presented by Amphitrite to the hero.

One further 'accessory' unique to performances of song and dance, the *schoinos* used of the chorus line at the beginning of Pindar's fr. 70b S.-M., belongs in this (partial) inventory of the woven objects punctuating choral lyric. The term chosen by the poet features a cord fashioned of plaited or woven reeds – a property brought out in a fragment of Aristophanes where a speaker pleonastically styles a woven basket a πλεκτήν ... σχοῖνον (fr. 36 K.-A.) – and Lawler may be correct when she understands the Pindaric image as predicated on the 'woven' nature of the choral ensemble, whose dancers interlinked their hands so as to form just such a woven chain.[155] Painters, among them the artist of the François Vase, repeatedly show choral dancers clasping hands in an arrangement that might call weaving to mind,[156] and that the patterns on many of the garments worn by the twice seven in the image could render in more schematic fashion (see Section 3). The Polledrara hydria from the Grotta of Isis at Vulci also cited in Section 1 for its representation of Theseus, Ariadne, the spiralling rope and a choral dance (the *geranos*?), portrays a more intricate manual 'network' that would reflect the performance's complex choreography: in this instance, each chorus member places one of her hands on the wrist of the next figure in the line, while reaching with the other past her neighbour so as to grasp the back-stretched arm of the next-but-one dancer.[157]

---

[155] Lawler 1950, 83–84. Weaving with the *schoinos* appears again in Theocritus: the boy who 'weaves' the cricket cage 'harmonizes' (ἐφαρμόσδων) the *schoinos* and the asphodel in what is patently an image for poetic composition (*Id.* 1.52–4).

[156] In light of Plato's later view that the warp represents masculine properties, and the weft feminine (*Pol.* 309b, with discussion in Section 4), the girl-boy alternation in this dance becomes particularly rich in meaning.

[157] See too the chorus in a fourth-century tomb painting from Ruvo for another such complicated manual design (Naples, Museo Nazionale 9352–57).

While choral poetry richly develops the equivalence between the weaver and *choreia* already sounded in Homeric epic in any number of virtuosic ways, it is a passage of Euripides that brings together many of the tropes and images reviewed in this section and returns to the spiders' webs which, I suggested, could be read as configurations of the dance staged by the Phaeacians in *Od.* 8. Redeploying the arachnid simile already present in the Odyssean episode, the chorus of the *Erechtheus*, here assuming the dramatic identity of old men, describes its renouncement of the martial sphere for the choral songs it hopes to perform, and, in this 'performative future', is currently enacting (fr. 369 K.):

> κείσθω δόρυ μοι μίτον ἀμφιπλέκειν ἀράχναις·
> μετὰ δ᾽ ἡσυχίας πολιῷ γήρᾳ συνοικῶν
> ᾄδοιμι κάρα στέφανοις πολιὸν στεφανώσας,
> Θρηκίαν πέλταν πρὸς Ἀθάνας
> περικίοσιν ἀγκρεμάσας θαλάμοις

> Let my spear lie idle for spiders to intertwine in their webs and may I, dwelling in tranquility with grey old age, sing, my grey hair garlanded with garlands, after hanging up a Thracian shield upon Athena's halls surrounded with columns.

In the analogies and oppositions that the lines construct, the old men's *choreia* stands to the now 'hung up' Thracian shield as the spiders weaving their webs stand to the idling spears around which their threads are intertwined; on both occasions a 'woven' good, the first the explicitly woven web fashioned on the spear-cum-loom, the second the more implicit cloth of the choral song, trumps war's arsenal.[158] But there is more to the chorus' choice of diction as its members cite items and actions that glance to the different elements of their ongoing performance. First, the emphasis on circularity already present in the Homeric account of Demodocus' song: not only are the spiders' webs woven 'around' the supports supplied by the spears in the manner of the Homeric chains wound about the bedposts, but the garlands, whose presence the pleonastic verb recapitulating the noun earlier in the line makes emphatic, would form woven circlets around the singer-dancers' aged heads. Fresh references – and another instance of the pillar/chorister analogy detailed in Chapter 6 – to things that circle about

---

[158] Just as in the vase paintings explored above, the garlands the elders now wear may parallel and replace the no longer carried circular shield.

come in the description of Athena's chambers, not merely equipped with porticos but, more literally, with pillars that 'go around'. Whether or not the chorus' motions in some way reflected these encircling objects, the language alone would prompt spectators to envisage a dance in the round.

3   Choral Song and Dance and Textile Design Past and Present

If, as I have argued, weaving and textiles stand in an intimate and marked relation to choral poetry, its design and execution, then does an underlying rationale exist for the two activities' alignment, and this in ways quite independent of the similar structural designs of loom and lyre and the several technical overlaps documented so far? The discussion of Anthony Tuck offers a novel approach to the 'web of song' conceit,[159] which he reads in the light of traditional weaving practices still visible today and that are used to generate complex textile designs or, to return to Nagy's term, 'pattern-weaving'. In Tuck's suggestion, epic texts depicting women singing while working at their looms offer an early example of how weavers in several socities (in Turkey, Afghanistan and India among them) commit to memory the numerical and colour information required for producing certain textile patterns by performing rhythmic, metrical pieces as they weave; since these individual songs encode particular numbers and sequences of stitches as well as the spacings between them and the thread colours, the choice of which song to sing depends on the specific pattern the weavers aim to create. Citing contemporary Afghan picture rugs, Tuck describes how their producers use 'coded rhythmic struc-tures to translate images into woven patterns', and, elaborating on this, explains that 'weavers reduce images to numerical grids that are then remembered and communicated throughout the course of production in the form of a chantlike song ... Information embedded within narrative structures, tonal shifts, or rhythmic changes, all in associ-ation with song, could conceivably provide the framework whereby the memorization and, equally important, the organization of numerical count sequences and colour codes that are repeated each time a pattern is reproduced'.[160] Picturing much this way of performing the

---

[159] Tuck 2006.

[160] Tuck 2006, 540 and 543. The author does add the caveat that 'without further study it is difficult to know precisely how these songs fully record such designs'.

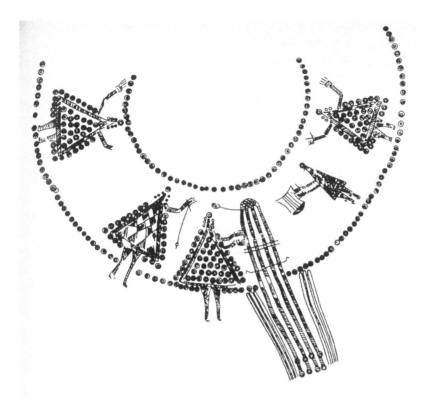

Fig. 7.16 Drawing of a seventh-century Hallstatt vase from Sopron. Vienna, Naturhistorisches Museum 35.424. Photograph: NHM, Vienna.

task is the seventh-century Hallstatt vase from Sopron, Hungary, which shows women spinning and weaving to musical entertainment (Fig. 7.16).[161]

The Hallstatt vase proves key to the extension and modification of Tuck's intriguing argument proposed here. Plainly visible on the pot is not only a male lyre-player but two female figures whose raised arms indicate that they are dancing, thereby adding to the song and music the third and kinetic element so central to the practice of *choreia* and one that goes unmentioned in Tuck's all but exclusively hexameter-focused account. Other practices apparent in ancient depictions of weavers further suggest that his model

---

[161] Vienna, Naturhistorisches Museum 35.424. Tuck 2006, 540 n. 8 describes an analogous scene he witnessed in northern India where younger members of the household worked at the large upright looms set up in the forecourt of the home (just like the site documented earlier) while another woman performed a chant-like song; the guide tells the author that the woman is 'singing the rug'.

better suits choral poetry than the hexameter genre from which he draws his several examples, and this on at least four grounds.

First, as the visual record and many of the passages already reviewed attest, weaving is predominantly, if not invariably, a group activity, an endeavour in which a single individual may also direct her companions or attendants, and where the production of a particularly broad and/or complex textile may involve weavers located at different sides of the loom, passing the weft bobbin between them, or performing different tasks simultaneously as they work on the same piece. On the Amasis lekythos (Fig. 7.9), the girl beating the weft stands towards the left while her companion moves the bobbin between the warp threads from the right side of the loom. An earlier small black-figure aryballos of ca. 590–560 from Corinth shows a scene (possibly the contest between Athena and Arachne) in which two groups of female weavers work at upright warp-weighted looms;[162] There is a clear division of tasks between the two figures standing on each side of the first of these: where the one on the left has a stick in each hand, the weaver on the right seems to hold up a two-pronged object. This plurality of participants is, of course, a defining feature of choral as opposed to monodic poetry, and is apparent in the several lyric interludes in fifth-century drama where the choreutes recall the songs they performed while at their looms.

Add to this the fact that, from the epic poems on, weavers rarely seem to perform their task while seated, at least not when weaving takes place on the upright loom and with multiple practitioners. Instead, as the common Homeric formula ἱστὸν ἐποίχομαι, 'to go back and forth at the loom' (e.g. *Il.* 1.31, *Od.* 5.62, 10.222), indicates, weaving involves motion first in one direction, and then in reverse, a bi-directionality made still more evident in the Pindaric expression, παλιμβάμους ... ὁδούς (*Pyth.* 9.18), which here describes the weaver's back-turning course. This back-and-forth trajectory maps neatly onto the strophic structure also characteristic of choral poetry, which requires choristers to perform the same sequence of steps twice, turning first in one direction and then the other.

A third signature property of choral poetry is the complexity of its metrical and rhythmic design and the variety of dance movements and *schêmata* that its shifting sequences generate. Choral compositions, whose changeable, alternating and 'variegated' quality (*poikilia*) their poets advertise, seem more likely than the comparatively simple hexameter genre (where a single metrical scheme structures each line of verse) to produce the similarly complex and richly patterned textiles cited by Tuck.

---

[162] Corinth, Archaeological Museum CP 2038; for this, see Barber 1991, 105–06 with her fig. 3.24.

Movement along the loom could itself generate this shifting metre and vocal line, whose variations and vocal rises and falls the foot fall simultaneously sounds out. On the aryballos from Corinth just cited, the female figures are equipped with platform clogs, which allow them to reach the upper portions of their looms; worn by the several participants in the task, and with two separate sets of individuals at each of the two upright structures, this footwear would sound out as the weavers moved across the floor, creating a variety of acoustic patterns and rhythms.

Finally, if the purpose of singing while weaving is, as Tuck proposes, to encode weaving information concerning thread colours, stitch counts and the rest, then dancing or at least moving in several different rhythms would facilitate the learning process and guarantee a more long-lasting ability to repeat an intricate design from one cloth to the next. According to this altered paradigm, the motions of the weavers as they witness or actually perform the steps would result in that form of bodily encoding and conditioning that scholars of dance observe, whereby the *kinêsis* becomes imprinted in the very neural structure of the participants and results in a 'movement thinking' that cannot be unlearned. Hands as well as feet are implicated in the 'embodied knowledge' that both dancers and weavers possess: passing the shuttle in and out of the warp threads and manipulating the pin beater or stick requires arm and hand to move in a swift, regular, sometimes recurrent and sometimes altered fashion, a motion that also possesses an audible dimension: the sound of the pin beater as it beats the weft or strums the threads generates a rhythm that in turn reflects the weavers' gestures.[163] In his description of contemporary pattern-weavers in the highlands of Bolivia, Gary Urton records an instance of this mode of somatic encoding: observing the practiced weaver at the loom, he notes that 'her movements are performed automatically without counting to herself, according to hand and body routines of movement that become habitual through long training'.[164] As he further describes this process of habituation, it results in 'the smooth flow of body movements and the feel of proper rhythms'.[165]

The weaving imagery devised by choral poets in references to playing intricate melodies on the lyre amd pipes acknowledges the role of the

---

[163] In similar fashion, ballet dancers use small hand motions to learn and imprint on the remainder of their bodies the sequence of gestures, steps and positions just performed by their choreographer-teacher and which they go on more fully to reproduce when they begin to move with their feet through space.

[164] Urton 1997, 118.   [165] Urton 1997, 125.

hands. The dithyrambist Telestes names Marsyas the first 'to fit together
the Lydian tune ... weaving around it on his reeds of variegated forms the
well-feathered breeze of his breath' (806 *PMG*), a conceit that positions the
(rectilinear) reeds as the vertical warp and the breath as the weft, and whose
sustained focus on manual action (ἅρμοσε, ἀμφιπλέκων) draws attention to
the aulete's hands, their rapid and changing passage along the instrument as
they work together with the player's breathing to produce the innovatory
nomos. The poet attributes this same skill to the player on the 'five-staffed'
magadis, a multi-stringed type of harp (808 *PMG*). Most pertinent to weaving
is the term selected for the actions of the harpist, 'swiftly running his hand up
and down around the turning post' (χέρα καμψιδίαυλον ἀναστρωφῶν
τάχος). In uncompounded form, στρωφάω (the frequentative form of
στρέφω) refers to the skilled Phaeacian wool-workers outside Alkinous'
palace, who wind the wool onto the distaff prior to weaving it into cloth (αἱ
δ' ἱστοὺς ὑφόωσι καὶ ἡλάκατα στρωφῶσιν, *Od.* 7.105).

Relevant to this match of elaborately patterned rugs and other textiles and
choral song and dance is Carruesco's discussion of the non-figurative designs
on Geometric pottery.[166] In his suggestion, the regular presence of these
commonplace elements – straight and zigzag lines, circles, grids or webs,
knots, whirls, maeanders, chevrons, diamonds, swastikas and the rest – both
within the representations of the dancers and in panels adjacent to these
establish close relations between these seeming 'space-fillers' and the figures
on the pot: the former serve as representations of the choral motions that the
artistic medium cannot otherwise render.[167] While Carruesco's focus is on
ceramics, he notes that woven cloths display the same ornamentation, and
observes in passing 'the importance of textiles and weaving patterns' in
suggesting the pictorial designs.[168] If he is correct (and there is, obviously, a
high degree of speculation here), then we could see the patterns on the textiles
as a form of choreographic notation, permanent records of the song and dance

[166] Carruesco 2016, 89.
[167] Many of the patterns cited by Carruesco exactly correspond to a system of dance notation
devised in the 1680s by Pierre Beauchamp, commissioned by Louis XIV for the Académie
Royale de Danse; in 1700, Raoul-Auger Feuillet's *Chorégraphie* offered a detailed description of
the system, subsequently modified by Pierre Rameau.
[168] Barber's work (Barber 1992, 112) spells out the exact equivalence between these textile
decorations and the patterns visible on Geometric pots, and particularly on the so-called
Dipylon vases. Describing the stick-figures of the mourners with their triangular shoulders as a
'debased version' of the weaving style used to produce the complex non-repeating patterns on
story-cloths, she also notes how the characteristic division of the painted vessels into thin
horizontal bands 'is the way a weaver's weft builds the cloth and which therefore is the most
natural way to build a picture when weaving'.

of those who made them. Pertinent to this notion is a representation of a seemingly dancing figure in a garden from Hagia Triada in Crete, dated to the Late Minoan I period. She wears a flounced skirt painted in red, white and blue, with elaborate pattern-weavings that include interlocked quatrefoils and edgings made up of snail-shell spirals.[169]

Ceramics and textiles coincide in the instance of the Boeotian doll-idol cited at this chapter's start, whose skirt combines a frieze of dancing women dressed in patterned cloths with geometric motifs. The mirroring relations between the dancing figures and the idol that I earlier observed now acquire an additional set of correspondences: taking his figurative and other motifs from the model supplied by woven garments, the artist has translated thread into the medium of paint while showing the end product of the weaver's art, the dress worn by the figurine. If the patterns on the doll's clothing have their origins in choral song and dance, then we witness a kind of *mise en abyme* or endlessly repeating loop: the singers' rhythmic motions in accordance with the metres that together determine their stitches generate the patterns of figurative and non-figurative elements painted on the terracotta cloth, including the image of the weavers themselves now transformed back into the chorus that first created the fabric with voice and motions in its song and dance at the loom. The design of this and other fabrics becomes a medium for recording *choreia*, a 'script' that can in turn prompt reperformances of the sounds and movements that accompanied their original production and are now replicated through the painted design. If the parallels between the ornamentation on metal goods and those on vases (both are made up of bands that vary and reproduce the patterns of other bands and panels) underpin the Homeric simile comparing the movement of the choreutes on Achilles' shield to the spins of the potter's wheel, then the two self-standing lines describing the clothing that the dancers wear reinforce that association (595–96):[170]

> τῶν δ' αἳ μὲν λεπτὰς ὀθόνας ἔχον, οἳ δὲ χιτῶνας   595
> εἵατ' ἐϋννήτους, ἧκα στίλβοντας ἐλαίῳ·

> And of these, [the girls] had delicate cloths, while the [youths] wore well-washed tunics, smoothly shining with oil.

---

[169] See Barber 1991, 318–19 and her pl. 2.

[170] A further, more rapid glance to another woven object, the headband worn by the maiden dancers, follows in line 597.

4 *Harmonia*: The End Product of *Choreia* and of Weaving

In a scene from Nonnus' *Dionysiaca*, Aphrodite comes to the home of
Harmonia while the goddess is working at her loom, weaving an elaborately
figured pattern cloth (41.294–302). A red-figure lekanis lid of ca. 410–400
attributed to the Meidias Painter anticipates the poet by combining
Harmonia with cloth-making implements:[171] here, placed at various points
in the visual field, are two kalathoi, one immediately adjacent to the seated
divinity. Some twenty years earlier, the Eretria Painter imagined a different
pairing between Harmonia and weaving, choosing a representation of her
marriage to Cadmos by way of image for an epinetron, the thigh device
worn by weavers to protect them from the grease the wool contained.[172]
Together, the text and lekanis lid position *harmonia* as the end product or
epiphenomenon of weaving, while the Eretria Painter's choice of the
weaving implement for this epithalamic scene suggests the institution of
marriage as the context in which that concordance is most fully realized.[173]

The pairing of *harmonia* with textile-making apparent in these diverse
sources and modes of representation makes good sense: as this chapter's
closing discussion goes on to suggest, weaving and woven cloths supply
symbols for the concordance and union of heterogeneous qualities that
harmonia signifies.[174] In fostering cohesion, the activity serves much the
same purpose as the institution of the chorus, which both the visual and
textual accounts cited in this chapter view as a means of reconciling hostile
and opposing forces that risk disturbing social and civic harmony. Insofar
as it is integral to both textile-making and choral song and dance, *harmonia*
also spans the two separate spheres to which, as earlier suggested, each
activity belongs, extending from the weaver's largely domestic domain to
the public world of the polis where choruses perform. While other scholars
have amply documented how, in their separate ways, cloth production and
choreia play critical roles in achieving *harmonia* in the home and public
space (whether in reality or in images used to articulate marital and
political consonance), my discussion focuses on the coincidence of the
two activities in practices and institutions aimed at the creation and

[171] Naples, Museo Nazionale SA 316; *ARV*² 1327.85.
[172] Athens, National Archaeological Museum 1629; *ARV*² 1250.34, 1688.
[173] Marriage is also intimated by the lekanis scene; the other seated figure is Aphrodite, shown together with Eros.
[174] In her divine personification, the goddess is of course the product of the commingling of antithetical forces, of Aphrodite and Ares, love and strife.

maintenance of concord and explores the shared processes and techniques that go into the realization of this political ideal.

4.1   Choral Performances and Textiles in the Oikos Economy

In my reading of the juxtaposition of scenes of wool-working and weaving with choral dance on the Amasis lekythos introduced in Section 1, I suggested that, together with the vase that forms its pair, the vessel demonstrates the place of the two activities in the context of the maiden's transition from girlhood to marriage. But there are other ways of understanding the co-presence of the motifs. As the work of Sheramy Bundrick has proposed, in fifth-century vase imagery, the frequent representations of the bride-to-be or newly wedded wife with cloth-making implements and/ or engaged in spinning and weaving express the idea of marriage as a cooperative, harmonious enterprise, husband and wife both contributing their industry – one by cloth-making in the home, the other by gathering money in the public space – to the domestic economy.[175] The choral dances that occur in conjunction with or independent of cloth-making on the two Amasis vases convey the same idea: they not only record the presence of the singer-dancers who would participate in the wedding, but more figuratively anticipate the *harmonia* that will exist between the future couple.[176]

Vases include more oblique pointers to the music-making and choral dancing that accompanied the marriage rite, combining these allusions with direct references to textile production. Wool-working appears alongside this musical theme (absent any suggestion of choral activity) on a lebes gamikos dated to ca. 430–420 by the Washing Painter, which shows on its body the seated bride surrounded by symbols and accessories of her nuptials;[177] since she is neither veiled nor garlanded, the scene may be set on the day following the rite, during the *epaulia* when relatives and friends visited the newly-wed in her home, bringing her gifts. The bride's two hands play on the strings of a harp, perhaps a reminder of the hymeneal songs that accompanied the previous day's events. Positioned on the base of the vase are two pairs of women equipped with wool baskets and sashes, among the items the bride would receive; one of the kalathos-carriers stands immediately below the bride as though better to equate the music produced on the harp with the loom at which she will also exercise her skills

---

[175] Bundrick 2008.   [176] Bundrick 2005, 179–92.

[177] New York, Metropolitan Museum of Art A 07.286.35; *ARV*² 1126.1; *Para.* 453, with Bundrick 2005, 188, whose reading I draw on.

in her new role. On a now-lost hydria by the Hephaistos Painter,[178] Eros carries a handloom and aulos case as he approaches the bride who sits with a kalathos in her hand.

A second look at the first of the two Amasis lekythoi reveals other continuities between *choreia* and cloth-making pertinent to this articulation of domestic *harmonia*. The image on the pot's body demonstrates the cooperative nature of textile production, the 'distributive cognition' required to produce the nuptial garment that the bride will wear; the choruses (made up of the erstwhile wool-workers) dancing on the neck reconfigure the allotment of specialized tasks down below by dividing themselves anew into subgroups, here just two, each of which performs a different sequence of steps and motions while joining together so as to form a continuous ring as the garment makers do around the body of the jar. The relations between the scenes are still closer when we recall that *ponos* and its cognates are used both of weavers and of choreutes, each group engaged in labours aimed at the creation of a cohesive and pleasing artefact. The representation of these two complementary forms of productive activity is, again, anticipatory insofar as the *parthenoi* rehearse the distribution of tasks characteristic of the domestic economy into which their companion now enters.

A projection of the harmonious *entente* that should, ideally, buttress a marriage may be of relevance to the series of single-mantle images earlier explored. As noted in Section 1, a subset of these vase representations places the mantle-wearing figures within a *Prozessionsschema*,[179] where the group (whether just one or often several such clusters) participates in what seem to be ritual events within a public setting and, in several examples, performs the gestures and motions that characterize chorus members as they advance in synchronized fashion. In some images we can securely identify the nature of the occasion: the celebration of a marriage. An aryballos of ca. 600, of Corinthian provenance but found in Vulci, shows the wedding of Heracles and Hebe;[180] among the divine attendants are two figures labelled Charites and two groups of three Muses, each collective covered by a common cloth. On another Corinthian vase, the wedding procession similarly includes three female triads, each group draped in one mantle, and resembling the nymphs shown on the Pitsa plaque (see Chapter 5). On the François Vase of a few decades later, female threesomes walk in the procession at the marriage of Peleus and Thetis; here the label Horai

---

[178] See Bundrick 2008, 323, fig. 15.   [179] The term belongs to the discussion of Buchholz 1987.
[180] See Larson 2001, 260 for this and the example that follows.

Fig. 7.17 Black-figure Erskine dinos by Sophilos, ca. 580–570 B.C.E. London, British Museum 1971, 1101.1. Photograph © The Trustees of The British Museum.

identifies one single-mantled group, whose hand movements, I earlier proposed, suggest a stately dance. From ca. 580–570 comes the large-scale black-figure Erskine dinos by Sophilos depicting the same occasion (Fig. 7.17).[181] Among the divinities conducting the newly-weds are several groups of females, made up of two to five individuals, all with their characteristic shared covering. Preceding Dionysus, two unidentified figures with cloaks extending from their shoulders to beneath their waists process, while a label designates a second set, five figures positioned in an arc behind the chariot carrying Ares and Aphrodite, as the Muses; frontality and the syrinx that she plays distinguish the central member of the pentad. Accompanying the next chariot, bearing Apollo playing the kithara and singing, are three more mantle-covered Muses, all facing right.

So contextualized, the artists' choice of iconographical scheme may not only – as earlier suggested – look to the cohesive character of the performance, the 'symphonic' quality of the choristers' assemblage of song and steps and their capacity to dance and sing as one. Reflecting the actual role of textiles within the marriage rite, the motif would also more broadly anticipate the creation of bonds between the bride and groom as joint

---

[181] London, British Museum 1971, 1101.1; *Para.* 19.16 *bis*

participants in the *oikos* they will share, and rehearse their future mutuality. As Margherita Guarducci proposes in her reading of these and the broader and more heterogeneous corpus of images that incorporate figures covered by a single mantle, including those that most probably show marital pairs,[182] the garment 'has the purpose of expressing the reciprocal union of the various figures that it joins',[183] drawn together by love, friendship or other types of bonds, including the erotic attraction and even cash nexus between the symposiast and hetaira or lower-class prostitute who on occasion shares the cloth.

A passage from a composition cited elsewhere in this study, Pindar's ninth *Pythian*, well illustrates how the expressly nuptial cloth that covers the two members of the bridal pair can serve as a metonym for the *harmonia* that should characterize marriage and relations within the home.[184] *harmozein* first appears when Aphrodite 'fits together' Apollo and Cyrene as groom and bride, an act that the goddess performs immediately after she 'casts *aidôs*' on their wedding bed (12–13):

> καί σφιν ἐπὶ γλυκεραῖς εὐναῖς ἐρατὰν βάλεν αἰδῶ,
> ξυνὸν ἁρμόζοισα θεῷ τε γάμον
>   μιχθέντα κούρᾳ θ᾽ Ὑψέος εὐρυβία·

> She cast on them loving *aidôs* over their sweet acts of love, fitting together in a marriage common to both parties the god and the daughter of mighty Hypseus, with whom he mingled.

Drawing on the commonplace notion of *aidôs* as a mantle or protective covering,[185] Pindar here gives that cloth greater specificity, figuring it in the form of the bedspread or *chlaina*, frequently woven by the bride-to-be, that covers and unites the newly-weds.[186] 'Harmonizing' then returns near the

---

[182] The most outstanding examples are, admittedly, quite remote from the images produced in archaic and classical Greece, and belong to a set of sarcophagi from Vulci. The first, dated to ca. 350–300 (Boston, Museum of Fine Arts 86.145a–b), shows on its lid a bearded, older man lying with a woman on an elaborately figured bed, both with their arms around each other and gazing into one another's eyes, in an evident commemoration of their enduring marriage. The single cloth wound round their lower and otherwise naked bodies is, most probably, not the commonplace blanket but the husband's cloak or *tebenna*, a rounded and frequently decorated mantle. Paired with this is a second, earlier sarcophagus of ca. 450–400 (Boston, Museum of Fine Arts 1975.799), portraying a younger married pair, clearly, like the first, of high social standing, that again lies beneath a single coverlet.

[183] Guarducci 1928–29, 61.

[184] Herodotus twice uses *harmozein* for the act of becoming engaged (5.32, 9.108).

[185] See Ferrari 1990.

[186] That covering conceit returns in the context of Apollo's desire to claim Cyrene's virginity by laying his hand on her then and there, and Cheiron's caution regarding the need to perform the act in private at 36–41.

end of the song, again in an epithalamic context, and in a scene that includes prenuptial choral dancing and, more glancingly, a garment. Seeking to resolve the problem of how to marry off his daughter, Antaios recalls how Danaus found grooms for his forty-eight daughters by staging a courtship competition (detailed in Chapters 1 and 5). Emulating the mythical example, this father similarly positions his daughter as the prize in the dance-cum-race in which the suitors will compete, thus devising a means of 'fitting' together the new pair (ἁρμόζων κόρᾳ / νυμφίον ἄνδρα, 117–18). Victorious in the contest, the successful suitor claims his bride and her maidenhood, as, in a patent echo of Apollo's wish to place his hand on Cyrene and 'cull the honey-sweet flower from the marriage bed' (36–37), he touches her bridal peplos (ἀμφί οἱ ψαύσειε πέπλοις, 120).

If the poet says nothing of the 'woven' quality of these figurative and literal garments, then a reference to weaving, or rather its absence, occurs in the preliminary account of Cyrene's rejection of the occupations that typify maidens poised on the threshold of marriage: choosing to spend her time combating wild beasts in the unacculturated realm, Apollo's future bride 'did not care for going back and forth at the loom or the pleasures of meals with her companions (ἑταιρᾶν) in the home' (18–19). In place of this activity, the *parthenos* substitutes another form of 'toil' (31a), which she performs in solitary fashion (μούναν, 27) rather than as part of the joint enterprise that weaving requires and that the presence of her *hetairai* in the home would allow. But for all Cyrene's attempt to turn her back on the conventional parthenaic trajectory, this weaver manquée does wed, with Aphrodite furnishing the nuptial cloth that the bride neglected to fabricate. Pindar would have no need to spell out the relevance of the activity to the sexual union that the poem repeatedly intimates. As Scheid and Svenbro observe, the term συμπλοκή, 'interlacing', belongs not only to the interweaving of the warp and weft but to the physical 'commingling' of the husband and wife,[187] whose marriage represents the conjunction and 'harmonization' (συναρμοσαμένη, Pl. *Plt.* 309c) of the masculine warp and feminine weft threads.

4.2   Weaving and Choral Dancing at the Heraia

Insofar as the union of Apollo and Cyrene stands figure for the seemingly harmonious joining of two formerly independent geographic bodies, Greece and Libya (in whose principal city, Cyrene, the Pindaric victor

---

[187] Cf. Pl. *Plt.* 281a.3, *Symp.* 191c.4.

lives), *Pythian* 9 illustrates how marital and domestic *harmonia* bears directly on the public, civic sphere and the juncture between potentially hostile communities. In its different way, Pausanias' extended description of the quadrennial festival celebrated on behalf of Hera at Olympia and overseen by a group called the 'sixteen women of Elis' offers another example of the intersections between weaving and choral dancing and their place in promoting concordance in the private and political realms. According to the account beginning at 5.16.2, 'every fourth year there is woven for Hera a robe by the sixteen women, and the same also hold games called Heraia. The games consist of foot races for maidens', these, as the periegete notes, divided into three age categories.

After supplying the aetiology of the races (see below) and the back history of the group of sixteen that administers them, Pausanias then resumes his account of the festival: 'Later on they [the sixteen women] were entrusted with the arrangement of the Heraian games, and with the weaving of the robe for Hera. The sixteen women also instituted two choral dances, one called that of Physcoa (beloved of Dionysus), and the other that of Hippodameia'. As the report makes clear, the two choruses celebrate different deities and at different sites; the choral tribute of the first, most likely involving a dithyramb, is addressed to Dionysus, in the context of his great festival, the Thyia, located at Elis,[188] while the second is performed on the occasion of the Heraia of Olympia. But absent from Pausanias is any indication of who danced in the two choruses (the sixteen women of Elis, perhaps divided in two rival groups of eight, the maidens who competed in the running races or other local women?), nor does he say anything about the composition of the group that wove the robe, whether it was made up of the Elean women, of the *parthenoi* who also competed in running contests or of some additional unspecified collective.

These omissions notwithstanding, we can nonetheless make some sense of the coincidence of elements that Pausanias does report, chiefly choral dancing, competing in running races, weaving and the celebration of Hippodameia, who, he relates, brought together the sixteen women so as to express her gratitude to Hera in sanctioning her union with Pelops. Beginning with the choruses and races, and although, again, nothing in the text establishes a parallel between the age divisions in the athletic contests and the make-up of the choruses or suggests that the same individuals participate in both, such continuities are apparent in Plato's prescripts for his city in the *Laws*. As the Athenian Stranger makes clear, Magnesia's

---

[188] For details, see Calame 1997, 24–25 and 136.

citizens will be divided into twelve *phylai* consecrated to the twelve gods (745d–e), and he later gives several indications that the three forms of choral performances, themselves organized according to age classes, involve these phyletic divisions.[189] Most apposite to Pausanias' description is a phrase at 828c2–3 describing how the city will celebrate twelve *heortai* for the twelve gods of each of the *phylai*, and noting that these festivals will involve 'choruses and musical competitions and also gymnastic ones'. As Lucia Prauscello interprets this portion of the text, 'in a society so obsessed with hierarchy based on biological seniority, it seems likely that at these *heortai* the age-class criterion would certainly have been respected'.[190]

Taken more as a whole, the activities cited by Pausanias together with the presence of Hippodameia also call to mind the individuals and actions found in the coming-of-age rituals celebrated by maidens elsewhere in Greece, among them those described in Alcman's first *Partheneion* where, according to most readings, the chorus members carry a robe (of their own weaving?) for presentation to the deity to whom their performance is addressed.[191] And while Artemis more frequently appears as the deity who presides over maturation rituals, Hera, as goddess of marriage, also plays a role, as she does in the myth of the Proitids whose story, detailed in Chapter 5, includes several of the activities present at the Heraia. Nor would it be unusual for older women to act as 'marshals' of the choruses; the expression 'to set up a chorus', used by Pausanias at 5.16.6 seems to present them fulfilling this function, and so too in Pindar's second *Partheneion* we witness the mother of the lead dancer preparing the chorus to participate in the Daphnephoria (fr. 94b.71–72 S.-M.); at the festival of Amyklai for Apollo, another occasion for choral perfomances, older women also have their part.

But the myth of origin concerning this Elean Heraia also includes an expressly political dimension, this visible in 'another story' (Paus. 5.16.5) concerning the origins of the group of sixteen that Pausanias relates. Following the death of the Pisan tyrant Damophon and his community's renunciation of his hostility and damage wreaking towards the neighbouring Eleans, the two cities decided to set their former differences aside. Central to the reconciliation was the choice of one woman, whoever was

---

[189] See Prauscello 2014, 154–55. [190] Prauscello 2014, 155.

[191] There are divergent views on what object the chorus carries (a robe, plough or perhaps a torch). For persuasive arguments in favour of the robe, see Priestley 2007. A weaving image immediately precedes the moment when the song pivots to its more self-referential section, where the chorus members speak of their own affairs and activities; at line 38, the term δι] ἀπλέκει appears, here applied to the individual who 'weaves out' a tearless day.

particularly 'venerable and sensible', from each of the sixteen Elean districts; the 'college' that resulted was then charged with making the peace and subsequently given responsibility for the organization of the races, the weaving of the robe and the choral dancing. Pausanias also comments that, in his own time, only eight *phylai* still existed from the original sixteen cities of Elis, and that each of these furnished two women so as to make up the sixteen. In the likely scenario suggested by Nagy,[192] these pairs could then have been assigned to one or the other of the choruses that danced in honour of the two cult figures, yielding 'eight choral performances entailing two rival choral subdivisions'.

The matrimonial elements so apparent in the story and that cluster around the figure of Hippodameia are also consistent with its political aspect: in similar fashion, marriage (which in itself serves a civic-cum-political end insofar as it promotes the propagation of new citizens) involves the union between two individuals, their families and larger polities. In the symbolic 'logic' informing the Elean festival, the marital conjunction for which the maiden participants are being readied supplies a reflection and articulation at the domestic level of the political concordance reaffirmed through the Heraia's regular celebration. The weaving of the cloth integral to the ritual, no less than the choral dancing, freshly expresses the 'coming together' of previously heterogeneous elements, their conjunction within a single product or performance.

4.3   Political Division and Recombination in Aristophanes and Plato

In their discussion of the Elean story,[193] Scheid and Svenbro cite another, much better known episode where the act of weaving proves symbolic of a political reconciliation between hostile states, now Athens and the other cities embroiled in the too long-lasting Peloponnesian War. In the fantasy devised by Aristophanes in *Lysistrata*, produced in 411 in the midst of the later stages of the struggle, the female protagonist aims to bring an end to the hostilities and famously uses an analogy from wool-working and weaving as she explains her plan to the *proboulos*, the city commissioner so skeptical of her stratagem. In response to his asking how she aims to resolve the 'confusion of affairs' and to 'untwine' (διαλῦσαι, 566) the mess, Lysistrata replies by equating the city at war with a tangled ball of wool (567) and compares the dispatch of embassies to the use of spindles to bring order to the skein. In her more detailed three-step proposal at 574–86, the

---

[192] Nagy 1990, 366.   [193] Scheid and Svenbro 1996, 9–34.

different stages of wool-working are made to correspond to the peace-making enterprise. Analogous with the washing of the raw fleece and its beating and the removal of burrs is the projected purge of the citizen body, which will rid it of criminals and venal politicians; the wool-carding that follows stands as counterpart to the women's plan to unite individuals well-disposed towards the city, whether citizens, metics, foreigners or the disenfranchised, all now joined 'into the common wool basket of concord'; the different colonies, currently 'lying around set apart like little flocks of wool' should, in the final stages, be added to the ball, from which the speaker then proposes to weave a cloak that will cover the entire populace.

As commentators regularly note, the speech draws on rituals and woven products familiar to the audience and that had long been symbols of civic harmony and the 'gathering into one' (συναθροίζειν εἰς ἕν, *Lys.* 585) of all elements making up the polis. Chief among these was the weaving and presentation of the peplos to Athena Polias, the city's tutelary goddess, at the culmination of the Panathenaia, a festival supposedly established by Theseus to celebrate his unification of Attica (cf. Plut. *Thes.* 24.1–3). The bestowal of the robe that would clothe the ancient image of the goddess marked the end point of the grand procession in which the diversified elements of the city – metics included – participated. The sources variously identify the different groups of individuals charged with the several stages in the creation of the robe.[194] Hesychius cites the *ergastinai* who, nine months before the Panathenaia and on the occasion of the Chalkeia, were responsible for hanging the warp onto the loom, dividing the threads and attaching the weights; another source notes that the Chalkeia coincided with the day when the priestess together with the Arrhephoroi (those girls of seven to eleven chosen to live on the Acropolis and to serve Athena for the year) 'also warp the peplos'.[195] Other women, including those desig-nated the 'priestesses', helped to card and spin the wool in preparation for the weaving. There is also evidence for the role of male weavers, respon-sible, in the view of some, for producing the larger and more elaborate 'sail-peplos' carried in the procession every fourth year. When these scattered pieces are assembled, the picture that emerges is of a sequence of ritual actions in which different segments of the female population, each arranged according to its age group, young girls, older girls and married women, variously took part, with men in a more occasional role.

---

[194] Barber 1992, 113–15 details the process.
[195] Pausanias Attikistes, *Attikôn Onomatôn Synagogê*, for which, see Barber 1992, 113 with her n. 23, and Connelly 2007, 39.

As Lysistrata's speech also specifies, division precedes the recombination on which the weaving of the communal cloak depends. In the preliminary words of the *proboulos*, the tangled affairs must be disentwined and in similar fashion the carding process untangles the wool and aligns the individual fibers in order to render them all alike. Lysistrata's description at 567–70 makes this act of differentiation and drawing apart explicit. Taking the tangled skein, and pulling it this way and that, she proposes that the different elements be disjoined or drawn asunder (διενεγκοῦσαι, 570; cf. the repetition of the prefix at 578 and 583).

Events at the Elean festival and the circumstances precipitating its foundation just described provide a parallel for this and demonstrate how the acts of division and assemblage detailed by Lysistrata also characterize the formation and conduct of the chorus, an institution already cited in the Aristophanic drama when the chorus leader notes that Athenian girls' participation in the (choral) rites at Brauron followed hard on the heels of their service at the Arrhephoria (641–45; see Section 2). The reconciliation between Elis and Pisa, which effectively unites the two previously warring communities, likewise involves a process a disaggregation then answered by the act of juncture in the creation of the collective 'college' charged with weaving the peplos for Hera. Not only are the women selected first from the sixteen different districts making up Elis, and later from the eight *phylai* that remain, but each may be (in Nagy's reconstruction) assigned to one of two separate choruses, an arrangement that resembles that found at the festival for Damia and Auxesia on Aegina. Here, as Herodotus reports at 5.83, 'there are ten men who are *chorêgoi* making public presentation for each of the deities' (χορηγῶν ἀποδεικνυμένων ἑκατέρῃ τῶν δαιμόνων δέκα ἀνδρῶν) who oversee the choruses of women as they compete in performances of mockery. Nagy also unpacks this too brief account: ten choruses, both presided over by their leader, would perform, further separated into rival choral 'subdivisions', each assigned to one of the two deities; so too at Elis, female choruses divided into two dance in celebration of two heroines, Hippodameia and Physcoa.[196]

Nagy further includes the Elean ritual in his discussion of the sources' use of *stasis*, a term that regularly refers to civic discord and internecine division and that can also describe the choral troupe.[197] In his account

[196] Nagy 1990, 364–65.
[197] Aesch. *Ag.* 1117, *Choeph.* 458, *Eum.* 309, each one in moments of pronounced choral self-referentiality, and again in the term *stasiarchos* used by the dramatist of Danaus in his capacity as *chorêgos* to his troupe of daughters (*Suppl.* 11); for these, see the discussion in Chapter 4 and

(cited in part in Chapter 4), the noun's seemingly contradictory meanings reflect the twofold process that goes into the establishment and marshalling of the chorus whether at the Heraia, or at Aegina or in Alcman's first *Partheneion*:[198]

> *stasis*, derivative of *histemi*, means not only "setting up, establishment, standing, station, status" both in general applications … and in more specific applications to the chorus … but also "division, conflict, strife" in general applications to the community at large (Theognis 51, 781, Hdt. 3.82.3) … I would argue that *stasis* in the negative sense of 'conflict' is a metaphor … for the ritualized interpersonal *divisions* that are acted out in the process of establishing or constituting choral performance; this constitution is in turn achieved through the literal *divisions* into which chorus members are systematically assigned when the chorus is organized … In sum, the ritual essence of the choral lyric performance is that it is *constitutive* of society in the very process of *dividing* it.

In this interpretation, the same choral activity whose core ritual purpose is the affirmation of social bonds achieves its end through a process of division, determined by age class, locality, deity or some combination thereof. We can witness this dynamic at Elis not only in the two choral groupings described by Plutarch, but also in the more complex, but parallel, divisions of the competitors into their age groups for the races.

Several commentators have noted how Plato's extended use of the statesman-weaver analogy of the *Politicus* is indebted to Aristophanes' *Lysistrata*, albeit with a change in emphasis and with the drama's central gender politics neutralized (the Platonic weaver is, of course, a man). For the Stranger, weaving supplies a handy example on two chief counts. First, because it offers a second paradigm (angling precedes the turn to textile-making) that demonstrates how to differentiate one skill from others akin to it, among them wool-carding, spinning, spindle-making and cleaning the clothes. While the *technê* of carding is a separative activity that involves 'undoing' the densely 'united' and matted materials so as to supply the thread for the warp and weft (τὸ δέ γε τῶν συνεστώτων καὶ συμπεπιλημένων διαλυτική, 281a5–6), weaving requires the very opposite and reversal of this: it is defined as the practice of *sumplokê*, intertwining, as manifested in the combination of the opposing warp and weft. Herein lies the further

---

Kavoulaki 2011, esp. 377–79. Note too the phrase στάσιν μελῶν at Ar. *Ran.* 1281, an expression glossed by a scholion as a stasimon.

[198] Nagy 1990, 366.

utility of the example and its particular pertinence to the statesmanship that the Eleatic visitor and his interlocutor are attempting to define; like the art of weaving, stewardship of the state necessitates the combination of opposites, not their elimination – the latter the work assigned to others – but rather their use for the city's advantage. The role of the statesman, it turns out, is to create order and harmony among the crafts and their practitioners subordinate to the weaver-king; directing others with their divided-up *technai*, he cleans and readies his 'human raw material, then weaves it into the fabric of the polis'.[199]

Indeed, the very tools used by the weaver supply metonyms for the co-presence of these twin processes of division and conjunction. As Socrates observes at *Cratylus* 389a–b, the *kerkis* serves to drive the threads of the weft close together while also keeping the threads of the warp and weft apart. In the more extended discussion of textile-making in the *Politicus*, the Stranger again comments on these complementary activities, noting that both weaving and spinning involve 'taking apart the things that lie close together' prior to their recombination or 'intertwining'. Where weaving is concerned, this act of separation falls to the *kerkis*, half of whose work it is (282b). Among the tasks performed by the pin beater that the speaker may have in mind could be its use in dividing the warps as it slips between them.[200] Aristotle names two separate objects belonging to the weaver, one of which divides, the other of which unites: the *kerkis*, he remarks, should be used in 'pushing apart' (a process characterized as δίωσις) while the *spathê*, a kind of broad, flat sword (cf. Aesch. *Choeph.* 231–32), is instead employed in pushing things together (σύνωσις, *Phys.* 243b6–11).

But if, as argued above, the art of weaving and the several processes it involves find parallels in the formation and morphology of the chorus, then neither the *Lysistrata* nor the Platonic texts do more than give that association a very passing glance,[201] and absent too from the *Politicus* is any consideration of chorality's role in uniting citizens into a single body (a motif writ so large in the *Laws*). These omissions notwithstanding, expressions of the three-way relations between weaving, *choreia* and civic concordance do exist, discernible in visual representations and texts that both pre- and postdate these classical sources. For the archaic age, I would return to the two images on the obverse and reverse of the cup from Argos in Fig.

---

[199] Blondell 2005, 55.   [200] See Edmunds 2012 for this and the Aristotle citation that follows.

[201] Note, however, that the language used to describe the weaving together of the contrasting qualities that different temperaments possess at *Pol.* 309a7–b7 strikingly anticipates Luc. *Salt.* 12, where the author explains that the 'necklace dance' interweaves the masculine and feminine attributes of its participants.

7.6, the first showing a group of nine, the second of seven maidens all grouped beneath a single pattern-woven cloth. The procession in which the mantled figures participate is a public, ritual event (note the three spectator figures, two men and a perhaps older woman, also wearing a flower-strewn, enveloping textile, who bracket the group on either side) that brings together the different members of the polis in a unified and well-ordered social body, for which these neatly configured choruses can serve as representatives.

Kowalzig, in what she calls an 'exercise of lateral imagination', takes this argument one step further, proposing that we might read the cloth in the image as a symbol for the walls that encompass and protect the polis in Plato's account of the structures at *Leg.* 778d–e.[202] A passage from the *Statesman* at 279c7–280a, which equates textiles with forms of protection at both the individual and societal level, not only supports Kowalzig's seemingly fanciful supposition, but can be set alongside a series of later texts that make weaving integral to the creation of the civic space and its public landmarks through which the chorus moves. As these post-classical sources suggest, the polis is not only, as Aristophanes and Plato variously imagine it, analogous to a woven cloth and/or the totality of citizens making up its 'fabric', but owes its very origins to the weaver's art. In Callimachus' formulation in his celebration of Apollo (*H.* 2.55–57), founding a city is an act of weaving:

Φοίβῳ δ᾽ ἑσπόμενοι πόλιας διεμετρήσαντο   55
ἄνθρωποι· Φοῖβος γὰρ ἀεὶ πολίεσσι φιληδεῖ
κτιζομένῃσ᾽, αὐτὸς δὲ θεμείλια Φοῖβος ὑφαίνει.

Following Phoebus, men measure out their cities; for Phoebus always delights in the founding of cities, and Phoebus himself weaves their foundations.

Just a few lines later, the poet presents Apollo engaged in the same activity, now 'pattern-weaving' (ἔπλεκε, 61) the altar of horns at Delos before casting about it walls of that material, a constructivist enterprise that Callimachus describes as supplying the template for the god's many future acts of city foundation. Detailing that Delian complex at 63–64, the poet patently imagines it as a cityscape in miniature, complete with the foundations (θεμείλια) introduced in the previous line, the walls that return so shortly afterwards when Apollo gives

---

[202] Kowalzig 2013, 200. That the choral institution was essential not just to civic harmony, but also to the defence of the polis in times of danger would give a particular charge to Aeschylus' *Septem*, which turns so centrally about the breaching of the Theban walls and juxtaposes the chorus of distraught maidens with the structures.

them to Cyrene (67) and the altars (80) also integral to the Libyan town, which receive offerings to the god on the occasion of the Karneia. That festival, moreover, features the re-enactment of the originary moment when Apollo witnessed 'the belted men of Enyo as they danced with the fair-haired Libyan women when the season of the Karneia came round' (85–87).

Others have detailed how central *choreia* is to the second *Hymn*, and how its proem already suggests a celebration of the god by an ephebic ensemble that the epiphanic god then joins as chorus leader. That choral motif, I suggest, continues to be visible in the references to Apolline weaving just cited. In emulating the divinity in their mirroring acts of city founding, men are literally those who have 'followed' (ἑσπόμενοι, 55) in the god's wake, much as chorus members do their *chorêgos*; and like those Spartan prisoners on the Tegean plain, its punitive dimension apart, their city-building enterprise takes the form of the rhythmic, 'metred' tread that these individuals dance out as members of Apollo's troupe (cf. Hdt. 1.66.4, διαμετρήσασθαι, with earlier discussion). Chorality is still more evident in the evocation of the Delian horn altar, the centrepoint around which Theseus and his twice seven danced in their originary performance of the *geranos*, and which the Iliaidic scholion figures as an act of weaving. Callimachus' return to Apollo and Delos in his fourth *Hymn* lingers on this performance, introducing the Athenian youths and maidens as one among the several choruses celebrating the god on the island (4.310–13; see too Chapter 6):

οἱ χαλεπὸν μύκημα καὶ ἄγριον υἷα φυγόντες   310
Πασιφάης καὶ γναμπτὸν ἕδος σκολιοῦ λαβυρίνθου,
πότνια, σὸν περὶ βωμὸν ἐγειρομένου κιθαρισμοῦ
κύκλιον ὠρχήσαντο, χοροῦ δ᾽ ἡγήσατο Θησεύς.

They, having scarcely fled the bellowing and savage son of Pasiphae and the coiling habitation of the crooked maze, lady [the island Delos], about your altar, after rousing the playing on the lyre, danced in a circle, and Theseus led the chorus.

To glance still futher into the post-classical future, the intercalation of weaving and city-founding apparent in the second *Hymn* would make another showing in Vitruvius' secularized 'anthropology', which identifies the moment when men start to build the *sine qua non* for all communal existence: 'and first, with upright forked props and twigs put between, they wove their walls' (2.1.3). More than just a large-scale configuration, as

Indra McEwen comments, 'of an upright Greek loom',[203] the city that results from their action may be understood as a woven textile, whose creation, in the argument this chapter has advanced, depends not only on the men who build, but on choruses that dance and sing, these chiefly made up of the maidens and women responsible for cloth production and who conjointly weave choral spectacles with body and voice.

[203] McEwen 1993, 113.

8 | Choreo-graphy: *Choreia* and Alphabetic Writing

'La danse, c'est la poésie avec des bras et des jambes.'

C. Baudelaire, *Petits Poèmes en prose*, 1868

Introduction

Sometime in the late fifth century the comic poet Callias produced what would come to be known as the *Letter Tragedy* (Γραμματικὴ Τραγῳδία) or *Letter Show* (Γραμματικὴ Θεωρία). According to Athenaeus' account of the drama at *Deipn.* 10.453c–54b, the chorus was composed of women representing the twenty-four letters of the Ionic alphabet. Following their introduction in the prologue, the chorus members then danced and sang out a series of two letter combinations of consonants and vowels that followed the order of the abecedarium, offering a 'jingle about syllabic phonology' and transporting to the stage pedagogic methods used to teach children how to read.[1] In the widely accepted argument of Pöhlmann,[2] the comedy would have been composed by way of humorous riposte to the debates generated by Athens' official adoption of the Ionian alphabet (involving the addition of three new letters to the public script) following the decree of one Archinus, enacted by the Athenian Assembly in 403/2 under the archonship of Eucleides. To make the words and actions of the 'letters' intelligible as they combined with one another in syllabic clusters while vocalizing the sound they made (this passage from the prologue is one among the four preserved by Athenaeus), each performer's costume or mask most likely carried some distinctive mark that would have alerted audience members to their individual identities.

Nor is this the first or only representation of the alphabet by a dramatic chorus. In Aristophanes' *Babylonians* of 427/26, a character remarks, 'The

---

[1] Rosen 1999, 152.

[2] Pöhlmann 1971; see too D'Angour 1999, Slater 2002 and Gagné 2013. See Gagné 2013, 309 for the suggestion of individuation in the choruses' costumes made below.

demos of the Samians how multi-lettered' (fr. 71 K.-A.). As Hesychius notes of the term πολυγράμματος, the description fits the Samians because their so-called Milesian or Ionic script included additional letters missing from the Old Attic alphabet,[3] and ancient commentators again cite the later reform of Archinus in glossing the line. In the suggestion of D'Angour, this production would have presented its twenty-four choreutes equipped with masks, each one displaying the letter that its wearer represented.[4] As in Callias' drama, audiences would witness letters personified in the form of the dancing-singing bodies, a veritable 'alfabeto figurato' such as Giovanni Battista Bracelli would represent in his print of 1632.[5]

In both dramatic instances, we could imagine chorus members performing motions that in some way corresponded to the individual letter shapes and gave physical, three-dimensional form to the distinguishing alphabetic marks that each one wore; when Callias' choreutes danced in pairs in their syllabic combinations, they may additionally have enacted a set of figures indicative of their design when now placed side by side in a word.[6] That such literal dancing out of alphabetic letters was a phenomenon not unknown to fifth-century Athenians, Sophocles' satyr-play *Amphiaraus* also suggests. According, once again, to Athenaeus, the dramatist brought on stage an individual tasked with 'dancing the letters' (τὰ γράμματα . . . ὀρχούμενον, fr. 121 R.). It seems plausible that dancing would also have accompanied several other passages in which letters are described as configurations, assemblages of different linear, circular and other shapes such as the body might assume through various *schêmata* and types of motions. So in a fragment from Euripides' *Theseus* (fr. 382 K.) an illiterate herdsman seeks to communicate the name 'Theseus' by describing the individual letter forms making up an inscription that he sees on the sails of a ship. After declaring himself unfamiliar with writing, he attempts to narrate the 'shapes and clear signs' (μορφάς . . . σαφῆ τεκμήρια) aligned in the word. The first (upper case) takes the form of a circle with a central element, the second that of two lines with another in between, the third features something like a curly (εἰλιγμένος) lock of hair, and the fifth 'two lines that begin from separate points and these run together into a single base'. Even as his account invites the audience to visualize the shapes, his

---

[3] Hesychius s.v., with discussion in D'Angour 1999, 113.   [4] D'Angour 1999, 113.

[5] The print appears in Bracelli's *Varie Figure*; for the illustration, see Franko 1993, fig 1.

[6] As Gagné 2013, 309 remarks, each letter would have been 'given physical shape through dancing by the group', while the two choristers that combined to make up each syllable might have executed 'some sort of characteristic dance'. Note Dion. Hal. *Comp.* 12.10, where he describes 'syllable weaving' as a process in which the syllabic components fashion just such figures, or *schêmata*. For this, see Section 4.

own bodily poses, now bent, now straight, and his movements, fashioning the links between the different *schêmata*, could accompany the spoken account and serve as a spur to mental visualization. The successive corporeal positions and the motions in between would also visibly depict how the letters were to be read sequentially.

Where most discussions of Athenaeus' report of the *Letter Show* concentrate on the identity of the dramatist, the date of the piece, its parodic relation to tragedy and the light that it casts on Greek reading practices, my concern is with a dimension of the *Theoria* that has gone largely unexplored: affinities between the art of alphabetic writing and choral dance and song.[7] Is Callias exploiting pre-existing connections between the two practices and how might they mutually influence one another in the performative, material and cognitive spheres? It is this relationship, or more literally choreo-graphy, that this chapter investigates, aiming to trace what will emerge as multiple and diverse links between the two phenomena that reach back to archaic times and to some of our earliest extant inscriptions. The exchanges documented here manifest themselves chiefly, although not exclusively, in the four areas treated in each section of this chapter. Section 1 presents a handful of self-standing inscriptions, absent any figurative elements, from archaic and early classical Greece which commemorate a variety of dance and choral performances and which showcase how the epigrams' composers and painters or incisors use the visible and material aspect of the letters, their arrangement on the surface of the clay and stone, their design and the manner in which they are painted or carved, so as to revisualize and generate re-enactments of the one-off performances they record.[8] As several analogies from the figurative vases and statues of the same period demonstrate,[9] these discussed in Section 2, artists and sculptors were also exploiting the affinity between these arts as they incorporated alphabetic elements into representations of choral dancers, alerting viewers to the properties that make alphabetic notations resemble, stand in for, prompt and actually dance with the figures. The chapter's third section turns to choral poetry, offering close

---

[7] Gagné 2013 does anticipate my approach, but the connections his illuminating treatment draws between choral activity and the role of writing are entirely different from those proposed here.

[8] For this dimension of the inscriptions, I will be referring to the distinction between 'sematography' and 'lexigraphy' proposed by Bennett 1963. In sematography, the painted or inscribed letters communicate through their visual appearance without direct correlation to speech; lexigraphy, by contrast, records speech. For discussion, see Pappas 2011, 45–46. Here too I draw on Day 2007, esp. 31–32, 39–40.

[9] Although the chapter treats the epigraphic and artistic instances separately, its underlying premise is that the inscriptions are every bit as 'artful' as these other works.

readings of several Pindaric pieces where the poet reflects on the interfaces between the song as written text and as a live choral performance; here fresh examples of epigraphic practices and writing technology occur, embedded in works that, like the inscriptions already explored, serve as catalysts for the transformation of the song's 'script' back into performative form. The chapter concludes in Section 4 with a discussion of passages from sources dating from the late fifth century on, where more theoretical accounts address, both directly and indirectly, the points of overlap that the earlier visual and poetic sources bring into play.

1 Song-dance in the Early Epigraphic Record

1.1 The Dipylon Oinochoe

I begin with a very simple observation and the question that it poses. For all that dance in ancient and modern times has largely escaped the transcription that music allows, from very early on the practice seems to have left an alphabetic trace; a striking number of our earliest extant examples of Greek alphabetic writing refer to what is competitive dancing, both solo and, perhaps, choral, and already suggest interrelations between the letters and the dancers. Among the most familiar of these is the so-called Dipylon oinochoe (Figs. 8.0, 8.1),[10] found northeast of the Dipylon gate in Athens and assumed to come from one of the numerous graves in the area. Dated to ca. 740–730, the hexameter inscription around the neck declares 'he who now of all dancers dances most delicately, of him this … ' (h ος νυν ορχεστον παντον αταλοτατα παιζει / το [=του] τοδε [sc. pot], *IG* I² 919; *IG* I Suppl. 492a), a phrase that allows us to identify the object as a prize awarded to the winner of a dancing competition, most probably in the context of a symposium; added on to this are a few more ungainly letters of a different style and hand that straggle upward toward the handle, perhaps, in the assessment of Barry Powell, 'an incompetent snippet from an abecedarium' scratched on by a second person trying to learn the new letter shapes.[11]

As the many discussions of the jug point out, the inscription forms an integral element of its larger decorative scheme and overall design; indeed, in the observation of Robin Osborne and Alexandra Pappas, were an

---

[10] Athens, National Archaeological Museum 192.   [11] See Powell 1988, 76–82 and 1991, 162.

Fig. 8.0 Dipylon oinochoe, ca. 740 B.C.E. Athens, National Archaeological Museum 192. Photograph © National Archaeological Museum, Athens.

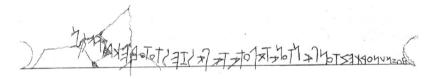

Fig. 8.1 Dipylon oinochoe, ca. 740 B.C.E. Detail of inscription. Athens, National Archaeological Museum 192. Drawing from B. Powell, 'The Dipylon Oinochoe Inscription and the Spread of Literacy in Eighth-Century Athens', *Kadmos* 27 (1988): 65–86.

illiterate viewer to come upon the oinochoe, its lettering would have seemed more a novel form of ornamentation than a message-bearing notation.[12] In accordance with the decorative concentric bands of black

---

[12] Osborne and Pappas 2007, 134.

slip surrounding the body, the arrangement of the letters on the solid black neck zone maintains the same circularity, while the saw-toothed design just below the inscribed shoulder introduces a shape that several of the letter forms echo and that reappears in the ornamentation on the neck in a somewhat altered form. The zigzags below the oinochoe's spout also reprise the geometric elements used to construct the letters immediately below, as does the combination of two diagonals adjacent to these.

But the inscription also stands distinct, and not just on the grounds of the diversity of its graphic signs – in contrast to the regularity and repetition that characterizes the other elements – and the different technique that incising as opposed to painting requires,[13] the former a device that gives the letters cut into the clay surface a depth and three-dimensionality absent from the painted designs. By contextualizing the object through its words, and the νῦν and deictic in the second partial hexameter that firmly anchor the vessel to the occasion, the inscription invites the viewer to place its message and other decorations within the prescribed frame: that of a dance competition. Here form and layout intersect with the message's content so as to engage in a complex form of the *mimêsis* that, in the later terminology, *enargeia* aims to achieve: not so much a narrative of an object or event but the effect of seeing that thing.[14] The spidery quality of the letters and thinness of the linear and circular notations, necessarily the product of a particularly sharp instrument requiring a dexterous inscriber, themselves evoke and match the 'delicacy' or 'friskiness' (in Powell's rendering) the winning dancer displays, the lightness of his trace, grace of his movements and diversity of his steps. As Carruesco suggests, the inscription circling the vessel 'through the form and direction of the letters and by echoing the movement of the bands below, seems to be trying to imitate the movement of the dance to which it alludes'.[15]

The mobility of the letters is more than merely latent: as the viewer rotates the vessel so as to read the entire text, the oinochoe itself goes into motion, circling about before returning to its place of origin. This corporeal engagement on the user's part extends to the *oinochoos* as he first fills the jug with wine drawn from the krater and then circumnavigates the room, serving each symposiast in turn: tipping the pitcher down and up, he not only observes the letter's correct orientation – from top to bottom – but makes the lettering enact the same bending back and rising motions performed by the two star Phaeacian dancers in their ball dance in

---

[13] Osborne and Pappas 2007 make both these points.
[14] *Enargeia* in reference to choral performances will be the topic addressed in Chapter 10.
[15] Carruesco 2016, 85.

Odyssey 8.370–79, a spectacle that elicits wonderment (384) on the part of the watching Odysseus. The image on the tondo of a late sixth-century red-figure cup by Oltos visualizes the interactions of bodily motion (even a dance?), enunciation, viewing and reading that I suggest:[16] to follow the letters around the interior space, quite independent of their meaning, is to recreate the dipping-pouring motion of the youth, whose vessel is positioned so as to form an element in the stream of *grammata*; indeed, the youthful *oinochoos* or komast, his feet resting lightly on the ground line of the cup which would be tipped up by the symposiast to drink the wine, seems poised to follow the letters' circular motion. The scenes on the cup's two sides develop the suggestion of komastic activity in the tondo, inviting the viewer to read the jug-bearer as a dancer: on one side a satyr plays the pipes, accompanied by a mule who seems to pick up its front hooves in a responsive dance, while on the other three dancing maenads appear, holding krotala in their hands.

We could, perhaps, interpret the dance performance commemorated on the Dipylon jug in a manner different from that proposed by most previous scholars.[17] While one individual is singled out as prize-winner, there is no need to assume a solo dance. Instead, the symposiasts or entertainers hired for the occasion might compete in impromptu or more organized displays of group or choral dancing at drinking parties, performances for which prizes could be awarded,[18] and that would resemble the more structured and formalized spectacles staged at civic celebrations and festivals, where they not infrequently formed part of larger agonistic programmes.[19] The Middle Corinthian aryballos of ca. 590–575 from the temple of Apollo in Corinth (Fig. 8.2),[20] which combines writing and an agonistic choral dance on an object similarly designed as a prize and commemoration of the lead dancer's win, offers an example of the latter type of intra-choral contestation in this more public and ritual context. If the competition recalled by the Dipylon oinochoe involved group dancing, then the *mimêsis* is closer still: forming a not quite complete chain around the shoulder of the pot, the letters suggest a sequence of figures both similar and disparate, that do not, as on the aryballos, so much accompany the dancers' bodies as visually substitute for them as they perform something akin to the ring dance so frequently depicted on vases, whose performers appear in circular

---

[16] Compiègne, Musée Antoine Vivenel 1093; *ARV*² 64.105.

[17] Henrichs 2003, 46 alone, as far as I am aware, makes the same suggestion as I do.

[18] See Plut. *Mor.* 747a–b for such prizes; cf. Eubulus fr. 2 K.-A.

[19] For images of choruses performing at symposia, see Smith 2000 and 2010.

[20] Corinth, Archaeological Museum C-54-1; I return to the aryballos in Section 2.

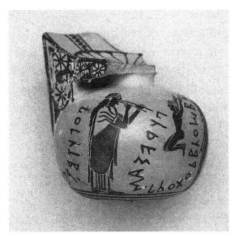

Fig. 8.2 Corinthian aryballos, ca. 590–575 B.C.E. Corinth, Archaeological Museum C-54-1. Photograph Ino Ioannidou and Lenia Bartzioti, American School of Classical Studies at Athens, Corinth Excavations, courtesy of N. Bookidis, *Corinth XX* (Princeton, 2003), pp. 249–50, fig. 15.1.

formations, often with their hands joined. The letters recall these circling painted choristers more narrowly. The shoulder area of the vase, and/or just below the beginning of the handles, is precisely where artists of the period may choose to position choral ensembles dancing or processing around the vessel, an arrangement found on a Late Geometric oinochoe where a chorus line made up of male and female figures dances in between bands of non-figurative designs that decorate the remainder of the pot.[21] And like other painted images of choruses too, as on a phiale in Athens by the Patras Painter dated to ca. 590–570, which includes women processing to the music of an aulos-player and a chorus of komast dancers,[22] the engraver has used the circular surface of the pot which in itself describes the rotational motions of the performers.[23]

By virtue of the letters' diverse grouping and positioning we can see more particularized elements of 'choreography' that also call a choral troupe to mind. Although they move in linear fashion, chorus members need not observe strict regularity; some turn towards one another, as in the mixed dance of youths and maidens on the neck of a Protoattic loutrophoros of ca. 690 by the Analatos Painter,[24] or on the oinochoe from

---

[21] Tübingen, Institut für Klassische Archäologie, Eberhard Karls Universität 2657. These dancers occupy an area rather lower than the Dipylon oinochoe inscription.

[22] Athens, National Archaeological Museum 536.

[23] See Lissarrague 2015, 239, who cites the phiale.   [24] Paris, Musée du Louvre CA 2985.

Pithekoussai cited in an earlier chapter, where the figures who may be performing the 'Crane Dance' are irregularly spaced and face in different directions (Fig. 3.0). The participants in the less regimented komastic choruses particularly at home at the symposium and depicted on Corinthian vessels from the late seventh century on before appearing in other areas (see below), supply fresh examples of these varied groupings and orientations. Comparable to these deployments is the letters' design on the Dipylon oinochoe, where the crooked iotas and sidelong alphas, modelled after their Phoenician prototypes, seem to be positioned backwards; so too, perhaps, again, with a chorus line in mind, the jug's inscriber has narrowed the spacing between some letters, placing them so that they seem to form a pair as they all but bump up against their neighbours while others proceed around the pot in more 'solo' fashion, with space on either side.

Irregular too on the oinochoe is the 'stance' of the individual letters vis-à-vis the base line formed by the area picked out in black; some rest on it while others rise above, more free-floating. In his analysis of a late eighth-century hydria from Aegina and now in Berlin (Fig. 5.2),[25] Roger Crowhurst observes how the painter introduces into his chorus line just these types of positional variations and ups and downs:[26] two in the procession of male figures rise up as though on their toes, while the remainder are shown more 'flat-footed'. Height differences further distinguish these Aeginetan dancers: one individual is shorter than his fellow chorus members, while two, their knees bent, are also given reduced dimensions. In similar fashion, some of the oinochoe letters appear elongated, while others 'squat', hugging the base line.

In terms of their aesthetics and patterning, lettering and choral morphology also exhibit matching designs: witness the alternating arrangement of the repeated 'a's, 't's and 'o's making up the words ατα̣λοτατα παιζει / το [=του] τοδε, and how the ταλοτ supplies an example of the visual symmetry found in images with identical figures at the start and end of chorus lines. This arrangement appears on the vase from Pithekoussai cited above, which presents two male dancers in identical position with the same dress and accoutrements at either end of a group of choristers that includes two female figures – these distinct from one another, although with only minor variations – while another differently positioned male, who is further singularized by his gesture, occupies the centrepoint. The Dipylon inscription builds in other units that form virtual mirror images, a harmonious arrangement corresponding to the orderly deployment of dancers in

---

[25] Berlin, Antikensammlung 31573.   [26] Crowhurst 1963, 32–36.

a chorus possessed of the *kosmos* that numerous sources ascribe to it[27] and that allowed the lead member of the ensemble to whom the oinochoe was awarded to claim the prize; the word ορχεστον accommodates the sequence εστο which then all but visually reappears (in alphabetic terms, the iota is different, but in shape and formation it closely resembles the earlier sigma) in the sequence of forms that occurs just before the legible portion of the inscription ends: ει/το.

Replacing the solo dancer with a choral ensemble also casts fresh light on one facet of the inscription that commentators tend to treat in cursory fashion:[28] the ungainly incisions at the sequence's close. If viewed as a tyro's attempt to practise his abc, then we have nothing more than an amateur's inept strivings to follow in the literal trace of a more skilled epigrapher. But what if these letters do not so much result from an attempt to gain alphabetic proficiency as present a second, analphabetic inscriber's desire to extend what he perceives as a chorus line and to add additional members to the ensemble? Insofar as they preserve the linearity, directionality and design of the more practised letters, these notations likewise offer stylized, schematic visualization of the dancers to whom the hexameter line refers (the ορχεστον of the *dipinto*). As Natasha Binek, on whose interpretation I draw,[29] persuasively points out, these additional ornamental elements respect the aesthetic principles observable on unlettered Geometric vases, those of 'symmetry and repetition' within a system, while also satisfying the viewer's desire to fill the visually displeasing still empty space on this portion of the jug and, in the interests of achieving symmetrical coherence, to complete the circular trajectory initiated by the first epigrapher.[30] Again, like the chorus members shown on the Geometric vessels already discussed, these supplementary notations are both similar and disparate. The final six traces also seamlessly breach the distance between the letters belonging to the hexameters and the remaining decorative devices on the oinochoe, which, as already noted, feature many of the same shapes, vertical lines, upside down v's and zigzags among them, visible in the inscribed band.

We can, perhaps, establish visual continuity between choral dancers and the two portions of the Dipylon inscription in one final respect. Viewed in

---

[27] E.g. Xen. *Oec.* 8.19–20; Plut. *Nik.* 3.4–7; Xenoph. *Eph.* 1.2.5. The term refers not just to the arrangement of the choreutes, but to their decking out (e.g. Pind. *Pyth.* 9.114–18).

[28] Binek 2017, for which see below, is one notable exception.

[29] Binek 2017. Where I differ from Binek is in my suggestion that all the graphic elements – whether alphabetic or not – are not just decorative but actual representations of the original dancers.

[30] Binek 2017, with citation from p. 430.

its entirety, the inscription on the oinochoe forms an undulating line, whose upward curvature becomes more pronounced in its final six signs.[31] Geometric pottery offers numerous instances of such maeanders placed above, below or alongside dancing groups: among the many instances, the serpentine decoration on an early seventh-century hydria in the Villa Giulia is positioned immediately below the maiden dancers encircling the vessel's neck,[32] while a second such motif reappears on the rim. Together the two elements frame the performance with their schematic revisualization of the girls' motions. Also comparable are the snakes 'serpentining' around the lower register of an Argive krater from Corinth (Fig. 2.4):[33] a panel in the upper register shows a chorus made up of three dancers. In another correspondence, the chevrons or upside-down v's prominent in both portions of the Dipylon inscription replicate the geometric designs, these in turn echoing the crooked elbows and joined arms of choral dancers on a steatite seal from the Argive Heraion, also with a snake positioned beneath the two performers.[34]

When read aloud, the Dipylon inscription still more closely re-enacts that winning dance. Like the message on the Corinthian aryballos, it takes the form of a hexameter which when vocalized, whether in recitative and/or to the accompaniment of the lyre, can give the lead to or echo the structure of the performance, both its regularity and passage through space and time, and the combination of arrest and motion that the Greeks assigned to its dancer's postures and transitions between them, the *rhythmos* that, as I detail later on,[35] our sources also attribute to alphabetic letters. In the Greek view of the art of *choreia*, following the formulation of Plato at *Leg.* 815d–816a, the corporeal movement materialized in the oinochoe lettering constitutes a physical projection and embodiment of the voice, whose attributes the motions of the dancers visibly take on in their enactment of the feelings and sensations it articulates.[36] Enunciating the inscription while the letters are viewed as a nonverbal configuration thus achieves a union between the latter-day reading and the winning dance, each a mirror image of the other, with the performers' movement made the substance of the text.

The letters' design further reflects or generates the tuneful reading. As noted earlier, while some rest on the base line, others are positioned above,

---

[31] As noted by Binek 2017, 434–35, who also observes the correspondence to the serpentine motif noted here.

[32] Rome, Museo Nazionale di Villa Giulia 1212.   [33] Corinth, Archaeological Museum T 2545.

[34] See Langdon 2008, 157, with her fig. 3.15.   [35] See the discussion in Section 3.

[36] For the Platonic view, see the discussion in Peponi 2009, 57–59.

suggestive both of the dancer's skips, leaps and the elevation and down beat of his feet and of the voice as it rises and falls in accord with the changes in pitch the vocalizer observes. The recreation of the acoustic element forms part of the larger function fulfilled by the mimetic dimension of the *grammata*. While the deictic and temporal 'now' seem to locate the pot at *this* particular symposium and to refer to *this* set of contestants, the inscription's reading will, of course, take place each time the oinochoe is used, long after that original contest has been decided and the prize awarded, and this on occasions, sympotic or otherwise, when there may be no dancers with whom to match its contents. The movement-filled and sounding letters remedy that absence. Insofar as their design and the sound of the reader's voice fully reproduce the spectacle of the dance, we are transported back both visually and acoustically to the original symposium – an early form of ecphrasis in which the reader and listener become viewers of the scene to which the text refers (see Chapter 10).

These multiple exchanges between the alphabetic elements and dancers participating in the contest also inform not so much the particularized message of the *grammata* as the inscriber's considered choice of diction, achieving an element essential, or so the later ancient theorists would teach, for the type of vivid, imaginative and engaged visualization that is the particular end of ecphrases: the generation of *phantasiai* or mental images of things imaginary and fictive as well as real. As Powell notes,[37] both the metre and the terms of the inscription necessarily put the reader in mind of Homeric verse, and he cites by way of close counterpart to its syntactical structure a phrase used by Odysseus to address his Phaeacian host at the paradigmatic banquet/symposium that Alkinous stages: 'lord Alkinous, most excellent of all men' (*Od.* 8.382). If we can assume that the correspondence goes beyond mere syntax and triggers remembrance of the line itself, then readers or hearers of the oinochoe message might recall the context of the hero's remark: this is the occasion for two pre-eminent displays of dancing on the part of the Phaeacian youths, the first a choral performance, the second a ball dance complete with leaping and acrobatics put on by the two most outstanding dancers in the group.[38] As Alkinous charges his guest with remembering at the symposia that Odysseus will celebrate at his own home,[39] the Phaeacians are dancers *sans pareils*, and

---

[37] Powell 1991, 160–61.

[38] Robb 1994, 31 modifies Powell insofar as he proposes that the precise referent intended by the phrase is Alkinous' statement at *Od.* 8.251–53, where the king issues the summons to the Phaeacian youths to put on a dance performance.

[39] *Od.* 8.241–48.

the jug's glance to that fictional world not only realizes his injunction but aggrandizes the skills of the winner of the oinochoe and the hospitality of the donor, a latter-day Alkinous who supplies his own sumptuous entertainment.

No less rich in associations is the exclusively epic adverb ἀταλώτατα, itself a pointer both to dancing and, perhaps, to the youthfulness of the performers capable of the litheness and grace requisite for carrying off the prize. At *Il.* 18.567, in the account of one of the shield bands forged by Hephaestus, ἀταλὰ φρονέοντες describes the youths and maidens who are 'skipping' down the path that leads to and from the vineyard, moving to the music supplied by the youth who plays the lyre and sings in their midst; elsewhere in the poem (20.222) ἀταλός appears of fillies who, as an earlier chapter illustrated, are themselves paradigmatic of lighthearted dancing. Through these echoes, the inscription thus realizes two forms of the visualization that allow the reader or hearer to think themselves back at the original scene: a *deixis ad oculos*, such as the indexicals convey and as we see the letters taking the part of the bodies competing for the prize, and a *deixis am phantasma* as we also witness the notional dancers on Scheria and the shield of Achilles.

1.2   The Graffiti from Thera

Dating from the early seventh century are the well-known graffiti from Thera, scratched onto rocks above the space that would become an ephebic gymnasium in the Hellenistic period.[40] Concentrated in an area known as the Agora of the Gods at the south-east end of the island, a significant proportion of these variously name and praise individuals not just for their role as purveyors of sexual gratification, but for their prowess in the dance and/or their skills as writers. To sample several of the declarations, some of which I explore at greater length below, *IG* XII 3.543 is a hexameter line written boustrophedon: 'Barbax dances well and he's given [me] pleasure (?)', and one of the three assertions making up *IG* XII 3.540 declares that 'Eumelos is best (*aristos*) in the dance'. In the third inscription included in 3.536, writing occurs in tandem with dancing: 'Enpedokles carved these things. And he danced, by Apollo' (*IG* XII 3.536c), an assertion which celebrates its author as skilled in these two domains.

Two insights from earlier discussions of these graffiti shape my discussion here: first, that inscriptions grouped together in close proximity

---

[40] For the most comprehensive and recent discussion of these, see Inglese 2008.

should be seen as existing in agonistic exchange, each one a response to the others in the set that attempts to cap its predecessors in a game of graphic one-upmanship.[41] And second, Pappas' demonstration that critical to our understanding of these lithic vaunts is their material aspect: the design of the letters, their placement on the rock, their self-positioning vis-à-vis the other inscriptions whose space they share and the visual impression they would make on the viewer as well as reader; as on the Dipylon oinochoe, physical form (and sound too, which conveys meaning aurally rather than semantically) turns out to play as critical a role in conveying the message's import as does the content. What I add to these accounts is a consideration of the role of dancing in the inscriptions, investigating how the graffiti fashion a series of connections between the dancer (perhaps as chorus leader), lover and writer that anticipate later sources' various equations of these several roles.

With the exception of Barbax's inscription, the graffiti cited above all belong to one of two clusters. The first in the series making up *IG* XII 3.536 (Fig. 8.3) boasts of the sexual conquests achieved by a series of named individuals and of the inscriber, so many notches on the stick: 'Pheidip(p) idas fucked. Timagoras and Enperes and I – we fucked too'.[42] As Pappas observes,[43] the emphasis falls, as it does in other instances of these assertions, on the verb: this is the point at which the line turns as it follows the rock edge downward before curving under and moving to the right. Not to be outdone, the second declaration in the triplet is placed in the space enclosed by the loop of the previous line, tucking itself into the curve: 'Enpylos [?] these things . . . *pornos*' (*Enpylos tade pornos* 536b).[44] Enpylos takes pains to coordinate his inscription with the one prior to it: the *en-* of his name appears, as Pappas points out, almost directly above the same combination of letters in the name Enperes toward the ending of the longer line, creating not just a visual reiteration but, when the line is enunciated, an audible one too.

Pappas and Powell diverge as to what activity is implied in the *tade* of this second statement: sex in Powell's account,[45] writing according to Pappas. If we adopt Powell's view, Enpylos simply seeks to insert

---

[41] Powell 1991, 171–80; Pappas (forthcoming).

[42] The illustration is from Inglese 2008, 470; I am most grateful to the author for generously allowing me to reproduce her photographs.

[43] Pappas (forthcoming).

[44] See Powell 1991, fig. 68 for clear illustration. The designation of Enpylos as 'faggot' belongs to a later hand, an addition that, situated above Enpylos' self-assertion, literally over-rides it even as it turns the whole phrase into a second loop and visual reiteration of the first inscription.

[45] Powell 1991, 180.

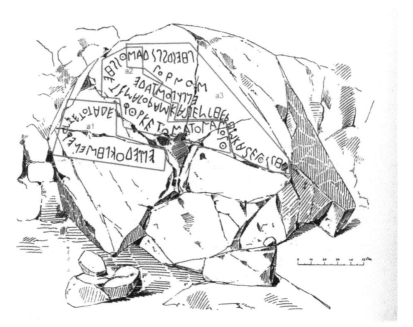

Fig. 8.3 The inscription cluster *IG* XII 3.536 from Thera. Photograph courtesy of Alessandra Inglese.

himself – quite literally – into the preceding list of sexual potentates, adding his name to the roster. But Pappas' reading not only respects the agonistic element that structures this and other graffiti clusters by introducing an element that ups the stakes by declaring Enpylos writer as well as fornicator, the latter the role already implied by the writing's material, visual and aural coordination with the line enclosing it; Enpylos' capacities as inscriber also give the cue for the opening assertion in the third of the series, which begins with an explicit claim of authorship:[46] 'Enpedokles carved these things (ἐνεϙόπτετο ταδε). And he danced (ϙορκⱨε͂το), by Apollo'. Again, this last individual has no need to spell out his membership of the fraternity of Theran *erastai*: as in the case of Enpylos, fresh echoes guarantee that status. The writer's name recapitulates the *en-* element found in the previous two instances, and establishes a visual and syntactical parallelism between writing and sex.[47]

---

[46] Pappas (forthcoming).

[47] As Pappas (forthcoming) notes, just as the author of the first inscription places in first position the name in the nominative case followed by the act that he performs – sexual penetration – so Enpedokles has replaced that verb with the act of carving, this again expressed by the third-person verb that follows the subject; and just as line 1 bends around at the verb, so does line 3. For the sexual innuendoes of carving, see Pappas and Ar. *Thesm.* 778–81.

But more important for my purposes is the no less patent relationship –
again brought out visibly and audibly by the reuse of many of the same letters in
a now-rearranged sequence, and by the imperfect in both clauses – that the
inscription establishes between writing and dancing. By virtue of the verbs'
close coordination, Enpedokles frames his carving as performative, a 'spectacular' display of expertise: no less than in the dance, primacy goes to the one
who writes best. Although the Theran graffiti exist outside a ritual setting and
their messages are addressed to other members of the local elite and only, in
passing, to a god ('by Apollo', an addition that appeals to a divine witness for
validation of the claim), a very similar view of writing as a status-enhancing
performance emerges from a more strictly religious context. Dating from ca.
700 to the early sixth century, several of the inscriptions found on potsherds
from the sanctuary of Zeus on Mount Hymettos and serving as dedications to
the god introduce their donors as writers, creators of objects whose value and
appeal depends on the presence of their written contents.[48] In self-referential
claims that recall Enpedokles' declaration, some inscriptions simply announce
'he wrote (εγραφσε/α)' while one spells out the relation between the giver's
'writerly' identity and his gift: 'I belong to Zeus. X wrote me'.[49] In two
instances, the sherds more emphatically draw attention to the act of inscribing
and foreground the donor as author: ℎοσπερ εγραφσεν ('as he wrote') and,
with a fresh burst of pride, – αι ταδ' αυτος εγ⟨ρ⟩αφ[σε ('he wrote this
himself').[50] As Merle Langdon comments in a discussion of these votives,
'writing must have been still so new that its accomplishment was being
stressed'.[51] The same phenomenon occurs elsewhere: the author of the
'postscript' to the message on the marble column cited in Chapter 6 enhances
the value of this already high-price artefact, a votive destined for a 'child of
Zeus', by advertising the donor's scribal skills: Ekphantos 'made this vow to
you and fulfilled it by writing (ετελεσε γροπℎον)' (*SEG* III 738). The act of
writing thus becomes one among the manifestations of technical expertise that
elevate more workaday objects to the ranks of *agalmata*.

Also suggesting the capping impetus motivating Enpedokles' inscription
is the visual extension of the line, which, exploiting the shape of the rock
surface, can travel further to the left than its two predecessors, claiming a

---

[48] For discussion with earlier bibliography, see Woodard 2014, 265–66 drawing on Langdon 1976,
18–21. As Woodard goes on plausibly to suggest (266–88), the emphatic role of writing in these
inscriptions may be particularly fitting for the worship of Zeus Semios, the deity celebrated at
the site: the sign-giving god is the one best able to appreciate these inscribed messages, and to
give answering signs.

[49] Langdon 1976, inscription 29.

[50] For the first, see Langdon 1976, inscription 30; for the second, Langdon 1976, inscription 27.

[51] Langdon 1976, 46.

hitherto vacant space. This 'stretching out' might implicitly reflect the superior duration of this individual's writing, dancing and sexual feats (recall the sympotic game whereby a prize went to the one still standing after a night's heavy drinking).[52] In a further sleight of the inscriber's hand, Enpedokles has appropriated part of the initial inscription so as to draw out his assertion still further. Its ending is so positioned that the eye sees the opening portion of that first graffito as part of the third inscription, which makes the lettering that covers the area to the right seem part of Enpedokles' space. The element of innovation – and what is new is always best – freshly declares itself in the line's design: the letters are retrograde, reversing the previous two inscriptions' directionality.

Where Pappas acutely signals the sexual 'subtext' implied by the verb chosen by Enpedokles for the act of inscription, literally 'to beat, pound in', I would note how the term additionally anticipates its author's role as dancer: as the previous chapter proposed, verbs of beating and striking can carry with them a reference to the sound made by the dancer as he hits the ground with his feet, a body part already apparent in the writer's name: Enpedokles is the individual famed for being 'in the ground, firm set on his feet'.[53] Taken together, name, dance and inscribing stand in relations of contiguity and contrast; where the alphabetic notations cut into the rock fix the boast for all times, Enpedokles' enduring renown also depends on his superior pedal mobility that adds a kinetic element to the otherwise static line, visibly enacted by its trajectory over the surface of the boulder which becomes, by virtue of the inscription and its contents, a dancing floor for the letters. If, following Pappas, the first inscription's curve around the term 'fornicate' visually replicates the bend of the sexual partners' bodies, so here a second curve introduces a new parallel between writing and the dance.[54] Inscribed retrograde, the letters literally bend back to form the loop, a particularly skilled move for a dancer and one executed by the two star Phaeacian performers in their ball dance (ἰδνωθεὶς ὀπίσω, *Od.* 8.375) and then again by the girl who entertains the company gathered at Callias' symposium: she bends backwards 'until she resembled a hoop (τροχοὺς ἐμιμεῖτο)' (Xen. *Symp.* 2.22). The addition of the appeal to Apollo in the context of Enpedokles' assertion of his role as dancer includes a further act of self-valorization. Already in the *Homeric Hymn* addressed to the divinity, we witness Apollo 'stepping finely and high' (καλὰ καὶ ὕψι βιβάς, *HHAp.*

---

[52] For this, see Węcowski 2014, 52–54, Bravo 1997, 115–18 and Steiner 2012, 137–38. Pappas (forthcoming) comments in passing on 'extension' but does not develop the idea.

[53] See Benveniste 1969 s.v. πέδον for the derivation of the term from πούς.

[54] As observed in passing by Pappas (forthcoming).

516) as he leads the Cretans in the paean; a fragment of Pindar (fr. 148 S.-M.) likewise celebrates Apollo as 'the dancer (ὀρχήστ') ruling over the festivities', using the noun cognate with the verb chosen by Enpedokles for the activity in which this graffitist emulates the divine performer.

A second cluster, *IG* XII 3.540 (Fig. 8.4),[55] also dating to the seventh century, again invites the viewer to perceive in the lettering's design and shape a re-enactment of a dance that stands in agonistic relation to previous performances. Three inscriptions in different hands also make up this set, beginning with the assertion *Lakydidas agathos*. Positioned next in the sequence, another inscriber outdoes his predecessor by writing boustrophedon and in two lines in place of one 'Eumelos is best (αριστος) in the dance'; the letters of the final term *orkesta[s]* are visually different from those in the line above it, more spaced out and many of exaggerated dimension as though to call attention to this activity. As noted above, it is the Phaeacians' prowess as dancers that Alkinous urges Odysseus chiefly to remember, asserting at *Od.* 8.250 that the Phaeacians are by far the best (ἄριστοι) at this, and that ὀρχηστύς is the sphere in which they excel (253); recapitulating two terms in the Homeric song, the author of the graffito may be signalling

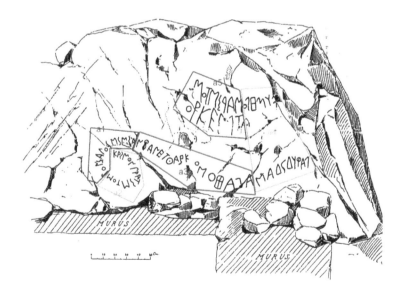

Fig. 8.4 The inscription cluster *IG* XII 3.540 from Thera. Photograph courtesy of Alessandra Inglese.

---

[55] The illustration is from Inglese 2008, 478.

his membership of an equivalent latter-day elite as well as his literary connoisseurship.

While Eumelos' declaration that he is 'best' obviously supersedes the merely 'good' quality of Lakydidas, now consigned to second place,[56] our third author manages to outdo even that superlative. In a line that Pappas describes as spiralling outward 'as if visually trumping' the less move-mented and briefer two-line inscription above it, Krimon – whose ten-dency for self-assertion and pre-eminence is visible in other inscriptions (537, 538b) – writes 'Krimon first (*pratistos*) in the *konialo*, has warmed/ melted Simias'. Krimon engages in the same scriptural 'hijacking' observed in the third inscription in 536: carved so that its opening coincides with the close of Lakydidas' message, it appears an extension of the first inscription, thereby covering more of the surface of the rock than any of its predeces-sors. Sheer length and spatial occupancy are themselves self-promoting moves in epigraphic competitions.

Where earlier commentators understood the activity in which Krimon scores his primacy as a type of obscene dance,[57] a re-examination of the cutting has put paid to that interpretation, and Alessandra Inglese suggests instead a proper name. But I would not abandon any reference to dancing here. Krimon's inscription begins with a claim to primacy, and the most obvious domain for him to assert this front-rank position is in the sphere in which Eumelos declared himself the 'best'. If the allusion to the dance remains implicit, a viewer of the line would witness its performance here as the inscriber demonstrates at one and the same time his skill as stone-cutter and as dancer. This final graffito is written in the so-called *Schlangenschrift*, where the writing uncoils in the manner of a snake and spirals round as though pirouetting at the end.[58] Contrasted with the design of Eumelos' inscription, it appears more fluid, replacing the squared-off, block-like or ranked arrangement of its neighbour with an undulating line ending in a circle or virtuosic spin.

For all the absence of any evidence that these inscribers were also members of choral ensembles that performed dances on civic or more private occasions, the designs of the two inscriptions closely match

---

[56] Pappas (forthcoming).

[57] Powell 1991, 176, citing Hesychius s.v. *konisalos*: 'a satyr-like leaping about of men with swollen sexual organs' or (dances?) 'to do with Aphrodite', suggests that we have here a reference to an obscene dance; both Scanlon 2002, 88 and Powell observe a link with athletics, and particularly the dust or residual substance (*konis*) scraped from athletes after exercise.

[58] The German designation is no mere modern construct; an Etruscan bucchero aryballos from the mid-seventh century (Rome, Villa Giulia 112765) displays an undulating snake on whose sinuous body the text is inscribed.

accounts of choral formations reaching back to the description of the movements of the choreutes on the shield of Achilles, where the *stichoi* alternate with circle dances (*Il.* 18.599–602). Following the linear-cum- 'processional' entrance of the first notations making up Eumelos' graffito, its last eight characters then position themselves so as to form just such a square, each element lined up in one of the two ranks that seem to face one another. Equally pertinent is Pindar's depiction of the old-style dithyramb, which took linear formation (fr. 70b.1–2 S.-M.) before assuming its more up-to-date circular structure. While this modification long postdates the Theran graffiti, what remains pertinent to my argument is the 'snake-like' quality of the Pindaric line, audible not only in the sibilants that, for all the letter's rejection, are foregrounded in its choice of terms and in the verb, ἔρπε, in the opening line.[59] Much as the Pindaric dithyramb semantically, audibly and visibly too describes a drawn-out, linear choral formation that may accommodate more maeandering, serpentine motions, so Krimon's assertion might consciously imitate a type of ensemble dance in which he participated and, perhaps, modify the pairing found on many Geometric vases (albeit ones from Argos), where snakes share the spaces occupied by choruses. Absent the temporal contrast between the two choral deployments that Pindar highlights, Krimon's graffito accommodates both that 'snaking' line and the expansive ring in which his alphabetic dance concludes.

If the references to the dance point not just to solo performances, but to dancers grouped in choruses[60] – and ὀρχηστύς clearly has a choral reference in Homer and later sources – then the terms ἄριστος and πράτιστος acquire fresh significance, suggesting the several authors' jockeying for the role of chorus leader. In conformity with visual and textual sources, Eumelos positions himself as the foremost of the bunch, the one who has the pre-eminent status, whether due to rank, beauty or dancing skill, reserved for the *chorêgos*. But Kimon's capping claim quite literally

---

[59] Lawler 1946, 124 would interpret the *ger-* root in the *geranos* dance as a reference to 'winding' and suggests that its motions were designed to imitate the winding path of the snake.

[60] Earlier discussions of the graffiti also cite choral dancing in association with the individuals who wrote the messages. Noting the presence of the cult of Apollo Karneios, celebrated in the temple erected on his behalf some 50–70m to the west of the site of the inscriptions, and the Hellenistic gymnasium that would later occupy the space, scholars propose the existence of 'coming-of-age' rituals for boys on Thera which, on the Dorian model, would have included pederastic relations, competitions and choral dancing; the importance of such choruses at the Spartan Gymnopaidia, also celebrated in honour of Apollo and featuring dances by youthful ensembles, supplies a possible equivalence to the Theran rites. But this equation proves anachronistic: all the evidence for cult activity and for choruses composed of boys postdates the rock inscriptions, whose language contains no reference to any ritual occasion.

displaces him, introducing this other individual at the head of the line. The superlative is derived from πρῶτος or πρᾶτος, the Doric form of the term,[61] used of the *chorêgos* in later sources: he is the πρωτοστάτης.[62]

While nothing allows us firmly to establish the nature of the dances in which the inscriptions' authors excelled, Inglese offers an approach that might explain the emphasis on the activity in the assertions cited above. Seeking to read the graffiti in their sociopolitical context and observing that many of the names on the rocks highlight their owners' aristocratic provenance and gesture towards positions of leadership within the emerging civic structure,[63] she suggests that the individuals and practices they mention can be aligned with the development of political institutions in Thera at this period. But I would modify this argument by noting that the three activities prominent in the more extensive graffiti – fornicating, writing and dancing – fit comfortably into the range of elite practices associated with the seventh-century symposium, where such one-upmanship and sharp elbowing for position would be played out in these and other domains, and where the ribald terminology to which the verb *ophein* chosen by the inscribers belongs appears in the iambic songs composed specifically for the occasion. One such piece of mockery and display of mastery by Archilochus takes its cue from its target's indecorous dance (fr. 185 W.) and contests his claim to primacy in the sympotic as well as civic domain (with a sexual subtext).[64]

1.3   The Ambracian Cenotaph

My third example moves from partying and sex to lamentation and features an inscription on a cenotaph in Ambracia, a Corinthian colony, of ca. 550 or shortly after. This takes the form of a funerary epigram of which eight of the original ten lines are still extant (*SEG* 41.540A):[65]

> ἄνδρας [τ]ούσδ' [ἐ]σλούς ὀλοφύρομαι hοῖσι Πυραιβὸν :
> παῖδες ἐμετίσαντ' ἀ[λ]γινόεντα φόνον :

---

[61] πρᾶτος appears in other inscriptions, where it forms the prefix of an individual name (*IG* XII 3, *Suppl.* 1446, 1616); used without suffix in 581, it may be an adjective describing one Meniadês, mentioned just above the term, or again be part of a proper name.

[62] Calame 1997, 41 citing Arist. *Met.* 1018b.26ff.; Phot. *Lex.* s.v. τρίτος ἀριστεροῦ.

[63] Inglese 2008, 122.   [64] See Steiner 2016a.

[65] For the text, see Cassio 1994, 103 and D'Alessio 1995, 26. The version here follows Bowie 2010, 361. My overall discussion owes much to the reading of the inscription in Day 2007, 31–40, with its central claim that 'writing symbolized performance, even became a kind of performance' (32).

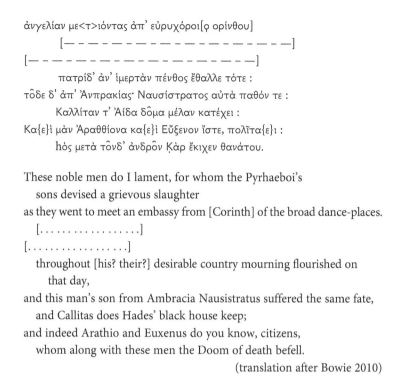

ἀνγελίαν με<τ>ιόντας ἀπ’ εὐρυχόροι[ο ορίνθου]
    [— — — — — — — — — — — — — — — — — —]
[— - — — - — — — — — — — — — — — — — —]
      πατρίδ’ ἀν’ ἱμερτὰν πένθος ἔθαλλε τότε :
τõδε δ’ ἀπ’ Ἀνπρακίας· Ναυσίστρατος αὐτὰ παθόν τε :
      Καλλίταν τ’ Ἀίδα δõμα μέλαν κατέχει :
Κα{ε}ὶ μὰν Ἀραθθίονα κα{ε}ὶ Εὔξενον ἴστε, πολῖτα{ε}ι :
      hὸς μετὰ τõνδ’ ἀνδρõν Κὰρ ἔκιχεν θανάτου.

These noble men do I lament, for whom the Pyrhaeboi’s
    sons devised a grievous slaughter
as they went to meet an embassy from [Corinth] of the broad dance-places.
    [. . . . .]
[. . . . .]
    throughout [his? their?] desirable country mourning flourished on
        that day,
and this man’s son from Ambracia Nausistratus suffered the same fate,
    and Callitas does Hades’ black house keep;
and indeed Arathio and Euxenus do you know, citizens,
    whom along with these men the Doom of death befell.
                                        (translation after Bowie 2010)

Before proposing that the appearance, layout and design of this inscription on the wall of the cenotaph in and of themselves enact a type of choral performance, in this instance a processional movement rather than a dance, I begin with the way in which its contents activates the reader and audiences’ sensory and emotional capacities, inviting them not just to see the events the language describes, but to experience the sounds, activities and sentiments from a bygone time. The deictic in the opening phrase already brings about this ‘presencing’ as it points towards the dead, a gesture all the more striking for the individuals’ absence: their bodies were never repatriated. The emphasis on the visibility of those who were conspicuously not perceptible in the *prothesis* that typically precedes burial both invites the audience to use its visual imagination and suggests the role of the inscribed monument as ‘stand in’ or replacement for the missing element. The first-person singular ὀλοφύρομαι then turns the laudatory description into a statement on the part of the reader and enunciator (the so-called ‘anonymous mourner’ familiar from other funerary epigrams and visible from the sixth century on) whom it positions in the role of witness to the monument and initial mourner over the absent bodies, and whose persona anyone who reads and responds to the message can assume in present and future times.[66]

The use of the imperfect ἔθαλλε gives the grief that this reader expresses a further temporal dimension, situating him or her at a time already future to the initial reception of the fact of death even as it collapses that past and the present, precipitating the narrator and audience into an earlier but still ongoing sensation whose expression we are listening to; as Egbert Bakker comments, 'the use of the imperfect is not so much a reference to an event as the displacement of its observer into the past',[67] to which Maria Ruffy adds, 'the imperfect presents the action as an experienced one. Indeed, it presupposes a personal point of view on the action since its non-completion depends on the point of view of the speaker'.[68] In the Ambracian inscription, the tense implies that the reader recalls his own past experience, a personal memory that the audience is invited to share. ἔθαλλε well suits this expression of continuity, ongoingness and self-propagation; more typically applied to vegetal fertility and flourishing growth, and hence packing a particular charge by transposing a normally healthful and life-giving process into the context of lamentation, the verb turns the grief into something whose past genesis and coming-to-fruition has gone on bearing its threnetic harvest from then to now.

But ἔθαλλε does more than declare the literally ever-burgeoning nature of the sorrow. Just as the inscription on the Dipylon oinochoe created for reader and audience the mental image, or *phantasia* in the phrasing of later theorists, of episodes of 'thaumatic' dancing in Homeric song, so here the choice of verb conditions the visualization of the dead by retrojecting the slain men into the world of epic heroism. The vegetal imagery so often used in the *Iliad* of youthful warriors – *ernos* describes Achilles among others, and θάλλω is a term of choice in similes likening young Trojan fighters to plants and trees –[69] inevitably foreshadows or accompanies these fighters' premature slaying on the field of battle; in the hypallage used in the inscription,

---

[66] This seems much more likely than the other possible speaker here, the monument. For discussion of this point, see Cassio 1994, 106; an anonymous speaker is also the assumption of Day 2007.

[67] Bakker 1997, 37.   [68] Ruffy 2004, 14.

[69] See, among other instances, *Il.* 18.54–60, 17.49–60, 473–76. The appropriation of the Homeric conceit supplies an instance of what Day 2007, 33–34 (drawing on the notion of 'traditional referentiality' in epic diction) terms 'thematization', a device by which an epigram frames and guides its reader's response.

the *floraison* normally assigned to heroic youth is transferred to the grief generated by these men's sudden death, suggestive of their still being in their prime. The application of the Homeric conceit gives the already signalled 'excellence' of these dead greater specificity, placing the lamented among those epic heroes who meet with what Jean-Pierre Vernant styles *la belle mort*, the battlefield demise that, by definition, makes the fallen, whatever their age and status, forever young and beautiful.[70] The 'lovely *patris*' (more Iliadic diction) in the same phrase recalibrates this Homeric ideology to the more recent civic ideal: what makes these individuals praiseworthy is death in the service of the state. Anticipating the assimilation of the objects of lamentation into the world of epic is the orthography (and consequent phonology) of ὀλοφύρομαι; as Day observes,[71] this is not the local form used elsewhere in the inscription, but Ionic spelling, which, when read out loud, places the reader and audience in the broader panhellenic tradition of death and its commemoration.

Another deictic opens the second half of the epigram (a third occurs in the final phrase) where we learn of the four Ambracians among the dead who are singled out for special mention. But most striking is the exhortation to a wider audience that introduces a third party to the twosome, the reader and the dead/their monument, encountered so far. The vocative πολῖται, identifying these listeners as the citizens of the polis to whom the slain belonged (and hence already emotionally engaged in their fate; since the monument would be raised at public expense, purse strings also heightened their 'investment'), expands the possible contexts for the inscription's delivery and adds a fresh element to what is being visualized here. Implying some kind of public setting, a commemoration of the dead before an assemblage of citizens, it recalls the occasion of the public inauguration of the cenotaph and the formal lamentation of the dead at that moment ('on that day'),[72] or perhaps at another city-wide gathering devoted, at some later time, to a renewed enactment of that memorializing event. One sepulchral epigram of ca. 500 from Thasos imagines just such a scenario, with the tomb's occupant Telephanes as apostrophizer here: 'Whoever wasn't there when I died and they carried me out, let him bewail me now' (*CEG* 159).

But much more frequent than this one-off or even cyclical occasion would be private, more haphazard encounters with the monument, as

---

[70] Vernant 1982.   [71] Day 2007, 40.

[72] ὀλοφύρομαι is used by Perikles at Thuc. 2.44.1 in the context of the funeral oration.

townsmen or visitors came across the cenotaph,[73] whose striking appearance, detailed below, would guarantee it attention. In these instances, no collectivity of citizens would be there and the address, like the opening evocation of the dead, would be to an absent presence, an apostrophe that introduces the addressee into the space and time occupied by the speaker and his auditors.[74] The effect of this, I suggest, is nothing less than the imaginative recreation on the part of both reader and audience of a past event, the original moment of the burial and the lamentation and celebration collectively performed on that occasion. Witnessing the cenotaph that substitutes for the dead, the anonymous mourner identifies himself and his real, or even imaginary audience, with the public mourners – whose voice the reader is assuming here – and the πολῖται gathered for the ceremony.

The ἴστε in the penultimate line carries two possible meanings: either 'do you know' or, in an instance of the use of the imperative common in funerary epigrams where the passer-by is exhorted to stop, look, mourn and learn,[75] the injunction 'know'. If the first, then the verb appeals to the audience's memory of the dead and their fate, or more probably to the collective occasion on which that recollection was made the stuff of public knowledge, whether or not the citizen audience was familiar with these men before. If ἴστε is an imperative, then what takes place here is the listeners' introduction to Arathio and Euxenus, who are brought no less vividly before their eyes than the citizens on whom they are to model their response. Just as in the case of the imperfect ἔθαλλε, the reader's capacity to perform this introduction gives him a kind of bi-temporality. By virtue of having known the individuals of whom he speaks, he must have participated in and been eyewitness to those past events.

But 'visualization' and 'presencing' also occur in a much more immediate form, effected through the viewing of the monument and of the lines inscribed on its surface.[76] The limestone wall is built of ashlar blocks with a moulding all around, a piece of costly and careful workmanship. Walls are in and of themselves objects worthy of aesthetic appreciation; in Aristotle's account, they are an adornment or *kosmos* for the city (*Pol.* 1331a12).[77] Forming a piece with this fine frame is the arrangement and design of the lettering, inscribed boustrophedon and in stoichedon style. While scholars

---

[73] This diversity of audience is already envisaged in the earliest surviving sepulchral epigram from Attica on behalf of Tettichos (ca. 575–550, *CEG* 13) with its opening reference to 'a citizen or foreigner coming from elsewhere'.

[74] Chapter 10 returns to the device.   [75] E.g. *CEG* 19 cited below; cf. *CEG* 27 and 161.

[76] Here I follow the reading of Day 2007, esp. 30–31 and 39–40.

[77] For this, see Stieber 2011, 80–81. Note too the discussion of walls at the close of the previous chapter.

continue to debate the origins of the epigraphic practice, and the degree to which it hinders legibility, stoichedon inscriptions are, Rosalind Thomas notes, 'highly ornamental, impressive and monumental',[78] their very impact (and perhaps the difficulty of deciphering them focuses attention on appearance alone) dependent on the inscription's symbolic, non-written dimensions. These letters are visually imposing;[79] set off in a separate space above the torus moulding, they measure 0.06 metres high, distinguishing this area from the remainder of the otherwise undecorated stone surface.

The impression of good order and regularity is reinforced by the numerical correspondence between the epigram's content and visual structure: a standard embassy has three members, and three verses are given to remembering these; three lines devoted to the four named Ambracians follow in the second half. Visible as well as audible isonometry exists between the first and final distichs, each made up of precisely the same sequence of longs and shorts; scan the lines whether with eye or voice, and the viewer encounters what one commentator describes as a 'regolarità quasi maniacale'.[80] Reinforcing the re-articulation and revisualization of the fate of the envoys and their escorts announced at the opening is the virtual mirroring in sound and appearance, with chiasmus, of two terms in lines 1 and 10: the ἄνδρας [τ]ούσδ' of the start turns around to form the τόνδ' ἀνδρῶν of the end.

The choice of stoichedon for the *grammata* bears directly on the monument and the epigram's eulogistic role. As Simonides, drawing on Pythagorean notions already current in the sixth century, would observe, to be perfect in body, mind and all the rest, is to be fashioned four-square (χερσίν τε καὶ ποσὶ καὶ νόῳ / τετράγωνον, ἄνευ ψόφου τετυγμένον, 542.2–3 *PMG*), just as these letters so visibly are. In the Ambracian instance, the notations not only invest the dead with this perfection, but also supply a visible corrective to the manner in which they died, one that carries the implication of violence written into φόνον.

The coalition of the monument and its inscription with the physical-cum-ethical virtues of the deceased finds many analogues from the period, whose inscribed grave markers variously announce their contiguity and even coalescence with the person buried beneath, the physical structure a literal embodiment of the inner worth of the individual whose death it

---

[78] Thomas 1992, 88.

[79] As Bousquet 1992 comments of the inscription, 'c'est un chef d'oeuvre technique et un tour de force d'organisation'; see too Cassio 1994.

[80] Cassio 1994, 105–06.

records: so *CEG* 161, where the *menêma* is designated καλόν, or, more fully and unequivocally, *CEG* 18, an epitaph on the base of a *korê* dated to ca. 550–540:

> [...? A parent] set up, for his/her dear child, me (the marker, beautiful to behold (καλὸν ἰδε̃ν). And Phaidimos fashioned (me).

Since the first person pronoun makes the *korê* the speaker of the epigram, she dictates the terms for her reception – admiration for the beauty of the image that reflects the deceased maiden's loveliness and value.[81] *CEG* 19, also mid-sixth century, achieves the same assimilation by creating an equivalence between the two terms to which the gaze of the passer-by is simultaneously directed – tomb and physical excellence (assuming the supplement is correct) – each located in the verse-emphatic positions of the second line's beginning and end:

> [... .τι]ς αἰχμετõ Χσενόκλεες, ἀνδρὸς | [ἐπισ]τὰς ⋮
> σῆμα τὸ σὸν προσιδὸν γνό[σετ]αι ἐν[ορέαν?]

> [He who] standing at [your tomb?] Xenocles, a spearman your marker will know, as he looks on it, your manliness

The well-known Kroisos epigram of ca. 540–530 (*CEG* 27) relies on another stratagem to prompt viewers to see the structure at the burial site as a declaration of the signal beauty of the dead, even as the mention of Kroisos' death while fighting (doubtless on the polis' behalf) 'in the front lines' – a sure-fire means of attaining *la belle mort* – affirms his aesthetic qualities:

> στε̃θι καὶ οἴκτρον Κροίσο παρὰ σε̃μα θανόντος
> hόν ποτ' ἐνὶ προμάχοις ὄλεσε | θõρος Ἄρες

> Stand and mourn near the marker of dead Kroisos whom raging Ares once destroyed in the front lines

Topping the base on which the lines are inscribed is the image of a *kouros*, the instantiation of youth in its beauteous prime. Reading the lines while looking at this *sêma*, the marker or stand-in that the lines bracket between mention of Kroisos and his death, makes clear that we witness in this resplendent figure none other than the object of remembrance and cele-bration (note the encomiastic relative pronoun). Here we apprehend the same relations of opposition between the violence of the fighter's death (so

---

[81] See Day 1989, 20.

'raging Ares') and the unblemished beauty of the *kouros* that the visually lovely Ambracian monument likewise alerts us to.

The stoichedon style of the cenotaph's inscription promotes the metonymy between marker and person in a very different respect. Confronted with the painstaking alignment of the letters in their linear and vertical ranks, the spectator sees the alphabetic notations assume the no less squared formation of the dead Ambracians as they escort the members of the Corinthian embassy. Already in the *Iliad*, those who form an escort, four in number in this instance too, although conducting cows not men, are arranged in *stichoi* with dogs positioned at the rear, all now in the form of figures materialized on the surface of the shield (Il. 18.577–78, with Chapter 4).

Besides the persons of the dead and the circumstances of their demise, layout and design visualize a third element, the funerary ritual that would include the *thrênos*, the sung lamentation performed by civic choruses.[82] As Day observes,[83] a complete viewing and decipherment of the inscription requires that individuals walk the length of the monument, which measures 12.40 m, and back again two and a half times so as to complete their reading; this movement would replicate 'a processional ritual, or perhaps choral performance with its back and forth motion of strophe/antistrophe, at the monument's founding' and so restage that original act of communal mourning and remembrance even as, through the act of reading, the sung or spoken eulogy is reperformed. Freshly dictating this mimetic and orderly progression common to the letters, the escort and the past and present participants in the rite is the identical scansion of the first and last distichs already noted, which means that the line's reader adopts the same rhythm, both vocal and kinetic, as he begins and ends his passage along the wall.

The diction of the cenotaph's epigram furnishes an additional prompt to the reader to reperform the *thrênos* at the earlier funerary event, a choral procession and sung performance whose contents the lines all but perfectly 'transcribe'. The characterization of the dead as 'good', [ἐ]σλούς, is very much at home in the language of the dirge, featured in Pindar's re-enactment of the funerary lament sung by the Muses at the burial of Achilles (*Isthm.* 8.60), while ὀλοφύρομαι, though often a generalized term for mourning, also refers more specifically to the formalized sung lamentation

---

[82] Day 1989, 23 notes how rituals at tombs, and sometimes the treatment of the stelai themselves, recreated the rites performed on the occasion of the burial. In what follows, I draw on many of the points and examples made through the course of his illuminating analysis.

[83] Day 2007, 40.

at the funeral of the dead: so the choice of the verb at *Od.* 24.58–61, where the Nereids, together with the Muses, perform the *thrênos* at the funeral of Achilles. *Penthos* is a third expression that fits this frame of civic funerary lament. In epic usage, the term not only refers to a collective emotion, but to 'the public ritual of mourning formally enacted with songs of lamentation'.[84] Again, a Homeric funeral, in this instance the preliminary rites performed before Hector's burial, offers a paradigmatic occasion. Responding to the *penthos* (*Il.* 24.708) suffered by those charged with laying out the corpse, the women standing by raise the ritual lament (οἵ τε στονόεσσαν ἀοιδὴν / οἳ μὲν ἄρ' ἐθρήνεον, 721–22).

Plentiful contemporary parallels also exist for the transcription of the words of the *thrênos* into epigrammatic form on the monument raised more lastingly to commemorate the dead. A near exact parallel for the Ambracian epigram's ὀλοφύρομαι, as well as for its characterization of the excellence of the dead, is the use of the same verb in an early Attic inscription on the base for a stele or *kouros* of ca. 560–550 (*CEG* 14):

> His father Amphichares set up this marker of the dead Chairedemos, mourning his good boy (ἀγαθὸν παῖδα ὀ|λοφυρόμενο[ς]).

As Day comments,[85] 'the epigram recalls the three typical features of funerals ... viz., lamentation, encomium, and the erection of a marker. Whoever reads it narrates the funeral Amphichares performed for Chairedemos' and, I would add, re-articulates the words that were sung or spoken there. The same conjunction of ὀλοφύρομαι and celebration occurs at the end of the inscription on a funerary monument from the Kerameikos of ca. 525 (*CEG* 43), erected for an individual whose Olympic victory the reader of the lines recalls in glorifying terms and the expression 'lamentory' (ὀλοφ|υδνόν) occurs on a memorial for Anaxilas (*CEG* 58). Integral to the continuity between epigram and *thrênos* is the elegiac metre that came to be the favoured mode for funerary inscriptions; if, *pace* Bowie,[86] threnodies at funerals were in this metre, then the epigram preserves the rhythm and processional linearity of that original song.

Before leaving the Ambracian monument, one final feature of this kinetic mimesis dependent on the motion and its arrest that the inscription compels its audience to reperform. We first meet the objects of lamentation as they encounter sudden death en route to meet the Corinthians. While

---

[84] Nagy 1979, 95.

[85] Day 1989, 25 n. 69 while also citing Eur. *Rh.* 896 and comparing to these examples Tyrt. 12.27 W.

[86] Bowie 1986, 22–27.

the deictic opening locates us in Ambracia, we then are prompted imaginatively to retrace the envoys' steps with our own as we first travel to where the ambush occurred, and later find ourselves in Corinth whose mention rounds out the triad, a sequence that recreates the full itinerary of those commemorated here. As the lines' viewer moves along the wall so as to read its content, he corporeally keeps pace with the letters' 'promenade "boustrophédique" ',[87] now forward and now back, that re-enacts the embassy's original journey.

The sudden termination of the writing at the midpoint of the line before a reader completes the third lap nicely parallels the abruptness of death's coming and the non-return it occasioned. Placed in final position, the term *thanatos*, whose immobilizing powers are already an epic commonplace, brings us to an unlooked-for stop mid-way along the wall as, like Euxenus, we are left, quite literally, still travelling, unable to complete our trajectory before, as other funerary inscriptions bid their reader do (e.g. *CEG* 13, 117), moving on. A simile at Il. 17.434–39 describing the sorrow of Achilles' horses at the death of Patroclus rehearses the immobility that claims the mourner afflicted with grief for the Ambracian dead, adding on to this the transformation of these preternaturally swift steeds into counterparts to the quintessentially static funerary monument that the inscription's reader contemplates:

> ἀλλ᾿ ὥς τε στήλη μένει ἔμπεδον, ἥ τ᾿ ἐπὶ τύμβῳ
> ἀνέρος ἑστήκῃ τεθνηότος ἠὲ γυναικός,   435
> ὣς μένον ἀσφαλέως περικαλλέα δίφρον ἔχοντες
> οὔδει ἐνισκίμψαντε καρήατα· δάκρυα δέ σφι
> θερμὰ κατὰ βλεφάρων χαμάδις ῥέε μυρομένοισιν
> ἡνιόχοιο πόθῳ·

> But like a stele stands firm rooted in the ground, which was set up on the tomb of a dead man or woman, even so they stood firmly staying the very beautiful chariot and bent their heads to the ground. And the warm tears ran to the ground down from their eyelids as they mourned, in longing for the absence of their charioteer.[88]

Patroclus' too early end proves relevant to the monument on a second count, and suggests a fresh coalescence between the present and past effected by the inscription, not just in its visual and material recreation of the events it describes – death and its ritual commemoration in speech, song and choral re-enactment – but in its generation of a visualization of

---

[87] Bousquet 1992, 606.   [88] Note the use of the imperfect for the tears' flow.

what happened and of imaginary events like to it. Enhancing the impression of regularity is the letter count and their arrangement so as to measure exactly 100 feet, then redivided in the ten lines of verse. Patroclus' pyre, a viewer might recall, is similarly ἑκατόμπεδον ἔνθα καὶ ἔνθα (*Il.* 23.164).[89] Pacing out the 100 feet 'this way and that', the mourner becomes a participant at that epic occasion, assimilating the dead anew to the heroic company more narrowly evoked in the ever-flourishing grief.

If the suggestion that a monument in all its craftsmanship, refinement and display of *kosmos* inscribed with letters invested with the same properties could prompt an enduring reperformance of a temporally remote choral procession seems unlikely, then a second monumental complex displays this same mimetic relation between an artefact and ritual. Detailing a series of images raised at Delphi, Pausanias supplies the monument's back history, observing that the construction resulted from what he styles a *sophisma* or tricky stratagem devised by the Orneatai from the Argolid (10.18.5).[90] In an attempt to repel a Sicyonian attack that threatened to displace them,

> they vowed to Apollo that, if they should drive the Sicyonians out of their native land, they would organize a daily procession in his honour at Delphi and sacrifice victims of a certain kind and a certain number. Well, they conquered the Sicyonians in battle. But finding the daily fulfillment of their vow a great expense and a still greater trouble, they devised the trick of dedicating to the god bronze figures representing a sacrifice and procession.

The Ambracian inscription does much the same, but with still greater economy: through the capacity of writing to prompt visualization and mimesis in the mental, verbal and kinetic/corporeal domains, the epigram turns readers and hearers into seers and empathetic participants at the original event whose perpetuation into present and future time it guarantees.

1.4   An Inscribed Dedication Following a Choral Victory

My fourth example concerns what is, perhaps, our 'earliest attestation of choral poetry in Athens',[91] a verse inscription (*IG* I³ 833*bis*) that occurs on a rectangular tripod base of Pentelic marble dated to c. 500–480; once set up

---

[89] Bousquet 1992, 604 cites the Iliadic example but without suggesting an allusion.

[90] See the discussion in Elsner 1996, 526–27.

[91] Martin 2007, 38. As the discussion will make clear, Martin's account has very much informed my reading.

on the Acropolis, the block would have formed part of a no longer extant more elaborate dedication set up by a victorious choral poet. The version presented here follows the reconstruction of Peppas-Delmousou, who made a new join between the different pieces and suggested a restoration of the opening lines.[92]

[νικέ]σας hό[δε πρõ]τον Ἀθένεσ[ιν χο]ρõι ἀνδρõ[ν] |
  [ἀσκε]τε͂ς σοφ[ίας τόνδ' ἀνέθε[κ]εν hόρον |
[εὐχσ]άμενο[ς· π]λείστοις δὲ [χ]οροῖς ἔχσο κατὰ φῦ[λα] |
  [ἀνδ]ρõν νι[κε͂]σαί φεσι π[ερ]ὶ τρίποδος.

[having won] first with a chorus of men at Athens this man dedicated this *horos* of (lovely? practiced?) poetic skill as he had vowed to; and he claims to have won with very many choruses of men overseas among nations for the honour of a tripod. (text and translation, with modifications, after Bowie 2010)

Recent scholars have documented the many paradoxes of the inscription, among them its hybrid form (midway between a choregic and personal dedication), its use and contravention of dedicatory conventions, its introduction of diction unparalleled in other votive texts.[93] But my concern is, again, chiefly with the alphabetic lettering as a locus of spectacularity, a repository of meaning in and of itself (see n. 8 for this 'sematography'), and, as corollary to this, the inscription's capacity to recreate a choral performance not only witnessed by the viewer/reader, but one in which he actively participates.

Placed at the close of the second line is the term *horos*, literally a 'boundary stone' and an expression that, previous discussions suggest, is found uniquely here in the votive repertoire.[94] While some would make the term describe the base alone or see in it a reference to the monument's shape, these accounts do not reckon with the rich set of meanings that the boundary stone has in its usage in the inscription, and its associations with other *horoi* familiar to an Athenian audience. Insofar as a *horos* establishes a limit that demarcates a certain space and can deny access to the closed-off area, its placement at the close of the second line exactly replicates the stone's actual and material function in the contemporary polis: it too marks a terminus, a point at which the writing stops before starting up again, and a chance for the reader to pause following his perusal of the first distich and to catch his breath before his eye moves back to its starting point to read line 3.

[92] Peppas-Delmousou 1971.   [93] Besides Martin 2007, see too Belis 2011.
[94] Martin 2007, 42. Note the reuse of the term in the strikingly similar epigram assigned to Parrhasius and cited in Athen. 12.543e.

The block set up by the boundary stone indicates movement arrested in a second sense. If we assume that the victory at Athens was the capstone to the *cursus honorum* that the inscription traces out,[95] and the most recent win that trumps the undifferentiated victories mentioned in the second distich (typical of epinician and 'catalogue' structures, we begin at the high point of the enumeration, the crescendo followed by lesser items), then the city indeed stands as the end point, the final term in the sequence of successful ventures. The *horos* positioned here in Athens encloses a space still more narrow and circumscribed in polis topography; raised on the Acropolis, the votive monument would have formed part of Athena's sacred *temenos* (perhaps even positioned at its outer limits), where its role is the same as that of a fourth-century Attic stone that explicitly declares itself a *horos temenous* and marks out ritual space accessible only to the select few.[96]

The placement of the *horos* in verse-final position also serves to reinforce the vaunt these lines articulate. If we understand the boundary stone as a physical and audible declaration of this capping manifestation of the dedicator's poetic *sophia*, then, as Richard Martin observes, its location blocks all attempts to top his victory: 'no going beyond this point'.[97] But no sooner does the viewer-reader encounter the limitation than the injunction is broken – and by the victor, inscriber and reader all in one. Despite the seeming boundary, the enjambed [εὐχσ]άμενος propels the phrase into line 3, calling the status of the monument as blockage into question; is its position reflective of the votive's role as *telos*, the fulfillment of a prayer and vow made prior to the competition in which our donor was victorious, or the materialization of the performative boast that εὔχομαι also signifies? The poet may still go on to further victories and what seemed a terminus might prove just a fresh departure point.

The epigram's second line offers another pointer towards the words' materiality, their physical reality as well as role as conduits of meaning. In calling itself a *horos*, the monument reminds the viewer that – like the boundary stones of ca. 500 B.C.E. that stood at the outer limits of the agora just down the hill from the Acropolis and carried the words 'I am the *horos* of the *agora*' –[98] the dedication categorizes itself as much an object fixed in

---

[95] Martin 2007, 41 and 59 also assumes this progression.

[96] For *horoi* demarcating sacred spaces, see *IG* I 858, 860; II² 2596–2612. Ober 1995 and 2006 offer additional discussions of these and other such boundaries.

[97] Martin 2007, 44–45.

[98] ΗΟΡΟΣ ΕΙΜΙ ΤΕΣ ΑΓΟΡΑΣ: agora inscription inv. nos. I 5510, I 7039, both of ca. 500; I 5675, a third such stone, was found displaced from its original location. See Thompson and Wycherley 1972, 117–19 and Martin 2007, 44.

the landscape, a 'fact on the ground',[99] as an inscription, and frames the written signs as things to be viewed as well as a text to be read. Reinforcing this focus on materiality is the expression *sophias . . . horon*. As Martin suggests,[100] if we understand σοφ[ίας] as a genitive of material or content, we are made to view the stone before us as something made of poetry – as indeed it is, since the poetic epigram is the material which constitutes the tangible matter of this *horos*.

The choice of the term *sophia* in and of itself directs attention to the monument as a tangible display of expertise; *sophia*, *sophos* and even the verb *sophizomai* all appear in the votive repertoire, where typically they belong to epigrams on dedications made by craftsmen whose finely worked offerings stand as visible statements of their artisanal skills. Among several possible examples, another dedication from the Athenian Acropolis of ca. 500, a red-figure vase, preserves the second line of an inscription on its still extant foot: '[These?] men made by their skills this beautiful *agalma*' (*CEG* 291).[101] It is not just the choral poet's prowess that the votive communicates and visualizes, but that of the stone's maker and message-writer as well.

Consistent with other dedications, the language of the epigram more narrowly defines this monument and its lettering as a view-worthy ensemble quite independent of its record-keeping function. Although only two letters of the word at the start of the second line still remain, commentators propose two possible supplements, *asketês*, finely wrought, or *himertos*, lovely, desirable. As in the examples discussed above, either adjective would add a new dimension to the visualization prompted by the lettered block. While the τόνδ' refers to *this* votive visible before the reader, the adjective would transport him back to a more notional artefact. *Asketês*, unique in the corpus of dedications, appears in an earlier and most fitting context, in a passage that combines a description of the superlative example of two master craftsmen's skills with an archetypal display of *thauma*-provoking choral dancing. In the lines prefacing the description of the dancers on the penultimate band of Achilles' shield, the poet compares Hephaestus' crafting of this *choros* – and here, as noted before, the noun can refer either to the fashioned chorus at it does later in the passage, or to the dancing floor itself – to that which Daedalus made for Ariadne; the term used of the

---

[99] The phrase belongs to Ober 2006.   [100] Martin 2007, 59–60.

[101] Bowie 2010, 326–29 offers other examples, including the very striking *CEG* 230 of ca. 500–480, an inscription on a marble column also from the Athenian Acropolis, whose text reads '[... .] for the skilled to exercise their skill (σο[φ]ίζεσθ[αι]) [...]) for he who has craft has [his skill] better'. Martin 2007, 40–41 n. 14 also cites this.

legendary artisan working the surface at 592 is ἤσκησεν.[102] If we follow the
second supplement, then the allusion to the Homeric scene remains; the
term occurs of the performance of or on this *choros* as the poet introduces
viewers to the spectacle, and the pleasure and even erotic attraction they
vicariously experience: 'a great crowd stood around the desirous/desire-
eliciting (ἱμερόεντα) chorus, taking delight' (603–04).

Again, taking my cue from Martin, and in accordance with the intimate
relations between the 'look' and material of the inscription and its contents,
I would suggest that the finely fashioned *horos* is consubstantial with the
chorus to a still greater degree. Just as the Iliadic χορός can refer to a
dancing floor, so here the marble surface becomes the space on which the
letters dance, performing anew the winning dithyramb complete with the
patterns, interchanges and different formations assumed by the members
of the troupe. As detailed elsewhere in this study, *marmaros*, 'marble', is
cognate with the term that evokes the sparkle of choral dancers' rapidly
moving feet in epic and choral poetry, *marmarugai*.[103] The letters cut into
the votive's surface possess the gleam of the matter into which they are
incised, a radiance heightened by their complex moves across the stone. As
for these moves themselves, we might first observe, as Martin suggests, the
perfect chiastic figure made by the r/o characters of *choroi* and the o/r of
horon (in the pre-Ionic Athenian alphabet, there is no distinction between
the letter forms for the long and short o); line 3 visibly repeats the sequence
of letters found at the start, with fresh rearrangement of its elements to
form the dative *chorois* as the dancers close the circle initiated in the
opening of their performance. In the first distich, *anetheken* placed directly
below *Athenesi* reverses syllables not letters (*the-ne/ne-the*) while the final
line takes the terms that framed the opening – being victorious and men –
and unites the two separated elements.[104]

The linear arrangement of the letters that record a victory in a dithyrambic dance whose characteristic element came to be, through the fifth
century's course, its circular formation and movements, does not obviate
the recreation of the prize-winning spectacle. In the patterns they describe,
where one arrangement of letters is then reversed in another line, the
alphabetic notations do 'circle'. As Hedreen has recently argued,[105] a

[102] See the discussion of finely worked dancing floors in Chapter 6.   [103] See Kurke 2012, 228.
[104] Martin 2007, 49–50. As Martin notes (49), the syntax of the phrase φῦλα / [ἀνδ]ρῶν is
      ambiguous – does the expression refer to the races of men or the choruses of men – and
      conjectures that 'the poet's desire for chiasmus and symmetry is what prompted this placement
      of the genitive'.
[105] Hedreen 2013.

processional deployment, with the dancers stretched out in the 'rope' that Pindar's second *Dithyramb* critiques, is also part of the dithyrambic performance.

The circles fashioned by the dithyrambic dancers prove pertinent to the diction of the epigram as well as to its physical appearance. The expression π[ερ]ὶ τρίποδος in final position in the closing line, while most obviously a reference to the prize for which the chorus competed and a glance towards the object that most likely topped the block, also has the literal sense 'around the tripod'.[106] Painted and poetic sources bear out the suggestion that dancers in competitions would circle around a central tripod or – in an arrangement that still more narrowly echoes the language of the epigram – that they would perform inside a space demarcated by a series of tripods surrounding the site. As the discussion in Chapter 2 noted, the upper portion of a large Geometric funerary vase found in the Kerameikos has among its many figurative elements a chorus of five youths dancing to the right (Fig. 2.8).[107] On either side of the line the painter has placed oversized Orientalizing cauldrons, equal in height to the youths, on highly orna-mented stands, which served as the prizes awarded at the event. In the image on a Geometric skyphos from Athens (Fig. 2.7), also cited earlier, a mixed chorus of youths and maidens performs a ring dance on the interior while a frieze of eight tripods circles the exterior.[108] Beyond the objects' likely role as the fruits of victory in the agonistic performance, their deployment, Papalexandrou suggests, may reflect the spatial dynamics of the tripod-circling dance represented here.[109] More simply, and as on the Kerameikos vase, these tripods delimit the dancing arena.

Visual accounts of tripods included in agonistic events realize a second role played by the verse-final *horos* that, as noted above, forms the point at which the reader must cast his eye back over the space already traversed. Representations of chariot competitions not only position tripods along the sides of the track (witness the depiction of Patroclus' funeral games on one band of the François Vase, and other images parallel the arrangement),[110] but show them mounted high on columns at the ends of the racecourse, where they serve as the τέρματα around which the charioteer must steer his team at the moment most demanding of his skill. On a fragment from a

---

[106] Wilson 2000, 217–18.

[107] Athens, National Archaeological Museum 810; for discussion, see Coldstream 2003, 119 and Papalexandrou 2005, 197–98 for this and the subsequent example.

[108] Athens, National Archaeological Museum 874.   [109] Papalexandrou 2005, 196–97.

[110] E.g. Paris, Musée du Louvre, E 875; Athens, National Archaeological Museum. 654b; for discussion of these and other images, see Wilson Jones 2002 and, with further examples, McGowan 1995, 621–26.

frieze on a relief pithos in Heraklion, dated to the second half of the seventh century and originally from Prinias, a monumental tripod cauldron stands between a rider and a chariot racing at top speed;[111] to a viewer, the arrangement, placed on the circular body of the vessel, could indicate the point at which each contestant turns the post. A later black-figure amphora from Munich, from around the middle of the sixth century, positions a single tripod and a group of three to delimit the beginning and end of a scene showing a race with warriors;[112] again, if the course comprised more than one lap, these could serve as turning posts. Aeolic columns with tripods towards which chariots are headed similarly appear on the surface of a Clazomenian sarcophagus from ca. 510–480, and a small mid-sixth-century black-figure amphora in Karlsruhe attributed to a painter of the Tyrrhenian Group shows riders racing towards a Doric column behind which stands a tripod cauldron that, elevated on extended legs, overtops the first of the two structures;[113] together both objects establish the terminus.

Presaging these visual examples is Nestor's detailed account of the marker designated as the turning point by Achilles in the chariot race in *Iliad* 23, which he describes as a tree stump flanked by two stones (327–30); these objects, 'planted firmly at the meeting point of the road', smoothed over and serving as 'a *sêma*', bear a marked likeness in both look and function to the *horoi* cited elsewhere in the poem and in later accounts, and foreshadow the composite of boundary stone and *terma* proposed by the epigram. In borrowing the language of the racecourse for a dance performance, the composer of the epigram also adopts a conceit very familiar from contemporary choral poetry, both epinician and in other lyric genres (e.g. Pind. fr. 107a S.-M., with Chapter 4).

But the 'turn around a marker' evoked by the combination of the material tripod and the inscribed term *horos* is more than merely metaphoric; instead it is experiential too, as the closing of the epigram invites the viewer not just to see the real and notional performances and contests revisited in its lettering but physically to participate and become one with the winning dancers – just the wizardry of choral dancing described in the *Homeric Hymn to Apollo* at 161–64.[114] Recall too how [Longinus] says that the aim of *phantasia* is to produce emotion (*pathos*) and *kinêsis* (*De subl.* 15.1–2), a twofold arousal that manifests itself in the motion that, in Plato's account at *Laws* 664e–665a, requires only the addition of *rhythmos* to

---

[111] Crete, Archaeological Museum of Heraklion AM 7652.
[112] Munich, Antikensammlungen 1471.
[113] London, British Museum 96.6–15.1; Karlsruhe, Badisches Landesmuseum B 2423.
[114] See Peponi 2009, 60–68 and Chapter 10.

become dance. With his reading now concluded, the viewer of the monument might treat the closing expression 'around the tripod' not just as descriptive, but as a prompt, an invitation similarly to circle about what was most probably a highly worked and decorated tripod, which might have included a figural design extending around its body. The best known of these is, of course, Lysikrates' choregic monument from well over a century after this dedication (complete with its frieze of the originary dithyrambic dancers, the chorus of dolphin-men that encircle the structure supporting the tripod) but earlier examples suggest the degree of elaboration that went into these commemorative objects.[115] In performing his circuit around the monument, the reader becomes enactor too, executing, albeit in solo fashion, the same movements as these 'many choruses' led by the *chorêgos*-cum-votary once performed.

1.5   Abecedaria and 'Letter-Weaving'

Central to the proposal advanced above is the notion that the letters and phrases in early inscriptions perform their own form of rhythmic procession or dance, reconstructing choral formations and movements familiar to viewers by means of their visual as well as semantic dimensions. Contemporary with, and sometimes preceding the sources reviewed so far, is a final set of artefacts consisting not of message-bearing inscriptions but more simply of abecedaria incised and painted on metal and clay surfaces and that supply the underpinnings to my larger argument. As these alphabetic sequences suggest, very early artists and scribes treat letters in ways that would predispose viewers to look for visual patterning and to see in an inscription's design and, on occasion, placement in a larger group artfully constructed assemblages that, perceived in their entirety, describe motions both diverse and repeated. Conditioned from the first (and from the methods in which instruction in reading and writing was carried out; see below) to regard writing according to aesthetic principles, the readers of the inscriptions treated above would more readily apprehend the coalescence of signs and chorus members that I have suggested.

The earliest instance consists of a series of copper plaques from the Fayum dated to the late ninth or early eighth century. Quite possibly the creation of scribes from the Ionic region of Greece and perhaps destined for some sacred context or cult purpose, these are inscribed with abecedaria that include letter forms of an archaic type and that frequently predate the

---

[115] See Wilson 2000, 207–18 for examples.

shapes current in the writers' own day. As Roger Woodard demonstrates in his book-length study of the plaques,[116] four chief and seemingly surprising phenomena occur in these alphabetic lines' design, anomalies for which, no less curiously, abundant parallels exist in the abecedaria and other types of inscriptions from the archaic period found in many regions of Greece.

First, many of the alphabetic lines include disruptions of the expected sequence; far from assuming fixed positions in the line, individual letters are sometimes displaced from their regular locations and appear out of order. Among the several instances cited by Woodard, *iota* may be inserted between *mu* and *nu*, *xi* may occur adjacent to *eta*, and both *kappa* and *lambda* and *lambda* and *mu* are sometimes inverted. On other occasions, a scribe might choose to omit single letters or whole clusters of these: again, *kappa* and *lambda* and *lambda* and *mu*, both singly and as a group, quite frequently disappear. Seemingly random too are choices between possible letter forms in individual lines: at a time when the alphabetic shapes are still fluid and come in a variety of different forms, the scribes use now one and now another of the available repertoire. Exemplary of this process is the frequent 'homography' of *eta* and *xi* and of *theta* and *omicron* on the copper plaques, a phenomenon also visible in the inscription on the rim of a bronze lebes from ca. 600–550 dedicated by one 'son of Dexippos' and found at Delphi (*CEG* 369). Here too both the *theta* and *omicron* assume a square rather than circular shape while the *theta* is like the so-called 'enclosed' *xi* of the copper plaques, which looks like a square with a grid inside. Both *theta* and *omicron* may also appear in dotted rather than the crossed forms also current. As these abecedaria further illustrate, the very placement of the alphabetic lines reveals a variety of possible configurations: forsaking strict linearity – one letter after the next – the sequence may break into two halves whose numerical make up, design and orientation suggest deliberate coordination.

According to Woodard's argument, those who inscribed the copper plaques and other abecedaria-hosting objects were guilty neither of carelessness nor of ignorance, nor did they select certain letter forms on account of their reluctance to attempt configurations demanding greater dexterity; instead they were following the principles of assimilation, dissimilation, 'allography' and symmetry that his study details and that recall exactly the axioms adopted by the individual who 'completed' the inscription on the Dipylon oinochoe. Later authors who comment on and variously explain the reasons for these arrangements acknowledge the cardinal

---

[116] Woodard 2014.

role of aesthetics. For Dionysius of Halicarnassus, the placement of the letters resulted from an author's attentiveness to their orthographic as well as phonological aspects, and proved fundamental to the creation not of these simple objects, but of a polished literary work: the construction of a harmonious sequence of words and phrases depends on 'the nature (φύσις) of the letters and the quality (δύναμις) of the syllables, from which the words are woven (πλέκεται)' (*Comp.* 13). A later passage in the same treatise returns to the idea: 'What is the chief point of my claim? That it is by the interweaving of letters (γραμμάτων συμπλοκάς) that the variegated effect of syllables comes about, that the combination of syllables produces the diverse nature of words, and that by the arrangement of words comes multiform (πολύμορφος) discourse' (*Comp.* 16). In this instance, and understanding the φύσις to which the rhetorician refers as 'outward form' as well as 'character', 'constitution' or 'disposition', Dionysius accommodates not just the acoustic properties of letters both individually and in combinations, but also the 'look' of the sequence; it is this that gives to *logos* its 'polymorphic' property, the shapeliness produced by the variegation in its elements.

For Jerome, more utilitarian and pedagogic purposes determine the design of written abecedaria and the breaks in the sequence they observe. Commenting on a practice also visible in the abecedaria (many of which predate the plaques) belonging to a variety of Near Eastern writing systems, he identifies and explains the so-called *atbash* arrangement, named from the pairing of the Hebrew letters *aleph* with *taw* and *beth* with *shin* (*In Jerem.* 25 v. 26):

> Among us, the Greek alphabet is recited all the way to the last letter in a straight sequence (*per ordinem*), that is *alpha*, *beta* and so on, all the way to *omega*; also, for the sake of children memorizing [the alphabet], we make it a practice to turn the line of recitation backwards and to intertwine the last with the first (*lectionis ordinem vertere et primis extrema miscere*), so that we say *alpha omega*, *beta psi*. In a corresponding way, among the Hebrews, the first letter is *aleph*, the second *beth*, the third *gimel*, all the way to the twenty-second and last letter, *taw*, before which is *shin*. Thus we recite *aleph taw*, *beth shin*, and when we make the turn in the middle, *lamed* comes face to face with the letter *kap*.

As proof that the creators of these abecedaria were well aware of the 'letter weaving' (in Woodard's phrase) that Jerome describes, and that is similarly apparent in the conceit of the woven literary text or, in the Latin term, *contextus*, Woodard cites line 16 from the reverse face of the second copper plaque, where the scribe explains what he is about: 'o abecedarium, may the stylus interweave you'.[117]

Building on Woodard's arguments, I would suggest that already in these very early instances letters are invested with the characteristics that the individuals responsible for the inscriptions on the Dipylon oinochoe, Theran graffiti, Ambracian cenotaph and choregic dedication in Athens would likewise introduce: in addition to possessing dynamism and mobility, the alphabetic signs in the abecedaria adopt configurations, dubbed *schêmata* by the alphabetic theorists treated in Section 4, that change from one line to the next and are arranged so as to create visual patterns both within single lines and from one row to the next, inviting us to view/read them as both linear and horizontal constructs. Two abecedaria from the archaic and classical period well illustrate these letter patterns while displaying other features pertinent to the affinity of writing to choral morphology.

Painted on the base of a Protocorinthian conical oinochoe from Cumae of ca. 700–675 (Fig. 8.5), the two partial alphabetic sequences that form the vessel's only decorative elements supply my first example.[118] The lower of

Fig. 8.5 Protocorinthian conical oinochoe from Cumae, ca. 700–675 B.C.E. Illustration in Jeffery 1961, 116–17, pl. 18 (2). Image reproduced courtesy of the Jeffery Archive, Centre for the Study of Ancient Documents, Oxford.

---

[117] Woodard 2014, 177–226. It should be noted that this interpretation is only one among many possibilities.

[118] Jeffery 1961, 116–17, pl. 18 (2), with discussion in Woodard 2014, 285–87 and Powell 1991, 156.

the lines is made up of eight letters in Cumaean (i.e. Euboean) script, running left to right and from *alpha* to *zeta*, with the final two letters in the sequence reversed so that *eta* precedes *zeta*. While the other letters uniformly observe the overall orientation of the line and face rightwards, the *gamma* is painted sinistroverse. Viewed as an ensemble, the sequence fashions a curve, moving from its lowest point up to the scored line that forms the axis between the two letter sets. The second abecedarium, also running left to right, offers a mirror image of the lower one. The six letters face leftwards and in this instance travel not up to the axis, but down instead, forming a curve whose angle is less pronounced than that of its pair. The painter has omitted both *alpha* and *epsilon* and again reversed the positions of *zeta* and *eta*. The first three letters adopt forms very different from those given to the same characters in the line below, and the twisted morphology of the *beta* here is quite unique. Together the two lines form a kind of 'meandering hybrid boustrophedon, looping at the point at which the two zetas meet ... with each individual grapheme paired, approximately, with an identical grapheme'.[119]

My second example, a Boeotian cup of ca. 420 now in Athens (Fig. 8.6),[120] includes two abecedaria, one painted on each of its faces and both divided into two horizontal lines that fill the space between the vessel's handles. Although the design lacks the complexity of that on the earlier oinochoe, it likewise demonstrates several of the features already noted and seems to be painted with an eye to creating a visually pleasing decorative arrangement that combines homogeneity and variegation. One of the abecedaria, made up of twenty-three letters, is incomplete: its first line runs from *alpha* to *lambda*, including twelve letters in all, while the second, shorter line of eleven begins at *mu* and ends with *chi*. On the reverse face, the painter supplies the full alphabet, dividing the two rows after the *mu*, thereby postponing the break by one position. In this instance too, the first line contains one more letter than the second, thirteen characters followed by twelve. On both faces, a series of dots runs beneath the lower row of letters, some positioned immediately beneath a character, others filling the spaces between them, and a sequence of short curvilear lines located just above a band of black circling around the entire vessel completes the decorative programme. Together these dots and serpentine lines, each of which begins to the left of where the previous one ends, nicely suggest the manner in which the individual letters and alphabetic sequence should be pronounced both individually and

---

[119] Woodard 2014, 286–87.

[120] Athens, National Archaeological Museum 9716. Jeffery 1961, 94 and pl. 10.20 with Woodard 2014, 251.

Fig. 8.6 Boeotian cup, ca. 420 B.C.E. Athens, National Archaeological Museum 9716. Photograph © National Archaeological Museum, Athens.

as an ensemble: pausing between each character, the reader coming to the end of the top row must then cast his or her eye back to the beginning of the next.

Important for my purpose is the overall design of the abecedaria on these two pots and the ways in which their formations and modes of progression over the terracotta surfaces mirror those visible in archaic and later representations of choral ensembles. The two convergent sequences shown on the oinochoe, both concluding with the same character, resemble the v-deployment of contemporary choruses, in which two lines, each one headed by its *chorêgos* and sometimes made up of unequal numbers, similarly meet at a centrepoint. The manner in which the artist has positioned his graphic characters duplicates the back-and-forth of the dancers who move first in one direction, and then reverse their steps while facing in the opposite direction. Travelling upwards in a left-to-right orientation, the same letters, albeit with some changes and omissions, then turn around so as to form a line that moves from right to left; the loutrophoros by the Analatos painter in Paris cited earlier offers just this arrangement, with identical dancers facing in opposite directions on either side of an aulete standing at their centre. On the Boeotian pot, we witness two sets of parallel lines, one with more letters than the other, and both divided into two rows of slightly unequal numbers. Even so on the seventh-century hydria from

Aegina, which also figured in the earlier discussion, the painter places a line of nine women on the upper portion of the neck while twelve men process in the same direction immediately below. The repetitions and variations included in the two abecedaria on the later cup, the one slightly different from the other, and that the partial alphabets on the oinochoe likewise display, also distinguish one chorus member from the next in vase images: like the *delta* on the jar, in one instance flat-topped and narrow, in the other more properly triangular, one of the dancers on the Aeginetan hydria wears a skirt patterned differently from the rest, while the painter of a line of dancers in a tomb painting in Ruvo dresses the five figures in individualized robes and shawls.[121]

But there is a more fundamental way in which the Fayum copper plaques and these other early abecedaria bear on the inscriptions this section has reviewed and that will continue to inform the objects and texts explored below. As noted of the Theran graffiti, the very act of writing is considered performative, equivalent to a (competitive) display of dancing where the individual who visibly does it best claims front rank. It is, moreover, this manifestation of a skill still at a premium that recommends inscribed artefacts for their role as votives, a function that may be assumed by abecedaria, several of which join their more sophisticated counterparts as dedications at the shrine of Zeus Semios on Mount Hymettos.[122] So too the very earliest abecedarium from eastern Greece appears on a cup found in the Samian Heraion, dated to ca. 660; as Powell comments of this gift, 'before giving it to the goddess, the inscriber made his modest vessel precious by writing on it his ABCs'.[123] Like a choral performance, a line of well-fashioned, diversely shaped and carefully arranged letters offers its own form of tribute.

2   Alphabetic Elements on Images and Vases Showing Participants in Choral Ensembles

Once we move to the figurative realm, where choruses appear on vases together with alphabetic lettering, or inscriptions accompany images of chorus members in stone and other media, relations between writing and the performers become at once more patent and complex. The written features on these representations can play two roles, frequently in tandem:

---

[121] Naples, Museo Nazionale 9352–57. See Kowalzig 2013, 188–89 for the larger point made here.
[122] See Powell 1991, 152–53 and Langdon 1976, 17–18 and 46 for these.
[123] Powell 1991, 157.

visually, through layout, orientation, the manner in which they are painted or incised and other properties dependent on their design, the letters, words and phrases may determine, demarcate, reiterate or complicate the movements of the dancers, in whose performance they may sometimes join; as units of meaning, the notations variously describe and define the mode of *choreia* and/or identify the participants. While the same points could be made of many instances of writing on images and in painted scenes more generally, these conjunctions of lettering and choruses none-theless stand distinct; by virtue of the graphemes' inclusion, the artist or statue-maker promotes the viewer's capacity to visualize and even re-enact this quintessentially 'spectacular' event, inviting the eye, voice and in some instances the entire body, to perform anew the historical or mythical dance-and-song.

2.1 Inscribed Korai

Dating to the first half of the sixth century, the offering set up by one Geneleos on the Sacred Way leading to the celebrated sanctuary of Hera on Samos depicts a family group that performs a series of cult activities (Fig. 8.7).[124] The figures would have stood in a row on a six-metre long base along the route that was the site for the erection of the most impressive dedications, placed one after the next, as though, in the attractive sugges-tion of Katerina Karakasi, engaged in a type of competition that invites viewers to judge the merits of each successive votive.[125] Three *korai* repre-sent the donor's daughters, distinctive for the individualization of their hairstyles and impressively heavy braids and the absence of the veils worn by all the other still extant Samian sculpted maidens. Each stands with one foot slightly forward while grasping her chiton in a somewhat different manner; on each occasion too, the folds of the gathered piece of cloth, carved so as to create a curve that forms a diagonal across the body in contrast to the linear lines used for the other folds, follow the movements of the wearer and vitalize the monumental representations. Adding to the sense of presence while ornamenting the images and freshly calling atten-tion to the motion of the garment, each one is identified by the name inscribed, after the Samian fashion, on the maiden's body; so the aligned lettering in the inscriptions on two of the girls, named Philippe and

---

[124] Vathy, Archaeological Museum of Samos 768. One of the figures, inscribed with the name Ornithe, is currently in Berlin (Berlin, Staatliches Museum 1739).

[125] Karakasi 2003, 24.

Fig. 8.7 Geneleos monument, ca. 560–550 B.C.E. Vathy, Archaeological Museum of Samos 768. Photograph © Luisa Ricciarini/Bridgeman Images.

Ornithe, occurs between the drapery folds, whose parallel lines determine the letters' height and form.

These evenly spaced and gridded letters bear on the context recreated by the monument. According to several recent discussions,[126] we can identify the role of the maidens here; they are choral dancers, processing along the Sacred Way as the living girls would once have done while *en route* to performing ring dances in honour of Hera at the sanctuary. An early sixth-century hydria found at the site, whose two groups of richly clad painted dancers, one on the vase's body, the other on its upper zone, resemble Geneleos' *korai* in their poses, clothing and hairstyles, may recall the event, confirming the place of choral dancing in the cult activities performed on the goddess' behalf.[127] The linear arrangement of the votive ensemble invites the viewer to pass from one figure to the next, enacting the same regularized step performed by the maidens as they processed and that finds its more miniaturized reflection in the carved letters' 'paratactic' layout.[128]

---

[126] Baughan 2011, 22; Day 2010, 193; Karakasi 2003, 28–29 with earlier bibliography.
[127] For the hydria, see Karakasi 2003, 29 and pl. 30.
[128] As Alexandra Pappas points out *per litteras*, the written notations on the *korai* bear on the larger meaning of the group and the progression that the monument requires in a further sense. Made up of various letters, when reconstituted by a reader, they become a sense-bearing unit, a series of names both similar and disparate; passage from one image to the next likewise requires that we 'string together' the individual members of the family, who then become the unified group of the choral ensemble.

A second family group from the same site, the gift of one Cheramyes, also shows a *kouros* and three *korai*, most likely originally displayed together, although their find spots were different. Here the inscriptions appear along the front line of the hem of the *epiblema*, the shawl worn by each of the maidens, a garment that forms a sinuous curve over the chest as the folds travel downwards from the right shoulder. On the matching pair, one now in the Louvre, the other still on Samos,[129] the carefully spaced and finely fashioned letters are cut vertically in a single line, running from top to bottom and to the left. Continuing on into a second line, the inscriptions again offer an early example of an incipient stoichedon style, as the letter forms in line 1 are placed above the six *stoichoi* below.[130] The remaining two images vary the arrangement, with inscriptions pointing in the opposite direction. As Day observes, 'if the four pieces were arranged so that the direction of the script alternated, the effect would be that of false boustrophedon',[131] causing the reader's eye to re-enact the back-and-forth movement of the erstwhile performers. The inscriptions on *korai* A and B issue the same message, 'Cheramyes dedicated me, the *agalma*, to Hera', while that on the maiden carrying a hare qualifies the term *agalma* with *perikalles*, individualizing this performer (together with her offering) as particularly worthy of admiration, as might suit a lead dancer or the triad's *chorêgos*.[132]

If we extend this reading to the well-known *korai* erected on the Athenian Acropolis, and understand these maidens as participants in choruses at the festival events staged at the site,[133] then their inscriptions might similarly play a role in defining and enhancing the movements that the statues' intricate carving already suggests. Day treats the inscription on the abacus of a dedication by one Aischines (*CEG* 202), who set up his offering in the final decade of the sixth century, and whose written lines are arranged horizontally on the rounded plinth that once supported a *korê*, her feet still extant, the left advanced before the right in a stepping gesture.[134] The inscription's two shorter opening lines are oriented toward the front of

---

[129] Paris, Musée du Louvre 686; Vathy, Archaeological Museum of Samos.   [130] Butz 2010, 91.

[131] Day 2010, 83 n. 281.

[132] The back-and-forth motion of the lettering appears similarly on the Nikandre dedication on Delos, in this instance incised below the belt on the figure's left side in two lines that travel from bottom to top and back and again.

[133] Budelmann and Power 2015 usefully gather the visual and more equivocal textual evidence for female choral activity on ritual occasions in the city. For references to parthenaic choruses performing in the vicinity of the Acropolis, see, among other instances, Eur. *Ion* 492–502 and *Hcld.* 777–83 (for which, see Chapter 6).

[134] For the inscribed capital and plinth with the *korê*'s feet, Athens, Acropolis Museum 3759 and 456, with Day 2010, 58, 195–96.

the image, while the longer third line extends to the right, prompting a reader to follow its trajectory after seeing the frontal view; does the writing suggest the movement of the erstwhile dancer, who first traces out the same sequence of steps twice over and then follows them with a lengthier one, moving from left to right? Just as a spectator at the original festival occasion where the maiden appeared would have seen her frontally and then in profile, so the image's later viewer/reader, prompted by the layout of the lettering to re-enact the motions of her dance, would encounter her in just these positions. Both in this and other instances, the coincidence between the performer's toes and the location of the inscription would further coordinate the out-stepping foot, the principal locus of movement, with the inscription, making the writing seem an extension and graphic expression of the figure's movements.

The inscription on a second Attic *korê*, this one dedicated by Euthydikos, moves around the circular base (*DAA* no. 56),[135] positioned so that the donor's name appears directly below the maiden's feet, perhaps the better to draw attention to this critical element of the message.[136] The stone-cutter has taken further pains to enhance not just the legibility of his writing, as Catherine Keesling notes, but to coordinate it closely with the image. Red paint makes the letters stand out against their background, and the same colour may – as its still traceable presence on other *korai* attests – have been used on the painted garments the *korê* wears, a continuity that would enhance the inscription's function as a revisualization or embodied textualization of the maiden's former activity. The letters in the inscription's second line are aligned vertically with those in the first in stoichedon-like style, again evoking the regularized motion of the *korê* and imposing on the reader the same orderly, even processional perusal. In this instance too the support's circularity works to artistic advantage; the lines' horizontal arrangement means that the viewer must move all around the image from left to right, travelling in the same direction as the letters and perhaps, again, re-enacting the circular dance to be performed by the maiden at the procession's end.

On the pillar supporting the *korê* dedicated by Luson of ca. 510–500, this too from the Acropolis, the lettering runs vertically and retrograde up the column, with different colours for different lines (*CEG* 205). The inscription both complements and contains the exuberant ornamentation of the *korê* with which the dedication has been associated (Figs. 8.8, 8.9),[137] and

---

[135] Athens, Acropolis Museum 686 and 609.   [136] For discussion, see Keesling 2003, 31–32.
[137] Inscribed pillar: Athens, Acropolis Museum 6503. Associated *korê*: Athens, Acropolis Museum 612 and 304.

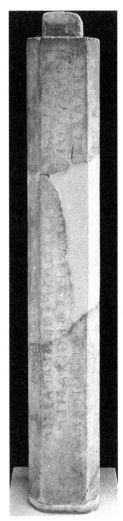

Fig. 8.8 Inscribed pillar supporting *korê* dedicated by Luson, ca. 510–500 B.C.E. Athens, Acropolis Museum 6503. Photograph © Erin Babnik, courtesy of Joseph Day and by permission of the Hellenic Ministry of Culture, First Ephorate of Prehistoric and Classical Antiquities.

whose visually dazzling, swirling patterns composed of various lines and shapes the written elements counteract with their regularity. The himation worn by the image over its chiton cascades down in a series of diversely shaped folds, from the narrowly spaced crinkles at the top to the diagonals below, which reach down to the gown's scalloped edge and seem to lead directly into the lines that demarcate the toes of the sandaled feet, making body and garment one. The column and plinth offer additional counterpoints

Fig. 8.9 *Korê* dedicated by Luson, ca. 510–500 B.C.E. Athens, Acropolis Museum 612 and 304. Photograph courtesy of the Deutsches Archäologisches Institut.

to the impression created by the image: the slab on which the *korê* stood was fitted into a capital with cavetto moulding, and rested on the rectangular pillar whose angularity plays against its bevelled edges. Again, the synthesis of the writing, its architectural framing and the figure topping the column suggest a diversity of movements, now circular and undulating, now linear, which turn an encounter with the inscribed monument into a snapshot of a performative event, and one designed to prompt the sensation that the inscription identifies: declaring that 'for Pallas Athena Luson set up a first fruits offering out of his own possessions, to be a *charis*-filled thing for the goddess', the text invites the reader to respond to the lithified spectacle as though present at the similarly grace-imbued occasion where the maiden had once appeared.

2.2   Dancing with Letters in Vase Painting

Writing's coordination with the images on vases from the archaic period on has been the object of much scrutiny, and, with François Lissarrague leading the way, many have detailed the dexterity of artists in manipulating the shape, orientation, placement and fashioning of the lettering so as both to reinforce its meaning and to emphasize the actions and properties of the individuals whom it accompanies; among the examples frequently cited in these discussions are representations of choruses, some processing, others dancing, which include alphabetic elements from as early as the first decades of the seventh century on. In light of the material presented in Section 1, which treated instances of writing that appeared quite independent of any accompanying scenes, my suggestion is that these pots do not merely form part of a larger vogue for reworking the combination of figural and non-figural elements typical of Geometric vase painting (although they do this too): instead these conjunctions freshly exploit the affinity that many different types of sources propose between the letter forms, whether singly or as parts of a longer word or phrase, the chorus member and/or his or her performance.

I begin with a vessel that belongs among the earliest instances of writing included in a figurative scene, and the first, despite its find spot on Aegina, of Athenian provenance. The so-called Menelas stand attributed to the Polyphemus Painter (Fig. 4.4, already treated in Chapter 4) dates to the first half of the seventh century and, as noted in my earlier discussion, displays just one word, the name Menelas, which appears between two of the five processing figures and above a large bird now only partially visible. Once thought to identify the figure it precedes, the inscription is now understood as a citation from the song sung by the members of the chorus shown advancing here.[138] But the presence of writing also has a different function, creating differentiation and even hierarchy among the otherwise seemingly identical members of the procession (contrast the Oltos psykter discussed below). Just as other painters might distinguish the *chorêgos* not just by placing the figure in lead position, but by investing him or her with distinctive dress, accessories or other singularizing features, so here the inscription assumes this function: is this the *exarchos*, the one who initiates the song before the others pick up the words? As lead-off singer, the figure might also be imagined as the one who heads the line; where the vase's conical shape necessarily makes the procession seem circular, the inscription matches the movement from left to right and allows the viewer to discern its structure, where the chorus line begins, and where it ends.

About a century stands between the Polyphemus Painter's vase and the Middle Corinthian aryballos from the temple of Apollo cited in Section 1,

---

[138] Ferrari 1987.

where the more extensive writing fulfills a diversity of functions (Fig. 8.2).[139] Designed as a prize and/or commemorative object for the *chorêgos* who carried off the victory in a musical *agôn*, it combines an inscription and the winning choral dance in minutely synchronized fashion. On the surface of the vessel, a formally dressed aulete on the left plays his double pipes from which the stream of writing issues; immediately to his right and facing him is a dancer with his arms thrown up in the air while performing a jump, most probably the so-called *bibasis*, which required a performer to touch his buttocks with his heels as many times as he could while jumping up high (see Aristoph. *Lys.* 82). Behind the leaper are three more pairs of dancers, separated one from the next by the serpentine inscription; they stand with their hands stiffly extended, waiting for the piper to give the musical cue.

The dipinto inscription – 'Polyterpos Pyrrhias, leader of the chorus and to him, himself, an *olpe*' – falls into two parts. The lettering of the first element, which identifies the aulete, retraces elements of the musician's design. Beginning as a straight line on the left, it echoes the patterns and shapes described by his features and garments: its linearity coincides with the straight lines into which his hair and the pleats of his dress fall, while the curve of the inscription mirrors the fold of the himation worn over the long robe. Beyond its contouring and reflective role, the lettering also highlights the relations between the different figures and distinctions between them. 'Polyterpos' is set off from the rest; curving away from the piper sinistroverse, it isolates him from the dancers who are joined into a single unit by the continuous letter stream that, beginning with the jumper's name, makes up the remainder of the message. While the right-to-left orientation of 'Polyterpos' and its subject's location between the inscription's two parts emphasize his separation from the company of dancers, the artist simultaneously uses the look of the lettering to indicate the close coordination between music and movement, piper and chorus leader: approached as purely visual elements, the letters forming the curve described by the aulete's name, and those that identify Pyrrhias and (the first part of) his function are in exact harmony, the second offering a mirror image of the shape and structure of the first. Visibly, and audibly too, should a viewer enunciate the message, the same series of letters opens and closes each name, reinforcing the two individuals' mutuality and skilled 'concordance'.

---

[139] For recent discussion, on which I draw, see Osborne and Pappas 2007, 145–46; for a full earlier treatment, see Roebuck and Roebuck 1955.

Vocalization would reveal a further distinction that sets the initial designation apart: while the remainder of the words make up, albeit with a slight irregularity in the fourth foot, a hexameter, the musician's name presents a different metrical element. The word's audible singularity suits not only the figurative design but also guides a viewing: the hexameter portion containing the line of performers displays the rhythmic regularity required of the music emitted by the piper and that determines the timing of the leader's leaps and the steps the dancers will soon perform; 'Polyterpos', by contrast, does not belong to the tune produced by the instrument. Differently too from the semantic import of the other alphabetic elements, the opening term describes the impact of the piper's playing on the original participants and audience for the dance, additionally serving by way of prompt for a latter-day viewer, who, for all the performers' absence, should feel a corresponding pleasure (*terpsis*) as he or she looks at the small-scale aryballos and admires the athleticism of the lead dancer and the artist and inscriber's corresponding skills.

As for the sinuous line formed by the letters that begin to the piper's right, here the writing is unmistakably coordinated with the dancing figures, executing the same motions, demarcating their order and calling attention to the contrast between the leaper and still static members of the ensemble. With his feet raised high above the ground, the airborne performer leaves ample space for the inscription to curve below his feet and follow his back and upraised arm as it winds its way up towards the next pair. But because the remainder of the chorus have their feet still firmly on the ground, when the stream of letters reaches the second of the groups, there must be a break in the graphic sequence; intervening between the two letters almost like caesuras or line dividers are the dancers' feet, whose affinity with the lettering the arrangement highlights as words, bodily motion (or its absence) and dance steps become indistinguishable. The letters shadow the ensemble on a further score; the repetition of certain alphabetic sounds and shapes brings out the homogeneity between the chorus members arranged in their groups of two, very similar in appearance, while their diversity recognizes each figure's individuality, signalled by the fact that no one dancer is identical to another. The representation of the letters also has a spatio-temporal dimension that measures out just how far the music has travelled; since the inscription ends just as it begins to curve upward towards the final pair, it is evident that these dancers are still waiting for the piping to reach them and to rouse them from their waiting pose.

Overall the different aspects of the image nicely illustrate and visually anticipate the paradigmatic choral scene that ushers in Pindar's *Pythian* 1.

Composed approximately a century later, with the lyre taking the place of the
aulos on the aryballos, the piece opens with the performers invoking the
instrument (1–4):

> χρυσέα φόρμιγξ, Ἀπόλλωνος καὶ ἰοπλοκάμων
> σύνδικον Μοισᾶν κτέανον· τᾶς ἀκούει
>   μὲν βάσις ἀγλαΐας ἀρχά,
> πείθονται δ᾽ ἀοιδοὶ σάμασιν
> ἀγησιχόρων ὁπόταν προοιμίων
>   ἀμβολὰς τεύχῃς ἐλελιζομένα.

> Golden lyre, joint possession of Apollo and the violet-tressed Muses, to
> you the footstep listens as it begins the splendid celebration and the
> singers heed your signals whenever with your vibrations you strike up
> the chorus-leading preludes.

The joint participation of Apollo and the Muses patently maps onto that of the
musician-*chorêgos* leading the Pindaric troupe, while the aggrandizing epithet
applied to the lyre makes the instrument a metonym of the player, typically
dressed – as suggested by the formal garments of the musician on the
aryballos – in costly fashion. The *sêmata*, a term regularly used for alphabetic
writing, correspond to the notations on the aryballos, while the anticipatory
stance of the Pindaric choristers, feet still firmly positioned on the ground as
their 'footsteps' wait to begin to dance after the lyre-player has 'struck up',
matches that of the three static painted pairs. Describing the instrument's
soundings as 'vibrations' or 'trillings', the poet invites us to interpret these not
just as musical notes but as additionally determining the choreographed
movements; here the lyre's rapid oscillations anticipate the quick-changing
motions of the dance, the whirligigs performed in response to the music's
summons as the choristers, in Euripides' later description, 'wind about their
lovely dance steps' (εἰλίσσουσαι καλλίχοροι, *HF* 690). The artist of the aryballos uses the lettering to convey this dimension of the performance too: circling
swiftly up and down over the 'dance floor' of the pot's similarly curved surface,
its design alerts the waiting dancers to the complex circles and ups and downs
which will replace their current linear formation. And where the Pindaric
audience could see at first hand a performance modelled after the ode's
opening description, the aryballos viewer would also play witness to a 'live'
spectacle: as Robin Osborne and Alexandra Pappas observe,[140] in tipping the
vessel up and down so as to dispense its contents, the *oinochoos* or other
individual handling the jug makes the letters enact the 'turning up and turning

---

[140] Osborne and Pappas 2007, 146.

back' motions that their arrangement visually displays; a further result of this action on the pourer's part is to cause Pyrrhias repeatedly to rise up before returning to the ground.

Where the prize jug shines the spotlight on one member of a choral troupe, no such primacy of place is accorded to any of the participants in the very different dance scene shown on a Corinthian kotyle, also from the start of the sixth century (ca. 595–570).[141] While Heracles accompanied by Iolaos (both labelled, as are the other figures in this scene) seeks to overcome the Hydra on the vessel's obverse, six padded figures, five of whom perform a free-form dance, disport themselves on its other side (Fig. 8.10). Here the names accompanying the revellers assume several functions: semantically, they comment on and describe the komasts' actions; visually they both enhance and reiterate their motions and gestures and suggest the interactions and distinctions between the members of the group. As Pappas notes in her detailed discussion,[142] the first figure in the sequence, named Lordios, alone does not dance, but, dipping his cup into a wine-filled dinos, prepares to drink; his name, forming a curve (Lordios means 'to toss the head back', a gesture that matches the letters' shape) leads down from his buttocks to the foot of the dancer next to him and so intimates his future

Fig. 8.10 Corinthian kotyle, ca. 595–570 B.C.E. Paris, Musée du Louvre CA 3004. Photograph © RMN-Grand Palais/Hervé Lewandowski.

---

[141] Paris, Musée du Louvre CA 3004.
[142] Pappas 2011, 44, whose larger discussion at 42–45 I build on here.

involvement in the spectacle; a draught of wine, it seems, as in *Od.*
14.462–65 where drinking impels a man to dance, is the prerequisite for
his joining the performers.[143] The next two komasts to appear, Whadesios
and Paichnios, form a matching pair, facing one another as each one lifts
his foot. The name of the first, 'Pleasure Giver', signals (in distinction to
the expression's more off-colour meanings) the delight that a dance
spectacle generates and cues the viewer's response to the scene; the
second, formed from the term παίζω, to play or dance, declares the overall
spirit and more particularized action displayed here. But the labels also
trace out the motions of the pair and their coordinated actions. To cite
Pappas, 'the raised foot of Whadesios is supported by his name, whose
retrograde arc recalls the passing swing of his foot. This carefully shaped
label also buoys the raised knee of his partner Paichnios',[144] an arrangement that complements the *pas de deux* shown by the painter. Paichnios'
name further links him to the next figure in the line, an unlabelled dancer
with his feet on the ground. Although his back is turned to 'Playful', the
curve formed by the preceding designation anticipates the similarly bent
knees of this fourth komast and draws him into the ensemble.

By so closely mirroring the revellers' motions and their interactions with
one another, the words themselves, each of which assumes an independent
shape and direction and fills in the still empty spaces of the scene, seem
simultaneously to participate in a performance of their own, whose dynamism and free-style, even riotous quality matches that of the komast
dancers. Like the individuals whom they accompany, some of the labels
are isolated, as though dancing solo, while others reflect the closer coordination between certain members of the group. Reinforcing this impression
of the presence of a second troupe, this one made up of alphabetic dancers,
are the links between the dipinti and the komasts' hands; rather than
grasping their neighbour in the line, both Paichnios and the fourth dancer,
this one labelled Komios (a commentary, of course, on the nature of this
choral band) reach down as though to hold onto the first letter in their
names, their partners and visual counterparts in the ongoing spectacle.

Standing in obvious contrast to the kotyle is a third, still more familiar
vessel from the same period, or perhaps a decade later. One outstanding
feature of the François Vase is the wealth of identifying inscriptions that
accompany virtually every noteworthy (and some less so) figure on the
different bands. But in the topmost scene, where Theseus leads the chorus

---

[143] The motion described by Lordios' name is as suited to the drinker as it is to the dancer.
[144] Pappas 2011, 44.

of Athenian youths and maidens (Fig. 0.5), the lettering seems to play a role beyond that of naming each member of the ensemble, whose identities this vase uniquely records. The labels are all placed in a broadly similar position, each situated above the dancer whom it designates, and all adopt much the same configuration.[145] Their conformity suits the no less cohesive nature of the Athenian choreutes; hands joined, all facing in the same direction, they form a chain behind Theseus, whose lyre-playing further coordinates their dance. Within this overall unity, heterogeneity is also visible; some names are written retrograde, each involves its own sequence of letters and of sounds, and slight differences exist in the shaping of individual designations. This variation finds its echo in the appearance of the chorus members; no two dancers are identically dressed and each maiden wears a differently patterned gown. The lettering also observes Theseus' pre-eminent role as *chorêgos* and leader of the expedition. Already singularized by his full-length robe (the other youths wear only a cloak and himation) and the lyre that he carries, his label exhibits its own distinctiveness: alone among the dipinti, it is placed beneath rather than above the figure.

A further image, dated to the sixth century's close, gives its alphabetic elements an additional function, deploying the writing so as to reinforce and comment on a signal aspect of choral song and dance: its acoustic dimension. On a much discussed red-figure psykter attributed to Oltos and dated to ca. 520–510 (Fig. 8.11),[146] six men equipped with spears, helmets, breastplates, greaves and shields ride on dolphins as they circle around the vase. Omitting the musician who frequently accompanies other dolphin-rider scenes, the artist has instead placed an inscription between each individual figure; issuing from the riders' mouths and curving downward, the words *epi delphinos* both indicate the contents of the choral song and closely complement and enhance the design of the participants in the representation. Each set of letters not only traces out the shape of the riders' helmet crests while following the line of the dolphins' heads, but the alphabetic sequence, repeated six times at regular intervals, corresponds to the performers' coordinated motions and united singing voices, promoting the cohesion of the ensemble that still allows for the performers' individualized poses and the particularized insignia on their shields. In contrast to the previous example, there is no hierarchy here but the

---

[145] Note, however, that unlike the labels given the remainder of the chorus members, the dipinti identifying the last two dancers in the line, Phaidimos and the maiden whom he follows, run horizontally. I return to this point at the chapter's end.

[146] New York, Metropolitan Museum of Art 1989.281.69; *ARV²* 1622.7 *bis*; *Para.* 326, 259.

Fig. 8.11 Red-figure psykter attributed to Oltos, ca. 520–510 B.C.E. New York, Metropolitan Museum of Art 1989.281.69. Gift of Norbert Schimmel Trust, 1989. Photograph © The Metropolitan Museum of Art.

isonomia additionally indicated by the riders' circularity and the absence of any *chorêgos* or pre-eminent performer.

The inclusion of the graphic notations serves one further purpose. The letters' dynamism (this reinforced by the psykter's oscillations as it floated in its liquid medium) combined with their conformity with the dolphins' plunging motion visually conveys a hallmark of *choreia* as described by Plato and other authors and noted elsewhere in this study: the inseparability of the kinetic and vocalic facets of a choral spectacle, where the chorister's movements are the embodiment of his or her song, the bodily projection of the audible voice (see Pl. *Leg.* 815d–816a). The dipinti on the psykter take on a mediating role, halfway between the song and dance, at once semantic elements sung by the chorus and, coordinated with the riders and their mounts, moving elements in the process of being corporealized. Peponi offers an example of this conjunction that proves particularly apposite to the psykter's aquatic scene,[147] the account given by the frog chorus of Aristophanes' drama of its ongoing performance, which it figures as an inseparable meld of sound and motion (*Ran.* 241–49):

---

[147] Peponi 2009, 58–59.

μᾶλλον μὲν οὖν
φθεγξόμεσθ', εἰ δή ποτ' εὐ-
ηλίοις ἐν ἀμέραισιν
ἡλάμεσθα διὰ κυπείρου
καὶ φλέω, χαίροντες ᾠδῆς
πολυκολύμβοισι μέλεσιν   245
ἢ Διὸς φεύγοντες ὄμβρον
ἔνυδρον ἐν βυθῷ χορείαν
αἰόλαν ἐφθεγξάμεσθα
πομφολυγοπαφλάσμασιν.

> Rather we will sound out the more, if ever on fine sunny days we leapt
> through the galingale and the wool-tufted reed, rejoicing in our many-
> diving-songs, or, fleeing the showers of Zeus, we sang underwater in
> the depth a choral song enlivened by bubbly splashy pops. (trans.
> Sommerstein modified)

On the psykter, diving and singing likewise form a unity as the words of the
song plunge into the depths together with the diving dolphins. We could
even imagine a corresponding alteration in pitch or drop in the voice, a
downward shift simultaneously embodied in the motions of the animal and
human figures, and preceding a move back up to a higher register, an up-
and-down, regularized musical, vocalic and verbal rhythm. For an illiterate
viewer, the painted letters might more closely call to mind something akin
to the Aristophanic account: these notations could be seen as nothing more
than 'bubbles and splashes', the product of the dolphins' movements
through the liquid element furnished by the water when the psykter was
filled, and by the breaths that issue from the animals' blow holes (styled
auloi, making redundant the piper's presence).

One among the several roles fulfilled by inscriptions on choral scenes
flagged above – that of designating the type of dance, pose and even
performance genre enacted by the figures on the pot – becomes both
more common and more particularized in the classical period. In
several instances these labels replace the need to show a dancer striking
a particular posture or performing a sequence of steps (difficult to
render in the medium of paint); in others, performers may adopt the
shapes and motions suggested by the inscriptions, serving more as
pictorial realizations or pictograms of the words. Already in evidence
on the kotyle, where one of the dancers has the name Komios, a second
Lordios, and the fifth of the company Loxios (crooked), these types of
notations return on a cup in Warsaw by the Eretria Painter dated to ca.

430–420 (Fig. 0.7, with earlier discussion in Chapter 6), whose artist portrays a Dionysiac *thiasos* made up of dancing satyrs and maenads. Accompanying these figures are a series of unusual identifying labels, most unparalleled and quite unlike the names more regularly given to the celebrants of Dionysus in the visual repertoire. As discussions of the pot suggest,[148] several of these are best understood as indicating the *schêmata* of the different performers, turning each of the figures into a statement of the particular pose and movement characteristic of his or her dance. For all that the satyr labelled Aietos, 'eagle', standing on the far left and holding up the kantharos on the obverse of the cup, lacks his companions' extravagant dynamism, his name suggests a dance evocative of flying, a conceit used by dramatists of Dionysus' followers, who in their swiftness are likened to birds. Were a drinker then to turn the vessel to its other side, he would encounter an unlabelled female figure who seems exactly to dance in the fashion intimated by Aietos' name: creating continuity between the scenes on the vessel's two faces, the maenad on the far right holds her two arms stretched out wide while her sleeves billow up as though filled with air.[149]

The name Kissos given a satyr in the scene on the obverse as he strikes a particularly exuberant pose most obviously evokes the signature ivy that is an identifying feature of so many Dionysiac occasions. But if the only partially preserved label Kin given the maenad partnering him (her hand rests on his bent knee) refers to her own capacity for movement, then, as Alexander Heinemann points out,[150] we might also think of the spiralling, twirling motion regularly associated with the plant and see in this name a comment on the dynamic properties of the individual she accompanies.[151] Two details in the representation of the maenad reinforce the two dancers' complementarity: she wears a garland of the ivy that also decorates her *thyrsos,* and the folds on the upper portion of her peplos describe multiple curlicues and swirls. A stamnos in New Haven gives further specificity to this type of movement, designating a nebris-clad maenad dancing to the

---

[148] See, most recently, Heinemann 2013, 285–90, whose reading I follow on a number of points; he also cites the satyrs shown on two cups by the same painter, both featuring groups of satyrs dancing (Taranto, Museo Nazionale 8266 and 8270; *ARV*² 1253.66 and 1253.67). Here the movements of the individual members of the ensemble are disparate, non-sequential and discrete. The labels on the Warsaw pot illuminate the nature of these several representations, confirming that the artist uses the figures to describe 'a series of dissected dancing *schêmata*' (p. 285).

[149] For these observations, see Heinemann 2013, 287.   [150] Heinemann 2013, 287.

[151] For this, see Csapo 2003, 93–94 and below.

music of a lyre-playing satyr Helike.[152] This suggestion of the circle dance typical of the dithyrambs performed in celebration of Dionysus finds further support in the identifications given to another group of one satyr and three maenads on the Warsaw cup: Lemnos, Delos, Euboia and Tethys. As detailed in Chapter 6, three of these are Cyclades, whose collective name indicates their circular formation and the rotating circle dances they stage in the sea, albeit in celebration not of Dionysus but Apollo.

In some instances, the label more simply identifies the genre of the dance-and-song and the ritual occasion to which it belongs. The word ΔΙΘΥΡΑΜΦΟΣ appears by the head of a lyre-playing satyr, behind whom Dionysus himself appears, on a mid-fifth-century krater fragment in Copenhagen attributed to the Group of Polygnotos;[153] he is positioned as the leader of a procession with Dionysus following immediately behind. On other vases of the period, we find fresh references to particular types of dances which likewise serve as tags for the mode in which the figures they accompany perform: these include Sikinnis or Sikinnos – the *sikinnis* is a particularly exuberant and unbridled dance that belongs to the *kômos* and is closely associated with satyrs (see Athen. 14.630b–c) – and the partially preserved name Dina, this suggestive of *dinein*, another term for whirling and also closely bound up with the dithyrambic dance and its patron deity.[154] In each instance, the label serves as a kind of synecdoche where the single word succinctly replaces or does the work of the succession of painted figures shown on other occasions, each of whom moves in a different fashion, or strikes his or her independent pose, so as to allow the viewer to recreate an entire dance sequence. This alphabetic 'economy' becomes evident if we juxtapose vases which include a written pointer to the *sikkinis* with those where individuals perform the dance, absent the notations;[155] in these latter instances, the viewer must translate the depiction of a single moment back into the much more extended sequence of poses and steps that make up the entirety of the performance.

Much of this later material suggests the more formal codification of different modes of dancing (perhaps buttressed by the appearance of those faintly discernible treatises on dance that can be dated to the fifth century's second half) and the development of a heightened sense of generic

[152] New Haven, Yale University Art Gallery 1913.132; *ARV²* 1035.4.
[153] Copenhagen, Thorvaldsens Museum H 597, *ARV²* 1055.78, with discussion in Heinemann 2013, 290.
[154] Heinemann 2013, 291 cites these several vessels.
[155] Examples include a red-figure cup painted by Makron of ca. 480 (Malibu, John Paul Getty Museum 86.AE.292; *Para.*379.326 *bis*).

distinctions among different forms of *choreia*, each linked with a particular god and/or ritual occasion. It coincidentally stands witness to a gradual evolution in the role fulfilled by writing, and to an increasingly literate audience, one predisposed to read alphabetic elements rather than to apprehend them in their more pictorial and ornamental aspect. Now chiefly restricted to its lexigraphic or discursive function, the lettering's sematography no longer plays the equal, or even dominant role that it did in earlier periods.

3 Inscribing *Choreia* in Pindaric Poetry

3.1 Olympian 6.87–92

Pindar's sixth *Olympian* traces the process of its own coming-into-being, pausing at several points to alert the audience to its inception, composition, enactment, dissemination and lasting preservation. An earlier chapter suggested that the grandiose golden columns rising at the poem's start served as figures for the choristers opening the performance, assembling their prelude in the manner of a colonnaded building even as their motions and poses embodied the verbal contents of their song. Typically Pindar then moves from the here-and-now of the work's performance at Syracuse to the mythical antecedents and origins of the occasion, using the conceit of a poetic journey in the Muses' chariot to evoke the process by which he gathers his material as he traces the victor's lineage back through time and space. The myth complete, the poem then pauses at Thebes, where the speaker receives fresh impetus for his epinician task by virtue of the waters that he will drink – a performative future which, as Calame remarks, 'collapses the moment of poetic inspiration into the performance-time of the epinician' –[156] in order to 'weave (πλέκων)' the variegated song now being sung (86–87). The account of the poetic draught also introduces Metope, Thebe's mother, who turns out to be the nymph of Stymphalus in Arcadia, the next stage on the itinerary; here the journey observes one final halt so as to introduce Aineas, the chorus leader and *didaskalos* as identified by our scholia, whom the speaker addresses, in another collapse of past and present, directly through apostrophe (87–92):

---

[156] Calame 2012, 310.

ὄτρυνον νῦν ἑταίρους,

Αἰνέα, πρῶτον μὲν Ἥραν

  Παρθενίαν κελαδῆσαι,

γνῶναί τ' ἔπειτ', ἀρχαῖον ὄνειδος ἀλαθέσιν

λόγοις εἰ φεύγομεν, Βοιωτίαν ὗν.   90

  ἐσσὶ γὰρ ἄγγελος ὀρθός,

ἠϋκόμων σκυτάλα Μοι-

  σᾶν, γλυκὺς κρατὴρ ἀγαφθέγκτων ἀοιδᾶν·

εἶπον δὲ μεμνᾶσθαι Συρα-

  κοσσᾶν τε καὶ Ὀρτυγίας·

Now rouse your companions, Aineas, first to celebrate Hera Parthenia
and then to know if by our truthful words we might escape the time-old
taunt, Boeotian swine. For you are an upright messenger, a message stick
of the fair-haired Muses, a sweet mixing bowl of loud-sounding songs.
Tell them to remember Syracuse and Ortygia.

As commentators note, the reference in line 88 is to the festival of Hera
Parthenia, for which Hagesias' Stymphalian relatives may have arranged
(and even financed) a performance of the ode.[157] The lines not only point
to another occasion for the current song's performance, but alert us to the
'technology' through which the multiple renditions reviewed by the piece
can be achieved. *Qua* baton or message stick – the *skutalê* in its technical
fifth-century meaning is a Spartan device for sending a coded message –
that supplies the holder for a written communication, the *chorodidaskalos*
is the vector for the poem as a text, the staff that carries it from place to
place. Implicit here too is an acknowledgement of the role that writing
would likely play in the training of the chorus, the existence of some kind of
script (or even score) prior to the rehearsals and stagings of the ode.

   But there is much more to the image, which effectively describes the way
in which this textual transcription becomes a live (re)performance. Since
deciphering the message depends on the recipient having a baton of the
same precise dimensions as the sender's (see further below), Pindar
imagines his chorus leader as exactly corresponding to the original composer; as the medium for the text, Aineas replicates the poet, matching up
to the initial generator of the piece. In a poem preoccupied with doubles
and things that 'fit' together,[158] the conceit could not be better chosen.
Orthos, so appropriate for the rectilinear baton about to be introduced,
points to the veracity of Aineas and the exactitude and integrity of his text,

---

[157] See Currie 2011, 288.   [158] As so skillfully demonstrated by Carne-Ross 1979.

the fact that, like the *theôros* of Theognis who must be 'straighter' (εὐθύτερον) than a carpenter's rule in order to carry back to his fellow citizens a precise transcription of the Pythia's words (805–10), this individual has made no alterations, additions nor subtractions from the song as originally composed (as the lines by Theognis spell out).[159]

The assertion of the messenger's 'rectitude' is carefully positioned in the structure of the lines. Aineas' straightness is both the precondition for the 'truthfulness' of the words just assigned to the celebrants and anticipates the song's textualization in the form of the *skutalê*: just as the stick protects the communiqué from those for whom it is not intended, so the 'matching' Aineas forestalls the risk of mendacity and the inclusion of the spurious and counterfeit that would result from an incorrect transcription of Pindar's work. The initial address to the chorus-trainer, in conjunction with the opening word of the antistrophe (εἶπον), points to another role that writing can play; not merely a means of exactly preserving and transmitting a song in the absence of its composer, but an *aide-mémoire*. By virtue of having the text, this *alter ego* can follow its script as he instructs his chorus members 'first to celebrate in song' and then 'to remember Syracuse and Ortygia'.

No less in play in the image is the technology of the *skutalê* that in and of itself choreographs the dancers' motions as they perform the song. As later sources explain, two identical round sticks would be fashioned, and a strip of leather on which the communication would subsequently be written then wound slantwise around one; when the leather was unwound, the message appeared scrambled. The one who possessed the second stick had only to rewind the text back onto his baton, and read off the now legible notations. Visualize this, and what we apprehend is a sequence of repeated rotations, which make the text move first in one direction as the strip is wound around the stick, and then reverse its course. The image, introduced as the strophe draws to an end and the dancers prepare to repeat the same set of steps (perhaps in reverse direction), invites us to see in these choreutes counterparts to the seemingly dynamic letters, likewise turning and turning about in their circling dance. William Mullen further notes the position of Aineas vis-à-vis the ensemble; as the upright stick supporting the text, he supplies the unmoving centre, positioned in the midst of the chorus as it surrounds him;[160]

---

[159] As so frequently, Pindar suggests by virtue of the 'cryptic' image that his composition may, like the oracular pronouncement, have a level of meaning comprehensible only to the select few. The 'veridical' nature of its words further emphasizes its unimpeachable nature. Note too the image at *Isthm.* 4.37–38, where Pindar imagines Homer as the one who, 'setting straight (ὀρθώσαις)' Ajax's achievement 'declared/indicated it with his staff (κατὰ ῥάβδον ἔφρασεν)'.

[160] Mullen 1983, 36; see too Kurke 2015, 3, who notes that the chorus 'materializes the leather tape with its written characters'.

indeed, without this guarantor of good order and arrangement, the dancers would remain scattered and random in their placement, an unintelligible and garbled 'text' or disparate sequence of letters, all misaligned.

The terms used in Plutarch's very full account of how the *skutalê* works allow us more precisely to perceive the equivalence between the device and the performance as envisaged by Pindar and staged by Aineas here (*Lys.* 19.7):

> δεξάμενος δὲ ἐκεῖνος ἄλλως μὲν οὐδὲν ἀναλέξασθαι δύναται τῶν γραμμάτων συναφὴν οὐκ ἐχόντων, ἀλλὰ διεσπασμένων, τὴν δὲ παρ' αὐτῷ σκυτάλην λαβὼν τὸ τμῆμα τοῦ βιβλίου περὶ αὐτὴν περιέτεινεν, ὥστε, τῆς ἕλικος εἰς τάξιν ὁμοίως ἀποκαθισταμένης, ἐπιβάλλοντα τοῖς πρώτοις τὰ δεύτερα, κύκλῳ τὴν ὄψιν ἐπάγειν τὸ συνεχὲς ἀνευρίσκουσαν.

> He (sc. the recipient), when he has received (the strip) cannot otherwise read it through since the letters have no connection but are scattered about, unless, taking his own message stick, he stretches the cut strip all around it so that, when the arrangement of the spiral is entirely restored and that which follows is placed next to that which precedes, he reads circle-wise around the staff and so discovers the continuity of the message.

While the opening portion presents a text that features disaggregation and disorder and lacks the requisite 'connection' or 'join' between the letters on the strip, the remainder of the passage describes how the original sequence is reconstituted, a process that involves re-conjoining and restoring what originally formed a circle or spiral. Even so do choral members first 'join' hands before dancing in a ring (see Aesch. *Eum.* 307, ἅψωμεν), and then perform the turns so frequently imagined as a *helix*, as rendered by the verb ἑλίσσω, before becoming realigned or 'continuous'.

Although the sources do not exploit the analogy, the spiral movements of the chorus also bear directly on the act of reading and on Pindar's glance towards a different and future type of audience. In a usage visible in Xenophon (*Mem.* 1.6.14), the verb ἀνελίσσω used by Plutarch describes the unrolling of the book scroll so as to read the text inside while an epigram by Meleager, placed at the *Garland*'s end, plays on the visuality of the coronis in its claim that the author has 'gathered the toil of all poets rolled up (ἐνελιξάμενον) into one in this book' (*AP* 12.257.3–4). Since Pindar's *skutalê* conceit necessarily presupposes a reader for this message-bearing baton, the terms of the image take on a second valence: divorced from a live performance, the 'message stick' maps onto the book-roll that a current reader holds, while the imperative εἶπον is addressed not to Aineas, who transmits the message to the Stymphalian chorus, but to the text that is being read and that effectively reminds the reader of Syracuse and Ortygia, the sites of the original choral spectacle.

The depiction of the song as a moving text, one in the process of being aligned by virtue of Aineas' exacting direction, is bracketed by references to its audible dimension, as though the transcription could yield sound as well as motion. In a more extravagant re-evocation of the ringing celebration introduced by κελαδῆσαι, line 88 presents Aineas in a second configuration, now as a krater filled with resonant song. No longer merely the conveyer of the message, and the unmoving centre around whom the choreutes dance, he becomes the actual container and generator of the performance, the source from which its many iterations can be drawn. Where the *skutalê* image invited us to visualize – and actually to witness within the current enactment – a process of sortition and sequencing, the mixing bowl suggests instead a coming together and synthesis, one in which, thanks to the *chorodidaskalos*, all the components are joined in a cohesive but variegated blend. The 'loud-sounding' facet of the songs follows naturally on from the conceit: the act of mixing water and wine in the krater not only sets the different elements swirling as they combine, but, as the liquid plashes and splashes in the metal bowl, is audible too (see Pind. *Ol.* 7.2, detailed below). With his choice of these two metaphors, each positing an action of a different kind, Pindar has effectively explained how the ode may self-replicate in performances at sites temporally and geographically remote.

3.2 Olympian 7

In the passage considered above, Pindar introduces a text-bearing object that can record his song and ensure its secure transmission and re-enactment at other occasions. The more diverse array of inscribed artefacts that punctuate *Olympian* 7 furnish fresh models for the perpetuation of the ode and demonstrate how things once sung and danced to musical accompaniment may take the form of inscriptions on objects that subsequently serve as catalysts for the work's recovery of its earlier performative status. Central to the reading of the poem proposed here is the unique 'twist' to the issue of textualization so inseparable from the poem's thematics, and which depends on a consideration of the *Nachleben* of this particular ode, the point with which my treatment begins.

In the familiar tradition surrounding the piece and reported by the scholia, 'Gorgon says that this ode is dedicated in the temple of Athena

Lindia in golden letters'.[161] Among the starting points for my discussion is the compelling suggestion of Leslie Kurke that in this piece we may encounter 'a poem commissioned and composed with the explicit intention of being set up as a lavish dedicatory monument'.[162] Substantiating her claim by showing that, contrary to received wisdom, there is no reason to assume that the ode's transcription occurred long after its original composition, and further arguing that its future dedication in the temple may have been projected by the celebrant Diagoras and/or his family in commissioning the ode from the first,[163] Kurke goes on to trace the multiple ways in which Pindar, cognizant of his patrons' intention, composes a poem that reflects on relations between commemorative goods, dedicatory practices and speech and song and so anticipates its transformation into monumental and votive form. As Kurke demonstrates, the composition is crowded with objects, many invested not just with a venerable ancestry but with the preciosity and talismanic powers that Pindar's own poem, *qua* gilded dedication, would come to possess.

Building on this insight, I want further to suggest that the ode's emphatic 'thingliness' – in Kurke's evocative phrase –[164] looks not just to its future reification but more narrowly to its preservation as an inscription that serves as both a votive offering and a written record of the original performance that had similarly furnished an *agalma* at a sacred site. In reviewing the sequence of objects featured in the poem's course, I focus on three outstanding aspects of their characterization: the epigraphic conventions and diction that shape their representation, their capacity as inscribed artefacts to preserve and generate the acts of speech and song that recall and restage earlier rituals, and their intimate connection to the physical fabric of Lindos and to its central temple. In brief, I argue that, to a degree perhaps unmatched elsewhere in Pindar, this ode reflects on what has been styled the Greek 'epigraphic habit' and, through its imagery and conceits, prompts future audiences to (re-)experience the original performance of the ode in the same physical setting that had first accommodated it.

My focus on the explicitly inscriptional and votive elements in the poem brings a further object into play, one erected at the Rhodian sanctuary of Athena Lindia many centuries after the celebration of Diagoras' triumph

---

[161] Σ *Ol.* 7, i.195 Dr. = *FGrH* 515 F 18; Gorgon has been identified as a local Rhodian chronicler or periegete for whom we have a possible terminus post quem of 306/5 B.C.E.

[162] Kurke 2015, 7.

[163] Carey 2007, 201 n. 13 entertains a similar scenario in passing: 'it is equally possible that Diagoras made a dedicatory gift of the ode to the temple analogous to the setting up of a statue'.

[164] Kurke 2015, 15.

and that turns out, retroactively, to bear on the Pindaric piece in multiple respects. Many of the goods cited through the course of the composition have their analogues – and, as I conjecture, models – in the *anathêmata* displayed in the temenos, which also housed the cult image of Athena, supposedly among the oldest in Greece, for whose *kosmêsis* some of the votive gifts were intended. Several centuries after the destruction of most of these in a fire in 392/91, the Lindians belatedly resolved to set up at the temple site a stele listing the treasures both lost and still remaining; the result was the erection of the so-called Lindian Chronicle of 99 B.C.E. Discussions of the Chronicle highlight its sheer monumentality and the painstaking labour and skill that its construction and incision required.[165] In its preamble, and promoting the ritualized aura surrounding the stone, the inscription records the stage-by-stage ordinances and prescriptions issued for its creation, and details the careful choice of personnel selected for the publicly financed and ratified enterprise; among their many resolutions, the Lindian citizens determined that 'Larian stone', prepared according to the architect's directions, was to be used for the inventory, specified the sources to be consulted in compiling the list and fixed the date on which the monument was to be erected. Standing 2.37m high, 0.85m wide and 0.32m deep, the stele originally itemized 45 objects (37 entries are still legible) and Athena's four epiphanies at the temple, these all demarcated by three columns with visible headings and narrow margins between them, with subsections signalled by short horizontal lines, which separated one entry from the next. As Verity Platt observes,[166] the impressive design and visuality of the stele and its own patent status as a fresh *anathêma* aimed to recreate the impression that the votives would once have produced and to invest the stone with the epiphanic potential that the object descriptions are designed to preserve: recording the prayers – complete with their direct addresses, deictics and other rhetorical devices that aim to summon the deity to the site – that had been pronounced when the donor first offered his gift, these texts' perusal and re-enunciation by latter-day readers could prompt fresh visitations. Giving additional lustre and religiosity to the Chronicle was its probable proximity to the venerable image of the goddess, a more immediate vehicle for direct contact with the divine.

The Chronicle is important to my argument in at least three ways; first, as noted above, because it serves as an invaluable source for the offerings that the temple would earlier have housed, and whose form, inscribed

---

[165] See particularly the detailed account in Higbie 2003 and the treatment of Platt 2011, 161–69, both with earlier bibliography.

[166] Platt 2011, 161–62.

content and capacity to 'presentify' the goddess may have informed Pindar's 'thingly' orientation as he, aware that his poem would assume votive and written form, set about composing his ode. Second, because, in the absence of the actual transcription of *Olympian 7* set up in its gleaming letters in the temple, the Chronicle, considered purely as a material and 'sematographic' object, offers a supersized example of how a dedication that took the form of a visually compelling text and transcription of earlier 'scripts' might function in the sacred space and could, through its design, layout, surface and lettering, restage past ritual practices. And third, because in gesturing towards the offerings already on display in the temple, both the poem and stone aim chronologically to record the 'historical' events in the Rhodian past, supplying audiences with a map or topographical 'guidebook' which creates experiential encounters with the votives that would confront a visitor to the temple, and in so doing may even retrace a kind of itinerary, a path of objects complete with words, from the present moment back to these earlier occasions.

My argument for the give-and-take between the Pindaric piece, as both performed and transcribed, and the offerings within the temple of Athena Lindia gains cogency given the likelihood that the work would have been first staged in this very space. While nothing allows us firmly to establish the performance site (indeed, events and images in the ode deliberately encompass diverse locations, some public and some more private), the poem's contents suggest two plausible venues. Kowalzig, proposing that the reference to the institution of the Tlepolemeia in lines 77–81 serves 'to create a continuity from the mythical past ... into the ritual present',[167] would see the Heliadic ancestors of the Rhodians featured there as the first celebrants of the festival for Tlepolemos and as paradigms for the current-day performers dancing and singing the ode at the festival whose aetiology the epinician narrates; the processions (complete with choral performances), games and sacrifices that occurred at the original event are those simultaneously witnessed by the present-day Pindaric audience. My reading privileges the second possible setting evoked within the ode, performance at the temple of Athena Lindia, the location that appears in the shape of the 'sanctuary on the Acropolis' that the Heliadai built in order to perform their 'fireless offerings' (48–49); the site would continue to host

---

[167] Kowalzig 2007, 247. Apart from this reference in the poem, we know almost nothing of the Tlepolemeia; as Higbie 2003, 80 notes, a second-century inscription from the island of Cedreae includes in its list of athletic victories a win at the Τλαπολέμεια (*SIG*³ no. 1067), most likely a reference to the Rhodian festival.

civic celebrations on the goddess' behalf in historical times.[168] If the objects that fill the song seem repeatedly to glance towards the famed and much visited votives that this sanctuary held, then the poet would, in his typical fashion, be both embedding the performance ever more fully into its physical location and sacred setting and spotlighting the centrality of the site to the ode's own future reification.

The extended and rococo simile with which the song begins sets the pattern for much that follows. Figuring the poetic ego's gift to his *laudandus* in the shape of a golden phiale used for drinking and libations, and given by a bride's father to the groom to seal the pledge or *enguê* that ratifies the marriage contract, the conceit proves apposite not just to the song's 'thingliness', but to its epigrammatic, dedicatory and performative concerns. Already in this prelude, Pindar rehearses the incorporation of terms from epigraphic diction, showcases the role of objects as both fixatives and cues for speech and song pronounced as part of ritual occasions and introduces an *agalma* that belonged together with other votive goods in the temple of Athena Lindia. Here, then, is that opening (1–12):

φιάλαν ὡς εἴ τις ἀφνειᾶς ἀπὸ χειρὸς ἑλών
ἔνδον ἀμπέλου καχλάζοισαν δρόσῳ
δωρήσεται
νεανίᾳ γαμβρῷ προπίνων
    οἴκοθεν οἴκαδε, πάγχρυσον, κορυφὰν κτεάνων,
συμποσίου τε χάριν κᾶ-   5
    δός τε τιμάσαις νέον, ἐν δὲ φίλων
παρεόντων θῆκέ νιν ζαλωτὸν ὁμόφρονος εὐνᾶς·

καὶ ἐγὼ νέκταρ χυτόν, Μοισᾶν δόσιν, ἀεθλοφόροις
ἀνδράσιν πέμπων, γλυκὺν καρπὸν φρενός,
ἱλάσκομαι,
Ὀλυμπίᾳ Πυθοῖ τε νικών-   10
    τεσσιν· ὁ δ᾽ ὄλβιος, ὃν φᾶμαι κατέχωντ᾽ ἀγαθαί·
ἄλλοτε δ᾽ ἄλλον ἐποπτεύ-
    ει Χάρις ζωθάλμιος ἀδυμελεῖ
θαμὰ μὲν φόρμιγγι παμφώνοισί τ᾽ ἐν ἔντεσιν αὐλῶν.

As when a man takes from his rich hand a phiale plashing within with the dew of the vine and presents it to his young son-in-law with a toast from one house to another, all golden, the topmost of all possessions, thereby honouring the joy of the symposium and his own alliance, and amongst friends who are present makes him envied for the harmonious marriage.

---

[168] For the cult, see Morelli 1959, 80–89.

So too I, in sending the poured out nectar, gift of the Muses, to prize-winning men, the sweet fruit of my mind, make recompense to victors at Olympia and Pytho. Fortunate is the man whom goodly repute holds. Now on one, now on another Charis who makes life bloom looks favourably, often with the sweetly singing lyre and pipes, every-voiced instruments.

Already visible in the description of the golden bowl is the use of votive terms, which position both the gift and the song for which the phiale stands symbol as (semi-)secular counterparts to dedications in the sacred sphere. δωρήσεται supplies the main verb in the opening clause; both in the epigraphic repertoire and in Pindar, the *dôron* denotes the votive object presented to the god.[169] The opening of *Ol.* 5, often flagged for its self-modelling on votive practice, offers a clear example of how Pindar employs the term in this ritual frame: here the tutelary goddess, 'daughter of Ocean', is asked to 'receive the sweet choicest prize of high achievements and crowns, those from Olympia, the gifts (δῶρα) of his cart and mules with untiring feet and of Psaumis' (1–3). Just as this equestrian ode then goes on to make explicit the votive frame at the prelude's end ('to you, he, having won, dedicated [ἀνέθηκε] his luxurious *kudos*', 7–8), so *Ol.* 7 postpones activation of the phiale's dedicatory resonances until the simile's second half: in Homer, Hesiod and others, ἱλάσκομαι (9), the verb in the antistrophe that answers to δωρήσεται in structure and metrical position, and that here refers to the bestowal of the song, regularly describes the propitiation of divinities, whether with sacrifices and other ritual acts or with material objects. So too the characterization of the bowl as the 'the choicest of possessions' proves consistent with the language of inscribed offerings; an inscription from the Athenian Acropolis of ca. 510–500 mentioned earlier in the chapter declares, 'For Pallas Athena Luson set up a firstfruits offering from his own possessions (κτ[εά]νον), to be a *charis*-filled thing for the goddess' (*CEG* 205). In both poem and inscription, the use of the term *kteanon* for the votive signals the value and high status of the proffered good; not just possessions, *ktêmata* are more particularly treasures stored away until their use as gifts, whether exchanged among the elite or given to the gods.[170] Both Pindar and Luson also include the critical term *charis*, as ubiquitous in the dedicatory sphere, and one of the absolutely standard elements in archaic and classical epigrams, as it is in the sympotic context featured in the prelude of the ode.

---

[169] Examples are listed in Day 2010, 62 n. 147; see particularly *CEG* 268 and *CEG* 351, this second from an inscription on a golden phiale of 458 or 457, which declares itself a *dôron*.

[170] See Day 2010, 236.

In the simile's turn to the *comparandum* for the golden cup, the speaker's corresponding 'gift' of song not only presents itself as a propitiatory offering (and note the hint of a libation that recalls the primary function of the phiale), but with its closing statement also reintroduces *charis*, now made a feature of a musico-choral performance. With that term, the poet equates the delivery and execution of the ode with that of explicitly religious songs, both hymns and in other genres, which regularly begin or close by invoking Charis and by inviting the deity to be present at and well-disposed towards the ongoing performance; as Day explains,[171] our sources imagine festivities in which interactions between gods and men occurred as *charis*-filled events, making integral to these exchanges a term found in the language more broadly used of gift-giving occasions. Nor is the more particularized diction of dedication absent from the Pindaric proem's final phrase. The second line of a couplet on a herm of ca. 480–475 from near Markopoulo similarly assumes the presence of the again attentive Charites when it declares that, in performing the dedication, the donor Leocrates 'did not escape the attention of the fair-tressed Graces' (*CEG* 312). Also noteworthy in Pindar's closing gnome is the segue from the presentation of this particular ode for Diagoras to a more generalized and potentially sacrosanct context; even as the mention of the pipes and lyre might look to the poem's current or potential instrumental accompaniment, the term θαμά, as it does in many epinicia and other choral works, turns this single performance into a recurrent event, suggesting the type of re-enactment that has its model in the *choreia* that forms part of the cyclical festival. If, as suggested above, *Ol.* 7 was first performed on just such a ritual occasion in the Lindian temple (with repeat performances both there and at symposia), then the conflation of the two choral moments, one for a private individual, the other for the gods, would be closer still.

While the simile may seem just an exercise in extravagant image-making, several commentators have proposed a possible real-world underpinning.[172] The first item cited in the Lindian Chronicle is the phiale that Lindos, the island's eponymous founder, presented.[173] Anticipating its primacy in the inventory, the bowl also stands as the starting point in Pindar's ode, a work that constructs, much like the chronological order followed in the later text and, perhaps, reflecting the physical arrangement of the *anathêmata* in the sanctuary, its own selective history of the island.

---

[171] Day 2010, esp. 232–79.   [172] Higbie 2003, 64, Kurke 2015, 21–22.
[173] The document's compilers duly note that they were unable 'to determine what it was made of'.

Besides Lindos, the Pindaric phiale could also take its impetus from the gift made by a second figure listed in the Chronicle, Telephos, the half-brother of Rhodes' chief heroes, Lindos and Tlepolemos; Telephos is cited for his dedication of another phiale, this one distinctive for its golden boss. Pindar's striking choice of ἱλάσκομαι for his bestowal of the gift of song might even direct the audience towards this second precious good, or towards others like it. As the chroniclers' description reads, 'Telephos, a phiale with a golden boss on which had been inscribed "Telephos a supplicatory offering (ἱλατή[ρι]ον) to Athena"'. As Higbie notes,[174] the term *hilatêrion* is extremely rare and confined to Rhodes, where it occurs on only one other occasion, also in an inscription. By aligning itself with these famed votives in its incorporation of their terminology, Pindar's phiale-ode not only claims a place among the votives; now dedicated in the form of a performance, it supplies both the latest gift to the god and a commemorative materialization of a fresh noteworthy event in Rhodian 'history', the Olympian victory of Diagoras, a feat that would (in the epinician account) attain a status equal to that enjoyed by those preceding it.

If Pindar's all-golden vessel suggests a votive complete with text so as to connect the poem with its sacred performance site, other message-bearing cups more anchored to the sympotic context inform this image too. For these we need to look more closely at the role assigned the phiale and how this is realized in the gesture imagined in the opening lines. As the poet describes the occasion, the bowl with which the father-in-law toasts his new connection serves to seal the agreement exchanged between the two parties to the betrothal. A second instance of such a marriage pledge occurs in Herodotus in a scene that clearly demonstrates that the agreement begins in spoken form: contracting his daughter to Megacles, Cleisthenes says 'I pledge myself (ἐγγυῶ)', to which Megacles replies in the middle voice (ἐγγυᾶσθαι), meaning either 'I accept the pledge' or 'I pledge myself in return' (6.130). The phiale exchanged between the two Pindaric parties furnishes the material marker of this verbal agreement, a treasure that, brought out on future occasions, sparks remembrance and the recreation of the moment when the contract was first ratified by the pronouncement of the verbal formula accompanied by the exchange of a valuable good. There may even be a play on the literal meaning of *enguê* in the Pindaric image, which further elides object and contents, making the spoken pledge as much a material phenomenon as the golden phiale. Already the ancient

---

[174] Higbie 2003, 83.

etymologists derived *enguê* from *guion*, the hollow or palm of the hand, and *gualon*, and understood it to refer to a 'handing over' or a placing in the hand, just the gesture Pindar describes as the bowl moves from donor to recipient.[175] Implicated here is the hollowed out shape of the container, filled with the wine whose drinking also seals the pledge. When reconfigured as the Pindaric song in the simile's second half, the 'poured out nectar' which the receptacle furnished by the poet's mind now contains, the ode retains its materiality: in order to be 'sent', it must have assumed physical shape and form.

Confirmation of the audible reactivation of the once-spoken pledge comes in the prelude's second line, where the speaker describes the wine as resonant: καχλάζω refers specifically to the plash or splash made by liquids. But it is also worth asking how a hearer would understand the image of this pledge-sealing vessel containing a song. The model that might come to mind is that of the cup incorporating sung elements in the form of the snatches of verse inscribed on its exterior or tondo. Whether these poetic texts, some metrical, others mere snippets, appear on tablets included in the vessel's iconography, or issue from a singing symposiast or instrumentalist shown in a sympotic context, the notations turn the larger artefact into just the singing cup imagined here. On the tondo of a red-figure cup by Douris of ca. 500,[176] the writing, albeit not in verse, comes directly from the krater positioned to the left of the scene while adjacent to it stands a lyre-playing singer. We might also look to the tondo of an unattributed red-figure cup in Athens of ca. 490,[177] where the words 'o most beautiful boy' coming from the mouth of the reclining singer recall the beginning of Theognis 1365, or those similarly placed on a red-figure amphora by Euphronius of ca. 520, where the phrase 'I suffer from longing' issuing from the singer's mouth suggests his performance of a song by Sappho.[178] Just as the nectar-like composition is 'poured out' in *Olympian* 7, so, in analogous fashion, the actual user of these vessels would cause the words on their surfaces to flow forth as he pours out the wine, drinks from the cup or uses it to play at kottabos.

If one common artistic practice informs the Pindaric image, then a second one also firmly anchored to a sympotic context is discernible

---

[175] In a fascinating discussion, Ferrari 2003b, 30 traces the etymology of the term – regularly connected with 'placing something in the hand' – and follows Benveniste in locating its origin with the cluster of words (*guê, guia, gualon*) referring to hollow structures. Nicely, the term *gualon* may also refer to a drinking vessel.

[176] Paris, Musée du Louvre G 127; *ARV²* 427.1.

[177] Athens, National Archaeological Museum 1357.

[178] Paris, Musée du Louvre G 30; *ARV²* 15.9, 1619; *Para.* 322.

here. Dionysius Chalcus' fr. 1 W. spells out how the 'toasting' gesture performed by the Pindaric father-in-law serves to 'seal' or ratify a pledge and, like Pindar before him, the poet seamlessly links the song and grace-and-favour imbued cup with the 'sending' motion the speaker performs:

> δέχου τήνδε προπινομένην
> τὴν ἀπ' ἐμοῦ ποίησιν· ἐγὼ δ' ἐπιδέξια πέμπω
> σοὶ πρώτῳ, Χαρίτων ἐγκεράσας χάριτας.
> καὶ σὺ λαβὼν τόδε δῶρον ἀοιδὰς ἀντιπρόπιθι,
> συμπόσιον κοσμῶν καὶ τὸ σὸν εὖ θέμενος.   5

> Receive this poem pledged as a toast from me. I am sending it from left to right for you first, having mixed in the delights of the Graces. And you taking this gift pledge me songs in return as a toast, adorning our symposium and making yourself of good repute (?).

Even as the sender of the poetic pledge-turned-cup sang out the lines, a vessel in use at the occasion might act by way of cue for the song's conceit and demonstrate how a seemingly *ex tempore* utterance could take more lasting textual form. A red-figure stemless cup in London and dated to ca. 470,[179] offers just one among a more extensive series of sympotic vessels inscribed with the pledges pronounced by kottabos players who whirl their cups and toss the wine lees towards the object of their desires, whom they name and call out to as they perform the throw.[180] While the Pindaric pledge in the prelude of *Ol.* 7 concerns matters more weighty than mere erotic dalliance, the phiale that ratifies the spoken agreement could similarly preserve the declaration in graphic form, ready for reactivation each time the vessel circulates at the drinking party.

This opening conceit of Diagoras' ode very much sets the terms for what follows. In lines 20–24 Pindar introduces a second set of ritualized events whose reperformance depends on a more explicitly inscribed object (albeit one that does not find its counterpart in the Chronicle). Here too, speech and physical fabric form a tight synthesis, each taking its cue from the other:

> ἐθελήσω τοῖσιν ἐξ ἀρχᾶς ἀπὸ Τλαπολέμου   20
> ξυνὸν ἀγγέλλων διορθῶσαι λόγον
> Ἡρακλέος
> εὐρυσθενεῖ γέννᾳ. τὸ μὲν γὰρ

---

[179] London, British Museum 95.10–27.2. For detailed discussion, see Csapo and Miller 1991; the cup also features a line of verse issuing from the mouth of the singer in the tondo.

[180] See Csapo and Miller 1991, 373 for a complete list of these.

πατρόθεν ἐκ Διὸς εὔχονται· τὸ δ' Ἀμυντορίδαι
ματρόθεν Ἀστυδαμείας.

> I am eager, in announcing for those from the beginning from Tlepolemos,
> to set up straight [or 'erect'] a common report, for the broad-strengthed
> lineage of Heracles, for they claim they descend from Zeus on their
> father's side, while on their mother's they are Amyntor's descendants
> through Astydameia.

As Kurke suggests, the phrase διορθῶσαι λόγον recalls other places where
the expression occurs in Pindar in explicitly dedicatory contexts; *Ol.* 3.1–4
and *Isthm.* 1.45–46 supply close counterparts.[181] As she also notes, here, as
in the first *Isthmian*, terms for speech transform these material record-
keepers into what I have elsewhere called *oggetti parlanti*,[182] object-cues for
discourse insofar as they include in their overall design the inscription that
the reader/performer's voice enunciates and turns back into audible speech
and song.

With the participle ἀγγέλλων folded into the phrase describing the
erection of the monumentalized account of Rhodian genealogical history,
the image also calibrates this commemorative and simultaneously epi-
taphic stone with objects whose iconography and inscriptions preserve
the solemn moment when the sacred herald at the athletic games pronounced the *angelia* or victory announcement as the winner stepped up to
claim his crown; by way of model for this synthesis of roles, there are the
sepulchral epigrams that include mention of an athletic triumph within
their eulogistic accounts of the deceased. From the second half of the sixth
century comes the *sêma* erected in Troezen by the mother of one
Damotimos, who recalls his victory in the running race as she mourns
her son (*CEG* 138):[183]

> For Damotimos his dear mother constructed this marker,
> Amphidama: for no children were born in her halls.
> And the tripod which he carried off running at Thebes [...]
> [...] is unharmed, and she set it up over her son.

So closely are voice and text intertwined in the Pindaric speaker's declaration that there is no establishing priority: does the originally heralded
logos become fixed in the word-made-object that the performance is setting

---

[181] As Kurke 2015, 20–21 concludes of the lines in *Ol.* 7, 'we might take Pindar's stated wish ... as an anticipation of the actual material dedication of the poem intended to follow its lavish public performance'.
[182] Steiner 1993.
[183] See too the epigram on behalf of Dandes of Argos attributed to Simonides (*AP* 13.14).

up, or is the *persona loquens* giving voice to the pre-existing text, announcing the contents of the stone? The same oscillation between written text and enunciation continues through to the lines' end: again, speech and inscription become indistinguishable as the descendants of Heracles commemorated by the materialized account make their claim through their stele, asserting or boasting of (εὔχονται) their lineage. Even so extant victory inscriptions cite not just the individual win but larger sets of family victories too.

Following this declaration, the performers then turn from the present day to the distant past, recalling signal instances when the gods intervened on the island's behalf. Twice Zeus made manifest his presence through miraculous meteorological phenomena, on each occasion causing golden rain to fall on Rhodes. Simultaneous with the second shower is the gift bestowed on the islanders by Athena, who grants them the skilled craftsmanship that allowed them to create quasi-animated objects; simply designating these ἔργα (51), Pindar's account of the distinctive properties of these fabrications ('like to things that walked') clearly gestures towards the images that Hephaestus and other legendary craftsman construct, ones that seem to move (and speak). As commentators note, here too the story assigns to the Heliadai the gift that more typically belongs to a different set of characters in Rhodian mythology, the Telchines, those magician-craftsmen and malignant wizards who settle the island and are best known for their capacity to fashion quasi-animated images. For all that these figures are not named, their oblique presence may orient us once again towards the sanctuary of Athena Lindia and to its array of votive goods, which accommodated not only sculpted images – the pharaoh Amasis includes statues among his gifts – but also a dedication from these mythical artisans. As the Chronicle reports, the Telchines, named second after Lindos in the list of donors, made an offering to the goddess: 'The Telchines, a vessel ... on which had been inscribed: "The Telchines to Athena Polias and Zeus Polieus, a tenth of their labours (δεκάταν τῶν ἔργων)". As Higbie comments of the phrase's closing clause, this is diction 'which one might expect craftsmen to use in making an offering';[184] it is also the expression that appears in Pindar's possible 'transcription'.

The gnome in line 52 (whose meaning is much debated) concerning the *sophia* belonging to the man who has 'learnt' not only points to the expertise, whether poetic or artisanal, needed for this work of simulated

---

[184] Higbie 2003, 70. Among other examples, see *CEG* 380 from Olympia of ca. 460 inscribed on the base for a set of bronze statues (a victory dedication) which declares: 'this is the shared work (ξυνόν ... ϝέργον) of Athanodoros and Asopodoros'.

vivification but continues to draw from the language of these craftsmen's dedications: from exactly the period of *Ol.* 7 comes a marble base from the Piraeus, which probably once supported a herm, on which the gift's donor acknowledges the contribution of the Parian sculptor who carved the work (*CEG* 316): 'Euphron fashioned it, not without learning (οὐκ ἀδαής), from Paros'. More commonplace still is a reference to the artisan's *sophia*; Dicon is both donor and maker of the large bronze strigil dedicated at Olympia ca. 450 (?), whose epigram boasts that he made it himself 'for he has this *sophia*' (*CEG* 387), and the potters or painters responsible for the red-figure vase dedicated on the Acropolis similarly likewise announce the *agalma* the product of their 'skills (σοφίαισιν)' (*CEG* 291).

So as to pivot from the mythical excurses back to the here-and-now and to praise Diagoras anew, the poet returns to the hero who appeared at the myth's inception, Tlepolemos, neatly shifting from a ritual occasion on Rhodes celebrating this founding figure to the athletic triumphs of his *laudandus*, now pictured as he received his crown at other sites. Almost imperceptibly, the song moves into one among the epinician's 'required elements', the victory catalogue (77–87):

> τόθι λύτρον συμφορᾶς οἰκτρᾶς γλυκὺ Τλαπολέμῳ
> ἵσταται Τιρυνθίων ἀρχαγέτᾳ,
> ὥσπερ θεῷ,
> μήλων τε κνισάεσσα πομπὰ   80
>   καὶ κρίσις ἀμφ' ἀέθλοις. τῶν ἄνθεσι Διαγόρας
> ἐστεφανώσατο δίς, κλει-
>   νᾷ τ' ἐν Ἰσθμῷ τετράκις εὐτυχέων,
> Νεμέᾳ τ' ἄλλαν ἐπ' ἄλλᾳ, καὶ κρανααῖς ἐν Ἀθάναις.
>
> ὅ τ' ἐν Ἄργει χαλκὸς ἔγνω νιν, τά τ' ἐν Ἀρκαδίᾳ
> ἔργα καὶ Θήβαις, ἀγῶνές τ' ἔννομοι
> Βοιωτίων,   85
> Πέλλανά τ'· Αἴγινά τε νικῶνθ'
>   ἑξάκις· ἐν Μεγάροισίν τ' οὐχ ἕτερον λιθίνα
> ψᾶφος ἔχει λόγον.

There, in sweet recompense for the lamentable disaster, is established for Tlepolemos, colony founder of the Tirynthians, as if for a god, a fragrant procession of flocks, and the judging of athletic contests, with whose flowers Diagoras has twice crowned himself. Four times did he succeed at the renowned Isthmus, and again and again at Nemea and in rocky Athens. And the bronze in Argos knew [or 'recognized'] him, and the works in Arkadia and Thebes, and the well-ordered games of the

Boeotians and Pellene; and Aegina knew him victorious six times. And in
Megara the stone counter has no other tale to tell.

That this catalogue, with its sequence of numbers and places, models itself
on inscriptions on victory monuments comes as no surprise, and follows
Pindar's practice on several other occasions.[185] But Kurke observes several
features of the list that distinguish it from other Pindaric catalogues and
that cohere with the ode's foregrounding of material objects complete with
the declarative, witnessing and commemorative powers focused on in my
reading. Among these singularities, Kurke suggests, is the emphasis on the
nature and physical matter of the prizes, beginning with the mention of the
'bronze' won at Argos.[186] Again Pindar may use dedications and their
formulaic inscriptions as his template here; epigrams similarly emphasize
the fabric of the gift, often placed in first position in the line as the text
directs the viewers' attention to a particularly attention-worthy aspect of
the offering. So the second line of the inscription on a bronze discus from
Cephallenia, tentatively dated to ca. 550–525, locates the bronze from
which the votive is made in verse-initial position (*CEG* 391),[187] while a
public inscription celebrating victory at Tanagra declares in its opening line
that the phiale given by way of thanks offering is made of gold (*CEG* 351).
The Lindian Chronicle follows the epigrammatic convention in foregrounding the material of the gift: 'Kadmos, a bronze lebes', 'Minos, a
silver drinking cup' are among the entry beginnings.

The second of the anomalies highlighted by Kurke, the agency given to
the objects, which are made the subjects of the verbs that follow, again
appears less of an outlier when read in the context of contemporary
epigraphic conventions.[188] Very familiar is the phenomenon of the speaking object, the self-styled stele, *sêma* or *agalma* that is similarly animated,
addressing the reader in its own voice through the medium of the inscription, whose written contents are the repository of the information that it
can impart (note Pindar's use of the imperfect, ἔγνω). The bronze that
'knew' Diagoras points to this diction in several further respects, among
them the phrase's resemblances (with variation) to the epigrams that urge

---

[185] Cf. *CEG* 346, set up at Delphi and dated to ca. 475–450: 'Twice winning at Pytho [...] seven
times at Nemea [...] and five times with crowns [...] o Pythodelos'. A stele from Sparta of ca.
530–500 similarly enumerates the wins (*CEG* 374): 'Aiglatas set up this *agalma* for the
Karneian god, having won the long race five times, and he added the dolichos three times [in]
the Athenian [contests] where the ?prize ... '.

[186] Kurke 2015, 16.

[187] Cf. *CEG* 58, whose speaking monument announces itself made of stone, λάινον.

[188] Kurke 2015, 17. For Kurke, this vivification coheres with the talismanic and all but animated
qualities assigned to the goods presented elsewhere in the ode.

knowledge or recognition on their readers. Many funerary and votive inscriptions enjoin the passer-by to apprehend the object and consequently to 'know', 'see' and 'recognize' the individuals and the achievements that they celebrate. An epigram from Attica of ca. 550–530 cited earlier (*CEG* 19) supplies a possible model for Pindar's choice of terms:

> [He who?] pauses and beholds your marker, Xenocles, the marker of a spearman, will know (γνό[σετ]αι) your manliness.

The more extended epigram inscribed on the Ambracian cenotaph treated in Section 1 addresses its audience of citizens, similarly urging them to 'know', and the practice would become still more widespread in the fourth century; *CEG* 597 from Rhamnous, and dated to ca. 330–320, bids the stranger passing by to 'note' (φράζεο) the *sêma* and injunctions to 'see', 'observe' and 'know' proliferate.

While most discussions of the Pindaric victory catalogue assume that the mention of the Argive bronze refers to the shield that Diagoras would have carried off as prize from the city's contests, the lines permit a different interpretation. Read together, the bronze and stone both look to self-standing victory lists, such as those publicly displayed in Zeus's Olympian sanctuary from at least the fifth century on; we also know of the preservation and display of local victory lists in Sparta and elsewhere. Although most of these catalogues were incised in the stone that the poem locates in Megara, bronze stelai and tablets appear at various sites and the Pindaric conceit finds its precedent in the votive repertoire as well as in civic contexts:[189] from ca. 500 B.C.E. comes a Cretan bronze mitra – an abdominal guard worn as a belt beneath a garment – flattened out so as to serve as a pinax and equipped with two holes for suspension, which records the honours given to the local scribe Spenthisios.[190]

Very much in keeping with the other objects featured in *Ol.* 7, the inscribed votives, athletic dedications and victory lists encompassed in the Pindaric passage freshly anchor the audience to the ode's performance site and to the offerings on show there. If shields are the (simultaneous) referents for the Argive bronze, then the Chronicle lists an inscribed bronze shield among the victory spoils presented by Heracles, and Tlepolemos similarly dedicates nine shields. As for tripod cauldrons, other objects that a scholion suggests as likely referents for the Pindaric phrase, Cadmus

---

[189] See Thomas 1992, 84, Liddel 2007, 185–86 and Sickinger 1999, 57, who offers a variety of other examples from the archaic and early classical period.

[190] London, British Museum 1969, 1402.1.

presents what the chroniclers style a λέβητα χά[λ]κιον, a votive also cited by Diodorus Siculus who, perhaps drawing on the Chronicle, calls it 'worthy of note, made in archaic fashion' and inscribed with 'Phoenician *grammata*' (5.58.3).

The final lines of the passage, which introduce the Megarian stone ψᾶφος that 'holds no other report', continue the song's incorporation of inscribed monuments and other message-bearing objects. As in the instance of the monumentalized genealogy earlier in the ode, Pindar's account of this ψᾶφος leaves indeterminate the precise nature of the *logos* that the marker preserves. The story/record may take written and/or spoken form, referring to the discourse inscribed on the stone, silent until a reader gives it voice, or to the stone that speaks in the first person (in *CEG* 108, an epigram on the monument erected by Timarete in Eretria of ca. 450, the viewer first hears the voice of the dead man, who subsequently yields his voice to that of the *stele* whose pronouncement we then hear). Our fifth- and fourth-century sources variously use *logos* of written accounts and of enunciating what the writing preserves.[191]

But there is more to the ψᾶφος chosen as record-keeper here. Commonly used to describe the pebble used for casting ballots, which, as the voting counters found in the Athenian agora illustrate and [Aristotle] confirms (*Ath. Pol.* 68), supplied surfaces for inscriptions, this counter suggests that the Megarians were of one accord in granting the athlete the honour of commemoration, voting in favour of a measure that would first be proposed *viva voce* and then receive official confirmation when the measure was declared as passed. But also critical here is the use of the ψῆφος in reckoning up accounts, a practice to which Pindar more clearly refers at *Ol.* 10.9, which features the same counting stone. Both in the prelude to that song, and in other fifth-century texts, the ψῆφος guarantees accuracy, a property integral to the Megarian pebble of *Ol.* 7: it holds this and no other *logos*.[192]

The emphasis on exactitude in *Ol.* 7, implicit too in the victory catalogue's precise enumeration, finds its counterpart in the statements issued by votive objects and sepulchral monuments endowed with voice: *CEG* 286, which always answers the same thing,[193] never deviates from the tale it has to tell, while a probably fourth-century inscription on the marble base of a

---

[191] For discussion, see Svenbro 1993.

[192] See Aesch. *Ag.* 570, 'to reckon by the pebble' with its parallel use of the term λέγειν, and Eur. *Rh.* 309–10.

[193] 'I perform an identical answer to all people, whoever asks who of men set me up: Antiphanes (did) as a tithe'.

statue of the Olympic victor Xenombrotos affirms the truth of its story in its opening line: 'if you would know, the tale is true (αὔτα ... ἐτύμα φάτις) that the most glorious victory ... '.[194] The inclusion of this accurate record as Pindar's poem heads towards its concluding prayer (and note that in lines 90–91 Diagoras will 'travel straight' in future times by virtue of his 'upright mind [ὀρθαὶ φρένες]') serves a larger purpose, offering a metonym for the composition's presentation and preservation of a similarly authenticated account.

By the time the ode draws to its end, the audience has encountered a plethora of material phenomena that are testaments to Rhodian history and that record both the glory of those who made, acquired, won and/or dedicated them and the enduring veneration enjoyed by the goddess to whom they now belong. If the work's transcription and transformation into a votive gift was Diagoras' design from the start, and part of the brief given Pindar by his patrons, then the song would implicitly rehearse the moment when it would take its place in this sequence of inscribed record-keepers and precious offerings, the latest object to join the record of wondrous achievements.

Nor would this be the only instance of works by Pindar (and of other poets) that took the form of texts destined for a votive role. According to Pausanias' report at 9.16.1, the Pindaric *Hymn to Zeus* was engraved on a stele at the temple of Ammon in Libya, and inscriptions from a number of temples and sanctuaries similarly preserve and display the texts of poems – particularly paeans – performed at the sites. In the fourth century, the paean to Dionysus composed by Philodamus formed the object of that poet's dedication at Delphi, and Isyllos similarly offered up his paean to Asclepius and Apollo at Epidauros: the inscribed stele preserving the piece together with a number of the poet's other works (*IG* IV² 1, 128, *CA* 133–36) includes a prose account of how Isyllos had it inscribed following directions issued by the Delphic oracle.[195] The start of a paean by Sophocles to Asclepius took monumental form when it too was inscribed on the left side of the Sarapion monument, tentatively dated to the early years of the third century C.E., and dedicatory inscriptions from a number of other sites include citations of songs and a short title.[196]

Several motives might prompt the dedication of the transcribed song in a sacred space, among them the poet's piety coupled with the desire to preserve the text for others to consult and copy. Both Ian Rutherford and

---

[194] *Inschriften von Olympia* no. 170.
[195] For discussion, see Rutherford 2001, 145 and Stehle 1996, 132–38. I return to these in Chapter 9.
[196] See Rutherford 2001, 145–46 for additional examples.

Bruno Currie supply a third and likely rationale.[197] Although Rutherford posits the author's desire to make a worthy offering as the prime mover here, he also proposes that the preservation of the text *qua* votive good would allow for a 'secondary performance', whether at the site that housed the text or, copied down in the form of a papyrus roll or book, at other locations. As he further suggests, the link between the dedication and live spectacle would be particularly close when the site preserving the transcription was also the venue, or starting point in the case of a processional song, for that re-enactment: so a piece composed for the Athenian Puthais at Delphi could have been kept in the temple of Zeus Astrapaios in the home city, Athens, from which the procession including the choruses who performed the piece set out, and Pindar's eighth *Paean*, with its emphasis on the matter from which the successive Delphic temples were built, might have been displayed on the last of these, part and parcel of the celebrated Parian marble used by the Alcmaeonids for its construction. For Currie too, the inscriptions would 'enable a publicly-owned text to serve as the basis for future, publicly organized performance' or rather reperformance.

Pindar's ode for Diagoras and Rhodes adds a further dimension to the scenario proposed by these scholars. The lines describing the foundation of the shrine of Athena Lindia and the offerings made on that originary occasion (in a practice which continues on to the time of the current celebration) establish the frame for the present and future performances guaranteed by the text's preservation, while the poem's oblique references to the objects also stored up at the sacred site, and whose inscriptions it embeds in its diction, supply a template for the role of Pindar's transcribed text: like these written declarations (which might further have been recorded, long before the Lindian Chronicle, in temple inventories, such as existed at Delphi, Delos and other sacred sites, and on which Herodotus would draw),[198] it too can generate re-enactments of that act of dedication, which might have been recorded in a preamble to the piece. The choice of the adjective ἐναργής, 'visible, brilliant' (42) for the altar erected by the Heliadai neatly spans the multiple roles played by the precious goods in the composition: it draws attention to the way in which an object offered up on a past occasion for sacred use remains manifest still today, gestures to what might have been the epicentre of the ongoing performance and that is visible to the audience, and anticipates the brilliance and far-shining quality that the poem with its gilded letters will likewise possess. Like

---

[197] Rutherford 2001, 144 and 176–77; Currie 2004, 64.
[198] See Kosmetatou 2013 for the Herodotean inventories.

Pindar's ode too, whose concluding portion invokes Zeus and bids him 'honour' the song (88), that altar furnishes a site where gods and mortals come together in an exchange of goods and favours.

4 Theoretical Discussions of Alphabetic Writing and Their Intersections with Choral Performances

Not surprisingly, in a society so permeated with these different expressions of relations between letters and choral performances, philosophers, rhetoricians and grammarians of various kinds offer additional, if more indirect, evidence of the affinities played out in the epigraphic, painted, sculpted, lyric and dramatic media. In closing with these abstract reflections on 'grammatology', my argument is not that the sources align writing with *choreia*, nor that they theorize the more particular analogies between choruses and alphabetic symbols; instead, I suggest, their discussions of letter and word formation and of what writers and readers do when they devise and vocalize texts draw on terms and conceits common to the two practices and allow us better to discern the linguistic and conceptual substructures of the pairings apparent in the literary and visual spheres. Singled out for particular investigation here is the capacity of letters, both singly and in combination, to strike poses that change in and over time, to move from one posture to the next, and to assume different and sometimes seemingly random placements and configurations in a written line. More broadly, like the chorus member and the ensemble to which he or she belongs, a letter and the sequence in which it occurs is treated as a visual object and one to be evaluated as much for its aesthetic properties and ability to harmonize, cohere and on occasion contrast with those adjacent to it as for its meaning.

One area where this common ground is, perhaps, particularly evident concerns conceptions of the shape of individual letters, and the potential spatio-temporal mutability they turn out to possess. Already in the sixth century, Pythagoras seems to have viewed the creation of letters as a matter of designing not just visually pleasing forms, but ones that possess dynamism too. Credited with the invention of several new alphabetic symbols, perhaps the supplemental letters of the Ionian alphabet, he paid close attention, a scholion to Dionysius Thrax's *Technê Grammatikê* reports, 'to the beauty of letters, creating well-rhythmed shapes (literally 'endowing then with *rhythmos* [ῥυθμήσας])')' by drawing them with angles, arcs and straight lines according to geometrical principles'.[199] A subsequent witness to the *rhythmos* characteristic of alphabetic letters is Herodotus, who observes that the Phoenicians were the first to teach the Ionian Greeks how to write, instructing them in the *grammata* that they subsequently used (5.58.5–10):

μετὰ δὲ χρόνου προβαίνοντος ἅμα τῇ φωνῇ μετέβαλλον καὶ τὸν ῥυθμὸν τῶν γραμμάτων. περιοίκεον δέ σφεας τὰ πολλὰ τῶν χώρων τοῦτον τὸν χρόνον Ἑλλήνων Ἴωνες· οἳ παραλαβόντες διδαχῇ παρὰ τῶν Φοινίκων τὰ γράμματα, μεταρρυθμίσαντές σφεων ὀλίγα ἐχρέωντο . . .

But afterwards, in the course of time, they [the Phoenicians] changed by degree their language and together with it the *rhythmos* of their letters. Now the Greeks who dwelled about those parts were chiefly Ionians. And they, taking up the letters from the Phoenicians after they had been taught, used them changing the shape of a few . . .

It is precisely *rhythmos* – a form in flux, a configuration without fixity in contrast to the static, rigid *schêma* –[200] that for Plato distinguishes choral dance from the unregulated motions that infants and animals perform; as the Athenian Stranger explains at *Laws* 664e–665a,

εἴπομεν, εἰ μεμνήμεθα, κατ' ἀρχὰς τῶν λόγων, ὡς ἡ φύσις ἁπάντων τῶν νέων διάπυρος οὖσα ἡσυχίαν οὐχ οἵα τε ἄγειν οὔτε κατὰ τὸ σῶμα οὔτε κατὰ τὴν φωνὴν εἴη, φθέγγοιτο δ' ἀεὶ ἀτάκτως καὶ πηδῷ, τάξεως δ' αἴσθησιν τούτων ἀμφοτέρων, τῶν ἄλλων μὲν ζῴων οὐδὲν ἐφάπτοιτο, ἡ δὲ ἀνθρώπου φύσις ἔχοι μόνη τοῦτο· τῇ δὴ τῆς κινήσεως τάξει ῥυθμὸς ὄνομα εἴη, τῇ δὲ αὖ τῆς φωνῆς, τοῦ τε ὀξέος ἅμα καὶ βαρέος συγκεραννυμένων, ἁρμονία ὄνομα προσαγορεύοιτο, χορεία δὲ τὸ συναμφότερον κληθείη.

We said at the beginning, if we recall, that all young things being fiery and mettlesome by nature are unable to keep their bodies or their tongues still – they are always making uncoordinated noises and jumping about. No other animal, we said, ever develops a sense of order in either respect; man alone has a natural ability to do this. Order in movement is called *rhythmos* and order in the vocal sounds, the combination of high and low notes, is called harmony; and the union of the two is called *choreia*.

As Plato's usage elsewhere in the *Laws* makes clear,[201] *rhythmos* does not just designate 'rhythm', but can also refer to something more particular, a 'dance movement'. Built into this relationship is the derivation of *rhythmos*

---

[199] Σ Vat. Dion. Thr. Hilgard 1.183.31–184.2.
[200] See the discussion elsewhere in this study and in Kowalzig 2013, 183.
[201] See the discussion in Chapter 6.

from ῥέω, 'to flow', and whose association with movement it retains. As Nagy comments of the term when used in the context of the dance, 'the basic idea inherent in *rhythmos* is that whatever bodily movement there is in dance has a "flow" to it. But the question remains, how does "flow" become "rhythm"? The answer has to do with the fact that the flow of movement in dance is counterbalanced by a holding up of the flow, as expressed by way of the noun *schêma*',[202] the regular term for a dance pose (see below) and which the *Laws* regularly couples with *rhythmos*. So, for example, at *Leg.* 669d6–7, the Athenian Stranger remarks on how the 'New Musical' poets whom he strictures 'tear apart *rhythmos* as well as *schêmata*', a conjunction that earlier appeared at 669c5–6, where poets compose both *rhythmoi* and the postures for what, in this context, must be choral dancing. Following the passage from the *Laws* cited above, rhythm involves the addition of order to movement, turning the uncoordinated elements into a 'configuration of movements organized in time' visible in the choreography as the dancer travels through space and over time.[203]

To return to Pythagoras' view, at least as preserved by a later commentator, a letter displays the beauty that comes about through achieving proper proportions, good alignment and shapeliness. In Herodotus' different but similarly phrased account, each alphabetic symbol possesses the potential to quit an earlier form (or *schêma*) and, in diachronic fashion, to adopt an altered one. The inscriptions, vases and images cited in earlier sections of this chapter, and which variously juxtapose or conflate written elements with choral dancers, demonstrate how the epigraphic and visual sources match letter and word *rhythmos* with the dancers' motions: the proximity of the moving bodies to the lines of writing with which they are so closely coordinated, and which can even on occasion replace them, invests the lettering with the performers' *kinêsis*, making them move and change one into the next even as the written line – which travels over the clay or stone surface – can 'dynamize' the necessarily static painted or fashioned bodies. On the Middle Corinthian aryballos, we know that the choreutes are just waiting for their musical-cum-alphabetic signal before they begin their fluid movements just as the letters' first up and then downward trajectory tells us that the now-leaping chorus leader will then return to the ground.

Pythagoras and Herodotus are not alone in attributing *rhythmos* to the alphabetic sign, to which they grant a capacity for motion that would be amply realized in late fifth-century drama when individual letters, syllabic

---

[202] Nagy 2010b, 373.   [203] Benveniste 1971, 287 cited by Kowalzig 2013, 184.

clusters, words and phrases are, in the words of Sophocles cited in this chapter's introduction, 'danced out' in their changing configurations on the stage. When *rhythmos* recurs in Aristotle, it does so in conjunction with several other 'grammatological' expressions that concern not the single letter but what happens when that element joins with others in word formation. In the course of an attack on the views of Leucippus and Democritus regarding *stoicheia*, elements, and the noun also regularly used for the individual letters of the alphabet, Aristotle discusses how his predecessors define three areas that can distinguish one *stoichos* from another (*Met.* 985b13–19):

> ταύτας μέντοι τρεῖς εἶναι λέγουσι, σχῆμά τε καὶ τάξιν καὶ θέσιν· διαφέρειν γάρ φασι τὸ ὂν ῥυσμῷ καὶ διαθιγῇ καὶ τροπῇ μόνον· τούτων δὲ ὁ μὲν ῥυσμὸς σχῆμά ἐστιν ἡ δὲ διαθιγὴ τάξις ἡ δὲ τροπὴ θέσις· διαφέρει γὰρ τὸ μὲν Α τοῦ Ν σχήματι τὸ δὲ ΑΝ τοῦ ΝΑ τάξει τὸ δὲ Ζ τοῦ Η θέσει.

> They hold that these differences are three – shape, arrangement, and position; being, they say, differs only in 'rhythm, touching, and turning', of which 'rhythm' is shape, 'touching' is arrangement, and 'turning' is position; for A differs from N in shape, AN from NA in arrangement, and Z from N in position. (trans. Kirk, Raven and Schofield, with their modification of the Greek text)

A second assessment of atomism employs the same terminology, now so as to illustrate the fallacy of Leucippus and Democritus' belief that the addition or subtraction of a single element could produce the appearance of an entirely different compound; by way of analogy, Aristotle again turns to the role of alphabetic signs combined within a word in what seems a citation from the earlier atomist sources (*De gen. et corr.* 315b6–15):

> Δημόκριτος δὲ καὶ Λεύκιππος ποιήσαντες τὰ σχήματα τὴν ἀλλοίωσιν καὶ τὴν γένεσιν ἐκ τούτων ποιοῦσι, διακρίσει μὲν καὶ συγκρίσει γένεσιν καὶ φθοράν, τάξει δὲ καὶ θέσει ἀλλοίωσιν. ἐπεὶ δ' ᾤοντο τἀληθὲς ἐν τῷ φαίνεσθαι, ἐναντία δὲ καὶ ἄπειρα τὰ φαινόμενα, τὰ σχήματα ἄπειρα ἐποίησαν, ὥστε ταῖς μεταβολαῖς τοῦ συγκειμένου τὸ αὐτὸ ἐναντίον δοκεῖν ἄλλῳ καὶ ἄλλῳ, καὶ μετακινεῖσθαι μικροῦ ἐμμιγνυμένου καὶ ὅλως ἕτερον φαίνεσθαι ἑνὸς μετακινηθέντος· ἐκ τῶν αὐτῶν γὰρ τραγῳδία καὶ κωμῳδία γίνεται γραμμάτων.

> They postulate figures and make alteration and coming to be the result of them, explaining coming to be and passing away by their dissociation and association but alteration by their arrangement and position. And since they thought that truth lay in the appearance, and that appearances are

conflicting and infinitely many, they made the *schêmata* infinite in number. Hence, owing to the changes of the compound, the same thing seems different and conflicting to different people; and having been transposed by a small additional ingredient, it appears utterly other by the transposition of a single constituent. For tragedy and comedy arise from the same letters of the alphabet.

One later passage selects this same set of terms in a discussion chiefly concerned with the sequencing and order that must be observed in combining individual letters into meaningful words. As a scholion to Dionysius Thrax's *Technê Grammatikê*, written some time in the second century B.C.E., comments of the grammarian's view (Σ Vat. Dion. Thr. Hilgard 1.197.17–23):

> and for this reason he says that [letters] are *stoicheia*, because they have a file (*stoichon*) and order (*taxis*), the ones in respect to the others; for in this case they are *stoicheia*. When they are not written in order, they are called *grammata* not *stoicheia*. As for instance *pros*, it is written correctly and in order (*kata taxin*); for this reason, they are called *stoicheia*, for as *stoicheia*, they produce *pros*. If, however, I change their order, writing *rpos*, they are called *grammata* and not *stoicheia* because they are not any more in order.[204]

While none of these passages looks even indirectly towards the chorus, the terms and properties their authors assign to *grammata* – *thesis, taxis* and *stoichos*, as well, of course, as *schêma* – appear repeatedly in accounts of how individual chorus members are marshalled, ordered and arranged in linear and other formations from archaic through to post-classical times. Discussions in earlier chapters have explored the dancer's 'placement', whether at the beginning or end of the line, or in the middle of the circle prior to the performance's start, and while ἵστημι is the much more common term for stationing the chorus member than τίθημι, the two verbs, as Benveniste notes, mutually influence one another and exchange their forms. *Taxis*, order, is also required of the well-regulated chorus, and its absence furnishes grounds for critique; in Xenophon of Ephesus' visualization of the procession at the festival celebrated on behalf of Artemis in his native city, the novel's heroine Antheia leads the parthenaic chorus as the maidens advance in their line: ἦρχε δὲ τῆς τῶν παρθένων τάξεως (*Ephes.* 1.2.5); later on at the same event, the maidens are faulted for breaking out of their linear deployment, abandoning their former good arrangement

---

[204] See Svenbro 2008, 209 for detailed discussion.

(1.3.3). A passage of Aelius Aristides also views the chorus line as a *taxis*, a term that appears combined with the notion of placement. Reflecting on how a mason aligns or places his stones (εἰς τάξιν τίθησιν) so as to assemble a wall, the orator cites the chorus-maker or χοροποιός by way of analogue (*Or.* 46.158).

Choral *taxis*, here combined with *stoichos*, appears again in a commentary on Aratus by an anonymous author, whose gloss suggests that the term reaches all the way back to Alcman and to an expressly choral context. Citing the hapax ὁμοστοίχους used by the Spartan poet, he explains that it refers to the parthenaic choristers dancing in their linear formation: τὰς ἐν τάξει χορευούσας παρθένους (Anon. I *ad Arat.* 2 (p. 91, 11 Maas) = Alcman fr. 33 *PMGF*).[205] The same Aratan commentator, albeit through a rather circuitous route, additionally links this usage to the *stoicheion* as a letter in the written line:[206] as he notes, Alcman chooses ὁμοστοίχους again, this time in a cosmological poem where it appears in an account of the four overlapping elements, ether, air, water and earth. In the commentary the exegete supplies, *stoicheia* also describe alphabetic letters because their elements are woven (πλέκεσθαι) by virtue of their orderly placement, τάξει. Just as the sources imagine the choral ensemble as a pattern-woven textile, so an alphabetic assemblage has the same character, with letters as the matter with which the writer weaves.[207]

The glossographer's remark points us back to the scholion to Dionysius Thrax cited earlier, where the annotator distinguishes letters, *stoicheia*, written in their correct sequence from mere *grammata*, which lack the requisite ordering and are positioned 'out of line'. In a preface to a discussion of the passage, Svenbro, following the same scholion, first observes the derivation of *stoicheion* from στείχω – the verb so often chosen for the processional movement of a chorus – and then goes on to suggest that the noun retains its 'connotations of alignment, rank, movement, which leaves us with the notion of sequence, of sequential movement';[208] reading, in his view, remains indissolubly linked to this marching or processional advance, a connection demonstrated by the scholiast who seeks to illustrate how one letter's shift from its correct position to another in the alphabetic formation renders a word unintelligible. The distinction between the *gramma* and *stoicheion* highlighted by the ancient commentator thus depends on the 'marked' quality that the latter has, its role as an

---

[205] See Calame 1997, 38–39.   [206] Here I draw again from Calame 1997, 39.
[207] Beyond the scope of this discussion is the whole motif of the text as a woven object; among many discussions, see Woodard 2014, 227–90.
[208] Svenbro 2008, 199.

element in an intelligible sequence, and pertains to the way that, in reading, we attend not to the letters' individual identity but to the way in which they follow one another through space.

To turn to the *schêma* selected by Aristotle and the fifth-century Atomists whom he cites in reference to the morphology of the alphabetic letter, the term concurrently appears in a source broadly contemporary with Leucippus and Democritus, a Hippocratic treatise that describes writing as a σχημάτων σύνθεσις, an assemblage of the 'poses' assumed by individual *grammata*: (γραμματικὴ τοιόνδε· σχημάτων σύνθεσις, *De victu* 1.23). The language chosen in a much later text grants to syllabic amalgams this same 'posturing': in the weaving of syllables, Dionysius of Halicarnassus remarks, the elements are arranged in diverse and changing combinations that involve their creation of shifting *schêmata* (παντοδαπῶς σχηματιζομένη, *Comp.* 12.10). There is little need to demonstrate the term's regular application, from the fifth-century sources on, to the poses assumed by dancers.[209] In lines apparently delivered by Aeschylus in a work by Aristophanes, the dramatist boasts that he single-handedly devised the *schêmata* for his choral dancers, remarking, 'it was I who gave the poses to the choruses' (Athen. 1.21e); Phrynicus, Callias and other dramatists similarly use *schêma* for both solo and group dances, and, outside the theatrical context, Herodotus selects the diminutive *schêmatia* for the 'Laconian figures' performed by Hippokleides in the course of his outrageous upside down dance on Cleisthenes' dinner table (6.129.13).

While many of the texts cited in this section long postdate the images and texts treated in the chapter's previous sections, one of the earlier visual accounts discussed there already illustrates many of the concerns and distinctions voiced by the theoreticians and allows us to view close up the common ground that writing and *choreia* share. To return to the first of the friezes on the François Vase and to its depiction of Theseus' disembarkation on Crete (Fig. 0.5), here Kleitias juxtaposes two sets of individuals, the crewmembers still on board the boat and the fourteen tributary youths and maidens in their chorus line led by the lyre-playing hero. As Chapter 5, building on Olsen's reading of the scene,[210] observed, the artist introduces marked distinctions between these groups that closely correspond to that between letters properly assembled in their words and phrases, and those that lack this necessary deployment and that, when read in sequence, remain meaningless. Whereas the young Athenians under Theseus' leadership are presented neatly aligned, hands linked with one another, all advancing from left to right with much the same motion and adopting

---

[209] See the exhaustive discussion in Catoni 2005, 124–33.   [210] Olsen 2015.

the same stance, and with regular girl-boy alternation too, no such homo-geneity belongs to the crew in their much more free-form and random dance; facing in different directions and performing a variety of gestures with their arms, they lack the cohesion, regularity and 'common choreog-raphy' of their land-bound counterparts.[211]

This orderliness and cohesion even extends, at the more minute level, to the tags that identify each of the chorus members: although made up of different letters and of varying lengths, these nonetheless are uniform in shape, all occupying the space to the left of the dancer whom they name and replicating the curve described by his or her arm.[212] Were a viewer to take a closer look, each set of letters would also yield an intelligible and even meaningful name. The crew members have no such labels, all remaining anonymous, unidentifi-able or, to extend the alphabetic analogy, impossible to 'read'. The presence of these dipinti not only, as I suggested in Section 2, invites us to dwell on the kinship between choral dancing and writing, the latter complementing the movement and properties of the figures with whom it is paired, but also prompts reflection on the cohesive and ordering quality that the writer, in the manner of the *chorêgos*, here Theseus who is both the 'internal leader of the dance, and choreographer',[213] imposes on his alphabetic matter. While het-erogeneity, individuality and changeability are admissible, even necessary, in the formation of letters, syllables, words and phrases, so too, as earlier noted, are differences in chorus members, who nonetheless share a group identity, a single performance mode and, most importantly, must remain 'in line'. Nothing better brings out the affinity between alphabetic writing and the choral body than the two figures shown on the far left of the chorus line, the youth (one Phaidimos) still in the act of stepping from the ship to shore,[214] and the maiden who, unlike her fellow dancers, cannot yet grasp his left hand since he has his arm raised up, as though gesturing to the remainder of the troupe as this 'late arrival' hastens to catch up with them. Even as the movements and stance of these two figures suggest that they are not fully assimilated into the choral collective and move more randomly than the rest, so too their labels stand out: in distinction to the curving design characteristic of the other names, the lettering runs horizontally, demarcated from the unified, homogeneous 'text' to which the remainder belong.[215]

---

[211] For the citation, see Olsen 2015, 112.   [212] Olsen 2015, 113.   [213] Olsen 2015, 117.

[214] Olsen 2015, 116 also comments on the distinction, noting Phaidimos' transitional status.

[215] The distinction between the horizontal and curved labels might reflect the transition from a linear, processional movement that precedes the circular ring dance signalled by the joined hands characterizing the other performers.

9 | Girls in Lines: Catalogues and Choruses

Introduction

Μουσάων Ἑλικωνιάδων ἀρχώμεθ᾽ ἀείδειν,
αἵ θ᾽ Ἑλικῶνος ἔχουσιν ὄρος μέγα τε ζάθεόν τε,
καί τε περὶ κρήνην ἰοειδέα πόσσ᾽ ἁπαλοῖσιν
ὀρχεῦνται καὶ βωμὸν ἐρισθενέος Κρονίωνος·
καί τε λοεσσάμεναι τέρενα χρόα Περμησσοῖο   5
ἢ Ἵππου κρήνης ἢ Ὀλμειοῦ ζαθέοιο
ἀκροτάτῳ Ἑλικῶνι χοροὺς ἐνεποιήσαντο,
καλοὺς ἱμερόεντας, ἐπερρώσαντο δὲ ποσσίν.
ἔνθεν ἀπορνύμεναι κεκαλυμμέναι ἠέρι πολλῷ,
ἐννύχιαι στεῖχον περικαλλέα ὄσσαν ἱεῖσαι,   10
(Hes. *Th.* 1–10)

Let us begin to sing from the Heliconian Muses, who possess the great and holy mountain of Helicon and dance with supple feet around the violet-dark spring and the altar of Cronus' broad-strengthed son. And having washed their tender skin in Permessus or the spring of Hippocrene or holy Olmeius, they perform fair, desire-instigating choral dances on highest Helicon and ply their feet. Setting out from there, enshrouded in much mist, they process by night, emitting their very beautiful voice . . .

Hesiod's *Theogony* opens in a manner that sharply differentiates it from its Homeric counterparts: in place of the singular 'goddess' or 'Muse' whom the *Iliad* and *Odyssey* proems invoke, Hesiod's divinities form a plurality. More than this, the opening vignette depicts the Muses engaged in a highly particularized and signature activity, performing a ring dance around a body of water and altar with the 'tender feet' distinctive of choral maidens in archaic epic and lyric poetry.[1]

The divinities' representation as an archetypal chorus continues through this opening visualization: a few lines on, we meet them 'making dances',

---

[1] Cf. Alcman fr. 3.10 *PMGF.*

plying their feet in the manner of Iliadic and other choral dancers,[2] and like the prototypical chorus on the shield of Achilles, and those that follow in the lyric corpus, the Muses' ensemble is both beautiful and desire-instigating.[3] Even as the performers sing – thereby satisfying the later Platonic definition of *choreia* as 'song-dance' (*Leg.* 654a) – their motion changes: now, marching (στείχω regularly denotes orderly, ranked movement) down from the Heliconian heights, the deities process. Here poetic content and choral formation coincide. Just as the Muses first sing a reverse theogony (*Th.* 11–21), beginning at the end of the succession struggle as they move from the mountain heights to lower land, so they invert the regular sequence that determines the movements of a chorus: first the linear procession to the sacred site, then the ring dance, typically performed around an altar or other centrepoint, when it reaches its destination. The Heliconian Muses, by contrast, quit the 'altar of Cronus' son' and the divinely inhabited bodies of water (so often the site of choral dancing, particularly that of the nymphs treated in Chapter 5) so as to descend into the mortal realm. The song sung by the goddesses as they journey downwards – an inventory of the Olympians and those preceding them – already supplies the generic template for the mode of discourse that Hesiod will adopt in much of the work that follows: the catalogue or list.

The *Theogony*'s opening scene succinctly exemplifies the larger phenomenon explored in this chapter, the co-presence of choruses and catalogues both here and elsewhere in archaic epic and lyric poetry. For all that the catalogue is typically viewed as an element integral to hexameter poetry and among the hallmarks of that strictly monodic genre, both in Hesiod's proem and elsewhere, choruses make regular appearances when such lists occur, whether as performers of the itemized accounts and/or as the subjects of a poet or internal narrator's 'catalogic' presentation. In the argument formulated here, the coincidence between troupes of singer-dancers and catalogues depends in no small part on the 'incipient chorality'[4] that the enumerative device possessed in early Greek thought and whose diverse expressions in art and text the successive sections of this chapter variously illustrate. Section 1 seeks simply to establish the premise of my proposal, offering its own selective 'catalogue' of passages from texts in hexameter and lyric compositions that underscore the relations between individuals or items presented as a list and the plurality and chorality of its

---

[2] E.g. *Il.* 24.616, *HHVen.* 261.
[3] Cf. *Il.* 18.590–601. For representations of maiden choruses in the lyric and dramatic corpus that recapitulate the terms used here, see Swift 2016.
[4] I borrow the expression, once again, from Power 2011, 75.

performers. Section 2 suggests some underlying reasons for the kinship, detailing continuities between the morphology of catalogues and choruses in the poetic and visual repertoires. In the chapter's third section, I offer close readings of three passages, one from hexameter epic, the other two from fifth-century choral poems, which demonstrate the exchanges argued for in the earlier discussions and highlight the indicators of the generic hybridity that results from these poetic interactions. The chapter's closing Section 4 focuses on catalogues in written form, and, developing points made in the previous chapter, takes up the question of the relations between choral ensembles and these itemized documents. For all the heterogeneity of the sources on which my argument draws, all share a common property: in each instance, to recite, sing, read, listen to or merely to cast a glance at a list is to participate in a choral performance, whether as one of the singing-dancing troupe or as an audience member and spectacle viewer.

1   Catalogues Become Choruses: Hexameter Epic and Archaic Choral Lyric

For early audiences, relations between the chorus and the catalogue might seem self-evident. Critics have long noted that Homer regularly invokes the Muses, sometimes in the singular, but more frequently as a plurality, before embarking on an extended list,[5] and cite issues of authority, comprehensiveness, mnemonic challenge and the poet's desire to emphasize the 'specialness', intensity or capstone nature of the enumeration by way of explanation. But Carruesco, noting the seemingly unmotivated switch from the single Muse of the *Iliad* proem to the invocation of the collective goddesses in the second preface before the show-stopping Catalogue of Ships, makes a different suggestion:[6] here, by virtue of the heterogeneity and sheer number of contingents requiring recitation, the poet spins out the idea of multiplicity, making evident that the human bard would have to undergo transformation into something equivalent to the divine chorus, equipped with the ten voices and ten tongues an ensemble naturally enjoys to achieve this superhuman feat. So too the poet stresses his own singularity in contrast to the first person plural used of the Muses and sets himself, a

---

[5]   See chiefly Minton 1962, Minchin 1996, Perceau 2002, Sammons 2010, these last two with other older and more recent bibliography.

[6]   Carruesco 2010, 172–73; I return to the Catalogue of Ships in Section 3.

lone ego, in opposition to the 'crowd' that he aims to list, closing the
invocation with a final declaration of multiplicity (*Il.* 2.484–93):

ἔσπετε νῦν μοι Μοῦσαι Ὀλύμπια δώματ' ἔχουσαι·
ὑμεῖς γὰρ θεαί ἐστε, πάρεστέ τε, ἴστέ τε πάντα,   485
ἡμεῖς δὲ κλέος οἶον ἀκούομεν οὐδέ τι ἴδμεν·
οἵ τινες ἡγεμόνες Δαναῶν καὶ κοίρανοι ἦσαν·
πληθὺν δ' οὐκ ἂν ἐγὼ μυθήσομαι οὐδ' ὀνομήνω,
οὐδ' εἴ μοι δέκα μὲν γλῶσσαι, δέκα δὲ στόματ' εἶεν,
φωνὴ δ' ἄρρηκτος, χάλκεον δέ μοι ἦτορ ἐνείη,   490
εἰ μὴ Ὀλυμπιάδες Μοῦσαι Διὸς αἰγιόχοιο
θυγατέρες μνησαίαθ' ὅσοι ὑπὸ Ἴλιον ἦλθον.
ἀρχοὺς αὖ νηῶν ἐρέω νῆάς τε προπάσας.

Narrate to me now, Muses having your home on Olympia, for you are
goddesses and are present and know all things, but we hear only hearsay
nor do we know anything, those who were the leaders of the Danaans and
the rulers; I would not be able to speak of nor to name the throng, not even
if I had ten tongues and ten mouths and a voice unbroken and a brazen
heart were within me, unless the Olympian Muses, daughters of aegis-
bearing Zeus, were to remember as many as came beneath Troy. I will
speak the leaders of the ships and all the ships.

That an individual might possess the capacity to speak or sing in multiple
voices seems pure poetic fantasy, but one Homeric character displays just
this skill. Witness Helen as she approaches the Trojan horse in Menelaus'
damning story in *Od.* 4.277–87:

τρὶς δὲ περίστειξας κοῖλον λόχον ἀμφαφόωσα,
ἐκ δ' ὀνομακλήδην Δαναῶν ὀνόμαζες ἀρίστους,
πάντων Ἀργείων φωνὴν ἴσκουσ' ἀλόχοισιν·
αὐτὰρ ἐγὼ καὶ Τυδεΐδης καὶ δῖος Ὀδυσσεὺς   280
ἥμενοι ἐν μέσσοισιν ἀκούσαμεν, ὡς ἐβόησας.
νῶϊ μὲν ἀμφοτέρω μενεήναμεν ὁρμηθέντε
ἢ ἐξελθέμεναι ἢ ἔνδοθεν αἶψ' ὑπακοῦσαι·
ἀλλ' Ὀδυσεὺς κατέρυκε καὶ ἔσχεθεν ἱεμένω περ.
ἔνθ' ἄλλοι μὲν πάντες ἀκὴν ἔσαν υἷες Ἀχαιῶν,   285
Ἄντικλος δὲ σέ γ' οἶος ἀμείψασθαι ἐπέεσσιν
ἤθελεν·

Three times you circled around the hollow ambush, feeling it, and you
called out, naming them by name, to the best of the Danaans, and made
your voice like to that of the wives of all the Argives. But I, and the son of
Tydeus and brilliant Odysseus sitting in the middle heard how you cried

out, and Diomedes and I both started up, both minded to go outside, or else to answer your voice from inside. But Odysseus restrained us and held us for all our yearning. And all the other sons of the Achaeans sat in silence, but there was only one, it was Antiklos, who was ready to respond.

On several counts, the singular performer seems to become a collective chorus: three times Helen walks around the trap in what could be seen as a choral circumambulation about an *agalma*,[7] calling out to each hero in turn by name – in effect an enumerative catalogue such as she performs at greater length for Priam in the *teichoskopia* of *Il.* 3.199–242, where, Muse-like in her omniscience, she lists the Achaean heroes whom she surveys. A second detail in the Odyssean scene further suggests chorality: Antiklos wishes to respond (ἀμείψασθαι, 286), the choral activity *par excellence*, as demonstrated by *HHAp.* 189 (Μοῦσαι μέν θ' ἅμα πᾶσαι ἀμειβόμεναι ὀπὶ καλῇ), and, still more appositely, *Od.* 24.58–62:

> ἀμφὶ δέ σ' ἔστησαν κοῦραι ἁλίοιο γέροντος
> οἴκτρ' ὀλοφυρόμεναι, περὶ δ' ἄμβροτα εἵματα ἕσσαν.
> Μοῦσαι δ' ἐννέα πᾶσαι ἀμειβόμεναι ὀπὶ καλῇ   60
> θρήνεον· ἔνθα κεν οὔ τιν' ἀδάκρυτόν γ' ἐνόησας
> Ἀργείων· τοῖον γὰρ ὑπώρορε Μοῦσα λίγεια.

And around you stood the daughters of the old man of the sea lamenting piteously and wearing immortal clothing; and the nine Muses sang the *thrênos*, all responding with beautiful voice. There you would perceive none of the Argives who was not weeping; such was the power of the shrill-voiced Muse to stir up.

As Martin, connecting the representation with the Helen episode, explains the switch from the choral Nereids and Muses to the singular goddess at the passage's end, 'one Muse leads the group and responds to them, as they respond to her and to one another . . .; if Helen is conceptualized as an *exarchousa* – a chorus leader – we might be able to imagine that she crystallizes the power of choral song, within her individual performance'.[8] As Martin further notes, like that Muse soloist, Helen is lead performer in what resembles a *thrênos*; her enumeration constitutes a roll-call of those about to die should the heroes hidden in the horse heed her invitation to respond, a point to which I will return.

---

[7] Carruesco 2012, 161. My discussion of the scene draws much from both Carruesco and Martin 2008.

[8] Martin 2008, 121.

But most uncanny in Menelaus' account is Helen's multiplication of her voice as she counterfeits the call of each warrior's wife. Closest to this mimetic feat is the performance by the Delian Maidens in the *Homeric Hymn to Apollo*, featured in another passage that highlights multiplicity and introduces the play between the singular bard and the choral ensemble that the hymnist will then develop. Where previously Apollo's celebrant has performed as a monodist, now he introduces a maidenly chorus (157–63):[9]

> κοῦραι Δηλιάδες Ἑκατηβελέταο θεράπναι·
> αἵ τ᾽ ἐπεὶ ἄρ πρῶτον μὲν Ἀπόλλων᾽ ὑμνήσωσιν,
> αὖτις δ᾽ αὖ Λητώ τε καὶ Ἄρτεμιν ἰοχέαιραν,
> μνησάμεναι ἀνδρῶν τε παλαιῶν ἠδὲ γυναικῶν   160
> ὕμνον ἀείδουσιν, θέλγουσι δὲ φῦλ᾽ ἀνθρώπων.
> πάντων δ᾽ ἀνθρώπων φωνὰς καὶ κρεμβαλιαστὺν[10]
> μιμεῖσθ᾽ ἴσασιν.

> The maidens of Delos, the handmaids of the Far-shooter, who, after first hymning Apollo, and then in turn Leto and Artemis arrow-pourer, turn their thoughts to the men and women of old and sing a song that charms the race of all people. They know how to mimic all people's voices and their rhythmic motions.

Here, as in the invocation in *Iliad* 2, the passage not only contrasts collectivity and individuation, drawing attention to the opposition between the *persona loquens*' solo status and the multiple numbers and voices of the participants at the Delian event, but again suggests an alignment between the plurality of chorus members and the several items that they must enumerate (three gods in place of one). The heterogeneous audience also forms a crowd (ἀθρόοι, 152), all sharing in the delight inspired by the performance (πάντων, 153 and 162; cf. πολλά, 155). A direct address to the Delian maidens follows their performance of what stands as a mini-catalogue – 'first' Apollo, and 'then again' Leto and Artemis (αὖτις δ᾽ αὖ, with double use of this typical catalogue 'connective' that establishes continuity between the different items)[11] – as the poet turns directly to address the markedly multiple chorus (ὑμεῖς πᾶσαι, 166). He then bids them fulfill the mnemonic role played by the catalogue before closing the passage with the contrast between his monodic recitation and the Delians' collective

---

[9] Martin 2008, 119–20 and Carruesco 2012, 159–60, both making different arguments from mine, cite the parallel.

[10] For this reading of the disputed κρεμβαλιαστὺν and the translation I propose, see Peponi 2009.

[11] Perceau 2002, 114 and 159–60; see too the example cited in Section 2.

voice. While they will respond as a group (171), his individual celebration (ἐγών, 177) features a single subject (Apollo).

On a second occasion in the *Odyssey*, where the protagonist treats his Phaeacian audience to an account of the heroines whom he encountered in the Underworld, it is Odysseus who assumes the cataloguer's role. In the preface to his list, he first describes the women whom Persephone has sent and who approach him in a disorderly mass and in great numbers (ὅσσαι, *Od.* 11.227, this a typical term for introducing a catalogue). Circling around the pit (so ἀμφ' at 228), and assembled in crowds (ἀολλέες ἠγερέθοντο, 228), they remain undifferentiated until Odysseus positions them in linear order (προμνηστῖναι, 'one by one', 233) so as to question each in turn. In much this way, as examples from choral poetry demonstrate, the poet-*chorêgos* might locate each chorus member in his or her place in a linear,[12] ranked or circular formation prior to the start of the performance, correcting those who, quite literally, step out of line.[13]

The question Odysseus then poses of each heroine offers a verbal equivalent to the group's spatial deployment, this further enforced by the temporal-cum-locational expressions 'first' and 'after' as, at the start of each successive entry, the speaker recounts how first one and then another came into view. Catching sight of his individual interlocutors in turn, Odysseus asks each heroine to recite her genealogy (ὃν γόνον ἐξαγόρευεν, 234), prompting the delivery of an ancestor list that offers an internal echo of the larger catalogue structure framing the encounters. The alternation between Odysseus and those from whom he seeks this information further resembles that between the *chorêgos* and collective choral voice, subdivided in episodes in later Attic drama where each chorus member might respond in turn to the leader.

To these examples one further, transgressive instance of a chorus-catalogue amalgam might be added. The Homeric *adynaton* of the pluralistic voice and tongue in the single performer finds realization in Hesiod's polycephalic Typhoeus, who not only multiplies the ten tongues imagined by the Iliadic poet into one hundred (*Th.* 825) but likewise possesses the imitative power of the Delian Maidens, able to make his *phônai* (the term used of the Deliades at *HHAp.* 162; the verb φθέγγομαι also appears in both passages) like that of any number of disparate beasts (829–35):

> φωναὶ δ' ἐν πάσῃσιν ἔσαν δεινῆς κεφαλῇσι,
> παντοίην ὄπ' ἱεῖσαι ἀθέσφατον· ἄλλοτε μὲν γὰρ   830
> φθέγγονθ' ὥς τε θεοῖσι συνιέμεν, ἄλλοτε δ' αὖτε

---

[12] Cf. Pind. *Pyth.* 9.113–14a.   [13] See Philostr. *Imag.* 2.1.3 with Chapter 10.

ταύρου ἐριβρύχεω μένος ἀσχέτου ὄσσαν ἀγαύρου,
ἄλλοτε δ' αὖτε λέοντος ἀναιδέα θυμὸν ἔχοντος,
ἄλλοτε δ' αὖ σκυλάκεσσιν ἐοικότα, θαύματ' ἀκοῦσαι,
ἄλλοτε δ' αὖ ῥοίζεσχ', ὑπὸ δ' ἤχεεν οὔρεα μακρά.   835

And there were voices in all his terrible heads, sending forth all sorts of
sounds, unspeakable; for at one time they uttered sounds as though for the
gods to understand, and at others a sound as great as that of a loud-
bellowing bull, unstoppable in strength and proud, and at other times that
of a lion with a reckless spirit, and at another like to those of pups, a
wonder to hear, and at other times he hissed, and the high mountains
echoed in accompaniment.

As Owen Goslin notes of what others read as a supreme instance of
disordering, or vocal *akosmia*, the Typhonomachy forms the closing element of the succession story that the Muses' performance in the preface
initiated, two episodes that focus centrally on the organization of sound.[14]
Particularly apposite to my argument is Goslin's observation that the poet
develops the opposition between the Muses and Typhoeus so as implicitly
to suggest proper choral performance and its contrary: 'the Muses
are separately named individuals, who are nevertheless "like-minded"
(ὁμόφρονας, 60), and produce a single voice in harmony. Typhon, on the
other hand, is a single entity of confused bodily forms …'.[15]
   Add to this the very structure of the Hesiodic representation of
Typhoeus as the poet seeks, through his Muses-sourced song, to tame
this monstrous perversion of the choral model: in emulation of his divine
instigators, the poet serves up a regular, orderly and rhythmically marked
enumeration, turning cacophony and jumble into a linear set of discrete
elements. Catalogue style and content are emphatic here: the fivefold
repetition of ἄλλοτε, in three instances in verse-initial position and accompanied by δ' αὖτε or δ' αὖ, prefaces each item in the delineation of the
confusion of divine and bestial sounds that the monster can imitate.[16] In
what is effectively an *agôn* between two rival manifestations of chorality,
one Olympian, the other the final manifestation and literal 'sounding' of
the heterogeneity and hybridity that characterized the earliest generation of
Titans and gods, the Muses emerge as the clear winners. The stratagem
recurs in the aftermath to the battle between Zeus and his challenger. While
the buried Typhoeus continues to generate what is multiple, the winds
described as so various and dissonant that they – unlike their Olympian

[14] Goslin 2010, 354.   [15] Goslin 2010, 361.
[16] For the strict organization underlying the passage, see Nooter 2018, 24.

counterparts, the three 'good' winds listed at 870 – 'rage with evil blast' (874), the Hesiodic account can accommodate these cacophonous phenomena within the second catalogue presented at 871–76. Built into the depiction of the fate visited on this final antagonist is not just the ordering of sound but of motion too: while the malignant Typhoean winds 'fall' on the seas, churn up the waters with their 'whirling' and 'scatter apart' (διασκιδνᾶσι) ships, the poet again subjugates this unregulated and disordered motion to syntactical structuring devices, using acoustic echoes and repeated terms additionally to temper their randomness.

The rule of thumb that these examples from archaic hexameter poetry suggest, that it takes a chorus to deliver a catalogue, finds confirmation in early choral lyric and in what is perhaps the most outstanding instance of the list's incorporation in that genre. As part of their passage of self-description, the chorus of Spartan maidens performing Alcman's first *Partheneion* includes a by-the-book catalogue, made up of both items and names (64–77):

> οὔτε γάρ τι πορφύρας
> τόσσος κόρος ὥστ' ἀμύναι,   65
> οὔτε ποικίλος δράκων
> παγχρύσιος, οὐδὲ μίτρα
> Λυδία, νεανίδων
> ἰανογ[λ]εφάρων ἄγαλμα,
> οὐδὲ ταὶ Ναννῶς κόμαι,   70
> ἀλλ' οὐ[δ'] Ἀρέτα σιειδής,
> οὐδὲ Σύλακίς τε καὶ Κλεησισήρα,
> οὐδ' ἐς Αἰνησιμβρ[ό]τας ἐνθοῖσα φασεῖς·
> Ἀσταφίς [τ]έ μοι γένοιτο
> καὶ ποτιγλέποι Φίλυλλα   75
> Δαμαρ[έ]τα τ' ἐρατά τε ϝιανθεμίς·
> ἀλλ' Ἀγησιχόρα με τείρει.

Neither of any help is a surfeit of purple, nor a chased golden snake-bracelet, nor a Lydian circlet, pride of violet-eyed maids, nor Nanno's tresses, not even godlike Areta or Thylaces and Cleesithera, nor will you go to Ainesimbrota's house and say: 'let Astaphis stand by me, and let Phillyla and Damareta and lovely Wianthemis look upon me, but Hagesichora effaces me'.

What the list presents is a group of eleven maidens, introduced in the form of three adornments – metonymns for their wearers – and then eight names (excluding the extra-choral Ainesimbrota). Like Hesiod and

Homer, the composer underscores plurality by setting against this group
of self-cataloguing girls a single *chorêgos*: Hagesichora. Here I adopt the
reading and interpretation of line 99 proposed by several commentators
on the piece:[17] because Hagesichora performs like a decad – in accordance with the model given in the proem to the Catalogue of Ships –
with her single voice, she can sing 'over and above' the eleven, the
number that should most likely be restored in the preceding line. Like
Helen and Typhoeus before her, this supremely skilled singer takes the
form of an ensemble, her vocal powers surpassing those of the chorus
whose performative and expressly choral skills their preceding inventory
put on show.

The elevenfold enumeration delivered by the chorus does not stand
alone in the poem. As Emmett Robbins' careful analysis details,[18] it
closely parallels the list with which our extant fragment opens. At the
start of the papyrus' legible portion is Polydeuces' name, followed by a
verb signalling the nature of what comes next, *alegô* – a negation of and
play on the cataloguing verb *par excellence*, *katalegô* –[19] that introduces
the list of Hippocoontidae. Not only do eleven members make up both
catalogues, but in each instance a pre-eminent pair, both invested with
equine associations, surpasses the ensemble, the Tyndaridae outmatching
the opposing fraternity, Agido and Hagesichora (likened to prize-winning coursers) their choristers. If, as commentators suggest, these two
chorêgoi are playing the part of the Leukippidae abducted by the Tyndarid
twins and worshipped in Spartan cult, then relations, equine and other,
become still more intimate. As for the maidenly aggregate, just as the
Hippocoontidae form a band of brothers, and are cousins of the
Tyndaridae, so kinship ties link the eleven-strong troupe that declares
Hagesichora their cousin (52). Through this act of choral projection, the
choreutes equate themselves with the members of this first catalogue
(while serving as correctives to their moral failings), instantiating each
of the names making up the list. Ferrari alerts us to a further feature of the
opening account, which she reads as a *thrênos*, an enumerative commemoration and celebration of the dead of the Spartan community.[20] An
heroic epithet would have accompanied each brother's name, creating
that rhythmic repetition characteristic of laments and that will be detailed
in Sections 2 and 3.

---

[17] See Robbins 1994, 10 with earlier bibliography.   [18] Robbins 1994, 13–15.
[19] Perceau 2002, 16–35 analyses the term closely.   [20] Ferrari 2008, 120–21.

2 Choral and Catalogue Morphologies

Postponing discussion of other catalogues embedded in choral poetry, I first return to the larger question addressed in this chapter: if, as argued above, archaic sources demonstrate tight connections between the 'set-piece' catalogue and its execution by a choral group, then how might we explain that affinity? Moving beyond the intuitive notion that a multiplicity of items requires plural performers, do deeper relations exist between catalogue poetry and choruses, and are these discernible in the ancient textual and visual evidence?[21] In attempting some answers, I begin with the morphology of the chorus – its make-up, the interactions between its different members, its organization, formations and movements through space – and demonstrate that catalogues in archaic and epic possess closely corresponding features.

In Benjamin Sammons' definition of a catalogue, whether made up of two or multiple members, it is 'a list of items which are specified in discrete entries … no explicit relation is made except for the shared suitability to the catalogue's specified rubric'. He further defines a rubric as 'a stated category or class which legitimates the involvement or exclusion of potential items'.[22] This 'rubric' squares with Calame's delineation of the three most broad-based features that determine membership of a maiden chorus: ties of kinship, locality and age (all the girls belong to one time of life).[23] These map still more narrowly onto the common criteria for inclusion in a catalogue: just as so many real and mythical choruses form sororities or find a parent or other relation by way of lead member (in addition to the Muses and Graces, we encounter the Pleiades, Nereids, Asopids and Hyades), so kinship ties unite the members of the extended family groupings that structure the *Catalogue of Women*, or the list of ancestors in Diomedes' genealogical recitation at *Il.* 6.146–211. There are any number of examples of 'epichoric' choruses, among them the Deliades, Karyatides and the maidens on Aegina featured in Bacchylides 13, who celebrate the local (ἐ[πιχω]ρίαν, 92) festival on their island in song and dance and are

---

[21] Here I build on the insights of Carruesco 2010, 386 and his more generalized and text-based explanation; the overlap is based on 'la similitud morfológica de una unidad articulada a partir de una pluralidad de miembros, como en el más profunda de la función, que es precisamente la capacidad activa de generar esa articulación'.

[22] Sammons 2010, 9. While he goes on to draw some distinctions between catalogues and lists, the former marked by a degree of elaboration, he grants that the division is a very narrow one, and here I do not differentiate between the two, using now one term, now the other.

[23] Calame 1997, 26–34.

also neighbours (89).[24] Analogous to these are the entries in some catalogues, or parts thereof, whose presence in the list is determined by geographical proximity: the suitors enumerated by Telemachus at *Od.* 16.247–53 all come from nearby islands (they belong to the same age class too) while the several women clustered at the start of Odysseus' list of underworld heroines share a Boeotian origin.

Beyond membership within an overarching 'rubric', studies of catalogues in early poetry have isolated a variety of syntactic principles that serve by way of armature or scaffolding device. Most simply, parataxis, sustained by bare connectives, these often repeated in a rhythmic sequence marked by the occurrence of the expressions in the same position in the hexameter line. While Dolon's list of the Trojan allies in *Il.* 10.428–34 uses the conjunctions καί and πρός to link the different contingents introduced one after the other, the expressions τε and καί, sometimes combined, coordinate the list of Nereid names at *Il.* 18.38–49. Enumerating his sequence of liaisons in *Il.* 14.317–27, Zeus introduces each conquest with the term οὐδέ, anticipating the structure of the second catalogue in Alcman's first *Partheneion*, that likewise prefaces the name of each chorus member with οὔτε and οὐδέ; as in the Iliadic instance, each term often occurs in first position in the line (cf. Tyrt. 12.1–9).

Compare to this the visual representation of choruses on Geometric and early classical vases, which similarly depict each chorus member as a discrete but interlinked item. In many instances only their joined hands connect the performers, a motif that serves as an iconographical equivalent to the verbal conjunctions.[25] Transposing this device to the animal realm, a black-figure Droop cup from the sixth century's final decade shows three men dressed as bulls who dance from left to right, each one holding on to the tail of the performer in front of him.[26] Just as poets frequently individualize the entries in a list through the addition of a distinguishing epithet, so artists use a variety of devices to singularize particular performers. The chorus of the 'twice seven' occupying the top frieze of the familiar François Vase of ca. 570 (Fig. 0.5), and whose storied bands stacked one on the other have been compared to the catalogue-like sequence of scenes on the Iliadic shield of Achilles,[27] offers a prime example of this simple

---

[24] Several of these examples receive more detailed treatment later on in the discussion.

[25] Just as parataxis is classified as what Aristotle terms εἰρομένη λέξις or the 'strung-along style' at *Rhet.* 1409a27, so Lucian views a chorus as the 'necklace' at *Salt.* 12, each chorister like a bead placed on a connecting string. For 'roped together' dancers, see Langdon 2008, 176 and my discussions in earlier chapters.

[26] Oxford, Ashmolean Museum 1971.903.

[27] Notopoulos 1949, 22 styles the vessel the '*locus classicus* for parataxis in vase painting'.

arrangement. Each chorister wears a different dress and bears a different name, while their clasped hands join each dancer to his or her neighbour. Much like the epithets given each Hippocoontid in Alcman's first maiden song are the different shield devices that distinguish the individual dolphin riders in the chorus on the red-figure psykter by Oltos of ca. 520–510 (Fig. 8.11); in this instance too, singularization coexists with the homogeneity established by the riders' identical poses, mounts and costumes and the refrain inscribed in the same position above each rider, which functions like the repeated elements observed in the shaping of poetic catalogues. Enunciation of the inscriptions would reinforce the collective quality of the chorus, the blending of all voices into one and their rhythmic unity: each dipinto reads 'on the dolphin'.

A second simple organizational device within epic lists is a 'first to last' structure, frequently marked by such temporal expressions as πρῶτος, ἔπειτα and τότε.[28] This enumeration may also coincide with another frequent feature of Homeric catalogues, the suggestion that the speaker visually scans a scene, whether in the mind's eye or as he or she performs the list.[29] As Dolon enumerates the Trojan allies at *Il.* 10.428–34, he presents the sequence of contingents according to their (recollected) localization in space (note the 'positioning' verb ἔλαχον at 430); similarly, the placement of each scene on the surface of Achilles' shield, one set after, above or below the next, seems to dictate the order of the Iliadic poet's cataloguing narrative. The *teichoskopia* in *Il.* 3 spells out the nature of the list as a visual survey: Priam questions Helen on what he sees on the plain beneath him while she, acting as 'focalizer' here, responds by enumerating the individual heroes as she also views them each in turn. Different forms of *εἴδω occur in lines 163, 169, 194, 225 and 226, a motif reinforced by the interlocutors' focus on each hero's appearance. Again choral morphology, with each chorister positioned one after the other, corresponds to this sequencing structure. In the case of Alcman's parthenaic ensemble, its second catalogue may form a piece with the performers' current deployment; quite plausibly, as the singers process or dance before their audience, they list their members' accessories and names in accordance with their positions in the chorus line, much as with the ordering of the inscribed names on the François Vase.

Beyond these primary devices, many lists display a more complex degree of artistry. Poets may introduce hierarchy and a progressive elaboration or

---

[28] Perceau 2002, 98 with examples.
[29] For discussion, see Perceau 2002, 108–09; this is also a point taken up in Section 4.

diminuendo through the addition or subtraction of epithets and/or by including additional information concerning the more privileged member(s). In the terms Christopher Faraone uses when a gradual *auxêsis* occurs, and one that manifests itself in the expanded space allotted to an item that stands solo in a line or extends over more than one, such lists culminate in a 'superlative name cap' flagged by the terms πλεῖστον, μάλιστα or other superlative.[30] There is a ranking here, a move from less significant objects, sites or individuals to those whose distinction depends, among other possible properties, on their high value and cost, outstanding artistry, social status and previous or subsequent importance in the narrative. Often the individual singled out occupies the first or last place in the birth order, a position that coincides with his or her place in the list; so the daughters of Celeus in the *Homeric Hymn to Demeter* 109–10, where final position is reserved for the eldest, or Hes. *Th.* 137; there Cronus is both the last born of the offspring of Okeanos and Gaia and the closing entry in that catalogue. Indeed, the passage well illustrates the ordering devices that Faraone observes: a bare connective joins the first eight names, distributed four per line, while only two names, complete with epithets as indicators of their greater importance, appear in the third line; allowed two lines and two superlatives is the final child, destined to succeed his father and who alone is the subject of the clause, the one to whom the poet uniquely gives agency and emotion (133–38):

Οὐρανῷ εὐνηθεῖσα τέκ' Ὠκεανὸν βαθυδίνην
Κοῖόν τε Κρεῖόν θ' Ὑπερίονά τ' Ἰαπετόν τε
Θείαν τε Ῥείαν τε Θέμιν τε Μνημοσύνην τε   135
Φοίβην τε χρυσοστέφανον Τηθύν τ' ἐρατεινήν.
τοὺς δὲ μέθ' ὁπλότατος γένετο Κρόνος ἀγκυλομήτης,
δεινότατος παίδων, θαλερὸν δ' ἤχθηρε τοκῆα.

Having bedded with Ouranos, she bore deep-eddying Okeanos and Koios and Kreios and Hyperion and Iapetos and Theia and Rhea and Themis and Mnemosyne and gold-crowned Phoebe and lovely Tethys. After these last-born was crooked-counselled Cronus, the most awesome of her children and he hated his vigorous father.

Just such hierarchical patternings structure the choral collective where we witness divisions between one or several members and the rest. Visual representations distinguish the *chorêgos* most simply by placing him or her in the lead or final position in the chorus line, a primacy sometimes underscored by the addition of an accessory, more elaborate clothing or increased stature. Hierarchy within an overall unity appears on the black-figure cup from Argos, dated to ca. 600–590 (Fig. 7.6) cited in earlier chapters,[31] where a single mantle covers the nine female choristers who all display the same hairstyle; at the line's head, the artist positions a maiden who is the only garland-carrier. A Geometric water pitcher in Munich shows a line of ten girls,[32] identically dressed in long robes; while the lead figure lacks any distinguishing feature, the last one wears a crown. The distinction accorded the third dancer on a late eighth-century Geometric hydria from Aegina (Fig. 5.2),[33] whose skirt is chequered differently from those worn by her fellow choreutes, might similarly supply a visual device for establishing leadership when the dancers form a ring.

Faraone well explains the privileging of Calliope, introduced last and given an entire line with superlative, in Hesiod's list of the nine Muses at *Theogony* 76–79, noting that it suits the thematic concerns of the passage in which she appears;[34] might the artist of a Corinthian aryballos of ca. 600 have had her primacy in that now-canonical poem in mind when he painted the Muses on his pot?[35] The vessel shows two groups, with three women in each, identified by the inscriptions Mousa and Mousai, while a further figure, labelled Kalliopa, is singled out from the rest; she appears separately, led by Apollo with his lyre. On the François Vase, dated to a decade or two later, Calliope likewise stands out among her fellow Muses, each identified by name: she not only leads the line, but the artist further establishes her pre-eminence by her frontality and by equipping her with an instrument, the syrinx. In this instance, as Luca Giuliani points out,[36] the artist seems both to echo and to revise the Hesiodic account. Where the poet reserves the final position for this capstone goddess, Kleitias has reversed the sequence by placing her in front. Since the other eight Muses process in exactly the order proposed in the *Theogony*, the change seems deliberate and, in Guiliani's view, suggests the artist's participation and intervention in an existing poetic tradition. More narrowly, the artistic design, which combines a chorus in procession with a sequence of names, brings out the chorus-catalogue affinity; following the prompt given by the dipinti, a viewer might read out the identifying tags and in so doing recite not the Hesiodic catalogue, but Kleitias' revisionary version.

---

[31] Berlin, Antikensammlung F 3993. See Chapters 6 and 7 for additional discussion.
[32] Munich, Antikensammlungen 6228 with Calame 1997, 22.
[33] Berlin, Antikensammlung F 31573.   [34] Faraone 2013, 300–01.
[35] See Wachter 2001, 57 for this and other vessels where the Muses are identified by name.
[36] Giuliani 2013, 122–24.

The topmost frieze of the François Vase (Fig. 0.5) anticipates the arrangement on the band below, again signalling the primacy afforded the *chorêgos*, the correlate to the singling out of the catalogue's first or last entry. Whereas the other youths wear cloaks over their tunics and process empty-handed, Theseus alone is dressed in a full-length robe under a richly decorated cloak and carries a lyre whose strings he plucks with his left hand. That he is group leader, and the most important, the diminutive figure of the nurse facing him further emphasizes; and while all the other names appear above the choreutes, his uniquely occurs beneath. This visual singling out of the pre-eminent name forms part of the larger catalogue which this scene also includes: like the 'catalogic' recitation elicited by the chorus of named Muses on the krater's shoulder, a viewer reading off the list of identifying labels, and even reciting these in rhythmic fashion so that the sounds coincide with the processional step of the participants, effectively performs a catalogue reminiscent of the enumeration of chorus members in Alcman's first *Partheneion*.[37] On the Corinthian aryballos cited in the previous chapter and dated to the early sixth century (Fig. 8.2), the distinction claimed by the lead dancer and *chorêgos* also declares itself; he too occupies the start of the chorus line, where, viewing from left to right, we encounter this prize-winner before the rest. A standout among his otherwise indistinguishable followers lined up in pairs behind him, 'Pyrrhias' alone is named in the accompanying inscription that accentuates the height of his leap.

Ring composition and internal patterning act as other structuring devices underpinning catalogues in poetic sources. We encounter the first several times in the *Theogony*, where the poet encloses the list of Nereids by the double mention of their father Nereus 'who bore them' at 240 and 263.[38] The name of the last listed daughter, Nemertes, prepares the way in sound and sense for the second mention of her 'infallible' father by introducing the property of 'unerringness' that he also possesses. A second, smaller ring occurs in the catalogue's first half, demarcated by the repetition of Amphitrite, first and last, at 243 and 254. Two rings, a larger one enclosing a smaller, likewise structure the itemization of Okeanos' progeny, his multiple daughters and sons; lines 337 and 365–66 delineate the larger circle, while 346 and 362–63 bookend the internal ring. A similar

[37] Cf. the black-figure cup showing a chorus of dancing Nereids treated in Chapter 5 (Fig. 5.4), where the inscription accompanying each of the differently costumed nymphs again suggests a catalogue of names that a viewer might recite. In this instance however, the artist creates only a simulation of a list since the dipinti are nonsense inscriptions.

[38] See Faraone 2013, 308–09.

arrangement is visible in Alcman's first *Partheneion*, where chorus line and catalogue design coincide. Prior to its self-introduction, the chorus draws attention to its *chorêgoi*, first Hagesichora, then Agido; following the closure of the list of the adornments and names of the individual members of the band, the singers return to their point of departure, now naming Hagesichora first and Agido second. The early seventh-century oinochoe from Pithekoussai cited in previous chapters (Fig. 3.0) supplies a visual parallel. Here the two all but identical male figures, both executing the same step, frame what may be a representation of the *geranos*; reinforcing the symmetrical design are the oars each youth holds, which form the boundaries to the scene.

Additional patterns in textual catalogues depend on verbal, acoustic and rhythmic relations between the different parts. Anadiplosis, homoioteleuton and isocola are common stylistic features that create affinities between two or more items that may be separated by other elements in the sequence. For all the apparent parataxis in the catalogue of Nereids at *Il.* 18.37–51, the poet introduces a series of internal combinations, repetitions, variations and progressions through the placement of the names and their assonance and alliteration: so Κυμοδόκη τε appears at the end of 39 while Κυμοθόη τε begins 41. Picking up on the suffix of her sister's name, but granted a new prefix, Ἀμφιθόη then enters at 42. The phrase καὶ Καλλιάνειρα forms the closing element in 44 while this nymph is then audibly paired with Καλλιάνασσα, who is also preceded by καί and likewise stands in verse-final position in 46.

Such internal forms of iteration and patterning also occur in visual representations of choral collectives, prompting viewers to perceive relations between discrete dancers sometimes adjacent, sometimes positioned at different points in the file. The painter of the chorus on the neck of a Late Geometric hydria in Rome duplicates features in some of the performers, and not in others:[39] while many carry only branches, others are additionally equipped with wreaths, establishing connections between dancers otherwise dispersed in the line. From ca. 550 comes an Attic black-figure krater by the BMN Painter (Fig. 4.5)[40] with a choral procession of men on the outside (the dolphins on the internal rim confirm the marchers' choral identity); different designs on the participants' gowns, as well as the alternation between those carrying staffs and those with drinking horns, construct visual echoes and variations. Paralleling the very intricate connections in the poetic catalogues devised by poets is the Polledrara hydria

---

[39] Rome, Villa Giulia 1212.   [40] Paris, Musée du Louvre CA 2988.

from the Grotta of Isis at Vulci, dated to ca. 575–550 and cited in Chapter 7 (Fig. 7.8),[41] which shows on its lower register the dance executed by the Athenian maidens (probably the *geranos* with its twists, turns and combination of linear and circular dancing) rescued by Theseus from the Cretan maze. Here the painter devises an interlinking arrangement evocative of the performance's intricacy: each chorister places one hand on the wrist of the next figure in the line while reaching with the other past her immediate neighbour so as to grasp the back-stretched arm of the next-but-one member of the troupe. To turn from choruses on vases to those on sacred architecture, the dancers on the metopes of the temple of Hera II at Foce del Sele adopt a variety of poses;[42] separated by another representation of a dancing pair occupying its own metope, two of the larger company lift up their skirts with their left hand so as to perform.

As the examples from Homer and Hesiod already cited demonstrate, two chief structural principles are visible in catalogues from the hexameter repertoire: one linear or paratactic, which may additionally involve the progressive amplification or diminishment of the members in a ranked arrangement, the other determined by the creation of units of repetition and association that turn linearity into several circles or one grand ring. These overarching structures not only neatly dovetail with the two principal choral formations, processional and circular, but their frequent co-presence within a single catalogue resembles the ways in which choral dancing so frequently involves alternations between the two modes of performance. The Hesiodic presentation of the Muses' circular dance followed by a processional descent cited at this chapter's start corresponds to the motions of the chorus on the shield of Achilles in *Il.* 18; here the youths and maidens sometimes turn in circles, as the simile of the spinning potter's wheel clearly indicates, and then switch off into their lines or 'ranks'.

The visual representations suggest a further choral formation: the convergence of two discrete choral lines, sometimes so as to fashion a 'v'.[43] In one early instance, two groups of choral dancers, one female, the other male, circle around the neck of a hydria of ca. 700 by the Analatos Painter; a phorminx-player appears at the juncture between the two.[44] More complex in its design is a Late Geometric skyphos from the Kerameikos (Fig. 2.6,

---

[41] London, British Museum 1859.0227.50.

[42] For discussion and illustration, see Marconi 2013.

[43] For discussion of this somewhat debated formation, see Calame 1997, 37 drawing on the treatment in Crowhurst 1963, 293–98.

[44] Athens, National Archaeological Museum 313.

with Chapter 2),[45] whose internal frieze displays three different choral ensembles; between a line of girls and one of boys a group of female figures appears, who seem to dance independently of the rest and who alone do not join hands; following the male dancers, a second line of girls appears. Again phorminx-players lead each of the segmentations. We might compare catalogues with gender divisions, such as that of the sons and daughters of Okeanos at Hes. *Th.* 337–70, where Tethys' role in giving birth to them (346) serves as the 'meeting point' between the two sets of progeny. On the diminutive lekythos by the Amasis Painter cited in Chapter 7 (Fig. 7.10), nine women divided into two groups, of three and six, perform a ring dance, their subdivision indicated by a seated aulete and a lyre-player who bracket each ensemble. Stephen Lonsdale notes further distinctions: the group on the lyre-player's left place their hands over the wrists of their fellow dancer, while those in the other chorus more simply link hands.[46] As in the hexameter examples of choral dancing, linear and circular motion here coexist: the interlinked hands of the six, together with the more vigorous step that three of their number perform, suggest a ring dance, while the smaller, more measured motions of the trio evokes a processional formation. The musicians are the place at which the lines converge. One final large-scale example, rendered in stone not clay, belongs to the representation of the chorus members in the frieze on the Hall of Choral Dancers, created in the fourth century's second half in Samothrace. According to a recent reconstruction,[47] the stone-cutters would have represented an unbroken sequence of dancers moving in two directions, one shorter and one longer, that comprised some 912–20 figures; converging towards the main façade as they moved from the south-west corner of the building, the two groups would have met up in the middle of the frieze.

No such juncture occurs in one final arrangement that characterizes both choruses and catalogues. In Homer and Hesiod, two uncoordinated lists may follow one another, as in the enumeration of top-rank horses that follows the catalogue of ships in *Iliad* 2. A comparable division occurs in the stacked presentation of a female and then male chorus on an Aeginetan hydria (Fig. 5.2), each occupying its separate band,[48] or on the mid-sixth-century Attic krater just cited, where the chorus of men processes on the outside while dolphins gambol around the interior rim. But for all their spatial separation, in this instance the artist has nicely suggested the affinities between the paradigmatic nature-based dolphin troupe and its human

[45] Athens, National Archaeological Museum 874.   [46] Lonsdale 1993, 215–17.
[47] Marconi 2010, 122.   [48] Berlin, Antikensammlung 31573.

counterparts in the civic sphere: tipping up the vessel so as to drink from it, the viewer would see the two choral collectives merged into one.

3   'Generic Contamination' in Homer, Bacchylides and Corinna

Two questions inform the close readings of three passages from archaic and classical poetry presented here. First, can we go beyond the broad-based parallels observed above and discern in these texts their composers' more explicit recognition and exploitation of the affinities between choruses and catalogues? And second, what in the epic passage points to its choral derivation or more properly coexistence in the form of a composition performed by a chorus before a collective audience, and, conversely, where do the choral poets acknowledge the hexameter tradition's use of the catalogue and their borrowings from that genre? Where most commentators assume that several of the catalogues in choral poetry, including those treated here, necessarily derive from prior hexameter sources, my discussion suggests more bilateral relations: the introduction of a catalogue within both hexameter epic and choral lyric offers an instance of what has been styled 'transgenericity' or boundary crossing, where a composer in one genre embeds within his or her piece a mode of discourse drawn from a very different performance tradition.

3.1   *The Homeric Catalogue of Ships*

For the chorality informing the most 'purple' of all Homeric catalogues, my reading takes its cue from a treatment of the passage by Bruce Heiden and builds on his discussion.[49] As part of a larger argument that aims to demonstrate the curiously populist or demotic orientation of the Catalogue and its privileging of the common soldier and the community that he has left behind over the aristocratic heroes who dominate the other portions of the poem, Heiden suggests that this extended enumeration does indeed conform to its prior characterization in Cedric Whitman's discussion.[50] This is, in Whitman's phrase, a 'hymn to the army' in more than a rhetorical sense insofar as it includes features more typical of lyric than of hexameter poetry, and most closely parallels a lyric lament, a threnody such as would be performed by a civic chorus at a funerary ritual

---

[49] Heiden 2008b, esp. 145–152.   [50] Whitman 1958, 262, cited by Heiden 2008b, 129.

on behalf of those who had lost their lives at Troy. Among the chief lyric fingerprints identified by Heiden are the use of refrains characteristic of choral laments and which give to the movements described a 'rhythmic performance dimension comparable to dance';[51] the ways in which the poet invites us to view the vessels not just as soldiers advancing in their ranks but as members of choral collectives processing in their 'stichic' formations (the expression νέες ἐστιχόωντο closes four of the lines); and the use of diction that suggests parallels between the structure of the crews and that of a choral ensemble and identifies those who assemble the contingents as their *chorêgoi*-like leaders.[52] While Heiden focuses all but exclusively on the appeal to the Muses and the inventory that follows, I want first to look at the events immediately preceding the invocation before noting some additional elements in the list of ships consistent with a lyric composition. Further support for the argument, I go on to suggest, can be found in later sources that, with evident echoes of the Homeric account, more patently 'choralize' naval armadas and/or their crews, and imagine these as participants in spectacles of song and dance.

The preamble to the Catalogue very much prepares the ground for what follows. Like Odysseus who cannot question his 'chorus' of heroines and identify its members before first placing them in line, so the Iliadic poet begins by sorting and demarcating the companies that his inventory will include.[53] Following Nestor's proposal that the mass of assembled but undifferentiated troops be separated by tribe and phratry (*Il.* 2.362), this followed by an interlude of a sacrifice and meal, the leaders then carry out the proposed division (κρίνοντες, 446). A simile allows the audience to visualize the action (474–76):

> τοὺς δ', ὥς τ' αἰπόλια πλατέ' αἰγῶν αἰπόλοι ἄνδρες
> ῥεῖα διακρίνωσιν, ἐπεί κε νομῷ μιγέωσιν,   475
> ὣς τοὺς ἡγεμόνες διεκόσμεον ἔνθα καὶ ἔνθα …

Just as goatherds easily divide up the broad herds of goats when they mingle in the pasturage, even so the leaders divided and marshalled them here and there …

The verb used in 476 means more than just 'to divide and marshal' and includes the aesthetic dimension more visible in its uncompounded form, κοσμέω. Thucydides would later use διακοσμέω of the organization-cum-

---

[51] Heiden 2008b, 149.   [52] Heiden 2008b, 149.

[53] Indeed, sorting and enumeration seem to dominate book 2 to an unprecedented extent; see in particular 125–29.

decking out of the Panathenaic procession (1.20.2.10; cf. 6.57.1.3), while, later still, Xenophon of Ephesus' description of the *pompê* celebrating the Artemisia selects the verb in uncompounded form for the simultaneous ornamentation and orderly positioning of the parthenaic chorus in its line (1.2.4). The fourth-century Athenian Xenophon, in a passage cited in an earlier chapter where he comments on how the exemplary housekeeper groups her different pots and pans according to their type prior to their enumeration, spells out connections between the act of division, the order-liness and aesthetic harmony that results and choral arrangement (*Oec.* 8.19–20):

> καλὸν δὲ καὶ ὃ πάντων καταγελάσειεν ἂν μάλιστα οὐχ ὁ σεμνὸς ἀλλ' ὁ κομψός, [ὅτι] καὶ χύτρας [φησὶν] εὔρυθμον φαίνεσθαι εὐκρινῶς κειμένας – τὰ δὲ ἄλλα ἤδη που ἀπὸ τούτου ἅπαντα καλλίω φαίνεται κατὰ κόσμον κείμενα· χορὸς γὰρ σκευῶν ἕκαστα φαίνεται, καὶ τὸ μέσον δὲ πάντων τούτων καλὸν φαίνεται, ἐκποδὼν ἑκάστου κειμένου· ὥσπερ καὶ κύκλιος χορὸς οὐ μόνον αὐτὸς καλὸν θέαμά ἐστιν,

> no serious man will smile when I claim that there is beauty in the order even of pots and pans set out in neat array . . . There is nothing, in short, that does not gain in beauty when set out in order. For each set looks like a *choros* of utensils, and the space between the sets is beautiful to see, when each set is kept clear of it, just as a circular chorus is a beautiful spectacle in itself . . .

Choral ordering frequently depends on the *chorêgos*, and so the troops' disposition in *Iliad* 2 ends by spotlighting this figure as he stands among the soldiery (477–81):

> μετὰ δὲ κρείων Ἀγαμέμνων
> ὄμματα καὶ κεφαλὴν ἴκελος Διὶ τερπικεραύνῳ,
> Ἄρεϊ δὲ ζώνην, στέρνον δὲ Ποσειδάωνι.
> ἠΰτε βοῦς ἀγέληφι μέγ' ἔξοχος ἔπλετο πάντων   480
> ταῦρος· ὁ γάρ τε βόεσσι μεταπρέπει ἀγρομένῃσι·

> Lord Agamemnon there among them, like to Zeus delighting in the thunderbolt with regard to his eyes and head, and to Ares in his waist and Poseidon in his chest, just as a bull is pre-eminent among the herds. For he is conspicuous among the gathered cows.

The term used of Agamemnon, μεταπρέπει, regularly signals the chorus-leader, likewise distinguishing Nausikaa as she leads her attendants in the dance in *Od.* 6.109. With a very similar expression, the chorus of Alcman's *Partheneion* styles Agido ἐκπρεπής (fr. 1.46 *PMGF*); and even as the hero-bull is conspicuous among the cows, so Agido 'appears outstanding as if one placed among a grazing herd a perfect horse, a prize-winner'.[54] It is, once again, the fourth-century Xenophon who explicitly compares a company of soldiers, where each man occupies his proper and predetermined place within the larger group, to a well-functioning choral ensemble. Approving his son Cyrus' suggestion that a general should arrange competitions in the warlike exercises required of soldiers in battle, Cambyses remarks that, by virtue of this regimen, 'you might see military companies that are just like choruses' (ὥσπερ χοροὺς τὰς τάξεις ... θεάσῃ,) (*Cyropaideia* 1.6.18). Still more apposite is Xenophon's return to the analogy in *Cyropaideia* 3.3.70: in disarray following the failure of their first assault, the troops 'halted in their regular position, knowing more accurately than a chorus each one the spot in which he should stand (ἔστησαν κατὰ χώραν, πολὺ μᾶλλον χοροῦ ἀκριβῶς)'.[55]

The Iliadic scene of the troops' sortition ends just before the invocation to the choral Muses, the point of transition between the narrative and the start of the Catalogue. In the divinely channelled list that follows, the chorality latent in the preceding episode becomes more marked. Not only, as Heiden notes, do the ships resemble members of choral collectives processing in their ranked formations, but we also witness the stationing of their crews when these reach their destination, where they now stand ready to resume the performers' part. In his account of the Boeotian contingent at 525, the poet notes how the ships' leaders 'placed the ranks' (στίχας ἵστασαν), an action that has a second sounding when Ajax similarly positions his twelve ships alongside those of the Athenians: στῆσε δ' ἄγων ἵν' Ἀθηναίων ἵσταντο φάλαγγες (558). As earlier chapters have detailed, the verb used for this stationing would acquire a choral dimension, assuming its place in the standard phrase that, from the late archaic period on, is used for the setting up, deploying or instituting of a chorus: χοροὺς ἱστάναι. The *kosmêsis* that occurred in the preliminaries to the Catalogue and that returns in the description of the Athenian Menestheus also suits a choral context; the Athenian hero receives special mention for his skill in arranging and adorning (κοσμῆσαι, 554) his company, an activity also placed in an agonistic context – only Nestor can 'vie' (ἔριζεν) with him – and which anticipates later rival *chorêgoi* and their ensembles who engage in competitive displays (see below). Consistent with the leaders' conduct is that assigned to the men making up their crews,

---

[54] See the discussion in Chapter 4.
[55] Note the verbal play between χώραν and χοροῦ. Cf. Xen. *Mem.* 3.4.4.

whose role it is to 'follow' these pre-eminent individuals: ἕποντο, regularly placed in final position in the line where it supplies one of the 'lyric' refrains, anticipates the choral deployment observed in Pindar's second *Partheneion*, where the *chorêgos*' daughter 'will follow' (ἕψεται) her father as he, 'stepping (στείχων) forth with his foot', is enjoined to 'lead (ἀγέῳ) the way' (fr. 94b.66–67 S.-M.).

If Heiden's larger claim is correct – that the Catalogue of Ships casts the vessels, their leaders and their crews in the role of choruses performing threnodies before civic audiences – then the Iliadic passage would offer our first extant example of an amalgam that becomes more visible in later literary and visual sources and that Chapter 5 already sampled; as the texts and images cited there illustrated, painters, poets and writers of prose accounts regularly equated sailing on and rowing ships and participating in choral troupes, fashioning multiple and detailed interfaces between the two activities. Also apparent in two of the literary sources where these parallels occur is the third element so foregrounded in the epic representation, the catalogue structure adopted by Homer for his review. The parodos of Euripides' *IA* not only unmistakably echoes the diction of the invocation prefacing the Catalogue of Ships, but prompts its audience to expect a Homeric-style enumeration of the vessels making up the Greek fleet: so the chorus' initial declaration at 164–73 that its desire to see 'the army of the Achaeans and the ships of the demigods' (cf. *Il.* 2.493) spurred its journey to Aulis, an eagerness then recalled at 231, where the singers again remark that they came 'for the count of ships' (ναῶν δ' εἰς ἀριθμὸν; cf. *Il.* 2.488, 493). Other verbal and structural cues also point the audience back to the epic model. In the first antistrophe, the chorus amends its opening list of the items it came to see, adding a third element; now the objects of its desirous spectatorship are not just the 'armament and the arms-bearing tents of the Danaans' but also 'the mass of horses' (189–91). Anticipating this, Homer follows up his enumeration of the ships with a brief coda, a list of the 'best of the horses' (*Il.* 2.763).

The description that follows continues to advertise its affinity not just with the Iliadic precedent, but with hexameter catalogues more broadly. Much as in Hesiodic and Homeric lists, ring composition undergirds the parodos,[56] whose second portion takes the shape of a smaller ring: Ajax heads the sequence of heroes initiated at 192, and a fresh mention of the hero closes out the song's descriptive portion at 288. Also reminiscent of the v-formation cited in Section 2 is Achilles'

---

[56] See Zeitlin 1993, 160.

capstone appearance as the final hero (as suits his pre-eminence in the expedition) in the epode concluding the first portion of the parodos; serving as a pivot between the two lists, it is Achilles whose ships then take the lead in the account's second part. At the very close of the final antistrophe, the singers re-sound the reference to the Homeric invocation of the Muses at the start of the poet's naval catalogue: where the bard completed his invocation with a renewed declaration of the impossibility of his task 'unless the Olympian Muses ... were to remember (μνησαίαθ') as many as came' (492), Euripides' choristers observe that they 'will guard the memory (μνήμην σῴζομαι) of the gathering of the host' (302; trans. Zeitlin).

Alongside the pronounced choral theme visible in Thucydides' report of the Sicilian armada mustered at the Piraeus that I earlier detailed is, once again, the conscious reuse of the Homeric template. The 'catalogic' and enumerative facet of the historian's account and its glances towards its Iliadic precedent emerge most clearly at 6.31.1, where Thucydides computes the '4,000 men of arms, 300 horse, and 100 galleys out of Athens itself' and goes on to reckon up the many ships that Lesbos and Chios contributed. Fresh cataloguing occurs when the historian turns his attention to the different kinds of vessels – there are one hundred empty galleys in all, sixty of one kind, forty of another – and the different categories of rowers offer fresh matter for another extended list. Together with the drawing up of this balance sheet, Thucydides also lards his description with emphatic declarations of the pre-eminent nature of the expedition, surpassing all that preceded it not so much in size as in its splendour and the length of its journey. Apparent in these statements is a challenge to and attempt to cap the Iliadic depiction of the fleet; if the Trojan armada constituted the largest gathering of Greek ships in 'historical' memory, then the present assemblage displaces it on multiple counts. In passing, Simon Hornblower suggests a different point of continuity and revisionism: like the list designed to showcase the virtuosity of the epic *aoidos*, this seemingly endless delineation might have similarly been composed for a kind of showpiece public display: 'it is ... worth asking if the description as a whole (30–32.3) might have been intended for recitation ... We can almost hear the burst of applause at a symposium or Olympia, when Th. reached the words ἠπείγοντο ἀφικέσθαι'.[57]

[57] Hornblower 2008, 390.

3.2   Catalogues in Choral Poetry: Enumerating the Asopids

The commingling of the two very different genres and performance traditions is no less evident in my examples from choral poetry, both featuring a
single parthenaic group, the nine daughters of the river god Asopos. As
Chapter 5 detailed, in compositions by fifth-century choral poets as well as
in a Euripidean stasimon and some visual representations, these maidens
repeatedly serve as objects of 'choral projection', supplying one among the
archetypal troupes of singer-dancers whom latter-day ensembles select as
choice paradigms. But chorality is not the only characteristic typically
assigned the Asopids. Instead, as the passages from works by Bacchylides
and Corinna treated here illustrate, poets may also place them within a
catalogue frame, introducing Asopos' daughters and their histories in the
form of a list. In the standard view, this mode of presentation results from
both composers' debt to a pre-existing hexameter source, the [Hesiodic]
Catalogue of Women, where, following Martin West's broadly accepted
view,[58] the Asopids were a central presence in the poem's fourth book. In
place of this straightforward act of appropriation, I will suggest that
Bacchylides and Corinna are no mere epigones: maintaining the sorority's
signature choral identity, they also draw on the hexameter tradition to
which the maidens simultaneously belonged, thereby engaging in that
'transgenericity' already practised in the Catalogue of Ships.

In Bacchylides' ninth ode (already treated in Chapter 5), which celebrates the Nemean victory of Automedes, an athlete from Phleious, Asopos
and his daughters form the focus of lines 47–65, where the singers make
this local riverine 'family' the object of their praise. Positioning the father as
their first *laudandus*, the singers hail their addressee before acknowledging
the daughters that contribute to his renown:

> στείχει δὶ εὐρείας κελε[ύ]θου
> μυρία πάντα φάτις
> σᾶς γενεᾶς λιπαρο-
>   ζώνων θυγατρῶν, ἃς θε.[ο]ί   50
> σὺν τύχαις ᾤκισσαν ἀρχα-
>   γοὺς ἀπορθήτων ἀγυιᾶν.
>
> τίς γὰρ οὐκ οἶδεν κυανοπλοκάμου
>   Θήβας ἐΰδμα[τον πόλι]ν,
> ἢ τὰν μεγαλώνυ]μον Αἴγιναν, μεγ[ίστ]ου   55
> Ζην]ὸς [ἃ πλαθεῖσα λ]έχει τέκεν ἥρω

---

[58] West 1985, 100–03. See too Larson 2002, 139–40.

...]δε σω[. . . . . . .]ου,
[ὃς γ]ᾶς βασά[νοισιν Ἀχ]αιῶν
    ]υ[   ]α.

τ[--◡---◡--]   60
α[. . . . . .]ω[. . . . . .ε]ὔπεπλον [..].[]

ἢ[δὲ Πειράν]αν ἑλικοστέφα[νον]
    κ[ούραν, ὅ]σαι τ' ἄλλαι θεῶν
ε[ὐναῖς ἐδ]άμησαν ἀριγνώτ[ο]ις π[α]λαι[οῦ]
[παῖδες αἰ]δο[ῖ]αι ποταμοῦ   65
    κε[λ]άδοντος·

on a wide path travel in all directions the countless reports of your progeny, the shining-girdled daughters whom the gods with good fortune have settled as rulers of unsacked streets. For who does not know of the well-built town of dark-haired Thebe or of the renowned Aegina, who (came to) the bed of great Zeus and bore the hero . . . who the land of the Achaeans by the tests..? . . . fair-robed . . . and (Peirene the maiden) of the twining garland, and all those others who won glory when bedded by gods, venerable daughters of the ancient sounding river.

Despite the lines' lacunose condition, we can assume that the chorus would have listed at least some of the river's progeny: with Thebe heading the enumeration, at least two or three other daughters would have then been named, each picked out by an epithet.[59] David Fearn suggests the inclusion of Cleona in line 61, and Peirene, the Corinthian spring, seems a likely candidate for 62.[60] The catalogue then ends in the fashion typical of hexameter lists, with a summary reference to 'all those other venerable daughters of the ancient sounding river'. As G. B. D'Alessio observes of the lines,[61] this is the 'passage which comes closest to a Hesiodic catalogue in the preserved song of Pindar and Bacchylides', and he further notes that the ἤ at the start of line 62 (the term retained by some editors although many prefer the ἢ[δέ proposed by Jebb, also used in my citation) suggests 'that the list may have been coordinated through the disjunctive particle, recalling the ἢ' οἵη formula' that gives the *Catalogue of Women* its other name. As argued earlier in Chapter 5, both these and the surrounding passages demonstrate the connections between this 'catalogued' ensemble and the current singer-dancers, and turn the Asopids into the originary performers onto whom the latter-day celebrants project themselves.

[59] Maehler 1982–97, 2.186 makes various proposals concerning the other names.
[60] Fearn 2003, 361.   [61] D'Alessio 2005, 237.

Corinna similarly looks back to the Hesiodic account, preserving both the catalogue structure and matching up the mythical maidens in the list to the members of her choral group. In her so-called 'Daughters of Asopos' fragment (fr. 654 *PMG*), the Asopids appear in the early portion of the work, presented in the manner of an enumeration that featured the abductions and marriages of at least some of the nine:

> ὧν Ἠγ[ιναν γε]νέθλαν
> Δεὺς[ἀ]γαθῶν
> πατρο[ἐ]ς,
> Κορκού[ραν δὲ κὴ Σαλαμῖ-]
> ν' εἰδ[' Εὔβοιαν ἐράνναν]   5
>
> Ποτι[δάων κλέψε πα]τείρ,
> Σιν[ώπαν δὲ Λατοῖδα]ς
> Θέσ[πιαν τ'   ἔστιν ἔχων·

> of these (daughters) Zeus, giver of good things, (took) his child Aegina ... from her father's ... while Corcyra (and Salamis) and (lovely Euboea) (were stolen) by father Poseidon, and (Leto's son) is in possession of Sinope and Thespia ...

The term ὧν, 'of these', suggests the start of the inventory, with Aegina in first position, then followed, in rapid succession, by Corcyra, Salamis, 'lovely Euboea', Sinope and Thespia and probably ending with Tanagra, whom Hermes stole. Fresh enumerative design follows in the more complete lines at 12–17:

> τᾶν δὲ πήδω[ν τρῖ[ς μ]ὲν ἔχι
> Δεὺς πατεὶ[ρ πάντω]ν βασιλεύς,
> τρῖς δὲ πόντ[ω γᾶμε] μέδων
> Π[οτιδάων, τ]ᾶν δὲ δουῖν   15
> Φῦβος λέκτ[ρα] κρατούνι,
>
> τὰν δ' ἴαν Μή[ας] ἀγαθὸς
> πῆς Ἑρμᾶς

> and of your daughters father Zeus, king of all, has three; and Poseidon, ruler of the sea, married three; and Phoebus is master of the beds of two of them, of one Hermes, good son of Maia

Apparent in the account is the repetition characteristic of catalogue structures. The phrase τὰν δέ stands at the start of three of the entries and, typically too, the presentation assumes a hierarchical arrangement, here a diminuendo: the conquests of Zeus, 'lord of all', occupy two full lines in contrast to the shorter phrases allotted the less exalted gods. The numbers also gradually diminish, three apiece for the first two 'top' and older gods, two for Apollo, one for Hermes – in effect a ranked and chronologically differentiated victory catalogue, observing ties of kinship and birth order. The close of the list is resumptive, as the divinities and sisters are reassembled into their original aggregate: following the dictates of love, the now collective gods will 'go in secret to [Asopos'] house and take for themselves nine maidens' (18–21).

As already noted in my earlier discussion, it has been commonplace to remark on the ways in which Corinna's extant poetry recalls the [Hesiodic] *Catalogue of Women*, and nowhere is this more apparent than in this fragment. The later poet's concern with genealogy and ancestry through maternity emphatic here recalls the *Ehoiai*, and Larson notes that a second likely reference to the Asopids in fr. 644 *PMG* 'hints at familiarity with the Catalogue'; in her further observation, 'both the Catalogue and Asopid daughters provide a marked, hierarchical catalogue of progenitor gods who beget a race of semidivine heroes'.[62] The enumeration of the Asopids also points back to the Odyssean catalogue of heroines, and not least for the Boeotian focus prominent in both; among those whom Odysseus encounters is Antiope, another daughter of Asopos according to Asios fr. 1 Davies, who has strong links to Boeotian sites and cults. The sequence of four that follows, Alkmene, Megara, Epikaste and Chloris, all share connections to the region.[63]

According to the suggestion made in Chapter 5, the present-day singers, whether the chorus of youths staging Bacchylides' epinician ode or the Tanagran *parthenoi* for whom Corinna most probably composed her songs, map their identities onto the mythic group of dancer-singers. If this is correct, then the performers of these works more narrowly assume the sequential and circular arrangements as well as the pairing and other combinations in which, as Section 2 explored, catalogue items regularly arrange themselves. One of the visual representations of the Asopids also cited in Chapter 5 further supports my claim that the sisters lend themselves to this inventory structure. The bronze statue group that Pausanias saw at Olympia (5.22.6) showed Aegina being abducted from the company of her sisters. In describing the monument, the periegete names Nemea, Harpina, Corcyra and Thebe, with Asopos seemingly positioned last in the line, as suits his leadership and paternal roles. As though reading off each identifying label as he might have encountered it, perhaps inscribed

---

[62] Larson 2002, 50–51 with additional parallels.   [63] As detailed in Larson 2000, 198.

beneath the successive images, Pausanias effectively performs a mini-catalogue, complete with internal repetition and a superlative name cap for the last item enumerated:

> ἀνέθεσαν δὲ καὶ Φλιάσιοι Δία καὶ θυγατέρας τὰς Ἀσωποῦ καὶ αὐτὸν Ἀσωπόν, διακεκόσμηται δὲ οὕτω σφίσι τὰ ἀγάλματα. Νεμέα μὲν τῶν ἀδελφῶν πρώτη, μετὰ δὲ αὐτὴν Ζεὺς λαμβανόμενός ἐστιν Αἰγίνης, παρὰ δὲ τὴν Αἴγιναν ἕστηκεν Ἅρπινα ..., μετὰ δὲ αὐτὴν Κόρκυρά τε καὶ ἐπ' αὐτῇ Θήβη, τελευταῖος δὲ ὁ Ἀσωπός.

> the Phliasians also dedicated a Zeus and the daughters of Asopos and Asopos himself: the images are divided and marshalled thus: Nemea is the first of the sisters and after her comes Zeus seizing Aegina; next to Aegina stands Harpina ... after her is Corcyra with Thebe next; last of all comes Asopos.

Striking here is the use of the verb διακοσμέω, also selected in the earlier sources for the division, marshalling and adornment of the choral ensemble. And visible too in Pausanias' report is both the disruption of the chorus line when Zeus intervenes to carry off Aegina, and the way in which a catalogue, in the manner of the chorus, can nevertheless assimilate new items: the expression that introduces the god, μετὰ δὲ αὐτήν, recurs in a subsequent phrase where the enumeration continues, μετὰ δὲ αὐτήν again.

4 Choruses and Catalogues as Objects of Display

So far I have explored a variety of continuities between choral performances and catalogues: whether chorus members are those who typically articulate the lists, or match the syntax and structures distinctive of the genre in their modes of self-presentation, organization and/or formations, or map their identities onto the particular items within the inventories they perform, the evidence offers multiple realizations of the affinities between these two disparate modalities. This closing section treats one further facet of their kinship, here located in the specific idioms applied to each and that are freshly realized when choral songs and catalogues (and combinations of the two) then undergo transformation into written form. As this specialized diction suggests, throughout their trajectories, catalogues and choruses present themselves as objects of display, artefacts that invite spectators' visual review and that preserve their signature visuality and material character when they assume documentary and specifically epigraphic form.

4.1 Displaying Choral Lyric

As both this study and many other recent works concerning chorality demonstrate, among the signature properties of performances of song and dance, whether as choice motifs in early vase painting, or in written sources where narrators, internal viewers and the chorus itself offer self-descriptions, is their outstanding visibility: *choreia* is, for all that the remnants we possess consist of no more than words or static images, an institution that, like the *agalmata* to which a chorus explicitly and implicitly likens itself, attracts attention and delight by virtue of its 'spectacularity', its appeal to the eyes and capacity to elicit what might be styled the 'choral gaze'.[64] For Laura Swift, this is a property that belongs more markedly to parthenaic ensembles than to those composed of youths or older men,[65] and while Swift's point is well taken, any chorus in performance would enjoy the same heightened visual allure and 'attractivity', whether this is expressly flagged or not.[66] A device regularly conveys this quality in both the painted and textual sources, the presence of an audience that watches and, in the verbal descriptions, not infrequently marvels at the spectacle. Vase painters have an even more economical way of signalling the chorus' visual appeal: the introduction of a painted eye into the scene.[67] Among the more striking instances of the motif occurs in the singular image on an oinochoe in Boston of ca. 735–720 showing, exactly aligned with its spout, two figures clasping hands, symmetrically positioned on either side of a warrior shown upside down (Fig. 9.0);[68] prominently placed in this inverted figure's mid-section is a wide-open eye, whose design the artist multiplies in the lines that make up the image's frames.[69] Generally viewed as a representation of an acrobatic

---

[64] I take the phrase from Carruesco 2016, 96. In the subsequent chapter, I expand this term to encompass the chorus' own particularized mode of seeing.

[65] Swift 2016; absent from the latter, she observes, are the self-descriptions that distinguish the former, with their focus on the choristers' garments, accessories and skilled movements. As Swift argues, these elements are all designed to draw attention to the girls, typically on the cusp of marriage and dancing in the ancient equivalents of the débutante ball, and to present them as attractive and compelling objects of spectatorship.

[66] Among numerous possible examples, all cited in other chapters, see *Il.* 18.506, Alcman's first and third *Partheneia*, Bacch. 17.102–06 and Eur. *IT* 1143–52.

[67] As observed by Carruesco 2016, 96–100, who cites the example given here together with others.

[68] Boston, Museum of Fine Arts, Richard Norton Memorial Fund 25.43.

[69] Carruesco 2016, 96.

Fig. 9.0 Black-figure oinochoe attributed to The Concentric Circle Group, ca. 735–720 B.C.E. Boston, Museum of Fine Arts, Richard Norton Memorial Fund 25.43. Photograph © Museum of Fine Arts, Boston.

dance,[70] the inclusion of the eye would incorporate the theme of viewing into the dance scene, effectively replacing the 'spectator figures' so frequent in other paintings depicting performing groups.[71]

Rather than rework this much travelled ground, we might look instead to a verbal expression all but unique to archaic and classical choral poetry and that demonstrates how this hallmark visuality is simultaneously embedded in the diction particular to the genre. As a discussion by Alexander Nikolaev documents,[72] choral poets from the archaic through to the late classical age imagine their song and dance performances as something that the composer/*chorêgos* 'shows' to his or her performers and to the larger audience at the spectacle: in the noun-verb expression reserved

[70] See Langdon 2008, 52 with earlier bibliography.
[71] In Chapter 10, I discuss a painting that is the subject of an ecphrasis; here the image of the chorus is similarly surrounded by eyes in the form of the jewelled border.
[72] Nikolaev 2012; the author's larger argument is entirely different from my own.

for this act of display, poets couple forms of *deiknumi* with an object referring to their compositions. Building on Nikolaev's account, I want both to review his several examples and additionally to focus on the other terms chosen in these passages so as to highlight the factural elements that their authors assign to *choreia* and that form a piece with the reifying verb; this objectification of the performance finds its counterpart in the representation of the items listed in the catalogues which, as the sequel to this discussion shows, draw on the same vocabulary.

The earliest examples of 'showing the song' belong to Alcman, and, on one of the two occasions where the phrase occurs, to the description of a *parthenos* whom the lines celebrate (fr. 59(b) *PMGF*):

> τοῦτο ϝαδειᾶν ἔδειξε Μωσᾶν
> δῶρον μάκαιρα παρσένων
> ἁ ξανθὰ Μεγαλοστράτα.

> the yellow-haired Megalostrata, one blessed among girls, displayed this gift of the sweet Muses.

In the view of Athenaeus, who preserves the lines (13.600f–601a), the passage stands evidence of how the poetess Megalostrata – with whom Alcman was supposedly passionately in love – exercised her charms through her conversational skills. But remove the erotic filter through which this much later reader (following Chamaeleon, who records the view of Archytas) approaches these lines, which he couples with a second and expressly amorous fragment, and they allow for a very different interpretation.[73] The reference to Megalostrata's status as *parthenos* makes it likely that she is imparting a *partheneion* to her maiden chorus. The 'gift' not only, as Calame observes,[74] involves the totality of the performance, its words, music and dance, but also assimilates that spectacle to an ostensible good, one that Megalostrata has been given by her divine patrons. In much this fashion, the poetic ego at the outset of Pindar's third *Nemean* proposes to 'share' (κοινάσομαι, 12) the *hymnos* that he has likewise received from the Muses with his waiting chorus of youths, who cannot begin their song without the wherewithal with which to perform or, in this instance, to 'build' since the opening of the ode imagines them as the 'craftsmen' (τέκτονες, 4) of the piece.

Alcman uses the phrase a second time, here describing another act of speech or, in this context, a performance of song (fr. 4.4–7 *PMGF*):[75]

---

[73] See Calame 1983, 561 and Nikolaev 2012, 544.   [74] Calame 1983, 562.
[75] NIkolaev 2012, 546 n. 13 cites other instances where γήρυμα is used of song.

σαυ]μαστὰ δ' ἀνθ[ρώποισ(ι)
γαρύματα μαλσακὰ[5
νεόχμ' ἔδειξαν τερπ[
ποικίλα

and wondrous soft utterances they showed new to men ...... intricately
fashioned

The four adjectives well suit the act of display and again align the verbal
contents of the composition with an object, here one that is precious and
intricately worked. In the hexameter sources and as other chapters have
noted, *thauma* is first and foremost the response that works of extraordinary craftsmanship, especially those able to simulate the appearance of
life (e.g. Pandora's crown in Hes. *Th.* 584, Odysseus' brooch in *Od.*
19.229), provoke in viewers and that audiences of choral dancing no
less frequently experience. Coupled here with the verb and noun, the
term alerts us to the middle ground occupied by these 'utterances' (the
γῆρυς from which the γαρύματα are derived typically refers to the sound
emitted by the human voice);[76] it indicates their potential materiality
even as we hear them sung in their current choral context. 'Softness', a
property twice used by Homer of *epea* (*Il.* 1.582 and 6.337) and then by
Pindar of song (*Nem.* 9.49), also gives to what is heard a haptic quality
that depends on its possession of a surface, its 'feel'. Applied to song in
Alcman's fr. 14.3 *PMGF*, νεόχμ' again looks in two directions. While
Telemachus deems best the song that is the newest (*Od.* 1.351–52),
elsewhere in Homer novelty enhances the value of a highly wrought
object, one so remarkable that it requires not the usual one or two, but
three epithets: Lykaon's eleven chariots are καλοὶ πρωτοπαγεῖς νεοτευχέες
(*Il.* 5.194). Neatly Timotheos would reprise the Homeric term in a phrase
which exactly brings out both its verbal and material dimensions and that
reimagines those chariots in the guise of song:[77] invoking Apollo, the
composer and citharode hails the god as 'you who foster the Muse newly
wrought (νεοτευχῆ) with the golden kithara' (fr. 791.202–03 *PMG*).
ποικίλα, describing something richly patterned that combines multiple
materials and designs, sounds this notion of skilled artisanship anew and
contributes to the ongoing objectification of the vocalizations.

Pindar follows the earlier usages when he introduces the formula at
Isthm. 8.47–48:

---

[76] As noted by Calame 1983, 423. In his suggestion, the lines would again refer to the poetic gift
bestowed on the singer by the Muses.

[77] See Ford 2013, 329–30, who suggests that the poet is drawing on the song-as-chariot motif.

καὶ νεαρὰν ἔδειξαν σοφῶν
στόματ’ ἀπείροισιν ἀρετὰν Ἀχιλέος

> and the voices of the wise revealed the youthful excellence of Achilles to
> those who had been unaware of it

Since Pindaric *sophoi* are invariably poets,[78] here imparting their knowledge to an as yet unschooled audience, and Achilles’ youthful exploits were as much a topic of choral as of hexameter verse, including of Pindar’s own, nothing prevents these singers from being composers and performers of lyric poetry. The act of ‘showing a song’ gains quasi-canonical, even hieratic status in Pindar’s second incorporation of the phrase in his fragmentary *Hymn to Zeus*, where Apollo puts his ‘upright *mousikê*’ on display, μουσικὰν ὀρθὰν ἐπιδεικνυμένου (fr. 32.1 S.-M.).[79] Context suggests the Muses as the god’s primary audience here, the divine chorus members who, like the maidens in Megalostrata’s troupe, will then freshly display in performance what their *chorêgos* has shown them, viz. the theogony-cosmogony that is his subject matter. The adjective ὀρθάν encompasses multiple facets of this Apolline *mousikê*; in addition to suggesting the visual, ethical and acoustical qualities of the divine art, it may also have a somatic dimension, looking to the person of the chorus leader who, like Aineas, the *chorodidaskalos* of *Ol.* 6 whom Pindar likens to the straight baton or *skutalê* (see Chapter 8 for the figure), is the still and upright centre around whom the Muses dance.

In a near contemporary example from choral poetry, Bacchylides introduces the phrase into what sources identify as a *hyporcheme*, a dance-song (fr. 15):

οὐχ ἕδρας ἔργον οὐδ’ ἀμβολᾶς,
 ἀλλὰ χρυσαίγιδος Ἰτωνίας
χρὴ παρ’ εὐδαίδαλον ναὸν ἐλ-
 θόντας ἁβρόν τι δεῖξαι (μέλος suppl. Blass)

> This is no time for sitting still or tarrying, but we must go to the richly
> built temple of Itonia of the golden aegis and display a delicate/luxuriant
> (song-dance)

---

[78] As noted, with additional examples, in Nikolaev 2012, 547.

[79] See Chapter 6. Σ *ad* Pind. *Ol.* 2.1a (i.58Dr.), picks up on the notion of this choral ‘showing’ in glossing the expression ‘lyre-ruling’ that modifies *humnoi* at the outset of that ode: ‘this means “those which rule over lyres”; for lyres follow hymns, by means of which they have been shown forth (ἀπεδείχθησαν)’.

The adjective used of this performance again signals a variety of properties, delicacy, fastidiousness and luxuriousness among them, and it also, as Nikolaev notes, appears in descriptions of playing on stringed instruments and of singing in several earlier poets (e.g. Anacr. 28.2, Stesich. 35.2). But most suggestive of its suitability for 'display' is the ongoing assimilation of the *melos* with a dedication. At its performance site, the temple of Athena Itonia, where the staging of the piece would have formed part of the celebration of the goddess, the song and dance and the choreutes who present it to their audience will take their place among other enduring artefacts, those material votives that likewise invite spectatorship and are set up for display in the correspondingly finely fashioned (εὐδαίδαλον) building. What we witness in the lines is the initial stage of this larger act of dedication, the processional departure of the celebrants equipped with their *choreia* as though it were an object that the lead performer were conveying to its destination point. In this ritual context, the character of the composition-in-performance coincidentally proves consistent with the quality that more broadly informs the larger occasion – its 'elegance, refinement, and luxury'.[80]

A further and later instance of 'showing a song' occurs in lines 110–14 of the fourth-century paean to Dionysus composed by Philodamus of Scarphea, where the gesture of ostentation fulfills the injunction of Apollo (Pindar's originary displayer of his *mousikê*):

> (θεὸς κελεύει...)
> δε[ῖξαι] δ᾽ ἐγ ξενίοις ἐτεί-   110
> οις θεῶν ἱερῷ γένει συναίμῳ
> τόνδ᾽ ὕμνον, θυσίαν δὲ φαί-
> νει[ν] σὺν Ἑλλάδος ὀλβίας
> πα[νδ]ήμοις ἱκετείαις.

(The god commands) to show this hymn for his brother to the family of gods on the occasion of the annual feast of hospitality and to make a public sacrifice at the panhellenic supplications of blessed Hellas.

Besides correlating the poetic votive with a second gift in the form of the 'public sacrifice', a correspondence made apparent by parallel syntax and diction ('show the hymn'/'display the sacrifice'),[81] there is a further twist to the usage here. Since the poem was preserved as an offering to the god in

---

[80] Mackil 2013, 160. Cf. Sappho's eight-line continuation to fr. 58 V. preserved in *P.Oxy.* 1787. In this undoubtedly choral composition that celebrates the (lost) delights of *choreia*, the poetic ego begins by declaring 'I love ἀβροσύναν', selecting a term that encompasses just these qualities.

[81] As noted by LeVen 2014, 312.

the form of an inscription on a stele set up at Delphi in 340/39, an individual encountering the lines would see the conceit realized: the text-cum-offering does indeed show in material, visible form the paean that once existed in performance, and that may do so again as the inscription receives a reading or is re-enacted by virtue of the text's existence.

While it could be objected that φαίνω and other 'showing' terms are used of epic recitations and non-choral songs, there are further reasons for positing a privileged relation between δείκνυμι, the pointing verb, and *choreia*. As already noted, *deiknumi* is never coupled with anything but choral lyric when song is the object of the verb, nor do any of the nouns for song and dance in the passages just cited appear together with the verbs for speaking or singing found with other types of poetry.[82] Strikingly too, as Nikolaev demonstrates, the comparative evidence from Vedic texts, where the cognate expression is found with nouns referring to 'songs of praise', contextualizes the phrase in the relations between *laudator* and *laudandus* and encodes the offering of praise in the form of song that the poet presents to the god on his patron's behalf.[83] With this Vedic material at hand, we can see a pre-existing relation between the composition that requires a showing and a more tangible gift to the gods and the role they share as visual phenomena that make manifest mortal celebrations of divinities and the services rendered them.

But there is a much later and non-poetic text (absent from Nikolaev, but frequently cited in this study) that adds a conclusive item to this inventory insofar as it conceives of the entirety of *choriea* as something both crafted and then displayed, while also taking us back to Hephaestus' chorus as an object being concurrently forged and viewed on the penultimate shield band. According to a scholion's gloss on *Il.* 18.591–92a, the metal-crafted scene recalls the original performance of the *geranos* devised on the occasion of Theseus' escape from the labyrinth with the 'twice seven':

> ἐξελθὼν δὲ μετὰ τὸ νικῆσαι ὁ Θησεὺς μετὰ τῶν ἠϊθέων καὶ παρθένων χορὸν τοιοῦτον ἔπλεκεν ἐν κύκλῳ τοῖς θεοῖς, ὁποία καὶ ἡ τοῦ λαβυρίνθου εἴσοδός τε καὶ ἔξοδος αὐτῷ ἐγεγόνει. τῆς δὴ χορείας τὴν ἐμπειρίαν ὁ Δαίδαλος αὐτοῖς ὑποδείξας ἐποίησε.

> Coming out after the victory, Theseus along with the youths and maidens wove just such a chorus in a circle for the gods in such a way that there was in it the going in and exiting of the labyrinth. And Daedalus showing them it, fashioned the skill of *choreia*.

---

[82] Nikolaev 2012, 556.   [83] Nikolaev 2012, 553.

Alongside the chorus leader as the weaver of his ensemble, Daedalus, the master mortal craftsman, 'makes' the reified craft of *choreia*, displaying it to the choristers so that they can perform the *geranos*. The scholion's choice of ποιέω positions this singular artisan, as Homer does, as paradigm for Hephaestus who, in the Iliadic account, similarly 'makes' many of the forged scenes prior to the choral one. The choice of the compound form, ὑποδείκνυμι, highlights the sense of actually pointing; among the meanings of the verb is that of 'to show by tracing out, mark out' and Aristotle selects it for a description of Homer as the one who first 'showed' the *schêma* – a reference often to the physical shape, the figures of the dance, a configuration – of comedy (*Poet.* 1448b36–37). Present in the scholion too is the votive dimension to the choral performance as an object of craftsmanship and display: Theseus constructs the chorus 'for the gods' by way of thanks offering for the safe escape from the labyrinth.

Before leaving the 'ostentatious' choral song behind, it is worth noting one further instance of the trope, albeit in a text that lacks the verb δείκνυμι and that stands as outlier to this study insofar as it most probably dates to first century B.C.E or C.E. and comes from the city of Susa. In a fragmentary inscription recording a hymn composed on behalf of Apollo,[84] here celebrated in his capacity as the Sun god ('Υπερίων, 4), the poet, the otherwise unknown Herodoros, a Greek who was native to the Parthian city, prefaces the transcription of his composition with a header that, I suggest, again positions the song as something 'shown' much in the manner of the works just documented: '[Herodoros, son of Artemon, from Seleukeia erected this] for Ap[ollo]' ([Ἀνέθηκ]ε Ἀπ[όλλωνι Ἡρόδωρος Ἀρτέμωνος Σελευκεύς]).

Reminiscent of Philodamus for the explicit mention of the hymn's status as a votive offering, something that the poet has 'set up' for his divine *laudandus*, the extant lines that follow offer a second indication, or more properly manifestation of the work's insistent visuality, its status as something designed not just for hearing but spectatorship too. In a reiteration of the author's name occupying the midpoint of the opening dedicatory inscription and a more expansive explanation of the circumstances prompting the raising of this terracotta plaque, the opening letters of lines 2–31 form an acrostic. Following the supplements suggested by Franz Cumont, the text's first editor, the whole reconstituted phrase would have spelled out

---

[84] For the text, see Cumont 1928, 89–96, whose version I follow here and Rougemont 2012, nos. 32–33; see too Canali De Rossi 2004, 125. Only fifteen legible lines remain of what would have been a much longer song, running to more than sixty lines. I owe many thanks to Hanna Golab for bringing the work to my attention and sharing her forthcoming discussion of the piece.

'Herodoros, son of Artemon, from Seleukeia on the Eulaios was victorious (νικητής) in …';[85] only an attentive viewer of the plaque, with an eye to letter size, placement and the layout of the stone, would be able to discern the message, effectively a statement of a win, complete with the victor's name, patronymic, place of origin and mention of the occasion – lost due to the inscription's lacunose state – framing the dedication. As Golab acutely observes,[86] the neatness of the acrostic device depends on the fact that its visible declaration of Herodoros' success was dependent on the very circumstances that it revealed: had the poet not taken first prize, his winning song would never have been transcribed this way and the acrostic would have remained indiscernible.

While there is no explicit indication of a choral performance in the extant lines, and the stichic priapeans selected by Herodoros could suit a variety of modes of delivery, there are several reasons for conjecturing a winning entry in a choral *agôn* and for reading the heading as a choregic type inscription, then elaborated in the lines that follow. Both Cumont and subsequent scholars have conjectured that the hymn would have been performed at a festival on behalf of Apollo, perhaps something, in Cumont's view,[87] akin to the Athenian Thargelia or Pyanepsia comprising musico-choral competitions. The mention of 'harvest wreaths' or 'decorated branches', rendered with the rare term εἰ]ρεσιώνας in line 5, might be a pointer to the garlanded performers or to the leafy branches that choristers typically carried and could even describe the dedication of the objects at the doors of the large-scale temple to Nanaia, where the hymn might have been performed (see Pind. fr. 75 S.-M., with discussion in Chapter 10, for a parallel gesture);[88] so too the assimilation of Apollo to the all-seeing sun, illuminating the landscape on which it diffuses its radiance, recalls the many choral tropes that position a divine and super-luminous *chorêgos* as leader of a dancing troupe, and suggestive too is the verb διελίσσ[ει], 'to unfold', in line 8, which echoes the many uses of this verb, typically uncompounded, for the circling chorus.[89] If the work was designed for choral delivery, then it would claim its place among the much earlier compositions considered above as evidence for the distinctive 'showiness' of *choreia* and its self-alignment with more tangible goods set up for display.

---

[85] As Golab 2018 cautions, the term νικητής is conjectural.   [86] Golab 2018.

[87] Cumont 1928, 96.

[88] No findspot is recorded for Herodoros' plaque, but the stones of the temple yielded numerous Greek epigraphic texts.

[89] The terms used by Herodoros for his celebration of Apollo are reminiscent in several ways of the opening of Pindar's first *Pythian*, where the god's power is expressly tied to his lyre, while also recalling Apollo's taming powers, similarly pegged to his musical emissions, in Eur. *Alc.* 578–87 treated in Chapter 4.

4.2   Showing the Catalogue; Cataloguing Choral Poetry

If a choral performance supplies a prime object of spectatorship, then, more curiously, so too does the catalogue. As Section 1 documented, whether the enunciator of the list is the narrative voice or an internal speaker, that individual frequently (although not invariably) depicts him- or herself as representing to an audience a sight either observed at first hand, or one that another eyewitness has earlier transmitted. To recall just a few instances, the Iliadic Muses whose list the poet relays are those whose presence allows them to *see* as well as know all things (so πάρεστέ τε, ἴστε τε πάντα, 2.485), and Odysseus introduces each of the individuals making up the catalogue of heroines at *Od.* 11.254–329 with the expression 'I saw'. The act of looking also frames fifth-century examples of the genre: in Euripides' *Electra*, the review of the decorative devices on Achilles' shield and other armour depends on the autopsy of an individual who came to Nauplia from Troy (452–53), and the chorus of the *IA* prefaces its catalogue of heroes and of ships by noting that it came 'so as to see' (ὡς ἐσιδοίμαν, 171), a theme elaborated at 231–34 and 274–75 and given one last sounding at the ending of the song, where the singers resume their itemizing account by noting that this was the nature of the fleet 'that I saw there' (299–300).

The catalogue's repeated self-presentation as an act of showing verbally what was originally seen by the inventory-maker helps elucidate Herodotus' use of a particular set of terms that all but replicates the formulaic phrase reserved for choral lyric: the expressions are *apodei-knumi*, to point, show or display, and *apodexis*, the noun derived from it.[90] An article by Athena Kirk examining the two expressions within the *Histories* makes several points directly relevant to my argument.[91] As she observes, both verb and noun typically appear in the context of itemized accounts, whether enumerations (e.g. 2.133, 7.118), lists of individuals introduced in chronological sequence (6.53) or various objects and phenomena presented in a catalogue format.

Particularly illuminating is a passage at 2.142 treated in Kirk's discussion,[92] where the historian uses *apodeiknumi* no less than three times in his account of the records of noteworthy people and deeds kept by the Egyptians and known to him from the verbal report in the form of a chronological review of 341 generations supplied by the priests at the temple precinct at Thebes. In this instance, Herodotus' informants are not just transmitting a narrative;

---

[90]   Casson 1914 and 1921 already noted how the two terms describe military inventories in Thucydides, while later epigraphic texts also apply the expressions to official catalogues.
[91]   Kirk 2014.   [92]   Kirk 2014, 28–29.

rather, 'they are making a formal display of generations of the past' in which *apodeiknumi* 'refers … to words, but of a ritualized and performative nature'. Still more important for my purposes is the fact that, as Kirk further notes, each individual included in the list has his 'material correlate on display in the temple in the form of a wooden likeness',[93] one of the *kolossoi* whom the priests simultaneously show their visitor at 2.143 and that seem to stand in a line or other sequential formation:[94]

> ἀριθμέοντες ὧν καὶ δεικνύντες οἱ ἱρέες ἐμοὶ ἀπεδείκνυσαν παῖδα πατρὸς
> ἑωυτῶν ἕκαστον ἐόντα, ἐκ τοῦ ἄγχιστα ἀποθανόντος τῆς εἰκόνος
> διεξιόντες διὰ πασέων, ἐς οὗ ἀπέδεξαν ἁπάσας αὐτάς.

> Thus counting them up and showing them, the priests pointed out to me each of them, being the child of the father, going through all of them from the likeness of the one who died most recently up until they had made a display of absolutely all.

A close parallel to this materialized and spatially linear enumeration appears in an earlier usage of *apodeiknumi*, in Pindar's sixth *Nemean*, where the singers turn to the task of praising the victor and Aegina, his native land (45–47):[95]

> πλατεῖαι πάντοθεν λογίοισιν ἐντὶ πρόσοδοι   45
> νᾶσον εὐκλέα τάνδε κοσμεῖν· ἐπεί σφιν Αἰακίδαι
> ἔπορον ἔξοχον αἶσαν ἀρε-
>   τὰς ἀποδεικνύμενοι μεγάλας

> Broad on all sides are the avenues for those versed in stories [or 'chroniclers'] to adorn this famed island, since for them the Aiakidae supplied an outstanding lot, displaying great deeds of excellence

On an island that was as famed for its sculptures as for its athletes, it seems likely that a home-based audience would think of sculpted images standing alongside the roadside, physical adornments that parallel this verbal display of the multiple paths from which the *laudator* can select. Since those monuments would, typically, accommodate inscriptions recording details of the athletic triumphs and of those who achieved them, they would more literally furnish the chroniclers with the materialized

[93] Kirk 2014, 28 and 29.
[94] For the particular role of *kolossoi*, ritual stand-ins for an absent individual whom the image has the power to re-present, see Steiner 1993.
[95] Also cited by Kirk 2014, 26 who also notes in passing the possibility of victory statues.

versions of the stories that they transform back into the verbal matter that maintains its 'adorning' role.

A second collection, again of objects presented in a spatial arrangement, offers a further instance of the visual display that underlies the verbal catalogues 'shown' by Herodotus, whether in the form of a verbal *apodexis* or in its fresh materialization in the substance of the written text. At 1.51–52, the historian inventories the offerings made by Kroisos at Delphi,[96] patently structuring his account as a 'one-after-the-other' catalogue made up of items whose locations the historian observes as we follow him through the sanctuary (so a silver bowl 'used to stand on the right-hand as you enter the temple'). Elizabeth Kosmetatou has demonstrated how closely in its style and contents the passage resembles the inventories preserved at the site, some stored in the temple archives, others set up for public viewing;[97] although all our extant documents postdate Herodotus, we can assume that earlier versions were available to the historian, who has seemingly drawn on their information and mode of presentation. Much later in the *Histories*, it turns out that the narrator was not the first to compile such a list: according to a report at 8.35, Xerxes had earlier dispatched a portion of his troops to 'inventory the treasures' (ἀποδέξαιεν τὰ χρήματα), presumably directing them similarly to produce a written account of the precious goods that they encountered at the sanctuary.

As Kirk concludes, for Herodotus, an *apodexis* constitutes an inventory or set of catalogued items that 'begins as an accompaniment to a collection, not an autonomous object' and that then devolves into the historian's purely verbal account, becoming a virtual collection that furnishes a 'facsimile of the physical or a usurpation' of what existed in material and visible form.[98] But where Kirk goes on to focus on how the *Histories*, as Herodotus presents his work in the text's well-known *prooimion*, becomes a both written and oral *apodexis* in and of itself, a supersized list of the phenomena and events detailed by the historian, I take for my ending point a handful of inscriptions, most Hellenistic, that bring lists and choral songs into particularly close proximity and that incorporate accounts of earlier choral performances into a strictly catalogue format. These documents, I suggest, offer a final illustration of a central contention of this chapter: that choral performances become the matter of lists while lists retain a latent performativity that may be realized when the events they record then recover their original spectacular and choral form.

---

[96] See Kirk 2014, 20–21 for discussion of the passage.   [97] Kosmetatou 2013, 69–70.
[98] See Kirk 2014, 23; see too 22, 32 and 37.

The combination of choral poetry and catalogue occurs most outstandingly on a document found at Delphi, whose entries are all written in the same third-century hand, and which would originally have listed no fewer than sixteen honorary decrees (in the view of some, all of these would have had poets as the recipients of the benefactions) covering three stelai if not more.[99] Whereas all the other decrees recorded on the stones were passed sometime in the first half of the third century, the one that bestows honours on the Corinthian poet Aristonous dates to ca. 338 and uniquely includes the citation of two of the songs that he composed for performances at Delphi, a paean that immediately follows the decree and a hymn to Hestia, already cited in Chapter 3, inscribed on what would have been the adjacent stele.[100] Within the compass of this document are 'scripts' for not one but three separate performances: the first the public declaration of Aristonous' honours, presumably delivered at a ritual event featuring the announcement of benefactors and that might itself occur in the course of song and dance spectacles,[101] the second and third belonging to the occasions on which choruses danced and sang the paean and hymn. Reading out the portion of the stelai concerning Aristonous, a visitor to the shrine would recreate those moments, celebrating anew the poet and the gods to whom the songs are addressed. The conferral of benefits not only exists as an entry in the larger catalogue of *euergetai*, but is itself presented as a list, an enumeration of the privileges the composer and his family are to enjoy in perpetuity, 'proxeny, the status of benefactor, priority in access to the oracle, privileged seating at games, priority in receiving justice, inviolability during both war and peace time, freedom from all taxes and the same rights as enjoyed by the Delphians'.

While this entry on the stelai supplies the only instance of a direct citation of a song within the larger inscription, the one immediately following it allows the individual who hears the proclamation, or encounters it in written form, to recover elements of the choral performances for which the honorand composed the works that earned him benefactor's

---

[99] *FD* 3:2 nos. 176–93; see *SIG* 449–51 for the texts considered here. For the issue of dating, see Vamvouri-Ruffy 2004, 211–15.

[100] See Alonge 2011, 218 for discussion.

[101] Chaniotis 2007, 54 cites a stele of ca. 130–110 (*SEG* 39, 1243 col. V 27–43) prescribing the order of events on a ritual occasion celebrated at the site, and preserving the words pronounced as a civic benefactor received his crown. The announcement of honours by the herald, the inscription notes, 'should be made during the performance of the *pyrrhiche* dance and the gymnical competitions forever'. In this instance the inscription, which goes on to cite the form the announcement should take, does very clearly supply a script for those regularized pronouncements.

status (the privileges he is to enjoy are listed in almost identical sequence and diction as those gained by Aristonous and would likewise have been declared aloud as the *euergetês* stepped up to claim his crown). According to the account preserved by the text, Kleochares of Athens, styled a ποιητὴς μελῶν, is celebrated for having written 'a processional song and a paean and a hymn for the god, so that the *paides* might sing them at the Theoxenia'.[102] As the entry goes on to detail, these youths, having been instructed in Kleochares' several songs by the *chorodidaskalos* also charged with leading them to the sacred space, should perform them each year at the same ritual event. Again, the terms of the inscription, these presented in linear and sequential format on the stone, invite those who encounter it mentally and visually to recreate the series of events leading up to the songs' performance and perhaps even to supply the element it omits: recalling these or other choral compositions familiar to him, he would supplement the inscription with his recollection of the type of song and dance in which the youths' training and processional movement culminate.

Comparable to this preservation of performance details within a catalogue rubric are a number of other inscriptions, chiefly dating to the second century C.E., recording the officials and other individuals who participated in the delegations sent by cites in Asia Minor to consult the oracle at Claros; included in these lists are the choral contingents who would perform at the sanctuary.[103] Seven choreutes typically accompanied delegates from the nearby Tabai, while Heraklea on the Salbake would send nine. The documents may also detail the nature of these choruses, distinguishing between those made up of *paides*, *êitheoi* and *parthenoi*. One of the more extensive documents from Tabai clearly illustrates the catalogue format, presenting one after the other the names of the delegates, including the priest, the scribe, a *theopropos*, a *didaskalos* and, collectively, the *paides* dispatched for the purpose of 'hymning the god'.[104] The sequential arrangement of the titles and names might plausibly reproduce the order in which the individuals and groups processed at the events in which such delegations participated during their consultation of the oracle and prompt visitors to Claros to witness in the text that original *pompê*. By accommodating the musico-choral element, the inscription also recovers the audible features of the spectacle and specifies the nature of the song appropriate to the event. As in the previous instances, the catalogue uses its different dimensions to recreate what it details: practising the 'readerly visuality' discussed in

[102] *SIG* 450.   [103] For these, see Ceccarelli 2010, 141.
[104] No. 192, with discussion in Robert and Robert 1954, 203–16.

Chapter 8, its succinct and purposefully selective record of events restages the spectacle and invests it with the *kosmos* and harmony that, in Plutarch's description, Nikias' theoric chorus at Delos so outstandingly possessed.

If all the examples just cited are chronologically remote from the archaic and classical age to which the other texts and images treated in this chapter chiefly belong, then a set of more nearly contemporary documents serves to connect these written catalogues from Hellenistic Greece with the earlier material and more particularly with the choralized naval inventories in Homer and Thucydides. This epigraphic cache consists of a series of stelai found in the Athenian agora that would originally have made up at least three documents. The earliest of these, dated to 357/56, are inscribed with small letters on marble blocks and belonged to a collection of records first erected at the Piraeus and subsequently moved to the agora (I 3227 and I 2012a–c).[105] Column II of 2012c lists some thirty-six ships, twenty-five of which are regularly classified as *exairetoi* or 'special'. Of the eleven remaining names, three belong to types of vessels that reappear only in later sources, three to ships of unfamiliar form, three to an unknown category and the two remaining are designated 'first' and 'second' class.[106] Here the emphasis falls not only on the vessel types, but on their equipment and specifically, in what can be discerned, their *pêdalia* or steering oars. A lost section in column V listed the *katablêmata* – hangings that covered the ships – and ropes. Two further fragments (7316 and 7450), from several years after, likewise record the equipment owed by the trierarchs.

For epigraphers, historians and prosopographers, the fragments' value depends on the evidence they supply for individuals, ship types, nautical equipment and the role of documents in fourth-century Athens. Revealing too is the light they shed on how the city financed its fleet: the inventories would have served in the auditing of accounts and the necessary calling in of debts following an individual's term of office, fulfilling much the same function as a second group of inscriptions, *IG* II² 1623, 1628 and 1631, found at the Piraeus and dated to 326/25.[107] As Peter Liddel comments, lists like these 'provided inventories of naval material in the docks and recorded the transactions between naval authorities and the trierarchs, and indicated the probity of the outgoing *epimelêtai*, as well as their fulfillment of obligations as outgoing magistrates about to undergo *euthuna* … As they detailed the conditions of the ships in the yards and the trierarchs responsible for returning them in that condition, they served also as

---

[105] Shear 1995 offers a detailed account that guides my reading here.   [106] Shear 1995, 180.
[107] For these, see the discussion of Laing 1965 and 1968. For more on these inscriptions, see below.

records and checks of obligations performed and debts owed by the trierarchs concerned'.[108] As typically occurs in documents of this kind, the 'book keeping units'[109] are not those who contracted for the boats, or the expeditions they undertook, but the ships themselves.

For my purposes, the fragments' interest depends on different features: first, the ship names recorded in each line. In Julia Shear's detailed analysis,[110] owners chose these designations so as to grant their vessels desirable attributes, flagging their beauty, good fortune, sea-worthiness, civic spirit and other properties that presaged successful ventures. Not only, consistent with the gender of ναῦς, are these ships uniformly feminine – some sharing names with mythological heroines, Procne, Thetis, Amphitrite among them – but many underscore their speed, ease of passage and, very prominently, radiance and 'spectacularity': Phôs, Phanera, Delia, Lampetia, Lampra, Theamosunê and Theama belong to this group. Somewhat more surprising, although a corollary to several other of their qualities, is the vessels' festive character: one boat is called Heortê, another Euphrosunê while Eris and Hamilla suggest participation in a festive no less than martial *agôn*. A further set of names, among them Phêmê, Seirên and Salpinx, assigns the ships vocal or instrumental powers.

A different dimension of the inscriptions illustrates stylistic correspondences between the oral catalogues in earlier hexameter sources and these written lists. For all the information-preserving and bookkeeping impetus determining these records' design, nonetheless regularity, patterning and a variety of internal relations between individual items characterize the stelai; each line of I 2012c, for example, contains two ships' names, with the exception of the final line of each section, where a single name appears; vessels equipped with exceptional features are also allotted an entire line. In this same document, variation distinguishes some anchors from the rest; in four instances they are made from iron while the remainder have no such specification. In columns II and III of 7316, each entry lists the names of the trierarchs in the accusative, followed by a pronoun standing for the equipment fitting out the ship whose name is then supplied; when these items belong to the first of the ships listed under the trierarch's name, a form of the verb 'to owe' precedes it. Shear's discussion of I 7316 and I 7450 notes the repeated use of the expression ἃ/ἃς/ὃν ἐπὶ τήν together with a ship's name, aptly designating these phrases 'formulas'.[111]

---

[108] Liddel 2007, 188–89.   [109] Davies 1969, 311.   [110] Shear 1995, 186–88.
[111] Shear 1995, 182.

Many of these elements reappear in the fragments of *IG* II^2 1623, which originally belonged to a single opisthographic structure erected at the Piraeus and which postdates the agora inscriptions by several decades.[112] Each segment of the reconstructed stone begins with a heading occupying several lines, listing the names, patronymics and demes of the outgoing and newly appointed boards of *epimelêtai* presented in their conventional tribal order; each individual is identified in the dative case, placed after the date by archon; numerical quantities – many of them the same, and positioned at the end of lines – create fresh internal connections, echoes and repetitions. Such pairing through recurrence, the presence of formulaic diction and 'refrains', the specialness of the item which occupies the final line, the distinction afforded certain pieces of equipment and syntactical repetitions, variation and patterning, are typical of hexameter catalogues, introducing the multiple small and larger internal links, audible and visible iterations and ring compositions that recent studies of the genre have illustrated.[113]

The features just described would be apparent even to an analphabetic viewer, and all the more so to the partially literate passer-by who, most likely, would have given these diminutive inscriptions no more than a cursory glance. Approached primarily as visual objects rather than as message-bearing documents, the lettering traversing the blocks of marble – the most eye-catching, translucent and light-emitting of all substances – presents a series of visual patterns and arrangements both similar and disparate displayed against a radiant backdrop. In his study of *IG* II^2 1628, Douglas Laing noted the stone-cutters' selection of Hymettian marble, whose colouring was a natural grey;[114] might some elements or portions of the text have been picked out with paint out so as to heighten their visibility, or simply to invest the block with a measure of artistry and visual appeal not usually associated with administrative documents? If, prompted by a more particularized concern, a viewer stopped to read the contents of a stele, articulating it aloud, the inscriptions' rhythmic and iterative character would become still more evident.

At the risk of pressing the interpretation, I would suggest that the impression conveyed by the stones' design and contents would be that of a large-scale maritime ensemble made up of companies of visually brilliant, swift, young, perhaps colourful and on occasion resonant maidens, each with her own singularity and even, in some instances, pre-eminence as well

---

[112] See Laing 1968.   [113] See Faraone 2013; cf. Sammons 2010, Perceau 2002.
[114] Laing 1968, 248.

as likenesses to the rest. Grouped in their linear and circular formations, the inscriptions enact what Richard Martin has described, à propos of the choregic dedication detailed in the preceding chapter, as 'a carefully choreographed visual ... performance on stone, a dance of the letters',[115] reminiscent of the spectacles devised by poets for live performance on the Attic stage and those depicted in the vase imagery reviewed in earlier portions of this study. To approach these and other written catalogues set up for public display in archaic, classical and post-classical Greece from this altered perspective is to see their performative potential, their capacity to quit their silent and static character and to become participants in spectacles of song and dance.

---

[115] Martin 2007, 50.

10 | Choral Envisioning: Archaic and Early Classical Choral Lyric and Post-Classical Accounts of *Enargeia*

Introduction

In a scene from the third book of Heliodorus' *Aethiopika*, a work generally dated to the early third century C.E., Calasiris, a priest of Isis from Memphis, treats his youthful interlocutor Cnemon to a description of the grand procession of the Thessalian Ainianians to the tomb of Neoptolemos at Delphi. The contents of the Pythia's surprise oracular pronouncement during the occasion, Calasiris observes, was of scant interest to the Delphians gathered for the event, who were much more eager to see the *pompê* that followed. Cnemon fully shares that sentiment. Frustrated by his informant's attempt to abbreviate his narrative by simply remarking, 'when the ceremony was over and the procession had gone by', Cnemon interrupts (3.1.1):

> καὶ μὴν οὐκ ἐτελέσθη πάτερ . . . ἐμὲ γοῦν οὔπω θεατὴν ὁ σὸς ἐπέστησε λόγος
> ἀλλ' εἰς πᾶσαν ὑπερβολὴν ἡττημένον τῆς ἀκροάσεως καὶ αὐτοπτῆσαι
> σπεύδοντα τὴν πανήγυριν ὥσπερ κατόπιν ἑορτῆς ἥκοντα, τὸ τοῦ λόγου,
> παρατρέχεις ὁμοῦ τε ἀνοίξας καὶ λύσας τὸ θέατρον.

> But it is not yet over for me, father . . . your tale has not yet made me (lit. 'set me up as') a spectator of it and when I am exceedingly overcome with eagerness to hear the whole story, and to see the panegyris myself with my own eyes, you pass me by and treat me like one who has come, in the words of the proverb, too late for the festival; as soon as you have opened the theatre, you shut the doors again.

Amending his account, Calasiris then indulges his listener's desire to be, in the older man's rejoinder, a θεωρός, ('spectator' or 'sacred envoy', 3.1.2), supplying Cnemon with a detailed account not just of the sacrificial victims, but of the chorus of Thessalian maidens that follows them, first processing and then performing in dance and song (3.2.1–3):

κόραι Θετταλαὶ διεδέχοντο καλλίζωνοί τινες καὶ βαθύζωνοι καὶ τὴν κόμην
ἄνετοι· διήρηντο δὲ εἰς δύο χορούς, καὶ αἱ μὲν ἔφερον καλαθίσκους – ὁ
πρῶτος χορός – ἀνθέων τε καὶ ὡραίων πλήρεις, αἱ δὲ κανᾶ πεμμάτων τε
καὶ θυμιαμάτων κανηφοροῦσαι τὸν τόπον εὐωδίᾳ κατέπνεον. ἠσχόλουν δὲ
οὐδὲν εἰς ταῦτα τὰς χεῖρας ἀλλ᾽ ὑπὲρ τῆς κεφαλῆς ἀχθοφοροῦσαι πρὸς χορὸν
στιχήρη καὶ ἐγκάρσιον ἀλλήλων εἴχοντο, ὡς ἂν βαδίζειν τε ἅμα καὶ χορεύειν
αὐταῖς ἐγγίνοιτο. τοῦ δὲ μέλους αὐταῖς τὸ ἐνδόσιμον ὁ ἕτερος χορὸς
ὑπεσήμαινεν, οὗτος γὰρ τὸν ὅλον ἐπετέτραπτο μελῳδεῖν ὕμνον· ὁ δὲ ὕμνος
ἦν, ἡ Θέτις ἐπῃνεῖτο καὶ ὁ Πηλεὺς κἀπὶ τούτοις ὁ ἐκείνων παῖς καὶ ὁ τούτου
πάλιν.

There followed some Thessalian maidens, beautifully and deeply girdled
and whose hair was flowing. They were divided into two choruses, of
which one, the first, carried baskets full of flowers and fruits, while the
second had vessels filled with cakes and incense which perfumed the air all
around. The bearing of these burdens, since they were carried on their
heads, did not prevent them from using their hands, but arranged in long
rows, some straight, some slanting, holding each other by the hand, they
marched or danced. The keynote to the melody was sounded by the first
company, to which was entrusted the singing of the whole hymn; this was
in praise of Thetis and Peleus, and then the son of this one in turn.

But the description is still not ample enough to satisfy the overeager youth.
Cnemon interrupts anew, objecting that the account has again fallen short
of its goal; by failing to let him actually hear the words of the hymn sung by
the girls, 'it seems that you want to make me a mere spectator (θεατήν) of
the ceremony, instead of sitting me down as auditor (ἀκροατὴν καθίσας)'
(3.2.3). Again Calasiris obliges, following his full citation of the song with a
more detailed report of the dance, whose impact on the viewers he also
describes (3.3.1):

τοσοῦτον δέ τι ἐμμελείας περιῆν τοῖς χοροῖς καὶ οὕτω συμβαίνων ὁ κρότος
τοῦ βήματος πρὸς τὸ μέλος ἐρρυθμίζετο, ὡς τὸν ὀφθαλμὸν τῶν ὁρωμένων
ὑπερφρονεῖν ὑπὸ τῆς ἀκοῆς ἀναπείθεσθαι καὶ συμπαρέπεσθαι
μεταβαινούσαις ἀεὶ ταῖς παρθένοις τοὺς παρόντας, ὥσπερ ὑπὸ τῆς κατὰ
τὴν ᾠδὴν ἠχοῦς ἐφελκομένους,

So well did the melody harmonize with the dance, and so well did the beat
of the steps suit the cadences, that sound caused the eyes of those watching
to overlook the spectacle and all who were present kept time with the
maidens in their paces as if carried away (lit. 'dragged along after') by the
sounding song ...

As the reader of the passage would perceive, Heliodorus has supplied nothing short of a 'novelized' discussion of how to devise an ecphrasis, filling the exchange with technical terms familiar from contemporary and earlier theoretical accounts of the rhetorical stratagem, and then going on to imagine Calasiris roundly satisfying the requirements that the imperial (and later) handbooks spell out: using *enargeia*, a pictorial and heightened 'visual vividness', the internal narrator effectively does what Cnemon asks of him, transforming him from a listener into a spectator (and back again).[1] Beyond the transition from hearer to seer – so Theon, the author of one rhetorical manual explains, 'ecphrasis is a descriptive speech which brings [literally 'leads'] the thing shown vividly (*enargôs*) before the eyes' (*Progymn.* 118.6, ed. M. Pantillon) while Nikolaos, another handbook writer, similarly states that 'ecphrasis seeks to fashion spectators out of hearers' (*Progymn.* 68, ed. J. Felten) – the exchange more narrowly echoes the terms and conditions of these formulaic definitions. Not only does Cnemon's objection that Calasiris has bypassed him and made him a latecomer pick up on the notion found in many of the theoreticians concerning the way in which the practitioner of ecphrasis should lead his listener by the hand. Also commonplace is the term *theatês* used of the hearer-turned-viewer, the theatrical analogy, the synaesthetic quality of the account together with its 'thick description' (the first-century B.C.E. critic Demetrios recommends just this type of *akribologia*, or fullness of detail, for the practice of *enargeia* at *Eloc.* 209–10) and repeated shifts from the visual to other senses. The inclusion of the response of the crowd, so literally transported by the spectacle that it is compelled to move in turn and follow in the maidens' wake as its engagement assumes bodily form, completes this list of standard features; among the cardinal properties of ecphrases is their ability to create this bond of empathy between the objects of the gaze and the internal focalizers whom descriptions invested with *enargeia* typically accommodate and who model the external reader/hearer's response (see Section 3).[2]

---

[1] In wishing to assume the status of listener again, Cnemon anticipates the Delphians' own passage from viewers to those who give themselves up to the pleasure of hearing alone. Note too how later in the two characters' exchange, Cnemon attributes his impassioned response to Calasiris' exacting description of Charikleia's dress by first remarking, 'It's them! It's Charikleia and Theagenes!' and then observing that the reaction was prompted by the *enargeia* of the account (*diêgesis*): 'I thought I could see them even though they are not here, so vividly and exactly as I have myself seen them did your account show them (θεωρεῖν αὐτοὺς καὶ ἀπόντας ᾠήθην, οὕτως ἐναργῶς τε καὶ οὓς οἶδα ἰδὼν ἡ παρὰ σοῦ διήγησις ὑπέδειξεν)' (3.4.7).

[2] In analogous fashion, the response of the hearer of a visually compelling narrative involves not just the senses but the body too.

Like the programmatic passage from Philostratus' *Imagines* treated at
this chapter's end, which also showcases a maiden chorus in performance,
Heliodorus chooses an expressly choral scene to demonstrate his familiarity with the ecphrastic genre and his ability to play on its conventions.
While Calasiris' revisualization of the procession continues on at considerable length, strikingly it is at the point of the chorus' appearance that the
novelist inserts this 'meta-narrative', in which the listener comments on the
rhetorical mode used by the speaker who witnessed the performance to
deliver his account. Together these two passages bookend this closing
chapter's central question: why, in the ancient view, do choral spectacles
seem to involve what would come, in the imperial period, to be labelled
enargeia, a complex form of envisioning that not only prompts a synaesthetic response and effects the transformation Cnemon seeks, replacing
hearing with autopsy; more than this, why does the archaic and classical
chorus so exactly anticipate what further distinguishes *enargeia*, its power
to bring about an imaginative immersion that allows the latter-day hearer/
reader to arrive at the same inner vision or *phantasia* – not just an image
that reproduces something seen but also one that brings to mind things
absent and remote, even mythical and non-existent – that the scene or
object described had originally elicited? In choosing to exhibit the chorus as
a privileged site for the exercise of *enargeia*, Heliodorus and Philostratus, I
suggest, stand heirs to a tradition that reaches back to some of the very
earliest textual and visual representations of choral spectacles.

While these two texts extend my discussion of *choreia* far beyond the
archaic and early classical period on which I have chiefly focused, they not
only most immediately pick up on the theme of 'spectacularity' explored in
Chapter 9, but also redirect us back to what has been perhaps the keynote
passage throughout this study: the image of the choral performance forged
by Hephaestus on Achilles' shield. Singled out by ancient and modern
readers alike as the 'originary' example of an ecphrasis,[3] this (as I have
argued) most technically virtuosic of the shield bands – and the verbal
description that it gives rise to, placed in penultimate position in the
narrative sequence – already seeks to turn the Homeric listener into one
who not only sees the scene on the metal artefact, but is granted an
experiential encounter with the look, sound, 'feel' and other sensory aspects

---

[3] For illuminating discussion of this rather divisive issue, see Squire 2013. Squire acknowledges the
strong caution of Webb 1999 and 2009 (in antiquity, an ecphrasis has little to do with verbally
describing a work of art), but offers a corrective in persuasively demonstrating that the shield
occupied a central place in ancient attempts to theorize relations between words and images;
note too Elsner 2002, 2.

of the choral performance materialized there. My suggestion is that the chorus was from the start a locus for exploring the passage from hearing words, whether performed or encountered in texts, to seeing, from spectacle to verbal articulation and back again. Anticipating the later theorists too are oscillations between verbalization and material objects and the invitation to practise an intensified kind of viewing that, following the choreutes' own exercise of their 'choral gaze', involves the generation of a quasi-visionary series of images of things unseen. In closing with this topic, I aim not to offer any conclusive or definitive statements about *choreia* in archaic and early classical Greece – the heterogeneity of the sources gathered here prohibits any such summary or synthesizing remarks – but rather to point the discussion towards a later stage in the ever-evolving notions or 'constructions' of *choreia* in antiquity and to review, from this fresh angle, some of the principal objects, texts and concepts presented through this study's course. The sources treated here illuminate the earlier material on one further count, allowing us, as it were, to look beneath the choral 'hood' and to see something of the mechanisms and internal workings that enabled a chorus to adopt its diverse roles and configurations and, most critically, to achieve the larger purpose that underwrites each and every choral spectacle: that of prompting an epiphany, of summoning the gods to attend, take pleasure in and join the ongoing performance as fellow dancers.

Each of this chapter's four sections details different facets of the powers and attributes of archaic and early classical choruses and of choral lyric more generally, aligning these with the chief tenets of *enargeia* and how these may, in the view of the later theoretical discussions, best be achieved. In Section 1, I begin with the two prime qualities repeatedly assigned the early chorus, its visual brilliance and mobility-cum-speed, which make it and its performances exemplary of the core sense of *enargeia* and would prove no less critical in the practice of this mode of discourse. Section 2 treats the distinctive and quasi-visionary powers of sight that a chorus possesses and observes the singers' use of the several rhetorical devices singled out by theorists as conducive to *enargeia* and to the stimulation of *phantasiai*. The eliciting of these images and their transmission to an audience, as Section 3 explores, subtends the creation of the bond of identification that exists between choruses and their spectators and that would come explicitly to characterize relations between practitioners of *enargeia* and their auditors and readers. The discussion's final portion turns to representations of the chorus as conduits to epiphanies, and correlates very early demonstrations of the power of *choreia* to attract the gods with much later expressions of the connections between *enargeia* and divine self-manifestations.[4]

1 Light and Motion

1.1 Enargeia, Dynamism and Illumination

In their discussions of how best to invest a scene with the vividness and *saphêneia* that characterize descriptions that possess *enargeia*, post-classical theoreticians and rhetoricians link the device to metaphor, attributing to both the capacity to provoke visualization or to 'place before the eyes'.[5] In Aristotle's discussion of the figure at *Rhet.* 1411b (to which I return in Section 2), he comments that metaphors that show their subjects in action, those with *energeia*, possess the capacity to place the image 'before the eyes (πρὸ ὀμμάτων)' to a heightened degree, surpassing those where the verbal figure remains static. As scholars note, an association seems already to have existed between *energeia*, variously construed as movement and its rendering of space through time, a dynamic, motional style, or an actualization in the form of perceptible movement, and its near homonym, *enargeia*.[6] In a remark in the passage referred to above, Aristotle more narrowly defines the expression 'before the eyes' and explicates this act of visualization's relation to *energeia*: 'I mean that things are set before the eyes by such things as signify actuality (ὅσα ἐνεργοῦντα σημαίνει)' (1411b24–25). As his subsequent citations of metaphoric language from the *Iliad* demonstrate, this quality in large part depends on infusing the inanimate with life and attributing to it the properties of living creatures: 'for in all these examples, there is the appearance of actuality since the objects are represented as animate (ἔμψυχα) ... and the rest express actuality (ἐνέργεια)' (1412a3–5).

<hr>

[4] In all but the closing discussion, I begin at the end of the chronological spectrum, moving from the post-classical rhetorical handbooks and discussions of *enargeia* in other late sources back to the realization of their recommendations and abstract concepts in choral performances; this structure is designed better to bring out the continuities.

[5] The *Progymnasmata* are less explicit, merely advising the use of figures without detailing what they mean.

[6] Note, however, that Aristotle never actually uses the term *enargeia* in either the *Rhetoric* or *Poetics* and instead selects the adverb ἐναργῶς, also using the expression 'before the eyes'; he thus seems to have the concept, but not the actual term, which only occurs once in his entire corpus, at *De anima* 418b24 in a passage where *energeia* also occurs and where the sense seems to be different from the later rhetorical use.

These examples fill out a remark made earlier in the text also concerning
the elements that most effectively contribute to 'placing something before
the eyes': these are metaphor (see below for more on this), antithesis and
energeia (1410b33–36). As Stijn Bussels handily glosses the larger argument, 'metaphors can achieve vividness since they can enable the visualization of inanimate matter as though it were animated by means of
presenting it in a state of actuality or *energeia*'.[7] Plato anticipates
Aristotle here, noting that we naturally desire to make visual representations conform as closely as possible to the living being, a property they
possess by virtue of their capacity for motion: 'on seeing beautiful creatures, whether works of art or actually alive but in repose, a man should be
moved with desire to behold them in motion (κινούμενα) and vigorously
engaged in some exercise as seemed suitable to their physique' (*Tim.* 19b).
Theon would echo the association of *enargeia* with activity in these earlier
sources when he explains that a speaker's creation of a *diatupôsis* – a term
regularly used of a vivid description – depends on his showing an event in
the moment of its enactment, ἐνεργούμενον (*Progymn.* 108–09). While
others have traced the sources' linkage of *enargeia* and *energeia* and tried
to tease out the somewhat elusive relations between them, I would suggest
that the two notions' proximity indicates how visual vividness depends in
no small part on the actively moving quality of the object described.[8]

Of no less concern to the individual seeking to achieve *enargeia* in
speech or writing is luminosity or spotlighting, a property that looks back
to the primary meaning of the adjective *enargês* in Homeric and other
archaic and early classical texts: 'in full light'.[9] Aristotle already suggests the
heightened visuality attendant on *enargeia* when he advises the poet to keep
his subject 'before the eyes' (πρὸ ὀμμάτων) so as to see it most clearly
(ἐναργέστατα), as though he were himself in its presence (*Poet.* 1455a23–
24). Light enters more explicitly into the philosopher's discussion of *phantasia*, where he first observes that mental visions engendered by *aisthêsis*
come about by means of *enargeia* and then derives *phantasia* from *phaos*,
'because it is not possible to see anything without light (ἄνευ φωτός)' (*De
an.* 429a1–4). A succinct statement of the role of illumination in phrases
invested with the requisite 'clarity' belongs to an observation, its author

---

[7] Bussels 2012, 74.
[8] See, among others, Webb 2009, 85–86 with earlier bibliography cited there.
[9] A passage from Pindar's seventh *Olympian* treated in Chapter 8 well demonstrates the
illumination that the adjective expresses and its link to the material object. In accordance with
the injunction of Helios, the 'divine bringer of light to mortals', the Rhodians set up an altar
qualified as 'distinct', 'brilliant', 'in clear view' (βωμὸν ἐναργέα, 42).

unknown, cited by Demetrios in his discussion of periods: 'clear expression (σαφὴς φράσις) diffuses much light over the hearer's mind' (*Eloc.* 17).

Lighting again proves an abiding concern in later Roman sources and their renditions of the Greek concept. In *Inst.* 6.2.32, Quintilian calls *illustratio* and *evidentia* the Latin equivalents of *enargeia* and adds that Cicero uses the nouns as synonyms. As commentators observe, contrary to Quintilian's assertion, Cicero never employs *illustratio*, but only the adjective *inlustris*, which identifies the particular clarity that results from the vividness that an orator grants his subjects and that characterizes a style that, Quintilian remarks, 'sets events almost before the eyes'. Derived from *in-lustrare*, the adjective means to 'throw light upon' or 'give lustre to', a literal highlighting which then draws an observer's attention (see Cic. *De orat.* 3.53.202). Cicero's praise of the style of Caesar's *Commentarii* recasts the idea, preserving the central role of illumination: 'it seems as if he had placed a well-painted picture in a good light (*in bona lumina*)' (*Brutus* 261). A brilliancy or splendour of expression, Cicero further remarks at *De orat.* 2.8.34, enhances and promotes the 'lighting up' of the phenomena the words describe (*res splendore inlustrata verborum*).

The second of Cicero's two nouns, *evidentia*, is formed from *ex-videre*, 'being seen by projecting, by shining', and applies to what is made manifest and distinct. As Quintilian goes on to observe in the passage at 6.2.32, the subject treated is not so much spoken as shown (*non tam dicere videtur quam ostendere*). To cite Bussels' account again, the contrast between *illustratio* and *evidentia* turns on the fact that in the first the observer of an object 'clarifies it by throwing a light' on it whereas in the second the trajectory is reversed; so etymologically speaking, *inlustris* refers to light thrown on the object by the observer, but *evidentia* describes the light derived from the object of observation.[10]

Famously, Livy selects *inlustris* when, introducing his history as a *monumentum* whose contents he invites his readers to look upon, he draws attention to its illuminated and illuminating or elucidating properties (*in inlustri posita monumento intueri, praef.* 10). The adjective possesses two meanings: matter styled *inlustris* is at once luminous and transparent, 'diaphanous' and light-refracting. While the historian does not specify the substance used for the construction of his notional *monumentum*, perhaps, given the transformations in the city landscape occurring all around him, marble is what he and his readers would most likely have in mind; as noted in other chapters, the stone is uniquely both a source of light

---

[10] Bussels 2012, 72.

due to its reflective properties and transparent, allowing light to pass through it. Just like that sparkling building material, Livy's text both casts light on the absent reality shining through it and makes it perceptible.

While these accounts of *enargeia* leave the connection between motion and brilliant light unexplored, the Byzantine commentators suggest that the properties exist in association. Echoing the *Suda*'s brief definition of *enargeia* as descriptive of the 'whiteness and luminosity (λευκότης καὶ φανότης) of discourse', the *Etymologicum Magnum* introduces a third element to the evidently standard gloss: *enargeia* is additionally the quality of 'swiftness (ταχύτης) in words'. Following a discussion of the earlier noted and hard to pin down connection between *energeia* and *enargeia* in the ancient sources, a more recent account of the latter property offers a possible way of understanding why, in the view of the author of the *EM*, the kinetic and luminous form two sides of the same coin, now turned to one face, now to the other:[11] where *energeia* describes actualization in the form of perceptible movement, *enargeia* is 'the potency of a visualized object prior to act once its state of rest is exchanged for one of movement'. The hearer-visualizer can only access the illuminating power of that object in the brief moments when, arrested by a verbal or graphic representation, it may be fully grasped and its details scrutinized in the course of an alternation between motion and *stasis*, a dynamic to which the discussion below returns.

1.2 Choral Motion and Luminosity in Archaic and Early Classical Accounts

If, as noted above, the adjective *enargês* in Homer literally means 'in full light', then the second element in the compound term has a semantic range that extends beyond the quality of luminosity and brightness and accommodates the movement and swiftness that come to be associated with *enargeia* in the later sources. Applying the epithet *argos* to dogs and other animals, the epic poet signals their rapid motion (the description of Odysseus' dog in *Od.* 17.296–306 plays on this with a triple reference to the current immobility of the once preternaturally speedy Argos, a name that might be rendered 'Flash').

---

[11] Collins 1991, 125–27. As he notes at 125, a 'lexical peculiarity' may be among the root causes of the link between the energic and enargic: the adjective *energôs* meaning 'active' or 'at work' originally had as its antonym the Homeric *aergôs*. After syncope caused the term's loss of its epsilon, the term that originally meant 'idle', 'quiescent', or 'out of work' became homonymous with *argos*, the same word used for 'bright'.

Indicative of the movement, most typically fast-paced, integral to the chorus is the archaic sources' focus on the dancers' feet, already styled 'knowing' and shown in the act of running in Homer's depiction of the performers on Hephaestus' shield band (*Il.* 18.599). A quick-stepped and vigorous *kinêsis* singularizes the dancer who claims the Dipylon oinochoe as his prize ('he who dances most friskily'), and the performers of a Pindaric hyporcheme engage in a 'race' with real or hypothetical rival choruses by 'whirling a competitive foot' (fr. 107a.3 S.-M.). Dramatic choruses likewise call attention to their quickness, a velocity made emphatic in the closing song in Aristophanes' *Thesmophoriazusai*, where the dancing choreutes bid themselves 'move lightly on your feet (κοῦφα ποσίν) ... move to the rhythm of the sacred dance. Come every one of us. Move with swift feet (καρπαλίμοιν ποδοῖν)' (953–56).

Typically, this swift-paced chorus is also luminous, one property reinforcing the other. Even before we witness what Hephaestus chooses to forge on the choral shield band, the narrator alerts his hearers to the combination of light and movement that, his initial choice of term suggests, distinguishes this most remarkable of the scenes. In François Frontisi-Ducroux's careful gloss of ποίκιλλε at *Il.* 18.590, she notes that both the verb and the cognate adjective ποικίλος not only describe objects of elaborate artistry but more specifically acknowledge their distinctive 'luminosité bigarrée et ... scintillement', a light that shifts and twinkles.[12] Everything in the Homeric representation works to enhance that moving sparkle; even the dancers' garments gleam with the oil used in Mycenaean times to keep linens supple and give them the desired sheen. Multiplying the play of light emanating from their clothing and metal-forged accessories, the youths and maidens are perpetually moving, their spins likened to the rotations of the potter's wheel, unceasing once given an initial push.

The combination of light and rapid movement returns in subsequent descriptions of choral performances, where the two again work in tandem. Radiance, often emitted by a metal surface, can in and of itself give the impression of motion (recall how Pindar ascribes *rhythmos*, form in flux, to the bronze walls and columns of the 'choralized' third temple at Delphi in his *Paean* 8), or be enhanced by the movement of an individual or object. Swiftness is, of course, the essence of the racehorse to whom the choristers of Alcman's first *Partheneion* compare their *chorêgos* Agido, already

[12] Frontisi-Ducroux 2002, 465. If, as argued in Chapter 7, the verb primarily refers to pattern-weaving, then speed also characterizes skilled practitioners in the art. One witness to weaving practices in a Bolivian village in the 1990s comments that 'weaving is usually performed extremely quickly by the master weaver' (Urton 1997, 118).

likened to the sun in her radiance, and light (and motion too) is no less prominent in the account of the second chorus leader, Hagesichora, whose hair 'blossoms like pure gold' (53–54). Since she is likewise equated with a racehorse, her tresses do double duty as the courser's mane, streaming out as the horse runs. More brilliance and motion belong to the all-golden snakes – creatures also styled ἀργοί in Homeric poetry – that Alcman's maiden performers wear. Here the adjective *poikilos* (66) also used of the bracelets refers not just to the light radiated by the gold but implicitly to the motion of the serpentine *comparanda* that coil around the dancers' arms.[13] In a final instance of the properties' coincidence in the song, the maidens also cite among their attributes the 'surfeit of purple (πορφύρας)' heightening their visual appeal; the colour's very name is related to *porphurô*, evocative of something that 'heaves' and 'swirls' and that itself recalls the technology that went into the dye's production, in which several colour changes would occur to achieve the desired shade. As purple-dyed objects shimmered in the light, they would seem to move, creating the impression of flashing motion and versi-colouration. Anticipating Alcman here is the Odyssean account of the *pas de deux* performed by the two Phaeacian youths, which opens with a lingering description of the purple ball that the dancers toss high into the air (8.372–74); the colour would in and of itself invest their choreographic feats with the shimmer otherwise absent from the visualization that follows.[14]

No less exemplary of two properties' co-presence is the sequence of images used by the maiden singers in Alcman's third *Partheneion* to portray Astymelousa, their lead dancer. Her likeness is, first off, that of a radiant star styled διαιπετής (67), an adjective well suited to the performer who, in a repetition of its prefix, 'goes through' (διέβα, 70) the crowd. In the ancient etymologies proposed for διαιπετής, light and motion form a pair; one account derives it from *dieros*, 'rapid, quick', and citing a phrase styling a woman διπετής, the *EM* glosses the expression with *diaugês*, 'dazzling'.[15] Also uniting star and dancer in the *Partheneion* is αἰγλά[ε]ντος (66), a descriptive term that illuminates the scene with the αἴγλη, that quasi-divine iridescence likewise belonging to Apollo (αἴγλη δέ μιν ἀμφιφαείνει) as he,

---

[13] That motion is visible in Homer's simile comparing Hector to a snake waiting to strike at *Il.* 22.95; the beast coils (ἐλισσόμενος) itself about in its hole.

[14] Democritus – the author of a work titled *On Colours*, whose content Theophrastus' *De sensibus* in part preserves – gives a theoretical underpinning to these accounts; for the atomist, the nature of colours depended on the interaction between daylight, itself a changing phenomenon, and an object's microphysical structure. For this, see Sassi 2015, 265.

[15] *Diaugês* coincides with luminosity in a description of the particular brilliance of the colour white at Theophr. *De sens.* 76–77.

'stepping high', leads the choral line in the *Homeric Hymn* (*HHAp.* 201–03). Pindar attributes that same glitter to the 'foot-racing' of the Olympic victory-winning father of his *laudandus*, an epiphenomenon of the athlete's swift-moving feet (*Ol.* 13.36). Assuming a second shape, Alcman's transmogrifying Astymelousa next resembles a 'golden branch' (68); a metallic glitter emanates from this, a fantastical version of the leafy shoot regularly carried by the real-world parthenaic dancer in contemporary visual accounts. The 'delicate feather' (68), whose epithet, ἀπαλό[ν, recalls the earlier description of the dancer's ἀπ]αλοὶ πόδες, closes the sequence. ψίλον is the Doric form of πτερόν, the wing or feather, a commonplace attribute of the choral dancer so frequently likened to a bird in art and text, and whose aerial quality circles back to the sky-travelling star first in this vertiginous run of similes.

In one last example of the conjunction of luminosity and dynamism in an early poetic representation of a choral performance, Anaktoria, the erstwhile premier dancer of Sappho's maiden chorus, possesses, in her companions' fond recollection, both a 'lovely step' (ἔρατόν τε βᾶμα, fr. 16.17 V.) and a 'sparklingly radiant' (κἀμάρυχμα λάμπρον, 18) countenance. The noun of the second phrase recalls the scintillating moves – μαρμαρυγαί – assigned to other choral dancers' feet in archaic poetry and to the flash-footed wrestler Automedes in Bacchylides 9.36. The suggestion of Anaktoria's transient gleam echoes the earlier representation of Helen, positioned, at least in some respects, as her mythical predecessor and paradigm. In the triple actions featured in line 9, Menelaus' bride moves from her marital home, departs and sails off to Troy (καλλ[ίποι]σ' ἔβα 's Τροΐαν πλέοι[σα), no sooner here than gone.

As already noted, the discussions of later philosophers and rhetoricians would again connect the two properties underscored in these archaic accounts, using the homonymity between *enargeia*, the visually brilliant, and *energeia*, the 'movemented', to devise a link between brightness, rapid motion and visibility.[16] If Christopher Collins is correct in proposing that a

---

[16] These several notions seem, as suggested above, to be bound up with the archaic and classical philosophers' discussions of colour (for which, see Sassi 2015), with their repeated emphasis on the brilliance and its eye-catching power that certain shades possess; indeed, at *Tim.* 68a7, Plato identifies the 'brilliant-and-glittering' (λαμπρόν τε καὶ στίλβον) as one of the four basic colours. Colour terms are also a repeated feature of post-archaic descriptions of choral dancers. See, for example, the passage of Philostratus cited in the final section of this chapter, where the author includes a whole digression on colour-mixing; there too the gems making up the picture's frame are not so much coloured as fashioned from light. For the connection between notions of brightness and movement, and the several Greek terms that convey a sense of both, see Sassi 2015, 267.

verbal representation or ecphrasis offers a means of arresting and closely examining what is otherwise a moving object, too fleeting in its passage for detailed perusal, then this alternation between motion and *stasis* maps readily onto an essential quality of *choreia*: choral dancing is a sequence of swiftly executed steps interspersed with the intervals of stillness when the performers strike their poses in moments of arrest.

2   *Enargeia,* Rhetorical Devices and the Stimulation of *Phantasiai*

2.1   *Figurative Language, Apostrophe, Deixis and Mental Images in the Theoretical Accounts*

In their recommendations to would-be practitioners of *enargeia* and their selections of and comments on passages of poetry and prose that exemplify the device, discussions of 'visual vividness' privilege certain rhetorical stratagems, recommending these as particularly conducive to turning hearers into viewers. Aristotle is just the first to flag metaphors as critical to the practice, explicitly observing, in the passage cited in Section 1, that they contribute to the act of putting things before the eyes (*Rhet.* 1411b). A discussion of how to devise a metaphor in *Poetics* 1459a7–8 adds a new element to the role of figuration in the promotion of verbal pictorialism and 'showiness'. Here Aristotle notes that success-fully to construct the verbal figure is the same as to practise perceptive or concentrated viewing, that intensive type of spectatorship that the sources particularize with the verb *theôrein*: 'for successful metaphor making is the apprehension of the similar' (τὸ γὰρ εὖ μεταφέρειν τὸ τὸ ὅμοιον θεωρεῖν ἐστιν). When we hear and grasp the meaning of a metaphor or a simile (which Aristotle treats on several occasions as interchangeable) we necessarily become those who view in this acute, heightened or even religiously inflected fashion.[17]

Bypassing other accounts and turning to the Romans, we find Quintilian also commenting at length on the role of images, and he places metaphor at the very head of his discussion of tropes at *Inst.* 8.6.4–5. In an account filled with terms pertaining to light (a metaphor is unmistakable, the rhetorician declares, because it 'illuminates itself by virtue of its own light [*clara proprio*

---

[17] A *theôria* is, of course, also a type of religious journeying or 'pilgrimage' that frequently involves acting as spectator at sacred sites and witnessing the rituals enacted there, which may include the visionary experiences that Pausanias and others so richly detail.

tamen lumine eluceat])', he concludes by drawing attention to the contribution that the figure makes to visualization: among its three functions is
that of 'placing things before the eyes' (8.6.19). The treatise has already
examined similes in an earlier part of book 8, where the author begins by
remarking that 'to throw light on descriptions, similes have been excel-
lently [lit. 'very clearly'] invented (*praeclare vero ad inferendam rebus lucem
repertae sunt similitudines*)' (8.3.72–73). He then narrows his lens to those
'adapted to give a lively representation of things' on the grounds that
comparisons of this kind are most applicable to his concern with vividness.
Several examples of effective and ineffective similes follow before the
discussion ends with a summary of its argument: such rhetorical figures
are designed 'not just to place things manifestly before the eyes, but to do so
with brevity and speed' (*non solum aperte ponendi rem ante oculos, sed
circumcise atque velociter*, 8.3.82); while the closing adverb refers chiefly to
the succinct quality of the selected similes, it simultaneously looks to the
image's display of rapid motion.

Cicero supplies additional evidence for the role of metaphoric language
in the practice of *enargeia*. In *De partitione oratoria*, he calls *inlustris* the
style of an orator who achieves vividness by presenting his protagonists
brilliantly, an achievement to which metaphor makes a central contribution: 'the style is illustrious [*inlustris*] if the words employed are chosen for
their dignity and used metaphorically and in exaggeration and adjectivally
and in duplication and synonymously and in harmony with the representation of facts' (6.20.1–5).[18] The link between metaphor and *enargeia*
proves more fundamental still since, as *De oratore* spells out, it is through
figurative language that the speaker elicits the visual powers centrally at
play in vividness (3.40.160–61):

> Every metaphor, provided it be a good one, has a direct appeal to the
> senses, especially the sense of sight, which is the keenest: for while the rest
> of the senses supply metaphors as in 'the fragrance of good manners', 'the
> softness of a human spirit' ... The metaphors drawn from the sense of
> sight are much more vivid, for they almost place in the eye of the mind
> such objects as we are unable to see and discern (*quae paene ponunt in
> conspectu animi, quae cernere et videre non possumus*).

Much less prominent in the Greek sources is a second rhetorical device
regarded by Roman authors as central to the practice and production of
enargeia, apostrophe. Understanding the term as a reference to the

---

[18] Cf. Cicero's return to the topic at 15.53.

moment when a speaker 'turns away' from the judge so as to address the accused or courtroom audience in forensic rhetoric, several discussions describe the practice in terms that closely echo those used in their and others' analyses of visual vividness. For the author of the *Rhetorica ad Herennium*, apostrophe may be defined as 'a figure that expresses grief or indignation by means of an address to some man or city or place or object' (4.15.22). The particular sentiments aroused by its exercise return, in almost identical terminology, in the author's subsequent discussion of *descriptio* – a device that parallels *enargeia* insofar as it too is a verbal account, or *demonstratio*, that causes 'the subject to pass vividly before our eyes (*res ante oculos esse videatur*)' (4.55.68) – whose purpose is expressly to arouse pity and indignation. *Indignatio* and *miseratio* are the two emotions identified by Cicero in his endorsement of vivid accounts, which place scenes or actions 'before the eyes' of the audience, and, by making the listeners think themselves present at the event, stimulate these sentiments (*De invent.* 1.54.104, 55.106; cf. *Rhet. Herren.* 4.39.51). When Quintilian likewise observes the emotive and persuasive power of apostrophe in the courtroom, he introduces vocabulary similar to that of the earlier authors, remarking that the turn from the judge to the adversary is 'exceedingly moving (*mire movet*), whether we attack our adversary . . . or turn to make some invocation . . . or to entreaty that will bring odium on our opponents' (*Inst.* 9.2.38).

In the examples of apostrophe that Quintilian goes on to offer, a further parallelism with *enargeia* becomes apparent: the speaker's deployment of the rhetorical figure allows him to make present the absent or abstract, whether he addresses the 'Alban hills and groves' or the 'Porcian and Sempronian laws' (9.2.38). This summoning of the remote and unseen proves consistent with what occurs when an orator conjures up mental images (*phantasiai* or *visiones*) in his mind so as to achieve *enargeia*, a process that enables him and those who listen to his speech to believe themselves in the presence of imperceptible things, whether real, fictional or non-existent. According to Quintilian's much cited definition at *Inst.* 6.2.29–30,

> what the Greeks call *phantasiai* – we will, if you allow, call them *visiones* – are the means by which the images of absent things are represented in the mind in such a way that we seem to see them with our eyes and to have them as present (*praesentes habere*). Whoever has good command of them will have a most powerful impact on the emotions. Some people call this

type of man who can imagine himself well in things, words and deeds in accordance with the truth 'good at imagining' (εὐφαντασίωτον).[19]

Quintilian immediately follows his discussion of apostrophe with a return to a figure already, as he reminds his reader, treated in book 8, the device of *evidentia* or *illuminatio* – the Latin equivalents for *enargeia* – 'which means a representation of things so fully expressed in words that it seems to be seen rather than heard' (9.2.40). While Quintilian draws no explicit connection between the two rhetorical stratagems, the shift from apostrophe to *enargeia* may reflect the kinship that their shared terminology likewise suggests.

The phrases cited by Quintilian at 9.2.38 to illustrate both apostrophe and pictorial vividness (now given the additional Greek name *hypotypôsis*) further resemble one another insofar as they almost all rely on the speaker's use of a third rhetorical device, albeit one neither explicitly named nor explored in the rhetorical handbooks or didactic treaties. Quintilian's first example, 'what was that sword of yours doing, Tubero, in the field at Pharsalus?' (*quid enim tuus ille, Tubero, in acie Pharsalica?*) deploys deixis (more fully defined below), as the speaker verbally points to *that* weapon belonging to the guilty party located in its telltale position; the second example, which appeals to the Alban topography (*vos enim iam ego, Albani tumuli atque luci*, 'on you I call, you hills and groves of Alba'), offers a twofold instance of what linguists call 'person deixis', where a speaker designates himself or an addressee or absent party. In the vivid description drawn from Cicero's *Pro Milone*, introduced in Quintilian's subsequent remarks to exemplify *enargeia*, the deictic *ipse* opens the visualization. Deixis and apostrophe (in the more recent sense) newly abound when Quintilian, now introducing the device of μετάστασις or the transmutation of time (for which he retains the Greek formulation) as an element of *hypotypôsis*, turns to a passage of Seneca where a father comes upon his son committing adultery with his stepmother, and promptly kills them both while invoking an absent presence: 'Lead, I follow, take this aged hand (*accipe hanc senilem manum*) and direct it wheresoever you please' (9.2.42–43).[20] A further instance of this act of deictic showing or more properly

---

[19] [Longinus] offers a similar formulation, explaining that *enargeia* is the result of the *phantasiai* stimulated by the orator and that these images occur 'when, under the effects of inspiration and passion, you seem to see what you are speaking about and place it beneath the eyes of your audience' (*De subl.* 15.1–2).

[20] Also indicative of the practice of deixis is the verb *ostendere* that Quintilian, citing Cicero, uses in the definition given in book 9 of 'placing things before the eyes' (9.2.40), and this same act of pointing is apparent in several other terms which Greek and Roman discussions variously substitute for *enargeia*, among them *demonstratio* used at *Rhetorica ad Herennium* 4.55.68. As

pointing occurs in the passage from Heliodorus, *Aeth.* 3.4.7 cited in n. 1; there, as Cnemon believes himself in the presence of the absent Charikleia and Theagenes, he acknowledges the power of Calasiris' rhetoric in bringing them onto the scene: 'so vividly did your description show (ὑπέδειξεν) them'; the same verb can refer to pointing to actual people and conjuring up a fictional character within a narrative.[21]

For [Longinus], a prime example of the 'enargic' poet's capacity to summon up sights beyond the bounds of normal human experience famously occurs when Euripides' Orestes thinks himself in the presence of the Furies, and, addressing his mother, follows his vivid description of the 'gore-faced maidens with their snakes' by citing an emphatically deictic line, 'here they are, here they are rushing upon me' (αὗται γὰρ αὗται πλησίον θρῴσκουσ' ἐμοῦ, *Or.* 257).[22] As the literary critic goes on to remark, 'here the poet has seen the Furies himself and has almost made his listeners see what he imagined (ἐφαντάσθη)' (*De subl.* 15.2). Quintilian places himself in the role of listener to whom the *phantasia* is shown when he cites the impact of a lost speech by Cicero featuring a vivid visualization of the aftermath to a night of debauched partying – 'I seemed to see some coming, others going, some reeling from the wine . . . ' (*Inst.* 8.3.66) – while his close reading of a second passage from Cicero details the transmission of these mental images from the orator to his audience or, in this instance, to the latter-day reader of the speech (8.3.64–65):

> Who could be so incapable of conceiving mental images that, when reading that passage in the *Verrines* . . . he does not just seem to see the characters themselves, and the place and their dress, but even constructs for himself some of the things which are not spoken? I indeed seem to see his face, his eyes, the couple's degrading caresses and the frightened shame of those who were present.

Again, this vivid picture which Quintilian is made to see, and which he can even amplify with fresh visual details that he 'constructs for himself', depends on the speaker's prior showing of its most striking features. Like other commentators on ecphrases and *enargeia* before him, however, Quintilian is careful to acknowledge the limits of their powers of presentification; repeatedly introducing the notion of his 'seeming' to see, he is in

---

the author of the treatise comments, 'it is *demonstratio* when an event is so described in words that the business seems to be enacted and the subject to be seen before the eyes'.

[21] See further Grethlein 2017, 110 and Hardie 1998, 27 on Calasiris' simultaneous immersion in his own narrative and its deceptive powers to make the absent present.

[22] The dramatist seems to take his cue from Aeschylus' version of the same appalling apparitions; at *Choeph.* 1054 and 1057, Orestes uses a series of deictics to signal the monsters' presence.

accord with such first-century C.E. critics as Theon, who qualifies his definition of ecphrasis as 'a speech that vividly (*enargôs*) brings the subject shown before the eyes' by noting that it has the capacity to achieve vividness (*enargeia*) 'which makes one almost (*schedon*) see what is spoken about' (*Progymnasmata* p. 118–19).[23]

2.2   The Visionary Chorus

To turn back to representations of choral performances in texts and vase paintings from the archaic through to the classical period is to encounter the practice of the same rhetorical devices that the later theoreticians single out and to observe how their presence results in precisely the production of the mental images or *phantasiai* that discussions of *enargeia* would foreground. Through close readings of two passages from choral lyric, and two painted scenes that stand in close relation to the second of these texts, my purpose is to illustrate how through their use of imagery, apostrophe and deixis, the performers can stimulate visions of the absent and unseen and, through the medium of their song together with the poses and movements of their dance, allow their audience to share in these perceptions to a still more heightened degree, without the limitations that the later accounts register.

The passage from Alcman's first *Partheneion* cited earlier in this chapter offers ample evidence for that particularized and more acute mode of viewing, what I would designate the 'choral gaze', as practised in an ongoing performance. Here the singers employ deictics, apostrophe and a dizzying proliferation of images so as to convey the audience repeatedly from the *hic et nunc* to a more visionary realm (a shift that Nancy Felson-Rubin nicely terms 'vicarious transport')[24] to which their outstandingly acute and even mantic powers of sight grant the performers and, through their mediation, those attending the performance access. When the song returns its spectators – as it regularly does through the interjections and other devices that punctuate the passage – to the actual scene before them, the audience's perceptions are not unchanged: instead, what it now apprehends is a bifurcated image, a palimpsest of the sense impressions most immediately transmitted to the eye, ear and other organs, and the remote, absent and imaginary within or behind these sensations. Lines 39–59 best exemplify the technique:

---

[23] Cf. Nicolaos, *Progymnasmata* p. 68, in whose view ecphrasis 'tries to turn listeners into spectators'.

[24] Felson-Rubin 1999.

ἐγὼν δ' ἀείδω
Ἀγιδῶς τὸ φῶς· ὁρῶ   40
ϝ' ὥτ' ἄλιον, ὄνπερ ἇμιν
Ἀγιδὼ μαρτύρεται
φαίνην· ἐμὲ δ' οὔτ' ἐπαινῆν
οὔτε μωμήσθαι νιν ἁ κλεννὰ χοραγὸς
οὐδ' ἁμῶς ἐῆ· δοκεῖ γὰρ ἦμεν αὔτα   45
ἐκπρεπὴς τὼς ὥπερ αἴτις
ἐν βοτοῖς στάσειεν ἵππον
παγὸν ἀεθλοφόρον καναχάποδα
τῶν ὑποπετριδίων ὀνείρων·

ἦ οὐχ ὁρῇς; ὁ μὲν κέλης   50
Ἐνετικός· ἁ δὲ χαίτα
τᾶς ἐμᾶς ἀνεψιᾶς
Ἁγησιχόρας ἐπανθεῖ
χρυσὸς [ὡ]ς ἀκήρατος·
τό τ' ἀργύριον πρόσωπον,   55
διαφάδαν τί τοι λέγω;
Ἁγησιχόρα μὲν αὔτα·
ἁ δὲ δευτέρα πεδ' Ἀγιδὼ τὸ ϝεῖδος
ἵππος Ἰβηνῷ Κολαξαῖος δραμήται·

I sing the light of Agido, I see it like the sun, which Agido affirms as witness to appear for us. But the glorious *chorêgos* forbids me either to praise or to blame her. For she appears to be outstanding, as if one were to place in the midst of a grazing herd a strong prize-winning horse with resounding hooves, one of the dreams that dwell beneath the rocks.

Don't you see? That one is an Enetic courser, while the hair of my cousin Hagesichora shines forth like unalloyed gold. Her face is of silver. Why do I tell you openly? Here she is, Hagesichora herself. Next will run Agido, her appearance that of a Colaxian horse following an Ibenian.

Most obviously, the opening remark offers an instance of the role of the chorus members, both leaders and followers here, as showers, even pointers: their initial task is to draw visual attention to Agido, a purpose which their subsequent remark, 'Don't you see', makes plain. The singers will enact the same gesture in their introductory praise of their second leader,

Hagesichora: 'Why do I tell you openly? Here she is, Hagesichora herself!'.[25]

But the sight that Alcman's choristers invite their audience to apprehend is anything but straightforward; instead what they do is to occlude the boundaries between the visible and what lies outside the immediate field of perception. This back-and-forth begins when the *parthenoi* declare that they see Agido 'as the sun', using the already distancing simile to draw attention at once to the beauty and special luminosity of what they observe (the equation of a girl's loveliness with light, φῶς, is already a commonplace). The next phrase, which introduces Agido as the one who 'summons [the sun] to witness for us and appear' (or, in other possible readings of the phrase, 'calls to shine on us as a witness', or 'attests as a witness to be shining'),[26] both transfers the 'showing' role to the *chorêgos* and, since φῶς regularly symbolizes the sun, draws on a second traditional conceit. But complicating the equivalence is the play between image and reality. The light/sun of the similes has now become the actual solar body, the agent that, in turn, makes things visible. Is this an instance of 'sympathetic magic', of Agido's sun-like beauty bringing about the appearance of the sun itself? Or do her 'Helios-like' and consequently surpassingly powerful faculties of sight – Helios is, of course, panoptic, the one who sees and reveals what remains invisible to mortals and even to the other gods – enable her to testify to the advent of what neither chorus nor audience can apprehend except metaphorically, through imaginative vision or second-order sight? While some commentators suggest that the light of day is becoming visible in the sky, in the view of many this event is yet to come; as later portions of the poem make clear, the end of the performance, still some way off, should coincide with the dawning of the day. If no such dawn is breaking now, then Agido seems to see and relay this still extrasensory realm. In an anticipation of the role assumed by later choruses and the poetic ego within their songs, the singers have positioned their leader as a

---

[25] Here the maidens verbally anticipate the device that Alberti would counsel the would-be artist to include in his scene: the better to draw the viewers' eyes to the central figure in the canvas, the one to whom they should direct their gaze, painters would do well to depict one of the secondary characters pointing in his or her direction (*De statua* 272–73). See too n. 1 for a parallel moment in Cnemon's reaction to Calasiris' narrative, where the characters' seemingly literal appearance before Cnemon's eyes depends purely on the *enargeia* of the verbal account.

[26] The issue of 'choral witnessing', already treated by Maslov 2015, 212–32, is one to which I would like to return. Differently from Maslov's juridical emphasis, I would highlight the connection between 'witnessing' and 'showing' what the witness has seen, a linkage apparent in the early uses of the term.

mantis or literally *prophêtês* (see Section 4), the one who can speak in advance of an event's coming.

A second and still clearer instance of this quasi-visionary choral gaze occurs in the next block of lines, where the singers liken first Agido and then Hagesichora to prize-winning horses. Again, the chorister-horse analogy seems no more than a simile, its hypothetical quality reinforced by δοκεῖ indicating a surmise, the indefinite *tis* and the optative verb in the opening part of the conceit.[27] But, as earlier chapters have proposed, the equine parallel has both a past and present performative reality as well as a traditional referentiality. While the description of 'someone' placing the horse among the herd may look back to the earlier 'stationing' of the *chorêgos* in the middle or at the head of the troupe prior to the song's commencement, the beat of the dancers' feet more immediately allows an audience to hear the sonorous hooves (καναχάποδα) of these two imagistic racers, the first presented in a simile, the second, more succinctly, in a metaphor: 'that one is an Enetic courser'. Since καναχή regularly refers to the 'ring' of music or song, the adjective additionally comprises the maidens' singing and its musical accompaniment. More than this, all the facets of the performance, its music, song and the dancers' rhythmic footfall and out-flowing locks render the attributes of these unseen horses perceptible to the ear and eye.

With the specification that the horse whom Agido resembles belongs to the dream realm, the here-and-now seems more fully to recede. But dreams, whether those seen in sleep or in daydreaming, possess a heightened visual clarity; they, alongside the gods themselves, are phenomena for which Homer reserves the adjective *enargês* (e.g. *Od.* 4.841; cf. Aesch. *Pers.* 179), and Quintilian would more explicitly link dreaming with *enargeia* when he remarks that dreams 'are the means by which images of absent things are represented in the mind in such a way that we seem to see them with our eyes and to be in their presence'. In the same passage, he recommends that the would-be orator practise daydreaming as a means of generating *phantasiai* (*Inst.* 6.2.30). Like the idealized speaker in Quintilian's account, Alcman's singers share their mental vision with their audience: the direct address, 'Don't you see?', assumes that the viewers envisage the same representation as the performers looking at their oneiric 'horsey' chorus leader. All distance between image and reality disappears when Agido takes the form of the Enetic racer whom the chorus then sets before our eyes with the deictic ὁ μέν.

---

[27] Peponi 2004, 314.

The next few lines develop the equine conceit and continue to make the audience party to the visionary world revealed by the maidens. Prompting us to see Hagesichora's hair in the likeness of gold, they turn that inanimate and static metal into something that lives and burgeons. Following one last invitation to enter into this intense mode of perception, the chorus again pauses to anchor its otherwordly realm in the immediate setting: 'Why do I tell you openly (διαφάδαν)? Here she is, Hagesichora herself'. Insofar as διαφαίνω, the verb from which the singers' adverb is derived, refers not just to the act of 'showing light' or 'shining through', but also means 'to let something be seen through something else', it exactly captures what the chorus has been doing all along: its words have shown the brilliance and moving light of the two *chorêgoi* while allowing the audience to look behind the surface and to perceive the multiple phenomena that the chorus-leaders' presence brings to the performance site.

Before leaving Alcman's maiden song, I would underscore its use of the two rhetorical devices already prominent in the lines cited, and that promote the vivid visualizing that the chorus invites the audience to practice. Deixis,[28] in which the speaker verbally points towards the extra-linguistic context framing the remark, 'is essentially – although not exclusively – a way of referring to sight',[29] and stands in particularly close relation to *enargeia* when it appeals not to what is visible to the eyes (a *deixis ad oculos*) but to the fictional, absent and/or imaginative realms (a *deixis am phantasma*), engaging the mental faculties as it gestures towards and makes present what otherwise remains invisible. This 'pointing' most obviously occurs at 50 and 51, with the appeal to the audience ('Don't you see'), which includes the viewers in the time and place that the chorus occupies, and the ἁ δὲ χαίτα that follows, most likely now directing our attention to Hagesichora's hair; in a further instance, the maidens close this portion of their song with their fresh interjections at 56–57. The device then introduces the subsequent passage as the singers open their reference to the Peleiades (stars, these most likely visible in the sky above and/or the unseen doves) with the indexical ταί (60).

Combined with this deictic accumulation is apostrophe, not the 'turning away' in the forensic context where the Roman rhetoricians would locate the rhetorical practice, but in the sense now regularly associated with it. Narratologists have amply detailed how the use of the second person contributes to *enargeia* in sources from the archaic to the imperial age,

---

[28] Most fully treated in reference to the *Partheneion* in Peponi 2004.

[29] Peponi 2004, 296, together with her discussion of lines 50 and 56 at 301.

allowing a poet or prose writer to practise 'a form of ventriloquism through which the speaker throws voice, life, and human form into the [absent] addressee, turning its silence into mute responsiveness'.[30] Breaching the barriers between the story and its distant time and place and the present of the ongoing performance, apostrophe can bring the dead, absent, mythical and divine into the audience's space. Where several examples treated in this and later sections of the chapter will exemplify this way of using the device, the second-person appeals to the viewer in Alcman's song reverse the trajectory: addressing not the absent but current audience, the singers shore up the presence and 'reality' of their visionary world by multiplying the numbers of those to whom it has become manifest.

The second stasimon of Sophocles' *Trachiniai* furnishes a later instance of a chorus that practises its distinctive mode of viewing and draws, again, on the rhetorical devices, diction and conceits characteristic of this choral spectatorship. In a vividly visualized account filled with synaesthetic effects (as detailed in Chapter 5), the singers recreate in word, choreography and sound the long-past encounter between Heracles and Achelous, a combat at which they could not have been present, and position Aphrodite as divine participant and internal viewer/regulator in the *agôn*.[31] In the closing portion of their song, the maidens then abruptly turn their gaze from the still interlocked contestants to the spotlighted 'far-gleaming (τηλαυγεῖ) hill' (524) where Deianeira sits, waiting for the end to an encounter that, she earlier confessed (22–23), she could not watch for fear that Heracles would not emerge victorious. Instead, as she remarked in an anticipation of the function now assumed by the dramatic chorus, it would be the task of another verbally to recount the nature of the struggle to an audience.

It is at this point in the stasimon that the singers, having already assumed the position of 'onlooker' renounced by Deianeira and allowed the audience in the theatre to become ringside spectators at the contest that hitherto lacked both a verbal and visual account, interject with an explicit definition of their function. Although the reading of the noun is disputed, according

---

[30] Johnson 1986, 30. Among the numerous discussions of the Greek material, see Bakker 1993 and De Jong 2009.

[31] Even as the chorus turns its theatre audience into those present at the combat by visualizing and re-enacting the event, the description 'choralizes' what it describes and invests the protagonists with the troupe's structure and hierarchy. Located 'in the middle' (ἐν μέσῳ, 515) of the two fighters where she holds the adjudicator's rod, Aphrodite seems to choreograph the dance-like motions that Heracles and Achelous perform. For a dancer-trainer with a rod, see the red-figure phiale attributed to the Phiale Painter showing just such a figure (Boston, Museum of Fine Arts 97.371; *ARV*² 1023.146, *Para.* 441).

to the emendation adopted by many editors the chorus seemingly styles itself a θατήρ (a noun cognate with *theatês*) and assigns to the practitioner of this intensified 'theoric' viewership a specific function: claiming that they 'indicate just as a spectator' (ἐγὼ δὲ θατὴρ μὲν οἷα φράζω, 526; note too the first-person deixis here), the choreutes further suggest that the *theatês* should also engage in reportage, turning the object of his or her spectatorship into the medium of speech. Where recent readers have, correctly, noted the coalescence within the phrase between the chorus and the theatre audience – a conceit that Cnemon, in the passage cited at this chapter's start applies to himself, albeit one whose attendance at the show Calasiris has blocked – no less important is Sophocles' choice of verb for what this viewer does. As usages of the 'marked' term φράζω in hexameter epic already illustrate, it exactly suits the dramatic context insofar as it stands midway between speech and a visual display, turning sights and visible objects into words and words back into things that are seen;[32] in many early instances too, the individual who communicates in this way is also an explicator, the one who reveals the hidden meaning of something seemingly apparent to all, whether a bird omen or some other phenomenon, but whose 'signifying' function he or she alone perceives.

Both the intensified mode of spectatorship practised by the θατήρ and the acts of display and revelation conveyed by φράζω find realization in the stasimon's closing lines. If, as Aristotle would suggest, a concentrated viewing – τὸ θεωρεῖν – involves the perception and expression of similarities,[33] then that is precisely what the turn to this manner of seeing allows the chorus to do. Introducing the song's first and only simile, the maidens liken Deianeira to the estranged and beleaguered calf bereft of its mother (529–30). Adopting that 'double vision' characteristic of performers of archaic choral lyric, these self-styled *theatai* allow us likewise to see in the bride-to-be the juvenile cow that, in so many ways, tropes the girl on the cusp of marriage.

The Sophoclean chorus' depiction of Heracles locked in combat with Achelous, complete with its cast of internal spectators who focalize the scene (or shirk that role), finds its precedent in the two vase images cited in the context of the drama in Chapter 5 (Figs. 5.3, 5.4), one showing the Nereids – or perhaps a chorus of men dressed as the nymphs – surrounding Peleus as he wrestles with Triton, the other the same combat with a line of

---

[32] For detailed discussion, see Steiner 1994, 17–26.

[33] The activity of concentrated observation is, in more general terms, central to Aristotle's broader definition of rhetoric at *Rh.* 1355b25–26, where he defines the art as the 'faculty of observing (τοῦ θεωρῆσαι) in any given case the available means of persuasion'.

viewers on each side and Poseidon who points towards the hero and monster. There, following the argument of Stansbury-O'Donnell, I suggested that these and other spectator figures who frame centrally positioned mythological episodes are choruses arranged in linear or circular formations, whose words, movements and gestures summon up remote and/or fictional events. In placing these images on vases, the artists have expanded the reach of the mythological exempla: taking the place of the original spectators who witnessed the chorus' performance, a second-tier viewer of the painted scene also gains access to heroic and divine actions, shaping his or her conduct according to the positive and negative paradigms that the chorus 'presentifies'. These scenes, I would add, are perhaps the most immediate demonstrations of the choral viewership practised by the painted figures' counterparts in lyric poetry, who similarly can see in a manner both visionary and 'ecphrastic', now translated into the medium of sung poetry.[34]

As Stansbury-O'Donnell notes,[35] Heracles' exploits supply Greek artists with their most frequent subject for such 'framed' spectatorship scenes, with any number of examples from the archaic and early classical period. An Attic black-figure neck amphora of ca. 520–510 in Como offers an instance of the common iconographical scheme while demonstrating the choral gaze with particular clarity (Fig. 10.0).[36] On the obverse of the pot, two figures viewing the *agôn* bracket the central mythological event, Heracles' encounter with the Nemean lion; to the right stands an armed Athena while on the left the artist positions a female figure in a patterned mantle and chiton similar to those worn by the goddess. Although she too carries a spear in her right hand, she lacks Athena's helmet and shield. With her left arm raised and fingers extended from her upright palm, this second bystander gestures towards the fighting pair, inviting us to participate in her spectatorship. Also included in the composition is a visual device to demarcate the objects of the internal viewers' attention: together the several spears equipping both the woman and goddess, one upwardly inclined, the others pointing downward, form diagonal lines that cordon off the hero and the lion and turn the representation of their struggle into the likeness of a framed image.

---

[34] Indeed, these choruses already realize the two meanings that the term ecphrasis acquires: it is quite literally, a 'speaking out' and, in the definitions offered in the *Progymnasmata*, Quintilian and other theorists, a type of discourse that, through its signature use of *enargeia*, 'makes visible' its subject matter.

[35] Stansbury-O'Donnell 2006, 39.

[36] Como, Museo Civico di Como D3359. Stansbury-O'Donnell 2006, 117–18 discusses the vase, and my interpretation builds on his.

Fig. 10.0 Black-figure neck amphora, ca. 520–510 B.C.E. Side A. Como, Museo Civico di Como D3359. Photograph courtesy of Museo Civico di Como.

Turning the vase to its other side (Fig. 10.1), or moving around it, a viewer would encounter three more figures whose dress and hairstyle echo those of the mortal spectator on the obverse, and whose back-turned heads indicate that they too are looking towards the combat. As their individualized gestures, movements and arrangement on the circular surface of the pot signal, they are dancing; the first hikes up her dress with one hand so as to allow her to lift her foot high in the air[37] while holding a lotus bud in the other, and the second steps forward, the back foot with the heel raised up, her arms positioned in a graceful *rond de bras*. The third dancer combines elements from the other two performers; she also carries a lotus bud while reprising her immediate neighbour's stance, moving swiftly to the right while pushing off with her back foot.

In Stansbury-O'Donnell's reading,[38] these dancing maidens are chorus members (one among the groups performing a dithyrambic song in the view of Ghiron-Bistagne),[39] whose varied postures, footwork and gestures

[37] Note how that upraised foot neatly responds to the lion on the obverse who performs an almost identical 'step'.
[38] Stansbury-O'Donnell 2006, 118.   [39] Ghiron-Bistagne 1976, 269.

Fig. 10.1 Black-figure neck amphora, ca. 520–510 B.C.E. Side B. Como, Museo Civico di Como D3359. Photograph courtesy of Museo Civico di Como.

offer the external viewer 'a synchronous picture of the different steps of the dance, arranged as a progression as the line moves through space' and who stage their spectacle under the leadership of the older *chorêgos* depicted on the other side. If, as he further observes, that figure's spatial 'apartness' signals her primacy, and her Athena-like spear freshly confirms her authority and even priestess-like status, then she also fulfills the mediating role typical of chorus leaders and that already characterized Agido in Alcman's first *Partheneion*. Equipoised between the divine and human characters in the image, she simultaneously occupies the realms of both Athena and her fellow dancers, transmitting the doings and perceptions of the goddess to the members of her choral ensemble.

Another Attic black-figure amphora from ca. 540–530 (Fig. 10.2), attributed to the Princeton Group and portraying a second of Heracles' canonical labours, his fight with the triple-bodied Geryon, follows the same general typology.[40] Unusually for the period, each of the antagonists

---

[40] New York, Metropolitan Museum of Art, The Bothmer Purchase Fund 2010.147.

Fig. 10.2 Black-figure amphora attributed to the Princeton Group, ca. 540–530 B.C.E. Side A. New York, Metropolitan Museum of Art, The Bothmer Purchase Fund 2010.147. Photograph courtesy © The Metropolitan Museum of Art, The Bothmer Purchase Fund 2010.

occupies his own side of the vase: Heracles, dressed in his now signature lion-skin, appears as an archer poised to dispatch an arrow; Geryon, whose three heads and bodies are superimposed one on another, each fully armed and moving in different directions (the artist makes space for all six limbs), fills the reverse (Fig. 10.3). Advancing around the amphora neck, one on each of its sides, two lines of men and youths process.[41] The scenes on the two faces are, in this instance, identical: each is composed of three figures, the last one bearded, all similarly dressed and equipped with elaborate crowns or wreaths as well as some type of cloth or fillet which they carry in their hands. A pipe-player, singularized by his different garments, leads each trio from left to right. Suggestive of a choral procession is not only the presence of the aulete and the marchers' regular stepping motion, but the youths and men have their mouths slightly ajar as though they were singing as they advanced. Where on the Como amphora the artist imagined the

---

[41] Cf. a third black-figure amphora of the same period (Naples, Museo Nazionale 81186) whose obverse shows Heracles and the Nemean lion while a line made up of six men and boys processes. Here too a pipe-player leads the group. For discussion, see Stansbury-O'Donnell 2006, 115–17.

Fig. 10.3 Black-figure amphora attributed to the Princeton Group, ca. 540–530 B.C.E. Side B. New York, Metropolitan Museum of Art, The Bothmer Purchase Fund 2010.147. Photograph courtesy © The Metropolitan Museum of Art, The Bothmer Purchase Fund 2010.

choristers dancing the episode into being, calling up the stance, movements and sounds of the struggle between Heracles and the lion with their choreography, here we should understand the hero's encounter with Geryon as the subject of the song performed by the sextet.

That Heracles' tenth labour could furnish the topic of a choral song and dance, Stesichorus' *Geryoneis*, probably composed in the first half of the sixth century and likely still performed at the time of the amphora's production, suggests. While there is no critical consensus on the question of the context for which the poem was designed, a recent discussion argues that a civic festival hosting competitive performances of 'epic-lyric' pieces, whether citharodic or choral, supplies the most likely venue.[42] Indeed, the myth selected by Stesichorus for his subject seems very well suited to this civic setting and to enactment by just such a group as the amphora proposes. Featuring its own more deadly competition by way of counterpart to the poetic-cum-choral *agôn* in which the poet and his troupe are engaged, the story offers a paradigmatic heroic episode which furnishes a

---

[42] Carey 2015, 53; for a more dissenting view, see West 2015.

model for the youths about to join the corps of citizen fighters as well as for
the more seasoned men in the choral ensemble; marching in formation,
they rehearse their participation in the hoplite ranks and victory over
antagonists inimical to their communities.[43]

While readers of the *Geryoneis* have commented on how well
Stesichorus has calibrated his seemingly innovative treatment of the
story – which presents us with a Geryon who more resembles an Iliadic
hero in ethos and sensibilities than a monstrous, bestial 'other' and
reserves cunning and the villain's role for Heracles – to the cultural
concerns of the community which likely supplied its original audience,[44]
the amphora suggests that this treatment of the myth may, by the time
that the artist conceived his design, be more widespread.[45] Much as
Stesichorus' poem does (at least as far as can be determined from its
fragmentary remains), the artist not only grants Geryon equal status with
the hero by allotting to the monster the reverse face, but additionally
chooses to depict him as a conventionally armed warrior, furnished with a
finely detailed shield, crested helmet and cuirass, albeit all in triplicate.
Indeed, if there is 'alterity' here, it belongs principally to Heracles: armed
with the bow that permits its user to avoid the more heroic type of close
combat for which Geryon is prepared, he wears his lion pelt, still complete
with its prominent tail and paws. Reinforcing the distinction between the
animalistic attacker and his impeccably armed antagonist is the recapitulation of the lion motif on the shield carried by the middle Geryon; the
beast's eye-catching white teeth, lolling tongue and shagginess highlight
its predatory nature while inviting the viewer to compare and contrast the
lions on each face; in the second instance, the bestial element is restricted
to a decorative device; in the first, it transforms, melding Heracles with
the victim of his predatory attack, and casting the confrontation more as
an ephebic-style hunt than a close encounter between hoplites on the field
of battle. The double chorus uniting the two sides might use the song that
they perform in processional fashion to accommodate the different
modes of combat and offer up both as models from which the community's fighting forces might draw.

---

[43] For an aulete accompanying hoplite lines, see the Chigi Vase (Rome, Villa Giulia 22679).

[44] See, most recently, Franzen 2009 and Noussia-Fantuzzi 2013.

[45] Since the provenance of the vase is unknown, it cannot be determined whether it was produced
for the south Italian export market, as a sizable number of neck amphorae were.

3　*Phantasia* and 'Fusion'

3.1　*'Only Connect':* Enargeia *and Empathetic Participation*

The powers and particularities of choral spectatorship detailed above do not exhaust a chorus' unique capacity to practice *enargeia avant la lettre*. Emphatic in later accounts of how to give a scene within a speech or text the desired visuality and consequent appeal to the audience's imagination was the need to create an intimate connection between the speaker and listener, this, perhaps, an extension of the notion of sight already found in Plato (most clearly expressed at *Phaedr.* 255a), which assumes the absence of a boundary between the perceiving subject and the object perceived and a coalescence of the two. In Quintilian's view, the first step towards achieving this bond was for the would-be practitioner of *enargeia* to imagine the episode for himself so as to stimulate the same sensations and emotions – these stored up by him, in Aristotle's earlier account, in the form of mental images that are not just visual but involve every kind of sensory perception (*De an.* 427b18–20) – experienced by the original participants (*Inst.* 6.2.31–32).[46] By virtue of entering into this state of empathy with individuals both real and fictional, and which then gives rise to verbalization, the speaker induces a matching response in those listening to his evocation and prompts them to entertain the same *phantasiai* that both arouse emotions and persuade them in turn. Refining this notion further, Quintilian suggests a somatic as well as 'psychic' element in the practice. Distinguishing between an ineffective speech that merely 'reaches the ears of the judge' and one 'expressed in full and displayed to his mind's eye' (8.3.62), the rhetorician seems to have in mind a process of bodily penetration, a passage from the surface to the interior which regards 'the human body as permeable'[47] to the quasi-physical force that words exercise (much as Gorgias had done in his delineation of the power of *logos* in his *Encomium to Helen*).

　　Two aspects of Quintilian's discussion prove particularly apposite to choral dynamics and to audience-performer interactions in much earlier times. The first concerns the context in which a speaker creates the bond of identification between his own multi-sensory perceptions and the emotional responses these generate and which he transmits to his audience. As Ruth Webb remarks, 'in his own examples of *enargeia*, Quintilian assumes

---

[46] For discussion, see Webb 2009, 94.　　[47] Webb 2009, 98.

a live performance situation in which the transmission of mental images and their concomitant emotions between a speaker and his audience is a vital part of rhetorical interaction in the forum or school'.[48] Consistent with this is [Longinus'] analysis of *phantasia*, which, he observes, is in contemporary usage 'predominantly applied to cases where, carried away by inspiration and emotion (ἐνθουσιασμοῦ καὶ πάθους), you think that you see what you describe and you place it before the eyes of your hearers'; so transported, the speaker is able to elicit his own sensations in the audience's visual imagination along with the attendant sensory and, in this instance, corporeal reactions (*De subl.* 15.1–2). Whereas poets, [Longinus] further observes, enter this quasi-frenzy so as to generate ἔκπληξις, the orator's aim is to achieve the *enargeia* that forms a critical part of the production of mental images. The language selected by [Longinus] at the end of his account signals the literally 'dynamizing' impact of the rhetorical stratagem: both poets and orators deploy the device with the intent of 'stirring up' (συγκεκινημένον), a verb whose literal meaning is to 'move along with' or 'together with'.

With equal bearing on the early chorus are the two facets of the state of empathy that Quintilian describes. Just as poets and artists so frequently include internal viewers in their depictions of choral performances and verbally and visually indicate the reciprocity of the actions, sensations and emotions of the perceiver and perceived, so the orator both takes the place of an original eyewitness of the scene and simultaneously assumes the role of the individuals who form the objects of his mental spectatorship, feeling, acting and responding as they had done. In those several instances where more peripheral viewers also appear in the account, as on the amphora in Como, these attendant figures furnish a second set of responders, galvanized by the sensations channelled by the primary spectator. The corporeal impact of mental images strikingly recalls not just the behaviour of the chorus-viewing crowd as Heliodorus' Cnemon described it (the audience moved along with the dancers), but also the response of the aged men similarly positioned as spectators to choral performances in Plato's *Laws*; in the account given by the Athenian Stranger of the pleasure that the elderly take in watching – and the verb again is θεωρεῖν – the chorus of younger men as it dances, the spectacle 'can best rouse us (ἐπεγείρειν), through recollection, to youth' (657d6). Like [Longinus'] συγκινεῖν, the verb refers to a literal 'awakening' or 'stirring up', a prompt for motion.

---

[48] Webb 2009, 96.

3.2 The 'Sympathetic' Chorus

Looking back to representations of choral performances in the archaic and early classical period, we can witness at first hand the creation of this bond of mutuality between performers and audiences, and find expressions of that visual, emotional and kinetic empathy explicated in the theoretical accounts and in the writings of the literary critics of the imperial age.[49] In a rich discussion of the aesthetics of listening in the early Greek sources, and more particularly of how audiences respond to aural beauty in the form of musical and vocal performances, Peponi introduces the term 'fusion' to describe the particular impact that instrumental music and song can have on an audience: 'by *fusion* I mean that condition whereby the forcefulness of auditory pleasure is conceptualized as keeping the listener united with the performer in such a transfixed manner that the boundaries separating the two recede'.[50] Using the Homeric account of Odysseus' encounter with the Sirens – who, as Peponi and others demonstrate, the epic poet already depicts in a manner that intimates the choral ensemble that they more emphatically become in later art and texts (see Chapter 3) – as her chief model, Peponi comments that, like the paradigmatic hero confronted with his irresistible singers, audiences are 'not simply fascinated by, but even forcefully drawn toward and attached to, the performers'.[51] A further element enters into the interactions that her discussion explores. In this collapse of boundaries between singer or musician and listener, the identification is so close that the hearer thinks him- or herself the performer.[52] Reworking Peponi's argument, I suggest that, in accordance with the archetypal Siren ensemble, our sources typically (although not exclusively) make this bond

---

[49] For a very different but complementary account of this reciprocity, here termed 'kinesthetic empathy', see the illuminating discussion of Olsen 2017; for Olsen, the response of the viewers of choral performances is a result of (in the definition of Sklar 2001, 199 n. 3 cited by Olsen on p. 154) 'the process of translating from visual to kinesthetic modes' which prompts the spectator 'to participate with another's movement'. Olsen's article treats several of the same passages cited here.

[50] Peponi 2012, 91.   [51] Peponi 2012, 89.

[52] As Peponi 2012, 89 details, the sources introduce a group internal to a song that models relations between the two parties to the auditory experience; as the parthenaic works of Alcman illustrate, the choreutes may be positioned as primary listeners to the 'lead' voice of the poet and/or *chorêgos*, describing and enacting their response, frequently one of *pothos* or *eros* as they witness the beauty of their pre-eminent member. Their status as both internal to and outside the performance offers a miniaturized version of the position of the external audience, 'listening while also being part of an evolving performance. They are in some way set apart while at the same time set in the midst. In other words, they are an integral part of a musical whole that is split only symbolically, so that their role *qua* listeners can be enacted effectively within the boundaries of the developing choral act'.

integral to their accounts of the response instigated by explicitly *choral* performances.

Two early texts (the second treated by Peponi) offer prime examples of this exchange between choristers and audience and the effacement of distinctions between the two. First, the choral band on Achilles' Iliadic shield that includes both performers and internal viewers. The youths and maidens in the image, as earlier chapters detailed, seem engaged in some kind of courtship dance;[53] hence the epithet ἀλφεσίβοιαι (18.593) assigned the girls, a term regularly used of those ready for the marriage that involves an exchange of goods, cattle among them. The nature of the performance gives a specificity to the adjective ἱμερόεντα (603) characterizing the chorus at the scene's close, an epithet which means at once 'desirous' and 'desire-arousing', this last in reference to the response of the audience that forms part of the forged representation and encircles the performers. The coincidence between the 'courting' character of the mixed chorus of youths and maidens, experiencing desire for one another,[54] and the impact of their dance on the similarly 'desirous' viewers is indicative of the correspondence and cohesion of the sensations of the two sets of participants in the scene.[55]

A much more explicit and wholesale account of this identification occurs in the *Homeric Hymn to Apollo*, also already cited in earlier chapters, where the Ionians gather on Delos to celebrate the divine object of the hymnist's praise.[56] Following a generalized description of the festival listing its various components, choral song and dance among them (treated below), the poet focuses more narrowly on the performance by the Delian maiden chorus (156–64):

πρὸς δὲ τόδε μέγα θαῦμα, ὅου κλέος οὔποτ' ὀλεῖται,
κοῦραι Δηλιάδες Ἑκατηβελέταο θεράπναι·
αἵ τ' ἐπεὶ ἄρ πρῶτον μὲν Ἀπόλλων' ὑμνήσωσιν,
αὖτις δ' αὖ Λητώ τε καὶ Ἄρτεμιν ἰοχέαιραν,

---

[53] See particularly Lonsdale 1995, 276–78.

[54] It is just such mixed performing groups that Plato and Lucian single out as occasions for pairing off and the formation of future marital bonds; see Chapter 7 for this.

[55] See Rawles 2011 on the collapse of distinctions not only between auditors and audience but those between the choral and authorial voices in their bond of shared *eros*. Note too that in the passage from Plato's *Laws* 657d already cited, the old men watching younger men as they dance in choruses experience *pothos*, albeit a desire directed not at the dancers but roused by the viewers' longing for their own lost youth when they too could participate in choral performances.

[56] Olsen 2017, 158–63 offers a rich but differently oriented discussion of the passage also drawing on Peponi's reading in her account.

μνησάμεναι ἀνδρῶν τε παλαιῶν ἠδὲ γυναικῶν 160
ὕμνον ἀείδουσιν, θέλγουσι δὲ φῦλ' ἀνθρώπων.
πάντων δ' ἀνθρώπων φωνὰς καὶ κρεμβαλιαστὺν
μιμεῖσθ' ἴσασιν· φαίη δέ κεν αὐτὸς ἕκαστος
φθέγγεσθ'· οὕτω σφιν καλὴ συνάρηρεν ἀοιδή.

And in addition, this great wonder, the fame of which will never perish: the maidens of Delos, the handmaids of the Far-shooter, who, after first hymning Apollo, and then in turn Leto and Artemis arrow-pourer, turn their thoughts to the men and women of old and sing a song that charms the races of humans. They know how to mimic all people's voices and their rhythmic motions; anyone might think that he himself was speaking, so beautifully is their song put together.

In Peponi's interpretation of the much debated term *krembaliastus* (both the reading and meaning are uncertain), the noun refers not just to the sound made by the castanets equipping the dancers which mark out their rhythm, but 'is mainly associated with kinetic activity, that is dance,' and 'denotes the act of generating, through *krembala*, rhythmic patterns that are meant to moderate patterned and stylized bodily movement, what the Greeks called *schêmata*'.[57] Drawing out the implications of this, Peponi concludes that the subsequent description of how 'anyone might think that he himself was speaking' refers not just to the Deliades' assumption of their viewers' voices but of their motions too. With the several dimensions of *choreia* operative in the phrase, we witness an exact blend of identities where performers and audiences move and speak as one, entering into a state 'where the line separating the act of performing from the act of attending tends to disappear' and 'the enchanted audience empathizes to such a degree that they attend as virtual performers'.[58]

The hymnist has, perhaps, already given something of a preview of the transfer between the Deliades and their viewers, and of the empathetic transformation – the 'great wonder' – that comes about expressly through the modality of *choreia*. In the earlier passage introducing the Ionian festival-goers and previewing events at the Delia, we hear the voice of an anonymous speaker, a figure who makes a second appearance in the passage concerning the Delian maidens (where the term φαίη again prefaces his remark). In the first of the two scenes, the individual comments on the properties assumed by those taking part in the pugilistic and choral spectacles (149–52):

[57] Peponi 2009, 55. [58] Peponi 2009, 67.

οἱ δέ σε πυγμαχίῃ τε καὶ ὀρχηθμῷ καὶ ἀοιδῇ
μνησάμενοι τέρπουσιν ὅταν στήσωνται ἀγῶνα.   150
φαίη κ' ἀθανάτους καὶ ἀγήρως ἔμμεναι αἰεὶ
ὃς τότ' ἐπαντιάσει' ὅτ' Ἰάονες ἀθρόοι εἶεν·

They take delight, remembering you, in boxing and dancing and song
whenever they take up position in the performance space and someone
might say that they are forever immortal and ageless if he came upon them
then when all the Ionians are together in a body.

As readers have observed, the two adjectives used of Ionians grant them
fully divine status, assimilating them to the gods whom they gather to
celebrate. While their momentary elevation – as the subsequent representation of the Olympians likewise dancing and singing in choral festivities
makes clear through its use of parallel diction (186–206) – seems chiefly to
depend on their emulation of a signature divine activity, this ability to
partake in the condition of the immortals might extend to those who watch
as well as those who perform.[59] If we follow the version of the lines
preserved by Thucydides at 3.104.4, then the hymnist has, as in the later
scenes where the Deliades and the Olympians sing and dance, included
spectators at the festivities. In the historian's citation of line 150, those not
actually participating in the various events have 'been seated in the performance space (καθέσωσιν ἀγῶνα)'. Assuming that the anonymous
speaker's observation concerns the entire assemblage and not just the
singer-dancers (the reference to the totality of those gathered, ἀθρόοι,
suggests as much), then the audience shares in the performers' divinization
within the charmed choral space that unites both parties to the event. Nor is
this internal commentator excluded from the Ionians' ontological unity
with the immortals: as he 'would take pleasure (τέρψαιτο) in his heart
looking at (εἰσορόων) the fair-girdled women' (153–54), both his spectatorship and sensations anticipate those of Zeus and Leto: they too will delight
their hearts while watching Apollo perform together with the other gods on
the Olympian heights (ἐπιτέρπονται θυμὸν μέγαν εἰσορόωντες, 204).

A passage from an early fifth-century text, whose other facets previous
chapters have explored, again illustrates, now with a malignant twist added
in, the bodily and psychic experience of hearing, viewing and becoming
indissolubly 'fused' with practitioners of *choreia*. In Pindar's evocation of
the third of the temples built in honour of Apollo at Delphi, we encounter

---

[59] Very apposite to this is Prauscello 2011, 157, who remarks of the description of the aged men
watching youthful choruses at Pl. *Leg.* 657d, 'to watch the dance and song *is* a way to participate
in it' (emphasis in the original).

the gable-decorating choral Keledones, on whose properties and powers
this portion of the paean lingers. As my previous discussions have
detailed, the poet patently models these Charmers on the Odyssean
Sirens, investing their voices with the same all-compelling quality and
capacity so utterly to enchant their listeners that they forsake all chance of
a home return. But in addition to drawing out the choral paradigm merely
latent in the epic singers, Pindar rings a further change on the Homeric
precedent when he details the fate of the spellbound audience: quite
literally transfixed by the performance, they 'hang up their spirits' on
the golden choristers' voice (μελ[ί]φρονι αὐδ[ᾷ θυμὸν ἀνακρίμναντες, fr.
52i.78–79 S.-M.). As Rutherford's translation cited here brings out, the
verb evokes the dedication of a votive good,[60] figuring the internal organ
– the locus of auditory pleasure in other accounts too – as one of the
commonplace plaques that, equipped with holes for that very purpose,
were regularly hung from a tree in proximity of the sanctuary, or affixed
to a wall, ceiling beam or temple column, or even suspended from the cult
image itself (Herodotus uses the verb in exactly this sense at 5.77.16 and
5.95.4).

The listener's self-transformation into a material offering additionally
involves an instance of the reflexivity or modelling outlined by Peponi,[61]
albeit of an extreme and disturbing kind, whereby an audience becomes
indistinguishable from the chorus members and assimilates him- or herself
to the actions, nature and role of the singer-dancers. Pindar's *Paean*
articulates this mirroring in several ways. Like the Keledones, the temple
visitors have become reified, permanent fixtures at the site and fresh
decorative devices in the Delphic complex; enchanted by the singing of
the existing architectural features, their emotional engagement makes them
an integral element of the overall temple ornamentation, part of its larger
kosmos. Whether the tern *daidalma* at 81 refers to the Keledones or,
following Pindaric practice on other occasions (e.g. *Ol.* 1.29, 105, *Nem.*
11.18, fr. 94b.32 S.-M.), to their song, the singers and/or their vocalizations
are clearly styled crafted objects, doublets of what their audiences will
become. The desirous element that the *Paean* seemingly attributes to the
Keledones' singing, styling their voice not merely 'honey sweet' (75) and
'like honey to the mind' (78) but also, if this is the meaning of the lacunose
phrase at 80–81, a 'cunningly worked artefact that causes mortals to

[60] Rutherford 2001, 220, noting the two facets to the experience described, comments that the
expression suggests 'both a religious dedication and psychological dependency'.
[61] See Peponi 2012, 77 for discussion of how the immobility of the singing Sirens imposes the same
stasis on Odysseus' ship.

dissolve (λυσίμβροτον)',[62] plays no small role in this reification and literal fusion. In his speech on Eros in Plato's *Symposium*, Aristophanes describes the ultimate if ineffable wish that forms the stuff of lovers' whimsies: were Hephaestus to come with his forging tools in hand to these besotted individuals and offer to 'weld you together and join you into something that is naturally whole, so that the two of you are made into one for as long as you lived' (ὑμᾶς συντῆξαι καὶ συμφυσῆσαι εἰς τὸ αὐτό, ὥστε δύ' ὄντας ἕνα γεγονέναι καὶ ἕως τ' ἂν ζῆτε, 192d8–e2), a state that would endure not just in life, but, as Aristophanes clarifies, in death as well, no lover would reject his offer. As the presence of Hephaestus with his welding instruments makes clear, such a process would involve the transformation of the pair into an enduring metallic artefact, two entities now lastingly fused into one.

Reinforcing the audience's inseparability from the Pindaric Keledones is, finally, the fate that claims them both. As argued in an earlier chapter, the sadly fragmentary text seemingly suggests that the gods punish the Charmers' abuse of the proper relations between this lyric chorus and its public (votives should be offered to the gods, not to those who celebrate them in song and dance)[63] by withdrawing or in some way suppressing the voice originally granted the golden singers.[64] There is little consensus concerning the meaning of line 87, which indicates that someone, most likely either Athena or her agent Mnemosyne, 'made breathless a cunning device of old'. Where Rutherford prefers to understand the line as part of a 'flash-back' to the original construction of the temple and the Keledones' manufacture,[65] I suggest that Pindar maintains the chronological progression observed so far and that the action forms part of the penalty exacted by the gods; in a move to strip the Charmers of the source of their transgressive power (just as supernaturally swift objects are turned to stone), they deprive them of the breath that, from Homer on, is the stuff of speech and song.[66] Indeed, the first extant usage of the closely cognate term ἄπνευστος describes exactly this speechlessness: barely sentient as he emerges from his buffeting by the waves, Odysseus washes up on the shore of Scheria 'breathless and speechless' (ἄπνευστος καὶ ἄναυδος, *Od.* 5.456). Since voice is, with motion, among the prime demarcators of a living being, and the incapacity to speak the hallmark of inanimate objects, the

---

[62] Cf. Alcm. fr. 3.61 *PMGF*, where the singers describe the erotic longing inspired by their lead performer as λυσιμελεῖ, limb-loosening.

[63] Power 2011, 93.

[64] Rutherford 2001, 229 imagines the Keledones' voice, now transformed into something beneficial, as continuing to sound from beneath the earth.

[65] Rutherford 2001, 222, following a review of the various interpretations.

[66] For discussion, see Clarke 1997/98.

Charmers are returned to the sphere of silent artefacts from which they have been permitted to emerge.

This same lack of voice may likewise belong to their plaque-turned-victims, who undergo a corresponding loss of breath that simultaneously figures the departure of the life spirit. Power acutely observes how the line describing the listeners 'hanging up their spirits in dedication to the voice like honey to the mind' includes one of the extremely rare instances of hiatus in Pindar, a pause which occurs right in the middle of the noun-epithet expression that the phrase includes.[67] For Power, the interruption of the flow of breath that the singers must observe reveals 'the gap between the singing voice of the "flawed", human, paeanic chorus and that of the flawless, deadly robotic Keledones',[68] signalling that while the song's current mortal performers are obliged to stop and catch their breath, the metal maidens continue to produce an unending stream of song. But could this 'hiatal glitch', in Power's phrase, instead flag the moment when the internal auditors suffering transformation into an inanimate object attempt to catch a final breath? Their condition not only foreshadows that to be visited on their beguilers but currently and audibly extends to the Pindaric chorus too: continuing this mimetic chain, the performers of the *Paean*, now forced momentarily to recover breath so as to proceed with their song, share in the condition of the original votary audience and the similarly 'breathless' Charmers.

Of particular pertinence to the notion of an audience's 'suspension' from the choral voice and the deeper connectivity that exists between auditors and choristers in *Paean* 8 is a later and more benign representation of relations between singers and those who attend their performances. In Plato's *Ion*, Socrates, seeking to establish that his interlocutor, the rhapsode of the dialogue's title, owes his ability to speak authoritatively of Homer to the Muse's inspiration, clarifies his meaning by citing the example of a magnet from which a chain of iron rings hangs down. While rhapsodic practice is Socrates' principal concern, here he expressly expands his explanatory paradigm to encompass lyric poets as well (533d1–e8):

> For as I was saying just now, this is not an art (τέχνη) in you whereby you speak well on Homer, but a divine power which moves you like that in the stone which Euripides named a magnet, but most people call 'Heraclea stone'. For this stone not only attracts iron rings, but also imparts to them a power whereby they in turn are able to do the very same thing as the stone and attract other rings; so that sometimes there is formed quite a

---

[67] Power 2011, 91–92.   [68] Power 2011, 92.

long chain of bits of iron rings, suspended one from another, and they all depend for this power on that of one stone. In the same manner also the Muse inspires men herself, and then by means of these inspired persons, the inspiration spreads to others and holds them in a connected chain. For all good epic poets utter all those fine poems not from art, but as inspired and possessed, and the good lyric poets (μελοποιοί) likewise.[69]

Following Ion's account of how, when he recites an epic scene, it is divine inspiration again that allows him to enter into the state of those whose actions and emotions he narrates, now weeping and now so terrified that his hair stands on end, and to transmit his sensations to an audience so that they act and feel that way in turn, Socrates returns to the magnet analogy and now, moving from the rhapsodic context, still more unequivocally pins it to a choral performance scenario (535e7–536a7):

οἶσθα οὖν ὅτι οὗτός ἐστιν ὁ θεατὴς τῶν δακτυλίων ὁ ἔσχατος, ὧν ἐγὼ ἔλεγον ὑπὸ τῆς Ἡρακλειώτιδος λίθου ἀπ' ἀλλήλων τὴν δύναμιν λαμβάνειν; ὁ δὲ μέσος σὺ ὁ ῥαψῳδὸς καὶ ὑποκριτής, ὁ δὲ πρῶτος αὐτὸς ὁ ποιητής· ὁ δὲ θεὸς διὰ πάντων τούτων ἕλκει τὴν ψυχὴν ὅποι ἂν βούληται τῶν ἀνθρώπων, ἀνακρεμαννὺς ἐξ ἀλλήλων τὴν δύναμιν. καὶ ὥσπερ ἐκ τῆς λίθου ἐκείνης ὁρμαθὸς πάμπολυς ἐξήρτηται χορευτῶν τε καὶ διδασκάλων καὶ ὑποδιδασκάλων, ἐκ πλαγίου ἐξηρτημένων τῶν τῆς Μούσης ἐκκρεμαμένων δακτυλίων.

Do you know that the spectator is the last of the rings that I spoke of as receiving from each other the power transmitted from the Heraclean lodestone? You, the rhapsode and actor, are the middle ring; the poet himself is the first; but it is the god who through the whole series draws the souls of men whithersoever he pleases, making the power of one depend on the other. And, just as from the magnet, there is a mighty chain of choreutes and masters and under-masters suspended by side-connections from the rings that hang down from the Muse.

Although this dialogue long antedates the detailed discussion of *choreia* in the *Laws*, the image of the chain that unites the Muse with the mortal practitioners of her arts and that permits these multiple transfers to occur strikingly resembles the Athenian Stranger's description of the golden chain operating in men and that makes them behave in the manner of 'a divine puppet' at *Leg.* 644d7–645c6. As Kurke's persuasive reading of this and later passages in the *Laws* demonstrates,[70] the Athenian Stranger's account then informs the subsequent more extended representation of the gods as chorus masters and of the

---

[69]   Trans. Lamb modified here and in the subsequent citations from the text.
[70]   Kurke 2013, 128–46.

humans who follow in their wake, attached to their *chorêgoi* in the manner of the puppets of the earlier description (653c7–654a5, cited in Chapter 7). The scene at the Apolline temple visualized by Pindar's eighth *Paean* anticipates the conceit in the *Ion* and *Laws* for more than the notion of receptivity and the physical attachment that structures choral relations: according to the sequence of events that the song traces out, the Keledones have also received a prior inspiration in the form of the *audê* that Athena seemingly has placed within them. It is this that stands as the source of the ineluctable power of attraction exercised by the voices that turn the Charmers into lookalike Sirens, creatures whose name ancient etymologists derived from *seira*, a rope.

4   *Enargeia* and Epiphany

The dimensions of *choreia* explored in the previous three sections – the brilliance and speed of choreutes and of the spectacles they stage, a chorus' capacity to exercise a 'second-order sight' in which an audience can participate and the 'attractive' powers that choral performers command – all contribute to the final area where archaic and early classical choruses already achieve the end to which, in Hellenistic and imperial accounts, the practice of *enargeia* also tends: that of stimulating an epiphany, or making audiences of viewers, hearers and, ultimately, readers believe themselves in the presence of the divine. Where, in the earlier period, the gods themselves seemingly attend and are participants in the choral song and dance, for later audiences, these encounters with the immortals more typically occur in the mediated and secondary forms and forums that self-consciously 'enargic' artistic and literary evocations supply.

4.1   *Epiphanic* Choreia *in Archaic and Early Classical Poetry and Art*

The better to illustrate the particular power of choral song and dance to prompt divine self-manifestations, I begin by looking back to a series of representations that long predate the material treated in this study's previous discussions and that stand behind many of the sources already addressed in Chapter 3. The first piece in my argument depends on a convention very familiar from Homeric epic and the broader mythical repertoire: the gods' propensity for assuming the shape of birds for their excursions from heaven down to the human realm. These avian deities are clearly visible already in Minoan and Mycenaean artefacts, where visual artists regularly include birds in scenes of cult activities and depictions of ritual spaces so as to indicate the presence of the divine – whether the god him- or herself, or some symbolic or secondary representation of the same – within the mortal setting. To cite just some of the many examples,[71] in the Post-Palatial period, goddesses with upraised hands from the Shrine of the Double Axes at Knossos and from Gaza, Kannia and Karphi wear headdresses with birds fixed to the top, and one among the many sealings from Zakro from the New Palace Period displays an eagle-headed female figure, suggestively posed with the wings with which she is equipped outstretched and her knees bent as though performing a Minoan version of a latter-day *plié*.[72] Mycenaean artists follow suit, albeit with differences in the modes of representation, and in several instances birds perch or stand behind the thrones reserved for divinities; in one such depiction, in a scene on the Homage Krater from Aradippo, Cyprus, showing warriors processing towards a divine figure seated on a throne, the artist includes a bird looking down from behind the seat towards the goddess, whose spotted garment its plumage reproduces.[73]

On many occasions, these birds are incorporated into scenes featuring rituals addressed to an already present or self-manifesting deity or seemingly appear in response to actions performed with the express intention of eliciting divine epiphanies.[74] That act of worship can take a variety of forms. On a gold ring from Tiryns, four genii advance with pitchers so as to present their liquid offerings to a goddess seated on a throne with a hieratic-looking bird placed behind her chair.[75] In other instances, artists include birds in scenes showing worshippers shaking or pulling trees or embracing a baetylic stone, two gestures similarly designed to stimulate a deity's advent;[76] so a ring from a tomb at Sellopoulou near Knossos includes a swallow that swoops down seemingly in response to the action performed by a man who kneels against a boulder with one arm outstretched towards the bird.[77] A ring from the necropolis at Kalyvia near Phaistos offers a similar combination of elements; a swallow flies from a pithos towards a man leaning over a boulder while a woman pulls at a tree growing from a container.

---

[71] For this and the examples that follow, I draw chiefly on Carter 1995, 290–91 with earlier accounts.

[72] Carter 1995, 290, with her fig. 18.2.

[73] Carter 1995, 290 discusses the bowl, illustrated in her fig. 18.3.

[74] As Lonsdale 1995, 279 and other discussions of these scenes regularly observe, any interpretation of this material is rendered problematic due to the lack of textual evidence.

[75] Athens, National Archaeological Museum 6208.

[76] For detailed discussion of this and the other artefacts cited here, see Foster 1995.

[77] Heraklion, Archaeological Museum, precious metal no. 1504.

Most apposite to the interface between *choreia* and epiphany are objects pairing these avian presences with what may be ritual dancing, often at architecturally specific sacred sites. A bronze votive tablet from the Psykhro cave includes three horns of consecration together with birds and other symbolic objects adjacent to a man who appears to be dancing,[78] while a gold ring from a chamber tomb at Midea shows two swallows, one above the other and moving in opposite directions, flying within the frame of what resembles a shrine-like structure. The actions of the two women placed in front of the building may generate the appearance of the birds: dressed in flounced skirts, and with their heads inclined upwards and arms positioned in an adoration gesture, the figures clearly dance.[79] In a Post-Palatial terracotta group from Palaikastro, music accompanies the occasion: here three women positioned on a circle-shaped base dance around a central female lyre-player (Fig. 10.4).[80] In Jane Carter's reading of the group, a direct link exists between the trio and an additional participant in the scene: 'as if in response, a bird alights on the circular base in front of the musician'. As she further suggests, depictions like these should be connected with the circular platforms unearthed by excavators at sacred sites and that would have served as dancing platforms.[81] Within this marked-off and sometimes decorated space, whose charged nature the presence of such sanctified objects as lions' heads, horns of consecration and altars indicates, dancing votaries use ritual movements to effect divine epiphanies.[82]

Reinforcing the arguments for seeing these birds as manifestations of the gods are the much debated glyptic images on other Minoan signet rings, which feature diminutive floating or flying figures, some male, others female, in the context of a variety of rituals, the boulder hugging, tree pulling and collective dancing described above; whether we read these airborne figures as actual divinities, or more as 'imagined visions' of the gods,[83] they are broadly (although there are several recent challenges to the view) interpreted as moments when deities declare themselves in response to the actions addressed to them by their human celebrants. Perhaps best known among the representations of this scenario is the Isopata signet ring on display in Heraklion in Crete (Fig. 10.5).[84] Dated on stylistic grounds to ca. 1550–1450 B.C.E., it shows

---

[78] Lonsdale 1995, 280.   [79] For this, see Foster 1995, 418 with her fig. 12.

[80] Heraklion, Archaeological Museum 3903.

[81] Carter 1995, 291. Other chapters treat evidence for dancing platforms.

[82] Lonsdale 1995, 280; see too Hägg 1986, 41–62.   [83] For this distinction, see Cain 2001, 36.

[84] Heraklion, Archaeological Museum, precious metal no. 424. Cain 2001 offers extensive analysis of this and related objects; see too Kyriakidis 2005 and Lonsdale 1995, 279–80, whose discussions also offer the basis for my account. As a caveat to what follows, and as Cain and Lonsdale both indicate, the whole question of whether or not we should interpret the motions performed by individuals on these rings as 'dancing' remains very much a matter of dispute.

Fig. 10.4 Post-Palatial terracotta group from Palaikastro, ca. 1400 B.C.E. Heraklion, Archaeological Museum 3903. Photograph: Zde/Wikimedia CC BY-SA 4.0.

Fig. 10.5 Isopata signet ring from the Isopata tomb near Knossos, ca. 1550–1450 B.C.E. Heraklion, Archaeological Museum AE 424. Photograph: Olaf Tausch/Wikimedia CC BY-SA 3.0.

four women in a landscape with flowering plants; all are bare breasted and wear long flounced skirts, and three have arm bracelets or short-sleeved jackets. Also visible is an eye-shaped oval element, and just above that a 'Heaven Line', a wavy symbol thought to indicate the separation of earth and sky in glyptic iconography. Other recognizable objects on the seal include some kind of vegetal branch and what some style a 'Sacred Heart' and others define as a vessel or chrysalis. Positioned off centre and at the top of the image a tiny female figure, also dressed in a flounced skirt, appears in profile with her right arm extended as she hovers in mid-air. Although some question our ability correctly to identify the nature of the activity depicted in the scene, most discussions of the ring assume that at least three of the larger figures, those on the left and the one located on the right, perform a dance; other images in Minoan art, the fresco known as the 'Sacred Grove and Dance' most particularly, show women with similarly positioned arms who appear to dance or at least to process as an ensemble.[85] Another dancer, albeit a solo performer, appears in a similar context on a gold ring from a tholos tomb in Vapheio,[86] where she forms part of a mixed group of men and women engaged in a variety of ritual gestures; again wearing a flounced skirt and moving with such vigour that her hair flies out horizontally behind her, she dances in close proximity to a man grasping a tree. As this scene suggests, the very act of moving rapidly in the dance could in itself summon deities into the mortal sphere where, as Nicola Cucuzza points out, they might also appear in the act of dancing.[87] Comparing the representation of the divinity on the Isopata ring with that of the goddess painted on the wall of room 14 from Hagia Triada, whose upturned arms and right foot pushing off the ground clearly designate her a dancer, Cucuzza concludes that a deity would on occasion engage in the same activity as her celebrants.

Before extending the paradigm suggested by these representations to the actions and words of choral dancers of the archaic and later periods, several other pre-Greek images can clarify the precise mechanisms at work in these epiphanic events and pinpoint the mimetic and persuasive rapports they construct between the worshipper and the god summoned to the occasion. As studies of Minoan ritual observe,[88] artists seem to depict two different forms of epiphany. In 'enacted' as opposed to 'visionary' divine advents, a mortal can perform the role of the deity, assuming his or her identity and receiving the gestures of worship that the other participants perform. A Minoan seal, this one a silver disc that shows a bird variously classified as a swallow, hawk or 'nonspecific' type, seems to conform to this first scheme. With its raptor beak and wings and clawless legs attached to the shoulder, the creature occupies the same ground line as the sprouting plant next to it

---

[85] Some scholars limit dancing to the woman on the left, noting the similarity in her pose to the two dancers who raise one arm while lowering the other on an Old Palace bowl from Phaistos in the presence of an armless figure with snaky loops, perhaps the Snake Goddess; for the bowl, see Carter 1995, 291.

[86] Athens, National Archaeological Museum 1801.   [87] Cucuzza 2013, 196–98.

[88] Hägg 1986, whose terms I use here, and Marinatos 1993.

and so forms part of the properly human, earth-bound realm. In Karen Foster's reading,[89] we should understand this curious figure as combining anthropomorphic and avian traits: the waist, codpiece and legs belong to a man while the wings and beak equate him with a bird. The position of the arm, raised high with elbow crooked, conforms to the standard 'gesture of adoration' and identifies the character as a worshipper rather than a god. In this instance, the individual performing the act of veneration emulates the appearance regularly assumed by the deity, perhaps in the hope that mimesis will prompt an answering avian epiphany.

This mimetic and avian frame accommodates a second Minoan representation. Decorating the three walls of Room 2 of Building Delta at Akrotiri on Thera is the familiar so-called Spring Fresco (Fig. 10.6),[90] a vividly rendered composition showing seven life-sized swallows set within a landscape of rocks and blossoming lilies; some of the seven are depicted in flight while others, forming pairs, seem to hover in mid-air. In the standard

Fig. 10.6 Spring Fresco from Room 2 of Building Delta, Akrotiri, ca.1500 B.C.E. Athens, National Archaeological Museum. Photograph © National Archaeological Museum, Athens.

---

[89] Foster 1995, 416–17.   [90] Athens, National Archaeological Museum.

view, these avian couples are engaged in a courting ritual, displaying the 'kissing' gesture that male swallows are known to perform in winning their mates; a revisionary account proposes agonistic relations instead, as the swallows fight one another for the feathers needed to line their nests.[91] But context should also help determine the significance of the birds and, although the question remains an open one, there is much to suggest the fresco's location in a space set aside for ritual activity. Excavators have discovered six or seven irregularly distanced holes drilled into the walls and interspersed among or above the birds and flowers as well as other more regularly spaced cavities used for the rods that supported a broad wicker-work shelf. In keeping with the practice observable at other sites, both the shelf and pegs fitted into the holes would have served for the display and suspension of the cult objects that accompanied the performance of rituals. Within this demarcated space, and in accordance with the presence of the swallows that so frequently signal divine epiphanies in Minoan art, the rites enacted within the room aimed to attract the god to the chamber; following this, the shelf and pegs would have held items associated with and symbolic of epiphanies, whether vegetal sprays, double axes, sacral knots or other winged creatures.

Additional features of the chamber corroborate this reading. Centrally located in the larger complex and with unusually thick exterior walls, the room restricts entry by virtue of its low-set door. Measuring only 1.6 m in height, its dimensions suggest that women might enter comfortably but that most men would be forced to stoop. From these disparate icono-graphic and architectural elements, Foster persuasively concludes that the room was designed 'as a cultic space for epiphanic rites',[92] a site where, I would further suggest, exclusively female participants might assume the role of the swallows, even dancing and singing in ways that emulated the painted templates on the walls surrounding them. By virtue, once again, of mimicking the look and actions associated with gods, and surrounded by visual representations of the same, the worshippers could by their gestures summon the divine presence into the space.

Whether through their simulation of the actions and appearances of birds, or the enactment of rituals that comprised music, dance and move-ments of other kinds, Minoan worshippers sought to bring about divine attendance at their rites. This impetus is no less apparent in archaic and early classical Greek choral lyric, whose hymns, paeans and songs in other genres are not only filled with direct addresses and summons to the gods

---

[91] Two detailed accounts are those of Foster 1995 and Hollinshead 1989.   [92] Foster 1995, 423.

that conjure up, hypostatize and compel their presence at and even leadership of the performance; also integral to these repeated appeals are the performers' declarations of the delight that their spectacle affords, the *charis* that adheres to their persons, song and dance, and that act as so many inducements that additionally attract deities to the site.[93]

Exemplary of choral songs that instigate divine appearances both through a proliferation of verbal summons and by highlighting the 'attractive' quality of the performers' ritual activities is the refrain of the Palaikastro Hymn (*IC* III.2.2), a song preserved in an inscription from the second century C.E., but dating back at least to the Hellenistic period and whose repeated portions may be older still.[94] The phrase that works by way of the first part of the refrain, 'o supreme child of Cronus, greetings on my part! Almighty over brightness [or 'quickening', γάνος], you have arrived leading (ἀγώμενος) the gods', draws attention at regular intervals to the advent of its chief addressee, Zeus in this instance, to the occasion, and, noting the god's affinity with its own hierarchical structure, where the mortal *chorêgos* leads the singer-dancers, invites him to respond to the actions of the performers at this time and place: 'come to Dicte at the turn of the year and take pleasure in our song-dance'. A second, simpler hymn performed by the choruses of women at the Heraia at Elis likewise opens by enjoining Dionysus to visit the site together with the Graces, who are, of all possible deities, those most likely to appreciate, model and participate in the dance: 'come, hero Dionysus, to the holy temple of the Eleans along with the Graces' (871 *PMG*). The cult songs of Pindar and Bacchylides similarly declare the power of the performance to compel not just divine attendance but sometimes the gods' assumption of the role of *chorêgoi* and their contribution to the dance; the maiden choristers of Pindar's second *Partheneion* simply announce that Apollo is already there at the Daphnephoria, 'Loxias is come, kindly, to mix immortal *charis* into Thebes' (fr. 94b.3–5 S.-M.), a statement that, as Day notes, 'was verified for the audience delighting in the performance's beauties'.[95]

Another work by Pindar, his fifth *Dithyramb* composed for the Athenians (fr. 75 S.-M.),[96] likewise takes as axiomatic the divine sponsorship and 'grace-infusion' requisite for the song and dance and, in much more detailed fashion, invites its audience to attend to the ever multiplying intimations of the gods' imminence that the opening injunctions, combined with the promise of reward in the shape of the ongoing choral tribute,

---

[93] See particularly Day 2010, 246–54; this is a theme addressed in other chapters of this study.
[94] For the problems of dating the work, see Allonge 2011, 224–26.   [95] Day 2010, 264.
[96] We have nineteen lines of what was doubtless a much longer song.

have already triggered. Freshly underscoring that an epiphany is in the making, and actually occurring, is the song's use of the term *enargês* and the self-characterization of the poetic ego as *mantis* as he engages in a particularly marked form of that 'choral seeing' discussed in Section 2 (1–19):

Δεῦτ᾽ ἐν χορόν, Ὀλύμπιοι,
ἐπί τε κλυτὰν πέμπετε χάριν, θεοί,
πολύβατον οἵ τ᾽ ἄστεος ὀμφαλὸν θυόεντ᾽
        ἐν ταῖς ἱεραῖς Ἀθάναις
οἰχνεῖτε πανδαίδαλόν τ᾽ εὐκλέ᾽ ἀγοράν·   5
ἰοδέτων λάχετε στεφάνων τᾶν τ᾽ ἐαρι-
        δρόπων ἀοιδᾶν,
Διόθεν τέ με σὺν ἀγλαΐᾳ
ἴδετε πορευθέντ᾽ ἀοιδᾶν δεύτερον
ἐπὶ τὸν κισσοδαῆ θεόν,
τὸν Βρόμιον, τὸν Ἐριβόαν τε βροτοὶ καλέομεν,   10
γόνον ὑπάτων μὲν πατέρων μελπόμεν<οι>
γυναικῶν τε Καδμεϊᾶν (Σεμέλην).
ἐναργέα τ᾽ ἔμ᾽ ὥτε μάντιν οὐ λανθάνει.
φοινικοεάνων ὁπότ᾽ οἰχθέντος Ὡρᾶν θαλάμου
εὔοδμον ἐπάγοισιν ἔαρ φυτὰ νεκτάρεα.   15
τότε βάλλεται, τότ᾽ ἐπ᾽ ἀμβρόταν χθόν᾽ ἐραταί
ἴων φόβαι, ῥόδα τε κόμαισι μείγνυται,
ἀχεῖ τ᾽ ὀμφαὶ μελέων σὺν αὐλοῖς,
οἰχνεῖ τε Σεμέλαν ἑλικάμπυκα χοροί.

Come join in our chorus, Olympians, and send over it glorious *charis*, you gods, who are approaching the much frequented, incense-filled navel of the city in sacred Athens, and the famed, all-ornamented agora. Receive a share of crowns bound with violets and songs plucked in the springtime, and look [with favour] on me as I proceed [or 'march'] from Zeus with the radiance of songs secondly to the ivy-knowing god, whom we mortals call Roarer and Loud-shouter, singing and dancing in celebration of the offspring of the highest of fathers and of Kadmeian women. And clear [signs] do not escape my notice, as if I were a seer, when, with the chamber of the red-robed Horai opened, nectar-bearing plants lead on the spring so that it is still more sweet smelling. Then, then the lovely locks of violets are cast upon the ambrosial earth, and roses are mingled with hair, and voices of songs resound to the accompaniment of pipes, and choruses approach Semele of the circling headband.[97]

[97] See Kurke and Neer 2014 for a thorough discussion of the fragment, and from whose reading I have drawn at several points.

Addressing Dionysus and his fellow gods, the choreutes solicit their attendance and the irradiating grace that comes with the luminous divine presence (cf. the answering radiance, ἀγλαΐα, of the choral song) through several rhetorical devices: the repeated imperatives, which further, by means of a deictic and ἴδετε, define the singers and their *choreia* as objects worthy of the immortals' spectatorship, the different naming terms, and the emphasis on the troupe's processional motion. The phrase at lines 7–8 (σὺν ἀγλαΐα . . . πορευθέντ' ἀοιδᾶν) has a triple frame of reference: it includes the hymnal practice of beginning a song with a mention/invocation of Zeus, overlord of the gods; observes the way in which the chorus, dancing around the Altar of the Twelve Gods where the performance is likely to have occurred (hence the references to the agora and *omphalos* at 3 and 5) verbally gestures to the sacred sites in close proximity even as the dancers' 'circular itinerary' might spatially coincide with each structure that the song identifies;[98] and suggests the Olympians' own sequential advent as each one of the divine company is named in turn. By means of such indications of a chorus' movements towards the ritual space that belongs to a divine addressee, or, in other instances, through descriptions of how that deity arrived on a previous occasion at the performance site, choral song and dance regularly offer mimetic representations to encourage and rehearse renewed divine visitations.[99] The trajectory can also work in the other direction. The singers' description of their marching-cum-conveying motion (πορευθέντ') may also be read together with the opening invocation Δεῦτ' ἐν χορόν: here the use of the middle/passive πορεύομαι, 'to be driven, moved along' suggests that the chorus advances under the impetus given it by the gods' simultaneous advent, as though the performers are spurred on so as to follow on the track that their song is laying out.

The twofold *epiklêsis* given Dionysus, 'Roarer and Loud-shouter' (τὸν Βρόμιον, τὸν Ἐριβόαν), further anticipates the looked-for appearance of the god to whom the dithyramb is most particularly addressed. In the *Homeric Hymn to Dionysus*, the deity no sooner turns the villainous sailors into the first performers of the Dionysiac dithyrambic dance than he casts off his several disguises and introduces himself to the remaining helmsman with the 'calling card' privileged by his celebrants in summoning him: 'I am Dionysus Eribromos' (56). Pindar thematizes the epithet in his second *Dithyramb* (fr. 70b S.-M.), which offers nothing less than a description of

---

[98] For this, see Kurke and Neer 2014, 566. The authors go on to suggest the precise location to which the phrase alludes: as noted below, there was an altar of Dionysus within a shrine of the same Horai featured in the poem.

[99] Furley 1995, 35–39 and 2007, 125–27.

an originary performance of the cacophonous and thundering dithyrambic song with the gods as the singer-dancers here. Confirmation for the efficacy of the designation in generating divine self-manifestations comes in Aeschylus fr. 355 R.: 'it is proper that the dithyramb, song mingled with shout (μειξοβόαν), should attend upon Dionysus and his fellow reveler'. The accumulation of epithets in fr. 75 S.-M. also makes an epiphany all the more probable, appealing to the god in each of the several guises he might choose to adopt.[100]

Following the prolonged account of the different features of the performance, the wreaths carried and/or worn by the chorus members of which the gods have already been invited to partake, turning them into doubling presences of the mortal choristers, the radiance of their appearance as realized in their songs, the kinetic and acoustic qualities of the spectacle and the dancing space complete with the altar around which the chorus would circle, the *persona loquens* goes on to declare himself *mantis*-like in his perception of things styled ἐναργέα.[101] Although the adjective comes without a referent, the term's close association with epiphanies together with the speaker's self-comparison to the individual best able to discern primary and secondary signals of the presence of a god suggests that the chorus now registers the success of its opening invocation and is observing the multi-sensory phenomena that typically accompany moments of divine self-revelation.[102] Built into the mantic identity is not just the notion of veracity – hence οὐ λανθάνει as the seer apprehends the truth of the signs (cf. *Ol.* 8.2 and *Pyth.* 11.6) – but the modality of sight as the choral ego answers the gods' hoped for spectatorship (ἴδετε) of the troupe with its more mediated vision of the divine. Most probably derived from μηνύω, to reveal or disclose, the Homeric *mantis* is the one who routinely 'brings to light' or 'sheds light on something'.[103]

The subsequent lines bear out what the seer's introduction heralds. By virtue of the chorus' mantic vision, we can witness not just actual indications of spring's arrival (the standard interpretation of the latter portion of

---

[100] The chorus performing Philodamus' later invocation to the god outdoes the Pindaric troupe, piling on no fewer than six asyndetic cult titles: 'Dithyrambos, Bacchus, Euios, bull, ivy-haired, Bromios' (*Coll. Alex.* 1–3).

[101] In the text of Dionysius of Halicarnassus (*Comp.* 23), to whom we owe the work's preservation, line 13 is incoherent, and has been subject to many emendations; here I follow the broadly accepted reading suggested by van Groningen 1955, 191.

[102] See Maslov 2015, 194–95. In his reading of fr. 75 S.-M. (see especially pp. 199–200) Maslov follows the more standard view that the speaker's 'mantic' function is limited to his perception of manifestations of springtime in the natural world.

[103] For this derivation, see the persuasive argument and Homeric examples included in Casewitz 1992, also cited by Maslov 2015, 194–95.

the passage)[104] but an instance of an epiphany declaring itself in its typically synaesthetic plenitude to the chorus and, through the singer-dancers' mediation, to those attending the performance. To read line 14 quite literally and with the poem's topographic specificity in mind, the seemingly spontaneous opening (no agent is mentioned here) of the doors to the innermost chamber of the shrine of the Horai, a site to which the song has already glanced and which, Philochoros reports (*FGrH* 328 F 5b and 173), also housed an altar to Dionysus Orthos,[105] supplies the first of the proliferating pointers to the gods' arrival. A close counterpart to the action of these sanctuary gates occurs in Callimachus' second *Hymn*, where the singers direct their audience to observe how, at the Delian shrine where they currently perform, 'the bolts of the gates are pushed back, the bars themselves', a phenomenon from which they infer that 'the god is no longer far off' (6–7).

Although the precise location of the Athenian temple to which the Pindaric chorus gestures remains unknown, and Philochoros is our only source for the building, the 'crimson-robed' Horai might find their real-world counterparts in images of the deities clothed in vibrant shades and erected in the innermost recess where access might be restricted and the sacred aura at its height.[106] Also familiar to the audience would be vase representations of the Horai, who typically appear as a triplet arranged in the processional formation characteristic of choral morphology and that styles them, like other triadic maiden deities, prototypical dancers.[107] Consistent too with the song, seasonal indicators, particularly fruit, flowers and foliage, regularly equip or surround the Horai in visual accounts. Insofar as the goddesses are among the prime performers and sponsors of choral dancing, they supply fitting paradigmatic doublets for the Athenian ensemble staging the dithyramb, an equivalence suggested by Pindar's diction at 15: no sooner do the singers evoke the plants that symbolize the goddesses in art and text (and these burgeoning elements act in the manner of *chorêgoi* as they 'lead in', ἐπάγοισιν, the spring) than

---

[104] Kurke and Neer 2014, 530 note the likely performance of the song on the occasion of the City Dionysia, celebrated just at spring's advent in late March.

[105] As detailed in Kurke and Neer 2014, 568–69.

[106] The opening of the doors of a shrine might, in some instances, be limited to one particular day of the year, making the otherwise hidden cult image visible (see Paus. 9.25.3 for an example). Such cult statues were designed to create the impression of divine *parousia* and offered a privileged site for close interactions with the gods whom they embody.

[107] See, for example, the red-figure cup by the Sosias Painter of ca. 500 (Berlin, Antikensammlung F 2278). For a later verbal representation of the dancing Horai, see the extended depiction in Philostr. *Imag.* 2.34.

they present themselves as iterations of that flower-filled season, decked out with the wreaths of roses whose colouring might plausibly match the ruddy shading of the Horai's garments.

The epiphanic signs go on to multiply, ever more abundant and insistent as the divine presence becomes increasingly perceptible to the senses and the song's own pace and, perhaps, the dancers' corresponding motions quicken, culminating in the *schema Pindaricum* of the fragment's close.[108] As Hesiod's *Theogony* attests (194–95), a burst of instantaneous and luxuriant vegetal activity is another harbinger of or testament to the advent of a god (indeed, Apollo's annual return to Delphi from the Hyperboreans occurs at precisely the springtime of the year, an arrival rehearsed and accompanied by the choruses performing at his shrine), and that is what then takes place in the dithyramb. The language of lines 15–17 conveys the supra-natural and divinity-infused quality of the blossoming witnessed by the chorus, and which it makes perceptible to the audience in turn. The plants are 'nectar-bearing', diffusing the fragrance that earlier belonged to the altar, a site in particularly close contact with the gods who might be indwelling and/or make it the object of their visitations, and whose incense-filled fumes allow us to apprehend the divine presence (see Heraclitus B67 DK for a properly riddling expression of the idea). This emanation is also a more direct testament to an epiphany: because gods smell exceptionally good, we can literally sniff them out, and flowers become more fragrant when a deity is in their midst.[109] Next in the sequence, the ground responds sympathetically to the ongoing event, becoming suddenly 'ambrosial'. Like the earlier νεκτάρεα, the adjective means both 'immortal' and 'fragrant'.[110] Exploiting the twofold frame of reference here, the song declares the divinization of the entire site, its entry into close contact with the gods,[111] thereby vicariously elevating us, through this choral envisioning, from the Athenian agora to the ever-vernal Olympian realm.[112]

This melding of the different spaces and of the divine and mortal continues as the singers then draw attention to further facets of the

---

[108] See Kurke and Neer 2014, 577 for this compelling suggestion.

[109] Examples include *HHCer.* 277, Eur. *Hipp.* 1391–94, Arist. *Pax* 520–38 and Philostr. *Her.* 3.3–4, 10.2 and 11.3, all cited in Clements 2015, 56–58. Note too that flowers were planted in temple gardens, a practice particularly suitable to the Horai.

[110] Clements 2015, 52.

[111] See van der Weiden 1991, 202–03 and Kurke and Neer 2014, 576–77.

[112] We might also be put in mind of Dionysus' well-attested ability to produce such spontaneous eruptions of fertility, not least the springs of milk and honey whose outpourings anticipate and accompany his arrivals.

performance and its occasion, cycling back to the elements in the fragment's opening phrase in what, Kurke and Neer suggest, might be a verbal counterpart to their circular dance in the agora.[113] Again the floral aspect proves important, now serving as a means of bringing together nature and the human and divine participants at the ritual event. The deliberate ambiguity of the term φόβαι endows the foliage with the same 'locks' (κόμαισι) that we encounter so shortly afterwards in the same line,[114] and that may belong to Dionysus as well as to his celebrants with whom he now mingles in their dance and song. As the choristers cast their wreaths of roses, part of their ritual trappings, to the ground, they enact their perception of the earth's seemingly spontaneous, but more properly god-instigated acquisition of its floral carpet, replicating Dionysus' act by adding new elements to the bouquet.[115] The description of the chorus that follows still more emphatically links the gods and celebrants: where earlier the Olympians were invited to 'approach', now the same verb is assigned the singers as they advance towards Semele, one of the 'Kadmeian women' earlier described.[116] It is as though, having recognized and displayed the signs of the gods' imminence through its reciprocal vision and embodiment, the chorus now more fully maps its actions onto those of the divinities who are simultaneously drawing ever nearer to the altar, the epicentre of their cult.

The 'sounds of song', instrumentation and dance all cited in the final extant lines offer a capping statement of the numinous presences: vocal and musical performances, an ever more vigorous and fast-paced dance, and the *realia* that indicate ongoing cult activities regularly frame moments when immortals reveal themselves to their celebrants.[117] Sappho fr. 2 V., an invocation to Aphrodite to come from Crete and participate in the current celebration, supplies just one of several precedents; complete with the incense, fragrance, nectar, roses, sounds, spring flowers, vegetal growth and 'mingling' that make Pindar's dithyramb so sensually vivid, the Sapphic fragment also reaches beyond the physically palpable and material and similarly closes with mention of the ongoing *thaliai*, the festivities that

---

[113] Kurke and Neer 2014, 576–78.   [114] As noted by Maslov 2015, 198.

[115] A poem from the *Palatine Anthology* attributed to Bacchylides or Simonides, and posing as a dedication by a chorus victorious in a dithyrambic competition, cites the 'headbands of finest roses' worn by the singers engaged in 'Bacchic struggles' (*AP* 13.28). Tsagalis 2009, 206 also suggests connections between Dionysus and roses in Bacch. 17, but more indirectly through the figure of Aphrodite.

[116] As observed in Maslov 2015, 198–99 and Kurke and Neer 2014, 576–77.

[117] See Tanner 2006, 45–48 and, more extensively, Day 2010.

include the concurrent choral song and dance.[118] It is Dionysius of Halicarnassus' discussion of the Pindaric dithyramb, which he cites as exemplary of the poet's 'austere style', that best expresses what the song puts into practice: analysing just the opening few lines, he observes how the verb and connective *en* in the very first phrase already 'have produced a not unpleasing *harmonia* by mingling and fusing together (συναλοιφῇ κερασθέντα)' (*Comp.* 22.92–93, trans. Usher). That small-scale 'fusion' at the verbal and syntactical level is what the fragment as a whole achieves.

Expressions of the power of choral song and dance to stimulate an epiphany in contemporary visual media, whether on vases or in wood or stone, are harder to track down. In many instances, it proves impossible to determine whether the female figures shown dancing in the company of Pan or another god on the wooden plaques and free-standing terracottas cited in Chapter 5 are nymphs (or other such deities), or whether they represent votaries whose activity results in the advent of their divine *chorêgos* to lead them in performance. But one set of objects, that become increasingly stylized and whose very proliferation might rob them of their earlier sacral 'charge', include scenes that seem more unequivocally to unite human chorus members with the deity celebrated in their song and dance and to suggest that a particularly well-fashioned and executed performance can precipitate an encounter between the members of a choral ensemble and the god. In the two examples cited here, the divinity does not so much enter human space as his choreutes gain access to the separate but contiguous realm in which he (or on occasion she, since Artemis figures in one instance)[119] dwells.

These representations, whose iconography contemporary Attic red-figure vases echo, occur chiefly on the now fragmentary choregic monuments raised in fifth- and fourth-century Athens following a win in the dramatic and dithyrambic competitions at civic festivals. In his study of the motifs included on both the dedications and painted pottery,[120] Csapo treats a series of so-called 'adoration-scenes', where chorus members, usually equipped with sacrifices or other offerings, approach a larger figure, whose

---

[118] Cf. Soph. *Trach.* 205–24, where the singers combine multiple choral genres (the paean, dithyramb, hymenaios and partheneion) in a song that summons Apollo and Artemis to participate in their celebration. Filled with details of the ongoing performance, its music, dance and the cult paraphernalia, the lines close by suggesting the success of the invocation and the divine advent stimulated by the song and dance: addressing the mortal witness to the scene, Deianeira, the choreutes declare 'you can see these things clearly (ἐναργῆ), right before your eyes'.

[119] See Munich, Glyptothek 552 with Vierneisel and Scholl 2002, 37–41.

[120] Csapo 2010, 82–103.

dress, accessories, sanctuary location and/or labelling securely identify him as Dionysus. While in some instances the victory garlands or masks held by the mortals moving towards the god establish their choral identity, on the so-called 'Actors' Relief' from the Piraeus of ca. 400 (Fig. 10.7) other features suggest that the three figures dressed in belted floor-length chitons advancing towards Dionysus, here labelled DIONYSOS and shown as a rhyton-equipped monosymposiast reclining on his *klinê*, similarly belong to a victorious chorus.[121] Countering the view that these are actors rather than choreutes, Csapo notes the uniformity in the figures' maenadic-style dress and the tympana held by two of the three, features 'that tie them together as a group, and also indicate that they are involved in music and dance'.[122] Brought into the Dionysiac presence, and allowed to witness the eternally feasting and drinking divinity, they are partially assimilated to the fawn-skin wearing female whose position and posture – she sits perched on the end of the god's couch and turns her head back to look at the threesome – allow this worshipper-cum-mythical companion to assume an intercessional role

Fig. 10.7 The 'Actors' Relief' from the Piraeus, ca. 400 B.C.E. Athens, National Archaeological Museum 1500. Photograph © National Archaeological Museum, Athens.

[121] Athens, National Archaeological Museum 1500. See Csapo 2010, 94–96 and Green 2008, 114–15 for discussion.
[122] Csapo 2010, 95.

between the two realms juxtaposed in the scene.[123] The banqueting imagery is important here: since the prizes awarded winning choruses included animals for sacrifice to Dionysus at his sanctuary, victory granted the members of the troupe entry into the space assigned to him and, more symbolically, the privilege of feasting on the meat from their sacrifice in divine company.

An earlier object, an Attic red-figure hydria attributed to the Pan Painter and dated to ca. 490–480 (Fig. 10.8),[124] incorporates motifs from the victory monuments while offering an especially suggestive account of the sensations of mortal choristers suddenly precipitated into the presence of the divine. Equipped with wreaths and the military corselets that costume other choreutes on contemporary vases,[125] and further characterized as chorus members by the nonsense inscriptions coming from their

Fig. 10.8 Attic red-figure hydria by the Pan Painter, 490–480 B.C.E. St. Petersburg, the State Hermitage Museum B 201 (St. 1538). Photograph courtesy of The State Hermitage Museum, St. Petersburg.

[123] In the inscriptions added long after the manufacture of the relief, this figure was labelled with a name whose last two letters, —IA, are still visible. 'Paidia' and 'Tragoidia' are among the suggested restorations.

[124] St. Petersburg, Hermitage B 201 (St. 1538), *ARV²* 555.95, *Para.* 387, 388 with discussion in Csapo 2010, 98–99 with earlier bibliography.

[125] Csapo 2010, 98 cites the tragic chorus shown performing on the Attic red-figure column krater (Basel, Antikenmuseum BS 415) also of ca. 490, where six figures dressed in just such corselets and with diadems on their heads dance in a rectangular formation.

mouths,[126] two 'awestruck' (in Csapo's phrase) figures standing in for the larger ensemble follow in the wake of Hermes (the god in many ways considered closest to men and a go-between) who seems to urge them on. Moving towards Dionysus, this mediator god looks back at the pair that lingers behind, grasping the wrist of one and visibly impelling him forward. As leader of the troupe, and the one positioned between his fellow god and mortals (his arms stretched to either side span both sets of figures), Hermes takes on the role not just of the one who presides over the choral competition in his capacity as Enagonios,[127] but also of *chorêgos*. For all that on this occasion Dionysus seems very ready to receive his guests, extending his right arm towards the new arrivals, and moving forward to meet and greet them, the artist takes pains to signal the reluctance of Hermes' two followers: one clings to the other and the second member of the pair tries to back away.[128] The visitors' hesitancy conveys something of the fear, what the sources style *tarbos*, experienced by mortals on epiphanic occasions.

The chronological gap between the two objects just cited may in part explain why, on the later Piraeus relief, the three figures approaching Dionysus show no signs of the tentativeness so apparent on the part of the hydria's back-hanging choreutes. By the fifth-century's end, monuments and vases uniting Dionysus and actors and chorus members typically represent the mortal protagonists as the god's 'close companions and assistants, the equivalent of satyrs and maenads',[129] who regularly participate in his activities on familiar terms (the Pronomos Vase from the fifth century's close exemplifies this more relaxed atmosphere). With the diffusion and increasingly conventionalized nature of the iconography, these dedications become more secularized, as much expressions of their donor's status and wealth as of his piety towards the tutelary god. But even in their more pallid and muted form, the later representations still preserve the idea whose expressions we find in the textual accounts: that participating in choral song and dance, and turning in an especially fine performance, allows choruses and their audiences alike a 'fast track' to an epiphanic encounter with divinity.

---

[126] The writing tablet that Hermes holds along with his kerykeion and whose significance Green 1995 considers at length may even hold the script containing the words of the song they perform as they advance, perhaps part of an ode celebrating Dionysus.

[127] See Csapo 2010, 99 for the identification; Hermes fulfilling his function as Enagonios is mentioned in several choregic dedications.

[128] Green 1995, 78 details their gestures and stance.

[129] Green 1995, 78, whose argument I draw on.

4.2 Enargeia, *Epiphany and the Chorus in Post-Classical Ecphrases*

Where in archaic and classical Greece *choreia* belonged among the prime movers in the generation of epiphanies through the medium's singular power to simulate and draw down the divine, in the post-classical period *enargeia* takes a novel turn: in this altered climate, the visual vividness operative in both texts and images comes more to depend on an artist or writer's *technê*, which assumes something of that catalytic and 'presentify-ing' role that choral performers earlier possessed.[130] This intimate link between *enargeia* and epiphany declares itself most clearly in developments in linguistic usage; the adjective ἐναργής comes increasingly to be applied to epiphanies and when, according to the *Suda*, the imperial author Aelian writes a treatise on epiphany, he titles it Περὶ θείων ἐναργειῶν.[131]

But the sources of the imperial age not only preserve the connection established in earlier accounts between divine self-manifestations and the 'enargic', this understood as a heightened, more acute and extra-ordinary mode of visuality that could access the reality within or behind appearances. In post-classical Greece, *enargeia* had also come to refer more narrowly to the power of language to stimulate the hearer/reader's synaesthetic perception of the object or occasion described, a duality of meaning most fully exploited and played on by contemporary authors of ecphrases. My final example features one such rhetorical exercise, here in the form of a highly self-conscious piece of writing that parades its use of *enargeia* even as it teases the reader with the power of the device to bring about – or to withhold – an epiphany. Like the passage from Heliodorus with which this chapter began, it also features a parthenaic chorus in performance for its exploration of how to transform the hearer-cum-reader of the discourse/text into a spectator at the original event, a choice which proves critical to our seemingly (but not) direct apprehension of the divine presence.

Cited here is the opening section of the programmatic passage that Philostratus places at the outset of his second book of *Imagines* (2.1.1–3), where (in the elaborate fiction constructed by the text) the narrator describes to his youthful interlocutor, the son of his host and gallery-

---

[130] *Technê* and a choral performance intersect in particularly complex and riddling ways in Philostr. *Imag.* 2.34.3, where the speaker describes a painting of the dancing Horai and remarks, '[the painter] seems to me, falling in with the Horai as they dance, to have been shaken to and fro by them into their artistry (εἰς τὴν τέχνην)'.

[131] For more on the link between *enargeia* and epiphany, see Platt 2011, esp. chapters 3 and 5; see too Koch Piettre 2005.

owner, and a group of slightly older boys one among the paintings hanging in the breezy portico of a home in suburban Naples:[132]

Ἀφροδίτην ἐλεφαντίνην <ἐν> ἁπαλοῖς μυρρινῶσιν ᾄδουσιν ἁπαλαὶ κόραι. διδάσκαλος αὐτὰς ἄγει σοφὴ καὶ οὐδὲ ἔξωρος· ἐφιζάνει γάρ τις ὥρα καὶ ῥυτίδι πρώτῃ, γήρως μὲν τὸ ὑπόσεμνον ἕλκουσα, τούτῳ δ' αὖ κεραννῦσα τὸ σωζόμενον τῆς ἀκμῆς. καὶ τὸ μὲν σχῆμα τῆς Ἀφροδίτης Αἰδοῦς, γυμνὴ καὶ εὐσχήμων, ἡ δὲ ὕλη συνθήκη μεμυκότος ἐλέφαντος. ἀλλ' οὐ βούλεται γεγράφθαι δοκεῖν ἡ θεός, ἔκκειται δὲ οἷα λαβέσθαι.

βούλει λόγου τι ἐπιλείβωμεν τῷ βωμῷ; λιβανωτοῦ γὰρ ἱκανῶς ἔχει καὶ κασίας καὶ σμύρνης, δοκεῖ δέ μοι καὶ Σαπφοῦς τι ἀναπνεῖν. ἐπαινετέα τοίνυν ἡ σοφία τῆς γραφῆς, πρῶτον μὲν <ὅτι> τὰς ἀγαπωμένας λίθους περιβαλοῦσα οὐκ ἐκ τῶν χρωμάτων αὐτὰς ἐμιμήσατο, ἀλλ' ἐκ τοῦ φωτός, οἷον ὀφθαλμῷ κέντρον τὴν διαύγειαν αὐταῖς ἐνθεῖσα, εἶτα ὅτι καὶ τοῦ ὕμνου παρέχει ἀκούειν. ᾄδουσι γὰρ αἱ παῖδες, ᾄδουσι, καὶ ἡ διδάσκαλος ὑποβλέπει τὴν ἀπᾴδουσαν κροτοῦσα τὰς χεῖρας καὶ ἐς τὸ μέλος ἱκανῶς ἐμβιβάζουσα.

Aphrodite, made of ivory, delicate maidens are hymning in delicate myrtle groves. The *didaskalos* who leads them is skilled in her art, and not yet past her youth, for a certain beauty rests even on her first wrinkle which, though it brings with it the gravity of age, yet tempers this with what remains of her prime. The type of the goddess is that of Aphrodite goddess of Modesty, naked and graceful, and the material is ivory, closely joined. However, the goddess is unwilling to seem painted, but she stands out as though one could take hold of her.

Do you wish us to pour something of a libation of discourse on the altar? For of frankincense and cinnamon and myrrh it has enough already, and it seems to me to give out a fragrance as of Sappho. Accordingly the artistry of the painting must be praised, first because the artist, in making the border of precious stones, has used not colours but light to depict them, putting a radiance in them like the pupil in an eye, and secondly, because he even makes us hear the hymn. For the maidens are singing, are singing, and the *didaskalos* frowns at one who is off key, clapping her hands and trying earnestly to bring her into tune.

The opening account of the goddess celebrated by the chorus members carefully observes the conventions of Hellenistic and imperial ecphrases: typical of these is the bifurcated emphasis on the statue's materiality (appropriately, it is fashioned from deceptive ivory) and the life latent within it, an oscillation amplified by the work's seeming possession of agency and unwillingness to remain a thing of stone and paint alone; the

---

[132] For discussion of the entire passage, see Platt 2011, 1–7; while my reading incorporates some of her many insights, my focus is much more squarely on the choral dimension.

speaker tracks this progressive animation by his description of Aphrodite's resistance to her painted (and written) status and her 'standing out', as if corporeally present in the viewer's space and endowed with depth and three-dimensionality as well as volition.[133]

But in this instance the goddess' capacity to manifest herself in living form depends on a further factor operative from the start. As the structure and diction of the opening passage make clear, any experiential encounter with Aphrodite, or rather with the seemingly vivified statue of the same, is accessible only by virtue of the choral performance that summons her into the text. The exegete's triadic arrangement of his phrases carries the point: we first encounter the deity as the inert object of the verb ᾄδουσιν; then, in intermediary position, the chorus members and their *chorêgos*; and, third, in the concluding clause of this initial overview, the goddess again, now in the subject position and given agency and thought. Absent the performers and their trainer, Aphrodite would remain beyond our sensory perceptions, triply encased in her stone, painted and written forms. Philostratus' use of συνθήκη more narrowly registers the role of the maidens' performance (further mediated through his text) in supplying the requisite lens for our discernment of the divine.[134] Derived from συντίθημι, to 'put together, combine, arrange, construct', the verb can variously refer to the composition of (this) discourse, the joining together of different elements in an artefact (its primary meaning here) and the assemblage of a song and/or dance. Both the appearance or shape (σχῆμα) of the statue and its cognate 'shapeliness' (εὐσχήμων) are also consubstantial with and even contingent on the chorus' performance, a reflection and product of the graceful dance figures, *schêmata*, which the narrator, albeit more implicitly at this point but more emphatically later on, also makes integral to his account.[135]

The choral spectacle continues to occupy centre stage as the pedagogue then focuses more closely on the nature of the song, now imagined in the form of the liquid libation that is so familiar a trope for an 'outpouring' of praise. Visible here too is a second conceit frequently found in choral poetry, and that addressed to a god more particularly, the song as a

---

[133]   The erotic element is also unmistakable here, as is the play with the levels of life and materialization and speech and text. The verb ἔκκειμαι means at once 'to be set up in public', as suits an image, 'to be exposed to, at the mercy of', as in a rape, 'to be expounded', and 'to project'.

[134]   Platt 2011, 4–5 also notes the term's relevance to the song as well as the image, albeit with a somewhat different emphasis.

[135]   This 'shapeliness' can, again, also inform the discourse/text that Philostratus is fashioning: as the several examples given in *LSJ* attest, the term is applied to words, speeches and written accounts.

drink, food or other offering placed on the altar and, in this instance, one whose fragrance engages the deity and audience's olfactory senses. With the revelation that the hymn's pleasing emanation is 'as of Sappho', the reader finds his initial expectations seemingly confirmed: the older but still seemly *chorêgos* leading her parthenaic troupe is none other than Sappho conducting her Lesbian chorus, or at least – since the song is not exactly that of Sappho, but more redolent of it (a kind of secondary emanation) – a latter-day *didaskalos* who stages a reperformance of her predecessor's piece.

Now the epiphanic quality of Aphrodite seeking to be more than a thing of paint and words (γεγράφθαι) also makes perfect sense: the chorus' song, we think, re-sounds the famous cletic hymn performed by the maidens whom Sappho once led and which recounted the goddess' epiphanies on previous occasions, a scenario reconfigured in the archaic poet's first fragment, which was placed at the head of the Alexandrian collection of her works (a position that Philostratus acknowledges with the prefatory location of his own passage).[136] Like the imperial author's ecphrasis, it was only by means of Sappho's no less synaesthetic account of Aphrodite's multiple advents that her audience might experience the goddess, brought into its contemporary space, or 'presentified', through her composition's invocation, its use of deictic terms and apostrophe and, most vividly of all, the way in which the singers ventriloquize the divine voice so as to make us hear her speak. Also more broadly 'Sapphic' here is the passage's reference to the 'delicate myrtle groves' and the fragrant offering: in fr. 2 V., the Lesbian choristers summon the deity anew, now to a 'graceful grove', its altars 'fuming with frankincense' (cf. fr. 44.30 V., where three perfumes, 'myrrh, cassia, and frankincense', all appear).[137] By virtue of this proliferation of allusions, we not only see the unknown performers depicted by the artist; practising that second-order type of sight that a chorus makes possible and that allows us similarly to witness the invisible and absent, we also apprehend in these painted figures those whose identities they assume and whose several songs and acts of worship they seem to enact anew.

But there is more to the transformation of the *logos* containing Sappho's song into the libation poured out on the altar (a gesture also described in Sappho fr. 141 V.). In turning the literary/musical tribute performed by the speaker and chorus into an offering, the conceit reminds us that both the

---

[136] See Platt 2011, 3–4 with additional bibliography on the intertextual reference.

[137] The flowers and libations that Philostratus introduces into his ecphrasis also appear in fr. 2 V.

choral performance and the painting would have once existed within that ritual context which involves multiple levels of re-enactment and aims to stimulate an epiphany in the processes rehearsed elsewhere in this study. The scene reproduced by the artist and redescribed in words resembles nothing so much as one that might be depicted on the dedicatory *pinakes* ubiquitous in sanctuaries from the archaic period on, which frequently combine a picture of the event and an inscription preserving the speech that accompanied the original giving of the votive (see particularly Chapter 5). Typically these plaques show mortals engaged in making an offering – sacrifices, presentations of goods and performances of song and dance – while visible in the same scene, although frequently differentiated by their appearance, stature and/or location, are the divinities who have come in response to the summons simultaneously issued by the epigraphic element and the ritual actions depicted by the tablet.

In a multiplication of the votive conceit, Philostratus' skilled piece of verbal artistry simultaneously becomes reified, calling the reader back to the physical object from which he or she now reads. As Chapter 8 detailed, choral poetry composed in celebration of a divinity could become a votive object at the performance site, enduringly recalling and replacing the original spectacle. But the expression λόγου τι introduced into the discourse-libation image distances the reader from the *hic et nunc* of the Lesbian occasion and its subsequent preservation within a sacred setting: if the *logos* includes a transcription of Sappho's hymn (now encountered by Philostratus' contemporaries in written form), then that work of representation is partial at best, introducing us not to Aphrodite *in propria persona*, but to that goddess as transmitted through a succession of images and texts and now no more than a thing made up of words.

Countering these estrangement devices, the sweet scent emanating from the altar and, by extension, from the page containing this passage from the *Imagines*, reinforces an audience's sense that an epiphany is shortly to occur: alongside the brilliant light emitted by the divine body, a pleasing smell, as noted in my discussion of the Pindaric dithyramb, was a sure marker of the gods' advent. That the transcription of poems into textual form can share in the attributes of the divine, in this instance chiefly their radiance but their fragrance too, Callimachus' fr. 7.13–14 Pf. affirms. Here the poet invites the Graces to 'wipe your shining hands on my elegies', an image that calls to mind the application of a sweet-smelling unguent that can preserve the written works (as the fragrant oils applied to divine images were in part designed to do) and invest them with the immortal ambience of their patron deities. But Philostratus again qualifies the mimetic potential of the textualized version of the song once given live performance. With a repetition of the τι just introduced, we are cautioned that the scent does no more than 'take breath from/exhale something of Sappho' (Σαπφοῦς τι ἀναπνεῖν), a phrase that taps into the notion common in Hellenistic and later epigrams, which views the book as a repository for the breath, voice or *pneuma* (complete with the notion of 'in-spiration') of the original poet, now dependent on the reader for its re-vivification. *AP* 9.186, apparently composed by Antipater of Thessalonika for an edition of Aristophanes, similarly alerts its audience to the limitations of transcription, bidding the reader observe 'how much of Dionysus the page contains (ὅσον Διόνυσον ἔχει σελίς)', this much, but not all.[138]

Before returning to the choral performance, the Philostratean gallery guide pauses to describe the painting's frame, a wondrous assemblage of precious and diaphanous stones that further objectify the ecphrasis, aligning it anew with a votive pinax while also, perhaps, calling to mind a text of Sappho's song, now surrounded by its 'illuminating' accretion of textual symbols, annotations and other marginalia designed to explicate the lines. These gems, it turns out, are no mere coloured daubs; in place of paint, the artist has fashioned them from light, making them resemble, in the narrator's phrase, 'the pupil in an eye'.[139] The stones' 'ocular' character not only casts them in the role of the spectators who so regularly surround or flank performers in archaic and classical depictions of choral spectacles; it also recalls how early artists might include eyes and eye-shaped elements within representations of performances, either integrating the features into the central field of an image and/or reserving them for its framing design (see Fig. 9.0, with discussion in Chapter 9). Following the logic of the internal narrator's description, we should also understand these phosphorescent gems as so many spotlights that irradiate the scene at which they look.[140] Whereas the earlier sources invest choreutes and the performances they

---

[138] For further examples and discussion, see Phillips 2016, 72–73 and 89–91, where he also supplies a fuller analysis of the epigram.

[139] As Platt 2011, 6 observes, this description of the ocular stone complete with its centrepoint or pupil (the curiously used κέντρον) also takes us back to the opening focus on the dancing *korai*; the term used at the start carries the secondary meaning 'pupil' of the eye, and is much more frequently applied to this feature than the more recondite noun selected by Philostratus later on. We might also imagine lozenge-shaped stones, whose shape would resemble that of an eye or, more fancifully, suppose that Philostratus plays on the notion of the gods' ability to lithify those who catch sight of them in unmediated form.

[140] This characterization well accords with one of the two dominant ancient theories of optics, the so-called 'emissionist' account, which understood the sense of sight as dependent on the fiery rays sent out by the eyes and which travelled towards the thing seen.

stage with brilliance and luminosity, here that dazzle depends on the light that the external viewers train on the maidenly dancers.[141]

But these lithified 'spectators' are not untouched by what they see; instead, and again like viewers of choral performances in much earlier images and texts, they actively respond to the internal scene and experience the sensation most apposite to the twofold objects of their gaze, the choral performers and the Aphrodite image. The participle ἀγαπωμένας, a highly singular way of expressing approbation for the artist's technique, attributes to these 'cherished' or 'beloved' stones the desire-instigating character that more regularly belongs to choral performers, whether to the 'desirous' and 'desiring' (ἱμερόεντα χορόν) chorus of *Il.* 18.603 or to Astymelousa, the *pothos*-arousing *chorêgos* moving through the singers' midst in Alcman's third *Partheneion*. Beyond observing the symbiosis that unites choristers and their audiences, making them feel and sometimes move as one, these love-eliciting objects also model that eroticized manner of spectatorship to be practiced by those who now view the painting or, more accurately, encounter it in Philostratus' narrative.[142] Confirmation of the desirous manner of viewing integral to *choreia* comes a little later in the exegesis, when the speaker alerts us to the presence of another set of amorous eyes that the scene includes: these, fittingly enough, belonging to Eros (see below).

Moving back to the image framed by the stones, Philostratus now redirects attention to the performance and to its auditory and kinetic elements. Not yet allowing us to hear the contents of the song, the exegete instead focuses on the quality of the sound and the vocal capacities of the singers. With the twofold repetition of ᾄδουσιν, the narrator achieves much the same effect in his *logos* that he credits the artist with doing as he too allows us to hear the hymn, in this instance its almost recitative and rhythmic character that turns the speech into something resembling a musical composition.[143] Just as in depictions of choruses on archaic vases, where some particularity in dress or movement may differentiate

---

[141] In directing the reader outwards to the border, the author also tacitly advertises his adherence to rhetorical convention as he puts into practice the handbooks' repeated definition of an ecphrasis as a λόγος περιηγηματικός, a speech that 'makes a tour' of something, or what Dubel (1997, 256–58) nicely terms a 'visite guidée'. As she explains the concept behind this 'going around', what permits the spatial passage is the moving gaze as the viewer's eye travels from one element of the scene to the next, exactly the type of spectatorship modelled by the ocular gems.

[142] See Webb 2006, 127 for discussion of the speaker's frequent appeal to the erotic element in the paintings.

[143] Webb 2006, 121 makes a similar point.

one performer from the rest, or the tyros of the group require instruction from more seasoned members, here one of the maidens attracts the eye of the *chorêgos* (another internal viewer), who casts her a reproving look because she fails to sing in tune. Dance is also written into the diction of the phrase used of this discordant girl: ἐμβιβάζουσα, the causal form of ἐμβαίνω, which here describes how the ill-sounding maiden is made vocally to rejoin the concord, simultaneously refers to bringing someone back into step or line (*melos* encompasses both song and dance). In its intransitive form, ἐμβαίνω appears in post-classical sources in the context of a step, dance or a march performed in a correct and synchronized motion.[144]

While still withholding the words of the song, Philostratus' lecture-giver goes on to detail elements of the choreutes' dress while also inviting us to take a closer look at the grove to which the opening more briefly referred (2.1.3.4–12):

> τὸ μὲν γὰρ τῆς στολῆς ἀπέριττον καὶ μὴ δι' ὄχλου αὐταῖς, εἰ ἀθύροιεν, ἢ τὸ ἐν χρῷ τῆς ζώνης ἢ τὸ εἰς βραχίονα τοῦ χιτῶνος ἢ ὡς ἀνυποδησίᾳ χαίρουσιν ἐφεστῶσαι ἁπαλῇ πόᾳ καὶ ἀναψυχὴν ἕλκουσαι παρὰ τῆς δρόσου, λειμών τε ὁ περὶ τὰς ἐσθῆτας καὶ τὰ ἐν αὐταῖς χρώματα, ὡς ἄλλο ἄλλῳ ἐπιπρέπει, δαιμονίως ἐκμεμίμηται· τὰ γὰρ συμβαίνοντα οἱ μὴ γράφοντες οὐκ ἀληθεύουσιν ἐν ταῖς γραφαῖς.

> For as to their clothing, it is simple and such as not to impede them, if they should disport themselves; so the form of the girdle close to the skin, of the chiton on the arm, and the way they take pleasure in treading barefoot on the tender grass and drawing coolness from the dew, and the meadow which is around the garments and the colours in these, how one is suited to another, these are awesomely imitated; for painters/writers who do not make things harmonize do not show them truthfully in their paintings/texts.

The many-coloured floral decorations on which the description lingers most immediately recall the gems that frame the image, which, the speaker claimed, were fashioned from what we should imagine as variously coloured bits of light, and newly convey the reflexivity and mutuality structuring relations between these lithified spectators and the performers whom they watch. But the observation also includes another pointer back

[144] Philostratus' phrasing here offers another instance of the notion treated in earlier chapters, the synthesis of voice and bodily motion in choral performances. Are we also meant to imagine the out-stepping girl moving out of the image, as Aphrodite seeks to do, her foot perhaps breaching the boundary between interior and frame and entering our space?

to Sappho's cletic hymn. In what the Lesbian poet likely intended as a *griphos* and display of Aphrodite's capacity for trickery (she is, of course, addressed as 'wile-weaver' in the same opening phrase), the epithet used of the deity, ποικιλόθρον' (fr. 1.1 V.), means at once 'of the skillfully worked throne' and 'with artfully worked pattern-woven flowers', a reference to Aphrodite's flower-strewn robe. Exploiting this second sense, Philostratus clothes his maidens in just such floral textiles so as to elide the goddess and her celebrants, turning the chorus members into stand-ins for the object of their praise, who is again made perceptible to the viewer by virtue of their role as intercessors.

But a concern with a different kind of 'facture' is also apparent here. The desire to maintain harmony and concordance that just prompted the *didaskalos* to intervene now reappears in the sartorial and painterly domains as the speaker first notes how well the girls' clothing is fitted to their bodies and then, in a second instance of the bringing together of disparate things so as to create a good 'fit', comments on the suitability of each colour used for the decorated garments to the rest so that they all harmonize. In the parenthetical remark that follows, the pedagogue takes up this notion of harmonious assemblage one further time: reflecting on what it is that allows artists to achieve the 'truthfulness' towards which paintings should tend, and choosing a verb (συμβαίνοντα) reminiscent of that just used for the audible and kinetic 'coming together' or juncture of one chorus member with the remainder of the troupe, he declares that truth in painting depends on the artist's ability to make each element cohere. Taken together, these several observations look back both to many representations of *choreia* in much earlier sources, where the motif of 'fitting together' so frequently occurs, and to Philostratus' own exercise of his skills: it is precisely through his ability to combine the many different features of the picture – the actors within it, the landscape, the frame, the spectators within the gallery – that permits the reader to believe in the reality of the scene and think him- or herself both eavesdropper and eyewitness.

It is not only the maiden dancers' robes that permit a sighting of the goddess in her living form. Just as, in a final comment on the performers' comeliness, we encounter Aphrodite – who as the opening remarked, wishes to be claimed – re-enacting her role in the Judgement of Paris, when she together with her fellow deities showed herself before men's eyes, so the chorus members now take her place as they participate in their own hypothetical beauty competition, itself a replication of and self-projection onto an imaginary event or *phantasia* which they share with their viewers.

In this portion of the text, it is the supposed judge, implicitly the narrator and the internal audiences of the boy and attendant youths in the gallery as well as the author and his readers, who plays the Paris role and is treated to his own more mediated type of epiphany with the girls replacing the original trio of divinities (2.1.3.12–16):[145]

> as to the figures (εἴδη) of the maidens, if we were to leave them to Paris or any other judge, I believe he would be at a loss as to how to vote, such is the rivalry among them in quick-glancing eyes and fair cheeks and in 'hon-eyed voices', to use the sweet expression (πρόσφθεγμα, lit. a salutation and sounding out) of Sappho.

With this fresh 'tease' and seeming promise to let the reader/hearer appre-hend the contents of the 'Sapphic' song, Philostratus introduces a final retardation (2.1.4.1–4). In a dazzling burst of enargic synaesthesia, the figure of Eros supplying the music for the performers as he strikes his bow-turned-lyre allows the artist of the image and author of the text to mix auditory, visual and kinetic elements anew. The instrument not only gains a 'panhar-monic' voice with which it sings together with the chorus (ἡ νευρὰ πανάρμόνιον ᾄδει), but the prosopopoeia becomes still more pronounced when that vocalizing bow string, asserting that it 'has as many notes as the lyre', supplants the narrator and assumes his role.[146] In a second appropri-ation of the exegetical function, the task of focalizing the chorus is also reassigned to the deity's eyes, which offer another refracted representation of the objects of their gaze. Moving swiftly just as an ecphrasis requires its audience's minds' eyes to do, these organs supply a kinetic counterpart to the music produced by the lyre as Eros 'lightly plucks' (παραψάλλει) the instru-ment, and, as the phrase 'swift are the eyes of the god as they perceive, I think, some sort of rhythm' (ταχεῖς τε οἱ ὀφθαλμοὶ τοῦ θεοῦ ῥυθμόν τινα οἶμαι διανοοῦντες, 4.4–5) also allows, seem to channel dance motions too.[147] If the 'rhythm' primarily belongs to Eros' lyre music, then it is no less suited to the movements performed by the girls whose own flashing-cum-whirling (ἑλικώπιδες) eyes earlier assumed the properties of their dance (cf. Alcm.

---

[145] The suggestion of a beauty competition among Lesbian choral *parthenoi* might call to mind a choral song by a different poet also from Lesbos. In fr. 130b V, Alcaeus describes the Kallisteia occurring in a Lesbian precinct even as the female chorus in the evocation performs the ritual *ololugê*.

[146] According to Quint. *Inst.* 9.2.31, prosopopoeia is a figure of speech that can 'bring down the gods from heaven'.

[147] The 'dance' of the visual faculties is made explicit in Philostratus' account of the Horai at 2.34.3, where the narrator comments that the Seasons' eyes 'are joining in the dance (συγχωροῦσιν)'. Their movement in turn dictates that of the painter, who seems to 'fall in with the Horai as they dance'.

fr. 1.69 *PMGF*, and the 'violet-eyed [ἰανογ[λ]εφάρων] choreutes). The choice of *rhythmos* may be doubly considered here; Plato speaks of vision 'flowing (*rhein*) through the eyes' (*Tim.* 45b7), and although for the philosopher the flow travels chiefly from the inside out, in the 'intromissive' theory of optics, that direction was reversed. Even as the sight of the girls impacts on Eros' eyes, these visual organs respond by replicating the movement perceived.

While, in paint and verbal rendering, the god offers another instance of the animation and 'presencing' that the rhetorical exercise can bring about, the description engages further with theoretical accounts of ecphrasis and reflects on the dynamics of the sense of sight so central to the device. In granting Eros' eyes the faculty of *noêsis* (διανοοῦντες), the speaker makes the god model the way in which, by virtue of its visuality, an ecphrasis causes the listener to conceive of the subject in his 'mind's eye'.[148] *Dianoia* is a key term in discussions of the workings of *phantasia*, where the mental image is produced by a sensory experience that is principally but not exclusively visual and comprises an intellectual element too. In Diogenes Laertius' report of the Stoic view (which is in part built on Aristotle), a *phantasia* 'arises first, and through thought (*dianoia*)' (7.49). Also operative in the choice of verb is the familiar notion that of all the senses, vision is the closest to *dianoia*.

As Diogenes Laertius' same report of concepts of *phantasia* among the Stoics goes on to observe, the *dianoia* instigated by a sense impression 'has the power of speech and expresses in language what it experiences by the agency of the *phantasia*'. Since there is no determining who poses the question 'what do they sing?' that comes immediately after the description of Eros' sentient eyes, Philostratus invites us to position the god or his visual faculties among the possible speakers here as he or they verbally respond to the impression left by the sight and sound of the performance. With that question, the account also returns one final time to the song by means of the refrain-like expression ᾄδουσιν that gives the spoken/written discourse its own musical character. Upending expectation, what the audience belatedly hears proves not to be Sappho's cletic hymn, or any another Sapphic composition. Instead, in this only partial transcription (the speaker prefaces his 'reading' by repeating the qualifying τι already twice used as he remarks 'something of the song has been painted/written', inviting us to wonder whether the painting is perhaps inscribed with an

---

[148] For an expression of this idea, see Sardianos, *Commentarium* 217.

incomplete citation), the performers present us with another, and ante-
cedent – in literary as well as biological chronology – instance of an
epiphany as they recall the birth of Aphrodite (2.1.4.6–13):

γέγραπται γάρ τι καὶ ᾠδῆς· τὴν Ἀφροδίτην ἐκφῦναι τῆς θαλάττης λέγουσιν
ἀπορροῇ τοῦ Οὐρανοῦ. καὶ ὅπου μὲν τῶν νήσων προσέσχεν, οὔπω
λέγουσιν, ἐροῦσι δὲ οἶμαι Πάφον, τὴν γένεσιν δὲ ἱκανῶς ᾄδουσιν·
ἀναβλέπουσαι μὲν γὰρ ἐμφαίνουσιν, ὅτι ἀπ' οὐρανοῦ, τὰς δὲ χεῖρας ὑπτίας
ὑποκινοῦσαι δηλοῦσιν, ὅτι ἐκ θαλάττης, τὸ μειδίαμα δὲ αὐτῶν γαλήνης ἐστὶν
αἴνιγμα.

For something of the song has been written/painted: they are telling the
birth of Aphrodite from the sea from an outpouring of Ouranos, and on
which of the islands she came to land they do not yet say, although I think
they will name Paphos, but of her birth they sing sufficiently; for by
looking upwards they make manifest that she is from the heavens, and
by slightly moving their upturned hands they show that she is from the
sea, and their smile is an intimation of the maritime calm.

This is an account that patently reworks not Sappho but a passage from
Hesiod with its now canonical representation of Aphrodite's birth (*Th.*
191–98):[149]

τῷ δ' ἔνι κούρη

ἐθρέφθη· πρῶτον δὲ Κυθήροισι ζαθέοισιν
ἔπλητ', ἔνθεν ἔπειτα περίρρυτον ἵκετο Κύπρον.
ἐκ δ' ἔβη αἰδοίη καλὴ θεός, ἀμφὶ δὲ ποίη
ποσσὶν ὕπο ῥαδινοῖσιν ἀέξετο· τὴν δ' Ἀφροδίτην   195
[ἀφρογενέα τε θεὰν καὶ ἐυστέφανον Κυθέρειαν]
κικλήσκουσι θεοί τε καὶ ἀνέρες, οὕνεκ' ἐν ἀφρῷ
θρέφθη·

And in [the white foam] there grew a maiden; and first she came to holy
Cythera and then from there she came to sea-girt Cyprus; she came forth,
the revered beautiful goddess, and under her slender feet the grass grew
up. Her gods and men call Aphrodite, and foam-born goddess and fair-
crowned Cytherea, because she grew from foam.

With this intertext belatedly in place, the *logos* engages in a fresh set of
appropriations and revisions of a 'primary' poetic depiction. The *Theogony*
narrative not only imagines the same moment of genesis and emergence,

---

[149] The scene also existed in various painted and sculpted forms, including, most famously, in the
bas-relief on the Ludovisi Throne, whose construction is dated to the first half of the fifth
century.

but more minutely anticipates details of the painting in Philostratus'
exegesis, which repeatedly acknowledges its secondary status and more
limited access to the epiphany. The picture in the gallery includes the grass
whose growth the divine birth precipitates in Hesiod, but relocates this to
the meadow where the chorus now performs; in place of the 'revered
goddess' herself, the ivory image painted by the artist offers just a *schêma*
of the same (σχῆμα τῆς Ἀφροδίτης Αἰδοῦς). As for the contents of the
maidens' song, where the newly inspired bard supplies a direct description
of Aphrodite's self-manifestation, the reader/hearer of this passage in the
Imagines sees and hears no more than a chorally embodied and verbal
mimesis of the Hesiodic scene on the written page.

But once again Philostratus goes on at least partially to grant access to
what has seemed irrecoverable, that direct encounter with divinity itself. As
the dancers' gestures and motions re-enact what their song describes, the
painted figures become multiple representations of the goddess whom their
choreia aims to call into our midst. Answering Aphrodite's up-down
movement (she is from the sky and sea) with their eyes and hands (their
cheironomia, or 'hand dance'), they complete their work of replication with
the smile that caps all previous allusions to what, despite the proliferation
of pointers, we have not heard, viz. the song of Sappho, where the goddess
similarly first comes into view 'smiling with her immortal countenance'
(μειδιαίσαισ᾽ ἀθανάτῳ προσώπῳ, fr. 1.14 V.).[150] But as throughout the
larger passage, so in this closing section Philostratus will not allow his
reader to forget the material aspect of the image and the secondary quality
of its depiction of a once live performance. Even the choral mimesis of
Aphrodite's epiphany cannot wholly remedy the gap between reality and
representation: the singers' smile only 'intimates' or hints at the sea that is
the medium of her birth. In the statement that closes the ecphrasis, the
facial expression is declared 'a riddle' or 'obscure saying' (αἴνιγμα) of a
moment of maritime calm, a stillness that returns us to the static picture
just described. In lingering on the chorus members' smiling countenances,
Philostratus introduces an additional element of estrangement: the painted
performers replicate not so much 'laughter-loving' Aphrodite's own physi-
ognomy as that belonging to a sculpted image, perhaps an archaic-style
korê with its characteristically indecipherable smile.

This caveat notwithstanding, the text continues to showcase what,
within limitations, *enargeia* can achieve. Just as a choral performance

[150] As also noted by Platt 2011, 4. That smile immediately precedes the moment when the lyric
poet allows us to hear the divine voice.

opens up a passage to phenomena otherwise imperceptible to the senses, so too does Philostratus' closing description of the song, which seems to fill in the absence just announced and remedy the omission of all that the performance once included.[151] Much as the speaker's conjecture (οἶμαι) had supplied the missing object of Eros' moving and sentient gaze, now too he reaches beyond the image and previews what the song will go on to describe, the goddess' arrival on Paphos, a nod to and modification of Hesiod, since Paphos is on Cyprus, which is the site of the last in the series of epiphanies punctuating her progress in the *Theogony*. This supplementation of the painted scene makes the performance, now permanently fixed and frozen within its frame of stones, ongoing, something with a future as well as past reality. Even as this opening discourse closes, the words of the painted, transcribed and re-enunciated song continue sounding on for other audiences and into future times.[152]

As noted through the course of my reading, at each and every stage of Philostratus' account, it is the singing, dancing and beautifully clothed maidenly chorus in its bucolic setting that transmits to us everything that we apprehend concerning Aphrodite and her presence within our space. But over and above its pertinence to the themes of *enargeia* and epiphany treated in this chapter, this late and vertiginously layered ecphrasis furnishes a fitting close to the discussion because it demonstrates both the continuities and sharp distinctions between Philostratus' representation of *choreia* and the much earlier material explored elsewhere in this study. For all that from the first it is so frequently maidens in the springtime of their lives dancing in ornamented garments in verdant sites who supply the paradigmatic practitioners of a ritual designed to bring the gods into the human realm, archaic and early classical authors, painters and other craftsmen would have had a first-hand familiarity with an institution in which, whether as performers or spectators, they had most likely taken part. For Philostratus and his readers, knowledge of *choreia*, still practiced in their time, but in very different forms, venues and organizational frames, was more remote, encountered chiefly through earlier verbal and artistic depictions or as the product of self-conscious attempts to revivify a performance mode still regarded as a hallmark of Greek culture.[153]

[151] See Dubel 1997, 262.
[152] The open-ended text recalls the stratagem with which the *Homeric Hymn to Aphrodite* also concludes: there the goddess darts up to the heavens while still speaking (ὣς εἰποῦσ' ἤϊξε, 291).
[153] For a helpful and succinct summary of the persistence of *choreia* and attitudes towards it in imperial Greece, see Bowie 2006.

These more attenuated engagements with the practice notwithstanding, in one narrower and one much broader respect song-dance in Philostratus' text retains the character it had possessed from the start of the 'story' that preceding chapters have traced out: as in *Iliad* 18, *choreia* continues to supply a choice subject for artistic representation, whether fashioned from metal, paint, stone or thread, that further lends itself to transmission and representation in verbal form; and also in keeping with its role in archaic and classical times, it lastingly provides a site for the exploration of existing and novel practices and techniques and for bridging boundaries between separate but overlapping orders of reality.

Bibliography

Ahlberg-Cornell, G. 1992. *Myth and Epos in Early Greek Art: Representation and Interpretation*. Studies in Mediterranean Archaeology 100. Jonsered.

Allan, W. (ed.) 2008. *Euripides: Helen*. Cambridge Greek and Latin Classics. Cambridge.

Alonge, M. 2011. 'Greek Hymns from Performance to Stone', in A. P. M. H. Lardinois, J. H. Blok and M. G. M. van der Poel (eds.), *Sacred Words: Orality, Literacy and Religion*. Orality and Literacy in the Ancient World 8. Leiden: 217–34.

Anderson, W. D. 1994. *Music and Musicians in Ancient Greece*. Ithaca.

Andújar, R. 2018. 'Hyporchematic Footprints in Euripides' *Electra*', in R. Andújar, T. R. P. Coward and T. Hadjimichael (eds.), *Paths of Song: The Lyric Dimension of Greek Tragedy*. Berlin: 265–90.

Ashmole, B. 1946. 'Kalligeneia and Hieros Arotos', *JHS* 66: 8–10.

Athanassaki, L. and E. Bowie (eds.) 2011. *Archaic and Classical Choral Song: Performance, Politics and Dissemination*. Berlin.

Bachvarova, M. R. 2009. 'Suppliant Danaids and Argive Nymphs in Aeschylus', *CJ* 104: 289–310.

Bakker, E. 1993. 'Discourse and Performance: Involvement, Visualization and "Presence" in Homeric Poetry', *CA* 12: 1–29.

　1997. *Poetry in Speech: Orality and Homeric Discourse*. Ithaca.

Barber, E. 1991. *Prehistoric Textiles: The Development of Cloth in the Neolithic and Bronze Ages with Special Reference to the Aegean*. Princeton.

　1992. 'The Peplos of Athena', in J. Neils (ed.), *Goddess and Polis: The Panathenaic Festival in Ancient Athens*. Princeton: 103–17.

Barker, A. 1984. *Greek Musical Writings. Vol. I: The Musician and His Art*. Cambridge.

　1995. '*Heterophonia* and *Poikilia*: Accompaniments to Greek Melody', in B. Gentili and F. Perusino (eds.), *Mousikê: Metrica ritmica e musica greca in memoria di Giovanni Comotti*. Pisa and Rome: 41–60.

　2004. 'Transforming the Nightingale: Aspects of Athenian Musical Discourse in the Late Fifth Century', in Murray and Wilson: 185–204.

Barrett, W. S. (ed.) 1964. *Euripides: Hippolytus*. Oxford.

Barringer, J. 1995. *Divine Escorts: Nereids in Archaic and Classical Greek Art*. Ann Arbor.

Baughan, E. P. 2011. 'Sculpted Symposiasts of Ionia', *AJA* 115: 19–53.

Beazley, J. D. 1928. *Greek Vases in Poland*. London.

Belfiore, E. S. 2000. *Murder among Friends: Violation of Philia in Greek Tragedy*. Oxford and New York.

Bélis, A. 1988. 'A proposito degli "Inni delfici" ad Apollo', in B. Gentili and R. Pretagostini (eds.), *La musica in Grecia*. Bari: 205–18.

Belis, Z. 2011. 'Pride and Paradox in IG I³ 833*bis*', *Mnemosyne* 64: 183–204.

Bellia, A. 2012. *Il canto delle vergini locresi: la musica a Locri Epizefirii nelle fonti scritte e nella documentazione archeologico (secoli VI–III a.C.)*. Nuovi saggi 116. Pisa and Rome.

Benediktson, D. T. 2000. *Literature and the Visual Arts in Ancient Greece and Rome*. Norman, OK.

Bennett, E. L. 1963. 'Names for Linear B Writing and Its Signs', *Kadmos* 2: 98–123.

Benveniste, E. 1969. *Le vocabulaire des institutions indo-européennes*. Vols. I–II. Paris.

1971. 'The Notion of "Rhythm" in its Linguistic Expression', in *Problems in General Linguistics*. Coral Gables, FL: 281–89.

Bergren, A. L. T. 1975. *The Etymology and Usage of πεῖραρ in Early Greek Poetry*. New York.

Bernsdorff, H. 2004. 'Schwermut des Alters im neuen Kölner Sappho-Papyrus', *ZPE* 150: 27–35.

Bierl, A. 2009. *Ritual and Performativity: The Chorus in Old Comedy*. Washington, DC.

2011. 'Alcman at the End of Aristophanes' Lysistrata: Ritual Interchorality', in Athanassaki and Bowie: 415–35.

2013. 'Maenadism as Self-Referential Chorality in Euripides' *Bacchae*', in Gagné and Hopman: 211–26.

2016. 'Visualizing the Cologne Sappho: Mental Imagery through Chorality, the Sun, and Orpheus', in V. Cazzato and A. Lardinois (eds.), *The Look of Lyric: Greek Song and the Visual*. Studies in Archaic and Classical Greek Song 1. Leiden: 307–42.

Billings, J., F. Budelmann and F. Macintosh (eds.) 2013. *Choruses, Ancient and Modern*. Cambridge.

Binek, N. 2017. 'The Dipylon Oinochoe Graffito: Text or Decoration?', *Hesperia* 86: 423–42.

Bing, P. 2008. *The Well-Read Muse: Present and Past in Callimachus and the Hellenistic Poets*. Rev. ed. Ann Arbor.

Blakely, S. 2006. *Myth, Ritual, and Metallurgy in Ancient Greece and Recent Africa*. Cambridge.

Blondell, R. 2005. 'From Fleece to Fabric: Weaving Culture in Plato's Statesman', *Oxford Studies in Ancient Philosophy* 38: 23–75.

Boedeker, D. 1974. *Aphrodite's Entry into Greek Epic*. Leiden.

1984. *Descent from Heaven: Images of Dew in Greek Poetry and Religion*. American Classical Studies 13. Chico, CA.

Borell, B. 1978. *Attisch Geometrische Schalen: eine spätgeometrische Keramikgattung und ihre Beziehungen zum Orient*. Mainz am Rhein.

Bosher, K. (ed.) 2012. *Theatre outside Athens: Drama in Greek Sicily and South Italy*. Cambridge.

Bousquet, J. 1992. 'Deux épigrammes grecques', *BCH* 116: 585–606.

Bowie, E. L. 1986. 'Early Greek Elegy, Symposium and Public Festival', *JHS* 106: 13–35.

    2006. 'Choral Performances', in D. Konstan and S. Saïd (eds.), *Greeks on Greekness: Viewing the Greek Past under the Roman Empire. PCPS* Suppl. 29: 61–92.

    2010. 'Epigram as Narration', in M. Baumbach, A. Petrovic and I. Petrovic (eds.), *Archaic and Classical Greek Epigram*. Oxford: 313–84.

    2011. 'Alcman's First *Partheneion* and the Song the Sirens Sang', in Athanassaki and Bowie: 35–65.

Bowra, C. M. 1938. 'The Daughters of Asopus', *Hermes* 73: 213–21.

Brann, E. 1961. 'Protoattic Well Groups from the Athenian Agora', *Hesperia* 30: 305–79.

Bravo, B. 1997. *Pannychis e simposio: Feste private notturne di donne e uomini nei testi letterari e nel culto, con uno studio iconografico di Françoise Frontisi-Ducroux*. Pisa and Rome.

Briand, M. 2009. 'La danse et la philologie: à partir du mouvement strophique dans les scholies anciennes à Pindare', in S. David et al. (eds.), *Traduire les scholies de Pindare*. Vol. I. *Dialogues d'histoire ancienne* Supplément 2: 93–106.

Brijder, H. A. G. 1986. 'A Pre-Dramatic Performance of a Satyr Chorus by the Heidelberg Painter', in H. A. G. Brijder, A. A. Drukker and C. W. Neeft (eds.), *Enthusiasmos: Essays on Greek and Related Pottery Presented to J. M. Hemelrijk*. Allard Pierson Series 6. Amsterdam: 69–82.

Brown, C. 1989. 'Anactoria and the Χαρίτων ἀμαρύγματα: Sappho fr. 16, 18 Voigt', *QUCC* 32: 7–15.

Buchan, M. 2012. *Perfidy and Passion: Reintroducing the Iliad*. Madison.

Buchholz, H. G. 1987. 'Das Symbol des gemeinsamen Mantels', *JdI* 102: 1–55.

Budelmann, F. and T. Power. 2015. 'Another Look at Female Choruses in Classical Athens', *CA* 34: 252–95.

Budin, S. 2008. *The Myth of Sacred Prostitution in Antiquity*. Cambridge.

Bundrick, S. 2005. *Music and Image in Classical Athens*. Cambridge.

    2008. 'The Fabric of the City: Imaging Textile Production in Classical Athens', *Hesperia* 77: 283–334.

Burkert, W. 1983. *Homo Necans: The Anthropology of Ancient Greek Sacrificial Ritual and Myth*. Berkeley and Los Angeles.

    1985. *Greek Religion: Archaic and Classical*. Oxford.

Burnett, A. P. 1985. *The Art of Bacchylides*. Cambridge, MA and London.

    2011. 'Servants of Peitho: Pindar fr. 122 S.', *GRBS* 51: 49–60.

Bussels, S. 2012. *The Animated Image: Roman Theory on Naturalism, Vividness and Divine Power*. Munich and Leiden.

Butz, P. A. 2010. *The Art of the Hekatompedon Inscription and the Birth of the Stoikhedon Style*. Leiden.

Cahill, N. 2002. *Household and City Organization at Olynthus*. New Haven.

Cain, C. D. 2001. 'Dancing in the Dark: Deconstructing a Narrative of Epiphany on the Isopata Ring', *AJA* 105: 27–49.

Cairns, D. 2005. 'Myth and the Polis in Bacchylides' Eleventh Ode', *JHS* 125: 35–48.

  2010. *Bacchylides: Five Epinician Odes (3, 5, 9, 11, 13). Text, Introductory Essays, and Interpretative Commentary*. Cambridge.

Calame, C. 1983. *Alcman. Introduction, texte critique, témoinages, traduction et commentaire*. Rome.

  1994/95. 'From Choral Poem to Tragic Stasimon: The Enactment of Women's Song', *Arion* 3: 136–54.

  1997. *Choruses of Young Women in Ancient Greece: Their Morphology, Religious Role, and Social Function*. Trans. Derek Collins and Janice Orion. Lanham, MD.

  2004. 'Choral Forms in Aristophanic Comedy: Musical Mimesis and Dramatic Performance in Classical Athens', in Murray and Wilson: 157–84.

  2009a. 'Apollo in Delphi and in Delos: Poetic Performances between Paean and Dithyramb', in L. Athanassaki, R. P. Martin and J. F. Miller (eds.), *Apolline Politics and Poetics*. Athens: 169–97.

  2009b. *Poetic and Performative Memory in Ancient Greece: Heroic Reference and Ritual Gestures in Time and Space*. Trans. H. Patton. Center for Hellenic Studies. Cambridge, MA.

  2012. 'Metaphorical Travel and Ritual Performance in Epinician Poetry', in P. Agócs, C. Carey and R. Rawles (eds.), *Reading the Victory Ode*. Cambridge: 303–20.

  2013. 'Choral Polyphony and the Ritual Functions of Tragic Songs', in Gagné and Hopman: 35–57.

Canali De Rossi, P. 2004. *Iscrizioni dello Estremo Oriente Greco: un repertorio. Inschriften griechischer Städte aus Kleinasien*. Bonn.

Carey, C. 1980. 'Bacchylides' Experiments. Ode XI', *Mnemosyne* 33: 225–43.

  2007. 'Pindar, Place and Performance', in S. Hornblower and C. Morgan (eds.), *Pindar's Poetry, Patrons, and Festivals from Archaic Greece to the Roman Empire*. Oxford: 199–210.

  2012. 'The Victory Ode in the Theatre', in P. Agócs, C. Carey and R. Rawles (eds.), *Receiving the Komos: Ancient and Modern Receptions of the Victory Ode*. London: 17–36.

  2015. 'Stesichorus and the Epic Cycle', in A. Kelly and P. Finglass (eds.), *Stesichorus in Context*. Cambridge: 45–63.

Carne-Ross, D. S. 1979. *Instaurations: Essays in and out of Literature, Pindar to Pound*. Berkeley and Los Angeles.

Carruesco, J. 2010. 'Prácticas rituales y modos del discurso: la coralidad como paradigma del catálogo en la poesía arcaica griega', in *Actas del XII Congreso Espanõl de Estudios Clásicos*. Vol. II. Valencia: 387–93.

2012. 'Helen's Voice and Choral Mimesis from Homer to Stesichorus', in X. Riu and J. Pòrtulas (eds.), *Approaches to Archaic Greek Poetry*. Messina: 149–72.

2016. 'Choral Performance and Geometric Patterns in Epic Poetry and Iconographic Representations', in V. Cazzato and A. Lardinois (eds.), *The Look of Lyric: Greek Song and the Visual*. Studies in Archaic and Classical Greek Song 1. Leiden: 69–107.

Carter, J. B. 1987. 'The Masks of Ortheia', *AJA* 91: 355–83.

1995. 'Ancestor Cult and the Occasion of Homeric Performance', in J. B. Carter and S. Morris (eds.), *The Ages of Homer: A Tribute to Emily Townsend Vermeule*. Austin: 285–312.

Casevitz, M. 1992. 'Mantis: le vrai sens', *REG* 105: 1–18.

Cassio, A. C. 1994. 'I distici del polyandrian di Ambracia e l' 'io anonimo' nell'epigramma Greco', *SMEA* 33: 101–17.

Casson, L. 1914. 'The Persian Expedition to Delphi', *CR* 28: 145–51.

1921. 'ΑΠΟΔΕΙΧΙΣ, "Inventory", in Herodotus and Thucydides', *CR* 35: 144–45.

Catoni, M. L. 2005. *Schemata: communicazione non verbale nella Greca antica*. Pisa.

Cazzato, V. and A. Lardinois (eds.) 2016. *The Look of Lyric: Greek Song and the Visual*. Studies in Archaic and Classical Greek Song 1. Leiden.

Ceccarelli, P. 2010. 'Changing Contexts: Tragedy in the Civic and Cultural Life of the City-States', in I. Gildenhard and M. Revermann (eds.), *Beyond the Fifth Century: Interactions with Greek Tragedy from the Fourth Century BCE to the Middle Ages*. Berlin: 99–150.

Ceccarelli, P. and S. Milanezi. 2007. 'Dithyramb, Tragedy – and Cyrene', in P. Wilson (ed.), *The Greek Theatre and Festivals: Documentary Studies*. Oxford: 185–214.

Chaniotis, A. 2006. 'Rituals between Norms and Emotions: Rituals as Shared Experience and Memory', in E. Stavrianopoulou (ed.), *Ritual and Communication in the Graeco-Roman World*. Liège: 211–38.

2007. 'Theatre Rituals', in P. Wilson (ed.), *The Greek Theatre and Festivals: Documentary Studies*. Oxford: 48–66.

Chantraine, P. 1999. *Dictionnaire étymologique de la langue grecque. Histoire des mots*. 2nd ed. Paris.

Clarke, M. 1997/98. 'πινύσκω and Its Cognates: A Note on Simonides, fr. 508 Page', *Glotta* 74: 135–42.

1999. *Flesh and Spirit in the Songs of Homer*. Oxford.

Clay, J. S. 1974. 'Demas and Aude: The Nature of Divine Transformation in Homer', *Hermes* 102: 129–36.

1992. 'Pindar's Twelfth *Pythian*: Reed and Bronze', *AJP* 113: 519–25.

Clements, A. 2015. 'Divine Scents and Presence', in M. Bradley (ed.), *Smell and the Ancient Senses*. London and New York: 46–59.

Cohen, B. 2006. *The Colors of Clay: Special Techniques in Athenian Vases*. The J. Paul Getty Museum. Los Angeles.

Coldstream, J. N. 1968. 'A Figured Geometric Oinochoe from Italy', *BICS* 15: 86–96.

2003. *Geometric Greece 900–700 B. C.* 2nd ed. London and New York.

Collins, C. 1991. *Reading the Written Image: Verbal Play, Interpretation, and the Roots of Iconophobia*. University Park.

Collins, D. 1999. 'Hesiod and the Divine Voice of the Muses', *Arethusa* 32: 241–62.

2006. 'Corinna and Mythological Innovation', *CQ* 56: 19–32.

Connelly, J. 2007. *Portrait of a Priestess: Women and Ritual in Ancient Greece*. Princeton.

2010. 'Excavations on Geronisos, Third Report: The Circular Structure, East Building, and the Square Houses', in *Report of the Department of Antiquities of Cyprus 2009*: 295–348.

2011. 'Ritual Movement through Sacred Space: Towards an Archaeology of Performance', in A. Chaniotis (ed.), *Ritual Dynamics in the Ancient Mediterranean: Agency, Emotion, Gender, Representation*. Stuttgart: 313–46.

Constantinidou, S. 1998. 'Dionysiac Elements in Spartan Cult Dances', *Phoenix* 52: 15–30.

Cook, A. B. 1902. 'The Gong at Dodona', *JHS* 22: 5–28.

Couprie, D. L., R. Hahn and G. Naddaf. 2003. *Anaximander in Context: New Studies in the Origins of Greek Philosophy*. Albany.

Cropp, M. (ed.) 2013. *Euripides: Electra*. 2nd ed. Oxford.

Crowhurst, R. 1963. *Representations of Performance of Choral Lyric on the Greek Monuments, 800–350 BC*. PhD diss., 2 vols. University of London.

Csapo, E. 1999/2000. 'Later Euripidean Music', in M. J. Cropp, K. Lee and D. Sansone (eds.), *Euripides and Tragic Theatre in the Late Fifth Century*. *ICS* 24–25. Champagne: 399–426.

2003. 'The Dolphins of Dionysus', in E. Csapo and M. C. Miller (eds.), *Poetry, Theory, Praxis: The Social Life of Myth, Word and Image in Ancient Greece. Essays in Honour of William J. Slater*. Oxford: 69–98.

2004. 'The Politics of the New Music', in Murray and Wilson: 207–48.

2008. 'Star Choruses: Eleusis, Orphism and New Musical Imagery and Dance', in M. Revermann and P. Wilson (eds.), *Performance, Iconography, Reception: Studies in Honour of Oliver Taplin*. Oxford: 262–90.

2010. 'The Context of Choregic Dedications', in O. Taplin and R. Wyles (eds.), *The Pronomos Vase and Its Context*. Oxford: 79–130.

Csapo, E. and M. C. Miller. 1991. 'The "Kottabos-Toast" and an Inscribed Red-figured Cup', *Hesperia* 60: 367–82.

Cucuzza, N. 2013. 'Minoan Nativity Scene? The Ayia Triada Swing Model and the Three-Dimensional Representation of Minoan Divine Epiphany', *Annuario della Scuola Archeologica di Atene* 91: 175–207.

Cumont, F. 1928. 'Inscriptions grecques de Suse', *Mémoires de la Mission Archéologique de Perse* 20: 77–98.

Currie, B. 2004. 'Reperformance Scenarios for Pindar's Odes', in C. J. Mackie (ed.), *Oral Performance and Its Context*. Leiden: 49–69.

    2005. *Pindar and the Cult of Heroes*. Oxford.

    2011. 'Epinician *Choregia*: Funding a Pindaric Chorus', in Athanassaki and Bowie: 269–309.

Curtis, L. 2017. *Imagining the Chorus in Augustan Poetry*. Cambridge.

D'Alessio, G. B. 1995. 'Sull' epigramma dal Polyandrion di Ambracia', *ZPE* 106: 22–26.

    2005. 'Ordered from the *Catalogue*: Pindar, Bacchylides and Hesiodic Genealogical Poetry', in R. Hunter (ed.), *The Hesiodic Catalogue of Women: Constructions and Reconstructions*. Cambridge: 217–38.

    2009. 'Re-Constructing Pindar's *First Hymn*: The Theban "Theogony" and the Birth of Apollo', in L. Athanassaki, R. P. Martin and J. F. Miller (eds.), *Apolline Politics and Poetics*. Athens: 129–47.

D'Angour, A. 1997. 'How the Dithyramb Got Its Shape', *CQ* 47: 331–51.

    1999. 'Archinus, Eucleides, and the Reform of the Athenian Alphabet', *BICS* 43: 109–30.

Davies, J. K. 1969. 'The Date of *IG* II^2 1609', *Historia* 18: 309–33.

Davies, M. and P. J. Finglass (eds.) 2014. *Stesichorus: The Poems*. Cambridge Classical Texts and Commentaries. Cambridge.

Day, J. W. 1989. 'Rituals in Stone: Early Greek Grave Epigrams and Monuments', *JHS* 109: 16–28.

    1994. 'Interactive Offerings: Early Greek Dedicatory Epigrams and Ritual', *HSCP* 96: 37–74.

    2000. 'Epigram and Reader: Generic Force as (Re-)activation of Ritual', in M. Depew and D. Obbink (eds.), *Matrices of Genre: Authors, Canons, and Society*. Cambridge, MA: 37–57.

    2007. 'Poems on Stone: The Inscribed Antecedents of Hellenistic Epigram' in P. Bing and J. S. Bruss (eds.), *Brill's Companion to Hellenistic Epigram down to Philip*. Leiden and Boston: 29–47.

    2010. *Archaic Greek Epigram and Dedication*. Cambridge.

De Jong, I. 2009. 'Metalepsis in Greek Literature', in J. Grethlein and A. Rengakos (eds.), *Narratology and Interpretation: The Content of Narrative Form in Ancient Literature*. Berlin: 87–115.

Depew, M. 1997. 'Reading Greek Prayers', *CA* 16: 229–58.

    2000. 'Enacted and Represented Dedications: Genre and Greek Hymn', in M. Depew and D. Obbink (eds.), *Matrices of Genre: Authors, Canons, and Society*. Cambridge, MA: 59–79.

Detienne, M. 1989. *L'écriture d'Orphée*. Paris.

Detienne, M. and J.-P. Vernant. 1978. *Les ruses de l'intelligence: la métis des Grecs.* Paris.

Diels, H. 1890. *Sibyllinische Blätter.* Berlin.

Dilke, O. A. W. (ed.) 2005. *Statius: Achilleid.* 2nd ed. Bristol.

Dillon, M. 2002. *Girls and Women in Classical Greek Religion.* London and New York.

Dougherty, C. 1993. *The Poetics of Colonization: From City to Text in Archaic Greece.* Oxford.

Dowden, K. 1989. *Death and the Maiden: Girls' Initiation Rites in Greek Mythology.* London.

Dubel, S. 1997. 'Ekphrasis et Enargeia. La description antique comme parcours', in L. B. Lévy and L. Pernot (eds.), *Dire l'évidence.* Paris: 249–64.

Dunbar, N. (ed.) 1995. *Aristophanes: Birds. With Introduction and Commentary.* Oxford.

Eckerman, C. 2014. 'Pindar's Delphi', in K. Gilhuly and N. Worman (eds.), *Place, Space, and Landscape in Ancient Greek Literature and Culture.* Cambridge: 21–62.

Edmunds, S. T. 2012. 'Picturing Homeric Weaving', in V. Bers, D. Elmer, D. Frame and L. Muellner (eds.), *Donum natalicium digitaliter confectum Gregorio Nagy septuagenario a discipulis collegis familiaribus oblatum = A Virtual Birthday Gift Presented to Gregory Nagy on Turning Seventy by His Students, Colleagues, and Friends.* Center for Hellenic Studies. Washington, DC.

Edwards, M. (ed.) 1991. *The Iliad: A Commentary. Vol. V: Books 17–20.* Cambridge.

Elsner, J. 1996. 'Image and Ritual: Reflections on the Religious Appreciation of Classical Art', *CQ* 46: 515–31.

2002. 'Introduction: The Genres of Ekphrasis', *Ramus* 31: 1–18.

Esrock, E. J. 1994. *The Reader's Eye: Visual Imaging as Reader Response.* Baltimore.

Faraone, C. 1992. *Talismans and Trojan Horses: Guardian Statues in Ancient Greek Myth and Ritual.* Oxford.

2013. 'The Poetics of the Catalogue in the Hesiodic *Theogony*', *TAPA* 143: 293–323.

Fearn, D. W. 2003. 'Mapping Phleious: Politics and Myth-Making in Bacchylides 9', *CQ* 53: 347–67.

2007. *Bacchylides: Politics, Performance, Poetic Tradition.* Oxford.

2011. 'The Ceians and Their Choral Lyric: Athenian, Epichoric and Pan-Hellenic Perspectives', in Athanassaki and Bowie: 207–34.

Fehr, B. 2009. '*Ponos* and the Pleasure of Rest: Some Thoughts on Body Language in Ancient Greek Art and Life', in D. Yatromanolakis (ed.), *An Archaeology of Representations: Ancient Greek Vase-Painting and Contemporary Methodologies.* Athens: 128–58.

Felson, N. 1999. 'Vicarious Transport: Fictive Deixis in Pindar's *Pythian* Four', *HSCP* 99: 1–31.

(ed.) 2004. *The Poetics of Deixis in Alcman, Pindar, and Other Lyric. Arethusa* 37.

Felten, J. (ed.) 1913. *Nicolai Progymnasmata. Rhetores Graeci* 11. Leipzig.

Fernandez-Galiano, M. (ed.) 1992. *A Commentary on Homer's Odyssey. Vol. III: Books XVII–XXIV*. With J. Russo and A. Heubeck. Oxford.

Ferrari, G. 1987. 'Menelãs', *JHS* 107: 180–82.

    1990. 'Figures of Speech: The Picture of *Aidos*', *Mètis* 5: 185–200.

    2002. *Figures of Speech: Men and Maidens in Ancient Greece*. Chicago.

    2003a. 'Myth and Genre on Athenian Vases', *CA* 22: 37–54.

    2003b. 'What Kind of Rite of Passage was the Ancient Greek Wedding?', in D. B. Dodd and C. A. Faraone (eds.), *Initiation in Ancient Greek Rituals and Narratives: New Critical Perspectives*. London and New York: 27–42.

    2008. *Alcman and the Cosmos of Sparta*. Chicago.

Fileni, M. G. 1987. *Senocrito di Locri e Pindaro (fr. 140b Sn.-Maehl.)*. Rome.

Fineberg, S. 2009. 'Hephaestus on Foot in the Ceramicus', *TAPA* 139: 275–324.

Fitzgerald, W. 1987. *Agonistic Poetry: The Pindaric Mode in Pindar, Horace, Hölderlin, and the English Ode*. Berkeley and Los Angeles.

Foley, H. P. (ed.) 1994. *The Homeric Hymn to Demeter: Translation, Commentary and Interpretive Essays*. Princeton.

    2016. 'Reconsidering "The Mimetic Action of the Chorus"'. Unpublished manuscript.

Forbes Irving, P. M. C. 1992. *Metamorphosis in Greek Myths*. Oxford.

Ford, A. 1992. *Homer. The Poetry of the Past*. Ithaca and London.

    2002. *The Origins of Criticism: Literary Culture and Poetic Theory in Classical Greece*. Princeton.

    2006. 'The Genre of Genres: Paeans and Paian in Early Greek Poetry', *Poetica* 38: 277–96.

    2010. '"A Song to Match My Song": Lyric Doubling in Euripides' *Helen*', in P. Mitsis and C. Tsagalis (eds.), *Allusion, Authority and Truth: Critical Perspectives on Greek Poetic and Rhetorical Praxis*. Berlin and New York: 283–302.

    2013. 'The Poetics of Dithyramb', in Kowalzig and Wilson: 313–31.

Foster, K. P. 1995. 'A Flight of Swallows', *AJA* 99: 409–25.

Franklin, J. C. 2013. '"Songbenders of Circular Choruses": Dithyramb and the "Demise of Music"', in Kowalzig and Wilson: 213–36.

    2015. *Kinyras: The Divine Lyre*. Cambridge, MA.

Franko, M. 1993. *Dance as Text: Ideologies of the Baroque Body*. Cambridge.

Franks, H. M. 2009. 'Hunting the Eschata: An Imagined Persian Empire on the Lekythos of Xenophantos', *Hesperia* 78: 455–80.

Franzen, C. 2009. 'Sympathizing with the Monster: Making Sense of Colonization in Stesichorus' *Geryoneis*', *QUCC* 92: 55–72.

Frontisi-Ducroux, F. 1975/2000. *Dédale: mythologie de l'artisan en Grèce ancienne*. Paris.

    1994. 'Athéna et l'invention de la flûte', *Musica e Storia* 2: 239–67.

2002. "'Avec son diaphragme visionnaire: ἰδυίῃσι πραπίδεσσι", *Iliade* XVIII, 481. À propos du bouclier d'Achille', *REG* 115: 463–84.

Führer, R. 2007. 'Responsion in Simonidesfragmenten', *ZPE* 159: 12.

Furley, W. D. 1995. 'Praise and Persuasion in Greek Hymns', *JHS* 115: 29–46.

2007. 'Prayers and Hymns', in D. Ogden (ed.), *A Companion to Greek Religion*. Oxford: 117–31.

Gagné, R. 2013. 'Dancing Letters: The *Alphabetic Tragedy* of Kallias', in Gagné and Hopman: 297–316.

Gagné, R. and M. Hopman. 2013. *Choral Mediations in Greek Tragedy*. Cambridge.

Gallet, B. 1990. *Recherches sur kairos et l'ambiguïté dans la poésie de Pindare*. Bordeaux.

Garvie, A. F. 1965. 'A Note on the Deity of Alcman's *Partheneion*', *CQ* 15: 185–87.

(ed.) 1994. *Homer: Odyssey Books VI–VIII*. Cambridge Greek and Latin Classics. Cambridge.

Gentili, B. 1958. *Bacchylide: Studi*. Rome.

Gernet, L. 1981. *The Anthropology of Ancient Greece*. Baltimore.

Ghiron-Bistagne, P. 1976. *Recherches sur les acteurs dans la Grèce antique*. Paris.

Giangrande, G. 1971. 'Interpretationen griechischer Meliker', *RhM* 114: 97–131.

Giuliani, L. 2013. *Image and Myth: A History of Pictorial Narration in Greek Art*. Trans. J. O'Donnell. Chicago and London.

Gleba, M. 2008. *Textile Production in Pre-Roman Italy*. Oxford and Philadelphia.

Golab, Hanna. 2018. *Postclassical Choral Performances*. Ph.D. dissertation, Princeton University.

Goldman, B. 1960. 'The Development of the Lion-Griffin', *AJA* 64: 319–28.

Gomme, A. W., A. Andrewes and K. J. Dover. 1992. *An Historical Commentary on Thucydides. Books V (25)–VII*. Oxford.

Goslin, O. 2010. 'Hesiod's Typhonomachy and the Ordering of Sound', *TAPA* 140: 351–73.

Grand-Clément, A. 2015. '*Poikilia*', in P. Destrée and P. Murray (eds.), *A Companion to Ancient Aesthetics*. Chichester: 406–21.

Graziosi, B. and J. Haubold (eds.) 2010. *Homer: Iliad Book VI*. Cambridge Greek and Latin Classics. Cambridge.

Green, J. R. 1985. 'A Representation of the *Birds* of Aristophanes', *Greek Vases in the J. Paul Getty Museum* 2: 95–128.

1995. 'Oral Tragedies? A Question from St. Petersburg', *QUCC* 51: 77–86.

2008. 'Theatre Production 1996–2006', *Lustrum* 50: 7–302.

Greene, E. 2009. 'Sappho 58: Philosophical Reflections on Death and Aging', in E. Greene and M. B. Skinner (eds.), *The New Sappho on Old Age: Textual and Philosophical Issues*. Hellenic Studies Series 38. Center for Hellenic Studies. Washington, DC: 147–61.

Greene, T. M. 2001. 'Labyrinth Dances in the French and English Renaissance', *Renaissance Quarterly* 54: 1403–66.

Gresseth, G. K. 1964. 'The Myth of Alcyone', *TAPA* 95: 88–98.

Grethlein, J. 2017. *Aesthetic Experiences and Classical Antiquity: The Significance of Form in Narratives and Pictures.* Cambridge.

Griffith, M. 2006a. 'Horsepower and Donkeywork: Equids and the Ancient Greek Imagination', *CP* 101: 185–246.

    2006b. 'Horsepower and Donkeywork: Equids and the Ancient Greek Imagination. Part Two', *CP* 101: 307–58.

    2013. 'Satyr-Play, Dithyramb, and the Geopolitics of Dionysian Style in Fifth-Century Athens', in Kowalzig and Wilson: 257–81.

Gronewald, M. and R. W. Daniel. 2004. 'Ein neuer Sappho-Papyrus', *ZPE* 147: 1–8.

Gruben, G. 1963. 'Das archaische Didymaion', *JdI* 78: 78–177.

Guarducci, M. 1928–29. 'Due o piu donne sotto un solo manto', *AM* 80: 52–65.

Hägg, R. 1986. 'Die göttliche Epiphanie im minoischen Ritual', *MdI* 101: 41–62.

Halliwell, S. 2002. *The Aesthetics of Mimesis: Ancient Texts and Modern Problems.* Princeton.

Hamilton, R. 1989. 'Alkman and the Atheian Arkteia', *Hesperia* 58: 449–72.

Harder, A. 2012. *Callimachus: Aetia. Introduction, Text, Translation and Commentary.* 2 vols. Oxford.

Hardie. A. 1996. 'Pindar, Castalia and the Muses of Delphi (the Sixth *Paean*)', *PLLS* 9: 219–57.

    2000. 'Pindar's "Theban" Cosmogony (the First Hymn)', *BICS* 44: 19–40.

    2005. 'Sappho, the Muses, and Life after Death', *ZPE* 154: 13–32.

Hardie, P. 1998. 'A Reading of Heliodorus, *Aithiopika* 3.4.1–5.2', in R. Hunter (ed.), *Studies in Heliodorus.* Cambridge: 19–39.

Haselberger, L. (ed.) 1999. *Appearance and Essence. Refinements of Classical Architecture: Curvature.* Williams Symposium on Classical Architecture. Ephrata, PA.

Haug, A. 2012. *Die Entdeckung des Körpers: Körper- und Rollenbilder im Athen des 8. und 7. Jahrhunderts v. Chr.* Berlin.

Heath, M. and M. Lefkowitz. 1991. 'Epinician Performance', *CP* 86: 173–91.

Hedreen, G. 1992. *Silens in Attic Black-figure Vase-painting: Myth and Performance.* Ann Arbor.

    2004. 'The Return of Hephaistos, Dionysiac Processional Ritual and the Creation of a Visual Narrative', *JHS* 124: 38–64.

    2011. 'Bild, Mythos and Ritual: Choral Dance in Theseus' Cretan Adventure on the François Vase', *Hesperia* 80: 491–510.

    2013. 'The Semantics of Processional Dithyramb: Pindar's *Second Dithyramb* and Archaic Athenian Vase-Painting', in Kowalzig and Wilson: 171–97.

    2016. *The Image of the Artist in Archaic and Classical Greece: Art, Poetry, and Subjectivity.* Cambridge.

Heiden, B. 2008a. *Homer's Cosmic Fabrication: Choice and Design in the Iliad.* Oxford.

    2008b. 'Common People and Leaders in *Iliad* Book 2: The Invocation of the Muses and the Catalogue of Ships', *TAPA* 138: 127–54.

Heinemann, A. 2013. 'Performance and the Drinking Vessel: Looking for an Imagery of Dithyramb in the Time of the "New Music"', in Kowalzig and Wilson: 282–309.

Henrichs, A. 1994/95. '"Why Should I Dance?" Choral Self-Referentiality in Greek Tragedy', *Arion* 3rd ser. 3: 56–111.

1996. 'Dancing in Athens, Dancing on Delos: Some Patterns of Choral Projection in Euripides', *Philologus* 140: 48–62.

2003. 'Writing Religion: Inscribed Texts, Ritual Authority, and the Religious Discourse of the Polis', in H. Yunis (ed.), *Written Texts and the Rise of Literate Culture in Ancient Greece*. Cambridge: 38–58.

Herrmann, H.-V. 1979. *Die Kessel der orientalisierenden Zeit*. Berlin.

Higbie, C. 2003. *The Lindian Chronicle and the Greek Creation of Their Past*. Oxford.

Highwater, J. 1996. *Dance: Rituals of Experience*. 3rd ed. Oxford.

Høgseth, H. B. 2013. 'The Language of Craftsmanship', in M. L. S. Sørensen and K. Rebay-Salisbury (eds.), *Embodied Knowledge: Perspectives on Belief and Technology*. Oxford and Philadelphia: 95–105.

Hoff, F. 1976. 'Dance to Song in Japan', *Dance Research Journal* 9: 1–15.

Hollinshead, M. B. 1989. 'The Swallows and Artists of Room Delta 2 at Akrotiri, Thera', *AJA* 93: 339–54.

Hopkins, C. 1960. 'The Origin of the Etruscan-Samian Griffin Cauldron', *AJA* 64: 368–70.

Hornblower, S. 2008. *A Commentary on Thucydides. Vol. III: Books 5.25–8.109*. Oxford.

Howe, T. 1954. 'The Origin and Function of the Gorgon-Head', *AJA* 58: 209–21.

Hubbard, T. K. 2011. 'The Dissemination of Pindar's Non-Epinician Choral Lyric', in Athanassaki and Bowie: 347–63.

Hunter, R. L. (ed.) 1999. *Theocritus, A Selection: Idylls 1, 3, 4, 6, 7, 10, 11 and 13*. Cambridge Greek and Latin Classics. Cambridge.

Hurwit, J. 1977. 'Image and Frame in Greek Art', *AJA* 81: 1–30.

1985. *The Art and Culture of Early Greece*. Ithaca.

2002. 'Reading the Chigi Vase', *Hesperia* 71: 1–22.

2016. *Artists and Signatures in Ancient Greece*. Cambridge.

Immerwahr, H. R. 1990. *Attic Script: A Survey*. Oxford.

Ingalls, W. B. 2000. 'Ritual Performance as Training for Daughters in Archaic Greece', *Phoenix* 54: 1–20.

Inglese, A. 2008. *Thera arcaica: le iscrizioni rupestri dell'agora degli dei*. Rome.

Jameson, M. 1990. 'Perseus, the Hero of Mykenai', in R. Hägg and G. Nordquist (eds.), *Celebrations of Death and Divinity in the Bronze Age Argolid, 11–13 June 1988* (Proceedings of the Sixth International Symposium at the Swedish Institute at Athens, June 11–13, 1988). Stockholm: 213–23.

Janko, R. 2005. 'Sappho Revisited', *TLS* 5360 (23/12/2005): 19–20.

Jebb, R. C. 1905. *Bacchylides: The Poems and Fragments*. Cambridge.

Jeffery, L. H. 1961. *The Local Scripts of Archaic Greece*. Oxford.

Johnson, B. 1986. 'Apostrophe, Animation, and Abortion', *Diacritics* 16: 29–47.

Johnston, S. I. 2008. *Ancient Greek Divination*. Walden, MA.

Jordan, B. 2000. 'The Sicilian Expedition was a Potemkin Fleet', *CQ* 50: 63–79.

Jørgensen, L. B. 2013. 'Spinning Faith', in M. L. S. Sørensen and K. Rebay-Salisbury (eds.), *Embodied Knowledge: Perspectives on Belief and Technology*. Oxford and Philadelphia: 128–36.

Jost, M. 1985. *Sanctuaires et cultes d'Arcadie*. École française d'Athènes. Études Péloponnésiennes 9. Paris.

Kaempf-Dimitriadou, S. 1979. *Die Liebe der Götter in der attischen Kunst des 5. Jahrhunderts v. Chr.* Basel.

Kallet, L. 2001. *Money and the Corrosion of Power in Thucydides: The Sicilian Expedition and Its Aftermath*. Berkeley and Los Angeles.

Karakasi, K. 2003. *Archaic Korai*. Los Angeles.

Karanika, A. 2014. *Voices at Work: Women, Performance, and Labor in Ancient Greece*. Baltimore.

Karouzou, S. 1954. *Corpus Vasorum Antiquorum. Grèce, Athènes-Musée Nationale*. Fasc. 2. Paris.

Karvouni, M. 1997. *Treading on the Rhythmos of a Greek Temple*. PhD diss. University of Pennsylvania.

    1999. 'Demas: The Human Body as a Tectonic Construct', in S. Parcell and A. Pérez-Gómez (eds.), *Chora Three: Intervals in the Philosophy of Architecture*. Montreal: 103–24.

Kavoulaki, A. 2011. 'Choral Self-Awareness: On the Introductory Anapests of Aeschylus' *Supplices*', in Athanassaki and Bowie: 365–89.

Keesling, C. M. 2003. *The Votive Statues of the Athenian Acropolis*. Cambridge.

Kirk, A. 2014. 'The Semantics of Showcase in Herodotus's "Histories"', *TAPA* 141: 19–40.

Koch-Harnack, G. 1989. *Erotische Symbole. Lotosblüte und gemeinsamer Mantel auf antiken Vasen*. Berlin.

Koch Piettre, R. 2005. 'La Chronique de Lindos, ou comment accommoder les restes pour écrire l'Histoire', in P. Borgeaud and Y. Volokhine (eds.), *Les objets de la mémoire*. Bern and Berlin: 95–121.

Kosmetatou, E. 2013. 'Herodotus and Temple Inventories', in P. Liddel and P. Low (eds.), *Inscriptions and Their Uses in Greek and Latin Literature*. Oxford: 65–77.

Kousoulini, V. 2016. 'Panhellenic and Epichoric Elements in Corinna's Catalogues', *GRBS* 56: 82–110.

Kowalzig, B. 2004. 'Changing Choral Worlds: Song-Dance and Society in Athens and Beyond', in Murray and Wilson: 39–65.

    2007. *Singing for the Gods: Performances of Myth and Ritual in Archaic and Classical Greece*. Oxford.

2013. 'Broken Rhythms in Plato's *Laws*: Materialising Social Time in the Chorus', in A.-E. Peponi (ed.), *Performance and Culture in Plato's Laws*. Cambridge: 171–211.

Kowalzig, B. and P. Wilson (eds.) 2013. *Dithyramb in Context*. Oxford.

Kurke, L. 1996. 'Pindar and the Prostitutes, or Reading Ancient "Pornography"', *Arion* 4: 49–75.

2005. 'Choral Lyric as "Ritualization": Poetic Sacrifice and Poetic *Ego* in Pindar's Sixth Paean', *CA* 24: 81–130.

2007. 'Visualizing the Choral: Epichoric Poetry, Ritual, and Elite Negotiation in Fifth-Century Thebes', in C. Kraus, S. Goldhill, H. P. Foley and J. Elsner (eds.), *Visualizing the Tragic: Drama, Myth, and Ritual in Greek Art and Literature*. Oxford: 63–101.

2012. 'The Value of Chorality in Ancient Greece', in J. K. Papadopoulos and G. Urton (eds.), *The Construction of Value in the Ancient World*. Los Angeles: 218–35.

2013. 'Imagining Chorality: Wonder, Plato's Puppets, and Moving Statues', in A.-E. Peponi (ed.), *Performance and Culture in Plato's Laws*. Cambridge: 123–70.

2015. Pindar's Material Imaginary: Dedications and Politics in Olympian 7. UCL Housman Lecture.

Kurke, L. and R. Neer. 2014. 'Pindar fr. 75 SM and the Politics of Athenian Space', *GRBS* 54: 527–79.

2019. *Pindar, Song, and Space: Towards a Lyric Archaeology*. Chicago.

Kyriakidis, E. 2005. 'Unidentified Floating Objects on Minoan Seals', *AJA* 109: 137–54.

Laing, D. R. 1965. *A New Interpretation of the Athenian Naval Catalogue, IG II^2, 1951*. PhD diss. University of Cincinnati.

1968. 'A Reconstruction of I.G. II^2, 1628', *Hesperia* 37: 244–54.

Langdon, M. K. 1976. *A Sanctuary of Zeus on Mt. Hymettos. Hesperia* Supplement 16. Athens.

Langdon, S. 1998. 'Significant Others: The Male-Female Pair in Greek Geometric Art', *AJA* 102: 251–70.

2001. 'Beyond the Grave: Biographies from Early Greece', *AJA* 105: 579–606.

2008. *Art and Identity in Dark Age Greece*. Cambridge.

Lardinois, A. 1996. 'Who Sang Sappho's Songs?', in E. Greene (ed.), *Reading Sappho: Contemporary Approaches*. Berkeley and Los Angeles: 150–72.

2009. 'The New Sappho Poem (*P. Köln* 21351 and 21376): Key to the Old Fragments', in E. Greene and M. B. Skinner (eds.), *The New Sappho on Old Age: Textual and Philosophical Issues*. Hellenic Studies Series 38. Center for Hellenic Studies. Washington, DC: 41–57.

2011. 'The *Parrhesia* of Young Female Choruses in Ancient Greece', in Athanassaki and Bowie: 161–71.

Larson, J. 2000. 'Boiotia, Athens, the Peisistratids, and the *Odyssey*'s Catalogue of Heroines', *GRBS* 41: 193–222.

2001. *Greek Nymphs: Myth, Cult, Lore*. Oxford.

2002. 'Corinna and the Daughters of Asopos', *Syllecta Classica* 13: 47–62.

Latte, K. 1913. *De saltationibus Graecorum capita quinque*. Giessen.

Lavecchia, S. 2000. *Pindaro: I ditirambi. Introduzione, testo critico, traduzione e commento*. Rome and Pisa.

Lawler, L. B. 1943. Ὄρχησις Ἰωνική', *TAPA* 74: 60–71.

1944. 'The Dance of the Ancient Mariners', *TAPA* 75: 20–33.

1946. 'The Geranos Dance – A New Interpretation', *TAPA* 77: 112–30.

1948. 'A Necklace for Eileithyia', *The Classical Weekly* 42: 2–6.

1950. '"Limewood" Cinesias and the Dithyrambic Dance', *TAPA* 81: 78–88.

1978. *The Dance in Ancient Greece*. 2nd ed. Middletown, CT.

Lee, K. H. (ed.) 1997. *Euripides: Ion*. Warminster.

Levaniouk, O. 1999. 'Penelope and the Pênelops', in M. Carlisle and O. Levaniouk (eds.), *Nine Essays on Homer*. Lanham, MD: 95–136.

LeVen, P. 2014. *The Many-Headed Muse: Tradition and Innovation in Late Classical Greek Lyric Poetry*. Cambridge.

Liberman, G. 2016. 'Some Thoughts on the Symposiastic Catena, *Aisakos*, and *Skolia*', in V. Cazzato, D. Obbink and E. E. Prodi (eds.), *The Cup of Song: Studies on Poetry and the Symposion*. Oxford: 42–62.

Liddel, P. 2007. *Civic Obligation and Individual Liberty in Ancient Athens*. Oxford.

Lissarrague, F. 1990. *The Aesthetics of the Greek Banquet: Images of Wine and Ritual*. Trans. A. Szegedy-Maszak. Princeton.

1993. 'On the Wildness of Satyrs', in T. H. Carpenter and C. A. Faraone (eds.), *Masks of Dionysus*. Ithaca and London: 207–20.

2013. *La cité des satyres. Une anthropologie ludique (Athènes, vi^e–ve siècle avant J. C.)*. Paris.

2015. 'Ways of Looking at Greek Vases', in P. Destrée and P. Murray (eds.), *A Companion to Ancient Aesthetics*. Chichester: 237–47.

Lonsdale, S. H. 1993. *Dance and Ritual Play in Greek Religion*. Baltimore.

1995. 'A Dancing Floor for Ariadne (*Iliad* 18.590–592): Aspects of Ritual Movement in Homer and Minoan Religion', in J. B. Carter and S. Morris (eds.), *The Ages of Homer: A Tribute to Emily Townsend Vermeule*. Austin: 273–84.

Lynn-George, M. 1988. *Epos: Word, Narrative and the Iliad*. Basingstoke.

Mack, R. 2002. 'Facing Down Medusa (An Aetiology of the Gaze)', *Art History* 25: 571–604.

Mackil, E. 2013. *Creating a Common Polity: Religion, Economy, and Politics in the Making of the Greek Koinon*. Berkeley and Los Angeles.

MacLachlan, B. 2009. 'Kore as Nymph not Daughter: Persephone in a Locrian Cave', www.stoa.org/diotima/essays/fc04/MacLachlan.html.

Maehler, H. 1982–97. *Die Lieder des Bakchylides*. 2 vols. *Mnemosyne* Supplements 62, 167. Leiden.

　2004. *Bacchylides: A Selection*. Cambridge.

Malagardis, N. 2008. 'A Chorus of Women *Ololyzousai* on an Early Attic Skyphos', in D. Kurtz (ed.), *Essays in Classical Archaeology for Eleni Hatzivassiliou 1977–2007*. Studies in Classical Archaeology 4. Oxford: 73–79.

Marconi, C. 2007. *Temple Decoration and Cultural Identity in the Archaic Greek World: The Metopes of Selinus*. Cambridge.

　2010. '*Choroi, Theôriai* and International Ambitions: The Hall of Choral Dancers and Its Frieze', in O. Palagia and B. D. Wescoat (eds.), *Samothracian Connections: Essays in Honor of James R. McCredie*. Oxford: 106–35.

　2013. 'Mirror and Memory: Images of Ritual Action in Greek Temple Decoration', in D. Ravagan (ed.), *Heaven on Earth: Temples, Ritual, and Cosmic Symbolism in the Ancient World*. Chicago: 425–66.

　2014/15. 'Pausanias and the Figural Decoration of Greek Sacred Architecture', *RES* 65/66: 179–93.

Marinatos, N. 1993. *Minoan Religion: Ritual, Image, and Symbol*. Columbia, SC.

　2000. *The Goddess and the Warrior: The Naked Goddess and Mistress of Animals in Early Greek Religion*. New York.

Martin, R. P. 2007. 'Outer Limits, Choral Space', in C. Kraus, S. Goldhill, H. P. Foley and J. Elsner (eds.), *Visualizing the Tragic: Drama, Myth, and Ritual in Greek Art and Literature*. Oxford: 35–62.

　2008. 'Keens from the Absent Chorus: Troy to Ulster', in A. Suter (ed.), *Lament: Studies in the Ancient Mediterranean and Beyond*. Oxford: 118–38.

Maslov, B. 2015. *Pindar and the Emergence of Literature*. Cambridge.

McEwen, I. K. 1993. *Socrates' Ancestors: An Essay on Architectural Beginnings*. Cambridge, MA.

McGowan, E. 1995. 'Tomb Marker and Turning Post: Funerary Columns in the Archaic Period', *AJA* 99: 615–32.

Mili, M. 2015. *Religion and Society in Ancient Thessaly*. Oxford.

Miller, J. 1986. *Measures of Wisdom: The Cosmic Dance in Classical and Christian Antiquity*. Toronto.

Minchin, E. 1996. 'The Performance of Lists and Catalogues in the Homeric Epics', in I. Worthington (ed.), *Voice into Text: Orality and Literacy in Ancient Greece*. Leiden: 3–20.

Minton, W. W. 1962. 'Invocation and Catalogue in Hesiod and Homer', *TAPA* 93: 188–212.

Mitchell, A. G. 2009. *Greek Vase Painting and the Origins of Visual Humour*. Cambridge.

Mitsopoulou, C. 2011. 'The Eleusinian Processional Cult Vessel: Iconographic Evidence and Interpretation', in M. Haysom and J. Wallensten (eds.), *Current Approaches to Religion in Ancient Greece: Papers Presented at*

a Symposium at the Swedish Institute at Athens, 17–19 April 2008.
Stockholm: 189–226.

Moore, M. B. 2004. 'Horse Care as Depicted on Greek Vases before 400 B. C.',
Metropolitan Museum Journal 39: 35–67.

2006. 'Hoplites, Horses, and a Comic Chorus', *Metropolitan Museum Journal*
41: 33–57.

Morelli, D. 1959. I culti in Rodi. *SCO* 8. Pisa.

Morris, I. 1992. *Death-Ritual and Social Structure in Classical Antiquity.*
Cambridge.

1998. 'Archaeology and Archaic Greek History', in N. Fisher and H. van
Wees (eds.), *Archaic Greece: New Approaches and New Evidence.*
Swansea: 1–91.

Morris, S. 1984. *The Black and White Style: Athens and Aigina in the Orientalizing
Period.* New Haven.

1992. *Daidalos and the Origins of Greek Art.* Princeton.

Muellner, L. 1990. 'The Simile of the Cranes and Pygmies: A Study of Homeric
Metaphor', *HSCP* 93: 59–101.

Mullen, W. 1982. *Choreia: Pindar and Dance.* Princeton.

Murnaghan, S. 2005. 'Women in Groups: Aeschylus' *Suppliants* and the Female
Choruses of Greek Tragedy', in V. Pedrick and S. M. Oberhelman (eds.), *The
Soul of Tragedy: Essays on Athenian Drama.* Chicago: 183–98.

2018. 'Penelope as a Tragic Heroine: Choral Dynamics in Homeric Epic',
Yearbook of Ancient Greek Epic 2: 165–89.

Murray, O. 2008. 'The *Odyssey* as Performance Poetry', in M. Revermann and
P. Wilson (eds.), *Performance, Iconography, Reception: Studies in Honour of
Oliver Taplin.* Oxford: 161–75.

Murray, P. and P. Wilson (eds.) 2004. *Music and the Muses: The Culture of Mousike
in the Classical Athenian City.* Oxford.

Myers, M. 2007. 'Footrace, Dance and Desire: The χορός of Danaids in Pindar's
Pythian 9', *SIFC* 5: 230–47.

Mylonas, G. E. 1961. *Eleusis and the Eleusinian Mysteries.* Princeton.

Mylonopoulos, I. 2006. 'Greek Sanctuaries as Places of Communication through
Rituals: An Archaeological Perspective', in E. Stavrianopoulou (ed.), *Ritual
and Communication in the Graeco-Roman World. Kernos* Supplément 16.
Liège: 69–110.

Naerebout, F. G. 1997. *Attractive Performances: Ancient Greek Dance. Three
Preliminary Studies.* Amsterdam.

2006. 'Moving Events: Dance at Public Events in the Ancient Greek World.
Thinking through Its Implications', in E. Stavrianopoulou (ed.), *Ritual and
Communication in the Graeco-Roman World. Kernos* Supplément 16. Liège:
37–67.

Nagy, G. 1973. 'Phaethon, Sappho's Phaon, and the White Rock of Leukas', *HSCP*
77: 137–77.

1979. *The Best of the Achaeans: Concepts of the Hero in Archaic Greek Poetry.* Baltimore.

1990. *Pindar's Homer: The Lyric Possession of an Epic Past.* Baltimore and London.

1994/95. 'Transformations of Choral Lyric Traditions in the Context of Athenian State Theater', *Arion* 3: 41–55.

1996. *Poetry as Performance: Homer and Beyond.* Cambridge.

2008/09. *Homer the Classic.* Washington, DC.

2009. 'The "New Sappho" Reconsidered in the Light of the Athenian Reception of Sappho', in E. Greene and M. B. Skinner (eds.), *The New Sappho on Old Age: Textual and Philosophical Issues.* Hellenic Studies Series 38. Center for Hellenic Studies. Washington, DC: 176–99.

2010a. *Homer the Preclassic.* Berkeley and Los Angeles.

2010b. 'Language and Meter', in E. Bakker (ed.), *A Companion to the Ancient Greek Language.* Chichester: 370–87.

2011. 'Asopos and His Multiple Daughters: Traces of Preclassical Epic in the Aeginetan Odes of Pindar', in D. Fearn (ed.), *Aegina: Contexts for Choral Lyric Poetry.* Oxford: 41–78.

2013. 'The Delian Maidens and Their Relevance to Choral Mimesis in Classical Drama', in Gagné and Hopman: 227–56.

Neer, R. 2001. 'Framing the Gift: The Politics of the Siphnian Treasury at Delphi', *CA* 20: 273–344.

2010. *The Emergence of the Classical Style in Greek Sculpture.* Chicago and London.

2018. 'Amber, Oil and Fire: Greek Sculpture beyond Bodies', *Art History* 41: 466–91.

Nightingale, A. 2018. 'The Aesthetics of Vision in Plato's *Phaedo* and *Timaeus*', in A. Kampakoglou and A. Novokhatko (eds.), *Gaze, Vision, and Visuality in Ancient Greek Literature.* Berlin and Boston: 331–53.

Nikolaev, A. 2012. 'Showing Praise in Greek Choral Lyric and Beyond', *AJP* 133: 543–72.

Nisetich, F. J. 1975. 'Olympian 1.8–11: An Epinician Metaphor', *HSCP* 79: 55–68.

Nooter, S. 2018. *The Mortal Voice in the Tragedies of Aeschylus.* Cambridge.

Notopoulos, J. A. 1949. 'Parataxis in Homer: A New Approach to Homeric Literary Criticism', *TAPA* 80: 1–23.

Noussia-Fantuzzi, M. 2013. 'A Scenario for Stesichorus' Portrayal of the Monster Geryon in the *Geryoneis*', *Trends in Classics* 5: 234–59.

Ober, J. 1995. 'Greek *Horoi*: Artifactual Texts and the Contingency of Meaning', in D. Small (ed.), *Methods in the Mediterranean: Historical and Archaeological Views of Text and Archaeology.* Leiden: 91–123.

2006. 'Solon and the *Horoi*: Facts on the Ground in Archaic Athens', in J. H. Blok and A. P. M. H. Lardinois (eds.), *Solon of Athens: New Historical and Philological Approaches.* Leiden: 441–56.

Olsen, S. 2015. 'Conceptualizing *Choreia* on the François Vase: Theseus and the Athenian Youths', *Mètis* 13: 107–21.

    2016. *Beyond Choreia: Dance in Ancient Greek Literature and Culture.* Ph.D. diss., University of California, Berkeley.

    2017. 'Kinesthetic *Choreia*: Empathy, Memory, and Dance in Ancient Greece'. *CP* 112: 153–74.

Osborne, R. 1988. 'Death Revisited, Death Revised: The Death of the Artist in Archaic and Classical Greece', *Art History* 11: 1–16.

    2008. 'Putting Performance into Focus', in M. Revermann and P. Wilson (eds.), *Performance, Iconography, Reception: Studies in Honour of Oliver Taplin.* Oxford: 395–418.

Osborne, R. and A. Pappas. 2007. 'Writing on Archaic Greek Pottery', in Z. Newby and R. Leader-Newby (eds.), *Art and Inscriptions in the Ancient World.* Cambridge: 131–55.

Page, D. L. 1952. *Corinna.* London.

Pantillon, M. and G. Bolognesi (ed. and trans.) 1997. *Theon Progymnasmata.* Paris.

Papalexandrou, N. 2003/04. 'Keledones: Dangerous Performers in Early Delphic Lore and Ritual Structures', *Hephaistos* 21/22: 145–68.

    2005. *The Visual Poetics of Power: Warriors, Youths, and Tripods in Early Greece.* Lanham, MD.

Pappas, A. 2011. 'Arts in Letters: The Aesthetics of Ancient Greek Writing', in M. Dalbello and M. Shaw (eds.), *Visible Writings: Cultures, Forms, Readings.* New Brunswick: 37–54.

    Forthcoming. 'Power Play: The Aesthetics of Ancient Inscription at Archaic Thera'.

Parker, R. 2005. *Polytheism and Society at Athens.* Oxford.

Pavlou, M. 2012. 'Bacchylides 17: Singing and Usurping the Paean', *GRBS* 52: 510–39.

Payne, H. 1971. *Necrocorinthia: A Study of Corinthian Art in the Archaic Period.* College Park.

Pemberton, E. G. 2000. 'Wine, Women and Song: Gender Roles in Corinthian Cult', *Kernos* 13: 85–106.

Peponi, A.-E. 2004. 'Initiating the Viewer: Deixis and Visual Perception in Alcman's Lyric Drama', *Arethusa* 37: 295–316.

    2007. 'Sparta's Prima Ballerina: *Choreia* in Alcman's Second *Partheneion* (3 *PMGF*)', *CQ* 57: 351–62.

    2009. 'Choreia and Aesthetics in the *Homeric Hymn to Apollo*: The Performance of the Delian Maidens (Lines 156–64)', *CA* 28: 39–70.

    2012. *Frontiers of Pleasure: Models of Aesthetic Response in Archaic and Classical Greek Thought.* Oxford.

    (ed.) 2013. *Performance and Culture in Plato's Laws.* Cambridge.

Peppas-Delmousou, D. 1971. 'Das Akropolis Epigram IG I² 673', *AM* 86: 55–66.

Perceau, S. 2002. *La parole vive. Communiquer en catalogue dans l'épopée homérique*. Louvain.

Pernice, E. 1892. 'Geometrische Vase aus Athen', *AM* 17: 205–28.

Petersen, E. A. H. 1917. *Rhythmus*. Abhandlungen der Königlichen Gesellschaft der Wissenschaften zu Göttingen, Philologisch-historische Klasse 16.5: 1–104. Göttingen.

Pettersson, M. 1992. *Cults of Apollo at Sparta: The Hyakinthia, the Gymnopaidiai and the Karneia*. Stockholm.

Pfeijffer, I. L. 1999. *Three Aeginetan Odes of Pindar: A Commentary on Nemean V, Nemean III, and Pythian VIII. Mnemosyne* Supplementum 197. Leiden.

Phillips, T. 2016. *Pindar's Library: Performance Poetry and Material Texts*. Oxford.

Platt, V. 2011. *Facing the Gods: Epiphany and Representation in Graeco-Roman Art, Literature and Religion*. Cambridge.

Pöhlmann, E. 1971. 'Die ABC-Komödie des Kallias', *RhM* 114: 230–40.

Pollitt, J. J. 1972. *Art and Experience in Classical Greece*. Cambridge.

  1974. *The Ancient View of Greek Art*. New Haven and London.

Poltera, O. (ed.) 2008. *Simonides lyricus. Testimonia und Fragmente: Einleitung, kritische Ausgabe, Übersetzung und Kommentar*. Freiburg.

Porter, J. I. 2010. *The Origins of Aesthetic Thought in Archaic Greece: Matter, Sensation, and Experience*. Cambridge.

Pouilloux, J. and G. Roux. 1963. *Énigmes à Delphes*. Paris.

Powell, B. 1988. 'The Dipylon Oinochoe and the Spread of Literacy in Eighth-Century Athens', *Kadmos* 27: 65–86.

  1991. *Homer and the Origins of the Greek Alphabet*. Cambridge.

Power, T. 2000. 'The "Parthenoi" of Bacchylides 13', *HSCP* 100: 67–81.

  2010. *The Culture of Kitharôidia*. Cambridge, MA.

  2011. 'Cyberchorus: Pindar's Κηληδόνες and the Aura of the Artificial', in Athanassaki and Bowie: 67–113.

Prauscello, L. 2011. 'Patterns of Chorality in Plato's *Laws*', in D. Yatromanolakis (ed.), *Music and Cultural Politics in Greek and Chinese Societies. Vol. I: Greek Antiquity*. Cambridge, MA: 133–58.

  2012. 'Epinician Sounds: Pindar and Musical Innovation', in P. Agócs, C. Carey and R. Rawles (eds.), *Reading the Victory Ode*. Cambridge: 58–82.

  2014. *Performing Citizenship in Plato's Laws*. Cambridge.

Priestley, J. M. 2007. 'The φάρος of Alcman's Partheneion', *Mnemosyne* 60: 175–95.

Prins, Y. 1991. 'The Power of the Speech Act: Aeschylus' Furies and Their Binding Song', *Arethusa* 24: 177–95.

Privitera, G. A. 1970. 'Pindaro, *Nem.* III 1–5 e l'acqua di Egina', *QUCC* 58: 63–70.

Pucci, P. 1997. 'The *Helen* and Euripides' "Comic" Art', *Colby Quarterly* 33: 42–75.

Rawles, R. 2005. 'Notes on the Interpretation of the "New Sappho"', *ZPE* 157: 1–7.

  2011. '*Eros* and Praise in Early Greek Lyric', in Athanassaki and Bowie: 139–59.

Renehan, R. 1969. 'Conscious Ambiguities in Pindar and Bacchylides', *GRBS* 10: 217–28.

Restani, D. 1983. 'Il *Cheirone* di Ferecrate e la "nuova" musica greca', *Rivista italiana di musicologia* 18: 139–92.

Revermann, M. 1998. 'The Text of *Iliad* 18.603–6 and the Presence of an ΑΟΙΔΟΣ on the Shield of Achilles', *CQ* 48: 29–38.

Richards, I. A. 1973. *The Philosophy of Rhetoric*. Oxford.

Richardson, N. J. 1974. *The Homeric Hymn to Demeter*. Oxford.

　　(ed.) 2010. *Three Homeric Hymns: To Apollo, Hermes, and Aphrodite, Hymns 3, 4, and 5*. Cambridge Greek and Latin Classics. Cambridge.

Richter, G. M. 1970. *The Sculpture and Sculptors of the Greeks*. New Haven.

Ridgway, B. S. 1977. *The Archaic Style in Greek Sculpture*. Chicago.

　　1999. *Prayers in Stone: Greek Architectural Sculpture (ca. 600–100 B.C.E.)*. Berkeley and Los Angeles.

Rinon, Y. 2006. 'Tragic Hephaestus: The Humanized God in the *Iliad* and *Odyssey*', *Phoenix* 60: 1–20.

Robb, K. 1994. *Literacy and Paideia in Ancient Greece*. Oxford.

Robbins, E. 1994. 'Alkman's *Partheneion*: Legend and Choral Ceremony', *CQ* 44: 7–16.

Robert, L. and J. Robert. 1954. *La Carie II: Le plateau de Tabai et ses environs*. Paris.

Roccos, L. J. 1995. 'The Kanephoros and Her Festival Mantle in Greek Art', *AJA* 99: 641–66.

Roebuck, M. C. and C. A. Roebuck. 1955. 'A Prize Aryballos', *Hesperia* 24: 158–62.

Rosen, R. 1999. 'Comedy and Confusion in Callias' *Letter Tragedy*', *CP* 94: 147–67.

Rosenmeyer, P. 2004. 'Girls at Play in Early Greek Poetry', *AJP* 125: 163–78.

Rothwell, K. 2007. *Nature, Culture, and the Origins of Greek Comedy: A Study of Animal Choruses*. Cambridge and New York.

Rougemont, G. 2012. *Inscriptions grecques d'Iran et d'Asie centrale*. Corpus Inscriptionum Iranicarum, Part II, Volume I. London.

Ruffy, M. V. 2004. 'Visualization and "Deixis am Phantasma" in Aeschylus' *Persae*', *QUCC* 78: 11–28.

Rutherford, I. 2001. *Pindar's Paeans: A Reading of the Fragments with a Survey of the Genre*. Oxford.

　　2004. 'χορὸς εἷς ἐκ τῆσδε τῆς πόλεως ... (Xen. *Mem.* 3.3.12): Song-Dance and State-Pilgrimage at Athens', in Murray and Wilson: 67–90.

Rykwert J. 1996. *The Dancing Column: On Order in Architecture*. Cambridge, MA.

Sabetai, V. 2009. 'The Poetics of Maidenhood: Visual Constructs of Womanhood in Vase-Painting', in S. Schmidt and J. H. Oakley (eds.), *Hermeneutik der Bilder: Beiträge zu Ikonographie und Interpretation griechischer Vasenmalerei*. Munich: 103–14.

Salapata, G. 2009. 'Female Triads on Laconian Terracotta Plaques', *ABSA* 104: 325–40.

Sammons, B. 2010. *The Art and Rhetoric of the Homeric Catalogue*. Oxford.

Sassi, M. 2015. 'Perceiving Colors', in P. Destrée and P. Murray (eds.), *A Companion to Ancient Aesthetics*. Oxford: 262–73.

Scanlon, T. F. 2002. *Eros and Greek Athletics*. Oxford.

Schachter, A. 1981. *Cults of Boiotia*. Vol. I. London.

Schechner, R. 1985. *Between Theater and Anthropology*. Philadelphia.

Scheid, J. and J. Svenbro. 1996. *The Craft of Zeus: Myths of Weaving and Fabric*. Trans. C. Volk. Cambridge, MA.

Schlesier, R. 2011. 'Presocratic Sappho: Her Use of Aphrodite for Arguments about Love and Immortality', *Scientia Poetica* 15: 1–28.

Schmitt Pantel, P. 1992. *La cité au banquet. Histoire des repas publics dans les cités grecques*. Rome.

Schörner, G. and H. R. Goette. 2004. *Die Pan-Grotte von Vari*. Mainz am Rhein.

Scodel, R. 1980. 'Hesiod Redivivus', *GRBS* 21: 301–20.

Seaford, R. 1988. 'The Eleventh Ode of Bacchylides: Hera, Artemis, and the Absence of Dionysos', *JHS* 108: 118–36.

Séchan, L. 1930. *La danse antique grecque*. Paris.

Seeberg, A. 1971. *Corinthian Komos Vases*. London.

Segal, C. 1998. *Aglaia: The Poetry of Alcman, Sappho, Pindar, Bacchylides, and Corinna*. Lanham, MD.

Shapiro, H. A. 1980. 'Jason's Cloak', *TAPA* 110: 263–86.

Shear, I. M. 1999. 'Maidens in Greek Architecture: The Origin of the "Caryatids"', *BCH* 123: 65–85.

Shear, J. L. 1995. 'Fragments of Naval Inventories from the Athenian Agora', *Hesperia* 64: 179–224.

Sickinger, J. 1999. *Public Records and Archives in Classical Athens*. Chapel Hill.

Silk, M. 1980. 'Aristophanes as a Lyric Poet', *YCS* 26: 99–152.

Simon, E. 1983. *Festivals of Attica: An Archaeological Commentary*. Madison.

Sinn, U. 1988. 'Der Kult der Aphaia auf Aegina', in R. Hägg, N. Marinatos and G. Nordquist (eds.), *Early Greek Cult Practice: Proceedings of the Fifth International Symposium at the Swedish Institute at Athens, 26–29 June 1986*. Stockholm: 149–59.

   1992. 'The Sacred Herd of Artemis at Lousoi', in R. Hägg (ed.), *The Iconography of Greek Cult in the Archaic and Classical Periods* (Conference, Delphi 16–18 November 1990). *Kernos* Supplément 1. Athens and Liège: 177–87.

Sklar, D. 2001. *Dancing with the Virgin: Body and Faith in the Fiesta of Tortugas, New Mexico*. Berkeley and Los Angeles.

Slater, N. W. 2002. 'Dancing the Alphabet: Performative Literacy on the Attic Stage', in I. Worthington and J. M. Foley (eds.), *Epea and Grammata: Oral and Written Communication in Ancient Greece*. Leiden: 117–29.

Smith, A. C. 2011. *Polis and Personification in Classical Athenian Art*. Leiden.

Smith, C. 1894. 'Polledrara Ware', *JHS* 14: 206–23.

Smith, T. J. 2000. 'Dancing Spaces and Dining Places: Archaic Komasts at the Symposion', in G. R. Tsetskhladze, A. J. N. W. Prag and A. M. Snodgrass (eds.), *Periplous: Papers on Classical Art and Archaeology Presented to Sir John Boardman*. London: 309–19.

2009. 'Komastai or "Hephaistoi"? Visions of Comic Parody in Archaic Greece', *BICS* 52: 69–92.

2010. *Komast Dancers in Archaic Greek Art*. Oxford.

2016. 'Instant Messaging: Dance, Text, and Visual Communication on Archaic Corinthian and Athenian Vases', in D. Yatromanolakis (ed.), *Epigraphy of Art: Ancient Greek Vase-Inscriptions and Vase-Paintings*. Oxford: 145–63.

Snyder, J. 1981. 'The Web of Song: Weaving Imagery in Homer and the Lyric Poets', *CJ* 76: 193–96.

Sourvinou-Inwood, C. 1987. 'A Series of Erotic Pursuits: Images and Meanings', *JHS* 107: 131–53.

Spantidaki, S. 2015.'Embellishment Techniques of Classical Greek Textiles', in M. Harlow and M.-L. Nosch (eds.), *Greek and Roman Textiles and Dress: An Interdisciplinary Anthology*. Oxford and Philadelphia: 34–45.

Squire, M. 2011. *The Iliad in a Nutshell: Visualizing Epic on the Tabulae Iliacae*. Oxford and New York.

2013. 'Ekphrasis at the Forge and the Forging of Ekphrasis: The "Shield of Achilles" in Graeco-Roman Word and Image', *Word and Image* 29: 157–91.

Stanford, W. B. (ed.) 1965. *Homer: Odyssey I–XII*. London.

Stansbury-O'Donnell, M. 2006. *Vase Painting, Gender, and Social Identity in Archaic Athens*. Cambridge.

States, B. O. 1996. 'Performance as Metaphor', *Theatre Journal* 48: 1–26.

Stehle, E. 1996. 'Sappho's Gaze: Fantasies of a Goddess and Young Man', in E. Greene (ed.), *Reading Sappho: Contemporary Approaches*. Berkeley and Los Angeles: 193–225.

1997. *Performance and Gender in Ancient Greece: Nondramatic Poetry in Its Setting*. Princeton.

Steiner, D. T. 1993. 'Pindar's "Oggetti Parlanti"', *HSCP* 95: 159–80.

1994. *The Tyrant's Writ: Myths and Images of Writing in Ancient Greece*. Princeton.

2001. *Images in Mind: Statues in Archaic and Classical Greek Literature and Thought*. Princeton.

2005. 'For Want of a Horse: Thucydides 6.30–2 and Reversals in the Athenian Civic Ideal', *CQ* 55: 407–22.

2009. 'Pot Bellies: The Komast Vases and Contemporary Song', in D. Yatromanolakis (ed.), *An Archaeology of Representations: Ancient Greek Vase-Paintings and Contemporary Methodologies*. Athens: 240–82.

2011. 'Dancing with the Stars: *Choreia* in the Third Stasimon of Euripides' *Helen*', *CP* 106: 299–323.

2012. 'The Swineherds' Symposium: *Od*. 14.457–533 and the Traditions of Sympotic Poetry', *QUCC* 100: 117–44.

2013a. 'The Gorgons' Lament: Auletics, Poetics and Chorality in Pindar's *Pythian* 12', *AJP* 134: 173–208.

2013b. 'The Priority of Pots: Pandora's Pithos Re-viewed', *Mètis* n.s. 11: 207–34.

2016a. 'Making Monkeys: Archilochus fr. 185–7 W in Performance', in V. Cazzato and A. Lardinois (eds.), *The Look of Lyric: Greek Song and the Visual*. Studies in Archaic and Classical Greek Song 1. Leiden: 108–45.

2016b. 'Harmonic Divergence: Pindar's fr. 140b and Early Fifth-Century Choral Polemics', *JHS* 136: 132–51.

Steinhart, M. 2007. 'From Ritual to Narrative', in E. Csapo and M. C. Miller (eds.), *The Origins of Theater in Ancient Greece and Beyond*. Cambridge: 196–220.

Stieber, M. 2011. *Euripides and the Language of Craft*. Leiden.

Svenbro, J. 1993. *Phrasikleia: An Anthropology of Reading in Ancient Greece*. Trans. J. Lloyd. Ithaca.

2008. '*Grammata* et *Stoikheia*. Les scholies à *La Grammaire* de Denys Thrax', *Kernos* 21: 197–210.

Swift, L. 2010. *The Hidden Chorus: Echoes of Genre in Tragic Lyric*. Oxford.

2011. 'Epinician and Tragic Worlds: The Case of Sophocles' *Trachiniae*', in Athanassaki and Bowie: 391–413.

2013. 'Conflicting Identities in the Euripidean Chorus', in Gagné and Hopman: 130–54.

2016. 'Visual Imagery in Parthenaic Song', in V. Cazzato and A. Lardinois (eds.), *The Look of Lyric: Greek Song and the Visual*. Studies in Archaic and Classical Greek Song 1. Leiden: 255–87.

Tanner, J. 2006. *The Invention of Art History in Ancient Greece: Religion, Society and Artistic Rationalisation*. Cambridge and New York.

Taplin, O. 1993. *Comic Angels: And Other Approaches to Greek Drama through Vase-Painting*. Oxford.

Themelis, P. G. 1992. 'The Cult Scene on the Polos of the Siphnian Karyatid at Delphi', in R. Hägg (ed.), *The Iconography of Greek Cult in the Archaic and Classical Periods* (Conference, Delphi 16–18 November 1990). *Kernos* Supplément 1. Athens and Liège: 49–72.

Thomas, E. 2015. 'The Beauties of Architecture', in P. Destrée and P. Murray (eds.), *A Companion to Ancient Aesthetics*. Chichester: 274–91.

Thomas, R. 1992. *Literacy and Orality in Ancient Greece*. Cambridge.

Thompson, D'Arcy W. 1936. *A Glossary of Greek Birds*. Oxford.

Thompson, H. A. and R. E. Wycherley. 1972. *The Agora of Athens: The History, Shape, and Uses of an Ancient City Center*. Vol. XIV. Princeton.

Topper, K. 2007. 'Perseus, the Maiden Medusa, and the Imagery of Abduction', *Hesperia* 76: 73–105.

2010. 'Maidens, Fillies and the Death of Medusa on a Seventh-Century Pithos', *JHS* 130: 109–19.

2012. *The Imagery of the Athenian Symposium*. Cambridge.

Trinkl, E. 2015. 'The Wool Basket: Function, Depiction and Meaning of the Kalathos', in M. Harlow and M.-L. Nosch (eds.), *Greek and Roman Textiles and Dress: An Interdisciplinary Anthology*. Oxford and Philadelphia: 190–206.

Trümper, M. 2012. 'Gender and Space, "Public" and "Private"', in S. L. James and S. Dillon (eds.), *A Companion to Women in the Ancient World*. Chichester: 288–303.

Tsagalis, C. 2009. 'Blurring the Boundaries: Dionysus, Apollo and Bacchylides 17', in L. Athanassaki, R. P. Martin and J. F. Miller (eds.), *Apolline Politics and Poetics*. Athens: 199–215.

Tuck, A. 2006. 'Singing the Rug: Patterned Textiles and the Origins of Indo-European Metrical Poetry', *AJA* 110: 539–50.

Umholtz, G. 2002. 'Architraval Arrogance? Dedicatory Inscriptions in Greek Architecture of the Classical Period', *Hesperia* 71: 261–93.

Urton, G. 1997. *The Social Life of Numbers: A Quechua Ontology of Numbers and Philosophy of Arithmetic*. With the collaboration of Primitivo Nina Llanos. Austin.

Vamvouri Ruffy, M. 2004. *La Fabrique du divin: les Hymnes de Callimaque à la lumière des Hymnes Homériques et des hymnes épigraphiques*. Liège.

van der Weiden, M. J. H. 1991. *The Dithyrambs of Pindar*. Amsterdam.

van Groningen, B. A. 1955. 'Ad Pindari Dithyrambi Fragmentum 75 S', *Mnemosyne* 8: 192.

Verdenius, W. J. 1987. *Commentaries on Pindar*. Vol. I. *Mnemosyne* Supplementum 97. Leiden.

Vernant, J.-P. 1982. *La mort, les morts dans les sociétés anciennes*. Paris.

Vestrheim, G. 2004. 'Alcman fr. 26: A Wish for Fame', *GRBS* 44: 5–18.

Vierneisel, K. and A. Scholl. 2002. 'Reliefdenkmäler dramatischer Choregen im klassischen Athen. Das Münchner Maskenrelief für Artemis und Dionysos', *Münchner Jahrbücher der bildenden Kunst* 53: 7–55.

Vlachou, V. 2016. 'Image and Story in Late Geometric Attica: Interpreting a Giant Pitcher from Marathon', in T. H. Carpenter, E. Langridge-Noti and M. D. Stansbury-O'Donnell (eds.), *The Consumers' Choice: Uses of Greek Figure-Decorated Pottery*. Boston: 125–51.

Wachter, R. 2001. *Non-Attic Greek Vase Inscriptions*. Oxford.

Watson, J. 2011. 'Rethinking the Sanctuary of Aphaia', in D. Fearn (ed.), *Aegina: Contexts for Choral Lyric Poetry*. Oxford: 79–113.

Webb, R. 1999. 'Ekphrasis Ancient and Modern: The Invention of a Genre', *Word and Image* 15: 7–18.

  2006. 'The *Imagines* as a Fictional Text: *Ekphrasis, Apatê* and Illusion', in M. Costantini, F. Graziani and S. Rolet (eds.), *Le défi de l'art: Philostrate, Callistrate et l'image sophistique*. Rennes: 113–33.

  2009. *Ekphrasis, Imagination and Persuasion in Ancient Rhetorical Theory and Practice*. Farnham.

Węcowski, M. 2014. *The Rise of the Greek Aristocratic Banquet*. Oxford.

Weiss, N. A. 2018. *The Music of Tragedy: Performance and Imagination in Euripidean Theater*. Oakland, CA.

West, M. L. (ed.) 1966. *Hesiod: Theogony*. Oxford.

1978. *Hesiod: Works and Days*. Oxford.

1985. *The Hesiodic Catalogue of Women*. Oxford.

2015. 'Epic, Lyric, and Lyric Epic', in A. Kelly and P. J. Finglass (eds.), *Stesichorus in Context*. Cambridge: 63–80.

Whitley, J. 1994. 'Protoattic Pottery: A Contextual Approach', in I. Morris (ed.), *Classical Greece: Ancient Histories and Modern Archaeologies*. Cambridge: 51–70.

Whitman, C. 1958. *Homer and the Heroic Tradition*. New York.

Willink, C. W. 1990. 'The Parodos of Euripides' *Helen* (164–90)', *CQ* 40: 77–99.

Wilson, P. 1999/2000. 'Euripides' "Tragic Muse"', in M. Cropp, K. Lee and D. Sansone (eds.), *Euripides and Tragic Theatre in the Late Fifth Century*. *ICS* 24–25. Champagne: 427–49.

2000. *The Athenian Institution of the Khoregia: The Chorus, the City and the Stage*. Cambridge.

2007. 'Performance in the Pythion: The Athenian Thargelia', in P. Wilson (ed.), *The Greek Theatre and Festivals: Documentary Studies*. Oxford: 150–82.

Wilson Jones, M. 2002. 'Tripods, Triglyphs, and the Origin of the Doric Frieze', *AJA* 106: 353–90.

2014. *Origins of Classical Architecture: Temples, Orders and Gifts to the Gods in Ancient Greece*. New Haven and London.

2015. 'Greek and Roman Architectural Theory', in C. Marconi (ed.), *The Oxford Handbook of Greek and Roman Art and Architecture*. Oxford: 41–69.

Wollheim, R. 1987. *Painting as an Art*. Princeton.

Woodard, R. 2014. *The Textualization of the Greek Alphabet*. Cambridge.

Yalouris, N. 1980. 'Astral Representations in the Archaic and Classical Periods and Their Connection to Literary Sources', *AJA* 84: 313–18.

Zeitlin, F. I. 1993. 'The Artful Eye: Vision, Ekphrasis, and Spectacle in Euripidean Theatre', in S. Goldhill and R. Osborne (eds.), *Art and Text in Ancient Greek Culture*. Cambridge: 138–96.

1996. 'Mysteries of Identity and Designs of the Self in Euripides' *Ion*', in *Playing the Other: Gender and Society in Classical Greek Literature*. Chicago and London: 285–338.

Zimmermann, B. 1992. *Dithyrambos: Geschichte einer Gattung*. Göttingen.

Index Locorum

Names in [ ] are Pseudo names.

Aelius Aristides
Or.
   43.13: 392
   46.158: 578
Aeschylus
Ag.
   50–51: 19
   1146–48: 121
   1186–92: 172
Choeph.
   232: 452
   794–95: 193
   796–99: 193–94
   1021–25: 195
   1025: 196
Pers. 1046: 329
Sept. 854–57: 329
Supp.
   11: 227
   223: 164
   463–65: 164
Fragments
   78 R.: 354
   312 R.: 170
Alcman (*PMGF*)
fr.1 (first *Partheneion*)
   fr. 1.39–59: 646–47
   fr. 1.40–41: 186
   fr. 1.46: 281, 602–03
   fr. 1.46–47: 29
   fr. 1.47: 186
   fr. 1.52: 590
   fr. 1.53–54: 41, 186, 639
   fr. 1.55: 350
   fr. 1.58–59: 98, 186
   fr. 1.60–63: 167
   fr. 1.64–76: 356
   fr. 1.64–77: 589
   fr. 1.66: 639
   fr. 1.66–67: 41
   fr. 1.67: 84

fr. 1.68–69: 187
fr. 1.87: 168
fr. 1.92–95: 189
fr. 1.96–101: 168
fr.3 (third *Partheneion*)
   fr. 3.1–3: 28
   fr. 3.8–9: 98
   fr. 3.64–72: 191
   fr. 3.66–67: 386
   fr. 3.67: 639
   fr. 3.68: 41, 384
fr. 4.4–7: 613–14
fr. 14.3: 614
fr. 26: 39–40, 119–20
fr. 59(b): 613
fr. 140: 452
Scholia
fr. 33 = Σ *ad* Arat. 2 (p. 91, 11 Maas):
   578
Anacreon (*PMG*)
   fr. 346: 191
   fr. 408: 240
   fr. 417.4–6: 191, 240
Anon.
   fr. 871 *PMG*: 347–48
Anthologia Graeca (AG)
   6.174: 430
   6.211: 451
Anthologia Palatina (AP)
   1.144: 561
   6.83.5–6: 453
   9.186: 692
Antigonus Carystus
   Mirabilia 23 = *De animalibus* fr. 54b
     Dorandi: 119–20
Antipater of Sidon
   AP
     6.160: 128–29
     6.287: 407
     7.745: 157
     9.151.7–8: 129

Antoninus Liberalis
Met. 1.1: 169
Apollodorus
Bibl.
  2.1.5: 298
  2.1.14: 287
  2.27.3: 229
  2.29.1: 229
Apollonius Rhodius
Argon.
  1.28–30: 55
  1.28–31: 394
  1.1123–31: 70
  4.1765–72: 275
Apuleius
De deo Socr. pr. 3: 356
Archilochus
fr. 185 W.: 510
[Arion]
fr. 939.5–7 *PMG*: 303
Aristonous (ed. Powell)
Hymn to Hestia: 91
Aristophanes
Av.
  203: 153
  209–22: 127
  250–51: 128
  924–25: 203
  925: 35
  1394: 152
Eq. 243–44: 338
Lys.
  566: 482
  567: 482
  567–70: 484
  574–86: 482
  585: 483
  642–45: 435
  1296–315: 204
  1304: 316
  1307–10: 316
  1309–15: 153
  1316–21: 252
Nub.
  271: 389
  333: 193
  333–38: 153
Ran.
  241–49: 547–48
  334: 112
  371: 314
  407: 315
  411: 315

445: 315
450–52: 314
1309–12: 123
Thesm.
947–1000: 52–53
953–56: 638
968: 373
985: 316, 353
986: 13
Vesp.
1509: 70
1523: 70
1529: 70
1531: 70
Fragments
fr. 36 K.-A.: 466
fr. 71 K.-A.: 490–91
Aristotle
De an.
427b18–20: 659
429a1–4: 635
Gen. corr., 315b6–15: 576–77
Hist. an. 488a3–4: 142n.8, 542b21: 137
Metaph. 985a13–19: 576
Ph. 243b6–11: 486
Poet.
1448b10–17: 15, 1448b36–37: 618
1459a7–8: 15, 641
Pol.
1331a: 514
Rh.
1410b33–36: 635
1411b: 641
1411b24–25: 634
1412a3–5: 634
[Aristotle]
Ath. Pol. 68: 570
Asios
fr. 1 Davies: 609
Athenaeus
Deipn.
1.15d: 66, 241
1.21f: 329
10.453c–454b:
    490
13.573e–f: 237
13.600d–601a: 613
14.617e–f: 246
14.628e: 194
14.631b: 308
14.631c: 182, 237
14.632f: 154
15e1: 241

Philochoros
  FGrH 328 F 5b, 173: 680
  FrGrH 328 F 173: 680
Philodamus
  Paean 110–14: 616
Philodemus
  AP 6.349: 300
  De pietate B 6529–33 Obbink: 224–25
Philostratus
  Imag.
    2.1.1–3: 687–88
      2.1.3.4–12: 694
      2.1.3.12–16: 696
      2.1.4.1–4: 696
      2.1.4.4–5: 696
      2.1.4.6–13: 698
    2.8: 300
Pindar (S.-M.)
  Isthm.
    1.45–46: 565
    5.4–6: 328
    8.1–4: 347
    8.16–24: 267
    8.47–48: 614–15
    88.60: 517
    8.66–67: 465
  Nem.
    2.2: 442
    2.11–12: 170
    3.3–5: 44
    3.3–7: 272
    3.4: 613
    3.4–5: 442
    3.11–12: 44
    3.12: 613
    3.12–16: 273
    3.76–79: 274
    4.5: 236
    4.44–45: 463
    5.1–2: 40
    5.53–54: 346
    6.45–47: 621
    7.77–79: 454
    8.15: 464
    9.49: 614
  Ol.
    1.8–9: 465
    1.29: 465
    1.101: 201–02
    1.105: 465
    2.61–62: 138
    2.71–74: 138
    2.81: 375

3.1–4: 565
3.1–6: 376–77
3.31–34: 398
3.33–34: 382
6.1–9: 340
6.86–87: 464, 551
6.87–92: 551–52
6.88: 555
6.90–91: 21
7.1–12: 559–60
7.20–24: 564–65
7.42: 572
7.48–49: 558
7.51: 566
7.77–87: 567–68
7.86–87: 570
7.88: 573
7.90–91: 571
9.13: 244
9.35–39: 459–60
10.9: 570
13.36: 640
14.8–9: 113
14.16: 113
14.17: 113
Pyth.
  1.1–4: 373, 461, 542–43
  1.4: 244
  1.81–82: 458
  2.15–19: 432
  2.69: 202
  3.311–14: 442
  3.17: 431
  3.17–19: 277
  3.77–79: 431–31
  3.78–79: 347
  4.95–96: 376
  5.90–91: 298
  6.1–3: 50
  6.14–18: 351
  7.1–3: 462
  9.12–13: 478
  9.18: 470
  9.27: 479
  9.31a: 479
  9.36–37: 479
  9.76–79: 457
  9.105–20: 293–94
  9.114: 29, 399
  9.114–16: 28–29
  9.117: 59
  9.117–18: 29, 479
  9.118: 30, 57

Pindar (S.-M.) (cont.)
  9.120: 479
  10.37–42
  12.8: 464
  12.8–10: 110
  12.19–27: 111
  12.25: 114
  12.25–27: 464
  Fragments
   fr. 29.1: 380
   fr. 29: 394
   fr. 30.2–4: 381
   fr. 32.1: 375, 615
   fr. 33c: 386
   fr. 33c.1: 379
   fr. 33c1–2: 383–84
   fr. 33c1–6: 386
   fr. 33d.1–9: 374
   fr. 35c: 379
   fr. 52b.96–102: 107
   fr. 52e.41: 387
   fr. 52f.1–5: 347
   fr. 52f.1–11: 258
   fr. 52f.7–8: 268
   fr. 52f.9: 367
   fr. 52f.15–18: 259
   fr. 52f.17–18: 447
   fr. 52f.58–61: 268
   fr. 52f.124–37: 387–88
   fr. 52f.125–29: 266–67
   fr. 52f.128–29: 268
   fr. 52f.134–35: 268
   fr. 52f.134–37: 267
   fr. 52f.135–36: 347
   fr. 52i.65–68: 351–52
   fr. 52i.65–90: 44–45
   fr. 52i.67–84: 107–08
   fr. 52i.75: 665
   fr. 52i.78–79: 665
   fr. 52i.80–81: 665–66
   fr. 52m.16–20: 378
   fr. 70b: 150, 459, 466, 678–79
   fr. 70b.1: 459
   fr. 70b.1–2: 166–67, 509
   fr. 70b.3: 460
   fr. 70b.4–5: 459
   fr. 70b.17
   fr. 70b.22: 182
   fr. 75.1–19: 677
   fr. 75.7–8: 678
   fr. 94a.13–19: 133
   fr. 94b.3–5: 676
   fr. 94b.13–19: 132

   fr. 94b.66–67: 604
   fr. 94b.66–70: 391
   fr. 94b.70: 376, 481
   fr. 94b.71–72: 62
   fr. 105a: 203
   fr. 107a: 192, 203, 241
   fr. 107a.2–3: 399
   fr. 107a.3: 638
   fr. 107b: 245
   fr. 112: 182
   fr. 122: 234–35
   fr. 140b: 463
   fr. 140b.11: 58
   fr. 148: 507
   fr. 194: 447
   fr. 215a.6–7: 450
  Scholia (ed. Drachmann)
   Nem.
    2.16: 137
    3.1: 273
   Pyth. 2.127: 241
Plato
  Crat.
   388a–b: 18
   389a–b: 486
  Euthphr. 6b–c: 444
  Grg. 472a6–7: 35
  Ion
   533d1–e8: 667–68
   535e7–536a7: 668
  Leg.
   644d7: 455
   644d7–645c6: 668
   644e1–645a5: 455–56
   645a: 455, 582
   653c7–d2: 455
   653c7–654a5: 409–10, 669
   654a1–5: 454–55
   654b3–4: 3
   655a: 108
   657d6: 660
   664–665a: 194, 526–27, 574
   669c5–6: 575
   669c–e: 194
   669d6–7: 575
   700d: 245
   745d–e: 481
   778d–e: 487
   790d–e: 173
   815a–b: 375
   815c–d: 173
   815d–816a: 500
   816a5: 16

Subject Index

Page numbers in italics are figures; with 'n' are notes; all 'Pseudo' authors will be found in [ ].

abduction, 294, 347
  at site of choral performance, 434
  of Aegina, 266–69, 279, 387–88, 609–10
  of Delos by Zeus, 387
  of Leukippidae, 168–69
  of maidens by Aristomenes, 164, 369
  of Medusa, 79–80
  of Paris by Aphrodite, 188
  of Thetis by Peleus, 80–81, 299, 304
  of Tithonus, 134–37
abecedaria, 527–33, *530*, *532*
Acanthus Column, *10*, 401–04
Acheloos Painter, pelike, 307
Achelous, 265, 307, 651, 652
Achilles
  in *Electra* (Eur.), 330–31
  funeral laments for, 517–18
  in *Iphigenia at Aulis* (Eur.), 197–200
see also Shield of Achilles
acroteria, 44, 107
Actor's Relief, *684*, *685*, 686
Aegina (island), 271–73
  temple of Aphaia on, 270–71, 278, 357
Aegina (nymph), 266–69, 273, 285, 387–88,
      609–10
Aelian, 186n.6, 687
Aelius Aristides, *Orationes*, 392, 578
Aeschylus
  Agamemnon, 19, 121, 172
  Choephoroi, 193–95, 196, 452
  Eumenides, Binding Song, 14n.25, 448
  fr. **312**, doves, 170
  fr. **355**, on Dionysus, 679
  Nereids, 299
  Persae, 329–30
  Septem, 329–30
  Suppliants, 164–65, 227, 291
  Thalamapoioi ('Chamber-makers'), 354
Afghan picture rugs, 468
agalma/agalmata, 187, 341
  see also votives

Agamemnon, 88, 602
Agido, 168, 169, 186, 189, 190, 192, 597,
      602–03, 647–50
agôn, 27–29
  see also competitions
Aiakos, 273–74, 346, 347
Aineas, 21, 551–55
Aischenes, 536–37
Ajax, in *Iphigenia at Aulis* (Eur.), 334–35
Akrotiri (Thera), Spring Fresco, *674*, *675*
Alcaeus, 90, 106, 696n.144
Alcmaeonidae, *Pythian* **7** (Pind.), 462, *see also*
      fr. 52i (Pind.)
Alcman
  fr. **1**
    catalogues, 589–90, 592, 593, 597, 602–03
    doves, 167–70
    enargeia, 646–51
    horses, 29, 98, 185–86, 187, 189, 638–39
    individualized participants, 356
    races, 153
    robe/plough, 481
    seasonality, 157
    silvery face, 350
    snake-like ornaments, 41, 84, 639
  fr. **3**
    agôn, 28
    Astymelousa, 41, 282, 384, 386, 387,
      639–40, 693
    branch, 384
    stars, 282, 386
  fr. **4**, 613–14
  fr. **14**, 614
  fr. **26**
    halcyons, 119–21
    and debility, 39–40
    maidens/parthenaic voice, 128–33
    mourning, 121–28
    rejuvenation, 134–41
      fr. **59(b)**, 613
      fr. **81**, 231

741

ololugê (cont.)
depicted on a skyphos, 415–17, *416*
Homeric Hymn to Apollo, 378
Paean **12** (Pind.), 378
Olsen, Sarah 322–23n.156
Oltos
cups, 242, 496
psykter, 311, 546–48, *547*, 593
Olynthos, 434
Orphelandros Painter, krater, 69
Oppian, *Halieutica*, cranes, 141
orchestra see floors, dancing
Orestes, 193–96, 248–49, 645
Orion, 47, 48, 53
Helen (Eur.), 152–53, 155
Iliad, 170
Nemean **2** (Pind.), 170
orthostates, 396
Osborne, Robin, 82, 218–19, 493–94, 543–44
ostriches, *179–80*
Ovid
Amores, 225n.92
Metamorphosis, 139

paint, in inscriptions, 627
Painter of Berlin 1686, amphora with horses, 216–18, *217*
Painter of Bologna, column krater, 190
Painter of London E 2, cup, 323–25, *324, 325*
Painter of the Louvre Centauromachy, pyxis, 433, *444*
Painter of Philadelphia, pyxis, 434
Palaikastro Hymn, 676
palm trees, 383–85
Pamphos, 314
Pan, 321
Pan Painter, hydria, *685*, 686
Panamyes, 570
pankration, 275, 276, 307–08
pannychis, 157, 314–16, 317, 371–72
Papalexandrou, Nassos, 28, 87, 93, 100, 525
Pappas, Alexandra, 493–94, 503–04, 506, 508, 543–45
parataxis, 592, 593
Paris Painter, amphora, 302
Parthenion (well), 314–15
Pasikles, 447
Patras Painter, phiale, 497
patterns
in catalogues, 597–98
weaving, 421, 442, 464, 468, 638–39n.13
Pausanias
Amymone in, 288

Asopid statue group, 269–70, 609–10
Celeus' daughters, 318–19
collective death of maidens in, 164n.145
daphnephoros, 99
Delphi, 520
fountain houses, 262
on the Heraia, 480–82
on the *Hymn to Zeus* (Pind.), 571
karyatids, 358–59
Polyboia, 141
purification ritual for Hera, 291
rites of Hera at Nauplia, 289
robe weaving ritual for Apollo, 439
throne of Apollo (Amyklai, Sparta), 368
pebbles (voting counters), 568, 570
Peleiades, 167–68
see also Pleiades
Peleus, abduction of Thetis, 80–81, 299, 304
Pemberton, Elizabeth, 413–15
Penelope, 159–67, 430, 462
Peponi, A.-E. 23, 29, 661–63
peristyle, 369–73
Perseus
and the Gorgons, 87, 88, 103
and maturation rites, 97–98
Petersen, Eugen, 353
Petrie Group, slim amphora, 117–18, *118*
phantasiai see mental images
Pheidias, shield of Athena, 444
Phelan, Amanda, 405
Pherecrates
Cheiron, 193
fr. **156**, 453
Pherecydes, 407, 420
Philo Mechanicus, *Syntaxis*, 352
Philochoros, 680
Philodamus of Scarphea, 571, 616–17, 679n.99
Philodemus, *De pietate*, 224–25
Philostratus (the Elder), 106, 300, 632, 687–701
Philostratus (the Younger), *Imagines*, 453
phorminx, 63, 91, 394–95, 446, 448–49, 461, 598–99
pick *see* plectrum
pillars
Ion (Eur.), 398–400
see also columns
pin beater *see* kerkis
pinax *see* plaques (*pinakes*)
Pindar
Apophthegmata, 7
in Athenaeus, 182
Isthmian Odes

CPSIA information can be obtained
at www.ICGtesting.com
Printed in the USA
LVHW062058050521
686585LV00006B/306

9 781107 110687